For Reference

Not to be taken from this room

The Reader's Adviser

The Reader's Adviser
A Layman's Guide to Literature
13th EDITION

Barbara A. Chernow and George A. Vallasi, Series Editors

Volume 1
The Best in American and British Fiction, Poetry, Essays, Literary Biography, Bibliography, and Reference
Edited by Fred Kaplan

Books about Books • Bibliography • Reference Books: Literature • Broad Studies and General Anthologies: Literature • British Poetry: Early to Romantic • British Poetry: Middle Period • Modern British and Irish Poetry • American Poetry: Early Period • Modern American Poetry • British Fiction: Early Period • British Fiction: Middle Period • Modern British Fiction • American Fiction: Early Period • Modern American Fiction • Commonwealth Literature • Essays and Criticism • Literary Biography and Autobiography

Volume 2
The Best in American and British Drama and World Literature in English Translation
Edited by Maurice Charney

The Drama • British Drama: Early to Eighteenth Century • Shakespeare • Modern British and Irish Drama • American Drama • World Literature • Greek Literature • Latin Literature • French Literature • Italian Literature • Spanish Literature • Portuguese Literature • German and Netherlandic Literature • Scandinavian Literature • Russian Literature • East European Literatures • Yiddish Literature • Hebrew Literature • Spanish American Literature • African Literature • Middle Eastern Literature • The Literature of the Indian Subcontinent • Chinese Literature • Japanese Literature • Southeast Asian and Korean Literature

Volume 3
The Best in General Reference Literature, the Social Sciences, History, and the Arts
Edited by Paula T. Kaufman

Reference Books: General • Dictionaries • General Biography and Autobiography • The Social Sciences • Education • Ancient History • United States History • Western Hemisphere: Canada and Latin America • British History • World History • Music and Dance • Art and Architecture • The Mass Media • Folklore and Humor • Travel and Exploration

Volume 4

The Best in the Literature of Philosophy and World Religions
Edited by William L. Reese

General Philosophy • Greek and Roman Philosophy • Medieval Philosophy •
Renaissance Philosophy • Modern Philosophy, 1600–1900 • Twentieth-Century
Philosophy • Ancient Religions and Philosophies • Eastern Religion and Philosophy •
Islamic Religion and Philosophy • Judaism • Early Christianity • Late
Christianity • The Bible and Related Literature • Minority Religions and
Contemporary Religious Movements

Volume 5

The Best in the Literature of Science, Technology, and Medicine
Edited by Paul T. Durbin

General Science • History of Science, Technology, and Medicine • Philosophy of
Science and Pseudoscience • Mathematics • Statistics and Probability • Information
and Computer Science • Astronomy and Space Science • Earth
Sciences • Physics • Chemistry • Biology • Ecology and Environmental
Science • Genetics • Medicine and Health • Illness and Disease • Clinical Psychology
and Psychiatry • Engineering and Technology • Energy • Science, Technology, and
Society • Ethics of Science, Technology, and Medicine

THE
Reader's Adviser

A Layman's Guide to Literature
13th EDITION

Volume 5

The Best in the Literature
of Science, Technology, and Medicine

Edited by Paul T. Durbin

Barbara A. Chernow and George A. Vallasi, Series Editors

R. R. BOWKER COMPANY
New York & London, 1988

Published by R. R. Bowker Company,
a division of Reed Publishing (USA) Inc.
Copyright © 1988 by Reed Publishing USA

International Standard Book Numbers
0-8352-2145-8 (Volume 1)
0-8352-2146-6 (Volume 2)
0-8352-2147-4 (Volume 3)
0-8352-2148-2 (Volume 4)
0-8352-2149-0 (Volume 5)
0-8352-2315-9 (Volume 6)
International Standard Serial Number 0094-5943
Library of Congress Catalog Card Number 57-13277

The paper used in this publication meets the minimum
requirements of American National Standard for
Information Sciences—Permanence of Papers for
Printed Library Materials, ANSI Z39.48-1984.

Contents

Preface

Over its thirteen editions, and since its first publication in 1921, chapters of *The Reader's Adviser* have been expanded and reorganized and new topics have been introduced, thus better to serve the needs of a growing and more diversified population. The first edition, entitled *The Bookman's Manual*, was based on Bessie Graham's course on book salesmanship given at the William Penn Evening High School in Philadelphia. Graham organized the book so that the chapters corresponded to the general classifications familiar to booksellers and, by providing publishers and prices in her text, she simplified book ordering for the bookseller. Since 1921, however, the book industry has experienced significant changes—comparatively few independent book dealers exist, information on titles is available from a wide variety of printed and computerized sources, and publishers are taking fewer risks by printing just enough copies of a title to meet immediate demands. At the same time that these changes were occurring, *The Reader's Adviser* was finding a broader audience; although still used by booksellers, the librarians, general readers, and high school and college students found that the topical organization of the volume with its annotated bibliographies also met their needs. For the nonspecialist who is interested in reading about a particular subject, *The Reader's Adviser* is a perfect starting point. The six-volume set provides annotated bibliographies arranged by subject, with brief biographies of authors, creative artists, and scientists worthy of special mention; in addition, it informs the reader of a book's availability, price, and purchasing source. Since the set is kept up to date by regular revisions, the volumes also serve as a reflection of the current state of the best available literature in print in the United States.

As a result of the growth of new fields of interest to the reading public and the continuing increase in the number of titles published, *The Reader's Adviser* has expanded with each succeeding edition. For this thirteenth edition, it has grown from three to six volumes. The first three volumes appeared simultaneously in 1986; the final three in 1988. The organization of the first two volumes is similar to that in the twelfth edition: Volume 1 covers mainly American and British fiction and poetry and Volume 2 covers drama, Shakespeare, and world literature in English translation. Volume 3, which covers the best in general reference literature, the social sciences, history, and the arts, has experienced the most significant changes—most chapters have been expanded, virtually new chapters have been created for the arts, and several chapters have been moved to form the nuclei of Volumes 4 and 5. Volume 4 covers the Bible, world religions, and philosophy; Volume 5 is devoted to science, technology, and medicine. Except for Volume 6, containing indexes to the entire set and a Publishers' Directory, each of the volumes has been edited by a specialist in the field, the whole project having been coordinated by the series editors.

Although the thirteenth edition of *The Reader's Adviser* retains the essential format and basic structure of the earlier editions, the editors and publisher have made a number of improvements designed to enhance the appearance and usefulness of the volumes. First, the design has been modified to increase readability and provide a more open look. The typeface is easier to read, biographies are printed in a larger face, and the titles in the "books about" sections following the biographies are in alphabetical order according to the authors' surnames. Finally, the authors and anonymous sagas that form the main headings in *The Reader's Adviser* are listed in alphabetical order within the chapters rather than the chronological order of previous editions. In the front matter of each volume, a Chronology of these individuals provides the reader with an overview of the development of a particular genre. For each chapter, the editors chose an eminent scholar or librarian with particular expertise in the subject area, so that the selection of bibliographies and main listings would reflect the best-informed judgment of a specialist in the field.

The greatest challenge was that of selection—which titles and authors to include. Since *The Reader's Adviser* is not a research tool for students and scholars, but rather a reference work designed for the nonspecialist, the editors' goal was to include those books generally available to an intelligent reader through the facilities of the library system of a moderately sized municipality. Books must be currently available in English from a publisher or distributor in the United States. Out-of-print titles are included for those major works which, because of their importance in the field, could not be excluded from the list. If a book is not presently available in English or cannot be purchased in the United States, it is considered out of print (o.p.) by the editors. In some disciplines, such as modern American poetry, publishers allow titles to go out of print quickly and the available literature was found to be surprisingly thin. The reader will also note that Volume 2 (the comparative literature volume) reveals how little of the world's non-English literature has been translated into English.

In selecting authors for main entries, contributing editors weighed a number of criteria—historical importance, current popularity as determined by the number of in-print titles, and space limitations. Particularly in American and British fiction, U.S. and world history, and the social sciences chapters, the necessity of adding new authors sometimes required eliminating authors who were previously the subjects of main entries in earlier editions of *The Reader's Adviser*. Most major authors are represented; other authors were selected as examples of particular movements or styles. The latter category is subjective; although these choices are valid, someone else's choices might have been equally valid. The constraints of space impose their own compromises.

The organization of each volume and of each chapter is designed to move the reader from the general to the specific, from reference books, books of history and criticism, and anthologies to specific authors, scientists, and creative artists. Each chapter opens with a brief introduction that provides a framework for the literature of a particular period or discipline, followed by general reading lists and then, with few exceptions, the main entries. In chapters covering more than one area of study, such as the social sciences, or more than one country, such as Southeast Asia, this pattern repeats itself for each major division. Each author selected as a main entry receives a brief biography followed by bibliographies of books by and about him or her. Wherever possible, the date of first publication follows the title of a work mentioned in the short biography or will instead appear, when available, as the first date in the "Books by . . ." entries below. In addition to *Books in Print, The New Columbia Encyclopedia* (1975) has served as the authority in verifying dates. The bibliographies of books by an author are mainly composed of collections of works and in-print titles of individual works in the particular genre covered by the chapter. Other titles may be mentioned in the biography, but only those works relevant to the genre under discussion appear in the bibliographies.

The bibliographic entries are so designed that the reader will be able both to locate a book in a library and to know where it is available for purchase and at what price. The editors have included the following information available or applicable for each title: author; title (translated titles or original titles are given in parentheses following the title); editor; series title; translator; authors of prefaces, introductions, and forewords; edition; number of volumes; reprint data; publisher (if more than one, publishers are listed alphabetically); date of publication; and price. The reader should be cautioned that the accuracy and completeness of information depends in large part on the information publishers supply to the *Books in Print* database and the information listed in individual publishers' catalogs.

If a date is listed directly after a title, this indicates the date of the publication of the first edition, regardless of whether that edition is still in print. For reprints, the date of the particular edition from which it was reprinted is given. If a title consists of more than one volume, and is listed with only one price, this is the price of the entire set. As book pricing changes so rapidly, some prices listed in *The Reader's Adviser* may have already changed. Although the editors considered the possibility of deleting prices from *The Reader's Adviser*, it was decided to retain them as an indication to the reader of the general price category into which an individual title falls and to assist the librarian in acquisition. Finally, the reader should be aware that not all in-print editions of a work are necessarily listed, but rather those selected by the editors because of their quality or special features.

To guide the reader through the volumes, *The Reader's Adviser* includes cross-references in three forms. The "see" reference leads the reader to the appropriate volume and chapter for information on a specific author or topic. "See also" refers the reader to additional information in another chapter or volume. Within any introductory narrative portions, the name of an author who appears as a main listing in another chapter or volume is printed in large and small capital letters. In each case, if the chapter cross-referenced is in a different volume from that being consulted, the volume number is also provided.

While the chapter organization of this book reflects, to a large degree, the traditional organization of scientific disciplines, those historical differences are becoming increasingly blurred. We are confronted today with a host of new disciplines that cut across these boundaries. As one example, artificial intelligence, far from being just a field of computer science, borrows heavily from psychology, linguistics, engineering, and mathematics. The reader is therefore advised to use the indexes and look for material across the chapter divisions.

Each volume of *The Reader's Adviser* has three indexes—one for names, one for book titles, and one for general subjects. The Name Index includes all authors, editors, compilers, composers, directors, actors, artists, philosophers, and scientists cited in *The Reader's Adviser*. If a name appears as a main listing in the text, the name as well as the first page number of the main listing appear in boldface type. The Title Index includes book titles with two exceptions: collected works or generic titles by authors who receive main listings (e.g., *Selected Prose of T. S. Eliot*) and "books about" titles that follow the main listings and include the name of the main-entry author (e.g., *Booker T. Washington* by Louis R. Harlan). (This does not hold true in the case of Chapter 3, "Shakespeare," in Volume 2, where all works by and about him are included.) Therefore, to ensure locating all titles by and about a main-entry author, the user should look up that author in the Name Index to locate the primary listing.

In preparing the thirteenth edition of *The Reader's Adviser*, the series editors are indebted to a great many people for assistance and advice. We are especially grateful to the many people at R. R. Bowker who have worked with us; in particular, to Olga S. Weber, who provided encouragement, support, and a critical eye in reading manuscripts; to Kathy Kleibacker, for her constant faith in the project; and to Marion Sader, Julia Raymunt, Iris Topel, Nancy Bucenec, and Glorieux Dougherty for their attention to detail and concern for quality in editing and production. We were fortunate in our choice of volume editors. Fred Kaplan, general editor of Volume 1, The Best in American and British Fiction, Poetry, Essays, Literary Biography, Bibliography, and Reference, is Professor of English at Queens College and at the Graduate Center, City University of New York; he is a distinguished Dickens and Carlyle scholar, the editor of *Dickens Studies Annual*, a member of the board of the Carlyle Papers, and is currently writing a biography of Dickens. The general editor of Volume 2, The Best in American and British Drama and World Literature in English Translation, is Maurice Charney, Distinguished Professor at Rutgers University in the department of English. His published works include *How to Read Shakespeare* and a biography of

Joe Orton. Paula T. Kaufman, who served as general editor of Volume 3, The Best in General Reference Literature, the Social Sciences, History, and the Arts, is director of the academic information services group, Columbia University Libraries. Volume 4, The Best in the Literature of Philosophy and World Religions, was developed under the general editorship of William L. Reese. He is Professor of Philosophy at the State University of New York, Albany. His publications include the *Dictionary of Philosophy and Religion*. Paul T. Durbin is general editor of Volume 5, The Best in the Literature of Science, Technology, and Medicine. He is Professor of Philosophy at the University of Delaware and editor of *A Guide to the Culture of Science, Technology, and Medicine*. All made invaluable suggestions for organizing their volumes, recommended contributing editors, and reviewed each chapter for substantive content. A special thanks to David B. Biesel, who first brought the project to us, and to Sanford Kadet, who provided invaluable assistance in coordinating many of the editorial aspects of Volumes 4 and 5. The editors also wish to thank Kathy Martin and Mae Liu who keyboarded many of the chapters, assisted with verification of bibliographic data, and maintained the project records. For special assistance and advice in the preparation of Volume 5, we also wish to thank Carl Mitcham and Fred Gregory.

In the 65 years since *The Reader's Adviser* first appeared, it has grown from a tool for booksellers to a standard reference work. In addition to bibliographic information, the introductions and biographies are enjoyable reading for someone just browsing through the volumes. *The Reader's Adviser* has a distinguished history; it is hoped that these latest volumes will continue in that tradition.

Barbara A. Chernow
George A. Vallasi

Contributing Editors

Judith A. Adams, SCIENCE, TECHNOLOGY, AND SOCIETY
Head, Humanities Department, Ralph Brown Draughon Library, Auburn University (Alabama); co-author of *Technology and Values in American Civilization: A Guide to Information Sources, Jules Verne: A Primary and Secondary Bibliography,* and co-editor of "Current Bibliography in the History of Technology," published annually in *Technology and Culture.*

Wendell Cochran, EARTH SCIENCES
Consultant and co-editor of *Geowriting: Writing, Editing, and Printing in Earth Science* and co-author of *Into Print;* honored in 1982 for "Outstanding Contributions to Editing and Publishing" by the Association of Earth Science Editors.

Stephen H. Cutcliffe, SCIENCE, TECHNOLOGY, AND SOCIETY
Director, Technology Studies Resource Center, Lehigh University (Pennsylvania); co-author of *Technology and Values in American Civilization: A Guide to Information Sources* and "STS, Technology Literacy, and the Arts Curriculum," *Bulletin of Science, Technology and Society* (1982); author of "The Emergence of STS as an Academic Field," *Research in Philosophy and Technology* (1988); editor of *Science, Technology and Society Curriculum Development Newsletter;* series co-editor of *Research in Technology Studies;* co-editor of "Current Bibliography in the History of Technology," published annually in *Technology and Culture.*

Joseph W. Dauben, MATHEMATICS
Professor, Department of History, Herbert H. Lehman College, City University of New York, and Ph.D. program in History, The Graduate Center, City University of New York; author of *Georg Cantor: His Mathematics and Philosophy of the Infinite;* editor of *Mathematical Perspectives, Essays on Mathematics and Its Historical Development, Festschrift in Honor of Kurt R. Biermann,* and *The History of Mathematics from Antiquity to the Present;* member, Institute for Advanced Study, Princeton University (1977–78); Guggenheim Fellowship (1980–81); Visiting Scholar, Harvard University (1980–81); IREX Exchange Scholar to the Soviet Union (1985); National Academy of Sciences Distinguished Professor Exchange with China (1987); Chairman, International Commission for History of Mathematics (1985–89); Teacher of the Year, Lehman College (1986).

Paul T. Durbin, GENERAL SCIENCE

Professor, Philosophy Department and Center for Science and Culture, University of Delaware; editor of *A Guide to the Culture of Science, Technology, and Medicine, Research in Philosophy and Technology,* and *Philosophy and Technology;* member of the board or editorial board of Society for Philosophy and Technology, Philosophy and Technology Studies Center, *Science, Technology, and Human Values,* Research in Technology Studies, and the National Association for Science, Technology, and Society.

Heyward Ehrlich, INFORMATION AND COMPUTER SCIENCE

Associate Professor of English and Director of American Studies, Rutgers University (New Jersey); author of *Light Rays: James Joyce and Modernism,* and "Burton's Gentleman's Magazine" and "Graham's Magazine" in *Collected Writings of Edgar Allan Poe;* President, Northeast Association for Computing in the Humanities (NEACH); member, Rutgers University Task Force on Information Resources.

Jean Dickinson Gibbons, STATISTICS AND PROBABILITY

Board of Visitors Research Professor of Statistics and Chairman of the Applied Statistics Program, University of Alabama; author of *Nonparametric Statistical Inference* and *Nonparametric Methods for Quantitative Analysis;* co-author of *Concepts of Nonparametric Theory* and *Selecting and Ordering Populations;* elected a Fellow of the American Statistical Association (1972); member of the International Statistical Institute (1980); recipient of the Burlington-Northern Faculty Achievement Award for Outstanding Scholarship (1985).

Amedeo Giorgi, CLINICAL PSYCHOLOGY AND PSYCHIATRY

Director of Research, Saybrook Institute, San Francisco; author of *Psychology as a Human Science;* editor of *Journal of Phenomenological Psychology* and Duquesne Series in Phenomenological Psychology; Fellow of APA (American Psychological Association), past president of Division 24 of APA (Theoretical and Philosophical Psychology), and current president of Division 32 of APA (Division of Humanistic Psychology).

Kathleen Kehoe Glass, BIOLOGY

Librarian, Biology Reference/Collection Development, Columbia University; book reviewer, life sciences, *Sci-Tech Libraries;* co-author of "Effect of Task Overload upon Cardiovascular and Plasma Catecholamine Responses in Type A and B Individuals," *Basic and Applied Social Psychology;* "Effects of Control over Aversive Stimulation and Type A Behavior on Cardiovascular and Plasma Catecholamine Responses," *Psychophysiology;* and "Stability of Individual Differences in Physiologic Responses to Stress," *Health Psychology.*

Anna Hamilton, GENETICS

Director of Information Resources and Services, National Center for Education in Maternal and Child Health, Georgetown University, Washington, D.C.; author of "Cytogenetically Speaking," *Gene Pool* (Winter Quarter 1983); co-author of "Networking: Toward a Strategy for Introducing Genetics Education in the Schools," Birth Defects Original Article Series (22[2]); and co-editor of *Resources for Teaching Medical Genetics.*

Robert A. Hatch, HISTORY OF SCIENCE, TECHNOLOGY, AND MEDICINE
Associate Professor in the Program for the History of Science, Technology and Medicine, and Associate Chairman, Department of History, University of Florida; author of *The Collection Boulliau (BN, FF. 13019–13059): An Inventory, The Correspondence Boulliau* (forthcoming), and *Respublica Scientarum: A Biographical Guide and Index to the Scientific Revolution* (forthcoming); co-editor of "History of Science," *The Eighteenth Century: A Current Bibliography*, 1981–present.

Jodith Janes, MEDICINE AND HEALTH; ILLNESS AND DISEASE
Librarian, University Hospitals of Cleveland; co-author of *The Consumer Health Information Source Book* and *The Money Management Information Source Book*.

Mary Kay, PHYSICS
Engineering Librarian, Columbia University.

Robert T. Kirkwood, ECOLOGY AND ENVIRONMENTAL SCIENCE
Retired Associate Professor of Biology, University of Central Arkansas; author of "The Back 40: Pine Bluff High School's Field Laboratory," *Nation's Schools*, and *Laboratory Exercises in Biology*; co-author of "Analysis of Effect on Wildlife of Various Plantings On Power Line Right of Way," *Proceedings of the Arkansas Academy of Science*; Arkansas Biology Teacher of the Year (1963); Arkansas Teacher of the Year (1965); Arkansas Wildlife Federation-Sears Roebuck Foundation Conservation Educator of the Year (1968); former president of Arkansas Academy of Science and Arkansas Audubon Society.

Maureen Welling Matkovich, CHEMISTRY
Manager, Library Services, American Chemical Society.

Patricia Davitt Maughan, ENGINEERING AND TECHNOLOGY
Head of the Science Libraries, University of California, Berkeley; author of "Facilities of the Kresge Engineering Library," *Science & Technology Libraries* (vol. 3, no. 4, Summer 1983); H.E.W. Title II Fellowship; member of Gamma Pi Epsilon and Beta Phi Mu.

Peter Meier, ENERGY
Chairman of the Energy Program at the State University of New York at Stony Brook; consultant and adviser on Energy and Economic Policy to the World Bank, UNDP, U.S. Department of State and governments in Africa and Asia; author of *Energy Policy in Developing Countries* and *Energy Systems Analysis*.

Carl Mitcham, ETHICS OF SCIENCE, TECHNOLOGY, AND MEDICINE
Director, Philosophy and Technology Studies Center, Polytechnic University, Brooklyn, New York; author of *Philosophy and Technology* and *Theology and Technology*; winner of the 1974 Abbot Payson Usher Prize of the Society for the History of Technology for *Bibliography of the Philosophy of Technology*.

Bruce Powell-Majors, GENETICS
Project Associate, National Center for Education in Maternal and Child Health, Georgetown University, Washington, D.C.; author of "Women's Worth," *The Ameri-*

can Spectator, and "Gun Control" in Annette T. Rottenberg's *The Elements of Argument*.

Michael Radner, PHILOSOPHY OF SCIENCE AND PSEUDOSCIENCE
Associate Professor of Philosophy, McMaster University, Hamilton, Canada; co-editor of *Analyses of Theories and Methods of Physics and Psychology;* co-author of *Science and Unreason*.

Daniel T. Richards, MEDICINE AND HEALTH; ILLNESS AND DISEASE
Assistant Health Sciences Librarian for Resources and Reference Services, Columbia University; author of numerous articles and papers on collection development in health sciences libraries; has served as consultant to the National Library of Medicine, Indiana University, and to commercial booksellers and publishers; an active member of the Medical Library Association, he was founding chairman of the Collection Development Section.

William Edward Rorie, GENETICS
Director of Technical Assistance, National Center for Education in Maternal and Child Health, Georgetown University, Washington, D.C.

Christine M. Roysdon, SCIENCE, TECHNOLOGY, AND SOCIETY
Head, Reference Department, Lehigh University (Pennsylvania); co-author of *American Engineers of the Nineteenth Century: A Biographical Index* and *Technology and Values in American Civilization;* co-editor of "Current Bibliography in the History of Technology," published annually in *Technology and Culture*.

Harry L. Shipman, ASTRONOMY AND SPACE SCIENCE
Professor of Physics, University of Delaware; author of *Space 2000: Meeting the Challenge of a New Era; Black Holes, Quasars, and the Universe; The Restless Universe: An Introduction to Astronomy;* Guggenheim Fellow (1980–81); NASA and NSF grantee; Excellence in Teaching award, University of Delaware (1984).

Abbreviations

abr.	abridged	Lit.	Literature
A.D.	in the year of the Lord	*LJ*	*Library Journal*
AHR	*American Historical Review*	ltd. ed.	limited edition
Amer.	America(n)	MLA	Modern Language Association
annot.	annotated	Mod.	Modern
B.C.	before Christ	*N.Y. Herald Tribune*	*New York Herald Tribune*
B.C.E.	before the common era		
bd.	bound	*N.Y. Times*	*New York Times*
bdg.	binding	o.p.	out-of-print
Bk(s).	Book(s)	orig.	original
B.P.	before the present	pap.	paperback
C.E.	of the common era	Pr.	Press
Class.	Classic(s)	pref.	preface
coll.	collected	pt(s).	part(s)
coll. ed.	collector's ed.	*PW*	*Publishers Weekly*
comp.	compiled, compiler	r.	reigned
corr.	corrected	repr.	reprint
cp.	compare	rev. ed.	revised edition
Ctr.	Center	*SB*	*Studies in Bibliography*
ed.	edited, editor, edition	sel.	selected
Eng.	English	Ser.	Series
enl. ed.	enlarged edition	*SLJ*	*School Library Journal*
fl.	flourished	*SR*	*Saturday Review*
fwd.	foreword	Stand.	Standard
gen. ed(s).	general editor(s)	Supp.	Supplement
ill.	illustrated	*TLS*	*Times Literary Supplement*
imit. lea.	imitation leather		
intro.	introduction	trans.	translated, translator, translation
lea.	leather		
lg.-type ed.	large-type edition	Univ.	University
Lib.	Library	Vol(s).	Volume(s)
lib. bdg.	library binding		

Chronology

Main author entries appear here chronologically by year of birth. Within each chapter, main author entries are arranged alphabetically by surname.

1. General Science
Bush, Vannevar. 1890–1974
Thomas, Lewis. 1913–
Medawar, Sir Peter Brian. 1915–
Asimov, Isaac. 1920–
Holton, Gerald. 1922–
Ziman, John M. 1925–
Gould, Stephen Jay. 1941–

2. History of Science, Technology, and Medicine

3. Philosophy of Science and Pseudoscience
Schlick, Moritz. 1882–1936
Carnap, Rudolf. 1891–1970
Reichenbach, Hans. 1891–1953
Nagel, Ernest. 1901–1985
Feigl, Herbert. 1902–
Popper, Sir Karl Raimund. 1902–
Hempel, Carl Gustav. 1905–
Kuhn, Thomas Samuel. 1922–
Feyerabend, Paul Karl. 1924–
Hesse, Mary Brenda. 1924–
Salmon, Wesley Charles. 1925–
Putnam, Hilary. 1926–

4. Mathematics
Apollonius of Perga. fl. 247–205 B.C.

Archimedes. c.287–212 B.C.
Euclid. fl. c.300 B.C.
Diophantus. fl. c.250
Descartes, René. 1596–1650
Fermat, Pierre de. 1601–1665
Newton, Sir Isaac. 1642–1727
Euler, Leonhard. 1707–1783
Gauss, Carl Friedrich. 1777–1855
Cauchy, Augustin Louis, Baron. 1789–1857
Weierstrass, Karl Wilhelm Theodor. 1815–1897
Cantor, Georg. 1845–1918
Poincaré, Jules Henri. 1854–1912
Hilbert, David. 1862–1943
Russell, Bertrand. 1872–1970
Noether, Emmy. 1882–1935
Gödel, Kurt. 1906–1978

5. Statistics and Probability

6. Information and Computer Science

7. Astronomy and Space Science
Copernicus (Kopérnik), Nicholas (Mikolaj). 1473–1543
Brahe, Tycho. 1546–1601
Galilei, Galileo. 1564–1642

11. Biology

Pliny the Elder (Caius Plinius Secundus). c. A.D. 23–A.D. 79

Linnaeus, Carolus. 1707–1778

Lamarck, Jean Baptiste (Jean Baptiste Pierre Antoine de Mondet Lamarck). 1744–1829

Cuvier, Baron Georges (Georges Leopold Chretien Frederic Dagobert Cuvier). 1769–1832

Audubon, John James. 1785–1851

Agassiz, Louis (Jean Louis Rodolphe Agassiz). 1807–1873

Darwin, Charles Robert. 1809–1882

Bernard, Claude. 1813–1878

Pasteur, Louis. 1822–1895

Fabre, Jean Henri. 1823–1915

Huxley, Thomas Henry. 1825–1895

Koch, Robert. 1843–1910

Bailey, Liberty Hyde. 1858–1954

Frisch, Karl von. 1887–1982

Huxley, Sir Julian Sorell. 1887–1975

Sinnott, Edmund Ware. 1888–1968

Haldane, John Burdon Sanderson. 1892–1964

Dubos, René Jules. 1901–1982

12. Ecology and Environmental Science

Aristotle. 384–322 B.C.

Darwin, Charles Robert. 1809–1882

Muir, John. 1838–1914

Frisch, Karl von. 1887–1982

Krutch, Joseph Wood. 1893–1970

Lorenz, Konrad. 1903–

Tinbergen, Nikolaas. 1907–

Goodall, Jane Van Lawick. 1934–

13. Genetics

Mendel, Gregor Johann. 1822–1884

Morgan, Thomas Hunt. 1866–1945

Muller, Hermann Joseph. 1890–1967

McClintock, Barbara. 1902–

Watson, James Dewey. 1928–

14. Medicine and Health

15. Illness and Disease

16. Clinical Psychology and Psychiatry

James, William. 1842–1910

Freud, Sigmund. 1856–1939

Ellis, Havelock. 1859–1939

Adler, Alfred. 1870–1937

Brill, A(braham) A(rden). 1874–1948

Jung, C(arl) G(ustav). 1875–1961

Binswanger, Ludwig. 1881–1966

Rank, Otto. 1884–1937

Horney, Karen. 1885–1952

Reik, Theodor. 1888–1969

Straus, Erwin. 1891–1975

Sullivan, Harry Stack. 1892–1949

Menninger, Karl Augustus. 1893–1966

Freud, Anna. 1895–1982

Allport, Gordon W(illard). 1897–1967

Fromm, Erich. 1900–1980

Erickson, Milton H. 1901–1980

Lacan, Jacques. 1901–1981

Erikson, Erik H. 1902–

Rogers, Carl Ransom. 1902–1987

Bettelheim, Bruno. 1903–

Boss, Medard. 1903–

Frankl, Viktor. 1905–

Maslow, Abraham H(arold). 1908–1970

May, Rollo. 1909–

Berne, Eric Lennard. 1910–1970

Ellis, Albert. 1913–

Van Den Berg, J. H. 1914–
Wolpe, Joseph. 1915–
Schafer, Roy. 1922–
Foucault, Michel. 1926–1984
Laing, R(onald) D(avid). 1927–

17. Engineering and Technology

18. Energy

19. Science, Technology, and Society

Mumford, Lewis. 1895–
Bronowski, Jacob. 1908–1974
Ellul, Jacques. 1912–

20. Ethics of Science, Technology, and Medicine

Introduction

This fifth volume of the thirteenth edition of *The Reader's Adviser* represents a new venture. It takes what was a relatively short—and some would say representative—chapter in the twelfth edition and expands it to an entire volume. The new venture also aims at being more representative, as well as more comprehensive. This expansion reflects the veritable explosion of interest in, and new publications on, science, technology, and medicine over the past decade.

When people think of science, it is often to the medical sciences—with the phenomenal success of their practitioners in the twentieth century in discovering the causes and cures of various diseases—that their thoughts turn. But students of the sciences, probing more deeply than the average layperson and cognizant of the contributions of pharmaceutical research (new "wonder" drugs) or of biomedical engineering (amazing new diagnostic equipment), as well as of public health initiatives (a crusade to wipe out smallpox worldwide), spread their thought-net more widely. When experts on, for example, philosophy or sociology of science, technology, and medicine, or on matters of science policy, discuss the nature of the sciences in their whole broad array, they are more likely to take their prime example to be something like the pure thought experiments of an Albert Einstein. For these experts, turning the implications of relativity physics into an atomic bomb is primarily a matter of applied science and engineering. But lest that judgment be understood as disparaging to applied scientists and engineers, defenders of these fields of endeavor would hasten to point out that good ideas—including under that heading scientific theories—are of no use whatsoever unless someone can put them into effect, by engineering and good management, for the betterment of humankind.

Confusing? All of this certainly suggests that the phenomena of the world of science, technology, and medicine are complex indeed. They have been studied assiduously—and, of course, criticized from ethics and values perspectives—by experts of all kinds. What this volume of *The Reader's Adviser* attempts to do is to make that body of scholarship accessible to the general reader.

Increasingly, the complexity of the interactions among scientists, engineers, and technical personnel such as computer experts, managers, and the public in modern society suggests something of the massive impact of science, technology, and medicine on society today. No one can be considered an enlightened citizen in today's world who does not know something about science and technology. The slogan for modern society's new need is "technological literacy," and this volume also attempts to solve this problem.

A focus on the social consequence of science and technology suggests, finally, still another dimension. Technological literacy is important because citizens in a modern democracy are called on with increasing frequency to make value decisions about major technological developments. Nuclear power and nuclear weapons are just the most obvious examples—with the issue of toxic wastes not far behind. These issues must be addressed not only at the global level, but, often even more urgently, at the local level. They will be better addressed if ordinary citizens are aware of the best literature on science, technology, and medicine—including the literature of criticism and challenge.

The authors who have contributed to this volume, and who have made it the useful intellectual tool that it is, are all well-known experts in their respective fields. Some are science librarians, performing the same useful service for the reader that they do in their prestigious universities and institutions for students, faculty, and practitioners. Others are renowned experts in particular sciences. And still others are among the leading scholars in fields studying the interactions of science, technology, medicine, and society. All of the authors deserve a word of appreciation for the way they have brought their expertise to bear on the problem of making science, technology, and medicine accessible—even understandable—to the interested reader.

Paul T. Durbin

The Reader's Adviser

CHAPTER 1

General Science

Paul T. Durbin

All men by nature desire to know.

—ARISTOTLE, *Metaphysics*

The aim of science is, on the one hand, a comprehension, as complete as possible, of the connection between sense experiences in their totality, and on the other hand, the accomplishment of this aim by the use of a minimum of primary concepts and relations.... The story goes on until we have arrived at a system of the greatest conceivable unity.

—ALBERT EINSTEIN, *Out of My Later Years*

Human knowledge and human power meet in one; for where the cause is not known, the effect cannot be produced. Nature to be commanded must be obeyed.

—FRANCIS BACON, *Novum Organum*

For many people today, medical science, because it offers so much promise of improving the human condition, is the preeminent science. For similar reasons, most people in technologically advanced societies barely distinguish between the so-called "pure sciences" and the products of engineering and technology. All the sciences are expected to solve human problems, from the conquest of disease to the conquest of space. Even among scientists, there is frequently a reflection of this popular view, embodied in their hope that research will lead to useful, if not to profitable, products.

But there is another side to science, and here it may be viewed above all as an intellectual pursuit. EINSTEIN's dream of an ever more comprehensive unified theory is the ultimate expression of this ideal.

One can be an intellectual, a member of the intelligentsia, by writing books and articles of the right sort—even by moving in the right circles in such "centers of thought" as Paris or New York City. But, for the most part, today's intellectuals work on university campuses or in other campuslike research facilities. This chapter focuses on one particular type of professional intellectual or "mental laborer": namely, people who systematize their theories by giving them a mathematical form, and who then subject these theories or hypotheses to tests (preferably experimental) that will satisfy their peers. Since scientists and engineers and other members of the technical community may go on to use their tested theories for the making of useful products and processes, science may be characterized as a set of

useful problem-solving skills. However, it is above all a matter of intellectual discipline.

These are the good sides of technology and science, but the scientific and
technological enterprise has also come under attack in recent decades. Environmental problems are associated with massive technological developments. In addition, there is widespread criticism of weapons technology, of
nuclear power, of gene technology, of what the critics view as the overly
hasty introduction of computers, automation, robotization, and so on.

Among the scientific disciplines, a customary division exists between the
social or behavioral sciences and the natural sciences. For the former, the
reader should consult Volume 3 of *The Reader's Adviser;* Volume 5 looks
primarily at the natural sciences. The natural sciences range from abstract
cosmological theorizing, closely akin to mathematics, to almost purely descriptive natural history; from theoretical physics to the so-called "engineering sciences"; and from basic biochemistry and biology to clinical trials in
medicine.

All facets of science and technology, including criticisms, are treated in
this volume. But in this particular chapter the focus is on science in general,
on the scientific-technological enterprise as a whole. The books listed here
emphasize the nature of scientific processes and products; scientists and
technical workers in terms of how they go about their work; the institutions
in which scientists work; and the policies that govern such work. In addition, both because the physical sciences are often taken to be the paradigm
of scientific rigor and because physical science in general is not treated
anywhere else in this volume, there is a section devoted to physical science
in general.

In the final section of this chapter, the emphasis is on science popularizers—writers who, by the clarity of their presentations, manage to convey to a general audience what it is like to be a practicing scientist.

REFERENCE BOOKS AND COLLECTIONS

Ever since DENIS DIDEROT (see Vols. 2 and 4) and his collaborators began
publishing the French *Encyclopédie* in 1751, the first place most people look
for scientific information is in the great multivolume encyclopedias that
exist in most languages. The modern storehouses of information for the layperson on how the world works, these encyclopedias are regularly updated—
and it would not be inaccurate to say that to initiate a scientific discovery or
advance means to become a candidate for inclusion in general encyclopedias.
These reference sources are not cited here, though the reader who wants to
know the latest findings in science ought to keep up with the annual encyclopedia supplements. What are included here instead are specialized scientific
encyclopedias.

The esoteric world of professional science also generates scientific journal
articles with wild abandon—almost all written in specialized jargon, and
usually accompanied by technical graphics, charts, and tables. As William

Broad and Nicholas Wade note, "The preoccupation with publication has resulted in a veritable ocean of journals and papers. As the *British Medical Journal* noted, today there are at least 8,000 journals in medicine alone" (*Betrayers of the Truth: Fraud and Deceit in the Halls of Science*). What the reader needs in this case are guides to the literature, sourcebooks that show where to begin a search, and general introductions or orientations to the vast body of technical scientific literature.

American Book Publishing Record (ABPR), a monthly publication, lists all books appearing in *Weekly Record* by Dewey Decimal classification; an annual cumulative index is also issued. (See also Chapter 1, "Reference Books: General" in Volume 3.) Science titles, formerly published in *American Scientific Books*, are now incorporated in ABPR.

Abbott, David, ed. *The Biographical Dictionary of Scientists*. P. Bedrick Bks. 5 vols. 1984–1986 ea. $28.00. Volume 1 is a list of over 200 astronomers from antiquity to the present, Vol. 2 gives a similar list of biologists, Vol. 3 of chemists, Vol. 4 of physicists, and Vol. 5 of engineers and inventors. The biographies are relatively short, but the effect of seeing individuals comparatively and in historical perspective is quite good. Especially useful for laypersons interested in the history of science seen through biographies.

Aluri, Rao, and Judith Shiek Robinson. *A Guide to U.S. Government Scientific and Technical Resources*. Libraries Unlimited 1983 $23.50. A guide to the literature, stressing accessibility to technical workers; useful also for the general reader.

American Men and Women of Science: Physical and Biological Sciences. 1906. Bowker 8 vols. 16th ed. 1986 $595.00. An indispensable work for academic, public, and special libraries; contains nearly 130,000 biographies of U.S. and Canadian scientists, alphabetically arranged.

American Men and Women of Science Cumulative Index: Volumes 1–14. Bowker 1983 $125.00.

Asimov, Isaac. (See Asimov's main listing in this chapter.)

Biographical Encyclopedia of Scientists. Ed. by John Daintith and others, Facts on File 1981 lib. bdg. $80.00. Covers 2,000 important scientists from earliest times to the present. Includes a chronology of the history of science, together with a list of about 250 of the most important books and papers in the history of science.

Bunch, Bryan H., ed. *Facts on File Scientific Yearbook*. Facts on File 1986 $24.95. Though aimed at high school students, this encyclopedic survey of life sciences, earth and space sciences, physical sciences, and mathematics is also useful for a broader audience; good illustrations, glossary, and indexes.

Chambers Dictionary of Science and Technology. Merrimack 1983 o.p. Standard source, with about 5,000 entries, covering a broad range of scientific fields; very helpful for the layperson.

Chen, Ching-Chih. *Scientific and Technical Information Sources*. MIT 2d ed. 1986 text ed. $55.00. Although primarily a guide for science and technology librarians, a useful guide to reference sources for the layperson.

Concise Science Dictionary. Oxford 1984 $27.50. Over 7,000 entries in areas from astronomy to human biology, with clear and understandable explanations. Very practical volume.

Dempsey, Michael W., ed. *Illustrated Fact Book of Science*. Arco 1983 $9.95. Popularized treatment notable for the illustrations.

Dictionary of Scientific Biography. Ed. by Charles C. Gillispie, Scribner 8 vols. 1970–

80 text ed. $750.00. Published under the auspices of the American Council of Learned Societies, this work is modeled on the prestigious *Dictionary of National Biography*.

Directory of Scientific Directories: A World Guide to Scientific Directories Including Medicine, Agriculture, Engineering, Manufacturing, and Industrial Directories. Ed. by J. Burkett, Gale 3d ed. 1979 $95.00. Allows one to find the current directories of scientists at work in a wide variety of fields. Covers national as well as international societies. Includes indexes of compilers and titles.

Durbin, Paul T., ed. *A Guide to the Culture of Science, Technology, and Medicine.* Free Pr. 1980 $65.00 1984 pap. $19.95. Although primarily a survey of academic disciplines that study science from the outside, provides a helpful look at all aspects of science as seen by historians, philosophers, and social scientists. Comprehensive bibliographies.

Eastern European Academies of Sciences: A Directory. National Acad. Pr. 1963 o.p. Important sourcebook. In Eastern Europe, the science academies are at the heart of the scientific enterprise.

Elliott, Clark A. *Biographical Dictionary of American Science: The Seventeenth Through the Nineteenth Centuries.* Greenwood 1979 lib. bdg. $60.50. A retrospective companion to *American Men and Women of Science;* focus is on scientists before 1900.

General Science Index. Wilson 7 vols. 1979–85 sold to libraries on service basis; consult publisher for price. A cumulative subject index to English-language periodicals covering scientific fields from astronomy to zoology. The *Reader's Guide* for scientific periodical literature.

Grogan, Denis. *Science and Technology: An Introduction to the Literature.* Shoe String 4th ed. 1982 $27.50 pap. $18.50. A textbook, rather than a guide, introducing the student to the forms of literature in science and technology.

Guide to American Scientific and Technical Directories. B. Klein 2d ed. 1975 $25.00. A comprehensive guide to more than 2,500 directories in social science, physical science, and technology.

The Harper Encyclopedia of Science. Ed. by James Roy Newman, Harper 1963 4 vols. in 1 rev. ed. 1967 o.p. Clear and correct, but now somewhat out-of-date.

Harvey, Anthony P. *European Sources of Scientific and Technical Information.* Gale 6th ed. 1984 o.p. Rather technical index of sources of scientific information, from patent offices to scientific and technical organizations.

How It Works: The Illustrated Science and Invention Encyclopedia. Cavendish 3d ed. 1983 lib. bdg. $324.95. Claims to be the first complete home reference library for the layperson that concentrates on how scientific and technical gadgets work. Excellent illustrations and clear descriptions.

Index to Scientific Book Contents: 1985 Annual. Institute for Scientific Information 1985 $400.00. Companion to the classic sources for citation indexing: *Science Citation Index* (begun 1961) and *SCI Journal Citation Reports.* These indexes attempt to provide an objective database for comparing or ranking scientists, science journals, and science books.

Ireland, Norma O. *Index to Scientists of the World from Ancient to Modern Times: Biographies and Portraits.* [*Useful Reference Ser. of Lib. Bks.*] Faxon 1962 lib. bdg. $13.00. Sources of information on scientists; for example, it lists more than 50 books on Isaac Newton (without annotation).

Jones, Bessie Z., ed. *The Golden Age of Science: Thirty Portraits of the Giants of 19th-Century Science by Their Scientific Contemporaries.* Intro. by Everett Mendelsohn, Simon & Schuster 1967 o.p. Entries, arranged by the birth dates of the biographees, give an excellent idea of the development of the sciences during the nineteenth century.

Kerrod, Robin. *The Concise Dictionary of Science.* Arco 1985 $11.95. Over 3,000 entries concentrating on the physical and engineering sciences. Good illustrations and clear text aimed at the layperson.

Longman Illustrated Science Dictionary. Longman 1981 o.p. Relatively small number of entries (about 1,500), and fairly short definitions of terms, but useful for laypersons wanting such brief definitions of basic scientific terms.

McGraw-Hill Concise Encyclopedia of Science and Technology. Ed. by Sybil P. Parker, McGraw-Hill 1984 $95.00. Shorter, more accessible version of *the* scientific encyclopedia, *McGraw-Hill Dictionary of Scientific and Technical Terms* (see below).

McGraw-Hill Dictionary of Science and Engineering. McGraw-Hill 1984 $36.00. Special version of the *McGraw-Hill Dictionary of Scientific and Technical Terms* aimed at the general public; more than 35,000 entries.

McGraw-Hill Dictionary of Scientific and Technical Terms. Ed. by Sybil P. Parker, McGraw-Hill 3d ed. 1983 $70.00. Contains at least 100,000 terms currently in use.

McGraw-Hill Encyclopedia of Science and Technology. McGraw-Hill 15 vols. 5th ed. 1982 $1,100.00. Continues to be the basic reference source; for annual updates, see the *McGraw-Hill Yearbook of Science and Technology* (below).

McGraw-Hill Modern Scientists and Engineers. McGraw-Hill 3 vols. 1980 o.p. Contemporary scientific biographies and, in some cases, autobiographies. Excellent sourcebook on leading figures.

McGraw-Hill Yearbook of Science and Technology. McGraw-Hill 1984 $46.00. Annual updates for 1982 edition (see above).

Malinowsky, Harold Robert, and Jeanne M. Richardson. *Science and Engineering Literature: A Guide to Reference Sources.* Libraries Unlimited 3d ed. 1980 lib bdg. $33.00 pap. $21.00. A guide for the librarian but also useful for students; well over 1,000 entries arranged by subject.

OECD Science and Technology Indicators, No. 2. R and D Invention and Competitiveness. OECD 1986 pap. $18.00. Does for world science and technology what *Science Indicators: The 1985 Report* does for the United States. Some aspects are technical, but gives an excellent statistics-oriented comparison of the scientific and technological establishment in key countries.

Owen, Dolores B. *Abstracts and Indexes in Science and Technology: A Descriptive Guide.* Scarecrow 2d ed. 1984 $17.50. A description of 235 titles useful in a literature search in the whole range of areas in science and technology. More useful for advanced students, but helpful for the general reader as well.

Pelletier, Paul A. *Prominent Scientists: An Index to Collective Biographies.* Neal-Schuman 2d ed. 1985 lib. bdg. $34.95. An index to other biographical indexes.

Primack, Alice Lefler. *Finding Answers in Science and Technology.* Simon & Schuster 1984 $22.50. A guide, arranged by subject matter, aimed at students at all levels, as well as the general public.

Pure and Applied Science Books, 1876–1982. Bowker 6 vols. 1982 $325.00. Truly comprehensive sourcebook, invaluable for science libraries. General readers might also find items here that were missed elsewhere.

Science and Technology Illustrated: The World Around Us. Encyclopaedia Britannica 32 vols. 1984 $223.75. Very attractive set aimed primarily at high schools but useful more generally for laypersons.

Science and Technology Indicators: Basic Statistical Series—Recent Results: Selected S and T Indicators, 1979–1984. OECD 1984 available free from publisher.

Chiefly tables, but contains invaluable data for those who can read them and who need to have objective indicators of the status of science and technology throughout the world.

Science Indicators: The 1985 Report. U.S. Government Printing Office 7th ed. 1985 o.p. Seventh in a series of biennial reports. This volume provides the most complete and accurate picture available (including some technical material) of the U.S. science and engineering community although it is almost exclusively an "insider" view.

Science Universe Series: An Illustrated Encyclopedia. Arco 8 vols. 1984 o.p. Basic encyclopedia of science and technology for schools.

Scientific and Technical Books and Serials in Print 1987. Bowker 3 vols. 1986 $159.95. Over 114,000 titles of in-print U.S. books are listed.

Sheehy, Eugene P., ed. *Guide to Reference Books.* American Lib. Association 10th ed. 1986 text ed. $50.00. Includes a section on pure and applied sciences, compiled by Richard J. Dionne and others.

Spiegel-Rosing, Ina, and Derek de Solla Price, eds. *Science, Technology and Society: A Cross-Disciplinary Perspective.* Sage 1977 $37.50. A monumental sourcebook on every aspect of science and technology policy; articles by leading philosophers, historians, and social scientists, with extensive bibliographies.

Uvarov, E. B., and Alan Isaacs. *The Penguin Dictionary of Science.* Penguin 6th ed. 1986 pap. $7.95. The standard "pocket" sourcebook on science for students and nonscientists.

Van Nostrand's Scientific Encyclopedia. Ed. by Douglas M. Considine, Van Nostrand 6th ed. 1984 2 vol. ed. $145.00 1 vol. ed. $112.00. A very reliable and useful work for both the scientist and the layperson. Recently brought up-to-date.

Walford, A. J. *Walford's Guide to Reference Material: Science and Technology.* Oryx 4th ed. 1980 $74.50. Guide to scientific and technical reference books and bibliographies, with special reference to Great Britain.

Who's Who in Frontiers of Science and Technology. Marquis 2d ed. rev. 1985 $94.00. Fourteen thousand leading scientists and technologists currently working in the United States; of limited utility because it is not truly representative.

Who's Who in Science in Europe: A Biographical Guide in Science, Technology, Agriculture, and Medicine. International Pubns. 3 vols. 4th ed. 1984 $500.00. About 30,000 entries cover industrial as well as academic scientists and engineers and those associated with scientific societies. The biographies, usually supplied by the biographees, are generally clear but not always complete. There is an index by country and area of research.

Who's Who in Technology Today. Res. Pubns. CT 5 vols. 4th ed. 1984 set $425.00. Claims to be the most informative, up-to-date biographical survey of leaders in U.S. technology.

Wolff, Kathryn, and Jill Storey, eds. *AAAS Science Book List Supplement.* Amer. Association for the Advancement of Science 1978 $16.50. Supplement to *AAAS Science Book List* (1970). One of a series of volumes published by AAAS to help keep laypeople, and especially students, up-to-date on nontechnical science books.

World Guide to Scientific Associations and Learned Societies. Ed. by Barbara Verrel and Helmut Opitz, Saur 4th ed. 1984 lib. bdg. $112.00. More than 22,000 associations and societies in all fields of science, technology, and the arts throughout the world. A sample page lists groups from the International African Institute to the International Commission for Orders of Chivalry, in several languages. Includes a useful subject index.

Young, Margaret L., ed. *Scientific and Technical Organizations and Agencies Direc-*

tory. Gale 2 vols. 1985 $150.00. Guide to about 12,000 agencies involved in physical science, engineering, and technological research. Lists directors, main activities, and publications.

————. *Scientific and Technical Organizations and Agencies Directory Supplement.* Gale 1986 lib. bdg. $80.00.

Yule, John-David. *Concise Encyclopedia of the Sciences.* Facts on File 1981 $29.95; Van Nostrand 1982 pap. $19.95. Useful scientific encyclopedia and dictionary of approximately 5,500 key words, together with excellent illustrations that make the volume more useful for laypersons than some other scientific encyclopedias and dictionaries.

SCIENTIFIC WORK: ITS NATURE AND PRODUCTS

Scientists are often thought of as relentlessly serious people, ever calculating, writing reports, working in laboratories or observatories or out in the field night and day, endlessly checking their results for accuracy. Although this stereotype surely captures something of what it means to be a scientist, there are other characteristics as well. Scientists and engineers want people to recognize the excitement of science, the creativity—not unlike that of art— that scientific discovery and engineering design require. Further, science to- day almost always involves teamwork, which very often means bureaucracy, whether in industrial research-and-development settings, government labora- tories, hospitals, or university research centers. And finally, science and tech- nology today involve interactions with the public: with government regula- tors, with the courts, with the media, and with citizen activists who want to slow down or even stop particular scientific or technological ventures. Science and technology constitute one of the major social institutions in modern soci- eties, which means that they are also subject to all the problems any major social institution faces in the modern world. The books in this section reflect these multiple facets of the scientific enterprise today.

Augros, Robert M., and George Staeuciu, eds. *The New Story of Science: Mind and the Universe.* Regnery-Gateway 1984 pap. $6.95. Attempts to spell out the implica- tions for psychology, religion, and the arts of twentieth-century physics.

Bernstein, Jeremy. *Experiencing Science.* Basic Bks. 1978 $12.50. Studies of physi- cists (Kepler and Rabi), biologists (Lysenko, Rosalind Franklin, and Lewis Thomas), and "innovators" (Arthur C. Clarke and Gödel), by a leading science popularizer.

Bowen, Mary E., and J. A. Mazzeo, eds. *Writing about Science.* Oxford 1979 text ed. pap. $9.95. A selection of scientific papers and popularizations to illustrate the rhetoric of science. Includes both historical and contemporary authors.

Brannigan, Augustine. *The Social Basis of Scientific Discoveries.* Cambridge Univ. Pr. 1981 $29.95 pap. $13.95. Study of psychological and sociological factors in the discovery process in science.

Broad, William, and Nicholas Wade. *Betrayers of the Truth: Fraud and Deceit in the Halls of Science.* Simon & Schuster 1983 pap. $6.95. Important and controver- sial book on fraud as a danger in contemporary "big" science; majority of cases are in medical research.

Bronwell, Arthur B. *Science and Technology in the World of the Future.* Krieger 1970 $24.50. Interesting collection of thinkers, from R. Buckminster Fuller to H. Guy-ford Stever, who look at the future of science and engineering and their potential impact on the world.

Buzzati-Traverso, Adriano A. *The Scientific Enterprise, Today and Tomorrow.* Unipub 1978 $59.50. A wide-ranging survey of science and related social problems, especially concerned with what motivates scientists. Also includes state-of-the-art surveys of a great many scientific fields aimed at a nonscientist audience.

Collis, John S. *The Vision of Glory: The Extraordinary Nature of the Ordinary.* Braziller new ed. 1973 $8.95. One-person survey, and synthesis, of the totality of recent science.

Crowley, Michael, ed. *Women and Minorities in Science and Engineering.* National Science Foundation 1977 o.p. Important survey focusing on a serious problem, the lack of women and minorities in science.

Darius, Jon. *Beyond Vision: One Hundred Historic Scientific Photographs.* Oxford 1984 $29.95. A fascinating survey, covering 150 years, of the importance of photography to science; thesis is that some discoveries can only be made through photography. A hundred examples, some in brilliant color.

Dickinson, John P. *Science and Scientific Researchers in Modern Society.* Unipub 2d ed. 1986 text ed. pap. $16.50. A commissioned study, very readable and especially informative about ethical codes and institutional support for scientific workers throughout the world. Helpful bibliography.

Dyson, Freeman. *Disturbing the Universe: A Life in Science.* [*Sloan Foundation Bk.*] Harper 1979 o.p. Physicist's popularized reflections on the nature of science.

Elkana, Yehuda, and Robert K. Merton, eds. *Toward a Metric of Science: The Advent of Science Indicators.* [*Science, Culture, and Society Ser.*] Wiley 1978 o.p. Proceedings of a conference sponsored by the Center for Advanced Study in the Behavioral Sciences and the Social Science Research Council; leading historians and sociologists of science look at the science indicators movement.

Friedman, Sharon M., and others, eds. *Scientists and Journalists: Reporting Science As News.* Free Pr. 1985 $24.95. One key to good popularization of science is good science journalism.

Gardner, Martin. *Fads and Fallacies in the Name of Science.* Dover 2d ed. 1957 pap. $5.95. More on pseudoscience than on science itself, but reveals a great deal indirectly; by one of the leading popularizers of science.

———. *Science: Good, Bad and Bogus.* Avon 1983 pap. $3.95. Leading science popularizer takes aim at the difference between good science and its fraudulent imitators.

Gibbons, Michael, and Philip Gummett, eds. *Science, Technology and Society Today.* Longwood 1984 $22.50 text ed. pap. $7.95. Focus on a variety of problems in science and technology in recent decades, such as energy, genetic engineering, and nuclear weapons.

Gibson, William C., comp. *The Excitement and Fascination of Science, Volume 2.* Annual Reviews 1978 text ed. $12.00 pap. $10.00. Collected essays from the Annual Review series. Mostly autobiographical by leading scientists, intended primarily to convey what the title suggests. An earlier volume (1965) with the same title covers much the same territory.

Gornick, Vivian. *Women in Science: Portraits from a World in Transition.* Simon & Schuster 1983 $15.95 1985 pap. $10.95. Interviews with more than 100 women scientists in a variety of fields reveal why they became scientists and what contributes to success in their work.

Harding, Sandra. *The Science Question in Feminism.* Cornell Univ. Pr. 1986 text ed. $35.00 pap. $9.95. Somewhat difficult but important philosophical discussion of feminist critiques of the bias in science.

Harrington, John W. *Discovering Science.* Houghton Mifflin 1981 text ed. pap. $13.95
Harrison, James, ed. *Science Now.* Arco 1984 $21.95. Covers recent developments in technology, space, basic science, natural resources, and the environment; short articles; well illustrated.
———. *Scientists as Writers.* MIT 1965 pap. $6.95. Focuses on literary style in addresses and lectures of leading scientists.
Holton, Gerald, and Robert S. Morison, eds. *Limits of Scientific Inquiry.* Norton 1979 $19.95 pap. $5.95. Originally a *Daedalus* volume based on an American Academy of Arts and Sciences seminar; many of the papers reflect the popular ambiguity toward science around the time of the recombinant-DNA gene-splicing debate in the middle to late 1970s.
Johnston, Ron, and Philip Gummett, eds. *Directing Technology: Policies for Promotion and Control.* St. Martin's 1979 $10.95. Science and technology policy in a critical period, with special reference to England.
Judson, Horace F. *The Search for Solutions.* Intro. by Lewis Thomas, Henry Holt 1980 $16.95. An ambitious attempt by a leading science journalist to characterize what it means to be a scientist; based on years of interviewing working scientists. Striking illustrations.
Keller, Evelyn F. *Reflections on Gender and Science.* Yale Univ. Pr. 1985 $22.50 1986 pap. $8.95. Questions scientific neutrality in terms of gender and explores the possibilities of a gender-neutral science.
Lenihan, J., and J. B. Fleming. *Science in Action.* International Pubns. 1983 pap. $8.50. Popularizations of scientific and technological advances.
Lomask, Milton. *A Minor Miracle: An Informal History of the National Science Foundation.* U.S. Government Printing Office 1976 o.p. Important document on the premiere government agency funding nonmedical basic science in the United States.
Mansfield, Richard S., and Thomas V. Busse. *The Psychology of Creativity and Discovery: Scientists and Their Work.* Nelson-Hall 1981 $19.95. Studies of creative ability in science.
Martin, Paul D. *Science: It's Changing Your World.* Ed. by Donald J. Crump [*Bks. for World Explorers*] National Geographic Society 1985 $6.95 lib. bdg. $8.50. Popularization.
Mitroff, Ian I. *The Subjective Side of Science: A Philosophical Inquiry into the Psychology of the Apollo Moon Scientists.* Fwd. by C. W. Churchman, Intersystems Pubns. repr. of 1974 ed. 1983 pap. $14.95. The title is an excellent indication of the contents of this worthwhile study.
Panati, Charles. *Breakthroughs: Astonishing Advances in Your Lifetime in Medicine, Science, and Technology.* Berkley Pub. 1981 pap. $3.25; Houghton Mifflin 1980 $12.95. Popularized and undocumented predictions of where medicine, science, and technology will be taking us in the near future. Fascinating, but it might be well to warn that Chapter 1 is entitled, "Holistic Health Breakthroughs."
Passmore, John. *Science and Its Critics.* Rutgers Univ. Pr. 1978 $15.00. A prominent philosopher attacks irrational ideas of the antiscience, antitechnology movement of the 1960s and 1970s in a set of lectures.
Petroski, Henry. *To Engineer Is Human: The Role of Failure in Successful Design.* St. Martin's 1985 $16.95. Claims that such failures as the Tacoma Narrows Bridge in Washington or the Hyatt Regency skywalks in Kansas City lead to better designs—and thus that engineering is a truly human, trial-and-error endeavor rather than a science.
Platt, John R. *The Excitement of Science.* Greenwood repr. of 1962 ed. 1974 o.p. Fine book by a scientist on the excitement of "doing science"; mostly essays that had appeared previously, several in popular magazines.

Quammen, David. *Natural Acts: A Sidelong View of Science and Nature.* Schocken 1985 $16.95. Thirty-one essays from *Outside* magazine, intended to clarify nature by taking a careful but offbeat look at science.

Rheingold, Howard, and Howard Levine. *Talking Tech: A Conversational Guide to Science and Technology.* Morrow 1982 $13.50 1983 pap. $6.70. Breezy attempt to supply basic knowledge needed to carry on a decent conversation on the sorts of science-related topics that come up frequently in daily life in today's world.

Rich, Robert F. *The Knowledge Cycle.* [*Focus Eds.*] Sage 1981 $25.00 pap. $12.50. Good anthology on knowledge creation, diffusion, and utilization; contributors are mostly specialists in science policy.

Robinson, Timothy C. *The Future of Science: 1975 Nobel Conference.* Wiley 1977 o.p. Proceedings of one of a series of conferences involving Nobel Prize winners at Minnesota's Gustavus Adolphus College in honor of Alfred Nobel; the future of science was chosen as the topic because of critiques of science and technology.

Roe, Anne. *The Making of a Scientist.* Greenwood repr. of 1953 ed. 1974 lib. bdg. $22.50. A classic on the background and development of scientists.

Sciences of the Times: A New York Times Survey. Intro. by Walter Sullivan, Ayer 1978 lib. bdg. $35.00. *The New York Times* science editor provides a survey of excellent science reporting.

Scientific Thought: Some Underlying Concepts, Methods, and Procedures. Mouton 1972 $19.20; Unipub 1972 $24.25. Articles by a dozen eminent scientists and philosophers of science from throughout the world; interesting diversity of perspectives.

Siegel, Patricia Joan, and Kay Thomas Finley. *Women in the Scientific Search: An American Bio-Bibliography 1724–1979.* Scarecrow 1985 $32.50. Aims to fill a gap, focusing on the women who have, despite a masculine stereotype, contributed to the U.S. scientific enterprise from the very beginning.

Trefil, James. *A Scientist at the Seashore.* Scribner 1985 $16.95. Using seaside phenomena as a focus, this is an intriguing popularization of many scientific findings.

Velikhov, E. P., J. M. Gvishiani, and S. R. Mikulinsky, eds. *Science, Technology and the Future: Soviet Scientists' Analysis of the Problems of and Prospects for the Development of Science and Technology and Their Role in Society.* Pergamon 1980 $43.00. View of Soviet scientists on the problems and prospects of scientific and technological development; also considers science, technology, and society.

Weintraub, Pamela, ed. *The Omni Interviews.* Ticknor & Fields 1984 $17.95 pap. $9.95. Twenty interviews with leading scientists; focuses on science and society as much as on the nature of scientific work.

Weissmann, Gerald. *The Woods Hole Cantata: Essays on Science and Society.* Fwd. by Lewis Thomas, Dodd 1985 $14.95; Raven 1985 text ed. $16.50. Essays on social aspects of science, especially biology.

INSTITUTIONAL STRUCTURES AND POLICIES FOR SCIENCE AND TECHNOLOGY WORLDWIDE

Because the scientific-technological enterprise is a major social institution in the modern world, it requires management in the same way that large corporations and government agencies do. Especially since World War II, a large body of literature has developed about science and technology policy or the management of scientists, engineers, and other technical professionals. This section includes such works, as well as cross-cultural comparisons of scientific and technical institutions, studies of science and technology in particular countries, of the transfer of technology from developed to developing countries, and of the claims made about the role of science and technology in improving the quality of life throughout the world. (For criticisms of science and technology in terms of their negative impacts on other cultures see Chapters 19 and 20 in this volume.)

Ailes, Catherine P., and Francis W. Rushing. *The Science Race: Training and Utilization of Scientists and Engineers, U.S.A. and U.S.S.R.* Crane-Russak 1982 $28.50. Includes surveys of scientists and engineers in the two countries; good bibliography.

Anderson, Alun M. *Science and Technology in Japan.* Longman 1984 text ed. $75.00. Invaluable survey of the entire science and technology enterprise in present-day Japan.

Andrews, Frank M., ed. *Scientific Productivity: The Effectiveness of Research Groups in Six Countries.* Unipub 1979 pap. $29.95. Useful comparative sociology perspective, though somewhat technical.

Baker, F. W. G. *The International Council of Scientific Unions: A Brief Survey.* Ed. by W. J. Whelan, ICSU Pr. 1985 consult publisher for information. Pamphlet describing this important international science advocacy organization.

Blume, Stuart S. *Toward a Political Sociology of Science.* Free Pr. 1974 text ed. $18.95. A useful introduction to the study of science and government from the perspectives of both political science and sociology.

Boffey, Philip M. *The Brain Bank of America: An Inquiry into the Politics of Science.* McGraw-Hill 1975 o.p. Focuses on National Academy of Sciences and National Research Council; somewhat critical account of the scientific establishment in the United States by a leading science journalist.

Caldwell, Lynton K. *Science, Technology, and Public Policy: A Selected and Annotated Bibliography.* Indiana Univ. Pr. 3 vols. 1968–72 o.p. The best bibliographical sourcebook available for a number of years; needs updating now.

Clarke, Robin. *Science and Technology in World Development.* Oxford 1985 $19.95 pap. $7.95. Discussion by a leading British science writer of the potential for world development of scientific and technological advances.

Cochrane, Rexmond Canning. *The National Academy of Sciences: The First Hundred Years, 1863–1963.* National Academy of Sciences 1978 $11.50. History of the most prestigious scientific institution in the United States; good bibliography.

Dean, Genevieve C. *Science and Technology in the Development of Modern China: An Annotated Bibliography.* Mansell 1974 $32.00. Important sourcebook on technological development in China since 1949 (with appendixes on earlier periods). Annotations are helpful and coverage is quite comprehensive.

Dickson, David. *The New Politics of Science.* Pantheon 1984 o.p. British "critical science" views on the nature of the scientific enterprise today. Dickson is the European correspondent for *Science* magazine.

———. *The Politics of Alternative Technology.* Universe 1975 $8.00 1977 pap. $4.50. Alternatives to "big" science and technology from the British "critical science" perspective.

Dupree, A. Hunter. *Science in the Federal Government: A History of Policies and Activities.* Ed. by I. Bernard Cohen, Ayer repr. of 1957 ed. 1980 lib. bdg. $39.00; Johns Hopkins Univ. Pr. repr. of 1957 ed. 1986 text ed. pap. $14.95. The classic source on the history of government involvement in science in the United States up to 1940.

Eisemon, Thomas. *The Science Profession in the Third World: Studies from India and Kenya*. Ed. by Philip G. Altbach [*Special Studies in Comparative Education*] Praeger 1982 $31.95.

European Research Centres: A Directory of Organizations in Science, Technology, Agriculture, and Medicine. Gale 2 vols. 5th ed. 1982 $350.00. A listing of research centers in 30 European countries; gives address, director, and scope.

Golden, William T. *Science Advice to the President*. Ed. by A. George Schillinger [*Pergamon Policy Studies*] 1980 $60.50. Important collection of papers on science advisers to the U.S. president after World War II.

Goodlad, J. S. *Science for Non-Scientists*. Oxford 1973 $14.50. Good source on the importance of scientific societies at various stages in the history of science.

Greenberg, Daniel S. *Politics of Pure Science*. New Amer. Lib. 1967 o.p. An iconoclastic look at the science establishment in the United States by a science journalist; written at the beginning of the period of antiscience and antitechnology sentiments among the general public.

Haberer, Joseph. *Science and Technology Policy: Perspectives and Developments*. [*Policy Studies Organization Bk. Ser.*] Univ. Pr. of Amer. repr. of 1977 ed. 1985 lib. bdg. $23.50. An early collection of papers on U.S. science and technology policy; helpful as an introduction to the field.

Huddle, Franklin P. *Science Policy: A Working Glossary*. U.S. Government Printing Office 1973 o.p. Prepared for the Subcommittee on Science, Research, and Development of the Committee on Science and Astronautics, U.S. House of Representatives, 93d Congress, first session. Though intended primarily for science policy students, a basic source for anyone interested in this field.

Kuehn, Thomas J., and Alan L. Porter. *Science, Technology and National Policy*. Cornell Univ. Pr. 1981 $45.00 pap. $14.95. Just about the best anthology on science and technology policy, with special reference to the U.S. government at all levels.

Lambright, W. Henry. *Governing Science and Technology*. [*Public Administration and Democracy Ser.*] Oxford 1976 text ed. pap. $5.95. An excellent analysis of the agencies in the U.S. government that support or control scientific and technological activity.

Layton, Edwin T., and others, eds. *The Dynamics of Science and Technology*. [*Sociology of the Sciences Ser.*] Kluwer Academic 1978 lib. bdg. $36.50 text ed. pap. $18.50. Proceedings of an important international symposium—involving historians, philosophers, and social scientists—on the topic of external control of science.

Libraries, Information Centers, and Databases in Science and Technology: A World Guide. Saur 1985 $100.00. Over 11,000 listings, from 139 countries, of science and technology information sources with the possibility of electronic linkups. Chiefly intended for other technical organizations, but also constitutes an interesting general reference source.

Long, T. Dixon, and Christopher Wright, eds. *Science Policies of Industrial Nations*. Praeger 1975 o.p. Case studies of science and technology policy in Great Britain, France, Japan, Russia, Sweden, and the United States.

Lubrano, Linda L., and Susan G. Solomon, eds. *The Social Context of Soviet Science*. [*Special Studies on the Soviet Union and Eastern Europe*] Westview Pr. 1980 o.p. Good collection of papers updating information on Russian science and technology.

Marcson, Simon. *The Scientist in Industry*. Princeton Univ. Pr. 1960 o.p. A pioneering sociological study of scientists in industrial research and development; stresses conflicts between the norms of "pure" and applied science.

Morgan, Robert P. *Science and Technology for International Development: An Assessment of U.S. Policies and Programs.* Westview Pr. 1985 pap. $16.95. Results of a conference; somewhat technical.

National Academy of Sciences, Committee on Science, Engineering and Policy. *Frontiers in Science and Technology: A Selected Outlook.* Freeman 1983 text ed. $32.95 pap. $16.95. Third in a series of five-year outlooks focusing on areas ripe for development; intended principally for science and technology policy experts.

Nayar, Baldev Raj. *India's Quest for Technological Independence.* Humanities Pr. 2 vols. 1983 text ed. $66.50. A leading Indian expert covers the whole field—from the ideal of technological independence through the Nehru years to the present, including specific technologies—in a masterly survey. Extensive but unannotated bibliographies.

Nelkin, Dorothy. *Controversy: Politics of Technical Decisions.* [*Focus Eds.*] Sage 2d ed. 1984 $29.00 pap. $14.95. Case studies of scientific and technological controversies with social and political ramifications; excellent introduction by Nelkin, a leading expert on the politics of science; very useful textbook.

Noble, David F. *America by Design: Science, Technology, and the Rise of Corporate Capitalism.* Oxford 1979 pap. $9.95. Marxist historian's account of the influence of scientific and technical managers on life in the United States in the twentieth century. Excellent use of public documents to indict capitalist managers with their own words. One of the most interesting books available on life in scientific-technological organizations and on the way those institutions have affected other institutions in American society.

Pecujlic, Miroslav, and others, eds. *Science and Technology in the Transformation of the World.* St. Martin's 1984 $19.95. Proceedings of an international symposium at Belgrade, Yugoslavia, in 1979.

Peer Review in the National Science Foundation: Phase One of a Study. National Academy of Sciences 1978 $11.75. Critical survey of the most important feature of the grants process in the most important nonmedical science funding agency in the United States.

Peer Review in the National Science Foundation: Phase Two of a Study. National Academy of Sciences 1981 $12.25. Completion of study (see entry above); though critical, the study concludes that peer review is probably the best system there is.

Price, Derek J. de Solla. *Little Science, Big Science . . . and Beyond.* Columbia Univ. Pr. 1986 $35.00 pap. $14.95. Essay on the structure of science by a historian especially interested in the measurement of scientific progress by way of counting scientific papers; Price strongly influenced the movement toward science citation indexes. Reprint of the 1963 classic includes a number of Price's later essays.

Price, Don K. *The Scientific Estate.* Harvard Univ. Pr. (Belknap Pr.) 1965 $22.50. Pioneering study of science and government in the United States. Still useful after two decades.

Primack, Joel, and Frank von Hippel. *Advice and Dissent: Scientists in the Public Arena.* New Amer. Lib. 1976 o.p. Classic book on the social responsibilities of scientists; the authors have been active in the American Association for the Advancement of Science's Committee on Scientific Freedom and Responsibility.

Ravetz, J. R. *Scientific Knowledge and Its Social Problems.* Oxford 1971 $42.00 pap. $9.95. Probably the best book available on the social dimensions of contemporary science; by a leader in the British "critical science" group.

Rescher, Nicholas. *Scientific Progress: A Philosophical Essay on the Economics of Research in Natural Science.* Univ. of Pittsburgh Pr. 1977 $26.95. Somewhat technical philosophical discussion of scientific progress; claims that, because of increasing technological dependency, it cannot continue indefinitely without extraordinary social commitment.

Research Centers Directory. Gale 10th ed. 1985 $340.00. A guide to over 8,000 university and nonprofit research organizations; includes nonscience as well as scientific research centers, arranged by field.

Rosenberg, Nathan. *Technology and American Economic Growth.* M. E. Sharpe 1972 pap. $9.95. The leading economic historian of American science and technology sums up his studies on that topic in a book that is accessible to all levels of readers.

Rotblat, Joseph, ed. *Scientists, the Arms Race and Disarmament: A UNESCO-Pugwash Symposium.* Unipub 1982 $24.95. Collection edited by one of the signers of the Russell-Einstein Manifesto that led to an ongoing series of conferences on science and world affairs at Pugwash, Nova Scotia, beginning in 1957.

Salomon, Jean-Jacques. *Science and Politics: An Essay on the Scientific Situation in the Modern World.* MIT 1973 $32.50. An account of today's "big" science by the leading European science-watcher.

Sardar, Ziauddin, ed. *Science and Technology in the Middle East: A Guide to Issues, Organizations and Institutions.* [*Longman Guide to World Science and Technology Ser.*] Gale 1982 $85.00. Covers science and technology policy for the area based on firsthand accounts. Some tables and lists of research institutions in countries from Afghanistan to Yemen.

Schafer, Wolf, ed. *Finalization in Science.* Kluwer Academic 1983 lib. bdg. $59.00. Translation of the proceedings of a conference on the topic: Can science be effectively directed toward external goals?

Shils, Edward, ed. *Criteria for Scientific Development: Public Policy and National Goals.* MIT 1968 pap. $6.95. An anthology of classic papers on science policy edited by a long-time defender of the role of science in modern culture.

Sklair, Leslie. *Organized Knowledge.* Beekman 1973 o.p. An account of contemporary science by a critic of antiscience critics.

Swannack-Nunn, Susan. *Directory of Scientific Research Institutes in the People's Republic of China.* National Council for U.S.-China Trade 1977–78 o.p. Introductions to and addresses of scientific research institutes in China; universities and social science research organizations are not included.

Technology on Trial: Public Participation in Decision-Making Related to Science and Technology. OECD 1979 $7.00. Perspectives on policy for science and technology at the height of antiscience, antitechnology criticisms; useful establishment view emanating from a leading science/technology advocacy international organization.

Teich, Albert H., and Ray Thornton. *Science, Technology, and the Issues of the Eighties: Policy Outlook.* [*Science, Technology, and Public Policy*] Westview Pr. 1982 lib. bdg. $28.00 text ed. pap. $13.50. A paper prepared for the National Science Foundation as a support document for the second five-year outlook report. Based on reports presented at a workshop sponsored by the American Association for the Advancement of Science in 1980.

True, Frederick W., and I. Bernard Cohen, eds. *The Semi-Centennial Anniversary of the National Academy of Sciences: And a History of the First Half-Century of the National Academy of Sciences. 1863–1913.* [*Three Centuries of Science in Amer. Ser.*] Ayer 2 vols. repr. of 1913 ed. 1980 lib. bdg. $49.00. See Cochrane (above) for a 100-year history.

Weinberg, Alvin M. *Reflections on Big Science.* MIT 1967 o.p. Reflections on post-

World War II science by the director of the Oak Ridge (Tennessee) National Laboratories; Weinberg is one of the leading defenders of science against antiscience critics.

Wilson, John T. *Academic Science, Higher Education, and the Federal Government: Programs and Policies, 1950 to 1983.* Univ. of Chicago Pr. 1983 lib. bdg. $10.00 pap. $3.50. Originally a seminar lecture on higher education and the government in the United States; bibliography.

World Dictionary of Research, Projects, Studies and Courses in Science and Technology Policy. UNESCO 1981 $21.75. Arranged by country, the directory lists science policy units throughout the world; also lists periodicals.

PHYSICAL SCIENCE

This section lists a mix of books detailing the nature of the physical sciences: popularizations, some textbooks, popularized introductions to physics for the nonscience student—even a book to relieve "science anxiety." The common note is that the books listed here give the general reader a picture of what physical science is all about, in terms of both process and product.

An Approach to Physical Science: Physical Science for Nonscience Students. Wiley 1969 o.p. An effort supported by the National Science Foundation to make physics and chemistry more accessible to nonscience undergraduate students.

Calder, Nigel. *The Key to the Universe: A Report on the New Physics.* Penguin 1978 pap. $8.95. A book related to a television program, "The Key to the Universe," first broadcast on BBC in 1977. Intended to capture some of the basic concepts in physical science and some of the excitement of the scientists responsible for discovering them. Calder is well known for his popularizations of science.

Cotterill, Rodney. *The Cambridge Guide to the Material World.* Cambridge Univ. Pr. 1985 $34.50. Covering a great many aspects of physical science—from atomic theory to biochemistry—from the perspective of materials science, this book amounts to a small encyclopedia useful for the general reader; good illustrations, notes, and index.

Daintith, John. *A Dictionary of Physical Sciences.* Rowman 1983 pap. $9.95. Handy definitions of most of the terms a student of physical science would need.

Feinberg, Gerald. *Solid Clues: Quantum Physics, Molecular Biology and the Future of Science.* Simon & Schuster 1985 $17.95 1986 pap. $8.95. An attempt by a physicist and philosopher of science to sum up the state of the art in key fields in science, and then to predict where science is most likely to take us in the future. Level is accessible to general readers.

Holton, Gerald. *Introduction to Concepts and Theories in Physical Science.* Rev. by Stephen G. Brush, Princeton Univ. Pr. 1985 text ed. pap. $19.95. Textbook in physical science for the nonscience major; strong historical orientation; grew out of efforts at Harvard to implement the 1945 Report on General Education.

Kemble, Edwin C. *Physical Science, Its Structure and Development: From Geometric Astronomy to the Mechanical Theory of Heat.* MIT 1966 o.p. Excellent survey using the historical approach pioneered by Kemble, Gerald Holton, and others at Harvard University around 1950. Aimed especially at nonscientists.

Klein, Margrete S., and F. James Rutherford, eds. *Science Education in Global Perspective.* Westview Pr. 1985 pap. $22.00. An examination of public school instruction in science and mathematics in Japan, the People's Republic of China, East and West Germany, and Russia. Partly intended to show, by contrast, how badly the United States does. Fairly technical and focuses on teaching methods rather than content.

Kone, Eugene H., and Helene J. Jordan, eds. *The Greatest Adventure: Basic Research That Shapes Our Lives.* Intro. by Isaac Asimov, Rockefeller Univ. Pr. 1974 $9.80. National Science Foundation-sponsored volume intended to let leading scientists from a variety of fields spell out how basic research has affected the lives of ordinary citizens.

Krauskopf, Konrad B., and Arthur Beiser. *The Physical Universe.* McGraw-Hill 5th ed. 1986 $35.95. Long a popular textbook in physical science for college level courses.

Larkin, Sonya, and Louise Bernbaum, eds. *The Penguin Book of the Physical World.* Penguin 1976 o.p. Excellent survey of the whole range of physical sciences aimed particularly at young people.

Lewis, John L., ed. *Teaching School Physics.* [*Source Bks. on Curricula and Methods*] Unipub 1972 pap. $11.50. A UNESCO survey of effective methods for teaching the physical sciences, primarily at the high school level. Includes a summary of organized efforts to improve physical science teaching throughout the world, e.g., Harvard Project Physics and the Nuffield Project in Britain.

Mallow, Jeffry V., and Joseph Howland, eds. *Science Anxiety: Fear of Science and How to Overcome It.* H & H Pub. 1986 $9.95

Pine, Jerome. *Contemporary Physics: An Introduction for the Nonscientist.* McGraw-Hill 1972 o.p. A college textbook in physics for the nonscience student.

Ripley, J. A., Jr. *The Elements and Structure of the Physical Sciences.* Wiley 1964 o.p. An early, fairly successful textbook in physical science for the liberal arts major.

Robertson, Barry C. *Modern Physics for Applied Science.* Wiley 1981 o.p. Though aimed at students who have already had physics and want to look at applications areas, this is an excellent introduction to modern physics that requires only a moderate level of mathematics.

Rothman, Milton. *The Laws of Physics.* Basic Books 1963 o.p. Interesting approach to the popularization of physics using the concept of laws of nature as the organizing device.

Shapiro, Gilbert. *Physics Without Math: A Descriptive Introduction.* Prentice-Hall 1979 text ed. $28.95. What the title says; scope includes applications such as radio and nuclear energy.

Trefil, James. *The Unexpected Vista: A Physicist's View of Nature.* Ed. by B. Lippman, Macmillan repr. 1985 pap. $7.95; Scribner 1983 $14.95. Popularization.

Vergara, William C. *Science in Everyday Life.* Harper 1980 $14.45. An attempt to clarify scientific concepts by showing how the various branches of science touch everyday lives.

Young, Louise B. *The Unfinished Universe.* Simon & Schuster 1986 $17.95. An effort to find meaning in the universe based on a survey of findings in the whole range of sciences.

ASIMOV, ISAAC. 1920–

Asimov has produced, alone or with others, more than 300 books. The best known are almost evenly divided between science fiction—he is generally regarded as one of the ten best science fiction writers ever (some even rank him first)—and science popularizer. Born in Russia, Asimov was brought to the United States at the age of three. He received a Ph.D. (1948) from Columbia

University in biochemistry and taught that subject—when he was not busy writing books or lecturing—at Boston University School of Medicine until 1958. Since then, he has been a full-time writer and lecturer, though still officially on the Boston University staff. Asimov's life can be followed in two autobiographical accounts (listed below). With so many books to his credit, only a handful can be listed here, and his science fiction works are not listed. A list of his popularizations of astronomy is included in Chapter 7 of this volume.

BOOKS BY ASIMOV

Asimov's Biographical Encyclopedia of Science and Technology. 1964. Doubleday 2d rev. ed. 1982 $29.95. A compilation of more than 1,500 vignettes of scientists from early Greek times to the present day. The entries are arranged chronologically according to the birth date of each major scientist, followed by biographies of other scientists who were closely related to his or her work. The index is organized by biography number to help give an idea of the interrelation of the sciences.

A Short History of Biology. 1964. Greenwood repr. of 1964 ed. 1980 lib. bdg. $32.50. Asimov at his best in bringing the history of biology, to the present, to a wide audience.

A Short History of Chemistry. 1964. Greenwood repr. of 1964 ed. 1979 lib. bdg. $29.50. Similar to his history of biology; not quite as successful.

Asimov's New Guide to Science. 1972. Basic Bks. rev. ed. 1984 $29.95. Probably the single best popularization of the sciences, across a broad range, that is available at the present time.

How Did We Find Out about Atoms? Walker 1978 $8.95. One of a series of about 30 informative books aimed primarily at schoolchildren.

In Memory Yet Green: The Autobiography of Isaac Asimov, 1920–1954. Avon 1980 pap. $7.95; Doubleday 1979 $19.95

In Joy Still Felt: Autobiography of Isaac Asimov, 1954–1978. Avon 1981 pap. $9.95

BOOK ABOUT ASIMOV

Miller, Marjorie M. *Isaac Asimov: A Checklist of Works Published in the United States.* [*Serif Ser.*] Kent State Univ. Pr. 1972 $11.00

BRONOWSKI, JACOB. 1908–1974

[SEE Chapter 19 in this volume.]

BUSH, VANNEVAR. 1890–1974

Though Bush had a distinguished career as an engineer, working on the development of the computer among other things, he is best known as an administrator of government science. It is not too much to say that Bush was more responsible than anyone else for the shape of governmental support for science after World War II—including in particular the National Science Foundation, the premiere funding agency for science in the United States. Bush was professor and then dean of engineering at MIT, president of the Carnegie Institution for Scientific Research, and, most important, director of the U.S. Office of Scientific Research and Development during World War II. His office gave him direct access to Presidents Roosevelt and Truman, and that access is what allowed him so singlehandedly to shape postwar science. His other writings were not numerous but were singularly influential in conveying to government figures and to the world at large his vision of science as *the* progressive influence in the modern world.

BOOKS BY BUSH

Science the Endless Frontier: A Report to the President. 1945. Ed. by I. Bernard Cohen [*Three Centuries of Science in Amer. Ser.*] Ayer repr. of 1945 ed. 1980 lib. bdg. $16.00. Reprint of Bush's most famous manifesto.
Pieces of the Action. Morrow 1970 o.p. An autobiographical account of his career.
Endless Horizons. [*History, Philosophy and Sociology of Science Ser.*] Ayer repr. of 1974 ed. 1975 $19.00. A collection of papers that includes *Science the Endless Frontier.*

GOULD, STEPHEN JAY. 1941–

Born in New York City, Gould received his Ph.D. in paleontology from Columbia University in 1967 and has been a professor at Harvard since that time. An outspoken advocate of the scientific outlook, Gould has been a vigorous defender of evolution against its "creation science" opponents in popular magazines such as *Discover.* A graceful writer, Gould has produced a remarkable series of books that admirably display the excitement of science for the layperson.

BOOKS BY GOULD

Ever Since Darwin: Reflections in Natural History. Norton 1977 $14.95 1979 pap. $4.95. Broad-ranging essays on themes related to Darwinian evolution; appeared originally in *Natural History.*
Ontogeny and Phylogeny. Harvard Univ. Pr. (Belknap Pr.) 1977 $25.00 1985 pap. $8.95. Somewhat technical essay on a theme—phylogeny recapitulates ontogeny—that most think discredited but Gould shows interesting parallels.
(ed.). *The History of Paleontology.* Ayer 20 vols. repr. 1980 lib. bdg. set $2,077.00. Important collection of major works.
The Panda's Thumb: More Reflections in Natural History. Norton 1980 $15.95 1982 pap. $4.95. Another set of essays from *Natural History,* focusing on the proof of evolution.
The Mismeasure of Man. Norton 1981 $17.95 1983 pap. $5.95. Somewhat difficult, though witty, attack on biological determinism and IQ testing.
Hen's Teeth and Horse's Toes: Further Reflections in Natural History. Norton 1983 $15.50 1984 pap. $5.95. Third collection from *Natural History,* compiled on the hundredth anniversary of Darwin's death.
The Flamingo's Smile: Reflections in Natural History. Norton 1985 $17.95 1987 pap. $8.95 Most recent collection from *Natural History;* includes an essay on Gould's own research on Bahamian snails.
An Urchin in the Storm: Essays about Books and Ideas. Norton 1987 $18.95. "Though the pieces . . . are technically book reviews, Mr. Gould tends to use the subject at hand as a jumping-off point for more general discussions, and as he notes in his introduction, the essays consequently share 'a particular view of nature and human life; the perspective of an evolutionist committed to understanding the curious pathways of history as irreducible, but rationally accessible' " (*N.Y. Times*).

HOLTON, GERALD. 1922–

Born in Berlin, Holton received his Ph.D. in physics from Harvard in 1946. Almost immediately, he launched into what would become a major part of his career, taking charge of the program to teach physical science to liberal arts majors at Harvard. Harvard Project Physics, as it was called, then became the model for an ambitious program to teach physics in a similar historical fashion in colleges and high schools throughout the United States. Later, he continued this same line of work in a different fashion, establishing a program for the public understanding of science that eventually grew into a journal, *Science, Technology, and Human Values* (published by Wiley). For many years, Holton was a coeditor of *Daedalus*, the journal of the American Academy of Arts and Sciences. More recently, he has also gained recognition as a biographer of Albert Einstein, and has worked tirelessly to demonstrate that science requires as much creative imagination as the arts and humanities.

BOOKS BY HOLTON

Thematic Origins of Scientific Thought: Kepler to Einstein. Harvard Univ. Pr. 1973 $17.50 pap. $9.95. Case studies illustrating Holton's "thematic" interpretation of the history of science.

(and William Blanpied, eds.). *Science and Its Public: The Changing Relationship.* [*Boston Studies in the Philosophy of Science*] Kluwer Academic 1975 lib. bdg. $37.00 pap. $17.50. Originally a *Daedalus* volume; important collection of essays on the new limits some people want to place on science.

The Scientific Imagination. Cambridge Univ. Pr. 1978 $47.50 pap. $15.95. New formulation of thesis about thematic origins; science requires imagination every bit as much as art.

(and Yehuda Elkana, eds.). *Albert Einstein, Historical and Cultural Perspectives: The Centennial Symposium in Jerusalem.* Princeton Univ. Pr. 1982 $42.00 1984 pap. $12.50. The major symposium on the centennial of Einstein's birth; proceedings volume includes provocative essays.

Introduction to Concepts and Theories in Physical Science. Rev. by Stephen G. Brush, Princeton Univ. Pr. 1985 text ed. pap. $19.95. One of the earliest, and probably still the best, introductions to physical science for nonscience students, in an updated version.

MEDAWAR, SIR PETER BRIAN. 1915–

A Nobel Prize winner in physiology and medicine (with Macfarlane Burnet in 1960), Medawar's scientific work has focused mainly on tissue compatibility and the immune system. Born in Rio de Janeiro, Brazil, but a British citizen, Medawar graduated from Oxford University in 1939 with a degree in zoology. He taught at the University of Birmingham, England, and University College, London, before becoming the director of the National Institute for Medical Research in Great Britain. This was followed by a position as head of the Division of Surgical Sciences at the Clinical Research Centre, simultaneously with a position as professor of experimental medicine at the Royal Institution. For all his scholarship and administrative experience, however, Medawar is almost equally well known for his popularizations of science.

BOOKS BY MEDAWAR

The Uniqueness of the Individual. Dover repr. of 1957 ed. 1981 pap. $5.95; Peter
    Smith 2d rev. ed. $13.50
The Art of the Soluble. Methuen 1967 o.p. Essays and book reviews reprinted from
    New Statesman; Mind; Nature; and elsewhere.
Advice to a Young Scientist. Harper 1979 $13.45 1981 pap. $5.95. Admirably captures
    the essence of Medawar's feel for the meaning of scientific work.
Induction and Intuition in Scientific Thought. [*Memoirs Ser.*] Amer. Philosophical
    Soc. 1980 $5.00. Attempts to explain how scientists' minds work in their scien-
    tific activities.
(and J. H. Shelley, eds.). *Structure in Science and Art: Proceedings at Taunus, May
    1979.* [*International Congress Ser.*] Elsevier 1980 $42.25. Important essay by
    Medawar on D'Arcy Thompson linked with other interesting essays on structure
    in art and science.
*Pluto's Republic: Incorporating "The Art of the Soluble" and "Induction and Intuition
    in Scientific Thought."* Oxford 1982 $27.50 pap. $9.95. Essays reprinted not only
    from earlier books but also from *Encounter* and *The Times Literary Supplement;*
    remarkable range of science-related topics.
(and J. S. Medawar). *Aristotle to Zoos: A Philosophical Dictionary of Biology.* Harvard
    Univ. Pr. 1983 $18.50 1985 pap. $7.95. More a collection of essays (of varying
    depth) for browsing than a reference work; about 170 biological topics.
The Limits of Science. Harper 1984 $11.45. Three essays on the nature and limits of
    science; mildly critical, but mostly favorable.
Memoir of a Thinking Radish: An Autobiography. Oxford 1986 $17.95

SAGAN, CARL. 1934–

[SEE Chapter 7 in this volume.]

SNOW, SIR CHARLES PERCY. 1905–1980

[SEE Volume 1.]

THOMAS, LEWIS. 1913–

A Harvard M.D. with specialization in internal medicine and pathology,
Thomas was born in Flushing, N.Y. He was a professor at several medical
schools, ending up at Yale where he also became dean of the School of
Medicine. Most recently he has been chancellor at the Memorial Sloan-
Kettering Cancer Center in New York City and a professor of medicine at
the Cornell Medical School. His literate and erudite books have gained him
a wide audience, making him one of the best-known advocates of science in
the United States in recent decades. (See also Volume 1.)

BOOKS BY THOMAS

The Lives of a Cell: Notes of a Biology Watcher. Bantam 1975 pap. $3.95; Penguin
    1978 pap. $3.95; Viking 1974 $10.95. Essays that appeared originally in *The New
    England Journal of Medicine* (1971–73).
The Medusa and The Snail: More Notes of a Biology Watcher. Viking 1979 o.p. More
    essays from the *New England Journal of Medicine* (1974–79).
Late Night Thoughts on Listening to Mahler's Ninth Symphony. Bantam 1984 pap.
    $5.95; Viking 1983 $12.95. Broad-ranging essays, mostly from *Discover* magazine.
The Youngest Science: Notes of a Medicine Watcher. Bantam 1984 pap. $6.95; Viking

1983 $14.75. Partly autobiographical survey of twentieth-century medicine; includes some earlier essays.

ZIMAN, JOHN M. 1925–

British physicist and philosopher of science, educated in New Zealand and at Balliol College, Oxford, Ziman has taught at several British universities, including Oxford, Cambridge, and the Imperial College of Science and Technology, London. Active in and chair of the Council for Science and Society, he is best known for a series of extremely lucid books on the nature of science. These have given him a reputation as the best British interpreter of science for college-level students, comparable to Gerald Holton in the United States.

BOOKS BY ZIMAN

Public Knowledge: An Essay Concerning the Social Dimension of Science. Cambridge Univ. Pr. 1968 o.p. Focus on the education of scientists, scientific communication, and science institutions.

Reliable Knowledge. Cambridge Univ. Pr. 1979 $29.95. Defense of science against critics, but with much sympathy for them.

The Force of Knowledge: The Scientific Dimension of Society. Cambridge Univ. Pr. 1976 $49.50 pap. $19.95. Based on a lecture series for undergraduate science students at Bristol University; excellent picture of science, technology, and society.

Teaching and Learning about Science and Society. Cambridge Univ. Pr. 1980 $27.95. What a science, technology, and society course ought to contain.

Puzzles, Problems and Enigmas: Occasional Pieces on the Human Aspects of Science. Cambridge Univ. Pr. 1981 $29.95. Book reviews, radio and public talks, and essays on a wide variety of topics, unified only in being about science.

An Introduction to Science Studies: The Philosophical and Social Aspects of Science and Technology. Cambridge Univ. Pr. 1985 $22.95. A remarkable tour de force; *the* one book to read to cover everything in this chapter and much in this whole volume.

CHAPTER 2

History of Science, Technology, and Medicine

Robert A. Hatch

We can add to our knowledge, but we cannot subtract from it.
—ARTHUR KOESTLER, *The Sleepwalkers*

The history of science is science itself.
—GOETHE, *Mineralogy and Geology*

Change is a constant and conspicuous fact of human experience. Long ago, in an effort to provide meaning and order to the past and to nature, human beings created history and science. In time, these too underwent change, only to become themselves additional objects of inquiry. So, having embraced the fact that all knowledge changes, we continue to add to our knowledge without subtracting from it.

The history of science, technology, and medicine adds to our knowledge by charting changes in the way we perceive, observe, and think about nature, and how we express, defend, and apply scientific ideas. Our subject, however, is in constant flux. From its first beginnings, science has built and built again on shifting conceptions—of space, time, and causality; of life, mind, and society; of man, nature, and God. Just as technology and medicine have modified our planet in shrinking space and time and diminishing disease and hunger, science has transformed our mental world, our sense of reality, truth, and value. In the end, science offers only knowledge; it provides provisional maps and charts, not a promised land. Like HERACLITUS's (see Vol. 4) flame or DARWIN's species, GOETHE's (see Vol. 2) *science* is a verb.

As a young discipline, the history of science, technology, and medicine is itself changing and growing. At the dawn of the century it enjoyed a childhood of heroes and dramatic discoveries, a youth of idealism and industry fostered by positive knowledge and the prospect of continued material and moral progress. Since the abrupt end to the last world war, however, the discipline has come of age in light of doubt, disillusionment, and a sharpened sense of identity. Venturing from its ancestral home, the carefully nurtured stepchild of the general practitioner and retired scientist has matured into a multidisciplinary specialty employing the instruments and skills of the sciences, social sciences, and humanities. Having been adopted in college curricula worldwide, it now claims over 120 regularly published journals, 200 learned societies, and an equal but growing number of programs for graduate study and advanced research.

Scholarly research and publication in the history of science, technology, and medicine cut across all categories of space, time, and topic, and opinions continue to vary on the nature of change, whether it is evolutionary or revolutionary, continuous or abrupt, independent of or integral to social and cultural developments. While the present chapter is devoted exclusively to historical aspects of the field, related materials can be found in chapters focusing on specific disciplines. See also especially Chapter 3, "Philosophy of Science and Pseudoscience"; Chapter 19, "Science, Technology, and Society"; and Chapter 20, "Ethics of Science, Technology, and Medicine." To assist the reader further, a substantial section on bibliography is included below. Finally, the present chapter follows the essential structure and format employed by *Isis*, the official international journal of the History of Science Society. Arrangement is topical by discipline and chronological period.

GENERAL WORKS

The history of science, technology, and medicine is woven into the very fabric of Western civilization. Given the complexity of this rich tapestry, historians have tended to specialize by selecting specific strands to trace through individual disciplines, time periods, and countries. The following general works, by contrast, have been selected for their breadth and scope. Drawing together several subjects and surveying large spans of time and space, the volumes listed below provide patterns and perspectives on the larger tableau.

Bernal, J. D. *Science in History.* MIT 4 vols. 1971 pap. $37.50. Standard survey of the social context of science by a prominent Marxist historian.

Boorstin, Daniel J. *The Discoverers: A History of Man's Search to Know His World and Himself.* Random 1985 pap. $9.95. Eminently readable and wide-ranging interpretation of the role of science in Western civilization by a Pulitzer Prize–winning historian.

Bronowski, Jacob. *The Ascent of Man.* Little, Brown 1974 $34.00 pap. $19.45. Brilliant "personal view" of the history of science in the broader context of Western culture; handsomely illustrated.

Burke, James. *The Day the Universe Changed.* Little, Brown 1986 $27.50. Provocative and witty interpretation of science for readers in an age of uncertainty; well illustrated.

Butterfield, Herbert. *The Origins of Modern Science.* Free Pr. rev. ed. 1965 text ed. pap. $10.95. Classic study emphasizing the central role of science in Western civilization and the discontinuity associated with the scientific revolution.

Cohen, I. Bernard. *Album of Science: From Leonardo to Lavoisier, 1450–1800.* Scribner 1980 $63.00. Handsome pictorial overview of science from the Renaissance to the Enlightenment.

———. *Revolution in Science.* Harvard Univ. Pr. (Belknap Pr.) 1985 $25.00 1987 pap. $9.95. Ambitious study of the concept of revolution arguing for incremental transformations in thought rather than discontinuous paradigm shifts.

Dampier, William C. *A History of Science.* Cambridge Univ. Pr. 1965 pap. $23.95.
   Useful but somewhat dated single-volume survey.
Daumas, Maurice, ed. *A History of Technology and Invention: Progress through the
   Ages.* Crown 3 vols. 1978 ea. $30.00; State Mutual Bk. 3 vols. 1980 ea. $60.00.
   Vol. 1, *The Origins of Technological Civilization;* Vol. 2, *The First Stages of Mecha-
   nization;* Vol. 3, *The Expansion of Mechanization, 1725–1860.* Comprehensive
   multiauthored survey treating all aspects of technology; well illustrated.
Derry, Thomas K., and Trevor I. Williams. *A Short History of Technology from the
   Earliest Times to A.D. 1900.* Oxford 1970 pap. $13.95. Perhaps the best single-
   volume survey of technology.
Dijksterhuis, E. J. *The Mechanization of the World Picture.* Trans. by C. Dikshoorn,
   Oxford 1961 o.p. Examines the development of physical science from antiquity
   to Newton, arguing that the mechanization of nature led to the mathemati-
   zation of science.
Gillispie, Charles C. *The Edge of Objectivity: An Essay in the History of Scientific
   Ideas.* Princeton Univ. Pr. 1960 pap. $14.95. Classic study of modern science,
   written with wit and insight, arguing that science offers a world embraced by
   measurement rather than penetrated by sympathy.
Hall, A. R., and Maria Boas Hall. *A Brief History of Science.* Signet 1964 o.p. Com-
   pact survey written by two founders of the discipline.
Holton, Gerald. *Thematic Origins of Scientific Thought: Kepler to Einstein.* Harvard
   Univ. Pr. 1973 $17.50 pap. $9.95. Traces themes in the physical sciences empha-
   sizing the role of creativity.
Jaffe, Bernard. *Men of Science in America: The Story of American Science Told
   Through the Lives and Achievements of Twenty Outstanding Men from Earliest
   Colonial Times to the Present Day.* Ed. by Bernard I. Cohen [*Three Centuries of
   Science in Amer. Ser.*] Ayer repr. of 1958 ed. rev. ed. 1980 lib. bdg. $62.00.
   Standard introductory survey from colonial times to the early twentieth cen-
   tury; somewhat dated.
Mason, Stephen F. *A History of the Sciences* (original title: *Main Currents of Scientific
   Thought*). Macmillan rev. ed. 1962 pap. $8.95. Enduring single-volume survey of
   the sciences, from antiquity to the twentieth century.
Nasr, S. H. *Science and Civilization in Islam.* Harvard Univ. Pr. 1968 o.p. Standard
   single-volume introductory to Arabic science.
Needham, Joseph. *The Grand Titration: Science and Society in East and West.* Univ.
   of Toronto Pr. 1979 o.p. Excellent collection of essays introducing the history of science in China and providing a comparative approach to its nature and
   development.
———. *Science and Civilisation in China.* Cambridge Univ. Pr. 5 vols. 1954–70. Vol.
   1, *Introductory Orientations* $65.00; Vol. 2, *History of Scientific Thought* $110.00;
   Vol. 3, *Mathematics and the Sciences of the Heavens and the Earth* $160.00; Vol.
   4, *Physics and Physical Technology* in 3 parts: Pt. 1, *Physics* $90.00 Pt. 2, *Mechani-
   cal Engineering* $125.00 Pt. 3, *Engineering and Nautics* $160.00; Vol. 5, *Spagyrical
   Discovery and Invention* $135.00. Monumental study of Chinese science and tech-
   nology by the acknowledged authority.
Ronan, Colin, and Joseph Needham, eds. *The Shorter Science and Civilisation in
   China.* Cambridge Univ. Pr. 1985 $49.50 1986 pap. $19.95. Useful abridgment of
   the magisterial parent edition.
Singer, Charles. *A Short History of Scientific Ideas to 1900.* Oxford 1959 pap. $9.95.
   Useful but dated survey by a pioneer in the field.
Singer, Charles, and others, eds. *A History of Technology.* Oxford 8 vols. 1955–84
   vols. 1–7 ea. $98.00 vol. 8 $45.00. Monumental study ranging over the breadth

and depth of the technical arts, technics, and technology from antiquity to the late nineteenth century.

Taton, René, ed. *A General History of the Sciences.* Thames & Hudson 4 vols. 1963–66 o.p. Useful multiauthored survey translated from the original French.

Thorndike, Lynn. *A History of Magic and Experimental Science.* Columbia Univ. Pr. 8 vols. 1923–58 ea. $70.00. Monumental study, rich in detail on minor figures and primary sources, placing the occult sciences and pseudosciences in historical context.

Whewell, W. *History of the Inductive Sciences from the Earliest to the Present Times.* Frank Cass 3 vols. repr. of 1837 ed. 1967 o.p. Classic and still largely dependable study.

Whitehead, Alfred North. *Science and the Modern World.* Free Pr. 1967 pap. $9.95; Irvington repr. of 1925 ed. 1987 text ed. $29.50 pap. $8.95. Brilliant philosophical perspective on the role of science in Western thought and culture.

Wightman, William. *The Growth of Scientific Ideas.* Greenwood repr. of 1966 ed. 1974 lib. bdg. $37.50; Telegraph Bks. repr. of 1953 ed. lib. bdg. $85.00. Survey of the development of science from antiquity to the twentieth century.

BIBLIOGRAPHY AND BIBLIOGRAPHICAL TOOLS

George Sarton, one of the pioneers in the history of science, once suggested that bibliographic extravagance is a sin rather than a virtue. Risking the appearance of sin, but avoiding hubris and self-contradiction, the following bibliographies are provided to assist readers with specialized interests in the history of science, technology, and medicine.

Black, George W., Jr. *American Science and Technology: A Bicentennial Bibliography.* Southern Illinois Univ. Pr. 1979 $15.95. Lists over 1,000 articles published during the American bicentennial that make reference to the history of science and technology.

Brush, Stephen G., and Lanfranco Belloni. *The History of Modern Physics: An International Bibliography.* [*History of Science and Technology Ser.*] Garland 1983 lib. bdg. $42.00. Provides annotated bibliography for scholarship focusing on the period since the discovery of X-rays in 1895.

Brush, Stephen G., and others. *The History of Meteorology and Geophysics: An Annotated Bibliography.* [*History of Science and Technology Ser.*] Garland 1985 lib. bdg. $70.00. Contains extensively annotated entries on all aspects of the history of geophysics and meteorology.

Dauben, Joseph W. *The History of Mathematics from Antiquity to the Present: A Selective Bibliography.* [*Reference Lib. of the Humanities*] Garland 1985 lib. bdg. $80.00. Provides over 2,000 carefully annotated entries compiled with the assistance of "49 scholars on five continents."

DeVorkin, David H. *The History of Modern Astronomy and Astrophysics: A Selected, Annotated Bibliography.* Garland 1985 lib. bdg. $79.00. Contains some 1,500 annotated entries for the period beginning with the invention of the telescope to the mid-twentieth century.

Dunbar, Gary S. *The History of Modern Geography: An Annotated Bibliography of Selected Works.* [*Reference Lib. of the Humanities*] Garland 1985 lib. bdg. $53.50. Emphasizing the period since 1750, the bibliography contains over 1,700 annotated entries reflecting scholarship in most major Western languages.

Durbin, Paul T., ed. *A Guide to the Culture of Science, Technology, and Medicine.* Free

Pr. 1980 $65.00 1984 pap. $19.95. Includes excellent introductory essays and useful bibliographies for all major specialties within the history of science, technology, and medicine.

Erlen, Jonathon. *The History of the Health Care Sciences and Health Care, 1700–1980: A Selective Annotated Bibliography.* [*Reference Lib. of the Humanities*] Garland 1984 lib. bdg. $100.00. Contains over 5,000 annotated entries reflecting historical scholarship in a variety of health-care sciences and specialties.

Gascoigne, Robert M. *A Historical Catalogue of Scientific Periodicals, 1665–1900.* Garland 1985 lib. bdg. $27.00. Lists some 900 scientific periodicals published between 1665 and 1900; arrangement is chronological by subject.

Hahn, Roger. *Bibliography of Quantitative Studies on Science and Its History.* Univ. of California Hist. Science Tech. 1980 pap. $5.00. Brief but useful bibliography on the role of quantitative methods in the history of science.

Home, R. W. (with the assistance of Mark J. Gittins). *The History of Classical Physics: A Selected, Annotated Bibliography.* [*History of Science and Technology Ser.*] Garland 1984 lib. bdg. $53.00. Focusing on the historical period from c.1700 to 1900, the volume provides annotated entries for some 1,200 books and articles.

Isis Cumulative Bibliography: A Bibliography of the History of Science Formed from Isis Critical Bibliographies 1–90, 1913–1965, ed. by Magda Whitrow, Mansell 5 vols. 1971–82 $212.00. Vol. 1, Pt. 1, *Personalities A–J*; Vol. 2, Pt. 1, *Personalities K–Z* Pt. 2, *Institutions*, 1975; Vol. 3, *Subjects*; Vol. 4, *Civilizations and Periods: Prehistory to Middle Ages*; Vol. 5, *Civilizations and Periods: Fifteenth to Nineteenth Centuries.*

Isis Cumulative Bibliography 1966–1975: A Bibliography of the History of Science Formed from Isis Critical Bibliographies 91–100 Indexing Literature Published from 1965 to 1974, Vol. 2, Pt. 1, *Personalities and Institutions,* ed. by John Neu, Mansell 1985 $125.00. The combined *Isis* cumulative bibliography volumes provide the most authoritative and comprehensive index of articles and books in the history of science and related fields; volumes are variously arranged by person, institution, and subject.

Knight, David. *Natural Science Books in English, 1600–1900.* David & Charles 1972 o.p. Presents essays on the history of science as reflected in prominent publications in science, 1600–1900.

Kren, Claudia. *Medieval Science and Technology: A Selected, Annotated Bibliography.* Ed. by Ellen Wells [*History of Science and Technology Ser.*] Garland 1985 lib. bdg. $53.00. Provides over 1,400 annotated entries emphasizing literature and scholarship on the medieval Latin West.

May, K. O. *Bibliography and Research Manual of the History of Mathematics.* Univ. of Toronto Pr. 1973 o.p. Provides a classified bibliography on the history of mathematics for materials published prior to 1965.

Molloy, Peter M. *The History of Metal Mining and Metallurgy: An Annotated Bibliography.* Garland 1986 lib. bdg. $55.00. Treats the history of metal mining, assaying, smelting, and related subjects, emphasizing scholarship from the late nineteenth through the twentieth centuries.

Multhauf, Robert P. *The History of Chemical Technology: An Annotated Bibliography.* Garland 1983 lib. bdg. $61.00. Provides over 1,500 annotated entries on all aspects of chemical technology.

Oleson, John Peter. *Bronze Age, Greek and Roman Technology: A Select, Annotated Bibliography.* Garland 1986 lib. bdg. $71.00. Contains over 2,000 annotated entries reflecting scholarship on all aspects of early technologies and technics.

Overmier, Judith. *The History of Biology: An Annotated Bibliography.* Garland 1986 lib. bdg. $35.00

Porter, Roy S. *The Earth Sciences: An Annotated Bibliography.* Garland 1983 lib. bdg.

$33.00. Provides over 800 annotated entries reflecting recent scholarship on the history of the earth sciences; thematically organized.

Rothenberg, Marc. *The History of Science and Technology in the United States: A Critical and Selective Bibliography.* Garland 1982 lib. bdg. $48.00. Contains 832 annotated entries surveying scholarship on the history of American science and technology, but excluding medicine.

Stapleton, Darwin H. (with the assistance of Roger L. Shumaker). *The History of Civil Engineering since 1600: An Annotated Bibliography.* Garland 1986 lib. bdg. $35.00. Lists secondary literature for the period since 1600, containing some 1,200 entries on various specialties within civil engineering.

Watson, Robert I., ed. *The History of Psychology and the Behavioral Sciences: A Bibliographic Guide.* Springer Pub. 1978 o.p. Contains annotated entries on historical resources, accounts, research, and historiographic fields in the history of psychology.

Wellcome Institute for the History of Medicine, London. *Subject Catalogue of the History of Medicine and Related Sciences.* Kraus Intl. 18 vols. 1979–80 $2,400.00. Useful multivolume guide to secondary sources in medicine and the life sciences.

BIOGRAPHICAL COLLECTIONS

In the final analysis, history is composed of individuals, their ideas, activities, and intersections in the natural and social worlds. The following segment provides information on biographical sources in the history of science, technology, and medicine. Individual volumes are usually arranged alphabetically, others are chronological.

American Men and Women of Science: Physical and Biological Sciences. Ed. by Jaques Cattell Press. Bowker 16th ed. 1986 8-vol. set $595.00. Complete biographical entries for 127,000 scientists in the physical and biological sciences in 10 major disciplines and 161 subdisciplines.

Asimov, Isaac. *Asimov's Biographical Encyclopedia of Science and Technology.* Doubleday 2d ed. rev. 1982 $29.95. Biographical guide arranged by birth date, antiquity to the twentieth century.

Concise Dictionary of Scientific Biography. Scribner 1981 $70.00. Standard quick reference; alphabetically arranged entries for 5,000 figures from the multivolume parent set.

Daintith, John, and others. *A Biographical Encyclopedia of Scientists.* Facts on File 2 vols. 1981 lib. bdg. $80.00. Contains some 2,000 entries on scientists living and dead, emphasizing the modern and contemporary periods.

Debus, A. G., ed. *World Who's Who in Science: A Biographical Dictionary of Notable Scientists from Antiquity to the Present.* Western Pub. 1968 o.p. Comprehensive dictionary containing brief entries for some 30,000 scientists, most from the twentieth century.

Elliott, Clark A. *Biographical Dictionary of American Science: The Seventeenth through the Nineteenth Centuries.* Greenwood 1979 lib. bdg. $60.50. Provides detailed entries on some 600 scientists omitted from the multivolume classic *American Men and Women of Science* (see above), which lists only living scientists.

Gillispie, Charles C., ed. *Dictionary of Scientific Biography.* Scribner 16 vols. 1970–80 text ed. $750.00. Monumental reference source for the history of science. Alphabetically arranged with excellent biographical entries and bibliographies for some 5,000 nonliving scientists throughout the world.

Herzenberg, Caroline L. *Women Scientists from Antiquity to the Present: An Index.* Locust Hill Pr. 1986 lib. bdg. $30.00. "Index to approximately 2,500 women who have contributed to the development of the sciences, medicine, technology, engineering, and some social sciences, the reader has a fair chance of obtaining the needed data. Featuring worldwide coverage from ancient times to the present, *Women Scientists* can be used to locate an individual by name or by scientific discipline" (*Booklist*).

Ogilvie, Marilyn B. *Women in Science: Antiquity through Nineteenth Century.* MIT 1986 $25.00. Contains brief entries, an introductory essay, and a useful bibliography.

Osen, Lynn M. *Women in Mathematics.* MIT 1974 pap. $5.95. Popular biographical approach from Hypatia to Emmy Noether.

Pelletier, Paul A., ed. *Prominent Scientists: An Index to Collective Biographies.* Neal-Schuman 2d ed. 1985 lib. bdg. $34.95. Provides an alphabetical index of some 12,000 names with coded keys to books published in English between 1960 and 1983.

Who Was Who in American History: Science and Technology. Marquis 1976 o.p. Contains perhaps 10,000 brief sketches on Americans prominent in all fields of science, invention, and technology.

Williams, Trevor I., ed. *A Biographical Dictionary of Scientists.* Wiley 3d ed. 1982 $31.95. Provides excellent entries for some 1,000 scientists, emphasizing the period since 1800, with brief lists of suggested readings.

PHILOSOPHY OF SCIENCE AND METHODS OF SCIENCE

It has been said that history without dates is philosophy. In fact, as in all areas of knowledge, the history and philosophy of science are cut from the same cloth. The following selections represent classic studies or standard introductions bearing directly on the history or historiography of science.

Blackwell, Richard J., ed. *A Bibliography of the Philosophy of Science, 1945–1981.* Greenwood 1983 lib. bdg. $85.00. Lists over 7,000 works published in the philosophy of science between 1945 and 1981; entries are topically and alphabetically arranged.

Duhem, Pierre. *To Save the Phenomena: An Essay on the Idea of Physical Theory from Plato to Galileo.* [*Midway Repr. Ser.*] Univ. of Chicago Pr. 1985 text ed. pap. $10.00. Brief but brilliant study by the pioneering historian of science applying his instrumentalist philosophy of science in examining the historical rift between descriptive astronomy and physical cosmology.

Feyerabend, Paul. *Against Method.* Schocken repr. of 1975 ed. 1978 pap. $7.95. The radical philosopher's first and perhaps boldest statement that "anything goes," that science is neither developed nor defended on rational grounds.

Gutting, Gary, ed. *Paradigms and Revolutions: Appraisals and Applications of Thomas Kuhn's Philosophy of Science.* Univ. of Notre Dame Pr. 1980 text ed. $18.95 pap. $9.95. Excellent selection of essays evaluating Kuhn's concepts and contributions.

Hanson, Norwood R. *Patterns of Discovery: An Enquiry into the Conceptual Foundations of Science.* Cambridge Univ. Pr. 1958 $49.50 pap. $13.95. Classic study emphasizing the role of perception in the act of observation, suggesting that perception is directed and restricted by theoretical expectation.

Kuhn, Thomas S. *The Essential Tension: Selected Studies in Scientific Tradition and*

Change. Univ. of Chicago Pr. 1979 lib. bdg. $25.00 pap. $13.00. Selection of articles, essays, and lectures written between 1959 and 1974 on historiographic and metahistorical themes.

————. *The Structure of Scientific Revolutions.* [*Foundations of the Unity of Science Ser.*] Univ. of Chicago Pr. 2d ed. 1970 $17.50 pap. $6.95. Brilliant and highly influential study of scientific and historical change, arguing that science normally develops cumulatively but periodically undergoes discontinuous paradigm shifts, that is, revolution.

Lakatos, Imre, and A. E. Musgrave, eds. *Criticism and the Growth of Knowledge.* Intro. by Thomas S. Kuhn, Cambridge Univ. Pr. 1970 $52.50 pap. $13.95. Traces the shift in themes and issues in the history and philosophy of science from Karl Popper to Thomas Kuhn.

Popper, Karl R. *Conjectures and Refutations: The Growth of Scientific Knowledge.* Harper 1968 pap. $8.95. Classic study providing an excellent introduction to Popper's philosophy of science.

Toulmin, Stephen. *Foresight and Understanding: An Enquiry into the Aims of Science.* Fwd. by Jacques Barzun, Greenwood repr. of 1961 ed. 1982 lib. bdg. $22.50. Classic introduction to Toulmin's approach, which argues for the historical underpinnings of a philosophy of science and the evolution of thought through conceptual natural selection.

HISTORIES OF THE SPECIAL SCIENCES

In an effort to aid and assist the reader, the following subsections are divided into scientific disciplines or subject areas. Readers will find historical surveys and introductions to subject areas that cut across two or more traditional time periods in the following sciences: mathematics, physical sciences, earth sciences, biological sciences, social sciences, medicine, and technology.

Following these subject divisions of individual sciences, a final section provides chronologically defined studies. These works are arranged by widely recognized periodizations, suggesting that the categories are commonly accepted by scholars and should be easily recognized and understood by lay people.

Mathematics

Ball, W. W. *A History of the Study of Mathematics.* Scholarly 1889 o.p. Classic survey tracing developments from medieval times to the early twentieth century.

Boyer, Carl B. *A History of Mathematics.* Wiley 1968 $42.95. Standard survey for students, covering primitive times to the twentieth century; includes problem exercises for students.

————. *The History of the Calculus and Its Conceptual Development.* Dover 1959 o.p. Standard and most comprehensive introduction to the history of the calculus.

Cajori, Florian. *History of Mathematical Notations.* Open Court 2 vols. 1951–52 o.p. Vol. 1, *Notations in Elementary Mathematics*; Vol. 2, *Notations Mainly in Higher Mathematics*. Still the best historical introduction to mathematical notations and the controversies surrounding their acceptance.

David, Florence N. *Games, Gods and Gambling: The Origins and History of Probability*

and Statistical Ideas from the Earliest Times to the Newtonian Era. Hafner 1962
pap. $14.25. Excellent introduction to the origins and early history of probabil-
ity and statistical thought.

Edwards, C. H., Jr. *The Historical Development of the Calculus.* Springer-Verlag rev.
ed. 1979 $33.00. Introduction for students; includes problem exercises.

Grattan-Guinness, Ivor. *The Development of the Foundation of Mathematical Analysis
from Euler to Riemann.* MIT o.p. Deals with the contributions of Euler, d'Alembert,
Lagrange, Cauchy, and others; excellent bibliography.

———, ed. *From the Calculus to Set Theory 1630–1910: An Introductory History.*
Biblio Dist. 1980 text ed. pap. $12.00. Multiauthored volume consisting of six
chapters on theories of the infinite.

Hacking, Ian. *The Emergence of Probability: A Philosophical Study of Early Ideas
about Probability, Induction, and Statistical Inference.* Cambridge Univ. Pr. 1975
$37.50 1984 pap. $12.95. Examines the philosophical context of early probability, emphasizing the seventeenth century.

Kline, Morris. *Mathematical Thought from Ancient to Modern Times.* Oxford 1972
$69.95. Perhaps the most comprehensive single-volume introduction from antiq-
uity to the early decades of the twentieth century.

———. *Mathematics and the Search for Knowledge.* Oxford 1985 $19.95 1986 pap.
$7.95. Thematic survey underscoring the importance of mathematics and the
mathematical imagination to scientific innovation.

———. *Mathematics in Western Culture.* Oxford 1953 $19.95 1964 pap. $12.95. Lively
and well-written introduction for the nonspecialist, arguing that mathematics is
central to the development of Western culture.

Scott, J. F. *History of Mathematics: From Antiquity to the Beginning of the Nineteenth
Century.* Fwd. by H. W. Turnbull, Barnes & Noble 2d ed. repr. of 1960 ed. 1975
$28.50. Solid survey particularly strong on English mathematicians.

Smith, David Eugene, and Jekuthiel Ginsberg. *A History of Mathematics in America
Before Nineteen Hundred.* Ed. by I. Bernard Cohen [*Three Centuries of Science in
Amer. Ser.*] Ayer repr. of 1934 ed. 1980 lib. bdg. $19.00. Introduction to the key
figures and concepts of mathematics.

Struik, Dirk J., ed. *Source Book in Mathematics: Twelve Hundred to Eighteen Hun-
dred.* [*Source Bks. in the History of the Sciences Ser.*] Harvard Univ. Pr. 1969 o.p.
Useful primary selections in algebra, geometry, and forms of analysis from
Oresme to Monge.

Todhunter, Isaac. *History of the Calculus of Variations in the Nineteenth Century.*
Chelsea Pub. 1961 $18.50. Dated but still useful study.

Van Heijenoort, Jean, ed. *From Frege to Godel: A Source Book in Mathematical Logic,
1879–1931.* [*Source Bks. in the History of the Sciences Ser.*] Harvard Univ. Pr.
1967 $35.00 pap. $15.00. Provides useful primary readings for the crucial 50-
year period at the turn of the century.

Physical Sciences: Astronomy, Physics, Chemistry

Berry, Arthur. *A Short History of Astronomy: From Earliest Times Through the 19th
Century.* Dover repr. of 1898 ed. 1961 pap. $8.95. Excellent single-volume survey
through the nineteenth century.

Cantor, G. N., and M. J. S. Hodge, eds. *Conceptions of Ether: Studies in the History of
Ether Theories, 1740–1900.* Cambridge Univ. Pr. 1981 $67.50. Multiauthored
volume including ten original essays and a useful bibliography.

Dick, Steven J. *Plurality of Worlds: The Extraterrestrial Life Debate from Democritus to*

Kant. Cambridge Univ. Pr. 1982 $39.50 pap. $13.95. Provocative survey of the philosophic, religious, and scientific issues in the history of this debate.

Dreyer, John L. *A History of Astronomy from Thales to Kepler.* Dover repr. of 1906 ed. 1953 pap. $8.50; Peter Smith 1953 $15.50. Still the most authoritative one-volume survey of planetary theory for the period up to c.1650.

Durham, Frank, and Robert D. Purrington. *Frame of the Universe.* Columbia Univ. Pr. 1983 $28.00 1985 pap. $12.50. Useful introduction by practicing astronomer-cosmologists.

Grant, Robert. *History of Physical Astronomy.* Intro. by H. Woolf, Johnson Repr. repr. of 1852 ed. 1966 $35.00. Detailed factual survey emphasizing post-Newtonian mechanics.

Heilbron, J. L. *Electricity in the Seventeenth and Eighteenth Centuries: A Study of Early Modern Physics.* Univ. of California Pr. 1979 $60.00. A model study of the development of physical sciences.

Herrmann, Dieter B. *The History of Astronomy from Herschel to Hertzsprung.* Trans. and ed. by Kevin Krisciunas, Cambridge Univ. Pr. 1984 $24.95. Examines classical astronomy, the development of astrophysics, and technological developments since the discovery of electromagnetic energy, c.1780–1930.

Hoskin, M. A., ed. *General History of Astronomy.* Cambridge Univ. Pr. 4 vols. consult publisher for information. Authoritative multiauthored study.

Ihde, Aaron J. *The Development of Modern Chemistry.* Dover repr. of 1964 ed. 1983 pap. $15.95. Classic encyclopedic survey with an excellent bibliographic essay.

King, Henry C. *The History of the Telescope.* Dover repr. of 1955 ed. 1979 pap. $9.95; Peter Smith 1979 $19.00. Still the best single-volume study of telescopes, observational instruments, and techniques from antiquity to the twentieth century.

King, Henry C., and John R. Millburn. *Geared to the Stars: The Evolution of Planetariums, Orreries and Astronomical Clocks.* Univ. of Toronto Pr. 1978 $80.00. Comprehensive and handsomely illustrated study of clocks and clock-driven instruments; excellent bibliography.

Leicester, Henry M., and Herbert S. Klickstein, eds. *A Source Book in Chemistry 1400–1900.* Harvard Univ. Pr. 1952 o.p. Useful primary selections from V. Biringuccio to Marie Curie.

Multhauf, Robert P. *The Origins of Chemistry.* Watson Pub. Intl. 1967 lib. bdg. $15.00. Traces themes from antiquity to the eighteenth century; excellent bibliography.

Pannekoek, A. *A History of Astronomy.* Rowman 1961 o.p. Perhaps the most comprehensive single-volume survey.

Partington, James R. *A History of Chemistry.* St. Martin's 4 vols. o.p. Erudite and classic multivolume reference source.

Shapley, Harlow, and H. E. Howarth, eds. *A Source Book in Astronomy, 1900–1950.* [*Source Bks. in the History of the Sciences Ser.*] Harvard Univ. Pr. 1960 o.p. Collection of primary readings and extracts emphasizing the nineteenth century.

Toulmin, Stephen, and June Goodfield. *The Architecture of Matter.* [*Phoenix Ser.*] Univ. of Chicago Pr. 1982 pap. $14.00. Eminently readable and intelligent study of theories of matter, alchemy, and the emergence of physical theories in chemistry and physics.

———. *Fabric of the Heavens: The Development of Astronomy and Dynamics.* Harper pap. $8.50. Dependable and provocative survey of astronomy, physical cosmology, and the emergence of modern dynamics.

Van Helden, Albert. *Measuring the Universe: Cosmic Dimensions from Aristarchus to Halley.* Univ. of Chicago Pr. 1985 lib. bdg. $30.00 1986 pap. $8.95. Superb study of the size and distances of planets and the limits of the cosmos, emphasizing the period after Kepler.

Van Melsen, Andrew G. *From Atomos to Atom: The History of the Concept of Atom.* Duquesne Univ. Pr. 1952 o.p. Surveys the concept of "atom" from antiquity to the twentieth century in philosophy and physical science; dated but still useful.

Warner, Deborah J. *The Sky Explored: Celestial Cartography, 1500–1800.* A. R. Liss 1979 $70.00. Handsomely illustrated survey of celestial cartography.

Earth Sciences: Geology, Geography, Meteorology, Oceanography, and Related Fields

Adams, Frank D. *The Birth and Development of the Geological Sciences.* Dover 1956 o.p. Survey of geological thought from antiquity to the early nineteenth century.

Blouet, Brian W., and Teresa L. Stitcher, eds. *The Origins of Academic Geography in the United States.* Shoe String 1981 $39.50. Contains 20 essays on the early intellectual and institutional history of academic geography in the United States.

Bowen, Margarita. *Empiricism and Geographical Thought: From Francis Bacon to Alexander Von Humboldt.* Cambridge Univ. Pr. 1981 $59.50. Surveys the impact of modern scientific methods on geography from 1600 to 1860.

Brown, Eric H., ed. *Geography Yesterday and Tomorrow.* Oxford 1980 $34.00. Surveys the history of the Royal Geographical Society and the current state of scholarly research in the history of geography.

Deacon, Margaret. *Scientists and the Sea 1650–1900: A Study of Marine Science.* Academic Pr. 1971 o.p. Traces the development of marine science from antiquity to the twentieth century, emphasizing the period since the seventeenth century and the interest in tides, navigation, and the gradual emergence of oceanography.

Frisinger, H. H. *The History of Meteorology to 1800.* Watson Pub. Intl. 1977 o.p. Brief introduction from Greek antiquity to about 1800.

Geikie, A. *The Founders of Geology.* Macmillan 2d ed. 1905 o.p. Classic survey still useful for breadth of perspective.

James, Preston E., and G. J. Martin. *All Possible Worlds: A History of Geographical Ideas.* Wiley 2d ed. 1981 text ed. $35.00. Introductory survey from antiquity through the twentieth century, focusing on the last century.

Kish, George, ed. *A Source Book in Geography.* [*Source Bks. in the History of the Sciences Ser.*] Harvard Univ. Pr. 1978 $35.00. Selections with notes from original geographical writings from Hesiod to von Humboldt.

Mather, Kirtley F., and Shirley L. Mason, eds. *A Source Book in Geology, 1400–1900.* Harvard Univ. Pr. 1970 o.p. Contains brief selections on geological topics from da Vinci to Van Hise, from the origin of the Earth to glaciation.

Middleton, W. E. Knowles. *The History of the Barometer.* Johns Hopkins Univ. Pr. 1964 o.p. Standard survey based on primary printed sources.

———. *A History of the Thermometer and Its Use in Meteorology.* Johns Hopkins Univ. Pr. 1966 o.p. Traces the development of the thermometer from the seventeenth century, emphasizing the problem of graduating scales.

Porter, Roy. *The Making of Geology: Earth Science in Britain, 1660–1815.* Cambridge Univ. Pr. 1977 o.p. Authoritative study arguing that attitudes toward Earth, and the foundations of geological thought, underwent great change in Britain prior to the flowering of geology as a science in the nineteenth century.

Schlee, Susan. *The Edge of an Unfamiliar World: A History of Oceanography.* Dutton

1973 o.p. Traces developments in Europe and America from the mid-nineteenth century through World War II, focusing on the scientific content but not excluding relevant instrumentation and technique; well illustrated.

Shirley, R. W. *Mapping of the World, 1472–1700: Early Printed World Maps.* Saifer $100.00. Superbly illustrated visual survey of the early history of cartography.

Tinkler, Keith J. *A Short History of Geomorphology.* Barnes & Noble 1985 $25.00. Compact and useful survey.

Wood, Robert M. *The Dark Side of the Earth: The Battle for the Earth Sciences, 1800–1980.* Allen & Unwin 1986 pap. $11.95. Recounts the heroic age of nineteenth-century geology before arguing that the twentieth-century decline was reversed only in the 1960s with plate tectonics.

Biological Sciences: Biology, Botany, Zoology, and Related Fields

Andrews, Henry N. *The Fossil Hunters: In Search of Ancient Plants.* Cornell Univ. Pr. 1980 $42.50. Traces the roots of paleobotany from the seventeenth century to the present; well illustrated.

Bulloch, William. *The History of Bacteriology.* Dover repr. of 1938 ed. 1979 o.p. Standard introductory survey.

Clay, Reginald S., and T. H. Court. *The History of the Microscope.* Longwood repr. of 1932 ed. 1977 lib. bdg. $30.00; Saifer $60.00. Still the best historical introduction to microscopy.

Cole, Francis J. *History of Comparative Anatomy: From Aristotle to the 18th Century.* Dover 1975 o.p. Chronicles the emergence of comparative anatomy through three stages: the recognition of the importance of the minutiae of anatomy, the development of technics for investigating and accumulating these details, and integrating the data into coherent patterns.

Farber, Paul. *The Emergence of Ornithology as a Scientific Discipline: 1760–1850.* Kluwer Academic 1982 $39.50. Argues that ornithology should be interpreted in the context of natural history and broader social and institutional developments.

Hall, Thomas S. *History of General Physiology, 600 B.C. to A.D. 1900.* Univ. of Chicago Pr. 2 vols. 1969 pap. ea. $6.50. Volume 1 traces the development of physiology from ancient Greece through the eighteenth century; volume 2 continues the survey to the end of the twentieth century.

———. *Ideas of Life and Matter.* Univ. of Chicago Pr. 2 vols. 1969 $50.00. Encyclopedic survey from antiquity to 1900.

———. *Source Book in Animal Biology.* [*Source Bks. in the History of the Sciences Ser.*] Harvard Univ. Pr. 1971 $45.00. Comprehensive selection of topically and chronologically arranged excerpts from original sources on all phases of animal life, research, and science from antiquity to the twentieth century.

Leicester, Henry M. *Development of Biochemical Concepts from Ancient to Modern Times.* [*Monographs in the History of Science Ser.*] Harvard Univ. Pr. 1974 text ed. $17.50. Traces concepts of the living organism and the emergence of biochemistry as a science, emphasizing developments since 1800.

Mayr, Ernst. *The Growth of Biological Thought: Diversity, Evolution, and Inheritance.* Harvard Univ. Pr. (Belknap Pr.) 1982 $35.00 1985 pap. $14.95. Useful survey from antiquity to the twentieth century, emphasizing the background, triumph, and defense of Darwinism.

Mayr, Ernst, and William B. Provine. *The Evolutionary Synthesis: Perspectives on the Unification of Biology.* Harvard Univ. Pr. 1980 text ed. $27.50. Collected symposium essays examining the background and emergence of the evolutionary synthesis.

Medvei, Victor C. *A History of Endocrinology*. Kluwer Academic 1982 text ed. $95.00.
  Extensive and useful survey of endocrinology.
Needham, Joseph. *A History of Embryology*. [*History, Philosophy and Sociology of
  Science*] Ayer repr. 2d ed. 1975 $30.00. Classic study by a pioneer in the history
  of science.
Nordenskiold, Erik. *The History of Biology: A Survey*. Trans. by L. B. Eyre, Scholarly
  Pr. 1935 $75.00. Standard single-volume survey translated from the original
  Swedish.
Persaud, T. V. N. *Early History of Human Anatomy: From Antiquity to the Beginning
  of the Modern Era*. C. C. Thomas 1984 $27.25. Brief but useful survey of anatomi-
  cal observation and investigation from earliest times to Vesalius in the sixteenth
  century; profusely illustrated.
Rothschuh, Karl E. *History of Physiology* (*Geschichte Der Physiologie*). Trans. by
  G. B. Risse, intro. by L. G. Wilson, Krieger 1973 lib. bdg. $28.50. Introductory
  survey from antiquity to the early twentieth century, focusing on German developments in the nineteenth century.
Rudwick, Martin J. S. *The Meaning of Fossils: Episodes in the History of Palaeon-
  tology*. Univ. of Chicago Pr. 2d ed. 1985 pap. $11.95; Watson Pub. Intl. 2d ed. 1977
  o.p. Examines the interpretation of fossils from sixteenth-century curiosities
  through eighteenth- and nineteenth-century debates touching on uniformity, revolution, progress, and the meaning of the fossil record in evolutionary theories.
Singer, Charles. *A History of Biology: A General Introduction to the Study of Living
  Things*. Henry Schuman rev. ed. 1959 o.p. Dated but still useful single-volume
  survey from Hippocrates to Mendel.
———. *Short History of Anatomy and Physiology: From the Greeks to Harvey* (*Evolution of Anatomy*). Dover 1957 text ed. pap. $4.95. Standard and enduring survey
  yet to be replaced.
Stresemann, Erwin. *Ornithology: From Aristotle to the Present*. Trans. by H. J. Epstein and C. Epstein, Harvard Univ. Pr. 1975 o.p. Standard single-volume survey
  defining the place of ornithology in the development of systematics, evolutionary theory, and the emergence of modern biology.
Thorpe, W. H. *The Origins and Rise of Ethnology*. Praeger 1979 $35.95. Traces the
  origins of the study of animal behavior from natural history to present
  ethological research.
Toulmin, Stephen, and June Goodfield. *The Discovery of Time*. Univ. of Chicago Pr.
  1976 pap. $9.95. Provocative and graceful study of the central component of
  science and history, from myth and memories to twentieth-century concepts of
  time and understanding.
Von Sachs, Julius. *History of Botany, 1530–1860*. Trans. by Henry E. Garnsey, Russell rev. ed. repr. of 1890 ed. 1967 o.p. Dated but still useful survey.

Social Sciences

Ackerknecht, Erwin H. *A Short History of Psychiatry*. Trans. by Sula Wolff, Hafner 2d
  ed. rev. 1970 pap. $8.95. Standard brief introduction.
Barnes, Harry E., ed. *Introduction to the History of Sociology*. Univ. of Chicago Pr.
  1948 $30.00. Massive collaborative study tracing the development of sociologi-
  cal thought from antiquity through the early twentieth century, emphasizing
  nineteenth-century thinkers.
Boring, Edwin G. *A History of Experimental Psychology*. Prentice-Hall 2d ed. 1950
  $47.00. Standard but dated single-volume survey from c.1860 to 1940.
Ellenberger, Henri F. *The Discovery of the Unconscious: The History and Evolution of*

Dynamic Psychiatry. Basic Bks. 1970 $29.95 1981 pap. $21.95. Expansive study of dynamic psychiatry focusing on contributions of Janet, Freud, Adler, and Jung.

Harris, Marvin. *The Rise of Anthropological Theory: A History of Theories of Culture.* Harper 1968 text ed. $31.95. Interpretive survey from the Enlightenment through twentieth-century cultural materialism.

Herrnstein, Richard J., and Edwin G. Boring, eds. *Source Book in the History of Psychology.* [*Source Bks. in the History of the Sciences Ser.*] Harvard Univ. Pr. 1965 $30.00 pap. $10.95. Excellent topical selections from original sources reflecting all phases of psychology from Aristotle to the early twentieth century.

Hodgen, Margaret T. *Early Anthropology in the Sixteenth and Seventeenth Centuries.* Univ. of Pennsylvania Pr. repr. of 1964 ed. 1971 text ed. pap. $3.95. Traces anthropological concepts from medieval times through the nineteenth century, focusing on sixteenth- and seventeenth-century developments.

Hothersall, David. *History of Psychology.* Temple Univ. Pr. 1984 $34.95. Introduction for students surveying developments from antiquity to the neobehaviorists.

Klein, D. B. *A History of Scientific Psychology: Its Origins and Philosophical Backgrounds.* Basic Bks. 1970 o.p. Traces the emergence of psychology as a science from antiquity to the modern period.

Leahey, Thomas H. *A History of Psychology.* Prentice-Hall 2d ed. 1987 text ed. $34.00. Introduction for students surveying all aspects of psychology from antiquity to the twentieth century.

Leakey, Louis S. B., and William S. Bester, eds. *Adam or Ape: A Sourcebook of Discoveries about Early Man.* Schenkman 1981 $24.50 pap. $16.95. Collected primary selections and essays on anthropology and paleontology from Darwin to the twentieth century.

Murphy, Gardner. *Psychological Thought from Pythagoras to Freud: An Informal Introduction.* Harcourt 1968 o.p. Popular survey and introduction.

Murphy, Gardner, and Joseph K. Kovach. *Historical Introduction to Modern Psychology.* Harcourt 3d ed. 1972 text ed. $25.95. Focuses on nineteenth- and twentieth-century developments and the transition to an experimental science based on research.

Penniman, T. K. *A Hundred Years of Anthropology.* Morrow repr. of 1935 ed. 1974 pap. $3.95. Standard survey of anthropological thought emphasizing the period c.1835 to 1935.

Reisman, John M. *A History of Clinical Psychology: Enlarged Edition of The Development of Clinical Psychology.* Irvington repr. of 1976 ed. 1983 text ed. pap. $19.95. Traces themes in clinical theory, technique, practice, and professional organization from the late eighteenth to the twentieth century.

Robins, R. H. *A Short History of Linguistics.* Longman 2d ed. 1980 text ed. pap. $13.95. Brief survey of linguistics from Greek antiquity to the mid-twentieth century.

Swingewood, Alan. *A Short History of Sociological Thought.* St. Martin's 1984 pap. $12.95. Compact and useful survey of the origins and development of sociology.

Watson, Robert I. *The Great Psychologists: From Aristotle to Freud.* Harper 4th ed. 1978 text ed. pap. $20.50. Brief primary selections from antiquity to the twentieth century.

Medicine and the Medical Sciences

Ackerknecht, Erwin H. *Therapeutics: From the Primitives to the 20th Century.* Hafner 1973 $18.95. Surveys therapeutics from antiquity to the present, focusing on internal diseases, diet, chemotherapy, and so on.

Cartwright, Frederick F. *A Social History of Medicine.* Longman 1977 o.p. Introduction to the history of medical science, eighteenth to twentieth centuries.

Castiglioni, Arturo. *A History of Medicine.* Aronson 1973 $40.00. Excellent survey of the history of medicine from antiquity to the twentieth century; particularly strong on the contributions of Italy and Britain.

Clendening, Logan, ed. *Source Book of Medical History.* Dover 1942 pap. $10.95; Peter Smith 1942 $15.50. Useful selected readings in the history of medical thought and practice.

Earle, A. S. *Surgery in America: From the Colonial Era to the Twentieth Century.* Praeger 2d ed. 1983 $58.95. Traces the early history of American surgery from primitive amputation techniques through the development of anesthesiology and mature surgical procedures.

Hopkins, Donald R. *Princes and Peasants: Smallpox in History.* Univ. of Chicago Pr. 1983 $25.00 1985 pap. $12.95. Traces the history of smallpox from Elizabethan times through the twentieth century and its virtual eradication.

Leavitt, Judith W., and Ronald L. Numbers, eds. *Sickness and Health in America: Readings in the History of Medicine and Public Health.* Univ. of Wisconsin Pr. 2d ed. rev. 1985 text ed. $32.50 pap. $14.95. Provides reprints and selections from authorities on all aspects of American medicine.

Rosen, George. *A History of Public Health.* MD Pubns. 1958 o.p. From Greek antiquity to the mid-twentieth century.

Shryock, Richard H. *Development of Modern Medicine: An Interpretation of the Social and Scientific Factors Involved.* Hafner repr. of 1947 ed. 1969 $16.25. Surveys medical developments from 1600 to the early twentieth century in Europe and America.

————. *Medicine and Society in America: 1660–1860.* Cornell Univ. Pr. 1962 pap. $6.95. Brief introduction to the origins of the profession, medical thought and practice, concepts of disease, and the modern transition, 1820–60.

Sigerist, Henry A. *A History of Medicine.* Oxford 2 vols. 1951–61 ea. $35.00. Vol. 1, *Primitive and Archaic Medicine;* Vol. 2, *Early Greek, Hindu and Persian Medicine.* Introductory survey of early medical practice and treatment; well illustrated.

Singer, Charles, and Ashworth E. Underwood. *Short History of Medicine.* Oxford 2d ed. 1962 o.p. Standard survey of the practice and science of medicine from prehistory to the early twentieth century.

Spink, Wesley W. *Infectious Diseases: A History of Their Control.* Univ. of Minnesota Pr. 1979 $34.50. Useful survey of the medical and social control of infectious disease.

Wagensteen, Owen H., and Sarah D. Wagensteen. *The Rise of Surgery: From Empiric Craft to Scientific Discipline.* Univ. of Minnesota Pr. 1979 $45.00. Useful survey of the development of surgical technique and practice from early times to the twentieth century.

Waterson, A. P., and L. Wilkinson. *An Introduction to the History of Virology.* Cambridge Univ. Pr. 1978 $49.50. Surveys the emerging recognition of the role of viruses in the course and spread of disease from 1850 to 1970.

Technology

Agassi, Joseph. *Technology: Philosophical and Social Aspects.* Kluwer Academic 1986 lib. bdg. $39.50 text ed. pap. $19.95. Examines the social and intellectual impact of technology and technological change.

Braun, Ernest, and Stuart MacDonald. *Revolution in Miniature: The History and Impact of Semiconductor Electronics Re-Explored.* Cambridge Univ. Pr. 2d ed.

1982 $32.50 pap. $10.95. Brief but detailed study of the development of postwar semiconductor electronics in America.

Calhoun, Daniel H. *The American Civil Engineer: Origins and Conflict.* MIT 1962 o.p. Standard study tracing the emergence of the profession in America to 1840; excellent bibliography.

Calvert, Monte. *The Mechanical Engineer in America, 1830–1910: Professional Cultures in Conflict.* [*Studies in the History of Technology*] Johns Hopkins Univ. Pr. 1967 o.p. Provides an overview and social analysis of the process of professionalization, emphasizing the role of activists and those who resisted reform.

Crouch, Tom D. *A Dream of Wings: Americans and the Airplane, 1875–1905.* Norton 1981 $15.95. Traces the early history of flight in America, emphasizing nineteenth-century engineering efforts and early gliders; well illustrated.

Eisenstein, Elizabeth L. *The Printing Press as an Agent of Change: Communications and Cultural Transformations in Early Modern Europe.* Cambridge Univ. Pr. 2 vols. 1979 $115.00. Superb study of the power of the printed word in the growth and dissemination of scientific ideas.

Emme, Eugene M., ed. *Two Hundred Years of Flight in America.* Intro. by Michael Collins, Univelt 2d ed. 1979 pap. $25.00. Collected essays on the history of flight and the heroic age of space exploration.

Goldstine, Herman H. *The Computer from Pascal to Von Neumann.* Princeton Univ. Pr. 1980 $39.00 pap. $10.50. Provides a solid survey of computer technology from the seventeenth to twentieth centuries.

Klemm, Friedrich. *History of Western Technology.* MIT 1964 o.p. Useful single-volume survey.

Kranzberg, Melvin, and Carroll W. Pursell, Jr., eds. *Technology in Western Civilization.* Oxford 2 vols. 1967 ea. $24.95. Vol. 1, *The Emergence of Modern Industrial Society, Earliest Times to 1900*; Vol. 2, *Technology in the Twentieth Century.* The best compact survey of the history of technology.

Landes, David S. *Revolution in Time: Clocks and the Making of the Modern World.* Harvard Univ. Pr. 1983 $20.00. Stimulating survey of timepiece technology and changing conceptions and attitudes about time.

Layton, E. T., and others, eds. *The Dynamics of Science and Technology.* Kluwer Academic 1978 lib. bdg. $36.50 text ed. pap. $18.50. Multiauthored volume containing cross-disciplinary essays on the interaction of science, technology, and medicine.

Leinwoll, Stanley. *From Spark to Satellite: A History of Radio Communication.* Scribner 1979 o.p. Popular introduction to the origins of radio technology and the development of radio and network communications.

Pursell, Carroll W., Jr., ed. *Technology in America: A History of Individuals and Ideas.* MIT 1981 pap. $9.95. Multiauthored collection surveying American technology from colonial times to the space age.

Ritchie, David. *The Computer Pioneers: The Making of the Modern Computer.* Simon & Schuster 1986 $17.95. Useful introduction for the layperson.

Rosenblum, Naomi. *A World History of Photography.* Ed. by Walton Rawls, Abbeville Pr. 1984 $39.95. Useful survey; well illustrated.

Rothschild, Joan, ed. *Machina Ex Dea: Feminist Perspectives on Technology.* Pergamon 1983 $27.50. Provides provocative essays on the place, role, and relationship of women and technology in Western culture.

Von Braun, Wernher, and Frederick I. Ordway, III. *History of Rocketry and Space Travel.* Crowell rev. ed. 1975 $29.45. Well-illustrated survey for the general reader.

Williams, Michael R. *A History of Computing Technology.* Prentice-Hall 1985 text ed.

$34.00. Brief but useful introduction to the history of number, computing, and computing devices, with particular emphasis on the last 50 years.

CHRONOLOGICAL STUDIES

The following section consists of seven subdivisions listing studies in the history of science, technology, and medicine by chronological period. Topical themes and geographical limits within these periods vary widely, from a synthetic history of science, technology, and medicine in antiquity to a study of eugenics in twentieth-century America.

Historical periodizations—convenient divisions on an imaginary chronological continuum—traditionally fall into three periods: ancient, medieval, and modern. Although finer conceptual lines have been drawn (often erupting into academic border disputes), the present chapter is essentially chronological. Other conceptual periodizations, however, merit brief mention.

According to tradition, Ancient science includes Egyptian, Babylonian (Mesopotamian), and Greek (classical) science, the latter often subdivided into Hellenic (from Thales, c.600 B.C., to the death of Aristotle, 322 B.C.) and Hellenistic science, symbolized by the Museum of Alexandria. Medieval science (Middle Ages) is usually understood to extend into the fifteenth century, and normally includes developments in Islam (Arabic science) and the Latin West before giving rise to the Renaissance and Reformation (c.1450–1600). In the modern period historians frequently speak of a Copernican revolution (sixteenth–seventeenth centuries), the scientific revolution, the Newtonian Synthesis (seventeenth century), the Industrial Revolution, Enlightenment science (eighteenth century), the age of science, the Darwinian revolution (nineteenth century), or the scientific revolution of the twentieth century (associated with Einstein, relativity, and quantum). Though conceptually colorless, the classification employed below for the modern period is by century.

In the end, the history of science does not follow the contours of chronology any more than it respects national boundaries or disciplinary empires. Should the reader fail to find a suitable path or desired destination, the Bibliography section above provides a series of topical maps and periodic charts.

Ancient and Classical

Aaboe, A. *Episodes from the Early History of Mathematics.* [*New Mathematical Lib.*] Mathematical Assn. 1964 pap. $8.75. Authoritative introduction for students.

Aristotle. *The Complete Works of Aristotle: The Revised Oxford Translation.* Ed. by Jonathan Barnes [*Bollingen Ser.*] Princeton Univ. Pr. 2 vols. 1984 $75.00. The most accessible collection of writings of "The Philosopher."

Broch, Arthur J., ed. *Greek Medicine: Being Extracts Illustrative of Medical Writing from Hippocrates to Galen.* AMS Pr. repr. of 1929 ed. 1977 $16.00. Intelligent selections of primary texts.

De Santillana, Giorgio. *Origins of Scientific Thought from Anaximander to Proclus,*

600 B.C.–500 A.D. NAL 1955 o.p. Brisk, breezy, but often brilliant survey of early scientific ideas.

Dicks, D. R. *Early Greek Astronomy to Aristotle.* [*Aspects of Greek and Roman Life Ser.*] Cornell Univ. Pr. 1985 text ed. pap. $9.95. Provides a philosophical and textual emphasis rather than technical analysis.

Euclid. *The Elements.* Ed. by Isaac Todhunter, Biblio. Dist. repr. of 1933 ed. 1967 $12.95; trans. by Thomas L. Heath, Dover 3 vols. repr. of 1926 ed. 1956 pap. ea. $8.95. The standard edition of one of the classics of ancient science and the history of mathematics.

Gillings, Richard J. *Mathematics in the Time of the Pharaohs.* Dover 1972 pap. $6.00. Offers a solid, nontechnical introduction.

Heath, Thomas L. *Aristarchus of Samos: The Ancient Copernicus.* Peter Smith $17.25. Although the title does not indicate this, Heath provides a brilliant study of ancient Greek astronomy through Aristarchus.

——. *A History of Greek Mathematics.* Dover 2 vols. 1981 pap. ea. $8.50. Still the best introduction to Greek mathematics.

Lloyd, Geoffrey E. *Early Greek Science: Thales to Aristotle.* Ed. by M. I. Finley, Norton 1974 pap. $5.95. Now the standard source for Hellenistic science.

——. *Greek Science after Aristotle.* Norton 1973 pap. $5.95. Companion to the above, a standard source for Hellenistic science.

——. *Magic, Reason and Experience: Studies in the Origin and Development of Greek Science.* Cambridge Univ. Pr. 1979 $62.50 pap. $19.95. Bold but balanced attempt to understand the emergence of Greek scientific thought in light of social, political, and anthropological models of development.

——. *Science, Folklore, and Ideology: Studies in the Life Sciences in Ancient Greece.* Cambridge Univ. Pr. 1983 o.p. Imaginative and insightful attempt to place ancient medicine and the life sciences in the broader context of knowledge represented by midwives and herbalists.

Lloyd, Geoffrey E., and G. E. Owen, eds. *Aristotle on Mind and the Senses.* [*Classical Studies Ser.*] Cambridge Univ. Pr. 1978 $44.50. Excellent introduction to "The Philosopher."

Neugebauer, Otto. *The Exact Sciences in Antiquity.* Dover 2d ed. repr. of 1957 ed. 1979 pap. $5.00; Univ. Pr. of New England 2d ed. 1957 text ed. $20.00. The best single volume for the technical rudiments of the exact sciences in antiquity. For advanced beginners.

——. *A History of Ancient Mathematical Astronomy.* Springer-Verlag 3 vols. 1975 text ed. $180.00. Definitive scholarly study by the acknowledged master.

Sarton, George. *History of Science.* Norton 2 vols. 1970 o.p. Vol. 1, *Ancient Science through the Golden Age of Greece*; Vol. 2, *Hellenistic Science and Culture in the Last Three Centuries B.C.* Standard but somewhat encyclopedic survey of ancient science.

Scarborough, John. *Roman Medicine.* Ed. by H. H. Scullard [*Aspects of Greek and Roman Life Ser.*] Cornell Univ. Pr. 1970 o.p. Solid introduction for serious students.

Singer, Charles J. *Greek Biology and Greek Medicine.* AMS Pr. repr. of 1922 ed. 1979 $20.00. Useful but somewhat dated classic.

Stahl, William H. *Roman Science: Origins, Development, and Influence to the Later Middle Ages.* Greenwood repr. of 1962 ed. 1978 lib. bdg. $37.50. Provides all you need to know about Roman science in antiquity.

Van der Waerden, Bartel L. *Science Awakening.* Oxford 1961 o.p. Excellent technical introduction to science in antiquity.

——. *Science Awakening 2: The Birth of Astronomy.* Oxford 1974 $45.00. Together with Neugebauer (*The Exact Sciences in Antiquity*), the most authoritative source on ancient science.

White, K. D. *Greek and Roman Technology*. Cornell Univ. Pr. 1983 $39.50. Surveys all aspects of classical technology, from agriculture to water transportation; excellent illustrations and diagrams.

Middle Ages

Clagett, Marshall. *The Science of Mechanics in the Middle Ages*. Univ. of Wisconsin Pr. 1959 o.p. Classic scholarly study tracing developments in mechanics, particularly impetus theory.

Dekosky, Robert K. *Knowledge and Cosmos: Development and Decline of the Medieval Perspective*. Univ. Pr. of Amer. 1979 text ed. $26.00 pap. $15.25. Survey of the conceptual foundations of the physical sciences from antiquity to the scientific revolution.

Gilson, Étienne. *Reason and Revelation in the Middle Ages*. Scribner text ed. pap. $8.95. Classic essay tracing the fundamental theme of knowledge and belief in medieval thought.

Gimpel, Jean. *The Medieval Machine: The Industrial Revolution of the Middle Ages*. Penguin 1977 pap. $6.95. Introduces medieval technology, arguing that medieval people produced an industrial revolution.

Grant, Edward. *Physical Science in the Middle Ages*. [*History of Science Ser.*] Cambridge Univ. Pr. 1978 pap. $10.95. Introduction to major themes in medieval physical thought stressing the role of the condemnations of 1270 and 1277; standard student introduction to medieval science.

———. *A Source Book in Medieval Science*. [*Source Bks. in the History of the Sciences Ser.*] Harvard Univ. Pr. 1974 text ed. $45.00. Contains excellent selections from over 150 authors in the period from the encyclopedic tradition to writers of the fifteenth century.

Haskins, Charles H. *The Renaissance of the Twelfth Century*. Harvard Univ. Pr. 1971 pap. $7.95. Classic study on the revival of learning in the Latin West.

Knowles, David. *The Evolution of Medieval Thought*. Random 1964 pap. $4.76. Standard introduction to the intellectual context of medieval science and learning.

Lindberg, David C., ed. *Science in the Middle Ages*. Univ. of Chicago Pr. 1979 pap. $15.00. Contains essays by authorities on all phases of medieval science and learning.

Murdoch, John E. *Antiquity and the Middle Ages*. Vol. 1 in *Album of Science*. Scribner 1984 $63.00. Superbly illustrated volume for an era dominated by the image rather than the written word.

Nasr, Hosein. *Science and Civilization in Islam*. NAL 1970 o.p. Presents the major developments of Islamic science and its legacy in the medieval Latin West.

Sarton, George. *Introduction to the History of Science*. Krieger 5 vols. 1975 $275.00. Encyclopedic volumes for reference. Extensive chronological survey of science and learning from Homer through the late fourteenth century; a classic compendium unparalleled for detailed reference.

Weisheipl, James A. *The Development of Physical Theory in the Middle Ages*. Univ. of Michigan Pr. 1971 pap. $3.95. Surveys themes in physical theory emphasizing the work of Albertus Magnus and Aquinas.

White, Lynn, Jr. *Medieval Technology and Social Change*. Oxford 1962 pap. $7.95. Classic study tracing the social dimension of medieval innovations such as the horse stirrup, collar, and three-field crop rotation.

Renaissance and Reformation, 1450–1600

Boas Hall, Maria. *The Scientific Renaissance 1450–1630.* Harper 1962 pap. $8.95. Standard single-volume survey of Renaissance science.

Copernicus, Nicholas. *Three Copernican Treatises: The Commentariolus and the Letter against Werner of Copernicus and the Narratio Prima of Rheticus.* Ed. by Edward Rosen, Hippocrene Bks. 3d ed. rev. repr. of 1939 ed. 1971 o.p. Brief primary readings that provide an excellent introduction to Copernican thought.

Debus, Allen G. *The English Paracelsians.* Univ. of Chicago Pr. 1968 $8.50. Evaluates the work and influence of Paracelsus on English thought, particularly chemistry and medicine.

———. *Man and Nature in the Renaissance.* [*History of Science Ser.*] Cambridge Univ. Pr. 1978 $29.95 pap. $10.95. Traces occult philosophies and their impact on the emergence of early modern science.

Drake, Stillman, and I. E. Drabkin, trans. *Mechanics in Sixteenth Century Italy: Selections from Tartaglia, Benedetti, Guido Ubaldo and Galileo.* Univ. of Wisconsin Pr. 1969 o.p. Excellent introduction to sixteenth-century mechanics and the contextual roots of Galileo's novelty.

Dreyer, John L. *Tycho Brahe: A Picture of Scientific Life and Work in the Sixteenth Century.* Peter Smith 1977 $13.25. Authoritative study of the prominent Danish astronomer.

Haydn, Hiram C. *The Counter-Renaissance.* Peter Smith 1950 o.p. Provides an intellectual context for interpreting the limits of Renaissance science and the "Scientific Reformation."

Johnson, Francis R. *Astronomical Thought in Renaissance England.* Hippocrene Bks. 1968 o.p. Standard introduction to Tudor astronomy and cosmology, focused in part on the reception of Copernicus; now somewhat dated.

Kocher, Paul. *Science and Religion in Elizabethan England.* Hippocrene Bks. repr. of 1953 ed. 1969 o.p. Traces themes of conflict and congruence in science and religion; compare with Westfall (see below under Seventeenth Century).

Nauert, Charles G., Jr. *Agrippa and the Crisis of Renaissance Thought.* Univ. of Illinois Pr. 1965 o.p. Examines the occult tradition from Ficino through Agrippa in light of the skeptical tradition.

O'Malley, C. D. *Andreas Vesalius of Brussels 1514–1564.* Univ. of California Pr. 1964 o.p. Standard study of the famous anatomist.

Popkin, Richard H. *The History of Scepticism from Erasmus to Spinoza.* Univ. of California Pr. 1979 $37.00 pap. $9.50. Brilliant study of the skeptical crisis and its impact on theology, philosophy, and science; argues that modern science was in part an intellectual compromise between dogmatism and skepticism.

Rosen, Edward. *Copernicus and the Scientific Revolution.* Krieger 1984 text ed. pap. $6.95. Somewhat polemical introduction to Copernicus's achievement.

Sarton, George. *Six Wings: Men of Science in the Renaissance.* Indiana Univ. Pr. repr. of 1957 ed. 1977 $19.50. Dated but useful introduction to Renaissance science.

Shirley, John W. *Thomas Harriot: A Biography.* Oxford 1983 $55.00. Detailed but largely descriptive biography of the English mathematician and physicist.

Swerdlow, Noel M., and Otto Neugebauer. *Mathematical Astronomy in Copernicus's De Revolutionibus.* Springer-Verlag 2 vols. 1984 $78.00. Scholarly analysis of Copernicus's magnum opus.

Vickers, Brian, ed. *Occult and Scientific Mentalities in the Renaissance.* Cambridge Univ. Pr. 1984 $49.50 1986 pap. $15.95. Collection of essays assessing the role and significance of the occult tradition in the emergence of modern science.

Walker, D. P. *Spiritual and Demonic Magic from Ficino to Campanella.* Kraus Repr. repr. of 1958 ed. $44.00. Classic study.

Wear, Andrew, and I. M. Lomie, eds. *The Medical Renaissance of the Sixteenth Century.* Cambridge Univ. Pr. 1985 $59.50. Collected conference papers focusing on medicine, particularly the Galenic tradition and medical education, in sixteenth-century Europe.

Westman, Robert S., and J. E. McGuire. *Hermeticism and the Scientific Revolution.* Univ. of California Pr. 1977 o.p. Excellent essays reevaluating the so-called Yates thesis that Hermeticism and other occult modes of thought helped direct or give impetus to Copernicanism and modern science.

Wightman, William P. *Science and the Renaissance.* Hafner 2 vols. 1962 $27.25. Standard survey of Renaissance science.

Yates, Frances. *Giordano Bruno and the Hermetic Tradition.* Random 1969 pap. $2.45; [*Midway Repr. Ser.*] Univ. of Chicago Pr. 1979 text ed. pap. $17.00. Brilliant but controversial study arguing that the emergence of modern science was stimulated by Hermetic philosophy, which provided the human will to understand and transform the natural and social worlds.

Seventeenth Century

Aiton, E. J. *The Vortex Theory of Planetary Motions.* Watson 1972 o.p. Excellent study of the legacy of Descartes's vortex theory as a cosmological alternative to Newtonian mechanics and action-at-a-distance.

Brown, Harcourt. *Scientific Organizations in Seventeenth Century France, 1620–1680.* Russell repr. of 1934 ed. 1967 $8.50. Classic study of the informal learned groups that gave rise to the French Academy of Sciences.

Burtt, Edwin A. *The Metaphysical Foundations of Modern Physical Science.* Humanities Pr. 2d ed. repr. of 1932 ed. 1980 text ed. pap. $12.50. Classic study arguing that the scientific revolution provided a new conception of truth, reality, God, man, and human value.

Caspar, Max. *Kepler.* Trans. by C. Doris Hellman, Abelard-Schuman 1959 o.p. The most authoritative and exhaustive biography of the prominent German astronomer.

Christianson, Gale E. *In the Presence of the Creator: Isaac Newton and His Times.* Free Pr. 1984 $27.50. Lively study of Newton's personality and career describing his major scientific achievements.

Cohen, I. Bernard. *The Birth of a New Physics.* Norton rev. & enl. ed. 1985 $17.95 pap. $5.95. Introduces the major themes in terrestrial and celestial physics during the scientific revolution.

Descartes, René. *Descartes Le Monde.* Trans. by Michael Mahoney, Abaris Bks. 1978 $20.00. English translation of Descartes's magnum opus, modestly entitled "The World."

————. *The Philosophical Writings of Descartes.* Trans. by John Cottingham, Robert Soothoff, and Dugald Murdoch, Cambridge Univ. Pr. 2 vols. 1985 ea. $47.50 pap. ea. $12.95. Destined to become the standard edition.

————. *Principles of Philosophy.* Trans. by Reese P. Miller and Valentine R. Miller, Kluwer Academic 1983 lib. bdg. $59.00 1984 text ed. pap. $19.50. Translated from the original Latin, the *Principia* was Descartes's most comprehensive statement of his physical hypotheses.

Dobbs, Betty J. *The Foundations of Newton's Alchemy: Or "The Hunting of the Greene*

Lyon." Cambridge Univ. Pr. 1983 pap. $17.95. Provocative study of Newton's alchemical interests.

Dobell, C., ed. *Antony van Leeuwenhoek and His "Little Animals."* Dover repr. of 1932 ed. 1960 o.p. Standard introduction to Leeuwenhoek and his early microscopic studies.

Drake, Stillman. *Galileo at Work: His Scientific Biography.* Univ. of Chicago Pr. 1978 o.p. Provides a useful chronology of Galileo's published work and intellectual development.

Eccles, Audrey. *Obstetrics and Gynaecology in Tudor and Stuart England.* Kent State Univ. Pr. 1982 $18.00. Brief but useful introduction to issues of reproduction, childbirth, and midwifery from c.1540 to 1740.

Frank, Robert G., Jr. *Harvey and the Oxford Physiologist: A Study of Scientific Ideas.* Univ. of California Pr. 1980 $34.00. Comprehensive study of the "English School" of physiology from Harvey to Lower in intellectual and institutional context.

Galilei, Galileo. *Dialogue Concerning the Two Chief World Systems, Ptolemaic and Copernican.* Trans. by Stillman Drake, Univ. of California Pr. 2d ed. rev. 1967 pap. $11.95. Standard translation of Galileo's scientific classic; an accessible masterpiece of science and literary style.

————. *Discoveries and Opinions of Galileo.* Trans. by S. Drake, Doubleday 1957 o.p. Excellent translations of Galileo's shorter writings on telescopic observation, science, and religion.

Gassendi, Pierre. *The Selected Works of Pierre Gassendi.* Ed. and trans. by Craig B. Brush, Johnson Repr. 1972 o.p. Selections, in English translation, written by Descartes's famous contemporary and critic.

Hall, Alfred Rupert. *Philosophers at War: The Quarrel between Newton and Leibniz.* Cambridge Univ. Pr. 1980 $39.50. Traces the war of words that erupted over the invention of the calculus, finally extending to the nature of God and the universe.

————. *The Revolution in Science 1500–1750.* Longman 1983 text ed. $18.95. Revised and expanded version of a standard work. "A thorough study of the theoretical and methodical developments in the early modern period and contains an up-to-date bibliography" *(Choice).*

Harvey, William. *De Motu Cordis: Anatomical Studies on the Motion of the Heart and Blood.* Trans. by Chauncey D. Leake, C. C. Thomas 5th ed. 1978 $20.75. Provides text and notes of Harvey's revolutionary *On the Motion of the Heart and Blood.*

Heilbron, John L. *Electricity in the Seventeenth and Eighteenth Centuries: A Study of Early Modern Physics.* Univ. of California Pr. 1979 $60.00. Model study of experimental physics in the seventeenth and eighteenth centuries.

Hooykaas, R. *Religion and the Rise of Modern Science.* Eerdmans 1972 o.p. Perhaps the best single study of science and religion in the seventeenth century.

Kargon, Robert H. *Atomism in England from Hariot to Newton.* Oxford 1966 o.p. Solid introduction to atomism, English science, and the mechanical philosophy.

Kepler, Johannes. *Epitome of Copernican Astronomy, Books 4 and 5.* Kraus Repr. 2 vols. in 1 1939 o.p. Provides a nontechnical summary of Kepler's views on celestial physics and his use of the archetype in science.

————. *The Secret of the Universe: Mysterium Cosmographicum.* Trans. by A. M. Duncan, Abaris Bks. 1981 o.p. Excellent translation of Kepler's first major work, with useful notes.

King, Lester S. *The Road to Medical Enlightenment, 1650–1695.* Watson 1970 o.p. Standard study of seventeenth-century English medical thought, emphasizing the works of Sylvius, Sydenham, Hoffmann, and others.

Koestler, Arthur. *The Sleepwalkers: A History of Man's Changing Vision of the Universe.* Putnam 1963 o.p. Lively but controversial biographical study of Copernicus, Kepler, and Galileo, arguing that scientific discovery involves periods of intellectual/psychological "sleepwalking."

Koyré, Alexandre. *The Astronomical Revolution: Copernicus–Kepler–Borelli.* Trans. by R. E. W. Maddison, Cornell Univ. Pr. 1973 o.p. Scholarly study aimed at the heart of the scientific revolution, the problem of the planets.

——. *From the Closed World to the Infinite Universe.* Johns Hopkins Univ. Pr. repr. of 1956 ed. 1968 pap. $6.95. Argues that the "geometrization of space" brought the destruction of Aristotle's closed cosmos.

Kuhn, Thomas S. *The Copernican Revolution: Planetary Astronomy in the Development of Western Thought.* Harvard Univ. Pr. 1957 $20.00 pap. $7.95. Provides historical, conceptual, and interpretive background to the so-called Copernican revolution.

Mandrou, Robert. *From Humanism to Science, 1480–1700.* Trans. by Brian Pearce [*History of European Thought Ser.*] Penguin 1979 pap. $6.95. Provides a broad social and cultural framework for understanding the scientific revolution.

Manuel, Frank E. *A Portrait of Isaac Newton.* Harvard Univ. Pr. 1970 o.p. Brilliant but controversial psychobiography focusing on Newton's character and psychological development.

Merton, Robert K. *Science, Technology and Society in Seventeenth Century England.* Fertig 1970 $35.00. Classic study by a prominent sociologist. "Merton argued that the spread of Puritanism (more specifically, Protestant asceticism), a religious event of the 17th century, effected the genesis of the scientific ethos and encouraged the initial growth of science" (*Choice*).

Middleton, W. E. Knowles. *The Experimenters: A Study of the Accademia Del Cimento.* Johns Hopkins Univ. Pr. 1972 o.p. Useful study of an early seventeenth-century scientific society.

Newton, Isaac. *Newton's Philosophy of Nature.* Trans. by H. S. Thayer [*Lib. of Class. Ser.*] Hafner 1953 text ed. pap. $7.95. Convenient selections from Newton's *Principia, Opticks,* and correspondence.

——. *Opticks, or a Treatise of the Reflections, Refractions, Inflections and Colours of Light.* Fwd. by Albert Einstein, Dover 1952 text ed. pap. $7.95; Peter Smith 1952 $16.00. Standard edition of Newton's classic—and perhaps most widely read—work.

Ornstein, Martha. *The Role of Scientific Societies in the Seventeenth Century.* [*History, Philosophy and Sociology of Science*] Ayer repr. 1975 $35.50. Remains the only inclusive one-volume study of seventeenth-century scientific societies.

Sabra, A. I. *Theories of Light from Descartes to Newton.* Cambridge Univ. Pr. 1981 $44.50 pap. $14.95. Traces the revolutionary developments of Descartes, Huygens, and Newton.

Santillana, Giorgio. *The Crime of Galileo.* [*Midway Repr. Ser.*] Univ. of Chicago Pr. 1955 pap. $14.00. Lively but somewhat polemical account of Galileo's condemnation for his heliocentric beliefs.

Shea, William R. *Galileo's Intellectual Revolution: Middle Period, 1610–1632.* Watson Pub. Intl. 1977 pap. $8.95. Focuses on Galileo's creative years, emphasizing his Aristotelianism against the Platonic interpretation of Koyré and the positivism of Drake.

Webster, Charles. *The Great Instauration: Science, Medicine and Reform 1626–1660.* Holmes & Meier 1976 text ed. $75.00. Comprehensive study emphasizing the religious, social, and institutional underpinnings of the radical shift in mid-seventeenth century English science, in which Puritan beliefs played a key role.

Westfall, Richard S. *The Construction of Modern Science: Mechanisms and Mechanics*. Cambridge Univ. Pr. 1978 $34.50 pap. $10.95. Excellent introduction to the scientific revolution, arguing that Newton reconciled the differences between the mechanical philosophy of Descartes and the mathematical tradition embodied by Galileo.

————. *Never at Rest: A Biography of Isaac Newton*. Cambridge Univ. Pr. 1981 $72.50 1983 pap. $22.95. Brilliant and definitive study of the life, intellectual development, and scientific achievement of Newton.

————. *Science and Religion in Seventeenth-Century England*. Univ. of Michigan Pr. 1973 pap. $4.95. Argues English scientists were uncertain about aspects of Christianity but remained committed to the harmony of science and natural religion.

Wolf, Abraham. *A History of Science, Technology and Philosophy in the Sixteenth and Seventeenth Centuries*. Peter Smith repr. of 1952 ed. 2 vols. $30.00. Encyclopedic classic rich in useful detail.

Eighteenth Century

Bedini, Silvio A. *Thinkers and Tinkers: Early American Men of Science*. Landmark Enterprises repr. of 1975 ed. 1983 $24.00. Excellent survey of colonial science and instrumentation emphasizing the role of mathematical practitioners rather than "pure" science; handsomely illustrated.

Burkhardt, Richard W., Jr. *The Spirit of System: Lamarck and Evolutionary Biology*. Harvard Univ. Pr. 1977 $18.00. Examines the structure and legacy of Lamarckian science.

Bury, John B. *The Idea of Progress: An Inquiry into Its Origin and Growth*. Dover repr. 1987 pap. $7.95; intro. by Charles A. Beard, Greenwood repr. of 1932 ed. 1982 lib. bdg. $39.75. Classic study in the history of ideas emphasizing the eighteenth-century conceptual shift from Providence to Progress.

Cohen, I. Bernard. *Franklin and Newton: An Inquiry into Speculative Newtonian Experimental Science and Franklin's Work in Electricity as an Example Thereof*. Amer. Philosophical Society 1957 o.p. Pioneering study tracing the impact of the Newtonian tradition exemplified by Newton's *Opticks*.

Darnton, Robert. *Mesmerism and the End of the Enlightenment in France*. Harvard Univ. Pr. 1968 $16.50 1986 pap. $7.95. Lively study of science and pseudoscience in intellectual, institutional, and political context.

Fox, Robert. *The Caloric Theory of Gases from Lavoisier to Regnault*. Oxford 1971 $32.00. Emphasizes the caloric theories of heat of Lavoisier, Laplace, and later Carnot.

Gelfand, Toby. *Professionalizing Modern Medicine: Paris Surgeons and Medical Science and Institutions in the Eighteenth Century*. [*Contributions in Medical History Ser.*] Greenwood 1980 lib. bdg. $35.00. Using Paris as a case study, examines the complex intellectual, social, and institutional elements giving rise to modern professional medicine.

Gillispie, Charles C. *Science and Polity in France at the End of the Old Regime*. Princeton Univ. Pr. 1980 $57.50. Monumental study of the "intersections" of the modern state and the emergence of modern science, pure and applied. Superb.

Hahn, Roger. *The Anatomy of a Scientific Institution: The Paris Academy of Sciences, 1666–1803*. Univ. of California Pr. 1971 $44.00 pap. $14.95. Detailed study of the academy, from its informal origins to its transformation into the Institut de France. Contains a comprehensive bibliography of individual academicians.

Hankins, Thomas L. *Jean d'Alembert: Science and the Enlightenment*. Oxford 1970 o.p. Award-winning study of d'Alembert in the intellectual context of his times; superbly written.

———. *Science and the Enlightenment*. [*History of Science Ser.*] Cambridge Univ. Pr. 1985 $29.95 pap. $9.95. Succinct and elegant introduction to eighteenth-century science, with particular emphasis on French developments.

Hindle, Brooke. *The Pursuit of Science in Revolutionary America, 1735–1789*. Norton 1974 o.p. Standard survey of the emergence of science in America from colonial naturalists and physicians to the development of national societies and cultural nationalism.

———, ed. *Early American Science*. Watson 1976 o.p. Multiauthored selection of articles, previously published in *Isis*, treating the period before c.1815.

Holmes, Frederic L. *Claude Bernard and Animal Chemistry*. Harvard Univ. Pr. 1974 text ed. $37.50. Detailed study of Bernard's life, work, and influence.

———. *Lavoisier and the Chemistry of Life: An Exploration of Scientific Creativity*. [*History of Science and Medicine Ser. 4*] Univ. of Wisconsin Pr. 1987 text ed. $38.50 pap. $15.75. Definitive study of Lavoisier's achievement and individual genius.

Hufbauer, Karl. *The Formation of the German Chemical Community, 1720–1795*. Univ. of California Pr. 1982 o.p. Rigorous examination of some 65 German chemists and their institutional affiliations.

King, Lester S. *The Philosophy of Medicine: The Early Eighteenth Century*. Harvard Univ. Pr. 1977 $30.00. Excellent introduction to emerging trends and themes in eighteenth-century medical theory and practice.

Lavoisier, Antoine L. *Elements of Chemistry*. Trans. by R. Kerr, Dover repr. of 1790 ed. 1984 pap. $11.95. The standard translation.

Lyon, John, and Philip Sloan, eds. *From Natural History to the History of Nature: Readings from Buffon and His Critics*. Univ. of Notre Dame Pr. 1981 text ed. $19.95. Translated selections from Buffon's *Histoire naturelle* and other writings prior to 1749.

McClellan, James E., III. *Science Reorganized: Scientific Societies in the 18th Century*. Columbia Univ. Pr. $47.50. Provides the first general survey of scientific academies and societies from 1660 to 1793.

Paul, Charles B. *Science and Immortality: The Éloges of the Paris Academy of Sciences (1699–1791)*. Univ. of California Pr. 1980 $26.95. Argues that published eulogies of the academy created a new hero and the myth of the disinterested scientist.

Porter, Roy, and Teich Mikulas, eds. *The Enlightenment in National Context*. Cambridge Univ. Pr. 1981 $44.50 pap. $16.95. Collected essays by specialists tracing historiographic themes from the intellectual and social history of Enlightenment science.

Roe, Shirley A. *Matter, Life and Generation: Eighteenth Century Embryology and the Haller-Wolff Debate*. Cambridge Univ. Pr. 1981 $39.50. Scholarly study of a key debate spanning the century and exposing rival theories of matter and life.

Rousseau, G. S., and R. Porter, eds. *The Ferment of Knowledge: Studies in the Historiography of Eighteenth-Century Science*. Cambridge Univ. Pr. 1980 $54.50. A useful series of essays appraising issues and historiographical themes in contemporary historical research.

Schofield, Robert S. *The Lunar Society of Birmingham: A Social History of Provincial Society and Industry in 18th Century England*. Oxford 1963 o.p. Standard study of the informal group powering the English Industrial Revolution, Boulton, E. Darwin, Priestley, Watt, and others.

———. *Mechanism and Materialism: British Natural Philosophy in the Age of Reason*.

Princeton Univ. Pr. 1970 $34.00. Traces Newton's impact in England arguing that a mechanist tradition eventually gave way to a materialist view based on fluid theories.

Thackray, Arnold. *Atoms and Powers: An Essay on Newtonian Matter-Theory and the Development of Chemistry.* Harvard Univ. Pr. 1970 o.p. Examines the development of Newtonian theories of matter through the eighteenth century.

Willey, Basil. *The Eighteenth Century Background: Studies on the Idea of Nature in the Thought of the Period.* Columbia Univ. Pr. 1941 o.p. Classic introduction to the intellectual context of eighteenth-century science.

Woolf, Harry. *The Transits of Venus: A Study of Eighteenth-Century Science.* Princeton Univ. Pr. 1959 o.p. Classic case study demonstrating the changing character of science through scientific institutions and expeditions.

Nineteenth Century

Appleman, Philip, ed. *Darwin.* Norton 2d ed. 1979 $24.95 pap. $9.95. Provides excellent primary selections on the background and impact of Darwin's thought on science, theology, philosophy, society, and letters.

Bowler, Peter J. *Evolution: The History of an Idea.* Univ. of California Pr. 1984 $29.95 pap. $11.95. Excellent introduction surveying the history and impact of evolution and evolutionary concepts; excellent bibliography.

Brooks, John L. *Just Before the Origin: Alfred Russel Wallace's Theory of Evolution.* Columbia Univ. Pr. 1983 $30.00. Examines the contribution of the co-discoverer of evolution.

Brush, Stephen G. *The Temperature of History, Phases of Science and Culture in the Nineteenth Century.* [*Studies in the History of Science*] Burt Franklin 1978 lib. bdg. $18.95. Examines theories of heat and molecular motion in the context of romanticism, radicalism, and neoromanticism.

Burchfield, Joe D. *Lord Kelvin and the Age of the Earth.* Watson 1975 o.p. Examines the late-nineteenth-century controversy about the age of the Earth.

Burrow, John W. *Evolution and Society: A Study in Victorian Social Theory.* Cambridge Univ. Pr. 1966 $39.50 pap. $13.95. Traces developments in social thought in the wake of Darwinian evolutionary theory.

Clark, Ronald W. *The Survival of Charles Darwin: A Biography of a Man and an Idea.* Avon 1986 pap. $5.95; Random 1985 $19.45. Wide-ranging and useful introduction to Darwin's life, times, and work.

Clerke, Agnes M. *A Popular History of Astronomy in the Nineteenth Century.* Scholarly repr. 1908 $39.00. Classic introduction to nineteenth-century astronomy and early astrophysics.

Coleman, W. *Biology in the Nineteenth Century.* [*History of Science Ser.*] Cambridge Univ. Pr. 1978 pap. $11.95. Standard single-volume survey tracing the emergence of modern biology through cell theory, the evolution debate, and issues surrounding form, function, and experiment.

Cosslett, Tess, ed. *Science and Religion in the Nineteenth Century.* Cambridge Univ. Pr. 1984 $42.50 pap. $14.95. Excellent essays reevaluating a complex and controversial subject.

Darwin, Charles. *The Autobiography and Selected Letters.* Ed. by Francis Darwin, Dover 1892 pap. $5.95; ed. by Francis Darwin, Peter Smith $14.00. Classic and telling introduction to Darwin's life and career.

———. *On the Origin of Species by Means of Natural Selection, or the Preservation of Favoured Races in the Struggle for Life.* Intro. by Ernst Mayr, Harvard Univ. Pr.

facsimile repr. of 1859 ed. 1975 pap. $8.95. The best edition for understanding Darwin's thoughts on evolution through natural selection.

Eiseley, Loren. *Darwin's Century: Evolution and the Men Who Discovered It.* Doubleday 1958 pap. $6.95. Excellent introduction to nineteenth-century natural history and the issues surrounding Darwin's achievement; beautifully written.

Fox, Robert, and George Weisz, eds. *The Organization of Science Technology in France, 1808–1914.* Cambridge Univ. Pr. 1980 o.p. Scholarly essays focusing on scientific research and educational institutions in nineteenth-century France.

Gillespie, Neal C. *Charles Darwin and the Problem of Creation.* Univ. of Chicago Pr. 1979 $16.50 1982 pap. $7.50. Best study of Darwin's religious beliefs.

Gillispie, Charles C. *Genesis and Geology: A Study in the Relations of Scientific Thought, Natural Theology and Social Opinion in Great Britain, 1790–1850.* [*Historical Monographs Ser.*] Harvard Univ. Pr. 1951 $22.50. Standard introduction.

Greene, John C. *American Science in the Age of Jefferson.* Iowa State Univ. Pr. 1984 text ed. pap. $27.50. Excellent introduction to American science in the early national period, stressing the slow development of institutional support and the influence of Jefferson.

———. *Death of Adam: Evolution and Its Impact on Western Thought.* Iowa State Univ. Pr. 1959 pap. $10.95. Traces the idea of evolution from the seventeenth through the nineteenth centuries.

Greene, Mott T. *Geology in the Nineteenth Century: Changing Views of a Changing World.* Cornell Univ. Pr. 1985 $36.50 pap. $14.95. Examines geological theories and controversies from Hutton and Werner to twentieth-century theories of continental drift and global tectonics.

Gregory, Frederick. *Scientific Materialism in Nineteenth-Century Germany.* Kluwer Academic 1979 o.p. Comprehensive study of German materialism in the second half of the nineteenth century, tracing the theme through Feuerbach, Buchner, and others.

Harman, Peter M. *Energy, Force and Matter: The Conceptual Development of Nineteenth-Century Physics.* [*History of Science Ser.*] Cambridge Univ. Pr. 1982 pap. $10.95. Traces broad themes in the transformation of nineteenth-century physics; a standard student introduction.

Himmelfarb, Gertrude. *Darwin and the Darwinian Revolution.* Norton repr. of 1959 ed. 1968 pap. $11.95; Peter Smith $16.25. Controversial study focusing on Darwin's method and the debate concerning the modern synthesis.

Hofstadter, Richard. *Social Darwinism in American Thought.* Beacon 1955 pap. $9.95; Braziller rev. ed. 1959 $7.95. Classic study now somewhat dated.

Howson, Colin, ed. *Method and Appraisal in the Physical Sciences.* Cambridge Univ. Pr. 1976 $52.50. Useful collection of essays.

Hull, David L. *Darwin and His Critics: The Reception of Darwin's Theory of Evolution by the Scientific Community.* Univ. of Chicago Pr. 1983 pap. $17.00. Presents selections and excerpts from Darwin's critics with brief introductory notes.

Huxley, Thomas H. *Autobiography and Essays.* Ed. by Brander Matthews, Kraus Repr. repr. of 1919 ed. 1969 $28.00. Self-evaluation by "Darwin's Bulldog."

Jones, Ernest. *The Life and Work of Sigmund Freud.* Basic Bks. 1953–57 3 vols. ea. $27.50 set $80.00. Detailed but classic study of the founder of psychoanalysis.

Kohn, David, ed. *The Darwinian Heritage.* Princeton Univ. Pr. 1986 $95.00. Multiauthored volume contains 31 chapters tracing Darwin's development as a theorist, the Victorian context of Darwinism, its global reception, and current historical perspectives.

Lenoir, Timothy. *The Strategy of Life: Teleology and Mechanics in 19th-Century Ger-*

man Biology. Kluwer Academic 1982 $59.00. Scholarly study turning on the question of life, mechanism, materialism, and the problem of purpose.

Merz, John Theodor. *A History of European Thought in the Nineteenth Century.* Peter Smith 4 vols. orig. pub. 1904–12. Vols. 1 and 2 o.p.; Vols. 3 and 4 ea. $16.50. Classic survey engulfing nineteenth-century thought; somewhat dated but yet to be replaced for breadth of vision and depth of perception.

Moyer, Albert E. *American Physics in Transition: A History of Conceptual Change in the Late Nineteenth Century.* Intro. by Daniel Siegal, Tomash Pubs. 1983 $30.00. Traces the shifting intellectual commitments of the American physics community from about 1870 to the appearance of relativity and quantum theory in the early twentieth century.

Paul, Harry W. *The Edge of Contingency: French Catholic Reaction to Scientific Change from Darwin to Duhem.* Univ. Pr. of Florida 1979 $15.00. Examines the Catholic reception of the breakdown of classical science, focusing on Darwinism.

———. *The Sorcerer's Apprentice: The French Scientist's Image of German Science, 1840–1919.* Univ. Pr. of Florida 1972 pap. $3.50. Analyzes French reevaluations of the nature of science in light of German developments.

Pernick, Martin S. *A Calculus of Suffering: Pain, Professionalism and Anesthesia in Nineteenth Century America.* Columbia Univ. Pr. 1985 $39.50 1987 text ed. pap. $14.50. Traces the reception of anesthesia among various ranks of American practitioners from its introduction in 1846 to the end of the century.

Reingold, Nathan, ed. *Science in Nineteenth-Century America: A Documentary History.* Hippocrene Bks. repr. of 1964 ed. 1979 lib. bdg. $19.50; Univ. of Chicago Pr. 1985 text ed. pap. $12.50. A standard introduction.

Rothstein, William G. *American Physicians in the Nineteenth Century: From Sects to Science.* Johns Hopkins Univ. Pr. 1972 $27.50. Provides a sociological interpretation of American medicine and medical practice in the nineteenth century.

Ruse, Michael. *The Darwinian Revolution: Science Red in Tooth and Claw.* Univ. of Chicago Pr. 1979 $25.00 pap. $12.00. Outlines themes and controversies surrounding the reception of Darwinism.

Sulloway, Frank J. *Freud, Biologist of the Mind: Beyond the Psychoanalytic Legend.* Basic Bks. 1979 pap. $13.95. Stimulating introduction to Freud and his work, arguing that many of his ideas were based on and rooted in nineteenth-century biological, particularly Darwinian, thought.

Turner, Gerald L'E. *Nineteenth-Century Scientific Instruments.* Univ. of California Pr. 1984 $65.00. Certain to become the standard.

Vorzimmer, Peter J. *Charles Darwin, the Years of Controversy: The Origin of Species and Its Critics, 1859–82.* Temple Univ. Pr. 1970 $17.95. Examines the immediate reception of Darwinism.

Williams, L. Pearce. *Album of Science: The Nineteenth Century.* Scribner 1978 text ed. $63.00. Handsomely illustrated survey of the "century of science"—the century that witnessed the emergence of modern science as a powerful national resource and world force.

———. *The Origins of Field Theory.* Univ. Pr. of Amer. 1980 lib. bdg. $22.25 text ed. pap. $8.75. Concise introduction to field theory and Faraday.

Twentieth Century

Allen, Garland E. *Life and Science in the Twentieth Century.* [*History of Science Ser.*] Cambridge Univ. Pr. 1978 $34.50 pap. $11.95. Standard single-volume study including post-Darwinian thought, embryology, heredity, genetics, biochemistry, and molecular biology.

Beyerchen, Alan D. *Scientists under Hitler: Politics and the Physics Community in the Third Reich.* Yale Univ. Pr. 1981 $34.00 pap. $10.95. Examines the response of prominent German scientists during the Third Reich.

Bliss, Michael. *The Discovery of Insulin.* Univ. of Chicago Pr. 1982 lib. bdg. $25.00 1984 pap. $10.95. Recounts the dramatic discovery of insulin and the career of Frederick Banting leading to the Nobel Prize; well illustrated.

Clark, Ronald W. *Einstein: The Life and Times.* Avon 1972 pap. $5.95. Comprehensive overview and introduction for the nonspecialist, with hundreds of photographs.

Cline, Barbara L. *The Questioners: Physicists and the Quantum Theory.* Crowell 1965 $5.00. Excellent introduction to the work of Thomson, Rutherford, Planck, and Heisenberg, emphasizing the differing views of Bohr and Einstein on quantum theory. This volume was later published in paperback under the title *The Men Who Made a New Physics* (Univ. of Chicago Pr. 1987 pap. $11.95).

Cravens, Hamilton. *Triumph of Evolution: American Scientists and the Heredity-Environment Controversy, 1900–1941.* Univ. of Pennsylvania Pr. 1978 $27.25. Examines the nature/nurture controversy in America during the early decades of the twentieth century.

Einstein, Albert. *Relativity: The Special and General Theory.* Trans. by Robert W. Lawson, Crown 1961 pap. $3.95. Einstein's classic introductory statement addressed to the layperson.

Einstein, Albert, and Leopold Infeld. *The Evolution of Physics: The Growth of Ideas from Early Concepts to Relativity and Quanta.* Simon & Schuster 1967 pap. $9.95. Provides background and an introduction to twentieth-century physics, particularly the theory of relativity.

Gingerich, Owen, ed. *Astrophysics and Twentieth-Century Astronomy to 1950.* [*General History of Astronomy Ser.*] Cambridge Univ. Pr. 1984 $32.50. Authoritative multiauthored study ranging through all aspects of astronomy and astrophysics.

Heilbron, John L. *The Dilemmas of an Upright Man: Max Planck as Spokesman for German Science.* Univ. of California Pr. 1986 $16.95. Recounts the dilemmas of a conservative thinker whose work had radical scientific and political implications.

Hirsh, Richard F. *Glimpsing an Invisible Universe: The Emergence of X-ray Astronomy.* Cambridge Univ. Pr. 1983 $44.50 1985 pap. $17.95. Traces the history of X-ray astronomy from the late 1950s, examining developments in technique and funding policy.

Hoffmann, Banesh, and Helen Dukas. *Albert Einstein: Creator and Rebel.* NAL 1973 o.p. Popular biography surveying Einstein's scientific and political activities.

Holton, Gerald, ed. *The Twentieth-Century Sciences: Studies in the Biography of Ideas.* Norton 1972 o.p. Collected essays both by and about major figures and themes in twentieth-century science, including essays by Erickson and Pauling.

Jammer, Max. *The Philosophy of Quantum Mechanics: The Interpretations of Quantum Mechanics in Historical Perspective.* Wiley 1974 $49.95. Detailed study based on primary documents.

Kevles, Daniel J. *In the Name of Eugenics: Genetics and the Uses of Human Heredity.* Knopf 1985 $22.95; Univ. of California Pr. 1986 pap. $9.95. Traces the development of eugenics and attendant social and ethical issues.

———. *The Physicists: The History of a Scientific Community in Modern America.* Knopf 1977 $15.95; Random 1979 pap. $10.95. Examines the internal and institutional development of the American physics community from the late nineteenth century.

Kuhn, Thomas S. *Black-Body Theory and the Quantum Discontinuity, 1894–1912.*

Oxford 1978 $26.50; Univ. of Chicago Pr. 1987 pap. $18.95. Scholarly study of the origins of the concept of quantum, emphasizing the contributions of Max Planck.

Lang, Kenneth R., and Owen Gingerich, eds. *A Source Book in Astronomy and Astrophysics, 1900–1975.* Harvard Univ. Pr. 1979 $60.00. Useful selection of original papers tracing the emergence of contemporary astronomy and astrophysics.

Layton, Edwin T. *The Revolt of the Engineers: Social Responsibility and the American Engineering Profession.* Johns Hopkins Univ. Pr. repr. of 1971 ed. 1986 text ed. $29.50 pap. $9.95. Traces the profession from the late nineteenth century, focusing on its efforts to establish professional criteria for social responsibility.

McDougall, Walter A. *The Heavens and the Earth: A Political History of the Space Age.* Basic Bks. 1985 $25.95 1986 pap. $11.95. Provides an excellent account of the space race in considering the broader issue of political involvement in technological and social change.

Mather, Kirtley F., ed. *Source Book in Geology 1900–1950.* Harvard Univ. Pr. 1967 o.p. Contains primary selections from over 50 authors, with useful introductory notes.

Metropolis, N., and others, eds. *A History of Computing in the Twentieth Century: A Collection of Essays.* Academic Pr. 1980 $39.50. Diverse collection of essays ranging from hardware and software to corporate warfare; includes contributions from historians as well as participants in the computer revolution.

Miller, Arthur I. *Imagery in Scientific Thought: Creating Twentieth-Century Physics.* Birkhäuser 1984 $24.95; MIT repr. of 1984 ed. 1986 text ed. pap. $8.95. Focusing on the work of Bohr, Boltzmann, Einstein, Heisenberg, and Poincaré, the author explores the roots of scientific innovation, the origin of ideas and their transformations.

Olby, Robert. *The Path to the Double Helix.* Univ. of Washington Pr. 1974 o.p. Provides intellectual and institutional background to the study of DNA and the double helix.

Pais, Abraham. *Subtle Is the Lord: The Science and Life of Albert Einstein.* Oxford 1982 $12.95. Scholarly biography filled with technical detail and insight.

Paul, Harry W. *From Knowledge to Power: The Rise of the Science Empire in France, 1860–1939.* Cambridge Univ. Pr. 1985 $49.50. Evaluates the state-stimulated growth of French science since the Second Empire.

Provine, William B. *The Origins of Theoretical Population Genetics.* [*History of Science and Medicine Ser.*] Univ. of Chicago Pr. 1971 $18.00 1987 pap. $11.95. Examines the resolution of the biometry-Mendelism controversy and the origins of theoretical population genetics in the early twentieth century.

Schilpp, Paul Arthur, ed. *Albert Einstein, Philosopher-Scientist.* Open Court 1973 o.p. Collection of essays on Einstein's life, thought, and influence in science, philosophy, and culture.

Skinner, B. F. *The Shaping of a Behaviorist.* New York Univ. Pr. 1985 pap. $11.95. Self-analysis of the pioneering behavioral psychologist.

Smith, Robert W. *The Expanding Universe: Astronomy's "Great Debate," 1900–1931.* Cambridge Univ. Pr. 1982 $34.50. Nontechnical treatment of the debate concerning the nature of our galaxy, the structure of the universe, and the specific contributions of Eddington, Shapley, and Curtis.

Snow, C. P. *The Two Cultures: And a Second Look.* Cambridge Univ. Pr. repr. of 1964 ed. 1969 $24.95 pap. $6.95. Classic statement and reevaluation of the controversial claim that scientists and humanistically trained individuals represent distinct cultures.

Struve, Otto, and Velta Zebergs. *Astronomy of the Twentieth Century.* Macmillan

1962 o.p. Comprehensive survey of astronomical research in the first half of the twentieth century.

Stuewer, Roger H. *The Compton Effect: Turning Point in Physics.* Watson 1975 o.p. Provides thorough analysis of the context and development of radiation physics culminating with Compton's discovery in 1922.

Watson, James D. *Double Helix: Being a Personal Account of the Discovery of the Structure of DNA.* Fwd. by L. Bragg, Atheneum 1968 $7.95 pap. $6.95; ed. by Gunther S. Stent, NAL 1969 pap. $3.95; Norton 1980 text ed. pap. $7.95. Autobiographical account of one of the great scientific developments of the century.

Will, Clifford M. *Was Einstein Right? Putting General Relativity to the Test.* Basic Bks. 1986 $18.95. Popular introduction to general relativity and the experimental ingenuity involved in its demonstration.

Williams, Trevor I. *A Short History of Twentieth-Century Technology, 1900–1950.* Oxford 1982 $29.95. Surveys the development of technology in the first half of the twentieth-century, touching on the economic, social, and political factors that gave shape to Western technological society.

CHAPTER 3

Philosophy of Science and Pseudoscience

Michael Radner

Scientific knowledge aims at being wholly impersonal, and tries to state what has been discovered by the collective intellect of mankind.
—BERTRAND RUSSELL, *Human Knowledge: Its Scope and Limits*

The Sciences, after all, are our own creation, including all the severe standards they seem to impose on us
—PAUL K. FEYERABEND, *Against Method*

Science is a complex, many-sided form of human activity. Some special disciplines have evolved just for the purpose of studying the scientific enterprise. Historians of science write about themes and episodes in the chronological development of the sciences. Sociologists of science examine the structure of scientific institutions and groups. Philosophers of science, too, take scientific activity for their subject matter. They ask questions about science that reflect certain long-standing philosophical concerns dating back to the ancient Greek philosophers PLATO (see Vols. 3 and 4) and ARISTOTLE (see Vols. 3 and 4): What is the nature of knowledge? Is it based on sense experience alone, or does it also require insights from the human intellect? Which patterns of reasoning are correct and which are erroneous? How are bits of knowledge systemized into coherent wholes?

Many other questions emerge when philosophers of science consider the impressive achievements of the sciences, especially in the period from the scientific revolution of the seventeenth century to the present: What special characteristics of scientific knowledge account for the great success of the natural sciences? What are the relations of the sciences to each other? Is there one fundamental science to which all the others ideally should be reduced? Do scientific theories, such as the physics of elementary particles, tell what really exists, or do they just supply useful fictions? How does scientific knowledge change and evolve? If it is genuine knowledge in the first place, how could it change?

Work in the philosophy of science may be roughly divided into two categories. (1) Investigations that consider the nature of science in general, or at least cut across different sciences. The above questions mainly belong to this first category. (2) Discussions focusing on one particular field of science, such as evolutionary biology or quantum physics. Here the philosopher examines basic concepts of the science, perhaps proposing definitions or criticizing some of the reasoning. In this category the work of the philosopher overlaps with that of the scientist. The topic of scientific method falls into the first category. In previous centuries, scientists and philosophers expressed the essence of science by that term. They hoped to extract the method inherent in the most successful science, physics, and apply it to other areas to generate equally reliable and accurate results. Most people today would agree that not all "sciences" are equal. The reliability and precision of research results vary widely from field to field. This suggests that something more than a simple set of rules is required for a science to be successful.

Even if scientific method is not going to provide a magic key for practicing science, philosophers of science want the clearest possible picture of how the sciences function. Much of the technical literature is concerned with making models to display the structure of systems of scientific knowledge. Philosophers of science frequently borrow concepts and formal apparatus from logicians in order to make their models of how scientific knowledge claims interrelate. Once one has a grasp of how a system of knowledge is organized, one can ask the important question: How does the information supplied by observation and experiment provide evidential support for the hypothetical or theoretical claims? Here not only the field of logic but also the subjects of probability and statistics become relevant for the philosopher of science.

Besides establishing a positive account of the proper functioning of science, philosophers of science have the negative task of criticizing pseudoscience (imitation science). Pseudoscientists twist or distort the methods of reasoning found in the legitimate sciences. They offer us unsupported ideas dressed up to resemble science. Investigations of how pseudoscientists go wrong not only supply needed critiques of misleading publications, but add to our understanding and appreciation of genuine science.

GENERAL BIBLIOGRAPHY

Achinstein, Peter, ed. *The Concept of Evidence.* Oxford 1983 pap. $8.95. Appearing in the series *Oxford Readings in Philosophy,* this very useful collection introduces the reader to controversies about how "experience" supports scientific theories. Three major viewpoints are presented: Popper's critical approach, nonprobabilistic confirmation (Glymour [see below] following Hempel), and the Bayesians (Salmon and others).

Armstrong, D. M. *What Is a Law of Nature?* [*Cambridge Studies in Philosophy*] 1983 $32.50 1985 pap. $9.95. Armstrong criticizes the doctrine that laws just express regular patterns of events and discusses laws as relations between "universals."

Asquith, Peter D., and Henry E. Kyburg, Jr., eds. *Current Research in Philosophy of Science.* Philosophy of Science Assn. 1979 $12.50 pap. $10.50. An excellent collection of review articles assessing progress on a number of problems.

Bergmann, Gustav. *Philosophy of Science.* Univ. of Wisconsin Pr. 1958 o.p. A distinguished analytic philosopher discusses basic concepts in philosophy of science, especially types of scientific laws.

Blake, Ralph M., Curt J. Ducasse, and Edward H. Madden. *Theories of Scientific Method: The Renaissance Through the Nineteenth Century.* Univ. of Washington Pr. 1960 o.p. Separate chapters on major figures in the history of scientific methodology. One of the few sources on the history of philosophy of science.

Bridgman, Percy W. *The Logic of Modern Physics.* Ed. by I. B. Cohen [*Three Centuries of Science in Amer. Ser.*] Ayer repr. of 1927 ed. 1980 lib. bdg. $21.00. Bridgman was the orginator of "operationism," the doctrine that scientific concepts are defined by how they are measured.

Bunge, Mario. *Causality and Modern Science.* Dover repr. of 1963 ed. 1979 pap. $8.95. (Printed in *Educational Studies*, vol. 11 [Fall 1980].) Bunge provides the reader with a useful survey of various concepts of causality in philosophy and science. He goes on to discuss causal determinism and delineates the role of causal concepts in modern physics.

———. *Formal and Physical Sciences.* Part 1 in Vol. 7 in *Treatise on Basic Philosophy.* Kluwer Academic 1985 lib. bdg. $39.00 text ed. pap. $22.00. Bunge's philosophical survey of the sciences includes an overview of classical and modern physics, chemistry, the earth sciences, biology, and neuroscience. The emphasis is on such questions as: Is quantum theory antirealist? Is chemistry reducible to physics?

———. *Metascientific Queries.* C. C. Thomas 1959 $24.50. In these essays on scientific method and the laws of physics, Bunge practices "metascience": the interplay of scientific, philosophical, and historical disciplines that enriches our understanding of science.

Cohen, Robert S., and Marx W. Wartofsky, eds. *In Memory of Norwood Russell Hanson.* Vol. 3 in *Boston Studies in the Philosophy of Science.* Kluwer Academic 1967 $45.00. This is one of the numerous volumes edited by Cohen and Wartofsky on behalf of the Boston Colloquium for the Philosophy of Science. This volume includes a symposium on "innate ideas."

———. Vol. 5 in *Boston Studies in the Philosophy of Science.* Kluwer Academic 1969 $42.00. Includes a lengthy reply by Adolf Grünbaum to Hilary Putnam's attack on his philosophy of geometry. The *Boston Studies* is a rich mine of articles in the philosophy of science.

Colodny, Robert G., ed. *Beyond the Edge of Certainty: Essays in Contemporary Science and Philosophy.* Univ. Pr. of Amer. 1983 text ed. $28.25 pap. $14.25. Includes an interchange on the significance of Newton's law of inertia, by Brian Ellis and Norwood Russell Hanson, and Feyerabend's "Problems of Empiricism" (Part 1).

———. *Frontiers of Science and Philosophy.* [*Philosophy of Science Ser.*] Univ. of Pittsburgh Pr. 1962 $24.95; Univ. Pr. of Amer. repr. of 1962 ed. 1983 text ed. $28.25 pap. $14.25. This is the first of a series of Pittsburgh Studies in Philosophy of Science edited by Colodny. Contributors include Hempel, Sellars, Scriven, and Grünbaum.

———. *Mind and Cosmos: Essays in Contemporary Science and Philosophy.* [*CPS Publications in Philosophy of Science*] Univ. Pr. of Amer. 1984 lib. bdg. $30.25 pap. $15.75. Wesley C. Salmon's long exposition on scientific inference appears here, and Dudley Shapere contributes an important article on conceptual change.

———. *The Nature and Function of Scientific Theories: Essays in Contemporary Science and Philosophy.* [*Philosophy of Science Ser.*] Univ. of Pittsburgh Pr. 1970 o.p. Abner Shimony contributes an important long essay on scientific inference.

Feyerabend's "Problems of Empiricism" (Part 2), and articles by Maxwell, Hesse, Salmon, and Hanson also appear. One of the best studies volumes.

Danto, Arthur, and Sidney Morgenbesser, eds. *Philosophy of Science*. New Amer. Lib. (Meridian Bks.) 1960 o.p. A fine collection that provides a good introductory survey of issues and doctrines.

Duhem, Pierre. *Aim and Structure of Physical Theory*. Atheneum 1962 text ed. pap. $5.95. The classic statement of the "instrumentalist" position, that physical theory tells about appearance, not about reality. (Originally published in 1906.)

Gale, George. *Theory of Science*. McGraw-Hill 1979 text ed. $28.95. A text that takes into account recent developments in philosophy of science.

Giere, Ronald N. *Understanding Scientific Reasoning*. Holt 2d ed. 1984 text ed. pap. $19.95. A very readable presentation of basic forms of reasoning in science, including an excellent section on correlation and causality.

Glymour, Clark. *Theory and Evidence*. Princeton Univ. Pr. 1980 $40.00 pap. $16.00. Glymour develops a doctrine in the Hempelian tradition of how explanations and predictions support the theories they are derived from.

Grandy, Richard E., ed. *Theories and Observation in Science*. Ridgeview repr. of 1973 ed. 1980 lib. bdg. $24.00 pap. $8.50. The issue of how theories affect observations is an important one; Grandy's collection provides the main doctrines.

Hacking, Ian. *Representing and Intervening: Introductory Topics in the Philosophy of Natural Science*. Cambridge Univ. Pr. 1983 $39.50 pap. $12.95. A thoughtful treatment of theory and observation and other matters.

————. *Scientific Revolutions*. [*Oxford Readings in Philosophy Ser.*] 1981 text ed. pap. $8.95. A balanced collection of the main contenders on "revolutions." Includes Popper, Kuhn, Feyerabend, Lakatos, and Shapere.

Hanson, Norwood Russell. *Patterns of Discovery: An Enquiry into the Conceptual Foundations of Science*. Cambridge Univ. Pr. 1958–65 $49.50 pap. $13.95. Hanson's influential book focuses on the pervasive effects of theory on observations.

————. *Perception and Discovery: An Introduction to Scientific Inquiry*. Ed. by Willard C. Humphreys, Freeman Cooper 1969 text ed. pap. $12.00. After Hanson's untimely death in 1967, Humphreys edited the manuscript. The result is a clear and easy-to-read introduction to Hanson's thought.

Harré, Rom. *Principles of Scientific Thinking*. Univ. of Chicago Pr. 1970 $22.50. Harré sets up a realist framework of understanding science that runs counter to some of the precepts of logical empiricism. The book is valuable for its thorough treatment of the concept of "models" of scientific theories.

Hesse, Mary B. *Models and Analogies in Science*. Univ. of Notre Dame Pr. 1966 o.p. For anyone investigating this topic, Hesse's book must be the starting point.

Körner, Stephan. *Experience and Theory*. Humanities Pr. 1966 text ed. $19.25. Körner argues for a distinction between theory and sense experience and then explores ways of bridging the logical gap.

Kurtz, Paul, ed. *A Skeptic's Handbook of Parapsychology*. Prometheus Bks. 1985 $25.95 pap. $14.95. Thirty critics and practitioners of parapsychology survey the history and current state of the field, with emphasis on the skeptical side. Includes most major commentators in this area.

Lakatos, Imre. *Philosophical Papers*. Ed. by J. Worrall and G. Currie, Cambridge Univ. Pr. 2 vols. 1978 ea. $39.50–$44.50 1980 pap. ea. $14.95–$15.95. Lakatos's philosophy is a unique blend of dialectical style and creative use of historical examples. His notion of "research programme" is especially valuable. Lakatos's essays are always lively, provocative, and worth reading. The second volume includes his articles on the problems of appraising scientific theories and inductive logic.

Lakatos, Imre, and A. E. Musgrave, eds. *Criticism and the Growth of Knowledge.* Cambridge Univ. Pr. 1970 $49.50 pap. $13.95. An indispensable volume for understanding the relation between Popper's and Kuhn's philosophies of science.

Laudan, Larry. *Progress and Its Problems: Towards a Theory of Scientific Growth.* Univ. of California Pr. 1977 $25.50 pap. $9.95. Laudan rejects traditional logical empiricist philosophies of science and proposes a doctrine based on the notion of "problems."

———. *Science and Values: An Essay on the Aims of Science and Their Role in Scientific Debate.* [*Pittsburgh Ser. in Philosophy and History of Science*] Univ. of California Pr. 1984 $14.95. Laudan's book is not about science and ethics, but about research goals of scientists. He attacks the view that has become identified with Thomas Kuhn.

Losee, John. *An Historical Introduction to the Philosophy of Science.* Oxford 2d ed. 1980 $14.95 pap. $7.95. A useful, elementary presentation of basic ideas in the philosophy of science. John Stuart Mill and other pioneers are included.

Naess, Arne. *The Pluralist and Possibilist Aspect of the Scientific Enterprise.* Universitet 1972 $30.00. A stimulating discussion of communication and change in science.

Pap, Arthur. *An Introduction to the Philosophy of Science.* Free Pr. 1962 o.p. A compendium of logical positivist philosophy of science by one of the clearest thinkers in the movement.

Poincaré, Henri. *The Foundations of Science: Science and Hypothesis, the Value of Science, Science and Method.* Trans. by George B. Halstead, Univ. Pr. of Amer. repr. of 1913 ed. 1982 lib. bdg. $33.50 text ed. pap. $20.75. The great French mathematician Poincaré assessed the significance of revolutionary results in geometry and physics for philosophy of science. The three books originally appeared in 1902, 1905, and 1908.

Putnam, Hilary. *Philosophical Papers.* Cambridge Univ. Pr. 3 vols. 2d ed. 1975–1983 ea. $39.50–$44.50 pap. ea. $15.95. Putnam, a logician and philosopher of language, has made a number of important contributions to philosophy of science. Putnam's papers on analytic and synthetic truths, and on realism, are especially notable.

Quine, Willard van Orman. *From a Logical Point of View: Nine Logico-Philosophical Essays.* Harvard Univ. Pr. 2d ed. rev. 1961 $14.00 pap. $5.95. "Two Dogmas of Empiricism," Quine's attack on the distinction between factual truths and truths based on "meaning," has been read by virtually every philosopher of science.

Rescher, Nicholas. *Methodological Pragmatism: A Systems-Theoretic Approach to the Theory of Knowledge.* New York Univ. Pr. 1977 $27.50. A clever treatment of the problem of establishing a "foundation" for scientific knowledge.

———. *Scientific Explanation.* Free Pr. 1970 $14.95. Rescher is a prolific writer on logic, philosophy of science, and related areas. His books are always clear and interesting.

———, ed. *Scientific Explanation and Understanding: Essays on Reasoning and Rationality.* [*CPS Publications in Philosophy of Science*] Univ. Pr. of Amer. 1983 lib. bdg. $23.75 text ed. pap. $10.50. Rescher has edited a series of these "studies" volumes, which extends the older series edited by Robert Colodny.

Russell, Bertrand. *Human Knowledge: Its Scope and Limits.* Simon & Schuster 1948 o.p. Russell's writings on logic and knowledge have exercised an enormous influence on twentieth-century philosophy of science. This is his last major book on theory of knowledge and includes his views on inductive inference.

Scheffler, Israel. *The Anatomy of Inquiry: Philosophical Studies in the Theory of Science.* Hackett 1981 lib. bdg. $19.50 text ed. pap. $9.95. Scheffler presents a well-organized compendium of philosophy of science in the later stages of the logical empiricist movement, focusing on the technical work of Hempel and Quine.

————. *Science and Subjectivity.* Hackett 2d ed. repr. of 1967 ed. 1982 lib. bdg. $17.50 text ed. pap. $6.95. Scheffler defends scientific objectivity against attacks from historically minded philosophers such as Kuhn and Feyerabend.

Sellars, Wilfred. *Science, Perception and Reality.* Routledge & Kegan 1963 o.p. An eminent U.S. philosopher discusses the relation of scientific knowledge to "common sense" and sense experience.

Shapere, Dudley. *Reason and the Search for Knowledge.* Kluwer Academic 1983 lib. bdg. $59.50 1984 text ed. pap. $19.95. Shapere attempts to formulate a philosophy of science to replace the logical empiricist approach. He has a wide knowledge of history of science as well as philosophy of science.

Suppe, Frederick. *Studies in the Methodology and Foundations of Science: Selected Papers, 1951–1969.* [*Synthese Lib.*] Kluwer Academic 1969 lib. bdg. $45.00. Suppe is an influential logician and philosopher of science who stresses the importance of statistical thinking in philosophy of science.

————, ed. *The Structure of Theories.* Univ. of Illinois Pr. 2d ed. repr. of 1974 ed. 1977 $35.00 pap. $14.50. A valuable review of research on what theories are and how they relate to experiment. The essays by Suppe, Kuhn, Putnam and others, together with an extensive bibliography, make the book especially useful.

Toulmin, Stephen. *Foresight and Understanding: An Enquiry into the Aims of Science.* Greenwood repr. of 1961 ed. 1982 lib. bdg. $22.50; Harper o.p. Toulmin's historical approach to scientific thinking overlaps with other postpositivist writers such as Kuhn.

————. *Human Understanding: Concepts.* Princeton Univ. Pr. 1972 $47.00 pap. $13.95. Toulmin's excellent grasp of intellectual history enables him to provide the reader with interesting insights into the evolution of scientific thought.

Van Fraassen, Bas C. *The Scientific Image.* Oxford Univ. Pr. 1980 text ed. $45.00 pap. $14.95. A sophisticated defense of instrumentalism (science as fiction). The book can be read as a response to Sellars' *Science, Perception and Reality.*

Watkins, John. *Science and Scepticism.* Princeton Univ. Pr. 1984 text ed. $44.00 pap. $14.50. Watkins attempts to defeat Hume's form of skepticism about the possibility of scientific knowledge.

Ziman, John M. *Reliable Knowledge.* Cambridge Univ. Pr. 1979 $29.95. Ziman is a physicist who expresses sociologically oriented views in philosophy of science.

INDUCTIVE INFERENCE

An ornithologist observes that 23 Northern Orioles have built finely woven nests hanging from branch tips, and predicts that the next Oriole observed will build a nest of the same type. Scientists and nonscientists alike commonly make such inductive inferences from observed cases to unobserved cases. All reasoning about matters of fact that reaches beyond the observed cases is uncertain. We are not sure that the next Oriole will behave according to form, whereas we are certain that 2 + 2 = 4. Philosophers of science are curious about inductive reasoning. First, are inductive inferences *reasonable?* Are they leaps of faith that people habitually make, and which are ultimately unjustified? Second, granting that they are reasonable, what are the general rules for inductive inferences? Third, the premises of an inductive inference make the conclusion *probable.* Does "probability" mean the amount of confidence in the conclusion or does it just indicate the proportion of cases in which the conclusion is true?

The subject of inductive reasoning is a live area for research, and controversies abound. Neither philosophers of science nor their cousins in the field of statistical inference have reached a consensus on foundations for inductive inference in science.

Earman, John, ed. *Testing Scientific Theories.* [*Minnesota Studies in the Philosophy of Science*] Univ. of Minnesota Pr. 1984 $39.50 pap. $16.95. This volume samples recent work in inductive reasoning. Clark Glymour's idea of "bootstrapping," which continues the work of Hempel on confirmation of theories, supplies a unifying theme. The Bayesian point of view is represented by some of its major practitioners. A number of historical case studies rounds out the collection.

Goodman, Nelson. *Fact, Fiction, and Forecast.* Harvard Univ. Pr. 4th ed. 1983 text ed. $10.00 pap. $4.95. Includes Goodman's classic puzzle of inductive inference and his proposed solution.

Hacking, Ian M. *Logic of Statistical Inference.* Cambridge Univ. Pr. 1966 $39.50 pap. $14.95. An attempt to locate the presuppositions of statistical reasoning.

Hesse, Mary. *The Structure of Scientific Inference.* Univ. of California Pr. 1974 o.p. A distinguished British philosopher of science analyzes scientific reasoning.

Horwich, Paul. *Probability and Evidence.* [*Cambridge Studies in Philosophy*] 1982 $29.95. A brief, clear introduction to inductive inference concepts, puzzles, and solutions.

Jeffrey, Richard C. *The Logic of Decision.* Univ. of Chicago Pr. 2d ed. 1983 lib. bdg. $22.00. One of the most eminent of current researchers supports a "decision theory" doctrine of scientific reasoning.

Kyburg, Henry E., Jr. *Epistemology and Inference.* Univ. of Minnesota Pr. 1983 $39.50 pap. $15.95. Nineteen essays, most of them previously published, and revised by the author, are collected here. Kyburg has divided the volume according to subject areas: some general philosophical essays, papers on probability, and papers on epistemology. This book gives the reader easy access to the range of views expressed by a leading inductive logician.

——. *The Logical Foundations of Statistical Inference.* [*Synthese Lib.*] Kluwer Academic 1974 lib. bdg. $60.50 pap. $25.00. The author proposes a common ground in which the divergent views on inductive reasoning can be compared. The book assumes mathematical sophistication but some parts are accessible to the less advanced reader.

——. *Theory and Measurement.* [*Cambridge Studies in Philosophy*] 1984 $39.50. This is a technically sophisticated treatment of measurement concepts. Kyburg stresses the role of measurements in the testing of scientific theories. A precise and rigorous analysis of an important topic.

Kyburg, Henry E., Jr., and Howard E. Smokler, eds. *Studies in Subjective Probability.* Krieger 2d ed. repr. of 1964 ed. 1980 pap. $12.50. The best collection of basic writings in subjective probability, from John Venn to L. J. Savage.

Levi, Isaac. *Decisions and Revisions: Philosophical Essays on Knowledge and Value.* Cambridge Univ. Pr. 1984 $34.50. In these papers, Levi explains his own doctrine and criticizes opposing views.

——. *The Enterprise of Knowledge: An Essay on Knowledge, Credal Probability, and Chance.* MIT 1980 text ed. $40.00 pap. $12.50. Levi contends that science is a body of knowledge with stringent standards of acceptance.

——. *Gambling with Truth: An Essay on Induction and the Aims of Science.* MIT 1974 pap. $5.95. Levi's earlier views on acceptance of scientific claims.

Maxwell, Grover, and Robert M. Anderson, Jr., eds. *Induction, Probability, and Confirmation.* [*Minnesota Studies in the Philosophy of Science*] Univ. of Minnesota Pr. 1975 $27.50

Rosenkrantz, Roger D. *Foundations and Applications of Inductive Probability.* Ridgeview 1981 lib. bdg. $29.00 text ed. pap. $15.00. An excellent text. Some parts are fairly elementary; other parts are highly mathematical.

——. *Inference, Method and Decision.* Kluwer Academic 1977 lib. bdg. $34.00 pap. $16.00. One of the best recent attempts to analyze scientific reasoning.

Salmon, Wesley C. *The Foundations of Scientific Inference.* 1966. Univ. of Pittsburgh Pr. repr. 1967 pap. $6.95. Extremely readable exposition of the basic problem of induction. Salmon develops Reichenbach's approach to induction.

——. *Scientific Explanation and the Causal Structure of the World.* Princeton Univ. Pr. 1984 text ed. $35.00 pap. $14.50. The most complete presentation of Salmon's theory of inductive inference.

Skyrms, Brian. *Causal Necessity: A Pragmatic Investigation of the Necessity of Laws.* Yale Univ. Pr. 1980 $31.00. The reader will not find here a general treatment or survey of causal necessity. Skyrms develops his own approach that depends on probability concepts rather than on "possible worlds" logic.

——. *Choice and Chance: An Introduction to Inductive Logic.* Wadsworth 3d ed. 1986 text ed. pap. $17.75. Probably the most elementary introduction to the subject.

——. *Pragmatics and Empiricism.* Yale Univ. Pr. 1984 text ed. $16.95. A more advanced adjunct to Skyrms's *Choice and Chance.*

Swinburne, Richard, ed. *Justification of Induction.* [*Oxford Readings in Philosophy Ser.*] 1974 text ed. pap. $8.95. A collection of readings on the most "philosophical" problem of inductive reasoning.

CRITIQUES OF PSEUDOSCIENCE

Philosophy of science is chiefly theory of science. It does not have the practical aim of teaching techniques for telling good science from bad, or fake science from genuine science. Yet people are consumers of scientific knowledge, and need to learn how to distinguish the genuine article from the phony. The ability to spot fake science is not automatically conferred by a scientific education either. Pseudoscientists often hoodwink scientists in fields that lie outside their own areas of expertise. Even within their specialties, scientists' training does not make them immune to deception and fraud.

The skills required for examining alleged scientific knowledge fall into an area that overlaps philosophy of science and "informal" logic. People publishing in this area employ a number of strategies, often in combination. These include: (1) explanations of what kinds of correct arguments scientists use to support their conclusions (e.g., Ronald Giere's *Understanding Scientific Reasoning* in the General Bibliography); (2) lists of logical and statistical fallacies (textbooks of critical thinking frequently take this approach, usually in rather fragmentary fashion); (3) investigations and criticism of particular cases of fraud, egregiously bad science, or imitation science (pseudoscience)—many books do this well; a number of them are listed below; (4) a systematic presentation of the characteristics of pseudoscience, so that readers can learn to diagnose individual cases for themselves (only one book at present pursues this strategy [Radner and Radner, *Science and Unreason*]).

Abell, George, and Barry Singer. *Science and the Paranormal.* Scribner 1983 pap. $9.95. Nineteen scientists and writers bring science to bear on a variety of fringe science and paranormal topics, including Kirlian photography, plant perception, and moon madness.

Alcock, James E. *Parapsychology: Science or Magic?* Pergamon 1981 $17.95. A skeptical psychologist presents criticisms of research methods in parapsychology and offers psychological explanations of tendencies to believe in "psi."

Bauer, Henry H. *Beyond Velikovsky: The History of a Public Controversy.* Univ. of Illinois Pr. 1984 $21.95. "Velikovsky's understanding, particularly of the physical sciences on which his theoretical arguments depend, is shown to be abysmal. . . . Many of the inept arguments used by the scientific critics of Velikovsky are also exposed, and in a most candid and direct way. . . . the book is rich in educational value, particularly as regards the nature of scientific thinking and inference" (*Science*).

Blackmore, Susan J. *Beyond the Body.* Academy Chicago pap. $5.95. A parapsychologist investigates the "out-of-body" experience. Sets a high standard of scientific rigor for research in this area.

Brandon, Ruth. *The Spiritualists: The Passion for the Occult in the Nineteenth and Twentieth Centuries.* Prometheus Bks. 1984 pap. $11.95. A detailed look at the famous mediums, from the Fox sisters to Madame Blavatsky.

Cazeau, Charles J., and Stuart D. Scott, Jr. *Exploring the Unknown: Great Mysteries Re-examined.* Plenum 1979 $18.95. A careful analysis, according to scientific principles, of pseudoscientific claims about the pyramids, Noah's Ark, Atlantis, and so on.

Cerullo, John J. *The Secularization of the Soul: Psychical Research in Modern Britain.* Institute for the Study of Human Issues 1982 text ed. $21.00. The history of the formative period of the psychical movement. Cerullo analyzes the attraction the paranormal exercised on Victorians.

Collins, H. M., and T. J. Pinch. *Frames of Meaning: The Social Construction of Extraordinary Science.* Routledge & Kegan 1982 $29.95. Discussions of the relationship of parapsychology to science, and the British case of alleged "metal-bending" by children.

Culver, Roger B., and Philip A. Ianna. *The Gemini Syndrome: Star Wars of the Oldest Kind.* [*Astronomy Quarterly Lib.*] Pachart 1979 $11.95; [*Science and the Paranormal Ser.*] Prometheus Bks. repr. of 1979 ed. 1984 $18.95 pap. $11.95. Two astronomers provide a critical survey of the history and practice of astrology.

Davies, John D. *Phrenology: Fad and Science; A Nineteenth Century American Crusade.* Shoe String repr. of 1955 ed. 1971 $22.50. Phrenology in nineteenth-century America was a pseudoscience based on the idea that the shape of a person's head provides information about his or her character. Davies's book is a well-documented study of the rise of phrenology in the United States and its influence on education, medicine, religion, and other areas of culture.

Eldredge, Niles. *The Monkey Business: A Scientist Looks at Creationism.* Washington Square Pr. 1982 $3.95. Eldredge, a noted paleontologist, has written a highly accessible and entertaining answer to creationist attacks on evolutionary science.

Franks, Felix. *Polywater.* MIT 1981 $20.00 pap. $5.95. A fascinating case study of pathological science.

Frazier, Kendrick, ed. *Paranormal Borderlands of Science.* [*Science and the Paranormal Ser.*] Prometheus Bks. 1981 pap. $15.95. A collection of 47 articles from the first four years of *Skeptical Inquirer*. Covers a wide range of topics in fringe science and the paranormal.

———. *Science Confronts the Paranormal*. Prometheus Bks. 1985 pap. $15.95. The companion volume to *Paranormal Borderlands of Science*. Recent articles from *Skeptical Inquirer*.

Gardner, Martin. *Fads and Fallacies (In the Name of Science)*. Dover 2d ed. 1957 pap. $5.95. A standard work in the field of debunking crank theories.

———. *Science: Good, Bad and Bogus*. Avon 1983 pap. $3.95. A collection of Gardner's articles, many on parapsychology.

Godfrey, Laurie R., ed. *Scientists Confront Creationism*. Norton 1984 pap. $7.95. "Many of the contributors to this critique of 'creation science' are established scientists associated with the Committee for the Scientific Investigation of Claims of the Paranormal—a group devoted to the exposé of pseudosciences in our culture. . . . Although this volume is not likely to make converts from the side of the creationists, it has a value beyond the scope of its polemic in that the diverse articles represent state-of-the-art reports in such fields as cosmology, paleontology, systematics, comparative biology, and stratigraphy" (*Choice*).

Goldsmith, Donald, ed. *Scientists Confront Velikovsky*. Cornell Univ. Pr. 1977 $19.95; Norton 1979 pap. $3.95. Papers by Carl Sagan and others from a 1974 symposium sponsored by the American Association for the Advancement of Science.

Gould, Stephen J. *Ever Since Darwin: Reflections in Natural History*. Norton 1977 $14.95 1979 pap. $4.95. Lively essays on a number of topics, including Velikovsky and racist theories of human nature.

———. *The Mismeasure of Man*. Norton 1981 $14.95 1983 pap. $5.95. Gould reveals the biases, bad science, and pseudoscience in major nineteenth- and twentieth-century theories of the nature of man.

Grim, Patrick, ed. *Philosophy of Science and the Occult*. State Univ. of New York Pr. 1982 $39.50 pap. $9.95. A collection of articles, some critical, some not, on a wide range of pseudosciences.

Hall, Trevor H. *The Enigma of Daniel Home: Medium or Fraud?* Prometheus Bks. 1984 $16.95. Daniel Home was a notorious medium who has intrigued and puzzled both scientists and parapsychologists for a century.

———. *The Medium and the Scientist: The Story of Florence Cook and William Crookes*. [*Science and the Paranormal Ser.*] Prometheus Bks. 1985 $18.95. An eminent British chemist, Crookes, of the late nineteenth century is taken in by Cook, a clever medium.

Hansel, C. E. M. *ESP and Parapsychology: A Critical Re-evaluation*. [*Science and the Paranormal Ser.*] Prometheus Bks. 1980 $18.95 pap. $12.95. The revised edition of the standard work on the subject.

Jerome, Lawrence E. *Astrology Disproved*. [*Science and the Paranormal Ser.*] Prometheus Bks. 1977 $18.95. Astrology has its origins in prescientific magical thought. Jerome argues that it has never been able to break free of its magical roots, and that there is no basis in astronomy, physics, or biology for astrological "predictions."

Kitcher, Philip. *Abusing Science: The Case Against Creationism*. MIT 1982 $20.00 pap. $7.95. Kitcher energetically rebuts the creationist arguments against modern evolutionary science. His style suits an intellectually sophisticated audience who are not necessarily well versed in science.

Klass, Philip J. *UFOs: The Public Deceived*. Prometheus Bks. 1986 $19.95 pap. $11.95. An authoritative treatment of UFOs by the senior editor of *Aviation Week and Space Technology*.

Kusche, Lawrence D. *The Bermuda Triangle Mystery—Solved*. Prometheus Bks. 1986 pap. $11.95; Warner Bks. 1975 pap. $2.50. Kusche is a technical writer (and pilot) who has made an exhaustive investigation of the triangle "mystery."

McGowan, Chris. *In the Beginning: A Scientist Shows Why the Creationists Are Wrong.* Prometheus Bks. 1984 pap. $11.95. "The book is not long, is easy to read, and is convincing in its arguments refuting those of the creationists against scientific truth and intellectual freedom" (*Choice*).

Marks, David, and Richard Kammann. *The Psychology of the Psychic.* [*Science and the Paranormal Ser.*] Prometheus Bks. 1980 $18.95 pap. $11.95. An exposé of the "psychics" Uri Geller and Kreskin, and technical criticism of Targ and Puthoff's "remote-viewing" experiments. The authors discuss biases that lead people to accept the fallacious claims.

Menzel, Donald H., and Lyle G. Boyd. *The World of Flying Saucers: A Scientific Examination of a Major Myth of the Space Age.* Doubleday 1963 o.p. Menzel and Boyd (Menzel was a prominent astronomer) present scientific analyses of famous UFO cases. Anyone seriously interested in "flying saucers" should become familiar with the elementary physics, astronomy, and meteorology so clearly explained by the authors.

Neher, Andrew. *The Psychology of Transcendence.* [*Transpersonal Ser.*] Prentice-Hall 1980 text ed. $13.95 pap. $7.95. Neher gives psychological analyses of mystical, psychic, and occult experiences, including auras, psychic healing, and Reichian orgone. Neher discusses the dangerous effects of occult practices.

Radner, Daisie, and Michael Radner. *Science and Unreason.* Wadsworth 1982 text ed. pap. $6.95. A short, clearly written book that presents rules for identifying pseudosciences. The rules are illustrated with a number of crank ideas from "flat-earth" to Velikovsky and biorhythm.

Randi, James. *Flim-Flam! The Truth about Unicorns, Parapsychology and Other Delusions.* Prometheus Bks. 1982 pap. $10.95. An incisive treatment, especially good on parapsychology.

————. *The Truth about Uri Geller.* Prometheus Bks. rev. ed. 1982 pap. $9.95. A prominent professional magician exposes Geller's tricks.

Sheaffer, Robert. *The UFO Verdict: Examining the Evidence.* [*Science and the Paranormal Ser.*] Prometheus Bks. 1981 $18.95. A careful look at UFO photographs, testimony, and the people of the UFO movement.

Stiebing, William H., Jr. *Ancient Astronauts, Cosmic Collisions and Other Popular Theories about Man's Past.* Prometheus Bks. 1984 $19.95 pap. $11.95. "Stiebing, armed only with the findings of modern scientific archaeology, takes on the Herculean labor of attempting to banish the humbug and pseudoscience from 'popular prehistory'. . . . Stiebing pursues his task of debunking systematically; he summarizes the thesis and evidence advanced for each of these ideas then counterposes the evidence and interpretations of mainstream science" (*Choice*).

Story, Ronald. *The Space-Gods Revealed: A Close Look at the Theories of Erich von Däniken.* Barnes & Noble 1977 pap. $1.75; Harper 1976 $13.45. "Story demolishes von Däniken's notion that visitors from outer space are responsible for all human progress. He also locates and drags into daylight the mixture of erratic reasoning and deliberate omission of fact by which von Däniken supports that notion" (*Atlantic*).

Vogt, Evon Z., and Ray Hyman. *Waterwitching U.S.A.* Univ. of Chicago Pr. (Phoenix Bks.) 1979 pap. $5.95. An anthropologist and a psychologist examine an old water-detecting practice that still has its devotees.

Zusne, Leonard, and Warren H. Jones. *Anomalistic Psychology: A Study of Extraordinary Phenomena of Behavior and Experience.* Erlbaum 1982 text ed. $45.00 pap.

$24.95. Psychologists Zusne and Jones explain supposed paranormal phenomena by thoroughgoing application of accepted psychological principles.

PHILOSOPHY OF SPACE, TIME, AND MODERN PHYSICS

The nature of space and time has concerned philosophers since ancient times. Philosophers of science approach the subject from the standpoint of up-to-date science. Thus EINSTEIN's Special and General Theories of Relativity occupy a central place in current studies. Inevitably some mathematics enters the discussion, though some presentations are quite elementary. Euclidean geometry formerly supplied a fixed framework for the events described by physics. With the advent of noneuclidean geometries, the relation of geometry to physics posed problems for physicists and philosophers. There are many "popular science" books that introduce the nonscientist to relativity and that are not listed here. The books listed below include only those with a philosophy of science orientation.

Quantum mechanics dominates twentieth-century physics of atoms, molecules, and subatomic particles. Like the subject of space and time, quantum physics demands some knowledge of mathematics, but again the sophistication required varies from book to book. The philosophical interest derives from the puzzling nature of the measurement process in quantum mechanics. Wheeler and Zurek's collection and Jammer's survey give the reader an idea of the problems associated with quantum measurement, which have led great physicists such as Einstein and SCHRÖDINGER to express dissatisfaction with the prevailing interpretations of quantum physics.

Bohm, David. *Causality and Chance in Modern Physics.* Univ. of Pennsylvania Pr. repr. of 1957 ed. 1971 pap. $9.95. Bohm on the interpretation of quantum physics. This is his 1952 essay on the topic.

———. *Wholeness and the Implicate Order.* Methuen 1980 $25.00 1983 pap. $6.95. Bohm, a prominent physicist-philosopher, explains his overall philosophy of nature.

Bohr, Niels. *Atomic Theory and the Description of Nature.* AMS Pr. repr. of 1934 ed. 1976 $12.50. Four papers from the 1920s in which Bohr discusses the relationship of quantum physics to the classical picture of nature.

Boltzmann, Ludwig. *Theoretical Physics and Philosophical Problems: Selected Writings.* [*Vienna Circle Coll.*] Kluwer Academic 1974 lib. bdg. $46.00 pap. $24.00. Boltzmann was an outstanding nineteenth-century pioneer in statistical thermodynamics.

Born, Max. *Physics in My Generation.* [*Heidelberg Science Lib.*] Springer-Verlag 2d ed. rev. 1969 pap. $12.95. The originator of the "statistical interpretation" of the quantum physics formulas treats a number of topics, including quantum mechanics.

Bub, Jeffrey. *The Interpretation of Quantum Mechanics.* [*Western Ontario Ser.*] Kluwer Academic 1974 lib. bdg. $26.00 text ed. pap. $16.00. Bub is one of the most knowledgeable interpreters of quantum physics. His book is not elementary.

Cartwright, Nancy. *How the Laws of Physics Lie.* Oxford 1983 pap. $9.95. Are physical laws and theories correct representations of real processes or are they idealizations that stray far from reality? Cartwright defends a view based on experimental physics.

Earman, John S., and others. *Foundations of Space-Time Theories.* [*Minnesota Studies in the Philosophy of Science*] Univ. of Minnesota Pr. 1977 $27.50. A collection of studies, some quite mathematical, on philosophical aspects of relativity.

French, A. P., and P. J. Kennedy, eds. *Niels Bohr: A Centenary Volume.* Harvard Univ. Pr. 1985 $27.50. Contains many papers by Bohr, including his discussion of his dialogue with Einstein on quantum theory. Also has material on Bohr's philosophy of physics.

Friedman, Michael. *Foundations of Space-Time Theories: Relativistic Physics and Philosophy of Science.* Princeton Univ. Pr. 1983 $35.00

Graves, John C. *The Conceptual Foundations of Contemporary Relativity Theory.* MIT 1971 o.p. Less mathematical symbolism than many other books on relativity. Also contains some general philosophy of science.

Grünbaum, A. *Boston Studies in the Philosophy of Science: Philosophical Problems of Space and Time.* [*Synthese Lib.*] Kluwer Academic 2d ed. 1973 $66.00 pap. $25.00. The second edition of Grünbaum's well-known book. He has set the pattern for work in this area.

———. *Geometry and Chronometry in Philosophical Perspective.* Univ. of Minnesota Pr. 1968 $12.50 pap. $3.45

Heisenberg, Werner. *Philosophical Problems of Quantum Physics.* Ox Bow Pr. repr. of 1952 ed. 1979 $16.00 text ed. pap. $10.00. According to critics, Heisenberg's interpretation of quantum mechanics is a mixture of classical and quantum concepts.

———. *Physics and Philosophy: The Revolution in Modern Science.* [*World Perspective Ser.*] Harper 1962 pap. $6.95. The eminent physicist Heisenberg formulated the "uncertainty principle" for quantum mechanics in the 1920s. He was deeply interested in the philosophical background of science.

Jammer, Max. *Concepts of Space: The History of Theories of Space in Physics.* Harvard Univ. Pr. 2d ed. 1969 $16.50. One of the few historical treatments available in English. Provides a good introduction to the subject.

———. *The Philosophy of Quantum Mechanics: The Interpretations of Quantum Mechanics in Historical Perspective.* Wiley 1974 $49.95. A valuable sourcebook for anyone studying the interpretation of quantum physics.

MacKinnon, Edward M. *Scientific Explanation and Atomic Physics.* Univ. of Chicago Pr. 1982 lib. bdg. $31.00. The evolution of fundamental theories in physics and concepts of explanation in physics are intimately related. MacKinnon traces theories of atoms from Newton and Kant up to the twentieth century. The modern quantum theory of the atom is seen through the debates between Bohr and Einstein.

Margenau, Henry. *The Nature of Physical Reality: A Philosophy of Modern Physics.* Ox Bow Pr. repr. of 1950 ed. 1977 $26.00 text ed. pap. $14.00. Margenau was a physicist-philosopher.

Meyerson, Emile. *The Relativistic Deduction: Epistemological Implications of the Theory of Relativity with a Review by Albert Einstein.* Kluwer Academic 1984 lib. bdg. $49.00. An eminent French philosopher and historian of ideas interprets relativity theory.

Nerlich, Graham. *The Shape of Space.* Cambridge Univ. Pr. 1976 $37.50. An excellent, readable text on the nature of space. Not heavily mathematical.

Newton-Smith, W. H. *The Structure of Time.* Routledge & Kegan 1980 $32.50 1984 pap. $14.95. "A very clear and readable book about the topological and metrical properties of time. . . . [It] is a very good introduction to these issues. Newton-

Smith brings in no more physics than Special Relativity. In general he defines his technical terms and explains the science clearly" (*TLS*).

Planck, Max. *Scientific Autobiography and Other Papers*. Trans. by Frank Gaynor, Greenwood repr. of 1949 ed. 1968 lib. bdg. $22.50. Like his colleague and friend Albert Einstein, Max Planck was a great physicist who pondered the philosophical basis of physics. These five essays, from the last years of Planck's long career, range from thoughts on his own professional life to the concepts of causality, the limits of science, and the relation of science to religion.

———. *Where Is Science Going?* Trans. by James Murphy, prologue by Albert Einstein, AMS Pr. repr. of 1932 ed. $18.50. The great German physicist Planck originated the "old quantum theory" around 1900.

Prigogine, Ilya. *From Being to Becoming: Time and Complexity in the Physical Sciences*. W. H. Freeman 1980 text ed. $27.95 pap. $15.95. This book provides a more rigorous technical basis for the ideas expressed in *Order Out of Chaos* (see below).

Prigogine, Ilya, and Isabelle Stengers. *Order Out of Chaos: Man's New Dialogue with Nature*. Bantam 1984 pap. $8.95; [*New Science Lib.*] Shambhala 1984 $18.95. A brilliant exposition of the Newtonian "static" worldview and how it is transformed by recent developments in theoretical mechanics and thermodynamics. The authors have managed to combine science, history of science, and philosophy of science into a fascinating essay.

Salmon, Wesley C. *Space, Time, and Motion: A Philosophical Introduction*. Univ. of Minnesota Pr. rev. ed. 1981 pap. $8.95. Salmon writes excellent expositions: easy to read and highly informative.

Schilpp, Paul A., ed. *Albert Einstein*. [*Lib. of Living Philosophers*] Open Court repr. of 1949 ed. 1970 $35.95 pap. $17.95. Einstein's "Intellectual Autobiography," which opens the work, is indispensable for understanding his philosophical orientation. Also contains Bohr's famous essay on his discussions with Einstein.

Schlesinger, George N. *Aspects of Time*. Hackett 1980 lib. bdg. $17.50 text ed. pap. $4.95. An astute analytic philosopher attacks some puzzles about time.

Sklar, Lawrence. *Philosophy and Spacetime Physics*. Univ. of California Pr. 1985 $25.00. The book is a collection of 12 reprinted articles that touch on many aspects of the philosophy of science. The central issue is the status of space-time geometry: should it be construed as a science on a par with other physical sciences?

———. *Space, Time, and Spacetime*. Univ. of California Pr. 1977 pap. $10.95. A very readable up-to-date introduction to philosophical problems of space and time. Requires little mathematics.

Van Fraassen, Bas C. *An Introduction to the Philosophy of Time and Space*. Columbia Univ. Pr. 1985 $25.00 text ed. pap. $10.00. Van Fraassen is a highly competent logician and philosopher of science who writes lucid expositions.

Wheeler, John A., and W. H. Zurek, eds. *Quantum Theory and Measurement*. Princeton Univ. Pr. 1982 $78.00 pap. $21.50. An 800-page sourcebook containing a large number of major papers on the experimental meaning of quantum physics. It presupposes some knowledge of quantum physics. The earlier papers are more accessible than the later, more mathematical articles.

Whitrow, G. J. *The Natural Philosophy of Time*. Oxford 2d ed. 1980 pap. $19.95. The revision of a classic book on the subject.

Wigner, Eugene P. *Symmetries and Reflections*. Greenwood repr. of 1967 ed. 1978 lib. bdg. $32.50; Ox Bow Pr. repr. of 1967 ed. 1979 text ed. pap. $10.00. Wigner is an eminent physicist who has developed von Neumann's approach to the philosophy of quantum physics.

PHILOSOPHY OF BIOLOGY

Biology presents special challenges for philosophers of science. Explanations in biology do not always fit the pattern established by explanations in physics or chemistry. Biology possesses a historical dimension in its exploration of the fossil record. The nonmechanical concepts of "purpose" and "organism" play a role in biological thought. Biology especially attracts philosophers now because it is a rapidly advancing science, with implications for technology, ethics, and social theory, as well as posing problems of scientific method. Philosophers of biology keep in touch with developments in the science, and even work with scientists to clarify definitions and principles.

Brandon, Robert N., and Richard M. Burian, eds. *Genes, Organisms, Populations: Controversies over the Units of Selection.* MIT 1984 text ed. $32.50. This collection includes such philosophers as Hull, Ruse, and Wright, and well-known biologists such as Mayr, W. D. Hamilton, and J. Maynard Smith.

Kitcher, Philip. *Vaulting Ambition: Sociobiology and the Quest for Human Nature.* MIT 1985 $25.00. A criticism, at length, of E. O. Wilson's approach to the unification of biology and social theory.

Monod, Jacques. *Chance and Necessity.* Random 1972 pap. $3.95. A pioneer of molecular biology discusses the implications of that discipline for the overall conception of biology.

Ruse, Michael. *The Philosophy of Biology.* Humanities Pr. 1973 text ed. pap. $12.50. The standard logical empiricist book on philosophy of biology.

———. *Sociobiology: Sense or Nonsense.* [*Episteme Ser.*] Kluwer Academic 2d ed. rev. 1984 $34.00 text ed. pap. $14.95. Ruse is sympathetic to E. O. Wilson's sociobiology.

Sober, Elliott, ed. *Conceptual Issues in Evolutionary Biology: An Anthology.* MIT 1983 text ed. $42.50 pap. $19.95. An excellent collection of recent work in the field. Both philosophers (Hull, Nagel, Ruse, Brandon, M. Williams) and biologists (Gould, Lewontin, Mayr) are represented.

———. *The Nature of Selection: Evolutionary Theory in Philosophical Forms.* MIT 1984 text ed. $25.00 pap. $12.50. A carefully reasoned treatment of important concepts in evolutionary biology (such as fitness and adaptation), in relation to the philosophical concepts of explanation, causation, and chance. Sober's writing is not on an elementary level, but definitely repays the reader's effort.

CARNAP, RUDOLF. 1891–1970

Carnap was the philosopher who revolutionized the philosophy of science by applying to it the results of modern logic. Born in Ronsdorf in Northwest Germany, Carnap attended the universities of Jena and Freiberg/Baden from 1910 to 1914, studying philosophy, mathematics, and physics. After World War I, he received his doctorate at Jena (1921) with a thesis on concepts of space. He researched on his own until his appointment as instructor in philosophy at the University of Vienna (1926–31). There he was a member of the Vienna Circle of Logical Positivists. He served as professor at the German University in Prague from 1931 to 1935. The rise of Hitler led to Carnap's emigration to the United States in 1936, where he was professor of philosophy at the University of Chicago (1936–52). In 1954 Carnap moved to the University of California at Los Angeles, occupying the professorship left vacant by the death of his friend Reichenbach. He retired from teaching in 1962, continuing his research until his death in 1970.

Carnap's immense influence on the philosophy of science stems not only from his many technical contributions to the field but also from his method, which others emulated. Carnap was a student of Gottlob Frege, a founder of the new symbolic logic, but BERTRAND RUSSELL (see also Vol. 4) had an even greater influence on him. Russell and ALFRED NORTH WHITEHEAD'S (see Vol. 4) *Principia Mathematica* introduced Carnap to the new "logic of relations," wherein phrases such as "father of," "greater than," and "between," received adequate treatment for the first time. Thus, Russell's logic could express complex mathematical and scientific propositions.

Carnap had felt strongly early in his studies that, outside of physics, the sciences did not attain sufficient clarity in their explanations of concepts and laws. Symbolic logic offered the means to reach the desired clarity. The turning point for Carnap came in 1921, when he read Russell's *Our Knowledge of the External World, as a Field for Scientific Method in Philosophy*. Russell demonstrated how symbolic logic could transform initially vague philosophical problems into precise questions admitting of definitive answers. All of Carnap's subsequent work follows this pattern. Carnap published several books on the logical structure of language, and made fundamental contributions to the field of inductive reference. His essays cover a wide range of topics: testability, observation and theory, and so on. Much of his writing is technical, requiring knowledge of symbolic logic. His "Intellectual Autobiography" in the Schilpp volume, though, provides an understandable survey of his thought.

BOOKS BY CARNAP

The Logical Structure of the World and Pseudoproblems in Philosophy. 1928. Trans. by Rolf A. George, Univ. of California Pr. 1967 pap. $9.95. The first is Carnap's early masterwork that builds knowledge-statements from statements about "slices" of sense experience.

Logical Foundations of Probability. 1950. Univ. of Chicago Pr. 2d ed. 1962 o.p. Carnap's great work on the logical relationship between evidence and theory. Mostly technical, though some parts are understandable without familiarity with the symbolism.

(ed.). *Introduction to the Philosophy of Science*. Ed. by Martin Gardner, Basic Bks. 1966 pap. $9.95. Probably the most readable Carnap book for the nonspecialist, thanks to Martin Gardner's editing.

BOOKS ABOUT CARNAP

Hintikka, Jaakko, ed. *Rudolf Carnap, Logical Empiricist: Materials and Perspectives*. [*Synthese Lib.*] Kluwer Academic 1975 o.p. After the Schilpp volume, this is the most valuable book for understanding Carnap. It includes insightful biographical comments by Feigl, Hempel, Jeffrey, and others; first-rate articles on Carnap's inductive logic; and a translation of a 1958 Carnap article.

Schilpp, Paul A., ed. *The Philosophy of Rudolf Carnap*. [*Lib. of Living Philosophers*] Open Court 1984 $44.95. Contains Carnap's "Intellectual Autobiography," an excellent essay on his life and thought. Carnap's "Replies" follow the essays contributed by outstanding scholars.

FEIGL, HERBERT. 1902–

Feigl was the first member of the Vienna Circle philosophers of science to take root in the United States. The Minnesota Center for Philosophy of Science, which Feigl founded and administered, set the pattern for cooperative research and for education of philosophers of science in the United States.

Born in Reichenberg (old Austria-Hungary) and educated at the universities of Munich and Vienna, Feigl studied with MORITZ SCHLICK (see also Vol. 4). With Friedrich Waismann, Feigl suggested to Schlick the idea of a discussion group; the group blossomed into the Vienna Circle. After Feigl completed his doctorate in 1927, he taught at the People's Institute in Vienna until 1930. During a visit to the United States in 1930, Feigl and Albert Blumberg wrote the article that put the label "logical positivism" on the new philosophy of science. (Later, Feigl and others preferred the tag "logical empiricism.")

In 1931, Feigl emigrated to the United States and accepted a post in the department of philosophy at the University of Minnesota. With the help of the Hill Family Foundation, he organized the Minnesota Center for Philosophy of Science and became its director in 1953. He has been professor emeritus since 1971.

The center invited distinguished scholars to pursue research and discussion. Inspired by the example of Schlick, Feigl always aimed at fruitful interchanges of ideas and cooperative efforts at solving philosophical problems. Feigl's influence on philosophy of science has several dimensions. First, his essays in the philosophy of science treat a number of topics, including scientific reasoning and the problem of induction. His most extensive work, however, lies in the philosophy of psychology. Feigl advocated an "identity theory" solution to the problem of the relation of the mental and the physical. Mental states and brain states are two aspects of a single underlying process. Second, Feigl was instrumental in communicating logical empiricism to English-speaking academics through his essays, edited collections, and Minnesota Center publications. His brand of logical empiricism is tolerant rather than strict. The "verifiability" theme is not pushed to extremes. The two "readings" books, on philosophical analysis and philosophy of science, which he edited with Wilfred Sellars and May Brodbeck, set the standard for such texts. The research at the center resulted in the publication of the *Minnesota Studies in the Philosophy of Science*, beginning in 1956. The volumes published under Feigl's supervision constitute essential sourcebooks for the development of philosophy of science in that period. The *Minnesota Studies* not only include important papers by Carnap, Hempel, Feigl, and others, but challenges to logical empiricism by authors such as Scriven and Feyerabend. Third, Feigl's Minnesota Center was the model for research institutions, publications format, and teaching of philosophy of science in the United States. Similar centers at the University of Pittsburgh and at Boston University are not thriving. Like the Minnesota Center, the Pittsburgh and Boston research groups publish series of "studies volumes."

BOOKS BY FEIGL

(and Wilfred Sellars), eds. *Readings in Philosophical Analysis.* 1949. Ridgeview 1981 lib. bdg. $25.00 text ed. pap. $15.00. A highly influential collection that begins with Feigl's classic essay summarizing logical empiricism.

(and May Brodbeck), eds. *Readings in the Philosophy of Science.* Appleton 1953 o.p. Still the best single collection of articles in philosophy of science, up to and including the logical empiricist period.

(and Michael Scriven), eds. *The Foundations of Science and the Concepts of Psychology and Psychoanalysis.* [*Minnesota Studies in the Philosophy of Science*] Univ. of Minnesota Pr. 1956 $22.50. Contains important papers by Feigl, Carnap, and Sellars.

(ed.). *Concepts, Theories and the Mind-Body Problem.* [*Minnesota Studies in the Philosophy of Science*] Univ. of Minnesota Pr. 1958 $25.00. Hempel, Scriven, Oppenheim and Putnam, Sellars, and Meehl all contribute major works to the volume. Feigl's "mental and physical" essay made its first appearance here.

(and Grover Maxwell), eds. *Scientific Explanation, Space and Time.* [*Minnesota Studies in the Philosophy of Science*] Univ. of Minnesota Pr. 1962 $25.00. Important work by Maxwell, Feyerabend, Hempel, Scriven, Brodbeck, Putnam, Grünbaum, and Sellars.

The "Mental" and the "Physical": The Essay and a Postscript. Univ. of Minnesota Pr. 1967 o.p. Feigl's most complete statement of his views of the mind-body problem.

(and Grover Maxwell), gen. eds. *Analyses of Theories and Methods of Physics and Psychology.* Ed. by Michael Radner and Stephen Winokur [*Minnesota Studies in the Philosophy of Science*] Univ. of Minnesota Pr. 1970 o.p. Includes essays by Feigl, N. R. Hanson, Hesse, Maxwell, Gunderson, and others, and 40 pages of discussion from a conference on the relation of theory to observation. Hempel contributes an important piece, and Feyerabend's notorious *Against Method* makes its first appearance here. The subsequent studies volumes are restricted to special topics.

Inquiries and Provocations: Selected Writings, 1929–1974. Ed. by R. S. Cohen [*Vienna Circle Coll.*] Kluwer Academic 1980 lib. bdg. $50.00 pap. $23.50. Includes papers on the mind-body problem, and Feigl's 1969 essay on the emigration of logical empiricists to America. Two selections from Feigl's early work are made available in English for the first time. Contains a bibliography of his writings through 1980.

BOOK ABOUT FEIGL

Feyerabend, Paul, and Grover Maxwell, eds. *Mind, Matter, and Method: Essays in Philosophy and Science in Honor of Herbert Feigl.* Univ. of Minnesota Pr. 1966 $17.50. The diversity of topics contained here reflects the great scope of Feigl's own philosophical work. The contributors, who include Popper, Grünbaum, N. R. Hanson, and Brodbeck, are grouped by subject matter: philosophy of mind, induction, and philosophy of physical science. The editors supply a bibliography of Feigl's publications to December 1965.

FEYERABEND, PAUL KARL. 1924–

Paul Feyerabend began his studies in the midst of "orthodox" philosophy of science and has evolved into the most prominent antiphilosopher of science. Feyerabend was born in Vienna. After serving in the German army during World War II, he completed his education in philosophy and physics at the University of Vienna (Ph.D., 1952). He absorbed the logical positivist doctrines and also Karl Popper's philosophy. Beginning in the mid-1950s, he taught in England (Bristol University) and the United States (University of California at Berkeley). From 1957 to 1963 he held fellowships at the Minnesota Center for Philosophy of Science. Since 1962 Feyerabend has been professor at Berkeley concurrently with holding a series of positions at the University of London, the Free University of Berlin, and the Federal Institute of Technology in Zurich.

Feyerabend advocates freedom and diversity in science, and disparages rationality, rules, and methodology. His views emerge from the mismatch between logical empiricist philosophy of science, with its emphasis on justification of theories, and history of science, with its stress on differences and idiosyncrasies. Feyerabend maintains that, in fact, scientists do not generally argue rationally. Instead, they resort to rhetoric, and concoct new principles to back up their ideas. Science does not run on a "scientific method." Feyerabend draws the moral that "anything goes," anarchy is the best policy (*Against Method*, 1975). Other philosophers of science, reading Feyerabend, extract a different lesson: Feyerabend offers us a choice between a rigid, oversimplified version of scientific method and total anarchy. Neither alternative is palatable. In effect, Feyerabend challenges philosophers of science to develop a third alternative: an account of scientific reasoning that does justice to both the logical and the historical aspects of science.

Books by Feyerabend

Against Method. 1975. Schocken repr. of 1975 ed. 1978 pap. $7.95. The original version appeared in the fourth volume of *Minnesota Studies in the Philosophy of Science.* Feyerabend challenges conventional philosophy of science and suggests a more flexible and open alternative.

Science in a Free Society. Schocken 1979 $8.00. Feyerabend elaborates on some aspects of *Against Method*, replies to critics, and tells us how he developed his philosophical ideas.

Philosophical Papers. Cambridge Univ. Pr. 2 vols. 1981 ea. $44.50–$57.50. In Volume 1, *Realism, Rationalism, and Scientific Method,* Feyerabend's articles offer a variety of themes and treatments, from quite formidable technical discussions to informal, even breezy essays. In Volume 2, *Problems of Empiricism: Philosophical Papers,* Feyerabend's long paper, "Problems of Empiricism," shows how he makes the transition from a more orthodox doctrine of scientific knowledge to his later radical phase.

HEMPEL, CARL GUSTAV. 1905–

Hempel's work is absolutely essential for understanding modern philosophy of science. His explanation of scientific explanation and his "paradoxes of confirmation" have stimulated research for decades.

Born in Oranienburg, Germany, Hempel has been a United States citizen since 1944. Like many other philosophers of science, he studied physics and mathematics at the universities of Göttingen and Heidelberg. In Berlin, he was a student of Hans Reichenbach and participated in the Society for Scientific Philosophy, the sister group of the Vienna Circle of Logical Positivists. Hempel left Germany for Brussels in 1934, and then came to the United States in 1937, where he held positions at the University of Chicago, City College of New York, Queens College, and Yale University. Hempel became professor of philosophy at Princeton University in 1955 and held the title of Stuart Professor from 1956 until he retired in 1973. The University of Pittsburgh appointed him professor of philosophy in 1977.

Hempel writes in a "scientific" style: clear, matter of fact, free of personal idiosyncrasies. The reader always has a sense of the goals, problems, and permissible means of solving the problems. In effect Hempel invites the reader to join him in research. Many philosophers of science have accepted his invitation. In conjunction with Paul Oppenheim, Hempel proposed the most influential model of scientific explanation (1948), that events are explained by *deducing* their descriptions from universal scientific laws and "antecedent conditions." Sociologists, political scientists, and historians have agonized over the question of whether their disciplines can possess such explanations. In 1945 Hempel published "Studies in the Logic of Confirmation." "Confirmation" is the *support* that evidence confers on a scientific theory. Hempel's investigation uncovered fundamental difficulties. He showed how accepted principles of confirmation lead to absurd results. Anyone who has since proposed an account of confirmation has had to demonstrate that his or her doctrine avoids Hempel's paradoxes. In 1965 Hempel published a collection of the above researches, *Aspects of Scientific Explanation*, which includes his more recent thoughts on confirmation and scientific explanation.

BOOKS BY HEMPEL

Fundamentals of Concept Formation in Empirical Science. [*Foundations of the Unity of Science Ser.*] Univ. of Chicago Pr. 1952 pap. $2.25. An early work that treats the ways in which scientific concepts are brought into the language of science. See also the later chapters of *Philosophy of Natural Science*.

Aspects of Scientific Explanation. 1965. Free Pr. 1970 text ed. pap. $14.95. A collection of Hempel's most important writings; indispensable for any philosopher of science.

Philosophy of Natural Science. Prentice-Hall 1966 pap. $13.95. An elementary textbook that sketches Hempel's positive views on scientific reasoning.

BOOK ABOUT HEMPEL

Rescher, Nicholas, ed. *Essays in Honor of Carl G. Hempel: A Tribute on the Occasion of His Sixty-fifth Birthday.* [*Synthese Lib.*] Kluwer Academic 1969 $29.50 pap. $22.00. Salmon, Jeffrey, Grünbaum, and Putnam are among the contributors who explore areas relevant to Hempel's work. Includes reminiscences about Hempel and a bibliography of his writings up to 1964.

HESSE, MARY BRENDA. 1924–

Mary Hesse possesses expertise both in the history of science and in the philosophy of science. She pursued her graduate studies at Cambridge University (M.A.) and the University of London (Ph.D.). She taught mathematics at the University of Leeds (1951–55), and then the history and philosophy of science at University College, London (1955–59). In 1960, she became a member of the faculty at Cambridge University where she was appointed Professor of Philosophy of Science in 1975.

Students and scholars in the United States have benefited from Hesse's teaching at Yale (1961), Minnesota (1966), and Chicago (1968). In addition, she edited the *British Journal for the Philosophy of Science* from 1965 to 1969.

Hesse has always stressed the need to compare abstract philosophy of science principles with concrete scientific case histories. *Forces and Fields* (1961) is a history of the "action at a distance" concept in physics, yet at the same time a philosophical exploration of the nature of physical theories. Hesse is well known for her analysis of analogical reasoning in *Models and Analogies in Science* (1963). This interest in analogy carries over into her work on inductive reasoning, *The Structure of Scientific Inference* (1974).

Some philosophers of science (such as Feyerabend) who are deeply immersed in the history of science have arrived at skeptical conclusions about scientific method. Hesse has consistently upheld the rationality of scientific practice against historians and others who try to undermine it. Some of her essays in defense of this position are collected in *Revolutions and Reconstruction in the Philosophy of Science*, published in London in 1980.

BOOKS BY HESSE

Forces and Fields: Action at a Distance in the History of Physics. 1961. Greenwood repr. of 1962 ed. 1970 lib. bdg. $24.75. Hesse draws philosophical conclusions from this historical study.

Models and Analogies in Science. 1963. Univ. of Notre Dame Pr. 1966 o.p. For anyone investigating this topic, Hesse's book must be the starting point.

The Structure of Scientific Inference. Univ. of California Pr. 1974 o.p. A thorough and wide-ranging study of the philosophical basis for scientific reasoning.

KUHN, THOMAS SAMUEL. 1922–

The name T. S. Kuhn is synonymous with "scientific revolutions." Trained as a physicist, Kuhn has made his mark in history and philosophy of science. Born in Cleveland and educated at Harvard, Kuhn earned his doctorate in physics in 1949. Already interested in the philosophy of science, he was introduced to the history of science by the historian (and president of Harvard) James B. Conant. With Leonard K. Nash, Kuhn was asked to teach a historically oriented course on science for nonscientists. He found that what he had learned in the philosophy of science did not fit the case studies central to the course in the history of science. For instance, "the discovery of oxygen" seen through the eyes of a historian looks different than the same episode seen from the point of view of present-day chemical theory. A postdoctoral fellowship at

Harvard enabled him to explore this interdisciplinary area. Subsequently Kuhn made the professional shift to history of science, retaining his philosophical interests. By 1956 he was teaching history of science at the University of California at Berkeley.

Kuhn was invited to contribute an essay on scientific revolutions for the *International Encyclopedia of Unified Science,* edited by Otto Neurath, Rudolf Carnap, and Charles Morris, a series of publications stemming from the logical empiricist movement. The resulting slim volume, *The Structure of Scientific Revolutions,* appeared in 1962. Kuhn's book asks: If scientists proceed by a scientific method that is definite and decisive, why are there dramatic disagreements among scientists, both during "revolutions" and in such disciplines as the social sciences? Kuhn proposes ideas that might answer the question. Successful, stable sciences possess "paradigms," which are "universally recognized scientific achievements that for a time provide model problems and solutions to a community of practitioners." Revolutions are changes from one paradigm to another. Lack of consensus, which occurs in the social sciences, indicates the absences of a paradigm. Conservatively, Kuhn is saying that logical empiricist philosophy of science needs to be supplemented by such other ideas as paradigm. Many readers, though, read Kuhn's book out of the context of the logical empiricist series in which it was published. They interpret him as proposing an entirely new approach to philosophy of science. Kuhn supplemented his 1962 book with a collection of historical-philosophical essays, *The Essential Tension* (1977); it is helpful in understanding Kuhn's thought.

BOOKS BY KUHN

The Structure of Scientific Revolutions. 1962. [*Foundations of the Unity of Science Ser.*] Univ. of Chicago Pr. 2d ed. 1970 $17.50 pap. $6.95. Kuhn applies lessons from the history of science to the philosophy of science in his most influential work.

The Essential Tension: Selected Studies in Scientific Tradition and Change. 1977. Univ. of Chicago Pr. 1979 lib. bdg. $25.00 pap. $13.00. Essays written both before and after *The Structure of Scientific Revolutions* help the reader to a fuller understanding of Kuhn's thought.

BOOK ABOUT KUHN

Gutting, Gary, ed. *Paradigms and Revolutions: Appraisals and Applications of Thomas Kuhn's Philosophy of Science.* Univ. of Notre Dame Pr. 1980 text ed. $18.95 pap. $9.95. "The theme, the impact of T. S. Kuhn's characterization of science and its dynamics, in philosophy, social studies, and humanities, is organized and justified by a brief but clear introduction. The authors chosen are eminent, and the opposing arguments are reasonably balanced. . . . The selections succeed in cross-disciplinary intelligibility as well as careful, expert criticism" (*Choice*).

NAGEL, ERNEST. 1901–1985

Ernest Nagel, who was one of the most eminent philosophers in the United States, has synthesized pragmatism and logical empiricism in his philosophy of science. Like the original logical positivists, Nagel was born in Central Europe (Nove Mesto, Czechoslovakia), but as a child of ten he emigrated to the United States. His teachers included MORRIS R. COHEN (see Vol. 4), JOHN DEWEY (see Vols. 3 and 4), and Frederick Woodbridge. From these men and from his reading of such other great American philosophers as C. S. PEIRCE (see Vol. 4) and GEORGE SANTAYANA (see Vol. 4), Nagel established a firm grounding in the tradition of American naturalism and pragmatism. Naturalists try to explain everything in terms of natural laws and processes, and deny that there is anything beyond the natural order. Natural means susceptible to scientific explanation, so naturalism is an overall philosophy rooted in science.

Nagel earned his doctorate in philosophy from Columbia University in 1930; he taught there from 1931 until his retirement four decades later. With Morris R. Cohen, Nagel wrote *An Introduction to Logic and Scientific Method* (1934), the first logic text to incorporate the new thinking in philosophy of science and mathematics. For 20 years it was the leading text in the field. In 1939, Nagel published *Principles of the Theory of Probability*, an essay that remains one of the basic sources for analysis of probability concepts. Much of the logical empiricist philosophy of science is located in articles and volumes intended for specialists. Fortunately, Nagel put many of those ideas into readable form in *The Structure of Science* (1961). The philosophical community immediately recognized the importance of Nagel's book. It served as a rallying point for advocates of "orthodox" philosophy of science and drew the fire of critics such as Feyerabend. *The Structure of Science* not only summarizes contemporary work in the philosophy of science but also reflects Nagel's own philosophical orientation. He describes the functioning of various components of scientific knowledge (laws, explanations, theories, and so on) and the interrelationships among scientific disciplines. He leaves the treatment of inductive inference to other philosophers of science. Nagel is especially interested in questions of explanation in biology and physics: determinism and indeterminism, teleology (purposive explanation), and whether one scientific theory can be "reduced" to another (e.g., chemistry as a subfield of physics).

BOOKS BY NAGEL

(and Morris R. Cohen). *An Introduction to Logic and Scientific Method.* Harcourt 1934 o.p. A pioneering and still highly readable textbook of deductive and inductive inference.

Principles of the Theory of Probability. 1939. Vol. 1, no. 6, in Otto Neurath and others, eds., *Foundations of the Unity of Science: Toward an International Encyclopedia of Unified Science.* Univ. of Chicago Pr. 1955 $25.00. Nagel presents the historical background of the theory of probability and an evaluation of the principal interpretations of its mathematics.

The Structure of Science. 1961. Hackett repr. of 1961 ed. 1979. lib. bdg. $35.00 text ed. pap. $13.75. Nagel combines pragmatism and logical empiricism in this influential account of scientific explanation.

Teleology Revisited and Other Essays in the Philosophy and History of Science. Columbia Univ. Pr. 1979 $30.00 pap. $15.00. Includes articles on the history of modern logic, the concept of determinism, and the title piece: the 1977 John Dewey Lectures at Columbia University.

BOOK ABOUT NAGEL

Morgenbesser, Sidney, Patrick Suppes, and Morton White, eds. *Philosophy, Science and Method: Essays in Honor of Ernest Nagel.* St. Martin's 1969 o.p. The first two parts of this volume concern philosophy of science issues pertinent to Nagel's thought. There, philosophers such as Hesse, Levi, and Black discuss inductive reasoning, and scientists (Feinberg, Dobzhansky) write on philosophical aspects of their fields.

POPPER, SIR KARL RAIMUND. 1902–

Popper's lively writing style, sharp wit, and strongly expressed views have made him the most widely read of major twentieth-century philosophers of science.

Although Popper was born and educated in Vienna, his academic career really blossomed in England. Popper received his Ph.D. from the University of Vienna in 1928. Although he was not a member of the Vienna Circle of Logical Positivists and he disagreed with some of their basic doctrines, there was a mutual influence between him and circle members. One of them, Herbert Feigl, encouraged Popper to write his ideas in book form. The long manuscript that emerged became *The Logic of Scientific Discovery* (1935) and is still the fundamental book for understanding Popper's thought.

In 1937, Popper left Austria to accept a post at Canterbury University College in New Zealand. After the war, he moved to the London School of Economics, where he was professor of Logic and Scientific Method from 1949 to 1969 and professor emeritus thereafter. He was knighted in 1965.

The period of Popper's prominence in philosophy of science begins with the publication of his 1935 book in English translation in 1959. A book of essays, *Conjectures and Refutations* (1962) followed. Other works have appeared since, on "evolutionary" theory of knowledge and philosophy of physics. While the logical positivists often stressed the experiential basis of scientific knowledge, Popper denied that there are absolute foundations for knowledge. Science is essentially a self-correcting progressive process, in constant flux. Against the proponents of inductive logic, Popper held that induction is never valid; science can only make "bold conjectures" and subject them to severe criticism. (See also Volume 4.)

BOOKS BY POPPER

The Logic of Scientific Discovery. 1935. Basic Bks. 1959 $10.75; Harper rev. ed. pap. $10.95. Popper's central ideas already appear here.

Conjectures and Refutations: The Growth of Scientific Knowledge. 1962. Harper 1968 pap. $8.95. This informally written book provides easy access to Popper's views for the general reader.

Objective Knowledge: An Evolutionary Approach. Oxford 1972 text ed. pap. $9.95. Popper's "evolutionary" theory is only distantly connected to biological evolution.

Popper Selections. Ed. by David Miller, Princeton Univ. Pr. 1985 $32.50 pap. $9.95.

Parts 1 and 2 reprint articles and sections of Popper's books on the theory of knowledge and philosophy of science. The collection has the advantage of juxtaposing extracts from different periods so that the reader can see both the continuity and the development of Popper's thought.

Unended Quest: An Intellectual Autobiography. Open Court rev. ed. 1985 $12.95 pap. $8.95. The revised edition of the autobiography that first appeared in the Schilpp volume. Popper's personality comes through clearly.

Realism and the Aim of Science. Ed. by W. W. Barley, III [*Postscript to the Logic of Scientific Discovery*] Rowman 1983 text ed. $38.50 1985 pap. $12.95. These writings, composed in the 1950s as appendixes to *The Logic of Scientific Discovery*, concern Popper's approach to the problem of induction and his propensity interpretation of probability.

BOOKS ABOUT POPPER

Bunge, Mario, ed. *The Critical Approach to Science and Philosophy.* Free Pr. 1964 o.p. Parts 1 and 3 are of special interest to philosophers of science. Paul Bernays, Herbert Feigl, David Bohm, and many other scientists and scholars contribute essays that pertain to Popper's doctrines and interests. The Popper bibliography runs up to 1964.

Burke, T. E. *The Philosophy of Popper.* Longwood 1983 pap. $12.50. A simple introduction to Popper's thought, which should be supplemented by further reading in more thorough commentators. About half of the book is devoted to issues in theory of knowledge and philosophy of science.

Magee, Bryan. *Philosophy and the Real World: An Introduction to Karl Popper.* Open Court 1985 pap. $8.95. Magee presents a vivid picture of Popper's philosophy, from the point of view of a believer.

O'Hear, Anthony. *Karl Popper.* Methuen 1982 pap. $10.95. "This book is not an introductory account of Popper's philosophy but a *critical* account of it. . . . O'Hear gives good criticisms of basic moves Popper *attempted* to make, such as to demarcate science from other activities in terms of falsifiability, to draw a good analogy between scientific society and society at large, to define verisimilitude, and to set up a clear conception of a third world [of ideas]" (*Choice*).

Schilpp, Paul A., ed. *The Philosophy of Karl Popper.* [*Lib. of Living Philosophers*] Open Court 1974 $39.95. An invaluable sourcebook about Popper's thought. It begins with his "Intellectual Autobiography," contains essays by distinguished scholars, and ends with replies by Popper.

PUTNAM, HILARY. 1926–

Hilary Putnam combines logic and the philosophy of language with philosophy of science. He was born in Chicago and educated at The University of Pennsylvania (A.B., 1948) and the University of California at Los Angeles (Ph.D., 1951). At UCLA, Putnam studied with Hans Reichenbach.

After holding a Rockefeller fellowship for a year, Putnam taught at Northwestern University (1952–53) and at Princeton (1953–61). He was Professor at the Massachusetts Institute of Technology from 1961 to 1965. Since 1965 he has been at Harvard University. He was appointed Walter Beverly Pearson Professor of Modern Mathematics and Mathematical Logic in 1976.

Putnam has ranged over a variety of philosophical topics rather than pursuing a single, narrow line of thought. He often brings a fresh outlook and a lucid, lively style to old controversies, mixing sharp criticism with interesting suggestions for solutions. For instance, he attacks the traditional distinction between observation and theoretical sentences in his essay "What Theories Are Not." In "The Analytic and the Synthetic," he defends a version of analytic-synthetic against critics such as Quine. Putnam's articles are readily accessible in the volumes of his *Philosophical Papers*.

Putnam tied together a number of ideas in his John Locke Lectures at Oxford University in 1976, published under the title *Meaning and the Moral Sciences*. There and in his recent book, *Reason, Truth and History* (1981), we see him grapple with recurrent themes in his thought: truth and rationality, realism and instrumentalism.

BOOKS BY PUTNAM

Philosophical Papers. Cambridge Univ. Pr. 3 vols. 2d ed. ea. $47.50–$49.50 pap. ea. $15.95. Includes Putnam's influential articles on theories, analytic and synthetic, and realism.

Meaning and the Moral Sciences. [*International Lib. of Philosophy and Scientific Method Ser.*] Routledge & Kegan 1978 $23.95 1979 pap. $7.95. The 1976 John Locke Lectures, principally on the concept of truth as correspondence with facts.

Reason, Truth and History. Cambridge Univ. Pr. 1981 o.p. In the course of these essays, centering on truth and rationality, Putnam comments on many issues in the philosophy of science.

REICHENBACH, HANS. 1891–1953

One of the great pioneers of twentieth-century philosophy of science, Reichenbach was colorful, incisive, and equally capable of writing successful popular books and abstruse technical tomes.

Reichenbach had a deep knowledge of physical science and engineering, gained during his student years and during his work in radio technology. Born in Hamburg, he studied with the eminent scientists PLANCK (Berlin), Sommerfeld (Munich), and HILBERT and BORN (Göttingen). His 1915 doctorate from the University of Erlangen was on the concept of probability. Afterward, working in engineering, he pursued his philosophical interests. He published his first book, *The Theory of Relativity and a Priori Knowledge* in 1920. A second followed on the axioms of space-time theory (1924). By then he was teaching a variety of scientific and philosophical subjects at the Technische Hochschule in Stuttgart. Reichenbach was appointed to a post at the University of Berlin in 1926. There he formed the Society for Scientific Philosophy in alliance with the Vienna Circle and published *Philosophy of Space and Time* (1928), one of Reichenbach's most influential works on space and geometry. It concerns the question of what aspects of the theory of space are true or false by experience, and what aspects are true by definition.

As the Nazi movement grew, Reichenbach left Germany for Istanbul (1933) and moved to the United States in 1938. Until his untimely death in 1953 he taught at the University of California at Los Angeles. His last German book, written in 1935, was his important work on the theory of probability in which he developed his approach to inductive inference. Thereafter all of his books were written in English, beginning with *Experience and Prediction* (1938), his theory of how sense experience supports knowledge claims. *The Rise of Scientific Philosophy* (1951) propagandized for the new philosophy of science, against the philosophy of past ages.

Reichenbach has had a major impact on the philosophy of science through his publications and through his teaching. Carl Hempel and Olaf Helmar were his students at Berlin. In the United States, Adolf Grünbaum, inspired by the 1928 space and time book, began a distinguished career in the 1950s in that special area. The logician and philosopher of language Hilary Putnam studied with Reichenbach at UCLA. And the inductive logician Wesley Salmon, who took his Ph.D. at UCLA, has taken up and advanced Reichenbach's work on the probability concept.

Books by Reichenbach

The Theory of Relativity and a Priori Knowledge. 1920. Univ. of California Pr. 1965 $34.00. Reichenbach's first book, in which he discusses the revisions in the notion of a priori knowledge necessitated by Einstein's theories of relativity. Maria Reichenbach's introduction provides useful background.

Philosophy of Space and Time. 1928. Dover 1957 text ed. pap. $5.50. The seminal book on the subject for twentieth-century philosophers of science.

The Theory of Probability: An Inquiry into the Logical and Mathematical Foundations of the Calculus of Probability. 1935. [*California Lib. Repr. Ser.*] Univ. of California Pr. repr. of 1949 ed. 1971 $42.50. A revised version of the 1935 German book. Presents Reichenbach's "frequency" interpretation of probability.

Experience and Prediction: An Analysis into the Logical and Mathematical Foundations of the Calculus of Probability. 1938. Trans. by E. H. Hutten and Maria Reichenbach, Univ. of California Pr. 2d ed. o.p. Reichenbach's theory of knowledge, which differs from the logical positivist "verifiability" theory in some respects.

The Rise of Scientific Philosophy. Univ. of California Pr. 1951 $34.00 pap. $7.95. A popular book in which Reichenbach tells us what is wrong with old-fashioned philosophy and what is right about the new philosophy of science.

Laws, Modalities, and Counterfactuals (*Nomological Statements and Admissible Operations*). Fwd. by Wesley C. Salmon [*Studies in the Logic of Science*] Univ. of California Pr. 1977 $37.50. Reichenbach proposed a logic to solve the persistent problem of how law statements function in science. Salmon's foreword aids the reader in understanding a difficult text.

Modern Philosophy of Science: Selected Essays. 1958. Ed. by Maria Reichenbach, Greenwood repr. of 1959 ed. 1982. lib. bdg. $24.75. Papers on relativity, space, causality, and ethics.

(and Maria Reichenbach). *The Direction of Time.* Univ. of California Pr. 1982 $31.00. Posthumously published writings that originally appeared in 1956. The Reichenbachs treat the problem of explaining the irreversible nature of temporal processes in a variety of physical theories, from classical mechanics through modern quantum physics.

Selected Writings, 1909–1953. Ed. by Maria Reichenbach and R. S. Cohen, trans. by E. H. Schneewind [*Vienna Circle Coll.*] Kluwer Academic 2 vols. 1978 o.p. Volume 1 includes a bibliography of Reichenbach's writings. The initial essays in that volume present a fascinating picture of Reichenbach's personality.

BOOK ABOUT REICHENBACH

Salmon, Wesley C., ed. *Hans Reichenbach: Logical Empiricist. [Synthese Lib.]* Kluwer
    Academic 1979 lib. bdg. $39.50

SALMON, WESLEY CHARLES. 1925–

Wesley Salmon is principally known for his development of ideas in the
philosophy of inductive inference. Born in Detroit, he came to philosophy of
science after studies in theology and metaphysics. Following an M.A. at the
University of Chicago (1947), Salmon began doctoral studies at the University of California at Los Angeles. There he encountered Hans Reichenbach
and completed his Ph.D. with him in 1950.

Thereafter, Salmon taught at several American universities, including
Northwestern and Brown, becoming professor of history and philosophy of
science at Indiana University in 1963. In 1967 he was named Norwood
Russell Hanson Professor at Indiana. From 1973 to 1981 he was professor at
the University of Arizona, and since 1981 he has been at the University of
Pittsburgh.

Salmon's essay, *The Foundations of Scientific Inference* (1966), exemplifies
many characteristics of his thought. He relates the problem of induction to
its historical roots and he explains some of the modern approaches to its
solution. His exposition is admirably clear and brings out the important
points. We see that the influence of Reichenbach remains strong.

Salmon's importance lies in his steady efforts to develop and improve
logical empiricism in the face of skeptical challenges. His 1984 treatise,
Scientific Explanation and the Causal Structure of the World, represents his
most fully worked out theory of inductive inference to date.

BOOKS BY SALMON

The Foundations of Scientific Inference. 1966. Univ. of Pittsburgh Pr. repr. 1967 pap.
    $6.95. Extremely readable exposition of the basic problem of induction. Salmon
    develops Reichenbach's solution to the problem.
Space, Time, and Motion: A Philosophical Introduction. Univ. of Minnesota Pr. 2d rev.
    ed. 1981 pap. $8.95. Salmon turns his expository skills toward this specialized
    and difficult topic.
Scientific Explanation and the Causal Structure of the World. Princeton Univ. Pr. 1984
    text ed. $35.00 pap. $14.50. The most complete presentation of Salmon's theory
    of inductive inference.

SCHLICK, MORITZ. 1882–1936

Modern philosophy of science may be said to begin with Schlick's Vienna
Circle. In the 1920s and 1930s, a small group of thinkers gathered around
Schlick to discuss issues in the philosophy of the sciences. The doctrines
they formulated later became known as logical empiricism, the philosophical starting point of present-day philosophy of science.

Schlick, born in Berlin, was educated in philosophy and science. He took
his doctorate in optics (Berlin, 1904) under the renowned physicist MAX
PLANCK. After teaching at Rostock and Kiel for a number of years, Schlick

was appointed (1922) to the "Chair in the Philosophy of the Inductive Sciences" at the University of Vienna.

Within a couple of years the discussion group that became known as the Vienna Circle began its meetings. The circle read and discussed current science as well as philosophical work, and hammered out tough-minded doctrines on the nature of science. Factual knowledge is the business of scientists alone. Philosophers should confine themselves to analyzing how science works, investigating basic concepts of science, and promulgating a worldview based on up-to-date science. Science succeeds because its claims are testable by observation, experiment, and calculation. Metaphysics is not knowledge at all; it is meaningless since its statements are completely unverifiable.

Circle members included the mathematician Hans Hahn, the sociologist Otto Neurath, Rudolf Carnap, and students (H. Feigl and F. Waismann). Wittgenstein and Popper were loosely affiliated with the group. Hans Reichenbach formed a sister group in Berlin with Richard von Mises and others.

Schlick not only published papers setting forth his ideas, but together with Philipp Frank, edited an important series of works by such authors as Neurath and Popper. The major impact of the circle, however, resulted from the dispersal of the group when the Nazis took power. Circle members found homes in other countries, preeminently the United States, which became the world leader in philosophy of science. Although Schlick was able to lecture at Stanford (1929) and Berkeley (1931), he did not live to emigrate from Austria. The meetings of the Vienna Circle ended with his death in 1936.

BOOKS BY SCHLICK

General Theory of Knowledge. 1918. Trans. by Albert Blumberg [*Lib. of Exact Philosophy*] Springer-Verlag 1974 $52.00. Schlick's masterwork of the early part of his career. Here his doctrines still relate closely to traditional philosophies such as that of Kant and his followers.

Philosophical Papers. Ed. by H. L. Muler and B. F. B. van de Velde-Schlick, trans. by P. Heath, and others [*Vienna Circle Coll.*] Reidel 2 vols. 1979 o.p. Exceptionally readable essays that provide a good introduction to the goals of the Vienna Circle.

BOOKS ABOUT SCHLICK

Ayer, Alfred J. *Logical Positivism.* Free Pr. 1966 pap. $14.95; Greenwood repr. of 1959 ed. 1978 lib. bdg. $32.50. An excellent collection that includes papers by Schlick and a number of his colleagues. One of the best sources from which to learn about logical positivism.

Kraft, Viktor. *The Vienna Circle, the Origin of Neo-Positivism.* Greenwood repr. of 1969 ed. 1985 lib. bdg. $50.00. Describes the history of the Circle and its philosophy. The author was himself a member of the Circle.

CHAPTER 4

Mathematics

Joseph W. Dauben

> Mathematics possesses not only truth, but supreme beauty—a beauty cold and austere, like that of sculpture, without appeal to any part of our weaker nature . . . sublimely pure and capable of a stern perfection such as only the greatest art can show.
>
> —BERTRAND RUSSELL

> No mathematician can be a complete mathematician unless he is also something of a poet.
>
> —KARL WEIERSTRASS

Mathematics has always been regarded as the supreme example of the rational power of the human mind. Along with the ability to speak and develop languages and alphabets, the creation of numbers, counting, and the invention of the most rudimentary arithmetic is associated with all human civilizations. From the earliest times, man recognized the need to measure distances and areas that led to geometry, or to count numbers of things that led to arithmetic.

It was the Greeks, however, who discovered in mathematics the great power of abstract reasoning based on axiomatic and deductive proof. The fact that one could establish, it seemed, for all time the necessary truth of mathematical propositions was extraordinary. The Pythagorean theorem, for example, which holds for all right triangles, no matter what their dimensions, asserts that the sum of the squares on the two sides of a right-angled triangle is equal to the area of the square on the hypotenuse:

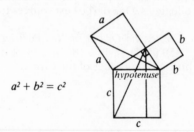

$$a^2 + b^2 = c^2$$

Ever since the Greeks, mathematical argument has been taken as the unique form of knowledge that, once rigorously established, could never be challenged. Consequently, some have argued that mathematics is the one branch of human knowledge that is truly cumulative. Unlike astronomy, physics, chemistry, or biology, mathematics rarely rejects its past. Mathematical "truth"—the positive results of arithmetic, geometry, and algebra that the ancients had established—remains true and is still used today.

Euclid has never been rejected or "replaced" the way Ptolemy, Galen, and even Newton (see also Vol. 4) were replaced by COPERNICUS, Harvey, and EINSTEIN (respectively). Even when something so startling as non-Euclidean geometry was discovered in the nineteenth century, it did not serve to nullify or replace the older Euclidean geometry. Instead, it supplemented the results of traditional geometry and shed new light on the nature and meaning of mathematics. Typically, whenever mathematics seems to undergo dramatic transformations, it does so through new discoveries or innovative theories that greatly enlarge its scope, generality, and power.

Apart from the purely intellectual interest of the subject for many theoreticians, mathematics has always been valued by primitive and advanced civilizations alike for its great power in applications. "Geometry," for example, literally means earth measurement, and was developed by the Egyptians to aid in the surveying of land. The oldest mathematical document that still exists, in fact, is the Rhind Papyrus that dates to about 1800 B.C. and is derived from a still earlier prototype written probably around 2000 B.C. It is replete with practical problems of everyday life solved by simple arithmetic, geometry, and even some rudimentary algebra.

Today the applications of mathematics are more complex, sophisticated, and varied. Everything from the precise measurement of time by atomic clocks to the synchronization of traffic lights or the simple tallying of a shopkeeper's bill involves some form of mathematics.

For mathematicians, however, what matters most is the highly abstract character of the concepts they use and the austere rigor of the results they achieve. When asked to define mathematics—what it is and what they do—mathematicians give a variety of answers. It has been defined by some as the science of quantity, now a rather old-fashioned view. It has also been equated with logic. Others regard it as a highly abstract enterprise, the study of "significant form." This may range from the familiar figures of geometry or the forms of numbers to various forms of logic itself. Rather than expect any one comprehensive definition to suffice, mathematics is perhaps most quickly defined by the various branches that comprise it. A short list of some major specialties includes: number theory, real and complex analysis, differential topology, group theory, algebraic geometry, operations research, computer science, combinatorics, and mathematical programming, to name only a few.

The following bibliography gives primary attention to elementary algebra, geometry, number theory, and calculus. The encyclopedias and handbooks described below will introduce readers to many of the other and more specialized branches of mathematics. The guides listed may also be used to provide helpful suggestions for further reading. Basically, the needs and abilities of general readers have been kept in mind when selecting books for this bibliography. Mathematicians will find other guides to more advanced and specialized literature, especially in *Mathematical Reviews*, published monthly by the American Mathematical Society.

All of the books listed here are in English, most are currently in print, and have been selected for their readability without presupposing any detailed knowledge of technical mathematics, unless otherwise noted. Anyone with a basic interest in the subject, and with a high school familiarity with geometry and algebra, should be able to read most of the books described below without unreasonable difficulty.

HANDBOOKS AND REFERENCE BOOKS

The books below represent readily available guides for readers interested in learning more about mathematics in general. Handbooks include compact introductions to the subject, whereas reference works comprise bibliographic aids and other resources of interest to mathematicians, or to those who wish to learn more about the subject.

Bronshtein, I. N., and K. A. Semendyayev, eds. *Handbook of Mathematics.* Trans. by K. A. Hirsch, Van Nostrand 3d ed. rev. 1985 $37.95. This work, originally in Russian, has actually gone through more than 20 editions in Russian and German. Many mathematicians have contributed new material as old sections were revised or new sections were added to the original *Handbook* to keep pace with recent advances in contemporary mathematics. Topics covered include tables and graphs, elementary mathematics, algebra, geometry, analysis (including calculus, calculus of variations, differential equations, and functions of complex variables), probability and statistics, linear optimization, numerical analysis and computation techniques (including computers), advanced analysis (including functional analysis, measure theory, tensor calculus, and integral equations), operations research, and data processing. Throughout, definitions are clearly labeled; examples and diagrams are frequently given to make explanations as clear as possible. An extensive bibliography of works in English is also included.

Fang, J. *A Guide to the Literature of Mathematics Today.* Paideia 1972 o.p. This book provides a comprehensive guide to international congresses of mathematicians, mathematical societies, a comparison of major topics in mathematics in 1900 versus 1970, and lists of major series (colloquiums, memoirs, proceedings, translations). A section is also devoted to the collected works of mathematicians. This is an excellent reference work for any reader wishing a concise overview of the most important sources used by mathematicians.

Gaffney, M. P., and L. A. Steen. *Annotated Bibliography of Expository Writing in the Mathematical Sciences.* Math Assn. 1976 $14.00. This reference work covers all major areas of mathematics, but limits itself almost exclusively to expository sources written mostly for readers with little or no knowledge of mathematics. Only a small portion of the works listed are annotated, leaving readers to judge the appropriateness of selections based on titles alone. Articles as well as books are included.

Gillispie, Charles C. *Dictionary of Scientific Biography.* Scribner 8 vols. 1970–80 text ed. set $750.00. Probably the single most important reference work in the history of science today, with signed biobibliographical articles on nonliving scientists and mathematicians who were deemed to have made an "identifiable difference to the profession or community of knowledge." The last volume contains a name and subject index and a list of scientists by field.

James, Glenn, and Robert C. James, eds. *Mathematics Dictionary*. Van Nostrand 4th ed. 1976 $32.95. This dictionary presents "a correlated condensation of mathematical concepts designed for time-saving reference work. Nevertheless the general reader can come to an understanding of concepts in which he has not been schooled by looking up the unfamiliar terms in the definitions at hand and following this procedure for familiar concepts" (Preface). The multilingual index provides English equivalents for mathematical terms in French, German, Russian, and Spanish. An appendix gives many useful tables and an extensive list of mathematical symbols, each with a brief explanation.

McGraw-Hill Encyclopedia of Science and Technology. McGraw-Hill 15 vols. 5th ed. 1982 $1,100.00. See especially the article on "Mathematics" by Solomon Bochner (Vol. 8, pp. 259–264). Copious illustrations, line drawings, and halftones contribute to the utility, clarity, and interest of the text. Most of the longer articles include bibliographies. Volume 15 contains both an analytical and topical index. It also provides a glossary of scientific notation that clarifies usage of symbols, abbreviations, and technical nomenclature. This encyclopedia is supplemented by an annual *McGraw-Hill Yearbook of Science and Technology*.

Millington, T. Alaric, and William Millington, eds. *Dictionary of Mathematics*. Harper 1971 $5.95. This dictionary seeks to convey *concepts*, as its compilers say, not just overly simplified definitions. Ample cross-references serve to guide readers to related topics and areas of interest. Historical references are also given when appropriate. The language of sets, groups, rings, fields, vectors, logic, and modern geometry are all explained, as well as standard terminology in the traditional branches of mathematics. Illustrations and diagrams are supplied throughout where suitable, and enhance the intelligibility of the explanations given.

Van Nostrand's Scientific Encyclopedia. Van Nostrand 2 vols. 6th ed. 1984 $145.00. A single volume edition is also available at $112.00. This concise reference work offers definitions and descriptions for more than 500 terms directly related to mathematics. Hundreds more are included under articles for the various branches of science. A table listing all topics related to mathematics appears on pp. 1840–1845; a list of mathematical symbols with brief definitions is given on pp. 1845–1846.

GENERAL MATHEMATICS

The following works represent a highly selective sample of the hundreds of books currently available that give broad summaries of all aspects of mathematics. In most cases they are designed for a general readership without any substantial background or familiarity with mathematics. In some cases, the authors have set themselves the task explicitly of conveying the nature of mathematics to an audience that has virtually no knowledge of what it is that mathematics is actually about in the twentieth century. Several works included here, however, like the series of books by A. D. Aleksandrov and his colleagues, will serve to give readers already familiar with mathematics a taste of what more advanced work at the college level and beyond has to offer.

Aleksandrov, A. D., A. N. Kolmogrorov, and M. A. Lavrent'ev, eds. *Mathematics—Its Contents, Methods and Meanings.* MIT 3 vols. 2d ed. 1969 $27.50 pap. ea. $9.95. This notable series of books is translated from the original work compiled by a group of Russian mathematicians. Viewing abstraction, proof, and applications as the most essential characteristics of mathematics, this series begins with a general overview of mathematics, including arithmetic, geometry, and elementary and contemporary mathematics. Other chapters cover analysis, analytical geometry, algebra, ordinary and partial differential equations, calculus of variations, functions of real and complex variables, prime numbers, theory of probability, linear algebra, abstract spaces, topology, functional analysis, groups, and other algebraic systems. Suggestions for further reading are supplied at the end of each chapter.

Benice, Daniel D. *Precalculus Mathematics.* Prentice-Hall 3d ed. 1986 pap. $28.95. This book aims to present standard introductions to algebra, trigonometry, geometry, and elementary functions with calculus-oriented examples. Thus the mathematics here goes beyond basic high school material to prepare the student for the kind of problems, methods, and thinking needed for a later course in calculus.

Courant, Richard, and Herbert Robbins. *What Is Mathematics? An Elementary Approach to Ideas and Methods.* Oxford 1978 $13.95. Originally published in 1941, this book remains a classic, one of the best expository introductions to a wide range of selected mathematical topics. The authors try to look beyond mathematical formalism and manipulation to grasp "the real essence of mathematics." Actual contact with the *content* of living mathematics is necessary, they believe, to convey any real understanding of it. Beginning with an historical and philosophical introduction, the book progresses to consideration of natural numbers, the number system in general of rational and irrational numbers, geometrical constructions, the algebra of number fields, projective geometry, axiomatics, non-Euclidean geometries, topology, functions and limits, maxima and minima, the calculus, and so on. This book presupposes only a good high school knowledge of basic mathematics. Excellent suggestions are offered for further reading.

Davis, Martin. *Lectures on Modern Mathematics.* Gordon & Breach 3 vols. 1967 $57.75. Davis explores a variety of topics in modern mathematics that he believes should be considered for incorporation into the teaching of high school mathematics. The topics are also developed well beyond that to give readers a sense of the serious content of contemporary mathematics. Major topics covered include algebra, geometry, calculus, sets, and computers.

Davis, Martin, and Reuben Hersh. *The Mathematical Experience.* Birkhäuser 1981 $27.95. This book sets out to give a sense, in nontechnical terms, of exactly what it is that professional mathematicians do and why they do it. It also tries to explain why the results of modern mathematics are of compelling importance. Rather than being a comprehensive introduction to mathematics, this work aims to display the extraordinary variety—and vitality—of modern mathematics. Both history and philosophy are used to demonstrate how mathematical knowledge arises and grows. As its authors say, the book should be regarded as an "impression" of what mathematics is. Although parts of the book were contributed by a variety of authors, Davis and Hersh are responsible for the bulk of material presented. Topics covered include general aspects of "the mathematical landscape" and "varieties of mathematical experience," as well as specific discussions of group theory, non-Euclidean geometry, nonstandard analysis, pedagogical issues, and aspects of "mathematical reality."

Kline, Morris. *Mathematics for the Non-Mathematician.* [*Popular Science Ser.*] Dover

1985 $10.95. This book attempts to present a basic understanding of what mathematics is for the nonmathematically inclined.

———, ed. *Mathematics: An Introduction to Its Spirit and Use*. W. H. Freeman 1979 $12.95. Selected readings from articles on mathematics that appeared in *Scientific American*.

Kramer, E. E. *The Nature and Growth of Modern Mathematics*. Princeton Univ. Pr. 1982 $12.50. This book provides a comprehensive overview of mathematics from the Babylonians to Bourbaki (the group of mathematicians who worked together in the twentieth century). Emphasis is placed on "mathematical content, history, lore and biography," integrated in order to offer "an overall, unified picture of the mother science" (Preface). Although Kramer surveys all of mathematics, emphasis is given to aspects of primary importance in the twentieth century. Written for nonspecialists, the book aims to convey a sense of the manifold aspects of modern mathematics, including connections with other branches of science.

Lang, Serge. *The Beauty of Doing Mathematics: Three Public Dialogues*. Springer-Verlag 1985 $19.80. This brief work presents three lectures in English given in Paris at the *Palais de la Découverte* (the old Museum of Science and Technology). The challenge to communicate to a general audience what mathematics is really all about is admirably met, although at times the level of mathematical detail strays beyond the grasp of nonmathematicians. Even so, by using examples of prime numbers, diophantine equations, geometry, and space, Lang explores the general question, "What does a mathematician do and why?"

Neuman, James R. *The World of Mathematics*. Simon & Schuster 4 vols. 1956 o.p. "A small library of the literature of mathematics from A^ch-mosé the scribe to Albert Einstein, presented with commentaries and notes" (Title Page). Volume 1 reprints articles and extracts from books considered to be of a general survey nature. Historical and biographical materials are presented here, as well as articles about arithmetic and the mathematics of space and motion. Volume 2 contains excerpts related to mathematics and the physical world, including probability, laws of chance, and aspects of mathematics applied to the social sciences. Volume 3 covers statistics and the design of experiments, group theory, infinity, mathematics, and logic. Volume 4 is a potpourri of articles on mathematics in warfare, literature, and music. To give a sense of how eclectic all of this is, Oswald Spengler on "the meaning of numbers" is included, along with an article on mathematics as a "culture clue." A section is also provided on "amusements, puzzles, and fancies." Each selection is preceded by an introduction, usually of several pages, setting the context of the article or excerpt, followed by the reading in question, with notes as necessary. The volumes are well illustrated. There are also short asides—on the vocabulary of mathematics, for example, or the "unreasonableness" of mathematics, or still another on mathematics as art.

Sawyer, W. W. *Prelude to Mathematics*. Dover 1983 $4.50. This book presents aspects of mathematics that are of intrinsic interest in themselves—mathematics that is unusual, out-of-the-ordinary, or seemingly impossible. Beginning with a discussion of the beauty and power of mathematics, Sawyer goes on to describe the qualities of a mathematician. He then presents ten chapters covering such subjects as pattern and generalization in mathematics, non-Euclidean geometry, matrix algebra, projective geometry, apparent impossibilities in mathematics, transformations, finite arithmetics and geometries, and group theory.

Steen, Lynn A., ed. *Mathematics Today: Twelve Informal Essays*. Random 1980 pap. $6.95; Springer-Verlag 1978 $29.50. This collection of essays by prominent

mathematicians is another attempt to survey contemporary mathematics, both
pure and applied, in order to give nonspecialists a sense of how mathematicians
work—not only their methods, but the different ways in which they go about
their work. Interviews and expository articles succeed in covering a range of
topics including the psychology of mathematical creativity and the relevance of
mathematics to contemporary society.

————. *Mathematics Tomorrow*. Springer-Verlag 1981 $22.00. A collection of articles
written by mathematicians reflecting their opinions and predictions about the
immediate future of mathematics research and education and the directions
they should take. The volume begins with six essays on aspects of what mathematics is and what it is not. A second substantial section covers the teaching
and learning of mathematics, followed by a shorter section, "Issues of Equality,"
which treats the special problems and challenges women face in mathematics.
The final section, "Mathematics for Tomorrow," takes up questions of curriculum and applications of mathematics, including issues proposed by the increasing use of computers by mathematicians and scientists in general.

Whitehead, Alfred N. *An Introduction to Mathematics*. Oxford rev. ed. 1959 pap.
$8.95. Worried that mathematics is viewed by the general public as too difficult
or impossible to understand, Whitehead blames this on the fact that "its fundamental ideas are not explained to the student disentangled from the technical
procedure which has been invented to facilitate their exact presentation in
particular instances." Thus, his approach is to offer general ideas first, without a
massive amount of technical jargon or intimidating notation. Although the book
does not profess to teach mathematics, it does seek to explain what it is about
and why it is an exemplar of exact thought as well as a necessity in studying
natural phenomena.

ALGEBRA

Algebra began as that branch of mathematics dealing with the general
properties of numbers and number systems, and above all with methods for
solving polynomial equations with one or more unknown quantities. Modern algebra, largely a product of the twentieth century, is highly abstract
and is primarily concerned with relations and properties of systems in
general, and not necessarily systems of numbers.

The word "algebra" itself is Arabic, and appears in a ninth-century work
by the Islamic mathematician Abū Ja'far Muhammad ibn Mūsā al-
Khwārizmī, namely his *Al-jabr wa'l-muqābala* (c.830). The word actually
means "restoration" or "completion," and is a reference to the way in which
simple equations may be solved by moving elements from one side of an
equation to another. For example, the equation $x - 2 = 5$ is solved by
"restoring" 2 to the right side of the equation: $x = 5 + 2 = 7$. This method of
"restoring" numbers shows the way in which algebra, in its earliest form,
arose through the study of numbers and number systems, and eventually
grew into a body of knowledge that was especially successful in facilitating
the solution of equations.

The history of algebra is in large measure the story of how mathematicians have invented methods for solving increasingly complex and general

forms of equations, establishing general forms of solutions for some and demonstrating the impossibility of general solutions under specified conditions for others. As a result of the increasing sophistication of algebra, negative, irrational, and complex numbers were eventually introduced to mathematics in order to "solve" such equations in the most general forms possible. Equations may contain any number of unknowns, and the coefficients may be integers, rational, real, or complex numbers. Prior to the modern period, it was the Arabs who developed most profoundly the ideas we associate with algebra today. Moreover, they were especially important in transmitting the Indian (or Hindu) decimal, place-valued number system to the West.

The European Renaissance found mathematicians like Chuquet, Pacioli, Recorde, Tartaglia, Cardano, Viète, Descartes, and Fermat making new and significant contributions to algebra. The most far-reaching discovery, however, was advanced by Descartes, who connected the discrete and general character of algebra with the continuous nature of geometry, thereby inventing analytic geometry. Descartes published this discovery as part of his general treatise on method, issuing *La Géométrie* in 1637. By referring points on a geometric curve to numerical scales on axes drawn perpendicularly (usually) to one another, he found it was possible to describe a curve in terms of an equation relating the horizontal and vertical elements of the curve, usually denoted by x and y respectively. Thus the geometric curve known as a simple parabola could be written in the algebraic form $y = x^2$. Not only could curves, as well as surfaces and even solids or objects of higher dimension, be represented by algebraic equations, but these in turn could be analyzed algebraically (or, later, by even more powerful means). Such methods were helpful in revealing properties of geometric curves not immediately or even necessarily obvious from examination of the actual curves themselves.

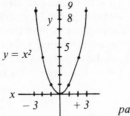

parabola $y = x^2$

By the end of the nineteenth century, algebra began its transformation to ever higher levels of generality. No longer was it simply concerned with the study of numbers and their properties, or even with the increasingly sophisticated problem of solving equations or systems of equations. For example, the French mathematician Galois, in trying to find a general solution to the quintic equation (equations of degree 5), helped to initiate research leading very quickly to a powerful but very abstract branch of modern mathematics, group theory. Others made equally far-reaching contributions, and by the end of the century, quaternions, vectors, determinants, and matrices had all been introduced as parts of the new algebra.

The twentieth century, however, has witnessed a wholly new level at which algebra has been studied both axiomatically and more abstractly than ever before. Today, modern algebra includes the study of such abstract structures as groups, rings, fields, lattices, and vector spaces, to name but a few of the most prominent areas of special interest.

The following books cover a wide range of material related to algebra, and represent available material at various levels of difficulty and sophistication. Most are general surveys and relatively simple introductions, but several works have also been included that will provide interested readers with a flavor of where current research is making some of its most important contributions.

Asimov, Isaac. *The Realm of Algebra.* Fawcett 1981 $2.50

Birkhoff, Garrett, and Saunders Maclane. *Survey of Modern Algebra.* Macmillan 4th ed. 1977 $42.95. A classic introduction to college algebra, the authors have revised and reworked the material presented for more than 40 years. Throughout, the authors "have tried to express the conceptual background of the various definitions used. We have done this by illustrating each new term by as many familiar examples as possible. This seems especially important in an elementary text because it seems to emphasize the fact that the abstract concepts all arise from the analysis of concrete situations." Numerous exercises are designed to encourage readers to think for themselves with new concepts as they are introduced. Applications to other fields, including analysis, geometry, physics, and philosophy, are also stressed. Integers, real and complex numbers, groups, vector spaces, matrices, linear groups, determinants, Boolean algebra, lattices, transfinite arithmetic, rings, ideals, algebraic number fields, and Galois theory are all covered.

Falstein, Linda D. *Basic Mathematics: You Can Count on Yourself.* Addison-Wesley 2d ed. 1986 $26.95. This textbook begins with a very rudimentary introduction to quantitative skills before covering the basics of elementary high school algebra. Quantitative skills are developed by understanding and using concepts, with concrete examples illustrating what is happening at every step. Topics include integers, fractions, decimals, percents, polynomials, linear equations and inequalities, word problems, radicals, exponents, quadratic equations, and graphs. This is a good place to begin for those who have little or no previous knowledge of algebra.

Greub, W. H. *Linear Algebra.* Springer-Verlag 4th ed. 1975 $42.00. An advanced textbook providing a detailed presentation of linear algebra based on an axiomatic treatment of linear spaces. Topics include vector spaces, linear mappings, matrices, determinants, algebras, gradations and homology, inner product spaces, symmetric bilinear functions, quadratics, unitary spaces, and polynomial algebra.

Herstein, I. N. *Abstract Algebra.* Macmillan 1986 $32.00. This widely used textbook provides a standard introduction to the fundamental concepts and methods of abstract algebra. Designed for college mathematics majors, it provides a solid foundation for the further study of modern algebra.

Hestenes, Marshal D., and Richard O. Hill, Jr. *Algebra and Trigonometry.* Prentice-Hall 2d ed. 1971 $29.95. Originally written as a text for an undergraduate linear algebra course at the Massachusetts Institute of Technology, this book is designed for mathematics majors at the junior level. Abstract ideas are avoided at the beginning. Examples and graded exercises, from routine applications to ones requiring considerable ingenuity, cover the basics of college algebra from linear equations, vector spaces, and linear transformations to polynomials, determinants, inner product spaces, and bilinear forms.

Keedy, Mervin L., and Marvin L. Bittinger. *Intermediate Algebra with Problem Solving.* Addison-Wesley 1986 pap. $25.95. For those who have had a year of algebra and need to prepare for college-level mathematics. Margin exercises, readiness checks, tests, and reviews provide aid to readers using this book on their own to learn the basics of algebra.

Kolman, Bernard, and Arnold Shapiro. *Algebra for College Students.* Academic Pr. 2d ed. 1986 $31.00. A precalculus text that takes an informal, intuitive approach. Exercises with answers make it possible for students to check their own progress. Calculator applications are also included.

Van der Waerden, B. L. *Algebra.* Ungar 2 vols. 1981 ea. $16.50. When Van der Waerden's *Algebra* first appeared in the 1930s, it inspired a new generation of mathematicians to utilize and explore further the many rich possibilities of mathematical abstraction it presented. This is an advanced introduction, suitable for college mathematics majors. Volume 1 covers the basics, introducing groups, rings, fields, vector spaces and tensors, polynomials, Galois theory, infinite field extensions, and real fields. Volume 2 develops valuation theory.

GEOMETRY

The meaning of the word "geometry" reflects the practical, applied origins of this branch of mathematics. It comes from the Latin words *geo* meaning "earth" and *metria* meaning "measure"—thus meaning "earth measurement." According to the ancient Greek historian HERODOTUS (see Vol. 3), mathematics arose first in Egypt because of the need to survey land quickly after the annual flooding of the Nile river. Other ancient writers (including Heron of Alexandria, Diodorus, Siculus, and Strabo) agree. The Egyptians, perhaps as a result of the annual flooding of the Nile, which would have obscured or even shifted property boundaries, may have found it necessary to measure parcels of land regularly in order to levy accurate taxes. The measuring was done by so-called "harpedonaptai"—the "rope stretchers" or royal surveyors of Egypt, who used their measuring ropes to survey the land.

From such simple origins, however, the study of geometric figures in general—not just of those that could be marked on the ground—quickly developed. Eventually this was gathered together into a single work by the great Greek geometer Euclid, whose *Elements of Geometry* remains to this day a classic of mathematical exposition.

One important branch of geometry is analytic geometry. This was a product of the seventeenth-century mathematicians, especially the insights of Fermat and Descartes. Both of these mathematicians found that by appealing to coordinate systems of perpendicular axes, it was possible to draw the "curve" of many equations, and likewise, it was possible to represent many "curves" (like the parabola) in terms of a corresponding algebraic equation, in this case $f(x) = y = x^2$ (see the introduction to "Algebra" above).

The eighteenth century developed both plane and solid geometry (two- and three-dimensional geometry), and began to explore the potential of projective geometry as well. Mathematicians in the nineteenth century generalized analytic geometry to spaces of even higher dimension. Here the works of Arthur Cayley, Hermann Grassmann, and Julius Plücker were most successful.

Among the most significant discoveries of the nineteenth century was the existence of what are today known as "non-Euclidean geometries." As the name implies, such geometries were not included in the traditional Euclidean geometry. This is because they violate one of Euclid's most basic postulates—his fifth—namely, that through any point only one line can be drawn parallel to a given line. In the nineteenth century, C. F. Gauss, János Bolyai, Georg Riemann, and N. I. Lobachevsky all discovered that perfectly consistent geometries could be developed in which this postulate was given up.

The possibility of non-Euclidean geometries was first realized when attempts to "prove" the parallel postulate (as Euclid's fifth postulate has come to be called) from the other axioms of geometry proved impossible. One elementary non-Euclidean geometry is that of the surface of the sphere. In Euclidean geometry, the sum of the angles of all triangles is 180°. On the surface of a sphere, however, the sum of all the angles of a spherical triangle is greater than 180°. Such geometries were called "hyperbolic" by F. Klein. Another form of non-Euclidean geometry is called "elliptic," and in such geometries, the sums of all the angles of a triangle are *less* than 180°.

Another major branch of geometry is trigonometry. The Greek word *trigonon* means triangle; trigonometry is really "triangle measurement." This involves the study of ratios of the sides of a right triangle. Among the most common trigonometric functions are the sine, cosine, and tangent. Various other trigonometric functions can also be defined, including cotangents, secants, cosecants, and inverse functions. Spherical trigonometry is a further generalization of plane trigonometry to figures drawn on the surface of a sphere.

Baker, Henry F. *Introduction to Plane Geometry.* Chelsea House 1971 $18.50. Baker develops geometry in an axiomatic fashion without assigning the notions of distance or congruence as axioms. It also gives equal standing to real and complex elements. Beginning with Euclid's theory of parallel lines, this introduction proceeds to cover involutions, conic sections, and linear transformations in detail, at a level suitable for readers with a general knowledge of basic Euclidean geometry.

Coxeter, H. S. *Introduction to Geometry.* Wiley 2d ed. 1969 $43.95. The first 11 chapters provide a basic introduction to geometry and some analytic geometry. Regular polygons, Platonic solids, and the "golden section" are studied, along with more general notions of similarity and isometry. Part 3 covers ordered, affine, projective, absolute, and hyperbolic geometries. Part 4 finishes the book with advanced topics, including differential geometry, combinatorial topology, and four-dimensional Euclidean geometry.

Coxeter, H. S., and S. L. Greitzer. *Geometry Revisited.* Math Assn. 1967 $10.00. This book is designed with high school and general readers in mind. Using the central notion of "transformation," it explores many elementary and some advanced results of basic geometry, and demonstrates its many links with other branches of mathematics. Chapter 6, on conic sections, for example, develops the geometric properties of focus, eccentricity, and so on, and shows their relevance in astronomy and physics, especially in studying the orbits of comets, planets, and satellites.

Eves, Howard. *Survey of Geometry*. Aliyn & Bacon rev. ed. 1972 text ed. $44.27. Believing that geometry is best learned by *doing* it, Eves's book offers a large number of problems to challenge its readers. Offering a comprehensive survey, this work includes an account of the historical origins of geometry along with overviews of elementary college geometry, transformation theory, projective geometry, non-Euclidean geometry, analytic geometry, differential geometry, and abstract spaces. The *spirit* of the book is geometric rather than algebraic, and emphasis has been given to conveying geometric *methods* along with specific results. Part 1 is synthetic and relatively elementary, easily read by anyone with a good high school level of mathematical training; analytical results and more advanced abstract approaches are reserved primarily for Part 2.

Holden, Alan. *Shapes, Space and Symmetry*. Columbia Univ. Pr. 1971 $26.00 pap. $13.00. This richly illustrated book makes extensive use of cardboard, wire, and other models of three-dimensional geometric objects, thereby giving readers a graphic, intuitive sense about geometry, space, and the properties of symmetry. Emphasis is given to the five so-called Platonic or perfect solids, namely the tetrahedron, cube, octahedron, dodecahedron, and icosahedron, as well as to more complicated regular and irregular polyhedra. The photographs reproduced here of hundreds of polyhedra are of great beauty, and help to impart a rich sense of the aesthetic as well as the theoretical fascination of the subject.

Middlemiss, Ross R., John L. Marks, and James R. Smart. *Analytic Geometry*. McGraw-Hill 3d ed. 1968 $38.95. Although it is often regarded primarily as a tool for the study and application of the calculus, analytic geometry has developed as a subject of increasing interest on its own. With this in mind, the authors have prepared this text with connections between analytic geometry and both higher geometry and modern abstract algebra. Calculus still receives attention, but this text emphasizes concepts along with a wide variety of applications. All of the basic theorems of analytic geometry are presented with proofs. Subjects covered include polynomials; rational, exponential, logarithmic, and trigonometric functions; graphs; vectors; parametric equations; polar, cylindrical, and spherical coordinates, as well as transformations of coordinates; algebraic, trigonometric, exponential, and logarithmic curves; conic sections; and analytic solid geometry.

Shafarevich, I. R. *Basic Algebraic Geometry*. Trans. by K. A. Hirsch, Springer-Verlag 1977 $29.50. This book is designed for mathematicians who want an overview of basic algebraic geometry in order to begin reading specialized literature on the subject. Although it assumes no prior knowledge of algebraic geometry, the first two parts of the book dealing with algebraic varieties in a projective space, along with schemes and varieties, does presuppose a college course in algebra and analytic geometry, with some knowledge of the theory of fields and commutative algebra. Part 3, devoted to algebraic varieties over the complex field and complex analytic manifolds, assumes an acquaintance with topology and the theory of analytic functions.

Stevens, Peter S. *Patterns in Nature*. Little, Brown 1974 $12.45. This is a striking book visually, full of stunning photographs illustrating the diversity of patterns and forms to be found in the natural world. Particularly numerous are spirals, meanders, branching patterns, and 120° joints in nature. Beginning with brief discussions of space, curvature, mosaics, polyhedra, and effects of scale, the book goes on to investigate basic patterns, topology, things that flow, spirals, meanders, explosions, models of branching, trees, soap bubbles, and patterns that turn up in packing and crating.

Stoker, James J. *Differential Geometry.* Wiley 1969 $48.50. This book, intended for readers with a minimum of mathematical training, nevertheless aims to provide a comprehensive introduction to the special area of differential geometry. Only linear algebra and basic elements of analysis are presupposed. Stoker has young students in mind, and makes a point of introducing (and applying) three important kinds of notation—vectors, tensors, and invariant differential forms.

NUMBER THEORY

Number theory is concerned with the character and properties of the natural numbers or integers. Its history goes back to antiquity and the origins of arithmetic, a word derived from the Greek *arithmetike*, which means "counting." Arithmetic is the study of whole numbers (integers) and the operations of addition, subtraction, multiplication, and division. Applying these operations eventually leads to fractions and negative numbers. Number theory limits itself to the study of integers and their properties.

As the history of mathematics has progressed, so too has the sophistication of number theory. Today it is a highly abstract and specialized subject, involving many still unanswered questions, among them the famous theorem of Fermat (i.e., there are no positive integers x, y, z, and n such that $x + y = z$ for $n > 2$). As the sophistication of mathematics has increased, tools drawn from diverse branches, including geometry, probability, and analysis, have all been used to advance and enrich the results of number theory.

Cassels, J. W. S. *An Introduction to the Geometry of Numbers.* Springer-Verlag 2d ed. 1971 $47.00. An advanced approach to a special part of number theory, this book covers the subject from lattices and distance functions to packings, automorphs, and a final chapter on inhomogeneous problems related to convex sets.

Dantzig, Tobias. *Number: The Language of Science.* Free Pr. 4th ed. rev. 1967 $10.95. A popular, if now somewhat dated, treatment of the history of the number concept, number systems, and their applications in diverse cultures, from antiquity to the present. Profusely illustrated; written for nonmathematicians.

Dudley, Underwood. *Elementary Number Theory.* W. H. Freeman 1978 $25.95. Designed as a one-semester or quarter introduction, with no prerequisites assumed except for some elementary algebra and a basic familiarity with properties of the real numbers. Proofs are presented clearly and all basic topics in number theory are covered. Numerical examples help to illustrate ideas and to show how playing with numbers may lead to important insights or discoveries.

Niven, Ivan M. *Numbers: Rational and Irrational.* Math Assn. 1961 $8.75. This book deals with one of the most fundamental structures in all of mathematics, the number system. It is written for anyone with a basic high school knowledge of mathematics and presupposes no preliminaries. Beginning with a straightforward coverage of natural numbers, integers, and primes, it goes on in a step-by-step way to introduce rational, irrational, trigonometric, logarithmic, and transcendental numbers. Answers and hints for solving the many problems set out in the book are especially helpful.

Niven, Ivan M., and Herbert S. Zuckerman. *An Introduction to the Theory of Numbers.* Wiley 4th ed. 1980 $39.50. This book is designed for undergraduate mathematics students wishing a comprehensive overview of basic number theory. Beginning with theorems about divisibility and congruences, the pace accelerates from quadratic reciprocity and Diophantine equations to continued fractions, algebraic numbers, the distribution of primes, and the density of sequences of integers.

Ore, Oystein. *Invitation to Number Theory.* Math Assn. 1967 $8.75. This book, described as a "simple little guide," gives the general reader a sense of the basic properties of numbers and why they are so fascinating. A short historical chapter is followed by material on prime numbers, divisors, and various number systems and their special properties, along with congruences and applications of congruences to problems involving the days of the week and tournament schedules.

Rademacher, Hans. *Lectures on Elementary Number Theory.* Krieger repr. of 1964 ed. 1977 lib. bdg. $12.50. Based on lectures given at Haverford College, Pennsylvania, in 1954 and 1955, the material presented here is thus suited to the abilities of most undergraduates. Although it does not presuppose any previous knowledge of number theory, this book uses algebra and analysis as background to introducing fundamental results of number theory, the uniqueness of prime number factorization, and the reciprocity law of quadratic residues.

Weil, André. *Basic Number Theory.* Springer-Verlag 3d ed. 1974 $33.00. The first part of this book was initially presented as a course for undergraduates at Princeton University, New Jersey, with basic theorems related to locally compact fields, adeles, algebraic number fields, the Zeta function, traces, and norms. The main features of both local and global class field theory are also given. The book incorporates important recent results in which compact groups, measure, and integration have all made important contributions to traditional number theory.

——. *Number Theory for Beginners.* Springer-Verlag 1979 $9.50. This book by one of the world's authorities on the subject was written from weekly notes taken by Max Rosenlicht at a summer course offered by Weil at the University of Chicago in 1949. The notes are very terse, but attentive reading with occasional guidance when needed from someone with a knowledge of number theory will help to make this a useful, quick survey to the subject for any student.

CALCULUS

Prior to the seventeenth century, mathematicians had enjoyed only limited success in treating physical problems of motion, or of any situation in which change occurred, whether of velocity, direction, temperature, and so on. The traditionally static mathematics of Greek algebra and geometry were severely limited for applications in such situations, especially when the change was highly variable or infinitesimal. What was needed was a new mathematics that could handle the problems of change and motion that were increasingly of interest in physics, including projectile motion, the natural acceleration of falling bodies (under the force of gravity), or the continuous elliptical motions of the planets and their satellites (also under the influence of gravitational forces).

Isaac Newton was one of two mathematicians in the seventeenth century who invented a new mathematics to deal with such situations—the calculus. LEIBNIZ (see Vol. 4), the German philosopher, was the other to develop the idea of an infinitesimal calculus at virtually the same time as Newton. Their new mathematics came to be known as the "calculus" because of the methods they derived for calculating areas of figures or for determining tangents to curves. Using the concept of infinitely small quantities (known as infinitesimals), both mathematicians found that they could deal with important and otherwise difficult-to-solve problems related to the lengths of curves, the areas of curved figures, rates of change, problems involving maxima and minima, as well as many other problems in physics and mathematics. The crucial realization, that finding the areas of curved figures was inversely related to the problem of finding tangents to the curve in question, represents a major advance. The latter, finding tangents to curves, came to be known as differentiation; the former, finding the areas under curves, integration.

In the eighteenth century, the power of the calculus was greatly enhanced when Euler approached it as part of a general theory of functions, appealing to infinitely small increments, namely differentials. The early development of the calculus culminated in the 1820s with major publications by the French mathematician A. L. Cauchy, who introduced new levels of rigor to the teaching of calculus by carefully defining the concepts of continuity and limit. This was improved on by the German mathematician Karl Weierstrass, who "arithmeticized" the calculus a generation later by adding a rigorous theory of real numbers as a foundation for the rest of the calculus. By the turn of the century, research due to Riemann, Lebesque, Denjoy, Stieltjes, and others further extended the concepts of the calculus, and of the integral in particular, to include wider and more general types of functions that could be handled.

Most recently, calculus has been further enriched by the approach of nonstandard analysis (the creation largely of Abraham Robinson), in which infinitesimals are rigorously defined and used. This makes it possible to develop many parts of mathematics more intuitively and with less complexity, appealing to infinitesimals directly instead of limits. This in turn provides the calculus with an alternative to the traditional use of $\delta-\epsilon$ methods favored by most mathematicians in the aftermath of the Cauchy-Weierstrass era as the only acceptably rigorous way to present definitions and proofs involving continuity and limits.

Apostol, Tom M. *Calculus.* Wiley 2 vols. 2d ed. 1984 ea. $44.95. Volume 1, subtitled *One-Variable Calculus with an Introduction to Linear Algebra*, attempts to strike a balance between introductions to calculus that regard it as a deductive theory, a branch of pure mathematics, and those that stress the physical origins and applications of calculus, making it more a part of applied mathematics. While proofs are often presented, they are usually preceded by some geometric or other intuitive background. Historical introductions precede the explanations of all major concepts. Early physical intuitions are later translated into precise and rigorous formulations. This volume presents the calculus of functions of one variable, including infinite series and a brief (one chapter) introduction to differential equations and linear algebra, along with applications to geometry and analysis. Volume 2, subtitled *Multi-Variable Calculus and Linear Algebra with Applications*, shares the same philosophy and format as Volume 1. It is devoted to multivariable calculus and to more advanced topics. It is divided into three parts—linear analysis, nonlinear analysis, and special topics, namely probability and numerical analysis.

Kline, Morris. *Calculus: An Intuitive and Physical Approach.* Wiley 1967 o.p. This introduction to calculus adopts an intuitive approach with many applications to real problems drawn largely from physics (although some from biology and the social sciences also appear). Only in the last chapter is a thoroughly rigorous treatment outlined. No knowledge of physics, however, is presupposed, and anyone with a basic knowledge of high school algebra can read this book with great profit, obtaining a good, intuitive understanding of such concepts as the derivative, integral, maxima and minima, trigonometric functions and their inverses, logarithmic and exponential functions, infinite series, partial differentiation, multiple integrals, and differential equations.

Lang, Serge. *A First Course in Calculus.* Springer-Verlag 5th ed. 1986 $39.95. This book aims to teach college-level students the basics of calculus, namely differentiation and integration, along with the most important techniques and applications related to them. Lange intends the book to provide "an immediate, and pleasant, access to the subject." Little in the way of previous knowledge is assumed. Beginning with an opening section on numbers, functions, graphs, and curves, differentiation of elementary functions precedes the subject of integration. This is followed by a section on Taylor's formula and series, and a final section on functions of several variables.

Niven, Ivan. *Calculus: An Introductory Approach.* Krieger repr. of 1966 ed. 2d ed. 1968 $13.50. This book provides a basic introduction to the calculus, along with the necessary background material from analytic geometry. Not as long or as comprehensive as many calculus texts, it focuses on a small number of central concepts. It is especially useful if only a brief introduction to the subject is desired. It may be used as a suitable course for liberal arts students in the social sciences, biological sciences, or business administration. Due to its conciseness, the book presupposes knowledge of basic high school algebra and trigonometry. Difficult problems are starred, and the answers are provided for all odd-numbered problems.

Sawyer, W. W. *What Is Calculus All About?* Math Assn. 1961 $8.75. Using simple nontechnical language, this book seeks to convey the basic elements of calculus. It proceeds intuitively, beginning with an analysis of speed, acceleration, and curvature, among other topics. The use of equations and other mathematical notation is minimal, while diagrams and physical situations help to illustrate graphically how and why the calculus is so important and useful.

HISTORY OF MATHEMATICS

Two basic reference works will serve to guide readers to the wide variety of materials relevant to the history of mathematics. These in turn will alert users to dictionaries, encyclopedias, bibliographies, periodicals, abstracting journals, handbooks, indexes, sourcebooks, and archival collections, along with major articles and books on the history of mathematics.

Dauben, Joseph W., ed. *The History of Mathematics from Antiquity to the Present: A Selective Bibliography*. Garland 1985 $80.00. This reference work was compiled by 49 experts drawn from five continents. Together they have pooled their individual expertise in specific areas of the history of mathematics to provide as wide a coverage of topics and time periods as possible. More than 4,000 years of mathematics are covered, as well as such topics as the history of specific branches of mathematics, the philosophy and sociology of mathematics, mathematics education, institutions, and regional studies of African and Asian mathematics. A separate section is devoted to women in mathematics.

May, Kenneth. *Bibliography and Research Manual of the History of Mathematics*. Univ. of Toronto Pr. 1973 o.p. This work aims to include all secondary literature in the field of the history of mathematics for the period 1868 to 1965. Arrangement is alphabetical under the following sections: biography, mathematical topics, epimathematical topics (e.g., the abacus, women, and so on), historical classifications (time periods, countries, cities, organizations), and information retrieval (bibliographies, historiography, information systems, libraries, manuscripts, museums, monuments, exhibits).

The following general surveys of the history of mathematics provide only a small sampling of the rich and diverse resources available to readers with historical interests. These books will suffice to orient readers, whatever their interests may be, to the major developments in the history of mathematics from antiquity to the present. These general surveys contain bibliographies, sometimes extensive ones, of the specialized literature in many languages dealing with specific aspects of the history of mathematics.

Boyer, Carl B. *A History of Mathematics*. Princeton Univ. Pr. 1985 pap. $12.50; Wiley 1968 $42.95. A college-level textbook, with chapter exercises; more extensive in scope than Eves's *An Introduction to the History of Mathematics* (below), and more historically oriented than Kline's *Mathematical Thought from Ancient to Modern Times* (below). Useful references include an extensive bibliography and a 12-page chronological table.

Eves, Howard. *An Introduction to the History of Mathematics*. Saunders 5th ed. 1983 $39.95. This book is intended to serve as "textbook for a one-semester undergraduate course which meets three hours a week." The mathematical level adopted assumes nothing more than the beginnings of calculus. Problems (with solutions) are presented in each section along with bibliographies. An eight-page chronological table and an index are appended.

Kline, Morris. *Mathematical Thought from Ancient to Modern Times*. Oxford 1972 $69.95. "Emphasizes the leading mathematical themes rather than the men," and gives primary emphasis to Western mathematics. This is the most complete and most modern in coverage of the general histories of mathematics currently available. In particular, it gives more attention than Carl Boyer's history does, for example, to the first few decades of the twentieth century. Chapter bibliographies and an index are provided.

——. *Mathematics in Western Culture*. Oxford 1964 $12.95. On an elementary level this work advances the thesis "that mathematics has been a major cultural force in Western civilization" by emphasizing mathematical applications in a range of subjects including painting, music, and relativity theory. Illustrated.

Struik, Dirk J. *A Concise History of Mathematics*. Dover 3d ed. 1967 text ed. pap.

$5.00. Though "concise," this book devotes two of its eight chapters to Oriental mathematics. It covers the history of mathematics up to the end of the nineteenth century and is probably the only modern history of its size and reliability. Generously illustrated; index and chapter bibliographies are provided.

Wilder, Raymond. *Evolution of Mathematical Concepts.* Taylor & Francis 1978 $10.00. Wilder regards mathematics as a "cultural entity," subject to laws that have directed and controlled its evolution as one of "the most important cultural components of every modern society."

PHILOSOPHY OF MATHEMATICS

Like the preceding section, History of Mathematics, the following works devoted to the philosophy of mathematics provide only a small sampling of the books currently in print on the subject. They will nevertheless serve to provide readers with a reasonable overview of major issues of interest to philosophers of mathematics, and these works will in turn provide bibliographies and references that will lead readers to further reading.

Benacerraf, P., and H. Putnam, eds. *Philosophy of Mathematics: Selected Readings.* Cambridge Univ. Pr. 2d ed. 1984 $19.95. Contains selections, among others, from Frege, Russell, Poincaré, Brouwer, and Hilbert. Two papers by Gödel, "Russell's Mathematical Logic" and "What Is Cantor's Continuum Problem?" are classic expressions of mathematical realism. Bernays's "On Platonism in Mathematics" is especially useful. "Hilbert's Program" by G. Kreisel remarks briefly on the development of Hilbert's views and the opposition between his approach and that of Brouwer to mathematics; Kreisel then proceeds to a reconstruction of Hilbert's program. There are also influential papers by W. V. Quine and C. G. Hempel, and a large section devoted to excerpts from and critical commentaries on Wittgenstein's philosophy of mathematics.

Beth, E. W. *Mathematical Thought: An Introduction to the Philosophy of Mathematics.* Kluwer Academic 1965 $22.00. This work serves the needs of mathematicians interested in philosophy, and of graduate students in philosophy without extensive knowledge of mathematics, logic, or foundations. It covers such topics as the foundations of arithmetic, traditional and symbolic logic, intuitionism, formalism, and the significance of logical and semantical paradoxes. A chapter on "recent developments" gives a flavor of Beth's thinking on recent issues of concern to philosophers of mathematics.

Kitcher, Philip. *The Nature of Mathematical Knowledge.* Oxford 1983 $25.00 pap. $9.95. This book is devoted to the nature of mathematics and to the problem of how mathematical knowledge grows. Basically, Kitcher argues against "mathematical apriorism," which holds that mathematical truth is about some abstract realm of ideal objects or forms. Instead, Kitcher argues that mathematics is no different from the natural sciences, and is basically a body of knowledge based on empirical evidence that then has an evolutionary history firmly rooted in aposteriori, rather than apriori, knowledge. Kitcher also draws on the sociology of knowledge in showing the extent to which mathematics is a social enterprise—passed on from one generation to another through teachers, journals, mathematical societies, and the "mathematical community" generally.

Korner, Stephan. *The Philosophy of Mathematics: An Introductory Essay.* Dover 1986 $5.95. This "essay" as Korner calls it was not written as an introduction to mathematical logic or the foundations of mathematics. It is rather more interested in the construction or reconstruction of mathematical theories, and in the relation between pure and applied mathematics. The early chapters are historical and expository, the latter ones are more critical, leading up to Korner's own introduction of a new philosophical position concerning the nature of pure versus applied mathematics in terms of perception, existence propositions, and other philosophical issues.

Lakatos, Imre. *Proofs and Refutations: The Logic of Mathematical Discovery.* Cambridge Univ. Pr. 1976 $10.95. Influenced by G. Polya and K. Popper, this book argues for a dialectical approach to the history of proofs in mathematics. Two case studies provide evidence for the thesis that mathematics grows through proofs challenged by counterexamples leading to revised proofs. These in turn are subjected to the same process of criticism and development in an unending series leading to successive revisions and progressive refinements.

Russell, Bertrand. *The Principles of Mathematics.* Norton 2d ed. 1964 $10.95. Originally published in 1903, this book gives Russell's most extensive philosophical presentation of logicism, the thesis that all mathematics can be reduced to logic. Throughout, Russell discusses the work of many of his predecessors, provides a lucid explanation of his famous antinomy, and describes attempts to deal with the paradoxes of set theory by various means. He also presents an exposition of his logic of relations, his analysis of the various number concepts, and much more. Russell, who opposed idealism, sought to refute the Kantian philosophy of mathematics. He was especially opposed to the Kantian doctrine that mathematics was not strictly formal, but always relied on intuitions. To this, Russell replied with his program, eventually embodied in the great work on which he and his colleague Alfred N. Whitehead collaborated, *Principia Mathematica*, which sought to reduce the major body of mathematical results achieved by the end of the nineteenth century to a system of symbolic logic.

Wilder, R. L. *Introduction to the Foundations of Mathematics.* Krieger repr. of 1965 ed. 1980 $24.50. This work grew out of an undergraduate course meant to give students some sense of modern mathematics, its foundations and the nature of its evolution. Following a presentation of basic concepts and methods, including the axiomatic method, set theory, transfinite numbers, and group theory, various views on the foundations of mathematics are presented. Logicism, intuitionism, and formalism are all covered. A final chapter presents mathematics from a "cultural" point of view and explores general features of the change and growth of mathematics.

OTHER TOPICS IN MATHEMATICS

The following works are a miscellany of different approaches to mathematics, some of them works by mathematicians reflecting on their careers and what being a mathematician has meant to them. Others deal with aspects of mathematical creativity and its origins, or with social approaches to questions about mathematics or mathematicians.

Hadamard, Jacques. *Psychology of Invention in the Mathematical Field.* Dover 1945 text ed. pap. $3.50. In this book one of France's most eminent mathematicians of the early twentieth century attempts to account for the genesis of abstract mathematical ideas based on his own introspection and the reports of others who have analyzed the sources of their mathematical creativity, including Pascal and Descartes. A letter by Albert Einstein about his own scientific creativity is appended.

Hardy, Godfrey H. *Mathematician's Apology*. Cambridge Univ. Pr. 1969 rev. ed. pap. $22.95. A famous apology for pure mathematics by one of England's greatest pure mathematicians. Hardy bases his defense of mathematics on its harmlessness, believing that unlike physics, chemistry, or biology, it could never be used to kill anyone. He also emphasizes the permanence of its achievements and the pleasure that "doing" mathematics provides.

Osen, Lynn M. *Women in Mathematics*. MIT 1974 $5.95. This book presents brief biographies of prominent women mathematicians, from Hypatia to Emmy Noether. Brief comments are also provided on contributions by contemporary women mathematicians. Also included: Agnesi, du Châtelet, Herschel, Germain, Somerville, and Kovalevskaya. The work is not a technical exposition of the mathematics produced by these women, but is written for a nonmathematical audience. References for further reading are provided.

Rademacher, Hans, and Otto Toeplitz. *The Enjoyment of Mathematics: Selections from Mathematics for the Amateur*. Princeton Univ. Pr. 1957 $24.00. Little previous mathematical knowledge is presupposed.

Steinhaus, Hugo. *Mathematical Snapshots*. Oxford 3d ed. 1969 $17.95. A series of mathematical vignettes that convey the nature of various mathematical notions with a minimal use of formulas and a liberal use of diagrams.

Wiener, Norbert. *I Am a Mathematician*. MIT 1964 $6.95. An autobiographical account of Wiener's mature years as a mathematician. This volume is a sequel to his earlier book (covering his childhood and adolescence), *Ex-Prodigy: My Childhood and Youth* (Simon & Schuster, 1953). Topics covered in *I Am a Mathematician* include quantum mechanics, the atomic bomb, and cybernetics. Wiener also includes recollections of many European and American mathematicians.

Zaslavsky, Claudia. *Africa Counts: Number and Pattern in African Culture*. Prindle 1973 $24.50. This book is devoted to an examination of mathematics in African cultures south of the Sahara. Emphasis is placed on mathematics and its connections with social and economic development. Drawing on both primary and secondary sources, topics covered include numeration systems, mystical attributes of numbers, time reckoning, currency, and measures. Geometric aspects of African art and architecture are also discussed, along with a section on mathematical games. In-depth studies of southwestern Nigeria and East Africa are also presented, along with many photographs, diagrams, tables, and maps.

PUZZLE BOOKS AND RECREATIONAL MATHEMATICS

Below are noted classics among books devoted to the genre of mathematical puzzles and games. The works listed here provide hundreds of hours of entertainment while teaching important lessons about mathematics itself at the same time.

Ball, W. W. *Fun with String Figures*. Dover 1971 $2.25. This book takes up the subject of string figures and various patterns that can be fashioned from loops of string wound between the fingers of both hands, and considers dozens of examples from a variety of cultures from antiquity on. The "cat's cradle" is but one example of such string figures that are of considerable interest. Although the present account does not go into any mathematical detail, interesting questions of geometry and topology are raised by such figures.

De Morgan, Augustus. *A Budget of Paradoxes*. Open Court 1915 $2.95. First published 30 years ago after De Morgan's death, this book examines such subjects as Newtonian physics, extensions of the number concept, and the impossibility of perpetual motion machines or of attempts to trisect angles or square the circle using straightedge and compass alone. The "Budget" reflects De Morgan's interests in literary, scientific, and social matters, and even today makes lively and entertaining reading.

Gardner, Martin. *Martin Gardner's New Mathematical Diversions from Scientific American*. Univ. of Chicago Pr. 1984 $7.95. A compendium of puzzles and problems drawn from Gardner's popular monthly column devoted to mathematical recreations in *Scientific American*.

———. *Unexpected Hanging and Other Mathematical Diversions*. Simon & Schuster 1972 $6.75. Twenty essays on mathematical recreations, considerable interest both for the historical and technical issues they raise.

Hunter, J. A., and Joseph S. Madachy. *Mathematical Diversions*. Dover 1975 pap. $3.95. Something old, and something new!—as the authors describe their purpose in presenting recreational mathematics for the fun of doing it. In 11 chapters Hunter and Madachy describe various problems and puzzles with interesting mathematical twists, including friendly numbers, mystic arrays, topological delights, inferential problems, alphametrics, probabilities, and a final section appropriately titled "Story Teasers." Answers and solutions are provided for most all of the problems proposed.

Lieber, Hugh G., and Lillian R. Lieber. *The Education of T. C. Mits*. Norton 1978 $5.95. T. C. Mits is "the celebrated man in the street," for whom this volume was written. It consists of challenging mathematical games and word problems that are designed to catch the uncritical reader off guard with the situations that are never as mathematically straightforward as they may seem at first. The many illustrations throughout are by Hugh G. Lieber.

O'Beirne, T. H. *Puzzles and Paradoxes: Fascinating Excursions in Recreational Mathematics*. Dover repr. of 1965 ed. 1984 pap. $4.95. Compares and analyzes popular puzzles and novelties, along with many historical references. River-crossing problems, jug-pouring problems, coin-weighing problems, as well as two-party strategic games, logical conundrums, and arithmetic problems, and many other subjects typical of recreational mathematics, are included here.

Salkind, C. T. *The Contest Problem Book: Annual High School Mathematics Exams*. Math Assn. 3 vols. 1961–73 ea. $8.75–$10.00. Volume 1 covers examinations administered between 1950 and 1960; Volume 2 covers 1961 through 1965; and Volume 3 covers 1966 to 1972.

Schaaf, William L. *A Bibliography of Recreational Mathematics*. NCTM 3 vols. 1970–73 ea. $9.00. From magic squares to complex cryptanalysis, mathematical puzzles have provided amusement and challenges for centuries. Testament problems, ferrying problems, coin problems, problems of pursuit and of arrangements remain today, as always, "old friends" as Schaaf puts it. Labyrinths, acrostics, tangrams, and palindromes are equally ageless. Recreational mathematics has generated an enormous literature, and these volumes survey most of it. Both popular articles and erudite memoirs are included, to offer something for everyone, from schoolchildren to scholarly mathematicians. Most entries are in English, but some French, German, and Italian titles are included. More than 50 headings cover such categories as arithmetical and algebraic recreations, geometric recreations, card tricks, chessboard problems, paper folding, and magic squares. Classical problems from antiquity are covered, as are cryptography and cryptanalysis, game strategy, symmetry, and so on. Volumes 2 and 3 update Volume 1 and fill gaps and omissions without repeating any of the material covered in the earlier publications. Volume 3 adds sections on classroom games and recreational activities of special interest to teachers. A chronological synopsis of Martin Gardner's popular column in *Scientific American* is also useful, as is a glossary of terms related to recreational mathematics. An appendix to Volume 3 gives a useful list of general works of mathematical recreations.

————. *Mathematics and Science: An Adventure in Postage Stamps.* NCTM 1978 $9.00. Believing that "the postage stamps of the world are, in effect, a mirror of civilization and that multitudes of stamps reflect the impact of mathematics and science on society," this book ranges over the entire history of science from the Egyptians and Babylonians to the present age of computers and space exploration. Hundreds of postage stamps devoted to scientific subjects are reproduced here, some in color. Two checklists are provided, one giving names of mathematicians and scientists who have been portrayed on stamps, the other noting applications of mathematics to science.

Schuh, Fred. *The Master Book of Mathematical Puzzles and Recreations.* Trans. by F. Göbel, Dover 1969 $5.95. A classic; comprehensive and scholarly, it is also illustrated.

Steinhaus, Hugo. *One Hundred Problems in Elementary Mathematics.* Dover 1979 pap. $3.95. For anyone who enjoys solving puzzles, the level of mathematical creativity and novelty displayed here will be refreshing. Most of the problems require clear thinking but nothing more complex mathematically than high school mathematics. Detailed answers are provided for each of the 100 problems presented, which succeed in conveying a considerable amount of significant mathematics. Problems are grouped into several major areas, including problems with numbers, geometric figures, problems on chess and pursuit, and even a section on "problems without solution."

Tietze, Heinrich. *Famous Problems of Mathematics.* Graylock 2d ed. 1965 $20.00. Solved and unsolved problems from antiquity to modern times. Emphasis is placed on problems from geometry and number theory. Tietze avoids proofs when they would require lengthy explanations and instead concentrates on a narrow selection of problems, emphasizing why at one time a problem resisted solution, and how it was that an answer was first advanced. Numerous portraits and even some color plates add greatly to the visual appeal of the book.

The following section of this bibliography provides brief biographical descriptions and works currently in print either by or about a selected group of the world's most important mathematicians. Coverage includes antiquity as well as the twentieth century.

APOLLONIUS OF PERGA. fl. 247–205 B.C.

The French geometer Chasles once contrasted Archimedes and Apollonius, describing the former as the master of *measurements* (by which he meant calculating areas and volumes, especially through the "method of exhaustion"), whereas Apollonius was adept at the "geometry of forms and situations." Consequently, Apollonius is often referred to as "the Great Geometer." Not only did he present the first systematic treatment of conic sections, but he coined the terms parabola, ellipse, and hyperbola, and explored their mathematical properties. Apollonius also made important contributions to astronomy, especially by applying his knowledge of geometry to theories about the motions of the planets.

BOOK BY APOLLONIUS

Apollonius of Perga. Treatise on Conic Sections. Edited in Modern Notation with Introductions Including an Essay on the Earlier History of the Subject. Ed. by T. L. Heath, Dover repr. of 1896 ed. 1971 o.p. This is the only version available in English of the seven surviving books of the treatise on conic sections by Apollonius. This is not, however, a direct translation, but takes such liberties as changing the order of propositions together and introducing modern (as of 1896) notation to express the theorems and proofs presented here.

ARCHIMEDES. c.287–212 B.C.

Archimedes is famous for his law of the lever, and for the ingenious catapults, burning parabolic mirrors, and other war machines he designed to defend the city of Syracuse during the Second Punic War between Rome and Carthage. It was there, in fact, during a siege of the city by the Romans that Archimedes met his death at the hands of a Roman soldier. Archimedes made fundamental contributions to hydrostatics, mechanics, and mathematical astronomy, but above all to theoretical mathematics. His method of exhaustion may be compared with later theories of integration in that it made possible the determination of areas, volumes, surfaces, and evolutes of curved figures. Archimedes ingeniously applied the method of exhaustion to find centers of gravity, and also used it to provide a very exact approximation for the value of π.

BOOKS BY ARCHIMEDES

The Works of Archimedes with the Method of Archimedes. Ed. by T. L. Heath, Dover repr. of 1897 ed. o.p. Based on Heiberg's edition of the Greek texts (1800–1801), this volume includes translations of Archimedes's treatises on the sphere and cylinder, on the measurement of the circle, on connoids and spheroids, on spirals, on the equilibrium of planes, on the quadrature of the parabola, on floating bodies, plus a book of lemmas, the cattle problem, and the "sand reckoner" in which the maximum number of grains of sand in the universe is calculated. A very thorough historical introduction (140 pages long) provides a biography of Archimedes, lists lost works, discusses his relation to earlier geometers, and investigates his use of arithmetics (including square roots). There is also a chapter on so-called "neusis" problems (involving constructions of lines needed to determine mean proportionals, trisection of angles, and so on). Chapters also cover Archimedes's solutions of cubic equations, his terminology, and a discussion of the extent to which Archimedes may be said to have anticipated the integral calculus of the seventeenth century. Also included in this edition is a translation by Heath of Archimedes's *Method*, presumed lost but rediscovered by Heiberg in Constantinople in 1906. This is the same work as listed below by Heiberg (with variations in the English translations due to Heath and Robinson).

Geometrical Solutions Derived from Mechanics. Ed. by J. L. Heiberg, trans. by Lydia G. Robinson, intro. by D. E. Smith, Open Court 1942 pap. $2.95. A short 28-page translation with a 6-page introduction. Here, in the form of a letter to Eratosthenes, Archimedes recounts his methods for investigating (and demonstrating or proving) mathematical questions using mechanical devices.

BOOK ABOUT ARCHIMEDES

Clagett, Marshall. *Archimedes in the Middle Ages.* Univ. of Wisconsin Pr. and Amer. Philosophical Society 5 vols. 1964–80 ea. $30.00–$120.00. A comprehensive set of volumes that analyzes medieval works, along with texts and translations. Extensive scholarly introductions, notes, and commentaries all serve to show the extent to which Archimedean and quasi-Archimedean techniques were used by medieval mathematicians and scholars. Volume 5, Part 5, contains a complete bibliography, diagrams, and indexes.

BOURBAKI, NICOLAS

Nicolas Bourbaki is the pseudonym for a group of mathematicians, mostly French, whose series of works on all aspects of modern mathematics, *Elements de mathematique,* emphasizes an axiomatic and abstract treatment. The first volume of *Elements* appeared in 1939, and since then a wide variety of topics have been covered, including works on set theory, algebra, general topology, functions of a real variable, topological vector spaces, and integration. One of the major aims of the Bourbaki series is devoted to making the logical structure of mathematical concepts as transparent and intelligible as possible. The works listed below are typical of volumes written in the Bourbaki spirit and now available (or expected to be) in English.

BOOKS BY BOURBAKI

Elements of Mathematics. Paris: Hermann; Addison-Wesley 1975 o.p. This series, in English, provides translations of some of the most important works by the Bourbaki group, all of which were originally published in French. So far, volumes on *General Topology* (1966 o.p.), *Theory of Sets* (1968 o.p.), *Commutative Algebra* (1972 o.p.) and *Algebra* (1973) have appeared. Several volumes are currently scheduled to appear, including *Algebra* (Pt. II), *Functions of a Real Variable, Integration, Lie Groups and Lie Algebras, Spectral Theories,* and *Topological Vector Spaces.* The general philosophy of the series is to present mathematics in an axiomatic, abstract framework, proceeding from the general to the particular. Each book starts "at the beginning," and gives complete explanations, as the preface to the first volume on *General Topology* says (p. v). This series is meant to provide a solid foundation for the whole body of modern mathematics.

BOOK ABOUT BOURBAKI

Fang, J. *Bourbaki.* Paideia 1970 o.p. This book represents Part 1 of the author's series *Towards a Philosophy of Modern Mathematics.* It provides a comprehensive overview of "Bourbaki"—the nom de plume of a group of mathematicians (mostly French). Special emphasis is given to the philosophy of mathematics underlying the group's prodigious and very influential books. Following a retrospective of the history of modern mathematics, the works, authors, contents, and formats of publications issued under the Bourbaki name are analyzed. The group's methods, including the abstract, the axiomatic, and the structural aspects of Bourbaki publications, are also examined. Three closing chapters are devoted to "anti-Bourbakians," to questions about mathematical creativity, and to the philosophy of modern mathematics.

CANTOR, GEORG. 1845–1918

Georg Cantor was born in St. Petersburg, Russia, but was educated and spent the rest of his life in Germany. He was the creator of set theory, and the founder of the theory of transfinite numbers. His most important work appeared between 1895 and 1897 (translated below by P. E. B. Jourdain). In addition to developing the philosophical implications of his transfinite set theory, Cantor was also concerned with the theological implications of his work. Cantor was also the founder of the German Mathematicians Union in 1891 and served as its first president.

BOOK BY CANTOR

Contributions to the Founding of the Theory of Transfinite Numbers. Trans. by P. E. B. Jourdain, Dover repr. of 1915 ed. 1955 pap. $4.95; Open Court 1952 $21.95. This work, originally issued in two parts, represents the culmination of Cantor's mathematical research and his most mature statement of transfinite set theory. Part 1 begins with the development of Cantor's theory of simply ordered sets; Part 2 goes on to develop the theory of well-ordered sets. The book contains a long, detailed, and informative introduction by Jourdain, with historical notes and an index adding further to the usefulness of this edition.

BOOK ABOUT CANTOR

Dauben, Joseph W. *Georg Cantor: His Mathematics and Philosophy of the Infinite.* Harvard Univ. Pr. 1979 o.p. This intellectual biography of the German mathematician Georg Cantor traces the origins of set theory from Cantor's early work on trigonometric series and his rigorous definition of real numbers through the discovery of nondenumerably infinite sets and his creation of transfinite numbers, resulting in his development of transfinite arithmetic and his theory of both transfinite ordinal and cardinal numbers. This book also considers the social and academic context in which Cantor's work was done, as well as the theological and psychological aspects of Cantor's interests, including the significance of his periods of manic depression and his theological interpretation of transfinite set theory for the development of his mathematics. This biography draws heavily on manuscripts, correspondence, and archival sources, and is well documented with photographs and previously unpublished material.

CAUCHY, AUGUSTIN LOUIS, BARON. 1789–1857

Cauchy was one of the great figures of French science in the early nineteenth century. Although he began his career as an engineer, and made diverse contributions to a wide variety of subjects in mathematical physics and applied mathematics, his most important advances were made in pure mathematics. As a mathematician, he made major contributions to the theory of complex functions, and his name is still attached to the Cauchy-Reimann equations, as well as to other fundamental concepts in mathematics, including the Cauchy integral theorem with residues, Cauchy sequences, and the Cauchy-Kovalevskaya existence theorem for the solution of partial differential equations.

As one of the professors at France's famous scientific school, the École Polytechnique, Cauchy was responsible for teaching mathematics to the country's most able future scientists. His interest in presenting fundamental concepts through clear definitions, and proofs through detailed and careful arguments, is reflected in the important textbooks he wrote from which many mathematicians first learned their mathematics in the nineteenth century. Cauchy was above all responsible for the famous δ−ε (delta-epsilon) method for defining many fundamental concepts in mathematics, including limits, continuity, and convergence, and by means of which he could establish rigorously basic propositions of calculus. He was also the first to give an existence proof for the solution of a differential equation, as well as for a system of partial differential equations.

BOOK BY CAUCHY

Ordinary Differential Equations. Intro. by Christian Gilain, pref. by Jean Dieudonne, Johnson Repr. 1981 $24.50. This volume reproduces a substantial fragment of the first 13 lectures (never previously published) presented by Cauchy as part of his course on ordinary differential equations presented at the École Polytechnique early in the nineteenth century. Gilain's lengthy introduction discusses in detail (in French) Cauchy's course at the École Polytechnique. Details are also provided about Cauchy's theory of differential equations, his method of successive approximations, his existence theorems, and his overall concept of analysis in general. The "Résumé des Leçons" comprises 136 pages of the rest of the book, with an appendix listing courses taught at the École Polytechnique between 1819 and 1824.

BOOK ABOUT CAUCHY

Grabiner, Judith V. *The Origins of Cauchy's Rigorous Calculus.* MIT 1981 $40.00. This book emphasizes the eighteenth-century concern for rigorous demonstrations in mathematics, especially where arguments using the infinite or infinitesimals in connection with the calculus were concerned. Grabiner shows in particular how Cauchy's treatment of such fundamental concepts as limits, continuity, convergence, differentiation, and so on, using the familiar δ−ε method, arose from approximation techniques, above all through the work of Lagrange (1736–1813).

DESCARTES, RENÉ. 1596–1650

Although best known as a philosopher, especially for his critical method of doubt and his enunciation of the so-called "mind-body" problem, Descartes was also one of the most prominent scientific minds of his time. In mathematics, he is especially remembered for his development of analytic geometry, which makes use of a coordinate system with which it is possible to refer geometric curves to algebraic formulas expressing relations between the points of a line, curve, surface, or solid. Descartes also did important work in meteorology, optics, and mechanics, although developments since the seventeenth century have greatly reduced his importance in these areas. (See also Volume 4.)

BOOK BY DESCARTES

The Geometry of René Descartes. Trans. by D. E. Smith and M. L. Latham, Dover repr. of 1925 ed. 1954 pap. $4.50. This book provides an English translation on facing pages to the original French version of Descartes's *Geometry* (1637, published as an appendix to his famous *Discours de la Method*). In addition to covering problems of construction using straightedge and compass, along with the analysis of curves, the major innovation of this book lies in Descartes's use of coordinates and his introduction of the basic methods of his analytic geometry. Descartes regarded this as an application of his general philosophical method, although today it represents one of the major branches of mathematics.

Books about Descartes

Clarke, Desmond M. *Descartes' Philosophy of Science*. Pennsylvania State Univ. Pr. 1982 $22.50. This book takes a fresh look at Descartes, and concludes that he was "a practising scientist who, somewhat unfortunately, wrote a few short and relatively unimportant philosophical essays" (Introduction). Thus the emphasis here is on Descartes as a working scientist. Experience, experiment, reason, metaphysics, physics, modes of explanation, theory confirmation, all lead up to a reconsideration of Descartes's two major methodological essays, *Regulae* and *Discourse on Method*. A final chapter, "Descartes: An Innovative Aristotelian," provides an overall summary of Clarke's conclusions concerning Descartes.

Federico, P. J. *Descartes on Polyhedra: A Study of the "De Solidorum Elementis."* Springer-Verlag 1982 $39.50. This book photoreproduces an original manuscript version (actually a copy made by Leibniz) of a text by Descartes, transcribes this into legible Latin, and then offers a translation with comments and notes of what amounts to a short work by Descartes that was unknown until 1860. The manuscript itself represents a general treatment of polyhedra and of figurate numbers related to regular and semiregular polyhedra. Federico's book begins with a short introduction, followed by a brief history of the manuscript. Background in geometry and Greek number theory is given, along with a review of Euler's papers on the subject of polyhedra. A comparison of Descartes's and Euler's approaches as well as their conclusions to the subject is also provided.

Gaukroger, Stephen, ed. *Descartes' Philosophy, Mathematics and Physics*. Barnes & Noble 1980 $30.00. This book contains ten essays whose central focus is Descartes's concern with providing a philosophical foundation for mathematical physics. Cartesian optics, geometry, algebra, Descartes's union of the latter two in analytic geometry, his *mathesis universalis*, as well as concepts of force, inertia, and comparisons of Descartes with Newton, Leibniz, and others, are all discussed.

Scott, J. F. *The Scientific Work of René Descartes (1596–1650)*. Beekman repr. of 1952 ed. 1976 $18.50. This book concentrates on the major discoveries in mathematics and physics due to the French philosopher Descartes. In particular, it traces the steps whereby Descartes was led to develop analytic geometry, his most influential discovery, along with his studies in geometrical optics. Also included is a brief biographical introduction to Descartes's early life and training, along with a survey of Descartes's scientific work in general. The book then proceeds to give detailed analyses of *Discourse on Method* and Descartes's contributions in dioptrics, meteorology, and geometry. The last three chapters analyze various aspects of Descartes's *Principia Philosophiae*. A concluding chapter provides a succinct evaluation of the importance of Descartes's work in the history of science.

DIOPHANTUS. fl. c.250

Diophantus was a Greek mathematician who many consider the father of algebra, largely because he developed many important methods and an accompanying symbolic notation for the solution of equations. Above all, Diophantus developed methods for solving both determinate and indeterminate equations that are exemplified in his *Arithmetica*. Because the solution of indeterminate equations represents an important branch of mathematics, it is still known today as Diophantine analysis.

BOOK BY DIOPHANTUS

Diophantus of Alexandria: A Study in the History of Greek Algebra. Ed. by T. L. Heath, Dover repr. of 1885 ed. 1964 o.p. This book analyzes the nature and influence of the Greek mathematician Diophantus. A long appendix presents abstracts of both problems and solutions to six books of *Arithmetica* and another work by Diophantus, *On Polygonal Numbers*. The Dover edition reprints the second edition of 1910, which added a supplementary section on approaches by Fermat and Euler to solutions of Diophantine problems.

BOOK ABOUT DIOPHANTUS

Sesiano, J., ed. *Diophantus' Arithmetica: Books IV to VI in the Arabic Translation of Qusta Ibn Luqa*. Springer-Verlag 1982 $79.00. Four of seven books presumed to be lost of *Arithmetica*, by Diophantus, were discovered in Arabic translation in the Shrine Library in Meshed in Iran. These have now been edited and published here with an English translation, together with a mathematical commentary. This critical edition includes bibliography and indexes. For conflicting views about this work, its merits and defects, see R. Rashed in *Mathematical Reviews* 85H (August 1985), Providence, Rhode Island: American Mathematical Society, review # 85h:01006, pp. 3254–55.

EUCLID. fl. c.300 B.C.

Almost nothing is known of the life of this important Greek mathematician. His compilation of the major results of ancient geometry in a comprehensive axiomatic framework, however, has remained a classic and easily the most influential scientific work of all time. Although the *Elements* was first translated into English by Sir Henry Billingsley in 1570, the standard translation from the authoritative text of Heiberg is that of Sir T. L. Heath. The *Elements*, beginning with definitions, axioms, and postulates, deduces hundreds of general theorems about plane and solid geometry, including the famous Pythagorean theorem.

BOOK BY EUCLID

The Thirteen Books of Euclid's Elements. Ed. by T. L. Heath, Dover 3 vols. repr. of 1926 ed. 1956 ea. $7.50. Based on Heiberg's definitive edition (1883–88), this has long been the standard version in English of Euclid's *Elements*. Heath's introductions, notes, and commentaries remain of value, and in his lengthy analysis of Euclid from the traditions about him to the commentators on him are included. Principal translations, editions (current to 1925 or so), and an analysis of the *Elements* as a mathematical work, including its definitions, axioms, postulates, theorems, problems, and the general nature of Euclid's methods are covered, together with most every aspect of scholarship pertaining to Euclid. Both Greek and English indexes are provided.

BOOKS ABOUT EUCLID

Greenberg, Marvin J. *Euclidean and Non-Euclidean Geometries: Development and History*. W. H. Freeman 2d ed. 1980 $26.95. This book aims to promote "a

rigorous, historically motivated presentation of the foundations of geometry"
(Preface). It goes on to present "the discovery of non-Euclidean geometry and
the subsequent reformulation of the foundations of Euclidean geometry as a
suspense story. The mystery of why Euclid's parallel postulate could not be
proved remained unsolved for over two thousand years, until the discovery of
non-Euclidean geometry and its Euclidean models revealed the impossibility of
any such proof. This discovery shattered the traditional conception of geometry
as the true description of physical space."

Knorr, Wilbur. *The Evolution of the Euclidean Elements: A Study of the Theory of
Incommensurable Magnitudes and Its Significance for Early Greek Geometry.* Kluwer Academic 1975 $66.00. This book presents a detailed analysis of the discov-
ery of incommensurable magnitudes, and the eventual development of a sophisticated theory of proportions due to Eudoxus and is meant to provide a satisfactory theory of irrationals. Works by the Pythagoreans, Theodoros, Theaetetos,
Archytas, and Eudoxus serve to evaluate the question of a "pre-Euclidean foundations crisis." This is a scholarly study and an essential work for anyone interested in the technical origins of Euclidean mathematics, especially the theory of
proportions constituting Book X of the *Elements.*

Mueller, I. *Philosophy and Deductive Structure in Euclid's "Elements."* MIT 1981
$47.50. A comprehensive study of the *Elements* using the tools of modern logic
to lay bare the deductive method as Euclid employed it. Mueller draws on a
vast amount of earlier literature, from Zeuthen to the more recent works of
Neugebauer and Neuenschwander, to present his views. He also takes advantage of modern philosophies of logic and mathematics, especially Hilbert's on
geometry, to elucidate Euclid's own view of the approach to mathematics.

Smith, Thomas. *Euclid: His Life and His System.* Foundation Class. repr. of 1902 ed.
1983 $67.85. A very discursive, chatty, not very technical discussion of Euclid
and the significance of his *Elements* through the ages. Digressions to such subjects as popular literature and evolution eventually return to the exactness and
significance of Euclid's methods and the impact of his great compilation.

Thomas-Stanford, Charles. *Early Editions of Euclid's Elements.* Wofsy Fine Arts 1977
$85.00. The first edition of this work was published in 1926. It covers incunab-
ula and books printed up to 1600. The preface provides brief information about
Euclid and the publishing history (including translations) of the *Elements.* The
annotated bibliography of editions lists those that included not less than the
first six books with demonstrations in Greek, Greek and Latin, or Latin; editions
of the Enunciations only; translations into Arabic and modern European languages; and fragmentary editions in various languages. Indexes of places, printers, and publishers are also provided along with plates reproducing frontispie-
ces and examples from especially noteworthy editions.

EULER, LEONHARD. 1707–1783

Leonhard Euler was one of the most prolific mathematicians of all time
(amassing nearly 900 publications over the course of his lifetime). Although
he was born in Basel, Switzerland, he spent substantial amounts of time
promoting mathematics at the courts of Berlin and St. Petersburg. Euler
was adept at both pure and applied mathematics. His textbooks on algebra
and calculus became classics and remained standard introductions to both
subjects for generations. He also made seminal advances in the theory of
differential equations, number theory, mechanics, astronomy, hydraulics,
and the calculus of variations.

BOOKS BY EULER

Opera Omnia. Birkhäuser 1975 $110.00. This is Volume IVA1 inaugurating the fourth series in the publication of Euler's *Opera Omnia* (a joint venture of the Swiss Society of Natural Sciences and the USSR Academy of Sciences). Section A will consist of seven volumes of Euler's correspondence. This first volume describes and summarizes nearly 3,000 letters in the correspondence, arranged alphabetically by correspondent, and then chronologically. A detailed introduction makes clear the pervasive significance of Euler through his correspondence with many of the greatest scientific figures of the eighteenth century. Also included here is a very important table listing all of Euler's papers and their location in the *Opera Omnia.*

Elements of Algebra. 1770. Springer-Verlag repr. of 1840 ed. 1984 $28.00. This book begins with a historical appreciation of Euler's life and work by C. A. Truesdell ("Leonhard Euler, Supreme Geometer") including an annotated bibliography of biographies, works, letters, manuscripts, and so on, either by or about Euler. This is followed by an excerpt from a "Memoir of the Life and Character of Euler" by Francis Horner and Bernoulli's preface to the French edition. The work itself was first published in German by the Royal Academy of Sciences in St. Petersburg. Additions to the work by Lagrange also accompany this edition.

BOOKS ABOUT EULER

Truesdell, C. A. *Essays in the History of Mechanics.* Springer-Verlag 1968 $54.00. This volume contains previously unpublished—as well as already printed—essays by C. A. Truesdell on the history of mechanics. Beginning with Leonardo da Vinci, they mainly concentrate on the eighteenth century, including the development of rational mechanics and such topics as stress, moment, momentum, and the early kinetic theory of gases. Two of the eight chapters are devoted to connections between the history of mechanics and modern research, and a survey of "recent advances in rational mechanics." Both name and subject indexes are included.

———. *Six Lectures on Modern Natural Philosophy.* Springer-Verlag 1966 $16.00. By natural philosophy Truesdell means mechanics—especially rational mechanics. In addition to rational mechanics, this includes the study of materials, polar and oriented media, thermodynamics and visco-elasticity, electrified materials, and the ergodic problem in classical statistical mechanics. A final chapter takes up the questions of "method and taste" in natural philosophy.

FERMAT, PIERRE DE. 1601–1665

Fermat was a contemporary of Descartes, and an equally prominent French mathematician. His best-known work is in algebra, probability, and number theory. He was particularly interested in the study of prime numbers and is famous for his conjecture (known as "Fermat's Last Theorem") that if x, y, and z are positive integers, then there are no integers $n > 2$ such that $x^n + y^n = z^n$. Fermat devised a method of treating geometric problems algebraically that is similar to Descartes's analytic geometry. He also made discoveries concerning problems of maxima and minima that are closely related to the methods of the calculus developed later in the seventeenth century by Newton and Leibniz.

BOOK ABOUT FERMAT

Mahoney, Michael S. *The Mathematical Career of Pierre de Fermat (1601–1665).* Princeton Univ. Pr. 1973 o.p. This book provides a comprehensive overview of

Fermat's life and works, with specific attention given to his development of number theory and his role in advancing the use of coordinates in dealing with geometric problems algebraically. His contributions to the early development of methods related to the infinitesimal calculus (later pursued so successfully by Newton and Leibniz) are covered in detail.

GAUSS, CARL FRIEDRICH. 1777–1855

While Euler was the most prolific mathematician of the eighteenth century, Gauss was the most profound. His motto, "pauca sed matura" (few, but ripe), reflected his belief that one should publish only the most developed and complete expositions of results as possible. His most influential work was in number theory, and his *Disquisitiones Arithmeticae* was not only remarkable in the number and difficulty of problems it solved, but it has served as an introduction and guide to development of the theory ever since. In addition to important contributions to physics and astronomy, Gauss was also an early contributor to the theory of statistics, where his method of least squares and results concerning the "Gaussian" or normal curve are still essential.

BOOK BY GAUSS

Disquisitiones Arithmeticae. Trans. by A. A. Clarke, rev. by W. C. Waterhouse (with C. Greither and A. W. Grootendorst), Springer-Verlag 1986 $58.00. The Waterhouse edition is reprinted from the edition by Yale University Press of 1966. This version was translated from the second German edition of 1870. Among topics covered are congruences, residues, sections of a circle, forms, and indeterminate equations. According to W. K. Buehler, the English translation is not "everywhere reliable" (see [below] Buehler, *Gauss*).

BOOKS ABOUT GAUSS

Buehler, W. K. *Gauss: A Biographical Study.* Springer-Verlag 1981 $19.80. This book traces the life of Gauss from his birth, childhood, and student years in Göttingen (1795–98), until his death in 1855. It presents contemporary political and social background, his family life and several marriages, but above all devotes separate chapters to Gauss's major contributions to mathematics in number theory, arithmetic, the orbit of Ceres, *Disquisitiones Arithmeticae*, modular forms, elliptic and hypergeometric functions, geodesy and geometry, physics, astronomy, dioptrics, and the method of least squares. Appendixes offer a survey of Gauss's collected works, along with an analysis of secondary literature about Gauss and an index of his works.

Dunnington, G. W. *Carl Friedrich Gauss: Titan of Science.* Exposition Pr. 1955 o.p. This study of Gauss's life and work is based on contemporary sources, both manuscript and printed. Emphasis here is on Gauss as a man and scientist, set against the times in which he lived. This work is expository with little detail given to Gauss's technical achievements in pure mathematics. The book is well illustrated.

Hall, T. *Carl Friedrich Gauss: A Biography.* Trans. by A. Froderbart, MIT 1970 o.p. This book keeps the mathematical technicalities to a minimum. Instead, it tries to give "Gauss's most important results by formulating the problems, saying something about their origin, and illustrating them with concrete examples."

Nevertheless, enough of the mathematics, including some equations and derivations, is provided to give readers a sense of how Gauss worked and the major results, both pure and applied, that he obtained.

Merzbach, Uta, ed. *Carl Friedrich Gauss: A Bibliography.* Scholarly Resources 1984 $95.00. This compilation includes a list of primary sources and translations, a guide to Gauss's correspondence, and an extensive list of secondary sources about Gauss with emphasis given to those related to the history of mathematics. Annotations are provided for general works, indicating their usefulness. Keyword indexing is also provided. Letter and manuscript locations (other than Göttingen) are given; indexes include a list of names known to Gauss, as well as an index of topics covered.

GÖDEL, KURT. 1906–1978

Kurt Gödel was easily the most outstanding logician of the first half of the twentieth century. Born in Czechoslovakia, Gödel came to the United States in 1940 as a member of the Institute for Advanced Study in Princeton. In 1953 he was made a professor at the institute, where he remained until his death in 1978. He is especially well known for his studies of the completeness of logic, the incompleteness of number theory, and the consistency of the axiom of choice and the continuum hypothesis. Gödel is also known for his work on constructivity, the decision problem, and the foundations of computation theory, in addition to his views on the philosophy of mathematics, especially his support of a strong form of Platonism in mathematics.

BOOKS BY GÖDEL

Collected Works of Kurt Gödel. Ed. by Solomon Feferman and others, Oxford 1986 vol. 1 $35.00. This is the first of a projected three volumes meant to present a comprehensive edition of the mathematical and philosophical works of the logician Kurt Gödel. Each article (or closely related group of articles) places Gödel's works in detailed historical contexts. English translations are provided for all works by Gödel originally in German. A detailed and highly informative biographical essay by Solomon Feferman constitutes the introductory chapter of Volume 1. Numerous photographs of Gödel, his family, friends, and colleagues also enrich this volume. Volume 1 covers Gödel's works through 1936, including his dissertation.

Consistency of the Continuum Hypothesis. Princeton Univ. Pr. 1940 $15.95. This volume was compiled from notes taken by G. W. Brown of lectures Gödel gave at the Institute for Advanced Study, Princeton, during the autumn terms of 1938 and 1939. It contains the essence of Gödel's famous work related to the axiomatic consistency of Cantor's celebrated continuum hypothesis, but actually does much more. In his lectures, Gödel provided that the axiom of choice and Cantor's generalized continuum hypothesis were both consistent with the other axioms of set theory (assuming the axioms of set theory were consistent) within the Zermelo-Fraenkel set theory. Five pages of notes and a revised bibliography were added at the second and subsequent printings.

On Formally Undecidable Propositions of Principia Mathematica. . . . Trans. by B. Meltzer, Basic Bks. 1962 o.p. In this famous work, Gödel showed that every system of arithmetic contains arithmetical propositions (e.g., propositions concerned solely with relations between whole numbers), which can neither be proved nor disproved within the system. A brief introduction by R. B. Braith-waite discusses among other things metamathematics, Gödel's method of "arithmetization," recursiveness, consistency, the unprovability-of-consistency theorem, as well as the syntactical character of Gödel's theorems.

BOOKS ABOUT GÖDEL

Gensler, Harry J. *Gödel's Theorem Simplified.* Univ. Pr. of Amer. 1984 $15.00. This book sets out to prove—in as simple and direct a way as possible—Gödel's famous proof that it is impossible to reduce basic arithmetic to an axiomatic system. This amounts to showing that no possible axiomatic system suffices to prove every truth (but no falsehood) of arithmetic. No more than high school algebra is presumed. Symbolic logic, to the extent that Gensler uses it, is explained as needed.

Mostowski, Andrej. *Sentences Undecidable in Formalized Arithmetic: An Exposition of the Theory of Kurt Gödel.* Greenwood repr. of 1952 ed. 1982 $27.50. "In the present booklet, an attempt is made to present as clearly and as rigorously as possible the famous theory of undecidable sentences created by Kurt Gödel in 1931." Drawing attention to Gödel's use of K-definability to develop his book, Mostowski adds that "in terms of the general theory of K-definable functions and relations it is possible to express clearly and conveniently the assumptions which are the common source of the various proofs of Gödel's incompleteness theorem formulated first by Gödel himself and then by Tarski and Rosser. It seems probable that the theory of K-definability will prove useful also in other logical researches" (Preface).

HILBERT, DAVID. 1862–1943

Hilbert was among the earliest adherents of Cantor's new transfinite set theory. Despite the controversy that arose over the subject, Hilbert always maintained that "no one shall drive us from this paradise (of the infinite)" (Hilbert, "Über das Unendliche," *Mathematische Annalen* [1926]). It has been said that Hilbert was the last of the great universalist mathematicians, that he was knowledgeable in every area of mathematics and made important contributions to them all (the same has been said of Poincaré). Hilbert's publications include impressive works on algebra and number theory (by applying methods of analysis he was able to solve the famous "Waring's Problem"). There are also many contributions of Hilbert to analysis, especially the theory of functions and integral equations, as well as mathematical physics, logic, and the foundations of mathematics. His work of 1899, *Grundlagen der Geometrie,* brought Hilbert's name to international prominence, for it was based on a wholly new understanding of the nature of axioms. Hilbert adopted a formalist view, and stressed the significance of determining the consistency and independence of the axioms in question. In 1900, he again captured the imagination of an international audience with his famous "23 unsolved problems" of mathematics, many of which became major areas of intensive research in this century, and some of which remain unresolved to this day. At the end of his career, Hilbert became engrossed in the problem of providing a logically satisfactory foundation for all of mathematics, and developed a comprehensive program to establish the consistency of axiomatized systems in terms of a metamathematical proof theory.

BOOKS BY HILBERT

Gesammelte Abhandlungen. Chelsea Pub. repr. of 1932–35 ed. 3d ed. 1981 $14.95. Volume 1 consists of papers by Hilbert on number theory, including his lengthy report for *Jahresbericht der Deutschen Mathematikervereinigung.* A detailed analysis and "appreciation" of Hilbert's "algebraisch-zahlentheoretischen" works by Helmut Hasse appears at the end of the volume. Volume 2 covers algebra, invariant theory, and geometry, with an overview of Hilbert's accomplishments in algebra and invariant theory by B. L. van der Waerden; Arnold Schmidt wrote the analysis of Hilbert's work in geometry. Volume 3 is devoted to analysis, foundations of mathematics, physics, and varia. There is a paper discussing Hilbert's work on integral equations by Ernst Hellinger, and another on foundations of mathematics by Paul Bernays. Volume 3 also contains a biographical article by Otto Blumenthal, including a list of Hilbert's lectures at Göttingen, dissertations written under him, and a list of works not reprinted in *Gesammelte Abhandlungen.*

Foundations of Geometry. Trans. by E. J. Townsend, Open Court 2d ed. 1980 $23.95. This translation by E. J. Townsend represents a course of lectures given by Hilbert at the University of Göttingen in 1898 and 1899, incorporating some additions made by Hilbert for a subsequent French edition. These lectures analyze the intuition of space in terms of definitions, axioms, and a study of their relations, with special attention to the logical development of Euclidean geometry. Of particular importance are questions of the independence of the axioms, consistency, and completeness. Also covered are plane areas, the theory of proportion, Desargues's theorem, Pascal's theorem, and geometric constructions. A substantive conclusion and appendix discuss the significance of non-Euclidean geometries and the important work of S. Lie, M. Dehn, G. Cantor, and C. Jordan.

BOOK ABOUT HILBERT

Reid, Constance. *Hilbert.* Springer-Verlag 1970 $29.50. This detailed and captivating biography was written, as Reid says, "largely from memory" (Preface). That is, it is based on extensive archival and other written and published resources. It covers everything from Hilbert's youth and childhood friends to interests in pure and applied mathematics, as well as Hilbert's long interest in the philosophy and foundations of mathematics, especially in axiomatic and logical foundations and in the nature and legitimacy of the infinite. The book is written in an expository, nontechnical style, and includes many illustrations. An appendix reprints a shortened version of Hermann Weyl's assessment of Hilbert's career, "David Hilbert and His Mathematical Work" from the *Bulletin of the American Mathematical Society,* 1944.

NEWTON, SIR ISAAC. 1642–1727

Newton ranks as one of the world's greatest scientists. He is best known for his theory of universal gravitation, first published in his book of 1687, *Mathematical Principles of Natural Philosophy* (often referred to as the *Principia*). As early as 1666, however, Newton had already worked out many of his most important ideas in physics and mathematics, including his discovery of the binomial theorem and invention of the infinitesimal calculus. Newton's calculus was developed in terms of fluxions and fluents—akin to what today are called differentiation and integration. Newton succeeded in relating a method of finding areas under curves with another for finding tangents to curves. This enabled him to calculate the lengths of curves and areas of plane figures, to solve basic problems of maxima and minima, and to advance new results through numerous applications to problems of velocity, acceleration, and other problems of mathematical astronomy and physics. (See also Chapter 9 in this volume and Chapter 5 in Volume 4.)

BOOKS BY NEWTON

The Mathematical Works of Isaac Newton. Ed. by D. T. Whiteside, Johnson Repr. 2 vols. 1964–67 ea. $32.00–$34.00. This edition (by a dozen scholars on the subject of Newton's mathematics) reprints in facsimile several important short works by Newton on mathematics or about his methods of quadrature of curves, fluxions, and infinite series, all related to the calculus. Volume 2 reprints three works on algebra, finite differences, and geometry, including Newton's famous "universal arithmetic." Brief historical and analytic introductions by D. T. Whiteside accompany each volume.

The Mathematical Papers of Isaac Newton. Ed. by D. T. Whiteside, Cambridge Univ. Pr. 8 vols. 1967–81 ea. $155.00–$210.00. This is a comprehensive, scholarly edition of the major mathematical manuscripts of Isaac Newton. General introductions to each of the volumes by D. T. Whiteside cover the substance and significance of Newton's mathematical papers; analytical tables of contents in turn describe in detail each of the papers; and introductions to individual sections of each volume provide even more comprehensive analysis of Newton's particular achievements and their importance in the history of science.

BOOK ABOUT NEWTON

Westfall, Richard S. *Never at Rest: A Biography of Isaac Newton.* Cambridge Univ. Pr. 1983 $24.95. This exhaustive 908-page biography covers every facet of Newton's life from cradle to grave. It gives a detailed account of the progress, meteoric rise, influence, and eventual decline of one of the world's greatest scientific figures. It pays ample attention to Newton's mathematics, including invention of the calculus and the infamous priority dispute with Leibniz, without becoming overly technical. A comprehensive bibliographical essay is a useful guide to major sources of material related to Newtonian studies. The book is also well illustrated.

NOETHER, EMMY. 1882–1935

Emmy Noether, the most important woman mathematician in the early twentieth century, studied at Erlangen and Göttingen in Germany, and taught at Göttingen, Moscow, and Frankfurt before emigrating to the United States (and Bryn Mawr College) in 1933 when Jewish professors were being dismissed from German universities by the Nazi government. Her most important work was in abstract algebra. She made notable contributions with her theory of primary ideals, and found that polynomial ideals had especially useful applications in algebraic geometry. Noether also made significant discoveries in the theory of noncommutative rings in linear algebra, and used the idea of the cross product to resolve major questions about noncommutative algebras.

BOOK BY NOETHER

Collected Papers. Ed. by Nathan Jacobson, Springer-Verlag 1983 $57.20. This volume contains 43 of Noether's papers, along with notes on lectures she gave at Göttingen on hypercomplex numbers in 1929 (containing her first account of crossed products), and a paper by H. Kapferer, part of which was jointly written by Noether. An address by P. S. Alexandrov, "In Memory of Emmy Noether," opens the book, followed by an introduction surveying her major achievements, mathematically, written by Nathan Jacobson.

BOOKS ABOUT NOETHER

Dick, Auguste. *Emmy Noether, 1882–1935.* Trans. by H. I. Blocher, Birkhauser 1970 $13.95. This English translation contains some additions by Dick to Noether's original German text of 1968. It is both a personal and professional account of Noether's life and her mathematics, presented with limited technical explanations and without full mathematical detail. Obituaries of Noether or notices of her life and work by A. Einstein, B. L. van der Waerden, H. Weyl, and P. S. Alexandrov are also included.

Srinivasan, Bhama, and Judith D. Sally, eds. *Emmy Noether in Bryn Mawr: Proceedings of a Symposium Sponsored by the Association of Women in Mathematics in Honor of Emmy Noether's 100th Birthday.* Springer-Verlag 1983 $30.00. This book contains scientific lectures about mathematics related to topics on which Emmy Noether had worked, along with a paper prepared for a panel discussion, "Emmy Noether in Erlangen, Göttingen, and Bryn Mawr." Also included are two articles, "The Study of Linear Associative Algebras in the United States, 1870–1927" by Jeanne La Duke and "Emmy Noether: Historical Contexts" by Uta Merzbach.

POINCARE, JULES HENRI. 1854–1912

Some have claimed that Poincaré was the last of the great universalist mathematicians, one who could comprehend and make significant contributions to virtually all branches of mathematics known in his day (the same has been said of Hilbert). Poincaré also did very important work in mathematical physics and astronomy. Above all, he opened many new fields to mathematicians, especially algebraic topology, and he made singular discoveries in the theory of complex variables (especially his discovery of automorphic functions), differential equations, and celestial mechanics. Poincaré wrote as well for general audiences, and made his own important contributions to both the philosophy and foundations of mathematics.

BOOK BY POINCARÉ

Papers on Fuchsian Functions. Trans. by J. Stillwell, Springer-Verlag 1985 $34.00. This is one of the areas in which Poincaré made important and original contributions that grew out of his dissertation on existence theorems for differential equations.

BOOK ABOUT POINCARÉ

Slosson, Edwin E. *Major Prophets of Today.* Ayer repr. of 1914 ed. $20.00. This work is comprised of brief biographies of significant personalities at the turn of the century; each is meant to serve as an introduction to the writings of each author. The chapter on Poincaré is somewhat rambling and concentrates more on philosophy than science. The question of where scientific inspiration and creativity come from is discussed. A critical bibliographic essay, "How to Read Poincaré," provides a very dated list of works about Poincaré.

RUSSELL, BERTRAND. 1872–1970

After writing his dissertation at Cambridge University on the foundations of geometry (published in 1897), Russell went on to a special lectureship in logic and philosophy of mathematics at Cambridge. His primary scientific interest at the time concerned a general study of the principles of mathematics, which he believed could be reduced to a small set of fundamental principles. Eventually, in collaboration with his colleague ALFRED NORTH WHITEHEAD (see Vol. 4), the two produced the monumental *Principia Mathematica*. Russell's interest in the paradoxes of set theory and logic led him to advance a theory of types that was unsuccessful in saving mathematical logic from the proof, later given by Gödel, that no axiomatic system can be proven to be self-consistent—one of the goals *Principia Mathematica* had set for itself. A nontechnical exposition of the major intent and significance of *Principia Mathematica* was written by Russell in his *Introduction to Mathematical Philosophy*. (See also Volume 4.)

BOOKS BY RUSSELL

Essays in Analysis. Ed. by D. Lackey, Allen & Unwin 1973 $8.95. This collection of essays by Russell focuses on the period from 1904 to 1913 leading up to his development of a mature theory of type and publication of his monumental effort with Whitehead, *Principia Mathematica*. Three previously unpublished papers (from the Bertrand Russell Archives at McMaster University, Ontario, Canada) are included, along with two English translations of articles originally published in French. A brief introduction sets Russell's work against the background of influences on his approach to mathematics and logic—namely figures like Peano, Frege, Cantor, Whitehead, and later Wittgenstein. A useful bibliography of Russell's writings on logic (published and unpublished) is appended.

The Principles of Mathematics. Norton repr. of 1903 ed. 1964 $10.95. Russell's major exposition of his philosophy of mathematics, namely logicism. It contains detailed discussions of many important mathematicians and their contributions to mathematics and logic at the turn of the century. Russell also explains his famous paradox, and draws the implications of the antinomies of set theory for the foundations of mathematics. The book contains an appendix on Russell's early ideas for a theory of types, later incorporated as a fundamental idea of *Principia Mathematica* written later in collaboration with Whitehead.

(and Alfred North Whitehead). *Principia Mathematica.* 1910–13. Cambridge Univ. Pr. 3 vols. 2d ed. 1925–27 $400.00

Introduction to Mathematical Philosophy. 1919. Simon & Schuster 1971 pap. $8.50

BOOK ABOUT RUSSELL

Grattan-Guinness, Ivor. *Dear Russell—Dear Jourdain: A Commentary on Russell's Logic, Based on His Correspondence with Philip Jourdain.* Columbia Univ. Pr. 1977 $31.50. This book provides running commentary and analysis by the author of an exchange of letters between two British philosopher-mathematicians during the early twentieth century—from March 1902 until Jourdain's early death in October 1919. Jourdain was especially concerned with attempts to resolve the paradoxes of set theory and prove the well-ordering principle (Zermelo's Axiom of Choice). At the time, Russell was also busy with his own interests in set theory and the paradoxes, and was engaged with Whitehead in writing *Principia Mathematica*.

WEIERSTRASS, KARL WILHELM THEODOR. 1815–1897

After an unhappy period as a high school teacher, Weierstrass was offered a position teaching in Berlin on the strength of his publication of a paper on Abelian functions. Later, at the University of Berlin, he became the center of an important circle of younger mathematicians who sought to carry out his approach to "arithmeticizing" mathematics, which was particularly influential in the latter part of the nineteenth century. In fact, supplying rigorous foundations to all mathematical arguments was one of his major preoccupations. Among the areas of research pursued by Weierstrass, the most important concerned analytic functions, elliptic and hyperelliptic functions, Abelian functions, and the calculus of variations.

BOOK BY WEIERSTRASS

Mathematische Werke. Berlin: Mayer and Müller 7 vols. 1894–1927; Johnson Repr. 7 vols. $210.00. Prepared by Weierstrass with remarks of his own to many of the papers and revisions to some papers by colleagues and former students (as acknowledged at the end of each volume). Volumes 1, 2, and 3 contain mathematical papers; Volumes 4, 5, 6, and 7, lectures on the theory of elliptic and Abelian functions, as well as the variational calculus.

CHAPTER 5

Statistics and Probability

Jean Dickinson Gibbons

A pinch of probably is worth a pound of perhaps.
—James Thurber

Collecting data is much like collecting garbage. You must know in advance what you are going to do with the stuff before you collect it.
—Mark Twain

Statistical thinking will one day be as necessary for efficient citizenship as the ability to read and write.
—H. G. Wells

The news media are full of statements about statistics and probability, but few people even understand what these terms mean, much less how to use them properly.

Probability is the likelihood of occurrence of a particular event or outcome. It is expressed as a number between zero and one, with zero indicating almost no chance of occurrence and one indicating an almost certain chance of occurrence. Probabilities are sometimes stated as percentages between 0 and 100, e.g., there is an 80 percent chance of rain. Probabilities are also sometimes given as odds. If the odds for an event's occurrence are given as "x to y," this means that the probability of the event occurring is x divided by $x + y$. The odds against the occurrence of this same event are "y to x." As an example, suppose the odds for State winning the football game are 4 to 1; then the probability that State wins is 4/5 or an 80 percent chance.

The word statistic (singular) refers to a number. A collection of numbers are data and are frequently called statistics (plural). However, statistics also has a meaning as a singular noun. Statistics is the methodology of collecting, describing, and analyzing data, and using data to make estimates, inferences, and decisions. The foundation of statistics is the theory of probability.

A statistician is a person who deals with numerical information or data. Statisticians have been trained to determine what kind of data to collect and how to collect those data, how to obtain useful information from the data in a scientific manner, and how to make informed decisions based on the data. A statistician is not a person who tabulates numbers. An example of a popular misuse of the term is a "baseball statistician," who is not really a statistician at all.

120

Computers are essential to the work of many statisticians. Calculations that once took weeks of time can now be done in a few seconds on a high-speed computer. Some statisticians use the computer to analyze data, others use it to help solve statistical problems whose mathematical complexity might be otherwise overwhelming, and still others use it to find statistical models to represent real-world situations. Almost everyone agrees that the computer is to the modern statistician what the test tube is to the chemist.

Professional statisticians generally have at least a master's degree in statistics. The best high school and undergraduate preparation for formal study in statistics is mathematics. Some colleges and universities offer a bachelor's degree in statistics, but most academic programs are at the graduate level. Some colleges and universities have a department of statistics. At other schools, statistics may be a subhead under mathematics, business, or interdisciplinary studies. People who like to work with numbers and to solve numerical problems generally like to study statistics.

The demand for professional statisticians has increased greatly in recent years in response to the increased need for the collection and interpretation of data, as well as the greater availability of high-speed computers. Statistical methodology is used widely in agriculture, biology, business, economics, education, engineering, insurance, medicine, political science, psychology, quality control, and all of the social sciences. State and federal governments employ many statisticians. Statisticians are in demand by lawyers to serve as expert witnesses in court cases. Many statisticians have a consulting practice with clients from business, industry, and government. A brochure on careers is available from the American Statistical Association (806 15th Street, N.W., Suite 640, Washington, DC 20005).

The origins of the theory of probability are in the middle of the seventeenth century as applied to games of chance. James Bernoulli (1654–1705) made major contributions to probability theory and claimed important applications existed in civil, moral, and economic affairs. The well-known normal curve was introduced by Abraham Demoivre (1677–1754) in 1733. Pierre La Place (1749–1827) and Carl Friedrich Gauss (1777–1855) (see Chapter 4 in this volume) made extensive use of the normal curve and thereby laid the groundwork for the development of statistics that began in the late nineteenth century with studies of the laws of heredity and genetics by Charles Darwin (1809–1882) (see Chapters 11 and 12 in this volume), Gregor Mendel (1822–1884) (see Chapter 13 in this volume), Sir Francis Galton (1822–1900), Karl Pearson (1857–1936), and others. The father of statistics in its present state is generally regarded to be Sir Ronald A. Fisher (1890–1962) because he solidified the concepts and theory. The twentieth century has seen countless new developments in the field, mostly by the Americans and English, although statisticians come from countries all over the world.

Even persons who do not want to become trained statisticians need to have a better understanding of how to interpret statistical evidence. The news media are flooded with quantitative measurements and evaluations, and supposed "facts" based on such statistics. Everyone, whether or not he or she likes it, is a lifetime consumer of statistics, and as such should be an informed consumer. The informed consumer will ask the following questions about any reported statistic:

1. Who is making the claim?
2. How unbiased is the claimant?
3. Is any needed information missing?
4. Has there been a verbal bait and switch?

As an example, consider an advertisement that claims pain reliever tablet *X* dissolves on the average twice as fast as tablet *Y*. Who is making the claim? The manufacturer, through the advertising agency. But the manufacturer's claim may be biased because the company obviously has a vested interest in making its product look good. Is any needed information missing? The manufacturer claims it recently completed a series of laboratory studies, but no details are given about the studies. Also missing is a definition of what is meant by "on the average." The "average" could be the mean, the median, or the mode. Is there a verbal bait and switch going on? Quite possibly. The rapid rate of dissolution of the tablet (i.e., the bait) may have nothing whatsoever to do with fast and effective pain relief. Hence, the claim that what the consumer is attracted by is not relevant to the effectiveness of the product that is advertised. If we learn to think like a statistician, we cannot be so easily fooled. We know that we have not been given enough information to know whether or not the advertising claim makes sense.

The following books can help the layperson learn to carry out this kind of critical assessment of reported quantitative "facts."

GENERAL BIBLIOGRAPHY

Brewer, James K. *Everything You Always Wanted to Know about Statistics, but Didn't Know How to Ask.* Kendall-Hunt 2d ed. 1978 text ed. pap. $9.95. Uses a question-and-answer format to explain the basic concepts of statistics.

Brightman, Harvey J. *Statistics in Plain English.* South-Western 1986 text ed. pap. $10.95. A user-friendly, self-teaching introduction to statistics.

Brook, Richard J., and others, eds. *The Fascination of Statistics.* Marcel Dekker 1986 $24.95. A collection of 30 interesting essays with illustrations about how statistical methods aid in answering questions of vital importance in many applied fields. The essays are written by experts in different fields, but are readable by nonexperts.

Campbell, Stephen K. *Flaws and Fallacies in Statistical Thinking.* Prentice-Hall 1974 pap. $16.95. A delightful book to read, aimed at helping consumers of information increase their ability to judge the quality of statistical evidence presented.

Cleveland, William S. *The Elements of Graphing Data.* Wadsworth 1985 $18.95. Explains the methods for displaying data effectively to give a clear understanding and interpretation to the reader; a good presentation that requires very little mathematical background.

Ehrenberg, A. S. C. *A Primer in Data Reduction: An Introductory Statistics Textbook.* Wiley 1982 $73.95 pap. $31.95. A nonmathematical introduction to traditional statistical methods and their limitations.

Fabricand, Burton F. *The Science of Winning: A Random Walk on the Road to Riches.* Van Nostrand 1979 o.p. Describes how to develop optimal strategies for betting or investing; well written, but not elementary.

Fairley, William B., and Frederick Mosteller. *Statistics and Public Policy.* Addison-Wesley 1977 text ed. $30.95. A collection of 18 essays by distinguished statisticians illustrating how important data, analysis, and models are to decision making on public policy issues.

Folks, J. Leroy. *Ideas of Statistics.* Wiley 1981 $32.95. Covers the history of statistics, gives information about well-known persons who contributed to the development of the field, and describes some of the famous controversies in statistics.

Friedman, Arthur, and Joel E. Cohen. *The World of Sports Statistics: How the Fans and Professionals Record, Compile and Use Information.* Atheneum 1978 o.p. Presents firsthand information about statistics in baseball, hockey, football, and basketball, along with personal anecdotes of experiences with the New York Mets and Rangers.

Gnanadesikan, Mrudulla, R. L. Scheaffer, and Jim Swift. *The Art and Technique of Simulation.* Dale Seymour 1986 $9.95. Shows how to solve practical probability problems through simple simulations.

Haack, Dennis G. *Statistical Literacy: A Guide to Interpretation.* Duxbury 1979 o.p. Emphasizes the proper interpretation of statistics so that readers can detect statistical doublespeak in the media and in various fields of study.

Hollander, Myles, and Frank Proschan. *The Statistical Exorcist: Dispelling Statistics Anxiety.* Marcel Dekker 1984 $17.95. A delightful book that explains through 26 vignettes how statistics is used in everyday life; clear, simple, and amusing, with many cartoons and quotations.

Hooke, Robert. *How to Tell the Liars from the Statisticians.* Marcel Dekker 1983 $17.75. Uses 76 vignettes as examples to show how statistical reasoning affects our lives significantly in many areas.

Huff, Darrell, and Irving Geis. *How to Lie with Statistics.* Norton 1954 pap. $1.95. A classic book that gives humorous examples of situations in which statistics can be very misleading; shows people how to recognize sound data and analysis; very easy to read and entertaining with delightful illustrations.

———. *How to Take a Chance.* Norton 1964 pap. $6.95. Pleasing illustrations and easy reading about probability theory, with chapters on the control of chance, strategy for winning, and caveats to look for in reported statistics.

Jaffe, Abram J., and Herbert F. Spirer. *Misused Statistics: Straight Talk for Twisted Numbers.* Marcel Dekker 1987 $29.75. Shows readers how to become critical observers of the statistical scene by giving many examples of misuses with explanations of why the conclusions are erroneous; includes some examples of proper uses.

Johnson, Allan G. *Social Statistics without Tears.* McGraw-Hill 1977 o.p. Introduces the reader to an understanding of statistical language, techniques, and principles important to the social sciences.

Kirk, Roger E. *Statistical Issues: A Reader for the Behavioral Sciences.* Brooks/Cole 1972 o.p. A collection of 55 essays dealing with conceptual issues of statistics as used in behavioral science research.

Kotz, Samuel, and Donna F. Stroup. *Educated Guessing: How to Cope in an Uncertain World.* Marcel Dekker 1983 $18.00. Gives a clear understanding of the concepts of probability and how they can be used in the real world.

Landwehr, James M., and Ann E. Watkins. *Exploring Data.* Dale Seymour 1986 $9.95. Encourages readers to learn to organize and display data so that patterns are evident.

Landwehr, James M., Jim Swift, and Ann E. Watkins. *Exploring Surveys and Information from Samples.* Dale Seymour 1987 $9.95. An elementary book that explains the basic techniques of obtaining information about a large group from a sample.

Larsen, Richard J., and Donna F. Stroup. *Statistics in the Real World: A Book of Examples.* Macmillan 1976 text ed. pap. o.p. A workbook of relevant substantive examples of applications of statistical procedures in anthropology, biology, economics, psychology, medicine, geology, political science, history, and sociology.

Levinson, Horace C. *The Science of Chance: From Probability to Statistics.* Rinehart 1956 o.p. The basic concepts of probability and statistics are developed by analyzing problems in games of chance; chances and strategies are given for poker, roulette, bridge, and craps. The same principles are then applied to real problems in government and business.

Lieberman, Bernhard, ed. *Contemporary Problems in Statistics: A Book of Readings for the Behavioral Sciences.* Oxford 1971 o.p. A collection of 45 articles from the behavioral science literature about some controversial issues involving applications of statistics and interpretations.

Light, Richard J., and David B. Pillemer. *Summing Up: The Science of Reviewing Research.* Harvard Univ. Pr. 1984 text ed. $17.50 pap. $7.95. Practical guidelines and step-by-step procedures for summarizing findings in quantitative research studies; well written.

Megeath, Joe D. *How to Use Statistics.* Canfield 1975 o.p. An intuitive introduction to the concepts of statistics, generally directed toward business applications.

Moore, David S. *Statistics: Concepts and Controversies.* Freeman 2d ed. 1985 text ed. $19.95 pap. $12.95. Focuses on the concepts of statistics and their impact on public policy and everyday life, i.e., the interaction of statistics and society.

Moroney, M. G. *Facts from Figures.* Penguin (Pelican) 1953 o.p. Provides a conducted tour through "the statisticians' workshop," explaining the jargon and the tools.

Moses, Lincoln E. *Think and Explain with Statistics.* Addison-Wesley 1986 $28.95. A lucid discussion of the uses and limitations of statistical techniques and concepts.

Mosteller, Frederick. *Fifty Challenging Problems in Probability.* Addison-Wesley 1965 o.p. A selection of problems with detailed solutions illustrating elementary probability and statistics in applications.

Mosteller, Frederick, Stephen E. Fienberg, and Robert E. K. Rourke. *Beginning Statistics with Data Analysis.* Addison-Wesley 1983 o.p. Intriguing real data examples are used to introduce readers to data handling and analysis, sampling, probability, and testing.

Mosteller, Frederick, and others. *Statistics by Example.* Addison-Wesley 4 vols. 1972–76 ea. $9.92. Vol. 1, *Exploring Data;* Vol. 2, *Weighing Chances;* Vol. 3, *Detecting Patterns;* Vol. 4, *Finding Models.* A four-part series of real-life interesting problems and examples prepared by the Joint Committee on the Curriculum in Statistics and Probability of the American Statistical Association.

Naiman, Arnold, and Robert Rosenfeld. *Understanding Statistics.* McGraw-Hill 3d ed. 1983 text ed. $36.95. An elementary book for persons with little mathematical background who want to learn how statistics is used properly.

Neft, David S., R. M. Cohen, and J. A. Deutsch. *The World Book of Odds.* Grosset & Dunlap 1978 o.p. An elementary book that gives odds on many, many things that can happen, e.g., the odds against having your letter published in a "Dear Abby" column are 600 to 1.

Nemenyi, Peter, and others. *Statistics from Scratch.* Holden-Day 1977 o.p. A readable introduction to statistics with many interesting examples of applications in real life.

Newman, Claire E., T. E. Obremski, and R. L. Sheaffer. *Exploring Probability.* Dale

Seymour 1986 $9.95. An elementary book that develops practical applications of probability through individual experiments.

Peters, William S. *Counting for Something.* Springer-Verlag 1987 $33.00. Teaches the principles of applied economic and social statistics in a historical context by interweaving personalities and descriptions of original applications.

Phillips, John L., Jr. *Statistical Thinking: A Structural Approach.* Freeman 1982 text ed. $18.95 pap. $11.95. Aims to teach persons to think logically and quantitatively about the concepts of statistics.

Reichard, Robert. *The Figure Finaglers.* McGraw-Hill 1974 o.p. A book for consumers of figures who want to learn how to separate fact from fiction, useful from useless, and how to recognize the signs of distortion.

Riechmann, W. J. *Use and Abuse of Statistics.* Penguin (Pelican) 1964 o.p. Discusses how and in what circumstances certain statistics can be used properly; emphasizes the dangers of misinterpretation; written in an interesting and entertaining style.

Rowntree, Derek. *Probability without Tears.* Scribner 1984 $7.95. A reader-friendly presentation of probability concepts for nonmathematicians; uses an interactive style; has exercises and solutions.

Runyon, Richard P. *Winning with Statistics: A Painless First Look at Numbers, Ratios, Percentages, Means and Inference.* Addison-Wesley 1977 text ed. pap. $12.95. An entertaining introduction to the ideas and concepts of statistics.

Slonim, Morris J. *Sampling: A Quick, Reliable Guide to Practical Statistics.* Simon & Schuster 1960 o.p. A technically sound book on sampling written for the layperson with amusing cartoons and many interesting examples of applications.

Splaver, Sarah. *Nontraditional Careers for Women.* Messner 1973 o.p. Covers statistics as a career.

Sprent, Peter. *Statistics in Action.* Penguin (Pelican) 1977 o.p. Explains the concepts of statistics and the work of statisticians through practical examples from many fields.

Stigler, Stephen M. *The History of Statistics: The Measurement of Uncertainty before 1900.* Harvard Univ. Pr. (Belknap Pr.) 1986 text ed. $25.00. Gives the early history of statistics and probability from 1700 to 1900; written by a science historian and statistician, with many illustrations.

Tanur, Judith M., ed. *Statistics: A Guide to Biological and Health Sciences.* Holden-Day 1977 text ed. pap. $8.95. A collection of 12 articles illustrating how statistics and probability help solve problems in the biological and health sciences.

———. *Statistics: A Guide to Business and Economics.* Holden-Day 1976 text ed. pap. $8.95. A collection of 12 articles illustrating how statistics and probability help solve problems in business and economics that are important to the nation, science, and persons in business.

———. *Statistics: A Guide to Political and Social Issues.* Holden-Day 1977 text ed. pap. $8.95. A collection of 12 articles illustrating how statistics and probability help solve problems in political science, sociology, and government.

———. *Statistics: A Guide to the Unknown.* Holden-Day 2d ed. 1978 text ed. pap. $14.00. A collection of 44 articles illustrating how statistics and probability help solve problems important to our biological, political, social, and physical world.

Tashman, Leonard J., and Kathleen R. Lamborn. *The Ways and Means of Statistics.* Harcourt 1979 text ed. $22.95. Shows how to communicate information through statistics in a precise and intelligible manner.

Tufte, Edward R., ed. *The Quantitative Analysis of Social Problems.* Addison-Wesley 1970 o.p. A collection of papers with real examples of how statistical studies have been used to solve social problems.

————. *The Visual Display of Quantitative Information.* Graphics Pr. 1983 $34.00. A
   beautiful and exquisitely designed book that gives a history of data graphics
   followed by a manual of how to display the maximum of information clearly
   and concisely using illustrations.

Waller, Ray. *Statistics: An Introduction to Numerical Reasoning.* Holden-Day 1979
   text ed. pap. $19.50. An introduction to the basic concepts and fundamentals of
   statistics.

Weissglass, Julian, and others. *Hands-on Statistics.* Wadsworth 1986 text ed. $54.00
   pap. $17.50. Introduces the reader to concepts of statistics with accompanying
   computer software supplied for "hands-on" learning.

Wheeler, Michael. *Lies, Damn Lies and Statistics: The Manipulation of Public Opinion
   in America.* Dell 1977 pap. $2.50. Explains how public opinion polls are carried
   out, demonstrates what polls can and cannot do, and discusses how to determine whether the results of polls can be trusted.

Willemson, Eleanor W. *Understanding Statistical Reasoning.* Freeman 1974 o.p. A
   book for persons who need to understand, review, and interpret statistical reasoning in research of the behavioral sciences.

Zeisel, Hans. *Say It with Figures.* Harper 6th ed. 1985 pap. $7.95. A practical descrip-
   tion of the analysis of sample surveys with much information about the history
   of statistics and measurement.

REFERENCE BOOKS

Freund, John E., and Frank J. Williams. *Dictionary/Outline of Basic Statistics.*
   McGraw-Hill 1966 o.p. Defines statistical terms and gives an outline of statistical
   formulas.

Kotz, Samuel, and Norman L. Johnson, eds. *Encyclopedia of Statistical Sciences.*
   Wiley 9 vols. 1982–87 ea. $85.00–$89.95 Information on a large number of
   topics in statistical theory and application of statistical methods. According to
   the Preface, "This information is intended primarily to be of value to readers
   who do not have detailed information about the topics but have encountered
   references . . . that they wish to understand."

Kruskal, William H., and Judith M. Tanur, eds. *International Encyclopedia of Statistics.* Macmillan 2 vols. 1978 $155.00. Includes approximately 70 articles on
   statistics proper, a number of articles on social science topics with strong statistical flavor, biographies of statisticians, and bibliographies.

CHAPTER 6

Information and Computer Science

Heyward Ehrlich

Computers and communication can help us create community.
—ALVIN TOFFLER

Any sufficiently advanced technology is indistinguishable from magic.
—ARTHUR C. CLARKE

The clerical error, as everyone knows, is now a thing of the past, but any net benefit to humankind is mitigated because the clerical error has been dwarfed by its technological successor, the computer error.

Indeed, during the last two or three decades, computers have rapidly taken over the task of handling more and more of the transactional, informational, and visual data, whether in numbers, words, or pictures, of each of the advanced nations of the world. The computer takes its name in English from World War II machines designed for massive military computations, but it is more appropriately named in some other languages: *ordinateur* in French and *elaboratore* in Italian suggest its additional powers to perform nonmathematical functions, such as to store, arrange, and retrieve information; to be a supercorrecting typewriter; to handle telecommunications; to control and design devices in industry; to create visual presentations on paper, film, and tape; and to do thousands of other tasks.

In a famous wrong guess, **IBM** decided not to make computers in the late 1940s because of its estimate that only six such machines could be sold in the entire world. There are now tens of millions of computers in operation—submicroprocessors, microcomputers, minicomputers, mainframe computers, and supercomputers, many of them linked to each other or to data banks by telecommunication lines, satellites, or optical fiber cables. Our military preparation, space exploration, national security, manufacturing and industry, agriculture, banking and finance, insurance, office work, service industries, advertising and publishing, education and research, even our cars and appliances, depend on computers. (One side-effect of nuclear explosions is the total erasure of the internal instructions and memory stores of any computers nearby.) In recent years, the quantity of computer data has increased so drastically that it is spoken of as the "information explosion." Moreover, this new computer data must be handled in such radically different ways as to constitute the "information revolution." These new economic and cultural vectors are taking us on a quantum leap into the "information society."

In *Profiles of the Future,* Arthur C. Clarke lists these unexpected and improbable inventions of the last hundred years that we now take for granted in the fields of communications and information: the telephone, phonograph, office machine, vacuum tube, radio, television, radar, tape recorder, electronic computer, transistor, laser, communication satellite, pocket calculator, and video recorder. Then, looking ahead to the next hundred years, Clarke foresees this list: pocket educators, new libraries, universal radiophones, telesensory devices, practical artificial intelligence, the detection of extrasolar intelligence, memory recording, and artifact coding. Other futurologists also see the paperless office, universal voice input and output instead of visual reading and manual keyboarding, automatic translation between human languages, two-way miniature televisions to connect to the libraries and data banks of the world, professional information centers with expert knowledge systems in the shop and office, and culture-creativity centers in the home. If they are right, we are in the springtime of an intellectual golden age.

It does not, however, feel like spring. Clarke's HAL in *2001* reveals our deep negative emotions about the future of intelligent computers. (Elsewhere Clarke—disagreeing with C. P. Snow—suggests that we will soon need two distinct human languages, one for counting and one for feeling.) Everywhere Cassandras warn us that new information technology threatens the rise of a two-class society based on access to data, sweeping unemployment and economic dislocation, painful losses of privacy and civil liberties, the trivialization of writing and speech, the loss or narrowing of perspective on Western ethical, philosophical, and intellectual traditions, and the degradation of scientific wisdom by the sheer mass of unmanageable data. Above all, we are warned that the growing technototalitarian state could base its extralegal power on the amalgamation of previously confidential information in the databanks that already contain our IRS, Social Security, Bell telephone, TRW bank and credit, FBI, police, real estate, tenant, political, educational, employment, membership, subscription, charity, mailing, and medical histories. We may never have imagined that some of these databases even existed.

Whichever version or versions of the information future will arrive, we will know soon enough. By the mid-1950s, there were already more persons employed in service industries than in factories in the United States. During the 1970s, large computers and satellite and telephone links were used to create huge information networks and data banks. In the 1980s, microcomputers and easy-to-use software, now possessing increased speed and capacity and reduced size and cost, facilitated the penetration of interactive computer information systems into every office, factory, institution—and a good many homes. At the same time, libraries abandoned the traditional card catalog, moving first to supplemental catalogs published in book form and then to selective online catalogs requiring the use of a computer terminal. The two familiar media that were standard before 1970 in information systems, the typed 8½" × 11" page produced on an electric typewriter and the standard 3" × 5" file card, were dethroned by the massive, rapidly produced, coded, hard to read (and sometimes harder to understand) computer printout on perforated, endless, zig-zag paper—and its electronic equivalent, an online, fully instantaneous, interactive, search-strategy accessible, password-secured, video-display and keyboard-equipped, hierarchically structured electronic database. The new Babel of information was not a tower of confused speech, but rather an underground web of branching, narrowing tunnels of specialist information technology. To understand one set of proprietary hardware, computer languages, or search strategies did not guarantee the understanding of any other. Moreover, the community of information workers, formerly a visible natural society, became an invisible network of remote initiates held together by expertise in documentation manuals, help and hot keys, and confidential 800-numbers—details and whole portions of which arise, change, or vanish each year.

The remedy for this Noah's flood of information may be much, much more information. It is widely argued that we must all become "computer literate," learning to write home computer applications in BASIC, replacing the medieval trivium of grammar, logic, and rhetoric with expertise in computer programming and artificial intelligence, and if possible updating the medieval quadrium of arithmetic, geometry, astronomy, and music with the latest microcomputer software applications packages for spreadsheets, turtle graphics, astrology, and synthetic music. The current fashion dictates that nothing has intellectual validity unless it was done on computer. Computers are very good at creating seas of information, but they do not automatically increase our knowledge or our wisdom. We do not need to know everything; we need first to discover exactly what we need to know, and in the process, feel comfortable with understanding both what we need and do not need to know.

This chapter is designed to help the reader find his or her way in the new world of information technology. It is divided into several parts: first, introductions to computing and information science, then computer programming and software applications, and finally artificial intelligence and current controversies. Although there are many works listed for the expert in business, professional, or academic applications, the headnotes in each section are designed to be most helpful to the novice.

Although many older works are still quite satisfactory in presenting the history or basic principles of their subject, in some fields the technology is changing very rapidly: Some microcomputer software packages are updated every year, and some hardware is improved almost as frequently. In certain growth areas—such as operating systems and chips, parallel processing, optical data storage and transmission, networking and connectivity, desktop publishing, laser printing, online searching and retrieval, scanning, laser disks, artificial intelligence, graphics and image processing, the human interface, extended memory, large disk storage, and microcomputer operating chips and systems—important changes may be so recent that quarterly, monthly, and weekly periodicals or even daily newspapers must be consulted. Do not overlook information and computer technology news in *Business Week, High Technology, New York Times, Newsweek, Psychology Today, Science, Scientific American, Wall Street Journal,* and *Whole Earth Review.*

INTRODUCTION TO COMPUTING

Beginner's Guides

The most successful beginner's guides to computing are well written, relaxed, and occasionally humorous. Many, written by authors who are also professional novelists, columnists, lecturers, or poets, avoid the off-putting effect of starting with excessively technical information or textbook approaches designed for the initiated. These books rightly treat the computer as a useful tool, not as an object of veneration, and are written for the user who is less interested in the engineering intricacies than in how to use the thing.

Bear, John. *Computer Wimp*. Ten Speed Pr. 1983 $14.95 pap. $9.95. A humorous introduction designed to take the formality and tension out of first encounters with microcomputers. The approach is anecdotal—"166 things I wish I had known before I bought my first computer."

Bernstein, Jeremy. *The Analytic Engine: Computers—Past, Present, and Future*. Morrow rev. ed. 1981 pap. $8.95. A series of highly readable articles on the history of computing, originally published in *The New Yorker* magazine. One of the best written introductions to computers and their history for people who claim they cannot understand them.

———. *Three Degrees above Zero: Bell Labs in the Information Age*. NAL 1986 pap. $4.50; Scribner 1984 $17.95. Splendidly written accounts of discoveries and developments at Bell Laboratories—including silicon chips, fiber optics, and a computer chess program called Belle. Originally published in *The New Yorker*.

Bradbeer, Robin. *The Beginner's Guide to Computers: Everything You Need to Know about the New Technology*. Addison-Wesley 1982 pap. $10.95. The history and working of computers, with some application programs in BASIC. The book originated as a text for the BBC "Computer Literacy Project," seen in the United States on PBS as "The Computer Programme."

Crichton, Michael. *Electronic Life: How to Think about Computers*. Ballantine 1984 pap. $3.95; Knopf 1983 $12.95. Crichton, a medical doctor best known as the author of several science fiction novels, produces an introduction to computers, and the result is not a hardware/software manual, but rather an interesting gathering of thoughts, feelings, and suggestions about encounters with a PC (personal computer).

Deken, Joseph. *The Electronic Cottage: Everyday Living with Your Personal Computer in the 1980's*. Morrow 1981 $15.95. What computers can do and how they operate, including computer logic, computer languages, decision support, simulations, feedback, and information management. The title is from Alvin Toffler's *The Third Wave*.

Evans, Christopher. *The Micro Millennium*. Viking 1980 $10.95. An enthusiastic and optimistic projection of the future of computers in our personal lives, homes, offices, schools, factories, and professions. Entertaining and easy to read.

Flock, Emil, and Howard Schulman. *The ShareWare Book: Using PC-Write, PC-File, and PC-Talk*. Osborne/McGraw 1986 pap. $14.95. "Shareware" is a merchandising technique perhaps unique to the computer world. Software developers who employ the concept encourage the free distribution of their programs and manuals through electronic bulletin boards and allow people to freely copy and pass them along to friends. If a user likes a program, he or she is expected to send a fee to the developer. This system of "try, then buy" has made at least one developer a millionaire. This book provides three manuals in one for well-tested, well-received, and inexpensive programs.

Forester, Tom. *The High-Tech Society: The Story of the Information Technology Revolution.* MIT 1987 $19.95. A significant survey of the history, dimensions, and problems of the computer revolution, including Silicon Valley, telecommunications, personal computers, factories, offices, and finance. Good bibliography.

Hansen, Dirk. *The New Alchemists.* Little, Brown 1982 o.p. An informal history of Silicon Valley industries in California, the microchip manufacturing business, and the microelectronics revolution.

Herbert, Frank, and Max Barnard. *Without Me You're Nothing: The Essential Guide to Home Computers.* Pocket Bks. 1983 $6.95. Early in the era of microcomputing, the author of the *Dune* science fiction novels wrote this introduction to home computing with a technical collaborator, Max Barnard.

Kidder, Tracy. *The Soul of a New Machine.* Avon 1982 pap. $4.50; Little, Brown 1981 $16.45. A Pulitzer prize-winning case history of the building of a new minicomputer at Data General, capturing the special dedication, euphoria, and work addiction of an engineering design team.

McCorduck, Pamela. *The Universal Machine: Confessions of a Technological Optimist.* Harcourt 1986 pap. $7.95; McGraw-Hill 1985 $16.96. A look at computers all over the world as the machine of the century that may produce beneficial results for society and culture globally. A well-written, upbeat panorama of the future applications and significance of the personal computer.

McWilliams, Peter A. *The Personal Computer Book.* Ballantine 1983 pap. $9.95; Doubleday 1984 pap. $9.95. One of a series of the author's highly popular introductions to PCs, word processing, and computing in business. McWilliams, a former bestselling poet, is always humorous, informal, and partisan, and he names names—both his favorite and unfavorite brands.

Martin, James. *The Telematic Society: A Challenge for Tomorrow.* Prentice-Hall 1981 text ed. $31.95; Telecom Lib. 1981 $33.95. A new edition of a classic (originally entitled *The Wired Society*), used as the basis for an international television special. An introduction to telecommunications in work, education, and leisure that was required reading for civil servants in the Thatcher government in England.

Meilach, Dona Z. *Before You Buy a Used Computer: A Practical Guide to Computer Shopping.* Crown 1985 pap. $10.95. Questions, procedures, decisions, and alternatives for persons purchasing their first personal computer.

Norton, Peter. *Peter Norton's DOS Guide.* Brady Comm. rev. ed. 1987 pap. $19.95. A standard introduction without excessively technical material on the operating system of the IBM PC and compatibles. Norton is a well-known computer columnist and commentator and the author of utilities software.

Ritchie, David. *The Computer Pioneers: The Making of the Modern Computer.* Simon & Schuster 1986 $17.95. A readable introduction to the development of computers from their prehistory through the decades after World War II and to the immediate present, seen through the eyes of the persons who made them.

Sandberg-Diment, Erik. *They All Laughed When I Sat Down at the Computer and Other True Tales of One Man's Struggle with Personal Computing.* Prentice-Hall 1986 pap. $7.95; Simon & Schuster 1985 $16.95. A chronicle of the microcomputer revolution from 1982 to 1984, collected from the author's columns in the *New York Times,* viewing industry events with old-fashioned wit and skepticism.

Shore, John. *The Sachertorte Algorithm and Other Antidotes to Computer Anxiety.* Penguin 1986 pap. $7.95; Viking 1985 $16.95. When is a Sachertorte recipe an algorithm? A sane and humorous introduction for beginners to the language and methods of computer programming.

Shurkin, Joel N., *Engines of the Mind: A History of the Computer.* Norton 1984 $17.50; Washington Square Pr. 1985 pap. $4.95. An introductory work for the nontechnical reader on computer inventions and innovations, their history, and the people who made them.

Sullivan, David R., and Curtis R. Cook. *Computing Today: Microcomputer Concepts and Applications.* Houghton Mifflin 1985 text ed. pap. $28.95. One of the first introductory textbooks to base itself not on programming in BASIC but rather on competence in standard PC software packages.

Understanding Computers: Input-Output. Time-Life 1986 $12.95. One of a series of introductory books, prepared by the editors of Time-Life, on computer basics, input and output, graphics, communications, artificial intelligence, and similar topics, each vertically explored in a few areas and accompanied by impressive graphics illustration. Each book in the series can be browsed on the coffee table, read for its essays by specialists in their fields, or used as a bibliography of books and periodical articles.

Walter, Russ. *The Secret Guide to Computers.* Russ Walter 3 vols. 1987. Do not be deceived by the homemade look, the weird jacket photo, the odd title, the "write-alike" contest, the sexual jokes, the bizarre examples, or the author's offer of his personal phone number. Walter expertly relaxes beginners and demystifies BASIC, hardware, popular applications, and arts and games, and then moves on to business applications, Advanced BASIC, FORTRAN, Pascal, COBOL, other languages, career opportunities, and much more.

Willis, Jerry, and Merl Miller. *Computers for Everybody.* Weber Systems 3d ed. 1983 pap. $4.95. An elementary and nontechnical introduction to computer hardware, software, purchasing, communications, and use in office and home.

Zinsser, William. *Writing with a Word Processor.* Harper 1983 $12.45. The author of *On Writing Well* recounts his experiences, fears, misadventures, and new discoveries about the nature of writing while mastering word processing on an IBM PC in the early 1980s.

REFERENCE WORKS, COLLECTIONS, DICTIONARIES

This section includes general anthologies, histories, dictionaries, guides to computer books and software, and collections of trivia and humor. The anthologies edited by Tom Forester provide fine panoramas of the fields of computing and information technology, and Stewart Brand has collected a very practical and sensible introduction to selecting and using PC software. Among the many histories of computers, Stan Augarten's book has the best collection of pictures and illustrations.

Augarten, Stan. *Bit by Bit: An Illustrated History of Computers.* Ticknor & Fields 1984 pap. $17.95. The interest in reading about computers is increased by the excitement of seeing their pictures at the same time.

Bates, William. *The Computer Cookbook: How to Create Small Computer Systems That Work for You.* Prentice-Hall 1983 o.p. A dictionary of hardware and software sources for small computers with information on a good many topics. The annuals are updated online via NewsNet.

Bowker's Complete Sourcebook of Personal Computing 1985. Bowker 1984 o.p. A single reference manual for software, hardware, glossary, books, magazines, user groups, and vendors.

Brand, Stewart. *Whole Earth Software Catalog 1986.* Doubleday 1985 pap. $17.50. A highly recommended introduction to what PC software can and cannot do, showing interesting differences of opinion among several expert users. This compendium arose from and is updated in the *Whole Earth Review.*

Burton, Philip. *A Dictionary of Minicomputing and Microcomputing.* Garland 1985 pap. $22.00. A concise and comprehensive dictionary of current hardware and software usage. In addition to the main alphabet, there are appendixes on structured programming, Pascal, magnetic bubble memory, printers, automatic control, multiprocessing, data communications, magnetic recording, and storage technology.

Computer Books and Serials in Print, 1985–1986. Bowker 1985 o.p. A guide to available books and magazines pertaining to computing.

Cortade, James W. *Historical Dictionary of Data Processing Organizations.* Greenwood 1987 $45.00. Short notes on the more important or prominent companies concerned with computer hardware and data processing. Arranged alphabetically, from Amdahl to Xerox.

Dertouzos, Michael L., and Joel Moses, eds. *The Computer Age: A Twenty-Year View.* MIT 1979 text ed. pap. $12.95. Future technological, economic, educational, and social issues as seen by Terry Winograd, Seymour Papert, Daniel Bell, Herbert A. Simon, Marvin Minsky, Joseph Weizenbaum, and others.

Ditlea, Steve, ed. *Digital Deli: The Lunch Group.* Workman 1984 pap. $12.95. A group of New York writers who met monthly for lunch began to write articles, cartoons, humor, and whatnots about their personal encounters with computing. The menu includes contributions by Howard Rheingold, Steve Wozniac, Ted Nelson, Esther Dyson, Peter McWilliams, Robert A. Moog, Mitchell Kapor, Timothy Leary, and William F. Buckley, Jr.

Downing, Douglas, and Michael Covington. *Dictionary of Computer Terms.* Barron 1986 pap. $6.95. Useful because of its practical examples and its pocketable format with durable soft covers and rounded corners.

Forester, Tom, ed. *The Information Technology Revolution.* MIT 1985 text ed. $32.50 pap. $14.95. A sequel to *The Microelectronics Revolution* (see below) that brings the record up to 1984, collecting new material on telecommunications; artificial intelligence; the "fifth-generation" computer; applications of information technology in schools, factories, offices, banks, and hospitals; and, finally, problems that computers pose in the areas of weapons systems, crime, and women's rights.

——. *The Microelectronics Revolution: The Complete Guide to the New Technology and Its Impact on Society.* MIT 1981 $40.00 pap. $13.50. A very useful collection of articles published before 1980 on computing and information technology, especially on aspects of its economic impact on industry, the office, employment, industrial relations, and society.

Freedman, Alan. *The Computer Glossary: It's Not Just a Glossary!* Computer Language 3d ed. 1983 $14.95; Prentice-Hall 1983 pap. $20.95. Intended for beginners and business people, 1,000 examples of technical jargon reduced to everyday language. With illustrations.

Goldstine, Herman H. *The Computer from Pascal to Von Neumann.* Princeton Univ. Pr. 1980 $39.00 pap. $10.50. A history of computing by a participant in many of the recent developments he describes.

Helms, H. L. *The McGraw-Hill Computer Handbook.* Intro. by Adam Osborne,

McGraw-Hill 1983 $84.50. Thirty sections by specialist contributors, written for the nonexpert. Many are adapted from textbooks issued by the same book publisher in the 1970s, with new chapters by Helms.

Hordeski, Michael. *The Illustrated Dictionary of Microcomputers.* Tab Bks. 1986 $24.95 pap. $14.95. The latest edition includes some 4,000 new items. With examples and illustrations.

Isaacs, Alan, ed. *The Multilingual Computer Dictionary.* Facts on File 1981 $22.50 pap. $12.95. About 1,600 terms in English, French, German, Italian, Portuguese, and Spanish, including British/U.S. variants, all combined in one alphabet.

Longley, Dennis, and Michael Shain, eds. *Dictionary of Information Technology.* Association for Information and Image Management 1983 $47.00; Oxford 2d ed. 1986 $29.95. More than 6,000 entries on computing, communications, and microelectronics, some of them fairly long, with 100 diagrams. The first edition was commended as outstanding by the American Library Association.

McGraw-Hill Dictionary of Electronics and Computers. McGraw-Hill 1983 $67.50. Ten thousand terms, including synonyms, acronyms, and abbreviations, in a compact desk volume, selected from the larger *McGraw-Hill Dictionary of Scientific and Technical Terms.*

Naiman, Arthur, ed. *Computer Dictionary for Beginners.* Ballantine 1983 pap. $6.95. Clear, often humorous, with illustrations and cartoons.

Newman, James R., ed. *The World of Mathematics.* Simon & Schuster 4 vols. 1956 o.p. Contains several brilliant, classic essays, including Alan Turing's "Can a Machine Think?" and John von Neumann's "The General and Logical Theory of Automata," both in Volume 4.

Nicita, Michael, and Ronald Petrusha. *The Reader's Guide to Microcomputer Books.* Golden-Lee Bk. 1983 pap. $9.95. Critical evaluations of more than 1,000 computer books. Although the work stops in 1984, the cross-indexing and subject score summaries are unusually useful.

Popenoe, Chris. *Book Bytes: The User's Guide to 1200 Microcomputer Books.* Pantheon 1984 o.p. Some 1,200 books on PC software and hardware on the market by January 1984, described and evaluated by levels of difficulty and by quality. Each chapter begins with useful highlights of recommended titles.

Rochester, Jack B., and John Gantz. *The Naked Computer: A Layperson's Almanac of Computer Lore, Wizardry, Personalities, Memorabilia, World Records, Mind Blowers, and Tomfoolery.* Morrow 1983 o.p. A compendium of anecdotes, trivia, facts, and world records about computers that is both entertaining and informative.

Rosenberg, Jerry M. *Dictionary of Computers, Information and Telecommunications.* Wiley 2d ed. 1987 pap. $18.95. A bestselling dictionary of more than 12,000 terms (usually briefly defined), symbols, acronyms, and abbreviations, plus glossaries of terms in Spanish and French. The second edition adds more than 2,000 new items.

The Software Encyclopedia, 1988. Bowker 2 vols. 1988 $149.95. A two-volume compendium of microcomputer software, specifying operating system, compatibility, and hardware and memory requirements for each. There are more than 27,000 software titles, 4,000 software publishers, 20 operating systems, and 900 application types.

Van Tassel, Dennie, and Cynthia L. Van Tassel. *The Compleat Computer.* Science Research Associates 2d ed. 1983 text ed. pap. $17.95. An unusual compendium of computer news, art, cartoons, and poetry, from scholarly, popular, and unexpected sources, including reprints of contributions by Norman Cousins, Claude Shannon, Michael Crichton, Ray Bradbury, Art Buchwald, Arthur C. Clarke, Stewart Brand, Sam Ervin, Jr., W. H. Auden, and John Kemeny.

INTRODUCTION TO INFORMATION AND LIBRARY SCIENCE

Guides and Introductions

While Eugene Sheehy's *Guide to Reference Books* remains the standard guide for library reference books, it may be supplemented by such introductions to computer and information automation and technology as those by Howard Fosdick, Dennis Reynolds, and Peter Zorkoczy. This section contains works on library and information science, information systems, library automation, information retrieval, library-based community computer literacy, information technology, print versus electronic storage issues, and library reference guides.

Burch, John G., and Felix R. Strater. *Information Systems: Theory and Practice.* Wiley 3d ed. 1983 o.p. A revised edition of a standard textbook.

Chen, Ching Chih, and Stacey E. Bressler. *Microcomputers in Libraries.* Neal-Schuman 1982 text ed. pap. $35.00. Using microcomputers in the routine tasks of the library.

Curtis, Howard, ed. *Public Access Microcomputers in Academic Libraries: The Mann Library Model at Cornell University.* ALA 1987 text ed. pap. $14.95. Based on the model of the Mann Library at Cornell University, a collection by nine contributors on planning, acquiring, staffing, and operating microcomputers for public use, with attention to software acquisition policies and information storage and retrieval. Policy statements, agreements, and legal notes are in the appendix.

Dewey, Patrick R. *Public Access Microcomputers: A Handbook for Librarians.* [*Professional Librarian Ser.*] Knowledge Industry 1984 $34.50 pap. $27.50. Advice on making an Apple, IBM compatible, or other personal computer freely available in a public library, with practical examples.

Encyclopedia of Library and Information Science. Dekker 40 vols. 1968–86 ea. $65.00–$75.00. A large international encyclopedia with signed articles containing bibliographies on all aspects of library and information science.

Fosdick, Howard. *Computer Basics for Librarians and Information Scientists.* Intro. by F. Wilfrid Lancaster, Information Resources Pr. 1981 text ed. $22.50. Chapters on hardware, personnel, storage, memory, system software, programming languages, and database systems.

Hills, Philip, ed. *The Future of the Printed Word: The Impact and the Implications of the New Communications Technology.* Greenwood 1980 lib. bdg. $29.95. Valuable essays from 14 contributors on electronic versus paper publishing, new printing technologies, microforms, videodisks, graphics, scientific and technical problems in publication, and economic and social factors.

Lancaster, F. Wilfrid. *Information Retrieval Systems: Characteristics, Testing and Evaluation.* [*Information Sciences Ser.*] Wiley 2d ed. 1979 o.p. A work that won the "Best Book on Information Science" award of the American Society for Information Science when it first appeared in 1968. The focus is on intellectual concepts, not equipment.

Lilley, Dorothy B., and Rose Marie Badough. *Library and Information Science: A Guide to Information Sources.* Gale 1981 $62.00. A selective guide in four parts: recent changes in technology, models for search strategies, information sources for various forms of material, and types of information sources.

Loop, Liza, and Julie Anton. *Computer Town: Bringing Computer Literacy to Your Community.* Prentice-Hall 1983 o.p. An implementation package for computer literacy at the community level, based on National Science Foundation research. The public computer plan centers the concept of the computer town on activities in public libraries.

Mathies, Loraine. *Computer-Based Reference Service.* ALA 1973 $15.00. On ERIC, MARC, and computer searching. Issued by the American Library Association.

Pepinsky, Harold B. *People and Information.* Pergamon 1970 o.p. About a dozen contributors. Old but still interesting for the variety of viewpoints reflected.

Purcell, Gary R., and Gail Ann Schlachter. *Reference Sources in Library and Information Services: A Guide to the Literature.* ABC-Clio 1984 lib. bdg. $45.00. A comprehensive guide to 700 general reference works and 500 subject reference works, each annotated.

Reynolds, Dennis. *Library Automation: Issues and Applications.* Bowker 1985 $37.50. Intended to serve librarians and administrators from beginners to experts who are interested in library automation, its history and background, planning and preparations, and practical applications.

Young, Heartsill. *ALA Glossary of Library and Information Science.* ALA 1983 $50.00. An attempt to develop a standard set of terms for workers in information science. Also includes terms from computer science, printing and publishing, telecommunications, and graphics and reprography.

Zorkoczy, Peter. *Information Technology: An Introduction.* [*Communications Lib.*] Association for Information and Image Management 1983 $35.95; Knowledge Industry 1983 $29.95; Van Nostrand 1984 pap. $19.95. A clear and concise introduction to telecommunications, optical communication systems, videotape and videodisk systems, computers, data protection, expert systems, microforms, voice communication with computers, data networks, electronic mail, information systems, and videotex/teletext.

Bibliographies, Indexes, Abstracts, Directories, and Handbooks

Several representative annuals are the *Annual Review of Information Science & Technology (ARIST)*, *Computing Information Directory*, and *Computing Reviews*, while an important bimonthly is the standard *Information Science Abstracts.* This section contains bibliographies, indexes, abstracts, directories, and handbooks to computing, microcomputers, information science, information management, and information technology.

Annual Review of Information Science and Technology. Ed. by Martha E. Williams, Knowledge Industry vol. 19 1984 $50.00. Known as *ARIST* and issued by ASIS (American Society of Information Science). Contains nine authoritative survey essays each year in three fixed domains of information science.

Cibbarelli, Pamela, and Edward J. Kazlauskas, eds. *Directory of Information Management Software for Libraries, Information Centers, Record Centers and Supplement 1984.* ALA 1985 pap. $49.00. Data on 85 specialist software packages, with 35 more listed in the appendix, representing various operating systems and software languages.

Computer Publishers and Publications: An International Directory and Yearbook, 1987–88. Ed. by Frederica Evan, Comm. Trends Inc. 1987 pap. $139.00. A major annotated guide to computer magazines, books, newsletters, and journals, with purchase recommendations for academic and public libraries, lists of bestselling computer books, guides to evaluating books for public libraries, and selected computer books indexed by author and title.

Computing Reviews. ACM 1960– $95.00/yr. The standard guide to computing literature from the Association for Computing Machinery, indexed by title, author, keyword, category, and terms.

Hildebrandt, Darlene M., ed. *Computing Information Directory (CID): A Comprehensive Guide to the Computing Literature.* Pedaro 4th ed. 1987 pap. $119.95. An important guide (annual in 1985 and 1986) to computer journals, computer center newsletters, books, dictionaries and glossaries, indexes and abstracts, software, reviews, hardware, directories, encyclopedias, handbooks, and computer languages. Information on more than 1,500 journals, 200 newsletters, 30 indexes or abstracts, and an especially useful section on book selection.

Micro Software Evaluations, 1986–1988. Ed. by Jeanne M. Nolan, Meckler 1987 text ed. pap. $95.00. Detailed narratives by users of various library software packages with practical evaluations and examples of each.

Public Management Institute. *Computer Resource Guide for Nonprofits.* Public Management 2 vols. 3d ed. 1985–86 pap. ea. $95.00. Evaluations of software packages for all systems. Unfortunately alphabetical by vendor only.

Online Sources and Information Utilities

A fairly inexpensive addition for a computer is a modem (MOdulator/DEModulator), which allows a computer to communicate with another computer over an ordinary telephone line. Thus a simple desktop microcomputer can access the information in a large mainframe computer across town or across the continent. From this ability has grown two important institutions—the electronic bulletin board and the online information service.

An electronic bulletin board is a computer with a modem and a lot of room to store files. It serves as a convenient place for people to leave questions, programs, or anything else that might be of interest to the computing community, to establish electronic pen-pal relationships, and to acquire new software programs that have been placed in the public domain. Some of these bulletin board systems charge for their use, but many are run by computer clubs and individuals as a free public service.

Online information services in recent years have become an important method for both scholars and businesses to acquire specific information—a demographic breakdown on single-child families in urban areas, a list of all *New York Times* articles in the past year dealing with aviation, the text of magazine articles in the popular sector on AIDS, all books in print that contain the words "plain language" in the title. Such research chores, which would be difficult if not impossible to do with traditional printed resources, are now the work of just a few keystrokes.

Introductions such as those by Elizabeth Ferrarini, Alfred Glossbrenner, and M. David Stone carry the beginner into the fields of telecommunications and online access. Guides to the various information utilities include the Data Base Directory, Datapro Directory, and Computer Readable Databases. Subjects covered in this section also include printed books that describe online databases, information services, online search and research procedures and strategies, telecommunications with personal computers, and proprietary databases.

Directory of Online Databases 1986–1987. New York Zoetrope rev. ed. 1986 pap. $39.95. A quarterly directory, begun in 1979, of online databases by type, subject, producer, conditions, content, coverage, and updating.

Ferrarini, Elizabeth. *Infomania: The Guide to Essential Electronic Services.* Houghton Mifflin 1985 pap. $14.95. How to access electronic information about money, news, science, careers, jobs, learning, bulletin boards, computers, shopping, travel, electronic mail, people, and commercial services.

Glossbrenner, Alfred. *The Complete Handbook of Personal Computer Communications: Everything You Need to Know to Go Online with the World.* St. Martin's 1983 pap. $14.95 rev. & enl. ed. 1985 pap. $14.95. A standard work on how to use modems in telecommunications and how to use information utilities.

———. *How to Look It Up Online: Get the Information Edge with Your Personal Computer.* St. Martin's 1987 $24.95 pap. $14.95. How to seek information about books, magazines, newspapers, business, employment, sales, marketing, and government. A clear and intelligible guide, with useful tips and graphics emphasis.

Howitt, Doran, and Marvin I. Weinberger. *Inc. Magazine's Databasics: Your Guide to Online Business Information.* Garland 1984 $27.00. Covers databases, searching, electronic mail, and business databases by subject, vendor, hardware, and software. Intended for the business user.

Katz, Bill, and Anne Clifford, eds. *Reference and Online Services Handbook: Guidelines, Policies and Procedures for Libraries.* Neal-Schuman 1986 lib. bdg. $39.95. Includes a collection of policy statements pertaining to online reference services in academic and public libraries.

Lambert, Steve. *Online: A Guide to America's Leading Information Services.* Microsoft 1985 pap. $19.95. A useful introduction to and handbook on the use of online data and information banks.

The North American Online Directory, 1987. Bowker 1987 $85.00. A guide to online information services available in the United States and Canada.

Stone, M. David. *Getting On-Line: A Guide to Assessing Computer Information Services.* Prentice-Hall 1984 o.p. Straightforward information on information utilities, hardware, software, search strategies, free services, and future prospects. The standard services listed and described include BRS and BRS/After Dark, Compuserve, DIALOG and Knowledge Index, Dow Jones News/Retrieval, Mead Lexis and Nexis, NewsNet, The Source, and others.

Williams, Martha E., ed. *Computer Readable Databases: A Directory and Data Sourcebook.* ALA 2 vols. 1985 pap. $157.50. Describes more than 5,000 databases, including both text and numerical databases. The first volume covers science, technology, and medicine, and the second volume includes business, law, the humanities, and the social sciences.

COMPUTER PROGRAMMING

A computer by itself (i.e., without software) is much like a car without a driver. The computer needs instructions to follow for the most trivial of tasks. Unfortunately, the type of instructions that computers can understand—"set the first, third, fourth, fifth, and sixth bits of the AH register high and the others low," "set the second bit of the AL register high and the others low," and so on—are not easy for human beings to work with. Computer languages solve this problem by allowing the programmer to use special codes that are simpler for human beings to follow but are then translated into instructions the machine can understand. Languages are very broadly categorized as either low-level or high-level. The former are little more than mnemonics for the very primitive machine-level instructions. Such languages, while tedious to work with and difficult to learn, are very powerful and economical on an operating level. The latter are far easier to learn and use, but generally produce slower-running, less-flexible programs.

Languages have been developed for a number of specific purposes: FORTRAN for scientific calculation, BASIC and Logo as teaching tools, SNOBOL and Icon for text processing, COBOL for business applications, and Pascal and C as structured languages. FORTRAN (FORmula TRANslation) was created to handle mathematical, scientific, and engineering procedures, but since it was the first language to establish itself widely on large computers, it has come to be used in all types of computing applications. BASIC (Beginner's All-purpose Symbolic Instruction Code) has been distributed with so many microcomputers and has been used in so many high school and "computer literacy" courses that it has become the language best known to the general public. Pascal (named for the French philosopher and mathematician) was intended to be only a demonstration language of strong structure and clear self-documentation, but is now very widely used in colleges and by professional programmers. The language called C is especially favored by programmers who require a language that is highly compact and extremely portable from one operating system or environment to another. Logo was created by Seymour Papert to teach the principles of programming to young children through the use of a movable turtle and other graphic visualizations. There are many other special-purpose languages, such as SNOBOL4 and Icon for handling text strings, LISP and PROLOG in artificial intelligence, and Ada (named for Ada, Countess of Lovelace) in Department of Defense programs. In addition, many programmers use proprietary software applications, such as dBase for database work or SPSS for statistics, in lieu of working directly in a programming language. Some mainframe computers and microcomputers provide proprietary programming languages that are virtually extensions of their operating systems. Programmers being inveterate tinkerers, most languages go through a series of implementations that add new features and all the established languages have increasingly grown very general in purpose.

Introductions, Surveys, and General Programming

Aho, Alfred V., and John Hopcroft. *Design and Analysis of Computer Algorithms.* Addison-Wesley 1974 text ed. $43.25. A text for a first course, emphasizing ease of understanding rather than advanced tips and tricks. Assumes some knowledge of FORTRAN and COBOL programming and linear algebra; with examples.

Aho, Alfred V., and Jeffrey D. Ullman. *Principles of Compiler Design.* Addison-Wesley 1977 o.p. General principles in the design and implementation of compilers, taking up universal problems, such as finite state techniques, context-free grammar, and syntax-directed translation schemes, applicable to any programming language or computer hardware. With exercises.

Aspray, William, and Arthur Burks, eds. *Papers of John von Neumann on Computing and Computer Theory.* MIT 1986 $65.00. A collection of von Neumann's papers on logical design, computer architecture, large-scale computing at high speed, and automata, with one explanatory essay by Donald Knuth. Excludes von Neumann's mathematical work, but includes a general bibliography of writing by and about him.

Babich, Wayne A. *Software Configuration Management.* Addison-Wesley 1986 text ed. pap. $18.95. Coordinating programmers on team projects for maximizing productivity and minimizing complications and delays. For software project leaders, senior programmers, and software managers; the approach is valid for any language, but many of the examples draw on UNIX or Ada.

Bailey, T. E., and Kris Lundgaard. *Program Design with Pseudocode.* [*Computer Science Ser.*] Brooks-Cole 2d ed. 1985 text ed. pap. $13.00. An introduction to problem-solving concepts and techniques for clearer thinking about programming. By emphasizing pseudocode, the approach encourages clearer thinking about program structure, modular design, and flowcharting without limiting itself to specific languages.

Baron, Naomi S. *Computer Languages: A Guide for the Perplexed.* Doubleday 1986 $27.50 pap. $17.95. A general overview and also a detailed individual review of 21 standard programming languages that considers their history, syntax, purpose, functioning, and possible future. An appendix takes up additional, less-known languages.

Barstow, David R., Howard E. Shrobe, and Erik Sandewall. *Interactive Programming Environments.* McGraw-Hill 1983 $37.95. Forty-two contributions on the subjects of programming methodology, interactive environments, software engineering, and artificial intelligence.

Birnes, W. J. *McGraw-Hill Personal Computer Programming Encyclopedia: Languages and Operating Systems.* McGraw-Hill 1985 $80.00. Signed articles on 19 programming languages. Contains several translation tables on languages and their principal dialects.

Brooks, Frederick P., Jr. *The Mythical Man-Month: Essays on Software Engineering.* Addison-Wesley 1974 text ed. pap. $17.95. Timely essays on software engineering, especially on the problems of attempting to speed up large projects. The "mythical man-month" principle is that six men working for one month to develop a software product do not have nearly the same output as one person working for six months.

Carberry, M. Sandra, and A. Toni Cohen. *Principles of Computer Science: Concepts, Algorithms, Data Structures, and Applications.* Computer Science Pr. 1986 text ed. $34.95. A survey of computer foundations, systems and languages, Pascal programming, applications, and social and cultural perspectives.

Chang, Shi-Kuo, ed. *Visual Languages.* Plenum 1987 $69.50. The new interdisciplinary field of visual languages involves computer scientists, engineers, graphic designers, psychologists, linguists, and philosophers. This work considers programming in visual languages, visual databases, how computer graphics can represent and process mental imagery, animation by children, cognitive aspects of processing Chinese characters, the computer-human interface, and visual information in human decision making.

Dijkstra, Edward W. *A Discipline of Programming.* Prentice-Hall 1976 $47.00. A classic text on methods of top-down programming, including the use of modules in any programming language, ways of thinking about programming and problem solving, and the uses of logic, mathematics, theory, and design in creating algorithms.

Held, Gilbert. *Data Compression: Techniques and Applications Hardware and Software Considerations*. Wiley 1983 $34.95. A discussion of rationales, utilizations, techniques, and software limitations in data compression. Includes IBM PC programs, available on an optional disk.

Hsu, Jeffrey. *Microcomputer Programming Languages*. Wiley 1987 pap. $16.95. A survey of some 20 languages for microcomputers, including BASIC, COBOL, FORTRAN, and Pascal, plus lesser-known languages including Ada, APL, C, FORTH, LISP, Logo, Modula-2, PILOT, PL/1, and PROLOG, showing advantages and disadvantages of each. The book includes two statistical packages, SPSS and SAS, as programming languages.

Kernighan, Brian W., and P. J. Plauger. *The Elements of Programming Style*. McGraw-Hill 2d ed. 1978 text ed. pap. $19.95. A classic text for programmers, establishing standards of clarity and expression.

———. *Software Tools in Pascal*. Addison-Wesley 1981 pap. $24.95. Mechanics of software engineering, with modules for structured programming and top-down design.

Knuth, Donald E. *The Art of Computer Programming*. Addison-Wesley 3 vols. 1974–81 ea. $39.95. One of the first systematic collections and discussions of algorithms: Volume 1, on fundamental algorithms, contains a wealth of material on data structures and their manipulation; Volume 2, on seminumerical algorithms, takes up issues of number representation and computer arithmetic; Volume 3, on searching and sorting, is useful for information structures. Knuth's exercises, graded in progressive difficulty, entail mathematical knowledge, and include some unsolved research problems.

Lancaster, Don. *Hexadecimal Chronicles*. Howard Sams 1981 o.p. Conversion tables for binary, octal, and decimal numbers as an aid to assembly language programming.

Mansuripur, Masud. *Introduction to Information Theory*. Prentice-Hall 1987 text ed. $40.00. The basic concepts and advanced implications of information theory and their relation to probability theory, continuous channels, and ergodic sources, including recent advances in universal source coding and rate distortion theory.

Pradhan, Dhiraj K. *Fault-Tolerant Computing: Theory and Techniques*. Prentice-Hall 1986 text ed. $47.00. Seven contributors on the subject of the much higher levels of reliability required in very critical applications, such as major telephone network operations and spacecraft missions. As theory demands much narrower margins for error, practice follows with new techniques for fault and error handling.

Pratt, Terrence W. *Programming Languages: Design and Implementation*. Prentice-Hall 2d ed. 1984 o.p. A comprehensive introduction, survey, and discussion of standard programming languages, explaining programming concepts and problems, comparing approaches and strategies, and indicating advantages and disadvantages of each language. With bibliographical comments in each chapter.

Press, William, and others. *Numerical Recipes: The Art of Scientific Computing*. Cambridge Univ. Pr. 1986 $39.50. Contributions from four collaborators from research and industry on subjects of interest to scientists, engineers, and social scientists using quantitative methods. Includes 200 routines in both FORTRAN and Pascal, usable on IBM PC compatibles, covering areas such as linear equations, evaluating splines, special functions, Fourier transforms, and statistical tests.

Price, Jonathan. *How to Write a Computer Manual: A Handbook of Software Documentation*. Benjamin Cummings 1985 text ed. pap. $26.95. A comprehensive text for writers, software managers, and educators, demonstrating through real-world examples how to schedule, write, edit, and self-evaluate software documentation and manuals.

Ralston, Anthony, and Edwin D. Reilly, Jr., eds. *Encyclopedia of Computer Science and Engineering.* Van Nostrand 1982 $89.95. An excellent reference tool for computing and computers, with signed articles, cross-references, and bibliographies. The appendix lists abbreviations, acronyms, American universities that offer doctoral degrees in computer science, and a glossary of major programming languages.

Sedgewick, Robert. *Algorithms.* [*Computer Science Ser.*] Addison-Wesley 1983 $34.95. Assumes prior knowledge of programming with Pascal. Forty chapters on such topics as mathematical algorithms, sorting, searching, string processing, geometric algorithms, graph algorithms, and other advanced topics.

Tennent, R. *Principles of Programming Languages.* Prentice-Hall 1981 $39.33. On programming language structure, design and implementation issues.

Tucker, Allen B., Jr. *Programming Languages.* [*Computer Science Ser.*] McGraw-Hill 2d ed. 1987 text ed. $38.95. A systematic treatment in depth of 11 programming languages: Ada, APL, C, COBOL, FORTRAN, LISP, Pascal, PL/1, PROLOG, SNOBOL, and Modula-2. The second edition stresses prominent languages now in use with microcomputers, but retains the initial emphasis on scientific, data processing, text processing, artificial intelligence, and systems programming.

Ward, Paul T. *Systems Development Without Pain: A User's Guide to Modeling Organizational Patterns.* Yourdon Pr. 1984 pap. $27.95. Offers ASML (A Systems Modeling Language) for communication between data processing professionals and end users, using the principles of structured analysis and integrating data and process modelling. Introduction by Edward Yourdon; with 200 diagrams.

Wasserman, Anthony I. *Programming Language Design.* IEEE Computer Society Pr. 1980 $30.00. A collection of papers that includes several critiques of the original Pascal design.

Wexelblatt, Richard L., ed. *History of Programming Languages.* Academic Pr. 1981 $49.50. Includes several contributions by authors of programming languages or by participants in design teams.

Wirth, Niklaus. *Algorithms and Data Structures.* Prentice-Hall 1986 text ed. $40.00. A collection of classical and basic problems in programming along with the solutions worked out logically.

Specific Programming Languages, Environments, Media

Alcock, Donald. *Illustrating FORTRAN (The Portable Variety).* Cambridge Univ. Pr. 1983 $19.95 pap. $12.95. A relaxed work, executed and illustrated by Alcock's own calligraphy and designs, for new programmers or those who know some BASIC, including methods of self-discipline, some introductory-level tips and tricks, and reference materials. The format is similar to the same author's *Illustrating BASIC.*

Cooper, Doug, and Michael Clancy. *Oh! Pascal!* Norton 1982 pap. $20.95. An excellent introduction to problem solving in Pascal, stressing dos and don'ts and emphasizing nonmathematical operations.

Crawley, J. Winston, and Charles E. Miller. *A Structured Approach to FORTRAN.* Prentice-Hall 2d ed. 1987 text ed. pap. $28.67. An introduction to programming, program design, and implementations, including the use of subprograms, pitfalls to avoid, and detailed explanations; contains exercises.

Dunteman, Jeff. *Complete Turbo Pascal*. Scott, Foresman 1985 pap. $19.95. A clear and explicit tutorial for Pascal, following principles of structured program design.

Dwyer, Thomas A., and Margot A. Critchfield. *BASIC and the Personal Computer*. Addison-Wesley 1978 pap. $16.30. A classic text, well written and profusely illustrated; recommended as an introduction to BASIC for nonprogrammers.

Etter, D. M. *Problem Solving with Structured FORTRAN*. Benjamin Cummings 1984 pap. $10.00. An introductory-level textbook, covering debugging and programming style, with key terms, a glossary, and frequent examples.

————. *Structured FORTRAN 77 for Engineers and Scientists*. Benjamin Cummings 2d ed. 1987 pap. $26.95. Top-down problem solving, with engineering and scientific applications, reference aids on syntax, FORTRAN statements, and self-testing features. Includes special attention to numerical methods for engineers.

Feingold, Carl. *Fundamentals of Structured COBOL Programming*. William C. Brown 4th ed. 1983 pap. $23.20. A useful textbook with flowcharts, program code, and reference appendixes. Each section covers tables, files, and writing reports.

Friedman, Daniel P., and Matthias Felleisen. *The Little LISPer*. Science Research Associates 1985 text ed. pap. $10.40. An elegant introduction to LISP and its recursive functions by one of its leading practitioners.

Goldberg, Adele. *Smalltalk-80: The Interactive Programming Environment*. Addison-Wesley 1984 $37.75. An introduction to the Smalltalk language, with sections on interfacing the system, support to find objects and information, class descriptions, error correction, and files and housekeeping.

Goldberg, Adele, and David Robson. *Smalltalk-80: The Language and Its Implementation*. Addison-Wesley 1983 text ed. $41.95. A more advanced work than the preceding title.

Grauer, Robert T., and M. Crawford. *The COBOL Environment*. Prentice-Hall 1984 text ed. $39.33. A discussion of program development, structured programming, top-down programming development and design, and COBOL implementations.

————. *Structured COBOL: A Pragmatic Approach*. Prentice-Hall 1981 pap. $32.00. Learning COBOL through a series of practical models and examples, unifying programming theory and commercial applications.

Griswold, Ralph E. *The Snobol4 Programming Language*. Prentice-Hall 2d ed. 1971 pap. $28.00. The standard reference work for the programming language used extensively in studies in literature and the humanities. A more elementary introduction is Ralph E. Griswold and Madge T. Griswold's *A Snobol4 Primer* (Prentice-Hall 1973 pap. $24.67).

Jensen, K., and N. Wirth. *Pascal User Manual and Report*. Springer-Verlag 3d ed. 1985 pap. $17.50. Since Wirth was the original author of Pascal, this volume stands as an authoritative basic reference manual as well as his own implementation of the language.

Kemeny, John G., and Thomas E. Kurtz. *BASIC Programming*. Wiley 3d ed. 1980 text ed. pap. $28.95. A standard introduction to BASIC by the creators of the original version of the program. This text features many specialized applications.

Kernighan, Brian W., and Dennis M. Ritchie. *The C Programming Language: Convergent Technologies Edition*. Prentice-Hall 1984 $13.42. A standard tutorial on C for experienced programmers. (For answers to and discussions of problems raised in this book, see Clovis L. Tondo and Scott E. Gimpel, *The C Answer Book* [Prentice-Hall 1985 text ed. pap. $20.33].)

McCabe, C. Kevin. *FORTH Fundamentals: Language Glossary*. Crown 2 vols. vol. 1 pap. $16.95 vol. 2 pap. $13.95; Dilithium Pr. 1983 pap. $16.95. A solid, traditional introduction to FORTH.

McCarthy, J., and others. *LISP 1.5 Programmer's Manual.* MIT 1962 pap. $7.95. The original LISP design.

Miller, Alan R. *BASIC Programs for Scientists and Engineers.* Sybex 1981 pap. $16.95. One of a series of texts of high quality that explains the use of BASIC as a programming language in science and engineering; companion volumes by the same author also treat FORTRAN or Pascal.

Seidel, Ken. *Microsoft COBOL.* Weber Systems 1983 pap. $9.95. Applying the mainframe file-handling capabilities of COBOL to microcomputers.

Weiner, Richard S., and Richard Sincovec. *Programming in Ada.* Wiley 1983 $30.95. Extensive examples of program listings for each concept presented. Intended for those with previous knowledge of programming.

Winston, Patrick Henry, and Berthold K. Horn. *LISP.* Addison-Wesley 1981 text ed. pap. $21.95 2d ed. 1984 $32.25 3d ed. 1988 $33.50. An introduction to basic elements of LISP programming, followed by a series of practical applications. Portions of the book supplement or replace Winston's previous work, *Artificial Intelligence* (MIT 2 vols. 1979 ea. $35.00 ea. pap. $16.50).

Wirth, Niklaus. *Programming in Modula-2.* [*Texts and Monographs in Computer Science*] Springer-Verlag 3d ed. 1985 $20.50. Wirth is the author of both Modula-2 and its predecessor, Pascal. This text continues the structured approach for which Modula-2 is known; revised editions contain Wirth's recent modifications of the language.

———. *Systematic Programming: An Introduction.* Prentice-Hall 1973 $44.00. Pascal applications, by the author of the Pascal and Modula-2 languages.

Yourdon, Edward. *Structured Walkthroughs.* Yourdon Pr. 3d ed. 1985 text ed. pap. $19.95. A standard work on using peer review as a procedure for facing the issue of clarity in programming.

Zaks, Rodnay. *Introduction to Pascal: Including Turbo Pascal.* Sybex 1986 pap. $19.95. A classic introduction to programming in Pascal, now including material on a new version of the language.

Operating Systems and Environments: New Media

There are many proprietary operating systems used on mainframe computers and minicomputers; in addition, there are several microcomputer operating systems that are specific to one manufacturer's hardware. In recent years, however, as personal computers became more powerful, three families of operating systems obtained important manufacturer and user support: IBM endorsed the MS-DOS (PC-DOS) and OS/2 standards of the Microsoft Corporation, AT&T supported the UNIX system created by Bell Telephone Laboratories, and Apple Computers introduced its own operating system for the Macintosh. Many single-task and single-user microcomputers used MS-DOS or PC-DOS in the earlier 1980s; by mid-decade, more powerful operating systems such as UNIX began to be applied to multi-user local networks connecting microcomputers, and in the late 1980s, IBM shifted its focus from PC-DOS to OS/2, a new and more advanced operating system for simultaneous multitasking. Microcomputers had already eclipsed the power, speed, and capacity of the classic vacuum tube computers of the 1940s and 1950s, and they were approaching the capacity of the minicomputers and mainframe computers of the 1970s. For several years IBM and compatible personal computers used a character-based display while Apple

Macintosh computers used a graphics-based display. The character display was adequate for words and numbers but the graphics display was superior for pictures and training. IBM introduced OS/2 to replace PC-DOS and to incorporate the idea of a graphical (pictorial) interface.

At the same time, compact disks (small laser disks) of enormous capacity were introduced for data storage. The CD-ROM could read only what the manufacturer put there (ROM stands for read only memory), but CD-I (compact disk–interactive) could also accept what the user created.

Andrews, Nancy. *Windows: The Official Guide to Microsoft's Operating Environment.* Microsoft 1986 pap. $17.95. An introduction for programmers using Windows to integrate multiple applications in MS-DOS and to create an operating environment that resembles the graphics capability of the Apple Macintosh.

Bell Laboratories. *UNIX Programmer's Manual.* Holt 1986 text ed. $37.95. The definitive work on the subject, prepared by its developers. Volume 1 is a reference manual and Volume 2 contains tutorials and applications.

Duncan, Ray. *Advanced MS-DOS: The Microsoft Guide for Assembly Language and C Programmers.* Microsoft 1986 pap. $22.95. For the advanced programmer using assembly language and C programs for maximum speed and compactness in MS-DOS. Duncan is a columnist for *Dr. Dobbs' Journal.*

Inside Macintosh. Addison-Wesley 1987 pap. $26.95. The official guide for programmers writing application programs, desk accessories, device drivers, and other projects. Follows the authorized requirements for the standard Macintosh user interface and explains the internal routines fixed in the Macintosh.

Lafore, Robert. *Assembly Language Primer for the IBM PC and XT.* NAL 1984 o.p. Treats assembly language for its speed, flexibility, and graphics routines, and covers DOS functions and programming with DEBUG and IBM Assembler ASM.

Lambert, Steve, and Suzanne Ropiequet. *CD ROM: The New Papyrus.* Microsoft 1986 $34.95 pap. $21.95. A pioneering compilation of more than 40 articles on the CD-ROM system and design, publishing, and other applications. A sequel is Suzanne Ropiequet and others, *CD ROM 2: Optical Publishing* (Microsoft 1987 pap. $22.95), which contains 15 more articles covering compact disk environments, text preparation and retrieval, image and sound preparation, disk production, data protection, and actual case studies.

McGilton, Henry, and Rachel Morgan. *Introducing the UNIX System.* McGraw-Hill 1983 pap. $24.95. Intended for professionals who already possess the UNIX system documentation and Programmer's Manual. This book uses UNIX version 7 primarily but also refers to the Berkeley version of UNIX.

Norton, Peter. *Inside the IBM PC: Access to Advanced Features and Programming.* Simon & Schuster 1985 pap. $19.95. A guide to the IBM PC microprocessor, DOS, ROM, programming, disk storage, and graphics.

———. *The Peter Norton Programmer's Guide to the IBM PC: The Ultimate Reference Guide to the Entire Family of IBM Personal Computers.* Microsoft 1985 pap. $19.95. Technical data and an explanation of the architecture of the IBM PC for intermediate and advanced programmers.

Norton, Peter, and John Socha. *Peter Norton's Assembly Language Book for the IBM PC, XT & AT.* Brady Comm. 1986 pap. $19.95. The two unusual features of this tutorial and reference guide to assembly language are the well-known authors and the optional diskette containing programs and utilities already on diskette.

Waite Group. *UNIX Primer Plus.* Howard Sams 1983 pap. $19.95. A good first reader on UNIX for the programmer who has some prior experience with other systems.

Wolverton, Van. *Running MS-DOS: The Microsoft Guide to Getting the Most Out of the Standing Operating System.* Microsoft 2d ed. 1985 pap. $21.95. All aspects of DOS, including file management, diskette administration, screen displays, and hard disks.

COMPUTER APPLICATIONS

Business and Professional

This section contains books for business use of computers in accounting, auditing and security, personnel, contract negotiation, cost estimation, executive computing, forecasts of future information, free-lancing and consulting, hiring and training computer personnel, information systems philosophy, introduction to business applications, investment and finance, management, marketing data, marketing and business management, microcomputer management, online business information, preventing fraud and unauthorized access, project management, purchasing software and hardware, small businesses, and spreadsheet uses. In addition, there are titles of interest in the professions of medicine and law. Although bookstores are well stocked with them, titles dealing mainly with particular business and spreadsheet software programs are not included here.

Anbar, Michael, ed. *Computers in Medicine.* Computer Science Pr. 1987 text ed. $32.95. Twelve essays on patient records and accounts, diagnostic techniques, clinical decisions, diet planning, and the psychology of doctor-nurse-patient interaction. Intended for doctors trained before computers were common, for current medical students, for computer science and engineering personnel interested in medical applications, and for health-care professionals concerned with the impact of automation.

Day, John. *Microcomputers in Business: Spreadsheet, Word Processing, and Database Management Systems.* Scott, Foresman 1986 pap. $8.85. An introduction to business applications through standard applications packages for IBM PC and compatible microcomputers.

Dayton, Doug. *Computer Solutions for Business.* Microsoft 1987 pap. $17.95. A refreshingly clearly organized overview of microcomputer possibilities for the small- to medium-sized business that concentrates on a systems approach to problems and solutions, not specific software packages.

Deutsch, Dennis S. *Protect Yourself: The Guide to Understanding and Negotiating Contracts for Business Computers and Software.* Wiley 1984 $21.95. The sometimes unusual nature of contracts, liability, and warranties in the area of acquiring business computer hardware and software, explained through concrete examples.

Frank, Judith. *Managing Business Microcomputer Systems.* Brady Comm. 1987 pap. $19.95. A comprehensive introduction, written for company microcomputer managers, to problems and issues in local area networks, multi-user systems, stand-alone personal computers, and the integration of computers into office automation and information technology.

Glossbrenner, Alfred. *How to Buy Software: The Master Guide to Picking the Right Program.* St. Martin's 1984 pap. $14.95. Comparative checklists of features of typical software packages, listing the criteria for selection in all standard areas of application packages.

Kanter, Jerome. *Computer Essays for Management.* Prentice-Hall 1987 text ed. $22.67. Ten essays, some of them developing ideas in John Naisbitt's *Megatrends* (Warner 1983 $17.00 pap. $4.50), on aspects of information systems (IS), including IS as a strategic tool, the IS executive, senior management, practical considerations in IS computing, IS long-range planning, managing risk in application development, and future developments in IS.

Kolve, Carolee N. *How to Buy (and Survive!) Your First Computer: A Guide for Small Business Success.* McGraw-Hill 1983 pap. $14.95. Advice for micro managers and for companies considering their first purchase, installation, training program, and systems integration for a micro- or minicomputer.

Kuong, Javier F. *Computer Security, Auditing, and Internal Control Manual.* Management Advisory Pubns. 1974 $25.00. On protecting electronic data processing (EDP) from error, accidents, fraud, theft, stress, and overload. How to plan and test an audit; evaluate weaknesses in EDP control organization, procedures, and staff; build effective control methods; handle emergency situations; provide insurance coverage; and solve special problems of networks and online databases.

Labelle, Charles, and others. *Finding, Selecting, Developing, and Retraining Data Professionals through Effective Human Resource Management.* Van Nostrand 1983 $31.95. The human approach to EDP that considers not the technical side of systems, hardware, and software, but rather the issue of supervising both new and long-term personnel in computer data operations.

Lobel, Jerome. *Foiling the System Breakers: Computer Security and Access Control.* McGraw-Hill 1986 $34.95. How to spot weaknesses in data communication networks through planning, organizing, and controlling direct access to information systems, while balancing the requirements of normal operations and the need for security control. With examples, charts, and graphs.

McCann, John M. *The Marketing Workbench: Using Computers for Better Performance.* Dow Jones-Irwin 1986 pap. $22.50. Marketing management philosophy for the consumer goods industry, with case histories of computer use at such companies as Pillsbury, Frito-Lay, and General Foods.

McClung, Christina J., and Kenneth A. McClung, Jr. *Microcomputers for Legal Professionals.* Wiley 1984 o.p. How personal computers can be used by both lawyers and paralegals in the law office, including word processing, forms for court papers, maintaining client records, time billing, and computer-assisted legal research.

McNitt, Lawrence. *The Art of Computer Management: How Small Firms Increase Productivity and Profits with Small Computers.* Simon & Schuster 1984 $15.95. Case studies from several representative business types explain how to undertake a computer needs analysis and make hardware and software selections.

McWilliams, Peter. *Personal Computers and the Disabled.* Doubleday 1984 pap. $9.95. Unique treatment of an often-neglected subject.

Martin, James. *Computer Networks and Distributed Processing: Software, Techniques, and Architecture.* Prentice-Hall 1981 text ed. $58.67; Telecom Lib. 1981 $59.95. Martin's early visible presence as a lecturer and his prolific book output in the 1970s earned him the epithet "the guru of DP," and this work, on software, techniques, and organization of distributed processing, is one of his comprehensive series for data processing managers.

———. *An Information Systems Manifesto.* Prentice-Hall 1984 text ed. $53.33. Lively, readable, state-of-the-art advice to data processing managers on productivity, personnel and organization structures, decentralized computing, fourth-generation very high level programming languages, application and report generators, database query languages, decision support microcomputer software, and the use of flexible corporate information centers.

Mellin, Michael, and Mia McCroskey, eds. *The Book of IBM Software*. Book Co. 3d ed. 1985 pap. $24.95. Lists and describes current software for the IBM PC and compatibles according to application categories.

Nevison, Jack M. *The Elements of Spreadsheet Style*. Brady Comm. 1987 pap. $12.95. Twenty-two rules for effective spreadsheet design and functioning, including correct structures free of hidden values, models capable of subsequent modification, and how to keep spreadsheet structure that is clear and explicit regardless of size. Not limited to specific software.

————. *Executive Computing: How to Get It Done on Your Own*. Addison-Wesley 1981 o.p. How executives can effectively use personal computers in such areas as project scheduling and forecasting.

Oppenheimer, Max Stul. *Chips! Strategic Issues in Computer Industry Negotiations*. Dow Jones-Irwin 1986 $25.00. How to negotiate with vendors for software products and services, and some of the prospects and pitfalls of contract negotiations.

Osgood, William R., and James F. Molloy, Jr. *Business Decision Making for Higher Profits: A 1-2-3 Business User's Guide*. Weber Systems 1984 pap. $19.50. An outstanding series of business computer application books, with individual volumes on Apple computers, the IBM PC, and several spreadsheet applications packages.

Perry, William E. *Survival Guide to Computer Systems: A Primer for Executives*. Van Nostrand 1982 $21.95. Computer systems explained for the business user by means of 50 rules for survival and success. The emphasis is on people and personnel.

Remer, Daniel. *Computer Power for Your Law Office*. Sybex 1983 o.p. An introduction to several aspects of computer applications for legal professionals, including word processing, databases, spreadsheets, and computer-directed printing of papers, correspondence, and legal research.

Rockhart, John F., and Christine V. Bullen. *The Rise of Managerial Computing: The Best of the Center for Information Systems Research*. Dow Jones-Irwin 1986 $30.00. A collection of 18 contributions on management information systems (MIS), originally part of the Working Papers Series of the Center for Information Systems Research of the Sloan School of Management of MIT.

Scheer, A. W. *Computer: A Challenge for Business Administration*. Springer-Verlag 1985 $22.50. Opportunities for business administration through electronic data processing and information technology, including trends in information processing, databases, interactive processing, office automation, factory automation, and artificial intelligence.

Schiller, Herbert I. *Who Knows: Information in the Age of the Fortune 500*. Ablex 1981 $29.50 pap. $17.95. Implications for business of many of the developments expected in the postindustrial era of the information society.

Schneider, J. Stewart, and Charles S. Bowen. *Microcomputers for Lawyers*. Tab Bks. 1983 $19.95. How personal computers can be used in the law office. A professional guide to using small computers to prepare court papers, handle correspondence, and undertake research.

Simon, A. R. *How to Be a Successful Computer Consultant*. McGraw-Hill 1985 pap. $16.95. Practical advice for software consultants and software designers on why people use consultants, some of the services and products offered, business negotiation, publicity, and how to update professional and technical knowledge.

Smedinghoff, Thomas J. *The Legal Guide to Developing, Protecting and Marketing Software: Dealing with Problems Raised by Consumers, Competitors and Employ-*

ees. Wiley 1986 $39.95. A survey of legal concepts and issues pertaining to software marketing. Explores law pertaining to copyright, trade secrets, trademarks, software contracts, vendor liability, and tax implications of software transactions, with citations of relevant cases, statutes, and government regulations.

Stewart, R. D. *Cost Estimating with Microcomputers.* McGraw-Hill 1985 $29.50. For cost estimators, designers, project and consulting engineers, university administrators, and owners of small businesses, on using spreadsheets, database application packages, and cost-scheduling systems.

Thomas, Terry, and Marlene G. Weinstein. *Computer-Assisted Legal and Tax Research: A Professional's Guide to Lexis, Westlaw, and Phinet.* Prentice-Hall 1987 pap. $40.00. Comprehensive guide to computer-assisted legal research (CALR), with suggestions on using terminals, personal computers, query formulas, blank search forms, office use and office integration, and time charges and other costs.

Waxman, Robert. *Moonlighting with Your Personal Computer.* Pharos Bks. 1984 pap. $7.95. Practical ideas and suggestions for starting and maintaining small businesses and business services in your spare time by using standard microcomputer hardware and software.

Weil, Ulric. *Information Systems in the 80s: Products, Markets, and Vendors.* Prentice-Hall 1982 $24.95. A guide to the impact of the information society on business, listing information system products, who sells them, and market targets for the information systems manager and professional.

Williams, Andrew T. *What If? A User's Guide to Spreadsheets on the IBM PC.* Wiley 1984 text ed. pap. $16.95. Principles and good practice of using spreadsheets with standard microcomputer software packages; maintaining documentation to expand or modify structures, preventing hidden values, and using macros.

Winston, Patrick Henry, and Karen A. Prendergast, eds. *The AI Business: Commercial Uses of Artificial Intelligence.* [*Artificial Intelligence Ser.*] MIT 1984 $15.95 1986 pap. $9.95. Artificial intelligence applications for oil, medicine, electronics, factory automation, and other fields. The discussion is especially relevant to project analysis, financing, and investment.

Woodwell, Donald R. *Automating Your Financial Portfolio: An Investor's Guide to Personal Computers.* Dow Jones-Irwin 2d ed. 1986 pap. $25.00. How to gather data on stocks and companies, screen stocks and bonds for buying opportunities, and manage investment portfolios with a personal computer.

Zboray, R., and D. Sachs. *Programs for Profit: How to Really Make Money with a Personal Computer.* McGraw-Hill 1984 pap. $9.95. On using a small computer for profit with a business of your own. Reviews software packages and what they offer for business applications.

Databases and Data Communications

This section contains books on connecting microcomputers and mainframe computers, data communications, database management systems (DBMS), design and structure, file management, relational databases, and telematics. Database software packages are continuing to become more powerful and more sophisticated while also becoming easier to use. Titles on standard proprietary database programs are not cited here, although they may be found in bookstores.

Atre, Shakuntala. *Data Base: Structured Techniques for Design, Performance and Management: With Case Studies.* [*Business Data Processing Ser.*] Wiley 1980 $39.95.

Real-world, practical information and case studies on high-quality database design and management. Covers database administration; relational, hierarchical, and network data models; DBMS, data storage and access, and performance issues.

Belitsos, Byron, and Jay Misra. *Business Telematics: Corporate Networks for the Information Age.* Dow Jones-Irwin 1986 $29.95. Management issues and telematic technology and applications, with actual corporate examples, surveying the fields of office integration, high-speed data communications, voice/data integration, office communications technology, local area networks, private branch exchanges, electronic mail, teleconferencing, micro-to-mainframe links, and videotex.

Chih-Yang, Chao. *Relational Databases.* Prentice-Hall 1986 text ed. $42.67. Advanced principles and practices of databases, including relational database models, relational algebra, tuple and domain relational calculus, and query languages.

Date, C. J. *Database: A Primer.* Addison-Wesley 1983 pap. $14.38. An introduction with practical exercises, detailed descriptions, and how-to-do-it information on microcomputer and mainframe databases. For more advanced treatment, see the same author's two-volume *Introduction to Database Systems* (Addison-Wesley 1981 vol. 1 $44.25 1983 vol. 2 $37.75), where Volume 1 covers basic concepts, examples of relational systems, relational database management, and database environments, and Volume 2 contains more advanced issues and applications.

————. *Relational Database: Selected Writings.* Addison-Wesley 1986 text ed. $33.95. Papers on relational database management, relational versus nonrelational systems, the SQL language, and database design.

Goley, George F., IV. *The Dow Jones-Irwin Technical Reference Guide to Microcomputer Database Management Systems.* Dow Jones-Irwin 1987 $49.95. Intended for application developers; an analysis of the capabilities, advantages, and disadvantages of most popular microcomputer DBMS packages, including the equivalent verbs, syntax, and functions of each package. In addition, there are practical tips and discussions of debugging and subroutines for each package.

Jones, J. A. *Databases in Theory and Practice.* Tab Bks. 1987 $28.95. How to maintain databases, the advantages and disadvantages of several database systems, their requirements, and sample case studies. For database administrators and systems analysts.

Kopeck, Ronald F. *Micro-to-Mainframe Links.* Osborne/McGraw 1986 pap. $18.95. A survey of file servers, local area networks, gateways, and bridge technologies, intended to be read by data processing managers and communications professionals. Discussions of installations in specific office environments, workstation/host relations, data transfer and data security, costs, and monitoring techniques.

Korth, Henry F., and Abraham Silberschatz. *Database System Concepts.* [*Computer Science Ser.*] McGraw-Hill 1986 text ed. $37.95. For readers with prior knowledge of programming and databases. Covers such subjects as entity/relationship; relational, network, and hierarchical models; their physical organization; indexing query processing; security; and applications of artificial intelligence.

Kruglinski, David. *Data Base Management Systems—MS-DOS: Evaluating MS-DOS Database Software.* Osborne/McGraw 1985 pap. $18.95. An update of Kruglinski's previous standard work on CP/M databases, valuable for its general discussion of database principles along with contemporary benchmarks for evaluating current database packages for business.

Laurie, Peter. *Databases: How to Manage Information on Your Micro.* Methuen 1985 pap. $19.95. A well-written introduction for beginners at the handling of computerized mailing lists, product information bases, and client data using microcomputer software packages. With ample diagrams and charts.

Maier, David. *The Theory of Relational Databases*. [*Principles of Computer Science Ser.*] Computer Science Pr. 1983 text ed. $39.95. Assuming some prior knowledge of programming and databases, this work discusses relational algebra, functional considerations, multivalued and joint dependencies, representation theory, query modifications, database semantics, and query languages.

Martin, James. *Principles of Data-Base Management*. Prentice-Hall 1976 $48.00. A pioneering volume on the subject, along with the same author's *Computer Data-Base Organization* (Prentice-Hall 2d ed. 1977 $49.95), stressing large computer systems; still useful for advanced users.

Turpin, John, and Ray Sarch. *Data Communications: Beyond Basics*. McGraw-Hill 1986 $28.95. Forty-three articles, originally published in *Data Communications* magazine in 1984 and 1985, on planning and design, new technology, applications, management, and future trends, with attention to digital transmission, data compression, transport protocols, and artificial intelligence. This volume supplements articles previously collected as *Basic Guide to Data Communications* (McGraw-Hill 1985 $29.95).

Ullman, Jeffrey D. *Principles of Database Systems*. Computer Science Pr. 2d ed. 1982 text ed. $34.95. Combines the treatment of actual database systems and query languages, such as ISBL, QUEL, Query-by-Example, and SEQUEL.

Word Processing, Desktop Publishing, and Typesetting

Peter A. McWilliams's books are a good place for the beginner in word processing; at the other end of the scale, Michael L. Kleper's handbook of desktop publishing and typesetting contains much that is useful to the professional. Bookstores are well supplied with titles on proprietary word processing programs, not discussed here, and their shelves are rapidly filling up with works on desktop publishing. The acceptance of the laser printer and the spread of better dot matrix printers has produced an unexpected marriage between the printing of text and graphics. Unlike previous printers, which produced characters and graphics formatted by lines, laser printers compose entire pages. Thus page description languages, such as PostScript, began to be necessary to bridge the double gap between three standards of computer printing: old typewriter-based daisy wheel printing, current laser (or near letter-quality dot matrix) printing, and professional typesetting.

Bove, Tony, and others. *The Art of Desktop Publishing*. Bantam 2d ed. 1986 pap. $19.95. An introduction to typesetting, newsletters, brochures, clip and generated art, laser printers and their software, page makeup, fonts, CD-ROM, and optical disks. For both IBM PC and Macintosh microcomputers.

Cole, B. C. *Beyond Word Processing: How to Use Your Personal Computer as a Processor*. McGraw-Hill 1985 $12.95. This useful book describes information storage in textbases and wordbases, how special programs work, and how existing software can be used for these language databases. Professional writers will still find the discussion of procedures useful although some of the software has been superseded.

Felici, James, and Ted Nace. *Desktop Publishing Skills*. Addison-Wesley 1987 text ed.

$21.50. A primer for typesetting, page makeup, font selection, hardware and software, laser printers, and cost evaluation, using the Macintosh or IBM PC.

Fluegelman, Andrew, and Jeremy Hewes. *Writing in the Computer Age: Word Processing Skills and Style for Every Writer.* Doubleday 1983 o.p. A standard book of advice to practicing writers on the basic mechanics of writing with a word processor and on how to use the computer to achieve and refine a personal style.

Heim, Michael. *Electric Language: A Philosophical Study of Word Processing.* Yale Univ. Pr. 1987 $19.95. A sophisticated view of word processing using the transformative theory of language of Wittgenstein and Eric Holbrook and the ontological theory of language of Martin Heidegger.

Kleper, Michael L. *The Illustrated Handbook of Desktop Publishing and Typesetting.* Tab Bks. 1987 $29.95. For both print-trade professionals and those new to desktop publishing, a comprehensive sourcebook on all current phases of personal computers, software, work stations, word processing, text formatters, telecommunications, data manipulation and conversion, typesetting hardware, typesetting software, desktop publishing, and output devices.

Knuth, Donald. *The $T_EX$book.* Addison-Wesley 1984 pap. $26.95. An introduction to T_EX (pronounced "tek" and spelled with block capitals, the E being lowered a partial line and spacing tightened so that its very name is a display of its versatility). This elementary volume is augmented by Knuth's *Computers and Typesetting* (Addison-Wesley 5 vols. 1986 ea. $32.25–$37.75), an advanced series including *T_EX: The Program* (Volume 2), *Metafont: The Program* (Volume 4), and *Computer Modern Typefaces* (Volume 5).

McWilliams, Peter A. *The Word Processing Book.* Ballantine 1984 pap. $9.95; Doubleday 1984 pap. $9.95. Probably the best book for beginners in computing and word processing for its feisty comments and no-nonsense approach. A sequel is the same author's *Questions and Answers on Word Processing* (Ballantine 1983 pap. $9.95).

Mitchell, Joan P. *The New Writer.* Microsoft 1987 pap. $8.95. A recent introduction to new developments, concepts, and technologies in word processing, and how to make the most of word processing as a writer.

Noble, David F., and Virginia D. Noble. *Improve Your Writing with Word Processing.* Que Corp. 1984 o.p. A more advanced work than the title suggests, this stimulating book offers parallels between block moves in word processing and how the writer can rearrange phrases, sentences, paragraphs, and sections.

Postscript Language Reference Manual. Addison-Wesley 1985 $22.95

Postscript Language Tutorial and Cookbook. Addison-Wesley 1985 $16.95. This and the above title are official manuals from Adobe Systems for their standard page description programming language. For software programmers, consultants, and other users employing laser printers for word processing, graphics illustration, or CAD/CAM.

Seybold, John, and Fritz Dressler. *Publishing from the Desktop.* Bantam 1987 pap. $19.95. A view of recent developments in desktop publishing technology, including type design, digital imaging, electronic typesetting, electronic page makeup and page design for professional results.

Will-Harris, Daniel. *Desktop Publishing with Style: A Complete Guide to Design Techniques and New Technology for the IBM PC and Compatibles.* Intro. by Peter A. McWilliams, And Bks. 1987 pap. $19.95. An introduction to software, hardware, basic graphics, typesetting, dot matrix printers, laser printers, clip art, and drawing programs.

Creativity in Art, Music, Film, and Language

Books in this section treat the use of computers in music, Musical Instrument Digital Interface (MIDI), fine art and commercial graphics, films and literature, interactive fiction and conversational games, computational stylistics, literary analysis, and linguistics.

Abercrombie, John R. *Computer Programs for Literary Analysis.* Univ. of Pennsylvania Pr. 1984 pap. $14.25. Programs in BASIC, Pascal, and IBYX for text conversion, indexing utilities, KWIC concordances, and other forms of literary analysis.

Boom, Michael. *Music Through MIDI: Using MIDI to Create Your Own Electronic Music System.* Microsoft 1987 pap. $19.95. How to use the standards and technology defined by MIDI to operate an electronic music system. Includes applications for home, education, and studio.

Butler, Christopher. *Computers in Linguistics.* Basil Blackwell 1985 $49.95 pap. $14.95. The use of computers in literary and linguistic research, with a long section on applications in the SNOBOL4 language. For readers interested in the quantitative analysis of literary data, see Butler's companion volume, *Statistics in Linguistics* (Basil Blackwell 1985 $39.95 pap. $14.95).

Chamberlain, Hal. *Musical Applications of Microprocessors.* Hayden 1983 pap. $21.95. A highly regarded text on analog, digital, and microprocessor sound and music systems, now in its second edition.

Deken, Joseph. *Computer Images: State of the Art.* Stewart, Tabori & Chang 1983 pap. $16.95. A beautifully illustrated book on graphics techniques, such as collage and transformations, input devices, visual communications, imagery construction, training simulations, fantasy, and the emulation of bioscientific processes.

Foley, James D., and A. van Dam. *Fundamentals of Interactive Computer Graphics.* Addison-Wesley 1982 $43.95. A standard tutorial covering hardware, interactive design, geometrical elements, and raster algorithms, employing BASIC concepts in Pascal and the new Core System of Standard Graphics of ACM-SIGGRAPH.

Harris, Mary Dee. *Introduction to Natural Language Processing.* Reston 1985 o.p. A useful work on natural language concepts and computer programming in the field of language and linguistics.

Hearn, D. Donald, and M. Pauline Baker. *Computer Graphics.* Prentice-Hall 1986 text ed. $48.00. Discusses algorithms for graphics display, programming examples in Pascal, and the Graphical Kernel System (GKS). Intended for those already adept in computer science.

Hockey, Susan. *A Guide to Computer Applications in the Humanities.* Johns Hopkins Univ. Pr. 1980 text ed. pap. $8.95. An international survey of academic uses of computing programs in literature, publishing, and linguistics. The sections describe how the programs actually work, and what their strengths and limitations are.

————. *SNOBOL Programming for the Humanities.* Oxford 1985 $32.50 pap. $14.95. A tutorial introduction to text analysis and string processing through programming in SNOBOL, useful for students without a background in math.

Kenny, Anthony J. *The Computation of Style: An Introduction to Statistics for Students and Readers of Literature.* Pergamon 1982 $33.00 pap. $16.50. A standard introduction to the concepts and techniques of computational stylistics.

Lewell, John. *A–Z Guide to Computer Graphics.* McGraw-Hill 1985 $29.95. An introductory survey to computer graphics, with a discussion of techniques and hardware, applications in graphics design, illustration, television and film, the sciences, architecture, and business, with 150 illustrations and examples in color.

Manning, Peter. *Electronic and Computer Music*. Oxford 1987 pap. $15.95. Critical perspective on the history of electronic and computer music, including studio developments, innovations in tape composition, live electronic performance, electronic rock and roll, and trends in computer composition of the last two decades, with bibliography and discography. The paperback version is a revised edition.

Mowshowitz, Abbe. *Inside Information: Computers in Fiction*. Addison-Wesley 1977 o.p. A collection of some three dozen works or excerpts from works of fiction that pertain to computers or computing; with bibliography. (The book was an outgrowth of the same author's study of information processing, *The Conquest of Will*.)

Newman, William M., and Robert F. Sproull. *Principles of Interactive Computer Graphics*. McGraw-Hill 2d ed. 1979 text ed. $49.95. An elementary survey of aspects of graphics design using Pascal, including point plotting, clipping, segments, and geometric elements.

Nicholls, Peter, ed. *The Science Fiction Encyclopedia*. Doubleday 1979 o.p. Informative articles on science fiction that treat such subjects as computers, communications, linguistics, information, intelligence, and technology.

Peterson, Dale. *Genesis II: Creation and Recreation with Computers*. Prentice-Hall 1983 o.p. A survey of creative work that has used the computer in North America in the fields of music, painting, literature, and games. The work, which is well researched and well illustrated, reflects considerable critical understanding, and has a bibliography of unusual sources.

Porush, David. *The Soft Machine: Cybernetic Fiction*. Methuen 1985 text ed. $29.95 pap. $10.95. A discussion in some detail of fiction about cybernetics and computers in such authors as Vonnegut, Burroughs, Pynchon, Barth, Beckett, and Barthelme. Bibliography.

Prueitt, Melvin L. *Art and the Computer*. Intro. by Carl Sagan, McGraw-Hill 1984 pap. $45.95. Introduces technical methods to produce professional and scientific computer graphics, stunningly illustrated with about 300 photographs, mostly in color.

Racter. *The Policeman's Beard Is Half Constructed*. Warner 1984 pap. $9.95. Racter, the author, is a computer program (written by Bill Chamberlain and Thomas Etter and available elsewhere as recreational software), and the book is therefore an interesting and amusing experiment.

Rivlin, Robert. *The Algorithmic Image: Graphic Visions of the Computer Age*. Microsoft 1986 pap. $24.95. A survey of professional applications of graphics by state-of-the-art producers, including NASA, the New York Institute of Technology, and Hollywood animation studios.

Roads, Curtis, and John Strawn, eds. *Foundations of Computer Music*. MIT 1987 pap. $17.50. High-level articles, reprinted from *Computer Music Journal*, on sound synthesis, digital signal processing, and perception. Each section is preceded by a summary.

Scott, Joan E. *Introduction to Interactive Computer Graphics*. Wiley 1982 $18.95. Help for professionals working in drafting, manufacturing, design, mapping, business reports, and scientific presentations, including equipment, organization, techniques, and career opportunities.

Waite, Mitchell, and Christopher Morgan. *Graphics Primer for the IBM PC*. Osborne/ McGraw 1983 pap. $21.95. An introduction in Advanced BASIC to business, education, and entertainment graphics, including charts, maps, forms, animations, and games.

Warrick, Patricia S. *The Cybernetic Imagination in Science Fiction*. MIT 1980 $30.00

pap. $8.95. A discussion of types of science fiction that have supported stories about automata, robots, computers. Includes bibliographies of studies, indexes, fiction, and anthologies.

Education

Subjects treated in education books include authoring languages, BASIC, computer acquisition and management in schools, computer applications from kindergarten through higher education, computer-assisted instruction (CAI), computer-assisted learning (CAL), guides to software and hardware, learning activities, the Logo language, and writing instruction.

Bork, Alfred. *Learning with Computers.* Digital Pr. 1981 $28.00; Harper 1986 text ed. $22.95. Papers based on ten years of experience with the use of computers in the teaching of physics in the Educational Technology Center at the University of California at Irvine. Includes sections on graphics, authoring languages, and future developments in higher education.

Daiute, Colette. *Computers and Writing.* Addison-Wesley 1985 pap. $16.95. Solid advice to teachers of writing on how computers should and should not be used at various levels of instruction. What distinguishes this work from others is its fine realization that writing is a cognitive and social process as well as a mechanical one.

Olsen, Solveig, ed. *Computer-Aided Instruction in the Humanities.* [*Technology and the Humanities Ser.*] MLA 1985 text ed. $27.50 pap. $14.50. Essays on college-level teaching in history, foreign languages, logic, and writing, with emphasis on software and courseware selection, microcomputer-mainframe connections, videodisks, and pitfalls in using computers. The bibliography and the list of personnel and programs are extensive.

Oulton, A. J., and J. J. Foster. *The Teaching of Computer Appreciation and Library Automation.* Longwood 1981 pap. $12.00. An informal pamphlet, drawing heavily on actual examples and anecdotes, on how to introduce and instruct university-level students in information and computer science. Issued by the British Library as Research and Development Report No. 5647.

Papert, Seymour. *Mindstorms: Children, Computers, and Powerful Ideas.* Basic Bks. 1982 $15.95 pap. $7.95. Papert invented Logo as a programming language to introduce schoolchildren to concepts of programming by enhancing their mental training according to the psychological and educational principles of Piaget. Logo is often used hands-on to manipulate a graphics turtle on a small computer, but there are also math and language applications.

Pea, Roy D. *Mirrors of Minds: Patterns of Experience in Educational Computing.* [*Cognition and Computing Ser.*] Ablex 1987 text ed. $42.50 pap. $19.95. Fifteen papers written between 1982 and 1986 at the Center for Children and Technology of Bank Street College, covering Logo, multimedia in the classroom, teaching science, the urban teacher, minority schools, the cognitive demands of programming, computers, and software design.

Schwartz, Helen J. *Interactive Writing.* Holt 1985 text ed. pap. $15.95. The first important college textbook for freshman composition courses to be based on the use of word processing and computer technology.

Sloan, Douglas, ed. *The Computer in Education: A Critical Perspective.* Teachers College Pr. 1985 text ed. pap. $11.95. A standard collection of articles on several aspects of computer applications in schools.

Tashner, John, ed. *Improving Instruction with Microcomputers: Readings and Re-*

sources for Elementary and Secondary Schools. Oryx 1984 pap. $31.00. A useful
anthology of 50 selections, originally published as articles or chapters in books.

Willis, Jerry, and Merl Miller. *Computers for Everybody.* Weber Systems 3d ed. 1983
pap. $4.95. For teachers and school administrators interested in CAI, computer-
managed instruction (CMI), computer testing, hardware, software, teacher training, and computer literacy. With tutorials in BASIC, PILOT, and Logo.

ARTIFICIAL INTELLIGENCE

Introductions

No issue in computing has aroused as many hopes, fears, and controversies
as has artificial intelligence (AI). Newcomers to the field will find the books
by Jeremy Campbell, Howard Gardner, George Johnson, Pamela McCorduck, Howard Rheingold, and Oliver Sacks to be unusually well written and
informative. The expectations of a decade or two ago that computers would
easily be able to imitate human thought and judgment have not been fully
met. Although computers have proved useful in manufacturing design, automation, and robotics, and have become standard in technical detection and
diagnosis procedures in the biological and physical sciences, other areas of
application, such as those in the humanities and social sciences, remain
unsettled. In the case of national defense and international treaties, the use
of artificial intelligence is a matter of continuing debate. Introductory
books here on artificial intelligence contain such subjects as cognitive psychology, games and decision making, fifth-generation languages, information representation, information theory, machine translation, natural language analysis, pattern recognition, popular introductions and surveys, programming languages for AI, robots and automata, self-referential loops, and
voice input/output.

Berry, Adrian. *The Super-Intelligent Machine: An Electronic Odyssey.* Salem House
1985 $14.95. An entertaining but serious introduction to computers and artifi-
cial intelligence; strong on quotable anecdotes and concrete examples. Useful
bibliography.

Brand, Stewart. *The Media Lab: Inventing the Future at MIT.* Viking 1987 $20.00. An
account, sometimes as euphoric as science fiction, of ongoing work at the Media
Lab at MIT, including the recent activity of such well-known figures as Marvin
Minsky and Seymour Papert, and some promising new developments, including
Danny Hillis's Connection Machine with 64,000 co-processors, a new design for
an electronic desk, a way of obtaining a custom-printed newspaper, and new
uses for videocassettes and compact disks.

Campbell, Jeremy. *Grammatical Man: Information, Entropy, Language, and Life.* Simon & Schuster 1982 $16.95 1983 pap. $8.95. A stimulating and wide-reaching
synthesis of information theory and its implications for people as grammar-
making animals who use both natural languages and computer programming
languages. Moreover, people are also grammar-made animals since genetic
DNA seems to operate as a kind of information channel.

Feigenbaum, Edward A., and Pamela McCorduck. *The Fifth Generation: Artificial
Intelligence and Japan's Computer Challenge to the World.* Addison-Wesley 1983
$15.95. Will the Japanese be first in the 1990s with a practical supercomputer

that combines government backing; a consortium of companies; fantastic speed, capacity, and versatility; expert knowledge systems; multiple processors; very high level programming languages; natural language operations in English and Japanese; and human voice input and output?

Frude, Neil. *The Intimate Machine: Close Encounters with Computers and Robots.* NAL 1983 $14.95. A highly readable book on the unusual thesis that people tend to grant to computers and robots those roles that make them resemble people.

Gardner, Howard. *The Mind's New Science: A History of the Cognitive Revolution.* Basic Bks. 1985 $22.50 1987 pap. $12.95. Although the human mind is turning out to seem less and less like a digital computer, computer and artificial intelligence modeling and simulation have been necessary to recent developments in cognitive psychology. Gardner traces connections between computing, cognitive psychology, and philosophy, psychology, information theory, linguistics, anthropology, mathematics, and theories of perception and representation.

Hart, Anna. *Knowledge Acquisition for Expert Systems.* McGraw-Hill 1986 $28.95. A clear and coherent account of how the knowledge engineer—a new specialization—elicits information from experts and places it into an expert system. The discussion covers project design, expert system organization, probability theory, fuzzy logic, machine induction, and some case histories.

Hartnell, Tim. *Exploring Artificial Intelligence on Your IBM PC.* Bantam 1986 pap. $14.95. An introductory book on several easy-to-understand aspects of artificial intelligence that use elementary AI programs written in BASIC.

Hopcroft, John E., and Jeffrey D. Ullman. *Introduction to Automated Theory, Languages, and Computation.* Addison-Wesley 1979 text ed. $35.95. An advanced work on such language-theory concepts as nondeterminism and complex hierarchies, and language-theory ideas, including regular expressions and context-free grammar in the design of computers and text processors.

Johnson, George. *Machinery of the Mind: Inside the New Science of Artificial Intelligence.* Microsoft 1987 pap. $9.95; Times Bks. 1986 $19.95. An unusually well written and well integrated survey of artificial intelligence, its movements, people, and controversies. Excellent selective bibliography.

Koestler, Arthur. *The Act of Creation.* Macmillan 1964 $9.95. Koestler, better known as a novelist and social critic, returned to his earlier scientific training to produce a highly suggestive and stimulating theory that humor, creativity, and insight occur at the intersection or "bisociation" of two mental frames in the mind.

Levine, Howard, and Howard Rheingold. *The Cognitive Connection: Thought and Language in Man and Machine.* Prentice-Hall 1987 $19.95. An attempt to connect computer languages to natural languages as common linguistic efforts of people, reminding us that a computer is essentially a symbolic manipulator that can emulate whatever processor structures its inventors can design.

McCorduck, Pamela. *Machines Who Think: A Personal Inquiry into the History and Prospects of Artificial Intelligence.* W. H. Freeman 1981 text ed. pap. $14.95. A standard introduction to artificial intelligence, delightful to read and based on personal knowledge and interviews, surveying the field from its forerunners in antiquity to its flowerings in the 1960s and 1970s. Highly recommended; with bibliography.

Michie, David, and Rory Johnston. *The Knowledge Machine: Artificial Intelligence and the Future of Man.* Morrow 1986 $16.95. An optimistic view of AI not merely as a method of handling routine tasks but also of solving the complex and pressing problems of our times.

Raphael, Bertram. *The Thinking Computer: Mind Inside Matter.* [*Psychology Ser.*]

W. H. Freeman 1976 text ed. pap. $15.95. An introduction to current work on robots and artificial intelligence with a brief history of the subject, emphasizing the nature and limits of the human mind.

Rheingold, Howard. *Tools for Thought: The People and Ideas Behind the Next Computer Revolution.* Prentice-Hall 1986 pap. $9.95; Simon & Schuster 1985 $17.95. The history and prospects of mind-expanding technology, told in lively fashion by following the people who made the most significant contributions.

Ritchie, David. *The Binary Brain: Artificial Intelligence in the Age of Electronics.* Little, Brown 1984 $14.45. Although much about the brain is neither binary nor digital, this treatment surveys the field of artificial intelligence.

Rose, Steven. *The Conscious Brain.* Random 1976 o.p. One of the best introductions to the study of the brain. Includes discussions of several philosophical issues pertaining to the physical brain, written from a humanistic viewpoint.

———. *Into the Heart of the Mind: An American Quest for Artificial Intelligence.* Harper 1984 o.p. An introductory survey of the field of artificial intelligence.

Rothfelder, Jerry. *Minds over Matter: A New Look at Artificial Intelligence.* Prentice-Hall 1986 pap. $7.95; Simon & Schuster 1985 $17.95. A useful survey of 30 years of developments in artificial intelligence.

Sacks, Oliver. *The Man Who Mistook His Wife for a Hat and Other Clinical Tales.* Harper 1987 pap. $7.95; Summit 1986 $16.95. Fascinating case histories, written with warmth by a clinical psychiatrist, about persons with partly defective cognitive faculties, reminding the reader that many invisible steps, wholly assumed in normal human information processing, cannot be taken for granted in AI machine simulations.

Schank, Roger C., and Peter Childers. *The Cognitive Computer: On Language, Learning, and Artificial Intelligence.* Addison-Wesley 1985 $12.95. A practical introduction to the field of artificial intelligence, written in nontechnical language for the beginner, warning very firmly that many of the promises of the 1960s and 1970s are still unrealized. One of Schank's successes is his model of multiple levels in human thought and its application to a practical system that can translate newspaper paragraphs between several human languages.

Schutzer, Daniel. *An Applications-Oriented Approach to Artificial Intelligence.* Van Nostrand 1986 $39.95. A survey of the fundamental tools of AI programmers, such as LISP, the PROLOG language, and special hardware and software, and their uses in expert systems, machine perception, natural language processing, vision and image processing, and robotics.

Staugaard, Andrew G. *Robotics and AI: An Introduction to Applied Machine Intelligence.* Prentice-Hall 1987 text ed. $43.00. The technology of AI and robotics in both home and industry, including very good coverage of the topics of speech synthesis and recognition, vision, navigation, and tactile sensing, with special attention to the distinction between automation and robotics.

Tanimoto, Steven L. *Elements of Artificial Intelligence: An Introduction Using LISP.* [*Principles of Computer Science Ser.*] Computer Science Pr. 1987 text ed. $37.95. The principles of artificial intelligence, illustrated through LISP as a programming language. Applications and discussions include a conversational simulation of Rogerian therapy, a calculus problem solver, inference, fuzzy logic, natural language understanding, computer vision, and expert systems.

Waldrop, M. Mitchell. *Man-Made Minds.* Walker 1987 $22.95 pap. $14.95. An informative current assessment of achievements, difficulties, promises, setbacks, and philosophical issues after several decades of development in the field of artificial intelligence, discussed through actual attempts to teach machines to learn, to reason, and to use language. Waldrop is a physicist and senior writer for *Science* magazine.

Winston, Patrick Henry. *Artificial Intelligence*. Addison-Wesley 1977 $24.95. A standard introduction to the field by an eminent member of the MIT faculty. The second half of the book contains an explanation of the LISP language.

Collections and Anthologies

Much of the original work in the AI field appeared as papers, not as books, and it is therefore very useful to have the collections and anthologies that have appeared since the 1950s. While some of the earlier anthologies cannot be ignored for the capture of classic papers or for the study of the history of the subject, many readers will be more interested in recent publications, such as the Barr and Feigenbaum handbook, the Shapiro encyclopedia, or the Hofstadter and Dennett compendium.

Barr, Avron, and others, eds. *The Handbook of Artificial Intelligence*. W. Kaufmann 3 vols. 1982 ea. $39.50–$59.50 1985 pap. ea. $27.95–$32.95. A standard reference collection, in three volumes. Volume 1 covers searching, knowledge representation, understanding natural language, and understanding spoken language; Volume 2 contains programming languages, applications in AI research in science, medicine, and education, and automatic programming; Volume 3 covers models of cognition, automatic deduction, vision, learning and inductive inference, and memory and problem solving.

Feigenbaum, Edward A., and Julian Feldman, eds. *Computers and Thought*. Krieger repr. of 1963 ed. 1981 lib. bdg. $33.50. Twenty reprinted articles on games, theorem proving, heuristics, baseball questions, pattern recognition, problem solving, verbal learning, decision making, and social behavior, reflecting the state of artificial intelligence in the early 1960s. There are distinguished contributions by Alan Turing and Marvin Minsky.

Haugeland, John C., ed. *Mind Design: Philosophy, Psychology and Artificial Intelligence*. MIT 1981 text ed. pap. $10.95. An anthology that collects articles on some of the major conceptual issues raised by developments in artificial intelligence.

Hofstadter, Douglas R., and Daniel C. Dennett, eds. *The Mind's I: Fantasies and Reflections of Self and Soul*. Bantam 1982 pap. $11.95; Basic Bks. 1981 $16.95. A collection of stimulating articles, fiction, and essays on mind, soul, and self in philosophy, literature, and artificial intelligence. Hofstadter later said its goal was "to probe the mysteries of matter and consciousness in as vivid and jolting a way as possible." The jolt comes from "the curious fact (or illusion) that something we call an 'I' is somehow connected to some hunk of matter floating somewhere and somewhen in the universe."

Schank, Roger C., and K. M. Colby, eds. *Computer Models of Thought and Language*. W. H. Freeman 1973 $35.95. An important collection of AI articles, accessible to the general reader, on simulation of mental processes, language understanding, translation, and related issues. Includes Kenneth M. Colby's PARRY program, which simulated a paranoid patient and passed the Turing test, and essays by Allen Newell, Terry Winograd, Roger C. Schank, and others.

Shapiro, Stuart C., ed. *The Encyclopedia of Artificial Intelligence*. Wiley 2 vols. 1987 $149.95. A professional compendium of more than 200 contributors on all aspects of artificial intelligence. The articles include their own bibliographies and thus amass more than 5,000 references overall.

Torrance, S. *The Mind and the Machine: Philosophical Aspects of Artificial Intelligence.* Halsted Pr. 1984 $31.95. Fifteen advanced essays about structure, limits, function, language, epistemology, intentionality, linguistics, methodology, reasoning, inference, meaning, creativity, and learning in artificial intelligence machines.

Winston, Patrick Henry, ed. *The Psychology of Computer Vision.* [*Computer Science Ser.*] McGraw-Hill 1975 o.p. Six articles by Winston, Marvin Minsky, and others on artificial intelligence, plus several programs that attempt to simulate human vision and the organization of knowledge.

Winston, Patrick Henry, and Richard H. Brown, eds. *Artificial Intelligence: An MIT Perspective.* [*Artificial Intelligence Ser.*] MIT 2 vols. 1979 ea. $35.00. The first volume contains expert problem solving, natural language understanding, intelligent coaching, problems of representation, and learning procedures; the second volume contains vision and manipulation, productivity, computer design, and symbol management.

Philosophy, Background, Context

Much of the early euphoria of AI writers—and partisanship of AI critics—has disappeared in favor of a more skeptical but still positive attitude. Among the classics of the 1970s, Margaret Boden's masterful discussion and the critical attacks by Hubert L. Dreyfus and Joseph Weizenbaum remain required reading. More recent works by Dennett, Hofstadter, and Winograd are highly recommended approaches to the current horizons in artificial intelligence. This section also includes works on game theory, information theory, current laboratory research, psychology and psychiatry, semantics and natural language processing, and computer vision.

Boden, Margaret. *Artificial Intelligence and Natural Man.* Basic Bks. 2d ed. rev. 1987 text ed. pap. $14.95. A well-written and clear introduction to AI from a philosopher's point of view. The concrete details on many programs make it easy to understand their strengths and weaknesses.

Cherry, Colin. *On Human Communication: A Review, a Survey and a Criticism.* MIT 3d ed. 1978 text ed. pap. $9.95. The entire range of media discussed from the point of view of an electrical engineer. A mathematical analysis of meaning in information theory, including implications for philosophy and communications practice.

Davis, Morton D. *Game Theory: A Nontechnical Introduction.* Basic Bks. rev. ed. 1983 $20.00 pap. $9.95. Excellent as an overview of the main ideas and some of the unresolved issues of game theory.

Dennett, Daniel C. *Brainstorms: Philosophical Essays on Mind and Psychology.* MIT 1980 text ed. pap. $12.50. Analyses of problems of mind, brain, and computer models of thought, perception, and sensation. Dennett's book has been justly praised for its clarity, grace, and freedom from jargon.

Dreyfus, Hubert L. *What Computers Can't Do: A Critique of Artificial Reason.* Harper 1979 pap. $8.95. A sustained attack on the methods and presuppositions of the AI field, especially its cognitive simulations of the late 1950s, semantic information processing in the 1960s, and automatic optimism of outlook. Written from the phenomenological point of view of a professional philosopher.

Gatlin, Lila L. *Information Theory and the Living System.* [*Molecular Biology Ser.*] Columbia Univ. Pr. 1972 o.p. An ingenious application of Claude Shannon's

information theory to DNA genetics as a living information channel, with fascinating discussions of the philosophical battle between mechanist reductionists
and their opponents, including the contributions of Francis Crick, Arthur Koestler, Michael Polanyi, and John von Neumann.

Hand, D. J. *Artificial Intelligence and Psychiatry.* [*Scientific Basis of Psychiatry Ser.*]
Cambridge Univ. Pr. 1985 $42.50. A serious reconsideration of the issues in such
AI programs as PARRY and ELIZA, hotly debated more than a decade ago by
Colby, Joseph Weizenbaum, and Hubert L. Dreyfus. In the process, recent devel-
opments in artificial intelligence are reviewed from unusual medical and profes-
sional perspectives.

Hofstadter, Douglas. *Gödel, Escher, Bach: An Eternal Golden Braid.* Basic Bks. 1979
$29.95. A stimulating and fascinating, but demanding, book on self-referential
loops in the mathematician Gödel, the painter Escher, and the composer Johann
Sebastian Bach, with fascinating implications for mathematical logic, DNA,
music, art, computer programming, and artificial intelligence. The author later
said: "In essence, *GEB* was one extended flash having to do with Kurt Gödel's
famous incompleteness theorem, the human brain, and the mystery of consciousness. It is well described on its cover as 'a metaphorical fugue of minds and
machines.' "

———. *Metamagical Themas: Questing for the Essence of Mind and Pattern.* Bantam
1986 pap. $14.95; Basic Bks. 1985 $24.95. Described on its dust jacket as 'An
Interlocked Collection of Literary, Scientific, and Artistic Studies," most of this
gathering of notions, puzzles, and queries, alternately profound and capricious
in the author's unique manner, was originally published in the columns of
Scientific American between 1981 and 1983. In book form it may be most rewarding if browsed at random; includes an excellent annotated bibliography.

Shannon, Claude, and Warren Weaver. *The Mathematical Theory of Communications.*
Univ. of Illinois Pr. 1963 pap. $6.95. A classic work that founded information
theory and introduced the terms *entropy* and *redundancy,* the basis of information handling not only in telecommunications and computers but also in linguistics, psychology, and DNA genetics. Nonmathematical readers will prefer to
read an introduction to Shannon, such as J. R. Peirce's *Symbols, Signals, and
Noise.*

Weizenbaum, Joseph. *Computer Power and Human Reason: From Judgment to Calculation.* W. H. Freeman 1976 text ed. pap. $13.95. Distressed that his experimen-
tal ELIZA program was taken as a serious attempt at psychological therapy,
Weizenbaum changed his views of the AI movement and wrote this powerful
critique on the dangers of artificial intelligence. A provocative book that is
required reading for anyone serious about computers.

Winograd, Terry. *Understanding Natural Language.* Academic Pr. 1972 $19.95. An
important and stimulating book that insists that language and language repre-
sentations cannot be separated from commonsense understandings of the ordinary world.

Winograd, Terry, and Fernando Flores. *Understanding Computers and Cognition.*
Ablex 1985 text ed. $24.95; Addison-Wesley 1987 pap. $12.95. A highly acclaimed recent work that argues that the AI movement has made the error of
pursuing the autonomous development of machine intelligence instead of developing artificial intelligence as an extension of natural human intelligence.

VIEWPOINTS AND INTERPRETATIONS
OF SOCIAL AND CULTURAL ISSUES

Beyond the technical questions they raise, changes in computer and information technology also pose several heated cultural and social issues. The
futurologists include Daniel Bell, Marshall McLuhan, John Naisbitt, and
Alvin Toffler, but the party of the past enlists David Burnham, Jacques
Ellul, Lewis Mumford, and Theodore Roszak. Analysts who have written
important works from the important middle ground include J. David
Bolter, Siegfried Giedion, Thomas S. Kuhn, and Sherry Turkle. Other books
in this section are on the arms race and national security, the belief in
automatic technological progress, computer literacy, cottage industry, defining technologies, failures in educational and home computing, the future of
computing, the information revolution, intellectual technology, the knowledge society, managerial surveillance, postindustrial society, the quality of
life, the social and cultural costs of information automation, social and
technological forecasting, threats of an informational "1984," threats to privacy and confidentiality, and unemployment and work issues.

Bell, Daniel. *Coming of Post-Industrial Society: A Venture in Social Forecasting.* Basic
    Bks. 1976 pap. $12.95. An essential book, a "venture in social forecasting" that
    sees the decline of corporate capitalism and the rise of a post-Marxist "knowl-
    edge society" where the new "intellectual technology" achieves "the codification
    of theoretic knowledge." As this society (using computers as its main tool)
    makes work more complex, more organized, and more impersonal, it separates
    itself further and further from personal intuition, moral and religious values,
    and the emerging sanctification of self in new forms of private culture.

Bolter, J. David. *Turing's Man: Western Culture in the Computer Age.* Univ. of North
    Carolina Pr. 1984 pap. $8.95. A major interpretation, by a classicist who is also a
    computer scientist, of the intellectual and philosophical impact of the computer
    on ways of thinking about basic concepts of time, memory, quantity, creativity,
    and intelligence. Each civilization tends to define itself by one technological
    image: Once it was the loom, the clock, and the steam engine, and now it is the
    computer.

Burnham, David. *The Rise of the Computer State.* Fwd. by Walter Cronkite, Random
    1983 $17.95. An investigative reporter discusses the threats to privacy and per-
    sonal liberty from the misuse and abuse of information in the data banks of
    telephone companies, credit checking services, the FBI, the IRS, the Social
    Security administration, and various police departments. Two shockers in
    Burnham's book: the National Security Agency (NSA) is the world's largest
    computer user, and professional and legal confidentiality are easily eroded by
    data technicians who are indifferent to professional and legal restraints.

Calder, Nigel. *1984 and Beyond: Into the 21st Century.* Viking 1984 $14.95. Fascinat-
    ing postscripts, two decades later, on computer and other technological predic-
    tions, originally made by contributors to Calder's symposium, *The World in
    1984* (published in 1964). All is told through an imaginary dialogue with a
    supercomputer named O'Brien (after George Orwell's villain in *1984*).

Ellul, Jacques. *The Technological Society.* Random 1967 pap. $4.95. The book that is
    the starting point for much criticism of modern technology and its negative
    impact on human culture and society.

Friedrichs, Guenter, and Adam Schaff, eds. *Microelectronics and Society: For Better or for Worse; a Report to the Club of Rome*. Pergamon 1982 $39.00 pap. $9.95. One of a series of reports to the international planning and advisory body known as the Club of Rome, with eleven contributions on technology, enterprise, the environment, the Third World, and information technology.

Giedion, Siegfried. *Mechanization Takes Command: A Contribution to Anonymous History*. Norton 1969 pap. $15.95; Oxford 1948 $25.00. "An approach to technology as culture. A training of perception in culture and technology" (Marshall McLuhan). A classic work on the historical, cultural, and social impact of mechanization on the factory, farm, and household since 1800.

Kuhn, Thomas S. *Structure of Scientific Revolutions*. [*Foundations of the Unity of Science Ser.*] Univ. of Chicago Pr. 2d ed. 1970 $17.50 pap. $6.95. A landmark work that demolishes the empiricist view of the history of science and argues that science leaps from one conceptual realm to another as new paradigms replace the old. Should be read as a warning that paradigms of increasing technological complexity may convey as much temporary fashion as permanent truth.

McLuhan, Marshall. *Gutenberg Galaxy: The Making of Typographic Man*. NAL 1969 o.p. Technological optimism that electronic information will be open, auditory, parallel, social, and global, replacing print information in books that has been closed, visual, serial, individual, and restrictive. An influential book.

Meadows, Donella H., and others. *The Limits to Growth: A Report for the Club of Rome's Project on the Predicament of Mankind*. Universe 2d ed. 1974 $10.00 pap. $5.00. The first of a series of important reports to the Club of Rome on the global and economic consequences of technological development and the distribution of finite resources.

Muller, Herbert J. *The Children of Frankenstein: A Primer on Modern Technology and Human Values*. Indiana Univ. Pr. 1970 o.p. A humanist approach to problems of technology in society and culture that acknowledges its starting point in previous works by Lewis Mumford and Jacques Ellul.

Mumford, Lewis. *Technics and Civilization*. Harcourt 1963 pap. $8.95; Peter Smith 1984 $16.75. The first important treatment in English of the history of machines and their impact on culture and society.

Naisbitt, John. *Megatrends: Ten New Directions Transforming Our Lives*. Warner Bks. 6th ed. 1983 $17.00 pap. $4.50. A successful corporation consultant looks at the states of California, Florida, Washington, Colorado, and Connecticut, and makes sweeping forecasts about the information society, high technology, political decentralization, a multiple-option culture, self-help, and other trends.

Nora, Simon, and Alain Minc. *The Computerization of Society: A Report to the President of France*. Intro. by Daniel Bell, MIT 1980 pap. $6.95. A report to the president of France revealing the special role information technology is playing in national planning in Europe.

Reinecke, Ian. *Electronic Illusions: A Skeptic's View of Our High-Tech Future*. Penguin 1984 $7.95. Reinecke, a professional technical editor, warns us against excessive confidence in computers and the technology of telephones, television, satellites, office work, schools, factories, and the information industry–pointing out that instead of salary increases we have gotten more managerial control and surveillance, unemployment, and the myth of automatic technocratic progress.

Roszak, Theodore. *The Cult of Information: The Folklore of Computers and the True Art of Thinking*. Pantheon 1986 $17.45 1987 pap. $7.95. This debunking book by the author of *The Making of a Counter Culture* (Doubleday o.p.) notes that we may be facing an information glut, the menace of hidden agendas in computer literacy programs, and dangerous data banks that can curtail our civil liberties. One of the best antidotes to overly optimistic books about the future of computing.

Simons, Geoff. *Computer Bits and Pieces: A Compendium of Curiosities*. Penguin 1985 pap. $5.95. Behind the humor and entertainment, a serious warning about the impact of intelligent machines on human life.

Toffler, Alvin. *The Third Wave*. Bantam 1981 pap. $4.95; Morrow 1980 $14.95. A sweeping forecast in the manner of Marshall McLuhan and Daniel Bell, seeing a global postindustrial information revolution and explosion. Toffler believes we will see a new human personality in the future "psycho-sphere," a new society centered around the "electronic cottage," and unique but appropriate patterns of culture.

Turkle, Sherry. *Second Self: Computers and the Human Spirit*. Simon & Schuster 1984 $17.95 1985 pap. $8.95. A remarkable and original book that applies six years of sociological and psychological research, as well as the principles of Jean Piaget and Sigmund Freud, to the question of what children, adolescents, adult beginners, and professionals feel about computers—and what they feel about themselves while using computers. The result, the notion of a "second self" or an extension of identity, is an important contribution to our understanding of what computer technology means to human personality and culture.

BIOGRAPHICAL AND HISTORICAL BIBLIOGRAPHY

The history of computing is often traced to the scientists and philosophers of the seventeenth century—to John Napier (1550–1617), who built logarithmic "bones" in 1617, to BLAISE PASCAL (1623–62) (see Vol. 4), who built the first workable calculating machine in 1643, to GOTTFRIED WILHELM VON LEIBNIZ (see Vol. 4), who improved Pascal's design and made a multiple-purpose calculating machine in 1694. The modern computer era actually begins with Charles Babbage (1791–1871), who designed and attempted to build a difference engine and an analytic engine in the mid-nineteenth century. Babbage's associate, Ada, Countess of Lovelace (1815–52), the daughter of Lord Byron, is sometimes called the world's first programmer. The nineteenth-century mathematician George Boole (1815–64) invented a new form of logic that broke with Aristotelian syllogisms and reduced statements to true or not-true states. In 1890, Herman Hollerith (1860–1929) designed for the U.S. census a machine that borrowed the punch-card design of the old Jacquard loom controllers; from Hollerith's company emerged the first manifestation of IBM.

In the 1930s Alan Turing (1912–54) contributed a design and a concept that have come to be known, respectively, as the Turing Machine and the Turing Test; the former provides a scheme of controlling and accessing data, and the latter proposes a method to know when machines can be said to think. The need for high-speed and complex computations stimulated the growth of electronic computers in the 1940s. The mathematician John von Neumann (1903–57) proposed what has come to be known as "Von Neumann architecture," a computer flexibly storing its own program in memory along with its data, not merely wired to do one task alone. Von Neumann, who did some of the computations for the original atom bomb tests, was also interested in analogies (and the lack of analogies), between computers and the human brain, in game theory, and in self-reproducing automata. At the same time Norbert Wiener (1894–1964), developing a computer program to direct anti-aircraft fire by means of continuous feedback corrections, invented the field known as cybernetics. During the same decade Claude Shannon (1916–   ), working with Boolean logic, developed information theory based on binary instead of digital values as the simplest form of guaranteed transmission along noisy lines, using the idea of individual bits with only two states, on and off, grouped into bytes. Since the 1970s, two companies have been prominent in the production of personal computers, Apple and IBM. The stories of many important figures remain to be told, but we can learn of Buck Rodgers's account of his years at IBM, of the founding of Apple in part by Steve Jobs and of John Sculley's displacement of him as head of that company. Other tales of heroes, hackers, programmers, and investors have come to be part of the legends of computing.

General Accounts

Carlston, Douglas G. *Software People: Inside the Computer Business.* Prentice-Hall 1986 pap. $9.95. Accounts of hackers, programmers, entrepreneurs, venture capitalists, and others who made major contributions to computer software as we know it today.

DeLamarter, Richard T. *Big Blue: IBM's Use and Abuse of Power.* Dodd 1986 $22.95. The dust jacket: "The Truth About IBM's Success and the Ominous Implications of Its Stranglehold on the Information Society." DeLamarter's accusations that IBM displays poor management, makes inferior products, frustrates its clients, and is ruthless to its competitors stem from his eight years of research as senior economist for the Justice Department in its antitrust suit against IBM, which was finally dismissed by the Reagan administration in 1982.

Fishman, K. D. *The Computer Establishment.* McGraw-Hill 1982 pap. $7.95. Well-researched, well-documented, and well-written history, largely of IBM. Portions first appeared in the *Atlantic Monthly;* the paperback edition has a postscript on the IBM antitrust suit.

Fjermedal, Grant. *The Tomorrow Makers: A Brave New World of Living-Brain Machines.* Macmillan 1987 $16.95. A euphoric panorama of the near future of artificial intelligence, based on interviews with pioneers working at the frontiers of the field and on in-depth profiles of their progress and projected success.

Freiberger, Paul, and Michael Swaine. *Fire in the Valley: The Making of the Personal Computer.* Osborne/McGraw 1984 pap. $11.95. The people and the events in the personal computer revolution, told entertainingly.

Gassée, Jean-Louis. *The Third Apple: Personal Computers and the Cultural Revolution.* Harcourt 1987 $14.95. A French view of the personal computer and its cultural revolution by a former European executive for Apple computers who counts Eve's and Newton's as apples one and two.

Lammers, Susan, ed. *Programmers at Work.* Microsoft 1986 $19.95 pap. $14.95. In interviews, 19 prominent programmers describe how they work, how well-known programs were developed, and what they see for the future.

Langley, Patrick, and Jan M. Zytkow. *Scientific Discovery: Computational Explorations of the Creative Processes.* MIT 1987 text ed. $25.00 pap. $9.95. A remarkable synthesis of philosophy, computer science, and the history of science into a computational model for the process of scientific discovery. By applying information processing technology, data-driven models simulate the scientific discoveries of Roger Bacon, John Dalton, Johann Rudolf Glauber, and Georg Ernst Stahl.

Levy, Steven. *Hackers: Heroes of the Computer Revolution.* Dell 1985 pap. $4.50; Doubleday 1984 $17.95. A highly readable account of the computer "whiz kids," hardware freaks, and games addicts, along with their adventures and misadventures with Ma Bell, Uncle Sam, and the Fortune 500.

Metropolis, N., ed. *A History of Computing in the Twentieth Century.* Academic Pr. 1980 $39.50. Actually a collection of papers by 39 eminent persons in the world of computing, originally presented at an international conference at Los Alamos in 1976.

Rodgers, Buck, and Robert Shook. *The IBM Way: Insights into the World's Most Successful Marketing Organization.* Harper 1986 $17.45 1987 pap. $8.95. Rodgers, who was at IBM from 1950 to 1984, reveals IBM's approach to marketing theory, employee relations, and corporate attitudes in this bestselling book for company managers.

Biographies

Austrian, Geoffrey D. *Herman Hollerith: Forgotten Giant of Information Processing.* Columbia Univ. Pr. 1982 $30.00 1985 pap. $15.50. A well-researched study by an employee of IBM who acquired access to the Hollerith family papers.

Babbage, Henry Prevost. *Babbage's Calculating Engines.* Tomash repr. of 1889 ed. 1983 $55.00. A modern reprint of a classic collection of papers by Charles Babbage, designer of the difference engine and the analytical engine, Victorian forerunners of the modern computer; first issued in 1889.

Baum, Joan. *The Calculating Passion of Ada Byron.* Shoe String 1986 $21.50. A recent biography of the Countess of Lovelace, who was perhaps the first thinker to insist that computers can do nothing except what they are instructed to do.

Butcher, Lee. *Accidental Millionaire: The Rise and Fall of Steve Jobs at Apple Computer.* Paragon 1987 $19.95. How Steve Jobs, the most improbable of all corporate executives, became a millionaire out of what he developed in his parents' garage, and how he left Apple Computer after a collision with its new head, John C. Sculley.

Buxton, H. W. *Memoir of the Life and Labours of the Late Charles Babbage Esq., F.R.S.* Intro. by Anthony Hyman, MIT 1987 text ed. $50.00. This classic biography has been reprinted under the editorship of Anthony Hyman.

Heims, Steve V. *John Von Neumann and Norbert Wiener: From Mathematics to the Technologies of Life and Death.* MIT 1980 pap. $11.95. The only book available that focuses on von Neumann—and the only one that also focuses on Norbert Wiener.

Hodges, Andrew. *Alan Turing: The Enigma.* Simon & Schuster 1983 $24.95 1984 pap. $10.95. A remarkable biography written with scientific understanding of the state of mathematics and logic during Turing's era, with drama for the tale of Turing's contributions to breaking the German code in World War II, and with compassion for the personal dilemmas faced by Turing as a homosexual during an era of repressive legislation and medicine in England.

Hyman, Anthony. *Charles Babbage: Pioneer of the Computer.* Princeton Univ. Pr. 1982 $30.50 1984 pap. $9.95. A recent account of Babbage's life and times, with an appendix containing Babbage's published works.

Moore, Doris L. *Ada, Countess of Lovelace: Byron's Legitimate Daughter.* Harper 1977 o.p. One of the first biographies of Byron's daughter, said to be the world's first computer programmer.

Sculley, John, and John A. Byrne. *Odyssey: Pepsi to Apple.* Harper 1987 $19.45. The story of Sculley's departure from the Pepsi-Cola Company after his success there, his retargeting the Apple Computer company, his conflict with Apple cofounder Steve Jobs and the consequent departure of Jobs, and Sculley's views of the future of Apple.

Stein, Dorothy. *Ada: A Life and Legacy.* [*Ser. in the History of Computing*] MIT 1987 pap. $9.95. An account of Ada, Countess of Lovelace, associate of Charles Babbage, that dispels the myths attributed to her in popular biographies as an epoch-making mathematician and programmer, and assigns to her a more plausible role in the light of available historical evidence about her working with Babbage and views of her in the context of English society and culture of the early and middle nineteenth century.

CHAPTER 7

Astronomy and Space Science

Harry L. Shipman

Twinkle, twinkle little star,
How I wonder what you are.

—Jane Taylor, *Rhymes for the Nursery*

Thus from these forces, by other propositions which are also mathematical,
I deduce the motions of the planets, the comets, the moon, and the sea.

—Isaac Newton, *Principia*

Astronomy and space science involve deep questions that human beings have asked ever since an ancestor gazed at the star-strewn nighttime sky and started to wonder. Where did the universe come from? Where is it going? Where are we? What are the stars made of? What kinds of worlds are the planets and their satellites? The answers to these questions have revealed a magnificently varied universe. There are planets that are rockballs like the earth and there are planets like Saturn, a huge ball of gas, so rarefied that it would float in water if it could be enclosed in a huge plastic bag that would prevent it from dissolving. There are tiny neutron stars, where a cupful of star-stuff would weigh a hundred billion tons. There are black holes, where gravity is so strong that something that comes too close to one will be trapped forever. And there are huge, gossamer clusters of galaxies, stretching 300 million light years from one end to the other. A light beam that left one end of such an object at the same time that our ancestors first crawled out of the primeval slime would only now have finished its trip across the cluster.

For thousands of years, thinkers were content to simply describe the universe, carefully tracking the motions of stars and planets without attempting to understand what they are or why they move in the way that they do. However, in a great intellectual movement, which started half a millennium ago and has accelerated enormously in the twentieth century, astronomers have been able to understand the universe and its contents, to reason why it works in the way that it does. Newton (see also Vol. 4), in the preface to the *Principia* (quoted above), refers to his achievement in explaining the extraordinarily complex motions of heavenly bodies by appealing to the simple laws of motion, laws that only take one or two typewritten lines to write down in the language of mathematics. Georges Lemaitre, in Munitz's *Theories of the Universe*, refers to the search for the underlying simplicity in a complex cosmos, and also makes the distinction between initial conditions and the force laws that govern the subsequent interaction of matter.

Astronomers can ask and answer a number of questions about various types of cosmic objects. What is it? How does it work? How does it evolve? As astronomy improves and becomes more sophisticated, astronomers progress from answering the first question to answering the second and even the third. At the beginning of this century, for everything but planetary motion, astronomers were stuck on the first question, simply describing, rather than understanding, the cosmos. But improvements in the understanding of physics and the capacity to measure the radiation from faint stars have allowed astronomers to unravel how planets, stars, and even the entire universe come to be the way that they are. The ability to hurl telescopes above the atmosphere and to send automated probes to other planets in the solar system has tied astronomy in with the space program and has resulted in an explosive growth of the field since the late 1950s.

Astronomy covers a wide range of subdisciplines, many of which are closely tied to other branches of science. Astronomers who study the sun and the effects of the solar wind on magnetized plasmas are basically plasma physicists who use the universe as a cosmic laboratory. Planetary scientists use insights from geology, geophysics, meteorology, and atmospheric chemistry in order to figure out how other planets work. And beyond the solar system, the astronomer or astrophysicist (there is no longer any real distinction between the two terms) applies the laws of physics on a cosmic scale. Space science, too, has become extraordinarily diverse, as scientists in many fields realize the different ways in which they can use the unique environment or vantage point that an orbiting laboratory provides. Some space scientists are astronomers who use planetary probes and telescopes orbiting above the atmosphere to measure the full extent of the electromagnetic spectrum. Others are oceanographers and earth scientists, who use the unique, orbital vantage point to make large-scale studies of our planet that are impossible from the ground. Still others are life scientists, who use the unique space environment and its absence of effective gravity to investigate the way in which humans and other organisms adapt to it. Materials scientists use space as a laboratory to investigate how fluids flow and solidify in the absence of gravity.

Astronomy appeals to the general public in a way that few other sciences do. Perhaps it is because anyone can look at what astronomers study by simply looking up on a clear night, in contrast to exotic chemicals that remain buried in laboratory sub-basements. Perhaps it is an innate human curiosity to explore further, to go where no human has gone before. In any event, there are a large number of popular books about various aspects of astronomy and the space program, which provide a solid supplement to the more visible aspects of astronomy popularization that appear in the broadcast media.

The nature of scientific research is such that many of the most important figures in a discipline make their contributions in the form of journal articles or in the form of books using so much jargon and mathematics that only specialists find them accessible. Consequently the astronomers and space scientists who are listed below cannot be regarded as a list of the "top" people of all time, because many of the top people did not write books. Some of the scientists listed in this section are world-class scientists who wrote a few accessible books or had a book written about them (for example, Copernicus, Halley, Herschel, and Hubble). Some scientists write more actively for nonspecialized audiences (e.g., Eddington and Gamow). A few people are listed here because of their role as popularizers of astronomy or space science (e.g., Patrick Moore).

As an indication of the limitations of this list of people, consider some figures who are not listed here because they did not write appropriate books. For example, Konstantin Tsiolkovsky (1857–1935), Robert H. Goddard (1882–1945), and Hermann Oberth (1894–   ), the three great rocket pioneers, are left out. Astronomers who have been omitted include the likes of George Ellery Hale (1868–1938), who pioneered the development of large telescopes, and Jan Oort (1900–   ), who discovered where comets come from and the rotation of the Milky Way Galaxy. Walter Adams (1876–1956) and Henry Norris Russell (1877–1957), who developed the use of spectroscopy to decode the temperature and composition of stars, are left out, but Cecilia Payne-Gaposhkin (1900–1979), involved in the same work and of comparable stature in the field, can be, and is, listed because several of her books are in print (see main entry in this chapter).

REFERENCE AND GENERAL BOOKS

A number of different types of books can provide a general overview of astronomy. Most accessible are those addressed exclusively to the general reader; these are often full of beautiful pictures, but they may not be absolutely comprehensive. A second type is the textbook. While a few are full of equations, most introductory texts are written for liberal arts students at the college level. These books generally have an absolute minimum of equations, and cover the field comprehensively. A third type of book is the handbook, which is a list of numbers and other pertinent astronomical data. While it is primarily serious students or professional scientists who use these, they are quite well indexed so that anyone can find a number or two in them.

Abell, George O. *Realm of the Universe*. Henry Holt 3d ed. 1984 $29.95; Saunders 3d ed. 1984 text ed. pap. $28.95. One of many college astronomy texts addressed to the nonscientist, it is comprehensive and nonmathematical.

Allen, Clarence W. *Astrophysical Quantities*. Longwood 1976 text ed. $65.00. This is the professional and amateur astronomers' guide to what's what in the cosmos. Lots of numbers.

Allen, Richard H. *Star Names: Their Lore and Meaning*. Dover rev. ed. 1963 pap. $7.95; Peter Smith 1963 $16.00. Star names are rooted deep in history, and this classic reference is a lovely source of information about their origins.

Annual Review of Astronomy and Astrophysics. Annual Reviews 1985 $44.00. Written for scientists, this series provides authoritative reviews of current research.

Asimov, Isaac. *The Universe: From Flat Earth to Quasar*. Avon 1976 pap. $3.95; Walker 1980 $15.95. A comprehensive survey, clear, entertaining, and accurate, as Asimov always is.

Audouze, Jean, and Guy Israel, eds. *The Cambridge Atlas of Astronomy*. Cambridge Univ. Pr. 1985 $75.00. "Imagine an accurate and lucid introductory astronomy text having a team of at least 26 competent authors and an apparently unlimited budget for color illustrations. If this sounds appealing, in fact it is" (*Sky and Telescope*).

Cornell, James, and Alan P. Lightman, eds. *Revealing the Universe: Prediction and Proof in Astronomy*. MIT 1981 pap. $8.95. In each chapter, a particular topic is addressed by an experimentalist, who in astronomy generally measures the amount, location, type, and variability of light and other forms of radiation from an object, and by a theorist who interprets what the experimentalist has found and suggests new, critical measurements to make. While not a comprehensive review, this book provides a good feeling for how astronomy is conducted.

Culver, Roger B., and Philip Ianna. *The Gemini Syndrome: Star Wars of the Oldest Kind*. [*Astronomy Quarterly Lib.*] Pachart 1979 $11.95; Prometheus Bks. repr. of 1979 ed. 1984 $18.95 pap. $11.95. The most comprehensive of a small number of books demonstrating that astrology just simply does not work.

Ferris, Timothy. *Spaceshots: The Beauty of Nature Beyond Earth*. Pantheon 1984 $24.45. Spectacular pictures, beautifully selected.

Fraknoi, Andrew. *Resource Book for the Teaching of Astronomy*. Freeman 1977 $6.50. While it was originally written as an instructor's manual for a particular textbook, this book has a number of suggestions for teachers, practical suggestions on audiovisual aids, and excellent references.

Friedman, Herbert. *The Amazing Universe*. [*Special Publications Ser.*] National Geographic Society 1975 $7.95 lib. bdg. $9.50. Although a bit dated, this short, well-illustrated survey of astronomy is an excellent introduction.

Ginzburg, Vitalii L. *Physics and Astrophysics: A Selection of Key Problems*. Pergamon 1985 $23.50 pap. $12.50. A well-known Russian astrophysicist reviews unanswered questions, summarizing each briefly, authoritatively, and largely nonmathematically.

Hartmann, William K. *Astronomy: The Cosmic Journey*. Wadsworth 1978 text ed. $24.95. Text for nonscientists; comprehensive and nonmathematical.

Hopkins, Jeanne, ed. *Glossary of Astronomy and Astrophysics*. Univ. of Chicago Pr. rev. ed. 1980 lib. bdg $19.00 2d ed. rev. & enl. 1982 pap. $10.00. The book to consult for definitions of astronomical jargon.

Illingworth, Valerie, ed. *Facts on File Dictionary of Astronomy*. Facts on File rev. ed. 1986 $19.95. A dictionary of astronomical terms that is, apparently, addressed more toward a lay audience than Hopkins's *Glossary*.

Jastrow, Robert. *Red Giants and White Dwarfs*. Norton 1979 $14.95; Warner Bks. 1980 pap. $3.95. Short, breezy, not too deep, but well-written overview.

Kaufmann, William J. *Universe*. Freeman 1985 $32.95. College text for nonscientists.

Lampton, Christopher. *Space Sciences*. [*Reference First Bk.*] Watts 1983 $9.40. A brief summary.

Lang, Kenneth R. *Astrophysical Formulae: A Compendium for the Physicist and Astrophysicist*. Springer-Verlag 1980 pap. $36.95. A handbook for scientists.

Lewis, Richard S., ed. *The Illustrated Encyclopedia of the Universe: Understanding and Exploring the Cosmos*. Crown $24.95. Profusely illustrated, authoritative, and comprehensive, this encyclopedia covers everything from the solar system to distant galaxies, including a brief section on the space program.

McGraw-Hill Encyclopedia of Astronomy. McGraw-Hill 1983 $54.50. Many short arti-

cles by professionals; a good complement to the other encyclopedias listed here
that have a smaller number of longer articles.

Malin, David, and Paul Murdin. *Colours of the Stars*. Cambridge Univ. Pr. 1984
$29.95. Spectacular color pictures and an excellent discussion of what makes
stars colored and how these colors can be represented in a reasonably accurate
manner.

Moche, Dinah L. *Astronomy: A Self-Teaching Guide*. [*Self-Teaching Guide Ser.*] Wiley
2d ed. 1981 text ed. pap. $9.95. A textbook for nonscientists with a self-directed
approach.

Moore, Patrick. *The New Atlas of the Universe*. Crown 2d ed. rev. 1984 $40.00. Spec-
tacular photos of space shuttles, satellites, stars, and galaxies tied together with
some brief text, more extensive than figure captions but much skimpier than a
basic text on the subject.

Morrison, Philip, and others. *Powers of Ten: About the Relative Size of Things in the
Universe*. [*Scientific Amer. Lib.*] Freeman 1982 $29.95 1985 pap. $19.95. A magnificently illustrated journey that starts with a picnic on the shores of Lake
Michigan and moves away from the earth to reveal the scope of the whole
universe, and then moves inward to show matter on the smallest scale. The
movie that this book is based on is an absolute classic.

Pasachoff, Jay M. *Astronomy: From the Earth to the Universe*. Saunders 2d ed. 1983
text ed. pap. $28.95. College text for nonscientists.

Robinson, J. Hedley, and James Muirden. *Astronomy Data Book*. Halsted Pr. 2d ed.
1979 $34.95. For amateur astronomers and general audiences.

Sagan, Carl. *Cosmos*. Ballantine 1985 pap. $4.95. Covers everything; breezy, well
written, and well illustrated; based on a very popular series on the Public
Broadcasting System.

Shu, Frank H. *The Physical Universe*. [*Astronomy Ser.*] Univ. Science Bks. 1982 text
ed. $36.00. For those who know basic physics and can handle algebra, this
textbook, a comprehensive survey of astronomy, is "becoming the book of
choice" (*Mercury*).

Snow, Theodore P. *The Cosmic Cycle*. Darwin Pr. 1984 $19.95. A very brief text that
is supplemented by some excellent, well-selected pictures and a short overview
of the universe.

——. *The Dynamic Universe: An Introduction to Astronomy*. West Pub. 2d ed. 1985
text ed. $35.95. College text for nonscientists.

Wagoner, Robert, and Donald Goldsmith. *Cosmic Horizons: Understanding the Universe*. Freeman 1982 $22.95 pap. $11.95. Wagoner and Goldsmith, in the course
of describing what we know about the evolution of the universe, also focus on
the way in which we have obtained this information; how the combination of
astronomical observations, laboratory experiments, and logical and mathematical reasoning has enabled us to understand how the universe came to be the
way that it is.

Zeilik, Michael. *Astronomy: The Evolving Universe*. Harper 4th ed. 1985 text ed.
$31.50. College text for nonscientists.

Zombeck, Martin V. *Handbook of Space Astronomy and Astrophysics*. Cambridge
Univ. Pr. 1983 $29.95. Virtually any astronomical number you ever wanted to
know about the universe.

TELESCOPES, TECHNIQUES, ASTRONOMERS, AND HISTORY

This section includes a number of books that describe what astronomers do and what they did in the past. Astronomy has a rich history, extending even before the time of writing, where ancient monuments are mute testimony to the enduring interest of humanity in the heavens. Some histories focus on particular figures; many such books can be found in the biographical section of this chapter. Others focus on pieces of equipment like telescopes. Autobiographies such as Clayton's and Cohen's can give someone who is thinking about a career in astronomy some idea of what it is like.

Asimov, Isaac. *Eyes on the Universe: A History of the Telescope.* Houghton Mifflin 1975 $8.95. Asimov's fascination for history comes through in a book that covers everything from the first Greek observations of the sky to the Space Telescope, scheduled for launch in the mid-1980s, after this book was completed.

Bauer, Henry H. *Beyond Velikovsky: The History of a Public Controversy.* Univ. of Illinois Pr. 1984 $21.95. Thirty years ago Immanuel Velikovsky made some fantastic claims about the history of the solar system, visualizing it as a gigantic pool table in which, for example, Venus nearly missed colliding with the earth in biblical times. Bauer makes no bones about dismissing this explanation as "nonsense," but "he also has some unkind, and perhaps unfair, words for some of Velikovsky's critics. Participants in and observers of the quarter-century-long Velikovsky controversy will find plenty to agree and disagree with here" (*Skeptical Inquirer*).

Clayton, Donald D. *The Dark Night Sky: A Personal Adventure in Cosmology.* Times Bks. 1975 o.p. An autobiography that illustrates what it is like to be a working astronomer.

Cohen, Martin. *In Quest of Telescopes.* Cambridge Univ. Pr. 1982 $13.95; Sky Publishing 1980 $13.95. In contrast to Clayton, who analyzes data collected by other people, Cohen is an observational astronomer.

Edge, David O., and Michael J. Mulkay. *Astronomy Transformed: The Emergence of Radio Astronomy in Britain.* [*Science, Culture and Society Ser.*] Wiley 1976 o.p. Edge, a radio astronomer by training, collaborated with a sociologist in this study of the growth of radio astronomy after World War II. The sociological conclusions are fascinating.

Gingerich, Owen, ed. *Astrophysics and Twentieth-Century Astronomy to 1950: Part A.* [*General History of Astronomy Ser.*] Cambridge Univ. Pr. 1984 $32.50. A compendium that emphasizes the development of instrumentation and the construction of large observatories as well as the growth of scientific ideas. "It should help the general reader understand how current discovery emerges from its recent past.... It may be trite to say so, but even in science we must learn from history or suffer from it" (Jesse L. Greenstein, *Sky and Telescope*).

Goldsmith, Donald, ed. *Scientists Confront Velikovsky.* Cornell Univ. Pr. 1977 $19.95; Norton 1979 pap. $3.95. "Articles by leading scientists on the colliding worlds theory; the definitive reference book in this field" (*Mercury*).

Harwit, Martin. *Cosmic Discovery: The Search, Scope and Heritage of Astronomy.* Basic Bks. 1981 $26.50; MIT 1984 pap. $9.95. A provocative account of the way in which astronomical research is conducted. It uses the historical record in an attempt to provide suggestions for the training of future astronomers and the selection of future facilities.

Krupp, Edwin C. *Echoes of the Ancient Skies: The Astronomy of Lost Civilizations.* Harper 1983 $19.45; New Amer. Lib. 1984 pap. $8.95. The study of ancient monuments like Stonehenge, which functioned as an ancient observatory, and other cultural artifacts constitutes the newly emerging field of archaeoastronomy.

Lang, Kenneth, and Owen Gingerich, eds. *A Source Book in Astronomy and Astrophysics, 1900–1975.* Harvard Univ. Pr. 1979 $60.00. Scientific results are generally first published as articles rather than books; this book reprints 132 important articles.

Lovell, Bernard. *The Jodrell Bank Telescopes.* Oxford Univ. Pr. 1985 $19.95. Lovell, who led the efforts to construct very large telescopes in Britain, provides an insider's view of a large project, and describes the challenges of constructing and financing the many different radio telescopes at the University of Manchester.

——. *Out of the Zenith: Jodrell Bank 1957–1970.* Harper 1974 o.p. A detailed account of the trials and tribulations of refurbishing the largest radio telescope of its time, and the discoveries made with it, often in collaboration with the Soviet Union.

Osterbrock, Donald E. *James E. Keeler, Pioneer American Astrophysicist: And the Early Development of American Astrophysics.* Cambridge Univ. Pr. 1985 $39.50. Keeler was one of the founders of astronomy and astrophysics in the United States.

Struve, Otto, and Velta Zebergs. *Astronomy of the Twentieth Century.* Macmillan 1962 $12.50. The astronomical discoveries of the first 60 years of the twentieth century and the personalities behind them.

ASTRONOMY WITHOUT INSTRUMENTS

Many books, including sky atlases and almanacs, are available to help identify objects seen without the aid of instruments in the nighttime sky. The motion of the moon and the planets is different from year to year, and an almanac provides information on their precise planetary positions. But to learn generally where a planet is, most books are updated often enough to offer current information. Note that some of these books are understandable by beginners (e.g., those by Moore, Ottewell, Pasachoff, Rey, and Whitney). Others (e.g., *Burnham's* and the more complex atlases and star catalogs) are useful to readers with some knowledge who want to learn more.

Budlong, John. *Shoreline and Sextant: Practical Coastline Navigation.* Van Nostrand 1977 $12.95. Many books on navigation treat it as an intellectual feat to be mastered in the most difficult way possible. Budlong's book is the one to consult to learn simply how to use the stars to find your way to port.

Burnham, Robert, Jr. *Burnham's Celestial Handbook: An Observer's Guide to the Universe Beyond the Solar System.* Dover 3 vols. 1979 ea. $9.95–$12.95. A comprehensive guide to what can be seen in the sky with a telescope. Not for beginners.

Covington, M. A. *Astrophotography for the Amateur.* Cambridge Univ. Pr. 1985 $24.95. Practical advice for taking pictures of the night sky.

Hirshfeld, Alan, and Roger W. Sinnott, eds. *Sky Catalogue 2000.* Cambridge Univ. Pr. 2 vols. 1982–1985 ea. $49.50-$52.50 pap. ea. $29.95–$32.50; Sky Pub. 2 vols. 1982–1983 ea. $49.95 pap. ea. $29.95. A list of all the bright stars and their properties, along with some explanation.

Moore, Patrick. *New Guide to the Stars.* Norton 1974 o.p. A nice combination of some chapters on "what's in the sky?" and some chapters that go beyond the naming of stars, discussing the basic nature of stars, galaxies, quasars, pulsars, and so on.

Muirden, James. *Astronomy with Binoculars.* Arco repr. 1983 pap. $7.95; Crowell 1979 $13.45. How to enjoy looking at the sky without spending a fortune on a telescope.

Norton, Arthur P., and J. Gall Inglis. *Norton's Star Atlas.* Sky Pub. repr. of 1919 ed. 1978 $24.95. A brief, compact atlas showing all the stars visible to the unaided eye, along with a number of deep-sky objects. This is the standard reference for visual observing, and has gone through 15 editions since its initial publication in 1910.

Ottewell, Guy. *Astronomical Calendar.* Astron. Wkshp. Published annually. pap. $12.00. Magnificently illustrated.

Pasachoff, Jay M., and Donald Menzel. *A Field Guide to the Stars and Planets.* [*Peterson Field Guide Ser.*] Houghton Mifflin 1983 $17.95 pap. $12.95. Introducing the sky to the beginner, this comprehensive, detailed guide, profusely illustrated in the spirit of the Peterson Field Guide series, is a good place to start learning about what is in the sky.

Rey, H. A. *The Stars: A New Way to See Them.* Houghton Mifflin 1976 pap. $8.95. Rey has ingeniously managed to draw lines between the stars to make most of the constellations look like their names.

Sherrod, P. Clay. *A Complete Manual of Amateur Astronomy: Tools and Techniques for Astronomical Observations.* Prentice-Hall 1981 $12.95. "The tools and techniques needed to make meaningful astronomical observations. Filled with useful tables, charts, references, addresses, and observing hints, it is an essential book for every serious amateur" (*Mercury*).

Tirion, Wil. *Sky Atlas 2000: Twenty-six Star Charts Covering Both Hemispheres.* Cambridge Univ. Pr. 1981 $39.50. One of the best and most attractive of the sky maps available, but a bit bulky to take at night just to pick out the constellations.

Whitney, Charles A. *Whitney's Star Finder.* Knopf 4th ed. 1985 $12.95. The title is a misnomer; there is very little about finding stars, but a lot of useful hints about where the moon is and how to recognize a planet when you are staring at one.

THE PLANETS AND THE SOLAR SYSTEM

Before the space age, scientists knew very little about the planets in their solar system. The many moons of Jupiter and Saturn were just dots with names; except for Mars, the other planets were cloud-enshrouded mysteries. One of the most spectacular, and visually exciting, results of the space program has been a series of missions that have at least flown by most of the planets in the solar system. By 1989, only Pluto will remain unprobed. Many planetary scientists are excellent writers, and a number of good introductory books are available.

Asimov, Isaac. *Mars: The Red Planet.* Lothrop 1977 $12.88. In a largely historical treatment of what we know about this enigmatic near neighbor, Asimov primarily recounts our knowledge from earth-based observations and includes a final chapter on the results from the Viking mission, which landed on Mars in 1976.

Beatty, J. Kelly, Brian O'Leary, and Andrew Chaikin, eds. *The New Solar System.* Sky Pub. 2d ed. 1982 $24.95 pap. $13.95. Twenty well-illustrated chapters on various aspects of solar system astronomy written by leading specialists in the field.

"This is *the* book to have if you want to find out what we know about the solar system" (*Mercury*).

Brown, Peter L. *Comets, Meteorites, and Men.* Taplinger 1974 o.p. An excellent source of anecdotes and comet lore.

Burgess, Eric. *Mars: The Red Planet.* Columbia Univ. Pr. o.p. An account of the Viking mission to Mars in 1976 and its predecessors.

———. *Venus, An Errant Twin.* Columbia Univ. Pr. 1985 $29.95. A mostly historical account of Venus, organized around the various missions (mostly Russian) to this planet, which is similar to the earth in size, but is much hotter and different in its surface features.

Calder, Nigel. *The Comet Is Coming: The Feverish Legacy of Mr. Halley.* Penguin 1982 pap. $6.95. This first of a flotilla of books that greeted the virtually invisible comet on its 1985 passage includes many historical anecdotes.

Carr, Michael H. *The Surface of Mars.* [*Planetary Exploration Ser.*] Yale Univ. Pr. 1984 pap. $24.95. A full summary, with 150 photographs, of what has been learned about the geology of Mars from the probes that have orbited and landed on the planet.

Chapman, Clark R. *Planets of Rock and Ice: From Mercury to the Moons of Saturn.* Scribner 1982 $13.95. An active planetary scientist provides a comprehensive account of the planets in our solar system that are smaller than the earth. Among these small planets and satellites are some of the most unusual worlds in the solar system, such as Jupiter's satellite Io with its eight active volcanoes and Saturn's satellite Titan with its thick, nitrogen atmosphere and a surface that may have lakes of liquid methane.

Chapman, Robert D., and John C. Brandt. *The Comet Book: A Guide for the Return of Halley's Comet.* Jones & Bartlett 1984 $14.95. The 1985–1986 appearance of Halley's comet prompted the publication of many books on comets. For readers interested in comets in general, in contrast to Halley's comet specifically, this is a good introduction.

Cooper, Henry S. F., Jr. *Imaging Saturn: The Voyager Flights to Saturn.* Holt 1985 $8.95. Cooper's books, written in the inimitable, readable *The New Yorker* style, present an accurate, intriguing picture of scientists at work. Here, the focus is on people—the scientists' reactions when they saw the Saturn pictures for the first time, and the great sense of adventure felt by everyone involved in a dramatic space project like Voyager.

———. *Moon Rocks.* Dial 1970 o.p. Describes the work of various teams who sweated under deadlines to make the most of the moon rocks.

———. *The Search for Life on Mars.* Henry Holt 1980 $10.95 1981 pap. $6.95. The role of Carl Sagan, and others, in the Viking mission to Mars.

Dodd, Robert T. *Thunderstones and Shooting Stars: The Meaning of Meteorites.* Harvard Univ. Pr. 1986 $24.95. "Referring to meteorites as the 'poor man's space probe' because they are the only extraterrestrial rocks that can be collected without leaving earth, Dodd explains the scientific data that can be extracted from meteorites, including what effect they have had on the earth and what they can tell us about the solar system" (*Booklist*).

Gehrels, Tom, and Mildred S. Mathews. *Saturn.* Univ. of Arizona Pr. 1984 $37.50. A compendium of articles, for the specialist, that will be up-to-date for a long time to come.

Hartmann, William K. *Moons and Planets.* Wadsworth 2d ed. 1983 text ed. $43.25. Hartmann goes beyond the usual descriptive treatment of what other solar system bodies look like to provide some indication of why they look the way that they do.

Marsden, Brian. *Catalog of Cometary Orbits.* Enslow Pubs. 1983 text ed. pap. $11.95. A list of numbers that can tell you all about the orbit of your favorite comet.

Morrison, David. *Voyage to Jupiter.* [*NASA Space Ser.*] U.S. Government Printing Office 1980 pap. $9.00. A participant in the Voyager mission presents his account of the mission and what has been learned about the giant planets and their satellites.

Murray, Bruce, Michael C. Malin, and Ronald Greeley. *Earthlike Planets: Surfaces of Mercury, Venus, Earth, Moon, and Mars.* Freeman 1981 text ed. $33.95 pap. $17.95. One of a very few books that compares several planets and goes beyond a merely descriptive treatment to demonstrate what happened to make the surfaces of these planets so different.

Noyes, Robert W. *The Sun, Our Star.* Harvard Univ. Pr. 1982 $20.00. A very readable survey of our understanding of the sun, ranging from the old type of solar physics (counting sunspots) to the new (space observations).

Washburn, Mark. *Distant Encounters.* Harcourt 1983 o.p. A journalist's account of the Voyager missions to Jupiter and Saturn. The experience of a journalist trying to cover this mission along with a thousand other reporters crowding around the Jet Propulsion Laboratory is as intriguing to read about as is the encounter itself.

STARS AND GALAXIES

The space age has also produced a dramatic improvement in the understanding of the distant universe. Telescopes, which are hurled above the atmosphere, measure the radiation that is blocked by the earth's atmosphere. In addition, the improvements in electronic technology have allowed astronomers to use ground-based telescopes more efficiently and to build bigger ones. Books in this section focus on a few subfields of astronomy. An author who does not feel the need to be comprehensive can bring the reader to the frontiers of current research and convey the excitement of modern science.

Asimov, Isaac. *The Collapsing Universe: The Story of Black Holes.* Walker 1977 $14.95. Not just about black holes, this book includes an accurate, readable (as always) account of the life and death of stars.

———. *The Exploding Suns: Secrets of Supernovas.* Dutton 1985 $18.95; New Amer. Lib. 1986 pap. $4.50. The dean of American science writers starts with fourth-century Chinese observations of supernovas, the violent death throes of massive stars in which a massive star, previously too faint for the unaided eye to see, becomes so much brighter that it may be visible in daylight for months. Asimov presents modern ideas of the origin of these celestial explosions and speculates about their possible effects on the solar system and on humanity.

———. *The Measure of the Universe.* Harper 1983 $15.34. Asimov starts with the human dimensions of various properties of cosmic objects—length, mass, speed, time, temperature, and so on—and leads readers, one step at a time, from familiar vistas to the unimaginably large and infinitesimally small.

———. *The Universe: From Flat Earth to Quasar.* Avon 1976 pap. $3.95. An excellent survey of astronomy.

Clark, David H. *The Quest for SS 433.* Penguin 1986 pap. $6.95; Viking 1985 $15.95. SS 433 is a very peculiar double star that ejects jets of matter traveling at more than one-quarter of the speed of light. This book tells the cosmic detective story, which led to the understanding of this object, with an only slightly exaggerated rendering of the excitement and drama of the chase.

Clark, David H., and F. Richard Stephenson. *The Historical Supernovae*. Pergamon 1977 text ed. $31.00 pap. $14.25. Chinese astronomers kept track of the sky and discovered a number of suddenly brightening "guest stars," at least some of which are now known to have been supernova explosions.

Disney, Michael. *The Hidden Universe*. Macmillan 1985 $17.95. It is likely that approximately 90 percent of the matter in the universe is invisible, and this book reviews what astronomers are doing to try to detect its existence directly.

Ferris, Timothy. *Galaxies*. Sierra 1980 $75.00; Stewart, Tabori & Chang repr. of 1980 ed. 1982 $27.50 pap. $16.95. This is not *just* a pretty picture book of galaxies, though the illustrations are its main feature. Ferris provides a lucid exposition of what is known about these huge star-swarms.

Greenstein, George. *Frozen Star*. Freundlich 1984 $16.95; New Amer. Lib. 1985 $8.95. A popular account of pulsars and black holes, two exotic types of stellar remnants. One of its strongest points is that Greenstein occasionally puts himself in the position of a journalist, describing not only scientific results, but what it is like to be a scientist as well, in very clear terms. The research careers of Stephen Hawking, Greenstein's faculty colleague Richard Huguenin, and Greenstein himself play a role in the book.

Kippenhahn, Rudolf. *One Hundred Billion Suns: The Birth, Life, and Death of the Stars*. Trans. by Jean Steinberg, Basic Bks. 1983 $25.00 1985 pap. $12.95. "We not only get the scientific record straight but also the priceless inside story and human history of those who brought about this intellectual achievement. . . [a] little masterpiece" (Dimitri Mihalas, *Sky and Telescope*).

Murdin, Paul, and Lesley Murdin. *Supernovae*. Cambridge Univ. Pr. 1985 $24.95. Historical and descriptive.

Shipman, Harry L. *Black Holes, Quasars, and the Universe*. Houghton Mifflin 2d ed. 1980 $18.95. This account of some selected areas of present research clearly separates current knowledge into fact, concrete theory, working model, and speculation. "An excellent account of the present status of astrophysical cosmology. . . . There is no nonsense in this book, and Mr. Shipman gives concise accounts of what is known and how it is known" (*The New Yorker*).

Shklovskii, Iosif S. *Stars: Their Birth, Life, and Death*. Trans. by Richard B. Rodman, Freeman 1978 text ed. $32.95. Readers who can handle a modest amount of mathematics will find this to be an excellent, comprehensive introduction to the life cycles of stars.

Spitzer, Lyman. *Searching Between the Stars*. [*Silliman Lectures Ser.*] Yale Univ. Pr. 1982 $32.00 1984 pap. $8.95. While it challenges the reader more than the typical bedtime book, this detailed, carefully reasoned account describes what is known about the wispy, tenuous gas that exists in the interstellar medium, the space between one star and another. When this gas condenses, it forms new stars and planets.

COSMOLOGY

Cosmology is the study of the entire universe and its origin. A hundred years ago, astronomers were little better off than the storytellers in primitive tribes whose myths are now so amusing. While scientists were beginning to understand how the universe worked, they had little or no idea where it came from. But the discovery of the expansion of the universe in the 1920s, followed by the accidental discovery of the echoes of the Big Bang (in the form of radio radiation that fills the universe) in 1965, were two high points in a very active field. Scientists now have access to a number of relevant facts which, if interpreted correctly, can reveal how the universe as a whole has evolved.

Because of the great human curiosity about the evolution of the universe, this subfield of astronomy has attracted a great deal of attention among science writers. Contemporary cosmology probably has the richest lay literature of any scientific subfield.

Barrow, John D., and Joseph Silk. *The Left Hand of Creation: Origin and Evolution of the Expanding Universe.* Basic Bks. 1983 text ed. $17.95 1986 pap. $7.95. A good, readable account of the astronomical cosmology.

Chaisson, Eric. *Cosmic Dawn: The Origins of Matter and Life.* Berkley Pub. 1984 pap. $3.95; Little, Brown 1981 $18.45. A very readable survey of cosmology, with a good treatment of biological and cultural evolution as well as the usual astronomy, but without detail and with less emphasis on the evidence that underlies our scientific belief in the Big Bang picture of cosmic evolution.

Cloud, Preston. *Cosmos, Earth and Man: A Short History of the Universe.* Yale Univ. Pr. 1978 $31.00 pap. $10.95. Geology, astronomy, and some evolutionary biology. The geology and biology is particularly strong.

Davies, Paul. *The Edge of Infinity.* Simon & Schuster 1983 pap. $7.95. Davies has written a large number of books on cosmology and particle physics, and there is considerable overlap between them. This one is a survey of cosmology.

Ferris, Timothy. *The Red Limit: The Search for the Edge of the Universe.* Bantam 1979 pap. $2.95; Morrow rev. ed. repr. of 1977 ed. 1983 pap. $9.70. The emphasis in this discussion of twentieth-century cosmology is on the history of the field and on the lives and achievements of those pioneering astronomers and physicists who developed scientific cosmology.

Harrison, Edward R. *Cosmology: The Science of the Universe.* Cambridge Univ. Pr. 1981 $34.50. A more or less standard treatment of Big Bang cosmology is expanded with discussions of the philosophical issues raised by modern cosmology: Where is the "center" of the universe? Does this term have any meaning? What are cosmic horizons?

———. *Masks of the Universe.* Macmillan 1985 $18.95 1986 pap. $9.95. A summary of the views of the universe held by different cultures. Any culture's view of the universe affects its philosophical, anthropological, and historical outlook on the human condition.

Islam, Jumal N. *The Ultimate Fate of the Universe.* Cambridge Univ. Pr. 1983 $15.95. If the universe expands forever, as seems to be indicated by the current evidence, then its general appearance will change as stars die out, galaxies collapse, and so on. The time scales are very long.

Jastrow, Robert. *God and the Astronomers.* Norton 1978 $9.95; Warner Bks. 1980 pap. $4.95. A good brief survey of cosmology, though despite the title there is rather little about the impact of modern cosmology on religion.

John, Laurie, ed. *Cosmology Now.* Taplinger 1976 $10.95. While this book is becoming a bit dated in this fast-moving field, this collection of essays by authorities is quite readable and a good introduction to cosmology in the mid-1970s.

Munitz, Milton K. *Theories of the Universe: From Babylonian Myth to Modern Science.*

Free Pr. 1965 pap. $10.95. A collection of short excerpts from a number of writings, primarily useful as a quick reference to various historical approaches to understanding the universe on a large scale.

Pagels, Heinz. *Perfect Symmetry: The Search for the Beginning of Time.* Bantam 1986 pap. $4.95; Simon & Schuster 1985 $18.95. The first few moments of creation can tell a lot about particle physics, the study of the fundamental nature of matter. Pagels writes very clearly about the very early evolution of the universe.

Reeves, Hubert. *Atoms of Silence: An Exploration of Cosmic Evolution.* Trans. by Ruth Lewis and John S. Lewis, MIT 1983 $14.95 1985 pap. $8.95. The cosmology is there, yes; but what makes this book special is Reeves's poetic approach. Reeves is a scientist, but he is also a human being who understands beauty, and this book conveys an appreciation of the beauty of the scientific view of the universe. His flowery prose retains its Gallic flavor in an excellent translation.

Trefil, James S. *The Moment of Creation: Big Bang Physics from Before the First Millisecond to the Present Universe.* Macmillan 1984 pap. $6.95; Scribner 1983 $15.95. An exciting development in the 1980s has been the use of elementary particle physics, the understanding of the fundamental forces of nature and the way that particles interact at very close distances, to probe what happened in the very early universe. While not an easy read, this book explains some very difficult concepts expertly and clearly.

———. *Space, Time, Infinity: The Smithsonian Views the Universe.* Pantheon 1985 $29.95. The Smithsonian's photo researchers have assembled one of the best sets of illustrations of the universe. Trefil's text weaves these pictures together and provides a comprehensive picture of the universe and efforts to understand it. A good overview of astronomy.

Weinberg, Steven. *The First Three Minutes: A Modern View of the Origin of the Universe.* Basic Bks. 1976 $14.95. Weinberg visualizes his reader as "a smart old attorney who does not speak *my* language, but who expects nonetheless to hear some convincing arguments before he makes up his mind." The details of classic Big Bang cosmology are presented here; the focus is not just on what people believe but on why they believe it scientifically. Because this book was written in the 1970s, it does not include an account of current speculations on the very early universe.

THE SPACE PROGRAM

On October 4, 1957, the world was astounded to hear beeping radio signals from an artificial satellite put into orbit by the Soviet Union. Since then astronauts, orbiting telescopes, spy satellites, communications satellites, and many other bits of orbiting hardware have been hurled into space atop flaming rockets. The impact of the space program on human culture is pervasive. Businesses, states like Alaska, and countries like Indonesia rely on space for their communications. The heroism of the space explorers, and the adventure of exploring the next frontier, are all a part of this human venture, a venture that has been compared to the Age of Discovery, the time when Columbus discovered America and Magellan sailed around the world.

Allen, Joseph P., and Russell Martin. *Entering Space: An Astronaut's Odyssey.* Stewart, Tabori & Chang rev. & enl. ed. 1985 $24.95 pap. $16.95. Astronaut Allen provides a lavishly illustrated account of his experiences in the Space Shuttle program, including Allen's own role in the mission of the Space Shuttle Discovery and the rescue of two satellites.

Cooper, Henry S. F., Jr. *Apollo on the Moon.* Dial 1969 o.p. Written before the first lunar landing, this is still "gracefully literate and offers a pleasant contrast to the technical jargon, the crackling voices and electronic beeps" of some other writers (Christopher Lehmann-Haupt, *N.Y. Times*).

————. *Thirteen: The Flight That Failed.* Dial 1973 o.p. "A near disaster in space is the theme of this readable account of Apollo 13's flight. . . . The account includes not only the astronauts but also the ground controllers and their differing concepts of the exciting events taking place" (*LJ*).

Cornell, James, and P. Gorenstein, eds. *Astronomy from Space: Sputnik to Space Telescope.* MIT 1983 $20.00 1985 pap. $8.95. A collection of articles by leading experts in the field, covering everything from planetary astronomy to space astronomy and beyond.

Gatland, Kenneth, and others. *The Illustrated Encyclopedia of Space Technology.* Ed. by Philipe de Ste. Croix, Harmony 1981 $24.95. Comprehensive, factual, and well illustrated, rather than critical or synthetic.

Grey, Jerry. *Beachheads in Space: A Blueprint for the Future.* Macmillan 1983 $14.95. Some of the predictions are quite visionary, so the word "blueprint" may be inappropriate, but this contribution by a knowledgeable participant in the space program offers some tantalizing possibilities of what might happen.

Hartmann, William K., Ron Miller, and Pamela Lee. *Out of the Cradle: Exploring the Frontiers Beyond Earth.* Workman 1984 $19.95 pap. $11.95. This magnificently illustrated visionary book shows what could, in principle, be done in space in the future. Not all these dreams will turn into reality, but some will.

Hecht, Jeff. *Beam Weapons: The Next Arms Race.* Plenum 1984 $17.95. A comprehensive, accurate, and balanced view of the technology behind the Strategic Defense Initiative (popularly called "Star Wars"), which may represent a significant step in the militarization of space.

Heppenheimer, T. A. *Colonies in Space.* Warner Bks. 1978 pap. $2.75. The proposal of establishing space colonies was quite popular in the late 1970s, and this well-illustrated book covers everything from space hardware to zero-g swimming pools.

Lewis, Richard S. *Appointment on the Moon: The Full Story of Americans in Space from Explorer One to the Lunar Landing and Beyond.* Viking rev. ed. 1969 o.p. This history of the Apollo program, written shortly after the first lunar landing in 1969, traces the turbulent history of the genesis of our space program.

————. *The Voyages of Apollo: The Exploration of the Moon.* Times Bks. 1974 o.p. Authoritative and complete.

McDougall, Walter A. *The Heavens and the Earth: A Political History of the Space Age.* Basic Bks. 1985 $25.95. "A narrative history of space activity, a political analysis of what caused Sputnik 1 and what Sputnik 1 caused, an exposition of the contradictions inherent in the Soviet socialist system and the American free enterprise system, and an essay on the eschatology of . . . the pursuit of power" (Alex Roland, *N.Y. Times Bk. Review*).

National Commission on Space. *Pioneering the Space Frontier.* Bantam 1986 pap. $14.95. A leading group of space scientists and engineers, largely working before the explosion of the Space Shuttle Challenger, developed an expansive vision of the future, placing humanity on Mars in the early part of the twenty-first century. This visionary, readable volume presents what could happen if the space program can recover from the effects of the Challenger tragedy.

Oberg, Alcestis R. *Spacefarers of the '80s and '90s: The Next Thousand People in Space.*

Columbia Univ. Pr. 1985 $24.95. Astronauts are a changing breed, ranging from the test pilots of the 1960s to the scientists, teachers, politicians, and journalists of the 1980s and 1990s. This book tells what it will take and what it will be like to be an astronaut in the future.

Oberg, James E. *Red Star in Orbit*. Random 1981 $16.95. This comprehensive and thoroughly researched history of the Soviet space program goes beyond the official press releases to penetrate the fog of disinformation that frustrates historians and writers.

O'Neill, Gerard K. *2081: A Hopeful View of the Human Future*. Simon & Schuster 1982 pap. $6.25. Largely drawing on O'Neill's concept of space colonies, this book describes a future era in which space technology plays a major role.

Presidential Commission on the Space Shuttle Challenger Accident. *Report to the President on the Space Shuttle Challenger Accident*. U.S. Government Printing Office 1986 $18.00. This report presents an unusually gripping, especially since it is a committee report, account of the tragic events of the morning of January 28, 1986, when the Space Shuttle Challenger exploded, the events that led up to it, and the committee's recommendations for future action.

Shapland, David, and Michael Rycroft. *Spacelab: Research in Earth Orbit*. Cambridge Univ. Pr. 1984 $22.50. The focus on one particular space mission means that the description of the space program is not particularly comprehensive, but even so, the wide range of human activities in space is described rather nicely in this account of a joint European-American mission.

Shipman, Harry L. *Space 2000: Meeting the Challenge of a New Era*. Plenum 1987 $19.95. This book focuses on what we do in space, not just on where we go, dealing with space activities that range from communications satellites to star wars, from space manufacturing to planetary exploration. It looks beyond the need to recover from the Challenger tragedy to explore what we could do in space in the early part of the next century.

Simpson, Theodore R., ed. *The Space Station: An Idea Whose Time Has Come*. Institute of Electrical & Electronic Engineers 1985 $19.95. A collection of essays by space station experts provides brief overviews of the historical background, the way that the space station decision was made, the likely uses of the station, and its long-term potential.

Stares, Paul B. *The Militarization of Space: U.S. Policy, 1945–1984*. Cornell Univ. Pr. 1985 text ed. $25.00. A comprehensive, authoritative description of the two superpowers' military space programs, including conclusions about past and future arms control negotiations.

Stine, G. Harry. *The Third Industrial Revolution*. Ace Bks. 1982 pap. $2.50. This visionary, speculative book is a good summary of the possibilities of manufacturing useful materials in space—but remember that the author is discussing possibilities and not certainties.

Von Braun, Wernher, and Frederick I. Ordway, III. *The History of Rocketry and Space Travel*. Crowell rev. ed. 1975 $29.45. "The coverage is international and ample, even exploring such fascinating side paths as science fiction and firecrackers" (*PW*).

Wolfe, Tom. *The Right Stuff*. Bantam 1984 pap. $4.50; Farrar 1983 $15.95. An informal, breezy, and very readable account of the space program, mostly concentrating on the period leading up to Apollo. In a way that few other writers have, Wolfe brings the Apollo generation of astronauts to life, superbly describing the heroism, the camaraderie, the tragedy, and many other human aspects of the space program.

THE SEARCH FOR EXTRATERRESTRIAL INTELLIGENCE

Philosophers have long speculated about the possibilities of life elsewhere. More recently, astronomers and a few biologists have reached the point where some estimates of the abundance of extraterrestrial life can be made. This whole field was greatly stimulated by an article by Giuseppe Cocconi and Philip Morrison that demonstrated, in principle at least, people's ability to send intelligible radio signals to other civilizations in the Milky Way Galaxy. Currently, a modest effort to listen for such signals is underway.

A more controversial side to the study of extraterrestrial intelligence is the persistence of reports of unidentified flying objects (UFOs). Unquestionably, people see things in the sky that they cannot readily identify. But many of the more puzzling UFO reports turn out to have an explanation that does not require, or even suggest, spacecraft piloted by intelligent aliens. Most of the available literature is written by UFO enthusiasts. The most rational book supporting this idea is by Hynek; other books listed below take a more skeptical approach to these reports.

Billingham, J., ed. *Life in the Universe*. MIT 1981 text ed. $25.00 pap. $12.50. A collection of essays by the leading lights in the search for extraterrestrial intelligence and the origin of life.

Dick, Steven. *Plurality of Worlds: The Origins of the Extraterrestrial Life Debate from Democritus to Kant*. Cambridge Univ. Pr. 1982 $39.50 pap. $13.95. An excellent historical perspective, containing references to the fictional literature predating the scientific discussion of this topic.

Goldsmith, Donald, and Tobias Owen. *The Search for Life in the Universe*. Addison-Wesley 1980 pap. $21.95. A recent summary of the optimistic view that extraterrestrial life is relatively common. Good comprehensive view of the field.

Hart, Michael, and Benjamin Zuckerman. *Extraterrestrials—Where Are They?* Pergamon 1982 $25.00. A collection of essays, many of which are thought-provoking. Several of the essays take the entirely respectable if not too well-popularized view that extraterrestrial life may not be abundant, and that earth may have the only civilization in the Milky Way Galaxy.

Hynek, J. Allen. *The UFO Experience: A Scientific Inquiry*. Ballantine 1978 pap. $2.25. If you want to read a book that supports the idea that UFO sightings are indications of aliens' visits to earth, this is the one to read. Although hysteria is kept to a minimum, Hynek goes overboard in interpreting "contactee" stories where witnesses claim to have had close contact with aliens. He is inclined to believe anything that a witness tells him.

Klass, Philip J. *UFOs: The Public Deceived*. Prometheus Bks. 1986 $19.95 pap. $11.95. "The noted UFO investigator holds the favorite theories of the UFO believers up to the cold light of day; an excellent summary of the current evidence (and lack of it)" (*Mercury*).

——. *UFOs Explained*. Random 1976 pap. $6.95. Klass is one of the leading skeptics on UFOs. This book contains an in-depth investigation of some of the leading cases cited by those who insist on believing that the evidence shows that some UFOs are spacecraft with aliens inside them. Klass demonstrates that many of these supposedly classic cases have simpler explanations that do not require aliens.

Menzel, D., and E. Taves. *The U.F.O. Enigma.* Doubleday 1977 o.p. An astronomer and a psychoanalyst demonstrate how slim the evidence is for interpreting this phenomenon as due to aliens. They also take on ancient astronauts, the Bermuda Triangle, and Uri Geller.

Regis, Edward, ed. *Extraterrestrials: Science and Alien Intelligence.* Cambridge Univ. Pr. 1985 $39.50. Many of the essays in this collection take novel approaches to this question, which differ from the standard viewpoints established by books like Sagan and Shklovskii, *Intelligent Life in the Universe* (see main entry for Sagan in this chapter).

Rood, Robert T., and James S. Trefil. *Are We Alone? The Possibility of Extraterrestrial Civilizations.* Scribner 1983 pap. $7.95. Since there is little evidence bearing directly on the question of whether intelligent life is abundant in the universe, two scientifically respectable views on this topic exist. Rood and Trefil ably present the viewpoint that life is relatively rare in the universe, because special conditions are needed in order to allow life to evolve.

Sheaffer, Robert. *The UFO Verdict: Examining the Evidence.* [*Science and the Paranormal Ser.*] Prometheus Bks. 1981 $18.95. A thoroughly researched, skeptical book on UFOs.

Stiebing, William H., Jr. *Ancient Astronauts, Cosmic Collisions, and Other Popular Theories about Man's Past.* [*Science and the Paranormal Ser.*] Prometheus Bks. 1984 $19.95 pap. $10.95. Readers have reportedly bought ten million copies of books by Erich von Däniken who claims on the basis of very flimsy "evidence" that ancient astronauts visited the earth in the past. This is one of a few books in which a professional confronts such ideas and shows how pseudoscientific and nonsensical they are. Stiebing deals with ancient astronauts, the lost continent of Atlantis, Velikovsky, pyramid power and other absurdities of "pyramidology," and early "discoveries" of America.

BOK, BART JAN. 1906–1983

Bok told the story of how his ignorance of the constellations in a Boy Scout examination kindled a lifelong interest in astronomy. After his education in Holland, he immediately moved to the Harvard College Observatory where he remained for nearly 30 years. His lifelong work was the study of the Milky Way Galaxy, its contents, and its spiral structure. He is best known for the recognition of "Bok globules," small patches of dust, which may be the sites for star and planet formation. After World War II, he led the pioneering efforts in radio astronomy that brought the United States into the field and, perhaps more importantly, trained a crop of graduate students who are now worldwide leaders. Subsequently he built up efforts in optical astronomy in Australia and in Arizona the same way that he had built up American radio astronomy. He was well known as a teacher, inspirational leader, and popularizer.

BOOKS BY BOK

(and Priscilla Bok). *The Milky Way.* 1941. Harvard Univ. Pr. 5th ed. 1981 text ed. $25.00. This classic work provides a comprehensive view of the Milky Way Galaxy, the collection of 100 billion stars in which we live. The nature of the stars in it, the spiral structure of this huge whirling disk, the gas between the stars, and the causes of spiral structure are laid out very clearly in this popular-level exposition.

(and Lawrence E. Jerome). *Objections to Astrology.* [*Science and the Paranormal Ser.*] Prometheus Bks. 1975 pap. $6.95. A slim volume, containing a statement denying the scientific validity of astrology signed by 182 scientists, and two articles by Bok and Jerome that provide the basis for the scientific criticism of this ancient practice.

BRAHE, TYCHO. 1546–1601

Despite the wishes of an uncle who wanted him to study law, Tycho Brahe's interest in astronomy developed while he was a student at the University of Copenhagen. His observation of an eclipse in 1560, which did occur at the predicted time, and his observation of a planetary conjunction in 1563, where Saturn and Jupiter came close together in the sky at a time quite different from the predicted one, represented the beginning of a career most notable for his ability to make extremely precise observations. In 1577 he established a household and a magnificent observatory on the island of Ven, where he and a retinue of assistants continued to measure planetary positions. When King Frederick II of Denmark died in 1588, Brahe lost favor with Danish royalty and moved south, settling in Prague in 1599. Although he never accepted Copernicus's suggestion that the sun rather than the earth was the center of the solar system, he made a key contribution to the Copernican revolution by making a comprehensive and precise set of observations of planetary positions put to good use by his successor Kepler. Brahe had a colorful personality, and stories about such things as his silver nose, which he wore because his nose was cut off in a duel, abound.

Book about Brahe

Dreyer, John L. *Tycho Brahe: A Picture of Scientific Life and Work in the Sixteenth Century.* Peter Smith 1977 $13.25. "The best single treatment of Brahe's life and work" (C. Doris Hellman, *Dictionary of Scientific Biography*).

CLARKE, ARTHUR CHARLES. 1917–

Clarke's career and education as a science writer and space pioneer began inauspiciously when he left Huish's Grammar School, Taunton, England, for a civil service position in the audit department of the British government. As a hobby he wrote several articles for the *Journal of the British Interplanetary Society,* and his wartime experience as a radio technician with the Royal Air Force gave him the background to suggest, in an article in *Wireless World* in 1945, that communications satellites in a 24-hour orbit could represent a significant application of the space program. After World War II, he went to King's College, London, graduating in 1949. For two years he abstracted articles for *Physics Abstracts* but gave up this job to be a free-lance writer, science popularizer, and underwater explorer and photographer. His early books on space and rocketry played a major role in building public support for the space program. He has written over two dozen science fiction novels and an equal number of science popularizations.

Books by Clarke

Ascent to Orbit: A Scientific Autobiography. Wiley 1984 text ed. $21.50. Contains
  some rarely seen works, including Clarke's 1945 article that led to the era of
  satellite communications.

The Exploration of Space. 1951. Pocket Bks. rev. ed. 1979 pap. $2.50. This was one of
  many works written in the 1950s that played a vital role in establishing popular
  support for the space program.

Profiles of the Future. 1962. Warner Bks. 1985 pap. $3.50. Clarke has developed a
  legendary reputation as a forecaster, as much through his science fiction as
  through his popular science writing. While this book is a bit dated, it shows
  how one author has tried to balance unbridled optimism with the need to keep
  one's feet on the ground.

1984 Spring: A Choice of Futures. Ballantine 1984 $14.95. This largely autobiographi-
  cal collection of Clarke's writings includes essays and speeches on the space
  program as well as on Clarke's life and his science fiction stories and novels.

COPERNICUS (KOPÉRNIK), NICHOLAUS (MIKOLAJ). 1473–1543

Copernicus was not trained as a scientist, nor was his job an officially
scientific one. He studied medicine and canon law at the University of
Kraków and in various universities in Italy, receiving a degree from the
University of Ferrara in 1506. He returned to Poland, eventually becoming
canon of the cathedral in Frauenberg, East Prussia, which is now part of
Poland. During his entire life he was preoccupied with understanding what
made the planets move, and his radical step was in proposing that the sun
rather than the earth was the center of the solar system. Except for a
preliminary version of his theory, which was privately circulated in 1514,
the first publication of his idea was in his magnum opus, *De revolutionibus
orbium coelestium* (*On the Revolution of the Heavenly Spheres*), now out of
print, published in the year of his death. This idea was not finally accepted
until more than 100 years later, when measurements and analyses by
Kepler, Tycho Brahe, Galileo, Newton, and others led to a detailed, quantitative comparison between predictions of the Copernican model and observation of planetary positions. This intellectual development, which kicked
humanity out of a central place in the old-fashioned cosmos and put it on a
rockball circling one of billions of stars, represented the most fundamental
change in the conception of the universe that has occurred in human history. Because of Copernicus's role in starting this change, it is referred to as
the Copernican revolution.

Book by Copernicus

On the Revolution of the Heavenly Spheres. 1543. Trans. by A. M. Duncan, Wiley 1974
  o.p.

Books about Copernicus

Adamczewski, Jan. *Nicholaus Copernicus and His Epoch.* Scribner 1974 o.p. "This
  brief scholarly volume... displays the context of Copernicus's lifetime in good
  color and velvety gravure, and in a meticulously detailed text" (*Scientific American*).

Armitage, Angus. *The World of Copernicus*. Beekman 1972 pap. $7.95. A short summary of Copernicus's life, concerned less with the philosophical or historical context.

Butterfield, Herbert. *The Origins of Modern Science 1300–1800*. Free Pr. rev. ed. 1965 text ed. pap. $10.95. While not strictly "about Copernicus," this description of the Copernican revolution was one of the first books to discuss this intellectual development in a larger context and to point out that Copernicus's physics was still quite similar to Aristotle's.

Kuhn, Thomas S. *The Copernican Revolution: Planetary Astronomy in the Development of Western Thought*. Harvard Univ. Pr. 1957 $18.50 pap. $7.95. A classic in the history of science.

Neyman, Jerzy, ed. *The Heritage of Copernicus: Theories "Pleasing to the Mind."* MIT 1974 pap. $14.95. A collection of essays on the intellectual impact of the Copernican revolution, written by leaders in physics, astronomy, biology, and other fields.

Rosen, Edward. *Copernicus and the Scientific Revolution*. Krieger 1984 pap. text ed. $6.95. Mostly biographical, it puts Copernicus's work in context.

EDDINGTON, SIR ARTHUR STANLEY. 1882–1944

Outside astronomy, Eddington is well known for his popular and semipopular books. But readers of these books may not realize that he is one of the pioneers of twentieth-century astrophysics, a founder of many important lines of research. Except for a few years spent at the Royal Observatory at Greenwich studying stellar motions, he spent his entire career at Cambridge University, where he was Plumian Professor of Astronomy for four decades. His early work on stellar motions laid the foundations for the subsequent work by Shapley and Hubble that demonstrated that the Milky Way is one of billions of spiral galaxies in the universe. But this work, however fundamental, pales in importance beside his contribution to relativity and to the understanding of stars. Eddington was perhaps the first person outside Germany to know of or appreciate Einstein's general theory of relativity, and he led an expedition to Principe, in South America, to test the theory experimentally.

Even though the source of stellar energy—nuclear fusion—had yet to be discovered, his analysis of stellar interiors in the 1920s demonstrated, correctly, what stars are made of and what makes them work. He predicted that nuclear energy was the source of the energy that we ultimately see as sunshine. In his later years he was very much preoccupied with establishing fundamental numerical relationships between various cosmic quantities, and it was Eddington who recognized the fundamental importance of a number called the fine structure constant, which is a measure of the strength of the electrical interaction (and which happens to be almost exactly 1/137).

BOOKS BY EDDINGTON

Space, Time, and Gravitation. Cambridge Univ. Pr. 1920 o.p. One of the first, and still one of the best, introductions to relativity. Like most of Eddington's books, it is useful not only to the scientist but also to the intelligent and patient general reader.

The Internal Constitution of the Stars. 1926. Cambridge Univ. Pr. 1930 o.p. The book is remarkable in that the existence of nuclear fusion, the source of energy in all stars, was still quite speculative when it was written. Nevertheless, it gives a quite accurate account of the interiors of stars (although a firm foundation for stellar evolution remained for the future).

The Nature of the Physical World. AMS Pr. repr. of 1928 ed. 1981 $27.50; Darby repr. of 1928 ed. 1981 lib. bdg. $30.00; Folcroft repr. of 1935 ed. o.p. This book describes the philosophical consequences of the new developments of early twentieth-century physics (particularly relativity and quantum theory); it is based on a lecture series.

Science and the Unseen World. Arden Lib. repr. of 1929 ed. 1980 lib. bdg. $12.50; Folcroft repr. of 1929 ed. 1979 lib. bdg. $12.50. A brief book, more like a pamphlet, in which Eddington, a lifelong Quaker, addresses a meeting of the Society of Friends on the reconciliation between science and religion.

BOOKS ABOUT EDDINGTON

Chandrasekhar, S. *Eddington: The Most Distinguished Astrophysicist of His Time.* Cambridge Univ. Pr. 1984 $12.50. A brief account of Eddington's scientific achievements by a Nobel Laureate.

Dingle, Herbert. *The Sources of Eddington's Philosophy.* Cambridge Univ. Pr. 1954 o.p. A brief treatment of Eddington's popularization of relativity and his ideas about time.

GALILEI, GALILEO. 1564–1642

Galileo is perhaps best known as the first person to use the telescope to probe the heavens. He constructed the first astronomical telescope and used it to view craters on the moon; spots on the sun; the phases of Venus; the moons of Jupiter; the oval appearance of Saturn, which is now known to be caused by the rings around this planet; and the myriads of stars that compose the Milky Way. It was not just a question of taking a Dutch military invention and turning it upward to the heavens; because Galileo improved the telescope significantly, his work was as valuable militarily as it was a key part of an intellectual revolution. Still further, his studies of pendulums and falling bodies were an important part of the development of modern physics, eventually synthesized by Isaac Newton in the late 1600s. A professor of mathematics at the universities of Pisa and Padua (1589–1610), Galileo moved to Florence in 1610, serving as chief mathematician to the Duke of Tuscany. His early works on astronomy, written in Latin, were primarily read by other astronomers. But his *Dialogue on the Two Chief World Systems* (1632) was written in Italian that ordinary people could understand and this widespread promotion of the Copernican model of the solar system, with the sun in the middle, brought him into conflict with the ecclesiastical authorities. He was tried in Rome in 1633 by the Inquisition, and forced to deny the truth of the Copernican system. Even after the trial, when he was under house arrest, he continued his investigations in physics, publishing another, less controversial *Dialogues Concerning Two New Sciences* (1638). (See also Chapter 9 in this volume and Chapter 4 in Volume 4.)

BOOKS BY GALILEO

Discoveries and Opinions of Galileo. Trans. by Stillman Drake, Doubleday (Anchor) 1957 pap. $5.95. These essays, written mainly between 1610 and 1620, include Galileo's first communications of his astronomical discoveries. Drake's essays explain the context of each of Galileo's works, placing them in a historical perspective.

Dialogue Concerning the Two Chief World Systems, Ptolemaic and Copernican. 1632. Trans. by Stillman Drake, fwd. by Albert Einstein, Univ. of California Pr. 2d rev. ed. 1967 $40.00 pap. $11.95. In Galileo's major work, ostensibly a dialogue between a proponent of the Copernican system, a proponent of the geocentric universe, and a moderator, the slant in favor of the Copernican view is only thinly veiled. Partly because it was written in Italian rather than Latin, it was the first book to promote the Copernican hypothesis outside of the narrow circle of intellectual astronomers.

Dialogues Concerning Two New Sciences. 1638. Dover 1914 text ed. pap. $5.50. Largely written after his trial, these dialogues establish some of the physical principles underlying the modern view of how things move.

BOOKS ABOUT GALILEO

Brecht, Berthold. *Galileo*. Trans. by Charles Laughton, ed. by Eric Bentley, Grove 1966 pap. $3.50. A fine play, quite controversial, in a version rewritten by Brecht after the bombing of Hiroshima. Brecht sees Galileo's recantation as the step by which science became irresponsible, and uses this as a metaphor for a criticism of science as irretrievably enmeshed with the military.

Drake, Stillman. *Galileo at Work: His Scientific Biography*. Univ. of Chicago Pr. 1981 pap. $9.95. Like many of Drake's books on Galileo, half is written by Galileo himself and half is Drake's commentary, brilliantly illuminating the significance of what Galileo did and its historical context.

Geymonat, Ludovico. *Galileo Galilei: A Biography and Inquiry Into His Philosophy of Science*. Trans. by Stillman Drake, fwd. by Giorgio de Santillana, McGraw-Hill 1967 o.p. A forceful argument that "Galileo's greatness lay in his appeal to empiricism rather than to a kind of Platonism" (*LJ*). "Admirably translated" and "very readable," this book "may be followed throughout by the nonscientist, while the extensive notes and references ensure its usefulness to the serious student of scientific history" (*N.Y. Times*).

Langford, Jerome J. *Galileo, Science, and the Church*. Univ. of Michigan Pr. rev. ed. 1971 pap. $6.95. An authoritative, balanced review of the factual circumstances surrounding Galileo's confrontation with the Catholic church.

Ronan, Colin. *Galileo*. Putnam 1974 o.p. "An informative yet simply written look at Galileo and his world" (*Booklist*).

Santillana, Giorgio de. *The Crime of Galileo*. [*Midway Repr. Ser.*] Univ. of Chicago Pr. 1955 pap. $13.00. The details of the confrontation between Galileo and the Catholic church, including a still controversial allegation that one of the key documents in the case against Galileo was forged.

GAMOW, GEORGE. 1904–1968

Gamow was born in Odessa, in the Soviet Union, and studied at the University of Leningrad. He left the U.S.S.R. permanently in 1933, coming to the United States, where he taught at George Washington University and the University of Colorado. His scientific work covered a very broad range, mostly related to nuclear physics, though he made forays into other fields, including one in which he suggested the triplet mechanism for coding DNA. With his associate Ralph Alpher, he developed a reasonably detailed model of the early stages of cosmic evolution in the Big Bang theory. Though his basic assumption that the universe started with neutrons was completely wrong, this work stimulated a great deal of subsequent work in cosmology.

He is the author of 30 popular books on astronomy, physics, and related sciences. His "Mr. Tompkins" series is one of the most famous. Here he used the figure of a curious, interested bank clerk as a protagonist for various journeys into quantum physics and gravity. His sense of humor comes through his books, and even entered his scientific career. One of the key papers on the Big Bang theory is called the alpha-beta-gamma paper. The original authors were Alpher and Gamow, but they added Bethe's name as an author to make the paper more memorable. UNESCO awarded Gamow the Kalinga Prize for science writing in 1956. (See also Chapter 9 in this volume.)

Books by Gamow

The Creation of the Universe. 1952. Viking rev. ed. 1961 o.p. An excellent popularization of the Big Bang theory, as it stood in the 1950s.

Gravity: Classic and Modern Views. Doubleday (Anchor) 1962 o.p. Still one of the best expositions of Einstein's general theory of relativity for the layperson.

Mr. Tompkins in Paperback. Cambridge Univ. Pr. 1967 $29.95 pap. $7.95. Based on *Mr. Tompkins in Wonderland* (1939) and *Mr. Tompkins Explores the Atom* (1945), part of a popular series.

Book about Gamow

Reines, Frederick, ed. *Cosmology, Fusion, and Other Matters: A Memorial to George Gamow.* Colorado Associated Univ. Pr. 1972 $22.50. Most festschriften like this are ponderous collections of serious essays about some scientific field written by a major figure's students. But here the impish sense of humor that was so much a part of Gamow comes through too.

HALLEY, EDMOND. 1656–1742

Halley is most famous for his recognition that several bright comets were appearances of the same object, now called Halley's comet, and his successful prediction that it would reappear in 1758. But he made many other important contributions to science. He played a key role in the publication of Newton's major work, the *Principia*, in 1687. He established the distance between the earth and the sun through measurements of the transit of Venus, and made the first discovery of stellar motion across the sky. Halley founded the science of geophysics by his studies of terrestrial magnetism and his demonstration that solar heating causes the trade winds and monsoons. He was also a diplomat and served as deputy controller of the Mint in 1696.

Book by Halley

Correspondence and Papers of Edmond Halley. [*History, Philosophy and Sociology of Science Ser.*] Ayer Co. 1975 $30.00. Some brief, some very old biographies of Halley, followed by letters by Halley written to a host of correspondents, including leading scientists of the seventeenth and early eighteenth centuries.

Book about Halley

Brown, Peter L. *Halley and His Comet.* Sterling 1985 $12.95. About half of this book is an engaging biography of Halley. The rest describes various appearances of Halley's comet in history.

HERSCHEL, WILLIAM. 1738–1822

Herschel's first profession was music. He began by playing in his father's German regimental band, and following his emigration to England became organist at Bath in 1766. But his interest in astronomy, and his ability to build large telescopes, led to a second career in astronomy, officially recognized by a royal appointment in 1782. Herschel built several monster telescopes, the largest in the world at the time. His most important astronomical achievement was establishing that the Milky Way was a flat galaxy through his studies of the distribution of stars in space, and his comprehensive work of mapping and cataloging the part of the sky observable from England. His discovery of the planet Uranus in 1781 marked the first use of the telescope to discover a new planet in the solar system. His younger sister Caroline (1750–1848) is not as well known as he, but her assistance in his projects was invaluable. (If proper twentieth-century customs had been followed then, she would have been a coauthor of many of his articles; the standards of the time rendered her role almost invisible.) His son John (1792–1871) established an observatory in South Africa and did the same job of cataloging and mapping the southern sky that William did in the northern hemisphere.

Book about Herschel

Whitney, C. A. *The Discovery of Our Galaxy.* Knopf 1971 o.p. A wide-ranging historical account of the ways in which we learned that we live on the outskirts of a huge star-swarm, containing a hundred billion stars. Most of this book is about Herschel's key role in that search.

HUBBLE, EDWIN POWELL. 1889–1953

As an undergraduate at the University of Chicago, Hubble's boxing abilities attracted the attention of a promoter who wanted to train him to fight the then heavyweight champion Jack Johnson. Instead, Hubble became a Rhodes Scholar. He practiced law for a short time, and finally, in 1914, found his niche in astronomy, going to the Yerkes Observatory for graduate work. He went to the Mount Wilson Observatory in 1919, where he remained for the rest of his career. His research work was on galaxies, and he was the first to determine that they were extragalactic swarms of hundreds of billions of stars. His discovery in the Andromeda Galaxy of a particular type of variable star allowed him to determine its distance. Using his own work and the work of others (principally Milton Humason and Vesto M. Slipher), he established that the relation between redshift and distance showed that the universe was expanding.

BOOKS BY HUBBLE

The Realm of the Nebulae. 1936. [*Silliman Memorial Lectures Ser.*] Yale Univ. Pr. 1982 $33.00 pap. $8.95. As astronomer James Gunn mentions in his foreword to the 1982 edition, this book's value is not just historical. While astronomers know far more now than in 1936, Hubble's lively prose makes this a good introduction to the study of galaxies, as long as the reader realizes that this is not the whole story.

The Hubble Atlas of Galaxies. Ed. by Allan Sandage, Carnegie Institution of Washington 1961 pap. $26.00. Allan Sandage, Hubble's student, produced this magnificent volume, working partly from Hubble's notes. It is a collection of photographs of galaxies, along with a description of the Hubble classification scheme in use today.

KEPLER, JOHANNES. 1571–1630

Kepler is perhaps best known for his three laws of planetary motion, but Kepler authority Owen Gingerich describes these as "only three elements in his search for cosmic harmonies and celestial physics." He began to think about astronomy and planetary motion when he was a schoolteacher in Graz, Austria, and published his first work, *Mysterium cosmographicum*, in 1596. He became an apprentice to Tycho Brahe, whose collection of astronomical observations was the best of its kind. Kepler's work on Mars was a long struggle to fit a theory to the observations, and led to his discovery that planets move in elliptical, rather than circular, orbits. His life was rather chaotic as a result of the repeated harassment of Protestant teachers in predominantly Roman Catholic Austria. Although some of his ideas about cosmic harmonies, such as the idea that the spacing of planetary orbits is related to the five regular polyhedrons, were incorrect, his basic approach of seeking a broad sense of order and harmony in the world led to the discovery of mathematical regularities in the motion of the planets and, ultimately, to the elegant simplicity of Newton's Laws of Motion. His *Somnium,* a fictional account of a voyage to the moon, was first published in German in 1898. It is often cited by historians of rocketry as an early work of science fiction that may have stimulated an interest in space travel.

BOOKS BY KEPLER

Mysterium cosmographicum. 1596. Trans. by A. M. Duncan [*Bilingual Eds. of Classics in Philosophy and Science Ser.*] Abaris Bks. 1981 $20.00. This is the first book Kepler wrote, and it is a curious collection that includes most of the key theories that Kepler was to develop later, along with some mysticism and some ideas that never worked out.

Kepler's Dream. Trans. by Patricia Kirkwood, ed. by John Lear, Univ. of California Pr. 1965 o.p. Includes the full text and notes of *Somnium, sive Astronomia Lunaris.*

BOOKS ABOUT KEPLER

Armitage, Angus. *John Kepler.* Roy 1967 o.p. Like Armitage's other biographies of figures in the Copernican revolution, this is short, readable, not necessarily too deep, but very valuable as an introduction.

Koestler, Arthur. *The Watershed: A Biography of Johannes Kepler.* Fwd. by John

Dursten, Univ. Pr. of Amer. 1985 text ed. pap. $12.00. While Koestler's own mysticism tends to color this work about one of the most mythical of scientists, he goes beyond a simple recitation of the facts to ask some fundamental questions about the nature of creativity in science.

MOORE, PATRICK (ALFRED). 1923–

Patrick Moore is one of the most prolific authors of popular astronomy books. He started publishing astronomy books in 1950 and has been extremely active ever since. He is director of the lunar section of the British Astronomical Association. He was director of the Armagh Planetarium in Northern Ireland from 1965 to 1968.

BOOKS BY MOORE

New Guide to the Stars. Norton 1974 o.p. Some material on "what's in the sky" is well mixed with some other chapters describing the basic nature, as well as the names, of stars, galaxies, and quasars.

Guide to Mars. Norton 1978 $14.95. Beginning with nineteenth-century visual observations of Mars, Moore leads the reader through the checkered history of modern investigation of this planet, complete through the Viking landing on its surface in 1976.

(and Garry Hunt). *Jupiter.* Rand McNally 1981 o.p. The publisher calls it an atlas; it is a superb collection of photos complemented by some authoritative, well-written text from Moore and Garry Hunt, a participant in the Voyager mission and an authority on planetary atmospheres.

Stargazing: Astronomy Without a Telescope. Barron 1985 $19.95. A month-by-month, comprehensive guide to what is in the sky, with a bit of sky lore to leaven the presentation of star names and places.

Patrick Moore's Armchair Astronomy. Norton 1986 $16.95. A collection of more than 100 one-page snippets (entertaining anecdotes) about the stars and the people who have observed them.

NEWTON, ISAAC. 1642–1727

[SEE Chapter 9 in this volume.]

PAYNE-GAPOSHKIN, CECILIA. 1900–1979

Born in England, Cecilia Payne earned an undergraduate degree from Cambridge University and went to the Harvard College Observatory in 1923. She remained there for the rest of her scientific career. She was one of the first scientists to analyze the spectra of stars in a quantitative way, doing such things as measuring their temperatures and chemical compositions with some degree of precision. Her radical proposal that the stars were mostly hydrogen turned out to be correct, even though at first she herself did not believe it. Her attention then turned—or, rather, was directed— to variable stars. Her sex was a barrier to her throughout her career; Cambridge University was unwilling to grant a Ph.D. degree to a woman, for example. Her position at Harvard was strictly as a researcher until the university appointed her as the first female full professor in 1956. While most of her writings are rather technical, she did occasionally write and lecture for popular audiences.

BOOKS BY PAYNE-GAPOSHKIN

The Galactic Novae. Elsevier 1957 $49.00. Novae are stars that suddenly increase in brightness, and this monograph, though old, is still used by astronomers.

Stars and Clusters. Harvard Univ. Pr. 1979 $22.50. Readers who want more than a brief introduction to the stars can find an excellent description of the inhabitants of our local stellar neighborhood, provided by an expert, who shows the local landscape in the same way as a tour guide shows a traveler the landmarks of a particular city.

Cecilia Payne-Gaposhkin: An Autobiography and Other Recollections. Ed. by Katherine Haramundanis, Cambridge Univ. Pr. 1984 $34.50. Payne-Gaposhkin's autobiography is preceded by three biographical essays written by people who knew her and the environment in which she worked.

SAGAN, CARL. 1934–

Carl Sagan is a respected planetary scientist who is best known outside the field for his popularizations of astronomy. He was educated at the University of Chicago, receiving his Ph.D. in 1960. Among his early scholarly achievements were the experimental demonstration of the synthesis of the energy-carrying molecule ATP (adenosine triphosphate) in primitive-earth experiments and the proposal that the greenhouse effect explained the high temperature of the surface of Venus. More recently, he was one of the driving forces behind the Viking mission to the surface of Mars, and he has been part of a team that investigated the effects of nuclear war on the earth's climate—the "nuclear winter" scenario. His role in developing the "Cosmos" series, one of the most successful series of any kind to be broadcast on the Public Broadcasting System, and his many popular books have established his career as a popularizer. His book *The Dragons of Eden* (1977) won the Pulitzer Prize.

BOOKS BY SAGAN

(and Thornton Page, eds.). *UFOs—A Scientific Debate.* Cornell Univ. Pr. 1973 $24.95; Norton 1974 pap. $7.95. Papers given in 1969 at a meeting of the American Association for the Advancement of Science, expressing a variety of viewpoints, mostly skeptical, about the idea that UFOs are craft-piloted by extraterrestrial beings.

The Dragons of Eden. 1977. Ballantine 1978 pap. $2.50; Random 1977 $10.95. Sagan, trained as an astronomer, takes on the fascinating question of the origin of human intelligence, and offers some speculations on the past, present, and future state of the single property that makes human beings so special: our ability to think.

(and I. S. Shklovskii). *Intelligent Life in the Universe.* Holden-Day 1978 text ed. pap. $17.95. This book has become a classic in the field, the first modern exposition of the idea that life is not too rare in the Milky Way Galaxy and that extraterrestrial civilizations would use radio signals to communicate with us.

Broca's Brain: Reflections on the Romance of Science. Ballantine 1980 pap. $3.50; Random 1979 $14.95. A collection of essays about a variety of topics, including debunking various pseudosciences.

The Cosmic Connection: An Extraterrestrial Perspective. Doubleday (Anchor) 1980 pap. $8.95. A Cook's tour of the universe, stopping briefly at a number of strange objects, and ending up on the question of extraterrestrial intelligence.

Cosmos. Ballantine 1985 pap. $4.95. A far-reaching, well-illustrated book about the universe, and a plentiful expression of Sagan's personality.

SHAPLEY, HARLOW. 1885–1972

Born in Missouri, Shapley became an astronomer by accident. As he told the story, he majored in astronomy after learning that the journalism school he wanted to attend at the University of Missouri was not to open until the following year. He earned his doctorate from Princeton, and then moved to the Mount Wilson Observatory where he did his most celebrated work. He demonstrated for the first time that the earth was not the center of the Milky Way Galaxy, but rather on the outskirts, once again dislodging humanity away from a central location in the cosmos. In 1921 he became director of the Harvard College Observatory, transforming it into the leading observatory of its time. He also continued his research program, which resulted in the discovery of the first small galaxies, called the Sculptor and Fornax dwarf galaxies after the constellations in whose direction they lie. Shapley was a public scientist; he played a major role in founding UNESCO and was well known as a writer and lecturer.

BOOKS BY SHAPLEY

Galaxies. 1943. Atheneum rev. ed. 1967 text ed. pap. $2.45. "The book is well apportioned among the various branches of the subject; it is clear, interesting, and very well illustrated" (*Science Progress*).

Of Stars and Men: Human Response to an Expanding Universe. 1958. Greenwood repr. of 1958 ed. 1984 lib. bdg. $24.75. Not recent, to be sure, but the cosmic questions Shapley deals with endure forever. An astronomer who thought more deeply than many scientists about the insignificant place of humanity in the universe presents a very readable account of the human perspective in the context of contemporary astronomy.

VON BRAUN, WERNHER. 1912–1977

Von Braun became technical director of the Nazi rocket program at Peenemünde, on the shores of the Baltic Sea, in 1937. His group was responsible for the development and production of the V-2 rockets, which were directed against England in the closing days of World War II. As the war ended, von Braun and most of his group chose to surrender to the United States. His team responded to congressional concern following the launch of Sputnik in October 1957 by hastily putting together the Explorer 1 rocket, which was the first successfully launched U.S. satellite.

BOOKS BY VON BRAUN

(and Frederick I. Ordway, III). *The History of Rocketry and Space Travel.* Crowell rev. ed. 1975 $29.45. Authoritative and complete.

(and Frederick I. Ordway, III). *New Worlds: Discoveries from Our Solar System.* Doubleday (Anchor) 1979 o.p. Two participants in the human venture to explore the solar system share their experiences and the findings from the planetary exploration in this well-illustrated book, written in the late 1970s.

BOOK ABOUT VON BRAUN

Ordway, Frederick I., III, and Mitchell R. Sharpe. *The Rocket Team.* MIT 1982 pap. $9.95. This story covers more than 50 years, starting with the fledgling German Rocket Society's involvement in a Fritz Lang film project (an unlikely source of funding for science) and extending through von Braun's leading role in the U.S. space program.

CHAPTER 8

Earth Sciences

Wendell Cochran

There may be heaven, there must be hell;
Meantime, there is our Earth here—well!
—ROBERT BROWNING, "Time's Revenges"

How easily shall we then examine the face of nature from one extremity of
the Earth to the other.
—SAMUEL JOHNSON, *The History of Rasselas*

They say it is to see how the world was made.
—SIR WALTER SCOTT, *St. Ronan's Well*

The last few decades have changed forever our view of the Earth.

In the late twentieth century, thousands of scientists were still working who had once been taught in school that the floor of the ocean was a featureless plain. They had learned that the continents simply could not drift, despite the close-fitting shapes of eastern South America and western Africa. That life forms evolved and took new forms at a pace almost infinitely slow. That the land is shaped gradually, by weathering, slow uplift, and decay. And that all forms of life ultimately depend on free oxygen and sunlight alone.

Now we know things are less simple and more exciting. On the global scale, most change really is slow and gradual, but exceptions do occur and they can be sudden and violent. The nature of things as we now see them is suggested by the title of a book by Nigel Calder, *The Restless Earth* (see under Geology in this chapter).

Our new view of the Earth's crust can be traced back to World War II, when a geologist turned Navy submarine commander changed his depth-sounder's readings into maps of the Pacific floor. After the war, large-scale mapping revealed great mid-ocean ridges that divide the Atlantic and virtually encircle the globe. Studies of rocks at the ocean bottom showed that molten rock was welling up from below and spreading away from the ridges, perhaps pushing apart the dozen or so great plates of the Earth's crust. The rate was perhaps only half an inch a year, but continents did drift after all. Thus plate tectonics was born, and scientists everywhere began considering what Tjeerd Van Andel has called "new views of an old planet."

Looking outward, the Apollo program took U.S. astronauts to the Moon and provided a new look at our old planet. (Studying lunar rocks extended the very meaning of the word "geology," which can never again mean only "knowledge of the Earth," and changed the names, and the subject matter, of university departments everywhere.) Apollo-related technology produced Landsat and other artificial satellites that gave geographers, and all people, new ways to examine our planet and its life and resources. Meteorologists gathered much new data about air masses, and modern computers gave them greater power to interpret the incredibly complex patterns of weather and climate. On the ocean floor, scientists in submarines discovered vents of hot water, apparently at boundaries of great crustal plates, and there found bacteria that seem to live without benefit of either sunlight or free oxygen. Elsewhere in the solar system, post-Apollo probes revealed vast canyons on Mars (clearly shaped by moving water), and volcanoes erupting on Jupiter's innermost moon, and scientists brought the evidence down to Earth in the fullest sense of geography and pun.

All of this amounts to a revolution in science. None of us can look at the world around us in quite the same way as we had only a few decades ago.

Life itself is being reexamined. Ever since DARWIN, evidence had been accumulating to show that life evolved throughout much of Earth's long history. If continents can move, however slowly, then such long-standing puzzles of how fossils came to be where we find them in the rocks can be solved. Now we wonder less about which animals and plants lived in former times, and more about how, when, where, and why. The ultimate origin of life may always remain a mystery, but we are finding out more and more about how physical laws have operated on that life throughout time.

Reading the rocks and reconstructing ancient environments lead to surprises: some dinosaurs were surely warm-blooded after all, they may have given live birth (rather than laying eggs), and they seem to have been quite intelligent despite the size of their brains. And even evolutionary change, apparently, now and then comes in bursts.

So upheavals in nature are acceptable, perhaps not even rare. A global catastrophe may explain an old problem, that of the extinction of the dinosaurs. A thin layer of clay, found on several continents and everywhere being of about the same age as the last of the dinosaurs, suggests that an asteroid collided with the Earth like a giant meteorite. If so, it spread dust and ash throughout the atmosphere and changed the worldwide climate— an environmental hazard that dinosaurs (and many other life forms) did not survive.

So much for the geologic past. Here in our own time, we must cope with the problems of industrialization and growing populations. Most of us realize that our oil is running out. We have mined our minerals until some are getting very hard to find. In places, even building stone and road materials are scarce. We need more clean water. Pollution is growing and wastes are building up. Earth science is often a matter of practical politics. Should we vote for a bond issue to finance a dam? What about zoning laws for building along beaches? Do we want oil wells near national parks?

Even the way we organize science and study it is changing. One example among many: early in this century almost any college or university had a Department of Geology. But new specialties have now developed and others merged, and so we find those departments called Earth Science, or Geology and Geophysics, or Planetary Science. There are many others. Academic classifications, like the Earth itself, are restless.

Problems are also opportunities, and our new knowledge of the Earth will at least add to our options. Everyone must adjust to the new worldview—perhaps the earth sciences most of all.

REFERENCE AND GENERAL BOOKS

The earth sciences literally cover the Earth, and often the Moon and the other planets, too. So for a first general view of the subject, consider the Earth as a planet and find a general work on the solar system. Atlases and collections of photographs from space show us at a glance more than COLUMBUS (see Vol. 3) and Magellan ever knew.

Encyclopedias of earth science, paleontology, and the like are useful—their introductory chapters often give good overviews and their lists of references lead to other sources. Also worth a close look are many works that at first seem forbiddingly technical. Curious readers should sample them carefully, for their early chapters may set the stage in simpler terms. Next are introductory textbooks. (This is like looking through a zoom microscope, turning the knob to increase the magnification and reduce the field of view.) Titles including "General" and "Elementary" may be misleading, but prefaces, introductions, indexes, and reference lists are usually helpful guides. Histories and biographies may tell even more about the science than about the people.

Much subject matter of the earth sciences can be seen and felt, so many authors find the topic easier to explain than, say, the physics of elementary particles. Thus we find many books—often collections of essays—on science and for nonscientists.

Long ago, JOHN DONNE (see Vol. 1) wrote that "no man is an island." Nor is any science: oceanography can never be seawater alone, and students of marine science will often find themselves wandering into geology or paleontology.

Bates, Robert L., and Julia A. Jackson, eds. *Dictionary of Geological Terms.* Anchor 3d ed. 1984 pap. $7.95. For nongeologists, definitions of the working vocabulary of the earth sciences; based on the much more comprehensive *Glossary of Geology* (see below).

———. *Glossary of Geology.* Amer. Geol. Inst. 2d ed. 1980 $60.00. Aided by approximately 150 other earth scientists, the editors here define 36,000 terms "as a bulwark against babelization." It is the most extensive work of its kind and it is useful in the other earth sciences as well.

Bramwell, Martyn, ed. *Rand McNally Atlas of the Oceans.* Rand McNally 1977 o.p. These things are basic: names, shapes, and locations of land and water bodies.

Couper, Alastair D., ed. *The Times Atlas of the Oceans.* Van Nostrand 1983 $79.95.

The oceans cover 71 percent of the globe, but until recently the topography of the basin floors was virtually unknown.

Fairbridge, Rhodes W., ed. *The Encyclopedia of Atmospheric Sciences and Astrogeology*. [*Encyclopedia of Earth Sciences Ser.*] Academic Pr. 1967 $101.00. This work was published before Apollo reached the moon, but many of the entries are as good as ever.

———. *The Encyclopedia of Geochemistry and Environmental Sciences*. [*Encyclopedia of Earth Sciences Ser.*] Van Nostrand 1972 $98.00. Though somewhat dated, this work covers an unusually wide range of topics.

———. *Encyclopedia of Geomorphology*. [*Encyclopedia of Earth Sciences Ser.*] Van Nostrand 1968 $105.00. Contains 410 articles, cross-indexed, on the land and the forces that shaped it.

———. *The Encyclopedia of Oceanography*. [*Encyclopedia of Earth Sciences Ser.*] Reinhold 1966 o.p. Fairbridge points out that in 1966 the ocean floor was "less well mapped than is the surface of the Moon."

———. *The Encyclopedia of World Regional Geology, Part 1: Western Hemisphere (Including Australia and Antarctica)*. [*Encyclopedia of Earth Sciences Ser.*] Academic Pr. 1975 $84.00. Useful for overviews of the geology of large areas.

Fairbridge, Rhodes W., and Joanne Bourgeois, eds. *The Encyclopedia of Sedimentology*. [*Encyclopedia of Earth Sciences Ser.*] Van Nostrand 1978 $105.00. More than 75 percent of the Earth's surface is covered by sediments and sedimentary rocks.

Fairbridge, Rhodes W., and David Jablonski, eds. *The Encyclopedia of Paleontology*. [*Encyclopedia of Earth Sciences Ser.*] Van Nostrand 1979 o.p. Includes a chapter on "post-plate tectonics."

Frye, Keith, ed. *Encyclopedia of Mineralogy*. [*Encyclopedia of Earth Sciences Ser.*] Van Nostrand 1981 $100.00. Mainly for nonmineralogists, but each article has references leading to advanced discussion.

Hallam, Anthony. *Atlas of Palaeobiogeography*. Elsevier 1973 $106.50. Shows where various fauna and flora lived in the geologic past, and when.

———. *Planet Earth: An Encyclopedia of Geology*. State Mutual Bk. 1977 $40.00. Earth and other planets, processes, landscapes, ocean floor, economic geology, rocks, Earth history (of life and the planet itself), and history of geology.

Hodgkiss, Alan G., and Andrew F. Tatham. *Keyguide to Information Sources in Cartography*. Facts on File 1986 $50.00; McGraw-Hill 1986 $50.00. Who mapped what, and where; what has been written about maps; where and how to find them.

Houghton, David D., ed. *Handbook in Applied Meteorology*. Wiley 1985 $84.95. Fundamentals, measurements, applications, societal impacts, resources—basic, thorough, and rather too technical for most readers.

Hunt, Lee M., and Donald G. Groves, eds. *A Glossary of Ocean Science and Undersea Technology Terms*. Compass Va. 1965 pap. $6.95. More than 3,500 terms, in underwater sound, oceanography, marine science, underwater physiology, and ocean engineering.

Hurlbut, Cornelius S., Jr., ed. *The Planet We Live On: An Illustrated Encyclopedia of the Earth Sciences*. Abrams 1976 $40.00. About 1,800 entries, covering the solid, liquid, and gaseous Earth, plus "space geology."

Keates, John S. *Cartographic Design and Production*. Halsted Pr. 1976 pap. $44.95. Mappers must look ahead and consider how ink goes on paper or they will not like their maps. This is particularly so for maps of geology, which tend to be more complex than most printers will believe.

Lapedes, Daniel N., ed. *McGraw-Hill Encyclopedia of the Geological Sciences*. Mc-

Graw-Hill 1978 o.p. About 560 alphabetically arranged articles cover the solid Earth and relevant aspects of the oceans and atmosphere.

Lowman, Paul D., Jr. *The Third Planet*. Univ. Pr. of Virginia 1972 $40.00. Large, high-altitude photos, mainly from Apollo 7 and 9, give a new perspective of our planet. It is a most useful starting point for studying any earth science.

Mitchell, Richard Scott. *Dictionary of Rocks*. Van Nostrand 1985 $29.95. Dictionaries of minerals are common, but this may be the only one for the aggregations of minerals called rocks.

Monkhouse, F. J. *A Dictionary of Geography*. Arnold 2d ed. 1965 o.p. Here "geography" is extended into several other earth sciences. The diagrams are especially helpful.

O'Donoghue, Michael, ed. *The Encyclopedia of Minerals and Gemstones*. Putnam 1976 o.p. Describes a thousand minerals, listed in alphabetical order. Separate sections cover their occurrence, geologic origin, and chemical composition.

Parker, Sybil P., ed. *McGraw-Hill Dictionary of Earth Sciences*. McGraw-Hill 3d ed. 1984 $47.50. Expands on 15,000 terms in the fields of climatology, crystallography, engineering, geochemistry, geodesy, geography, geology, geophysics, hydrology, mapping, meteorology, mineralogy, mining engineering, oceanography, paleobotany, paleontology, petroleum engineering, and petrology.

Redfern, Ron. *The Making of a Continent*. Times Bks. 1983 $27.95 1986 pap. $16.95. This book, and the Public Broadcasting System film based on it, shows the building of North America over geologic time.

Roberts, Willard Lincoln, George Robert Rapp, Jr., and Julius Weber. *Encyclopedia of Minerals*. Van Nostrand 1974 o.p. Approximately 2,200 species are described, with perhaps a thousand color photos. The editors say that nearly a third of the mineral species are described in print with conflicting data—conflicts they have attempted to resolve here.

Seltzer, Leon E., ed. *The Columbia Lippincott Gazetteer of the World*. Lippincott 1962 o.p.

Sheriff, Robert E. *Encyclopedic Dictionary of Exploration Geophysics*. Soc. of Expl. Geophysicists 1973 o.p. In general this is geophysics as used in seeking geologic structures that might hold oil and gas. It overlaps geology and earthquake studies.

Small, John, and Michael Witherick. *A Modern Dictionary of Geography*. Arnold 1986 pap. $12.95. The terms defined and explained illustrate the wide range of modern geography, and its overlap with (say) geology. Perhaps the best of its kind.

Smith, David G., ed. *The Cambridge Encyclopedia of the Earth Sciences*. Cambridge Univ. Pr. 1982 $37.50. By 32 scientists, mostly British. The earth sciences transcend political boundaries.

Times Atlas of the World. Times Bks. 7th ed. comprehensive ed. 1985 $139.95. Here are approximately 210,000 place names, with pinyin used for most of the Chinese.

Todd, David K., ed. *The Water Encyclopedia*. Water Info. 1970 o.p. Covers climate and precipitation, and many aspects of water, including pollution and management.

Tver, David F. *Ocean and Marine Dictionary*. Cornell Maritime 1979 $18.50. From sailing ships to seaweeds.

Webster's New Geographical Dictionary. Merriam-Webster 1984 $19.95. More than 200 maps and 47,000 entries. For the United States and Canada, most towns included have a minimum population of 2,500; for the United Kingdom, 10,000; the Soviet Union, 40,000; China, 100,000.

Wood, Elizabeth A. *Science from Your Airplane Window*. Dover 2d ed. rev. 1975 pap.

$4.95. A window seat is the observation point. Earth, air, and water constitute the laboratory. Subjects include standing water, coastlines, running water, weather, and rock structures.

GEOGRAPHY

Geography is a shifting field. Many people still think of it as consisting mainly of maps, political boundaries, and the distribution of life, land, water, and resources. It is all that, but any reader who explores the map of geography will find its boundaries vague and far away. As one example, geology and geography both concern mineral resources, and geography and meteorology both concern climates. Books on "physical geography" and "physical geology" may be much the same. The exploration may begin with one of the many books outlining the study of geography, or describing geographers at work, or asking "What is geography?"

Readers should consider tools such as atlases and geographical dictionaries. Next should be an introductory textbook, to be read for an idea of the range of modern geography. Artificial satellites, for instance, aid geographers in mapping land and sea, and in evaluating natural resources. More and more, geography's arena includes the continental shelves and the ocean bottom itself, so books on marine geology and oceanography may match the reader's needs and interests.

Alexander, John W., and L. Gibson. *Economic Geography.* Prentice-Hall 2d ed. 1979 $38.95. From agriculture through mining, manufacturing, transportation, and trade to services, and the theory of "the new geography."

Bagrow, Leo. *History of Cartography.* Rev. by R. A. Skelton, Precedent Pub. repr. of 1964 ed. 1985 $64.95. Inseparable, of course, from traditional geography, as well as geology and other fields.

Balchin, W. G. V., ed. *Geography: An Outline for the Intending Student.* Routlege & Kegan 1970 o.p. How geography is now studied in the universities of the United Kingdom. Very useful.

Berry, Brian J., ed. *The Nature of Change in Geographical Ideas.* [*Perspectives in Geography Ser.*] Northern Illinois Univ. Pr. 1978 $17.50 pap. $7.50. Concerns the social aspects of the field and various philosophical approaches.

Boyce, Ronald Reed. *Geographic Perspectives on Global Problems: An Introduction to Geography.* Wiley 1982 $34.95. Boyce proceeds from the general (Earth as a planet) to the particular (urban areas) and goes on to the future (resources).

Brewer, J. Gordon. *The Literature of Geography: A Guide to Its Organisation and Use.* Shoe String 2d ed. 1978 $25.00. What is available, what is useful, how it is organized, and how it relates to other fields.

Buttimer, Annette. *Values in Geography.* Assn. of Amer. Geographers 1984 pap. $31.95. Examines the relations between humankind and geography.

Campbell, John. *Introductory Cartography.* Prentice-Hall 1984 $37.95. The basics of mapping with an eye to the printed product.

Church, Martha, Robert E. Huke, and Wilbur Zelinsky. *A Basic Geographical Library: A Selected and Annotated Book List for American Colleges.* Assn. of Amer. Geographers 1966 o.p. Organized under general works and aids, geographic methods, thematic geography, and regional geography.

Clark, Audrey N. *Longman Dictionary of Geography, Human and Physical.* Longman

1984 $35.00. "Geography," once mainly physical and political, now straddles the humanities and the natural and social sciences.

Dickinson, R. E., and O. J. R. Howarth. *The Making of Geography.* Greenwood repr. of 1933 ed. 1976 $22.50. A history of geography, beginning with the Greek philosophers (and a few even earlier).

Dunbar, Gary S. *The History of Modern Geography: An Annotated Bibliography of Selected Works.* [*Reference Lib. of the Humanities*] Garland 1985 lib. bdg. $53.50. Original intent aside, it helps define geography's range.

Freeman, T. W. *The Geographer's Craft.* Longwood 1967 $30.00. Freeman uses the achievements of several eminent geographers as case histories.

Goddard, Stephen, ed. *A Guide to Information Sources in the Geographical Sciences.* Croom Helm 1983 $27.50. Geomorphology; historical, agricultural, and industrial geography; major regional sources; tools (roughly, maps, air photos, statistics, and archives).

Goudie, Andrew, ed. *The Encyclopedic Dictionary of Physical Geography.* Basil Blackwell 1985 $60.00. Aimed at professionals and secondary-level teachers, but the cross-references and index are useful to anyone searching the field of geography and also other earth sciences.

Gould, Peter. *The Geographer at Work.* Methuen 1985 pap. $16.95. Emphatically not a compilation of job descriptions, but a highly readable account of what geography has become in the last 30 years.

Grim, Ronald E. *Historical Geography of the United States and Canada: A Guide to Information Sources.* [*Geography and Travel Information Guide Ser.*] Gale 1982 $62.00. The subject is "the Europeanization of the American landscape," with cartographic sources, archives, and other historical works, and selected literature.

Hammond, Kenneth A., George Macinko, and Wilma B. Fairchild, eds. *Sourcebook on the Environment: A Guide to the Literature.* Univ. of Chicago Pr. 1978 $27.50. Approximately 3,800 references.

Haring, L. Lloyd, and John F. Lounsbury. *Introduction to Scientific Geographic Research.* William C. Brown 3d ed. 1982 $12.76. Techniques for defining the problem, devising an approach, gathering data and analyzing it, and writing a report.

Harris, Chauncey D., ed. *A Geographical Bibliography for American Libraries.* Assn. of Amer. Geographers 1985 $32.45. Harris focuses on the years 1970 to 1984.

Hartshorne, Richard. *The Nature of Geography: A Critical Survey of Current Thought in the Light of the Past.* Assn. of Amer. Geographers 1961 pap. $4.95. Historical development of the science leading up to the question: What kind of a science is geography?

James, Preston E., and Geoffrey J. Martin. *All Possible Worlds: A History of Geographical Ideas.* Wiley 2d ed. 1981 pap. $37.95. A survey, with bibliography and biosketches of influential geographers.

Kates, Robert W., and Ian Burton. *Geography, Resources, and Environment: Selected Writings of Gilbert F. White.* Univ. of Chicago Pr. 1986 pap. $25.00. An eminent geographer discusses natural resources, hazards, and human environment.

King, Cuchlaine A. *Physical Geography.* Barnes & Noble 1980 $34.50. King arranges topics according to scale: local (meteorology, hydrology, and so on), regional and continental, and global.

Kish, George, ed. *A Source Book in Geography.* Harvard Univ. Pr. 1978 $30.00. Among the 123 selections: Socrates explains the nature of the Earth, the Venerable Bede describes seventh-century Britain, Jefferson asks Humboldt about the nature of Louisiana.

Lounsbury, John F., and Frank T. Aldrich. *Introduction to Geographic Field Methods and Techniques.* Merrill 1979 pap. $14.95. Despite photos and other imagery from space, often geographers must still gather data in the field—mapping, measuring, counting, and recording. Elementary but vital.

Muriel, C. B. *Geography and Cartography: A Reference Handbook.* Linnet Bks. 3d ed. 1976 o.p. Covers "the main focal points of geographical study"—mainly organizations (as the Geological Society of London), sources (Library of Congress), publications (*Canada in Maps*), and subjects (maps, globes, map librarianship).

Prescott, John R. *The Maritime Political Boundaries of the World.* Methuen 1986 $48.00. Measurement, claims, zones, continental shelves, the high seas. Of special interest since the United States and other nations extended their claims to 200 miles.

Stamp, Dudley, and Audrey N. Clark. *A Glossary of Geographical Terms.* Longman 3d ed. 1979 text ed. $42.95. Long the standard reference, and still among the best.

Strahler, Arthur N., and Alan H. Strahler. *Modern Physical Geography.* Wiley 2d ed. 1983 $36.95. Encyclopedic in scope; treats the Earth as a globe, with major sections on the atmosphere and hydrosphere; climate, soils, and plants; and landforms.

Wheeler, Jesse H., and others. *Regional Geography of the World.* Holt 3d ed. 1975 $37.95. A solid traditional textbook, systematically describing the world we live in—physiography, climate, political boundaries, populations.

Whittow, John B. *The Penguin Dictionary of Physical Geography.* Penguin 1984 pap. $8.95. Whittow takes into account the "fundamental and conceptual changes" in the 1960s and 1970s.

Wilford, John Noble, Jr. *The Mapmakers.* Knopf 1981 $20.00. A thorough and engaging history of mappers and their work from the earliest times.

GEOLOGY

Geology is most set apart from other sciences by the concept of geologic time. Earth is about 4.5 billion years old, and that gives geology a lot of scope—the materials and shape of the Earth, its natural forces, its life forms, and the history of all those things. Now plate tectonics and the accentuated view of the Earth as a planet have forced reassessment of many long-held beliefs. Many findings of science have been reconfirmed, others modified, some disproved. And there are great surprises.

Geology relies heavily on the record of the past. Not only the record in the rocks, but also the observations recorded for decades and even centuries past. That is to say the history of the science, too, is useful. Thus anyone exploring geology must look back in time, and also consult works in other fields that authors, libraries, and schools may treat as a part of geology.

For an overview, seek an introductory text, though that may mean two: some introductions stick to physical geology and leave historical geology to be treated separately. After that, the most obvious step is to find a book on rocks and minerals and another on fossils. Thereafter individual interest usually sets the course.

Or, as an alternative, begin with field guides to fossils and to rocks and minerals, and then consult introductory textbooks. Use encyclopedia articles, too, if only for their lists of cross-references, which suggest new routes of study.

Adams, Frank Dawson. *Birth and Development of the Geological Sciences.* Dover repr.
of 1938 ed. 1954 o.p. Outlines various concepts of the Earth throughout history,
and tells how old ideas gave way to the new.

Ager, Derek V. *The Nature of the Stratigraphical Record.* Halstead Pr. 2d ed. 1981
$19.95. Ager is a respected geologist, and though the title seems harmless he
questions some ideas generally accepted. Provocative.

Albritton, Claude C. *Abyss of Time: Changing Conceptions of the Earth's Antiquity
after the 16th Century.* Freeman Cooper 1980 $16.50 pap. $9.50. Perhaps geologists' greatest contribution to science is the concept of geologic time.

———, ed. *The Fabric of Geology.* Freeman Cooper 1963 o.p. Surveys the history of
geology, examines its status, and considers future direction.

Blatt, Harvey, Gerard V. Middleton, and Raymond Murray. *Origin of Sedimentary
Rock.* Prentice-Hall 2d ed. 1980 $42.95. An advanced text stressing the "pro-
found ideas and new evidence" of the previous decade.

Burchfield, Joe D. *Lord Kelvin and the Age of the Earth.* Natural History Pr. 1975 o.p.
About a century ago, Kelvin calculated that the Earth could be no more than 24
million years old. The relative youth shocked geologists who believed much
more time was needed for normal physical forces to produce geologic features.
Discovery of radioactivity proved Kelvin wrong.

Calder, Nigel. *The Restless Earth: A Report on the New Geology.* Penguin 1978 pap.
$9.95. Volcanoes, earthquakes, drifting continents, and erosion transform the
Earth as they have throughout geologic time.

Cattermole, Peter, and Patrick Moore. *The Story of Earth.* Cambridge Univ. Pr. 1985
$24.95. Tells how the Earth was formed from a cloud of dust and gas circling
the primitive Sun.

Cloud, Preston. *Cosmos, Earth, and Man: A Short History of the Universe.* Yale Univ.
Pr. 1978 $35.00 pap. $11.95. From the "Big Bang," several billion years ago,
down to the time of creatures capable of trying to reconstruct the history.

Craig, Gordon Y., and E. J. Jones, eds. *A Geological Miscellany.* Princeton Univ. Pr.
1984 pap. $7.95. These snippets from the life and times of earth scientists con-
firm Toepfer's comment (in 1841) that "geologists are charming company—
particularly for other geologists."

Fenton, Carroll Lane, and Mildred Adams Fenton. *Giants of Geology.* Doubleday
1952 o.p. Biographical sketches outline the development of geological ideas.

———. *Story of the Great Geologists.* Ayer repr. of 1945 ed. 1974 $22.00. History of
science through biography: Eratosthenes measures the Earth (third century
B.C.); James Hutton finds no need of the Flood (A.D. 1795).

Geikie, Sir Archibald. *Charles Darwin as Geologist.* Gordon 1977 $59.50. Nowadays
Darwin's name evokes evolution, but he was among the first to recognize
changes in sea level and to see that the shape of the land did not depend on
catastrophic events.

———. *Founders of Geology.* Macmillan 2d ed. 1905 o.p. From the ancient Greeks to
the petrographic microscope. Geikie (1835–1924), a Scottish geologist and popularizer of geology, was also a historian.

———. *Types of Scenery and Their Influence on Literature.* Associated Faculty Pr. repr.
of 1898 ed. 1970 $16.50. Geikie dominated geology in his time and described it
lucidly for nonscientists.

Gilluly, James, Aaron C. Waters, and A. O. Woodford. *Principles of Geology.* W. H.
Freeman 4th ed. 1975 $30.95. Long popular and widely respected, and with
reason.

Hallam, Anthony. *Great Geological Controversies.* Oxford 1983 pap. $14.95. The age
of the Earth has long been disputed, as has the reading of the record in its rocks and

the mechanism of geologic forces. Hallam tells tales of conflict among neptunists, volcanists, plutonists, catastrophists and uniformitarians, and drifters.

———. *A Revolution in Earth Science, from Continental Drift to Plate Tectonics.* Oxford 1973 pap. $9.95. Apparently the first to suggest that the New World and the Old World had drifted apart was Francis Bacon (1561–1626). Nearly three centuries passed before the idea was seriously revived, by Alfred Lothar Wegener (1880–1930), and general acceptance came only in the 1960s (with a rush). Hallam sums up the story well.

Harland, W. B., and others. *A Geologic Time Scale.* Cambridge Univ. Pr. 1982 pap. $11.95. The most distinctive feature of geology as a science is the concept of geologic time. As usually depicted, the geologic time scale looks something like a ladder, with rungs at various distances corresponding to the duration of eras and periods. Harland discusses the ladder.

Leveson, David. *A Sense of the Earth.* Natural History Pr. 1971 $18.00. A geologist as philosopher describes his work and comes to terms with the only Earth we have.

Longwell, Chester L., ed. *Sedimentary Facies in Geologic History.* Geol. Soc. of Amer. 1949 o.p. These discussions are quite technical, but the concept is important: it has to do with the relationships of sedimentation and geologic time.

McAlester, A. Lee. *The Earth: An Introduction to the Geological and Geophysical Sciences.* Prentice-Hall 1973 $29.95. Physical aspects dominate; life of the past is left, mainly, for another book.

McCall, G. J. H., ed. *Astroblemes-Cryptoexplosion Structures.* Van Nostrand 1979 $57.95. This collection of papers concerns geologic structures of imperfectly explained origin. Some were surely produced by meteorites; others may have some kind of pseudovolcanic origin.

———. *Meteorite Craters.* Van Nostrand 1977 $68.00. A collection. Among the "craters" is one that is not: the Tunguska event of 1908, in which many people observed a great fireball over Siberia and heard it explode from a thousand kilometers away. Investigators found a forest flattened and many reindeer killed, but no crater.

McPhee, John. *Basin and Range.* Farrar 1981 $10.95 pap. $6.25. This is the first of a series from *The New Yorker,* published under the overall title "Annals of the Former World." Geologists praise McPhee's understanding of their science; nongeologists praise his writing.

———. *Encounters with the Archdruid.* Farrar 1971 $16.95 pap. $5.95. Invigorating interviews with extremes among exploiters and environmentalists, represented by the Sierra Club, the Bureau of Reclamation, a developer, and a geologist.

———. *In Suspect Terrain.* Farrar 1983 $12.95 pap. $6.95. From the foundations of Manhattan to the glacial drift of Indiana. McPhee's unifying theme is plate tectonics, but as he notes it does not fit all the geology everywhere—that insures interest for a long time to come.

———. *The Pine Barrens.* Farrar 1981 $10.95 pap. $6.25. Almost within sight of the Empire State Building is one of our most sparsely populated areas, and under the barrens is one of our greatest sources of fresh water. McPhee reports on the interaction of people and geology.

———. *Rising from the Plains.* Farrar 1986 $15.95. Science of and in the northern Rockies, told mainly in terms of a man who grew up in Wyoming and became the acknowledged expert on the region's geology.

Mahaney, William C., ed. *Quaternary Dating Methods.* Elsevier 1984 $72.25. The Quaternary period includes our own time, including the most remote hominids, and the study of evolution requires precise ages for fossil remains. Various methods are used to fix those ages.

Mason, Shirley L., and Kirtley F. Mather, eds. *Source Book in Geology, 1400–1900*. Harvard Univ. Pr. 1970 $40.00. A remarkable collection of writings on geology, many of them out of print and nearly all difficult to find.

Matthews, William H., III. *Geology Made Simple*. Doubleday 2d ed. 1982 pap. $5.95. After the first brick comes out of a sidewalk the others seem easy. Matthews pulls out the first brick.

Matthews, William H., III, and others. *Investigating the Earth*. Houghton Mifflin 3d ed. 1978 o.p. This junior high text, developed in the early years of the plate-tectonics revolution, covers an unusually wide range of the various earth sciences. Geologists give copies of this work to their neighbors.

Merrill, George Perkins. *Contributions to a History of American State Geological and Natural History Surveys*. [*History of Geology Ser.*] Ayer repr. of 1920 ed. 1978 $49.50. In the opening of the West (and the East), exploration and surveys were mainly organized by the federal and state governments. No one else has condensed the history so well.

————. *The First One Hundred Years of American Geology*. Lubrecht & Cramer repr. of 1924 ed. 1969 $15.75. Depicts the development of a new science in a new land.

Miller, Hugh. *The Old Red Sandstone, or New Walks in an Old Field*. Ed. by Claude C. Albritton, Jr. [*History of Geology Ser.*] Ayer repr. of 1851 ed. 1978 $34.50. In planning canals in England, Miller (1802–1856) found that each bed of rock had its own fossils and that helped him find the same bed elsewhere. Now it is a fundamental principle.

Moore, Ruth. *The Earth We Live On*. Knopf 2d ed. 1971 o.p. Moore tells how science changed and some "natural philosophers" came to be called "geologists."

Nininger, H. H. *Arizona's Meteorite Crater—Past—Present—Future*. Amer. Meteorite Lab. 1956 pap. $4.50. This crater, the most famous of its kind, is 4,000 feet across. Many iron fragments have been found, but drilling has failed to find any central mass.

Parker, Ronald B. *Inscrutable Earth: Explorations in the Science of the Earth*. Scribner 1984 $14.95. "Geology is the root of the family tree of sciences." This is not a text, but essays introducing concepts, discoveries, and puzzles.

Pearl, Richard M. *Guide to Geologic Literature*. McGraw-Hill 1951 o.p. Essays on methods of research and library facilities, stressing specific kinds of literature.

Peterson, Morris S., and J. Keith Rigby. *Interpreting Earth History*. William C. Brown 3d ed. 1982 $14.40. The rocks bear evidence showing changes in land and water and their life throughout hundreds of millions of years. This book is historical geology and complements a text on physical geology.

Pettijohn, Francis J. *Memoirs of an Unrepentant Field Geologist*. Univ. of Chicago Pr. 1984 $25.00. "A candid profile of some geologists and their science, 1921–1981," by an expert on sands and sandstones.

Picard, M. Dane. *Grit and Clay*. Elsevier 1975 o.p. A geologist irreverently reviews not only works on geology but also novels and movies that depict geologists at work and play.

Press, Frank, and Raymond Siever. *Earth*. W. H. Freeman 3d ed. 1982 $29.95. Physical geology only—no history of life, but the text is one of the biggest and best around.

Raup, David M., and Steven M. Stanley. *Principles of Paleontology*. W. H. Freeman 2d ed. 1978 $31.95. As the theory of evolution evolves. fossils provide new clues bearing on plate tectonics and much else.

Rhodes, Frank H. T. *Geology.* [*Golden Guide Ser.*] Western Pub. 1971 pap. $2.95. Rhodes may have aimed at children, but he did not write down to them. This is a case of one size fits all.

Rhodes, Frank H. T., and Richard O. Stone, eds. *Language of the Earth.* Pergamon 1981 text ed. $39.00 pap. $19.25. The language is really *about* the Earth, by geologists, novelists, humorists, reporters, engineers, historians, and others. Many of the samples are very hard to find elsewhere.

Rossbacher, Lisa A. *Recent Revolutions in Geology.* Watts 1986 $10.90. Many secondary schools and general science texts scant recent developments. Among them are plate tectonics, new discoveries on the ocean floor, premonitory signs of earthquakes and volcanic eruptions, theories of mass extinctions, and new Earth-based technology for studying the geology of other planets.

Sarjeant, William Antony S. *Geologists and the History of Geology: An International Bibliography from the Origins to 1978.* Arno 5 vols. 1980 $350.00. Huge, expensive, important, and unduplicated elsewhere.

Schneer, Cecil J., ed. *Two Hundred Years of Geology in America: Proceedings of the New Hampshire Bicentennial Conference.* Univ. Pr. of New England 1979 $35.00. Surveys the science on the nation's bicentennial.

Skinner, Brian J., ed. *Earth's History, Structure, and Materials.* Kaufmann 1980 pap. $9.95. Covers measurement of geological time, plate tectonics, and volcanic chains.

Snelling, N. J. *The Chronology of the Geological Record.* Blackwell Pubns. 1985 text ed. $99.00. Despite any difficulties, the science of geology can hardly exist without a chronology of rocks, events, and life.

Stokes, W. Lee. *Essentials of Earth History.* Prentice-Hall 4th ed. 1982 text ed. $33.95. Seafloor spreading and global tectonics have been verified, forcing reinterpretation of evolutionary changes in life forms. Pairing this book with another on physical geology makes a solid basis for further study.

Ward, Dederick C., Marjorie Wheeler, and Robert A. Bier, Jr. *Geologic Reference Sources: A Subject and Regional Bibliography of Publications and Maps in the Geological Sciences.* Scarecrow Pr. 2d ed. 1981 $39.50. More than most scientists, geologists depend on the record of the past, whether in rocks or on paper.

Weiner, Jonathan. *Planet Earth.* Bantam 1986 $14.95. A respected Public Broadcasting System series by WQED, Pittsburgh, led to this companion text.

Wyatt, Antony. *Challinor's Dictionary of Geology.* Oxford 1986 $35.00 pap. $15.95. "Challinor" proves worthwhile when reading about British geology, for regional terms do exist.

Wykoff, Jerome. *The Story of Geology: Our Changing Earth Through the Ages.* Golden Pr. 1960 o.p. Not so rigorous as, say, an introductory textbook, but more readable than most.

LANDSCAPE

Everyone who goes outdoors and looks around soon notices the lay of the land. Walking down a hill or across a bridge makes us conscious of the landscape, and we may wonder how things came to be that way.

The study of the landscape and the natural forces that shaped it is called geomorphology and it is a field of science all its own. However, it is sometimes considered a part of geology, and sometimes a part of geography, and it is closely linked with glacial geology or Quaternary geology or both. So, readers must watch for cross-references to other fields of earth science. Whatever its academic classification, the landscape strongly affects the way we live. We enjoy the scenery of national parks, avoid building on flood-plains, use estuaries as seaways, fly higher over mountain chains, and avoid active volcanoes—all this takes into account geomorphology.

The remarks above include keywords for seeking out pertinent books. An introductory text may be the best starting point, though a first work on physical geology or physical geography may do. Less obvious are regional guides to geology, descriptions of national parks, and works on beaches and coastlines (which are reshaped rapidly by waves).

Butzer, Karl W. *Geomorphology from the Earth*. Harper 1976 $34.50. Space exploration has shown that the face of the Earth is unique and Butzer describes features and processes from that point of view.

Daly, Reginald A. *The Changing World of the Ice Age*. Hafner repr. of 1934 ed. 1963 $21.75. A readable and standard approach to glacial geology, which necessarily includes much geomorphology.

Feldman, Rodney M., and Richard A. Heimmlich. *Geology Field Guide: The Black Hills*. Kendall-Hunt 1980 pap. $11.95. Geomorphology and paleontology help decipher a popular scenic area.

Flint, Richard F. *Glacial and Quaternary Geology*. Wiley 1977 $52.95. The Quaternary period began two to three million years ago and extends to our own time. Most of it is sometimes called, loosely, the Ice Age.

Flint, Richard F., and Brian J. Skinner. *Physical Geology*. Wiley 2d ed. 1977 $40.95. An excellent textbook, and it is no criticism to say that the reader needs a book on historical geology too.

Foster, Robert J. *General Geology*. Merrill 5th ed. 1985 pap. $9.95. Concerns "the solid rock Earth," especially the processes that formed its surface features.

Frye, Keith. *Roadside Geology of Virginia*. Mountain Pr. 1986 pap. $9.95. Travelers pass over and through the geologic record, and highway cuts strip away vegetation and soil, providing a clearer view.

Gilbert, Grove Karl. *Report of the Geology of the Henry Mountains: U.S. Geographical and Geological Surveys of the Rocky Mountain Region*. [*History of Geology Ser.*] Ayer repr. of 1877 ed. 1978 $21.00. In his work, Gilbert (1843–1918) stressed the power of running water, pointing out that a stream adjusts its gradient precisely to enable it to just carry the sediment deposited in it. He was noted for his clear explanations of geologic phenomena and the book listed here is a classic analysis of a newly explored region.

Harris, Ann, and Esther Tuttle. *Geology of National Parks*. Kendall-Hunt 3d ed. 1983 pap. $27.95. Acceptance of global tectonics provoked this revision, showing that the "new geology" extends far from plate boundaries.

Harris, David V., and Eugene P. Kiver. *The Geologic Story of the National Parks and Monuments*. Wiley 3d ed. 1980 pap. $30.95. Often the main reason for preserving an area is its geology on display, and so many parks are painless and dramatic lessons in Earth materials and geologic processes.

Hill, Mary. *Geology of the Sierra Nevada*. Univ. of California Pr. 1974 pap. $7.95. The Sierra ranks among the Earth's great ranges and is a key to understanding many other mountain systems.

Hunt, Charles B. *Death Valley: Geology, Ecology, Archaeology*. Univ. of California Pr. 1975 $19.95 pap. $9.95. As the subtitle suggests, one science seldom stands alone.

————. *Natural Regions of the United States and Canada.* W. H. Freeman 1974 $31.95.
A "region" has characteristic geology, topography, climate, flora, and fauna.

Krutch, Joseph Wood. *Grand Canyon: Today and All Its Yesterdays.* Peter Smith 1958
$13.75. An essay on one of the great features of the Earth, one whose canyon
walls represent nearly two billion years. Illustrated.

Lobeck, Armin K. *Geomorphology: An Introduction to the Study of Landscapes.*
McGraw-Hill 1939 o.p. "Lobeck" is a permanent classic, with text facing illustrations in units of two or four pages and showing how natural forces shape the
landscape. Many unsurpassed early photos of the American West by William H.
Jackson, pioneer photographer.

McKee, Bates. *Cascadia: The Geologic Evolution of the Pacific Northwest.* McGraw-
Hill 1972 o.p. Mount Rainier alone illustrates volcanology, glacial geology, the
power of running water, and meteorology. *Cascadia* covers far more than one
mountain and is a model for geological field guides.

Pethick, John. *An Introduction to Coastal Geomorphology.* Arnold 1984 pap. $17.95.
Where land and ocean meet, nature moves beaches and otherwise, usually,
defeats anyone who opposes it.

Redfern, Ron. *Corridors of Time: 1,700,000,000 Years of Earth at Grand Canyon.*
Times Bks. 1980 $55.00. The Grand Canyon provides a panorama of Earth his-
tory extending back to a time before the earliest known life. Redfern provides
panoramic photos.

Shelton, John S. *Geology Illustrated.* W. H. Freeman 1966 $31.95. Earth features are
often best shown from the air, as in these photos and diagrams. The text explains the natural forces responsible.

Shimer, John A. *This Sculptured Earth: The Landscape of America.* Columbia Univ.
Pr. 1959 $36.00. Depicts the workings and results of natural sculptors—wind,
water, waves, ice.

Sullivan, Walter. *Landprints: On the Magnificent American Landscape.* Times Bks.
1984 $22.50. Pictures show the geologic record of the United States as any
traveler can see; the text explains geologists' interpretation for nongeologist
readers.

ROCKS, MINERALS, AND GEOCHEMISTRY

In the earth sciences, chemistry usually means the chemical composition
of the Earth's materials—mainly rocks, minerals, and water—and is formally known as geochemistry. Most books, and most fields of academic
study, treat separately the fields of mineralogy, petrography, and petrology (roughly, rocks and minerals), but the relationships are clear. All those
subjects are discussed in books about volcanoes, magma (molten material), and metamorphism.

To learn about the chemical composition of materials of the Earth, a
reader should begin with a standard chemistry textbook, then a book on
physical geology, and then one on rocks and minerals. Cross-references and
natural curiosity should then show the way. Another approach is to go to
one of the big encyclopedias of mineralogy for a general view of the huge
variety of minerals (several thousand are known). Then use a field guide to
rocks and minerals to find out more about the much smaller number of

minerals anyone can find in fields, road cuts, and the walls of downtown buildings. From there proceed to books on chemistry, geology, and mineralogy, to learn how the rocks and minerals came to be that way.

Agricola, Georgius. *De Re Metallica*. Trans. by Herbert Clark Hoover and Lou Henry Hoover, Dover repr. of 1912 ed. 1950 $19.95. For more than two centuries, Agricola's work was the leading guide to mining and technology, and even now it remains fascinating history.

Barnes, Virgil E., and Mildred A. Barnes. *Tektites*. Van Nostrand 1973 $57.95. Tektites are glassy fragments that are found in groups in widely scattered regions of the Earth's surface. Their origin is unclear, although they seem to be meteoritic; one theory is that they were splashed onto the Earth by meteoritic impact on the Moon.

Chesterman, Charles W. *The Audubon Society Field Guide to North American Rocks and Minerals*. Knopf 1979 $13.50. A handbook on discovery, identification, and labeling of specimens. Perhaps more important, it is an elementary introduction to geology and mapping.

Colman, Steven M., and David P. Delthier. *Rates of Chemical Weathering of Rocks and Minerals*. Academic Pr. 1986 $95.00. Very technical, but illustrates the importance of weathering as a powerful geologic agent.

Cooper, Henry S. F., Jr. *Moon Rocks*. Dial 1970 o.p. The first geological field trips to the Moon provided hand specimens for mineralogists and petrographers whose work had always been purely theoretical.

Desautels, Paul E. *The Mineral Kingdom*. Grosset & Dunlap 1968 o.p. A coffee-table book, but also much more: history of mineralogy and crystallography, occurrences, and collecting.

Fleischer, Michael. *Glossary of Mineral Species 1983*. Mineralogical Record 1983 o.p. Catalogs mineral names, including synonyms, varieties, and discredited names, with chemical composition—and, often, reference to first descriptions.

Freedman, Jacob. *Trace Element Geochemistry in Health and Disease*. Geol. Soc. of Amer. 1975 $31.50. In Deaf Smith County, Texas, the drinking water can mottle teeth. That is only one example of hundreds in which tiny amounts of naturally occurring substances affect the health of inhabitants.

Frye, Keith. *Modern Mineralogy*. Prentice-Hall 1974 $36.95. A textbook on minerals—their formation, occurrence, properties, composition, and classification. Technical but useful.

Krauskopf, Konrad B. *Introduction to Geochemistry*. McGraw-Hill 2d ed. 1979 $49.50. More technical than some other introductory textbooks, but chemistry is essential to understanding the Earth.

McDivitt, James F., and Gerald Manners. *Minerals and Men: An Exploration of the World of Minerals and Metals Including Some of the Major Problems That Are Posed*. Johns Hopkins Univ. Pr. 1974 rev. ed. pap. $11.95. For nonspecialists; as suggested by the subtitle, the problems are economic and political as well as scientific.

Mason, Brian, and Carleton B. Moore. *Principles of Geochemistry*. Wiley 4th ed. 1982 $42.95. The principles remain, but the subject matter changes as new data arrives from deep-sea cores and from imagery of the extraterrestrial planets.

Mitchell, Richard Scott. *Mineral Names: What Do They Mean?* Van Nostrand 1979 $15.95. Names link minerals to persons, places, chemical composition, and a host of tribes, fictional characters, and so on.

Ollier, C. D. *Weathering*. Elsevier 1975 pap. $22.95. Weathering is the breakdown of materials on or near the Earth's surface and their alteration to suit more closely their new environment. We all recognize rust, but seldom think of it as a powerful and pervasive geologic agent.

Pough, Frederick H. *A Field Guide to Rocks and Minerals.* [*Peterson Field Guide Ser.*] Houghton Mifflin 4th ed. 1976 $17.95 pap. $12.95. Photos, descriptions, classifications, and simple chemical and blowpipe tests.

Sorrell, Charles A. *A Field Guide and Introduction to the Geology and Chemistry of Rocks and Minerals.* Western Pub. 1973 pap. $7.95. The title is unwieldy but accurate.

Sutulov, Alexander. *Minerals in World Affairs.* Univ. of Utah Ptg. Servs. 1972 o.p. A better title might be "Minerals and Economics." It can be argued that minerals very nearly lead the list of motives for war.

Tomkeieff, S. I., and others, eds. *Dictionary of Petrology.* Wiley 1983 $140.00. The arrangement is alphabetical, but each term is cross-indexed to tables that regroup related items.

Wilk, Harry. *The Magic of Minerals.* Springer-Verlag 1986 $45.00. The choice is selective, with 110 full-page photos. There are thousands of known minerals, but only mineralogists or museum-goers are likely to ever see more than these.

Williams, Howel, and others. *Petrography: An Introduction to the Study of Rocks in Thin Sections.* W. H. Freeman 2d ed. 1983 $38.95. One of the most efficient ways to identify rocks is to examine, by microscope, thin slices of samples. More than other books on the subject, this one stresses sedimentary rocks.

GEOPHYSICS

Geophysics, like geology, has outgrown its Earthbound origin. Even on our own planet, geophysics covers a lot of ground, and most people (among them scientists, authors, and librarians) permit the term to incorporate volcanology, seismology, and magnetism. Some add meteorology and oceanography to the list, and planetary physics, too. Here let us say the physical properties of Earth and other objects circling our Sun.

With that range of subject matter, a first book in geophysics must be very general—perhaps one on the solar system itself. Physical geology is needed too. Thereafter the path lies in the direction of increasingly specialized fields, for example, toward plate dynamics, or volcanology, or seismology, or terrestrial magnetism.

Studying geophysics in detail soon requires mathematics, chemistry, and physics. However, those tools are not needed to gain a general understanding of many fascinating phenomena. We can easily see that the Pacific Plate, grinding northward against the North America Plate, causes earthquakes along the San Andreas Fault. Further understanding may require learning to use the tools, but encyclopedia articles and bibliographies will guide the way.

Bullard, Fred M. *Volcanoes of the Earth.* Univ. of Texas Pr. 1984 2d rev. ed. $47.00. This, probably the most comprehensive of books on volcanoes, ranks with the most readable.

Bullen, K. E., and Bruce A. Bolt. *An Introduction to the Theory of Seismology.* Cambridge Univ. Pr. 4th ed. 1985 pap. $24.95. Not observation but theory, and technical; nevertheless, fundamental.

Carr, Michael H., ed. *The Geology of the Terrestrial Planets.* NASA 1984 consult publisher for information. As recently as the early 1960s, we knew nothing of the
geology of the other planets, and very little about the rocks of the Moon.

Darden, Lloyd. *The Earth in the Looking Glass.* Anchor 1974 o.p. Remote sensing—
the examination of the Earth from space, or at least from high altitudes. The
means can be photographs using visible light, but are likely to involve instruments sensitive to infrared and other wave lengths.

Decker, Robert, and Barbara Decker. *Volcanoes.* W. H. Freeman 1981 pap. $11.95.
Along with much else, the authors list 101 of the Earth's most notorious volcanoes.

Eicher, Don L., A. Lee McAlester, and Marcia L. Rottman. *The History of the Earth's
Crust.* Prentice-Hall 1984 $21.95. Earth history is shown most clearly in its
crust—the outer layer we can examine directly and with seismic waves.

Elder, John. *The Bowels of the Earth.* Oxford 1976 $21.95 pap. $9.95. The Earth is a
"vast machine, insatiably consuming itself." Mathematical formulas are abundant, but Elder's way with words compensates for any difficulty.

French, Bevan M. *The Moon Book: Exploring the Mysteries of the Lunar World.* Penguin 1977 o.p. Astronomy, rocketry, and mineralogy meet on Earth's satellite.

Glen, William. *The Road to Jaramillo: Critical Years of the Revolution in Earth Science.* Stanford Univ. Pr. 1982 $40.00. Widely scattered work cumulated in the
plate-tectonics revolution—work on rock dating, geomagnetic reversals, and
seafloor spreading.

Iacopi, Robert, ed. *Earthquake Country: California.* Lane Bks. 1971 pap. $7.95. To
many Americans, "earthquake" means California, the San Andreas Fault, and
the San Francisco Earthquake of 1906. Iacopi gives the science and facts for
nonscientists.

Menard, Henry W., ed. *Oceanic Islands.* W. H. Freeman 1986 $29.95. From *Scientific
American,* by scientists, for curious nonscientists. Changes in the sea level may
drown islands or form them; if the Pacific were evaporated, the Hawaiian islands would be taller than Everest.

Mission to Earth: Landsat Views the World. NASA 1976 consult publisher for information. Landsat is a satellite designed to assess the natural resources of the United
States. It was spectacularly successful, and also transmitted images of other
countries: neither satellites nor science respect political boundaries.

Redfern, Ron. *The Making of a Continent.* Times Bks. 1983 $27.95 1986 pap. $16.95.
This book, and the Public Broadcasting System film based on it, shows the
making of North America over geologic time.

Simkin, Tom, and others. *Volcanoes of the World: A Regional Directory, Gazetteer, and
Chronology of Volcanism During the Last 10,000 Years.* Van Nostrand 1981
$31.95. The data is from the Smithsonian Institution, and there is no other
source like it.

Simon, Ruth B. *Earthquake Interpretations: A Manual for Reading Seismograms.* Kaufmann 1981 pap. $9.95. A primer for reading records of seismographs for clues to
the internal structure of the Earth. This way lies earthquake prediction.

Sullivan, Walter. *Continents in Motion: The New Earth Debate.* McGraw-Hill 1974
o.p. Sullivan, science editor for *The New York Times,* was one of the first to
explain the "New Geology" to nonscientists.

Takeuchi, H., S. Uyeda, and H. Kanamori. *Debate About the Earth.* Freeman Cooper
1970 $10.00. General acceptance of continental drift forced geoscientists to reap-
praise many aspects of geology and geophysics.

Van Andel, Tjeerd. *New Views of an Old Planet: Continental Drift and the History of
the Earth.* Cambridge Univ. Pr. 1985 $19.95. Earth is dynamic, with "a history of
many brief intervals of dramatic change between longer times of relative quies-

cence." The major changes have been in "drifting of continents, fluctuations of climate, the precession of life."

Veverka, Joseph, and NASA's Planetary Geology Working Group. *Planetary Geology in the 1980s.* NASA 1985 consult publisher for information. "In the 70s," the authors say, "the bizarre nature of Titan's surface was hardly suspected; we were not aware of the intense volcanic activity of Io [Jupiter's innermost moon], or of the possibility that Neptune's Triton may have an ocean of liquid nitrogen." We can no longer consider the Earth's rocks unique in their composition and history, and must review the accepted wisdom with that in mind.

Wahrhaftig, Clyde. *A Streetcar to Subduction and Other Plate Tectonic Trips by Public Transport in San Francisco.* Amer. Geophysical Union rev. ed. 1984 pap. $7.50. Plate tectonics did much to shape the Bay Area and produced the San Francisco Earthquake of 1906. Here is an ideal way, and setting, for a self-guided tour of geology you can see and touch.

Williams, Howel, and A. R. McBirney. *Volcanology.* Freeman Cooper repr. of 1979 ed. 1982 $37.00. The authors are less concerned with descriptions of eruptive peaks than with the physics and chemistry of the magma involved.

Windley, Brian F. *The Evolving Continents.* Wiley 2d ed. 1984 $69.95. Continental drift became respectable in the 1960s. Now the geodynamics of plate tectonics is being elucidated.

HYDROLOGY AND OCEANOGRAPHY

Earth is known as the blue planet—blue mainly because of its water. The principal sciences of water are called oceanography and hydrology, the latter including surface water (on land) and ground water (under the surface). Most books about water concern one of the three: oceanography, surface water, or ground water. But traps for the unwary abound. "Marine science" tends to include marine life. "Oceanography" tends to concentrate on composition and wave mechanics. "Marine geology" tends to stress the coasts and the ocean floor.

Whatever the name, the study of water often leads deeply into chemistry, physics, and mathematics. Even so, many introductory texts are both readable and worth reading. Informal works are numerous, too, as are books on even fairly specialized topics such as rivers and submarine geology. Somehow—perhaps because water is so familiar to all of us?—the technical level of most works on water is easy to judge.

Books about physical geology always discuss water (solid, liquid, and gas) in the hydrologic cycle and as an agent of erosion and transport. No books on meteorology or geography can neglect water, none on natural hazards and few on natural resources. Water is as pervasive in books as in nature.

Anikouchine, William, and Richard W. Sternberg. *The World Ocean: An Introduction to Oceanography.* Prentice-Hall 2d ed. 1981 text ed. $33.95. Based on the important fact that on the surface of the globe there is much more water area than land.

Bascom, Willard. *Waves and Beaches: The Dynamics of the Ocean Surface.* Doubleday (Anchor) rev. ed. 1980 pap. $9.95. The ocean still sets the rules for humanity's use of land and water along the shore.

Carson, Rachel. *The Edge of the Sea.* Houghton Mifflin 1979 pap. $9.95. Here Carson, most widely known for *Silent Spring* (Houghton Mifflin 1962 $16.95), turns to the coastal zone and its biology, geology, oceanography, and meteorology.

——. *The Sea Around Us.* New Amer. Lib. 1954 pap. $4.95. The oceans from the beginning: history, mystery, and facts. Deceptively easy reading.

Davis, Stanley N., and Roger J. M. DeWiest. *Hydrology.* Wiley 1966 $42.95. A textbook on the chemistry and physics of water.

Flemming, N. C., ed. *The Undersea.* Macmillan 1977 o.p. Not a text on oceanography, but a discussion of the ocean floor, water, fauna and flora, resources, use of oceans, underwater archaeology, submarines, and marine law.

Geraghty, James J., and others. *Water Atlas of the United States.* Water Info. 3d ed. 1973 $45.00. Charts and graphs show, more effectively than words, where the water is—in rivers, lakes, aquifers—and how much, and so on.

Gross, M. Grant. *Oceanography.* Merrill 4th ed. 1980 pap. $9.95. An introduction to the composition of seawater and the mechanism of waves, and related subjects.

Heezen, Bruce C., and Charles D. Hollister. *The Face of the Deep.* Oxford 1971 pap. $21.95. Many photos and diagrams. Heezen was among the first to map large areas of the ocean floor, thus contributing to the discovery and explanation of seafloor spreading.

Kaufman, Wallace, and Orrin H. Pilkey, Jr. *The Beaches Are Moving: The Drowning of America's Shoreline.* Duke Univ. Pr. 1983 pap. $9.75. The sea level is rising, inexorably, and the works of man only increase the damage.

Kennett, James P. *Marine Geology.* Prentice-Hall 1982 $43.95. The word "geology" indicates emphasis on rocks and sediments at the expense of water.

Leopold, Luna B. *Water: A Primer.* W. H. Freeman 1974 $22.95. Really a primer, and really informative. It may well be the best starting point for the innocent and interested.

Marx, Wesley. *The Oceans, Our Last Resource.* Sierra 1981 $13.95. "Resource" means food, minerals, energy, recreation, scenery, and gene pool.

Maury, Matthew F. *The Physical Geography of the Sea, and Its Meteorology.* 1855. Ed. by John Leighly, Harvard Univ. Pr. 1963 pap. $9.95. The first textbook of modern oceanography. Matthew Fontaine Maury (1806–73) was an officer in the U.S. Navy, first superintendent of the U.S. Naval Observatory, produced the first bathymetric chart of the Atlantic floor (to show the feasibility of a submarine telegraph cable), and was an early student of the Gulf Stream (like Benjamin Franklin before him, he collected records from ships' captains). He is remembered as both oceanographer and meteorologist, as suggested by his widely known *Wind and Current Charts* (many versions, concerning several oceans).

Menard, Henry W. *Anatomy of an Expedition.* McGraw-Hill 1969 o.p. Here is what an oceanographer does for a living; in this case, from desk to sea on the Nova Expedition.

Powledge, Fred. *Water: The Nature, Uses, and Future of Our Most Abused Resource.* Farrar 1982 $13.95 pap. $7.95. From chemistry through water-resource management.

Schumm, Stanley A. *The Fluvial System.* Wiley 1977 $45.50. Mark Twain described the vagaries of the Mississippi; now Schumm describes the ways and means of rivers doing such things.

——, ed. *River Morphology.* Van Nostrand 1972 pap. $45.95. This wide-ranging survey includes classic papers hard to gather elsewhere.

Sheaffer, John R., and Leonard A. Stevens. *Future Water: An Exciting Solution to America's Most Serious Resource Crisis.* Morrow 1983 $14.95. "Polluted water," the authors say persuasively, "are really valuable resources out of place."

Shepard, Francis P. *Earth Beneath the Sea.* Atheneum rev. ed. 1968 pap. $3.95.

Shepard pioneered the direct study of the ocean bottom and its sediments, replacing theory with observed fact.

——. *Geological Oceanography: Evolution of Coasts, Continental Margins, and the Deep Sea Floor.* Crane Russak 1977 o.p. Coastlines, continental margins, and the deep ocean floors differ markedly, but are interrelated.

Steinbeck, John, and Edward F. Ricketts. *Sea of Cortez: A Leisurely Journal of Travel and Research.* Appel repr. of 1941 ed. 1986 $30.00. Ricketts was the original for "Doc" of Steinbeck's Cannery Row novels (*Cannery Row* and *Sweet Thursday*), and the expedition to the Gulf of California was real, too.

Van Andel, Tjeerd. *Tales of an Old Ocean: Exploring the Deep-Sea World of the Geologist and Oceanographer.* Norton 1978 pap. $8.95. The adventures of an oceanographer at work as the science changes all around him.

Vetter, Richard C., ed. *Oceanography: The Last Frontier.* Basic Bks. 1973 o.p. The specialists represented here wrote for radio broadcast, so the technical level is low and the readability high.

White, Gilbert F. *Strategies of American Water Management.* Univ. of Michigan Pr. 1969 o.p. Particularly in the American West, the demand for water leads to political, legal, and economic problems.

ATMOSPHERIC SCIENCE

Life on Earth exists because of water, a suitable distance from the Sun, and free oxygen. Oxygen means air, and the science of air is called atmospheric science or meteorology. Most of us say weather and climate. Geophysicists and geographers often claim meteorology for their own, but readers who know about the overlapping claims will not be confused. One place to start exploring is in a field guide to the weather. Books on physical geography discuss climates and perhaps weather, and usually suggest further reading.

Titles of introductory textbooks in this field are likely to include "meteorology" or "climatology." Those books are likely to provoke interest in forecasting, satellite imagery, weather modification, or violent storms. Further specialization leads to advanced mathematics and computer-aided manipulation of data from artificial satellites.

Weather and climate touch everything around us. That means it is important to watch other earth sciences for works on atmospheric phenomena. Who would expect a book called *Volcano Weather?* (see Stommel and Stommel below).

Barry, Roger G., and Richard J. Chorley. *Atmosphere, Weather, and Climate.* Methuen 2d ed. 1982 $38.00 pap. $14.95. Wide ranging without being excessively technical.

Barth, Michael C., and James G. Titus, eds. *Greenhouse Effect and Sea Level Rise.* Van Nostrand 1984 $24.50. Global warming seems sure to raise the sea level enough to drown thousands of square miles in the United States, including several major cities.

Battan, Louis J. *Fundamentals of Meteorology.* Prentice-Hall 2d ed. 1984 $31.95. An introductory text, sparing of mathematics, physics, and chemistry, and stressing what we already know and what we need to know.

Calder, Nigel. *The Weather Machine: How Our Weather Works and Why It Is Chang-*

ing. Penguin 1977 pap. $4.95. The easy reading disguises the amount of information.

Cole, Franklyn W. *Introduction to Meteorology.* Wiley 3d ed. 1980 $38.95. Serious, sound, and thorough.

Conway, H. McKinley, and Linda L. Liston, eds. *The Weather Handbook.* Conway Data rev. ed. 1974 $29.95. "A summary of weather statistics for selected cities throughout the U.S. and around the world." A reference work to use in preparing to move or travel, or to fill in your mental picture of places in the news.

Critchfield, Howard J. *General Climatology.* Prentice-Hall 4th ed. 1983 text ed. $33.95. Straightforward and readable introduction, and not intimidating.

Donn, William L. *Meteorology.* McGraw-Hill 4th ed. 1975 $39.00. Donn notes that this introductory text retains its "marine flavor" even though he has cut back a chapter on the oceans because of the publication of more textbooks on oceanography.

Minnaert, M. *The Nature of Light and Colour in the Open Air.* Dover 1948 text ed. pap. $6.00; Gannon 1954 lib. bdg. $13.50. Describes and explains hundreds of natural phenomena (rainbows, sun dogs, the green flash); some are easily recognizable as probable explanations of reported sightings of UFOs.

Oliver, John E., and John J. Hidore. *Introduction to Climatology.* Merrill 1984 $29.95. As usual, physics and dynamics, regional aspects, and paleoclimates; not so usual, applied studies.

Pearce, E. A., and C. G. Smith. *The Times Books World Weather Guide.* Times Bks. 1984 $22.50. Arranged by country, region, city. The authors describe the climate for each region; then for each city is a chart showing monthly extremes and averages of temperature, precipitation, and humidity. Few books of charts are so easy to pick up and so hard to put down.

Riehl, Herbert. *Introduction to the Atmosphere.* McGraw-Hill 3d ed. 1974 $42.95. The third edition adds a discussion of artificial satellites as observation tools and takes into account humankind's increasing disturbance of the environmental equilibrium.

Schaefer, Vincent J., and John A. Day. *A Field Guide to the Atmosphere.* Houghton Mifflin 1983 $13.95 pap. $10.95. How to identify clouds, describe meteorological phenomena, understand storms, and (loosely) predict weather.

Sloane, Eric. *Look at the Sky . . . and Tell the Weather.* Dutton 1979 pap. $4.95. Anecdotal commonsense science.

Stommel, Henry, and Elizabeth Stommel. *Volcano Weather: The Story of 1816, the Year Without a Summer.* Seven Seas Pr. 1983 $15.00. In 1815, Mount Tambora (in present-day Indonesia) erupted catastrophically and ejected 100 cubic kilometers of debris—by far the greatest eruption in the last 10,000 years. For at least a year it disrupted the weather and life all around the Earth.

Trewartha, Glenn T. *The Earth's Problem Climates.* Univ. of Wisconsin Pr. 2d ed. 1981 $27.50. Some climates are stable and inhospitable; others are erratic and unpredictable.

Trewartha, Glenn T., and Lyle H. Horn. *An Introduction to Climate.* McGraw-Hill 5th ed. 1980 $38.95. Climate is the normal weather pattern for a region—but climates do change, as shown by the evidence of archaeology and geology, and they have changed faster than civilizations could handle.

Weather of United States Cities. Ed. by James A. Ruffner and Frank E. Blair, Gale 2 vols. 1981 $160.00. For each city there is a narrative summary and approximately two pages of tables showing temperature, precipitation, heating-degree days.

Wigley, T. M. L., M. J. Ingram, and G. Farmer. *Climate and History: Studies in Past Climates and Their Impacts on Man.* Cambridge Univ. Pr. 1981 pap. $24.50. Over geologic time, climates shift and change, leaving evidence in sediments, pollen (in rocks and glaciers), and tree rings. How climate detectives find the facts.

Zim, Herbert S., and others. *Weather.* [*Golden Guide Ser.*] Western Pub. 1987 pap. $3.95. For a novice of almost any age or background. Deceptively informative.

NATURAL RESOURCES AND APPLIED SCIENCE

What is science good for? Sometimes the answer is fairly obvious. Sometimes the answer is "nothing—yet." Sometimes it is an intellectual challenge, training for the brain. Practical results may come along later. Our civilization depends on soil for agriculture, on rocks and minerals for materials, and on oil, gas, and coal for energy. For building and safety, we need knowledge of natural hazards (such as earthquakes, landslides, and tornadoes) and of the mechanical properties of rock and soil (as for bridge footings and road building).

That is applied science. It is also quite a mixture, with many of the pieces found under geography, geology, geomorphology, geochemistry, hydrology, and seismology. A book on any of those subjects is likely to have a chapter on use in everyday living. Also, consult the index and reference list for topics such as economic geography, engineering geology, geologic hazards, natural resources, and rock mechanics. Look, too, for books on the practice of various professions—case histories, field mapping, career opportunities.

An old newspaper rule says, "Tell how people live." Add to that "Find how an earth science helps people live."

Basile, Robert M. *A Geography of Soils.* William C. Brown 1981 o.p. A basic introduction to a resource so common we sometimes forget that it is vital.

Bates, Robert L. *Geology of the Industrial Rocks and Minerals.* Dover 1969 pap. $8.50. To many, economic geology means oil and gas and the major ore minerals. Bates concentrates on materials that become brick, concrete, talcum powder, and other everyday artifacts.

————. *Stone, Clay, and Glass, Basics for Building.* Enslow Pubs. 1986 $11.95. Everyday geology of the most practical kind.

Bates, Robert L., and Julia Jackson. *Our Modern Stone Age.* Kaufmann 1982 $18.95. Here are about two dozen of the most common rocks and minerals used in everyday life—how they are formed, found, and converted to useful products.

Blyth, F. G., and M. H. DeFries. *A Geology for Engineers.* Crane-Russak 6th ed. 1974 pap. $24.50. Engineers are concerned primarily with immediately practical aspects of earth materials.

Bolt, Bruce A., and others. *Geological Hazards.* Springer-Verlag 2d ed. 1977 $29.50. As population grows and concentrates in urban areas, a single windstorm threatens more people and property. And not only storms—earthquakes, seismic sea waves, storm waves, volcanoes, avalanches, landslides, uneven settlement of the ground, and floods.

Clark, Edwin H., Jenniver A. Haverkamp, and William Chapman. *Eroding Soils: The Off-Farm Impacts.* Conservation Foundation 1985 pap. $15.00. Every year, erosion takes six billion tons of soil from U.S. land and moves it into lakes and streams. Humans cause much of that loss and can control it.

Coates, Donald R. *Environmental Geology*. Wiley 1981 $39.95. This is geology as applied to water, sewage, scenery, and similar concerns—humankind versus nature. A handbook for modern living.

————. *Geology and Society*. Methuen 1985 $49.95. Nowadays they masquerade as "environment": minerals, fuels, water, geologic hazards (eruptions, quakes, slides, floods), engineering geology, pollution, waste, resource management, political regulation. Coates has gathered together a handbook for citizens.

Compton, Robert R. *Geology in the Field*. Wiley 1985 $23.95. Compton stresses the high cost of fieldwork and the importance of recognizing key geologic features the first time around. This is a handbook of techniques and surely an essential tool for anyone who goes out to look at the rocks in place. Anyone at all interested in rocks or the land should consult this book early.

Couniham, Martin. *A Dictionary of Energy*. Routledge & Kegan 1981 $16.95. Not only fuels, but power from the Sun, wind, tides, and underground steam. Technology too.

Crozier, Michael J. *Landslides: Causes, Consequences, and Environment*. Croon Helm 1986 $43.00. Here is how landslides work, where they occur, when, and who cares? and why. Practical geology for the engineer and for anyone living near slopes.

Eckes, Alfred E. *The United States and the Global Struggle for Minerals*. Univ. of Texas Pr. 1979 $20.00 pap. $9.95. Oil and gas—fuel minerals—are the most obvious examples for Americans, but we must import many others such as cobalt, platinum, and chromium.

Epstein, Samuel S., Lester O. Brown, and Carl Pope. *Hazardous Waste in America*. Sierra 1982 $27.50. More and more, our waste affects our environment—landfills, ground water, and scenery. Empty aluminum cans and spent uranium rods have an expensive and troublesome afterlife.

Frazier, Kendrick. *The Violent Face of Nature: Severe Phenomena and Natural Disasters*. Morrow 1979 $12.95. Thunderstorms, tornadoes, lightning, hail, floods, hurricanes, blizzards, volcanoes, earthquakes—how they happen and what can be done about them.

Gere, James M., and Haresh C. Shah. *Terra Non Firma: Understanding and Preparing for Earthquakes*. W. H. Freeman 1984 pap. $12.95. Written by earthquake engineers at Stanford University, California, for potential victims. Given the information, mere common sense can help.

Griggs, Gary B., and John A. Gilchrist. *Geologic Hazards, Resources, and Environmental Planning*. Wadsworth 1983 $26.00. Industrialization and population growth increase the risk of death and destruction and also the demand for water, minerals, and energy. Thus environmental planning, with legal aspects, is needed.

Jensen, Mead L., and Alan M. Bateman. *Economic Mineral Deposits*. Wiley 3d ed. rev. 1981 $40.95. The location and nature of ore bodies is a geological problem that must be solved before mining can be considered. A textbook, not overly technical.

Kiersch, George A., and others, eds. *Engineering Geology Case Histories*. Geol. Soc. of Amer. 1974 $12.50. How knowledge of geologic materials and natural forces affected various construction projects—and, in some cases, their catastrophic collapse and failure.

Lahee, Frederic H. *Field Geology*. McGraw-Hill 6th ed. 1961 $58.95. A handbook of conventions and methods of mapping rocks as they occur in the field.

Langenkamp, Robert D. *The Illustrated Petroleum Reference Dictionary*. PennWell
    Bks. 3d ed. 1985 $55.95. Little science—mainly engineering and business.
Menard, Henry W. *Geology, Resources, and Society: An Introduction to Earth Science*.
    W. H. Freeman 1974 text ed. $30.95. Menard stresses practical applications.
Moseley, Frank. *Methods in Field Geology*. W. H. Freeman 1981 $32.95 pap. $17.95.
    The "black boxes" of computer-age technology have not entirely displaced field
    boots, rock hammer, and compass.
Odell, Peter R. *Oil and World Power*. Penguin 7th ed. 1983 pap. $9.95. Of politics,
    economics, and resources, here at home and in the Middle East.
Pitts, John. *A Manual of Geology for Civil Engineers*. Halsted Pr. 1985 $24.95. Stresses
    the mechanical properties of rocks and soil, effects of weathering and erosion,
    and how to read geologic maps, record drill cores, and describe rocks.
Ross, Charles A., and June R. Ross. *Geology of Coal*. Van Nostrand 1983 $38.95.
    Many books on coal are limited to individual beds, mines, or basins. This collec-
    tion ranges much more widely.
Rossbacher, Lisa A. *Career Opportunities in Geology and the Earth Sciences*. Arco 1983
    $12.95 pap. $7.95. The major employers are government, industry, and schools.
    Here are job descriptions, some by working scientists themselves.
Skinner, Brian J., ed. *Earth's Energy and Mineral Resources*. Kaufmann 1980 pap.
    $9.95. Papers from *American Scientist* explore the question of where, in the next
    few decades, can we find fuels and minerals for more than five billion people.
Weston, Rae. *Strategic Minerals: A World Survey*. Rowman 1984 $34.50. Nickel and
    titanium (among many others) are essential to advanced technology but their
    ore deposits are scarce and isolated.
White, Gilbert F., ed. *Natural Hazards: Local, National, Global*. Oxford 1974 o.p.
    Researchers studied human response to such natural events as floods in New
    Zealand, volcanic eruptions in Hawaii, and the earthquake threat in California.
Whittow, John. *Disasters: The Anatomy of Environmental Hazards*. Univ. of Georgia
    Pr. 1980 $22.00 pap. $9.95. Knowing how such things happen is the first step in
    preventing or avoiding them.

PALEONTOLOGY

Paleontology is the science of ancient life. In a word, fossils. Questions like
these are natural: What is the name of this shell? Here is a bone—what did
the whole animal look like? Paleontologists ask much more: When did it
live? Under what conditions? In water? How deep? What salinity? With
what other life? In short, paleontologists use the evidence of fossils to reconstruct former environments.

For perhaps a billion years, life forms have been immensely varied. Nowa-
days, so are books about animals and plants of the geologic past. Some
elementary guides to fossils do exist, but most describe only a limited range
of fossils or those found in a limited area. Those may suffice, but a reader
wanting to know much about fossils should begin with a biology book
describing life in our own time, and also one on general geology. Next
should be an introduction to historical geology, which will outline the physical history of the Earth and also describe the animals and plants that lived
at different times in the geologic past.

Studies of paleontology normally go from the simple to the complex. First invertebrate animals, then vertebrates. Beyond that are reconstructions of ancient environments, studies of assemblages (fauna and flora that lived in the same environment), and the great mysteries of earliest life and evolutionary change.

"Evolution" remains a provocative word, though paleontologists think of it as a mechanism following present-day physical laws rather than as an alternative to ultimate origin. Readable and informative books on the subject are rampant.

Bakker, Robert. *The Dinosaur Heresies: New Theories Unlocking the Mystery of the Dinosaurs and Their Extinction.* Ed. by Maria Guarnaschelli, Morrow 1986 $19.95. Bakker contradicts the long-held notion that all dinosaurs were cold-blooded, laid eggs, and had little intelligence. Brontosaurs in particular seem to have borne their young live and otherwise resembled today's mammals.

Case, Gerard R. *A Pictorial Guide to Fossils.* Van Nostrand 1982 $32.95. Case arranges fossils by their zoological classification.

Charig, Alan. *A New Look at the Dinosaurs.* Facts on File 1983 $15.95 pap. $5.95. Charig gives us a good mix of scholarship, writing, and artwork.

Colbert, Edwin H. *A Fossil-Hunter's Handbook: My Life with Dinosaurs and Other Friends.* Dutton 1980 o.p. Autobiography of a vertebrate paleontologist. Colbert (born in 1905) is one of the most widely known vertebrate paleontologists and was for many years curator at the American Museum of Natural History (1930–70), New York, before moving to the Museum of Northern Arizona. He specialized in fossil mammals of North and South America and Asia, and in describing them for fellow scientists and also for nonspecialists who simply like dinosaurs and other life of the past. Among his books (most of them out of print) are *The Dinosaur Book* (1951), *Dinosaurs: Their Discovery and Their World* (1961), *The Age of Reptiles* (1965), *Man and Dinosaurs* (1968), and *Evolution of the Vertebrates* (1980).

Darwin, Charles. *Voyage of the Beagle.* Anchor 1962 $6.95. Charles Robert Darwin (1809–82) is known everywhere as author of *On the Origin of Species by Means of Natural Selection* (1859), but as Sir Archibald Geike has pointed out he was a self-taught geologist, his training ground being the HMS *Beagle,* a survey ship for the British Admiralty, and its ports of call (1831–36) in Patagonia, Chile, Peru, and many islands in the Pacific. His textbook was the first volume of Sir Charles Lyell's *Principles of Geology* (1830), which he had been warned to distrust because it contradicted the prevailing belief that catastrophic events explained everything in geology. During the five-year cruise, Darwin found evidence in the rocks that convinced him Lyell was right: that the physical laws of the present sufficed to explain all geologic phenomena. His experience during the voyage of the *Beagle* led to the publication of *Coral Reefs* (1842), which invoked changes in sea level to explain many features of the Pacific islands. Life on the *Beagle* also laid the groundwork for *Origin of Species* and a storm of controversy that still lingers on in our own time. Darwin published much more, and is himself the subject of many books and essays. (See Alan Moorehead, *Darwin and the Beagle,* 1969.)

Eldredge, Niles. *Unfinished Synthesis: Biological Hierarchies and Modern Evolutionary Thought.* Oxford 1985 $24.95. Evolution is much more than merely a gradual development of species throughout geologic time. It also concerns distribution and adaptation to environment, and may involve episodic changes.

Glut, Donald F. *The New Dinosaur Dictionary.* Citadel Pr. 1982 $12.95. An earlier version by the same author was merely adequate; this one is much improved. Many drawings.

Gould, Stephen Jay. *Ever Since Darwin: Reflections in Natural History.* Norton 1977 $14.95. An innovative thinker in evolutionary theory, Gould discourses on Darwin, recounts Cambrian history, and evicts Velikovsky (a later-day catastrophist). Stephen Jay Gould (1941–   ) is professor of geology at Harvard University, a vertebrate paleontologist, somewhat controversial but widely respected by fellow scientists, and widely admired by readers of his monthly column in *Natural History.* He is one of the advocates, and originators, of a modification of the Darwinian version of evolution: changes in species sometimes occur quite abruptly, geologically speaking. (A parallel: rocks flanking the San Andreas Fault creep slowly in opposite directions, but for a time they do not slip and the strain builds up—and the inevitable sudden adjustment comes as an earthquake.)

——. *The Flamingo's Smile: Reflections in Natural History.* Norton 1985 $17.95 1987 pap. $8.95. This work, and also the one below, consists of wide-ranging essays on topics, including the earth sciences.

——. *Hen's Teeth and Horse's Toes: Further Reflections in Natural History.* Norton 1983 $15.50 pap. $5.95. "Probes controversies, oddities and discoveries in modern evolutionary biology in a wonderful collection of essays, rich in ideas. . . . These diverse essays, at once erudite and conversational, deal with Teilhard de Chardin's bizarre involvement in the Piltdown hoax; Darwin, Agassiz, Hutton and Cuvier at work; the politics of the census; and the revival of pseudoscientific Creationism" (*PW*).

——. *The Mismeasure of Man.* Norton 1981 $17.95 pap. $5.95. Mistakes—honest and otherwise—in the practice of science.

——. *Ontogeny and Phylogeny.* Harvard Univ. Pr. 1977 $25.00. This is Gould in the professional mode: the history of evolutionary theory revisited. Technical, but irresistible reading.

——. *The Panda's Thumb: More Reflections in Natural History.* Norton 1980 $15.95. Gould revisits Piltdown, describes episodic evolution, speculates on the dumbness—or otherwise—of dinosaurs.

Johanson, Donald, and Maitland Edey. *Lucy: The Beginnings of Humankind.* Warner Bks. 1982 pap. $9.95. Fossils of early Man—earliest man?—turn up in east Africa. Discovery and controversy.

Laporte, Leo, ed. *The Fossil Record and Evolution.* W. H. Freeman 1982 pap. $14.95. These articles from *Scientific American* are semitechnical but provide a readable overview of the evolution of life.

McFall, Russell P., and Jay C. Wollin. *Fossils for Amateurs: A Guide to Collecting and Preparing Invertebrate Fossils.* Van Nostrand 2d ed. 1983 $17.95 pap. $11.95. From conodonts to mammoths, this is a *practical* guide, giving advice on reading maps, collecting specimens, and labeling them. (Mislabeling can render a fossil quite worthless.)

McKerrow, W. S., ed. *The Ecology of Fossils: An Illustrated Guide.* MIT 1981 pap. $12.50. McKerrow shows and discusses assemblages—animals and plants that occurred together in life—in a typical environment for every geologic system since the Precambrian.

Matthews, William H., III. *Fossils: An Introduction to Prehistoric Life.* Barnes & Noble 1962 o.p. A useful, reasonable handbook for the casual fossil hunter who wants to know more.

Norman, David. *The Illustrated Encyclopedia of Dinosaurs.* Crescent Bks. 1985 o.p. All children, apparently, are fascinated by dinosaurs. In works like this, anyone can take the text or leave it alone.

Raup, David M., and Steven M. Stanley. *Principles of Paleontology.* W. H. Freeman
2d ed. 1978 $31.95. As the theory of evolution evolves, fossils provide new clues
bearing on plate tectonics and much else. An introduction, and a good one.

Rhodes, Frank H. T., and others. *Fossils.* [*Golden Guide Ser.*] Western Pub. 1962 pap.
$2.95. Rhodes manages to make the subject intelligible to young readers and
also informative to adults.

Sattler, Helen Roney. *The Illustrated Dinosaur Dictionary.* Lothrop 1983 $17.50. Of
the 300 or so kinds of dinosaurs described here, nearly 100 were discovered and
named since about 1960.

Schopf, Thomas J. M. *Paleoceanography.* Harvard Univ. Pr. 1980 $25.00. Books de-
voted exclusively to the history of the oceans—their physics, chemistry, climatology, and biology—are few.

————, ed. *Models in Paleobiology.* Freeman Cooper 1972 $14.00. Schopf says paleon-
tologists should turn from collecting and describing fossils and stress interpretation of the evolution and distribution of life. That seems to be the trend.

Simpson, George Gaylord. *Fossils and the History of Life.* W. H. Freeman 1984
$27.95. An eminent paleontologist cites evidence in the rocks for evolution. The
name George Gaylord Simpson (1902–84) is known widely, and well, both
among professional vertebrate paleontologists and the vicarious kind. He spent
most of his career at the American Museum of Natural History (1924–59), New
York, and at Harvard University (1959–70) and then, like Edwin H. Colbert,
moved to the Southwest—in Simpson's case, to the University of Arizona. He
specialized in fossil mammals, especially those found in early Tertiary rocks of
North and South America, and penguins. Many of his books are readable by
people lacking a doctorate in comparative anatomy, among them *Concession to
the Improbable: An Unconventional Autobiography* (1978). Among others are *Life
of the Past* (1953), *This View of Life* (1964), *Penguins: Past and Present, Here and
There* (1973), and *Discoverers of the Lost World* (1984).

————. *Horses: The Story of the Horse Family in the Modern World and through Sixty
Million Years of History.* Oxford 1951 o.p. Horses, like dinosaurs and trilobites,
rank as favorites among fossil hunters and students of evolution.

————. *Meaning of Evolution: A Study of the History of Life and Its Significance for
Man.* Yale Univ. Pr. 1967 pap. $9.95. A readable and influential account for
nonspecialists.

Skinner, Brian J., ed. *Paleontology and Paleoenvironments.* Kaufmann 1981 $10.95.
Experts discuss (in *American Scientist*) life in the geologic past, where the ancient animals and plants lived, how they evolved, and what became of them.

Stanley, Steven M. *The New Evolutionary Timetable: Fossils, Genes, and the Origin of
Species.* Basic Bks. 1981 $17.50 1984 pap. $8.95. Nearly all paleontologists agree
that the fossil record proves Darwin essentially right. Now some say the *tempo* of
evolution included changes in short rapid bursts (rapid as geologic time goes).

Steel, Rodney, and Anthony P. Harvey, eds. *The Encyclopedia of Prehistoric Life.*
McGraw-Hill 1979 o.p. Largely descriptive (e.g., brachiopods) but also expository (e.g., evolution). In depicting fossils the line drawings used here are often
more informative than photographs. Charts and brief lives, too.

Stewart, Wilson N. *Paleobotany and the Evolution of Plants.* Cambridge Univ. Pr.
1983 $32.50. The text is rather technical, but references are extensive and useful.

Thompson, Ida. *The Audubon Society Field Guide to North American Fossils.* Knopf
1982 $13.50. Maps, descriptions, and other aids to identification; color plates.

Tiffney, Bruce H., ed. *Geologic Factors and the Evolution of Plants.* Yale Univ. Pr.
1985 text ed. $25.00. Ancient environments may have been quite different from
now, even though controlled by the same physical laws.

Wilford, John Noble, Jr. *The Riddle of the Dinosaur.* Knopf 1985 $22.95. Since the
   1960s, paleontologists have found evidence that some dinosaurs, at least, were
   warm-blooded, and that they may have died out quite rapidly after an asteroid
   struck the Earth.

CHAPTER 9

Physics

Mary Kay

> To observe the facts first, to vary their circumstances as much as possible, to accompany this first task with exact measurement so as to deduce from them general laws based solely upon experience, and to deduce from these laws independently of any hypothesis on the nature of the forces that produce the phenomena, the mathematical value of these forces, that is, the formula that represents them—such is the procedure that Newton followed. In general, it has been adopted . . . by the savants to whom physics owes the immense progress it has made recently, and it has served as my guide in all my research.
>
> —ANDRÉ MARIE AMPÈRE

The word *physics* comes from the Greek word *physos*, meaning nature. Dating from ancient Greece, physics can legitimately claim to be the basic experimental science, and the first to exemplify the scientific method of proposing a theory that then is verified or rejected on the basis of experiment.

Physics is that branch of natural science which deals with the most general properties of matter and energy. The objects of its studies are the characteristics of heat, light, electricity, magnetism, sound, and of matter itself, thus including atomic and nuclear processes. It is the most autonomous physical science, with laws unlikely to be derived from other sciences in the way that laws of, say, chemistry and geology are derived from physics. At the same time, physics is very closely linked to other sciences, with much overlap in spheres of interest.

Special branches of science encompassing such borderline areas include, for example, astrophysics, which treats physical phenomena as they occur in regions beyond the earth's immediate vicinity, and which is included in this chapter. Other such areas, perhaps more appropriately classed with the science on the other side of the border, include chemical physics, geophysics, and biophysics.

Many areas of engineering are closely related to physics. As enough knowledge about a topic is accumulated for everyday or industrial use to be made of it, the topic tends to pass over to engineering, as has occurred for example with atomic power, atomic weapons, and magnetic resonance imaging. In general, physicists study basic phenomena while engineers tend to solve problems generated by specific applications.

Major advances have been made in the past generation, especially in understanding subatomic constituents of matter and in discovering new phenomena such as superconductivity. In the near future, physicists expect to see substantial progress made in grand unified theories (GUTs), which it is hoped will finally provide an adequate theory explaining the elementary particles of matter. More powerful accelerators will possibly assist in this effort. Superconductivity is in a revolutionary state at present as current theories are overturned by discoveries of materials whose behavior violates predictions. Astrophysics and cosmology are very active areas as physicists seek explanations for such phenomena as quasars, neutron stars, and black holes, and as particle physics uses evidence of the early universe to extend knowledge of the nature of matter.

GENERAL PHYSICS

Alvarez, Luis W. *Alvarez: Adventures of a Physicist*. Basic Bks. 1987 $19.95. "Luis Alvarez's career in experimental physics reads like a scientific adventure story.... Science on the cutting edge where life and the laboratory meet" (*American Libraries*).

Bernstein, Jeremy. *The Life It Brings: One Physicist Remembers*. Ticknor & Fields 1987 $16.95. "Thoroughly charming story of how one young man, under the influence of some remarkable teachers, came to feel the powerful lure of modern physics and its manifold mysteries" (*American Libraries*).

Cadogan, Peter H. *From Quark to Quasar*. Cambridge Univ. Pr. 1985 $24.95. Pictorial journey from the subatomic blur of elementary particles to the furthest and largest astronomical objects known.

Cole, K. C. *Sympathetic Vibrations: Reflections on Physics as a Way of Life*. Fwd. by Frank Oppenheimer, Bantam 1985 pap. $9.95; Morrow 1984 $16.95. A science writer describes the scientific approach and aesthetic, and reflects on how physical principles relate to the everyday world. Impressionistic.

Davies, P. C. *The Physics of Time Asymmetry*. Univ. of California Pr. 2d ed. 1985 $9.95. An established physicist discusses the conceptual difficulties inherent in a science that explains experience, clearly time-dependent, in terms of fundamental physical laws that are time-independent.

Fairbank, J. D. *Near Zero: Frontiers of Physics*. W. H. Freeman 1987 $35.95. Original papers on "near zero" physics where by pushing a single physical variable toward zero new phenomena are sought. Temperature, pressure, electric and magnetic fields, gravity, and thermal noise are among the control variables discussed. Somewhat technical, but interesting for a view of physics frontiers.

Feinberg, Gerald. *Solid Clues: Quantum Physics, Molecular Biology and the Future of Science*. Simon & Schuster 1985 $17.95 1986 pap. $8.95. Concentrating on the rapidly advancing fields of physics and molecular biology, Feinberg assesses where science has been over the last 40 years, and attempts to give a sense of where it will be going in the next four decades. An authoritative account useful for the general reader and in considerations of public policy.

Gleick, James. *Chaos: Making a New Science*. Viking 1987 $19.95. "Gleick chronicles the work of various maverick scientists who have discovered that nature does not fit within linear formulas and predictable patterns" (*American Libraries*).

Landsberg, P. T., ed. *The Enigma of Time*. International Pubns. 1984 pap. $19.00. Anthology of reprinted essays on cosmology, irreversibility, quantum theory, black holes, and even literature and art. A good introduction and index enhance the book's utility.

Morrison, Philip, and Phyllis Morrison. *Powers of Ten: The Relative Size of Things in the Universe.* W. H. Freeman 1985 pap. $19.95. A beautifully illustrated and printed book that graphically presents the familiar idea that natural phenomena range in linear dimensions across 42 orders of magnitude, and that their characteristics vary accordingly.

National Research Council, Physics Survey Committee. *Physics Through the 1990s.* National Research Council 8 vols. 1986 $160.00 An introductory volume and seven subject volumes present a nontechnical but authoritative survey of recent advances in each major field of pure and applied physics together with statements of current important problems. Unfortunately, names of prominent researchers and references are not furnished. However, these volumes and the annual survey of physics published in each January issue of *Physics Today* are the only available concise sources for this type and level of information.

Rigden, John S. *Rabi: Scientist and Citizen.* Basic Bks. 1987 $21.95. "This biography of one of America's leading men of science captures the adventure, the romance, and the excitement of twentieth-century physics" (*American Libraries*).

Spielberg, Nathan, and Byron D. Anderson. *Seven Ideas That Shook the Universe.* Wiley 1987 $22.95. 1986 pap. $14.95. Two Kent State University physicists discuss seven ideas basic to modern physics: Copernican astronomy, Newtonian physics, quantum theory, conservation principles, symmetries, relativity, and entropy.

Trefil, James. *The Unexpected Vista: A Physicist's View of Nature.* Ed. by B. Lippmann, Macmillan 1985 pap. $7.95. Presents physical explanations for a variety of everyday phenomena so as to demonstrate that they can be reduced to a handful of general laws.

Weisskopf, Victor F. *Knowledge and Wonder: The Natural World as Man Knows It.* MIT 2d ed. 1979 text ed. pap. $7.95. A stimulating qualitative presentation of scientific methods at work. Weisskopf, a well-known physicist, takes the reader through many examples of scientific problem solving as he presents a survey of what is known about the natural world.

Wilczek, Frank, and Betsy Devine. *Longing for Harmonies: Themes and Variations from Modern Physics.* Norton 1988 $19.95. "Wilczek and Devine draw compelling analogies between physics and music, both of which thrive on a simple structure based on themes and variations" (*American Libraries*).

Zee, Anthony. *Fearful Symmetry: The Search for Beauty in Modern Physics.* Macmillan 1986 $22.50. A well-known physicist explains how the notion of symmetry forms the intellectual and aesthetic foundations of modern physics. The arcane and abstract symmetries of particle physics and cosmology are presented for the layperson.

History

Crease, Robert P., and Charles C. Mann. *The Second Creation: Makers of the Revolution in Twentieth Century Physics.* Macmillan 1985 $25.00. A well-reviewed and up-to-date history of twentieth-century physics, concentrating on personalities rather than theories. It emphasizes the effort in the last two decades to fulfill the old dream of developing an ultimate, unified theory.

Kevles, Daniel J. *The Physicists: The History of a Scientific Community in Modern America.* Harvard Univ. Pr. 1987 pap. $12.95; Knopf 1977 $15.95; Random 1979 pap. $10.95. A landmark study detailing the process whereby American professional physics came to maturity. In the late 1800s American physics came to be built on institutions for the training of physicists rather than, as in the European model, around research problems and research production. In the 1920s science became the object of public attention in America, as exemplified by the Einstein boom. The 1930s saw the infusion of Hitler's emigrés and the beginning of big science, which continues to this day. Kevles details the public face of the American physics community through these changes rather than the content of ideas it pursued.

Moyer, Albert E. *American Physics in Transition: Conceptual Shifts in the Late Nineteenth Century.* Intro. by Daniel Siegal, Tomash 1983 $30.00. A readable account of the late nineteenth century in American physics, a time when the nation was coming to scientific maturity. The attitudes of ten important representative American scientists are examined to illustrate the process.

Snow, C. P. *The Physicists.* Intro. by W. Cooper, Little, Brown 1981 $15.95. A brief, well-illustrated history of the development of the atomic bomb, written from personal recollections by a contemporary physicist active during this period and an outspoken critic of nuclear armaments.

Reference Books

Abbott, David, ed. *The Biographical Dictionary of Scientists: Physicists.* Bedrick Bks. 1984 $28.00. A volume of Bedrick's Biographical Dictionary of Scientists series, the book is composed of 200 short biographies of important physicists both contemporary and historical. No bibliographies are included, but the book does contain a convenient glossary and also a subject index.

Anderson, Herbert L., ed. *Physics Vade Mecum.* Amer. Institute of Physics 1981 $25.00. For each of 22 fields of physics, the editors attempt to supply the professional with ten pages of the most useful numerical data, definitions, and formulas that would also be of use to the interested layperson.

Beiser, Arthur. *Concepts of Modern Physics.* McGraw-Hill 3d ed. 1981 text ed. $39.95. Textbook introducing modern physics to the reader with some knowledge of calculus and elementary classical physics. Relativity, quantum mechanics, elementary particles, radioactivity, and solid state physics are covered. Intended for the nonscience major or lay reader.

Besancon, Robert M., ed. *The Encyclopedia of Physics.* Van Nostrand 3d ed. 1985 $99.95. Excellent one-volume encyclopedia incorporating the work of about 300 contributors, and recently revised. Articles are signed, illustrated, cross-referenced, and offer bibliographies for further reading.

Dictionary of Physics. McGraw-Hill 1985 $15.95. Brief definitions of technical terms.

Directory of Physics and Astronomy Staff Members, 1984–85. Amer. Inst. of Physics 1984 pap. $30.00. Faculty at academic institutions and staff members of research organizations are listed, together with addresses and phone numbers. Additionally, physics departments and research laboratories throughout the country are listed, with their faculty and research scientists.

Driscoll, Walter G., ed. *Handbook of Optics.* McGraw-Hill 1978 $98.00. Standard handbook.

Halliday, David, and Robert Resnick. *Fundamentals of Physics.* Wiley 2d ed. rev. 1986 $50.85. Standard college text presuming a knowledge of calculus; probably the most widely used physics textbook in history.

Handbook of Chemistry and Physics. CRC Pr. annual $69.95. The standard bench ready-reference handbook of physical and chemical reference data.

International Who's Who in Energy and Nuclear Sciences. Gale 1983 $195.00. Brief biographical entries on workers involved in the generation, storage, and efficient use of energy in 70 countries.

Kaye, G. W., and T. H. Laby. *Tables of Physical and Chemical Constants: And Some Mathematical Functions.* Wiley 15th ed. 1986 $39.95. Compact and useful set of tables for quick reference.

Olenick, Richard, and others. *Beyond the Mechanical Universe: From Electricity to Modern Physics.* Cambridge Univ. Pr. 1986 $24.95. The Annenberg Foundation granted $6 million to the California Institute of Technology to develop a new sequence of introductory physics classes, incorporating video technology into a textbook presentation. The Mechanical Universe series, shown on public television, was the widely hailed result. The textbooks can be read independently or used in conjunction with the video series, and include much interesting historical information as well as a good presentation of basic physics.

————. *The Mechanical Universe: Introduction to Mechanics and Heat.* Cambridge Univ. Pr. 1985 $24.95.

Parker, Sybil, ed. *McGraw-Hill Encyclopedia of Physics.* McGraw-Hill 1983 $69.50. Composed of selected articles from the *McGraw-Hill Encyclopedia of Science and Technology,* 1982 edition. Articles are authoritative and illustrated, and include bibliographies.

Pasachoff, Jay M., and Marc L. Kutner. *Invitation to Physics.* Norton 1981 text ed. $23.95. Well-recommended text for the nonscience major. Classical and modern physics are covered by two astronomers. The text emphasizes the relationships between astronomy and physics, and covers basic topics such as the physics of the atom and the structure of the universe.

Sears, Francis W., and Hugh D. Young. *College Physics.* Addison-Wesley 6th ed. 1985 text ed. $37.95. Standard introductory college text, no calculus required.

World Nuclear Directory. Gale 7th ed. 1985 $180.00. Descriptive international directory of world's nuclear organizations.

ELEMENTARY PARTICLE PHYSICS

Since the time of the ancient Greeks, men have tried to identify the elementary constituents of matter. The contemporary form of this effort is the field of elementary particle physics, which identifies the smallest building blocks of matter and investigates the laws governing their interactions.

The electron and proton were the first two elementary particles to be discovered, as the constituent parts of atoms began to be identified at the end of the nineteenth century. Quarks are unusual particles having charges one- to two-thirds the strength of those of electrons and protons and are suspected by some researchers to be a more elemental particle of which all others are formed. The present catalog of dozens of elementary particles falls into several families, such as protons, leptons, messons, baryons, quarks, and gluons. Most are unstable and decay quickly. The wide variety of interactions between them can be understood in terms of three basic interactions—strong (nuclear), electromagnetic, and weak—all thought to be mediated by specific particles.

The current goal of particle physicists is to produce a grand unified theory to explain how this multiplicity of elementary particles interacts to form the world around us. Much work remains to be done, but particle physicists for the first time are optimistic that a unified, definitive theory will soon be found.

Close, Frank, and Christine Sutton. *The Particle Explosion.* Oxford 1987 $35.00. An
   illustrated tour of the subatomic world, containing hundreds of photographs of
   personalities, machines, and particle images.
Davies, P. C. W. *The Forces of Nature.* Cambridge Univ. Pr. 2d ed. 1986 $39.50 pap.
   $12.95. Clear and well-organized introduction to fundamental particles and in-
   teractions of matter. The conceptual basis of modern subatomic physics is given
   particularly careful attention.
Dodd, James. *The Ideas of Particle Physics: An Introduction for Scientists.* Cambridge
   Univ. Pr. 1984 $47.50 pap. $18.95. Briefly presents the discoveries of recent
   high-energy physics for readers with a technical background. A bibliography of
   nonspecialist technical references is included.
Fritsch, Harald. *Quarks: The Stuff of Matter.* Basic Bks. 1983 $19.00. Fritsch, a phys-
   ics professor at the Max Planck Institute, describes the complex and costly
   experiments involving particle accelerators that have illuminated the quark
   substructure of matter.
Herbert, Nick. *Quantum Reality.* Doubleday 1987 pap. $9.95. Description of the
   world of subatomic particles and their interactions.
Parker, Barry. *Einstein's Dream: The Search for a Unified Theory of the Universe.*
   Plenum 1986 $18.95. Popular account of twentieth-century attempts to produce
   a unified field theory.
Perkins, Donald H. *Introduction to High Energy Physics.* Addison-Wesley 3d ed. 1986
   $38.95. A clear, balanced presentation on high-energy physics suitable for self-
   study and accessible to beginners.
Squires, E. *To Acknowledge the Wonder.* Taylor & Francis 1985 $42.00 pap. $20.00. A
   survey of the world of atomic particle physics that introduces and develops
   essential concepts such as quantum electrodynamics and quantum chromody-
   namics. The "standard model" as it existed as recently as 1985 is described.
   Particle physics is linked with cosmology, and concepts such as the inflationary
   universe and the anthropic principle (the idea that many of the local and global
   properties of the universe can be derived from the fact of human existence) are
   explored. Altogether, a fine survey and an excellent place to commence reading
   for those curious about the field.
Trefil, James S. *From Atoms to Quarks: The Strange World of Particle Physics.* Scribner 1980 $12.95 1982 pap. $8.95. A qualitative survey of the twentieth-century
   search for the ultimate building blocks of matter. Includes glossary, but no
   references.

History

Brown, Laurie M., and Lillian Hoddeson, eds. *The Birth of Particle Physics: Proceedings of the International Symposium on the History of Particle Physics, May, 1980.*
   Cambridge Univ. Pr. 1983 $47.50 1986 pap. $18.95. A volume of papers about
   the evolution of particle physics out of cosmic ray and nuclear physics from
   1930 to 1950. Such figures as Paul Dirac, Victor Weisskopf, and Robert Marshak
   reflect on their contributions.
McCusker, Brian. *The Quest for Quarks.* Cambridge Univ. Pr. 1984 $15.95. In a short
   historical account of the search for the fundamental material of nature, Mc-
   Cusker first discusses atomic theory, then subatomic particles and their constituent quarks. A chapter is devoted to the "quest for the free quark," an enterprise
   in which the author is an active researcher. An interesting presentation, although the reader may become confused by the swarm of particles and symbols.

A table of particles and their symbols would have helped, since these are used freely in the book.

Ne'eman, Yuval, and Yoram Kirsh. *The Particle Hunters.* Cambridge Univ. Pr. 1986 $49.50 pap. $13.95. An interesting nontechnical history of twentieth-century particle physics by a leading theorist in the field. Very readable.

Pickering, Andrew. *Constructing Quarks: A Sociological History of Particle Physics.* Univ. of Chicago Pr. 1986 pap. $19.95 lib. bdg. $37.50. An account of the development of high-energy physics, beginning with a survey of "old physics" (1945–64) and then describing the rise of the "new physics of the subsequent decade." The objective is to give the general reader some knowledge of what scientists do and to point them to further reading by means of a 40-page bibliography.

Sutton, Christine. *The Particle Connection: The Most Exciting Scientific Chase since DNA and the Double Helix.* Simon & Schuster 1984 $16.95. A detailed nontechnical description of the circumstances surrounding the 1933 discovery of the W and Z particles at CERN (European Centre for Nuclear Research), a discovery that confirmed the theory of weak interactions.

Taubes, Gary. *Nobel Dreams: Power, Deceit, and the Ultimate Experiment.* Random $19.95. An account of how Carlo Rubbia and Simon van der Meer of CERN came to win the 1984 Nobel Prize in physics for experimentally discovering the W and Z particles, the theoretically predicted mediators of the weak interaction. Politics, passions, and personalities all play a role in "big science," Taubes concludes.

Watkins, Peter. *Story of the W and Z.* Cambridge Univ. Pr. 1986 $44.50 pap. $13.95. Watkins gives a personal account of the 1983 experiment at the CERN laboratory near Geneva that searched for the W and Z bosons predicted by the Weinberg-Salam electroweak theory, using state of the art detectors and colliders. He also presents a review of some of the most current ideas and experiments in particle physics. The book is written for the general reader.

NUCLEAR PHYSICS

Modern nuclear physics, similar to atomic physics, owes its beginning to Ernest Rutherford's famous 1911 experiments, in which he established the existence of a massive central core within the much larger diameter of the atom. While atomic physics focuses on the structure and external interactions of atoms, nuclear physics studies the structure, composition, and forces within the nucleus itself. In the 1930s, it became known that the nucleus was composed of protons and neutrons, and it was theoretically predicted that a new elementary particle acted as an agent to bind them together to form the nucleus. The binding particle was finally identified in 1947 as the pion, completing the first phase in the description of the nuclear structure. Since then a host of additional elementary particles have been discovered.

Wartime use was made of this knowledge, as the world knows. The discovery of the process of nuclear fission in 1939 led to the development of the nuclear bomb and of fission power reactors. The fusion process, the mechanism by which stars generate their energy, was the basis for development of the hydrogen bomb in the 1950s and for intense energy research under the rubric of plasma physics.

Nuclear physics has provided many practical applications, such as radioactive isotopes and nuclear magnetic resonance techniques in medicine, tracers for geological and archaeological dating, and tracers for atmospheric and water flow patterns. At present, much attention has shifted to the nuclear substructure, in particular to the constituents of the protons and neutrons, the quarks.

Cottingham, W. M., and D. A. Greenwood. *An Introduction to Nuclear Physics*. Cambridge Univ. Pr. 1986 $44.50 pap. $14.95. An introductory undergraduate-level survey of modern nuclear physics from the viewpoint of basic physics, including discussions of nuclear power generation and nuclear astrophysics.

Sutton, Christine, ed. *Building the Universe*. [*New Scientist Guides Ser.*] Basil Blackwell 1985 $29.95 pap. $9.95. A reprise of articles on articles originally published in *New Scientist* on recent developments in nuclear physics.

Turnbull, R. M. *The Structure of Matter: An Introduction to Atomic Nuclear and Particle Physics*. Trans-Atlantic 1979 text ed. pap. $22.50. A concise account of atomic, nuclear, and elementary particle physics for the beginning student. The emphasis is on explaining basic physics principles rather than on experimental considerations.

History

Groves, Leslie M. *Now It Can Be Told: The Story of the Manhattan Project*. Intro. by Edward Teller [*Quality Pap. Ser.*] Da Capo repr. of 1962 ed. 1983 $39.50 pap. $9.95. Personal account of involvement in the project to build the first atomic bomb, by an administrative officer on the project.

Keller, Alex. *The Infancy of Atomic Physics: Hercules in His Cradle*. Oxford 1983 $29.95. Traces the unfolding of theories about internal atomic structure during the period from the middle of the nineteenth century through the 1930s. The author successfully delineates contemporary scientific culture, showing the flow of opposition and discussion that preceded each advance.

Rhodes, Richard. *The Making of the Atomic Bomb*. Simon & Schuster 1987 $22.95. Well-written and thoroughly researched work on the making of the first atomic bomb. The first third of the book lays out the scientific background of this massive effort, and the balance gives a detailed account of its execution. The emphasis is on politics and personalities rather than science. A National Book Award winner.

QUANTUM PHYSICS

Quantum mechanics is a theory that was developed in the 1920s to explain and predict the behavior of the microscopic world. It represented a sharp break with classical mechanics, and came about as a response to observational discoveries. Werner Heisenberg and Erwin Schrödinger were prominent in its development.

In classical mechanics the present and future state of a system can be completely specified by the position and momentum of all particles in a system. However, the quantum state is less specific, and can at most determine probabilities for the time evolution of a system. Moreover, the theory precludes exact measurement of even present conditions for the system. The uncertainties inherent in quantum mechanical predictions, as contrasted with the determinism of classical mechanical predictions, slowed the acceptance of the theory. Yet, to date its utility is proven, and there is no better theory explaining the mechanics of the atomic world.

Atkins, P. W. *Quanta: A Handbook of Concepts.* Oxford 1977 pap. $28.95. A brief encyclopedia composed of about 200 illustrated articles with bibliographies that explain various concepts of quantum theory. Useful for all levels of reader.

Brandt, Siegmund, and Hans D. Dahmen. *The Picture Book of Quantum Mechanics.* Wiley 1985 $40.00. Extensive computer-generated graphics help convey important aspects of quantum theory. Intended for the reader with some knowledge of physics.

Davies, P. C. W. *The Ghost in the Atom: A Discussion of the Mysteries of Quantum Physics.* Cambridge Univ. Pr. 1986 $29.95 pap. $9.95. This book developed from a BBC radio program in which the author interviewed eight well-known physicists with divergent interpretations of quantum mechanics. The statements are here expanded and developed and demonstrate that there is no recognized uniformity in the scientific community on this question.

———. *Other Worlds: Space, Superspace and the Quantum Universe.* Simon & Schuster. 1981 $11.95. Assesses the impact of quantum theory on our modern conception of the world, including implications for philosophical questions such as the nature of reality, uniqueness and indeterminism of the universe, and the structure of space and time. The author contends that these implications have gone largely unnoticed by the general public.

———. *Quantum Mechanics.* Methuen 1984 $9.95. A concise first survey of quantum mechanics, including many problems.

Eisberg, Robert, and Robert Resnick. *Quantum Physics of Atoms, Molecules, Solids, Nuclei and Particles.* Wiley 2d ed. 1985 $52.20. The book presents properties of important quantum systems as a way to teach elementary quantum mechanics to beginning science students. Calculus and elementary physics are assumed, and the treatment is detailed.

Hey, A. J., and P. Walters. *The Quantum Universe.* Cambridge Univ. Pr. 1987 $47.50 pap. $16.95. Hey and Walters seek to convey to the nonscientist the way quantum mechanics underlies our current understanding of the physical world, in chemistry, solid state phenomena, superconductivity, lasers, stars, black holes, and cosmology. Although no one really *understands* quantum mechanics, nevertheless it works, as the authors demonstrate in any number of ways.

Martin, J. L. *Basic Quantum Mechanics.* Oxford 1981 $42.50 pap. $19.95. A good, well-written introductory book for science students, with a modern, nonhistorical approach.

Pagels, Heinz. *The Cosmic Code: Quantum Physics as the Law of Nature.* Simon & Schuster 1982 $16.95. Quantum views of nature are described from earliest appearances to recent particle physics developments. Intended for the general reader, or to supplement the reading of a beginning physics student.

Polkinghorne, J. C. *The Quantum World.* Longman 1984 text ed. $14.95; Princeton Univ. Pr. 1985 pap. $6.95. Polkinghorne contends that of the two great discoveries of modern physics (the second great discovery is the theory of relativity), the theory of quantum mechanics is the more important, since it introduced probability into fundamental physical explanation. The theory is explained with a minimum of mathematics, and long-standing problems of interpretation are explained. A glossary and a mathematically more demanding appendix are included.

Popper, Karl R. *Quantum Theory and the Schism in Physics*. Ed. by W. W. Barley, III [*Postscript to the Logic of Scientific Discovery*] Rowman 1984 pap. $10.95. A famous philosopher of science and critic of scientific realism explains his idea that contemporary physics is in a crisis of understanding, despite its apparent successes. This is due, he argues, to the intrusion of subjectivism into modern physics and to the pervasive notion that quantum theory is basically completed.

Resnick, Robert, and David Halliday. *Basic Concepts in Relativity and Early Quantum Theory*. Wiley 2d ed. 1985 pap. $28.05. Introductory text by bestselling textbook authors.

History

Cline, Barbara L. *Men Who Made a New Physics: Physicists and the Quantum Theory*. Univ. of Chicago Pr. 1987 pap. $11.95. An account of the revolution in physics during the first three decades of the twentieth century, with emphasis on the personalities involved, notably Rutherford, Planck, Heisenberg, Einstein, and Bohr. The author attempts to show science as a human enterprise.

Feuer, Lewis S. *Einstein and the Generations of Science*. Transaction Bks. 2d ed. 1982 pap. $12.95. Examines the social roots of the burst of scientific creativity in physics of the early twentieth century. He contends that the work of Einstein, Bohr, and Heisenberg was part of a "generational rebellion," and attempts to relate the motivation for their scientific discoveries to the philosophical enthusiasms of the day.

PLASMA PHYSICS

A plasma is a gaseous state of matter produced by the application of high temperature. In this special state, the material becomes a fully ionized gas, that is, nuclei and electrons of atoms detach from each other and assume chaotic behavior that can be predicted only by using techniques and concepts of classical statistical mechanics, electromagnetics, numerical analysis, and computer modeling. Matter in a plasma state loses all of its characteristic properties. That is, a plasma of neon gas has the same properties as a plasma of sodium gas, for example.

Plasmas are interesting because of their unique physical properties, the variety of roles they play in the universe, and their many applications. Much of the matter in the universe exists in this form, in the interiors of stars and as intergalactic space plasmas. Understanding these phenomena has a practical goal, since stars have as their energy source sustained thermonuclear or fusion reactions. Much activity in plasma physics today centers around magnetic fusion research, as physicists struggle to produce controlled fusion reactions that can be used as a clean and virtually limitless energy source.

Such a reaction requires that the plasma in question be heated to a temperature in excess of one million degrees. Clearly such a gas cannot be confined by normal vessels, so techniques have been developed to confine the hot plasmas by electromagnetic forces rather than by a physical vessel. Plasma is the state of matter in which atoms have lost all of their electrons and therefore lose all of their characteristic properties. There is no characteristic radiation, but rather complete chaos. Such a condition is obtained under very high temperatures, such as occur in stars. At such temperatures, quantum mechanics does not apply, and it is necessary to apply classical statistical mechanics and electromagnetics. Plasma physics primarily studies details of plasmas in stars, including their motion, rate of energy production, and magnetic properties.

Artsimovich, L. *A Physicist's ABC on Plasma*. Imported Pubns. 1978 pap. $3.95; State Mutual Bk. 1985 $39.75. A quick survey of the elements of plasma physics.

Bittencourt, J. A. *Fundamentals of Plasma Physics*. Pergamon 1986 $75.00 pap. $29.50. A somewhat advanced but very up-to-date textbook.

History

Bromberg, Joan L. *Fusion: Science, Politics and the Invention of a New Energy Source*. MIT 1982 $40.00 pap. $9.95. A history of the U.S. magnetic fusion energy program. The book concentrates on the four largest programs—in California, Tennessee, New Mexico, and New Jersey—and explains the intermingling of science and politics that created the fusion program's strategy.

MECHANICS

Classical mechanics, or Newtonian mechanics, is the study of the motions of objects of ordinary experience, for example, falling stones, planets, or dust particles. NEWTON (see also Volume 4) identified the basic laws of motion and gravity, and applied them to a variety of physical systems with great success. For example, Newtonian mechanics was made in this century by Adam in 1915 when from a detailed analysis of the perturbations in the orbits of the outer planets of the solar system he predicted the existence of the planet Uranus.

It is difficult to underestimate the influence of Newtonian mechanics in human civilization. It was the first grand scientific theory worthy of the name. It not only became the model for other physical theories, but provided the basis for the philosophical rationalism of the Enlightenment in the eighteenth and nineteenth centuries. The entire field of mathematical analysis developed in response to problems posed by Newtonian mechanics.

Asimov, Isaac. *Understanding Physics: Motion, Sound and Heat*. NAL 1969 pap. $6.50. "The topics cover the complete span of physics, historically developed with ample examples to instill basic rudiments of the principles. The ease with which the reader is able to assimilate the different topics is a compliment to the author" (*LJ*).

SOLID STATE PHYSICS

A solid consists of atoms or molecules held together in close proximity by a variety of forces. Although only an infinitesimal proportion of the universe is in the solid state, solids constitute most of the world around us. Moreover, most modern technology is based on special characteristics of solid materials.

Solid state is perhaps the most rapidly developing field of physics, with many applications in computer technology, the key technology of our time. Solid state physics is not a fundamental field, but is rather primarily an applied field. It investigates the detailed properties of solid matter, especially of metals and silicon. For example, although general properties of metals at the fundamental atomic level are known, there is much still to learn about various combinations of metals fused at different temperatures or conditions. Solid state physicists work to devise new metals with desirable properties such as lightness, strength, and conductivity.

In the two postwar decades, solid state physicists primarily explored the electronic properties of crystalline solids and constructed a comprehensive picture of electron energy levels, optical properties of simple metals, insulators, and semiconductors. Today, the field concentrates primarily on surfaces and interfaces, and systems with strong fluctuation or varying degrees of disorder.

The hottest field in solid state physics currently is that of superconductivity. The search is on for materials that exhibit virtually no resistance at relatively normal temperatures, a phenomenon that, until 1987, was to be found only in certain materials when cooled to a few degrees above absolute zero.

Bernstein, Jeremy. *Three Degrees above Zero: Bell Labs in the Information Age.* NAL 1986 pap. $4.50; Scribner 1984 $17.95. Physicist Jeremy Bernstein, who is the science writer for *The New Yorker,* here discusses in detail important research at AT&T's Bell Laboratories. The areas of research include telephony and the discovery of cosmic background radiation by Robert Wilson and Arno Penzia. Most importantly, he gives the early history of solid state physics' finest hour, the invention of the transistor at Bell Labs. The book is thus a good source for those interested in the process and personalities of industrial science as well.

Kittel, Charles. *Introduction to Solid State Physics.* Wiley 6th ed. 1986 $43.95. Standard text in the field.

Papacosta, Pangratios. *The Splendid Voyage: An Introduction to New Sciences and New Technologies.* [*Frontiers of Science Ser.*] Prentice-Hall 1987 pap. $10.95. Although the print is large and the language of this book highly simplified, it contains many excellent diagrams and photographs to illustrate its discussion of such topics as lasers and the invention of the transistor.

Rudden, M. N., and J. Wilson. *Elements of Solid State Physics.* Wiley 1980 $36.60. Intended for the beginning college student, but better for the reader with some physics background.

History

Braun, Ernest, and Stuart MacDonald. *Revolution in Miniature: The History and Impact of Semiconductor Electronics Re-explored.* Cambridge Univ. Pr. 2d ed. 1982 $32.50 pap. $10.95. The focus of this book is on technology and application, but it also contains excellent discussions of the foundations and early development of solid state physics.

Mott, Nevill, ed. *The Beginnings of Solid State Physics.* [*Royal Society Ser.*] Scholium Intl. 1980 lib. bdg. $30.00. A collection of reminiscences by men who created the field, for example, Bloch, Bethe, Wilson, and Mott. Generally entertaining for the personal and historical information conveyed.

ATOMIC AND OPTICAL PHYSICS

Throughout the twentieth century, the study of atoms, their internal structure, and their interactions with electromagnetic radiation and other particles, has been central to scientific efforts to understand the physical world. The concept of the atom as the building block of nature must be attributed to the ancient Greeks, but modern atomic physics began with the discovery of the electron by J. J. Thomson in 1897. In 1911, Ernest Rutherford discovered the existence of the atomic nucleus and the search was on to discover how atoms can be stable when the laws of classical mechanics predicted the immediate decay of such entities. The pursuit of the answer occupied several decades.

A by-product of atomic studies was renewed interest in optics when the maser and then the laser were invented, the latter in 1960. This invention made use of the fact that in a given population of atoms capable of two energy states, there are more atoms in the higher state than the lower. It is thus possible to make an oscillator tuned to an atomic spectral line, resulting in an optical beam of high intensity at a single frequency. The laser in its various forms has revolutionized optical technique, making possible innumerable investigations of atomic states, chemical reactions, atomic collisions, and the like. Information from these investigations is heavily used by physicists in other fields, such as astrophysics and elementary particle theory.

Asimov, Isaac. *Understanding Physics: The Electron, Proton and Neutron.* NAL 1969 pap. $4.50.

Falk, David S., and others. *Seeing the Light: Optics in Nature, Photography, Color, Vision and Holography.* Harper 1986 $37.50. The book first presents the fundamental principles of light and geometric optics, and then uses them to discuss and explain everyday phenomena. Well-illustrated, informative, intended for the nonscientist.

Hecht, Jeff. *The Laser Guidebook.* McGraw-Hill 1987 $49.50. A guide to the wide variety of lasers available commercially. The book includes a brief overview of the history of lasers and of the basics of laser theory.

Klein, Miles V., and Thomas Furtak. *Optics.* Wiley 2d ed. 1986 $55.10. Standard introduction to the field of modern optics.

Lawrence, Clifford L. *The Laser Book: A New Technology of Light.* Prentice-Hall 1986 $19.95. An introduction to lasers for the layperson, the book is written essentially without mathematics. Included are not only the what and how of lasers, but discussions of types and applications.

Optics Today. [*Readings from Physics Today Ser.*] Ed. by John N. Howard, Amer. Inst. of Physics 1986 text ed. pap. $25.00. Reprinting of more than 50 articles and news items originally published in *Physics Today* and meant for a general scientific audience. The book is intended to illustrate the progress of the last decade in this field. Such topics as X-rays and tomography, lightwave communications technology, and laser applications are covered.

Shimoda, Koichi. *Introduction to Laser Physics.* Springer-Verlag 2d ed. 1986 pap. $35.00. A first-rate introductory treatment for students with a mathematical background written by a prolific contributor to the field.

Tarasov, L. V. *Laser Age in Optics.* Imported Pubns. 1985 $6.95. Covers topics such as holography and nonlinear optics, and the elementary theories required to explain the topics. A short historical survey of the development of modern optics is included. Intended for lay people who want a summary rather than a comprehensive treatment.

History

Bertolotti, Mario. *Masers and Lasers: An Historical Approach.* International Pubns. 1983 $39.00. A history of the discovery and development of the laser and its precursor the maser, tools essential to much of modern science and technology. The book also provides an introduction to the statistical properties of light, which are an important general feature of lasers. Although any curious reader will learn from this book, its intended audience is other scientists, and technical formulations are integral to the text.

Brush, Stephen G. *Statistical Physics and the Atomic Theory of Matter, from Boyle and Newton to Landau and Onsager.* Princeton Univ. Pr. 1983 $45.00 pap. $14.50. Brush surveys the last three centuries of attempts to understand macroscopic properties of matter in terms of its microscopic constituents. The book is unique in emphasizing modern developments such as theories of superconductivity and superfluidity, but often requires a physics background in its reader.

RELATIVITY

The theories of special and general relativity arise from certain requirements of the laws of nature. Speaking intuitively, the requirements state that all frames of reference for relative motions, whether linear or accelerated, are equivalent. Speaking more technically, the requirements are that the forms of the laws of nature must be invariant under certain transformations, or groups. Special relativity assumes that the speed of light is constant for all observers, and predicts that time will be delayed and distances shortened for an observer in motion. Both of these effects have been experimentally verified. General relativity was the first physical theory that utilized already existing mathematical theories, in particular Riemann geometry, instead of the required mathematical theory being developed with the physical theory, as in Newtonian mechanics. This successful utilization set physicists looking for other areas of mathematics to mine in a similar way, and the mathematization of physics is still proceeding. The special theory of relativity is used to study objects moving close to the speed of light, and general relativity is used to study large masses.

These are subtle ideas indeed, and as a result contemporaries of Einstein had a difficult time comprehending and accepting his theories. Although proposed in 1905, relativity was a controversial theory until the early

1920s. The controversy and misunderstanding were so great that Einstein received his Nobel Prize not for relativity theory but for his explanation of the photoelectric effect, a far less fundamental accomplishment. Once controversial, relativity theory has come to be a routine tool. Both special and general theories are indispensable to modern physicists.

Calder, Nigel. *Einstein's Universe.* Penguin 1980 pap. $6.95; Viking 1979 $15.95. Einstein revolutionized scientific ideas of space, time, and motion by his theories of special and general relativity. This book explains them to all comers on the occasion of the centenary of Einstein's birth. The author is one of the most skillful writers of popular science working today, and this book is a fine example of his work.

Geroch, Robert. *General Relativity from A to B.* Univ. of Chicago Pr. 1978 lib. bdg. $17.50 pap. $7.95. Intended for the nonscientist. Geroch explains what relativity is, how it works, to what physical phenomena it applies, and what it predicts, all in a straightforward and thorough way. He takes the reader through some of the chains of argument that justify the theory, to help the general reader understand the construction of the theory as well as its content.

Kaufmann, William J., III. *Relativity and Cosmology.* Harper 2d ed. 1977 pap. text ed. $13.50. Kaufmann is an effective and skillful writer on astrophysics for the layperson. Here he discusses relativity theory and its applications to astrophysics. White holes, wormholes, and similar notions are discussed. Now somewhat dated.

Rindler, W. *Essential Relativity.* Springer-Verlag rev. ed. 1980 pap. $25.00. A simplified treatment of relativity theory for the advanced undergraduate. Covers special and general relativity and cosmology.

Schwinger, Julian. *Einstein's Legacy.* Scientific Amer. 1985 o.p. Schwinger is well known for his contributions to quantum electrodynamics, for which he shared a Nobel Prize with Feynman. Here he offers a fine contribution to popular physics, explaining the complex concepts of relativity theory to the layperson using mathematics no higher than elementary algebra. The book is well illustrated.

Will, Clifford M. *Was Einstein Right? Putting General Relativity to the Test.* Basic Bks. 1986 $18.95. The development of general relativity was motivated by theoretical considerations, with very little experimental verification possible. This book surveys the surge of interest in the postwar years in experimentally verifying the theory, emphasizing the personalities and narrative elements of each experiment. Includes an excellent summary of the theory for the general reader.

History

Goldberg, Stanley. *Understanding Relativity: Origin and Impact of a Scientific Revolution.* Birkhauser 1984 $24.95. Einstein's theory of special relativity and historical uses of the term in scientific contexts.

ASTROPHYSICS

A field that bridges astronomy and physics, astrophysics studies nonterrestrial physical phenomena. The term is generally understood to include all aspects of celestial objects save the measurement of direction, thus it includes velocity, composition, temperature, and other physical conditions.

Objects studied include the planets, sun, and comets of our solar system as well as the stars and other objects we commonly associate with astrophysics. These studies are conducted by means of optical, radio, X-ray, gamma-ray, and spectroscopic detection, with special detectors developed as needed for other portions of the electromagnetic spectrum and for other waves or particles. So many observational and theoretical discoveries have been made in astrophysics in recent years that many scientists think this period will come to be known as the "golden age" of astrophysics.

Cameron, A. G. W., ed. *Astrophysics Today*. Amer. Inst. of Physics 1984 $25.00. An anthology of articles and new items originally published in *Physics Today* in the last decade reporting on the frontiers of research in the field including the physics of black holes, white dwarfs, galactic physics, and the like. For the interested layperson.

Golden, Frederic. *Quasars, Pulsars, and Black Holes: A Scientific Detective Story*. Scribner 1976 $9.95. Discussion of some of the most exciting discoveries of modern astrophysics, and the scientists who made them. The author was the science editor at *Time* magazine, and chronicled this news as it broke. This adds an exciting and personal dimension to the story.

Kaufmann, William J., III. *Black Holes and Warped Spacetime*. Bantam 1980 pap. $3.50. An interesting account of the process whereby the existence of black holes was theoretically predicted. Also discussed are stellar evolution, general relativity, wormholes, quasars, and the fate of the universe.

——. *The Cosmic Frontiers of General Relativity*. Little, Brown 1977 text ed. pap. $16.50. Extensive discussion by a skillful expositor of black holes and related topics on the frontier of general relativity. Kaufmann was himself heavily involved in these investigations. Diagrams and pictures, rather than mathematics, are used to convey ideas.

——. *Discovering the Universe*. W. H. Freeman 1986 text ed. pap. $24.95. A beautiful, up-to-date, and thorough introductory text. Makes extensive use of algebra and geometry but no calculus is required. Brief essays by practicing astronomers and astrophysicists are included.

——. *Galaxies and Quasars*. W. H. Freeman 1979 text ed. $21.95. Historical survey for the lay reader of how we came to know what we know about galactic and extragalactic phenomena. The book concludes with a strong justification for basic research in astronomy and astrophysics.

Narlikar, Jayant V. *The Structure of the Universe*. Oxford 1977 pap. $9.95. A summary of modern astronomy and astrophysics concentrating on fundamental questions, such as the nature of gravity, inertia, and time. Narlikar includes new observational information about the nature of the universe, and makes a special effort to list all alternate explanations for phenomena rather than only the standard one.

COSMOLOGY AND GRAVITATION

Cosmology discusses the universe in the large scale of distance and time, and with respect to the problems of the origin, structure, and evolution of the universe. The distances are on the order of the radius of the Milky Way galaxy, and the time spans on the order of billions of years. Einstein in his special and general theories of relativity showed that on these scales ordinary Newtonian mechanics is false.

With the help of Einstein's theories, much insight has been obtained into the structure of the universe. For example, for a given density of matter it is known that the universe must expand infinitely, while for other values the same universe must eventually collapse. If experimentalists are ever able to determine a reasonably accurate value of the density of matter in the universe, one of the basic human questions will have finally been answered.

Since the discovery of the expansion of the universe in the 1920s, one goal of cosmology has been to trace the history of the universe. Unresolved problems in particle physics have incited the development of a new type of physical theory, gauge theory, resulting in an immense simplification of our view of the subatomic world. In recent years, the overlapping area between high energy physics and astronomy has been one of the most exciting fields of modern science, as knowledge of the early universe has been pushed back in time to somewhere around 10 to 40 seconds of the big bang itself (see also Chapter 7 in this volume).

Barrow, John D., and Joseph Silk. *The Left Hand of Creation: The Origin and Evolution of the Expanding Universe.* Basic Bks. 1986 $7.95. An informal, simply written, discursive survey of current problems and theories in cosmology. Its essay style makes the material easy to assimilate, and its speculative cast adds interest.

Barrow, John D., and Frank N. Tipler. *The Anthropic Cosmological Principle.* Oxford 1986 $29.95. The authors set out to describe the modern anthropic principle, which seeks to link global properties to the universe with local structure. The book explores the notion that many of the local and global properties of the universe can be derived from the fact of human existence. Most of the book is intelligible to the layperson and will interest the thoughtful reader.

Bernstein, Jeremy, and Gerald Feinberg. *Cosmological Constants: Papers in Modern Cosmology.* Columbia Univ. Pr. 1986 $38.00. A translated collection of landmark papers in cosmology written between 1917 and 1982.

Boslough, John. *Stephen Hawking's Universe.* Morrow 1984 $12.95. Summarizes Hawking's biography and contributions to fundamental physics and cosmology. As an appendix, the book includes Hawking's essay "Is the End in Sight for Theoretical Physics?"

Contopoulos, G., and D. Kotsakis. *Cosmology.* Springer-Verlag 1987 pap. $32.50. Extremely up-to-date undergraduate text introducing modern cosmology. The book is divided into sections surveying observational data that must be explained by any theory; current theories and concepts of modern cosmology including the impact of high-energy physics; and deeper considerations such as the universality of physical laws, inflation and causation, and the anthropic principle.

Davies, P. C. W. *The Accidental Universe.* Cambridge Univ. Pr. 1982 $23.95 pap. $11.95. An interesting exploration of how sensitive features of the universe are to the values of fundamental constants. For example, if the force of gravity were slightly greater, what would the universe look like? A fascinating and broad use of thought experiments.

———. *The Search for Gravity Waves.* Cambridge Univ. Pr. 1980 $17.95. A well-written book explaining experimental efforts to detect gravity waves. Difficult and abstract concepts are discussed without mathematics, to enable the uninitiated reader to understand the point of the experiments.

————. *Space and Time in the Modern Universe.* Cambridge Univ. Pr. 1977 $15.95. A readable and stimulating account for the layperson or the undergraduate of the nature of space and time and of modern cosmology, covering such subjects as the arrow of time, the big bang, and thermodynamics.

————. *Superforce: The Search for a Grand Unified Theory of Nature.* Simon & Schuster 1984 $8.95. A professor of theoretical physics guides a tour of his field's frontiers, starting from a knowledge base of high school physics. His goal is to elucidate the progress being made toward a unified theory linking all natural forces. He thus explains the latest progress toward a theory that unifies the three nongravitational forces, and the "supersymmetric" models that additionally incorporate gravitational forces.

Disney, Michael. *The Hidden Universe.* Macmillan 1985 $17.95. One of the great open questions of cosmology continues to be the end of the universe, and its answer seems to depend on an accurate estimate for the mass of the universe. This book discusses the presence of hidden material, detected only by its gravitational effect, and techniques in astronomy and physics that may resolve these mysteries.

Feinberg, Gerald, and Robert Shapiro. *Life beyond Earth: The Intelligent Earthling's Guide to Extraterrestrial Life.* Morrow 1980 o.p. A statement of the possibilities of alternate chemistries and habitats for life forms in the universe, highly speculative at times but always interesting. Feinberg is a theoretical physicist at Columbia and Shapiro a biologist at New York University.

Fritsch, Harald. *The Creation of Matter: The Universe from Beginning to End.* Basic Bks. 1974 $19.95. An authority on particle physics here offers a brief introduction to the history of the universe from the big bang to its end. In the process, he gives presentations of key concepts from physics and astronomy that are required to understand this process, such as relativity, quantum theory, and stellar evolution. A current, concise treatment for the layperson.

Harrison, Edward R. *Cosmology: The Science of the Universe.* Cambridge Univ. Pr. 1981 $34.50. An exciting, thorough, and generally excellent textbook at the elementary level. The book includes a review history of cosmology and the basics of stellar astronomy, space and time, and the frontiers of contemporary cosmology. The best available survey of the field.

————. *Masks of the Universe.* Macmillan 1985 $18.95 1986 pap. $9.95. Taking as his scope all science and human history, Harrison locates modern rationalist models of the universe and its origins in an ancient historical sequence. He argues that when a worldview fails to satisfy human needs, others will fill the vacuum. Thus, modern science refuses to endow life with a purpose, encouraging the survival of medieval worldviews. About half of the book inventories and describes modern scientific cosmologies. An interesting study, but painted in terribly broad, speculative strokes.

Heller, Michael. *Encountering the Universe.* Trans. by J. Potocki [*Astronomy Quarterly Lib.*] Pachart 1982 $9.95. A qualitative, historical discussion of scientific attempts to model the universe. The book contains no bibliography, but does expose the reader to many modern cosmological models and their references.

Henbest, Nigel. *Mysteries of the Universe.* Van Nostrand 1983 o.p. A review by a British science writer of what is known and unknown concerning stellar and planetary formation, the origins of life, and high-energy phenomena such as pulsars, quasars, and black holes. Many interesting facts and their relationships are examined, and important unanswered problems are explored, for example, the "missing mass" of the universe.

Islam, Jumal N. *The Ultimate Fate of the Universe.* Cambridge Univ. Pr. 1983 $15.95.

The author attempts to answer for the general reader the question of the long-term future of the universe and its ultimate fate. In the process he discusses its large-scale structure and the evidence for a closed or open universe.

Layzer, David. *Constructing the Universe.* W. H. Freeman 1984 $29.95. This book is structured around Newton's and Einstein's two great modern theories of space, time, and gravity, and about the theories of cosmic structure and evolution that have been built around them. The level is somewhat technical for the average reader, but the book's splendid illustrations and diagrams are a real strength.

Narlikar, Jayant V. *Introduction to Cosmology.* Jones & Bartlett 1983 text ed. $45.00. An excellent advanced-level introduction to cosmology. A particular strength is Narlikar's thorough presentation of the weaknesses as well as strengths of the various competing cosmological theories, notably the hot big bang and steady state theories.

————. *The Lighter Side of Gravity.* W. H. Freeman 1982 text ed. $20.95 pap. $12.95. A nontechnical presentation of the principles of modern theoretical physics, concentrating on the wide range of astronomical phenomena controlled by gravity.

Pagels, Heinz. *Perfect Symmetry: The Search for the Beginning of Time.* Simon & Schuster 1985 $18.95 1986 pap. $4.95. Another explication of early-universe cosmology. Included are a solid introduction to the present state of the universe, a treatment of the early universe, and a survey of the frontiers of speculation in cosmology and unified field theories. Pagels is particularly adept at explaining relations among theories.

Reeves, Hubert. *Atoms of Silence: An Exploration of Cosmic Evolution.* MIT 1983 $22.50 1985 pap. $8.95. Assuming that the universe has a history that can be narrated, the author, who is a Canadian astrophysicist, gives an account of its origin and evolution, and also of its parallels with the development of life.

Ronan, Colin. *Deep Space: A Guide to the Cosmos.* Macmillan 1982 $25.95. A British astronomer explains the concepts of gravity and relativity, and discusses cosmological theories and the question of extraterrestrial life. Well illustrated.

Rowan-Robinson, Michael. *The Cosmological Distance Ladder.* W. H. Freeman 1985 $35.95. Clearly explains the methodology and problems of distance estimates. Somewhat technical, but will satisfy the curiosity of anyone who has wondered how extragalactic distances are determined.

————. *Cosmology.* Oxford 2d ed. 1981 $36.50 pap. $17.95. Describes the visible universe and summarizes cosmological theory for the beginning student. In particular, the book discusses the big bang cosmological models together with their observational implications.

Silk, Joseph. *The Big Bang: The Creation and Evolution of the Universe.* W. H. Freeman 1980 text ed. $19.95 pap. $13.95. In a nontechnical presentation, a Berkeley astronomer conveys first the specific evidence for the big bang origin of the universe, and then describes the standard physical models of evolutionary cosmology. Additionally, the book offers yet another presentation of the development of the universe from its first seconds. (See also *The First Three Minutes* in the Steven Weinberg biography, and James Trefil's *The Moment of Creation* [below]).

Trefil, James. *The Moment of Creation: Big Bang Physics from Before the First Millisecond to the Present Universe.* Macmillan 1984 pap. $6.95. Increasing insight into the structure and behavior of elementary particles and recent advances in unification theory have given rise to an enormous expansion in our knowledge of the early universe. The author gives a clear account of the problems connected with conventional big bang theory and the most recent progress in understanding the universe's first millisecond.

Wagoner, R., and D. Goldsmith. *Cosmic Horizons: Understanding the Universe.* W. H. Freeman 1982 $22.95 pap. $12.95. Another readable and informative presentation of cosmology. Wagoner and Goldsmith emphasize the development of concepts and the meaning of theories as opposed to simple exposition, in an attempt to present the scientific method in action.

History

Durham, Frank, and Robert D. Purrington. *Frame of the Universe.* Columbia Univ. Pr. 1983 $28.00 1985 pap. $12.50. A history of Western cosmological ideas from ancient to modern times for the general reader. Although not original in its approach and omitting discussions of Eastern cosmologies, the book is nevertheless interesting and well written.

Koyré, Alexandre. *From the Closed World to the Infinite Universe.* Johns Hopkins Univ. Pr. repr. of 1956 ed. 1968 pap. $8.95. Landmark lectures detailing the sixteenth- and seventeenth-century revolution in cosmology, as the heliocentric view of creation came to replace the geocentric, and the scientific worldview, the religious.

Lovell, Bernard. *Emerging Cosmology.* Ed. by Ruth N. Anshen [*Convergence Ser.*] Praeger 1984 pap. $9.95. Lovell, a well-known elder statesman of astronomy, surveys cosmological beliefs in the West since opinions on this subject began to be based on mensuration, in an attempt to identify important factors in the development of scientific cosmologies. Along the way he naturally discusses the major examples proferred by Copernicus, Galileo, Newton, and modern astronomers led by Sir William Herschel.

BACON, ROGER. c.1214–1294?

An English philosopher and scientist as well as a Franciscan monk, Bacon was more notable in the first area. His modest contributions to physics were mainly in the field of optics.

He was educated in mathematics and philosophy at Oxford, then lectured at the Faculty of Arts in Paris for about six years. After 1247, he returned to Oxford, where he began to study the modern topics of the day: astronomy, alchemy, optics, and languages. His writings were mainly compendia, a three-volume encyclopedia of all known science commissioned by Pope Clement IV and written in 1266 and 1267: *Opus Majus, Opus Minus,* and *Opus Tertium.* However, in these works he made some notably successful predictions of future inventions, such as the automobile and the airplane.

Having become acquainted with Alhazen, the Iraqi giant of medieval physics, Bacon proposed that lenses could be used as magnifying glasses to improve weak sight, and could also be used to make an instrument of great magnifying power for distant objects—in other words, a telescope. He also described some of the properties of gunpowder (not its potential as a propellant), discerning that it could be used in warfare.

However, Bacon is most famous as one of the first proponents of the use of experiment to prove an argument, an idea essential to the scientific method that was to fully appear later in the sixteenth century. He argued for the practical benefits of science and described the laws of optics as universally applicable natural laws, an assumption vital to the development of modern science. (See also Volume 4, Chapter 3.)

BOOK BY BACON

The "Opus Majus" of Roger Bacon. Ed. by Robert B. Burke, Oxford 2 vols. 1928 o.p. Bacon's famous encyclopedia.

BOOKS ABOUT BACON

Bridges, John H. *The Life and Work of Roger Bacon.* AMS Pr. repr. of 1914 ed. 1982 $21.50. Useful older biography, especially good for its analysis of Bacon's important writings.

Easton, Stewart C. *Roger Bacon and His Search for a Universal Science.* Greenwood repr. of 1952 ed. $22.50. Scholarly biography giving a balanced presentation of Bacon's life and work, in his contemporary context. Includes an extensive bibliography and index.

Newbold, William R., and Roland G. Kent. *The Cipher of Roger Bacon.* Century Bookbindery 1983 $85.00. Newbold was an early twentieth-century classics scholar who attributed a thirteenth-century manuscript in cipher, the "Voynich manuscript," to Roger Bacon. This book details his proposed solution to the cipher, and his reading of its contents, ranging from the medicinal properties of plants to the astral origin of the soul. This attribution is today considered highly questionable.

Westacott, Evelyn. *Roger Bacon in Life and Legend.* Folcroft repr. of 1953 ed. 1974 $30.00. Readable summary of available evidence concerning Bacon's life.

BETHE, HANS ALBRECHT. 1906– (NOBEL PRIZE 1967)

The son of a university professor in Strasbourg, Hans Bethe was educated in Frankfurt and Munich. From 1928 to 1933 he lectured in physics at various German universities, but moved to Britain when Hitler came to power. In 1935 he emigrated to the United States to join the physics faculty at Cornell University. He remained at Cornell as a professor of physics until his retirement in 1975. From 1943 to 1946 he was also director of the Theoretical Physics Division of the Los Alamos Laboratory, working on the Manhattan Project to develop the atomic bomb.

In 1938 Bethe succeeded in working out the sequences of nuclear reactions that power the stars, and for this work he received the Nobel Prize in 1967. This problem had remained unsolved for 75 years since William Thomson Kelvin and Hermann Helmholtz first described it. Bethe has also worked on a wide range of other problems, from electron densities in crystals to operational conditions in nuclear reactors.

Bethe has been active in science policy discussions for decades. In 1958 he served as a delegate to the first International Test Ban Conference at Geneva, and has continued to be a leader in the nuclear disarmament movement since then. At present, he is active in the national debate on the "Star Wars" defense proposal.

BOOK ABOUT BETHE

Bernstein, Jeremy. *Hans Bethe: Prophet of Energy.* Basic Bks. 1980 $12.95. Based on two years of extensive interviews with the subject, this profile was originally published in *The New Yorker.*

BLOCH, FELIX. 1905– (NOBEL PRIZE 1933)

A Swiss-American physicist, Bloch spent most of his career at Stanford University. He is best known for introducing the technique of nuclear magnetic resonance imaging (NMR) as an analytical tool. He has also worked extensively in solid state physics, developing a detailed analysis of the behavior of electrons in crystals.

NMR uses the fact that atomic nuclei will interact with a magnetic field in such a way that the nuclei will assume particular spatial orientations, representing slightly different energies. The technique was first used to study nuclear particles, but has become a basic tool for analyzing complex organic molecules, and now has medical imaging and industrial applications. Bloch was awarded the Nobel Prize in physics in 1933 for his work on NMR.

BOOK ABOUT BLOCH

Gutfreund, H., ed. *Felix Bloch and Twentieth-Century Physics*. Rice Univ. 1980 $25.00 pap. $15.00.

BOHR, NIELS HENRIK DAVID. 1885–1962 (NOBEL PRIZE 1922)

Niels Bohr was a Danish physicist who laid the foundation for quantum mechanics and explained the process of nuclear fission. He is therefore one of the century's most important theoretical physicists.

He was born into a distinguished scientific family, and spent most of his life in Copenhagen. After receiving his doctorate there in 1911, Bohr went to England to work with J. J. Thomson, discoverer of the electron, and then with Ernest Rutherford, who had just shown that an atom consists of a small central nucleus surrounded by relatively distant electrons (1911). At this time, it was not understood how electrons could continually orbit the nucleus without radiating energy, as classical electrodynamics demanded. In 1913, Bohr proposed an explanation. Ten years earlier Max Planck had argued that radiation is emitted or absorbed by atoms in discrete units or quanta of energy. Bohr applied this quantum theory to the atom, proposing that electrons are limited to exchanging energies in quanta only. Using this idea, he derived a theoretical formula for the series of lines in the hydrogen spectrum, long observed but never yet explained. His formula matched the empirical formula, thus verifying the theory. Bohr received the Nobel Prize in physics in 1922 for this work.

Among his many additional contributions to the early development of quantum theory, he formulated the "correspondence principle" (1916) and the "complementarity principle" (1927). The first requires that the quantum theoretical description of the atom correspond to classical physics at large magnitudes, and the second that it is impossible to distinguish between the actual behavior of atomic objects and their interaction with the measuring instrument. These ideas have been of interest to philosophers as well as to physicists.

In 1910 the government of Denmark created the Institute for Theoretical Physics for Bohr, and he continued as its director until his death. The institute under his leadership became a world center for the exchange of ideas and information on nuclear physics.

In 1940, when Denmark was occupied by the Germans, Bohr became active in the resistance movement. In 1943 he and his family escaped to Sweden in a fishing boat. Traveling to the United States, he assisted in the effort to develop the atomic bomb, working in Los Alamos. After the war, he became a passionate advocate of nuclear disarmament. In 1952 he was instrumental in creating the European Centre for Nuclear Research (CERN) in Geneva, Switzerland. In 1955 he organized the first Atoms for Peace Conference in Geneva.

BOOKS BY BOHR

Atomic Theory and the Description of Nature. AMS Pr. repr. of 1934 ed. 1976 $17.00; Ox Bow Pr. 1987 $20.00 pap. $10.00. Contains four republished essays on quantum theory and the atom. After an introductory survey of quantum mechanics, Bohr discusses fundamental concepts including quantum states, the correspondence principle, and the uncertainty principle.

Essays 1958–1962 on Atomic Physics and Human Knowledge. Ox Bow Pr. 1987 $20.00 pap. $10.00. Discussions of the philosophical implications of modern atomic physics, and its relevance to other fields of human knowledge.

BOOKS ABOUT BOHR

French, A. P., and P. J. Kennedy, eds. *Niels Bohr: A Centenary Volume.* Harvard Univ. Pr. 1985 $27.50. A stimulating collection of essays for a wide audience on Bohr and his work, including many interesting photographs. Some of Bohr's own essays are included, such as his 1950 "Open Letter to the United Nations" on the future of atomic energy.

Hendry, John. *The Creation of Quantum Mechanics and the Bohr-Pauli Dialogue.* Kluwer Academic 1984 $34.50. Traces the historical development of modern quantum mechanics, and can also serve as an introduction to these ideas. The author makes little attempt to portray personalities, professional circumstances, or the cultural or political environment.

Moore, Ruth. *Niels Bohr: The Man, His Science, and the World They Changed.* MIT 1985 $9.95. Originally published in 1966, this book is still the only full-length biography of Bohr in English. The most important concepts of atomic and quantum physics necessary to understand Bohr's work are discussed throughout the text, making the work accessible to the nonscientist. Also described are Bohr's political life, anti-Nazi activities, and postwar efforts to avert a nuclear arms race.

Rozental, S., ed. *Niels Bohr: His Life and Work as Seen by His Friends and Colleagues.* Elsevier 1985 $24.95. A "collective book" on Niels Bohr comprised of essays by friends, family, and professional colleagues describing and evaluating his life and work.

BOLTZMANN, LUDWIG. 1844–1906

Ludwig Boltzmann was born and educated in Vienna. A theoretical physicist, he moved from post to post throughout Europe and even visited the United States three times. Boltzmann developed the kinetic theory of gases independent of Maxwell, and went on to establish a firm theoretical foundation for statistical mechanics. In particular, he successfully interpreted the second law of thermodynamics in terms of order and disorder. His famous equation, $S = k \log W$, which relates the entropy S of a system to its probability W, is engraved on his tombstone. He also derived from a thermodynamic basis the law governing the radiation rate of a black body. Boltzmann was a champion of the atomic theory of matter, a subject of controversy in the late nineteenth century. Seriously depressed from these bitter debates, he committed suicide in 1906 just as the last of his opponents conceded the truth of atomic theory.

BOOK BY BOLTZMANN

Theoretical Physics and Philosophical Problems: Selected Writings. Kluwer Academic 1974 $24.00

BORN, MAX. 1882–1970 (NOBEL PRIZE 1954)

Max Born was a German physicist who made many significant contributions to quantum physics as he sought a mathematical explanation for Niels Bohr's successful application of quantum theory to the behavior of electrons in atoms.

After receiving his doctorate in physics and astronomy from the University of Göttingen in 1921, he taught at the universities of Göttingen, Berlin, and Frankfurt-am-Main. Returning to Göttingen in 1921, this time as a professor, he made it a world center for theoretical physics. With his students and colleagues, he introduced a theory called matrix mechanics to account mathematically for the position of an electron in an atom, building on the work of his student Werner Heisenberg. This theory was soon replaced, however, by Erwin Schrödinger's theory of wave mechanics. Nevertheless, Born was later able to link the wave function of a particle to the probability of finding it, using wave mechanics to interpret quantum theory statistically. For this discovery, published in 1926, he belatedly was awarded the Nobel Prize in 1954.

BOOKS BY BORN

Einstein's Theory of Relativity. Dover repr. of 1962 ed. 1986 pap. $6.00. A simple but deep exposition of the physical principles of both the special and general theories of relativity, intended for the serious student but requiring little formal mathematics.

My Life: Recollections of a Nobel Laureate. Scribner 1978 $17.50. Personal reminiscences of a curiously timid and self-deprecating Nobelist.

My Life and My Views. Scribner 1968 o.p. Two brief essays treat Born's own education and work, but more of the book concentrates on the social responsibilities of scientists.

Physics in My Generation. Springer-Verlag 1969 $12.95. A selection of Born's views on a wide range of subjects, including reflections on the nature of the new physics and his bleak view of the role of science in society.

Restless Universe. Dover 2d ed. 1951 $6.95. Discusses concept of atomic and molecular physics from the nineteenth century to quantum mechanics. Along the way, Born explains important concepts such as temperature, mole, mass, energy, spectral line, and the Pauli exclusion principle.

BRIDGMAN, PERCY WILLIAMS. 1882–1961 (NOBEL PRIZE 1946)

Percy Bridgman, born in Cambridge, Massachusetts, a graduate of and professor at Harvard, was best known in physics for his work in high-pressure physics. He explored the properties of many liquids and solids, and designed innovative experimental equipment. Bridgman proposed a process for synthesizing diamonds, which was finally successfully implemented in 1955. This technique was favorably applied to other problems of mineral synthesis, and his work became the basis for a new school of geology based on experiments conducted at high pressures and temperatures.

Bridgman is also widely known as a philosopher of science. Realizing that many ambiguities arise in an examination of scientific methodology, he published *The Logic of Modern Physics* in 1927 to argue his view that a scientific concept is really a set of operations ("operationalism"), a view that is still widely discussed.

BOOKS BY BRIDGMAN

The Logic of Modern Physics. Ayer repr. of 1927 ed. 1980 $9.95. Central exposition of operationalism; not suitable for the beginner. Rather, it should be read after works such as Born's *Restless Universe* (see above).
Reflections of a Physicist. Ayer repr. of 1955 ed. 2d ed. 1980 $48.50. Collection of Bridgman's nontechnical writings, discussing characteristics of the operational method, applications of this method to scientific situations, science in a social environment, and future possibilities for science.
Sophisticates Primer of Relativity. Wesleyan Univ. Pr. 2d ed. 1982 $9.95. This book is meant for the reader who, after assimilating an introduction to the special theory of relativity, seeks a more critical exposition of the subject.

BROGLIE, LOUIS VICTOR, PRINCE DE. 1892–1987

Louis De Broglie, a French physicist, developed the principle that a particle such as an electron can be considered to behave as a wave as well as a particle, which is a fundamental law governing the structure of the atom.

In 1922, using the particle theory of light, De Broglie was able to derive Planck's formula relating energy to the frequency of the radiation. This prompted the question of how a particle could have a frequency. Then, using Einstein's famous equation $E = mc^2$, which also related energy to momentum, he was able to relate a particle's momentum to its wavelength. The existence of De Broglie waves was confirmed experimentally in 1927, when electron diffraction patterns or "matter waves" were first observed.

BOOKS BY DE BROGLIE

New Perspectives in Physics. Basic Bks. 1962 o.p. Offers an exposition of the concepts of modern physics and some of their implications for old philosophical problems such as "determinism."
Physics and Microphysics. Hutchinson 1955 o.p. Concepts of modern physics are explained, and are compared and contrasted with concepts of classical physics. The book also contains a discussion of scientific philosophy and the history of science in general terms.
Revolution in Physics: A Nonmathematical Survey of Quanta. Greenwood repr. of

1953 ed. $22.50. This famous physicist successfully surveys all of quantum mechanics in plain English. All major topics that are required to understand quantum mechanics are covered, such as classical mechanics, optics, and relativity.

CURIE, MARIE SKLODOWSKA. 1867–1934 (NOBEL PRIZE 1903, 1911)

Marie Curie, a Polish-born physicist and chemist, spent her adult life studying and working in France. The focus of her work was the study of radioactivity, a phenomenon discovered by Henri Becquerel in 1896. Married to the physicist Pierre Curie and working in his laboratory, she had demonstrated by the end of 1898 the existence of three new and radioactive elements—uranium, radium, and polonium—as well as some characteristics of their radioactivity. However, a successful explanation of radioactivity was proposed not by the Curies but by Rutherford and his students. In 1903 she received the Nobel Prize in physics jointly with her husband and Becquerel for their pioneering work on radioactivity. In 1911 she was awarded a second Nobel Prize, in chemistry, for her discovery of radium and polonium. Despite these and many other honors, as a foreign-born woman she had to contend throughout her life with the refusal of the French academic community to recognize her scientific eminence.

BOOKS ABOUT MARIE CURIE

Curie, Eve. *Marie Curie.* Doubleday 1939 o.p. Written by Marie Curie's daughter, and drawing on family recollections and papers. Contains a detailed index and lists of Madame Curie's prizes and decorations.

Giroud, Francoise. *Marie Curie: A Life.* Holmes & Meier 1987 $34.50. Informal, emotive biography translated from the French *Une Femme Honorable,* for the general-interest lay reader. Emphasizes personal life and social issues.

Reid, Robert. *Marie Curie.* NAL 1975 o.p. Solid narrative biography, based on research done in four countries.

DIRAC, PAUL ADRIEN MAURICE. 1902–1984 (NOBEL PRIZE 1933)

Paul Dirac, a British theoretical physicist, was a central figure in the development of quantum electrodynamics, introducing important concepts like the magnetic monopole and electron spin. He also predicted the existence of antiparticles.

Dirac was well known for his creativity. After reading Heisenberg's first paper on relativity in 1925, he promptly devised a more general form of the theory. The next year, he formulated Wolfgang Pauli's exclusion principle in quantum mechanical terms. He developed useful statistical rules for particles that obey the Pauli exclusion principle. Most importantly, in 1928 he joined special relativity to quantum theory. The result was a theory of the electron that permitted its spin and magnetic moment to be calculated, and also predicted the existence of positively charged electrons, or positrons. These particles were actually observed in 1932. Dirac's theoretical considerations in predicting the positron were sufficiently general to apply to all particles, and hence constituted an argument for the existence of antimatter. In later years, Dirac worked on what he called "large-number coincidences," that is, relationships that appear to exist between some cosmological constants.

He shared the 1933 Nobel Prize in physics with Erwin Schrödinger for his theory of the electron and prediction of the positron.

BOOKS BY DIRAC

The Principles of Quantum Mechanics. Oxford 4th ed. 1958 text ed. pap. $19.95. "Dirac's classic textbook . . . first appeared in 1930 but it remains incomparably the best book on the fundamentals of quantum theory" (*Nature*). However, the book is quite difficult.

The Development of Quantum Theory. Gordon & Breach 1971 $22.00. An anecdotal short account of the development of quantum mechanics, informative for those who wish to know more about the individuals who played roles in its development and about their contributions.

General Theory of Relativity. Wiley 1975 $30.95. Concise treatment of general relativity for the reader with some physics background.

EINSTEIN, ALBERT. 1879–1955 (NOBEL PRIZE 1921)

A Swiss theoretical physicist, Einstein is the dominant figure in modern physics, and comparable in historic importance to Archimedes, Galileo, and Newton. Born of Jewish parents in Ulm, Germany, he studied in Switzerland and was graduated (1909) from the Federal Institute of Technology, Zurich. He became a Swiss citizen, and it was not until 1914, when he assumed the post of director of theoretical physics at the Kaiser Wilhelm Institute in Berlin, that he resumed his German citizenship. While he was visiting professor at the California Institute of Technology (1933), Hitler became Chancellor of Germany. Einstein did not return to Germany, and in 1934 his property was confiscated by the Nazi government and he was deprived of his German citizenship.

Einstein proposed that light has a dual character, composed of particles as well as wave properties, thus closing the 250-year long debate on that question. He explained the phenomena of the photoelectric effect and of Brownian motion. He revolutionized the world's understanding of space, time, and matter through his theories of special and general relativity. Predictions of his theories have been confirmed by many types of observations, leading to their acceptance as the standard model of physical phenomena.

Einstein's first major contribution was his solution of the photoelectric effect problem, published in a short paper in 1905. Experimental physicists had observed that shining light on the surface of certain metals liberated electrons. However, it did not depend as much on the intensity of light as on its color (frequency). This was successfully explained by Einstein by assuming that light energy travels in discrete packets or quanta, called photons.

Einstein is perhaps most famous for his theory of relativity, special and general. By assuming the constancy of the speed of light, special relativity shows that in describing laws of nature all frames of reference in relative nonaccelerated ratios with respect to each other are equivalent and general relativity shows the same result for accelerated frames of reference. These ideas are fully explained in his *Relativity: The Special and the General Theory*.

Einstein spent the last 30 years of his life trying without success to develop a model of nature that would derive electromagnetic and gravitational forces from one force, a grand unified theory. He believed in the basic simplicity of nature as is evident in his famous remark "God may be subtle but He is not malicious." However, today, as in the year he died, the prospect for a unified theory is as elusive as ever.

BOOKS BY EINSTEIN

Albert Einstein Autobiographical Notes: A Centennial Edition. Ed. by Paul A. Schilpp, Open Court 1979 $10.95. A 43-page essay written at age 67 as a conscious examination of his own life and work. Text of German original included in the volume.

Albert Einstein, the Human Side: New Glimpses from His Archives. Ed. by Helen Dukas and Banesh Hoffmann, Princeton Univ. Pr. 1979 $20.50. Modest anthology of excerpts from Einstein's letters, journal entries, and other commentaries written during his late years in Princeton. Compiled by two personal friends.

Essays in Physics. Philos. Lib. 1985 $3.95

(and Leopold Infeld). *Evolution of Physics: The Growth of Ideas from Early Concepts to Relativity and Quanta*. 1938. Simon & Schuster 1961 o.p. A thorough exposition of the concepts of quantum mechanics together with all prerequisites, such as central ideas of classical physics and relativity.

Ideas and Opinions. Outlet 1954 $4.98. Selected essays drawn from three previously published compendia, including *The World as I See It* (1934) and *Out of My Later Years* (1950). He describes his first impressions of the United States, comments on ethics and social values, and discusses some of the burning political issues of his times.

Meaning of Relativity. Princeton Univ. Pr. 5th ed. 1956 $7.50. A concise treatment of topics in relativity, both special and general. The level is advanced although formulas do not appear in the text.

Out of My Later Years. Greenwood repr. of 1950 ed. $22.50. Sixty collected short essays from the period 1934 to 1950 on science, public affairs, education, Judaism, and Zionism.

Relativity: The Special and the General Theory. Crown 1961 $3.95. No better introduction to the theory exists, in the opinion of many physicists.

Sidelights on Relativity. Dover 1983 $2.25. Contains two articles, the first concerning ether and its relation to relativity, and the second about geometry and its connection to experience.

The World as I See It. Citadel Pr. 1979 $2.95. Collected short essays written between 1922 and 1934 on topics including politics and pacifism, Germany in 1933, Jews and Zionism, and scientific matters.

BOOKS ABOUT EINSTEIN

Barnett, Lincoln. *The World and Dr. Einstein*. Foreword by Albert Einstein, Bantam 1968 o.p. Originally published in a shorter form in *Harper's Magazine*, this enormously popular book saw at least 25 printings. It offers a clear exposition of relativity accessible to a wide audience.

Bernstein, Jeremy. *Einstein*. Penguin 1975 pap. $4.95. The author, a theoretical physicist though not a personal associate of Einstein, outlines Einstein's life and work in this brief introduction.

Born, Max. *Einstein's Theory of Relativity*. Dover rev. ed. 1962 $14.50. A simple but deep exposition of the physical principles of both the special and general theories of relativity, intended for the serious student but requiring little formal mathematics.

Calder, Nigel. *Einstein's Universe*. (See section above on Relativity.)

Clark, Ronald W. *Einstein, the Life and Times: An Illustrated Biography*. Abrams 1984 $28.50. A substantial book in terms of the wealth of material presented concerning Einstein's external life, nevertheless essentially unsuccessful in its treatment of the subject's scientific work and motivations.

Dukas, Helen, and Banesh Hoffmann, eds. *Albert Einstein, the Human Side: New Glimpses from His Archives*. Princeton Univ. Pr. 1979 $20.50 pap. $8.95. "Featuring bits of unpublished letters chosen by Einstein's secretary and his collaborator/biographer, this modest volume illuminates Einstein's character rather than his scientific theories" (*LJ*).

Fine, Arthur. *The Shaky Game: Einstein, Realism, and the Quantum Theory*. Univ. of Chicago Pr. 1986 $25.00. "The essays, most of which have been previously published, are clear, well-reasoned and appropriate settings for the gems they are studded with, quotes from the Einstein archives at Princeton" (*Nature*).

Frank, Philipp. *Einstein: His Life and Times*. Knopf 1947 o.p. Still an excellent scientific biography, emphasizing Einstein's scientific work rather than biographical detail.

Hoffmann, Banesh, and Helen Dukas. *Albert Einstein: Creator and Rebel*. NAL 1973 $6.95. The authors, long-time associates of Einstein, try to convey the form and flavor of his work and show how it compared with contemporary work. Concepts are accessible to the general reader since they are reliably communicated by analogies and drawings rather than by mathematics.

Pais, Abraham. *Subtle Is the Lord: The Science and Life of Albert Einstein*. Oxford Univ. Pr. 1982 $12.95. Written at an advanced level by a distinguished physicist, this is a truly scientific biography, and excludes philosophical issues. The work successfully complements the biographies by Frank (above) and Hoffmann and Dukas (above).

Rosenthal-Schneider, Ilse. *Reality and Scientific Truth: Discussions with Einstein, von Laue, and Planck*. Ed. by Thomas Braun, Wayne State Univ. Pr. 1980 $20.00. The author-editor carried on a correspondence with Einstein, Planck, and Max von Laue for many years concerning the nature of scientific truth and physical reality, as well as on lighter topics. Selections of the correspondence are here published together with connecting text.

Schilpp, Paul A., ed. *Albert Einstein: Philosopher-Scientist*. Open Court 2 vols. 1970 $17.95. Nearly all aspects of Einstein's scientific and philosophical discoveries are discussed in this collection of essays. Contributors to the work include many of the twentieth century's most distinguished physicists.

Whitrow, G. J., ed. *Einstein: The Man and His Achievement*. Dover 1973 $2.95. Published form of three BBC broadcasts on Einstein's life and work. The intention was to put both into perspective while many who had known him personally were still alive, and to convey the content of his theories in nonspecialist language.

FARADAY, MICHAEL. 1791–1867

Michael Faraday, a British physicist and chemist, was one of the greatest experimentalists of the nineteenth century. The son of a blacksmith, he received a minimal education, including almost no mathematics. Nevertheless, in 1812 his native talent brought him to the attention of Sir Humphry Davy at the Royal Institution, who invited him as a laboratory assistant. Faraday remained at the Institution until retirement in 1862, and it was here that he made his contributions to the study of electricity. Faraday produced the basic laws of electrolysis in 1834. He discovered that the circular lines of magnetic force produced by the flow of current through a wire deflect a nearby compass needle. In fact, either the magnet or the conductor can be made to move. By demonstrating this conversion of electrical energy into motive force, Faraday identified the basic principles governing the electric motor. Simultaneously with Joseph Henry, he discovered electromagnetic induction, and then Faraday went on to build the first electric generator, following up on a suggestion from British mathematician and physicist Lord Kelvin. After a series of experiments using polarized light, he proposed an electromagnetic theory of light that was later developed by Maxwell and is fundamental to the later development of physics. Famous as a popularizer of science, Faraday regularly lectured to lay audiences from 1825 to 1862, though just as regularly he declined honors bestowed in recognition of this fame, such as a knighthood and the presidency of the Royal Society. (See also Chapter 10 in this volume.)

BOOK BY FARADAY

The Chemical History of a Candle: A Course of Lectures Delivered Before a Juvenile Audience at the Royal Institution. Larlin repr. of 1861 ed. 1978 $13.95. An example of Faraday's famous popular Christmas lecture series, with this set of six focusing primarily on combustion.

BOOKS ABOUT FARADAY

Agassi, Joseph. *Faraday as a Natural Philosopher.* Univ. of Chicago Pr. 1971 $23.00. Agassi argues that Faraday viewed himself not as a discoverer but primarily as a theoretician. He wanted to be remembered as a natural philosopher, in other words, but was frustrated because his theoretical constructions were not understood. It was left to Maxwell to systematize his discoveries.

Tricker, R. A. *Contributions of Faraday and Maxwell to Electrical Science.* Pergamon 1966 $25.00. Thorough account of the scientific work on electromagnetic induction of Faraday and Maxwell, conveying historical, biographical, and anecdotal information. Gives a quick overview of electromagnetic phenomena as well.

Tyndale, John. *Faraday as Discoverer.* 1868 o.p. Tyndale was a pupil and close personal friend, and describes Faraday as a great discoverer of important facts of nature.

Williams, L. Pearce. *Michael Faraday: A Biography.* Basic Bks. 1965 o.p. Definitive biography of Faraday, making extensive use of Faraday's own writings to tell his story, so that the book is nearly an autobiography. Assesses Faraday's own work in terms of modern science.

FERMI, ENRICO. 1901–1954 (NOBEL PRIZE 1938)

Enrico Fermi was born in Rome and trained in Pisa, Göttingen, and Leiden, working with leading figures in the new quantum mechanics. Returning to Rome in 1926, he spent several years working on the statistical mechanics of particles and wrote the first textbook on modern physics to be published in Italy. In 1934 he began a series of experiments producing new radioactive isotopes by neutron bombardment. This was the work for which he was awarded the Nobel Prize in 1938. After the prize ceremony Fermi did not return to Italy, because of the Fascist regime, but emigrated with his wife and two children to the United States. As part of the atomic bomb effort, Fermi directed the design and construction of the first nuclear reactor at the University of Chicago, which began operating in December 1942. He spent the next two years with Arthur Compton leading the American team that constructed the first atomic bomb. One of the few modern physicists to excel in both theory and experiment, Fermi died of cancer in 1954. The next year the newly discovered element with atomic number 100 was named fermium in his honor.

BOOKS ABOUT FERMI

Fermi, Laura. *Atoms in the Family: My Life with Enrico Fermi.* Amer. Inst. of Physics 1987 $32.00. Biography and family portrait of this physicist's physicist.

Lichello, Robert. *Enrico Fermi: Father of the Atomic Bomb.* [*Outstanding Personalities Ser.*] Samuel Harcourt Pr. 1972 $1.95. Brief biography.

Segre, Emilio. *Enrico Fermi: Physicist.* Univ. of Chicago Pr. 1972 $2.95. Segre was a compatriot, lifelong friend, and coworker of Fermi, and himself a Nobelist. He has written a nontechnical, professional portrait of his colleague. Four appendixes include letters from Fermi, the Nobel acceptance speech, and two addresses describing the Manhattan Project to develop the atom bomb.

FEYNMAN, RICHARD PHILLIPS. 1918–1988 (NOBEL PRIZE 1965)

Richard Feynman, an American theoretical physicist, received his Ph.D. from Princeton in 1942. From 1945 to 1950, he taught at Cornell University. In 1950, he became professor of theoretical physics at the California Institute of Technology. Feynman has made important contributions to quantum electrodynamics (QED). This is the part of quantum mechanics that treats electromagnetic interactions, for example, interactions among electrons. In Feynman's approach, these interactions are treated as exchanges of virtual particles. For example, the interaction of two electrons is explained as an exchange of virtual photons. The final theory has proved to be accurate in its predictions. The Nobel Prize for physics in 1965 was awarded to Feynman, Julian Schwinger, and Sin-Itiro Tomonaga, all pioneers in quantum electrodynamics.

BOOKS BY FEYNMAN

Character of Physical Law. MIT 1967 $5.95. An informative book about physics in simple English by an outstanding expositor. The notions of a physical theory, conservation laws, and quantum mechanics are discussed.

Feynman Lectures on Physics. Addison-Wesley 3 vols. text ed. pap. ea. $20.95. Classic undergraduate treatment.

QED: The Strange Theory of Light and Matter. Princeton Univ. Pr. 1985 $18.50. Principles of quantum theory and in particular of quantum electrodynamics are explained simply and without mathematics. The book is the published form of a series of public lectures. It is witty and will reward readers of all levels.

(and Ralph Leighton). *"Surely You're Joking, Mr. Feynman!": Adventures of a Curious*

Character. Norton 1985 $16.95. Based on tapes of conversations over the years with his friend Ralph Leighton, this book is not an autobiography. Rather it displays the flamboyant and outrageous personality of this famous physicist.

FRANKLIN, BENJAMIN. 1706–1790

Benjamin Franklin was the first great American scientist, making a major contribution to physics by developing an understanding of electric charge as a presence or absence of electricity. Additionally, in a classic experiment, he proved that lightning is electrical in nature, and later invented the lightning rod. Additional useful inventions included bifocal spectacles. His rejection of the particle theory of light inspired researchers to work on wave theory later in the century. In the United States, of course, Franklin is perhaps better known among historians as a diplomat and statesman who was active in the drafting of the Declaration of Independence, the peace treaty of 1783, and the Constitution of the United States. Other achievements include the founding of the American Philosophical Society in 1743 and a college in 1749 that later became the University of Pennsylvania. (See also Volume 3.)

BOOKS BY FRANKLIN

The Autobiography of Benjamin Franklin: A Genetic Text. Univ. of Tennessee Pr. 1981 $31.50. A critical edition of the autobiography.
The Ingenious Dr. Franklin: Selected Scientific Letters of Benjamin Franklin. Ed. by Nathan G. Goodman, Univ. of Pennsylvania Pr. 1974 $23.00. A reprint of a collection first published in 1931, this volume is a lively collection of brief letters and papers by this remarkable man, commenting on everything from meteorology to marsh gas.

BOOKS ABOUT FRANKLIN

Clark, Ronald W. *Benjamin Franklin: A Biography.* Random 1983 $22.95. Only incidentally a scientific biography, this book details a very different and more colorful life from the carefully doctored account of the *Autobiography.*
Crowther, J. G. *Famous American Men of Science.* Bks. for Libraries 1969. o.p. A book-length narrative biography of Franklin is included in this volume.
Scudder, Evarts S. *Benjamin Franklin: A Biography.* Ayer repr. of 1939 ed. $21.00
Seeger, Raymond J. *Benjamin Franklin.* [*Selected Readings in Physics*] Pergamon 1973 $17.75. After a short biographical account, this book presents selected scientific letters on heat, static electricity, surface tension, lightning, and meteorology.

GALILEI, GALILEO. 1564–1642

The methods and results of Galileo, an Italian physicist and astronomer, are usually considered the beginning of modern science. That is, he is credited with establishing the effectiveness of the scientific method of deriving mathematical laws to explain experimental observations. He was perhaps the most revolutionary scientist who ever lived. The ideas that he proposed and defended were often in direct conflict with the accepted theories of his time. These were basically theories of ARISTOTLE (see also Volumes 3 and 4), integrated into religion. For example, Aristotle thought that more massive bodies fall faster than less massive ones and that men have more teeth than women. Galileo, who must be recognized as the father of the scientific method, put these ideas to the test of objective experiment.

Although Galileo did not develop a comprehensive theory as Newton was to do later, nonetheless without him Newton could not have accomplished this feat. Formulation of a comprehensive theory requires as a prerequisite a massive amount of scientific and detailed observation of nature. Galileo provided the rules and motivation for scientists to gather this data, and began the process. In applying this method he discovered the pendulum, invented the thermometer, and was the first to use a telescope to make astronomical observations. With his telescope, for example, he observed mountains on the moon, sunspots, and the phases of Venus. He concluded that heavenly bodies were made of the same substances and processes as the earth. It then became possible for a Newton to treat celestial and earthly phenomena from a unified point of view. Galileo is most widely known today for his famous experiment at Pisa demonstrating that bodies of different weights fall at the same speed. From these observations he formulated the laws that govern the motion of falling bodies, and published his ideas in *De Motu* (*On Motion*) in 1590. He also formulated a notion of inertia, later to be incorporated into Newton's first law of motion.

Galileo was a pugnacious and argumentative man. Publicly espousing the heliocentric theories of Copernicus, he aroused the wrath of the church. In 1616 Galileo was instructed to abandon Copernican theory, but he continued to be personally convinced. When Urban VIII became pope in 1624, Galileo obtained permission to present the rival heliocentric and geocentric theories in an impartial way. Instead, he wrote a polemical dialogue called *Dialogue Concerning the Two Great World Systems*, which was immediately banned. Galileo was tried for heresy, and sentenced to life imprisonment. Working under house arrest in his villa near Florence, he summed up his life's work in *Discourses and Mathematical Discoveries Concerning Two New Sciences*. The manuscript was smuggled out of Italy and published in Holland in 1638. (See also Chapter 7 in this volume and Chapter 4 in Volume 4.)

BOOKS BY GALILEO

Dialogue Concerning the Two Chief World Systems, Ptolemaic and Copernican. 1632. Ed. by Stillman Drake, Univ. of California Pr. 2d ed. rev. 1967 $11.95. A Galilean-style dialogue incorporating a new English translation of Galileo's *Bodies That Stay Atop Water, or Move in It.* This is the first English translation since 1665 of Galileo's first, controversial work on hydrostatics. Additionally, contemporary documents have been translated and incorporated into the unusual format.

Dialogues Concerning Two New Sciences. 1639. Dover repr. of 1914 ed. 1952 pap. $5.50

Discoveries and Opinions of Galileo. Anchor 1957 pap. $5.95. Several famous short works, including "The Starry Messenger," letters on sunspots, and other selections.

Books about Galileo

Brophy, James, and Henry Paolucci, eds. *The Achievement of Galileo*. New College Univ. Pr. 1962 $7.95. Edited selections from the writings of Galileo, contemporaries such as Bellarmine, and modern commentators.

Campanella, Thomas. *The Defense of Galileo*. Ayer 1975 $14.00

Drake, Stillman. *Galileo*. Oxford 1981 pap. $3.95. In this short book, the author sets forth a new view of Galileo's relation to his contemporary philosophers and scientists, and to the church. Drake argues that Galileo, in his search for freedom of inquiry, feuded with his fellow philosophers, and that it was they who sought a pretext for censuring him.

————. *Galileo at Work: His Scientific Biography*. Univ. of Chicago Pr. 1981 $9.95. Drake presents a chronological reconstruction of Galileo's scientific studies, year by year. Many contemporary documents and passages, newly translated, are incorporated into the text. Anecdotes are plentiful, and an appendix of 200 capsule biographies is included. The book is a fine first introduction to Galileo, and strongly recommended for a general audience.

————. *Telescopes, Tides and Tactics: A Galilean Dialogue about the "Starry Messenger" and Systems of the World*. Univ. of Chicago Pr. 1983 $22.50. Galileo's first astronomical work, "The Starry Messenger," is presented in the context of an imaginary dialogue among three of his friends.

Fahie, J. J. *Galileo: His Life and Work*. Irvington repr. of 1903 ed. 1981 $57.00. Older biography with extensive coverage of the famous trial.

Gebler, Karl von. *Galileo Galilei and the Roman Curia from Authentic Sources*. Richwood Pub. repr. of 1897 ed. 1977 $28.50. "Its general effect is to dissipate some of the popular exaggerations . . . concerning Galileo's treatment by the Roman authorities. The torture and the rigorous imprisonment are disproved, but the torture was certainly threatened, and the movements of the philosopher were certainly watched with unceasing jealousy" (*The Spectator*).

Langford, Jerome J. *Galileo, Science and the Church*. Univ. of Michigan Pr. rev. ed. 1971 $6.95. The condemnation of Galileo is examined in this historical context, in light of contemporary theological, philosophical, and scientific issues. Galileo is described as an impatient defender of Copernican theory before sufficient evidence had accumulated, and his opponents as using the Bible as a scientific textbook.

McMullin, Erwin. *Galileo: Man of Science*. Basic Bks. 1968 o.p. A collection of essays gathered for Galileo's quadricentennial, each on a different aspect of his life and work, such as astronomy, dynamics, and scientific methodology.

Poupard, Paul, ed. *Galileo Galilei: Toward a Resolution of 350 Years of Debate, 1633–1983*. Duquesne 1986 $28.00

Santillana, Giorgio de. *The Crime of Galileo*. Univ. of Chicago Pr. 1955 $14.00. Focuses on Galileo's trial before the Inquisition, and on events leading to it. The book is based on a detailed scrutiny of original texts and transcripts.

Seeger, Raymond J. *Galileo Galilei: His Life and His Works*. Pergamon 1966 o.p. Primarily comprised of selections from Galileo's writings, introduced by Seeger. Seeger is a physicist, and tends to emphasize those of Galileo's conclusions that remain valid today rather than the process by which those conclusions were reached.

Shea, William R. *Galileo Intellectual Revolution*. Science History Pubns. 1973 o.p. Concentrates on Galileo's fruitful period, 1610 to 1632, detailing the contemporary debates, discussions, science, and philosophy that formed the context for his work.

GAMOW, GEORGE. 1904–1968

George Gamow, a Soviet-American physicist, worked primarily in theoretical nuclear physics and cosmology, but made substantial contributions to molecular biology as well. He was also widely known as the author of valuable and exciting popular science books, notably the "Mr. Tompkins" series, in which he used the figure of a curious bank clerk for a layperson's exploration into quantum physics and gravity.

His early scientific work dealt with alpha- and beta-decay, and the liquid drop model of nuclear structure. However, his work on the early universe is better known. The Big Bang theory of the universe had first been proposed by Georges Lemaitre. Gamow considered the state of the universe prior to the postulated Big Bang, and predicted that the original explosion would produce a uniform background radiation. In 1964 this radiation was observed by Arno Penzias and Robert Wilson, which gave considerable experimental support to the Big Bang theory of the origin of the universe.

Gamow turned from astronomy to molecular biology. He theorized that the sequences of four nucleic acid bases that constitute the DNA chain could control the construction of proteins. He demonstrated that a sequence of three bases was sufficient to act as a code for all known amino acids. In 1961 the genetic code was solved, and the 64 triplets identified with the respective amino acids. (See also Chapter 7 in this volume.)

BOOKS BY GEORGE GAMOW

Mr. Tompkins in Paperback. Cambridge Univ. Pr. 1967 pap. $7.95. Includes two of the most popular of Gamow's Mr. Tompkins series: *Mr. Tompkins in Wonderland* (1939) and *Mr. Tompkins Explores the Atom.* The works were updated to include more information on advances in physics that occurred after their original publication.

One, Two, Three . . . Infinity. 1947. Bantam 1971 o.p. Facts and theories about the universe in its microscopic and macroscopic manifestations by a skillful popularizer.

Thirty Years That Shook Physics: The Story of Quantum Theory. Dover repr. of 1966 ed. 1985 pap. $4.95. Still a charming introduction to the development of quantum theory, covering the period from 1900 to 1930. The author knew many of the important figures who made these discoveries, and includes personal recollections and impressions to provide a popular and anecdotal presentation that nonetheless conveys a good deal of information about physics.

My World Line: An Informal Autobiography. Viking 1970 o.p. A fragmentary and charming autobiography, "a collection of short stories, all of them pertaining to me, and all of them completely true."

HAMILTON, SIR WILLIAM ROWAN. 1805–1865

An Irish mathematician, Hamilton provided some of the basic mathematical tools of modern physics. For example, working in dynamics, he developed a set of equations to describe the positions and other characteristics of a collection of particles. These equations utilize the Hamiltonian function, which is widely used in quantum mechanics problems. He created what was later to be transformed into modern vector analysis. The Hamilton-

Jacobi equation is also commonly used in mechanics. Hamilton also made a number of contributions to optics.

A child prodigy, he was appointed astronomer royal for Ireland at the age of 22 so that he could continue his research unhindered by teaching obligations. He received many honors for his scientific work throughout his life, and was intimate with the English romantic poets, notably Coleridge and Wordsworth. In later life he drank increasingly, eventually dying of gout.

BOOK ABOUT HAMILTON

Hankins, Thomas L. *Sir William Rowan Hamilton.* Johns Hopkins Univ. Pr. 1980 $39.50. An excellent example of a scientific biography, including thorough explanations of everything from Irish politics to quaternions. Includes a useful bibliography and index.

HEISENBERG, WERNER. 1901–1976 (NOBEL PRIZE 1932)

Werner Heisenberg, a German physicist, is thought of as the founder of quantum mechanics, the explanation of atomic structure in mathematical terms.

In the 1920s quantum theory abounded in controversies following the proposal of Niels Bohr's successful model for the hydrogen atom. Heisenberg, uneasy with the prevalent mechanical models of the atom, conceived an abstract approach using matrix algebra. Helped by Max Born and Pascual Jordan, in 1925 he developed this approach into a theory, matrix mechanics. However, the theory was difficult to assimilate, providing no means of visualization for the phenomena it sought to explain. Erwin Schrödinger's wave formulation, proposed in the following year, proved more successful. In fact, Heisenberg's and Schrödinger's formulations were finally shown by JOHN VON NEUMANN (see Volume 3) to be mathematically equivalent in 1944.

In 1927, Heisenberg made the discovery for which he is best known, namely the uncertainty principle. According to this principle, it is impossible to specify simultaneously both the position and the momentum of a particle such as an electron. This is due to interference with those quantities by the radiation that must be used to make the observation. The principle was demonstrated by means of a thought experiment rather than by physical observation. Heisenberg also explained ferromagnetism by tracing it to an origin in atomic structure. He was awarded the Nobel Prize in 1932.

Heisenberg was one of the few great modern German physicists to remain in Germany during World War II. During the war he was in charge of atomic research in Germany, with the goal of constructing a bomb. Whether by intent or by circumstance this effort proved unsuccessful, and contradictory statements by Heisenberg have not fully explained the outcome of the project. After the war, Heisenberg publicly declared that he would not take part in the production or testing of atomic weapons.

BOOKS BY HEISENBERG

Physics and Philosophy: The Revolution in Modern Science. Harper 1962 pap. $6.95. A general discussion of physics, its philosophy, and its relation to other sciences.

Stylistically, somewhat roundabout. In particular, Heisenberg answers criticisms of his uncertainty principle by Einstein and others.

Physics and Beyond. Harper 1971 $7.50. A collection of 20 recollected conversations primarily with great scientists of the atomic age, such as Wolfgang Pauli, Bohr, and Planck. No claim is made to accurate transcription; rather, the conversations are reconstructed from what Heisenberg knew of his fellow scientists as well as from his memories.

Physicist's Conception of Nature. Trans. by Arnold J. Pomerans, Greenwood repr. of 1958 ed. $22.50. A collection of essays, including "The Idea of Nature in Contemporary Physics" and "Atomic Physics and Causal Law," together with observations on education and the beginnings of modern science.

Tradition in Science. Harper 1983 pap. $10.95. "These essays begin with a deceptive simplicity but move quickly into the abstractions of theoretical physics. . . . Heisenberg's metaphysics and his explorations into the intuitions of creative physicists in formulating 'closed systems' make him more akin to Plato than to Aristotle: the Really Real may be the idea, the abstraction" (*Kirkus Reviews*).

BOOKS ABOUT HEISENBERG

Heisenberg, Elisabeth. *Inner Exile: Recollections of a Life with Werner Heisenberg.* Birkhauser 1984 $16.95. Werner Heisenberg's life and his decision to stay in Germany during World War II are explained and defended by his wife.

MacPherson, Malcolm. *Time Bomb: Fermi, Heisenberg, and the Race for the Atomic Bomb.* Dutton 1986 $18.95. "Conveys in nontechnical terms the theories and lab experiments that brought Heisenberg to the brink of success in Germany, and in America led Fermi to the first self-sustaining chain reaction in uranium on Dec. 2, 1942" (*PW*).

HELMHOLTZ, HERMANN LUDWIG FERDINAND VON. 1821–1894

A German physicist and physiologist of broad interests, Helmholtz made the first precise formulation of the principle of conservation of energy. During physiological studies of muscle action and animal heat, Helmholtz developed this idea following up his conclusion that the energy required for life processes in animals is derived entirely from the oxidation of food. In his formulation, he was helped by having available the precise determination of the mechanical equivalent of heat made by English physicist James Joule. His formulation led to the first law of thermodynamics, which states that the total energy of a system and its surroundings remains constant even if it may change form. Other areas of contributions to physics include hydrodynamics and electrodynamics, where he attempted to produce a general unified theory.

Helmholtz's physiological studies were also significant. He made many discoveries in the physiology of vision and hearing, in particular inventing the ophthalmoscope, and reviving the three-color theory of vision to investigate color vision and color blindness.

By the enormous breadth of his scientific contributions and the exactness of his work, Helmholtz dominated German science in the middle of the nineteenth century and made it the focus of attention for the world's scientific community. He and his students took classical mechanics to its limits, helping to set the stage for the revolution in physics at the beginning to the twentieth century represented by quantum theory and relativity. This revolution was mainly the creation of German scientists, applying the rigorous mathematical and experimental standards set by Helmholtz. Helmholtz was also active as a popularizer of science.

Books by Helmholtz

Popular Scientific Lectures. Appleton 1900 o.p. Contains articles on medicine, physiology, and physics. The article on conservation of energy is particularly important due to the influence of its author on the formulation of this fundamental law of physics.

Selected Writings of Hermann Von Helmholtz. Ed. by Russell Kahl, Wesleyan Univ. Pr. 1971 $37.50. Collection of 20 readable shorter papers and lectures on such topics as perception, medicine, electricity, the solar system, and the origins of mathematics.

HENRY, JOSEPH. 1797–1878

An American physicist, Joseph Henry carried out early experiments in electromagnetism, anticipating Michael Faraday's discovery of electrostatic induction although not publishing his own results until later. Henry developed a greatly improved form of the electromagnet, constructed the first practical electrical motor, and developed the relay (used in telegraphy).

As the first secretary of the Smithsonian Institution, he made that organization a liaison between scientists and government. His meteorological studies while at the Smithsonian led to the founding of the U.S. Weather Bureau.

Books about Henry

Crowther, James G. *Famous American Men of Science.* Ayer 1937 $27.50. Includes a 75-page essay on Joseph Henry's life and work.

Molella, Arthur P., and others. *A Scientist in American Life: The Essays and Lectures of Joseph Henry.* Smithsonian 1981 $7.95. Several of the essays included were first published in Henry's lifetime. Henry's effort to articulate the relationship of pure science to technology is discussed.

HUYGENS, CHRISTIAAN. 1629–1695

A Dutch physicist and astronomer, Huygens worked extensively on optics and dynamics. His greatest achievement was his development of the wave theory of light published in 1678 in his *Traite de la Lumiere* (*Treatise on Light*). This was written to counter Newton's particle (or "corpuscular") theory of light. Huygens proposed that light travels in successive spherical shells from its source in space and that when one shell hits a barrier the point of contact becomes another source of light, in turn radiating light spheres. Using these ideas he successfully deduced Snell's law and explained the phenomena of interference. His wave theory became accepted over Newton's corpuscular theory when it correctly predicted a decrease in the speed of light when refracted into a medium denser than air.

In 1657, Huygens invented a reliable pendulum clock, succeeding where many had failed, including Galileo himself. He worked on the more general theory of harmonic oscillating systems throughout his life, finally publishing his *Horologium Oscillatorium* (1673).

Essentially a solitary man, Huygens did not attract students and disciples. As was common in the seventeenth century, he was slow to publish. Nevertheless, in seventeenth-century science he was second only to Newton in stature.

BOOK BY HUYGENS

The Pendulum Clock, or Geometrical Demonstrations Concerning the Motion of Pendula as Applied to Clocks (Horologium Oscillatorium). 1673. Iowa State Univ. Pr. 1986 $38.95

BOOK ABOUT HUYGENS

Baker, Bevan Braithwaite, and E. T. Copson. *The Mathematical Theory of Huygens' Principle*. 1950. Oxford 2d ed. 1969 $6.25. "Devoted almost exclusively to a *mathematical* analysis of Huygen's Principle, this text will be found of value to those physicists who wish to explore various ways of solving wave theory problems from a theoretical point of view" (*Choice*).

KAPITZA, PETER LEONIDOVICH. 1894–1984. (NOBEL PRIZE 1978)

A Soviet experimental physicist, Kapitza is best known for his work in low-temperature physics with the form of liquid helium that exists at temperatures close to absolute zero. He found that helium in this temperature exists in a "superfluid" state that conducts heat better than copper, the best conductor known at normal temperatures. His investigations showed that this form of helium is highly viscous and also displays an unusual form of internal convection.

Related to this work, he developed a process for liquefying helium. The subsequent availability of liquid helium permitted the production of electric semiconductors and much other low-temperature work. The early equipment that he designed and built was far superior to anything else of its day. As an example, in the course of an experiment in 1924 he produced a record high pressure that was not surpassed until 1956.

Like many other twentieth-century physicists, Kapitza was caught up in political turmoil. As a young man in 1919 he traveled to England to work on magnetic research under Rutherford at the Cavendish Laboratory of Cambridge University, eventually becoming deputy director of the laboratory. In 1930 he was made director of the Royal Society's Mond Laboratory at Cambridge, which was built for him. In 1934 he paid a visit to the Soviet Union for a professional meeting, as he had done previously. However, this time the Stalinist government ordered Kapitza detained and his passport seized. The next year Kapitza was made director of a new research institute in Moscow, and the Mond Laboratory was sold to the Soviet government and transported to Moscow for his use. Kapitza worked there until 1946, when he refused to work on the development of nuclear weapons and was put under house arrest only to be released after Stalin's death in 1953. He was then restored to his old post as director of the institute. He was belatedly awarded the Nobel Prize for physics in 1978.

BOOKS BY KAPITZA

Experiment, Theory, Practice. Kluwer Academic 1980 $14.95. Collection of articles
and speeches on physics education, Russian physics institutions, and science
and society. Also included are comments on notable scientific figures both contemporary and past, such as Rutherford, Lomonosov, Landau, and Franklin.
Society and the Environment: A Soviet View. Imported Pubns. 1977 pap. $3.45

BOOK ABOUT KAPITZA

Badash, Lawrence. *Kapitza, Rutherford and the Kremlin.* Yale Univ. Pr. 1985 $20.00.
Recent work drawing on Kapitza's recently released letters to his family written
during the period immediately after his detention in 1934.

MACH, ERNST. 1838–1916

Ernst Mach, an Austrian physicist, made important contributions not
only to physics but also to the psychology of sensation and perception and
to what is now considered the philosophy of science. In physics, Mach is
best known for defining the Mach number, a familiar term in today's world
of supersonic aircraft. While studying the shock wave produced in a gas
around the tip of a projectile, he found that the flow of gas changes radically as the projectile reaches the speed of sound. The Mach number describes the ratio of the velocity of an object to the speed of sound in the
medium in which the object is moving. Thus, an aircraft flying at Mach 2 is
flying at twice the speed of sound in air.

Mach's name has also been given to his cosmological principle of inertia.
Rejecting Newton's assumption of absolute space and time independent of
matter, Mach argued that the concept of inertia acquires quantitative meaning only via Newton's laws and that only motion relative to a background
or framework exists. Hence, inertia exists only relative to the background of
fixed stars. This relativism heavily influenced Einstein.

More widely, Mach is known today as a tough exponent of a view of
science that sought to understand knowledge in the context of the psychological, sensory, and historical processes that govern its acquisition. He
tended to oppose mechanical explanations of the universe that could not be
adequately observed in favor of more mathematical or conceptual explanations capable of at least indirect observation. Throughout his life this insis-
tence led him to reject as metaphysics the crude atomic theory of his day,
as well as Einstein's later relativity theory. However, his critical objections
helped push theoretical physicists to develop more mathematical and statistical descriptions of the atom, thus aiding the development of quantum
mechanics.

BOOKS BY MACH

The Science of Mechanics. 1893. Open Court 6th ed. 1960 $12.95. A landmark work in
the history of physics, this is a critical evaluation of mechanics, which was
perhaps the major branch of physics in Mach's time. Not for the beginner.
Popular Scientific Lectures. Open Court 1986 $10.95. A dated exposition of various
concepts of physics by a nineteenth-century master. The work treats the topics
of symmetry and electrostatics, and the principle of the conservation of energy.

BOOKS ABOUT MACH

Cohen, R. S., and R. J. Seeger, eds. *Ernst Mach: Physicist and Philosopher.* Kluwer Academic 1970 $29.00. A collection of essays by 12 authors dealing with Mach's work from historical, biographical, and critical points of view.

Musil, Robert. *On Mach's Theories.* Catholic Univ. Pr. 1983 $34.95. A translation of the 1913 collection of essays, discussing natural laws, space and time, electrostatic and quantum theories of matter, and science and ethics.

MAXWELL, JAMES CLERK. 1831–1879

James Clerk Maxwell was a British physicist who developed the standard theoretical model for the modern understanding of electricity and magnetism, showing that these two phenomena are two aspects of the same force. With this work he unified and systematized a vast field of experiment, taking many diverse observations and qualitative concepts developed by Faraday and others, and formulating them into a system of powerful differential equations. This unified theory was developed between 1864 and 1873. On the basis of this theory, Maxwell predicted that electromagnetic waves should exist and travel with the speed of light. He also identified light as a form of electromagnetic radiation. These predictions were experimentally confirmed.

Maxwell's other great contribution to physics was to provide a mathematical basis for the kinetic theory of gases. Using a statistical approach, he related the velocity of the molecules in a gas to its temperature, showing that heat results from the motion of molecules. This result had been conjectured for some time but had never been proven. Maxwell then expanded his approach to treat viscosity, diffusion, and other properties of gases.

Maxwell also gave the first satisfactory account of Saturn's rings, establishing on theoretical grounds that the rings are not solid but are composed of many small bodies that orbit Saturn. This conclusion of course had been experimentally confirmed by observation.

BOOKS ABOUT MAXWELL

Campbell, Lewis, and William Garnett. *Life of James Clerk Maxwell.* Johnson Repr. repr. of 1882 ed. 1970 $50.00. Official biography written by an old school friend together with Maxwell's laboratory assistant.

Tricker, R. A. *Contributions of Faraday and Maxwell to Electrical Science.* Pergamon 1966 $25.00. Thorough account of the scientific work on electromagnetic induction of Faraday and Maxwell, conveying historical, biographical, and anecdotal information. Gives a quick overview of electromagnetic phenomena as well.

MICHELSON, ALBERT ABRAHAM. 1852–1931 (NOBEL PRIZE 1907)

Albert Michelson was an American experimental physicist who performed crucial experiments in optics. In 1882 he made a precise measurement of the velocity of light, and refined this precision ten years later with improved equipment. As part of this set of experiments, he developed an extremely sensitive interferometer, a device that can divide a beam of light, send the two subbeams in different directions, and then reunite them. If the two beams travel different distances at the same speed, or the same distance at different speeds, the light waves are no longer synchronized and interference patterns result.

At this time, many physicists believed that the earth must be moving through a static substance, the ether, that was thought to fill all space. The existence of the ether was assumed as a necessary carrier for the propagation of light waves, since waves implied a medium or carrier in classical physics. Using his new interferometer, Michelson devised an experiment to test for the existence of the ether. In the experiment, a beam of sunlight was split so that part would travel in the direction of the earth's motion and the rest in a direction perpendicular to that motion. If there were an ether medium, an interference pattern would be obtained from which the existence of the ether could be detected. In his first trials, Michelson could detect no difference in the speed of light, whatever the direction. Working with American scientist Edward Morley, he built a more sensitive interferometer, but even when working under near-perfect conditions in 1887, once again he could not detect the presence of ether.

Physicists therefore were forced to consider the likelihood that the ether did not exist, and the way was open for Einstein to develop the theory of special relativity to explain the constant speed of light. Michelson was awarded the Nobel Prize in 1907 for his work, the first American scientist to receive this honor.

BOOK BY MICHELSON

Studies in Optics. 1927. Univ. of Chicago Pr. 1962 pap. $2.45

BOOKS ABOUT MICHELSON

Jaffe, Bernard. *Michelson and the Speed of Light.* Greenwood 1979 $22.50
Livingston, Dorothy Michelson. *The Master of Light: A Biography of Albert A. Michelson.* Univ. of Chicago Pr. 1979 $6.95. Written by Michelson's youngest daughter, this is a well-organized scientific biography based on personal recollections, much reading, and interviews. The man and his achievements are described, as well as the growth of physics in the United States from a few individuals in 1880 to a developed discipline in 1930.

MILLIKAN, ROBERT ANDREWS. 1868–1953 (NOBEL PRIZE 1923)

An American experimental physicist, Millikan made the first determination of the charge of the electron and of Planck's constant. He was awarded the 1923 Nobel Prize in physics for these contributions. The determination of the charge on the electron proved experimentally that electrons are particles of electricity. Millikan accomplished this feat by designing an experiment studying the fall of oil droplets in an electric field. He conjectured that the droplets would take up integral multiples of electrical charge. By measuring the strength of the field required to counteract the gravitational force on the droplets, he was able to compute a highly accurate unit charge for the particle.

Millikan also studied the photoelectric effect experimentally, in 1916 confirming Einstein's equation relating the kinetic energy of a particle emitted by incident radiation to the frequency of that radiation. By measuring the strength of the field required to counteract the gravitational force on the droplets, he was able to compute a highly accurate unit charge for the particle. After World War I, Millikan studied cosmic rays and the ultraviolet spectra of many elements until his retirement.

BOOKS BY MILLIKAN

Science and Life. Ayer repr. of 1924 ed. $14.00. Essays on the practical value of pure science, and science related to religion and society.

Evolution in Science and Religion. 1927. Arden Lib. repr. of 1929 ed. 1976 $17.50. Published version of a series of lectures on the evolution of twentieth-century physics and of religion. Millikan emphasizes the lack of dogmatism in modern physics.

Science and the New Civilization. Ayer repr. of 1930 ed. $18.00. "A collection of addresses previously published in various magazines, and which carry the same essential message: a defense of scientific knowledge against its detractors" (*Isis*).

The Autobiography of Robert A. Millikan. Ayer repr. of 1950 ed. 1980 $26.50. A detailed autobiography, detailing events of the life of the man who was for many years the central figure in American physics.

BOOK ABOUT MILLIKAN

Kargon, Robert H. *The Rise of Robert Millikan: Portrait of a Life in American Science.* Cornell Univ. Pr. 1982 $28.50. Study of the life and work of one of America's most prominent physicists. This is a "selective essay" on Millikan's career and modern American science, focusing on selected personalities and episodes rather than covering the entire story.

MOSELEY, HENRY GWYN JEFFREYS. 1887–1915

The brilliant career of Moseley, a British physicist, was brief, cut short by World War I. Consequently, he is mainly known for his work with X-ray spectra. As X-rays are produced by an element, it will emit powerful radiation at a few characteristic wavelengths. Moseley obtained data for consecutive elements of the periodic table, and was able to infer a relationship between the X-ray wavelengths of an element and its atomic number (the number of protons in its nucleus). This permitted him to correct ambiguities in contemporary atomic number assignments, and to predict the existence of several then-unknown elements. Moseley soon realized that there are important links between his discovery and Niels Bohr's atomic model. Until his work, only electrons and negatively charged particles were known to occur in discrete or quantized energy packets. Atoms themselves are observably neutral in charge. His work showed that the positive charge in the nucleus that neutralizes the negative charge of the atom's electron shell is also quantized. This gave an early insight into nuclear structure.

When World War I broke out, Moseley enlisted in the British Army, and was commissioned in the Royal Engineers. In 1915 he was sent to Turkey on a disastrous campaign, where he was killed at the age of 27.

BOOK ABOUT MOSELEY

Heilbron, John L. *H. G. J. Moseley: The Life and Letters of an English Physicist, 1887–1915.* Univ. of California Pr. 1974 $41.00. A balanced account of a short, spectacular career, treating Moseley's scientific achievements as well as other aspects of his life. Half the volume is devoted to reprinting Moseley's letters.

NEWTON, SIR ISAAC. 1642–1727

A British physicist and mathematician, Newton is universally assessed as one of the greatest scientists of any period or culture. In physics, he discovered the laws of motion that are named for him and was the first to explain gravitation. He made fundamental discoveries in optics and invented the reflecting telescope. In mathematics he formulated the calculus and derived the binomial theorem. Taken together, these accomplishments constitute an intellectual achievement that only a handful can equal.

In 1665–66, Newton was forced by the plague to leave Cambridge, where he was a professor of mathematics, for his country home. Many of Newton's discoveries were made during this so-called *annus mirabilis* (miraculous year). The year saw the foundations laid for his work in mathematics, dynamics, celestial mechanics, and gravitation theory, as well as his first optics experiments. However, the results of much of this work were not published until 20 years later. Finally, in 1687, his greatest single work appeared, the *Philosophiae Naturalis Principia Mathematica (Mathematical Principles of Natural Philosophy*, commonly known as the *Principia*). It took even longer for him to publish much of his work in optics, which he finally compiled in his *Opticks* of 1704.

Newton's work on gravitation, dynamics, and mechanics provides the foundation for classical physics. He had previously developed ideas of centrifugal force and of how force and inertia affect motion. When he was inspired by a falling apple to consider the problem of gravity, it occurred to him that the force that pulled the apple might also extend into space and pull the moon into orbit. He conjectured that two bodies attract each other with a force that depends on the product of their distances and falls off as the square of their distance apart. In 1679, when an accurate value for the radius of the earth became available, he calculated the moon's motion on the basis of this theory of gravitation and obtained a correct result, thus verifying his conjecture. He also found that his theory explained Johannes Kepler's empirically derived laws of planetary motion, discovered earlier in the century.

In his *Principia* of 1687, Newton created the subject of classical mechanics by stating, proving, and applying his three laws of motion. The first law states that every body remains at rest or in motion in a straight line unless it is acted on by a force. This is the concept of inertia, which finally replaced Aristotle's notion that force is required to keep anything moving. The second law states that a force accelerates a body by an amount proportional to its mass. This was the first clear definition of force, and the first time mass was distinguished from weight. The third law states that action and reaction are equal and opposite, thus demonstrating how things can be made to move. By stating and applying these laws, Newton established a unified system that explained diverse phenomena from a basic set of laws.

Newton created the differential and integral calculus, or as he called it, the "method of fluxions," to facilitate his studies of mechanics and dynamics. This was the basis not only for much of modern mathematics, but also for the most famous priority dispute in the history of science, as Newton fought Leibniz's claims to co-discovery. In another major contribution to mathematics, he stated and proved the binomial theorem.

Finally, Newton's *Opticks* gave a systematic and highly organized account of his theory of the nature of light and its effects. For example, in a series of elegant experiments in 1666, Newton had used prisms to show that white light is a compound of colored light, each color with a different index of refraction. Although he held that light rays were corpuscular in nature, and therefore capable of being analyzed by the universal forces discussed in the *Principia*, he integrated the concept of periodicity into his treatment as well. This view showed tremendous physical intuition, since light has since been shown by Einstein to have a dual wave-particle nature.

Newton's supreme achievement was his thorough demonstration that scientific principles are of universal application. In the *Principia* he built a model of the universe from mathematical premises and experimental evidence that is still valid 300 years later. His example initiated an explosion of discovery in modern science that continues to the present day. (See also Chapter 4 in this volume and Chapter 5 in Volume 4.)

BOOKS BY NEWTON

Demonstrations of Some of the Principal Sections of Sir Isaac Newton's Principles of Natural Philosophy. Ed. by John Clarke, Johnson Repr. 1972 $28.00. Selections from the *Principia*.

Mathematical Principles of Natural Philosophy and His System of the World. 1687. Trans. by Andrew Motte, Greenwood 1962 $32.50. Includes Volume 1, *The Motions of Bodies*, and Volume 2, *The System of the World*. Translated text of the *Principia*.

Newton's Philosophy of Nature: Selections of His Writings. 1687. Ed. by H. S. Thayer, Hafner 1953 $9.95. Selections from the *Principia*.

Opticks. 1704. Dover 1952 $7.95

BOOKS ABOUT NEWTON

Andrade, E. N. *Isaac Newton*. Folcroft repr. of 1950 ed. 1979 $12.50. Solid short biography by a modern physicist.

Brodetsky, Selig. *Sir Isaac Newton*. Richard West repr. of 1927 ed. $20.00. A charming short biography by an applied mathematician, meant for the general public and emphasizing Newton's scientific work.

Burtt, Edwin A. *Metaphysical Foundations of Modern Physical Science*. Humanities Pr. 2d ed. 1967 $29.00. Classic intellectual history of early modern science, with Newton as its climax.

Christianson, Gale E. *In the Presence of the Creator: Isaac Newton and His Times*. Free Pr. 1984 $27.50. The first major popular biography of Newton in 50 years, incorporating modern scholarship and the author's study of original sources. However, the author, a historian, fails to offer serious descriptions of Newton's philosophical work.

Cohen, I. Bernard. *The Newtonian Revolution*. Cambridge Univ. Pr. 1983 $17.95. Newton's technique of successively developing mathematical models and comparing these with experiment and observation in a continual process of refinement until an accurate model of nature is obtained. Cohen sees this technique as the truly revolutionary feature of the *Principia*.

Manuel, Frank E. *The Religion of Isaac Newton*. Oxford 1974 $24.95. Lectures on Newton's theology. Apparently Newton spent many of his later years studying writings of theologians who had "corrupted" the primitive creed by injecting metaphysical speculations.

Pullin, V. E. *Sir Isaac Newton: A Biographical Sketch*. Arden Lib. repr. of 1927 ed. 1979 $15.00. Short biographical sketch.

Westfall, Richard. *Never at Rest: A Biography of Isaac Newton*. Cambridge Univ. Pr. 1983 $19.95. A massive study that directly confronts Newton's scientific endeavors, and the first major biography of Newton since 1855. The biography of choice for the serious reader.

OPPENHEIMER, J. ROBERT. 1904–1967

An American physicist, born in New York City, Oppenheimer made significant contributions to the development of quantum mechanics and was the key figure in the rapid development of the first atom bomb. After extensive study with key researchers in Britain and Germany (he received his Ph.D. in 1927 from the University of Göttingen), Oppenheimer returned to the United States to establish and run simultaneously two influential schools of theoretical physics, at the California Institute of Technology and at Berkeley. Theoretical physics had never before been studied with such intensity in the United States. During the 1930s, he made numerous contributions to atomic and nuclear physics, working with the mass of an electron. This particle was detected in 1932 and called the positron. Oppenheimer also published early papers theoretically discussing black holes and neutron stars. These papers were ignored by astronomers for many years.

Oppenheimer is best known to the general public as the leader of the successful American effort to develop the atom bomb at Los Alamos, New Mexico (1942–45). In 1947 he was appointed director of the Institute of Advanced Study at Princeton, New Jersey. After the war, Oppenheimer made powerful enemies by his opposition to the development of the hydrogen bomb and by his public proposals for international control of atomic energy. In 1954, during the McCarthy era, the Atomic Energy Commission (AEC) declared him a "security risk," thereby greatly disturbing many scientists. In 1963, AEC reversed its position, nominating Oppenheimer for its Fermi Prize in recognition of his many achievements.

BOOKS BY OPPENHEIMER

Science and Common Understanding. Simon & Schuster 1966 o.p. A series of six lectures delivered in 1953 over the BBC on the development of modern physics, with conclusions drawn on the role of science in the modern world.

Robert Oppenheimer: Letters and Recollections. Harvard Univ. Pr. 1981 $8.95. Includes 167 letters, all but a few written by Oppenheimer himself, covering the years from 1922 to 1945. A parallel narrative draws on reminiscences of friends and a series of oral history interviews recorded in 1963. There is little scientific material.

BOOKS ABOUT OPPENHEIMER

Davis, Nuel P. *Lawrence and Oppenheimer*. Da Capo 1986 $11.95. Based on published documents and personal interviews with about 100 associates of American physicist Ernest Lawrence and Oppenheimer, Davis gives an account of the roles they played in the development of the atom bomb.

Goodchild, Peter J. *Robert Oppenheimer: Shatterer of Worlds*. Fromm Intl. Pub. 1985 $10.95. Competent biography, brisk, readable, well illustrated.

Kunetka, James W. *Oppenheimer: The Years of Risk*. Prentice-Hall 1982 o.p. Enjoyable first introduction to Oppenheimer's life story, but contains little on the nature and significance of his own scientific work.

Major, John. *The Oppenheimer Hearing*. Stein & Day 1983 pap. $9.95. Analysis of the secret hearings held in 1954 that resulted in Oppenheimer's removal from his post as AEC consultant. Oppenheimer's political and ethical motivations as well as the hearings' procedural shortcomings are detailed.

U.S. Atomic Energy Commission. *In the Matter of J. Robert Oppenheimer: Transcript of Hearing before Personnel Security Board and Texts of Principal Documents and Letters*. MIT 1971 pap. $9.95. Complete transcript of the dramatic secret hearings.

PLANCK, MAX. 1858–1947 (NOBEL PRIZE 1918)

Max Planck, a German physicist, discovered in his study of black-body radiation that energy is not continuous, but is emitted or absorbed in fundamental, individual units called quanta. Quantum theory originated from his 1900 paper, representing a radical break with classical physics that Planck himself could not wholly accept. With Albert Einstein, Planck ranks as one of the two founders of modern physics. For this work Planck was awarded the 1918 Nobel Prize in physics.

Following up on his revolutionary idea, others were able to apply the quantum concept. Einstein's 1905 paper explaining the photoelectric effect and Niels Bohr's 1913 model of the hydrogen atom were two such applications.

Planck was the acknowledged leader of German science in the 1930s, having been appointed president of the Kaiser Wilhelm Institute. However, he resigned his post in 1937 to protest Nazi treatment of Jewish scientists, having raised the issue previously with Hitler himself. He remained in Germany through the war years. After the war the Institute was renamed the Max Planck Institute, and he served as its president once more until his death in 1947.

BOOKS BY PLANCK

Scientific Autobiography and Other Papers. Greenwood repr. of 1949 ed. 1968 $19.75. Besides the autobiography, the volume reprints philosophical essays on such topics as causality, the meaning and limits of science, and religion and natural science.

Where Is Science Going? Prologue by Albert Einstein, AMS Pr. repr. of 1932 ed. 1981 $19.50. A discussion of many philosophical topics such as free will, causality, and the reality of the external world, from the point of view of an important theoretical physicist.

Books about Planck

Heilbron, J. L. *The Dilemmas of an Upright Man: Max Planck as Spokesman for German Science*. Univ. of California Pr. 1986 $18.95 1987 pap. $7.95. With his solution of the problem of black-body radiation, Planck came to be the most respected authority in German science. This book concentrates on his courageous efforts to oppose Nazi policies on behalf of German science.

Rosenthal-Schneider, Ilse. *Reality and Scientific Truth: Discussions with Einstein, von Laue, and Planck*. Ed. by Thomas Braun, Wayne State Univ. Pr. 1980 $20.00. The author-editor carried on a correspondence with Einstein, Planck, and Max von Laue for many years concerning the nature of scientific truth and physical reality, as well as on lighter topics. Selections of the correspondence are here published together with connecting text.

POINCARE, JULES HENRI. 1854–1912

A gifted and wide-ranging French mathematician, Henri Poincaré made important contributions to physics as well. In the context of mathematical astronomy, he extensively studied problems of calculating the motions of celestial objects in mutual interaction, for example, of planetary systems. This is the so-called n-body problem. He was able to make significant advances in methods by which solutions could be approximated, developing the theory of asymptotic expansions and integral invariants.

His great contribution was his creation of the qualitative theory of differential equations. These equations are heavily used in all fields of physics, and interesting for that reason. The qualitative study of differential equations becomes necessary when an exact solution of such equations proves to be impossible, and a numerical solution inconvenient or also impossible. Even though a given differential equation may not be solvable, it still may be possible by using qualitative methods to say important things about the system the equation describes. For example, without a solution it may be possible to say that the equation has a stable solution, so that if the initial conditions vary slightly, so will the solution. These techniques greatly enhance the physicist's ability to interpret theoretical results, and originated with Poincaré.

Poincaré's clear expositions of the scientific method and the role of hypothesis in science are still studied today by practitioners and philosophers alike.

Book by Poincaré

The Foundations of Science: Science and Hypothesis, the Value of Science, Science and Method. 1902, 1904, 1908. Univ. Pr. of Amer. 1982 $20.75. Thorough treatment of several topics in the philosophy of science, divided into sections on science and hypothesis, the value of science, and science and method.

Book about Poincaré

Dantzig, Tobias. *Henri Poincaré, Critic of Crisis: Reflections on His Universe of Discourse*. Greenwood repr. of 1954 ed. 1968 $15.00. An attempt to interpret the mid-century issues of science in light of Poincaré's thought. A short biographical essay is included.

RUTHERFORD, ERNEST. 1871–1937 (NOBEL PRIZE 1908)

Ernest Rutherford, a British experimental physicist, was one of the dominant figures of early modern physics. He was the first to explain that radioactivity is produced by the disintegration of atoms. Distinguishing among alpha, beta, and gamma rays, he was able to identify alpha rays as helium nuclei. For these two early achievements he won the Nobel Prize in chemistry in 1908. He was the first to clarify the structure of the atom with his nuclear model. He did extensive work with the natural and artificial transmutation of radioactive elements, and was the first to suggest the presence of a neutral particle in all atomic nuclei, although neutrons were not isolated until 1932. After this tremendous record of accomplishment, he became the director of Cambridge University's Cavendish Laboratory, where he attracted the best young physicists in research projects that rapidly enlarged understanding of the atomic nucleus he had discovered.

When Rutherford began to explore the phenomena of radioactivity, little more was known than that it was a phenomenon that characterized not just uranium but other elements as well. Working with the English chemist Frederick Soddy at McGill University on samples of the element thorium, he explained radioactivity as an atomic phenomenon caused by the breakdown of atoms in the radioactive element to produce a new element. The two men discovered that the intensity of the radioactivity decreases at a rate determined by the element's half-life. The notion that atoms could change their identity was a revolutionary idea, yet Rutherford's explanation was so satisfactory that it found immediate acceptance in the scientific community.

He utilized the notion of natural transmutation of elements to calculate the ages of mineral samples, arriving at figures greater than a billion years. This was the first proof of the great age of the earth's rocks, and radioactive dating has been developed and applied to fossils and archaeological remains as well.

Rutherford continued to study alpha particles. With Hans Geiger, he developed particle counters to measure radioactivity. In 1907, he finally proved that alpha particles are helium atoms by trapping some in a tube and observing a helium spectrum when the content was sparked.

Perhaps his greatest discovery came in 1909. Before Rutherford's work, an atom was pictured as a sphere of positive charge occupying the whole volume of the atom. Negatively charged electrons were thought to be embedded in the volume, rather like raisins in a raisin cake. This model had to be abandoned when Geiger and Rutherford's student Ernest Marsden made a series of measurements of the unexpected scattering of alpha particles by thin metal foils. They observed that a few of the particles bombarding the foil were even reflected back. As Rutherford remarked, "It was as incredible as if you fired a 15-inch shell at a piece of tissue paper and it came back and hit you." To explain this, Rutherford was forced to assume that most of the atom's mass was concentrated in a small space, or nucleus. Gradually, this new model came to be the accepted one.

BOOK BY RUTHERFORD

(and Bertram Boltwood). *Rutherford and Boltwood: Letters on Radioactivity.* Ed. by Lawrence Badash, Yale Univ. Pr. 1969 o.p. Letters exchanged between Rutherford and American chemist and physicist Bertram Boltwood over 20 years. Scientific matters are discussed, but additionally the two comment extensively on their private lives and on other scientific giants of the early twentieth century. Also included is a brief history of radioactivity, and biographies of the two men.

BOOKS ABOUT RUTHERFORD

Andrade, E. N. *Rutherford and the Nature of the Atom.* Peter Smith $11.25. Outstanding short biography by a contemporary and colleague, primarily dealing with the Manchester years.

Feather, Norman. *Lord Rutherford.* Priory Pr. 1973 o.p. Classic and definitive biography, written with authority and personal knowledge by a coworker at the Cavendish Laboratory. Shows how Rutherford and his work were regarded by contemporaries and is filled with interesting anecdotes.

Oliphant, Mark. *Rutherford: Recollections of the Cambridge Days.* Elsevier 1972 o.p. Reminiscences by a coworker at the Cavendish Laboratories. Letters and photographs are included.

Shea, William R., and M. A. Bunge, eds. *Rutherford and Physics at the Turn of the Century.* Watson Pub. Intl. 1979 $20.00. A collection of essays that conveys a picture of Rutherford and his times. Includes Feather's Memorial Lecture telling the story of the alpha particle.

Wilson, David. *Rutherford: Simple Genius.* MIT 1983 $30.00. A wide-ranging and interesting account of Rutherford's life and work, written by a former science correspondent for BBC television news.

SCHRÖDINGER, ERWIN. 1887–1961 (NOBEL PRIZE 1933)

Erwin Schrödinger, an Austrian physicist, developed the theory of wave mechanics (1925–26). This theory finally furnished a solid mathematical explanation of quantum theory, and for this achievement he shared with P. A. M. Dirac the Nobel Prize in physics for 1933.

Schrödinger was dissatisfied with Bohr's early quantum theory of the atom, objecting to the many arbitrary quantum rules the theory imposed. Building on De Broglie's idea that a moving atomic particle has a wave character, he developed a famous wave equation that describes the behavior of an electron orbiting the nucleus of an atom. When this equation was applied to the hydrogen atom it yielded all the results of Bohr and De Broglie, and additionally was used as a tool to solve a wide range of new problems in which quantization occurs.

Schrödinger fled Austria in 1938 under the threat of Nazi arrest, and was invited to Dublin's newly established Institute for Advanced Studies. He remained there until his retirement in 1956, when he returned to Austria.

In 1944 Schrödinger published *What Is Life?*, a book that had a tremendous impact on a new generation of scientists. Reading it, young physicists who were disillusioned by the Hiroshima bombing were directed to an unexplored discipline free of military applications, molecular biology. In it,

Schrödinger proposed the existence of a molecular code as the genetic basis of life, inspiring a generation to explore this idea.

BOOKS BY SCHRÖDINGER

What Is Life? Mind and Matter. 1944. Cambridge Univ. Pr. 1968 pap. $12.95

My View of the World. Ox Bow Pr. 1983 $10.00. Discusses the limits of science and the value of its study.

Space-Time Structure. Cambridge Univ. Pr. 1985 $12.95. Addresses and essays on science and society, including his Nobel Prize acceptance speech, "The Fundamental Idea of Wave Mechanics."

BOOKS ABOUT SCHRÖDINGER

Kilmister, C. W., ed. *Schrödinger: Centenary Celebration of a Polymath.* Cambridge Univ. Pr. 1987 $54.50. Collection of essays, some biographical and some technical.

Mehra, Jagdish. *Erwin Schrödinger and the Rise of Wave Mechanics.* [*Historical Development of Quantum Theory*] Springer-Verlag 1987 $50.00. Part 1: *Schrödinger in Vienna and Zurich, 1887–1925.* The first of two volumes on Schrödinger planned for this fine series. Part one details Schrödinger's youth and education, early scientific work, and research leading to the development of wave mechanics.

Scott, William T. *Erwin Schrödinger: An Introduction to His Writings.* Univ. of Massachusetts Pr. 1967 $11.00. First comprehensive study of Schrödinger's scientific and philosophical works. Included are a biographical sketch, several interpretive chapters on the foundations of wave mechanics and quantum mechanics, and a discussion of Schrödinger's other diverse intellectual endeavors.

WEINBERG, STEVEN. 1933– (NOBEL PRIZE 1979)

Steven Weinberg, an American physicist, has devised a theory that unifies two of the four known fundamental forces of physics. He did this work independently of but simultaneously with Abdus Salam, who shared the 1979 Nobel Prize for physics with him.

The electroweak theory, as this unification is known, gives a single explanation of the electromagnetic interaction between charged particles and the weak interaction, which is involved in certain radioactive decay processes. Additionally, the two types of forces are very different in scale, one being 10 billion times stronger than the other. Weinberg showed that at a primitive level, both forces are aspects of a single interaction mediated by four massless particles. The formulation of this theory is considered to be an intellectual feat comparable to Maxwell's in the nineteenth century. It is the first step toward the long-sought "unified field theory," a single theory explaining the strong, weak, electromagnetic, and gravitational interactions sought by Einstein, Schrödinger, and many more. The Weinberg-Salam theory has received experimental verification in the observation of two phenomena predicted by the theory: the Z particle and "neutral currents."

BOOKS BY WEINBERG

The Discovery of Subatomic Particles. W. H. Freeman 1983 $27.95. This book developed from a course intended to introduce nonscientists to the achievements of twentieth-century physics, and primarily covers the discoveries made prior to

World War II. The author uses "flashbacks," which may be skipped if desired, to explain needed physics concepts and history as the need arises in the description. These sections, however, occupy about half the text. The book is well written and beautifully illustrated. It concludes with a brief survey of the extensive contemporary particle physics family.

The First Three Minutes: A Modern View of the Origin of the Universe. Basic Bks. 1976 $14.95 1988 pap. $7.95. Weinberg literally details the "standard model" of what is known about the universe's first moments. He includes a mathematical supplement for those who want to see the basic computations as well. Although old now, the book was the first of its type, and is still useful.

YUKAWA, HIDEKI. 1907–   (NOBEL PRIZE 1949)

Hideki Yukawa, a Japanese physicist, has done important theoretical work on elementary particles and nuclear forces. In particular, he predicted the existence of the pi-meson (pion) and the short-range nuclear force associated with this particle. He received the 1949 Nobel Prize for physics for this work, the first Japanese to receive this honor.

In the early 1930s, Yukawa tackled the problem of what holds the atomic nucleus together despite the repulsive forces its protons exert on each other. The interaction, though extremely strong, has limited range. Yukawa eventually proposed an explanation in terms of an exchange between nucleons of a similar intermediate mass observed in studies of cosmic rays. However, this particle, later named the "muon," did not interact strongly with nuclei as required by the theory. In 1947, the pion particle, or pi-meson, was discovered, possessing Yukawa's predicted properties. The pion was additionally observed to undergo rapid decay into the muon, which explained the mystery.

BOOK BY YUKAWA

Tabibito, the Traveller. World Scientific 1982 $14.00. Yukawa was invited by a major Japanese newspaper to write his autobiography to commemorate his fiftieth birthday. In 1957, the work appeared, was wildly popular, and subsequently went through 36 printings. Now it has been translated for Western audiences.

CHAPTER 10

Chemistry

Maureen Welling Matkovich

It is the great verity of our science, CHEMISTRY, that advancement in it . . . instead of exhausting the subjects of research, opens the doors to further and more abundant knowledge, overflowing with beauty and utility to those who will be at the easy personal pains of understanding its experimental investigation.

—MICHAEL FARADAY, *Experimental Researches in Electricity*

Chemistry is one of the physical sciences. Its practitioners study the composition, properties, and structure of matter—that part of the universe that has mass and occupies space—at the atomic and molecular levels. Chemists also study the changes in composition and structure of matter and measure the energy changes causing and resulting from these changes. Chemistry is an experimental science, one that constantly tests results of experiments on the physical world against the results predicted by theory. The four major branches of the traditional study of chemistry are analytical, inorganic, organic, and physical.

The modern science of chemistry was preceded by the medieval practice of alchemy, a synthesis of fakery, experimentation, and mysticism, which rested on the classical Greek theories in which earth, water, air, and fire were the basic elements of the universe. Paracelsus added the principles of sulfur, mercury, and salt to these basic elements.

Although alchemy has been firmly associated with chemistry in the popular mind, at least one chemical historian, Aaron J. Ihde, in *The Development of Modern Chemistry* (see below under History of Chemistry and the Chemical Industry), has argued that medieval medicine and technology, particularly that area now called metallurgy—the obtaining of metals from ores, contributed more to the science of modern chemistry than did alchemy. Distillation, a basic method of purifying substances, came from medieval medicine. From metallurgy came the attempt to quantify the amounts of precious metals obtainable from a particular ore. This introduced another important scientific concept, the necessity for measurement. The importance to any science of this necessity to measure and quantify was expressed eloquently generations later by a physicist, William Thompson, Lord Kelvin: "When you can measure what you are speaking about, and express it in numbers, you know something about it; but when you cannot measure it, when you cannot express it in numbers, your knowledge is of a meager and unsatisfactory kind: it may be the beginning of knowledge, but you have scarcely, in your thoughts, advanced to the stage of Science" (*Popular Lectures and Addresses, 1891–1894*).

From the period of the alchemists through the formulation of the periodic table, chemists struggled to develop the basic tools of a modern science, to understand the true nature of the chemical elements, and to postulate how chemical compounds were produced from these elements. Short biographies of representative contributors to chemical knowledge are included here. In the biographies one sees that these scientists not only contributed to chemistry, but also lived active lives in the political and religious spheres.

Chemical compounds differ from each other in their chemical composition, molecular structure, and stereochemistry. Chemists represent these compounds by using certain types of chemical formulas and by a highly structured system of nomenclature. The nomenclature, with its accompanying conventions necessary to represent and univocally identify the myriad of chemical compounds, is a significant stumbling block to the layperson's understanding of chemistry. This problem is the most troublesome in organic chemistry and, therefore, several basic study guides to organic nomenclature have been included in the reading list.

To simplify considerably, chemists use the following types of formulas to describe the chemical composition of matter: (1) empirical formulas identify the elements present and the correct proportions; (2) molecular formulas identify the elements, the proportions, and the size of the molecule; and (3) structural formulas, represented as diagrams, give all the above information as well as indicate how the atoms are linked to each other. Compounds with the same molecular, but differing structural, formulas are called isomers. Isomers may differ substantially from each other in physical properties, chemical reactivity, and effects on biological substances.

In conclusion, modern chemistry does not exist independently of the other sciences. Chemistry is indebted to many of the concepts of modern physics. Chemists use mathematical models to express their theories. Chemistry and biology meet in biochemistry, which is now the most exciting science frontier. Inorganic chemists, metallurgists, and solid state physicists all study metals, and chemists contribute to toxicology, the study of poisons. Modern geology and archaeology use the newest analytical chemistry techniques.

GENERAL BIBLIOGRAPHY

General reference sources for the chemical sciences abound. Scientific and chemical encyclopedias and dictionaries are used by the chemist and nonchemist alike. The practicing chemist requires handbooks with physical and chemical data on large numbers of chemicals. Specialty handbooks on chemical toxicity and lists of regulations covering chemical use are products of the last 20 years. Many standard sources contain biographical data on significant chemists, and histories on the development of chemistry, although uncommon, do exist. Because of the importance of the chemical industry, encyclopedias on chemical technology and industrial processes as well as sourcebooks of chemical suppliers are available. Finally, there are even guides to the literature of chemistry intended for the bench or laboratory chemist.

Careful attention to these general sources of information may instruct the layperson more than dogged persistence in reading the more detailed texts.

Directories, Dictionaries, Encyclopedias

Ash, M., and I. Ash, eds. *Encyclopedia of Industrial Chemical Additives*. Chemical Pub. 3 vols. 1984–85 ea. $82.50. A compilation of trade-name products used as additives. Arranged by use, such as antioxidants, catalysts, and chelating agents.

―――. *Encyclopedia of Plastics, Polymers and Resins*. Chemical Pub. 3 vols. 1981–83 ea. $75.00. Compiles practical information on trade-name plastic, polymer, and resin products. Entries are arranged by trade name and include manufacturers, brief chemical descriptions, and mechanical properties.

Ballentyne, D. W., and D. R. Lovett. *Dictionary of Named Effects and Laws in Chemistry, Physics and Mathematics*. Methuen 4th ed. 1980 $19.95. Useful for its section on common names for organic chemicals and the tables giving systematic names and formulas.

Bennett, H., ed. *Chemical Formulary Series: With Cumulative Indexes*. Chemical Pub. 27 vols. 1933–87 ea. $45.00. A 27-volume set, with a collection of formulas for chemical compounding.

―――. *Concise Chemical and Technical Directory*. Chemical Pub. 4th ed. 1986 $95.00. Chiefly covers trademarked chemical products.

―――. *Encyclopedia of Chemical Trademarks and Synonyms*. Chemical Pub. 3 vols. 1981–83 ea. $65.00. A three-volume set covering trademarked products. One of several sets by this publisher identifying these hard-to-find products. (See also the two titles by Ash above.)

Best's Safety Directory. A. M. Best 1987 $20.00. Intended to be used as a buyer's guide for safety products and as a safety training aid. It gives summaries of the federal Occupational Safety and Health Administration (OSHA) requirements. Invaluable and inexpensive. Contains advertising for products.

Bretherick, Leslie. *Handbook of Reactive Chemical Hazards*. Butterworth 3d ed. 1985 text ed. $99.95. Compilation of reports from the chemical literature of hazards encountered while using these chemicals. Specifically good in determining conditions under which chemicals have exploded. Well-indexed. Necessary for chemists, but the National Fire Protection Association (NFPA) manual of all types (see below) may be adequate for others.

Chem Sources U.S.A. Directories Publishing 28th ed. 1987 $200.00. The most comprehensive buyer's guide for chemicals of all types for sale in the United States. Contains an alphabetical list of 104,400 chemicals produced or distributed by 855 firms. Codes indicate bulk and high-purity chemical producers.

Chemcyclopedia. Amer. Chemical Society 1987 $40.00. Another buyer's guide for chemicals in the United States. Chemicals are arranged alphabetically within large divisions by use. Much product advertising.

Clansky, Kenneth B., ed. *Suspect Chemicals Sourcebook: A Guide to Industrial Chemicals Covered under Major Federal Regulatory and Advisory Programs*. Roytech 6th ed. 1987. Federal regulations for more than 3,000 industrial chemicals arranged by CAS registry numbers. Cross indexes and mid-year supplement. The best ready reference available to answer the question, "Is this chemical federally regulated?"

Considine, Douglas M., ed. *Chemical and Process Technology Encyclopedia*. McGraw-Hill 1974 $89.50. A good compilation of industrial chemical processes. Strongest in its articles on processes such as distillation, drying of solids, and adsorption.

——. *Van Nostrand Reinhold Encyclopedia of Chemistry*. Van Nostrand 4th ed. 1984 $94.95. Excellent summaries of chemical concepts such as valence and radioactivity. Brief discussion of organic nomenclature.

Dean, J. A. *Lange's Handbook of Chemistry*. McGraw-Hill 13th ed. 1985 $59.50. Physical and chemical data of chemical compounds. Also has nomenclature guides and cross-references for trivial and mineral names.

Directory of American Research and Technology, 1988. Bowker 1987 $199.95. Contains more than 11,000 research laboratories in the United States. The standard directory of the work place for chemists and allied scientists.

Encyclopedia of Physical Science and Technology. Ed. by Robert A. Meyers, Academic Pr. 15 vols. 1987 $149.00. A more scholarly and mathematical treatment than the *McGraw-Hill Encyclopedia* (see below). Because this publication's emphasis is on the physical sciences, chemistry subjects comprise a higher percentage of the overall material. Good combination of mathematics, physics, and chemistry.

Farm Chemicals Handbook. Meister 1987 $50.00. Intended primarily for the agricultural industry, this title is extremely useful in answering basic questions about fertilizers and, more importantly, pesticides. Describes toxicity, handling and storage cautions, and recommended uses with extensive coverage of trade names. Also has information about pesticides currently banned in the United States.

Gardner's Chemical Synonyms and Trade Names. Ed. by Jill Pierce, Gower Pub. Co. 9th ed. 1987 $149.95. Covers trade-named chemicals in commerce in Britain extremely well. It is also quite useful for chemicals produced or sold in the United States. Included is an alphabetical list of trade names and synonyms with brief descriptions and manufacturers' designations.

Gerhartz, Wolfgang, ed. *Ullmann's Encyclopedia of Industrial Chemistry*. VCH 5th ed. 1985 ea. $190.00. Presently 7 volumes of this 36-volume set are available in English. The entire fifth edition of this standard set on industrial chemistry is being published in English rather than German. Its coverage is similar to *Kirk-Othmer Encyclopedia of Chemical Technology* (see below).

Kent, James A., ed. *Riegel's Handbook of Industrial Chemistry*. Van Nostrand 8th ed. 1983 $65.95. Excellent summary of chemical technology with an emphasis on the economic aspects of the chemical and related industries.

Kirk-Othmer Concise Encyclopedia of Chemical Technology. Ed. by Martin Grayson, Wiley 1985 $99.95. This one-volume reference covers the subjects of the complete *Kirk-Othmer Encyclopedia* in abbreviated form. The best substitute for the larger encyclopedia.

Kirk-Othmer Encyclopedia of Chemical Technology. Ed. by Martin Grayson and David Eckroth, Wiley 26 vols. 1978–84 $4,550.00. The classic multivolume set on industrial chemical processes. In comprehensive articles, each author introduces the subject, covers the industrial production and uses of the chemical, and then discusses it in greater depth. Bibliographies are included. An excellent reference set for specialist and nonspecialist alike.

McGraw-Hill Concise Encyclopedia of Science and Technology. McGraw-Hill 1984 $95.00. A substitute for the *McGraw-Hill Encyclopedia of Science and Technology*. The publisher notes that the material in this title was taken from the longer set.

McGraw-Hill Dictionary of Chemistry. McGraw-Hill 1984 $36.00. Provides good coverage of basic chemical terms. The material has been published previously in the *McGraw-Hill Dictionary of Scientific and Technical Terms.*

McGraw-Hill Encyclopedia of Science and Technology. McGraw-Hill 20 vols. 1984 $1,600.00. An excellent general reference for most phases of science and technology, including chemistry.

National Fire Protection Association. *Manual of Hazardous Chemical Reactions.* NFPA 1986 $18.50. This title, available from the American National Standards Institute, compiles reports about hazardous chemicals and reactions. Less expensive and perhaps not so comprehensive as Bretherick's book (see above).

National Research Council. *Prudent Practices for Disposal of Chemicals from Laboratories.* National Academy Pr. 1983 $16.50. An excellent source of information, but not truly comprehensive.

———. *Prudent Practices for Handling Hazardous Chemicals in Laboratories.* National Academy Pr. 1981 $16.95 text ed. pap. $9.95. Again, a fine authoritative source of information, but its coverage is of necessity limited.

Orchin, Milton, and Hans Zimmer. *The Vocabulary of Organic Chemistry.* Wiley 1980 $49.50. Not a dictionary, this book should be read chapter by chapter. It is extremely useful for learning the vocabulary and concepts of organic chemistry.

Reagent Chemicals. Amer. Chemical Society 7th ed. 1986 $89.95. Specifications for procedures and chemicals used in analytical chemistry.

Sax, N. Irving, and Richard J. Lewis, Sr., eds. *Hawley's Condensed Chemical Dictionary.* Van Nostrand 11th ed. 1987 text ed. $46.75. Covers chemical processes, equipment, and famous chemists. The best chemical dictionary ever for general collections.

Sax, N. Irving, and Elizabeth Weisberg. *Dangerous Properties of Industrial Materials.* Van Nostrand 6th ed. 1984 $239.95. Written for the specialist or serious amateur, this book is an all-around compilation of data on chemical hazards. The introduction and early chapters on toxicology, industrial air contamination control, and occupational biohazards interpret the data in the main chapter of the book. Data for approximately 20,000 chemicals.

Sigma-Aldrich Library of Chemical Safety Data. Ed. by Robert W. Lenga, Sigma-Aldrich 1985 $195.00. Typical entry includes name, registry number, toxicity, health hazards and first aid, incompatibilities and decomposition, and recommended storage and handling. Limited to the materials that this manufacturer sells, but still an extremely valuable source of information.

Weast, Robert C., ed. *Handbook of Chemistry and Physics.* CRC Pr. 68th ed. 1987 $69.95. The best known and most widely used of the compilations of physical data of compounds. Includes boiling points, melting points, densities, solubilities, and refractive indexes of many compounds. Issued annually.

Windholz, Martha. *Merck Index: An Encyclopedia of Chemicals, Drugs, and Biologicals.* Merck 1983 $28.50. An indispensable compendium of information about chemicals, drugs, and biological substances. It also has a section on named organic chemical reactions.

Wolman, Yecheskel. *Chemical Information: A Practical Guide to Utilization.* Wiley 1983 $26.95. A good introduction to chemical information systems.

World of Learning. Europa 2 vols. 36th ed. 1986 $150.00. Covers learned organizations and universities in a range of disciplines, including chemistry.

Chemistry in Perspective

Asimov, Isaac. *Asimov's New Guide to Science.* Basic Bks. rev. ed. 1984 $29.95. Chapters on the elements and the molecule summarize two basic concepts of chemistry. The remainder of the book covers fundamental concepts from other branches of science.

Cavalieri, Liebe F. *Double-Edged Helix: Science in the Real World.* Ed. by Ruth N. Anshen, Columbia Univ. Pr. 1981 $20.00. Thoughtful study of the interaction between science and society.

Kieffer, William F. *Chemistry: A Cultural Approach.* Harper 1971 o.p. Unique and generally successful attempt to relate the science of chemistry to other cultural influences. Freshman chemistry text for nonscientists.

Morris, Richard. *Dismantling the Universe: The Nature of Scientific Discovery.* Simon & Schuster 1983 $14.95 1984 pap. $6.95. Most of the examples concerning scientific discoveries come from physics, but the author's conclusions apply also to chemistry.

National Research Council. *Opportunities in Chemistry.* National Academy Pr. 1985 $28.50 pap. $18.50. A report on the benefits to society provided by chemistry and the current scientific frontiers. It also identifies priority areas and opportunities in chemistry and makes recommendations for federal involvement (particularly the National Science Foundation) in these areas.

Office of Technology Assessment, U.S. Congress. *Regulatory Environment for Science: A Technical Memorandum.* USGPO 1986 pap. $6.00. Certainly the discussion is not limited to chemical research, but this thoughtful document examines the social and legal forces that restrict or regulate scientific and engineering research in the United States, from regulations on the use of animals in experiments to land-use prohibitions on the storage, use, and disposal of toxic and flammable chemicals.

Porterfield, William W. *Concepts of Chemistry.* Norton 1972 o.p. "A must for all college libraries, public libraries, and collections dealing with chemistry" (*Choice*).

Guides to the Chemical Literature

Aluri, Rao, and Judith S. Robinson. *Guide to U.S. Government Scientific and Technical Resources.* Libraries Unlimited 1983 lib. bdg. $23.50. This guide follows the information flow from research proposal to the production of the secondary sources such as abstracting and indexing services.

Dodd, Janet S., ed. *The ACS Style Guide: A Manual for Authors and Editors.* Intro. by D. H. M. Bowen, Amer. Chemical Society 1986 $24.95 pap. $14.95. Good chapter on the literature of chemistry. Interesting for its discussion of the ethical obligations of editors, authors, and reviewers. Also discusses the ethical obligations of scientists publishing outside the scientific literature.

Maizell, Robert E. *How to Find Chemical Information: A Guide for Practicing Chemists, Teachers and Students.* Wiley 2d ed. 1986 $55.00. Intended for the professional, but the lay reader can gain an understanding of the shape of the literature in chemistry. Useful discussion on patents and chemical marketing information.

Schoenfeld, Robert. *The Chemist's English.* VCH 2d ed. 1987 $17.95. "It is strongly recommended that everyone contemplating the preparation of a scientific article should first purchase and study this splendid little book" (*Carbohydrate Research*).

Skolnik, Herman. *The Literature Matrix of Chemistry.* Krieger 1982 $40.00. Covers books, encyclopedias, numerical data compilations, patents, the journal literature, abstracting and indexing services, and computerized databases. Useful for chemical industry libraries.

HISTORY OF CHEMISTRY AND THE CHEMICAL INDUSTRY

The modern science of chemistry grew from several major traditions, those of alchemy, primitive metallurgy, and medicine. Chemistry is an experimental science with a strong underpinning of theoretical concepts developed by physicists and mathematicians. As with all modern sciences, the study of chemistry is a cooperative endeavor. Individuals can make outstanding contributions to theory or practice, but always they are indebted to the body of scientific thought that preceded them. Or, as SIR ISAAC NEWTON (see also Vol. 4) wrote to Robert Hooke (1634–1703) in 1676, "If I have seen further [than you and Descartes], it is by standing on the shoulders of giants." One of Robert Boyle's outstanding contributions to chemistry was his clear grasp of the fact that the secrecy, fakery, and sorcery so prevalent in medieval alchemy had no place in modern science. Jons Jakob Berzelius and Justus Liebig (1803–73), in addition to their own substantial scientific contributions, also founded important scientific journals to spread the results of scientific research.

The following reading list does not emphasize individual chemists. Instead it emphasizes the development of chemical concepts, industrial processes, and experimental methods as well as a major theme in the history of chemistry—the discovery of the elements.

American Men and Women of Science: Physical and Biological Sciences. Bowker 8 vols. 16th ed. 1986 $595.00. The standard biographical dictionary of approximately 127,000 living U.S. and Canadian scientists.

Asimov, Isaac. *Asimov's Biographical Encyclopedia of Science and Technology.* Doubleday 2d ed. rev. 1982 $29.95. Selection is not limited to chemistry, but the book has an alphabetical index of individuals and also a subject index. Both living and dead individuals are included.

————. *The Search for the Elements.* Basic Bks. 1962 o.p. The periodic table has changed since this book was written, but it is an extremely readable and easily understood history of chemistry.

Burland, C. A. *The Arts of the Alchemists.* Macmillan 1967 o.p. A sympathetic study of alchemy that does not try to relate it to modern-day chemistry.

Dictionary of Scientific Biography. Ed. by Charles C. Gillispie, Scribner 8 vols. 1970–80 $750.00. A set that covers the careers of scientists from antiquity to the present in many scientific endeavors including chemistry. Living scientists are excluded. Bibliographies are included for each entry.

Farber, Eduard. *Evolution of Chemistry: A History of Its Ideas, Methods, and Materials.* Ronald Pr. 1952 o.p. For readers who have some knowledge of chemistry, because the author follows the development of specific ideas and concepts.

Goldwater, Leonard J. *Mercury: A History of Quicksilver.* York Pr. 1972 o.p. The origins and uses, properties and behavior, of mercury from Aristotle to the present.

Goran, Morris. *Story of Fritz Haber.* Univ. of Oklahoma Pr. 1967 o.p. Haber (1868–1934) developed a method of combining nitrogen from the air with hydrogen to produce ammonia, which could be used for the production of chemicals from fertilizers to gunpowder. Though he also invented the poison gas that Germany used in World War I, he was forced to leave Germany after Hitler's rise to power because of his Jewish background. Haber's life poignantly illustrates the tragedies made possible by modern science.

Great Chemists. Ed. by Eduard Farber, Wiley 1961 o.p. More than 100 biographies of chemists. No living chemists are included.

Haber, L. F. *Chemical Industry during the Nineteenth Century: A Study of the Economic Aspect of Applied Chemistry in Europe and North America.* Oxford 1958 o.p. A serious, well-documented study of the rise of the chemical industry.

——. *Chemical Industry, 1900–1930: International Growth and Technological Change.* Oxford 1971 o.p. A continuation of the preceding title. The coverage is comparatively better for the European and British chemical industries than the rapidly growing American chemical industry.

Hochheiser, Sheldon. *Rohm and Haas: History of a Chemical Company.* Univ. of Pennsylvania Pr. 1985 text ed. $19.95. One of the best historical studies of an American chemical company.

Ihde, Aaron J. *The Development of Modern Chemistry.* Dover repr. of 1964 ed. 1983 pap. $15.95. History of chemistry from before 1750 to the mid-twentieth century. Fine bibliography and appendixes that cover the chemical elements (1982) and Nobel Prize winners in chemistry, physics, and medicine (1983).

Leicester, Henry M. *Historical Background of Chemistry.* Dover repr. of 1956 ed. 1971 text ed. pap. $6.00; Peter Smith $14.50. Chemistry from the history of iron extraction. A good one-volume text covering the ideas and practices before the era of modern chemistry.

——. *Source Book in Chemistry, 1400–1900* and *Source Book in Chemistry, 1900–1950.* [*Source Bks. in the History of Science*] Harvard Univ. Pr. 2 vols. text ed. ea. $18.50. Selections from the writings of the chief contributors to chemical thought. The basis for inclusion was that the particular selection influenced the understanding of chemical concepts. Short synopses of the lives and times of the contributors are given.

Li Ch'iao-p'ing. *The Chemical Arts of Old China.* AMS Pr. repr. of 1948 ed. 1979 $24.50. Covers the development of applied chemistry during the period from approximately 400 B.C. to the early twentieth century. Includes chapters on the production of gunpowder, ceramics, and dyes.

Multhauf, Robert P. *Neptune's Gift: A History of Common Salt.* [*Studies in the History of Technology*] Johns Hopkins Univ. Pr. 1978 text ed. $32.50. Follows the history of the technology and production of common table salt and related compounds from antiquity to the mid-twentieth century.

——. *The Origins of Chemistry.* Watson Pub. Intl. 1967 lib. bdg. $15.00. A "most engaging book" (*LJ*) on the history of scientific knowledge to the seventeenth century. The book begins with the use of iron and manganese oxides in paleolithic paintings.

Nobel Prize Lectures: Chemistry. Elsevier 1963–70 $92.75. Each entry includes the presentation speech, the Nobel lecture, and a brief biography of the laureate's life and scientific contributions. The Nobel lectures were translated into English, where necessary.

Partington, James R. *A History of Chemistry.* St. Martin's 4 vols. o.p. A thorough, scholarly, and heavily referenced work on the history of chemistry from the early Greek philosophers to G. N. Lewis and his generalized theory of acids and bases.

Sherwood, M. *The New Chemistry.* Basic Bks. 1973 o.p. A very readable account for the lay reader of the discovery of industrial chemical products, such as nylon, plastics, and food products.

Skolnik, Herman, and Kenneth M. Reese, eds. *Century of Chemistry: The Role of Chemists and the American Chemical Society.* Amer. Chemical Society 1976

$15.95. History commemorating the one hundredth anniversary of the founding of the American Chemical Society.

Smith, Richard Furnald. *Chemistry for the Millions.* Scribner 1972 o.p. "Chapters cover such themes as ancient origins and alchemy, metals, Lavoisier, oxygen, inert gases, the Periodic Table, halogens, nonmetals, and carbon" (*LJ*).

Stillman, John Maxson. *The Story of Alchemy and Early Chemistry.* Dover 1960 o.p. First published as *The Story of Early Chemistry* in 1924, it relates the story of the development of chemistry from the early use of metals through the time of Lavoisier. An intriguing feature is the author's liberal use of quotations describing laboratory procedures and his accompanying explanations.

Thackray, Arnold. *Atoms and Powers: An Essay on Newtonian Matter—Theory and the Development of Chemistry.* Harvard Univ. Pr. 1970 o.p. A thought-provoking examination by one of today's leading historians of science.

Weeks, Mary Elvira. *Discovery of the Elements.* Rev. by Henry M. Leicester, Journal of Chemical Education 1968 o.p. A scholarly one-volume summary of the discovery of the elements beginning with the precious metals discovered before history began and ending with those elements made possible by controlled radioactive methods.

GENERAL CHEMISTRY

Lay readers without, or perhaps many years removed from, a rigorous grounding in the language and principles of chemistry often find difficulty in reading even the most innocuous texts that assume a general knowledge of chemistry. Therefore several self-study texts are included here.

Arem, Joel E. *Man-Made Crystals.* Smithsonian 1973. Somewhat dated in a swiftly moving technology, but covers the growth of synthetic crystals, man-made gems, and the electronic revolution made possible by the transistor. Attractive illustrations.

Bliss, Anne. *A Handbook of Dyes from Natural Materials.* Scribner 1981 $14.95. Uses an elementary knowledge of chemistry and chemical formulas and techniques in one of the earliest forms of chemical technology, the art of dyeing.

Cotterill, Rodney. *The Cambridge Guide to the Material World.* Cambridge Univ. Pr. 1985 $34.50. This book is not strictly a chemistry book, but it covers the properties of materials ranging from crystals to plastics.

Hess, Fred C. *Chemistry Made Simple.* Rev. by Arthur L. Thomas, Doubleday 1984 pap. $5.95. Perhaps slightly more elementary than *Chemistry Made Easy* (see Nentwig below), it explains basic concepts including the gas laws, oxidation-reduction reactions, and chemical equilibria.

Lippy, John D., Jr., and Edward L. Plader. *Modern Chemical Magic.* Stackpole 1959 o.p. Contains certain experiments that are no longer considered safe for amateurs to perform. However, for the recipes for invisible inks, colored flames, and materializing ghosts, it is fascinating. Many of these experiments are better read about than performed.

Nentwig, Joachim. *Chemistry Made Easy.* Trans. by D. H. Roureay, VCH 2 vols. 1983 vol. 1 pap. $19.00 vol. 2 pap. $22.50. A self-study course utilizing programmed instruction techniques to teach basic chemistry.

Pauling, Linus, and Roger Hayward. *Architecture of Molecules.* W. H. Freeman 1970 o.p. Explains to a lay audience chemical bonding and how it determines molecular structure.

Richards, W. Graham. *The Problems of Chemistry.* Oxford 1986 $24.95 pap. $8.95. A readable little book that introduces the layperson to some of the basic concepts of chemistry and then relates these concepts to parts of the physical world that the reader already knows.

Ryschkewitsch, George E. *Chemical Bonding and the Geometry of Molecules.* Reinhold 1963 o.p. Discusses chemical bonding and molecular geometries and their dependence on electronic structure. The usefulness of the book for the lay reader is in its emphasis on a single topic.

Sisler, Harry H. *Electronic Structure, Properties, and the Periodic Law.* Reinhold 1963 o.p. Explains the chemical properties of elements in terms of their electronic structure. An extremely useful introductory book on a topic of fundamental importance.

ORGANIC CHEMISTRY

Organic chemistry can be defined as the study of chemicals that contain, or that are analogous to compounds that have, at least one carbon-carbon bond. However, this definition includes carbides that are usually not considered organic compounds. Another definition states that organic chemists study only hydrocarbon derivatives. The first definition stresses the unique property of carbon—its ability to form chains—that makes possible the seemingly infinite variety of organic compounds. Organic chemicals can be broadly categorized by the type of molecular structures present, either rings or chains.

All living organisms contain and can synthesize organic chemicals and, at one time, this distinction was used to separate chemistry into two major classes—namely, inorganic (not derived from living species) and organic (containing carbon and derived from living species).

Carbon has the ability to make four bonds—a fact that the German organic chemist Friedrich August Kekulé von Stradonitz (1829–96) published in 1858. These bonds are covalent rather than ionic. Carbon can bond with up to four other carbon or other element atoms to form straight, branched, and cyclic chains containing single, double, and triple as well as aromatic bonds. It should be noted that almost all organic chemicals contain hydrogen in addition to carbon. Nitrogen, oxygen, and sulfur also frequently occur bonded to carbon.

The state of knowledge of organic chemistry in 1800 contained knowledge of the medicinal properties of some naturally occurring compounds. People had developed methods of extracting these naturally occurring chemicals for use. A theory called vitalism postulated that a vital force, which was present only in living organisms, was necessary to produce organic chemicals. Berzelius (see biographical entry at end of chapter) believed in vitalism and that a chemist in the laboratory could not produce an organic chemical from an obviously inorganic material, until proved wrong by German chemist Friedrich Wöhler (1800–82). Until Wöhler's laboratory synthesis in 1828 of urea, chemists believed that organic chemicals could be synthesized only by living organisms. Today, the vast majority of organic chemicals are made in a laboratory or chemical manufacturing plant. Many of these chemicals have never occurred naturally.

Because of the multitude of organic chemicals, chemists have found it necessary to develop elaborate classification schemes. Usually, these chemicals are classified by structure because chemicals of like structure tend to react in similar ways. The functional group concept is by far the most widely used classification scheme. For example, acetic acid contains the carboxyl group, which means that it should behave as a weak acid and ionize to the anion (negatively charged ion) and the cation (a positively charged hydrogen ion). One can predict that it will react with an alcohol to produce an ester. The major functional groups are listed below.

Hydrocarbons are compounds of only carbon and hydrogen. Due to the multiple bonding capability of carbon as already discussed, there are thousands of hydrocarbons. They can be straight chains such as butane, branched chains such as isooctane, and cyclic structures such as cyclohexane. Because of this diversity in structure, chemists often use drawings called structural formulas to represent organic compounds. In addition, a very elaborate system of nomenclature exists for naming these compounds according to their structure. Hydrocarbons are further classified based on the bonds in the molecule. Alkanes contain only single bonds, alkenes contain one or more double bonds, and alkynes contain one or more triple bonds. Aromatic hydrocarbons contain one or more rings with a unique mix of single and double bonds. The primary source of these hydrocarbons is the processing of petroleum.

Many organic chemicals have oxygen in the molecule as well as hydrogen and carbon. Alcohols (including ethyl alcohol) have a hydroxy or (OH) group. Ethers such as diethyl ether have an oxygen atom with single bonds to two carbon atoms. Aldehydes have a carbon atom at the end of the chain with a double bond to an oxygen and a single bond to a hydrogen. Ketones have a carbon atom with a double bond to an oxygen and with the other bonds to other carbon atoms. Carboxylic acids consist of a terminal carbon atom with a double-bonded oxygen and a singly bonded oxygen bonded to a hydrogen atom.

Carboxylic acid derivatives consist of acyl halides consisting of a carbon double-bonded to an oxygen with a single bond to the halide atom; acid anhydrides with two carbon atoms double-bonded to oxygen atoms with an oxygen atom bonded between them; esters that are produced by the reaction of an alcohol and an acid; and amides that have a carbon double-bonded to an oxygen atom and with the same carbon single bonded to a nitrogen atom.

Nitrogen containing organic compounds can be categorized by nitriles, amines, and nitro compounds.

Benfey, O. Theodor, ed. *Kekulé Centennial.* Amer. Chemical Society 1966 $19.95. A collection of ten papers on various historical aspects of Kekulé's benzene ring postulation.

Cahn, R. S., and O. C. Dermer. *Introduction to Chemical Nomenclature.* Butterworth 5th ed. 1979 text ed. $39.95. Useful basic book on chemical nomenclature, with the rules for naming both organic and inorganic compounds.

Fessenden, Ralph J., and Joan S. Fessenden. *Organic Chemistry*. Brooks-Cole 3d ed. 1986 text ed. $36.00. Organic chemistry text that attempts to show the relationship between organic chemistry and biology by the selection of problems and material.

Flory, Paul J. *Principles of Polymer Chemistry*. Cornell Univ. Pr. 1953 $49.50. Classic discussion of polymer chemistry by a great contributor to the science.

Mislow, K. *Introduction to Stereochemistry*. Benjamin Cummings 1965 pap. $31.95. Mislow covers stereochemistry in organic chemistry in three sections: structure and symmetry, stereoisomerism, and separation and configuration of stereoisomers.

Morawetz, Herbert. *Polymers: The Origins and Growth of a Science*. Wiley 1985 $47.50. "A well-documented chronology of the origins and growth of polymer science based on obviously careful readings, excerpts, and annotation of the original literature—more than 1,000 references in all, and all mostly important references, coupled with a lifetime of experience between the author and contemporary scientists and their work" (*Choice*).

Morrison, Robert T., and Robert N. Boyd. *Organic Chemistry*. Allyn & Bacon 4th ed. 1983 $36.00. Organic chemistry text stressing reaction mechanisms and functional groups.

Pine, Stanley H., and George S. Hammond. *Organic Chemistry*. McGraw-Hill 5th ed. 1987 text ed. $49.95. Organic chemistry text with emphasis on chemical structures and reactions.

Traynham, James G. *Organic Nomenclature: A Programmed Introduction*. Prentice-Hall 3d ed. 1985 text ed. pap. $13.95. An excellent self-study program for the beginning student of organic nomenclature.

Woodward, R. B., and R. Hoffmann. *The Conservation of Orbital Symmetry*. VCH 1970 pap. $17.95. The classic approach to the problem of symmetry in chemical bonding.

BIOCHEMISTRY

Biochemistry, the chemistry of living organisms, rests on the twin foundations of biology and organic chemistry. Possibly the most exciting work occurring in science today is being done in biochemistry. The basic textbooks on this reading list approach biochemistry from the perspective of chemistry.

Boikess, Robert, and Edward Edelson. *Elements of Chemistry: General, Organic and Biological*. Prentice-Hall 1986 text ed. $35.95. Nonmathematical text for use in the agricultural or biological sciences. Useful to the general reader interested in the principal concepts of chemistry.

Cairns-Smith, A. G. *Seven Clues to the Origin of Life: A Scientific Detective Story*. Cambridge Univ. Pr. 1985 $17.95 1987 pap. $8.95. An examination of the origin of life using the conceit of a detective story. (The author seems to be quite a Sherlock Holmes fan.) Entertaining and informative. Based on the author's book for a technical audience, *Genetic Takeover and the Mineral Origins of Life* (Cambridge Univ. Pr. 1982 $39.50).

Coombs, Jim. *Biotechnology Directory 1986*. Stockton Pr. 1986 pap. $140.00. Directory of suppliers and biotechnology products in the world.

Gregory, Richard P. *The Biochemistry of Photosynthesis*. Wiley 1977 $44.95. "Stimulating comparisons between analogous systems in plant and animal life, e.g., processes in the chloroplast and in the mitochondrion" (*Choice*).

Holum, John R. *Elements of General and Biological Chemistry: An Introduction to the Molecular Basis of Life.* Wiley 7th ed. 1987 $41.20. Text for students of chemistry in the allied health care fields.

Rawn, J. David. *Biochemistry.* Harper 1983 text ed. $37.00. A textbook designed for a comprehensive introductory course in biochemistry. One year of college organic chemistry is the assumed prerequisite. Not for beginners.

Watson, James D. *Double Helix: Being a Personal Account of the Discovery of the Structure of DNA.* Atheneum 1968 $7.95 pap. $5.95; NAL 1969 pap. $3.50; ed. by Gunther S. Stent, Norton 1980 text ed. $7.95. This is a first-person account of the research and personalities that won a Nobel Prize and started the biotechnology revolution.

INORGANIC CHEMISTRY

Inorganic chemistry studies the more than 100 noncarbon elements and the properties and reactions of those elements to form compounds. The reactions are primarily of an ionic type in which compounds dissociate into positively or negatively charged ions, which react with one another to form new compounds held together by ionic bonds. Usually these chemicals are acids, bases, or salts.

Acids and bases are very important classifications of chemicals. Sulfuric acid is the major manufactured chemical in the world. It is used in the production of everything from fertilizers and hydrochloric acid to detergents and other household products. Bases such as ammonia and sodium hydroxide are also produced in large quantities. The chemicals called acids display some properties that are common to all acids. For example, acids are sour to the taste, e.g., acetic acid (an organic acid) gives vinegar its sour taste and citric acid (another organic acid) gives lemon its characteristic taste. Acids also can dissolve many metals and liberate hydrogen in the process. (Early chemists studied this reaction thoroughly.) Bases, on the other hand, tend to precipitate metals.

One of the properties shared by acids is the ability to change the color of certain naturally occurring and some synthetic dyes. For example, litmus paper, which is paper impregnated with litmus, turns red on exposure to acids and blue when exposed to bases. The ability to change color on exposure to acids or bases imparts the property of being an indicator to the litmus. Indicators such as litmus, phenophthalein, bromothymo blue, and bromocresol are still widely used to distinguish acids. Acids have been defined as chemicals that can donate hydrogen ions. Incidentally, many dyes used to color textiles are to some extent acid-base indicators and can suffer permanent color changes.

Swedish chemist Svante August Arrhenius (1859–1927) in the late 1800s developed a theory of acids and bases based on the ability of a chemical to conduct electricity. An acid in water dissociates into hydrogen ions and the remaining characteristic anion. Because these particles are charged, the water can then efficiently conduct electricity.

Bases were postulated to contain the hydroxide ion (OH⁻) and to behave in a similar fashion when dissolved in water. The base dissociated into a hydroxide ion and the corresponding base cation. For example, potassium hydroxide will dissociate in water to potassium ions with positive charges and hydroxide ions with negative charges. The hydroxide ions give the characteristic properties to the base.

The Arrhenius theory of acids and bases was quite useful, but it failed to explain some observed phenomena. For example, ammonia was known to be a base even though it did not possess a hydroxide group. Hydrochloric acid and ammonia when dissolved in benzene still reacted to form a salt, ammonium chloride, just as these two chemicals would if dissolved in water. In the early 1920s, Johannes Bronsted (1879–1947) and Thomas Lowry (1874–1936) modified the Arrhenius theory. Their concept was that an acid was a hydrogen ion donor and that a base was a hydrogen ion acceptor. Thus, ammonia, without a hydroxide group, was a base because it could accept a hydrogen ion and acid-base reactions could occur without water. Later, G. N. Lewis (1875–1946) would further modify the acid-base theory in terms of electron pair donors and acceptors.

The formation of salts from acids and bases, such as ammonium chloride as mentioned above, is one of the more important chemical reactions. Salts are very important commercially. For example, the salts of acids such as nitric and phosphoric acids are used as fertilizers. The salts do not demonstrate the same properties as the acids or bases from which they are derived, but instead display properties that are characteristic of salts. Salts cannot dissolve or precipitate metals, do not taste sour or bitter, and can, as the acids and bases, conduct electricity when dissolved in water. This latter fact demonstrates that salts also dissociate or ionize when dissolved in water to the corresponding negatively and positively charged ions. For example, ammonium chloride in water dissociates to the ammonium ion and the chloride ion. Sodium chloride, or common table salt, dissociates to the sodium ion and the chloride ion.

Allen, Thomas L., and Raymond M. Keefer. *Chemistry Experiment and Theory.* Harper 2d ed. 1982 text ed. $35.50. A solid freshman chemistry text with an emphasis on the physical phenomena of chemistry.

Asimov, Isaac. *The Noble Gases.* Basic Bks. 1966 o.p. One of the many books on science for the lay reader by this author and one of the few books devoted to the noble gases. It examines their history from their discovery by Ramsey and Rayleigh to the preparation of the first noble gas compounds in 1962.

Brown, Theodore L., and H. Eugene LeMay, Jr. *Chemistry: The Central Science.* Prentice-Hall 3d ed. 1985 text ed. $37.95. A freshman chemistry text that shows the relevance of chemistry to everyday life.

———. *Chemistry: The Central Science, Qualitative Inorganic Analysis.* Prentice-Hall 3d ed. 1985 text ed. pap. $9.95. A companion to the preceding title.

Coulson, Charles. *Coulson's Valence.* Ed. by Roy McWeeney, Oxford 1979 $59.00 pap. $25.95. One of the classic descriptions of chemical bonding.

Holden, Alan, and Phyllis S. Morrison. *Crystals and Crystal Growing.* MIT repr. of

1960 ed. 1982 pap. $9.95. A fascinating book for the nonspecialist that describes crystal symmetry, cleavage, and classification as well as vacancies and grain boundaries.

Kieffer, William F. *Mole Concept in Chemistry*. Van Nostrand 2d ed. 1973 o.p. This book, intended for freshman chemistry students, explains thoroughly the fundamental concept of the "mole" or Avogadro's number of molecules.

Pauling, Linus. *The Nature of the Chemical Bond and the Structure of Molecules and Crystals: An Introduction to Modern Structural Chemistry*. 1939. Cornell Univ. Pr. 3d ed. 1960 $45.00. Reprint of his classic work concerning the behavior of the electron in chemical bonding.

PHYSICAL CHEMISTRY

Physical chemistry most clearly illustrates the theoretical and mathematical basis of modern chemistry. Physical chemists solve scientific problems using mathematical models to quantify and predict the behavior of matter. Brief illustrations of two questions that have concerned physical chemists and physicists follow.

John Dalton first proposed the modern atomic theory in the early 1800s. Throughout much of the nineteenth century, scientists supposed that the atom was indivisible. Later in the century, scientists started to consider the possibility that the atom itself consisted of smaller particles. Experimental work by physicist ERNEST RUTHERFORD and his coworkers in the early 1900s contributed to the idea of a nuclear atom with a positive charge at the nucleus surrounded by a negative charge. NIELS BOHR, another physicist, using his knowledge of Rutherford's work and MAX PLANCK's quantum theory, in which he assumed that energy could be emitted in discrete units, developed a model for the electronic structure of the atom. Later, the work of LOUIS DE BROGLIE on the wave theory of matter and WERNER HEISENBERG's postulate that it is impossible to know both the position and velocity of the electron at the same time contributed to the current quantum mechanical view of the electronic structure of the atom.

Theories of chemical equilibrium and thermodynamics have been extremely important in the development of modern chemistry. During the nineteenth century, the caloric concept of heat was abandoned and the interconvertibility of heat and mechanical work was established. Julius Mayer first calculated the mechanical equivalent of heat. Hermann von Helmholtz (1821–94) postulated the principle of the conservation of energy and that the universe had a constant amount of energy. Clausius (1822–88) defined a term for the disorder in the universe—*entropy*—and said that the entropy of the universe always tends to increase. The law of mass action, proposed by Cato Guldberg and Peter Waage, defined an equilibrium constant in terms of the concentrations of reactions and products. The development of the Clausius-Clapeyron equation applied thermodynamic principles to chemical equilibria. Josiah Gibbs, the first significant American chemist, developed the phase rule, which allowed the calculation of the degrees of freedom in a heterogenous system. In 1884, Henri Louis Le Châtelier (1850–

1936) stated that imposed changes on a system in equilibrium causes the equilibrium to readjust in the direction necessary to offset the change.

Many of the physical chemistry texts are difficult for the reader without a strong mathematical background. However, much useful information can be gleaned from the introductory material contained in even the most mathematical treatments.

Alberty, Robert A. *Physical Chemistry*. Wiley 6th ed. 1983 text ed. $45.00. The standard textbook on physical chemistry. Not for the beginner. The four sections cover thermodynamics, quantum chemistry, chemical dynamics, and structure of compounds.

Lewis, G. N., and M. Randall. *Thermodynamics*. McGraw-Hill 2d ed. 1961 o.p. The classic exposition on the interconvertibility of heat and work. However, this is a highly mathematical treatment.

Prigogine, Ilya, and Isabelle Stengers. *Order Out of Chaos: Man's New Dialogue with Nature*. Bantam 1984 pap. $10.95; Shambhala 1984 $18.95. "The 1977 Nobel laureate in chemistry and a former co-worker and scientific journalist have written a dazzling and profoundly optimistic book . . . in which . . . they envisage a universe where chance becomes a partner of determinism—a universe which may under certain conditions become spontaneously self-organizing, achieving 'order out of chaos' " (*LJ*).

Seaborg, Glenn T., ed. *Transuranium Elements: Products of Modern Alchemy*. Van Nostrand 1978 $64.95. A selection of the original papers on the production of the transuranium elements. The editor's comments are extensive and placed throughout the book. These comments are worth reading in themselves even if the actual papers may be too technical.

Spielberg, Nathan, and Byron D. Anderson. *Seven Ideas That Shook the Universe*. Wiley 1987 pap. $14.95. The seven ideas—Copernican astronomy, Newtonian mechanics, the concept of energy, entropy and probability, relativity, the quantum theory, and conservation of principles and symmetries—are properly concepts of physics. However, the concepts of energy and entropy and the quantum theory have a major impact on physical chemistry. One of the best current explanations of these topics for the lay reader.

ANALYTICAL CHEMISTRY

Analytical chemistry, the fourth traditional branch of chemistry, defines techniques used to gain information about the chemical composition of materials. Improved instrumentation has made possible the detection of trace quantities of chemicals undetectable even 20 years ago. The advancement of these analytical techniques has greatly improved the ability of chemists to determine minute contaminants in industrial processes such as semiconductor manufacture and to trace amounts of chemicals in the environment. Because of the current use of improved analytical techniques in toxicological studies, the several titles related closely to toxicology are included in this section.

Bender, Gary. *Principles of Chemical Instrumentation*. Saunders 1987 $18.50. Instrumental analysis as it is practiced in clinical chemistry and molecular biology. Useful to the more general reader because it does not require knowledge of either physics or calculus.

Christian, Gary D. *Analytical Chemistry*. Wiley 4th ed. 1986 $37.90. One of the fundamental undergraduate texts on analytical chemistry. Useful elementary chapter on data handling.

Furman, N. Howell, and Frank J. Welcher. *Standard Methods of Chemical Analysis*. Krieger 3 vols. 6th ed. repr. of 1962–66 ed. 1975 set $422.50. A somewhat dated but comprehensive set of fundamental analytical separations and methods. Contains methods of preparation for many reagents and standard and indicator solutions.

Official Methods of Analysis of the Association of Official Analytical Chemists. Ed. by S. Williams, Assn. of Official Analytical Chemists 14th ed. 1984 $148.50. Membership in this organization is by institution and includes government agencies such as federal and state departments of agriculture. A compendium of analytical methods used in the enforcement of the food, feed, and pesticide laws.

Szabadvary, Ferenc. *History of Analytical Chemistry*. Trans. by Gyula Svehla, Pergamon 1976 o.p. Demonstrates the importance of analytical chemistry to the development of modern chemistry. Postulates that the development of suitable analytical methods was necessary for most new results in chemistry. Evaluates the contributions of Lavoisier, Berzelius, and Ostwald, among others.

Vogel, A. I. *A Textbook of Quantitative Inorganic Analysis Including Elementary Instrumental Analysis*. Wiley 1978 $54.95. The most comprehensive one-volume compilation of a large number of analytical methods.

ENVIRONMENTAL CHEMISTRY
AND APPLICATIONS OF CHEMISTRY

Anderson, Kim, and Ronald Scott. *Fundamentals of Industrial Toxicology*. Ann Arbor Science 1981 $24.95. Intended for a more general audience than Doull (see below), this book gives a good background for the understanding of toxicology, or the study of poisons. Not a catalog of chemical hazards, but rather a discussion of the underlying principles.

Berger, Melvin. *Hazardous Substances: A Reference*. Enslow Pubs. 1986 $13.95. "A concise, alphabetically-arranged, guide to 230 dangerous materials and other environmental hazards that are encountered at home and in the workplace. . . . Technical terms are kept to a minimum, and a handy glossary at the front of the volume defines those which are used in the annotations" (*SLJ*).

Brodner, Paul, ed. *Asbestos Hazard*. New York Academy of Sciences 1980 o.p. Based on the proceedings of a conference held in New York in June 1978, by the New York Academy of Sciences, on the health hazards of asbestos exposure. Written for the general public.

Crone, Hugh. *Chemicals and Society: A Guide to the New Chemical Age*. Cambridge Univ. Pr. 1987 $39.50 pap. $14.95. A book that discusses the benefits and disadvantages of the current uses of chemicals. One of the few books for the layperson that notes the improvements in analytical techniques.

Doull, John, and others, eds. *Casarett and Doull's Toxicology: The Basic Science of Poisons*. Macmillan 3d ed. 1986 $54.95. Basically a textbook in toxicology, but two chapters entitled "Origin and Scope of Toxicology" and "Principles of Toxicology" are useful to the nonspecialist.

Epstein, Samuel S., and Carl Pope. *Hazardous Waste in America: Our Number One Environmental Crisis*. Sierra 1983 $27.50 pap. $12.95. Well-documented discussion on the problems of hazardous waste and legal and technical remedies for those problems.

Goffer, Zvi. *Archaeological Chemistry: A Sourcebook on the Applications of Chemistry to Archaeology.* Wiley 1980 $60.00. Discusses the use of newer analytical techniques in archaeology.

Gough, Michael. *Dioxin, Agent Orange: The Facts.* Plenum 1986 $17.95. A scholarly treatise of the studies on the health of dioxin-exposed people. Gough's conclusion that the effects of dioxin on human health have been overdrawn may be controversial.

McCann, Michael. *Artist Beware.* Watson-Guptill 1979 $18.95. Artists are exposed to a number of chemicals that can be hazardous. Because many artists work by themselves, they need to be responsible for their own safety. This book and the next describe correct ventilation and safety equipment, and the hazards of materials used as dyes and pigments.

——. *Health Hazards Manual for Artists.* N. Lyons Bks. 3d ed. rev. 1985 pap. $7.95. A somewhat technical, but nevertheless interesting, compendium of information about naturally occurring compounds that can be poisonous. This set documents naturally occurring teratogens and carcinogenic toxins, as well as the compounds that cause contact dermatitis.

National Research Council. *Regulating Pesticides in Food: The Delaney Paradox.* National Academy Pr. 1987 $29.95. This book results from a study by the Board of Agriculture of the National Research Council on the impact of the Delaney Clause of the Food, Drug, and Cosmetic Act on the Environmental Protection Agency's methods for allowing pesticide residues in food. Examines the contradictions inherent in barring any pesticide residue that has been found to cause cancer in animals and the law's requirement for "an adequate, wholesome, and economical food supply."

Nriagu, Jerome O. *Lead and Lead Poisoning in Antiquity.* Wiley 1983 $65.95. This interesting book contains the controversial hypothesis that the decline of the Roman Empire was caused by lead poisoning of the ruling class.

O'Neill, Peter. *Environmental Chemistry.* Allen & Unwin 1985 $25.00 pap. $13.95. An overview of the operation of natural systems and the movement of the chemical elements and their compounds. The chemistry covered is similar to that of a freshman chemistry text, but without the interruptions caused by problems and exercises.

Ottoboni, M. Alice. *The Dose Makes the Poison: A Plain-Language Guide to Toxicology.* Vincente Bks. 1984 $15.95 pap. $9.95. This is a balanced discussion for nonscientists of the basic tenets of toxicology and its application to chemical exposures.

Rushefsky, Mark. *Making Cancer Policy.* State Univ. of New York Pr. 1986 $44.50 pap. $14.95. Studies the controversies surrounding cancer policy and risk-assessment procedures. Discusses significant choices and the assumptions used in making those choices. Introductory chapter concerns "science, uncertainty, and politics."

Sittig, Marshall. *Handbook of Toxic and Hazardous Chemicals and Carcinogens.* Noyes 2d ed. 1985 $96.00. Another compendium of industrial chemicals and their hazards and regulations. Usually describes harmful effects and symptoms in graphic detail.

REPRODUCTIVE HAZARDS AND CHEMICALS

The public has recently become concerned about the effects of some chemicals on human reproduction. These substances, called teratogens, under some circumstances may cause fetal and developmental deformities. The following two titles cover this subject quite well for the lay audience and are highly recommended.

Office of Technology Assessment, U.S. Congress. *Reproductive Health Hazards in the Workplace*. USGPO 1985 pap. $19.00. This is an excellent and balanced discussion of the current knowledge of hazards and suspected hazards to the reproductive health of American men and women. It reviews the basic principles of reproductive biology and development as well as the legal and ethical issues surrounding the subject. It is not a catalog of suspected teratogens.

Shepard, Thomas H. *Catalog of Teratogenic Agents*. Johns Hopkins Univ. Pr. 5th ed. 1986 $45.00. A definitive list of agents that have been studied as possible teratogens in man and animals. For use in answering the question, "Does this agent cause congenital defects?" It has nonchemical entries such as emotional stress and the rubella virus. A good complement to the preceding title.

BERZELIUS, JONS JAKOB. 1779–1848

Although John Dalton used certain symbols to represent elements and compounds, it was Berzelius who introduced the series of chemical nomenclature used today. He was a Swedish chemist who performed many analyses to prove Proust's law of multiple proportions. Perhaps in order to help with his own record keeping, he invented a system of abbreviations for the elements and compounds. He published this system of nomenclature as part of a work entitled *Essay on the Cause of Chemical Proportions, and Some Circumstances Relating to Them, Together with a Short and Easy Method of Expressing Them*. Berzelius recommended that the elements be expressed as letters and that the combining ratios be included in the formula. He dominated the infant science of chemistry from 1815 to 1835. He published the journal *Jahres-Bericht*, in which he reviewed the chemical reports of the year.

BOOK BY BERZELIUS

Essay on the Cause of Chemical Proportions (Essai sur la Theorie Des Proportions Chimiques et Sur L'influence Chimique De L'electricite). Johnson Repr. repr. of 1819 ed. $36.00

BOOKS ABOUT BERZELIUS

Jorpes, J. Erik. *Jacob Berzelius: His Life and Work*. Trans. by Barbara Steele, Univ. of California Pr. 1970 o.p. A small but lavishly illustrated book that, contrary to its title, concentrates on the work, not the man.

Melhado, Evan M. *Jacob Berzelius: The Emergence of His Chemical System*. Univ. of Wisconsin Pr. repr. 1982 $45.00. An understanding of the man and the chemist.

BOYLE, ROBERT. 1627–1691

Born in Munster, Ireland, of English parents, Boyle must certainly be numbered among the earliest scientists who studied nature and drew conclusions justified by the experiments. A son of a wealthy man, he received a good education, and in 1654 he had the money necessary to set up a laboratory in Oxford, England, and hired Robert Hooke (1634–1703) as his laboratory assistant. He and Hooke designed a greatly improved air pump, which enabled them to study the behavior of air by creating a reasonably good vacuum. Boyle published *Spring and Weight of the Air* in 1660, in which he articulated Boyle's Law, describing the inverse relationship between the temperature and the pressure of a gas.

In 1661, Boyle published *The Sceptical Chymist*. Here, he challenged the alchemists' belief in the four elements of earth, air, fire, and water. He also attacked the three principles of Paracelsus: salt, sulfur, and mercury. In this work he described his concept of an element as follows: "Certain Primitive and Single, or perfectly unmingled bodies which not being made of any other bodies, or of one another, are the ingredients of which all those called perfectly mixed bodies are immediately compounded." Boyle also studied the effects of air in combustion and respiration of animals, and reported his findings in *Suspicions about Some Hidden Qualities of the Air* in 1674. However, the discovery of oxygen would wait for Joseph Priestley.

Boyle experimented with the calcination of tin in a sealed container, but because he weighed only the resultant tin oxide, he did not get the data to interpret the results correctly. Instead, when the tin oxide proved to weigh more than the original tin, he theorized that something had passed into the glass container. Lavoisier would later repeat the experiment, weigh the container, and realize that something in the air had combined with the tin.

Boyle became somewhat of a celebrity and enjoyed King Charles II's favor with his discovery of Boyle's Law. He contributed to the founding of the Royal Society of London for Improving Natural Knowledge in 1662, and died in London.

BOOKS BY BOYLE

Robert Boyle on Natural Philosophy: An Essay with Selections from His Writings by Maria Boas Hall. Fwd. by Norman Russell, Greenwood repr. of 1965 ed. 1980 lib. bdg. $42.50. "Hall places Boyle's contributions in the stream of scientific thought. This essay also serves as a prelude to the wide selection of Boylean writings which constitute the second part of the volume" (*LJ*).

The Sceptical Chymist. 1661. Biblio Dist. 1964 o.p.

Robert Boyle's Experiments in Pneumatics. Ed. by James Bryant Conant, Harvard Univ. Pr. 1950 o.p.

Experiments and Considerations Touching Colours. Johnson Repr. repr. of 1664 ed. 1964 o.p.

Origin and Virtues of Gems. 1672. Macmillan 1972 o.p. "This facsimile reprint . . . makes a valuable addition for historians of geology, historians of science and medicine, and for the general historian of the 17th century" (*Choice*).

BOOKS ABOUT BOYLE

Hall, Maria Boas. *Robert Boyle and Seventeenth-Century Chemistry.* Kraus Repr. repr. of 1958 ed. $23.00. Hall was an eminent historian of science who spent most of her career studying Boyle.

Scootin, Harry. *Robert Boyle: Founder of Modern Chemistry.* Watts 1962 o.p. A detailed discussion of the personal life and scientific contributions of Robert Boyle. It includes diagrams of Boyle's experimental apparatus.

DALTON, JOHN. 1766–1844

Dalton was born at Eaglesfield, Cumberland, in England. A practicing Quaker, he studied many areas of physical science, including chemistry and physics. In 1794, he published the first study of color blindness, *Extraordinary Facts Relating to the Vision of Colors*. Perhaps not surprisingly, he was color blind. Dalton is best remembered for his ideas on atomic theory, which he began formulating beginning about 1800. In 1808, he published *A New System of Chemical Philosophy*, in which he expounded the basic laws of the atomic theory:

1. Small particles, which he called atoms after the ancient Greek philosopher Democritus's terminology, exist and compose all matter.
2. These atoms are indivisible and indestructible.
3. Atoms of the same chemical element have the same chemical properties. They do not transmute or change into atoms of a different element. The atoms of one element differ from the elements of another element because their masses are different.
4. Elements form compounds in constant combining ratios consisting of integral ratios of one type of atom to another.

Dalton, because of his religious beliefs, at first refused to be nominated to the Royal Society. Later, in 1822, he was elected without his knowledge.

BOOK BY DALTON

A New System of Chemical Philosophy, 1808–1827. Beekman 2 vols. repr. of 1827 ed. 1953 o.p.; Philos. Lib. 1964 o.p.

BOOK ABOUT DALTON

Patterson, Elizabeth C. *John Dalton and the Atomic Theory: The Biography of a Natural Philosopher*. Doubleday 1970 o.p. A readable biography of Dalton's life and scientific achievements. Ample notes and illustrations.

DAVY, SIR HUMPHREY. 1778–1829

An indifferent student, the young Davy pursued his interest in hunting, fishing, and hiking in the great outdoors of his native Cornwall, England. He began to study medicine, but spent a good deal of time composing poetry. Then he discovered chemistry and his life's work became clear.

He brought remarkable energy and intellectual gifts to his studies. Davy frequently used himself as a guinea pig in his study of gases and in one incautious experiment with water gas, a mixture of mainly hydrogen and carbon monoxide, nearly lost his life. Work in agricultural chemistry led him to write a book that stood as the standard text in the field for more than 50 years. His studies in electrochemistry produced the first arc lamp and the first incandescent electric light (Edison's was merely the first practical one) as well as the discovery of sodium and potassium, among other elements.

In 1815 he invented the miner's safety lamp, for which he refused to take out a patent so that it might be manufactured and used without impediment. He was already one of the most popular lecturers of his day, and this selfless act won him even greater public esteem.

Illness in the last few years of his life forced him to abandon many activities, including the presidency of the Royal Society. Finally he withdrew from England itself and sought unsuccessfully to restore his health on the continent. There he wrote a lyrical examination of the joys of fishing called *Salmonia*, a final demonstration to the world of both his lifelong love for nature and his great gifts as a writer.

Books by Davy

Collected Works. Ed. by John Davy, Johnson Repr. 9 vols. repr. of 1839–40 ed. 1972 $260.00. Edited by Davy's brother. "Davy was one of the great 19th-century chemists, known especially for his discovery of sodium and potassium, his electrochemical analyses, his standard text on agricultural chemistry, and his invention of a safe miner's lamp. These volumes originally appeared in 1839–40 and contain the major parts of his scientific writings and lectures" (*Choice*).
Salmonia. Freshet 1970 $10.75

Books about Davy

Fullmer, June Z. *Sir Humphrey Davy's Published Works*. Harvard Univ. Pr. 1969 text ed. $10.00. "This annotated bibliography 'lists all of Davy's published writings, including translations, critical reviews, and reports of experimental findings printed prior to the official versions' " (*LJ*).
Hartley, Sir Harold. *Humphrey Davy*. Morrow 1970 o.p. "Davy's place in the history of science is secure. From the discovery of nitrous oxide ('laughing gas') at Bristol in 1799 to the invention of the miner's safety lamp in 1815 there stands to his credit an immense record of achievement which is not merely of theoretical interest but has also had a profound effect upon the modern world. . . . Hartley's . . . excellent assessment of Davy's life and achievement leaves nothing to be desired in orderliness of presentation, freshness of writing and sureness of judgment" (*TLS*).

FARADAY, MICHAEL. 1791–1867

Faraday contributed the basic concepts of electrochemistry now known as Faraday's laws. He came from a poor family and had little formal education. Apprenticed to a bookbinder, he came to the attention of Sir Humphrey Davy, who carried out a variety of studies on chemistry and its relationship to electricity. Faraday's scientific achievements surpassed those of Davy when he related the quantity of electricity to electrochemical equivalents. Faraday's two laws describe the relationship first that "the mass of an element involved in an electrolysis reaction is directly proportional to the quantity of electricity employed" and that "the same quantity of electricity produced chemically equivalent quantities of all substances" (Hamm, *Chemistry*). (See also Chapter 9 in this volume.)

Books by Faraday

Chemical Manipulation. 1827. Wiley 1974 $35.00. "A reproduction of the copy Faraday presented to the Royal Institution, with his own handwritten dedication and corrections. Nobel Prize winner Sir George Porter has written a new foreword for this edition. As he points out, this book was a landmark in chemical techniques. Much of what Faraday describes is still applicable today, and what is no longer applicable is well founded for its time and lends a bit of nostalgia for chemists trained before World War II" (*Choice*).

Experimental Researches in Electricity. 1839–55. Dover 3 vols. in 2 1962 o.p. "This work is one of the masterpieces of scientific literature, setting forth with wonderful clarity and in explicit detail the step-by-step records of Faraday's investigations and discoveries, among them electromagnetic induction, . . . the laws of electrolysis, the identities of different forms of electricity, the electrical capacities of various substances, the effect of magnetism on polarized light and diamagnetism" (*Scientific American*).

Experimental Researches in Chemistry and Physics. 1859. International Pub. 1969 o.p.

On the Various Forces of Nature (A Course of Six Lectures on the Forces of Matter and Their Relations to Each Other). 1860. Crowell 1961 o.p. Lectures for young people on gravity, electricity, and magnetism.

The Chemical History of a Candle. Ed. by William Crookes, Crowell 1957 o.p. Lectures for young people, given at the Royal Institute.

The Achievements of Michael Faraday. Ed. by L. Pearce Williams, Johnson Repr. 1973 o.p. Letters and other writings.

BOOKS ABOUT FARADAY

Agassi, Joseph. *Faraday as a Natural Philosopher.* Univ. of Chicago Pr. 1971 $23.00. An interesting biography by a leading philosopher and historian of science.

Gooding, David, ed. *Faraday Rediscovered: Essays on the Life and Work of Michael Faraday, 1791–1867.* Intro. by George Porter, Stockton Pr. 1986 $70.00. "Research on Faraday can draw on an enormous manuscript record of correspondence and laboratory notebooks as well as his experimental apparatus itself. . . . Though not quite an industry in itself, this excellent volume, which brings together essays by some dozen scholars, could claim to have 'rediscovered' Faraday in three basic ways: as experimentalist, as member of the Royal Institution, and as Sandemanian" (*Science*).

Jeffreys, Alan E. *Michael Faraday: A List of His Lectures and Published Writings.* Academic Pr. 1961 $39.00. "The bibliography is a model of clarity, both in the presentation as a whole and in that of the individual items. The latter, which are arranged in chronological order under each year, are numbered from 1 (1816) to 489 (1932), the last seven being works, e.g. the *Diary*, published subsequently to Faraday's death in 1867. Titles are given in full, followed by bibliographical details (in smaller type) and brief notes by the author, including references to later reprints, e.g. in the *Experimental Researches*" (*Annals of Science*).

Ludwig, Charles. *Michael Faraday: Father of Electronics.* Herald Pr. 1978 $7.95

Williams, L. Pearce. *Michael Faraday: A Biography.* Simon & Schuster 1971 o.p. "Dr. Williams has written a definitive study of the man and his work. Although the subject matter is necessarily of a technical nature, the book's clear and vivid prose style should make it appealing to a wider audience" (*LJ*).

GIBBS, JOSIAH WILLARD. 1839–1903

Possessor of one of the greatest minds of American science, Gibbs led the most unassuming of lives. The son of a Yale Divinity School professor, he showed early promise as a scholar, winning prizes in Latin, Greek, and mathematics during his undergraduate days at Yale. In 1863 Yale awarded him the first doctorate in engineering in the United States. After serving several years as a tutor, he traveled to Europe in 1866 for three intensive years of postdoctoral study. Returning to New Haven and the house where he was born, he took up his teaching duties at Yale, never to leave again. His studies behind him, he began to single-handedly develop several whole new fields of science.

His *On the Equilibrium of Heterogeneous Substances* formed the basis of chemical thermodynamics. The phase rule, one of the principal and enduring tools of this new field, opened up new and lucrative avenues of industrial production and metallurgy. For the first time, chemists were able to precisely calculate, and thus vary, the conditions under which different forms of compounds could exist. As just one consequence, great strides were made in the development and production of alloys. Gibbs was aware of the potential value of his work, but made no effort to gain from it, preferring instead the quiet life of the bachelor scholar.

So diffident was he and so difficult the nature of his papers that he was largely unrecognized by the scientific community of his time. When he developed vector analysis, a mathematical tool of critical importance to physics and engineering, he did not even bother to publish his work, but merely circulated several papers among his students.

His final legacy was the development of statistical mechanics, which found wide application in physics, chemistry, and engineering and prepared the way for the great developments in quantum mechanics in the early decades of this century.

BOOKS BY GIBBS

Scientific Papers of J. Willard Gibbs. 1906. Peter Smith repr. 1961. 2 vols. $21.00. "That Josiah Willard Gibbs advanced science the world over more than it has ever been given to any other American researcher to do, can hardly be questioned. [Except for] 'Elementary Principles in Statistical Mechanics' . . . his only other printed remains are the papers now collected, which are few but fundamental. They are substantially limited to three, not counting an unusually small number of preliminary and supplementary outputs" (*The Nation*).

Elementary Principles in Statistical Mechanics. 1902. Ox Bow 1982 $22.00 pap. text ed. $12.00. The only separate book (as opposed to writings in collections) published by Gibbs, this appeared in the Yale Bicentennial Series the year before his death.

BOOKS ABOUT GIBBS

Seeger, Raymond J. *Josiah Willard Gibbs: An American Physicist Par Excellence.* [*Men of Physics Ser.*] Pergamon 1974 $41.00. A very readable book from an established writer of scientific biography.

Wheeler, Lynde Phelps. *Josiah Willard Gibbs: The History of a Great Mind.* Shoe String repr. of 1962 ed. 1970 $18.50. The definitive biography. Contains an extensive bibliography.

LAVOISIER, ANTOINE LAURENT. 1743–1794

Born in Paris of a well-to-do family, Lavoisier received a good education and, at an early age, became interested in science. He had the genius of making accurate measurements and of conducting careful experimentation.

He made the measurement that Boyle had not: He weighed the tin oxide and the retort (particularly the air inside the retort) and noted that the total system did not gain or lose weight; he then concluded that during the calcination, the metal got a substance from the air. Lavoisier realized that the true state of Priestley's "dephlogistonated air" consists of at least two substances—one that supports combustion, oxygen; and another, nitrogen.

Because of his part ownership of a tax-collecting firm, Lavoisier was sent to the guillotine on May 8, 1794. According to tradition, the presiding judge responded to a plea on Lavoisier's behalf by saying, "The Republic has no need for scientists. Let justice take its course."

BOOKS BY LAVOISIER

Essays: Physical and Chemical. Trans. by H. Thomas Pope, Biblio Dist. repr. of 1776 ed. 1970 $45.00. "The *Essays* are therefore historically valuable, as a sort of uncalcinated Lavoisier; but they are not for the uncommitted. They are not for those who are likely to be taken unawares by the theory that there might be either fixed or indeed fixable air in calcareous earths. The reader must know his phlogisticated air from mephitic gas, his acidum pingue from spiritus sylvestris. Granted a very little chemical knowledge, and a vocabulary, however, one can study not only Lavoisier's chemistry, but the man himself—a much more complicated affair" (*TLS*).

(and Pierre Simon LaPlace). *Memoir on Heat.* Ed. by Henry Guerlac, Watson 1981 $14.95

Elements of Chemistry in a New Systematic Order, Containing All the Modern Discoveries. 1790. Dover 1984 pap. $11.95. "Scientists tend to assume that present theories are substantially correct whereas older assumptions were obviously erroneous. This accurate 1790 Kerr translation is a valuable antidote. It demonstrates Lavoisier's ability to create a practical science on experimental facts. It also underscores difficulties still encountered in the interpretation of nature" (*Choice*).

BOOKS ABOUT LAVOISIER

Guerlac, Henry. *Antoine-Laurent Lavoisier: Chemist and Revolutionary.* Scribner 1975 pap. $2.95. The best general text on the life and scientific achievements of Lavoisier. Drawn from Gillispie's *Dictionary of Scientific Biography* (see above under History of Chemistry and the Chemical Industry).

Holmes, Frederic L. *Lavoisier and the Chemistry of Life: An Exploration of Scientific Creativity.* [*History of Science and Medicine Ser.*] Univ. of Wisconsin Pr. 1984 text ed. $38.50. Emphasizes Lavoisier's interest in physiological chemistry.

MENDELEEV, DMITRII IVANOVITCH. 1834–1907

Mendeleev was born in Tobolsk, Siberia. He was educated at St. Petersburg, and became a professor of chemistry at the university. His liberal political views kept him from receiving full credit for his scientific discoveries. In 1869, he devised a periodic table in which the clear repetition of the properties of the elements was shown. Using his understanding of the law of periodicity, Mendeleev correctly predicted in 1871 the properties of a then yet undiscovered element, which he called ekaaluminum. Gallium was discovered in 1875, and quite closely resembled the element that Mendeleev had predicted. The periodic table, unlike the natures of the elements themselves, has been dynamic. It has been rearranged as new elements have been synthesized (in the case of the transuranium elements) or as fashions have changed as to the correct presentation of chemical information.

BOOK BY MENDELEEV

Principles of Chemistry. 1868–71. Ed. by Thomas H. Pope, trans. by George Kamensky, Kraus Repr. 2 vols. 3d English ed. repr. of 1905 ed. $60.00. A standard text for many years.

BOOK ABOUT MENDELEEV

Petryanov, I. V., and D. N. Tifonov. *Elementary Order: Mendeleev's Periodic System.* Imported Pubns. 1985 pap. $3.95

OSTWALD, WILHELM. 1853–1932 (NOBEL PRIZE 1909)

Born in Riga, Latvia, Ostwald was raised in a flourishing German enclave. He received a degree from the University of Dorpat and taught at the University of Riga. In 1877 he moved to Leipzig to become director of the Physicochemical Institute. There he busied himself as scientist, teacher, administrator, and chief publicist for the burgeoning field of physical chemistry. In 1887 he founded the *Zeitschrift für physikalischer chemie (Journal of Physical Chemistry)* with contributions from Svante August Arrhenius, Jacobus Hendricus van't Hoff, and himself.

Ostwald's study of chemical affinities led to his pioneering work on catalysis. While his fundamental understanding of the nature of catalysts— that they take no direct part in the reactions that they influence—has been shown to be incorrect, he did produce significant results. The most famous is a process for producing nitric acid from ammonia using platinum as a catalyst. This Ostwald process gave the chemical industry a means to economically produce both fertilizers and explosives.

A prolific writer, he authored more than 500 papers and 45 books. Among the other interests in his crowded life was painting, which motivated him to study the chemistry of color.

BOOK BY OSTWALD

Electrochemistry: History and Theory. Amerind Pub. 1980 o.p.

BOOK ABOUT OSTWALD

Slosson, Edwin E. *Major Prophets of To-Day.* Ayer repr. of 1914 ed. 1982 $20.00. Interesting but very dated view of Ostwald and his work.

PARACELSUS, PHILIPPUS AUREOLUS. 1493?–1541

Scholars have sharply divided opinions as to the value of Paracelsus's contributions to modern chemistry. Clearly, Paracelsus, the Swiss physician who was born Theophrastus Bombastus von Hohenheim, left a large number of influential writings on medicine and chemistry. The chemical historian Aaron J. Ihde, in *The Development of Modern Chemistry* (see above under History of Chemistry and the Chemical Industry), minimizes Paracelsus's contributions on the grounds that he did not add any empirical knowledge and only introduced theoretical concepts that were incorrect. Burland (see above under History of Chemistry and the Chemical Industry), in *The Arts of the Alchemists*, postulates that Paracelsus left "books and ideas behind him which sealed the fate of the chemical side of alchemy." In the chapter "Medical Chemistry" from *The Origins of Chemistry* (see above under History of Chemistry and the Chemical Industry), Multhauf discusses many of the activities of sixteenth-century European medical practitioners. An illustrative footnote describes the use of sulfuric acid by Paracelsus for treating a variety of ailments. Multhauf notes that Paracelsus may have described the preparation of diethyl ether (the anesthetic gas) from sulfuric acid and wine. However, Multhauf ascribes to Valerius Cordus (1515–1544) the honor of having first noted clearly the preparation of diethyl ether from sulfuric acid and alcohol. In conclusion, much of the problem in assessing Paracelsus's contributions lies in the confusing and obtuse nature of his numerous writings. This style, of course, was standard for the alchemists. (See also Chapter 4, Volume 4.)

BOOK BY PARACELSUS

Selected Writings. Ed. by J. Jacoby, trans. by Norman Gutterman, Princeton Univ. Pr. 1958 o.p. Covers selections from Paracelsus's major writings, including *Archidoxes*, his single most important work.

BOOK ABOUT PARACELSUS

Pachter, Henry M. *Magic into Science: The Story of Paracelsus.* Arden Lib. repr. of 1951 ed. 1982 lib. bdg. $35.00. A reasoned approach to his work.

PAULING, LINUS (CARL). 1901– (NOBEL PRIZE 1954, 1963)

This American winner of two Nobel Prizes, the first in chemistry for his discoveries on the structure of the molecule and the nature of the chemical bond, did pioneering work in many areas of his field, includings its medical applications. His books on chemistry are basic to understanding the subject. He did research and taught at the California Institute of Technology (1922–64), was research professor at the Center for the Study of Democratic Institutions in California (1963–67), and taught at the University of California, San Diego. Understanding as he did the threat to the human system from radioactive fallout in the postwar days of indiscriminate atomic-bomb testing, he conducted a personal crusade in the 1950s and early 1960s seeking a halt to the tests, for which he suffered considerable persecution at the hands of the U.S. government in the form of denial of passport—and similar limitations—as a dangerous radical. He was certainly one of the people most responsible for the change in American public opinion that resulted in the 1963 international ban on above-ground testing. He received the Nobel Prize for peace in recognition of his efforts—from an international community that had admired him throughout, threatened as it felt itself from fallout experiments by the two major nuclear powers. His *No More War* (1958), written in this cause, is still a valuable primer on the nature of the three giant bombs of which we know—atomic, hydrogen, and thermonuclear—and of the effects of radiation on human beings. He was instrumental in securing the signatures of 52 Nobel laureates for the "Mainau Declaration of Nobel Laureates" in 1955, which ended: "In extreme danger no nation will deny itself the use of any weapon that scientific technology can produce. All nations must come to the decision to renounce force as a final resort of policy. If they are not prepared to do this they will cease to exist."

BOOKS BY PAULING

The Nature of the Chemical Bond and the Structure of Molecules and Crystals: An Introduction to Modern Structural Chemistry. Cornell Univ. Pr. 3d ed. 1960 $39.95

No More War. 1958. Dodd 1983 pap. $7.95; Greenwood repr. of 1962 ed. 1975 lib. bdg. $20.00

(and Peter Pauling). *Chemistry.* W. H. Freeman 1975 $13.95. "Although much is borrowed from the elder Pauling's texts, there is also much that is new in the way of recent advances, especially in biochemistry. Coverage of the Watson-Crick model and its ramifications is the clearest and most thorough this side of a course in biochemistry. The excitement of modern molecular biology, conveyed through excellent illustrations as well as text, will captivate any intelligent student with some bent in that direction" (*Choice*).

(and E. Bright Wilson). *Introduction to Quantum Mechanics with Applications to Chemistry.* Dover 1985 pap. $9.95. A classic text for chemists. Lucid for its kind, but heavily mathematical.

Vitamin C, the Common Cold, and the Flu. W. H. Freeman 1976 pap. $10.95. In this, his most controversial work, Pauling argues that massive doses of vitamin C will prevent these common maladies. Pauling's findings are disputed by many medical professionals.

(ed.). *Centennial Lectures.* Oregon State Univ. Pr. 1969 $8.95 pap. $6.95

BOOK ABOUT PAULING

White, Florence M. *Linus Pauling: Scientist and Crusader.* Walker 1980 $9.95

PRIESTLEY, JOSEPH. 1733–1804

Born in Leeds, England, Priestley received an education for the dissenting ministry. However, throughout his life, his religious views were far more liberal than those of his fellows, and so part of the time he earned his living as a schoolmaster and, later, as the librarian for Sir William Petty, the second Earl of Shelbourne. During those six years, Priestley systematically studied a variety of gases, including nitrogen oxides, ammonia, and oxygen. In 1774, he prepared and collected oxygen by heating mercuric oxide and collecting the gas over mercury. During separate experiments with mice and burning candles in closed systems, he noted that the "dephlogistonated air" or oxygen supported combustion and respiration better than air or nitrogen. Priestley was an amateur scientist; he focused much of his effort on the religious and political issues of late eighteenth-century England. During the Birmingham riots of 1791, he was a target of the mobs because of his liberal religious views. Finally, in 1794, he emigrated to the United States and for the last ten years of his life lived in Northumberland, Pennsylvania.

BOOKS BY PRIESTLEY

Autobiography of Joseph Priestley. Fairleigh Dickinson Univ. Pr. 1971 $20.00. "Starts . . . from the time of his birth, including a brief account of his family's background, and continues it in chronological order up to the time of his self-imposed exile in the United States. . . . [It] ends with a short account of the last few years before his death, given by his son. This book can be appreciated not only by historians of science but also by the general reader interested in Priestley or in the beginnings of Unitarianism" (*LJ*).

Considerations on the Doctrine of Phlogiston and the Decomposition of Water. Ed. by William Foster, Kraus Repr. repr. of 1929 ed. 1968 $20.00

Experiments and Observations on Different Kinds of Air. Kraus Repr. 3 vols. repr. of 1790 ed. $108.00

The History and Present State of Discoveries Relating to Vision, Light and Colours. Ed. by Bernard I. Cohen, Ayer 1981 lib. bdg. $70.00; Kraus Repr. repr. of 1772 ed. $90.00

The History and Present State of Electricity, with Original Experiments. Johnson Repr. 2 vols. 3d ed. repr. of 1975 ed. $46.00

A Scientific Autobiography of Joseph Priestley. MIT 1966 o.p. A good discussion of Priestley's scientific contributions with several letters from his correspondence with his friend Benjamin Franklin.

Priestley in America, 1794–1804. Ayer repr. of 1920 ed. 1980 lib. bdg. $16.00. Priestley's noteworthy experimental work was done nearly two decades before in England, but nevertheless this is an interesting tract.

BOOK ABOUT PRIESTLEY

Kieft, Lester, and Bennett R. Willeford, Jr., eds. *Joseph Priestley: Scientist, Theologian, and Metaphysician.* Bucknell Univ. Pr. 1980 $15.00. A collection of papers revealing the diverse interests of this man. "Three recognized authorities from Harvard University . . . give a renewed appreciation of the contributions of Joseph Priestley . . . Unitarian minister, theologian, teacher, historian, chemist, and physicist. . . . 'His life's objective,' says Erwin N. Hiebert [one of the contributors], 'was to generate a polymorphic synthesis of natural science and revealed religion.' To him 'religion and science were compatible domains' " (*Zygon*).

CHAPTER 11

Biology

Kathleen Kehoe Glass

The great tragedy of science—the slaying of a beautiful hypothesis, by an ugly fact.

—T. H. HUXLEY

Biology is the study of living things and the processes within them. Traditionally, biology is divided into two branches—zoology and botany. Each branch has further subdivisions according to the plant or animal studied. Recently areas of study in the biological sciences have been redefined. The specialties now correspond to different levels of structural organization of living organisms and the focus of the work is defined by the concepts and methods used.

The beginnings of biology informally date back to prehistoric times, with the observation and handling of plants and animals by man. As a systematic science, biology existed in ancient Egypt, Babylonia, and Greece. The decline of Greek civilization was followed by a long period of scientific inactivity, and a loss of codified knowledge. This period lasted until about the mid-seventeenth century, when the development of the microscope sparked an interest in the observation of cells and tissues, which now could be seen for the first time. The eighteenth century was characterized by the collection, classification, and analysis of exotic fauna and flora brought to Europe by the many expeditions of explorers. The nineteenth century saw the development of modern biology as we know it. The Darwinian theory of evolution had revolutionized biology and determined the course of that science for the next century.

During the first half of the twentieth century, Mendelian genetics dominated biological research. By the 1950s another revolution had taken place in biology—the discovery of deoxyribonucleic acid (DNA) and the growth of molecular biology.

Many researchers believe that we are now in another "Golden Age," as revolutionary and productive as the seventeenth and eighteenth centuries were, for the biological sciences. Advances made in biology are providing the basis for enormous progress in medicine. This is contrary to the earlier history of biology, when medicine provided the impetus and understanding that enabled the biological sciences to develop and progress.

As a result of the great activity in biological research, the literature is

306

vast and continually growing. More than 70 percent of the literature is highly technical, and is published in the form of journal articles. Fortunately, there are scientists and science writers who publish books that are meant for, or understandable to, the general reader. The general bibliography that follows contains reference books, and a representative group of recent titles from all the specialties of biological literature. (See also Chapter 12, Ecology and Environmental Science, and Chapter 13, Genetics, both in this volume.)

BIOLOGY

General Bibliography

Ahmadjian, Vernon, and Surindar Paracer. *Symbiosis: An Introduction to Biological Associations.* Univ. Pr. of New England 1986 text ed. $32.50. A good introduction to the concept of symbiosis in all life forms.

Bernischke, Kurt, and Andy Warhol. *Vanishing Animals.* Springer-Verlag 1986 $49.50. Fifteen chapters on animals belonging to endangered species, each concentrating on an animal's biology and ecology, with silk screens by Andy Warhol.

Bleier, Ruth. *Science and Gender: A Critique of Biology and Its Theories on Women.* Pergamon 1984 $12.50. A critique of the role that science has played in supporting the myth that women are biologically inferior. Bleier provides an objective background for the biological and evolutionary basis of sexual differences.

Bowler, Peter J. *The Eclipse of Darwinism: Anti-Darwinism Evolution Theories in the Decades Around 1900.* Johns Hopkins Univ. Pr. 1983 $30.00. "The 1982 centenary of Darwin's death renewed interest in the scientific thought of his day. . . . Bowler discusses the many alternate theories of the day, including Lamarckism, mutation theory, and others, introducing some of the noted scientists of the late 19th Century." (*LJ*).

Cairns-Smith, A. G. *Seven Clues to the Origin of Life: A Scientific Detective Story.* Cambridge Univ. Pr. 1985 $17.95. "A clear, readable overview of evolutionary thinking as it is applied to the origins of life that will appeal to the informed reader" (*LJ*).

Campbell, Neil A. *Biology.* Benjamin Cummings 1987 text ed. $39.95. Presents basic material in a meaningful way.

Catton, Chris, and James Grey. *Sex in Nature.* Facts on File 1985 $19.95. A popular introduction to reproductive biology.

Cohen, I. Bernard. *Revolution in Science.* Harvard Univ. Pr. (Belknap Pr.) 1985 $25.00. A wonderful introduction to the history of science, with exceptional coverage of the changes in biology brought about by Darwin's theories.

Dawkins, Richard. *The Blind Watchmaker: Why the Evidence of Evolution Reveals a Universe without Design.* Norton 1986 $18.95. "A lovely book. Original and lively it expounds the ins and outs of evolution with enthusiastic clarity, answering at every point the cavemen of creationism" (Isaac Asimov).

Depew, David J., and Bruce H. Weber. *Evolution at the Crossroads: The New Philosophy of Science.* MIT 1985 $25.00. A collection of essays by ten acclaimed biologists, addressing the conceptual side of their work. "Knowledgeable readers will find this challenging and worthwhile" (*LJ*).

Douglas, Matthew M. *The Lives of Butterflies.* Univ. of Michigan Pr. 1986 $45.00. "The perfect book for someone who wants to learn about butterflies without becoming bogged down in the technical literature. It is not long; it is written in very readable and lucid English; and the reader is referred to the literature at every point in case one wishes to pursue a topic further. Glossary of terms; 18-page bibliography; species index; subject index" (*Choice*).

Dunne, Peter. *Tales of a Low Rent Birder*. Rutgers Univ. Pr. 1986 $15.95. An amusing and engaging collection of reminiscences of interest to all bird-watchers.

Eldredge, Niles. *Life Pulse: Episodes from the Story of the Fossil Record*. Facts on File 1987 $19.95. "Eldredge (and his frequent collaborator S. J. Gould) may be approaching Darwin himself for the total number of words produced concerning topics relating to evolution. This spicily written volume concentrates on paleontological vignettes that, for the most part, emphasize the apparent cyclical phenomenon of widespread periodic extinctions" (*Choice*).

Fausto-Sterling, Anne. *Myths of Gender: Biological Theories about Men and Women*. Basic Bks. 1986 $18.95. Presents evidence to support Fausto-Sterling's contention that the biological differences between men and women are trivial.

Fisk, Erma J. *Parrots' Wood*. Norton 1985 $15.95. A lively and well-written account of an 80-year-old amateur ornithologist's expedition to Belize.

Forsyth, Adrian, and Ken Miyata. *Tropical Nature: Life and Death in the Rain Forests of Central and South America*. Scribner 1984 $17.95. "An introduction to the natural history of the New World tropical forests that provides the most recent information available on tropical biology. The authors, who did most of their field study in Costa Rica and Ecuador, give an overview of essential ecological features of rain forests, with closer examination of topics they found particularly interesting, epiphytes, the forest floor, army ants, etc." (*LJ*).

Garstand, William. *Larval Forms and Other Zoological Verses*. Univ. of Chicago Pr. 1985 pap. $5.95. A collection of rhymes and writing about phylogeny and ontogeny.

Gormley, Gerald. *A Dolphin Summer*. Taplinger 1985 $14.95. Traces the story of the first eight months of a dolphin's life, basing the story on biological fact and weaving in interpretive material on behavior and feelings.

Gould, Stephen Jay. *Ever Since Darwin*. Norton 1977 $14.95 pap. $4.95. The first of Gould's collections of essays for the general reader. This volume won him acclaim as a writer of popular science.

———. *The Flamingo's Smile: Reflections in Natural History*. Norton 1985 $17.95 1987 pap. $8.95. This collection of Gould's essays on evolutionary theory is well written and thought provoking. "Quirkiness and meaning are my not so contradictory themes."

———. *Hen's Teeth and Horse's Toes: Further Reflections in Natural History*. Norton 1983 $15.50 pap. $5.95. Another excellent collection of essays by Gould on evolution and sundry matters. "The essays range widely, from a discussion of the evolution of the Hershey bar or an appraisal of Teilhard de Chardin's role in the Piltdown forgery to the parental behavior of Galapagos Island boobies" (*LJ*).

Grant, Peter R. *Ecology and Evolution of Darwin's Finches*. Princeton Univ. Pr. 1986 $55.00 pap. $22.50. "Can anyone with an interest in biological science not have heard of Darwin's finches? . . . Because they are so central to evolutionary theory, numerous studies of behavioral, morphological, and biochemical aspects of their life histories have been made. . . . The volume provides a description of the [Galápagos] islands, and the characteristics of the finches with emphasis on their beak size and shape, the two features critical to Grant's long-term study of their evolution" (*Choice*).

Griffin, Robert D. *The Biology Coloring Book*. Harper 1986 pap. $9.95. A step-by-step presentation of the fundamental concepts of biology, with diagrams for the reader to color. The author believes that coloring the diagrams aids in the retention of information, as well as entertaining the reader.

Hay, John. *The Immortal Wilderness.* Norton 1986 $14.95. Twenty well-written essays on the natural world and its creatures, including man.

Heinrich, Bernd. *In a Patch of Fireweed.* Harvard Univ. Pr. 1984 $18.50. Discusses what motivates nature studies in general and his own entomological interests and experiences, in particular.

Janovy, John, Jr. *On Becoming a Biologist.* [*Series on the Professions*] Harper 1986 pap. $6.95. A very readable book about life in the biological sciences. "Provides a realistic view of its topic" (*LJ*).

Kanigel, Robert. *Apprentice to Genius: The Making of a Scientific Dynasty.* Macmillan 1986 $19.95. Clearly written book about several outstanding neuroscientists and their mentors. The general reader will have no trouble grasping the biologic principles that are discussed in the context of the scientist's work.

Keeton, William, and James L. Gould. *Biological Science.* Norton 4th ed. 1986 text ed. $36.95. This lucid and well-organized text is the standard by which new biology textbooks are judged.

Kurten, Bjorn. *How to Deep Freeze a Mammoth.* Columbia Univ. Pr. 1986 $16.95. A collection of 14 graceful essays on prehistoric life. The title is derived from the essay of a bison discovered in Alaska in 1979 that had been frozen 36,000 years ago.

La Bastille, Anne. *Women and Wilderness.* Sierra 1984 pap. $8.95. "The first part of the book explains how American women initially experienced the wilds.... The second part deals with 15 biographies of modern outdoorswomen. Among these are a caver, an Alaskan homesteader, a hunter, a zoologist, a white-water rafter and such notable personalities as Dr. Eugenie Clark, the 'shark lady,' and author Margaret Murie" (*SLJ*).

Lawrence, Gale. *A Field Guide to the Familiar.* Prentice-Hall 1984 pap. $9.95. One in a series of guides designed for the amateur naturalist. The book is organized by seasons and the author presents the fauna and flora that characterize each time of the year.

Levins, Richard, and Richard Lewontin. *The Dialectical Biologist.* Harvard Univ. Pr. 1985 $20.00. Essays selected to illustrate dialectical thinking. Written for biologists, but with careful reading could be enjoyed and valuable to the informed nonspecialist.

Lopez, Barry. *Arctic Dreams: Imagination and Desire in a Northern Landscape.* Bantam 1985 $4.95. "Lopez presents a whole series of raptures and riffs on the subject of musk oxen, ivory gulls, white foxes, polar bears, icebergs and sea currents" (*N.Y. Times Bk. Review*).

Luria, Salvador E. *A Slot Machine, A Broken Test Tube.* Harper 1984 $17.95 1985 pap. $6.95. "Forthright and appealing memoir [of the] pioneering molecular biologist ... the sections on his work and on serendipity in the scientific process are particularly engrossing" (*LJ*).

———. *Thirty-Six Lectures in Biology.* MIT 1975 $19.50. A collection of the author's classic lectures on biology and genetics.

Luria, Salvador E., Stephen Jay Gould, and Sam Singer. *A View of Life.* Benjamin Cummings 1981 text ed. $37.95. A fine introductory textbook for general biology written by three distinguished scientists—a microbiologist, a paleontologist, and a physician.

McGowan, Chris. *In the Beginning: A Scientist Shows Why the Creationists Are Wrong.* Prometheus Bks. 1984 pap. $10.95. McGowan very fairly works through the areas of dispute between creationists and evolutionists. The book is written with great clarity in a style appropriate for the general reader.

Maienschein, Jane. *Defining Biology: Lectures from the 1890's*. Harvard Univ. Pr. 1986 $27.50. A collection of ten lectures from the 1890s that were delivered at the Woods Hole, Massachusetts, research center by famous biologists. An introduction puts each lecture's content in the perspective of the times. Includes photographs of each lecturer.

May, John, and Michael Martin. *The Book of the Beasts*. Viking 1983 $12.95. Discusses unusual characteristics of different species of animals, with an emphasis on animal behavior. "Both entertaining and educational, the book will be enjoyed by a wide, diverse audience" (*LJ*).

Mayr, Ernst. *The Growth of Biological Thought: Diversity, Evolution, and Inheritance*. Harvard Univ. Pr. 1982 pap. $12.95. A classic work on the history of biology, its theories, and the philosophical views that have developed within the discipline.

Medawar, Peter. *Memoir of a Thinking Radish: An Autobiography*. Oxford 1986 $17.95. "In this autobiography the Nobel-prize winning scientist provides a witty and discerning view of biological research" (*LJ*).

Medawar, Peter, and J. S. Medawar. *Aristotle to Zoos: A Philosophical Dictionary of Biology*. Harvard Univ. Pr. 1983 $20.00. Not a dictionary in the usual sense, this is a book for browsing, with descriptions and commentary on biological phenomena and concepts.

Monaghan, Charles A. *The Reluctant Naturalist: An Unnatural Field Guide to the Natural World*. Atheneum 1984 $10.95. A humorous guide to nature in the familiar environments of backyards and nearby woods.

Montagu, Ashley, ed. *Science and Creationism*. Oxford 1984 pap. $19.95. This collection of essays includes contributions by such notable scientists as Isaac Asimov and Stephen Jay Gould. The essays attempt to refute the creationist viewpoint and take a strong stand against the teaching of creationism in the public schools.

Morgan, Elaine. *The Descent of Woman: A New Edition*. Souvenir Pr. 1985 $20.00. "Morgan's book was enjoyed by many, welcomed as a breath of fresh air by feminists and was found stimulating by at least some evolutionary biologists" (*Nature*).

Morowitz, Harold J. *Mayonnaise and the Origin of Life*. Berkeley 1986 pap. $3.95. "Morowitz is a sage celebrant at heart and we share his pleasure as he contemplates the beauty of biochemistry, mathematics, beetles, bacteria" (*PW*).

Olby, Robert. *The Origins of Mendelism*. Univ. of Chicago Pr. rev. ed. 1985 pap. $14.95. A revised and updated edition of Olby's classic work on the history of genetics and evolution.

Page, Jake. *Pastorale: A Natural History of Sorts*. Norton 1985 $13.95. A collection of essays about nature and natural phenomena, written in a comfortable style.

Preston, Douglas J. *Dinosaurs in the Attic: An Excursion into the American Museum of Natural History*. St. Martin's 1986 $18.95. A charming book, which provides a fascinating insider's view of the collectors and collections, the explorers and the expeditions, that were instrumental in amassing the museum's treasures.

Purcell, Rosamund Wolff, and Stephen Jay Gould. *Illuminations: A Bestiary*. Norton 1985 $35.00. A beautiful work, composed of Purcell's photographs of fossil specimens accompanied by an elegant text by Stephen Jay Gould.

Purves, William K., and Gordon H. Orians. *Life: The Science of Biology*. Sinauer 2d rev. ed 1987 text ed. $39.95 workbook $14.95. A good introductory text to all of biology.

Quammen, David. *Natural Acts: A Sidelong View of Science and Nature*. Schocken

1985 $16.95. "Well-informed, witty, irreverent and sometimes outrageous" (*Quarterly Review of Biology*).

Re, Richard Noel. *Bioburst: The Impact of Modern Biology on the Affairs of Man*. Louisiana State Univ. Pr. 1986 $19.95. An interesting description of the advances made by modern biology and the resulting impact on medicine, agriculture, and technology.

Ricketts, Edwards F., and others. *Between Pacific Tides*. Stanford Univ. Pr. 1986 $29.50. A well-written presentation of the organisms that live in the intertidal zone of Pacific waters.

Roessler, Carl. *Coral Kingdoms*. Abrams 1986 $35.00. This around-the-world undersea journey has 250 brilliant color photographs of coral reefs and the life around them.

Schullery, Paul. *Mountain Time*. Schocken 1984 $17.95. Contains 21 short, well-written essays on the natural history of Yellowstone National Park.

Shapiro, Robert. *Origins: A Skeptic's Guide to the Creation of Life on Earth*. Bantam 1987 pap. $9.95; Summit Bks. 1986 $17.95. "Shapiro, a professor of chemistry and an expert on DNA research, takes the reader on a quest to explain 'what science does and does not understand about how life first began.' Rejecting both the belief that a supernatural power endowed life and also that life evolved from clay, Shapiro describes other explanations and manages to entertain and educate in the process" (*LJ*).

Shaw, Evelyn, and Joan Darling. *Female Strategies*. Walker 1985 $14.95. "*Female Strategies* is an interesting, sometimes entertaining book, and the authors' points are generally valid ones that merit presentation to a popular audience" (*Quarterly Review of Biology*).

Skutch, Alexander F. *Life Ascending*. Univ. of Texas Pr. 1985 $22.50 pap. $10.95. An overview of "life ascending" from its simplest beginnings to man. Chosen by *Library Journal* as one of the best sci-tech books of 1985.

Smith, John Maynard. *The Problems of Biology*. Oxford 1986 $16.25. An interesting presentation of the fundamental ideas of biology and its major unsolved problems.

Swain, Roger B. *Earthly Pleasures: Tales from a Biologist's Garden*. Penguin 1985 pap. $5.95. An amusing and informative collection of essays that cover an unusual range of subjects regarding plants, animals, and natural phenomena.

Thomas, Lewis. *Late Night Thoughts on Listening to Mahler's Ninth Symphony*. Bantam 1984 $5.95; Viking 1983 $12.95. "An especially interesting chapter is concerned with the 'Seven Wonders'—not the usual Seven Wonders of the World but with such wonders as a certain bacterial species, a species of beetle, a virus, an olfactory receptor cell, the termite, a human child, and the greatest wonder of all: the plant Earth. The short chapters of the book reflect the usual 'Thomas style'—captivating, unusual, provocative. The book is again meant for the curious reader who appreciates original, interesting, and probing writing mainly in the area of science" (*Choice*).

——. *The Lives of a Cell: Notes of a Biology Watcher*. Bantam 1975 pap. $3.95; Penguin 1978 pap. $3.95; Viking 1974 $10.95 pap. $3.95. "A brilliant but humble scientific mind is at work in this collection of 29 short essays by the president of the Sloan-Kettering Center for Cancer Research. Thomas can look at recent biological discoveries on tiny microorganisms and relate them to the totality of human society. He has perceptive and surprising things to say. . . . A National Book Award winner" (*PW*).

——. *Medusa and the Snail: More Notes of a Biology Watcher*. Bantam 1979 $3.95. Another collection of engrossing essays on nature by Lewis Thomas. "In essay after essay, Thomas shows us that all forms of life are interconnected, especially *Homo sapiens*. . . . A leading figure in the medical establishment [he] blames our superexpensive health care system on 'societal propaganda,' defends the pre-medical curriculum's de-emphasis of liberal arts, dismisses laetrile and acu-puncture as 'magic' and calls for massive basic biological research. His essays, even when arguable, charm with their easy grace, digestibility, wit" (*PW*)

Trefil, James S. *The Unexpected Vista: A Physicist's View of Nature*. Scribner 1983 $14.95. An interesting and unusual volume, as a physicist contemplates nature.

Truett, Joe C., and Daniel W. Lay. *Land of Bears and Honey: A Natural History of East Texas*. Univ. of Texas Pr. 1984 $12.95. A beautifully written book presenting biotypes in vignettes over periods of time, from American Indian days to the present.

Wallace, David Rains. *The Untamed Garden and Other Personal Essays*. Ohio State Univ. Pr. 1986 $15.95. The author has written 26 essays on all forms of natural life from minnows to coyotes.

Weissmann, Gerald. *The Woods Hole Cantata: Essays on Science and Society*. Dodd 1985 $14.95. "Written by a man who is both a physician and an experimental marine biologist, these 18 essays aimed at general readers explore issues touch-ing on modern biology and the inadequacies of our social organization" (*LJ*).

Wertheim, Anne. *The Intertidal Wilderness*. Sierra 1985 $25.00. "The wonderful photo-graphs of the plant and animal life in the Pacific Northwest intertidal zone deserve recognition on their own, but each is enriched by accompanying text which spells out the biological principle depicted" (*LJ*).

Wolken, Jerome J. *Light and Life Processes*. Van Nostrand 1986 $39.95. Wolken explores light in relationship to living things and physiologic processes. A com-prehensive overview of photobiology.

Young, Louise B. *The Unfinished Universe*. Simon & Schuster 1985 pap. $8.95. "Her book is informative, intelligent and sensitive. It was the force of Mrs. Young's imagery, not her logic and theories, that increased my awe of nature as I read" (*N.Y. Times Bk. Review*).

Zimmer, Kevin J. *The Western Bird Watcher: An Introduction to Birding in the United States*. Prentice-Hall 1985 $21.95. A beginning guide for the amateur ornitholo-gist.

Reference Books

Abercrombie, M., C. J. Hickman, and M. L. Johnson. *The Penguin Dictionary of Biology*. Viking 2d ed. 1977 $6.95. A good dictionary for the student or general reader.

Adelman, George. *Encyclopedia of Neuroscience*. Birkhauser 2 vols. 1987 $125.00. This encyclopedia covers all the fields of study in neuroscience and is a valuable tool for specialists and nonspecialists alike. The contributors include distin-guished researchers, such as Francis O. Schmitt.

Allaby, Michael. *Oxford Dictionary of Natural History*. Oxford 1985 $26.00. An excel-lent dictionary for the layperson, with 12,000 concise, jargon-free definitions. "This dictionary will clearly help us to better understand our natural world, and will make it possible for us to communicate that understanding to others" (*Choice*).

Ammirati, Joseph F., James A. Traquair, and Paul A. Horgen. *Poisonous Mushrooms of the Northern United States and Canada*. Univ. of Minnesota Pr. 1985 $75.00. A field guide to poisonous mushroom species for the botanist and the amateur naturalist.

Anderson, Sydney, and J. Knox Jones, Jr., eds. *Recent Mammals of the World.* Wiley 1984 $54.95. An invaluable reference book on mammalogy that contains authoritative summaries on 21 orders and 131 families of living mammals.

Asimov, Isaac. *Asimov's New Guide to Science.* Basic Bks. 1984 $29.95. "An updating of the author's 1972 version, consisting of a series of chapters collectively covering the physical sciences, the biological sciences, and mathematics" (*LJ*).

Audubon Society Field Guide to North American Fishes, Whales and Dolphins. Knopf 1983 $13.50. An excellent identification guide.

Banister, Keith, and Andrew Campbell. *Encyclopedia of Aquatic Life.* Facts on File 1985 $35.00. This illustrated encyclopedia surveys animals of many species, fresh- and salt-water habitats. "Although the ground has been covered before, the excellent presentation makes this book special.... The photographs are clear, have informative captions, and frequently not only show the animal but illustrate behavior. The drawn and painted illustrations depict body features in a way often impossible in photographs.... One of the best encyclopedias on this topic" (*LJ*).

Barnes, R. S. K. *A Synoptic Classification of Living Organisms.* Blackwell Scientific 1984 $14.95. A pocket guide to the classification of living things, including kingdoms, phyla, classes, and orders of plant and animal life.

Barrett, James, ed. *Contemporary Classics in Plant, Animal and Environmental Sciences.* Institute for Scientific Information 1986 $39.95. This is a collection of classic science articles, which includes a useful bibliography containing many references to recent botanical works.

Barrett, Paul H., and others, eds. *A Concordance to Darwin's "Expressions of Emotions in Man and Animals."* Cornell Univ. Pr. 1986 $45.00. A thorough and invaluable reference to Darwin's *Expressions of Emotions in Man and Animals.* Each of Darwin's words is indexed with references to every occurrence in that work.

Bull, John. *Audubon Society Guide to North American Birds: Eastern Region.* Knopf 1977 $13.95. The standard field guide to eastern birds.

Campbell, Bruce, and Elizabeth Lack, eds. *A Dictionary of Birds.* Buteo 1985 $75.00. This dictionary lists bird species and provides extensive information, photographs, and illustrations for each species. Short bibliographies and biographies of amateur and professional ornithologists are included.

Coombs, J. *Dictionary of Biotechnology.* Elsevier 1986 $39.50. An important aid to understanding the terminology of the recently developed area of biotechnology, that field of biology, especially genetics, which applies biological theory, method, and data to industrial and technological problems.

Corbet, G. B., and J. E. Hill. *A World List of Mammalian Species.* Facts on File 2d ed. 1986 $56.50. A very useful list that includes more than 4,000 species of living and recently extinct mammals giving Latin names, common names, and habitat for each one.

Farrand, John, Jr., ed. *Audubon Society Master Guide to Birding.* Knopf 1984 3 vols. ea. $13.95 set $41.85. Vol. 1, *Loons-Sandpipers;* Vol. 2, *Gulls-Dippers;* Vol. 3, *Old World Warblers-Sparrows.* A well-organized and comprehensive work on American birds for serious bird-watchers.

Fielding, Alan. *Computing for Biologists.* Benjamin Cummings 1985 $22.50. A guide to writing BASIC programs for use in analyzing biological data.

Freeman, Richard Burke. *British Natural History Books, 1495–1900: A Handlist.* Archon 1977 o.p. Lists all the books written on the fauna and flora of Britain, Ireland, and the Channel Islands during this time period.

Friday, Adrian, and David S. Ingram, eds. *Cambridge Encyclopedia of the Life Sciences.* Cambridge Univ. Pr. 1985 $45.00. This excellent encyclopedia, which covers all the life forms in authoritative and well-written articles, is illustrated with fine drawings, micrographs, and photographs.

Frodin, D. G. *Guide to the Standard Floras of the World.* Cambridge Univ. Pr. 1984 $175.00. An annotated bibliography of standard botanical works, including books written up to 1980.

Frost, Darrel R. *Amphibian Species of the World: A Taxonomic and Geographical Reference.* Assn. of Systematics Collections 1985 $85.00. The most authoritative guide to amphibian life forms. This book includes 4,014 species giving the scientific name, locality, distribution, protected status, and authority.

Gray, Peter. *The Encyclopedia of the Biological Sciences.* Van Nostrand 2d ed. 1970 $59.50. In spite of its age, this encyclopedia is still a fine reference work for the biological sciences.

Grzimek, Bernhard. *Grzimek's Animal Life Encyclopedia.* Van Nostrand 1974 o.p. A comprehensive encyclopedia of animal life in 13 volumes. Volume 1 covers lower animals; Volume 2, insects; Volume 3, mollusks and echinoderms; Volume 4, fishes; Volume 5, fishes and amphibia; Volume 6, reptiles; Volumes 7–9, birds; Volumes 10–13, mammals.

——. *Grzimek's Encyclopedia of Evolution.* Van Nostrand 1976 o.p. Includes articles covering paleontology, paleogeology, and the evolution of man.

Hancock, James, and James Kushlon. *The Heron's Handbook.* Croon Helm 1984 $20.00. "A work of major importance to bird biologists and conservationists. Birdwatchers will find it a highly readable guide, which will not only aid in identification but introduce the reader to a detailed natural history of the heron family" (*Quarterly Review of Biology*).

Harding, Keith A., and R. G. Welch. *Venomous Snakes of the World: A Checklist.* Pergamon 1980 $52.50. This checklist is organized taxonomically. It gives descriptions, geographical distribution, and original description reference for each species.

Harrison, Peter. *Seabirds: An Identification Guide.* Houghton Mifflin 1984 $29.95. "A definitive guide to more than 300 species of seabirds found the world over, this volume is designed to become a classic" (*LJ*). The guide includes color photographs, line drawings, distribution maps, and keys to the identification of each species.

Herbert, W. J., and P. C. Wilkinson, eds. *A Dictionary of Immunology.* Blackwell Scientific 2d ed. 1977 $28.50. The dictionary includes a broad variety of terms used in the immunological literature that are of use in biology, biochemistry, and immunology.

Hodge, Walter H., and Les Line. *Audubon Society Book of Wildflowers.* Abrams 1978 $50.00. A beautifully illustrated guide to wild flowers, a fine coffee-table book.

Holt, John G., Noel R. Krieg, and Peter H. A. Sneath, eds. *Bergey's Manual of Systematic Bacteriology.* Williams & Wilkins 2 vols. 1984–86 ea. $82.50. This is the definitive manual of bacterial taxonomy and provides uniform conventions for the naming of newly discovered organisms. For the nonscientist it is extremely useful as a source of information on specific types of bacteria.

Hora, Bayard. *Oxford Encyclopedia of Trees of the World.* Oxford 1971 $27.50. An introduction to trees for the general reader. The book includes information on 2,200 species, including color photographs to aid in the identification of trees.

Hoyt, Erich. *Whale Watcher's Handbook.* Doubleday 1984 $12.95. A fine field guide for the novice observer, the book includes a worldwide list of species, their locations, and drawings to aid in identification.

Jolivet, Pierre. *Insects and Plants: Parallel Evolution and Adaptations.* Flora and

Fauna 1986 pap. $19.95. "This fascinating handbook covers in an abbreviated manner almost all types of insect and plant relationships. . . . Some of the topics discussed are diets and food selection, biological control of weeds, galls, carnivorous plants, myrmecophilous and myrmechorous plants, and insect pollination" (*Choice*).

Kavanagh, Michael. *A Complete Guide to Monkeys, Apes and Other Primates.* Viking 1984 $19.20. A useful reference guide containing a photograph of every living genus of primate and a series of distribution maps for each genus.

King, Wayne. *Audubon Society Field Guide to North American Reptiles and Amphibians.* Knopf 1979 $13.50. A reliable field guide to reptiles and amphibians.

Kress, Stephen W. *Audubon Society Guide to Attracting Birds.* Scribner 1985 $24.95. Tips on how to attract local bird species to your yard or windowsill.

Kulik, Stephen, and others. *The Audubon Society Field Guide to the Natural Places of the Northeast.* Pantheon 2 vols. 1984 ea. pap. $11.95. "These volumes aim to provide information to enhance a reader's enjoyment and exploration of selected sites in the northeast, organized by geological and ecological region. After comments on the geology, vegetation, and wildlife found in the region, practical information is provided about each site" (*LJ*).

Lampe, Kenneth F., and Mary Ann McCann. *AMA Handbook of Poisonous and Injurious Plants.* Amer. Medical Assn. 1985 $24.95. A useful field guide to poisonous plants and their toxic effects on humans.

Landau, Sidney, and others, eds. *International Dictionary of Medicine and Biology.* Wiley 3 vols. 1986 $395.00. The most extensive dictionary of medicine and biology currently available (more than 159,000 definitions and 30,000 etymologies). Disciplines covered include cell biology, anatomy, botany, ecology, biochemistry, genetics, histology, microbiology, and marine biology, among others.

Leatherwood, Stephen, and Randall R. Reeves. *The Sierra Club Handbook of Whales and Dolphins.* Random 1984 $12.95. The handbook was written by two biologists and includes a wealth of information on the many dolphin and whale species. This is an excellent guide for learning how to identify these animals in the field.

Levy, Charles K. *A Field Guide to the Dangerous Animals of North America.* Stephen Greene Pr. 1983 pap. $9.95. This volume is illustrated with photographs and pictures of dangerous animals of the American wilderness.

Lillanger, David B. *A Field Manual to the Ferns and Fern Allies of the United States and Canada.* Smithsonian 1985 $45.00 pap. $29.95. An excellent field guide to ferns and related plants, with ample color photographs to aid in identifying ferns.

Lincoff, Gary F. *Audubon Society Field Guide to North American Mushrooms.* Knopf 1981 $13.50. A guide to edible and inedible mushroom species.

Little, Elbert I., Jr., ed. *Audubon Field Guide to Trees: Eastern Edition.* Knopf 1980 $13.50. An authoritative guide to trees of the eastern region of the United States.

———. *Audubon Field Guide to Trees: Western Edition.* Knopf 1980 $13.50. A useful and authoritative guide to western American trees.

Little, R. John, and C. Eugene Jones. *A Dictionary of Botany.* Van Nostrand 1980 $18.50. The dictionary includes concise definitions of 5,500 botanical terms.

Locquin, Marcel, and Maurice Langeron. *Handbook of Microscopy.* Butterworth 1983 text ed. $130.00. An introduction to microscopes and their use. The book includes the types of light and electron microscopes, instruction for specimen preparation, and general methodology.

Macdonald, David, ed. *The Encyclopedia of Mammals.* Facts on File 1984 $45.00. A comprehensive reference book to mammalia, including a vast amount of detailed information on the major mammalian orders. The 700 articles by research scientists are well written and elegantly illustrated.

Macura, P., ed. *Elsevier's Dictionary of Botany II: General Terms.* Elsevier 1982 $117.00. A polyglot dictionary of botanical, horticultural, agricultural, and taxonomic terminology in English, French, German, and Russian.

Martin, E. A. *A Dictionary of the Life Sciences.* Macmillan 2d ed. rev. 1984 $25.00. A concise, authoritative, and well-written dictionary, illustrated with helpful line drawings, diagrams, and charts.

Meinkoth, Norman A. *Audubon Society Field Guide to North American Seashore Creatures.* Knopf 1981 $13.50. A standard guide to fiddler crabs, snails, and such.

Milne, Lorus. *Audubon Society Field Guide to Insects and Spiders.* Knopf 1980 $13.50. The standard field guide to insects and spiders.

National Academy of Sciences Staff. *Frontiers in Science and Technology: A Selected Outlook.* W. H. Freeman 1983 $32.95 pap. $16.95. "Third in a series of reports on the five-year outlook for science and technology. . . . Areas in which future developments are considered particularly important are studied, including genetic engineering, hormones, psychobiology, fluid turbulence, lasers, robots, and others. . . . Brief bibliographies are provided for each area" (*LJ*).

Nelson, Joseph S. *Fishes of the World.* Wiley 2d ed. 1984 $44.95. An updated and revised edition of the excellent 1977 work. The book includes basic information and many photographs of all types of fishes.

Parker, Sybil P. *McGraw-Hill Concise Encyclopedia of Science and Technology.* McGraw-Hill 1984 $95.00. A good reference source for information on major biological concepts, structures, organisms, and other basic questions.

Perrins, Christopher M., and Alex L. Middleton, eds. *The Encyclopedia of Birds.* Facts on File 1985 $45.00. "Provides succinct, up-to-date coverage of the world's birds, organized by family and groups of closely related families. . . . Superb color photographs are used to illustrate behaviors and skills, and are complemented by expert line drawings and color paintings" (*LJ*).

Peterson, Roger Tory. *Peterson's First Guide to Birds.* Houghton Mifflin 1986 pap. $3.95. A reprint of the well-known bird guide.

———. *Peterson's First Guide to Wildflowers.* Houghton Mifflin 1986 pap. $3.95. A reprint of Peterson's well-known wildflower guide.

Pyle, Robert M., ed. *Audubon Society Field Guide to North American Butterflies.* Knopf 1981 $13.50. An excellent field guide for butterfly watchers.

———. *The Audubon Society Handbook for Butterfly Watchers.* Scribner 1984 $17.95. "A confirmed butterfly watcher shares his knowledge. . . . Entertaining anecdotes illustrate his points as Pyle moves through chapters on butterfly biology, watching equipment, names and identification, field notes, behavior, butterfly gardening, and conservation, to name a few" (*LJ*).

Rehder, Harold A. *Audubon Society Field Guide to North American Seashells.* Knopf 1981 $13.50. An invaluable companion for beachcombing.

Ride, W. D. L., and others. *International Code of Zoological Nomenclature.* Sabbot-Natural History Bks. 3d ed. 1985 $26.50. The international standard for nomenclature conventions, which provides maximum universality and continuity in the naming and classification of animals.

Roe, Keith E., and Richard G. Frederick. *Dictionary of Theoretical Concepts in Biology.* Scarecrow Pr. 1981 $24.00. A very helpful reference book for the general reader. Major concepts and scientific "laws" are listed by the names used to identify them in the biological literature. A bibliographic citation accompanies each entry.

Scott, James A. *The Butterflies of North America: A Natural History and Field Guide.* Stanford Univ. Pr. 1986 $49.50. The author fulfills his purpose "to write a book that would give all the important natural history information for all the species of North American butterflies in a scientifically accurate form, but would present it in such a fashion that it is accessible to everyone."

Simon, James E., Alena F. Chadwick, and Lyle E. Craker. *Herbs: An Indexed Bibliography, 1971–1980.* Archon 1984 $69.50. This bibliography provides easy entry into the literature on herbs. It includes works dealing with the chemistry, botany, horticulture, culinary uses, and pharmacological uses of herbs.

Sims, R. W., ed. *Animal Identification: A Reference Guide.* Wiley 3 vols. 1980 $90.00. These volumes were compiled for the purpose of providing the nonspecialist with a way to identify any animal from any part of the world.

Singleton, Paul, and Diana Sainsbury. *Dictionary of Microbiology.* Wiley 1978 $97.95. Includes concise definitions for the subfields of microbiology, including bacteriology, mycology, and virology.

Smith, Roger C., W. Malcolm Reid, and Arlene E. Luchsinger. *Guide to the Literature of the Biological Sciences.* Burgess 9th ed. 1980 $9.95. A good guide to the literature for students and general readers. The book includes coverage of primary and secondary sources, ready reference sources, databases, thesis preparation, and thesis writing.

Sugden, Auden. *Longman Illustrated Dictionary of Botany: The Elements of Plant Science Illustrated and Defined.* Longman 1984 pap. $6.00. This dictionary covers all of botany: morphology, plant physiology, evolution, ecology, and classification. It is illustrated with extensive charts, tables, and diagrams to facilitate the understanding of the concepts that are defined.

Terres, John K., ed. *The Audubon Society Encyclopedia of North American Birds.* Knopf 1980 $75.00. A comprehensive one-volume encyclopedia on the birds of North America with contributions by distinguished ornithologists.

Thompson, Ida, ed. *The Audubon Society Field Guide to North American Fossils.* Knopf 1982 $13.50. An excellent tool for the novice interested in identifying fossils. Photographs (many in color), maps, and line drawings are included.

Toothill, Elizabeth. *The Facts on File Dictionary of Biology.* Facts on File 2d ed. 1984 $16.95 pap. $5.95. An excellent dictionary with comprehensive coverage of biological terminology and concise, lucid definitions.

Toothill, Elizabeth, and Stephen Blackmore. *The Facts on File Dictionary of Botany.* Facts on File 1984 $16.95 pap. $5.95. An excellent dictionary of botanical terms for the scientist or general reader.

Udvardy, M. D. *Audubon Society Guide to North American Birds: Western Region.* Knopf 1977 $13.95. The standard field guide to western birds.

U.S. Department of Agriculture Soil Conservation Service. *National List of Scientific Plant Names.* USGPO 2 vols. 2d ed. 1982 consult publisher for information. This helpful list includes species names, plant distribution, and other general information for plants of the United States and Canada.

Wells, Susan M., Robert M. Pyle, and N. Mark Collins. *The IUCN Invertebrate Red Data Book.* Unipub 1983 text ed. $20.00. Living invertebrate species are listed and each entry contains a description, a summary of the organism's habits, distribution, and conservation status.

Whitfield, Phillip, ed. *Macmillan Illustrated Animal Encyclopedia.* Macmillan 1984 $35.00. A good ready-reference tool for the general reader, this volume provides the common name, Latin name, range, habitat, and size of each animal as well as pictures for identification. A short summary for each species includes breeding habits, diet, and other general information.

BOTANY

Botany is the study of all plant life—marine, terrestrial, one-celled, many-celled, living, and fossilized. Botanists study individual plants and groups of plants, in relationship to each other and the environment.

Early work in botany consisted primarily of collecting, describing, and classifying plants. Modern botanical science had evolved by the nineteenth century, when the first work in plant cell biology was done and Mendelian genetics was rediscovered and pursued by botanists. At this time, the experimental method was employed in plant physiology and botanists began to use biochemical techniques.

Today, a new world of botanical research is developing in the field of biotechnology. Molecular biologists are pursuing research that could revolutionize agriculture. Through genetic engineering, plants have already been developed that are resistant to specific crop diseases and herbicides. Other problems that researchers are studying are ways to improve the nutritional quality of certain plants, to increase plant size, to heighten different species' resistance to drought, and to make crops more resistant to fungal diseases.

Andrews, Jean. *Peppers: The Domesticated Capiseums.* Univ. of Texas Pr. 1984 $35.00. A well-researched and beautifully illustrated volume that encompasses the history, biology, speciation, and cooking of peppers.

Barth, Friedrich G. *Insects and Flowers: Biology of a Partnership.* Princeton Univ. Pr. 1985 $35.00. This book on basic pollination biology is written in a sprightly and engaging manner, and is illustrated with excellent color plates, line drawings, and electron micrographs.

Brookes, John. *The Indoor Garden Book.* Crown 1986 $24.95. A general guide to house plants for apartment or house dwellers. A well-organized, informative, and well-illustrated book.

Burgess, Jeremy. *An Introduction to Plant Cell Development.* Cambridge Univ. Pr. 1985 text ed. $39.95. A good introductory textbook for undergraduates or the nonspecialist.

Cox, Donald D. *Common Flowering Plants of the Northeast: Their Natural History and Uses.* State Univ. of NY Pr. 1984 $29.95. A good source of general information on the flowering plants of the American Northeast.

Cumminghan, Isabel Shipley. *Frank N. Meyer: Plant Hunter in Asia.* Iowa State Univ. Pr. 1984 $29.95. Meyer was a true explorer and a rugged individualist who devoted his life to the collection of new plant material. This well-written book documents the dangers and rigors of plant exploration at the turn of the century.

Elias, Thomas S., and Peter A. Dykeman. *Field Guide to North American Edible Wild Plants.* Van Nostrand 1983 pap. $19.95. "Amateur botanists will enjoy this authoritative treatment of more than 200 native species and the good color photographs that support it. . . . Includes helpful guides to the identification of toxic and inedible plants that closely resemble those that can be eaten" (*LJ*).

Freethy, Ron. *From Agar to Zenry: A Book of Plant Uses, Names, and Folklore.* Longwood Pub. Group 1985 $24.95. A charming book for reference or browsing.

Friedman, Sara Ann. *Celebrating the Wild Mushroom: A Passionate Quest.* Dodd 1986 $18.95. Friedman offers practical information on mushroom identification, chemistry, biology, and cooking techniques. Line drawings and a bibliography are included.

Gibbons, Bob. *How Flowers Work: A Guide to Plant Biology*. Sterling 1984 $17.95. A good overview of plant physiology, morphology, ecology, and evolution for the layperson.

Gibson, Arthur C., and Park S. Noble. *The Cactus Primer*. Harvard Univ. Pr. 1986 $39.95. An authoritative book on primitive cacti by two biology professors. It includes a new generic taxonomy of Cactaceae, and the biology, chemistry, and evolutionary relationships of members of this family.

Hobhouse, Henry. *Seeds of Change: Five Plants That Transformed Mankind*. Harper 1986 $19.95. Hobhouse focuses on the role of sugar, quinine, tea, opium, and the potato in terms of their impact on history and society. "Highly recommended" (*LJ*).

Huxley, Anthony. *Green Inheritance: The World Wildlife Fund Book of Plants*. Doubleday 1985 $19.95. "Raises the reader's appreciation for and knowledge of the earth's vegetation with emphasis on the many ways in which survival depends on the diversity of plants. Lots of illustrations, including maps, drawings, and color photographs enhance the message" (*LJ*).

Johnson, Warren T., and Howard H. Lyon. *Insects That Feed on Trees and Shrubs*. Cornell Univ. Pr. 1976 $49.50. A comprehensive work on pests and pest damage to ornamental plants. Excellent for the amateur or professional horticulturalist.

Koreshoff, Deborah R. *Bonsai: Its Art, Science, History and Philosophy*. Timber 1984 $39.95. A guide to the care and design of Bonsai plants by an authority.

Lima, Patrick. *The Harrowsmith Illustrated Book of Herbs*. Camden House 1986 $19.95. A guide on selecting, starting, and propagating herbs written by a Canadian authority. The text is engaging and the book is illustrated with color photos and watercolors.

Loughmiller, Campbell, and Lynn Loughmiller. *Texas Wildflowers: A Field Guide*. Univ. of Texas Pr. 1984 $19.95 pap. $10.95. An above-average-quality field guide that was written for the amateur naturalist. The book is an enjoyable pictorial tour of Texas wildlife.

Margulis, Lynn, and Karlene V. Smith. *Five Kingdoms: An Illustrated Guide to the Physics of Life on Earth*. W. H. Freeman 1981 $31.95. An overview of all the life forms. The book is organized by phyla, and the material on each phylum includes a brief essay, photographs, and an anatomical drawing.

Meeuse, Bastiaan, and Sean Morris. *The Sex Life of Flowers*. Facts on File 1984 $19.95. Wonderful book for the lay reader who wants a better understanding and appreciation of floral ecology.

Moldenke, Harold N. *Plants of the Bible*. Dover rev. ed. 1986 pap. $8.95. A good reference source to plants mentioned in the Bible.

Prance, Ghillean Tolmie. *Leaves: The Formation, Characteristics, and Uses of Hundreds of Leaves Found in All Parts of the World*. Crown 1985 $35.00. This is the first leaf book of its kind. It includes information on leaf structure, function, fossil leaves, leaf identification, and leaf collecting. Illustrated with 300 magnificent color transparencies. "The clearly written text by a respected botanist at the New York Botanical Garden provides a setting for the vivid color photographs, many showing magnified detail, of leaves from around the world by a noted photographer [Kjell B. Sandved] at the Smithsonian Institution" (*LJ*).

Rost, T. L., and others. *Botany: A Brief Introduction to Plant Biology*. Wiley 1984 text ed. $33.95. An unusually well written textbook for introductory botany.

Rush, Werner. *The Wonderful World of Succulents: Cultivation and Description of Selected Succulent Plants Other Than the Cacti*. Smithsonian 1984 $49.50. An excellent introduction to the species of succulents and their care and cultivation. Beautifully illustrated with color and black-and-white photographs.

Schofield, W. B. *Introduction to Bryology*. Macmillan 1985 $45.00. A new introduction to the diversity and biology of the mosses and liverworts. The only recent English-language book to cover the morphology, ecology, fossil record, and taxonomy of the bryophytes.

Stewart, Wilson N. *Paleobotany and the Evolution of Plants*. Cambridge Univ. Pr. 1983 $29.95. This excellent and reasonably priced book is a fine introduction to paleobotany for the nonspecialist.

Stone, Doris M. *The Lives of Plants: Exploring the Wonders of Botany*. Scribner rev. ed. 1983 $15.95. An introduction to the anatomy and physiology of seed plants.

Swartley, John. *The Cultivated Hemlocks*. Timber 1985 $24.95. The first comprehensive treatment of the cultivated hemlocks. This book contains a wealth of information of interest to gardeners and horticulturalists.

Wilson, Brayton F. *The Growing Tree*. Univ. of Massachusetts Pr. rev. ed. 1984 $20.00 text ed. pap. $8.95. A readable overview of tree biology at the introductory level.

ZOOLOGY

Zoology is the study of animal life. Early zoologists, like botanists, were primarily interested in describing and classifying fauna. The zoological specialties were defined by the phylum studied. These included herpetology (the study of reptiles), icthyology (the study of fishes), ornithology (the study of birds), entomology (the study of insects), and mammalogy (the study of mammals).

By the late nineteenth century, zoology had taken on its modern form as a discipline. The experimentalists changed the focus of zoology from the study of species types to the study of biological processes, structures, and their functions. The processes of inheritance and development became important areas of inquiry.

A broad range of research issues is being studied in zoology today. Traditional pursuits such as the classification of animals continue, using new techniques developed by molecular biologists, such as the analysis and comparison of the amino acid sequences of two species. Some zoologists are working in genetic engineering research, developing new animal subspecies by transferring (cloned) DNA from one animal species to another. Others work on live animal populations, studying such phenomena as communication, for example in whales' songs and dolphin language.

Anderson, E. W. *Animals as Navigators*. Van Nostrand 1983 $19.50. "Discusses various external influences on animal migration behavior (predation, seasonal weather, etc.) and describes how different animal groups respond to external and internal stimuli by changing their habitats" (*LJ*).

Barth, Friedrich G. *Neurobiology of Arachnids*. Springer-Verlag 1985 $69.50. "Most of the chapters provide well researched reviews as well as detailed accounts of each author's own work. Distinguished by bountiful half-tone illustrations and a beautiful layout" (*Science*).

Bright, Michael. *Animal Language*. Cornell Univ. Pr. 1984 $24.95 pap. $12.95. A well-written, nontechnical book that summarizes the research on animal sounds.

Carr, Archie. *The Sea Turtle: So Excellent a Fishe*. Scribner 2d ed. 1985 $15.95; Univ. of Texas Pr. 1986 rev. ed. pap. $9.95. A revised edition of this classic work on the biology of sea turtles.

Cook, L. M., ed. *Case Studies in Population Biology*. Longwood Pub. Group 1985 $35.00. A good overview of population biology, based on material drawn from the work of field zoologists.

Davidson, R. H., and W. F. Lyon. *Insect Pests of Farm and Orchard*. Wiley 8th ed. 1986 $20.00. A wealth of information on pests that afflict agricultural crops, humans, domestic animals, and the home.

———. *The Zoology Coloring Book*. Harper 1982 pap. $8.95. This really is a coloring book, with diagrams.

Duellman, William E., and Linda Trueb. *Biology of Amphibians*. McGraw-Hill 1985 $40.00. A delightful, accurate, informative, and lively book.

Dukelow, Richard W., and J. Erwin. *Reproduction and Development*. Vol. 3 in *Comparative Primate Biology*. Alan R. Liss 1987 $190.00. A comprehensive compilation of all the primates in terms of reproduction and development.

Ewer, R. F. *The Carnivores*. Cornell Univ. Pr. 1985 pap. $17.95. "To anyone who likes carnivores and wants to learn interesting facts about them, whether the size of the home range of a wolf, or the hunting methods of lions, this book will be interesting."

Forsyth, Adrian. *Mammals of North America*. Camden House 1985 $29.95. A good basic source on American mammals for the general reader.

Goodall, Jane. *The Chimpanzees of Gombe: Patterns of Behavior*. Harvard Univ. Pr. 1986 $30.00. Synthesizes Goodall's 25 years of chimpanzee research working in the field at Lake Tanganyika as well as recent laboratory work with chimpanzees. Illustrated with attractive photographs of the chimps; also includes tables of data to help organize the information that is presented.

Gotch, A. F. *Reptiles: Their Latin Names Explained*. Sterling 1986 $43.00. A guide to reptile taxonomy for the nonspecialist.

Hill, J. E., and J. D. Smith. *Bats: A Natural History*. Univ. of Texas Pr. 1986 $24.95. Hill and Smith have transformed a mountain of data into a very readable, well-organized book that is beautifully illustrated and includes scientific and vernacular name indexes.

Hosking, Eric, and Bryan Sage. *Antarctic Wildlife*. Facts on File 1983 $22.95. "Provides a pictorial overview of the Antarctic and its fauna. That best known inhabitant of the continent, the penguin, is given the most attention, but other birds and seagoing mammals are also discussed" (*LJ*).

Johnsgaard, Paul A. *Diving Birds of North America*. Univ. of Nebraska Pr. 1987 $45.00. This book covers three bird families—loons, grebes, and auks. The author focuses on comparative biology and species accounts. Although technical, the book is accessible to serious birders.

———. *The Pheasants of the World*. Oxford 1986 $75.00. A fine, scholarly volume on pheasant biology, illustrated with exquisite watercolors. Johnsgaard provides information for all 49 pheasant species.

Jones, Dick. *Spider: The Story of a Predator and Its Prey*. Facts on File 1986 $12.95. A general overview of spider biology and behavior.

Jones, Mary Lou, and Stephen L. Schwartz. *The Grey Whale, Eschrichtius Robustus*. Academic Pr. 1984 $75.00. The most current review of the research and summary of knowledge on the grey whale.

Kevles, Bettyann. *The Female of the Species: Sex and Survival in the Animal Kingdom*. Harvard Univ. Pr. 1986 $20.00. An interesting book surveying the behavior of females of all species in the animal kingdom.

King, J. E. *Seals of the World*. Cornell Univ. Pr. 1983 $24.50. An authoritative introduction to seals, sea lions, and walruses. The book includes geographical and subject indexes and is illustrated with color and black-and-white illustrations.

Kirevald, Barbara C., and Joan S. Lockhart, eds. *Behavioral Biology of Killer Whales.* Alan R. Liss 1986 $65.00. A thorough overview of the biology and behavior of killer whales.

Knowler, Donald. *The Falconer of Central Park.* Bantam 1986 pap. $8.95; Karz-Cohl 1984 $14.95. "This offers quite a different view of New York City than one usually gets. An amateur ornithologist visits Central Park daily over one year, always on the lookout for any of the 200 species of birds in residence at any one time. Experienced birders and armchair naturalists will enjoy reading about his adventures" (*LJ*).

Lofgren, Lars. *Ocean Birds.* Knopf 1984 $27.50. This book provides a survey of ocean bird biology, behavior, and evolution. "An homage to ocean birds as the 'last great adventurers on earth' that will appeal to bird lovers and amateur naturalists" (*LJ*).

Moss, Sanford A. *Sharks: An Introduction for the Amateur Naturalist.* Prentice-Hall 1984 $21.95 pap. $10.95. "Serious study of sharks began in 1958 and this book brings together what has been learned about shark biology since that time. A primary focus is the ways in which sharks, skates, and rays have adapted to their varied environments. Well-labelled black and white illustrations add to the educational value" (*LJ*).

Napier, J. R., and P. H. Napier. *The Natural History of the Primates.* MIT 1985 $25.00. A fine introduction to primates. The material includes primate anatomy, characteristics, classification, diet, distribution, evolution, and social behavior. Illustrations, glossary, references, and a list of books for further reading are included.

Nowak, Ronald M., and John L. Paradiso. *Walker's Mammals of the World.* Johns Hopkins Univ. Pr. 4th ed. 1983 $65.00. The most recently revised edition of the basic reference book on mammal systematics, description, and natural history. Seventeen new genera are included.

Oberman, Laloa. *The Pleasures of Watching Birds.* Prentice-Hall 1986 $17.96. Another worthwhile introduction to bird watching.

O'Connor, Raymond J. *Growth and Development of Birds.* Wiley 1984 $39.95. The most current review of the literature on avian growth patterns and the factors that regulate them.

O'Toole, Christopher, ed. *The Encyclopedia of Insects.* Allen & Unwin 1985 $19.00. This is not an encyclopedia or reference book, but a good introductory text on entomology with excellent illustrations.

Peters, Roger. *Dance of the Wolves.* Ballantine 1986 pap. $3.50; McGraw-Hill 1985 $16.95. "While qualifying as a record of animal behavior, this is also an 'impressionistic' and 'subjective' record of the author's experiences studying packs of free-ranging wolves near Lake Superior. . . . The reader will learn a lot about pack social organization, territorial defense, and courtship. An entertaining and informative book" (*LJ*).

Preston-Mafham, Rod, and Ken Preston-Mafham. *Spiders of the World.* Facts on File 1984 $19.95. An excellent introduction to the biology of spiders, most suitable to the amateur entomologist or general reader.

Schaller. George B. *The Deer and the Tiger: A Study of Wildlife in India.* Univ. of Chicago Pr. 1967 $14.00. A classic study of predator-prey relationships.

Schaller, George B., and others. *The Giant Pandas of Woolong.* Univ. of Chicago Pr. 1985 $25.00. This beautifully illustrated book gives a detailed account of the biology and natural history of the panda. "The finest study completed on the panda" (Stephen Jay Gould).

Scheffer, Victor B. *Adventures of a Zoologist.* Scribner 1980 pap. $5.95. A distinguished scientist reviews his 50 years' experience as a researcher of marine mammals. A very enjoyable book.

Seeley, Thomas. *Honeybee Ecology: A Study of Adaptation in Social Life*. Princeton Univ. Pr. 1985 $39.50 pap. $13.50. "A masterly statement of what we know about honeybee behavior" (Edward O. Wilson, *Science*).

Shear, William A., ed. *Spiders: Webs, Behavior, and Evolution*. Stanford Univ. Pr. 1986 $55.00. Collection of papers by 16 internationally recognized experts that gives a detailed overview of webs and their significance and variations. Illustrated.

Sinclair, Sandra. *How Animals See*. Facts on File 1985 $24.95. Summarizes what is known about vision in animals, including fishes, mammals, amphibians, reptiles, and insects. Splendid photographs of the eyes of these animals accompany the text.

Steel, Roger. *Sharks of the World*. Facts on File 1985 $17.95. A good sourcebook for information on the many different varieties of sharks.

Swindler, Daris R., and J. Erwin, eds. *Systematics, Evolution and Anatomy*. Vol. 1 in *Comparative Primate Biology*. Alan R. Liss 1986 $190.00. The first in a series of books, each of which comprehensively covers an area of primate research for use by specialists and nonspecialists. The second and third volumes are *Behavior, Conservation and Ecology* and *Reproduction and Development*.

Terborgh, John. *Five New World Primates: A Study in Comparative Ecology*. Princeton Univ. Pr. 1983 $42.00 pap. $14.50. "This is one of the most well reasoned and thoughtful studies of primate ecology ever written. It is also delightful reading" (*Quarterly Review of Biology*).

Tyrrell, Esther Quesada, and Robert A. Tyrrell. *Hummingbirds: Their Life and Behavior. A Photographic Study of American Species*. Crown 1984 $35.00. A beautiful and invaluable work that includes 235 photographs of hummingbirds in all activities and all settings.

Wharton, David A. *A Functional Biology of the Nematodes*. Johns Hopkins Univ. Pr. 1986 $30.00. A good general overview of the biology of different families of worms.

Winn, Lois King, and Howard E. Winn. *Wings in the Sea: The Humpback Whale*. Univ. Pr. of New England 1985 $25.00 pap. $15.00. The authors recount their 20 years of experience observing and researching humpback whales.

Wootton, Anthony. *Insects of the World*. Facts on File 1984 $17.95. This book was designed for adult readers with no prior knowledge of entomology, who want a brief introduction to the world of insects.

Young, J. Z. *The Life of Vertebrates*. Oxford 3d ed. 1981 text ed. $29.50. An overview of vertebrate anatomy, physiology, and paleontology that covers all the vertebrate families that exist or ever existed and draws general conclusions on the evolution of the vertebrates.

ANATOMY, HISTOLOGY, AND PHYSIOLOGY

Anatomy is the science of the structural organization of any life form—plant or animal. General anatomy combines the gross and microscopic anatomy of the organs, tissues, and fluids of the body. Anatomy includes such subspecialties as developmental anatomy (the structures of embryonic organism) and comparative anatomy (the systematic comparison of structures within groups of plants or animals).

Histology is the study of plant or animal tissues, and is actually a subfield of anatomy. Histologists study the molecular cellular and intracellular makeup of the tissues, the chemical processes that take place in the tissues, and the individual tissue's function in the organs' and body's physiology.

In the eighteenth century, Haller described physiology as a "vitalized anatomy." This remains a succinct description of the discipline. Physiology encompasses the physical structures and internal processes that maintain life in the plant or animal organism. General physiology studies functions common to all life forms, such as respiration and circulation. Cell physiology studies the processes within the cell without regard to the whole organism. Molecular biology, biophysics, and biochemistry are all related to physiology.

Clemente, Carmine D., ed. *Anatomy of the Human Body.* Lea & Febiger 30th ed. 1984 $68.50. Still the definitive general anatomy text after 125 years. The writing is elegant, succinct, and appropriate to the general reader.

Crapo, Lawrence. *Hormones: The Messengers of Life.* W. H. Freeman 1985 $19.95 pap. $11.95. A witty, literate, authoritative account of the substances that regulate life.

Despopoulus, Agamemnon, and Stefan Silbernagl. *Color Atlas of Physiology.* Thieme Med. Pubs. 3d ed. 1986 text ed. $17.00. An economical and concise overview of physiology with helpful charts, anatomical maps, and illustrations.

Eckert, Roger, and David Randall. *Animal Physiology.* W. H. Freeman 2d ed. 1983 text ed. $35.95. An introduction to the physiology of animals as a reflection of biological adaptation.

Gartner, Leslie P., and James L. Hiatt. *Atlas of Histology.* Williams & Wilkins 1987 $21.95. This atlas was designed for use by beginning students and is therefore useful to readers without a background in histology.

Kristic, R. V. *Illustrated Encyclopedia of Human Histology.* Springer-Verlag 1984 $38.50. A general reference guide to histology. The book is in encyclopedic format with very brief general entries and accompanying illustrations.

Leeson, C. Roland, and others. *Text-Atlas of Histology.* Saunders 1988 $49.00. Presents basic human histology and relevant background information on the cell and microscopy.

Restak, Richard M. *The Brain.* Bantam 1984 $24.95. Restak, a neurologist, presents a history of research on the brain and its functions. Well written and appropriate to the nonspecialist, the book is "an outgrowth and expanded version of the popular, eight-part public television series on the brain. . . . The information, presented in an interesting manner, includes discussions of right brain/left brain research, biological rhythms, learning and memory, stress and emotions, vision and movement, and mental illness. The text is nicely complemented by over 150 color and black and white illustrations" (*LJ*).

Romer, Alfred S., and Thomas S. Parsons. *The Vertebrate Body.* Saunders 6th ed. 1986 text ed. $38.95. A newly revised edition of the classic textbook on comparative vertebrate anatomy.

Ross, Michael H., and Edward J. Reith. *Histology: A Text and an Atlas.* Harper 1985 text ed. $62.00. This introductory text covers all of histology and relevant material in cell biology.

Sadler, T. W. *Langman's Medical Embryology.* Williams & Wilkins 1985 $25.95. A concise but comprehensive text and atlas to prenatal human development. Contains photographs, drawings, and anatomical maps to illustrate the fetus and body systems in different stages of development.

Salisbury, Frank B., and Cleon W. Ross. *Plant Physiology.* Wadsworth 3d ed. 1985

$47.25. Reviews the background material needed to understand the concepts of plant physiology and is a fine introductory text.

Shek, Judy W., and others. *Atlas of the Rabbit Brain and Spinal Cord.* S. Karger 1986 $237.50. Very fine photographs of the brain and spinal cord constitute the basis of this atlas, the only one on the rabbit nervous system.

Thompson, Richard F., ed. *Progress in Neuroscience: Readings from Scientific American.* W. H. Freeman 1986 $21.95. A collection of articles from recent editions of *Scientific American* that provide an overview of new discoveries and theories in neuroscience.

Vander, Arthur J., James H. Sherman, and Dorothy S. Luciano. *Human Physiology: The Mechanism of Body Function.* McGraw-Hill 4th ed. 1985 text ed. $37.95. This is a beginning text for human physiology. It is accessible to any reader with or without a background in biology.

BIOCHEMISTRY

Biochemistry is the study of the chemical substances that occur within living organisms. Biochemists identify chemical substances in plants and animals and analyze their structures, explain their function, and investigate the roles they play in physiological processes. Examples of biochemical problems are the process of nitrogen fixation in plants and the structure of proteins in DNA.

Allport, Susan. *Explorers of the Black Box: The Search for the Cellular Basis of Memory.* Norton 1986 $17.95. "Allport, a science writer, has provided a very interesting account of the inroads made by neurobiologists to explain the mechanisms of memory" (*LJ*).

Baker, Jeffrey, and Garland E. Allen. *Matter, Energy and Life: An Introduction to Chemical Concepts.* Addison-Wesley 4th ed. 1980 pap. $15.95. Designed for beginning students in biology and medicine, this book presents the basic principles of chemistry and physics necessary to understand biology.

Durden-Smith, Jo, and Diane DeSimone. *Sex and the Brain.* Arbor House 1983 $16.95; Warner Bks. 1984 pap. $3.95. "A serious, scholarly treatment of gender differences in brain structure and development and their implications for mathematical, spatial, and verbal abilities in men and women. . . . An excellent treatment of a subject that has received much recent attention from sociologists, biochemical researchers, and behaviorists" (*LJ*).

Freifelder, David. *Physical Biochemistry.* W. H. Freeman 2d ed. 1982 text ed. $47.95 pap. $26.95. The author's aim was to prepare a textbook that would enable a student to read and understand the current biochemical literature. This is an excellent text, for which the reader requires a basic background in chemistry and biology.

Gunstone, Frank D., John L. Hardwood, and Fred B. Padley. *The Lipid Handbook.* Chapman & Hall 1986 $200.00. The major reference compendium. It covers all aspects of occurrence, isolation, chemical identification, and technological applications of lipids.

Lehninger, Albert L. *Principles of Biochemistry.* Worth 1982 text ed. $40.95. The best basic textbook in biochemistry. A background in general chemistry and biology is needed to understand it.

Palmer, Trevor. *Understanding Enzymes.* Halsted Pr. 2d ed. 1985 $45.00. This is a general introduction to the theoretical and applied aspects of enzyme biochemistry.

Smith, Emil L. *Principles of Biochemistry: General Aspects.* McGraw-Hill 7th ed. 1983 text ed. $36.00. A good introductory text in biochemistry that is accessible to readers with a background in general chemistry and biology.

———. *Principles of Biochemistry: Mammalian Biochemistry.* McGraw-Hill 7th ed. 1983 text ed. $42.00. A good general textbook for mammalian biochemistry. Some background in biology and chemistry is needed for this book to be accessible to the reader.

BIOCLIMATOLOGY

Bioclimatology is an interdisciplinary field that combines biology, climatology, and ecology. Bioclimatologists study the relationship between climate and living organisms. Among the most important climatic conditions studied are variations in the atmospheric conditions that affect the lives of animals and plants and limit their geographical distribution. Marine organisms are studied as well as terrestrial life forms. Salinity, temperature, and light are among the climatological factors that affect sea life. Bioclimatology became prominent in the 1960s due to an increasing awareness of the environment and environmental concerns. Today, although work continues in this area, the discipline is not as active as it was in the past.

Hadlow, Leonard. *Climate, Vegetation and Man.* Philos. Lib. $7.95. A good introduction to climatological research that focuses on man.

Johnson, H. D. *Progress in Animal Biometeorology: The Effects of Weather and Climate on Animals.* Swets North Am. 1976 vol. 1 $115.00. A good review of the research done on the effect of weather on animal life.

Monteith, J. L. *Vegetation and the Atmosphere.* Academic Pr. 1976 $69.00. A good overview of basic bioclimatology.

Schneider, Stephen H., and Randi Londer. *The Coevolution of Climate and Life.* Sierra 1984 $25.00. An authoritative and understandable account of theories regarding the coevolution of climate and living life forms. "This is a thoroughly professional, sparkling piece of writing that will bring pleasure as well as enlightenment to the person interested in bioclimatology of paleobioclimatology" (*Quarterly Review of Biology*).

Smith, L. P., ed. *The Effect of Weather and Climate on Plants (1963–1974).* Swets North Am. 1975 $88.00. A comprehensive review of significant bioclimatological work.

Sulman, Felix G. *The Effect of Air Ionization, Electrical Fields, Atmospherics and Other Electric Phenomena on Man and Animals.* C. C. Thomas 1980 $44.75. An interesting work on the effects of physical phenomena on animal life.

BIOPHYSICS

Biophysics encompasses theories and methods from both chemistry and physics, and applies them to biological problems. The development of biophysics is due to the development of such technological innovations as X-ray diffraction equipment, which enables work at the molecular level.

Subspecialties are molecular, radiation, physiological, and mathematical (theoretical) biophysics.

Berg, Howard C. *Random Walks in Biology*. Princeton Univ. Pr. 1983 $16.50. A fine introduction to biophysical phenomena that will be most accessible to readers with some background in biochemistry and biology.

Cerdonio, M., and R. W. Noble. *Introduction to Biophysics*. Taylor & Francis 1986 $29.95. Emphasizes the application of chemical and physical methods to the study of biological systems.

Franks, Felix. *Biophysics and Biochemistry at Low Temperatures*. Cambridge Univ. Pr. 1986 $44.50. This book covers a broad sweep of problems relevant to low-temperature phenomena. The purpose is as much to provide the uninitiated reader with a new and broad perspective as to educate about any specific subject.

CELL BIOLOGY

Cytology is now more commonly called cell biology. The cell as a unit is the focus of study. Cytochemistry (the study of chemical processes within the cell) and cytophysiology (the study of physiologic processes within the cell) are cell biology's main subdisciplines. The most closely related specialties are molecular biology, biochemistry, and biophysics.

Becker, Wayne M. *The World of the Cell*. Benjamin Cummings 1986 $39.95. This is a comprehensive introduction to molecular and cell biology with substantial background material on microscopy.

De Duve, Christian. *A Guided Tour of the Living Cell*. Scientific Amer. 1985 $33.95. De Duve takes the reader on a tour of the eucaryotic cell and presents what is currently understood in cell biology with a simplicity suitable for reading by the student or layperson.

Gray, Peter. *Encyclopedia of Microscopy and Microtechnique*. Krieger repr. of 1973 ed. 1983 $42.50. A comprehensive manual on specimen preparation and microscope use.

———. *The Microtomists' Formulary and Guide*. Krieger 1975 $47.50. A manual for staining and specimen-preparation techniques that would be an aid to anyone who uses a light microscope.

Karp, Gerald. *Cell Biology*. McGraw-Hill 2d ed. 1984 text ed. $44.95. The experimental approach to cell biology is stressed in this introductory text.

Kimball, John W. *Cell Biology*. Addison-Wesley 1984 text ed. $45.00. An introductory textbook for cell biology that is intelligible to the reader with a minimal background in chemistry and biology.

Lackie, J. M. *Cell Movement and Cell Behavior*. Allen & Unwin 1986 text ed. $45.00 pap. $19.00. All locomotion and all behavior are important, growing areas of biological research. This is the best current introduction to the research.

McKinnell, Robert Gilmore. *Cloning of Frogs, Mice and Other Animals*. Univ. of Minnesota Pr. 1985 $12.95. A layperson's guide to cloning—this is an overview of how nuclear transfer and related experiments are carried out.

Margulis, Lynn. *Symbiosis in Cell Evolution*. W. H. Freeman 1981 $30.95. This book presents the idea that eucaryotic cells evolved from bacterial ancestors. It is well written and accessible to the general reader.

Margulis, Lynn, and Dorion Sagan. *Microcosmos: Four Billion Years of Evolution from Our Microbial Ancestors*. Summit Bks. 1986 $17.95. "A beautifully written explanation of evolutionary theory now emerging regarding the origins of life on earth. . . . Margulis and Sagan provide the general reader with an excellent overview of current thought on evolution as informed by research in the areas of biochemistry, paleontology, and microbiology. A short glossary will help readers, while in general the writing style works well and should please and inform those new to this area of biology" (*LJ*).

Thorpe, Neal O. *Cell Biology*. Wiley 1984 $41.95. The central theme of this text is the structure and function of the cell and its organelles.

DEVELOPMENTAL BIOLOGY

Developmental biology was formally founded at a conference in 1939, but the first independent journal was not established until 1959. Thus, it is a very new area of research. Developmental biologists seek to go beyond the mechanics of fertilization to understand the processes that govern the development of living things.

Dworkin, Martin. *Developmental Biology of the Bacteria*. Benjamin Cummings 1986 $22.50. This is an excellent overview of the developmental biology of bacteria written for readers with a general background in biology and biochemistry.

Gilbert, Scott F. *Developmental Biology*. Sinauer 1985 text ed. $36.75. This is the best developmental biology textbook now available at the introductory level. It presents descriptive and analytic aspects of animal embryology at the organismal, biochemical, and molecular biologic levels.

Guidics, Giovanni. *The Sea Urchin Embryo: A Developmental Biological System*. Springer-Verlag 1986 $49.00. This is a review of the problems studied and literature published by developmental biologists who used the sea urchin embryo as a model. It is representative of developmental research and is accessible to readers with a general biology background.

Raff, Rudolph A., and Elizabeth C. Raff, eds. *Development as an Evolutionary Process*. Alan R. Liss 1987 $58.00. A collection of papers that summarize the work in a new area of study—the experimental study of developmental mechanisms in evolutionary development. The papers are the product of a symposium of developmental biologists held at Woods Hole, Massachusetts, in 1985.

Rossant, Janet, and Roger A. Pedersen. *Experimental Approaches to Mammalian Embryonic Development*. Cambridge Univ. Pr. 1987 $70.00. This book provides a review of the recent work done in cellular, molecular, and biochemical aspects of research in mammalian development.

MICROBIOLOGY AND VIROLOGY

Microbiology is the study of the following microorganisms: bacteria, algae, fungi, and rickettsiae. Microbiologists study the organisms' structures, physiology, biochemistry, and pathology. Virology, the study of viruses, is an independent subdiscipline, although originally it was a subspecialty of microbiology. Viruses are not complete cells; they are DNA fragments that require a host cell in order to multiply. Viruses were not "discovered" until the twentieth century because their small size made them impossible to see with a light microscope. The electron microscope, which uses electrons instead of light to create the images seen, made it possible to view viruses for the first time.

Brock, Thomas D., David W. Smith, and Michael T. Madigan. *Biology of Microorganisms*. Prentice-Hall 4th ed. 1984 text ed. $42.50. This textbook includes coverage on basic microbiology, as well as material on immunology, biotechnology, and biochemistry.

De Kruif, Paul. *Microbe Hunters*. Harcourt repr. of 1924 ed. 1986 pap. $5.95. This classic book on the history of early biology will provide enjoyable reading.

Gabriel, Barbra L. *Biological Electron Microscopy*. Van Nostrand 1982 $36.95. A basic introduction to the use of the electron microscope, specimen preparation, and related topics. A good general overview of electron microscopy.

Herbert, R. A., and G. A. Codd. *Microbes in Extreme Environments*. Harcourt 1986 $74.00. This work is a collection of papers on how microorganisms adapt to different types of extreme environments, a topic of increasing research interest in academic and biotechnological study.

Leadbetter, Edward R., and Jeanne S. Poindexter, eds. *Bacteria in Nature, Vol. 1: Bacterial Activities in Perspective*. Plenum 1985 $39.50. The first in a series of books intended to provide a survey of the issues in bacteriological research. The book gives an overview of all classes of bacteria.

Lee, John J., and others, eds. *An Illustrated Guide to the Protozoa*. Allen Pr. 1985 $80.00. "For the nonprotozoologist this book serves as a valuable reference to identify organisms, learn about their biology, and the relations of the genera" (*Quarterly Review of Biology*).

Postgate, John. *Microbes and Man*. Penguin rev. ed. 1975 pap. $9.95. "The book is so well written that its elegance can only be appreciated after that rewarding journey. The book is a pleasure from first to last" (*New Scientist*).

Scott, Andrew. *Pirates of the Cell: The Story of Viruses from Molecule to Microbe*. Basil Blackwell 1985 pap. $12.95. Designated by *Choice* as an outstanding academic book of 1985–86. A good introduction to viruses.

MOLECULAR BIOLOGY

Molecular biology is one of the most recently developed specialties in biology. Molecular biologists study cellular processes in the form of molecular behavior. The major questions that specialists in this discipline address are the cell's uptake and transformation of energy, the intracellular production and use of energy, and the molecular representation of information that governs the cell's metabolic activities. Biochemistry, biophysics, and genetics all overlap with molecular biology.

Changeux, Jean-Pierre. *The Neuronal Man: The Biology of Mind*. Pantheon 1985 $19.95. A translation of *L'Homme neuronal*, the winner of the 1983 Broquette-Gonin Literary Award. This book is at once neuroscience, molecular biology, and psychology. Accessible to the informed general reader.

Darnell, James, Harvey Lodisch, and David Baltimore. *Molecular Cell Biology*. Scientific Amer. 1986 text ed. $43.00. This text integrates basic material from cell biology, biochemistry, and genetics to form the basic introduction to the study of molecular biology.

Denton, Michael. *Evolution: A Theory in Crisis*. Adler & Adler 1986 $19.95. Evolutionary theory explained from the point of view of molecular biologists.

Nei, Masatoshi. *Molecular Evolutionary Genetics.* Columbia Univ. Pr. 1987 $45.00.
"Nei has made a significant scholarly contribution, presenting the leading edge
of evolutionary thought" (*Quarterly Review of Biology*). Recommended for readers with a background in basic biology and chemistry.
Rees, A. R., and M. J. E. Sternberg. *From Cells to Atoms: An Illustrated Introduction
to Molecular Biology.* Blackwell Scientific 1984 pap. $12.95. This is a good intro-
duction to molecular biology that can be understood by anyone with a general
biology background.
Scientific American. *The Molecules of Life.* W. H. Freeman 1985 $21.95. pap. $12.95.
The author describes in simple terms the range of instruments and techniques
now available in electron microscopy and illustrates how these techniques are
employed.

AGASSIZ, LOUIS (JEAN LOUIS RODOLPHE AGASSIZ). 1807–1873

"The exact description of things seen, on which so many twentieth-
century writing is found, was a craft developed as recently as the nineteenth century, and not by men of letters but scientists. Agassiz was quite
possibly the greatest master of this art who ever lived" (Hugh Kenner). As a
penurious student and professor in Paris, this Swiss naturalist and geologist
studied fish classification and produced the monumental five-volume treatise on extinct life forms of the sea, *Recherches sur les poissons fossiles*
(1833–43). His second period of research was devoted to the study of Swiss
glaciers (the results published as *Etudes sur les glaciers,* 1840); he made
important discoveries about the Ice Age in Europe. The widespread hunger
for scientific knowledge in the early nineteenth century brought him to the
United States in 1846, where he became a professor of zoology and geology
at Harvard University. A skillful lecturer and popular and devoted teacher,
Agassiz revolutionized the study of natural history by urging and practicing
the fresh observation and interpretation of nature, as opposed to reliance on
traditional classification systems. The Agassiz approach was adopted by an
entire generation of scientists. With his usual industry and enthusiasm he
established a museum of comparative zoology, now the Agassiz Museum at
Harvard. His second wife, Elizabeth Cabot Cary, a pioneer in the higher
education of women, played a major role in the founding of Radcliffe College. His famous "Essay on Classification" is included in his four-volume
Contributions to the Natural History of the United States (1857–62, o.p.). EZRA
POUND (see Vol. 1) once said of him, "Agassiz, apart from his brilliant
achievement in natural science, ranks as a writer of prose, precise knowledge of his subject leading to great exactitude of expression."

BOOKS BY AGASSIZ

Geological Sketches. Amer. Biography Service repr. of 1885 ed. 1985 $39.00
*The Intelligence of Louis Agassiz: A Specimen Book of Scientific Writings; Selected,
with an Introduction and Notes.* Ed. by Guy Davenport, Greenwood repr. of 1963
ed. 1983 $42.50
Louis Agassiz: His Life and Correspondence. 1885. Somerset 2 vols. o.p.

BOOKS ABOUT AGASSIZ

Gould, Alice B. *Louis Agassiz*. Folcroft repr. of 1900 ed. 1981 o.p.

Lurie, Edward. *Louis Agassiz: A Life in Science*. Univ. of Chicago Pr. 1960 o.p.

————. *Nature and the American Mind: Louis Agassiz and the Culture of Science*. Watson 1974 pap. $7.00

Marcou, Jules. *Life, Letters and Works of Louis Agassiz*. Gregg Intl. repr. of 1896 ed. $82.80

Paton, Lucy A. *Elizabeth Cary Agassiz: A Biography*. Ayer repr. of 1919 ed. 1974 $32.00. Among the most interesting features of the book are the accounts of Elizabeth Cary Agassiz's travels with her husband. She was the first president of Radcliffe College.

Robinson, Mabel L. *Runner of the Mountain Tops: The Life of Louis Agassiz*. Gale repr. of 1939 ed. 1971 $40.00

Tiner, John H. *The Ghost Lake: The True Story of Louis Agassiz*. Baker Bks. 1983 pap. $3.95

AUDUBON, JOHN JAMES. 1785–1851

The great American ornithologist was born in Haiti, educated in France, and came to the Audubon estate ("Mill Grove") near Philadelphia in 1803. As a youth he enjoyed observing birds and organizing bird-banding flights, the first in this country. He began by painting portraits and teaching drawing, then conceived the idea of painting every species of American bird in its native habitat. Audubon spent years traveling through the wilderness and enduring incredible hardships. His drawings and paintings of bird life "represent a rare combination of artistic talent and scientific observation and remain one of the great achievements of American intellectual history" (*Columbia Encyclopedia*). Despondent at being unable to provide for his family, he went to Great Britain in search of a publisher in 1826, and *The Birds of America*, in elephant folio size, was published in parts between 1827 and 1838. The accompanying five-volume text, called *Ornithological Biography* (1831–39), was prepared largely in Edinburgh in collaboration with William MacGillivray. *The Viviporous Quadrupeds of North America*, which he began in collaboration with John Bachman, was completed by Audubon's two sons.

BOOKS BY AUDUBON

The 1826 Journal of John James Audubon. Ed. by Alice Ford, Abbeville Pr. 2d rev. ed. repr. of 1966 ed. 1987 $27.50. This is the first unabridged version to be published of Audubon's journal describing his search in England and Scotland for a publisher for *Birds of America*. Audubon was a painstaking diarist, and this eight-month memoir, written in the form of letters to his wife in Louisiana, shows him at his best—naive, sincere, proud, and above all, ebullient. "Ford's notes . . . are excellent, but it should be added that the index is not perfectly reliable. Illustrated with sketches and drawings done by Audubon during his trip" (*The New Yorker*).

The Birds of America. 1827–38. Macmillan 1985 $39.95; Peter Smith 7 vols. repr. of 1840 ed. 1985 $73.50

The Audubon Notebook. Ed. by Maria F. Audubon, Ayer 2 vols. repr. of 1897 ed. $56.50; Dover 2 vols. repr. of 1897 ed. pap. ea. $8.95; Running Pr. $12.90 pap. $5.95

Audubon and His Journals. Ed. by Maria F. Audubon, Ayer 2 vols. repr. of 1897 ed.
    set $56.50; Dover 2 vols. repr. of 1897 ed. 1986 pap. ea. $8.95
Delineations of American Scenery and Character. Ed. by F. H. Herrick, Ayer repr. of
    1926 ed. 1970 $24.50. Extracts from Audubon's pictures of American frontier
    life.
Audubon Reader: The Best Writings of John James Audubon. Ed. by Scott R. Sanders,
    Midland Bks. 1986 $29.95; Indiana Univ. Pr. 1986 pap. $9.95

BOOKS ABOUT AUDUBON

Dock, George, Jr. *Audubon's Birds of America.* Abrams 1979 o.p.
Durant, Mary, and Michael Harwood. *On the Road with John James Audubon.* Dodd
    1980 $19.95. "Durant and Harwood have given us a fascinating journal. They
    manage, at every step, to evoke the time past to supply us with interesting facts
    and to guide us through the inconsistencies in Audubon's work" (*Natural History*).
Fries, Walderman H. *The Double Elephant Folio: The Story of Audubon's Birds of
    America.* Amer. Lib. Assn. 1973 o.p. Thirty of the plates of the engravings for the
    elephant folio are reproduced in color with a simple accompanying text.
Herrick, F. H. *Audubon the Naturalist.* 1917. Peter Smith 2 vols. 1980 o.p.
Peterson, Roger Tory. *Audubon Birds.* Abbeville 1980 pap. $4.95
A Selection from the Birds of America by John James Audubon. North Carolina Mu-
    seum of Art 1976 $4.00
Warren, Robert Penn. *Audubon: A Vision.* Random 1969 o.p. "With irony Warren
    develops Audubon's passage in time—his birth, life and death—into a story of
    deep delight, a story both intellectually and emotionally moving" (*LJ*).

BAILEY, LIBERTY HYDE. 1858–1954

This American botanist and horticulturalist is noted for his basic works in
both fields. He was instrumental in raising the stature of horticulture to
that of an applied science and in bettering the living conditions and education of farmers. A professor of horticulture at Cornell University (1888–
1903), he also held many administrative positions. "Bailey was a man of
driving energy. As a diversion from administrative burdens and research in
science he wrote two volumes of poetry and nine in the fields of sociology,
religion, and philosophy" (*Encyclopaedia Britannica*). He wrote more than
60 books on botany, horticulture, and agriculture.

BOOKS BY BAILEY

The Standard Cyclopedia of American Horticulture. 1914–17. Gordon 6 vols. $600.00.
    This book is a "complete record of the status of North American Horticulture as
    it exists at the close of the nineteenth century" (Preface).
Sketch of the Evolution of Our Native Fruits. Scholarly Resources repr. of 1898 ed.
    1973 $39.00
*Cyclopedia of American Agriculture: A Popular Survey of Agricultural Conditions, Prac-
    tice and Ideals in the United States and Canada.* 1907–09. Ayer 2 vols. 4th ed.
    repr. of 1912 ed. 1975 $65.00. The cyclopedia is too out of date to be a useful
    reference tool anymore. It is a collection of articles with bibliographies written
    by agricultural specialists.
Manual of Cultivated Plants. 1924. Macmillan rev. ed. 1954 $15.95. This is the stan-
    dard manual of cultivated plants that are common in North America.
How Plants Get Their Names. Dover repr. of 1933 ed. 1963 pap. $3.95; Peter Smith
    repr. of 1933 ed. $12.75

Pruning Manual. Ed. by E. P. Christopher, Macmillan rev. ed. 1954 $15.95
Nursery Manual. Macmillan rev. ed. 1967 o.p. This is the classic plant nursery man-
    ual and it is still useful as a guide to plant cultivation.
The Holy Earth. Gordon $59.95; NY State College of Agriculture 1980 pap. $4.95
(and Ethel Z. Bailey). *Hortus Third: A Concise Dictionary of Plants Cultivated in the
    United States and Canada.* Macmillan 1976 $125.00. *Hortus Third* includes the
    description and correct botanical name with its author or authors for 281 fami-
    lies, 3,301 genera, and 20,397 species of North American plants. This is the
    standard American horticultural reference work. It was preceded by *Hortus,*
    published in 1930, and followed by *Hortus Second* in 1941.

Book about Bailey

Rodgers, Andrew D., III. *Liberty Hyde Bailey.* 1949. Hafner 3d ed. 1965 o.p. "Mr.
    Rodgers alternates between the romantic and the pedantic. Documents and
    letters are lavishly quoted and footnoted. But through this musty material
    steals the soft breath of orchards in bloom and of fields turning green in the
    spring. Especially is this true in the description of Bailey's Michigan boyhood"
    (*N.Y. Times*).

BERNARD, CLAUDE. 1813–1878

Claude Bernard, the father of modern experimental physiology, was born
in France. In his early years, as a student in Lyon, he studied to become a
playwright. His work was rejected by critics and this experience ended his
dramatic aspirations. He became instead a physician and an exceptional
biological scientist.

His investigations in physiology were very fruitful, and wide in scope. In
1855 he was appointed full professor of medicine at the Collège de France.
By this time he had already explained the chemical and nervous system
control of digestion, demonstrated the role of the pancreas in fat metabolism, and discovered the role that bile plays in the digestion of proteins. In
the years that followed, he identified the liver as the site of glycogenesis and
explained the processes governing vasodilation.

His most important theoretical contribution was proposing the concept of
"homeostasis," which he called the *milieu interieur.* Homeostasis is the principle that all of the body's systems are in a constant state of adjustment,
and that these adjustments maintain a balanced state within the body.
Also, Bernard was the first physiologist to demonstrate that the theories
and methods of chemistry and physics could contribute to the study of
biology. This first use of interdisciplinary techniques broadened the base of
physiology, and foreshadowed the form that future research in biology
would take.

Books by Bernard

The Cahier Rouge of Claude Bernard. Trans. by Hebbel E. Hoff, Lucienne Guillemin,
    and Roger Guillemin, Schenkman 1967 o.p. The translated notebooks of Claude
    Bernard; the original is held by the archives of the Collège de France.
An Introduction to the Study of Experimental Medicine. 1865. Trans. by Henry C.
    Greene, Dover 1957 pap. $3.95. This work is accessible to the general reader.
Lectures on the Phenomena of Life Common to Animals and Plants. Trans. by Hebbel

E. Hoff, Roger Guillemin, and Lucienne Guillemin, C. C. Thomas 1974 $34.75.
Bernard's treatise on biology and general physiology.

*Memoir on the Pancreas and on the Role of Pancreatic Juice in Digestive Processes:
Particularly in the Digestion of Neutral Fat.* Trans. by John Henderon, Academic
Pr. 1985 $48.00. This is Bernard's classic work elucidating the functioning of the
pancreas; it is very technical for the general reader.

BOOKS ABOUT BERNARD

Bergson, Henri. *An Introduction to Metaphysics: The Creative Mind.* Littlefield repr.
of 1965 ed. 1975 pap. $5.95

Hirst, Paul O. *Durkheim, Bernard and Epistemology.* Methuen repr. of 1975 ed. 1980
pap. $7.95

Holmes, Frederic L. *Claude Bernard and Animal Chemistry.* Harvard Univ. Pr. 1974
$37.50. A fine scholarly account of the life of Claude Bernard, based largely on
his diaries and notebooks.

Parvez, H., ed. *Advances in Experimental Medicine: A Centenary Tribute to Claude
Bernard.* Elsevier 1980 $96.50. This is a collection of addresses, essays, and
lectures on Claude Bernard's work by distinguished biologists.

Robin, E. D. *Claude Bernard and the Internal Environment: A Memorial Symposium.*
Dekker 1979 $44.75

CUVIER, BARON GEORGES (GEORGES LEOPOLD CHRETIEN FREDERIC DAGOBERT CUVIER). 1769–1832

Georges Léopold Chrétien Frédéric Dagobert Cuvier was born in France.
This great paleontologist and zoologist had no formal scientific training. He
studied at the military academy at Stuttgart in order to qualify for the
French civil service.

Cuvier worked as a tutor on the north coast of France while he waited for
a civil service appointment. There, he became fascinated with the forms of
sea life that he saw on the beaches, and began to study them. He dissected
mollusks and fishes, and drew them and their various parts. His understanding of anatomy and his drawings were so superior that he was offered a
chair at the University of Paris in the Department of Comparative Anatomy.

At the University of Paris he turned to studying the great apes as a way of
understanding human anatomy. As a result of his studies, he proposed the
revolutionary idea that all life forms descended from a single species. His
most notable theory of comparative anatomy was the "correlation theory."
He recognized that all body structures are related to each other, and that
therefore a single organ or structure could be used to predict the form of the
rest of the animal's parts. This concept provided the basis for future work in
the reconstruction of fossils. Thus Cuvier originated modern paleontological
theory and method.

Cuvier's work led him to reject theories of continuous evolution and he
developed a theory whereby all evolutionary changes were caused by "cataclysmic" geological events. Darwin and later evolutionists were to disprove
this idea.

During later life Cuvier was recognized by Napoleon as one of France's
foremost thinkers. Napoleon conferred a baronetcy on him (1819) and appointed him director of the Department of Education of France. Cuvier

made many reforms and innovations in the French educational system, and founded many new universities. He died of cholera in 1832.

BOOKS BY CUVIER

The Class Mammalia: The Animal Kingdom Arranged in Conformity with Its Organization by the Baron Cuvier. Ed. by Keir B. Sterling, Ayer 5 vols. repr. of 1827 ed. 1978 ea. $43.00 set $217.00. This set includes an English translation of volume 1 and the entire French editions (1827–35) of *Regne Animal.*

The Animal Kingdom, Arranged after Its Organization: Forming a Natural History of Animals and an Introduction to Comparative Anatomy. Kraus Repr. repr. of 1863 ed. 1979 $63.00. Cuvier's work illustrating the use of his principle of the correlation of body parts.

Essay on the Theory of the Earth. Arno repr. of 1817 ed. 1978 $32.00. The text of this reprint is in English and French.

Memoirs on Fossil Elephants and on Reconstruction of the Genera Palaeotherium and Anoplotherium (Recherches sur les ossemens fossiles des quadrupèdes). Ed. by Stephen Jay Gould, Arno repr. of 1812 ed. 1980 $80.00. This is a reprint of volumes 2 and 13 of the 1812 edition, including memories I–II. The text is in French.

BOOK ABOUT CUVIER

Outram, Dorinda. *Georges Cuvier: Vocation, Science and Authority in Post-Revolutionary France.* Longwood 1984 $42.00

DARWIN, CHARLES ROBERT. 1809–1882

Darwin's interest in the study of evolution began when he was official naturalist on the HMS *Beagle,* which sailed around the world from 1831 to 1836. After his return he continued his research on animal and plant forms, concluding that "selection was the key to man's success." His theory of evolution, soon known as Darwinism, held that beneficial variations of species were preserved, while others, unfavored by their environments, were eliminated in the struggle for existence. Darwin used findings from anatomy, geology, embryology, and paleontology. Although later research made it necessary to modify some of Darwin's statements, his discoveries were corroborated by Mendelian genetics and became the "prime cornerstone of modern scientific teaching." The storm aroused by the first publication of *On the Origin of Species* (1859) and its sequel, *The Descent of Man,* 12 years later is still raging in some parts of the world. Darwin is remembered as a warm and modest man. Always poor in health, he spent the last 40 years of his life studying and writing at his home in Down, Sussex. Darwin had the faculty of writing simply on abstruse matters, and his use of reminiscence or a discursive anecdote lends great color to his scientific expositions. (See also Chapter 12 in this volume.)

BOOKS BY DARWIN

Works. AMS Pr. 18 vols. repr. of 1897 ed. 1972 $765.00. This is a facsimile edition of the complete works of Charles Darwin.

Autobiography of Charles Darwin. Ed. by Nora Burlow, Norton 1969 pap. $6.95; ed. by Thomas H. Huxley and Gavin De Beer, Oxford 1974 o.p. The Norton edition restores Darwin's comments on religion, omitted from the original 1887 version because of family sentiment. "Some of the passages formerly suppressed are the most revealing he ever wrote concerning his own estimate of the bearing of his famous theory on religion, morals and philosophy" (J. W. Krutch, *N.Y. Times*).

The Collected Papers of Charles Darwin. Ed. by Paul H. Barrett, Univ. of Chicago Pr. 2 vols. 1977 $40.00 pap. $12.50

(and others). *The Correspondence of Charles Darwin: Vol. 1, 1821–1936.* Ed. by Frederick Burkhardt and Sydney Smith, Cambridge Univ. Pr. 1985 vol. 1 $37.50 vol. 2 1987 $37.50. "The 338 letters in this first volume begin when Darwin was 12 years old and end as he returns from the *Beagle* voyage. . . . Includes letters from family and friends as well as scientific colleagues, giving the reader a full view of Darwin's personal life, the social mores of the time, and the nature of his particular creative genius. Enriched with a list of books on the *Beagle* and a biographical register of the correspondents" (*LJ*).

Book of Darwin. Intro. by George Gaylord Simpson, Washington Square Pr. 1983 pap. $6.95

The Essential Darwin. Ed. by Kenneth Korey, Little, Brown 1984 $19.95 pap. $10.95. "This will be welcomed by readers who want to understand more precisely what Darwin said and where his theories stand today. Excerpts from Darwin's *Autobiography, The Voyage of the Beagle, The Origin of Species,* and *The Descent of Man* are interspersed with overviews and critical notes" (*LJ*).

Metaphors, Materialism, and the Evolution of the Mind: Early Writings of Charles Darwin. Annot. by Paul H. Barrett, Univ. of Chicago Pr. 1980 pap. $6.95

Journal of Researches into the Natural History and Geology of the Countries Visited during the Voyage of the H.M.S. Beagle round the World under the Command of Captain Fitz Roy. 1839. AMS Pr. 1972 $42.50; Norwood 1977 $40.00. All of Darwin's later work stemmed from observations he made during the Beagle voyage. The first volume focuses on his geological observations and the second on natural history.

On the Structure and Distribution of Coral Reefs. Richard West repr. of 1842 ed. 1985 $65.00. Darwin's theories on the development of coral reefs, based on his observations and theorizing during the Beagle voyage, are explicated here. He argued that coral reefs resulted when the ocean floor dropped and that corals grow upward continuously over time.

Geological Observations on the Volcanis Islands and Parts of South America Visited During the Voyage of the H.M.S. Beagle. 1844–46. AMS Pr. 1972 $42.50. Darwin's work on geology and geological evolution has been eclipsed by his theory of the origin of species. This work is fundamental to all of his later writings and is much neglected.

The Fossil Lepadidae. Johnson Repr. repr. of 1851 ed. pap. $6.00

A Monograph of the Sub-Class Cirripedia. Johnson Repr. 2 vols. repr. of 1851–54 ed. set $88.00

The Fossil Balanidae and Verrucidae. Johnson Repr. repr. of 1854 ed. pap. $6.00

The Origin of Species by Means of Natural Selection. 1859. AMS Pr. 2 vols. 1972 $85.00; intro. by Ernst Mayr, Harvard Univ. Pr. facsimile ed. 1975 pap. $8.95; Macmillan 1962 pap. $4.95; NAL pap. $3.50; ed. by Phillip Appleman, Norton abr. ed. 1975 pap. $3.95; Richard West 2 vols. in 1 repr. of 1914 ed. $57.00; ed. by Charlotte Irvine and William Irvine, Ungar pap. $6.95. Six editions were issued under Darwin's direction between 1859 and 1872. Each edition embodied the author's own revision of his theory as new evidence presented itself. By 1872 about 75 percent of the first edition had been rewritten.

The Illustrated Origin of Species. Intro. by Richard Leakey, Hill & Wang 1979 $25.00
   pap. $12.50
The Various Contrivances by Which Orchids Are Fertilised by Insects. 1862. AMS Pr.
   1972 $42.50; Coleman repr. of 1862 ed. 1980 $27.50; Univ. of Chicago Pr. 2d ed.
   1984 $20.00 text ed. pap. $9.95. In this monograph, Darwin illustrates the principle that all changes in the form of a species are adaptations that improve the
   plant's chances of survival. Orchids and all other plants fertilized by insects
   show physical adaptations different from the adaptations of plants fertilized by
   wind-borne pollen.
On the Movements and Habits of Climbing Plants. 1865. Richard West repr. of 1891
   ed. $40.00. In this volume Darwin explored the specific adaptations of plants to
   climbing. Tendrils that enable plants to climb help them to reach light. The
   mechanisms that govern the direction in which the tendrils grow (movement)
   maximize the plants' exposure to needed light. His research formed the basis for
   the later elucidation of the mechanism of plant growth hormones.
Variation of Animals and Plants Under Domestication. 1867. AMS Pr. 2 vols. 1972
   $85.00; Richard West 2 vols. 1986 $200.00. This is a detailed study by Darwin on
   the origins of cultivated plants and domesticated animals.
The Descent of Man and Selection in Relation to Sex. 1871. Princeton Univ. Pr. repr. of
   1871 ed. 1981 $50.00 pap. $12.50. In the *Descent of Man,* Darwin applied the
   principles of evolution and natural selection to man. "Natural selection" is replaced by the concept of "sexual selection."
The Expression of the Emotions in Man and Animals. Longwood repr. of 1872 ed.
   1979 pap. $20.00. This is the first work in the field of ethology, the study of
   comparative animal behavior.
Insectivorous Plants: Works of Charles Darwin. 1875. AMS Pr. 2 vols. 1972 $42.50.
   This monograph focuses on the adaptations of meat-eating plants, such as "fly-
   catching" plants. The various anatomical and physiological features of these
   plants, which are specific to snaring and consuming prey, are described and
   discussed.
The Different Forms of Flowers on Plants of the Same Species. 1877. Univ. of Chicago
   Pr. 1986 pap. $13.95
The Power of Movement in Plants. 1880. AMS Pr. repr. 3d ed. 1972 $42.50; Da Capo
   repr. of 1881 ed. 1966 $55.00; Richard West repr. of 1892 ed. $49.00
*The Formation of Vegetable Mold, Through the Action of Worms with Observation of
   Their Habits.* 1881. Fwd. by Stephen Jay Gould, Univ. of Chicago Pr. 1985 pap.
   $11.95. This is one of the first complete treatises on plant ecology. Darwin
   characterizes and quantifies the changes in soil that are brought about by earthworms, and that benefit plants.
The Effects of Cross and Self-Fertilisation in the Vegetable Kingdom. Richard West
   repr. of 1889 ed. $49.00. Darwin did a series of experiments comparing plants
   that are cross-fertilizers (the species has two sexes) with plants that are self-
   fertilizers (one sex). Darwin demonstrates the advantages of cross-fertilization
   (which involves the interchange of different sets of genes) in terms of developing
   adaptations.
Foundations of the Origin of Species. Ed. by Francis Darwin, Kraus Repr. repr. of
   1909 ed. $21.00
Natural Selection. Ed. by Robert C. Stauffer, Cambridge Univ. Pr. 1975 $100.00.
   "This book is probably the publishing event of the decade in history of science. . . . I cannot praise highly enough the meticulous work of Stauffer and a
   staff of assistants in rendering the text right down to the details of Darwin's

misspellings. And it was no easy task. . . . *Natural Selection* is a joy to read. It is full of insights and subtle observations" (*Science*).

The Voyage of Charles Darwin: His Autobiographical Writings. Ed. by Christopher Ralling, Mayflower Bks. 1980 $12.50 pap. $4.50; Parkwest Pubns. 1986 $17.95

The Substance of the Descent of Man. Richard West repr. of 1926 ed. 1978 $32.50

BOOKS ABOUT DARWIN

Alland, Alexander, Jr. *Human Nature: Darwin's View.* Columbia Univ. Pr. 1985 $27.50

Armstrong, Patrick. *Charles Darwin in Western Australia.* International Specialized Bk. 1986 pap. $9.95

Berry, R. J. *Charles Darwin: A Commemoration, 1882–1982.* Academic Pr. 1982 $22.50

Clark, Ronald W. *The Survival of Charles Darwin: A Biography of a Man and an Idea.* Avon 1986 pap. $5.95. An excellent biography of Darwin's life and summary of Darwin's ideas on evolution.

Darwin, Francis, ed. *The Life and Letters of Charles Darwin.* 1887. Arden Lib. repr. of 1891 ed. 2 vols. 1981 $125.00. This is the most authoritative "life" of Darwin, written by his son, Francis. It contains extensive personal information about Darwin and his family.

Gale, Barry G. *Evolution Without Evidence: Charles Darwin and the Origin of Species.* Univ. of New Mexico Pr. 1982 $21.00

Ghiselin, Michael. *The Triumph of the Darwinian Method.* Univ. of Chicago Pr. repr. of 1969 ed. 1984 pap. $9.95. Research biologist Ghiselin has written this book about an important but neglected subject—Darwin's methodology. "It has much to recommend it" (*LJ*).

Gillespie, Neal C. *Charles Darwin and the Problems of Creation.* Univ. of Chicago Pr. 1982 pap. $7.50

Grene, Marjorie, ed. *Dimensions of Darwinism: Themes and Counterthemes in Twentieth Century Evolutionary Theory.* Cambridge Univ. Pr. 1986 pap. $14.95

Hamrum, Charles L., ed. *Darwin's Legacy.* Harper 1983 pap. $5.95. A collection of essays derived from the Darwin Centennial Symposium, held in San Francisco in 1983.

Howard, Jonathan. *Darwin.* Oxford 1982 pap. $4.95. Howard is a prominent zoologist. He has written a scholarly work that assesses Darwin's ideas on natural selection, heredity, and evolution.

Hull, David L. *Darwin and His Critics: The Reception of Darwin's Theory of Evolution by the Scientific Community.* Univ. of Chicago Pr. 1983 pap. $17.00. "Writing clearly and cogently, [Hull] skillfully combines five of his own brief essays with an anthology of 16 contemporary reviews of 'The Origin of Species' and adds helpful comments" (*Choice*).

Irvine, William. *Apes, Angels, and Victorians: The Story of Darwin, Huxley, and Evolution.* Intro. by Julian Huxley, Univ. Pr. of Amer. 1983 pap. $18.75. A skillful blending of information and humor about Charles Darwin, T. H. Huxley, and the impact of Darwinism on the nineteenth-century world.

Livingstone, David N. *Darwin's Forgotten Defenders: The Encounter between Evangelical Theology and Evolutionary Thought.* Eerdmans 1987 pap. $9.95

Smith, John M., ed. *Evolution Now: A Century after Darwin.* W. H. Freeman 1982 $23.95. This is a fine collection of review articles originally printed in *Nature* and other journals.

Stebbins, G. Ledyard. *Darwin to DNA, Molecules to Humanity.* W. H. Freeman 1982 text ed. pap. $19.95. Stebbins is one of the fathers of modern evolutionary thought and a plant scientist. "His book is a marvel of clear and graphic exposition, a fine choice of material and a flowing, lucid style" (*Quarterly Review of Biology*). "This is a readable book with an apt title for modern ideas concerning the evolutionary origin of human beings" (*Choice*).

Sunderland, Luther. *Darwin's Enigma*. Master Bks. 1984 pap. $6.95

Young, Robert M. *Darwin's Metaphor: Nature's Place in Victorian Culture*. Cambridge Univ. Pr. 1985 $47.50 pap. $15.95

DUBOS, RENE JULES. 1901–1982

René Dubos was a famous microbiologist as well as a writer, educator, and environmentalist. Born and educated in France, Dubos came to the United States in 1924 to join the research staff of Rutgers University. In 1927 he was invited to join the staff of Rockefeller University. At Rockefeller he pioneered research in commercially produced antibiotics for commercial use during the 1940s. As he grew older, his interests shifted from microbiology to humanistic and social-environmental issues. He devoted much of his writing to environmental problems and their impact on human life.

Dubos served as president of several professional organizations in the sciences. The author of some 20 books, he was awarded more than a score of prizes by the scientific community. As an emeritus professor at Rockefeller University he continued to write up until the time of his death.

BOOKS BY DUBOS

Louis Pasteur: Free Lance of Science. Da Capo repr. of 1960 ed. 1986 pap. $11.95

Dreams of Reason: Science and Utopias. Columbia Univ. Pr. 1961 $22.50 pap. $11.00. "Dubos develops his theme with wit, irony, art and facts" (*The New Yorker*).

Torch of Life. Simon & Schuster 1962 o.p.

The Unseen World. Rockefeller Univ. Pr. 1962 o.p. "The story of microorganisms, both disease producing agents and 'domesticated' microbes that yield beer, cheese, antibiotics, etc." (*N.Y. Times Bk. Review*).

Man Adapting. 1965. Yale Univ. Pr. 1980 $37.50 pap. $12.00. "An incisive analysis of the situation in organized medicine, which continues to define all minute particulars of life without adapting to the new problems posed by the modern social conflict" (Oscar Handlin, *Atlantic*).

So Human an Animal. 1968. Scribner 1984 $8.95. Dubos "asserts that we are as much the product of our total environment as of our genetic endowment . . . that we can change our suicidal course by learning to deal scientifically with the living experience of man" (Publisher's note).

Reason Awake: Science for Man. Columbia Univ. Pr. 1970 $28.00 pap. $12.00. "Dubos attempts to determine the role of science in human life and the growth of civilization . . . [and] indicates new attitudes and directions that could help man to find his place within nature" (*LJ*).

Mirage of Health. Harper 1971 o.p.

(and Barbara Ward). *Only One Earth: The Care and Maintenance of a Small Planet*. Norton 1972 $13.95 1983 pap. $5.95. A study done for the United Nations giving background information on the "fact of environmental interrelationships—air, water, land, energy resources—and the consequences of policies which ignore these interrelationships" (*America*).

A God Within. Irvington 1974 $29.50

The Professor, the Institute, and DNA. Rockefeller Univ. Pr. 1976 $15.00

The Wooing of Earth. Scribner 1980 pap. $6.95. "In a rebuttal to those who equate ecological and environmental purity with unspoiled wilderness, Dubos argues in this extended essay that humankind irretrievably changes the natural world and that the results do not have to be detrimental" (*LJ*).
Celebrations of Life. McGraw-Hill 1981 $12.95

FABRE, JEAN HENRI. 1823–1915

The French entomologist worked directly from nature. After a period teaching at French universities, he spent all his time observing and writing about insect behavior. His well-known essays on the life and habits of various insects are imaginative and charming. Now out of print is his well known *The Marvels of the Insect World* (1938), selected translations from his main ten-volume work *Souvenirs entomologiques* (1879–1907).

BOOKS BY FABRE

The Life of the Spider. Norwood 1912 $45.00. Selections in English from his principal work, *Souvenirs entomologiques.*
Social Life in the Insect World. Ayer repr. of 1912 ed. $23.50. This is a monograph on familiar insects, their habits and life stages. Fabre presents his observations in a romantic and "humanized style." A good popular introduction to insect life.
The Insect World of J. Henri Fabre. Ed. by Edwin Way Teale, Dodd 1949 o.p. This book includes some of the most vivid and perceptive insect studies ever written. It is a fine overview of Fabre's studies, accessible to the layperson.

FRISCH, KARL VON. 1887–1982 (NOBEL PRIZE 1973)

"*Man and the Living World,*" wrote Ruth Moore in the *New York Times*, "is at once a broad, scientific summary of biology and a book to engage and delight the mind." Written for the general reader, but with the authority of a lifetime of study and original research, it offers "captivating and memorable accounts of the form and development of many of the world's myriad plants, insects and animals, including man."

The Austrian zoologist achieved international recognition for his pioneer research on sense functions in fish and for his discovery of the "language" of the bees, which he describes in his great book *The Dancing Bees.* In this work he explains how these insects are able to communicate to their fellow colonists the direction, quantity, and quality of food through dances.

As a student, von Frisch studied medicine and zoology in Vienna and Munich. In 1910 he joined the faculty of the University of Munich and was associated with it intermittently until his retirement as professor of zoology in 1958. He spent many years as the director of the Zoological Institutes in Rostock, Breslau, and Munich. He was active in the international scientific community, lecturing in the United States and Europe.

In 1959 von Frisch was awarded the Kalinga Prize and in 1963 a Balzan Prize. In 1973 he shared the Nobel Prize for physiology or medicine for his contributions in sociobiology. Karl von Frisch died at the age of 96, ending a productive and rewarding life. (See also Chapter 12 in this volume.)

BOOKS BY VON FRISCH

The Dancing Bees: An Account of the Life and Senses of the Honey Bee. Trans. by Dora
   Ilse and Norman Walker, Harcourt 1961 pap. $5.95
Dance Language and Orientation of Bees. Harvard Univ. Pr. 1967 $30.00. This is still
   the major source on bee communication.
Bees: Their Vision, Chemical Senses and Language. Cornell Univ. Pr. 2d ed. 1971
   $25.00 pap. $5.95
Man and the Living World. Harcourt 1963 o.p. This is a fine introduction to biology
   for the layperson.
Twelve Little Housemates. Pergamon 1979 $17.00 pap. $7.75. This is a book on insects
   that are common household pests; written for a popular audience.

HALDANE, JOHN BURDON SANDERSON. 1892–1964

J. B. Haldane, an eccentric genius, was once described as "the last man
who might know all there was to know." A student of classics at Oxford, he
became a brilliant biochemist, physiologist, and geneticist—and Marxist
revolutionary (until he broke with the Communist party over its uncritical
reverence for the Russian biologist Lysenko). During his Communist period
he did important work in science for the British government. An officer in
World War I, he later taught at the University of London, and made remarkable discoveries in the application of mathematics and statistics to biology.
Upset by the British attack on Egypt over Suez, Haldane spent his last few
years pursuing his research and holding various scientific posts in India,
though he traveled back to England on several occasions and on one of
those saw his own obituary on BBC television.

Haldane was known for trying dangerous experiments on himself and for
his lucid and enthusiastic expositions for the layperson. "This ability to
entrance," writes Ronald Clark in *JBS* (see below), "was due partly to his
humble wonder at the world around him [and partly to] his facility for
linking the facets of one science with those of all of the rest: beneath this
there lay the touchstones of personal integrity, honesty and courage."

BOOKS BY HALDANE

Daedalus, or Science and the Future. 1923. Quaker City Bks. $27.00. Haldane prophe-
   sizes here about the future of the sciences and the subsequent impact on human
   life. "Mr. Haldane's is a brilliant little book, sparkling here and there with a
   witty thought or turn of phrase, often daring in some casual statement" (*N.Y.
   Tribune*).
Possible Worlds and Other Essays. Richard West 1927 $35.00. This is a collection of
   lectures, broadcasts, and essays expressing a Marxist point of view on biological
   and sociological issues.
The Philosophical Basis of Biology. Richard West 1931 $25.00. This book was based
   on a series of lectures Haldane delivered at Trinity College in 1930. He presents
   his view of the "nature of life" based on his own observations as a biologist.
Science and Human Life. Ayer repr. of 1933 ed. $19.00. The concept that unifies this
   collection of essays, addresses, and lectures is, once again, how science affects
   human life. "Only a man of independent thought, originality of view and exceptional literary gifts could be sure that a miscellany of this type would be read

with interest. He is as fascinating to himself as any of the dahlias, fruit flies, mice and other organisms with which he experiments" (*N.Y. Times*).

Marxist Philosophy and the Sciences. Ayer repr. of 1939 ed. $15.00. Here Haldane deals with mathematical, biological, and sociological problems from a Marxist point of view.

Keeping Cool and Other Essays. Richard West repr. of 1940 ed. $25.00

The Philosophy of a Biologist. Richard West 1955 $25.00

On Being the Right Size and Other Essays. Ed. by John M. Smith, Oxford 1975 pap. $5.95

Science and Everyday Life. Ayer 1975 $25.50

Books about Haldane

Clark, Ronald. *JBS: The Life and Work of J. B. S. Haldane.* Oxford 1984 pap. $8.95. "J. B. S. Haldane loomed larger than life in so many ways that is difficult to compress his accomplishments and personality into a brief biography. Ronald Clark, who based his work on primary sources . . . has met the challenge, however, in this delightful, balanced, well-written study of both the man and his work. He presents scientific explanations with a lucidity likely to have pleased Haldane himself. He includes the details of Haldane's often flamboyant life without sensationalism but also without sloughing over highly controversial works. . . . I cannot recommend this book too highly" (*LJ*)

Dronamraju, K. R., ed. *Haldane and Modern Biology.* Johns Hopkins Univ. Pr. 1968 o.p. "A truly fascinating" (*LJ*) collection of essays by an international group of scientists.

HUXLEY, SIR JULIAN SORELL. 1887–1975

Sir Julian, elder brother of Aldous Huxley (see Vol. 1), was born in London, the eldest son of Leonard Huxley, biographer and historian; "the nephew of Mrs. Humphrey Ward"; the grand nephew of Matthew Arnold (see Vol. 1); and the grandson of the great scientist Thomas Henry Huxley. Julian Huxley began gathering honors while at Balliol College, Oxford, where he lectured on zoology for two years. He was a gifted master of lucid prose and wrote innumerable articles and books, many on science for the unscientific, on subjects ranging from "the evolutionary conception of God to the politics of ants." He advocated a scientific humanism as a substitute for the mysticism of the past. He interested himself in politics as well as science and was director-general of UNESCO (1946–48). In January 1960, Sir Julian received the New York University Medal following his lecture entitled "Evolution in Our Time." "My final belief is life," was his philosophy.

Books by Sir Julian Huxley

Essays of a Biologist. Arden Lib. $10.00; Ayer repr. of 1923 ed. $19.00; Telegraph Bks. repr. of 1923 ed. 1986 $45.00. This is a collection of addresses, lectures, and essays on progress in biology and sociology, and the relationship of science and religion. "The book covers a wide field and Mr. Huxley shows himself to be a man of many parts . . . attractive style of writing" (*N.Y. Times*).

Africa View. Greenwood repr. of 1930 ed. 1968 $25.00. Huxley spent four months traveling in East Africa, during which time he kept a daily record of his thoughts, activities, and observations. Huxley wrote this book from his daily record and enriched it with his views on imperialism, education, and science.

Ants. AMS Pr. repr. of 1930 ed. 1985 $20.00. "The ants are of all the social insects the most successful and perhaps the most extraordinary." Huxley takes this view of ants and his essays on the various aspects of ant life are surprisingly interesting as well as being gracefully written.

Science and Religion. Ayer repr. of 1931 ed. $14.25

Man Stands Alone. Ayer repr. of 1941 ed. $22.00. A collection of essays on natural science, evolution, humanism, and religion originally published in London under the title *The Uniqueness of Man.*

Heredity, East and West: Lysenko and World Science. Kraus Repr. repr. of 1949 ed. 1969 $21.00

Religion Without Revelation. Greenwood repr. of 1967 ed. 1979 $24.75

BOOK ABOUT SIR JULIAN HUXLEY

Baker, J. R. *Julian Huxley: Scientist and World Citizen, 1887–1975. A Bibliographic Memoir.* Unipub 1978 pap. $7.00

HUXLEY, THOMAS HENRY. 1825–1895

Huxley, "the great agnostic," the living example of the high ethical standard of the true evolutionist and the true rationalist, devoted himself almost exclusively to the defense and exposition of Darwin's theory of evolution. Like Darwin he started his scientific investigations while on a voyage to far places. He was assistant surgeon on the H.M.S. *Rattlesnake*, sent to explore Australia and the Great Barrier Reef, and stayed with the ship throughout the voyage (1846–50). Although he was one of the foremost anatomists of his time, his lectures and books were almost entirely on Darwinism. He had the "gift for the apt and acid phrase" and his "pure, rapid, athletic English" has stood as a model for all scientific writers. Huxley was later active as secretary and president of the Royal Society and as a member of many royal commissions. His period on the London school board had an important impact on British educational reform.

BOOKS BY THOMAS HENRY HUXLEY

Autobiography and Essays. Ed. by Brander Matthews, Kraus Repr. repr. of 1919 ed. 1969 $28.00

Collected Essays. 1894. Greenwood 9 vols. repr. of 1902 ed. 1969 $138.00. These fine essays are a neglected part of Huxley's contribution. They include his thoughts on science, religion, and education.

Critiques and Addresses. Ayer repr. of 1873 ed. $15.50

Darwiniana. AMS Pr. repr. of 1896 ed. 1985 $39.50. This is a collection of articles and essays that Huxley wrote in defense of Darwin's theory of evolution.

Man's Place in Nature and Other Essays. 1863. Richard West repr. of 1906 ed. 1979 $20.00. Contests the anatomist Richard Owen's view that man differs from other animals in the structure of his brain.

Diary of the Voyage of the H.M.S. Rattlesnake. Kraus Repr. repr. of 1936 ed. $29.00. The *Rattlesnake's* voyage in the Pacific waters north of Australia provided a natural laboratory that Huxley used to study medusae and plankton. On this voyage, Huxley's work led him to be a master at invertebrate zoology, and his later work and thought stem from this trip.

Huxley: Selections from the Essays. Ed. by Aubrey Castell, Harlan Davidson 1948 text ed. pap. $4.95. Huxley's essays are valuable to any reader interested in the history and philosophy of science.

BOOKS ABOUT THOMAS HENRY HUXLEY

Ainsworth-Davies, James R. *Thomas H. Huxley.* AMS Pr. repr. of 1907 ed. 1974 $21.50

Clodd, Edward. *Thomas Henry Huxley.* Folcroft repr. of 1902 ed. $17.00

DiGregorio, Mario A. *T. H. Huxley's Place in Natural Science.* Yale Univ. Pr. 1984 $25.00

Irvine, William. *Thomas Henry Huxley.* British Bk. Ctr. pap. $1.95

Marshall, A. J. *Darwin and Huxley in Australia.* Verry 1971 $11.00

Peterson, Houston. *Huxley: Prophet of Science.* AMS Pr. repr. of 1932 ed. 1975 $26.00

KOCH, ROBERT. 1843–1910 (NOBEL PRIZE 1905)

Robert Hermann Heinrich Koch was born in Clausthal, Germany. He first studied the natural sciences at Göttingen University and then switched to the medical school. In 1866 he graduated, went to Berlin, and worked in charity clinics.

Koch practiced medicine in a rural community for a short time, and then joined the army to serve as a field physician. He gained valuable experience serving on the battlefield during the Franco-Prussian War. Upon leaving the army, he obtained a post as district physician in Wollstein, Austria. There, in 1876, during a severe anthrax outbreak, Koch made his first important discovery. He identified the bacillus that causes anthrax—the first time a specific pathogen was proven to cause a specific disease. This breakthrough earned Koch an appointment to the Imperial Health Service in Berlin.

Koch's next achievement was the identification of the tuberculosis bacillus, and the explanation of its mode of transmission. In 1905 Koch won the Nobel Prize for physiology and medicine for his work on tuberculosis.

Berlin was Koch's headquarters for most of his lifetime, and he was promoted to higher ranks in the Imperial Health Service. Throughout the years he traveled extensively to the sites of different epidemics in Europe and Africa. He identified the organism that causes cholera, as well as bacteria that cause other human and animal epidemics.

Koch's work established him as the founder of modern bacteriology, tropical medicine, and public health. Among his major contributions are "Koch's Postulates," the principles that have been used to diagnose disease agents. He also developed the methods used for culturing and staining bacteria, growing pure bacterial cultures, and using steam as a sterilizer. Koch had an enormous impact on the development of the field of public health. He was responsible for much early public health legislation in Europe, and for developing public awareness of disease control through hygienic and immunologic measures.

BOOK BY KOCH

Founders of Modern Medicine. Ed. by Ilia Ilich Mechnikov, Louis Pasteur, Joseph
Lister, and Robert Koch, trans. by D. Berger, Ayer repr. of 1939 ed. $21.00.
Three essays, one by Pasteur, one by Lister, and "The Etiology of Wound Infec-
tions" by Robert Koch, comprise this volume.

LAMARCK, JEAN BAPTISTE (JEAN BAPTISTE PIERRE ANTOINE DE MONET LAMARCK). 1744–1829

Lamarck made significant contributions to the disciplines of botany, zoology, and paleontology. Born in Picardy, France, he studied at a Jesuit semi-
nary, but he never completed his training for the priesthood. Lamarck
joined the army, and fought in the Seven Years' War. During this time he
developed an interest in botany and began to do botanical research. The
first recognition Lamarck received as a scientist was due to his design of a
new classification scheme for plants. This was published in 1778 as *Flore
française.* His two other major botanical works were *Dictionnaire botanique,*
an encyclopedic work finished in 1795, and *Introduction á botanique,* published in 1803. Lamarck had begun work in zoology and paleontology in the
1790s. In 1801 he published his most significant work on invertebrate
zoology—*Système des animaux sans vertèbres.* His major paleontological
work, *Memoires sur les fossiles des environs de Paris,* was written between
1802 and 1806.

Lamarck's evolutionary theories were presented in *Recherche sur l'organisation des corps vivans* (1802). Lamarck believed that over long periods of
time, life forms evolved and grew increasingly complex. He attributed these
changes in form to the inheritability of acquired traits. This theory was
widely publicized and had great impact on the future of biology. Although
his theories were proven fallacious by the work of other evolutionists,
Lamarck paved the way for Darwin and Alfred Russel Wallace (1823–1913).

During the later years of his life, Lamarck's reputation declined. He proposed theories in chemistry and physics that were ridiculed. Ten years
before his death, Lamarck went blind, but continued to work despite pov-
erty and blindness. He was beset by tragedy throughout his life. He was
widowed three times. He had two sons: one was deaf, and one was insane.
Lamarck died in 1829.

BOOKS ABOUT LAMARCK

Barthelemy-Madaule, Madeleine. *Lamarck the Mythical Precursor: A Study of the
Relations Between Science and Ideology.* Trans. by Michael Shank, MIT 1982
$25.00. "The thesis is established that Lamarck was an heir of the enlighten-
ment and founder of a new science, but the many references make the book
difficult to read" (*Choice*).

Burkhardt, Richard W., Jr. *The Spirit of System: Lamarck and Evolutionary Biology.*
Harvard Univ. Pr. 1977 $18.00. "All in all Burkhardt has given us an important
and reliable study, no doubt the major source now on the topic" (*Science*).

Cannon, H. Graham. *Lamarck and Modern Genetics.* Greenwood repr. of 1959 ed.
1975 $27.50

Jordanova, L. J. *Lamarck.* Oxford 1984 $13.95 pap. $4.95. "Jordanova provides not only an effective introduction to Lamarck's work, but also a highly original interpretation" (*TLS*).

McKinney, H., ed. *Lamarck to Darwin: Contributions to Evolutionary Biology, 1809–1859*. Coronado Pr. 1971 pap. $7.50

Packard, Alpheus S. *Lamarck: The Founder of Evolution; His Life and Work; with Translations of His Writings on Organic Evolution.* Ayer repr. of 1901 ed. $39.00

Palmer, Katherine. *The Unpublished Velins of Lamarck, 1802 to 1809: Illustrations of Fossils of the Paris Basin Eocene.* Paleo Research 1977 $15.00

LINNAEUS, CAROLUS. 1707–1778

Linnaeus was a botanist, physician, teacher, writer, and administrator. He was the most influential naturalist of his time, and the father of biological taxonomy. His eminence is due to the development of the biological classification systems for plant and animal life.

Carolus Linnaeus, also known as Carl von Linné, was born in Rashult, Sweden. He studied at the universities of Lund and Uppsala, and at Harderwyck, where he received a degree in medicine. At the age of 25, Linnaeus undertook an expedition to Lapland to collect exotic plants. This was the most adventurous exploit of his life. It was also the beginning of a project that would involve him for 20 years: naming, describing, and classifying every organism known to the Western world.

While pursuing his botanical and taxonomic research, Linnaeus practiced medicine to earn a living. As his research progressed he published numerous works. Among them are 12 editions of *Systema Naturae* (1735), *Species Plantarum* (1753), *Philosophia Botanica* (1751), and *Genera Plantarum* (1737). In 1741 he was appointed to a chair at Uppsala, and in the following year he accepted a chair in botany at the same institution. By 1758 he had completed his taxonomic project by classifying 4,400 species of animals and 7,700 species of plants. In his middle age he became a university administrator. In 1770, Linnaeus became ill and remained sick until his death in 1778.

Linnaeus's enduring contributions were to develop the principles and methods for defining taxonomic groups, and to establish the need for the use of uniform taxonomic systems. His systems have been used until the present with modifications and revisions.

BOOKS BY LINNAEUS

Bibliotheca Botanica. Lubrecht & Cramer 1968 $10.00. This was the second important bibliography of botany to be compiled and printed.

Hortus Cliffortianus. Lubrecht & Cramer repr. of 1751 ed. 1968 $108.00

Philosophia Botanica. Lubrecht & Cramer repr. of 1751 ed. 1960 $67.50

A Facsimile Reprint of Systema Naturae by Carolus Linnaeus. 1753. Meckler 1983 $95.00 *Systema Naturae Regnum Vegetable* introduced the Linnaen classification system.

Species Plantarum: A Facsimile of the First Edition 1753. British Museum of Natural History 2 vols. 1956 $84.00. In *Species Plantarum*, the Linnaen classification system was applied to all known plants. This was the starting point for internationally accepted nomenclature.

Caroli Linnaei: A Photographic Facsimile of the First Volume of the Tenth Edition

(1758) Regnum Animale. British Museum of Natural History repr. of 1956 ed. 1978 $36.00. The first volume of *Regnum Animale* is the first use of Linnaen zoological classification, which also became internationally accepted.

Miscellaneous Tracts Relating to Natural History, Husbandry, and Physick: Calendar of Flora Is Added. Ayer repr. of 1762 ed. 1978 $29.00

Mantissa Plantarum, 1767–71. Lubrecht & Cramer 2 vols. 1970 $67.50

Select Dissertations from Amoenitates Academicae: Supplement to Mr. Stillingfleet's Tracts, Relating Natural History. Ayer repr. of 1781 ed. $38.50

Index Kewensis Plantarum Phanerogarum (Linnaeus to the Year 1885). Ed. by J. D. Hooker and B. D. Jackson, Lubrecht & Cramer 2 vols. 1977 $636.00

Carl von Linnaeus' Travels. Ed. by David Black, Scribner 1984 o.p.

BOOKS ABOUT LINNAEUS

Broberg, Gunnar, ed. *Linnaeus: Progress and Prospects in Linnean Research.* Hunt Inst. Botanical 1980 $49.50

Frangsmyr, Tore, and others, eds. *Linnaeus: The Man and His Work.* Univ. of California Pr. 1983 $30.00. "This book is important reading for all biologists and science historians and will interest informed layreaders" (*LJ*).

Gjertsen, Derek. *The Classics of Science: A Study of Twelve Enduring Scientific Works.* Barber Pr. 1984 text ed. $24.95 text ed. pap. $12.95

Lewis, Arthur M. *Evolution—Social and Organic: Linnaeus, Darwin, Kropotkin, Marx.* C. H. Kerr 1984 $17.95

Smith, James E., and Keir B. Sterling. *A Selection of the Correspondence of Linnaeus and Other Naturalists: From Original Manuscripts.* Ayer 2 vols. repr. of 1821 ed. 1978 $99.00

Soulsby, Basil H., ed. *A Catalogue of the World of Linnaeus Preserved in the Libraries of the British Museum of Natural History.* British Museum of Natural History 1933–36 o.p.

Stearn, W. T. *Three Prefaces to Linnaeus and Robert Brown.* Lubrecht & Cramer 1962 pap. $8.50

Weinstock, John. *Contemporary Perspectives on Linnaeus.* Univ. Pr. of Amer. 1985 $12.75 pap. $12.25. This book includes expanded papers from a biological history symposium and a bibliography.

West, Luther S., and Oneita B. Peters. *Annotated Bibliography of Musca Domestica Linnaeus.* Northern Michigan Univ. Pr. 1973 $38.95

PASTEUR, LOUIS. 1822–1895

This many-sided scientific genius spent most of his life teaching at various universities throughout France, including the Sorbonne (1868–69) and the Ecole Normale (1857–67) in Paris. He had a passion for work, whose virtues he liked to extol, and was able to combine his teaching with research of tremendous consequence. His discoveries about bacteria demolished once and for all the ancient theory of the "spontaneous generation" of disease; his "pasteurization" process became the widely used method of decontaminating milk; with it, among other services to his country, he saved the wine and beer industries of France from endemic souring. He did valuable work on diseases of the silkworm (which threatened the French silk industry) and on rabies, to which the Pasteur Institute in Paris, of which he became the first director, was devoted. He lived to receive many honors but declined all temptations to wealth.

BOOKS BY PASTEUR

Studies on Fermentation. 1879. Trans. and ed. by James B. Conant, Harvard Univ. Pr. 1952 o.p. Pasteur discovered yeast as the cause of fermentation in beer and isolated the microorganism that ferments wine. The pasteurization process was an outcome of these fermentation studies, which he did in order to address the problems of spoilage in the wine and beer industries.

Founders of Modern Medicine. Ed. by Ilia Ilich Mechnikov, Louis Pasteur, Joseph Lister, and Robert Koch, trans. by D. Berger, Ayer repr. of 1939 ed. $21.00. Three essays, one by Pasteur, one by Lister, and "The Etiology of Wound Infections" by Robert Koch, comprise this volume.

BOOKS ABOUT PASTEUR

Conant, James B. *Pasteur's and Tyndall's Study of Spontaneous Generation.* Harvard Univ. Pr. 1953 o.p. Pasteur's fermentation research enabled him to prove that the yeast in fermented beer did not arise spontaneously. He added important evidence to the refutation of the spontaneous-generation theory.

Dubos, René. *Louis Pasteur: Free Lance of Science.* Da Capo repr. of 1960 ed. 1986 pap. $11.95

Eastman, Fred. *Men of Power: Thomas Jefferson, Charles Dickens, Matthew Arnold, Louis Pasteur.* Ayer 5 vols. repr. of 1938 ed. ea. $18.00 set $88.00

Hume, David. *Bechamp vs Pasteur.* Blackwell 1981 $15.95

Keim, Albert, and Louis Lumet. *Louis Pasteur.* Folcroft repr. of 1914 ed. 1981 o.p. An illustrated conventional biography of Louis Pasteur, and a summary of his work.

Koprowski, Hilary, and Stanley A. Plotkin. *World's Debt to Pasteur.* Alan R. Liss 1985 $39.50

Radot, Rene V. *The Life of Pasteur.* Richard West 1923 $35.00

Wood, Laura N. *Louis Pasteur.* Messner 1948 o.p. This biography emphasizes Pasteur's scientific work and his contributions to medical and industrial research.

PLINY THE ELDER (CAIUS PLINIUS SECUNDUS). C.A.D. 23–A.D. 79

This Roman scholar and naturalist wrote many works in the fields of natural science and military tactics. Only his great work, *Natural History,* the oldest encyclopedia (in 37 books) is extant. It deals with the nature of the physical universe: geography, anthropology, zoology, botany, mineralogy, and allied subjects. Pliny was credulous; his *History* contains many unsubstantiated marvels and many, many errors of fact. He hated to waste time, and his prolific output was considered authoritative for several centuries after his lifetime. It offers information on ancient art and general culture that is to be found nowhere else. He died of asphyxiation near Naples during a massive eruption of Vesuvius.

BOOKS BY PLINY THE ELDER

The Elder Pliny's Chapters on Chemical Subjects. Scholarly 2 vols. repr. of 1929 ed. o.p. Translated excerpts from Pliny's *Naturalis Historia.*

Natural History. Ed. by Paul Turner, Centaur 1983 $65.00; ed. by E. H. Warmington, Harvard Univ. Pr. 10 of 11 vols. ea. $12.95–$13.95

The Elder Pliny's Chapters on the History of Art. Ed. by K. Jex-Blake and Eugenie Sellers, Ares 1974 $15.00

BOOK ABOUT PLINY THE ELDER

French, Roger, and Frank Greenaway. *Science in the Early Roman Empire: Pliny the Elder, His Sources and Influence.* Barnes & Noble 1986 $28.50

SINNOTT, EDMUND WARE. 1888–1968

One of the world's leading botanists, Sinnott was particularly interested in problems of biological philosophy. In *The Biology of the Spirit,* his main thesis is that "protoplasm, the basic stuff of plants and animal life, has a biological purpose." In man, this "goal-seeking" protoplasm, which seems to direct human motivation, is an extension of a universal reality—"God" ("Spirit," "Force," or "Personality"). In *Matter, Mind and Man,* he provides answers for man's perennial questions—about himself and his world—that will form a unified and logically harmonious framework of concepts about man and his relation to life and to the universe. "Our aim," he writes, "has been to fit man into the universe of matter, mind, and spirit without the necessity of dismembering him." He sees man steadily and sees him whole, and believes that "only in God can man be fulfilled" (*SR*). He is the author of many textbooks.

BOOKS BY SINNOTT

Matter, Mind and Man: The Biology of Human Nature. Atheneum 1963 pap. $2.75

Plant Morphogenesis. Krieger repr. of 1960 ed. 1979 $36.50. Sinnott was a botanist who specialized in the morphology (physical form) of vascular plants. In this book, he presents a comprehensive discussion of the phenomena of morphogenesis in plants and the main physiological factors governing plant development.

CHAPTER 12

Ecology and Environmental Science

Robert T. Kirkwood

Each of us . . . is an observer of the myriad worlds about us . . . we are in some way . . . constantly responding to our environment . . . ; a Cape Cod saltwater marsh, or the majestic redwood forests of the West Coast; the night sky sequined with stars, or a dragonfly flashing in the summer morning sun.

—WILLIAM D. MCELROY AND CARL P. SWANSON,
Foundations of Biology (1968)

Ecology, the study of the environment in which a plant or animal lives and of the ways the plant or animal interacts with other factors in that environment, was a practical art long before it was a science. Members of a hunter-gatherer society relied on their knowledge of ecology for survival. Hunters had to know where prey was most likely to be and when it was most likely to be there; gatherers had to learn to interpret the appearance of a landscape so they would know where to look for edible plant material. Ecological information may have been the subject matter of the first teachers as one generation attempted to prepare the next to survive.

The first step in the development of the science of ecology, at least in the Western world, occurred in Greece. ARISTOTLE (see also Vols. 3 and 4), called the Father of Biology, gathered a tremendous amount of information (and misinformation) about animals, which he divided into four categories. One of them—*bioi*, or "modes of living"—was ecological information. However, neither the Greek philosophers nor the average Greek citizen attempted to apply ecological principles to themselves or their surroundings; following the pattern of many other people, they used their environment as if it were an inexhaustible resource. The thistle-covered, eroded hills of Attica are their descendants' heritage.

Ancient Rome, *Roma Aeterna*, failed to last eternally, at least in part, because its citizens, too, had no concern for their environment. Trees were removed, erosion filled irrigation canals with silt, and farming became more and more difficult. At one time, so many people left the land that farms were offered free to those who would work them.

Ecology shared the fate of other sciences during the Middle Ages. When truth is dictated rather than discovered, science has no place. Many church leaders of that time shared the view of the third-century church father Tertullian, who wrote, "We do not need to wonder since Jesus Christ, nor to ask questions." He went on to assert that Thales of Miletus, the early philosopher, had gotten what he deserved when he fell into a well while his eyes were raised to the heavens in astronomical study.

The first tentative steps of the modern science of ecology were not taken until individuals, many of them trained in theology, decided that studying nature was another way to learn about God.

NATURAL HISTORY

A naturalist differs from an ecologist in that the work of the naturalist is primarily descriptive while that of the ecologist is quantitative. One observer has asserted that the difference is that the ecologist considers what he does to be work while the naturalist insists that he is having fun. Many current workers, such as Marston Bates and Howard E. Evans in the following list, are effective combinations of ecologist and naturalist.

Ardrey, Robert. *The Territorial Imperative: A Personal Inquiry into the Animal Origins of Property and Nations.* Atheneum 1966 $10.95; Bantam 1978 pap. $2.50; Dell 1968 pap. $3.25. Robert Ardrey is a writer (playwright) who became interested in the role of territoriality in the lives of animals. He describes various types of territory and speculates about the impact of territoriality on human life.

Bates, Marston. *The Forest and the Sea.* Random 1965 o.p. Marston Bates begins this book with a wide-ranging look at the place of biology in the whole of human knowledge. He points out some of the artificial barriers that work against understanding ourselves: (1) The words "ecology" and "economics" come from the same Greek root, but we keep the natural science "ecology" and the social science "economics" isolated from each other. (2) We are dealing with a continuum of phenomena and any attempt to divide knowledge into physical sciences, biological sciences, social sciences, and humanities is artificial and often leads us to "think small" when we should be doing the opposite. The final chapter is a discussion of the place of the human species in nature. Bates notes, "The danger of complete man-centeredness in relation to nature is like the danger of immediate and thoughtless selfishness everywhere: the momentary gain results in ultimate loss and defeat." The other chapters deal with organisms in a variety of habitats, the natural history of disease, and aspects of animal behavior.

———. *Jungle in the House: Essays in Natural and Unnatural History.* Walker 1970 $7.50. What do you do if you were born in southern Florida, lived for many years in the tropics, and suddenly find yourself in a university town in Michigan in the winter? Marston Bates has answered the question by bringing a bit of the tropics to his house. First, a porch was converted into a conservatory by replacing screens with thermopane windows and adding fluorescent lights. Bates began to accumulate plants and animals for the conservatory, many of them as gifts. He immediately started to learn some previously unreported aspects of animal behavior: iguanas are incompatible with many kinds of plants, for instance. (His iguanas—Abelard and Heloise—devastated poinsettias. He began to select plants carefully so the conservatory would contain only those species that iguanas did not like.) When it became obvious that the conservatory was just not large enough, a 30-foot greenhouse was added along one side of the house.

This was divided into two separate areas providing, with the converted porch, three rooms. Having the three rooms made possible the separation of incompatible species among the birds, lizards, tree frogs, and plants. There is one exception to the previous statement. Mrs. Bates has a chapter in which she discusses the invasion of the house by various species of cockroaches hatched from egg cases brought in on plants collected for the greenhouse. A biologist's spouse must be a long-suffering individual with infinite patience and an incredible sense of humor.

————. *Man in Nature*. Prentice-Hall 2d ed. 1964 o.p. Bates has wide-ranging interests and writes well in many areas of biology. This volume is a collection of essays on various topics in ecology. It is well written and easy to read.

Durrell, Gerald, and Lee Durrell. *The Amateur Naturalist*. Knopf 1983 $24.95. The Durrells not only help the reader to do what a naturalist does but also to think as a naturalist thinks. Nothing would help the conservation of our natural resources as much as having many Americans become amateur naturalists. Everyone is more concerned about what happens to friends than about what happens to strangers. This book will help the potential naturalist get started.

Evans, Howard E. *The Pleasures of Entomology: Portraits of Insects and the People Who Study Them*. Smithsonian 1985 pap. $14.95. This book is not only a source of information about insects but also a gold mine of ideas for the person who would like to observe nature and record what he or she observes but is not sure where to start. Evans demonstrates that insects are fascinating and that the more one knows of their natural history the more fascinating they are.

Fabre, Jean H. *Social Life in the Insect World*. Trans. by Bernard Miall [*Select Bibliographies Repr. Ser.*] Ayer repr. of 1912 ed. 1978 $23.50. Fabre was a French naturalist who demonstrated to biologists the benefits of lying flat on your stomach in a vacant lot and observing what goes on before your eyes. He had a particular interest in social insects.

Garber, Steven D. *The Urban Naturalist*. Wiley 1987 pap. $14.95. "As well as describing . . . a lot of plants and animals that manage to inhabit American cities, Mr. Garber addresses the environmental pressures and opportunities that make them do so" (*N.Y. Times Bk. Review*).

Holden, Edith. *The Country Diary of an Edwardian Lady*. Holt 1977 $20.00 pap. $9.95. This book is a facsimile copy of the diary of an English woman who lived during the reign of Edward VII. She had not only curiosity and a keen eye but also a talent for drawing. The diary includes her observations, appropriate citations from poetry, and her drawings of plants and animals. A charming book.

Hubbell, Sue. *A Country Year: Living the Questions*. Harper 1987 pap. $6.95; Random 1986 $17.95. Move Edith Holden 81 years ahead in time and 5,000 miles west, and the Edwardian lady becomes the Ozarkian lady. Sue Hubbell has the same keen eye and knack for description that Holden had, and she also includes more comments about her personal life. She describes the activities and interactions of reptiles, mammals, insects and other arthropods, and birds. Another charming book.

Kastner, Joseph. *A World of Watchers*. Knopf 1986 $25.00. Anyone who has ever answered the phone at first light and heard someone say "I just saw the first scissortail (or prothonotary warbler or indigo bunting or something else)" will appreciate this book. The history of birding, the people who have encouraged birders, organizations of birders, and the contributions of birders to avian biology are all included.

Kieran, John. *A Natural History of New York City*. Fordham Univ. Pr. 2d ed. 1982 pap. $9.95. Those of us who think of a city as a concrete and asphalt desert, and of

New York as the biggest desert of all, will find we must completely change our vision of a city after we have read this book. Kieran begins with some history of the New York area, including the explorations of Verrazano, Gomez, and Henry Hudson. He also quotes some seventeenth-century writers who listed some of the native plants and animals of the area. Kieran then begins to discuss the plants and animals that can be found today, and there are many. He points out, "within the city limits there are springs, brooks, streams, ponds, and lakes, fresh- and salt-water marshes, and . . . more than seventeen miles of wonderful sea beach." He then lists and describes some of the myriad forms—from algae and protozoa to crabs and sand dollars—that can be found in these waters. Kieran has chapters on nonflowering plants, flowers, trees and shrubs, reptiles and amphibians, birds and mammals. Apparently a biologist could devote a lifetime to the study of the life-forms of New York City and still have work left to do.

McLoughlin, John. *The Animals among Us: Wildlife in the City.* Viking 1978 o.p. McLoughlin begins the preface of this book by describing the ecology of a shag carpet. He had rented a house and the first change he made after moving in was to pick up a shag carpet to put it in storage. He happened to see a small beetle in the fibers of the rug and took time to find what else was there. He identified animals from 3 classes, 7 families, and 12 genera of the phylum Arthropoda living in the carpet. He wondered about the ecology of the "shag community," especially about where the animals got their energy; a basic principle of ecology is that energy must come into a community from outside it. (Hint: The carpet was in a room where people gathered to watch television.) McLoughlin discusses other animals that have found niches in man-made environments. These animals include house (English) sparrows, which were deliberately brought to the United States by Brooklynites of English ancestry who were homesick for some of the birds with which they were familiar, and starlings, which became U.S. citizens because a Mr. Eugene Scheiffin wanted every bird named in the plays of Shakespeare to be here, and so had the first starlings imported. McLoughlin points out that rats came over on their own, climbing down mooring lines to get ashore. In speaking of rats he says that they are "actually the finest . . . product that nature has managed to create on this planet to date." By this he means that they can live in a variety of habitats, eat many kinds of food, and produce many offspring in these habitats while eating these kinds of food. McLoughlin also discusses mice, pigeons, brown recluse spiders, and many other animals that have become the bosom companions of human beings by finding niches in human communities.

Mitchell, John H. *A Field Guide to Your Own Backyard.* Norton 1985 $14.95 1986 pap. $5.95. Many people insist that nature can be observed only in an area such as a national park or game preserve. Mitchell demonstrates that this is not so. He writes of birds, wildflowers, salamanders, and trees in urban and suburban areas.

Seton, Ernest T. *Two Little Savages.* Amereon repr. of 1903 ed. 1962 $16.95; Century Bookbindery repr. of 1903 ed. 1982 lib. bdg. $45.00; Darby repr. of 1903 ed. 1983 lib. bdg. $35.00; Dover repr. of 1903 ed. 1962 pap. $5.95; Peter Smith 1967 $13.50. Born in South Shields, England, in 1860, Seton moved to Canada while quite young and lived in the backwoods. He demonstrated talent as an artist and studied at the Royal Academy, London, and in Paris. Seton was fascinated by nature and Indian life. In addition to writing many books, he worked with youth groups, such as the Boy Scouts, and established the Seton Institute in New Mexico for boys and girls interested in nature, nature crafts, and Indians. One must be careful in reading Seton because he can at times be very anthropomorphic—that is, he interprets animal behavior in human terms. This mind-set, considered a moral sin by biologists a generation ago, is much less disturbing to younger animal behaviorists. All boys, and most girls, should have read this book at least twice by the time they are 14 years old. It is semiautobiographical, based on the time Seton spent in the Canadian backwoods. Two boys learn from an old frontiersman to build a teepee from a tattered wagon cover, to make a bow and arrows, and to identify many of the plants and animals they see. The book is richly illustrated with Seton's drawings. Woven through all of this is an exciting story of robbers, a rendezvous at the crossroads at midnight, an old woman who knows strange secrets, a raccoon that turns out to be a lynx, games, mathematics, and reminders that "in one hour them pigs has got to be fed." Don't miss it!

Teale, Edwin W. *Autumn across America; Journey into Summer; North with the Spring; Wandering through Winter.* Dodd 1981 pap. ea. $8.95. All these books are reports on close observations of plants and animals and commentary on relationships. Teale must have traveled more than 80,000 miles as he gathered the information for them.

————. *The Golden Throng: A Book about Bees.* Universe repr. 1982 $16.50. In this book Teale deals with honeybees, their social organization, and their activities.

Thelwell, Norman. *A Plank Bridge by a Pool.* [*Encore Ed. Ser.*] Scribner 1979 o.p. This book, like Edith Holden's *The Country Diary of an Edwardian Lady* (see above), is of a kind for which the British seem to have a special knack. Thelwell describes his experiences when, as a child, he went to Raby Mere and got to ride in a rowboat. He writes, "There is no restriction, thank goodness, to dreams, and the dreams of childhood are untouched by the tired dust of experience. I dreamed of having a lake of my own—deep, quiet and beautiful." The rest of the book is about a "lake of his own." He and his wife bought an old cottage in Hampshire in the valley of the Test River. He had a lake dug and stocked it with rainbow trout, later replaced with native brown trout, and ducks. He describes a remarkable instance of animal behavior in the competition of the trout and the ducks for trout pellets. He also tells about . . . but read it for yourself.

Thompson, Gerald, and Jennifer Coldrey. *The Pond.* MIT 1984 $30.00. A pond is an excellent unit for ecological study. Unless one is overly zealous in making a selection, a pond is small enough that relationships among organisms are more obvious than they would be in a larger area. This book provides the amateur (using the original meaning of the word: "one who does something for the love of it") with information necessary to do his or her own pond study. The writing is nontechnical and the color illustrations are marvelous.

White, Gilbert. *The Natural History of Selborne.* Darby repr. of 1898 ed. 1981 lib. bdg. $39.50 [*Penguin Eng. Lib. Ser.*] 1977 pap. $4.95; State Mutual Bk. 1984 $20.00. White was one of the early naturalists whose example helped to give rise to ecology. Born in Selborne, a village in Hampshire, England, in 1720, he received an A.B. degree from Oxford University in 1743 and took holy orders. He served very little as a priest but spent most of his life in the village where he was born. White had the two characteristics essential for a naturalist or ecologist—a lively curiosity and the ability to observe carefully. His observations of the natural history of his native village are recorded in the letters that make up this book. White wrote of soils, climate, landforms, animal behavior; he was the epitome of the complete naturalist. He kept accurate records of the arrival and departure dates of various species of migratory birds. Some of his most interesting observations are about relationships between animals of different species—a horse and a hen, for instance.

Wilson, David Scofield. *In the Presence of Nature.* Univ. of Massachusetts Pr. 1978

$17.50. "Nature is present to naturalists the way God is to saints or the past is to humanists—not simply as a matter of fact but as an insistent and live reality. To come face to face with a flying spider or a rattlesnake in the road unhinges habit and intensifies awareness, just as stumbling upon an ancient rune does, or encountering a burning bush." These are the words with which Wilson opens this book. As the words indicate, Wilson is not a naturalist, an ecologist, or a biologist; he is a humanist who is attempting to place "nature reporters" (his term) in their proper place in the cultural history of this country. As an outsider examining naturalists, ecologists, and biologists under the microscope of scholarship he is able to reveal to these people things about themselves they do not suspect. He sees them as agents of an evolutionary change from a "cosmos of culture" to a "cosmos of nature." I know of no other book that holds before biologists a mirror in which they can see themselves as others see them. It is well worth the time and concentration that reading it demands.

ARISTOTLE. 384–322 B.C.

Aristotle was the son of the court physician to Amyntas II, the father of Philip of Macedon. According to Galen, the Roman anatomist and physician, Aristotle's father taught the boy some anatomy before sending him to Athens to become the pupil of PLATO (see Vols. 3 and 4). This may account for his interest in biology.

Aristotle was an able and dedicated student. After Plato's death in 347 B.C., Aristotle apparently considered himself to have all the formal schooling he needed and looked around for a place to put his education to use. He went to the court of Hermeias, another former student of Plato, married his adopted daughter Pythias, and was preparing to settle in Assus when political events forced his departure. He fled to Lesbos where he spent some time studying the plants and animals of the island.

In 340 B.C., Philip asked Aristotle to undertake the education of his son Alexander. The result of this assignment was that rare phenomenon—a ruler who, although not a scholar, had a great respect for scholarship. Alexander is reputed to have written Aristotle, "I would rather surpass others in the knowledge of what is excellent, than in the extent of my power and domination."

Aristotle returned to Athens in 334 B.C. and began to teach rhetoric and philosophy in a school he established called the Lyceum, held among the covered walks of one of the most elegant gymnasia in Athens. Aristotle liked to move along these walks while talking to his students, and thus earned the title "the Peripatetic Philosopher," from the Greek peripateo, "to walk." Aristotle had a large library, developed a zoological garden, and gathered specimens, collected by himself or sent to him by his students, in a museum of natural history.

In a very real way, Aristotle was more of a biologist than a philosopher. He was concerned with reasoning as a process, and his discussion of logic, the Organon, was the standard text up to modern times. However, he was one of the few philosophers of his time and for hundreds of years who espoused inductive as well as deductive reasoning and the use of experimentation. (See also Volumes 3 and 4.)

BOOKS BY ARISTOTLE

The Complete Works of Aristotle: The Revised Oxford Translation. Ed. by Jonathan Barnes [*Bollingen Ser.*] Princeton Univ. Pr. 2 vols. 1984 $75.00. The reader will find Aristotle's *History of Animals* in Volume 1 of this collection.

Historia Animalium. [*Loeb Class. Lib.*] Harvard Univ. Pr. 1965 3 bks. ea. $13.95. One must remember that Aristotle was writing some 2,500 years ago to people who lacked the scientific viewpoint that is our major frame of reference today. Some of his errors are monumental: "Twins with sheep and goats may be due to richness of pasturage, or to the fact that either the ram or the he-goat is a twin-begetter or that the ewe or the she-goat is a twin-bearer. Of these some animals give birth to males and others to females; and the difference in this respect depends on the waters they drink and also on the sires. And if they submit to the male when the north winds are blowing, they are apt to bear males; if when the south winds are blowing, females." That is powerful interaction of organism and environment! In another place, Aristotle asserts, "Serpents have an insatiate appetite for wine." Although ecological information is scattered throughout *Historia Animalium,* it is concentrated in Books 8 and 9. These two books are worth reading as history and as information, but one should evaluate the information.

BOOKS ABOUT ARISTOTLE

Grene, Marjorie. 1963. *A Portrait of Aristotle.* Univ. of Chicago Pr. 1979 text ed. pap. $8.00. A portrait of Aristotle's thought might be a more appropriate title for this book. I enjoy the opening lines of Chapter 1. Grene asserts in the first paragraph that a person is known to another person through his/her expressions, gestures, words, and actions. Then she declares in the second paragraph that philosophers can be known in the same way that we can know people! Grene discusses the problem of Aristotle's development, especially as the understanding of his development has been impacted by the writing of Werner Jaeger. She objects to the method of Jaeger and his followers by saying, "instead of leading the student to do his best to understand the philosopher in question, it makes him try his utmost to dissolve the thinker he is studying into many opposing thinkers and finally to legislate him out of existence altogether." She devotes the rest of the book to revealing the thinker rather than to dissolving him. Unless one has the time and the enthusiasm really to come to grips with Aristotle's thought, it would be better to depend on McKeon.

McKeon, Richard, ed. *Introduction to Aristotle.* Random 1965 text ed. pap. $5.00; Univ. of Chicago Pr. 2d ed. rev. & enl. 1974 text ed. $13.50. The name of this work indicates exactly what it is—an introduction to the thinking of Aristotle. The editor indicates in the preface that one cannot just pick up one of Aristotle's works and expect to derive a great deal from reading it. Some understanding of the man and his overall thought is necessary. The purpose of this introduction is to prepare the reader for individual works. The general introduction includes biographical material and a discussion of the times in which Aristotle lived as well as an overview of his thinking about art, science, and experience. Although *Historia Animalium* is not included, this volume provides the background against which one may understand the content of those books. The sections "Physics" and "Psychology and Biology" will be most useful to the student of biology.

DARWIN, CHARLES ROBERT. 1809–1882

Born in Shrewsbury, England, descended from two noted families, Darwin clearly had the proverbial silver spoon in his mouth. However, he showed so little promise in his early schooling that his father told him, "You care for nothing but shooting, dogs, and rat catching, and you will be a disgrace to yourself and all your family."

For his college work Darwin first went to Edinburgh to study medicine. Here again he was a poor student and could not stand the operating theater where surgery was performed without an anesthetic. When he returned home there appeared only one career choice left open—the ministry. Darwin went to Christ's College, Cambridge, to study theology. The British biologist Julian Huxley observed that if Darwin were living today he would not get into a good university. He may have entered Cambridge a poor student, but while he was there the faculty made sure that he learned something. He had extra tutoring, special assignments, and whatever else was necessary for him to know something before he was granted his A.B. degree.

Darwin's big break came shortly after graduation. A nonpaying position as a naturalist on His Majesty's Ship *Beagle* was available, and Darwin was recommended for the post by John Henslow, botany professor at Cambridge. Darwin's observations of natural history on this five-year voyage led eventually to his theory of evolution and the publication of *The Origin of Species* (1859). We will limit our interest here to those of his publications that had an ecological component. (See also Chapter 11 in this volume.)

BOOKS BY DARWIN

Journal of Researches into the Natural History and Geology of the Countries Visited during the Voyage of the H.M.S. Beagle round the World under the Command of Captain Fitz Roy. 1839. AMS Pr. 2 vols. repr. of 1892 ed. 1972 $42.50; Norwood repr. of 1892 ed. 1977 lib. bdg. $40.00. One of the benefits of being born with a silver spoon in your mouth is that you can afford to do interesting things even if you get paid nothing for them. Darwin's interest in natural history, stimulated by people he met at Cambridge, led to his appointment as naturalist on the *Beagle*. As one would expect from a person with Darwin's eye for detail, his reports are quite interesting. The *Beagle* was involved in surveying the coast of South America, and Darwin had plenty of leisure ashore to make observations. His enthusiasm can be seen time after time in his descriptions. Darwin observed human beings as well as other species and was violently indignant at what he observed of slavery. He wrote later, "I thank God that I shall never again visit a slave country." And in another place, "It makes one's blood boil, yet heart tremble, to think that we Englishmen and our American descendants, with their boastful cry of liberty, have been and are so guilty." Reading this book is a good way to spend an afternoon.

Fertilization of Orchids by Insects. 1862. Intro. by Norris H. Williams, E. M. Coleman repr. of 1862 ed. 1980 text ed. $27.50. We are so accustomed to certain bits of information heard over and over during our school years that we forget that someone had to make the first observations of the phenomena. That "someone" had always to be a person who saw what other people passed over. Observations of the ways in which flowers are adapted to profit from the visits of bees are especially interesting.

Darwin on Earthworms: The Formation of Vegetable Mould through the Action of Worms. 1881. Bookworm Pub. repr. of 1881 ed. 1976 $7.95 pap. $5.95. In *The Natural History of Selborne* Gilbert White had noted the importance of earthworms in soil formation. Darwin concentrated on two aspects of worm activity: He studied the way worms use leaves as food or to line or cover the openings of burrows, and he estimated the rate at which worm castings can cover objects lying on the surface of the field.

BOOKS ABOUT DARWIN

Appleman, Philip, ed. *Darwin.* [*Norton Critical Eds.*] 2d ed. 1979 $24.95 pap. $8.75. Norton Critical Editions deal with the history of ideas. This volume deals with the impact that Charles Darwin's theory of evolution has had on all aspects of life. Appleman selected papers from outstanding people in many fields. Some of these papers reflect the misuses of Darwinian thought and serve to illustrate why many people are concerned about the ultimate impact of sociobiology. These papers are in Part 5, "Darwin and Society." One of these, from Richard Hofstadter's book *Social Darwinism in American Thought* (see Vol. 3, Ch. 7), demonstrates how the ideas of Herbert Spencer were used to defend the premise that a few starved children were to be expected because we live in a world of "survival of the fittest." Spencer understood Darwin's ideas so poorly that he never did see that the environment decides which organisms are the fittest; if you vary the environment, you select for different organisms. Another paper in this section, "Mutual Aid" by Prince Peter Kropotkin, consists of interesting observations on animal behavior and human relationships. Although the whole book is stimulating, the reader will find Part 5 especially so.

Irvine, William. *Apes, Angels, and Victorians: The Story of Darwin, Huxley and Evolution.* Univ. Pr. of Amer. 1983 text ed. pap. $18.75. Irvine is able to communicate the intellectual and social atmosphere of the time in which Charles Darwin lived. The reader can feel as if he or she were in the audience as the good Bishop "Soapy Sam" Wilberforce was demolished by Thomas Henry Huxley, the commander of Darwin's "shock troops," and the central character in this book. Bishop Wilberforce turned to Huxley and "begged to know, was it through his grandfather or his grandmother that he claimed his descent from a monkey?" When the bishop finished, the audience, which was strongly anti-Darwin, called on Huxley to respond. Slowly he rose, walked to the podium, trenchantly destroyed all of the bishop's arguments, and ended by saying that he would not be ashamed of a monkey ancestry but he would be "ashamed to be connected with a man who used great gifts to obscure the truth." Irvine writes, "A hostile audience accorded him nearly as much applause as the Bishop had received." Irvine continues, "Huxley had committed forensic murder with a wonderful artistic simplicity, grinding orthodoxy between the facts and the supreme Victorian value of truth-telling." The book has both heroes and villains as did those times—or any times. It also has a tender love story between Huxley and Henrietta Heathorn. It is worth reading—by men or monkeys.

Montagu, Ashley. *Darwin: Competition and Cooperation.* Greenwood repr. of 1952 ed. 1973 lib. bdg. $24.75. Ashley Montagu has been a humane voice in the United States for many years. In this book he demonstrates clearly the differences between Darwinism and the theory of evolution. These beliefs often have no relationship to the actual content of the theory. Montagu describes his purpose in this way: "What is solid in Darwin's work will endure. Nothing that anyone can say or wish to say can detract from the greatness of what is sound in Darwin's achievement. There are, however, certain aspects of Darwin's thought and work that are unsound and some that are only partly true. It is these aspects of Darwin's achievement, which have had such disastrous consequences for mankind, with which I am concerned in the pages which follow." This is probably the most important book that I have reviewed in this chapter. Not only does it point to the fallacies of popular ideas about Darwinism, but it also provides a warning to those who would read their own psychic hungers into the theories of sociobiology.

KRUTCH, JOSEPH WOOD. 1893–1970

Joseph Wood Krutch demonstrated that the Renaissance man was not someone merely to read about. Born in Knoxville, Tennessee, he received his B.A. from the University of Tennessee and M.A. and Ph.D. degrees from Columbia, where he remained to teach as a member of the English department and later occupied an endowed chair of dramatic literature. He was also an editor and a drama critic. His biographical work includes books on EDGAR ALLAN POE (see Vol. 1), SAMUEL JOHNSON (see Vol. 1), and HENRY DAVID THOREAU (see Vol. 1). We will be concerned with some of his writing in natural history.

BOOKS BY KRUTCH

The Twelve Seasons. 1949. [*Essay Index Repr. Ser.*] Ayer repr. of 1949 ed. $16.00. Krutch's first book on natural history.

The Desert Year. 1952. Univ. of Arizona Pr. repr. of 1952 ed. 1985 pap. $9.95. Many of us see in our mind's eye pictures of the most desolate parts of the Sahara when we hear the word "desert." Krutch replaces that picture with another as he leads the reader to take a close look at a desert environment and to see the beauty that is a part of that ecosystem.

The Forgotten Peninsula: A Naturalist in Baja California. Fwd. by Ann Zwinger, Univ. of Arizona Pr. repr. 1986 pap. $9.95. Most Americans who hear a reference to Baja California probably think of the television commercials in which the advantage of one vehicle or another is demonstrated by showing it powering its way through the rugged desert area of the Baja. Actually, Baja California is a land of interesting environments from the nursery waters of the gray whale along the shore to the rugged areas of the interior. Krutch describes these environments.

Grand Canyon. Morrow 1968 pap. $5.95. The Grand Canyon can serve to illustrate many of the great principles of ecology, and Krutch uses it for this purpose. He points out that as a great barrier the canyon separates the Abert and Kaibab squirrels and, undoubtedly, led to the formation of the two separate species. He also describes the plant succession of aspen and pine. Aspen seeds are able to germinate in the ashes of a forest fire and the young trees to stand exposure to the full rays of the sun. The pines, which are a climax type, germinate in the aspen shade and eventually replace the broadleaf trees. I know of nothing that conveys the sense of the canyon as well as his description of a mule-back journey to Phantom Ranch: "The entire journey down has been through scenes indescribably grandiose, often between colorful hillocks and buttes but always austere and sometimes, especially within the inner gorge, somber almost to the point of gloominess. Vegetation was sparse and obviously just surviving: animal life extremely scanty. One was constantly reminded of terrific forces, vast stretches of time, and the depth of whole races of once flourishing living creatures now reduced to a few mineralized skeletons or a few impressions in the hardened mud, and it is easy to realize how terrifying it all was to those earlier explorers who were completely alone in a forbidding, seemingly accursed land where nature was many things but certainly not kindly."

MUIR, JOHN. 1838–1914

Muir was born in Scotland, moved to the United States when he was 11, and lived on a Wisconsin farm where he had to work hard for long hours. He would rise as early as one o'clock in the morning in order to have time to study. At the urging of friends, he took some inventions he had made to a fair in Madison, Wisconsin. This trip resulted in his attending the University of Wisconsin. After four years in school he began the travels that eventually took him around the world. Muir traveled primarily on foot carrying only a minimum amount of food and a bedroll. His lively descriptions of many of the natural areas of the United States contributed to the founding of its national parks.

Books by Muir

My First Summer in the Sierra. Berg 1972 lib. bdg. $19.95; Houghton Mifflin 1979 pap. $8.95; Penguin 1987 pap. $6.95. Muir was hired to oversee a shepherd who was taking a flock into the high country for the summer with the promise that he would have plenty of time for exploring. This is an account of that summer. A typical entry in his diary: "July 8—Now away we go toward the topmost mountains. Many still, small voices, as well as the noon thunder, are calling, 'Come higher.' "

Stickeen. Heydey Bks. repr. of 1909 ed. 1981 pap. $3.95; Outbooks repr. of 1897 ed. 1978 pap. $2.00; Richard West repr. of 1916 ed. 1977 lib. bdg. $15.00. Alaska was one of the sites of Muir's walks. (Muir Glacier indicates his passing through that area.) *Stickeen* is an account of a dog, a tramp across a glacier, and a violent, potentially dangerous but exhilarating storm.

The Yosemite. Intro. by Michael P. Cohen, Univ. of Wisconsin Pr. repr. of 1912 ed. 1987 text ed. $32.50 pap. $10.95. Muir's name has been intimately associated with Yosemite. This volume describes some of his many hikes during which he explored the area. Muir was one of the first explorers to postulate the role of glaciers in forming Yosemite.

The Story of My Boyhood and Youth. Berg 1975 $15.95; fwd. by V. Carstensen, Univ. of Wisconsin Pr. repr. of 1913 ed. 1965 $15.00 pap. $7.95. One reviewer said that this is about the only biographical book that boys like. Muir did have an interesting early life. It should be especially interesting today because few, if any, people alive today will have had the types of experiences of which Muir writes.

ECOLOGY

The name "ecology" was first applied to this branch of biology in 1886 by Ernst Haeckel. The Greek root *oikos* means "home" or "household." The first college courses in ecology in the United States were established by H. C. Cowles at the University of Chicago, Charles C. Adams and Victor E. Shelford at the University of Illinois, and J. E. Weaver and Frederic E. Clements at the University of Nebraska. (Clements was later at the University of Minnesota.)

Allee, Warder C. *Animal Aggregations: A Study in General Sociology.* AMS Pr. repr. of 1931 ed. 1978 $28.00. This book is not for casual reading. It is a study of loosely integrated animal groups. Allee was interested in the physiological effects of crowding on individuals, whether the crowding involved physical contact or not.

Allee, Warder C., and others. *Cooperation among Animals with Human Implications (Social Life of Animals).* Schuman repr. of 1938 ed. 1951 o.p. Allee cites Empedocles's idea that earth, air, fire, and water are acted on by the combining power of love and the disrupting power of hate to form the universe. He goes on to say, "Widely dispersed knowledge concerning the important role of basic cooperative processes among human beings may lead to the acceptance of cooperation as a guiding principle in social theory and as a basis for human behavior. Such acceptance will alter the course of human history."

——. *Principles of Animal Ecology.* Saunders 1949 o.p. This text is easier to read than some dealing with animal ecology. The reader will find that Section 1 is a good summary of the history of ecology.

Andrewartha, H. G., and L. C. Birch. *Distribution and Abundance of Animals.* Univ. of Chicago Pr. 1954 $35.00

——. *The Ecological Web: More on the Distribution and Abundance of Animals.* Univ. of Chicago Pr. 1986 lib. bdg. $40.00 pap. $25.00. This second volume is an expansion and update of the first. Neither is easy reading. An interesting inclusion in the 1954 volume is the "envirogram," a graphic representation of modifiers in an animal's environment.

Ayensu, Edward S., and others. *Our Green and Living World.* Smithsonian Bks. 1984 $25.00. "Our love for and dependence upon the plant kingdom have existed since the beginning. The question addressed here is whether we can stop the damage that is being done in the name of conquering nature and exploiting the earth's resources" (*LJ*).

Boulding, Kenneth E. *Ecodynamics: A New Theory of Societal Evolution.* Sage 1978 $29.95 1981 pap. $14.95. Boulding is an economist who is concerned with integrating human ecology and economics. Both disciplines deal with *oikos,* "households," and related problems.

Braun-Blanquet, J. *Plant Sociology: The Study of Plant Communities.* Trans. and ed. by C. D. Fuller and H. C. Conrad, Lubrecht & Cramer repr. of 1932 ed. 1983 lib. bdg. $55.20. This book looks at communities in terms of the plants that are present, just as the early animal sociology or animal ecology texts looked at the animals. Braun-Blanquet was one of the first plant ecologists to look carefully at plant relationships. The reader will be able to appreciate the rapid development of plant ecology by reading a current text after *Plant Sociology.*

Browne, Janet. *The Secular Ark: Studies in the History of Biogeography.* Yale Univ. Pr. 1983 $32.00. "A history of the study of the distribution of species around the world and how that early thought contributed to Darwin's evolution theories" (*LJ*).

Clements, Frederic E. *Plant Competition: An Analysis of Community Functions.* Ed. by Frank N. Egerton [*History of Ecology Ser.*] Ayer repr. of 1929 ed. 1978 lib. bdg. $37.50. As the title indicates this text deals with the interactions of plants in a community. Technical.

——. *Plant Succession and Indicators: A Definitive Edition of Plant Succession and*

Plant Indicators. Hafner repr. ed. 1973 $23.95. A basic principle of plant ecology is, as Heracleitus of Ephesus said, "All things flow, nothing abides." Only change is permanent. The change in plants in a particular area is called succession. Clements discusses these changes and indicates plants that are indicators of change.

Craighead, Frank C., Jr. *Track of the Grizzly.* Peter Smith 1985 $15.75; Sierra repr. of 1979 ed. 1982 $10.95 pap. $9.95. The killing of campers by grizzly bears has led to a call by some people for the killing of all grizzlies in any area in which they might come into contact with humans. Craighead describes the life history and ecology of this species and makes some suggestions about management.

Craighead, John J., and Frank C. Craighead, Jr. *Hawks, Owls, and Wildlife.* Dover repr. of 1956 ed. 1969 pap. $7.95; Peter Smith 1969 $16.00. "If it flies, it dies" is a motto embraced by too many Americans, as the numbers of dead and wounded hawks, owls, and eagles attest. The Craigheads look at the relationships between these carnivorous birds and other wildlife.

Daubenmire, Rexford F. *Plant Communities: A Textbook of Plant Synecology.* Harper 1968 o.p.

———. *Plants and Environment: A Textbook of Plant Autoecology.* Wiley 3d ed. 1974 $39.95. Autoecology is the study of a species in a community or communities; synecology is the study of communities as parts of ecosystems. This, the first of these books, is a technical study and is not intended for recreational reading. Both books are intended for the reader who wants to delve deeply into the study of plant ecology.

Dethier, Vincent G. *The Ecology of a Summer House.* Univ. of Massachusetts Pr. 1984 lib. bdg. $15.00 pap. $7.95. Like John McLoughlin in *The Animals among Us,* Dethier demonstrates that one need not go to Africa to find an interesting collection of animals. These range in size from ants to squirrels.

Elton, C. S. *Animal Ecology.* Methuen 1966 pap. $8.95. One of the first texts in animal ecology, this book was revised and used in college courses for more than 20 years.

———. *The Pattern of Animal Communities.* Methuen 1966 pap. $19.95. Elton writes that the idea for the studies that led to this book "came to me from gazing at the intricate pattern of landscape out of railway train windows, from walking slowly in woods, from observing . . . Arctic fjaeldmark soils and vegetation, from lying flat at the edge of ponds . . . and from analysing sand dunes, sea-cliff slopes and rocky shores."

Fitzharris, Tim. *The Wild Prairie: A Natural History of the Western Plains.* Oxford 1983 $27.50. Fitzharris points out that the North American prairie once extended from the area of Edmonton, Alberta, to just north of Mexico City. He notes that this immense grassland once supported 45 million bison, nearly as many pronghorns, many mule deer, white-tailed deer, elk, plains grizzlies, foxes, lynx, bobcats, coyotes, cougars, and huge populations of smaller mammals. After a short discussion of the main characteristics of the grassland, Fitzharris describes many of the organisms. These organisms are divided into those of the typical grassland, those of the wetland, and those of the riverland. The text is complemented by many beautiful pictures. There are sunsets and bull thistles, coyotes and pincushion cacti, and a great many other organisms. My favorite shows a prairie falcon just in the act of leaping into space from a rock ledge.

Goldsmith, Donald. *Nemesis: The Death Star and Other Theories of Mass Extinction.* Berkley Publ. 1986 pap. $3.50. Companion volume to the books on extinction by Ehrlich and Ehrlich and by Kaufman and Mallory (see below under Environmentalism). Although the subject matter is specifically astronomy, it is also about a major ecological phenomenon, the extinction of a number of species of organisms.

King, Lester C. *Wandering Continents and Spreading Sea Floors on an Expanding Earth*. Wiley 1984 $47.95. This work would not usually be considered ecological, but in one sense it is basic ecology. The present position of the continents, where they were in the past, and the results of the interaction of the tectonic plates on which they ride all contribute to the ecological conditions of the present. King postulates an expanding earth and discusses how this expansion could have affected the continents and seas that are the present homes of plants and animals.

Kirk, Paul W., Jr., ed. *The Great Dismal Swamp*. Univ. Pr. of Virginia 1979 $25.00. Dismal Swamp is an undrained, peaty area of southwestern Virginia and north-western North Carolina. Because of the topography of the area the swamp is essentially an island surrounded by completely different types of countryside. A symposium dealing with the natural history of the swamp was held June 9, 1911, aboard a steamship traveling from Washington, D.C., to Norfolk, Virginia. Members of the group were then to make an excursion into the swamp. The agenda included six topics. This book consists of the papers presented at a symposium held 67 years later. It includes 20 papers dealing with geology, hydrology, birds, mammals, forest dynamics, ferns, insects, ticks, amphibians, reptiles, and human inhabitants of the swamp. Until I read this book I associated bolas, weapons that are essentially a cord with weights at both ends, with gauchos of South America. Bottoms and Painter, who have collected extensively and have previously published a paper on bolas, note that "hundreds of bola weights have been encountered on Archaic sites in the dismal swamp area." Although these are technical papers, they are worth reading by anyone interested in unusual habitats.

Perry, Donald. *Life above the Jungle Floor: A Biologist Explores a Strange and Hidden Tree Top World*. Simon & Schuster 1986 $16.95. A little-known community exists among the understory and canopy trees of a tropical rain forest. Donald Perry decided that the only way to know what was there was to be there. He used technical climbing equipment to get up into this community and then built a platform from which he could observe who was there and what was going on. Perry's descriptions are as colorful as the photographs with which the book is illustrated.

Powledge, Fred. *Water: The Nature, Uses, and Future of Our Most Precious and Abused Resource*. Farrar 1982 pap. $7.95. A very readable overview of water conservation for the layreader.

Shelford, Victor E. *Animal Communities in Temperate America: Illustrated in the Chicago Region, Study in Animal Ecology*. Ed. by Frank N. Egerton [*History of Ecology Ser.*] Ayer repr. of 1937 ed. 1978 lib. bdg. $32.00. This early study in animal ecology describes relationships among animals in a particular geographic area around Chicago. Shelford wrote of lakes, streams, flood-plain forests, and a variety of other habitats. The writing is technical and provides detailed descriptions of the habitats that are discussed.

———. *The Ecology of North America*. Univ. of Illinois Pr. 1978 o.p. In this monumental work Shelford provides a look at the ecology of a continent, no small task. Looking at the big picture is good background for closer looks at smaller pictures.

Stokes, Donald W. *A Guide to Nature in Winter: Northeast and North Central North America*. Little, Brown 1976 $16.45 pap. $8.70. The ecologist knows no seasons. Living things are out there at any time of the year, and the ecologist is anxious to study them and their relationships under a variety of conditions. *A Guide to Nature in Winter* will help the amateur ecologist to study these living things during the severe conditions of winter. Stokes has keys to and discussions of weeds, snow crystals, trees, insects, birds, mushrooms, tracks in the snow, and woodland evergreen plants. The book is well illustrated by Stokes and Deborah Prince. It would be ideal to have along on a winter hike. You could then determine that those tracks were made by a mink or a muskrat, or that the dried plant protruding above the snow was dock, or that the patch of green was Christmas fern. Then, back home by the fire with a cup of hot chocolate, you could read about mink, muskrat, dock, and Christmas fern from the same book.

ENVIRONMENTALISM

Any scheme of classification presents difficulties. Separating naturalists, ecologists, and environmentalists is especially difficult. An environmentalist may or may not also be a naturalist or an ecologist. The environmentalists listed here have displayed particular concern for the maintenance and intelligent use of natural resources. In recent years environmentalists have been concerned with two major problems: (1) the effects of a burgeoning population on the global environment, and (2) the effects of nuclear war on the global environment. A number of the titles below address these issues.

Addkison, Roy, and Douglas Sellick. *Running Dry: How to Conserve Water Indoors and Out.* Stein & Day 1982 $12.95 pap. $8.95. The physiology of living organisms is a water-based collection of chemical reactions. This means that the importance of water to living organisms cannot be overstated. Water is a critical factor in any environment. The authors use examples to demonstrate the importance of water and discuss methods of conserving this essential resource.

Allin, Craig W. *The Politics of Wilderness Preservation.* Greenwood 1982 lib. bdg. $29.95. Those Americans who have the opportunity to stand silent, listening to the heartbeat of nature in some area of wilderness, owe a great debt to our forebears who lived not for themselves alone but for those of us who would come after them. Allin describes their efforts and the efforts of people in our time to continue to preserve something as it came from the hand of God. He discusses the exploitation mind-set of earlier times and the gradual development of a different view of our natural environment. There is considerable discussion of the period from 1964 to the present.

Ashworth, William. *The Late, Great Lakes: An Environmental History.* Knopf 1986 $17.95. This work combines biography (of our Great Lakes), sociology (what we have done and the consequences), meteorology (lake effects and weather), industrial concerns (manufacturing and results), and ecology (how all of these fit together). The reader will also feel that this is primarily an obituary.

Berger, John J. *Restoring the Earth: How Americans Are Working to Renew Our Damaged Environment.* Knopf 1985 $18.95. Not all Americans have decided that nothing can be done to restore our environment. Berger describes how people in different parts of the United States are involved in restoration. One might say that the theme of these people is: "It is better to plant one seed than to curse the Destroyers."

Bourassa, Robert. *Power from the North.* Simon & Schuster 1985 o.p. When he was premier of Quebec, the author was instrumental in getting a power-generating facility built at James Bay. This book describes the development of this complex, which exports surplus power to the United States, and points out the potential for many similar facilities, which would have a minimal impact on the environment. Generating plants of this type are more cost-effective than other sources of electricity.

Burroughs, John. *Camping and Tramping with Roosevelt*. [*Amer. Environmental Studies*] Ayer repr. of 1906 ed. 1970 $13.50. Burroughs was born and grew up on a farm near Roxbury, New York. He was successively a teacher, a clerk in the Treasury Department, Washington, D.C., and a bank examiner. After his retirement he lived on a fruit farm. Burroughs was a good friend of John Muir and, like Muir, was involved in conservation activities in the United States. His writings are wide-ranging, including a book on the American poet Walt Whitman and several books on the world of nature. Burroughs, Muir, and Theodore Roosevelt shared a love for the outdoors. Roosevelt and Burroughs spent more time together than with Muir, because both lived in the East and neither was as likely to be hiking in sheer wilderness as was Muir. These are fascinating accounts of their times together.

————. *John Burroughs' America*. Ed. with an intro. by Farida A. Wiley, fwd. by Julian Burroughs, Devin-Adair 1951 o.p. There are samples of some of Burroughs's best writing here. Reading this book is a good introduction to the wrtings and can lead the reader to try some of the complete works.

Carson, Rachel. *The Edge of the Sea*. Houghton Mifflin 1979 pap. $9.95. The zone between the high- and low-tide marks along a beach is one of the most challenging environments in which an organism can live. An organism that lives in this habitat will spend part of the time covered with salt water and part exposed to the air. The length of time spent under each of these conditions depends on the position of the organism in this zone; the higher in the zone the organism lives the more time it will spend exposed to the air. If the organism lives near the mouth of a fresh-water stream, it must contend with variations in salinity. Silt and sand present a problem as they are carried in by incoming tides. These same tides bring in food, which is available only when the zone is covered with sea water. Carson devotes this entire book to descriptions of many of the myriad organisms that live in this zone despite the great challenges. She describes how the animals protect themselves from wave action, sand, and silt; how they time their reproductive cycles to enhance the survival rates of young offspring; and how predator and prey interact with each other and in the interaction hone the traits necessary for both species to maintain themselves.

————. *The Sea Around Us*. New Amer. Lib. 1954 pap. $4.95; Oxford rev. ed. 1961 $19.95. In this book, Carson deals primarily with the physics, chemistry, and geography of the oceans, but one cannot write of these characteristics without indicating how they affect living organisms, so the book is a study of the oceans as ecological biomes. The Gulf Stream, North Atlantic Drift, Canary Current, and North Equatorial Current form a giant, wind-driven whirlpool in the Atlantic Ocean. Carson discusses them and the Sargasso Sea, the large area of essentially motionless water defined and confined by these great rivers of the sea. She points out that similar currents are found in the Pacific Ocean and that the organisms found in one current vary from those in another.

————. *Silent Spring*. Fawcett 1978 pap. $2.95; Houghton Mifflin 1962 $16.95. Carson used a worst case scenario to show possible outcomes of the unwise use of a variety of environmental contaminants. Many people who were unaware of the problem stopped to think. The shock wave is still being felt.

Cohen, Michael P. *The Pathless Way: John Muir and American Wilderness*. Univ. of Wisconsin Pr. 1986 pap. $12.95. This is the latest book dealing with John Muir, the great naturalist. The author is primarily interested in interpreting or revealing Muir, not in writing his biography. The book might mean more to the reader who had just finished two or three of Muir's own books.

Dansereau, Pierre, ed. *Challenge for Survival: Land, Air, and Water for Man in Megalopolis.* Columbia Univ. Pr. 1970 $31.00 pap. $16.00. One look at the shack-towns that are part of most of the world's major cities will convince a reader of the relevance of this book. Future historians may recognize ecologists as the prophets of our time.

Durrell, Lee. *State of the Ark: An Atlas of Conservation in Action.* Doubleday 1986 $22.95 pap. $14.95. "A beautifully written, informative, and most enjoyable book that gives excellent coverage of the conservation front. . . . Durrell treats the major issues of genetic diversity, acid rain, endangered species, tropical rain forest destruction, desertification, and soil erosion clearly and knowledgeably" (*Choice*).

Ehrlich, Paul R. *The Cold and the Dark: The World after Nuclear War—The Report of the Conference on the Longterm Worldwide Biological Consequences of Nuclear War.* Ed. by Walter Orr Roberts, fwd. by Lewis Thomas, Norton 1984 $12.95 1985 pap. $7.95. At one time, the federal government stockpiled emergency rations, water, and Geiger counters in many public buildings. It also circulated how-to-do-it diagrams for the construction of fallout shelters. We were told that in the event of a nuclear war we would have to stay in the fallout shelters for two weeks and then we could come out and carry on as before. Many people at that time knew this was a hoax. This book indicates just how cruel a hoax.

———. *The Machinery of Nature.* Simon & Schuster 1986 $18.95 1987 pap. $8.95. As the reviews of his other books indicate, no one has done any more than Paul Ehrlich to convince the average citizen that we are in a crisis situation in our relations with our environment. In this book Ehrlich goes back to fundamentals to help readers understand just what is involved in the discipline called ecology. He describes methods of fieldwork, how fieldwork leads to the development of hypotheses, how more fieldwork results in hypotheses becoming principles, and how the entire field interacts with other areas of biology.

———. *The Population Bomb.* Amereon rev. ed. 1975 lib. bdg. $16.95; Ballantine rev. ed. 1976 pap. $2.50. Ehrlich began in the 1960s to point out the consequences of uncontrolled increase in the human population. He was another prophet without honor in his own country.

Ehrlich, Paul R., and Anne H. Ehrlich. *Extinction: The Causes and Consequences of the Disappearance of Species.* Ballantine 1983 pap. $4.50; Random 1981 $16.95. Although many species have become extinct throughout the history of life on earth, the process has never occurred on a global scale or as the result of the activities of a single species of organism as it is happening at the present time. All of us should be aware of the disaster and of possible consequences.

Ehrlich, Paul R., and John P. Holdren. *Ecoscience: Population, Resources, Environment.* W. H. Freeman 1977 o.p. The point of focus is similar to that in the preceding work, but this is more wide-ranging. The main thrust is an examination of the consequences of increasing numbers of people.

Errington, Paul L. *Of Men and Marshes.* Iowa State Univ. Pr. 1957 pap. $9.45. Errington writes of those marshes that exist where the final (Wisconsin) stage of the Pleistocene ice sheet left an environment in which they could form. My favorite chapter is "of marshes and spring." Even the reader who has not seen, in person, the transition of the marsh under the aegis of spring can feel it in Errington's writing. One can see in his mind's eye mink and skunk, great horned owls and muskrats emerging into a still wintry world under the drive of an increasing titer of reproductive hormones in the bloodstream. Errington then describes the marsh throughout the other seasons and the relations of men and marshes. One of the most powerful sentences in the book is: "The principal moral that the lives of muskrats may have for us may be that the biological foundation of peace is moderation."

Firestone, David B., and Frank C. Reed. *Environmental Law for Non-lawyers.* Butterworth 1983 $32.95. The title probably should have included the phrase "and Non-ecologists." The treatment of some of the ecological-environmental principles and problems is rudimentary. The book presents the general reader with information about those facets of the law that apply to environmental concerns. Information about the process of using environmental law is also included.

Franklin, Kay, and Norma Schaeffer. *Duel for the Dunes: Land Use Conflict on the Shores of Lake Michigan.* Univ. of Illinois Pr. 1983 $22.95. This book is a thorough discussion of the problems associated with different ideas as to proper use of the fragile environment of the dune areas along Lake Michigan. The authors have included history, demography, ecology, and politics in their discussion.

Gold, John, and Jaquelin Burgess, eds. *Valued Environments.* Allen & Unwin 1982 text ed. $39.95. This book is the result of, but not the proceedings of, a symposium held at Hull University, England. Papers presented at the symposium were expanded and other papers added. Although the contributors are all British, the premises they present and defend are applicable to other countries as well. One of several strengths of this collection of papers is the authors' assumption that people may feel an attachment to environments other than natural ones. They discuss the "why" of attachments and point to attempts to become reattached to a personal past, the desire "to be aware . . . that one is part of an immense unbroken stream that has flowed over this scene for more than a hundred years," and the belief that life in earlier days was better. The papers present a wide-ranging study of human ecology and therefore include psychology, sociology and history.

Hardin, Garrett, ed. *Population, Evolution, and Birth Control: A Collage of Controversial Ideas.* W. H. Freeman 2d ed. 1969 text ed. pap. $13.95. Hardin has included work from many authors who present various viewpoints. One that I particularly remember is from the *Panchatantra* (a fourth-century collection of Sanskrit literature): "Unless a mortal's belly pot is full, he does not care a jot for love or music, wit or shame, for body's care or scholar's name, for virtue or for social charm, for lightness or release from harm. For godlike wisdom, youthful beauty, for purity or anxious duty."

Hardin, Garrett, and John Baden, eds. *Managing the Commons.* W. H. Freeman 1977 text ed. pap. $12.95. What everybody owns, nobody owns. Hardin has been trying for at least two decades to convince all of us that we must look at common property—national parks, national forests, state parks, and so on—as if it were a personal possession. Apparently, we have not been listening. The essays that make up this book deal with major problems in human ecology.

Kaufman, Les, and Ken Mallory, eds. *The Last Extinction.* MIT 1986 $16.95. The person who thinks "So what, if a few dickey birds cease to exist" needs to read both this book and the Ehrlichs' *Extinction* (see above). No other animal in the history of life on earth has had the influence on other life-forms that man has exerted. Each contributor to this book has the credentials to write of the causes and results of extinction.

Koopowitz, Harold, and Hilary Kaye. *Plant Extinction: A Global Crisis.* Stone Wall Pr. 1983 $18.95. There cannot be too many books awakening us to the worldwide crisis of extinction of living organisms in our time. This volume illustrates the many ways in which humans depend on plants and recounts the tragic loss of plants, species after species.

Lee, James A. *The Environment, Public Health, and Human Ecology: Considerations for Economic Development.* Johns Hopkins Univ. Pr. 1986 text ed. pap. $14.95. A massive amount of data confronts anyone involved in developing an approach to planning for national growth that will include a consideration of the impact on public health and general human well-being. This book is not for experts in ecology, but for laypersons who find themselves charged with the responsibility of making decisions that may have an ecological impact. The thrust of the book is: "Hopefully, humans are going to be living here for a long time; let's give them a reasonable place in which to live."

Leopold, Aldo. *A Sand County Almanac: With Other Essays on Conservation from Round River.* Oxford 1966 $17.95. Aldo Leopold stands with John Muir and Rachel Carson among the great leaders in efforts to protect the American environment from thoughtless exploiters. Born in Iowa, Leopold joined the U.S. Forest Service and became associate director of the Forest Products Laboratory. The University of Wisconsin made him its first professor of game management. He was serving as an adviser on conservation to the United Nations when he died in 1948 while helping to fight a grass fire on a neighbor's farm. "Like winds and sunsets, wild things were taken for granted until progress began to do away with them. Now we face the question whether a still higher 'standard of living' is worth its cost in things natural, wild and free. For us of the minority, the opportunity to see geese is more important than television, and the chance to see a pasque-flower is a right as inalienable as free speech." In these words Leopold expresses the mind-set of all people who enjoy things as they came from "the hand of God."

Louw, G. N., and M. K. Seely. *Ecology of Desert Organisms.* Longman 1982 text ed. pap. $18.95. The picture on the cover shows a sidewinder rattlesnake leaving its unique signature on barren sand. All we see is the snake, the ladder marks, and sand. The authors spend the rest of the book telling the reader what a desert is, where deserts are found, why they are found there, what organisms live in a desert, how these organisms are adapted so they can live there, and how the snake was able to survive heat, cold, a shortage of water, and a high level of thermal radiation. This is a technical discussion of the principles of desert ecology, not something to read on a sleepy Sunday afternoon. It is, however, well worth reading. The illustrations—drawings, graphs, and photographs—help the reader to understand the text.

Malin, James C. *History and Ecology: Studies of the Grassland.* Ed. by Robert P. Swierenga, Univ. of Nebraska Pr. 1984 $28.50 pap. $13.95. This collection of papers by Malin is another contribution to human ecology. Malin was a pioneer in asserting that all history must be understood in ecological terms. He knew practical ecology as it can be known only by a person who has lived on a farm and experienced it day by day. He learned economics by working during his teen years in his father's store. He knew the folklore, the mind-sets, and the problems of the people of the grasslands of central Kansas. He also was trained in history and ecology and, therefore, could produce his synthesis of these disciplines. The ideas presented in the book will be stimulating to the person who wonders why we are as we are and is willing to accept the fact that we did not get this way just because we or our ancestors decided this is the way we should be.

Milbrath, Lester W., and Barbara V. Fisher. *Environmentalists: Vanguard for a New*

Society. [*Environmental Public Policy Ser.*] State Univ. of New York Pr. 1984 $44.50 pap. $14.95. This book is much more than a plea for the preservation of dickey birds. Milbrath and Fisher report the results of sociological investigations in which the attitudes toward environmental questions of individuals in three different countries were ascertained. The data are reported to show different attitudes according to age, socioeconomic status, public office, and so forth. The results are controversial, subject to various interpretations, and fascinating.

National Research Council. *The Effects on the Atmosphere of a Major Nuclear Exchange.* Natl. Acad. Pr. 1985 text ed. pap. $14.50. "This informative and authoritative report . . . represents a survey by some of the best minds in the country on the so-called 'nuclear winter'. . . the effects of this exchange are examined in terms of major constituents—dust, fires, chemistry, and atmospheric effects and interactions . . . will serve a purpose in many capacities ranging from social to research" (*Choice*).

Norwood, Christopher. *Protecting Children from Environmental Injury.* Penguin 1980 o.p. There was a time in the United States when, because we loved them, we put our children on the fluoroscope machine at the shoe store to be sure the new shoes fit properly. Now we know better, and fluoroscope machines have been banned from shoe stores. Norwood writes of the many other environmental contaminants that may be having an effect on children. She includes discussions of lead poisoning, microwaves, PCBs and other synthetic chemicals, diethylstilbestrol (DES), asbestos, and so on. The list appears endless. Anyone who reads this book will begin to wonder how any of us gets to celebrate a twenty-first birthday. Parents who read this book will become aware of the many environmental hazards their children face.

Osborn, Fairfield, ed. *Our Crowded Planet: Essays on the Pressures of Population.* Greenwood repr. of 1962 ed. 1983 lib. bdg. $29.75. This book is a series of papers dealing with various aspects of the population problem.

Pinchot, Gifford. *Breaking New Ground.* Intro. by George W. Trow, Univ. of Arizona Pr. 1946 o.p. Gifford Pinchot studied forestry in Europe after he graduated from Yale University. He became involved in politics, was twice elected governor of Pennsylvania, served on many public boards and commissions, was chief of the U.S. Forest Service, and was a good friend and supporter of Theodore Roosevelt. Pinchot was also an ardent conservationist and, as late as 1945, gave President Truman his plans for the worldwide conservation of natural resources. In this book Pinchot expanded his vision and wrote of conservation problems from a worldwide perspective.

Sale, Kirkpatrick. *Dwellers in the Land: The Bioregional Vision.* Sierra 1985 $14.95. Sale essentially says that since the impact of the human animal on the global environment is greater than all other animals taken together it is time for us to stop thinking and acting like "just another animal." He asserts that it is time for the human species to shift from domination to preservation.

Sanborn, Margaret. *Yosemite: Its Discovery, Its Wonders and Its People.* Random 1981 $17.50. Members of a party of explorers and trappers who made their way across the Sierra Nevada in 1833 were the first men, other than native Americans, to see Yosemite valley. Sanborn tells the story of the valley up to the poignant Indian-Roman Catholic funeral in 1931 of Totuya, a native American, last survivor of the Ahwahneeche tribe, which had been driven from its home in the valley. The chapter "John Muir: The Lure of Yosemite" includes photographs of Muir and President Theodore Roosevelt and Muir and John Burroughs.

Scheaffer, John R., and Leonard A. Stevens. *Future Water.* Morrow 1983 o.p. Like Addkison and Sellick in *Running Dry*, these authors predict that the greatest long-term environmental problem in the United States will be to provide water for a growing and more demanding population. Their recommended solution is drastic, an "order of magnitude" more drastic than most proposed solutions, but it may be the only solution that will solve the problem.

Schrepfer, Susan R. *The Flight to Save the Redwoods: A History of Environmental Reform, 1917–1978.* Univ. of Wisconsin Pr. 1983 $27.50. One of the bitterest and longest-running conservation struggles in the United States has been for the protection of the giant redwood trees. Schrepfer illuminates the various facets of the struggle and discusses the adverse interests that have been involved. She also uses the fight for the redwoods as a framework through which to observe the conflicting interests that become involved in any attempt at conservation of natural resources.

Stone, Roger D. *Dreams of Amazonia.* Penguin 1986 pap. $6.95; Viking 1985 $17.95. In *Life above the Jungle Floor* Donald Perry discusses the organisms that make up the community of the canopy of a tropical rain forest; in this book Stone describes the impact of one species, humans, on that same environment. "Slash and burn" agriculture and many other human activities are rapidly destroying this extremely fragile biome. Slash and burn agriculture is effective when there are so few people involved that any area of the rain forest has time to recover before the people return, or when there is an infinite supply of rain forest to be slashed and burned. Neither of these conditions is being met at the present time. Stone documents the destruction that is occurring.

Thomas, Keith. *Man and the Natural World: A History of Modern Sensibility.* Pantheon 1983 $19.45. Thomas revised and added to material he presented in the Richard Macaulay Trevelyan lectures at the University of Cambridge in 1979 to produce this book. Reading the work of a genuine scholar is always a pleasure, but usually a pleasure to be taken in small doses. However, when I first read this book I sat up until 3:00 A.M. to finish it. The subtitle is "A History of the Modern Sensibility," and this history is the primary message of the book. Thomas is even more wide-ranging than Malin. He includes theology as well as psychology, sociology, and ecology in this history. Quoting from innumerable sources, he demonstrates the change in attitudes about our relation to nature that has occurred in English-speaking countries. He also demonstrates that many of the attitudes of the past are still with us, but are held by minorities. In his discussion of the widely held Christian idea that human beings are the sole reason for the creation of the universe and that all things, inanimate as well as animate, are for man's use, Thomas writes, "Vegetables and minerals were regarded in the same way. Henry More [a seventeenth-century British philosopher and one of the Cambridge Platonists] thought that their only purpose was to enhance human life. . . . Without metals, men would have been deprived of the 'glory and pomp' of war fought with swords, guns, and trumpets; instead there would have been 'nothing but howlings and shoutings of poor naked men belabouring one another . . . with sticks or dully falling together by the ear at fisticuffs.' " A great book!

Wilson, Edward O. *Biophilia.* Harvard Univ. Pr. 1984 $15.0 1986 pap. $6.95. *Bios* is a Greek word meaning "life or living" and *phileo* is a Greek word meaning "love." Wilson demonstrates in this book that he has a love for both life and living. His love for life extends to the many forms in which life manifests itself on earth. His love for living shows itself in his accounts of his childhood and of some of the fieldwork in which he has been involved. The book includes a strong plea for a conservation mind-set that is considerably less strident than many similar pleas.

Worster, Donald, ed. *American Environmentalism: The Formative Period, 1860–1915.* Wiley 1973 o.p. This collection of the work of several authors ranges from George Perkins Marsh's assertion that man was meant to dominate all things, through John Burroughs's plea that, although we must accept the contributions of science, we must not lose our souls in the process, to Liberty Hyde Bailey's "A constructive and careful handling of the resources of the earth is impossible except on a basis of large cooperation and of association for mutual welfare." Many viewpoints are expressed in the book.

ANIMAL BEHAVIOR

Animal behavior has been one of the most rapidly developing fields of ecology for the last 25 years. The discipline was given legitimacy in 1973 when Konrad Lorenz, Karl von Frisch, and Nikolaas Tinbergen shared the Nobel Prize in physiology and medicine. A by-product of the study of animal behavior has been an increasing understanding of human nature. Three terms used over and over in discussions of animal behavior are territory, display, and imprinting. Territories are of different kinds and have different functions, but in all circumstances they are areas that are defended by an organism or a pair of organisms against members of the same species. A display is a behavior pattern an animal carries out hoping to influence another member of the same species. Displays can be involved in courtship, defense of territory, or some other interactive behavior. Imprinting is the process by which an organism learns what organism it is. At a certain critical period while it is quite young the organism becomes imprinted on whatever is moving or is making a sound near it. Usually this will be the mother, but ducks and geese have been imprinted on wooden blocks, cats, and humans. The process can be carried on with other animals.

Altman, Stuart A., ed. *Social Communication among Primates.* [*Midway Repr. Ser.*] Univ. of Chicago Pr. 1982 text ed. pap. $18.00. Vocalization is only one way by which animals can communicate with other members of their species. Even humans use a variety of other methods. Altman indicates that other primates also have many ways of keeping in touch.

Bliss, Eugene L., ed. *Roots of Behavior: Genetics, Instinct, and Socialization in Animal Behavior.* Hafner repr. of 1962 ed. 1969 $22.95. When you feel you would really like to get involved in a broad-range, in-depth study of animal behavior, this is the book for you. The authors make up a "who's who" of animal behaviorists. The chapter by Harry Harlow, "Development of Affection in Primates," is interesting in itself and because of its application to humans. The importance of touch in primate development is clearly indicated. Vincent Dethler's chapter, "Neurological Aspects of Insect Behavior," is also interesting. So are Hess's "Imprinting and the 'Critical Period' Concept" and Carpenter's "Field Studies of a Primate Population." As a matter of fact, the entire book is interesting.

Burton, Robert. *Bird Behavior.* Ed. by Bruce Campbell, Knopf 1985 $18.95. This would be a good book to read right after reading *A World of Watchers* by Joseph Kastner. After you have read *Bird Behavior* you will have new ideas of what to watch to observe various aspects of bird behavior. A birder is always looking for interesting new facets of bird biology.

Caras, Roger. *The Endless Migrations: The Epic Voyages of Living Things across the*

North American Continent. Dutton 1985 $20.00. When the average person thinks of migration he or she thinks of birds, but birds are only one of many species of animals that migrate. Caras tells about insects, reptiles, birds, and mammals that migrate, and discusses some factors that may trigger migration.

Errington, Paul L. *Of Predation and Life.* Iowa State Univ. Pr. 1967 pap. $12.75. Most of us tend to favor the bunny rabbit over the fox that is eating the bunny. Errington's thesis is that predation is a natural phenomenon: the fox, as well as the rabbit, must eat. If "the lion shall eat straw like the ox," the lion is going to starve to death because it lacks the enzymes to digest straw. Predators are important in any community. Because some people have used the fact that predation is a natural phenomenon to justify predatory conduct among humans, Errington is careful to stipulate: "I wish to restrict my usage [of the word predation] to exclude such political and social activities of civilized man as may be called predatory." This book is well worth reading.

Hahn, Emily. *On the Side of the Apes.* Crowell 1971 o.p. Many research projects dealing with primates other than man are being conducted in the United States as well as in other parts of the world. Hahn visited many of the research sites in the United States, interviewed many of the researchers, and here reports what she found. There is an especially good discussion of behavior studies.

Lockley, Ronald M. *Flight of the Storm Petrel.* Eriksson 1983 $16.95. Those of us who are landlocked may need to be told that a storm petrel is a very small seabird, some species of which migrate a great distance. Lockley is a British naturalist and author of natural history books. As often happens to a naturalist, Lockley has developed some kind of interaction with the birds about which he is writing, and they come alive: "Love, for a species that meets intimately and mates only by night, is but a familiar voice, a presence (and in the petrels a familiar smell) in the darkness." The illustrations by Noel Cusa add a great deal to the book.

McFarland, David, ed. *The Oxford Companion to Animal Behavior.* Fwd. by Niko Tinbergen, Oxford 1982 $39.95 1987 pap. $19.95. One may find information on topics from abnormal behavior to wildlife management in this volume, which is as useful to the animal behaviorist, professional or amateur, as is *The Oxford Companion to English Literature* (see Vol. 1, Chs. 3 and 4) to the student of literature, professional or amateur. There is an excellent short "History of the Study of Animal Behavior." Among the many other topics included are imprinting, territoriality, conditioning, operant behavior, and releaser mechanisms.

Markowitz, Hal, and Victor Stevens, eds. *Behavior of Captive Wild Animals.* Nelson-Hall 1978 text ed. $24.95. This volume consists of papers by several scientists who conduct research on captive wild animals. They deal with topics such as the control of predatory behavior, operant research in a zoo, vocal communication of sea lions, fur seals, and walruses, and a variety of others. These are technical reports. Included in an account of operant research is a report on work with camels by Victor Stevens. He reports that there was some concern about the loud slap made by the mechanism dispensing food for the camels, but that the camels became habituated to the sound faster than the researchers. Stevens writes, "It should be added that contrary to their reputation, we found camels very easy to work with. No researcher was ever threatened or attacked, and the animals were never observed to spit on anyone."

Mead, Christopher. *Bird Migration.* Facts on File 1983 $19.95. There is good reason to believe that bird migration was one of the first behaviors of wild animals that human beings noted. The return of a food supply after a season of short rations must have been a sight to look forward to. Christopher Mead has been with the

British Trust for Ornithology for more than 20 years, and during that time he has been working primarily in its bird-banding programs. His book is comprehensive, including quotations referring to migration from the Bible, Aristotle, and Pliny, and information about observing migration, as well as more technical material. The discussion includes American as well as European species. (The American reader will have to remember that the author uses British names: a redwing is not a redwinged blackbird, for instance.) The maps are very useful.

Teleki, Geza. *The Predatory Behavior among Wild Chimpanzees.* Bucknell Univ. Pr. 1973 $28.50. At one time chimpanzees were thought to be nearly entirely herbivorous. Jane Goodall demonstrated that they are carnivorous to some extent. This book discusses in greater detail the role of these primates as predators.

FRISCH, KARL VON. 1887–1982 (NOBEL PRIZE 1973)

Karl von Frisch was born in Vienna, Austria, in 1887, received a Ph.D. from the University of Munich, and honorary degrees and awards from many institutions, foundations, and other groups. His particular research area was the behavior of honeybees. (See also Chapter 11 in this volume.)

BOOK BY VON FRISCH

The Dancing Bees: An Account of the Life and Senses of the Honey Bee. Trans. by Dora Ilse, Harcourt 1961 pap. $5.95. Worker bees communicate the location of food to other worker bees by dancing. Von Frisch discovered this fact and a great deal more about honeybees by doing some very elegant experiments using simple equipment, essentially saucers and colored water. This book reports the results of those experiments.

GOODALL, JANE VAN LAWICK. 1934–

Jane Goodall, a young English student, followed the advice of S. F. B. Leakey that a field study of some of the higher primates would be a major contribution to the understanding of animal behavior. She went to the Gombe Stream Preserve in Tanzania to study the chimpanzees.

BOOKS BY GOODALL

My Friends the Wild Chimpanzees. Natl. Geog. 1967 o.p. It was not easy, but Jane Goodall finally got the chimpanzees to accept her. She then devoted her time to observing all aspects of their lives. She kept records of mother-offspring interactions, sibling interactions, interactions with other species, and of the hierarchy of males in a group. A colleague of mine, who insists that males are good for nothing but to provide sperm and make noise, is especially taken with the account of the male who worked his way up the social ladder by banging two stolen gas cans together while he was displaying.

In the Shadow of Man. 1967. Houghton Mifflin 1983 pap. $9.95. This book also is a report on the lives of the chimpanzees. There is a poignant account of a male, which Goodall called Mr. McGregor, who was very close to a younger male, probably his brother or half-brother. When Mr. McGregor was stricken with polio and his lower legs were paralyzed, the younger male could not understand why Mr. McGregor could not keep up. Goodall very movingly describes the devotion of the younger male.

The Chimpanzees of Gombe. Harvard Univ. Pr. 1986 $30.00. This is the technical account of Goodall's 25 years of work with chimpanzees. As with most technical reports, information is presented in charts and graphs as well as in narrative form. Charts and graphs are effective tools for demonstrating relationships or for summarizing statistical information. Readers of Goodall's other books will encounter old friends among the chimpanzees discussed here.

LORENZ, KONRAD. 1903–

Born in Vienna, Austria, Lorenz studied medicine at the University of Vienna and Columbia University, before receiving a Ph.D. in zoology from the University of Munich. He has served in various academic and research positions and has been involved in the study of animal behavior for most of the last 40 years. His studies led to the discovery of imprinting, an early and centrally important learning process for many animal species. His works benefit from his rare talent of being able to write for both general and technical audiences.

Books by Lorenz

King Solomon's Ring. 1952. Fwd. by Julian Huxley, Harper 1979 pap. $5.95. Lorenz believes that the way to study animal behavior is to have intimate contact with animals as they are "doing what comes naturally." Readers often argue about which incident recounted in this book is the most hilarious. A large fraction insists that nothing could be funnier than Lorenz, standing on the roof of his house in devil costume (he wore the party costume so that the jackdaws—a kind of crow—would not later be frightened of him), banding young jackdows in the bird cote, with the adults flying noisy circles around him. Another large fraction asserts that the funniest is the scene in which Lorenz is crawling across his front yard quacking like a mama mallard with a batch of baby mallards strung out behind him. The ducklings believed him to be their mother because they had been imprinted on him. A smaller fraction insists that visualizing Lorenz, who had been selected as a mate by a newly mature male jackdaw that was imprinted on him, resisting the attempts of the jackdaw to place earthworms in his mouth, is also worth a chuckle. Many similar events give this book a real sparkle.

On Aggression. 1966. Trans. by Marjorie K. Wilson, Harcourt repr. ed. 1974 pap. $8.95; Peter Smith 1986 $16.50. Lorenz believes that we must study the aggressive drives of other animals in order to understand them in ourselves. He also believes that understanding these drives in ourselves may be essential to our survival as a species.

TINBERGEN, NIKOLAAS. 1907–

Born in The Hague, Netherlands, Tinbergen received a Ph.D. from Leiden University in 1932 and remained there to teach, becoming professor of zoology in 1947. Two years later he moved to Oxford University. He has studied the behavior of animals, and some of his reports on the behavior of sea gulls are exceptionally interesting.

Books by Tinbergen

Curious Naturalists. Univ. of Massachusetts Pr. 1956 rev. ed. 1984 pap. $10.95. Tinbergen recounts some of his experiences in the field with various observers studying the behavior of many types of animals. The book is easy to read and recounts some interesting events in the lives of curious naturalists.

Social Behavior in Animals: With Special Reference to Vertebrates. Methuen 1965 pap. $9.95. Students of animal behavior are always particularly interested in relationships among animals. Tinbergen discusses this area of animal behavior and describes a variety of social behavior.

SOCIOBIOLOGY

Sociobiology is properly a subfield of animal behavior. Sociobiologists hold that there is a genetic component to the behavior of all animals, including humans, and they try to determine just how large this component is. As far as humans are concerned there are two extreme positions: (1) All human behavior is genetically controlled; and (2) all human behavior is the result of culture. (In earlier times, and in philosophic rather than scientific terms, this was called the nature-nurture controversy.) Individuals from many disciplines are accumulating data and developing theories that, we may hope, will lead to an understanding of human behavior. As is true with any developing field of human thought, there has been resistance to ideas propounded by animal behaviorists. One result of the sociobiology controversy is that it has destroyed forever the idea of scientists as dispassionate searchers for truth. There is more of the "You did!—I didn't!" kind of argument than could be found in all the third-grade classrooms in the United States.

Barash, David. *The Whisperings Within.* Harper 1979 o.p. I was first attracted to this book by its title. The fact that a person interested in and knowledgeable about sociobiology would even consider that there was something "within," other than genes, was intriguing. It is a good book. Though Barash presents a great deal of information showing a genetic component in behavior, he includes these words in his final chapter: "But, as with its predecessors, sociobiology will not by itself tell us what is good, or what we should do with our lives. Evolution is not a program for social or political action. It is less a message than it is a mirror: gaze in it and you will see your own biases and preconceptions. Do not look to it for advice or guidance, for it will only reflect what is already in you."

Breuer, Georg. *Sociobiology and the Human Dimension.* Fwd. by Mary Midgley, Cambridge Univ. Pr. 1983 $39.50 pap. $16.95. In her foreword to this book, Mary Midgley says that Breuer has done "the first thing needful—to keep one's head and one's temper, get rid of irrelevancies and sort out the different issues." Breuer asks the important questions: (1) How could unselfish behavior evolve at all? (2) Can one extrapolate from animals to man? (3) Is sociobiology a reactionary science? He provides detailed answers to the questions and also discusses "sex and family in animals and man." This is one of the best discussions of sociobiology.

Caplan, Arthur L., ed. *The Sociobiology Debate.* Fwd. by Edward O. Wilson, Harper 1979 pap. $10.00. This is the best presentation of firsthand information available about the sociobiology debate. Caplan has included materials from background documents as well as from the protagonists in the debate.

Gregory, Michael S., Anita Silvers, and Diane Sutch, eds. *Sociobiology and Human Nature: An Interdisciplinary Critique and Defense.* [*Social and Behavioral Sciences*

Ser.] Jossey-Bass 1978 text ed. $25.95. This book consists of papers presented at a conference, "Sociobiology: Implications for Human Studies," sponsored by NEXA, the Science-Humanities Convergence Program. Edward O. Wilson wrote the introduction in which he defines sociobiology and surveys some of the history of its development. Other papers include Garrett Hardin's "Nice Guys Finish Last," David L. Hull's "Scientific Bandwagon or Traveling Medicine Show," and Donald R. Griffin's "Humanistic Aspects of Ethology." One of the best of these papers is "The Human Condition" by George Wald, Nobel Prize winner in physiology and medicine. All of these contributors have great minds; Wald also has a great heart, not just a pump in his thoracic cavity.

King's College Sociobiology Group. *Current Problems in Sociobiology.* Cambridge Univ. Pr. 1982 $59.50 pap. $19.95. These papers are the result of what must have been a time of stimulating interaction among participants in the sociobiology group at the research center at Cambridge University. The papers are somewhat more technical than those in similar volumes and, therefore, probably less interesting to persons not involved in the field. Members of the study group were careful to limit their work to what they were supposed to work with. As Patrick Bateson writes in the preface, "They would tolerate neither sloppy argument nor extravagant generalizations from studies of animals to humans." Although this is not an easy book, it is worth the time and effort necessary to read it.

Kitcher, Philip. *Vaulting Ambition: Sociobiology and the Quest for Human Nature.* MIT 1985 $25.00. If someone were to ask me, "Which of these books on sociobiology should I read?" I would reply, "All of them." If he or she persisted that the number would have to be reduced to a bare minimum, I would recommend David Barash's *The Whisperings Within* and Kitcher's book. They take different looks at sociobiology and reach different conclusions in many cases, but between the two of them a reader can get a fairly complete picture of this discipline. This book is longer than most of the others but repays the reader for the extra time spent on it.

Lewontin, R. C., and Leon J. Kamin. *Not in Our Genes.* Pantheon 1984 $21.45 pap. $8.95. The authors write to challenge the sociobiologists who hold that our genetics exerts an inexorable influence on the way we behave. Lewontin was a member of the first group to challenge some of the conclusions advanced by Edward O. Wilson in *Sociobiology: The New Synthesis.* I have already recommended Barash's and Kitcher's books as the two to read to get an understanding of sociobiology; the reader who wants to hear from the two extremes should add this book and the title by Lumsden and Wilson that follows.

Lumsden, Charles J., and Edward O. Wilson. *Promethean Fire: Reflections on the Origin of Mind.* Harvard Univ. Pr. 1983 $17.50 1984 pap. $6.95. To meet some of the more cogent objections to the sociobiological theories stated earlier by Wilson and others, the authors here postulate a gene-culture coevolution of human social behavior. The stridency of some of the earlier comments about the Science for the People group has been moderated; the authors even write, "The Science for the People representatives were well-meaning." Nevertheless, they still use emotionally loaded terms ("radical left," for instance) in speaking of those who differ with them. They could simply have said that "other biologists and sociologists differed." They attempt to free sociobiology of the charge of being sexist, but in describing the inheritance of genes for particular traits, they explain only how these genes come from the father. (The procedure is the same for the mother's genes, but males wrote the book.)

Trigg, Roger. *The Shaping of Man: Philosophical Aspects of Sociobiology.* Schocken 1983 $14.95. Trigg includes philosophic and religious concerns as he looks at sociobiology. He examines Socrates, Jesus, Hume, Heidegger, Sartre, and many others, relating their teachings to sociobiology. Referring to Wilson's dismissal of the altruism of Mother Theresa as "the cultural inflation of innate human properties," Trigg writes, "Apart from the cynicism involved in this view of apparently great personal self-sacrifice, there is a theological objection. According to Christianity, even if personal salvation is gained through loving others at the expense, if necessary, of one's own interests, loving them merely as a means of salvation is wrong. In fact the use of others for one's own ends cannot be Christian love." His view of sociobiology is different enough to make this book worth reading, along with another of a more standard viewpoint, whether pro or con.

Wilson, Edward O. *Sociobiology: The New Synthesis.* Harvard Univ. Pr. (Belknap Pr.) 1971 o.p. It is seldom that a book dealing with some aspect of biology causes such a ferment as *Sociobiology.* The resulting discussion has involved biologists, philosophers, politicians, and theologians. Most of the sometimes acrimonious discussion resulted from different interpretations of material in one chapter, "Man: From Sociobiology to Sociology." Essentially, Wilson claimed that aspects of human behavior have a genetic component. The book is a thorough, technical discussion of the entire field. The chapter "Man" is worth reading by itself if one lacks the background in animal behavior or time to tackle the entire book.

CHAPTER 13

Genetics

Anna Hamilton, Bruce Powell-Majors,
and William Edward Rorie

> It requires some courage to undertake a labour of such far-reaching extent;
> this appears, however, to be the only right way by which we can finally
> reach the solution of a question the importance of which cannot be overesti-
> mated in connection with the history of the evolution of life forms.
> GREGOR MENDEL, *Experiments in Plant Hybridization*

Fundamental questions about the variety and variability of living things
can only be answered through a study of genetics—the science of heredity.
This field traces its origins to Gregor Mendel, who through his systematic
experimentation and observation proposed a theory of heredity in 1865.
Unfortunately Mendel's work was ignored until 1900 when three botanists,
Hugo De Vries (1848–1935), Carl Correns, and E. Von Tschermak (1871–
1962), essentially repeated his experiments and revived interest in his theories. During the first years of the twentieth century the term *genetics* was
coined (by William Bateson [1861–1926]) and Mendelian laws were applied
to humans (by W. E. Castle and A. E. Garrod).

Studies of fruit flies, corn, bacteria, and viruses have all added to the
body of genetic knowledge. The delineation of the molecular structure of
DNA by James Watson, Francis Crick, and Maurice Wilkins was certainly a
milestone paving the way for the intense interest in molecular genetics
today.

There has been a burgeoning interest in human genetics (including medical genetics) in recent years, and over 4,000 inherited disorders have been
cataloged. Prenatal diagnosis is now possible for many of these disorders as
well as many chromosomal abnormalities. The potential for genetic testing
both prenatally and postnatally will certainly increase, but the availability
of testing has already furthered the development of a new profession—
genetic counseling. Such counselors are responsible for collecting enough
information to apprise families or individuals of their risk or their offspring's risk for a genetic disorder, as well as for explaining fully whatever
risks exist and whatever testing may be necessary.

Because of the increasing role that genetic technology now has in medicine and agriculture and the subsequent ethical and legal issues that may
arise, a basic knowledge of genetics has become a necessity.

REFERENCE AND GENERAL

Readers new to the field of genetics will find that a good grasp of issues involved in medical genetics, genetic counseling and genetic engineering, and the ethical and legal quandaries that arise from these, requires an understanding of basic principles and terminology of genetics.

Biass-Ducroux, Francoise, and others, eds. *Glossary of Genetics.* Elsevier 1970 $76.75. This volume is a multilanguage translation dictionary of genetic terminology. The first section is an alphabetized and numerically indexed list of almost 3,000 terms in English. Each term is followed by its equivalent in French, Spanish, Italian, German, and Russian, without definition. The remainder of the volume consists of alphabetized lists of terms segregated by language, each term followed by the index number for its equivalent in the English-language section.

Bornstein, Sandy, and Jerry Bornstein. *New Frontiers in Genetics.* Messner 1984 $10.79. Written by a geneticist and a journalist, this volume focuses on the practical aspects of the latest genetic technology.

Brennan, James R. *Patterns of Human Heredity: An Introduction to Human Genetics.* Prentice-Hall 1985 text ed. $31.95. A textbook, clearly written and well illustrated. Suggested readings, review questions, chapter summaries, and a glossary are included. Key terms appear in bold type.

Carlson, Elof Axel. *Human Genetics.* Heath 1983 text ed. $26.95. A basic genetics text. Includes material on the ethical issues of genetics and the political history of eugenics.

Davern, Cedric I., ed. *Genetics: Readings from Scientific American.* W. H. Freeman 1981 text ed. pap. $12.95. These articles selected from the pages of *Scientific American* "comprise a series of vignettes that capture the essence of significant problems that have characterized the field of genetics" (Introduction). Also includes Mendel's classic 1866 paper "Experiments in Plant Hybridization."

Edlin, Gordon. *Genetic Principles: Human and Social Consequences.* Jones & Bartlett 1983 text ed. $25.00. This textbook, written for readers with little or no scientific background, presents basic genetic principles and emphasizes the potential effects on society of current research. Particularly informative are chapters on recombinant DNA technology (genetic engineering) and screening and counseling for genetic disorders. Edlin presents factual information clearly and also outlines the ethical and legal implications inherent in many aspects of human genetics.

Hartl, Daniel L. *Our Uncertain Heritage: Genetics and Human Diversity.* Harper 2d ed. 1984 text ed. $31.95. Written by a genetics professor for students who wish to gain some familiarity with the field, this volume approaches genetics topics as a lively and challenging part of any student's general education. This edition has incorporated many suggestions of students and teachers, resulting in a shorter but more current and readable text.

Judson, Horace Freeland. *The Eighth Day of Creation.* Simon & Schuster 1979 $40.00 pap. $13.95. The result of extensive interviews with leading contemporary scientists, this book is a history of molecular biology's investigation of DNA from 1930 to 1970, covering the careers of T. H. Morgan, Francis H. C. Crick, and James D. Watson. Photographs, illustrations, notes, and index.

King, Robert C., and William D. Stansfield. *A Dictionary of Genetics.* Oxford 3d ed. 1985 $29.95 pap. $17.95. In addition to offering 5,920 definitions and 225 illustrations, there are four appendixes that provide the complete classification of all living organisms by kingdom, phylum, class, order, family, genus, and species; an alphabetical list, by popular name, of domestic species, with genus and species names given; a chronology of events in biology and genetics from 1590 to the present (with name index and bibliography); and an alphabetized address list of journals and multijournal publishers. Also included is a list of foreign words (with translation) commonly found in scientific titles.

Kowles, Richard V. *Genetics, Society and Decisions.* Scott, Foresman 1985 text ed. $28.95. This book is intended for students majoring in disciplines such as psychology, anthropology, and philosophy. Readers are given the basic concepts of genetics but are also alerted to the course of events in genetics and society that lead to controversial issues and problematic situations. Unique to this volume are chapters on the genetic consequences of inbreeding, heredity and aging, and genetics and politics.

McCarty, Maclyn. *The Transforming Principle: Discovering That Genes Are Made of DNA.* Norton 1985 $14.95 1986 pap. $5.95. "McCarty, along with Oswald T. Avery and Colin M. MacLeod, discovered in 1944 that genes are made of DNA, thereby paving the way for many more advances in the field of genetics. This is their story, and it yields all the fascinating intricacies of doing science" (*LJ*).

Maxson, Linda R., and Charles H. Daugherty. *Genetics: A Human Perspective.* William C. Brown 1985 text ed. pap. $25.80. Intended for nonscience majors. Includes chapters on immunogenetics, genetic technologies, and agricultural genetics.

Pai, Anna C. *Foundations of Genetics: A Science for Society.* McGraw-Hill 2d ed. 1984 $29.95. Since Pai feels that many genetics textbooks for the nonscientist omit basic genetic principles, she has covered them thoroughly here while keeping technical language for the most part simplified.

Portugal, Franklin H., and Jack S. Cohen. *A Century of DNA: A History of the Discovery of the Structure and Function of the Genetic Substance.* MIT 1977 $35.00 pap. $7.95. This account begins with the Swiss physiologist Friedrich Mischer (1844–95) and his isolation of "nuclein" in 1869, and recounts the discovery of the double helix model of DNA, and the formulation of the genetic code, the information-bearing sequences of DNA molecules.

Rieger, R., and others. *Glossary of Genetics and Cytogenetics: Classical and Molecular.* Springer-Verlag 4th rev. ed. 1976 pap. $20.00. Although this volume has not been kept up-to-date as have other genetics dictionaries, it does have a unique and valuable feature. For many entries there is a reference to the author and year of publication in which a term was first employed. Includes a bibliography of publications cited.

Singer, Sam. *Human Genetics: An Introduction to the Principles of Heredity.* W. H. Freeman 2d ed. 1985 text ed. pap. $13.95. This second edition is longer and more detailed than its predecessor, published seven years earlier. The fundamentals of human genetics are presented with clarity.

Sutton, H. Eldon, and Robert P. Wagner. *Genetics: Human Concern.* Macmillan 1985 $27.50. This text provides ample information on human genetics topics while devoting several chapters to genetics of other organisms.

Suzuki, David T., and others. *An Introduction to Genetic Analysis.* W. H. Freeman 3d rev. ed. 1985 text ed. $35.95. In the first half of this balanced view of genetics as practiced today, classical genetics is treated in general; the second half introduces molecular techniques and information. An emphasis is placed on the techniques of analysis and modes of inference rather than on the various uses of genetic information.

Tiley, N. A. *Discovering DNA: Meditations on Genetics and a History of the Science.* Van Nostrand 1983 $21.95. Tiley's history of the discovery of DNA begins with the ancient Greek philosophers and continues through Watson and Crick. Her section on "Applying Genetics" includes an extensive discussion of the promises and controversies associated with genetic engineering. Tiley's most original contribution is the speculative association of mythology and symbolism with genetics.

Voeller, Bruce R., ed. *The Chromosome Theory of Inheritance: Classic Papers in Development and Heredity.* Plenum 1968 pap. $15.00. Papers of historic significance in the study of the chromosome theory of inheritance, from the eighteenth through the early twentieth centuries, are reprinted here, many translated for the first time.

Winchester, A. M. *Human Genetics.* Merrill 1982 $19.95. Winchester presents a very well organized discussion of genetics topics, beginning with the nature of genes and ending with some of the more complicated aspects of population genetics, with an emphasis on the medical applications of genetics.

HEREDITY VERSUS ENVIRONMENT

Whether we are the product of our genes or of our environment, or some ratio of both, has been and is variously a hot, inflammatory, or explosive topic of discussion in the twentieth century. From GEORGE BERNARD SHAW's (see Vol. 2) *Pygmalion* to the movie *My Fair Lady* in the arts, to political controversies about ethnicity and intelligence or the value of early and special education for children from families of lower socioeconomic status, the issue of whether nature or nurture determines our destiny has captured the modern imagination.

Cravens, Hamilton. *The Triumph of Evolution: American Scientists and the Heredity-Environment Controversy, 1900–1941.* Univ. of Pennsylvania Pr. 1978 $27.25. In the United States, the rediscovery of the Mendelian laws of genetics in 1900 coincided with large-scale social changes: the expansion of higher eduction, the professionalization of science, urbanization, increased immigration, the migration of southern blacks to northern cities, and the Progressive Era with its new faith in the special competency of experts to solve social problems. This volume explores the debates among scientists and others over the primacy of heredity (including race and ethnicity) or of environment in the causation of poverty, criminality, psychopathology, and intelligence.

Karlsson, Jon L. *Inheritance of Creative Intelligence.* Nelson-Hall 1978 text ed. $20.95 pap. $10.95. Karlsson, a pediatrician and geneticist at the Human Genetics Laboratory in Reykjavik, Iceland, discusses the evidence for inheritance of intelligence, creativity, myopia, alcoholism, diabetes, schizophrenia, and a variety of personality traits, as well as that for relationships among these characteristics. Much of the research on which Karlsson draws consists of studies conducted in Iceland, although studies from Denmark, Finland, the United States, and other countries are also covered. Lucid but dry, the text includes some statistical tables.

Lewontin, Richard. *Human Diversity.* W. H. Freeman 1982 $27.95. Lewontin, a geneticist and author of many popular and technical works on heredity, argues in this very well-written, albeit somewhat polemical, book that human pheno-

types, capacities, and tendencies are not intelligible as genetically determined.
Profusely and attractively illustrated, with an index.

Prosser, C. Ladd. *Adaptational Biology: Molecules to Organisms*. Wiley 1986 $99.00
pap. $49.50. "It is highly commendable when a reference work can both review
a broad sphere of information and provide a new synthesis of ideas, as Prosser
has done impressively in this overview of evolutionary theory from the molecular to organismal level" (*Choice*).

Robinson, Daniel N., ed. *Heredity and Achievement: A Book of Readings*. Oxford 1970
text ed. pap. $7.95. This anthology is divided into four sections: heredity and
learning; heredity and personality; intelligence, ability, and race; directions for
the future. Although all of the contributions are by and primarily for researchers and teachers, only the section on heredity and learning, which deals with
rodent experiments, would be inaccessible to the intelligent lay reader new to
the study of genetics.

Tributsch, Helmut. *How Life Learned to Live: Adaptation in Nature*. MIT 1983 $22.50
pap. $7.95. "The remarkable adaptation by animals to their environment in the
evolutionary struggle for survival is explored in this good translation from the
original German. . . . Focuses on the relationship of principals of physics expressed in animal physiology and behavior" (*LJ*).

Watson, Peter. *Twins: An Uncanny Relationship?* Viking 1982 $12.95. This volume
surveys twins in history, myth, and literature, and provides a number of contemporary, usually sensational, accounts of twins (the most memorable being that
of identical twin brothers of half-Jewish ancestry, one raised by his German
mother to be a Nazi sympathizer, the other raised as a Jew in Israel). Research
on the etiology of multiple births, and research conducted on twins indicating
genetic determination of mental and physical illness, sexuality, and mundane
and seemingly trivial habits is summarized and discussed.

HEREDITY AND EVOLUTION

Together heredity and evolution explain both constancy and change in the
history of life on earth, and comprise much of the core of biological theory.
Heredity and evolution are also the veins of biology most often mined by
philosophers, anthropologists, sociologists, political scientists, and other social scientists.

Dawkins, Richard. *The Selfish Gene*. Oxford 1976 pap. $6.95. Dawkins, a zoologist,
attempts to ground ethology (the study of animal behavior) in genetics, by
means of the idea that "an organism is just a gene's way of making another
gene." Written at a popular level.

Dillon, Lawrence S. *The Genetic Mechanism and the Origin of Life*. Plenum 1978
$59.50. This study begins with the assumption that molecular genetic mecha-
nisms must have preceded single-cell organisms in the evolutionary process.
Dillon uses viruses as models for these precellular stages.

Dobzhansky, Theodosius. *Genetics and the Origin of Species*. Ed. by Niles Eldredge
and Stephen Jay Gould [*Classics of Modern Evolution Ser.*] Columbia Univ. Pr.
1982 pap. $18.00. A classic of basic genetics, based on lectures delivered in 1936.
Integrates genetics and evolutionary theory.

Eldredge, Niles. *Time Frames: The Rethinking of Darwinian Evolution and the Theory
of Punctuated Equilibria*. Simon & Schuster 1986 pap. $8.95. "With Stephen Jay

Gould, Eldredge developed the still-controversial notion that species, once evolved, 'tend to remain remarkably stable, recognizable entities for millions of years,' and that evolutionary change occurs in quick bursts rather than by a gradual, continuous process" (*LJ*).

Lerner, I. Michael, and William J. Libby. *Heredity, Evolution and Society*. W. H. Freeman 2d ed. 1976 text ed. $27.95. Lerner and Libby intend this textbook to be of use to humanities students in core biology courses. A closing chapter covers the history of genetics in the Soviet Union. Key terms in bold type.

Nagle, James J. *Heredity and Human Affairs*. Mosby 3d ed. 1983 pap. $20.95. Contains sections on reproduction and evolution (including an excellent 17-page history of evolutionary theory), as well as a section on genetics. Some algebra and statistics in the genetics section.

Provine, William B. *Sewall Wright and Evolutionary Biology*. Univ. of Chicago Pr. 1986. $30.00. "Best known for developing the theory of genetic drift, Wright was one of a select few who helped flesh out Darwin's theory of evolution by natural selection. . . . Provine has done an exceptionally good job of presenting Wright's contributions to this field" (*LJ*).

Schwartz, Jeffrey H. *The Red Ape: Orang-utans and Human Origins*. Houghton Mifflin 1987 $18.95. "Schwartz is one of the principal proponents of the close relationship of the orang and *Homo*. His account of the origins and relationships of primates covers a vast range of studies including paleontological, biochemical, anatomical, and behavioral. The book could and should be read with ease and pleasure by readers interested in human evolution" (*Choice*).

Stebbins, G. Ledyard. *Darwin to DNA, Molecules to Humanity*. W. H. Freeman 1982 pap. $19.95. A nontechnical volume that takes novel approaches to the discussion of evolution. Natural selection and heredity are interwoven. In the introduction Stebbins compares the framework of the book to a classical symphony. The analogy fits nicely.

Vines, Gail, and Linda Gamlin, eds. *The Evolution of Life*. Oxford Univ. Pr. 1987 $35.00. "An excellent introduction for the novice who wishes to learn what Darwin was all about. . . . Includes a discussion on the diversity of life and adaptation to ecological niches, and a summary of research since Darwin. An explanation of DNA, RNA, and the genetic code is particularly welcome" (*LJ*).

MEDICAL GENETICS

Virtually every week a different human ailment is revealed to have a genetic aspect. From different forms of senility, mental illness, and emotional problems, to predispositions to breast cancer or differences in susceptibility to the virus that causes AIDS (acquired immune deficiency syndrome), the disorders that have a genetic component promise to make medical genetics an awesome, powerful, complex, and explosive field.

Goodwin, Donald. *Is Alcoholism Hereditary?* Natl. Coun. on Alcoholism 1976 $10.95; Oxford 1976 pap. $4.95. This volume provides an extremely readable history of alcohol and alcoholism, a résumé of research on the causes of alcoholism, an account of current treatments, and a chapter on new prospects in alcoholism treatment research. Goodwin, an American academic psychiatrist, here recounts his studies in the United States and Denmark that concluded that alcoholism is hereditary.

Harsanyi, Zsolt, and Richard Hutton. *Genetic Prophecy: Beyond the Double Helix—Genes That Predict the Future.* Rawson 1981 pap. $3.95. The authors, the project director of the genetics section of the Office of Technology Assessment, and a science journalist, survey current and prospective means for identifying genetic markers for disease, longevity, IQ, depression, alcoholism, schizophrenia, and so on, and consider the potential uses and abuses of this information by employers, governments, medical professionals, insurers, and others.

Jolly, Elizabeth. *The Invisible Chain: Diseases Passed on by Inheritance.* Nelson-Hall 1972 $18.95. A very simple and clear discussion of the most common genetic diseases: diabetes, arthritis, disorders of vision, anemias, mental illnesses, epilepsy, and mental retardation. Jolly, a physician, concludes with a chapter on treatment and prevention. This book could be read by many high school and some junior high school students.

Moraczewski, Albert S., ed. *Genetic Medicine and Engineering: Ethical and Social Dimensions.* Catholic Health 1983 pap. $17.50. The ethical issues raised by reproductive technologies predominate, but other issues, including the increased involvement of biotechnology corporations and academia, are discussed.

Riccardi, Vincent M. *The Genetic Approach to Human Disease.* Oxford 1977 text ed. $25.95 pap. $14.95. Covers chromosome, Mendelian, and polygenic disorders, inborn errors of metabolism, teratology, counseling, therapies, and pharmacogenetics.

Thompson, James S., and Margaret W. Thompson. *Genetics in Medicine.* 4th ed. Saunders 1986 $19.95. The authors, one a professor of anatomy and one a professor of medical genetics and pediatrics, present an introduction to medical genetics in 19 chapters, with photographs, illustrations, glossary, references, name and subject indexes, and chapter review questions that are answered in an appendix. Topics covered include heredity, structure and function of chromosomes and genes, single-gene inheritance, biochemical genetics, chromosomal aberrations, sex chromosomes, immunogenetics, blood polymorphisms, somatic cell genetics, linkage and mapping, multifactorial inheritance, genetic aspects of development, mathematical and population genetics, twin studies, dermatoglyphics, prenatal diagnosis and genetic counseling. In order to grasp the chapter on mathematical genetics the reader must be prepared to acquire a basic knowledge of algebra and probability. Fortunately this chapter presents the material with examples and step-by-step, so that the reader receives a review course in the mathematics involved.

Tsuang, Ming T., and Randall Vandermey. *Genes and the Mind: Inheritance of Mental Illness.* Oxford 1980 text ed. $16.95. An introduction to psychiatric genetics for the intelligent lay reader, this volume summarizes what is known about the inheritance of schizophrenia, manic depressive disorders, Huntington's disease, and alcoholism; contains a chapter on psychiatric genetic counseling; and offers a clearly written 19-page exposition on general "human genetics for beginners."

GENETIC COUNSELING

Along with medical genetics, genetic screening and counseling promise to be rapidly growing fields. Providing counseling to people about their reproductive decisions and their children's futures while taking into account diverse religious practices and opinions, cultural values, and other considerations, is a delicate task. Philosophers, psychologists, social workers, and the clergy have addressed the issues from a variety of perspectives.

Applebaum, Eleanor G., and Stephen K. Fierstein, eds. *A Genetic Counseling Casebook.* Free Pr. 1983 $19.95. An annotated collection of 24 varied genetic counseling cases provided by 26 practitioners and one client. Provides excellent insights into the work of the counselor and the different responses of patients to the counseling experience.

Atkinson, Gary M., and Albert S. Moraczewski, eds. *Genetic Counseling, the Church, and the Law.* Pope John Center 1980 pap. $9.95. This work is the result of an interdisciplinary Task Force on Genetic Diagnosis and Counseling assembled by the Pope John Center, Massachusetts, to examine the moral issues engendered by genetic counseling.

Capron, Alexander M., and others, eds. *Genetic Counseling: Facts, Values and Norms.* A. R. Liss 1979 o.p. An anthology of articles on genetic counseling covering concepts in human medical genetics, roles and qualifications of genetics counselors, and moral and legal issues.

Emery, Alan E. H., and Ian Pullen, eds. *Psychological Aspects of Genetic Counseling.* Academic Pr. 1984 $32.00 pap. $14.00. A comprehensive presentation of various components of genetic counseling; emphasizes the psychological impact of genetic disease on the family.

Fletcher, John C. *Coping with Genetic Disorders.* Harper 1982 $14.45. Written by an Episcopal priest, this is a guide for the clergy who must counsel couples already having or at risk of having a child affected with a genetic disorder. Many sections of the book are also informative for those interested in genetic counseling and in the dilemmas created by genetic technology.

Hilton, Bruce, and others, eds. *Ethical Issues in Human Genetics: Genetic Counseling and the Use of Genetic Knowledge.* Plenum 1973 $35.00. Thirty contributors explore the ethical problems raised by genetic screening/prenatal diagnosis.

Hsia, Y. Edward, and others, eds. *Counseling in Genetics.* A. R. Liss 1979 $34.00. Provides a comprehensive view of genetic counseling. Also includes a chapter on basic human genetics.

Kelly, Thaddeus E. *Clinical Genetics and Genetic Counseling.* Year Book Medical 1980 $39.95. A clinically oriented text written for health professionals, but chapters on genetic screening, genetic counseling, and case studies are useful for the general reader.

Kessler, Seymour, ed. *Genetic Counseling: Psychological Dimensions.* Academic Pr. 1979 $33.50. A very well written collection of papers on the psychosocial aspects of genetic counseling. The editor writes that "the book is based on two premises: first, genetic counseling deals with human behavior and psychological functioning, and. . .a strong kinship exists between genetic counseling and other forms of counseling."

Lubs, Herbert A., and Felix de la Cruz, eds. *Genetic Counseling.* Raven 1977 o.p. An anthology covering genetic counseling, the organization and delivery of genetic counseling services, special techniques in counseling, and prospects for the future. A few of the articles require knowledge of algebra, statistics, and probability theory.

Milunsky, Aubrey, and George J. Annas, eds. *Genetics and the Law II.* Plenum 1980 o.p. An anthology of articles covering pollution, family and adoption law, mutagenesis, teratogenesis, public attitudes toward the handicapped, eugenics, government control of science, counseling and screening, and legal and moral issues.

GENETIC ENGINEERING

Genetic engineering represents a union of high theory and high technology, a culmination of the modern turn away from science as contemplation. The results are a number of new types of individuals and institutions: the scientist-businessperson, the professor-consultant, and the corporate affiliated and funded university laboratory. The seventeenth-century natural philosophers who gave the original impetus to modern science proposed to "render ourselves as masters and possessors of nature." Genetic engineering raises special ethical and political issues in that the nature at whose mastery and possession it chiefly aims is that of human beings.

Cavalieri, Liebe F. *The Double-Edged Helix: Science in the Real World.* Columbia Univ. Pr. 1981 $22.50. A critical evaluation of recombinant DNA technology and its impact on society.

Cherfas, Jeremy. *Man-Made Life: An Overview of the Science, Technology and Commerce of Genetic Engineering.* Pantheon 1982 $15.45. Despite the subtitle, this book focuses on the tools, methods, and techniques used by molecular biologists in the historically significant experiments in the investigation of DNA. The book is useful for this reason in that most of the works on "genetic engineering" concern themselves largely with ethical, social, and political issues. Illustrations, notes, glossary, and index.

Grobstein, Clifford. *A Double Image of the Double Helix: The Recombinant-DNA Debate.* W. H. Freeman 1979 text ed. $20.95 pap. $11.95. A history of the debate, discussion of the dangers of recombinant DNA research technology, and an appendix of documents from the mid-1970s. Includes a glossary and list of periodicals in the field.

Jackson, David A., and Stephen P. Stich, eds. *The Recombinant DNA Debate.* Prentice-Hall 1979 text ed. $38.95. An interdisciplinary anthology on the debate. Includes a glossary and part of the National Institutes of Health guidelines for recombinant DNA research.

Krimsky, Sheldon. *Genetic Alchemy: The Social History of the Recombinant DNA Controversy.* MIT 1982 pap. $9.95. In the late 1960s and early 1970s biochemists and molecular biologists began to consider using viruses that infect bacteria in order to recombine DNA (the substance from which genes are constituted) from one bacterium to another, altering the genetic endowment of the latter. The possible hazard of releasing new and lethal bacteria into the environment, as well as more lurid speculations about the manipulation of the genetic endowments of higher species, including humans, led to a debate on the need to regulate recombinant DNA research. Krimsky provides a thorough, if dry, history of these 15 years of controversy.

Lappe, Marc. *The Broken Code: The Exploitation of DNA.* Sierra 1985 $17.95. Lappe, a pathologist and professor of public health, discusses environmental and other dangers of recombinant DNA technology.

Nossal, G. J. V. *Reshaping Life: Key Issues in Genetic Engineering.* Cambridge Univ. Pr. 1985 pap. $11.95. Detailed coverage of current and prospective uses of genetic technology, including such recent areas as AIDS vaccine research.

Rifkin, Jeremy. *Algeny: A New Word—A New World.* Viking 1984 pap. $6.95. A popularizing and wide-ranging essay on genetic technology, its dangers, and its antecedents in intellectual and cultural history.

Rosenfeld, Albert. *Prolongevity II: An Updated Report on the Scientific Prospects for*

Adding Good Years to Life. Knopf 1985 $18.95. "This substantial revision of the earlier work reports a positive trend toward consensus and convergence among gerontologists. The rapid development of genetic engineering figures in on this trend and receives considerable attention" (*LJ*).

Sylvester, Edward J., and Lynn C. Klotz. *The Gene Age: Genetic Engineering and the Next Industrial Revolution.* Scribner 1983 $15.95. Klotz, a physical biochemist, and Sylvester, a journalist, report on the genetic engineering industry in the early 1980s. Though this book covers technical, ethical, and legal issues, its primary emphasis is on the economics of the industry. This coverage is of a nontechnical sort, much like the business pages of a daily newspaper. Might be of special interest to business administration students. Illustrations, notes, and index.

Zimmerman, Burke K. *Biofuture: Confronting the Genetic Era.* Fwd. by Francis Crick, Plenum 1984 $16.95. Clearly explains genetics in lay terms, surveys current technology, covers contemporary controversies, evaluates the ethical issues, and concludes with a history of recombinant DNA research.

REPRODUCTIVE TECHNOLOGY: ETHICAL ISSUES

With the advent of reproductive technology, the old phrase "making babies" takes on new meaning. New technologies that allow prospective parents to circumnavigate or heal infertility, to control the timing of reproduction and the sex of their offspring, and to judge the health, wholeness, and desirability of the gestating fetus are constantly developing, and continue to generate new moral and legal questions.

Ames, David A., and Colin B. Gracey, eds. *Good Genes? Emerging Values for Science, Religion and Society.* Forward Movement Pubns. 1984 pap. $3.60. A group study guide on screening, fetal therapy, and reproductive technology, written by officials of the Episcopal Church.

Blank, Robert H. *The Political Implications of Human Genetic Technology.* Westview Pr. 1981 text ed. lib. bdg. $28.50 pap. $12.95. Although a scholarly volume, this lucid exposition of the public policy alternatives for governing human genetic technology is accessible to the general reader.

Carney, Thomas P. *Instant Evolution: We'd Better Get Good at It.* Univ. of Notre Dame Pr. 1981 text ed. pap. $6.95. Carney, an organic chemist and the founder of a high-technology company, gives a critical evaluation of the ethics of reproductive and other technologies.

English, Darrel, ed. *Genetic and Reproductive Engineering.* Irvington 1974 text ed. $29.75 pap $9.50. This anthology is divided into three broad areas: a survey of human genetics, especially the genetics of disease; the prospects for gene therapy; and the possibilities and dilemmas involved in the scientific control of reproduction. The reader should note that this volume was published before the first human child conceived in vitro was born (1978), and so many of the discussions of "future" ethical problems are now present.

Hall, Stephen S. *Invisible Frontiers: The Race to Synthesize a Human Gene.* Atlantic Monthly 1987 $19.95. "An absorbing narrative of the first demonstrations that bacterial cells could be made to clone mammalian genes and to express their protein products. It is also an illuminating rendition of the technical and entrepreneurial beginnings of Genentech, now one of the country's leading biotechnology companies, and, by extension, of the birth of the biotechnology industry from the academic womb of molecular biology" (*N.Y. Times Bk. Review*).

Kass, Leon R. *Toward a More Natural Science: Biology and Human Affairs.* Free Pr. 1985 $23.50. Kass argues that genetic and reproductive technologies are eroding our concepts of human nature, normality, equality, integrity, birth, parenthood, gender, lineage, selfhood, and individuality. This volume also contains sections on medical ethics and its ground, and on the philosophy of nature.

Lebacqz, Karen, ed. *Genetics, Ethics and Parenthood.* Pilgrim Pr. 1983 $7.95. Examines moral and religious issues raised by advances in genetic technology. Designed as a workbook of exercises and reflections to be used by church groups. Provides an interesting theological perspective.

Lipkin, Mack, Jr., and Peter T. Rowley, eds. *Genetic Responsibility: On Choosing Our Children's Genes.* Plenum 1974 $27.50. This anthology focuses on the ethical issues and social outcomes involved in prenatal genetic screening.

The New Technologies of Birth and Death: Medical, Legal and Moral Dimensions. Pope John Center 1980 pap. $8.95. Four contributions on issues related to genetic screening address the subject from the standpoint of Catholic moral theology.

Packard, Vance. *The People Shapers.* Little, Brown 1977 $12.50. A popular discussion of biotechnology in general.

Ramsey, Paul. *Fabricated Man: The Ethics of Genetic Control.* Yale Univ. Pr. 1970 pap. $5.95. An early and classic statement of the view that reproductive technologies endanger our concepts of parenthood, humanity, and so forth.

Singer, Peter, and Deane Wells. *Making Babies: The New Science and Ethics of Conception.* Scribner 1985 $14.95. Singer, a professor of philosophy at Monash University (Victoria, Australia) and Wells, a member of the Australian parliament, survey the state of reproductive technology in the United States, Great Britain, and Australia, discuss current regulations of these technologies, and evaluate the different positions of those debating the ethical issues involved.

Snyder, Gerald S. *Test-Tube Life: Scientific Advance and Moral Dilemma.* Messner 1982 $10.29. This book would be accessible to some junior high school readers. Covers recombinant DNA, in vitro fertilization, surrogacy, cloning, and the moral dilemmas posed by biotechnologies.

Williams, Roger J. *Free and Unequal: The Biological Basis for Individual Liberty.* Liberty Pr. 1980 $8.00 pap. $3.50. Williams, a biochemist by training, was moved to pen this popular essay on the biological basis and social value of human diversity in response to political criticisms of genetics.

Because genetics is a comparatively young science, it is still possible for the reader to make a thorough study of works by and about the major discoveries in the field and the scientists who made them.

McCLINTOCK, BARBARA. 1902– (Nobel Prize 1983)

McClintock discovered anomalies in pigmentation and other features of corn (*Zea mays*) that led her to question the prevailing picture of the chromosome as a linear arrangement of fixed genes. Her proposed picture of the chromosome involved a process of "transposition" in which the chromosome released chromosomal elements (genes and groups of genes) from their original positions (this subprocess is named "dissociation") and reinserted them into new positions. Though her original work was published in the 1940s and 1950s, it was not until the advent of molecular biology and its confirmation of her theories that she received professional recognition, including ultimately a number of honorary doctorates and other awards, among them the Nobel Prize in 1983.

BOOK ABOUT MCCLINTOCK

Keller, Evelyn Fox. *A Feeling for the Organism: The Life and Work of Barbara McClintock.* W. H. Freeman 1983 text ed. $17.95 pap. $8.95. This volume begins with a short psychobiography of the reclusive McClintock. Her giftedness, unconventional parents, and native capacity to be alone, self-entertained, and absorbed in whatever project she chose to pursue, are called on to explain the hermetic life-style that almost caused her work to go unremarked.

MENDEL, GREGOR JOHANN. 1822–1884

Mendel, the Austrian biologist, was a Roman Catholic priest whose classic article on the breeding of peas (1866), published in an obscure journal, was ignored in his lifetime and only rediscovered at the turn of the century 16 years after his death. It described Mendel's crucial discoveries in genetics, based on intensive experimentation; these discoveries, now known as Mendel's laws, concern the incidence of dominant and recessive characteristics and other factors in the offspring of plant and animal families. Besides their importance for the understanding of human biological inheritance, they have been of great practical assistance in the breeding of animals and plants.

BOOK BY MENDEL

Experiments in Plant Hybridization. 1866. Fwd. by Paul Christopher Mangelsdorf, Harvard Univ. Pr. 1965 pap. $3.50. Mendel's original paper recounting the experiments that led him to formulate his laws of inheritance is in this translation easily accessible to the undergraduate. The foreword gives a brief history of the rediscovery of Mendel's work.

BOOKS ABOUT MENDEL

Olby, Robert C. *The Origins of Mendelism.* Univ. of Chicago Pr. 2d ed. 1985 lib. bdg. $38.00 pap. $14.95. Olby recounts the history of hybridization experiments and related studies before Mendel by such men as Georges Louis LeClerc du Buffon, Rudolph Camerius, Carl Linneaus, Johann Hedwig, Augustin Sageret, and especially Joseph Gottlieb Koelreuter and Carl von Gaertner. He then turns to the work of Mendel, Darwin, Naudin, and Galton, and the rediscovery of Mendel's work by De Vries, Correns, and Tshermak. Photographs, illustrations, notes, appendixes, and index.

Stern, Curt, and Eva R. Sherwood, eds. *The Origin of Genetics: A Mendel Source Book.* W. H. Freeman 1966 text ed. pap. $10.95. An anthology of the original papers and correspondence of the Austrian monk, teacher, and botanist Gregor Johann Mendel, and one of those who rediscovered his work 34 years after its publication and 16 years after his death. Of the three European botanists who simultaneously and independently rediscovered Mendel's work in 1900, Hugo De Vries of Holland, Carl Correns of Germany, and E. Von Tschermak of Austria, papers of the first two are included in this volume.

MORGAN, THOMAS HUNT. 1866–1945 (NOBEL PRIZE 1933)

Thomas Hunt Morgan was at the center of genetics research in the first half of the twentieth century. Morgan won the Nobel Prize in 1933 for work that he had begun in 1910 with the fruit fly (*Drosophila melanogaster*). Coming to sexual maturity 12 to 14 hours after birth, the fruit fly had a number of visible heritable traits, primarily variations of wing shape and eye color, as well as large chromosomes easily visible under the microscopes of the time. The results of the experiments conducted in "The Fly Room," Morgan's laboratory at Columbia University, showed that two apparently different approaches to heredity, the chromosome theory (which identified the chromosomes of the cell nuclei as agents of heredity), and the Mendelian laws of inheritance, were one. Morgan's contributions to genetics included the ideas that Mendel's factors or determinants of characteristics (now called "genes") were grouped together on chromosomes, that some characteristics are sex-linked, and that the position of genes on chromosomes can be mapped.

BOOKS BY MORGAN

(and Hermann Joseph Muller). *The Mechanism of Mendelian Heredity.* 1915. Johnson Repr. repr. of 1915 ed. 1972 $35.00

The Theory of the Gene. Richard West repr. of 1926 ed. 1985 lib. bdg. $100.00. Covers Mendelian principles, particularly theories and theories of mechanism in heredity, the relationship of chromosome to gene, mutation, tetraploids, haploids, triploids, polyploids and heteroploids, sex determination, intersexes, and sex reversal.

Embryology and Genetics. Greenwood repr. of 1934 ed. 1975 lib. bdg. $22.50. Covers such topics as the gametes, egg cleavage, gastrulation, twinning, parthenogenesis, sex determination, and larval and foetal types. Illustrations, notes, and index.

BOOKS ABOUT MORGAN

Allan, Garland E. *Thomas Hunt Morgan: A Scientific Biography.* Princeton Univ. Pr. 1978 text ed. $48.50

Shine, Ian B., and Sylvia Wrobel. *Thomas Hunt Morgan: Pioneer of Genetics.* Univ. Pr. of Kentucky 1976 $15.00 pap. $6.95. This short (160 pages) biography is accessible to some high school students. Contains an illustration of the Morgan family tree, photographs, a chronology, notes, and index.

MULLER, HERMANN JOSEPH. 1890–1967 (NOBEL PRIZE 1946)

Muller was one of Thomas Hunt Morgan's students at Columbia, and a coauthor with Morgan of *The Mechanism of Mendelian Heredity* in which they codified their view that chromosomes contained Mendel's factors or determinants of the characteristics of organisms. Muller received the Nobel Prize in 1946 for work that grew out of Morgan's "Fly Room." Muller's work demonstrated that radiation was mutagenic—that it caused changes in the genes of irradiated cells.

BOOKS BY MULLER

The Modern Concept of Nature: Essays on Theoretical Biology and Evolution by H. J. Muller. Ed. by Elof Axel Carlson, State Univ. of New York Pr. 1973 $34.50. Ten scientific papers first published from 1922 to 1958. This volume includes a chronology of Muller's life, a list of his honors and awards, and a glossary of genetics terminology.

Man's Future Birthright: Essays on Science and Humanity. Ed. by Elof Axel Carlson, State Univ. of New York Pr. 1973 $29.50. Nine papers from 1939 to 1967 in which Nobel laureate Muller discusses the eugenics movement, mutagenic dangers of radiation, and speculates on the prospects for extraterrestrial life.

(and Thomas Hunt Morgan). *The Mechanism of Mendelian Heredity.* 1915. Johnson Repr. repr. of 1915 ed. 1972 $35.00

Out of the Night: A Biologist's View of the Future. Ed. by Charles Rosenberg, Garland repr. of 1935 ed. 1984 $24.00

Genetics, Medicine, and Man. Cornell Univ. Pr. 1947 o.p.

Studies in Genetics: The Selected Papers of H. J. Muller. Fwd. by Joshua Lederberg, Indiana Univ. Pr. 1962 o.p. Papers in this anthology are sorted into nine chapters: the chromosome basis of heredity and linkage; genotype-phenotype relations; gene theory; spontaneous mutation; radiation induced mutations; chromosome properties; heterochromatin; evolution; and human genetics. Index.

BOOK ABOUT MULLER

Carlson, Elof Axel. *Genes, Radiation and Society: The Life and Work of H. J. Muller.* Cornell Univ. Pr. 1981 $37.50. Carlson recounts Muller's criticism of the American eugenics movement, his proposal for a reformed eugenics movement, his Communist party activities in the United States, and his sojourns abroad, including his life in the U.S.S.R., where he debated with T. D. Lysenko, Soviet biologist and agronomist, and other leaders of the antigenetics movement.

WATSON, JAMES DEWEY. 1928–   (NOBEL PRIZE 1962)

Watson, American biologist and educator, was born in Chicago, Illinois. He was a graduate of the University of Chicago and received his Ph.D. at the University of Indiana where he was a pupil of H. J. Muller. It was while he was at the Cavendish Laboratory of Cambridge University, England, in 1951 that he began, with British molecular biologist Francis H. C. Crick, his research on the molecular structure of DNA. The 1962 Nobel Prize in Medicine and Physiology was awarded to them and to M. H. F. Wilkins (Irish biophysicist on whose work their studies were partly based) as a result of their published research findings.

BOOKS BY WATSON

The Double Helix: Being a Personal Account of the Discovery of the Structure of DNA. Atheneum 1968 pap. $6.95; New Amer. Lib. 1969 pap. $3.95; ed. by Gunther S. Stent, Norton 1980 text ed. pap. $7.95. The Norton Critical Edition of Nobel laureate James Watson's partial autobiography includes his account of the decipherment of DNA, as well as articles, correspondence, and reviews of the original volume. "Watson's account of the events leading up to the discovery unabashedly discloses the competitive atmosphere within the scientific community, the amoral tactics employed, and the less-than-logical procedures that eventually led to the discovery of the double-helical structure of DNA" (*Choice*).

Molecular Biology of the Gene. W. A. Benjamin 3d ed. text ed. 1976 $39.95. This text
is derived from introductory undergraduate course lectures in biochemistry and
molecular biology. Topics covered include Mendelian laws, cell chemistry, the
chemistry of *E. coli*, weak chemical interactions, coupled reactions and group
transfers, template surfaces, gene arrangement, structure and function, DNA
replication, RNA transcription, protein synthesis, the genetic code, viral replication, embryology at the molecular level, cell proliferation, antibody synthesis,
and the viral origin of cancer.

Recognition and Regulation in Cell-Mediated Immunity. Ed. by John Marbrook, Dekker 1985 $75.00. An anthology whose 17 contributions cover cell biology and the
thymus, development of recognition and the T cell receptors, mediators and T
cell maturation, and regulation of T cell induction.

(and John Tooze). *The DNA Story: A Documentary History of Gene Cloning.* W. H.
Freeman 1983 text ed. $29.95 pap. $19.95. Provides a documentary history of
the debates about recombinant DNA and cloning that began in the 1960s, a
history here presented in memoranda, articles, letters, and photographs.

(and John Tooze). *Recombinant DNA: A Short Course.* W. H. Freeman 1983 text ed.
$27.95 pap. $17.95. Covers the role of genes in the life of the cell, the nature of
DNA, the genetic code, gene expression, recombinant DNA methods, viral vectors, cloning, in vitro mutagenesis, and the use of recombinant DNA in treating
genetic diseases. Illustrations, reading list, dateline (with photographs), appendixes on enzymes, and index.

CHAPTER 14

Medicine and Health

Jodith Janes and Daniel T. Richards

The amount of writings of a profession is a measure of its vitality and activity, whilst their quality is a rough indication of its intellectual state. Medical literature ... is the currency or medium of exchange by which a man contributes to or borrows from the common stock of knowledge and experience, and the volume of this currency and the character of its mettle are of the greatest importance to us all.
—SIR ROBERT HUTCHINSON, *Lancet* (1939)

As a rule, disease can scarcely keep pace with the itch to scribble about it.
—JOHN MAYOW (1678)

The health care field is the nation's second largest industry, and the publication of books on medical topics constitutes a substantial segment of the publishing business. With the growth of the nation's "health conscience" have come large numbers of books on many aspects of health, particularly on exercise, physical fitness, and nutrition. There has also been an increase in the number of "life-style" books focused on the way one's routine activities affect one's individual health. The explorations of the brain and the nervous system have produced bulges in the popular literature, as has the expanding American waistline and the truly phenomenal advances in medical technology. A litigious society produces a need for informed and authoritative information on many topics, including medical treatment.

Growing out of the nation's concerns for the escalating costs of medical treatment and hospitalization, there has been a spate of publishing activity dealing with the wide range of viewpoints on social aspects of health care. There is a substantial interest too in the aging process, family planning, birth techniques, and child development, and each is well represented by vigorous and prolific authorship. The number of books dealing with pregnancy and infant care has resulted in separate sections devoted to these topics in many bookstores.

Television specials on health issues and specific diseases have created a demand for supplementary readings written for the intelligent layperson. Finally, the renewed interest in things historical, perhaps abetted by national and local celebrations and markings of anniversaries, has produced a lengthy list of well-written, easily readable historical and biographical titles.

These developments overall have resulted in what can truly be called a flood of books about virtually all facets of health care. Medical publishing is second only to the social sciences in the number of titles produced annually. Because the rate of advances in medicine is so rapid, there is little that stays current for any length of time. This chapter, therefore, can only serve as an introduction to the many books that are available.

Works included here concentrate on the functioning of the normal, healthy body, its organs and their functions, the physiological aspects of human development, and the maintenance of health. (Diseases are treated in Chapter 15, Illness and Disease, in this volume). This chapter also includes works describing the various health care professions, education for those professions, and a small list of historical treatments of medical subjects. No compilation of books on medicine and health would be complete without the inclusion of information on the continuing debate concerning health care costs, and the organization, management, and economics of various health care delivery systems. The relatively lengthy section of such books includes discussions, comparisons, criticisms, and descriptions of the economics and philosophies of health care delivery systems both in the United States and in other countries.

We have attempted to select authoritative and informative works as well as a representative number of works that serve to introduce a topic. The criteria used for the selection process included clarity and accessibility of the information presented, the ease of use of the physical volume, the significance and validity of the content, the authorship, and the scope of the title in treating its subject. The opinions of critics, reviewers, colleagues, and, in some instances, physicians themselves have also been used.

The categories are introduced with a brief definition and, where possible, a statement about publishing activity in the particular area. Several factors have been taken into account in selecting subjects—their usefulness in organizing library collections, the general availability of books in the subject, and the concept of the way readers might approach the literature of the health sciences. As a consequence, the subjects vary to some degree in their level of specificity.

REFERENCE BOOKS

From the many dictionaries, guides, and directories available, the following list includes only representative titles of each type. Most are directed at, or written specifically for, the medical consumer.

American Society of Hospital Pharmacists. *Consumer Drug Digest.* Facts on File 1982 $19.95 pap. $9.95. Arranged by type of malady, this digest provides descriptions of the ailment along with names of drugs appropriate for the problem. Contains information about side effects and possible allergic reactions.

Bosco, Dominick. *The People's Guide to Vitamins and Minerals from A to Zinc.* Contemporary Bks. 1980 $12.95 pap. $8.95. Lists individual vitamins and minerals, their specific functions in the body, problems of insufficiency and overdose, toxic qualities, and utility in disease prevention.

Brace, Edward R. *A Popular Guide to Medical Language.* Van Nostrand 1983 $19.50.

Easily understood information on more than 1,000 medical terms, tests, procedures, and diseases.

Bressler, Rubin, and others. *The Physician's Drug Manual: Prescription and Nonprescription Drugs.* Doubleday 1981 $17.95. Comprehensive compendium of medication informateion arranged by type of disease. Color illustrations and index of brand and generic names.

Bricklin, Mark. *Rodale's Encyclopedia of Natural Home Remedies.* Rodale Pr. 1982 $19.95. Compilation of advice from *Prevention* magazine on everything from acne to warts. No questionable or potentially hazardous remedies are included.

Complete Home Medical Guide. Columbia Univ. College of Physicians and Surgeons 1985 $25.00. A comprehensive and encyclopedic approach to health care advice containing information from medical experts on the diagnosis, prevention, treatment, and cure of many common diseases and ailments. It also contains information about health and wellness, drugs, and medical emergencies.

Dox, Ida, John Melloni Biagio, and Gilbert M. Eisner. *Melloni's Illustrated Medical Dictionary.* Williams & Wilkins 2d ed. 1985 text ed. $22.50. An excellent dictionary with clear illustrations and comprehensible definitions.

Health, United States 1985. U.S. Gov. Printing Office 1985 pap $6.50. From the Department of Health and Human Services, this is a superb source for basic health statistics and information on health topics of particular current interest.

Karlin, Leonard. *Medical Secretary's and Assistant's Encyclopedic Dictionary.* Prentice-Hall 1984 $19.95. Though designed for the medical assistant, this book contains brief definitions, in layperson's terms, of many medical procedures, disease states, terms, and drugs (generic and proprietary).

Kunz, Jeffrey R. M., ed. *The American Medical Association Family Medical Guide.* Random 1982 $29.95. Divided into four sections (health maintenance, self-diagnosis, diseases, and caring for the sick) and written for the layperson, this reference work on family medical care constitutes a very useful guide for home use. The AMA (American Medical Association) imprimatur testifies to its reliability as a source for health advice and the book includes understandable explanations of anatomy, diseases, and surgical operation.

Lampe, Kenneth F., and Mary Ann McCann. *American Medical Association Handbook of Poisonous and Injurious Plants.* Chicago Review Pr. 1985 pap. $18.95. Arranged alphabetically by botanical name, descriptions are accurate and brief; among the best books available for information on human poisoning from plants.

Napoli, Maryann. *Health Facts: A Critical Evaluation of the Major Problems, Treatments, and Alternatives Facing Medical Consumers.* Overlook Pr. 1983 $18.95 pap. $8.95. Derived from the newsletter of the same name, this directory is designed to assist consumers to take responsibility for and to make their own health care decisions. Contains historical and current viewpoints, statistics, suggestions, and recommended readings.

Pantell, Robert, and David Bergman. *The Parent's Pharmacy.* Addison-Wesley 1982 $16.95 pap. $8.95. Advice from two pediatricians about over-the-counter drugs, home remedies, and prescription medicines for children.

U.S. Pharmacopeial Convention, Inc. *Advice for the Patient.* USPC 1988 $35.00 Provides, in nontechnical language, information for the patient on about 3,000 prescription drugs, including allergic reactions, contraindications, and interactions with other drugs.

Zimmerman, David R. *The Essential Guide to Nonprescription Drugs.* Harper 1983 $27.50 pap. $10.50. Well-organized, alphabetical guide to the wide range of drug categories and their purported therapeutic values. Includes information about the status of all medically active ingredients available for purchase within the United States.

BIOGRAPHY AND HISTORY OF MEDICINE

Writing in the history of medicine is dominated by erudite treatments directed at other scholars. There has been, however, a significant growth in the number of titles published for the intelligent lay reader and the following list provides a sample. Autobiographies reflecting training experiences are included with the Health Professions section later in this chapter. (See also Chapters 2 and 15.)

Anderson, Odin W. *Health Services in the United States: A Growth Enterprise Since 1875.* Health Admin. Pr. 1985 $29.00. An excellent study of an extraordinary period in the history of health care in America showing the evolution of health services from a predominantly private enterprise to one involving the federal and state governments on a large scale.

Bean, William N. *Walter Reed: A Biography.* Univ. Pr. of Virginia 1982 $14.95. The first full-length biography of the discoverer of the transmission mechanism for yellow fever. An important piece of U.S. Army history as well.

Bell, Whitfield J. *The Colonial Physician and Other Essays.* Watson Pub. Intl. new ed. 1975 text ed. $16.00. Bell examines the education, demeanor, and attitudes of the American physician during the colonial and revolutionary periods.

Brieger, Gert H., ed. *Theory and Practice in American Medicine.* Science History 1976 o.p. A collection of historical studies arranged in five categories—medical education, medical theory and research, medical practice, surgery, and medical care. The majority of papers deal with nineteenth-century developments.

Cassedy, James H. *American Medicine and Statistical Thinking, 1800–1860.* Harvard Univ. Pr. 1984 text ed. $22.50. Well-written account of the medical use of statistics and the social development of medicine in the United States.

Cournand, Andre F. *From Roots . . . to Late Budding: The Intellectual Adventures of a Medical Scientist.* Gardner Pr. 1986 $19.95. Autobiography of the Nobel prize winner in physiology in 1956.

Dobkin, Bruce H. *Brain Matters: Stories of a Neurologist and His Patients.* Crown 1986 $17.95. An autobiographical description of clinical neurology.

Drachman, Virginia G. *Hospital with a Heart: Women Doctors and the Paradox of Separatism at the New England Hospital, 1862–1969.* Cornell Univ. Pr. 1984 $19.95. A full and rich description of the evolution of a hospital from an institution of medical charity to one of medical science.

Franklin, Jon, and John Sutherland. *Guinea Pig Doctors: The Drama of Medical Research Through Self-Experimentation.* Morrow 1984 $17.95. A physician, John Sutherland, and a Pulitzer Prize-winning journalist, Jon Franklin, describe physicians in history and their autoexperimentation.

Gifford, George E., ed. *Physician Signers of the Declaration of Independence.* Science History Pubns. 1976 o.p. Biographical essays on the five physicians who signed the Declaration of Independence—Josiah Bartlett, Matthew Thornton, Oliver Wolcott, Lyman Hall, and Benjamin Rush.

Harden, Victoria A. *Inventing the NIH: Federal Biomedical Research Policy, 1887–1937.* Johns Hopkins Univ. Pr. 1986 $32.50. The story of the long legislative effort to implement a program of federal biomedical research.

Harvey, A. McGhee. *Science at the Bedside: Clinical Research in American Medicine,*

1905–1945. Johns Hopkins Univ. Pr. 1981 text ed. $37.50. A scholarly examination of the rise of the various contributors to clinical research efforts in the United States in the first half of the twentieth century.

Helman, Ethel. *An Autumn Life: How a Surgeon Faced His Fatal Illness.* Faber 1986 pap. $6.95. A loving portrait by the surviving widow of a South African surgeon.

Hudson, Robert P. *Disease and Its Control: The Shaping of Modern Thought.* Greenwood 1983 lib. bdg. $29.95. A review of the major concepts leading to the present theories of disease and its control in the West, following a conceptual rather than a chronological organization.

Kanigel, Robert. *Apprentice to Genius: The Making of a Scientific Dynasty.* Macmillan 1986 $19.95. A very readable account of research in the fields of neuroscience and neuropharmacology and the way leaders in the field were mentors for each other.

Kaufman, Martin. *American Medical Education: The Formative Years, 1765–1910.* Greenwood 1976 lib. bdg. $29.95. Traces the evolution of American medical education from colonial times to the period immediately following publication of the influential Flexner Report.

King, Lester S. *Medical Thinking: A Historical Preface.* Princeton Univ. Pr. 1984 $27.50 pap. $11.50. Presents a wide-ranging account of the problems faced by physicians and the development of the critical judgment needed to solve them. Analyzes changing and constant elements of the definitions of important medical concepts such as signs and symptoms, syndromes, fact and theory, disease entity, and clinical entity.

———. *The Philosophy of Medicine: The Early Eighteenth Century.* Harvard Univ. Pr. 1978 $27.50. Places eighteenth-century medicine in the setting from which it emerged and examines the assumptions on which the physicians worked.

Kramer, Mark. *Invasive Procedures: A Year in the World of Two Surgeons.* Penguin 1984 $6.95. An intelligent view of dedication to task, obsession with technical perfection, peer relationships, and ambivalent involvement with patients of two successful surgeons. Told in an easily readable way by a medical writer who is not a physician.

Leavitt, Judith W. *The Healthiest City: Milwaukee and the Politics of Health Reform.* Princeton Univ. Pr. 1982 $25.00. A social history documenting Milwaukee's transformation from a typically unhealthy American city to one acclaimed as its healthiest.

Levenson, Dorothy. *Montefiore: The Hospital as Social Instrument, 1884–1984.* Farrar 1984 $19.95. A fascinating study of a hospital, social change, and philanthropy in New York City.

Levin, Beatrice S. *Women and Medicine.* Scarecrow Pr. 1980 $16.00. A light, humorous approach to the topic that includes a historical overview of the challenges, cultural attitudes, riots, and discrimination that women have faced in the medical profession.

McLaughlin, Loretta. *The Pill, John Rock, and the Church: The Biography of a Revolution.* Little, Brown 1983 $15.95. A biography of the man who discovered the birth control pill.

Marks, Geoffrey, and William K. Beatty. *The Story of Medicine in America.* Scribner 1972 $10.00. A succinct and highly organized literature review of medicine in the United States from the founding of Jamestown through medical advances of the twentieth century.

Medawar, Peter. *Memoir of a Thinking Radish: An Autobiography.* Oxford 1986 $17.95. The 1960 Nobel prize winner for physiology and medicine provides a witty and discerning view of biological research through his career in immunology.

Morantz, Regina M., Cynthia Pomerleau, and Carol H. Fenichel. *In Her Own Words:*

Oral Histories of Women Physicians. Greenwood 1982 $29.95; Yale Univ. Pr. 1982 pap. $9.95. Interviews with nine female physicians, over three generations from the 1920s to the 1970s, coupled with extensive editorial commentary. Covers their obstacles, triumphs, and disappointments with an especially telling analysis of the reconciliation of career and family.

Morantz-Sanchez, Regina M. *Sympathy and Science: Women Physicians in American Medicine.* Oxford 1985 $19.95. A major intellectual achievement tracing women in American medicine from the colonial period through the early decades of the twentieth century.

Morse, Thomas S. *A Gift of Courage.* Doubleday 1982 $16.95. A narrative of the experiences of a pediatric surgeon.

Pappas, Charles N. *The Life and Times of G. V. Black.* Quintessence 1983 text ed. pap. $28.00. A biography of the father of scientific dentistry.

Patterson, Jane, and Lynda Madaras. *Woman Doctor: The Education of Jane Patterson, M.D.* Avon 1983 pap. $3.95. A vivid portrayal of the stresses of medical training in obstetrics and gynecology and of one woman's journey to self-acceptance.

Sacks, Oliver. *A Leg to Stand On.* Summit Bks. 1984 $14.95. An account of the experience of the author, a neurologist, when he lost the use of his leg as the result of a mountain fall.

Selzer, Richard. *Letters to a Young Doctor.* Simon & Schuster 1982 $14.50 1983 pap. $5.95. This and his earlier *Confessions of a Knife* (1979) constitute a collection of essays and vignettes on medical topics.

Sheehan, John C. *The Enchanted Ring: The Untold Story of Penicillin.* MIT 1982 $22.50. Though other books have been written on penicillin, this describes the American production of the drug during World War II.

Sidel, Victor W., and Ruth Sidel. *Reforming Medicine: Lessons of the Last Quarter Century.* Pantheon 1984 $19.45 pap. $9.95. A collection of essays documenting the postwar reform in the American health care system.

Silverstein, Arthur M. *Pure Politics and Impure Science: The Swine Flu Affair.* Johns Hopkins Univ. Pr. 1981 text ed. $17.50. The application of Murphy's first law to the nation's preparation for the 1976 swine flu epidemic that never came.

Starr, Paul. *The Social Transformation of American Medicine: The Rise of a Sovereign Profession and the Making of a Vast Industry.* Basic Bks. 1983 $24.95 1984 pap. $11.95. A landmark work tracing the evolution of the American health care system over two centuries.

Thomas, Lewis. *The Youngest Science: Notes of a Medicine-Watcher.* Bantam 1984 pap. $6.95; G. K. Hall 1983 lib. bdg. $15.95. The memoir of a distinguished scientist and educator.

Weisse, Allen B. *Conversations in Medicine.* New York Univ. Pr. 1984 $24.95. A collection of interviews with 16 physicians who were involved in the major medical advances of the twentieth century.

Whorton, James. *Crusaders for Fitness: A History of American Health Reformers.* Princeton Univ. Pr. 1982 $25.00 1984 pap. $10.95. A chronicle of the health reform movements in the United States from the early 1800s to the present day.

AGING

Though there is a very large literature dealing with aging as a social phenomenon, the emphasis in the following list is on the clinical and psychological aspects of the aging process and health services for the aged. Books on nutrition and aging are included under Nutrition and Diet in this chapter.

Arie, Tom, ed. *Health Care of the Elderly*. Johns Hopkins Univ. Pr. 1981 o.p. A reference book rather than a text, this book of essays by distinguished experts is readable and thought-provoking. It presents a critical evaluation of the current status of several aspects of aging as a social issue.

Berghorn, Forrest J. *The Dynamics of Aging: Original Essays on the Processes and Experience of Growing Old*. Westview Pr. 1981 $32.50 pap. $13.50. An up-to-date multidisciplinary survey of the field of aging, this volume addresses the biology of aging, social roles, public policy, service delivery, and other topics.

Bosse, Raymond, and Charles L. Rose. *Smoking and Aging*. Lexington Bks. 1984 $30.00. An excellent reference source with a primary focus on the relationship between smoking, aging, and disease in the elderly.

Breitung, Joan. *Care of the Older Adult*. Lippincott 2d ed. text ed. 1982 $12.50; Mosby 1977 text ed. pap. $13.95. A useful idea-packed text for families of aging individuals as well as for home health care workers.

Brody, Elaine M. *Mental and Physical Health Practices of Older People: A Guide for Health Professionals*. Springer Pub. 1985 $25.95. Despite its subtitle, a useful book for the educated layperson as well as the health professional.

Burdman, Geri Marr. *Healthful Aging*. Prentice-Hall 1986 $23.95. A discussion of the factors that prevent aging people from realizing their wellness potential. This useful book also includes a "Resources" section that lists organizations, periodicals, and so on.

Busse, Ewald W., and George L. Maddox. *The Duke Longitudinal Studies of Normal Aging, 1955–1980: Overview of History, Design, and Findings*. Springer Pub. 1985 $26.95. Readable, well written and clearly organized, this work describes the classic Duke research on aging.

Duncan, Theodore G. *Over 55: A Handbook on Aging*. Erlbaum 1982 $19.95. A comprehensive manual that examines the sometimes-overlooked medical, emotional, financial and social interests of the elderly.

Futrell, May, ed. *Primary Health Care of the Older Adult*. Duxbury Pr. 1980 o.p. With a broad approach, this book presents detailed information about the health care of persons 65 and older. It is useful for professionals and for caregivers but less so for the individual.

Hall, David A. *The Biomedical Basis of Gerontology*. PSG Pubns. 1984 $27.60. A compact and integrated study of all aspects of the aging process from a scientific point of view.

Hallowell, Christopher. *Growing Old, Staying Young*. Morrow 1985 $18.95. A report on the aging process as it affects both the individual and society, with special attention to the effect that a large-aged population will have on the United States.

Haug, Marie R., ed. *Elderly Patients and Their Doctors*. Springer Pub. 1981 text ed. $20.95. An interesting compilation of articles on a frequently overlooked aspect of gerontology, the physician-patient interaction.

Health in an Older Society. Natl. Acad. Pr. 1985 text ed. pap. $19.50. Contains the landmark papers from the 1983 symposium on societal health that focus on specific topics such as cardiovascular aging, depressive illnesses, dementias, and so forth, as well as the life-style and care of the elderly as determinants of health status.

Henig, Robin M. *The Myth of Senility: Misconceptions about the Brain and Aging*. Doubleday 1981 $13.95. A timely reexamination and redefinition of senility, this book identifies the differences between the normal effects of aging and the very different effects of cerebral illness or damage.

Horne, Jo. *Caregiving: Helping an Aged Loved One.* Amer. Assn. of Retired Persons and Scott, Foresman 1985 $13.95. Provides valuable home health care information for the caregiver.

Hostel, Mildred O. *Nursing Care of the Older Adult: In the Hospital, Nursing Home, and Community.* Wiley 1981 $27.50. A blend of clinical experience and scientific fact, this book would be useful for caregivers in all settings.

Kastenbaum, Robert. *Old, Sick, and Helpless: Where Therapy Begins.* Ballinger 1981 $24.50. A holistic approach to geriatric care that encompasses the history of care of the aging, the therapeutic relationship, and a series of case histories.

Lammers, William W. *Public Policy and the Aging.* Congr. Quarterly 1983 pap. $9.50. Reports the political agenda for the aging, the history of the three White House Conferences on Aging, and discusses at length the health, long-term care, social services, and housing policy for the elderly.

Leutz, Walter N., and others. *Changing Health Care for an Aging Society: Planning for the Social Health Maintenance Organization.* Lexington Bks. 1985 $27.00. This discussion of the evolution of a SHMO for the elderly is a solid foundation for those interested in improving the delivery of health care services to the elderly.

Morgan, Robert F., with Jane Wilson. *Growing Younger: Adding Years to Your Life by Measuring and Controlling Your Body Age.* Stein & Day 1983 $16.95. Morgan, a psychologist, suggests that hypnosis, yoga, graphotherapy, diet, and so on, can all promote longevity.

Murray, Ruth B., M. M. W. Huelskoetter, and Dorothy L. O'Driscoll. *The Nursing Process in Later Maturity.* Prentice-Hall 1980 text ed. $28.95. A comprehensive survey of the needs and problems of senior citizens, this volume is an excellent resource for individuals involved in geriatric care.

Oberleder, Muriel. *The Aging Trap.* Acropolis 1982 $11.95. A thoughtful examination of the aging process designed to dispel many of the myths associated with it.

Ogle, Jane. *Ageproofing.* NAL 1984 $16.95. A refutation of the notion that degenerative processes associated with aging are inevitable. Ogle advocates that proper nutrition and exercise can do much to delay the aging process.

Pagels, C. Carl. *Health Care and the Elderly.* Aspen 1981 text ed. $31.00. A good introductory reference source and overview of health care policymaking and its financing for the aging population.

Palmore, Erdman. *International Handbook on Aging: Contemporary Developments and Research.* Greenwood 1980 lib. bdg. $45.00. A substantial sourcebook for the field of aging.

Phillips, Harry T., and Susan A. Gaylord, eds. *Aging and Public Health.* Springer Pub. 1985 $27.95. This volume stresses the important role to the public health movement and practitioner in improving the well-being of the elderly. A comprehensive and thorough treatment.

Pizer, Hank. *Over Fifty-Five, Healthy, and Alive: A Health Resource for the Coming of Age.* Van Nostrand 1983 o.p. A manual focusing on the health concerns of people over the age of 55 with chapters written by a variety of health professionals.

Walford, Roy L. *Maximum Life Span.* Avon 1984 pap. $3.95; Norton 1983 $15.50. A timely book that focuses on the historical and the current implications of longer life spans.

Williamson, John B., Judith Shindul, and Linda Evans. *Aging and Public Policy: Social Control or Social Justice?* C. C. Thomas 1985 $34.75. A review of health delivery in the United States and an examination of the profits and cost containment of long-term care with limited funds.

ALTERNATIVE HEALTH CARE
AND OTHER SPECIAL SYSTEMS

This section is highly selective and contains works that discuss alternatives to traditional clinical medicine. The holistic health movement in particular has spawned a great many publications, and, with the opening of China in the 1970s, there is a renewed emphasis on oriental therapies. The inclusion of titles here does not constitute endorsement of the techniques, but rather an effort to include nontraditional approaches to health care.

Achterberg, Jeanne. *Imagery in Healing: Shamanism and Modern Medicine.* Shambhala 1985 pap. $9.95. An exploration of the meaning of shamanism in worldwide cultures past and present.

Albright, Peter, and Beth Parker Albright. *Body, Mind, and Spirit: The Journal Toward Health and Wholeness.* Stephen Greene Pr. 1980 o.p. "A collaborative work on holistic health, which testifies for the triune wholeness of the person in whom the components are unified into a matrix of love and naturalistic health practices" (*Choice*).

Becker, Robert O., and Gary Selden. *The Body Electric: Electromagnetism and the Foundation of Life.* Morrow 1985 $17.95. A description of Becker's more than 30 years of research, the insights derived from it, and the personal and political experiences of a working scientist challenging accepted views.

Berkeley Holistic Health Center. *The Holistic Health Lifebook: A Guide to Personal and Planetary Well-Being.* And/Or Pr. 1981 pap. $12.95; Stephen Greene Pr. 1984 pap. $12.95. An extension of *Holistic Health Handbook* (1979) attempting to extend the concept of holism beyond health to one's entire life-style.

Bliss, Shepherd, ed. *The New Holistic Health Handbook: Living Well in a New Age.* Stephen Greene Pr. 2d ed. rev. 1985 pap. $14.95. A wide-ranging compilation of articles on all aspects of the holistic health movement.

Chinese Massage Therapy: A Handbook of Therapeutic Massage. Shambhala 1984 o.p. Following an explanation of Chinese massage therapy principles, this book describes 24 commonly used techniques, illustrates important acupoints, and so on. Text is detailed but clear and accompanied by line drawings.

Deliman, Tracy, and John S. Smolowe. *Holistic Medicine: Harmony of Body, Mind, Spirit.* Reston 1982 text ed. $23.95 pap. $17.95. Sixteen contributors discuss a holistic helping process designed to increase the harmony of mind, body, and spirit.

Dever, G. E. Alan. *Community Health Analysis: A Holistic Approach.* Aspen 1980 text ed. $36.50. A comprehensive, well-written, well-documented text that provides a philosophical approach to holistic health.

Eisenberg, David. *Encounters with QI: Exploring Chinese Medicine.* Norton 1985 $16.95. Told from the viewpoint of a Western physician, this balanced account presents many Chinese ideas and practices worthy of careful examination for their therapeutic value.

Freund, Peter E. S., and Miriam Fisher. *The Civilized Body: Social Domination, Control, and Health.* Temple Univ. Pr. 1983 text ed. $19.95. An important book on the relationship between social structure and disease. The first to carefully integrate the individualistic literature of the holistic health movement with sociological concepts of social control and stratification.

Griggs, Barbara. *Green Pharmacy: A History of Herbal Medicine.* Viking 1982 $14.95. A history of botanical medicine, or herbalism, from Galen to the present.

Hand, Wayland D., ed. *American Folk Medicine: A Symposium.* Univ. of California Pr.

1976 pap. $5.95. A classic and fascinating work that includes the papers from a landmark symposium held at the University of California at Los Angeles. Includes folk practices among various ethnic groups.

Hastings, Arthur C., James Fadiman, and James S. Gordon. *Health for the Whole Person: The Complete Guide to Holistic Medicine.* Westview Pr. 1980 o.p. A comprehensive summary of world health practices in the holistic health vein covering the diverse field of holistic health practices with clarity and excellent documentation.

Hittleman, Richard. *Yoga for Health: The Total Program.* Ballantine 1983 pap. $7.95. A manual of Hatha yoga exercises, vegetarian nutrition, and meditation.

Inglis, Brian, and Ruth West. *The Alternative Health Guide.* Knopf 1983 $19.95. A compendium of historical backgrounds, procedures, research findings, and typical applications for some 66 physical, psychological, and paranormal therapies ranging from osteopathy to spiritualism.

Kaptchuk, Ted J. *The Web That Has No Weaver: Understanding Chinese Medicine.* Congdon & Weed 1984 $19.95 pap. $9.95. A detailed readable work emphasizing the basic differences of approach to recognizing and treating disharmony in the human body.

Lawrence, D. Baloti, and Lewis Harrison. *Massageworks: A Practical Encyclopedia of Massage Techniques.* Putnam 1983 pap. $8.95. A beginner's guide to massage self-care for a variety of complaints.

LeShan, Lawrence. *The Mechanic and the Gardener: Making the Most of the Holistic Revolution in Medicine.* Holt 1982 o.p. A book aimed at the health care consumer which asserts that both allopathy and holistic treatment are necessary to the healing process.

Lillyquist, Michael J. *Sunlight and Health.* Dodd 1985 $15.95. Sunlight is both health-giving and a health hazard. A well-documented summary of current knowledge.

Lowe, Carl, and Jim Nechas. *Body Healing.* Rodale Pr. 1983 $21.95. A guide to selected alternative therapies, exercise, and self-care, notable for its clear straightforward instructions.

Otto, Herbert A., and James W. Knight. *Dimensions in Wholistic Healing: New Frontiers in the Treatment of the Whole Person.* Nelson-Hall 1979 $29.95. An important collection of writings focusing on the various aspects of holistic health care as it has developed in the United States and its early historic framework.

Pizer, Hank. *Guide to the New Medicine: What Works, What Doesn't.* Morrow 1982 $10.95. A consumer's guide to alternative health care, this work evaluates various techniques, for example, homeopathy, acupuncture, meditation, and biofeedback based on a review of scientific findings.

Salmon, J. Warren, ed. *Alternative Medicines: Popular and Policy Perspectives.* Methuen 1984 $25.00 pap. $12.95. Essential for those interested in the future direction of health care and delivery this is the first forthright treatment of the several alternative medicines in one volume.

Sofowora, Abayomi. *Medicinal Plants and Traditional Medicine in Africa.* Wiley 1983 $37.95. Covers the fundamental procedures of traditional African healing methods and compares their advantages and disadvantages to methods used in modern medicine.

Stalker, Douglas, and Clark Glymour. *Examining Holistic Medicine.* Prometheus Bks. 1986 $20.95. A collection of 20 essays that critically analyze the philosophy, methodology, and practice of holistic medicine.

Steiner, Richard P., ed. *Folk Medicine: The Art and the Science.* Amer. Chemical

Society 1986 $22.95 pap. $12.95. Contributors examine the folk medicine traditions of nine countries, encompassing nine cultures, to establish the scientific basis for remedial actions of treatment.

Trotter, Robert T., and Juan A. Chavira. *Curanderismo: Mexican American Folk Healing.* Univ. of Georgia Pr. 2d ed. 1981 $18.00 pap. $9.00. A comprehensive work on the theory and practice of curanderismo also dealing with its characteristics and social nexus.

Weil, Andrew. *Health and Healing: Understanding Conventional and Alternative Medicine.* Houghton Mifflin 1984 $13.95. This thoughtful and stimulating book challenges Western ideas of orthodox medicine and considers homeopathy, osteopathy, naturopathy, chiropractic, Chinese medicine, and so on. It is the most important book available in English on the subject.

Weiss, Gaea, and Shandor Weiss. *Growing and Using the Healing Herbs.* Rodale Pr. 1985 $19.95. The history of herbal healing in many cultures with practical hints for growing and manufacturing your own herbs.

West, Ruth, and Joanna E. Trevelyan. *Alternative Medicine: A Bibliography of Books in English.* Mansell 1985 $31.00. A quality work of its kind, this bibliography brings together English-language books on therapies outside the mainstream of medicine.

ANATOMY

[SEE the section on The Healthy Body in this chapter.]

CARDIOLOGY

[SEE Chapter 15, under Cardiovascular Diseases, in this volume.]

CHILDCARE AND DEVELOPMENT

As in libraries, the reader will find in many bookstores a separate section dealing with the topic of childcare, one which produces an astonishingly large number of titles each year. This list is very representative.

Anastasiow, Nicholas J. *The Adolescent Parent.* P. H. Brookes 1982 $15.95. A concise review of the worldwide problems of adolescent pregnancy and a thorough but readable summary of knowledge about physical and intellectual development in adolescents.

Arnold, L. Eugene, and Donna Esteicher. *Parent-Child Group Therapy: Building Self-Esteem in a Cognitive-Behavioral Group.* Lexington Bks. 1985 $25.00. The description of a successful method to build the self-esteem and improve the functioning of learning- and behavior-disordered children.

Auckett, Amelia D. *Baby Massage: Parent-Child Bonding Through Touching.* Newmarket 1982 pap. $6.95. Presents massage as a positive experience for parents and children that results in improved communication.

Batshaw, Mark L., and Yvonne M. Perret. *Children with Handicaps: A Medical Primer.* P. H. Brookes 1981 text ed. $22.95. Easy-to-read, clear, and sensitive, a singularly important book about the medical aspects of handicaps in children.

Baum, Andrew, and Jerome E. Singer. *Issues in Child Health and Adolescent Health*. Erlbaum 1982 text ed. $29.95. A collection of works on the study of behavioral disorders including reviews of the literature and relevant research findings.

Brazelton, T. Berry. *Working and Caring*. Addison-Wesley 1985 $16.95. An excellent book by the renowned Harvard pediatrician focusing on working parents and the issues they confront.

Brown, Jeffrey L. *The Complete Parents' Guide to Telephone Medicine, How, When, and Why to Call Your Child's Doctor: A Ready Reference for Childhood Illnesses, Common Emergencies, Newborn Infant Care, Psychological and Behavior Problems*. Putnam 1982 pap. $6.95. Presents advice similar to that of major child development physicians such as Spock, Brazelton, and Dodson.

Caplan, Theresa, and Frank Caplan. *The Early Childhood Years: The Two to Six Year Old*. Bantam 1984 pap. $4.50; Putnam 1983 $9.95. Even more so than their earlier books, *The First Twelve Months of Life* (Bantam 1978 pap. $4.95) and *The Second Twelve Months of Life* (Bantam 1980 pap. $4.95; Putnam 1979 pap. $10.95), this is a sourcebook for parents.

Collins, W. Andrew. *Development During Middle Childhood: The Years from Six to Twelve*. Natl. Acad. Pr. 1984 text ed. $28.50. Topics include biological development and physical health, cognitive development, self-understanding and self-regulation, family relationships, peer relationships, schooling, and psychopathology.

Cuthbertson, Joanne, and Susie Schevill. *Helping Your Child Sleep Through the Night*. Doubleday 1985 pap. $7.95. A useful book arranged in chapters by age, and positive in tone, the authors spell out specific day-by-day plans of action.

DeLorenzo, Lorisa, and Robert DeLorenzo. *Total Child Care: From Birth to Age Five*. Doubleday 1982 $29.95. A comprehensive book on childrearing by a physician and a psychologist.

Dickens, Monica. *Miracles of Courage: How Families Meet the Challenge of a Child's Critical Illness*. Dodd 1985 $14.95. In a style that is vivid, compassionate, and emotionally wracking, Dickens relates the experiences of people who have faced critical illness in their children.

Dodson, Fitzhugh, and Ann Alexander. *How to Parent*. NAL 1973 pap. $3.95. A commonsense combination of love and discipline, Dodson's approach to childrearing offers a creative, complete, and mutually enjoyable program for guiding the child from birth to five years of age. An alternative to Spock.

Ferber, Richard. *Solve Your Child's Sleep Problems*. Simon & Schuster 1985 $15.95. By a medical expert, a good discussion of the physiology of sleep and uncommon sleep problems. Presents systematic approaches to these problems.

Goldberg, Susan, and Barbara Divitto. *Born Too Soon: Preterm Birth and Early Development*. Freeman 1983 text ed. $19.95 pap. $12.00. A useful summary of what is known about premature babies citing numerous studies from medical and academic sources.

Haessler, Herbert A. *How to Make Sure Your Baby Is Well—And Stays That Way: The First Guide to over 400 Medical Tests and Treatments You Can Do at Home to Check Your Baby's Daily Health and Growth*. Rawson 1984 $17.95 1985 pap. $7.95. Not a diagnostic manual, but an understandable guide to routine tests and treatments that parents can do to assess and maintain the health of a child.

Harrison, Helen, and Ann Kositsky. *The Premature Baby Book: A Parents' Guide to Coping and Caring in the First Years*. St. Martin's 1983 $24.95 text ed. pap. $15.95. A splendid book presenting clinical and technical information exhaustively but succinctly.

Henig, Robin M., and Anne B. Fletcher. *Your Premature Baby: The Complete Guide to*

Caring for Your Premie During That Crucial First Year. Ballantine 1984 pap. $7.95; Rawson 1983 $14.95. Written by a medical writer and a physician, this book offers clear, practical, and comforting advice for parents on a wide range of topics associated with premature children.

Hillman, Sheilah, and others. *The Baby Checkup Book: A Parents' Guide to Well Baby Care.* Bantam 1984 pap. $3.95. An excellent, well-presented book on baby checkups with an unusual emphasis on the physical examination.

Jones, Monica Loose. *Home Care for the Chronically Ill or Disabled Child: A Manual and Sourcebook for Parents and Professionals.* Harper 1985 pap. $12.95. Well-researched book with an emphasis on details of care for ill children.

Kagan, Jerome. *The Nature of the Child.* Basic Bks. 1984 $22.50. An eloquent look at issues of child development which suggests that many popular notions about parenting are askew.

Kelly, Paula. *First Year Baby Care: An Illustrated Step-by-Step Guide for New Parents.* Meadowbrook Pr. 1983 pap. $5.95. A concise how-to-do-it and what-to-use manual of baby care. Also includes a symptoms index of health problems and emergencies.

Lieberman, Adrienne, and Thomas Sheagren. *The Premie Parents' Handbook: A Lifeline for the New Parents of a Premature Baby.* Dutton 1984 pap. $10.95. Thorough coverage of causes of premature birth and treatments for premature infants. Of special importance is the discussion of what the parents can contribute to the well-being of the hospitalized infant and of considerations for subsequent pregnancies.

Nance, Sherri, and others. *Premature Babies: A Handbook for Parents.* Arbor House 1982 $15.95. An account by parents of premature babies, hospital staff who deal with premies and parents, and grandparents and friends. Topical arrangement.

Pfister, Fred, and Bernard Griesemer. *The Littlest Baby: Handbook for Parents of Premature Children.* Prentice-Hall 1982 $12.95 pap. $5.95. Written by the grandfather and physician of a premature infant, this book provides information for parents and medical personnel.

Restak, Richard M. *The Infant Mind.* Doubleday 1986 $18.95. A description of the normal development of the brain in infants and children.

Samuels, Mike, and Nancy Samuels. *The Well Child Book.* Summit Bks. 1982 pap. $10.95. A sequel to their *The Well Baby Book* (1979), this is a clearly written, well-illustrated medical self-care manual for parents and children.

Spock, Benjamin, and Michael B. Rothenberg. *Dr. Spock's Baby & Child Care.* Dutton 40th anniversary ed. 1985 $19.95. The classic baby book.

Worth, Cecilia, with Anna Marie Brooks. *New Parenthood: The First Six Weeks.* McGraw-Hill 1985 $16.95 pap. $8.95. A welcome addition to the new-parent literature, this is a concise, positive, and well-designed source of basic information about normal infant care.

DEATH AND DYING

[SEE Chapter 15 in this volume.]

DENTAL CARE

[SEE the section on The Healthy Body in this chapter.]

DENTISTRY

[SEE the section on Health Professions, Dentistry in this chapter.]

DERMATOLOGY

[SEE the section on The Healthy Body in this chapter;
for skin diseases, see Chapter 15 in this volume.]

DIAGNOSTIC TESTING

The medical consumer of the 1980s is subjected to an everincreasing array of tests as part of routine physical examinations and as part of the office visit for illness. The tests and technologies are becoming increasingly more sophisticated and this section serves to introduce many of the more common techniques.

Byrne, C. Judith, and others. *Laboratory Tests: Implications for Nurses and Allied Health Professionals.* Addison-Wesley 1981 $21.95. An excellent book for allied health practitioners and the students of these disciplines that provides, in a clear and concise format, information on many current laboratory tests.

Culyer, A. K., and B. Horisberger, eds. *Economic and Medical Evaluation of Health Care Technologies.* Springer-Verlag 1983 $22.00. Illustrates the great necessity for the public at large to become better informed on the technological bases of health care. This book, which is well edited, is comprehensible to the layperson.

DeMarre, Dean A., and David Michaels. *Bioelectric Measurements.* Prentice-Hall 1983 $29.95. A well-written book and concise overview of the present status of bioelectronic measurement. Of value to individuals interested in learning about some of the instrumentational aspects of medical care.

Gofman, John W. *Radiation and Human Health.* Sierra 1981 $29.95. A sourcebook containing practical information needed for individuals to make personal and family decisions about voluntary exposures to medical and dental radiation as well as occupational exposures.

Lenburg, Carrie B. *The Clinical Performance Examination: Development and Implementation.* Appleton & Lange 1979 $24.95. This well-written, well-indexed book has the distinction of being the first volume on clinical performance examinations based on comprehensive research and not on trial and error.

Lutz, Harald, and R. Meudt. *Manual of Ultrasound.* Springer-Verlag 1984 pap. $26.00. The conciseness of style, the diagrams, and the extensiveness of the topics covered make this an excellent book for the technologist, health care personnel, and students interested in the fundamentals of ultrasound.

McFarland, Mary B., and Marcia M. Grant. *Nursing Implications of Laboratory Tests.* Wiley 1982 pap. $16.50. Chapters of this very useful book focus on the body's physiological functions rather than test types/groups, as most other "test guides." Consequently, descriptions of single laboratory tests that test multiple functions are frequently repeated under each function.

McNeil, Barbara J., and Ernest G. Cravalho, eds. *Critical Issues in Medical Technology.* Auburn House 1981 $28.00. The record of an interesting and thought-provoking conference of known experts in the field who carefully address social and ethical implications of technological advances and applications in medicine.

Pinckney, Cathy, and Edward R. Pinckney. *Do-It-Yourself Medical Testing.* Facts on File 1983 $16.95 pap. $7.95. This book offers valuable information for those persons interested in taking an active role in their health care. Medical tests are described thoroughly.

Reiser, Stanley M. *Medicine and the Reign of Technology.* Cambridge Univ. Pr. 1981 pap. $12.95. Examines the influence that the growth of technology has had on physicians' ability to diagnose disease more precisely.

Tresler, Kathleen M. *Clinical Laboratory Tests: Significance and Implications for Nursing.* Prentice-Hall 1982 $20.95. An outstanding book for individuals studying and practicing health care delivery.

Williams, A. Roy. *Ultrasound: Biological Effects and Potential Hazards.* Academic Pr. 1983 $49.50. A useful and informative presentation of physical, biological, and epidemiological aspects of ultrasound exposure and its potential risk.

DIET

[SEE the section on Nutrition and Diet in this chapter.]

DRUGS AND PHARMACEUTICAL PREPARATIONS

[SEE the section on Pharmacology and Toxicology in this chapter.]

ENDOCRINOLOGY

[For endocrine diseases see Chapter 15 in this volume.]

EPIDEMIOLOGY

[SEE Chapter 15 in this volume.]

EXERCISE AND PHYSICAL FITNESS

The fitness boom has brought with it a deluge of titles dealing with specific kinds of exercise, and aimed at specific audiences, for example, children, the aged, and so on. This section includes some representative titles of each type.

Alter, Judy. *Surviving Exercise.* Houghton Mifflin 1983 $11.95 pap. $5.95. The goal of all exercise should be to tone muscles, not to stress ligaments, grind joints, or fray tendons, says the author. This book provides well-illustrated recommended exercises and sound advice on what exercises not to do and why.

Binney, Ruth. *The Complete Manual of Fitness and Well-Being.* Viking 1984 $25.00. Whole life programs to help individuals assess their lives and life-styles in terms of fitness and preventive health care make up the bulk of this recommended family fitness guide.

Bland, Jeffrey. *Nutraerobics: The Complete Individualized Nutrition and Fitness Program for Life after 30.* Harper 1983 $16.95. Written by a physician, this book is a good general discussion and guide to the benefits of an improved life-style. Emphasis is on nutrition.

Bove, Alfred A., and David T. Lowenthal. *Exercise Medicine: Physiological Principles and Clinical Applications*. Academic Pr. 1983 $47.00. Provides an excellent reference source for physicians and individuals involved in exercise programs.

Broccoletti, Pete. *Thirty-Five and Holding: Complete Conditioning for the Adult Male*. Icarus 1982 $10.95. The strength here is in the weight training section, which provides helpful routines for general fitness and individual sports.

Brown, Millie. *Low-Stress Fitness*. HP Bks. 1985 pap. $8.95. A book crammed with useful tips and philosophy to help the sedentary person develop a sane fitness program.

Cannon, Geoffrey, and Hetty Einzig. *Dieting Makes You Fat: A Guide to Energy, Food, Fitness and Health*. Simon & Schuster 1985 $15.95. Advocates a food regimen that increases metabolic rate combined with aerobic exercise. Cites numerous studies and reports.

Cooper, Kenneth H. *The Aerobics Program for Total Well-Being*. Bantam 1983 pap. $10.95; M. Evans 1982 $16.95. Recommended title providing a program for balancing nutrition, exercise, and emotional health. Includes directory of sports medicine clinics and descriptions of medical examinations.

DeVries, Herbert, with Dianne Hales. *Fitness after 50*. Scribner 1982 $12.95 pap. $5.95. Combining sense and readability, DeVries and Hales present an excellent book that explains the relationship between continued fitness and aging.

Dietrich, John, and Susan Waggoner. *The Complete Health Club Handbook*. Simon & Schuster 1983 $9.95. An amazingly complete manual that tells how to determine what type of health club best suits one's needs. Includes, with candid reviews, a directory of facilities in ten major U.S. cities.

Dusek, Dorothy. *Thin and Fit: Your Personal Lifestyle*. Wadsworth 1982 o.p. A clear and concise introduction to a holistic plan for changing one's life-style to promote thinness, Dusek presents a readiness/self-responsibility profile to help readers assess their independence, spontaneity, assertiveness, and emotions.

Hales, Dianne, and Robert E. Hales. *Be All You Can Be! The U.S. Army Total Fitness Program*. Crown 1985 $14.95. An eight-week exercise regimen based on the U.S. Army's Fit to Win program. The program can be individually tailored using the self-assessment test provided.

Jameson, Robert H. *Exercise for the Elderly*. Emerson 1982 o.p. Large-print book that describes and demonstrates simple limbering, stretching, and strengthening exercises, including those for bedridden or wheelchair-bound individuals.

Katz, Jane. *The W.E.T. Workout: Water Exercise Techniques to Help You Tone Up and Slim Down, Aerobically*. Facts on File 1985 $8.95. A progressive three-month illustrated program of stretching and toning exercises for use in the water.

Layman, Donald K. *Nutrition and Aerobic Exercise*. Amer. Chemical Society 1986 $34.95. Written for an audience with a basic knowledge of physiology and metabolism, this symposium volume provides current research information on specific topics within nutrition and exercise, for example, responses to exercise, skeletal muscle adaptations to exercise, and so forth.

McArdle, William D., and others. *Exercise Physiology: Energy, Nutrition, and Human Performance*. Lea & Febiger 1981 text ed. $23.00. In layperson's language, the authors emphasize the interrelationships of body composition, obesity, weight control, and the role of exercise in these areas. Appendixes include useful data on the nutritive value of foods, the amount of energy used in various forms of exercise, and so on.

National Board of YMCAs. *The Official YMCA Fitness Program*. Rawson 1984 $18.95

pap. $9.95. A good all-around illustrated program geared toward helping achieve individual fitness through calisthenics, proper nutrition, and good mental health.

Peters, Jane S. *The Indoor Bicycling Fitness Program: A Complete Guide to Equipment and Exercise*. McGraw-Hill 1985 $8.95. This handbook provides a consumer's checklist of available equipment, exercise programs for cardiovascular fitness, muscle tone, and so forth. Useful appendixes of books, periodicals, catalogs, manufacturers, and so on.

Van Orden, Naola, and S. Paul Steed. *The Bio-Plan for Lifelong Weight Control*. Dial 1983 $10.95. This book combines nutritional advice with a vigorous program of exercise. Includes nutritional information on the composition of foods and recommended daily allowances of proteins, carbohydrates, and fats.

FORENSIC MEDICINE

[SEE the section on Medicine and the Law in this chapter.]

GERONTOLOGY/GERIATRICS

[SEE the section on Aging in this chapter.]

GYNECOLOGY

[SEE the section on Women's Health in this chapter.]

HEALTH CARE

General

This section deals with the philosophy and organization of health care. The past, present, and future organization, financing, and management of health care delivery is examined. It includes works on Health Maintenance Organizations (HMOs) and Preferred Provider Organizations (PPOs).

Aaron, Henry J., and William B. Schwartz. *The Painful Prescription: Rationing Hospital Care*. Brookings 1984 $26.95 pap. $9.95. "Attempts to predict the consequences of financial barriers to medical care that will result from the budgetary limitations being imposed, at the state and federal levels, in an attempt to restrict the heretofore unlimited increase in the costs of hospital care. Highlights issues of concern to patients and physicians alike" (*Choice*).

Barocci, Thomas A. *Non-Profit Hospitals: Their Structure, Human Resources, and Economic Importance*. Auburn House 1981 $24.95. "A rather unfocused compilation of information about the particular sample of hospitals that may or may not be generalizable to the total population of hospitals in the U.S." (*Choice*).

Bell, Roger, ed. *Assessing Health and Human Service Needs: Concepts, Methods and Applications*. [*Community Psychology Ser.*] Human Sciences Pr. 1983 $39.95. "After a brief introduction to the concepts of needs assessment comes discussion of conceptual issues, methodological techniques, the use of these methodologies in actual program planning, and a summary that includes a very useful annotated bibliography" (*Choice*).

Boland, Peter. *New Healthcare Market: A Guide to PPOs for Purchasers, Payors and Providers.* Irwin 1985 $75.00. "A comprehensive treatment of the phenomena of competitive marketing in health care known as preferred provider arrangements or preferred provider organization (the PPO in the title). Presents 16 case studies of operational PPO's sponsored by physician groups, hospitals, insurance companies, and private investor groups" (*Choice*).

Braverman, Jordan. *Crisis in Health Care.* Acropolis rev. ed. 1980 pap. $7.95. "Presents a picture of where American medicine [stood in 1980] and describes realities confronting the physician and other health care providers. National Health Insurance, health maintenance organizations, professional standard review organizations, drug substitution laws, anti-trust investigations, public fraud and abuse, medical malpractice law suits, and other issues are confronted" (*Choice*).

Brickner, Philip, and Linda Scharer. *Health Care of Homeless People.* Springer Pub. text ed. 1985 $29.95. "Defines the homeless population, introduces historical background of experiences, discusses medical disorders, explains that consideration of homeless populations is based on impressions rather than on types of illness, deals with access to care, health care teams and hospital experiences" (*Choice*).

Brown, Lawrence D. *Politics and Health Care Organization: HMO's as Federal Policy.* Brookings 1983 $33.95 pap. $16.95. "The complexity and, on occasion, the incomprehensibility of the American health care system are nowhere better shown than in this detailed study. This is an analysis of the origins of health maintenance organizations (HMOs) in the dual context of progressive federal involvement through Medicare and Medicaid" (*Choice*).

Dowling, Harry F. *The City Hospitals: The Undercare of the Underprivileged.* Harvard Univ. Pr. 1982 text ed. $25.00. "Traces the development of city hospitals through four periods: the almshouse period, lasting until approximately 1860 in the larger eastern cities; the practitioner period, from 1860 to 1910; the academic period, from about 1910 to 1965; and the present community period" (*Choice*).

Duffy, John. *The Healers: Rise of American Medicine.* McGraw-Hill 1976 o.p. "Deals, often very briefly, with the whole range of medical and public health. Rich in insights about the social aspects of medicine" (*Amer. Scientist*).

Falkson, Joseph L. *HMOs and the Politics of Health System Reform.* Amer. Hospital 1980 o.p. "Describes the emergence of health maintenance organizations (HMO's) as an instrument of national health policy in the years 1969–1978" (*Choice*).

Feder, J., and T. Marmor, eds. *National Health Insurance: Conflicting Goals and Policy Choices.* Urban Institute Pr. 1980 text ed. $28.00 pap. $14.95. "Considers the choices that policymakers (legislators and administrators) must make in enacting and implementing any national health insurance program" (*Choice*).

Foltz, Anne-Marie. *An Ounce of Prevention: Child Health Politics Under Medicaid.* [*Health and Public Policy Ser.*] MIT 1982 $39.95. "A highly critical and at times cynical case study of the Early and Periodic Screening, Diagnosis, and Treatment (EPSDT) Program under Medicaid from its first inauspicious beginning in 1968 to the present day [1982]" (*Choice*).

Ginzberg, Eli, and Edith M. Davis. *Local Health Policy in Action: The Municipal Health Services Program.* Rowman 1985 $28.50. "The book represents the findings and recommendations based on the Municipal Health Services Program, which remained in existence from 1978 to 1984, as a demonstration of primary health care delivery to urban populations in Baltimore, Cincinnati, Milwaukee, St. Louis, and San Jose" (*Choice*).

Greer, Ann Lennarson, and Scott A. Greer. *Cities and Sickness.* Sage 1983 pap. $14.95. "Economists, sociologists, political scientists, and health planners focus on the implications of urbanization for human health and the prevention and care of illness" (*Choice*).

Haddad, Amy Marie. *High Tech Home Care: A Practical Guide.* Aspen 1987 $32.00. A significant contribution to home care covering the broad scope of home care management, delivery, and services, this book provides to the consumer a wealth of useful facts and sound advice about frequently bewildering medical technology.

Hassinger, Edward W. *Rural Health Organization: Social Networks and Regionalization.* Iowa State Univ. Pr. 1982 text ed. pap. $12.95. "Basic thesis is that, in order to understand the delivery of medical services in rural areas, one must consider both the cultural aspects of rural life and the organizational aspects of the health system" (*Choice*).

Havighurst, Clark C. *Deregulating the Health Care Industry: Planning for Competition.* Ballinger 1982 $39.95. "Basic premise is that shortsighted, if not stupid, regulatory controls have led to excessive costs, monopolistic practices, and reduced quality. Examines the condition necessary for a greater reliance on market forces to correct these problems" (*Choice*).

Health Planning in the United States: Selected Policy Issues. Natl. Acad. Pr. 2 vols. 1981 pap. ea. $9.75–$11.75. "The final report of a two-year study commissioned by the Health Resources Administration" (*Choice*).

Imershein, Allan W., ed. *Challenges and Innovations in U.S. Health Care Policy.* Westview Pr. 1981 o.p. "Papers given at a 1979 meeting of the Health, Health Policy and Health Services Division of the Society for the Study of Social Problems. The U.S. health-care scene is assessed and health policies are presented from various viewpoints" (*Choice*).

John, J., and others, eds. *Influence of Economic Instability on Health.* Springer-Verlag 1983 pap. $34.00. "Contains 22 papers presented at the GSF-MEDIS symposium of the same name held in Munich in 1981. The symposium was organized around the pioneering work of M. Harvey Brenner, who demonstrated a positive relationship between economic dislocation, unemployment in particular, and mortality rates in Great Britain" (*Choice*).

Kark, Sidney L. *The Practice of Community-Oriented Primary Health Care.* Appleton & Lang 1980 o.p. "A thorough treatment of all that community health encompasses; identifies problems and needs for programming; describes successful programs in detail" (*Choice*).

Margulies, N., and J. D. Adams. *Organizational Development in Health Care Organizations.* Addison-Wesley 1982 $27.50. "A comprehensive description of the current state of the art of health care organization" (*Choice*).

Miller, Irwin. *The Health Care Survival Curve: Competition and Cooperation in the Marketplace.* Irwin 1984 $35.00. "Analyzes current health policies, innovative community strategies, and industrialization of health delivery and the benefits of voluntarism. Contends there must be a balance between competition and operation if institutions are to succeed and communities are to be well served" (*Choice*).

Milner, Murray, Jr. *Unequal Care: A Case Study of Interorganizational Relations.* Columbia Univ. Pr. 1980 $32.00. "A sociologist examines the source of inequality in the delivery of health care in the U.S." (*Choice*).

Morris, Jonas. *Searching for a Cure.* Universe 1984 $27.50. "Provides a detailed account of the battle over national health insurance during the last 20 years. Good exploration of the legislative process" (*Choice*).

Numbers, Ronald L., ed. *Compulsory Health Insurance: The Continuing American Debate.* [*Contributions in Medical History Ser.*] Greenwood 1982 $29.95. "Papers by historians and social scientists originally presented at a 1979 symposium at the University of Wisconsin" (*Choice*).

Rutkowski, Arthur D., and Barbara Conway Rutkowski. *Labor Relations in Hospitals.* Aspen 1984 $35.95. "The title is somewhat misleading, since it implies a more comprehensive treatment of hospital labor relations than is provided. Does a good job of providing practical guidelines for managing the hospital labor relations function" (*Choice*).

Sidel, Victor, and Ruth Sidel, eds. *Reforming Medicine: Lessons from The Last Quarter Century.* Pantheon 1984 $19.45 pap. $9.95. "Experts in social medicine describe reforms in the health care delivery system—Medicare, Medicaid, women's health care, medical education, occupational health and safety" (*LJ*).

Thompson, John D., and Grace Goldin. *The Hospital: A Social and Architectural History.* Yale Univ. Pr. 1975 o.p. "A handy source for information about hospitals and how they have functioned" (*Amer. Scientist*).

U.S. Dept. of Health and Human Services, Task Force on Health Risk Assessment. *Determining Risks to Health: Federal Policy and Practice.* Auburn House 1986 pap. $16.95. "One of the first accounts to promote general public understanding of the role of the U.S. Department of Health and Human Services in the assessment of health risks. Discusses various approaches used in studying risk assessments, results found through surveys and analysis, and recommendations for improving the present policies and practices" (*Choice*).

Vogel, Morris J. *The Invention of the Modern Hospital: Boston, 1870–1930.* Univ. of Chicago Pr. 1980 lib. bdg. $15.50 1985 pap. $6.95. "Explores the evolution of the hospital from a voluntary organization assisting charity patients into a primary supplier of health care for all social classes" (*LJ*).

Waitzkin, Howard B. *The Second Sickness: Contradictions of Capitalist Health Care.* Free Pr. 1983 text ed. $19.95 1986 pap. $11.95. "A frustrating, nettlesome, and in parts, significant critique of health care organization in capitalist countries, most specifically the U.S. First part establishes the author's Marxist perspective; second explores specific problems with capitalist health care; third covers policies for social change" (*Choice*).

Williams, Stephen J., ed. *Issues in Health Services.* Wiley 1980 o.p. "Introduces the concept of health services; raises questions about the effects of medicine on health and mortality; deals with the utilization of services and meeting the demand for services; discusses how to assess and effect performance of health service systems; and explores different organizational forms for health services delivery" (*Choice*).

Williams, Stephen J., and Paul R. Torrens, eds. *Introduction to Health Services.* Wiley 2d ed. 1984 $29.95. "Divided into five parts: an introduction to health service systems of this country; factors associated with the utilization of health services; providers of health services; organizations and programs that provide health care; and setting of priorities of health services, as well as use of regulatory and planning mechanisms to achieve social goals" (*Choice*).

Wilson, Florence, and Duncan Neuhauser. *Health Services in the United States.* Ballinger 2d ed. rev. 1982 $17.95. "Captures the breadth of the health-care industry in a concise yet comprehensive manner. Includes health-care services such as mental retardation, nursing homes, and mental-health services" (*Choice*).

Wohl, Stanley M. *The Medical Industrial Complex.* Crown 1984 $14.95. "A lucid, thoughtful, balanced, and erudite exposition of the background, history, evolution, virtues, and dangers of the almost total monetarization of the health care system" (*Choice*).

Work in America Institute. *Improving Health-Care Management in the Workplace.* Pergamon 1985 $19.25. "Intended to help both employers and unions select health plan options that are cost effective, not just inexpensive" (*Choice*).

Zawadski, Rick T., ed. *Community-Based Systems of Long-Term Care.* Haworth Pr. 1984 text ed. $22.95. "Reports of eight federally funded community-based projects that offered elderly persons an alternative to nursing home care. A critical review of past successes and errors" (*Choice*).

Comparative Studies

This section includes books dealing with the organization and economics of health care delivery systems both international and national. Includes analysis and comparison of health care delivery systems around the world.

Akin, John S., and David K. Guilkey. *The Demand for Primary Health Services in the Third World.* Rowman 1985 $39.95. "Combines economic variables with data from medical anthropology, sociology, and geography, and organizes them within an economic framework. Selected simple and complex theoretical models of demand for medical care are critically reviewed, and the authors also formulate their own model. The book's joining of economic and noneconomic variables and its questioning of widespread assumptions about Third World primary health care constitute significant contributions to international health work" (*Choice*).

Chacko, G. K., ed. *Health Handbook: An International Reference on Care and Cure.* Elsevier 1979 $170.25. "Fifty-seven papers contributed by over 100 authors dealing with environmental management for improved health services; national organization of health services; computer augmentation of health service operations; diagnostics to decision-making; educational innovation in health services; and health indicators and health services utilization" (*Choice*).

Ehrlich, Isaac, ed. *National Health Policy: What Role for Government?* Hoover Inst. Pr. 1982 $27.95. "Includes economic theorizing about government and health care; descriptions of national health insurance proposals and health insurance in Germany and Australia; an analysis of access to medical care in the U.S.; a statement of a business perspective on health costs; an agenda for increasing the role of competition in health services; and an after-dinner speech" (*Choice*).

Fox, Daniel M. *Health Policies, Health Politics: The British and American Experience, 1911–1965.* Princeton Univ. Pr. 1986 text ed. $25.00. "Although specialists may want more evidence than the author provides, the book is valuable as the first comparative study of 20th-century health policy" (*Choice*).

Goodman, John C. *National Health Care in Great Britain: Lessons for the U.S.A.* Fisher Inst. 1980 lib. bdg. $11.95 pap. $6.95. "A conservative polemic on all that ails the British National Health Service. The book provides a brief historical background of developments leading to the creation of the NHS in 1946, and then takes a sector-by-sector view of the Service, its administration, financing, and delivery of care. Although it is subtitled 'Lessons for the U.S.A.,' the volume spends just 4½ pages on this important topic" (*Choice*).

Heidenheimer, Arnold J., and Nile Elvander, eds. *The Shaping of the Swedish Health System.* St. Martin's 1980 $27.50. "Covers the historical roots of the Swedish health care system. Uses cross-national comparisons to bring a sense of perspective and to explain the organization of the Swedish system" (*Choice*).

Lanza, Robert, ed. *Medical Science and the Advancement of World Health.* Praeger 1985 $42.95. "Argues that physicians and health professionals have the tools and obligation to arouse world powers from their apathy and to organize a concerted international effort in the areas of individual and public health. A well-balanced, intelligent, unbiased overview of the problem" (*Choice*).

Maxwell, Robert. *Health and Wealth: An International Study of Health-Care Spending.* Fwd. by Brian Abel Smith, Lexington Bks. 1981 o.p. "Studies the health-spending habits of ten developed countries: Australia, Canada, France, West Germany, Italy, Netherlands, Sweden, Switzerland, Britain, and the U.S." (*Choice*).

Mirzahi, Andree, and others. *Medical Care, Morbidity and Costs: Graphic Presentation of Health Statistics.* Pergamon 1983 $35.00. "Provides graphic and pictorial representation of a wide range of health-related statistics: 81 annotated charts cover historical trends and current data for France in the areas of mortality and morbidity, medical expenditures, health service utilization, and supply of health care providers. A limited number of French/U.S. charts give the volume an international flavor" (*Choice*).

Raffel, Marshall, ed. *Comparative Health Systems: Descriptive Analyses of Fourteen National Health Systems.* Pennsylvania State Univ. Pr. 1984 $29.95. "Reviewed in considerable detail are the systems of Australia, Belgium, Canada, China, Denmark, England, France, Germany, Japan, Netherlands, New Zealand, Sweden, USSR, and U.S." (*Choice*).

Sidel, Ruth, and Victor W. Sidel. *The Health of China.* Beacon 1983 pap. $11.95. "A comprehensive and detailed summary of changes in health care in the People's Republic of China from 1971 to 1979, with primary emphasis on the last few years" (*Choice*).

Stone, Deborah A. *The Limits of Professional Power: National Health Care in the Federal Republic of Germany.* Univ. of Chicago Pr. 1981 lib. bdg. $21.00. "Focuses on the power of physicians' organizations, governmental and consumer groups, and the limits of each. Deals with some policy questions and answers" (*Choice*).

Consumerism and Health Promotion

This brief list of books examines the increasing role of consumers in the medical marketplace, and the organization and implementation of patient and consumer health education programs.

Corry, James M. *Consumer Health: Facts, Skills, and Decisions.* Wadsworth 1983 o.p. "Beginning with major concerns of the medical marketplace and those psychosocial factors relating to consumerism, the author considers all phases of consumer health practices, including individual and societal responsibilities" (*Choice*).

Haug, Marie, and Bebe Lavin. *Consumerism in Medicine: Challenging Physician Authority.* Sage 1983 $27.50. "Two medical sociologists discuss how patients have grown more skeptical about the ability of the physician to 'cure' and use sampling techniques to determine attitudes of both physician and patient" (*Choice*).

Huttman, Barbara. *The Patient's Advocate.* Viking 1981 o.p. "Hints on how to cope with hospitalization as well as insight into what to expect and demand as a patient" (*LJ*).

Mailick, Mildred, and Helen Rehr, eds. *In the Patient's Interest: Access to Hospital Care.* Watson Pub. Intl. 1982 text ed. $17.50. "An excellent book dealing with the needs of the consumer of hospital-based services. Organized in four parts: access to hospital-based services; community-based programs; patient adversary; and conclusions and recommendations needed to deal with obstacles to services needed by consumers" (*Choice*).

Squyres, Wendy. *Patient Education and Health Promotion in Medical Care.* Mayfield 1985 text ed. $29.95. "A resource in matters of program implementation, beginning with establishing a department in a medical setting. Includes needs assessment, educational methods and evaluation, and recognizing that information alone seldom changes behavior" (*Choice*).

Sutherland, Ian, ed. *Health Education: Perspectives and Choices.* Allen & Unwin 1980 o.p. "An excellent and wide-ranging consideration of health education, its values, uses, and practical applications in many settings and situations. . . . Though written in terms of problems, services, and agencies in the United Kingdom, the basic tenets would be quite applicable to their counterparts here in the U.S." (*Choice*).

Economics

How and by whom the health care system is to be financed is a constant and continuing debate. Books in this section examine economic, philosophical, and organizational considerations, and the roles played by the medical profession, the hospital industry, and government and private insurance.

Altman, Stuart H., and others, eds. *Ambulatory Care: Problems of Cost and Access.* Lexington Bks. 1983 $26.50. "An analytical look at ambulatory care, its successes and shortcomings. Contains analyses and reports on the problems of access and cost. Areas addressed include access to care, payer's perspective, organizational considerations, choice of ambulatory-care settings, and research findings" (*Choice*).

Brown, Jack H. U. *The High Cost of Healing: Physicians and the Health Care System.* Human Sciences Pr. 1985 $29.95. "Provides an overview of the costs of the health care system and then examines the factors that influence the costs of medical care with particular attention to the role of the physician in private practice, in the hospital, in the technological scene, and in medical education. Ancillary factors that affect the practice and cost of medicine (e.g., ethics and insurance) are also examined" (*Choice*).

Califano, Joseph A., Jr. *America's Health Care Revolution: Who Lives? Who Dies? Who Pays?* Random 1986 $17.95. "Filled with up-to-date statistics on the costs of the health care system and information on efforts to control those costs. Individual chapters detail the current status of what Califano describes as an incredibly inefficient and wasteful system and explore the medical profession, the hospital industry, medical supplies industries, long-term care, government, and other third-party payment systems" (*Choice*).

Christianson, Jon B., and Kenneth R. Smith. *Current Strategies for Containing Health Care Expenditure: A Summary of Their Potential, Performance and Prevalence.* SP Medical 1985 text ed. $24.95. "One of the most comprehensive overviews of health cost-containment issues available in print" (*Choice*).

Feldstein, Martin S. *Hospital Costs and Health Insurance.* Harvard Univ. Pr. 1981 text ed. $25.00. "A compilation of 12 papers dealing with the behavior of hospitals and hospital costs, the role of private insurance, and national health insurance" (*Choice*).

Fuchs, Victor R. *Economic Aspects of Health.* Univ. of Chicago Pr. 1982 lib. bdg. $35.00. Papers presented at the Second NBER conference on Health Economics held in Stanford, California, on July 30 and 31, 1980. "[Covers] determinants of health, consequences of ill health, and health and public policy" (*Choice*).

———. *The Health Economy*. Harvard Univ. Pr. 1986 $25.00. "Compilation of previously published articles and essays on a wide range of health-related topics such as national health insurance, health promotion, cigarette smoking, time preferences, market competition, physician control, and other economic aspects of health and medical care" (*Choice*).

Ginzberg, Eli, ed. *From Health Dollars to Health Services: New York City, 1965–1985*. Rowman 1986 text ed. $29.50. "Codifies, organizes and elucidates data into an eminently readable and comprehensible account. The principal actor in the tale is Medicare, with strong support from Medicaid, private insurance, and the ever increasing and expensive medical technology" (*Choice*).

Gray, Bradford H., ed. *The New Health Care for Profit: Doctors and Hospitals in a Competitive Environment*. Natl. Acad. Pr. 1983 $17.50. "Part of a two-year Institute of Medicine study, provides general background for an examination of the ethical, legal and financial questions raised by the growth of the for-profit health care sector" (*Choice*).

Sloan, Frank A., and James M. Perrin, eds. *Uncompensated Health Care: Rights and Responsibilities*. [*Contemporary Medicine and Public Health Ser.*] Johns Hopkins Univ. Pr. 1986 text ed. $25.00. "Raises questions about individual rights to health care and how to finance services provided to those who cannot afford to pay for them. Recommends that a way must be found to relieve the health care providers of the financial burden of the nation's uninsured indigents" (*Choice*).

Sorkin, Alan. *Health Care and the Changing Economic Environment*. Lexington Bks. 1985 $25.00. "Evaluates the impact of the changing economic environment upon our health care system, including the effects of federal expenditures, inflation, alterations in manpower, malpractice costs, and the growth of for-profit organization. Discusses in detail the increased competition from the increased numbers of physicians, nurses, and physician extenders. The problems and future directions of the Medicare and Medicaid programs are given careful consideration" (*Choice*).

Yaggy, Duncan, and William G. Anlyan, eds. *Financing Health Care: Competition vs. Regulation*. Ballinger 1982 $35.00. The papers and proceedings of the Sixth Private Sector Conference, March 23 and 24, 1981. "Debates the relative merits of regulation and competition in allocating health care services" (*Choice*).

Legislation/Governmental Role

This section includes descriptions of the responses of state and federal government to the challenge of providing and funding health care.

Bovbjerg, Randall R., and John Holahan. *Medicaid in the Reagan Era: Federal Policy and State Choices*. Urban Inst. Pr. 1982 pap. $7.95. "Two events occurred in 1981 that shook Medicaid to its foundations: the onset of the deepest recession since the Great Depression and passage of the Omnibus Budget Reconciliation Act. Chronicles these events in concise, nontechnical prose and then goes on to analyze how the states have coped in a time of rising demands and declining resources" (*Choice*).

Health Policy: The Legislative Agenda. Congr. Quarterly 1980 o.p. "A concise historical description of the problems, the issues, the executive and legislative proposals introduced to control health care costs, to provide a more effective delivery system and to promote personal and environmental health" (*Choice*).

Kronenfeld, Jennie J., and Marcia L. Whicker. *U.S. National Health Policy: An Analysis of the Federal Role.* Praeger 1984 $31.95. "Describes the American health care system, with an emphasis on increased use of technology, rising costs, and the difficulty of evaluating the benefits. Focuses on national health policy" (*Choice*).

Home Health Care and Nursing Homes

This section offers a brief look at the past, present, and future of home health care services and nursing homes.

Buckingham, Robert W. *Complete Book of Home Health Care.* Continuum 1984 $19.50 pap. $9.95. "Outlines the history and economics of home health care, criteria and marketing for home health care agencies and the kinds of services home care should provide" (*LJ*).

Ginzberg, Eli, and Miriam Ostow. *Home Health Care: Its Role in the Changing Health Services Market.* Rowman 1984 text ed. $29.50. "[This] final report of a study conducted on home health care by the Conservation of Human Resources, Columbia University, includes a review of the literature, results of patient and agency studies, and a discussion of short- and long-range futures of home health care. Its particular strength is in describing detailed patient needs and services rendered" (*Choice*).

Jones, C. Clyde. *Caring for the Aged: An Appraisal of Nursing Homes and Alternatives.* Nelson-Hall 1982 text ed. $18.95. "As the exposition of a philosophy, the book is fine: as a resource it is limited" (*LJ*).

Vladeck, Bruce C. *Unloving Care: The Nursing Home Tragedy.* Basic Bks. 1980 pap. $7.50. "Details the history of nursing home policies, touching upon such things as reimbursement systems, real estate loopholes, and regulatory legislation" (*LJ*).

Trends

This section provides an overview of the present and future structure and organization of health care delivery.

Ginzberg, Eli. *American Medicine: The Power Shift.* Rowman 1985 text ed. $32.50. "Ginzberg's historical perspective lends rationale for the current monetarized status of health care; his visionary approach affords ideas for preventing further erosion of the eleemosynary purpose in meeting the health care needs of people in all socioeconomic sectors" (*Choice*).

——, ed. *The U.S Health Care System: A Look at the 1990s.* Rowman 1985 $36.50. Cornell University Medical College Conference on Health Policy, 1985. "Five papers presented at a 1985 conference, provide a range of perspectives, and focus on policy choices for the 1990s, organizational innovations in health care, the changing role of the hospital, the impact of new technology, and health care financing in the 1990s" (*Choice*).

Leyerle, Betty. *Moving and Shaking American Medicine: The Structure of a Socioeconomic Transformation.* [*Contributions in Economics and Economic History Ser.*] Greenwood 1984 lib. bdg. $32.95. "Traces changes within the structure of the American health care system that have been both a cause and a consequence of a transformation in the occupational authority enjoyed by physicians" (*LJ*).

Mechanic, David. *From Advocacy to Allocation: The Evolving American Health Care System.* Free Pr. 1986 $24.95 pap. $12.95. "Exceptionally useful to anyone interested in the present and future state of the U.S. health care system. Divided into four major areas: issues in health policy, promotion of health and management of illness, the health profession, and the health of special populations (the elderly, the mentally ill, etc.)" (*Choice*).

Meltzer, Judith, Frank Farrow, and Harold Richman, eds. *Policy Options in Long-Term Care.* Univ. of Chicago Pr. 1982 lib. bdg. $28.00 pap. $12.50. Papers from a National Symposium on Long-Term Care Policy Options held in Williamsburg, Virginia, June 1980. "Emphasizes that although personal support systems often exist for some disabled persons, their resources for long-term care are unpredictable and largely unsupported financially" (*Choice*).

Miller, Alfred E. *Options in Health and Health Care: The Coming of Post-Industrial Medicine.* [*Health, Medicine, and Society Ser.*] Wiley 1981 o.p. "Describes some of the pertinent trends in the history of medicine and then thoroughly examines the free-market, public-service, and regulated-utility aspects of our current system" (*LJ*).

HEALTH PROFESSIONS

This section contains books about all health and allied health occupations and professional issues related to those occupations, such as licensing and education. Also included are some representative titles, written in the first person, which are autobiographical in nature.

General

Alperin, Stanley, and Melvin Alperin. *120 Careers in the Health Care Field.* Ballinger 1980 o.p. Includes valuable introductory information on potential careers in health care for high school and college students whose interests and capacities are in areas other than professional preparation in medicine, dentistry, nursing, and pharmacy. Important as a resource for concise information and further exploration.

Gross, Stanley. *Of Foxes and Hen Houses: Licensing and the Health Professions.* Greenwood 1984 lib. bdg. $35.00. An effective book on a very complex and important public issue, i.e., does self-regulation in the health care field protect the public?

McGuire, Christopher H., and others. *Handbook of Health Professions Education.* Jossey-Bass 1983 o.p. Presents a comprehensive critical review, by leading scholars, of where we have been and where we are going in health professions education in the United States. Very readable.

Mechanic, David, ed. *Handbook of Health, Health Care, and the Health Professions.* Free Pr. 1983 text ed. $49.95. An impressive compilation of essays that contains a wealth of information on determinants of health and illness in the United States and on the organization and provision of health care.

Dentistry

Calisti, Louis J. P., Jacob B. Silversin, and Henry Wechsler. *Handbook of Dental Specialties.* Arandel 1979 o.p. A useful compilation of data on dentistry and its several specialties, for example, public health dentistry, endodontics, oral surgery, and so on. Information is provided on required education and certification training in each field; includes a list of dental schools and programs.

Davis, Peter. *The Social Context of Dentistry*. Croom Helm 1980 $27.50. An excellent book that examines the major institutional features of contemporary dentistry within a broad social and historical context.

Peterson, Haller Alvarey. *Preparing to Enter Dental School*. Prentice-Hall 1979 text ed. $13.95 pap. $6.95. A complete guide for applying to dental school and being accepted. Explains selection of schools and gives information about the Dental Admissions Test (DAT); tables and appendixes.

Wiles, Cheryl B., and William J. Ryan. *Communication for Dental Auxiliaries*. Reston 1982 text ed. $18.95 pap. $14.95. A thorough presentation of communication as it applies to dentistry.

Medicine

Broadhead, Robert S. *The Private Lives and Professional Identity of Medical Students*. Transaction Bks. 1983 $24.95. An interesting study, by a sociologist, of the effects of medical school on the private lives and functioning of medical students.

Colombotos, John, and Corinne Kirchner. *Physicians and Social Change*. Oxford 1986 $35.00. A readable examination of how physician attitudes vary according to social background, professional profile, and medical specialty.

Ginzberg, Eli, ed. *From Physician Shortage to Patient Shortage: The Uncertain Future of Medical Practice*. Westview Pr. 1986 $25.00. A timely and informative contribution to the literature on the rapidly changing problems facing medical practice, this volume is based on a conference on health policy.

Hoffman, Stephen A. *Under the Ether Dome: A Physician's Apprenticeship at Massachusetts General Hospital*. Scribner 1986 $18.95. The sensitive, literate, and compelling story of a medical internship at one of America's greatest teaching hospitals.

Illich, Ivan. *Medical Nemesis: The Expropriation of Health*. Pantheon 1982 pap. $8.95. A classic and very controversial call for reform in the delivery of health care.

Israel, Lucien. *Decision-Making: The Modern Doctor's Dilemma—Reflections on the Art of Medicine*. Random 1982 o.p. A brief but important commentary on the use of decision-making techniques for the optimization of medical performance.

Johnson, David G. *Physicians in the Making*. Jossey-Bass 1983 text ed. $29.95. A report on the personal, social, economic, and educational characteristics of contemporary medical students that suggests guidelines for reforms in the admission and training of America's future physicians.

Kelman, Steven. *Improving Doctor Performance: A Study in the Use of Information and Organizational Change*. Human Sciences Pr. 1980 $34.95. An analysis of how various administrative and data systems can improve physician performance in hospital practice.

Konner, Melvin. *Becoming a Doctor: A Journey of Initiation in Medical School*. Viking 1987 $19.95. A critical and self-critical account of the clinical experiences of medical school and how those experiences mold the practitioner.

Kra, Siegfried J. *Examine Your Doctor: A Patient's Guide to Avoiding Medical Mishaps*. Ticknor & Fields 1982 o.p. Well written in nontechnical language, this book discusses appropriate pre- and postsurgical care and covers major medical problems.

LeBaron, Charles. *Gentle Vengeance: An Account of the First Year at Harvard Medical School*. Penguin 1982 $4.95. Well written and engrossing, this book has become a classic of its kind. A somewhat condemning but realistic description of what happens in medical education.

Ludmerer, Kenneth M. *Learning to Heal: The Development of American Medical Edu-*

cation. Basic Bks. 1985 $21.95. An engrossing narrative history of the rise of the modern medical college and teaching hospital.

Morgan, Elizabeth. *The Making of a Woman Surgeon.* Berkeley Pub. 1981 $3.95. A gripping first person account of one woman's medical school (Yale University) experience and residency in surgery.

Rosen, George. *The Structure of American Medical Practice, 1875–1941.* Univ. of Pennsylvania Pr. 1983 o.p. Examines the changes in doctors' attitudes and actions and discusses the reasons for the transfer of the doctor's activity from the patient's home to the office or the hospital.

Sarason, Seymour B. *Caring and Compassion in Clinical Practice.* Jossey-Bass 1985 $19.95. A wise and important book by the dean of clinical psychologists, this work examines the lack of care and compassion that too often characterizes clinical professional services.

Wechsler, Henry, and Barbara Gale. *Medical School Admissions: A Strategy for Success.* Ballinger 1983 $24.95 pap. $14.95. A compendium of practical information on the logistics, mechanics, and determinants of admission to medical school.

Nursing

Aiken, Linda H., and Susan R. Gortner, eds. *Nursing in the 1980s: Crises, Opportunities, Challenges.* Lippincott 1982 text ed. $13.95. An interdisciplinary work of excellent quality, this book examines issues, dilemmas, and challenges facing the nursing profession.

Archer, Sarah E., and Patricia A. Goebner. *Nurses: A Political Force.* Wadsworth 1982 $15.25. A specific, well-written overview of nursing and politics.

Armstrong, Penny. *A Midwife's Story.* Arbor House 1986 $15.95. The autobiography of a twentieth-century midwife in Lancaster County, Pennsylvania.

Bullough, Vern L., and Bonnie Bullough. *The Care of the Sick: The Emergence of Modern Nursing.* Watson Pub. Intl. 1978 $17.50. "Nursing has included a diverse collectivity, from priests and attendants in the temples of ancient Greece to maids and servants in wealthy households" (*Amer. Scientist*).

Chaska, Norma L., ed. *The Nursing Profession: A Time to Speak.* McGraw-Hill 1983 $28.00. A current, comprehensive view of the state of the nursing profession—its research, education, practice, theory, and administration. Includes predictions about the future for the nursing profession.

Davitz, Joel R., and Lois L. Davitz. *Inferences of Patients' Pain and Psychological Distress: Studies of Nursing Behaviors.* Springer Pub. 1981 text ed. $25.00. A comprehensive, well-written, well-documented text dealing with nursing behavior related to patient pain and psychological distress.

DelBueno, Dorothy J., and Cynthia M. Freund. *Power and Politics in Nursing Administration: A Casebook.* Rynd Comm. 1986 text ed. $25.00. A creative, practical reference work for nursing administrators in organizational settings, and for students in health care settings.

DeVries, Raymond G. *Regulating Birth: Midwives, Medicine and the Law.* Temple Univ. Pr. 1985 $29.95. A sociological examination of laws regulating midwives and the impact of those laws on the practice of midwifery.

Gino, Carol. *The Nurse's Story.* Bantam 1983 pap. $3.95; Simon & Schuster 1982 $14.95. An autobiography based on 16 years' experience in several hospitals.

Gow, Kathleen M. *How Nurses' Emotions Affect Patient Care: Self-Studies by Nurses.* Springer Pub. 1982 text ed. $24.95. An analysis of the nurse-patient relationship.

Heron, Echo. *Intensive Care: The Story of a Nurse.* Atheneum 1987 $18.95. A moving and personal account of a nurse's life from training to practice to burnout.

Huttman, Barbara. *Code Blue: A Nurse's True-Life Story.* Berkley Pub. 1984 pap. $3.50; Morrow 1982 $12.50. The story of a 40-year-old corporate wife and mother who decides to become a nurse.

Janosik, Ellen H., and Lenore B. Phipps. *Life Cycle Group Work in Nursing.* Wadsworth 1982 $15.75. An important contribution to the field of nursing and one of the few works written by and for nurses on the subject of group process and treatment.

Kalisch, Beatrice J., and Philip A. Kalisch. *Politics of Nursing.* Lippincott 1982 $14.50. An excellent handbook for the nursing profession, the major point of which is to advocate that nurses be politically active.

Litoff, Judy B. *The American Midwife Debate: A Sourcebook on Its Modern Origins.* Greenwood 1986 lib. bdg. $35.00. In a historical context, Litoff identifies the origins of the ongoing debate about the value of midwife management as opposed to medical management of normal labor and delivery.

Melosh, Barbara. *The Physician's Hand: Work Culture and Conflict in American Nursing.* Temple Univ. Pr. 1982 text ed. $29.95 1983 pap. $9.95. Analysis of one of nursing's most persistent controversies. The schism between professionalization and apprenticeship culture that began with the founding of American schools of nursing in the late nineteenth century.

Petrowski, Dorothy D. *Handbook of Community Health Nursing: Essentials for Clinical Practice.* Springer Pub. 1984 $24.00. A well-written comprehensive, easy-to-read basic text for community health nursing students and others interested in the profession.

Yedidia, Michael J. *Delivering Primary Health Care: Nurse Practitioners at Work.* Auburn Hse. 1981 $23.00. A brief historical summary of the evolution of primary health care precedes an in-depth differentiation between the "cure" concept of medicine and the "care" concept of nursing. Though recommended for nurses, this work will have interest and relevance for other allied health professions.

Other Health Professions

Cromwell, Florence S. *The Changing Roles of Occupational Therapists in the 1980s.* Haworth Pr. 1984 text ed. $19.95. Deals with the emerging roles that are being undertaken in this decade by a significant health care profession. Important reading not only for occupational therapists, but also for health care administrators, vocational sociologists, and others working in collaboration with occupational therapists.

Cummings, Stephen, and Dana Ullman. *Everybody's Guide to Homeopathic Medicines.* Houghton Mifflin 1984 $9.95. An introduction to the rudiments of homeopathic practice in which the authors are careful to point out symptoms that contraindicate the home remedy approach. Includes a list of the most important medicines and their corresponding physiological and psychological symptoms.

Gevitz, Norman. *The D.O.'s: Osteopathic Medicine in America.* Johns Hopkins Univ. Pr. 1982 $18.50. An exploration of the field of osteopathy from its founding in the late nineteenth century to modern osteopathy. Includes principles of current practice and a good summary of the relationship between the American Medical Association and the American Osteopathic Association.

Kaufman, Martin. *Homeopathy in America: The Rise and Fall of a Medical Heresy.* Johns Hopkins Univ. Pr. 1971 o.p. The best history of homeopathy and the bitterness with which the nineteenth-century medical establishment attempted to stop the homeopathy movement.

Langone, John. *Chiropractors: A Consumers' Guide.* Addison-Wesley 1982 o.p. An objective, well-organized guide to chiropractic, this book covers the history, principles, educational requirements, most common treatments, fees, and so forth of the specialty. Also included is an appendix of state laws, schools, and associations.

Serrett, Karen D. *Philosophical and Historical Roots of Occupational Therapy*. Haworth Pr. 1985 $22.95 pap $17.95. A compact volume tracing the development of occupational therapy, especially in mental health. Useful both for historical purposes and for a perspective on current practice.

Sexton, Patricia Cayo. *The New Nightingales: Hospital Workers, Unions, New Women's Issues*. Enquiry Pr. 1982 $12.95 pap. $7.95. Examines the nature of nonprofessional work in a hospital from a feminist perspective. Written in a journalistic style and easily read, this work is recommended for general readers.

Weston, Alan J. *Survey of Allied Health Professions*. College-Hill 1980 $12.50. Discusses the various allied health professions with regard to employment trends and professional publications. Well written and informative.

Zarbock, Sarah F., and Kenneth Harbert. *Physician Assistants: Present and Future Models of Utilization*. Praeger 1986 $35.00. A useful summary of the education, role, and utilization of physician assistants in modern medical practice.

THE HEALTHY BODY

Books that provide basic, authoritative, and reliable information about the body, its organs, and systems, are plentiful. The following list includes representative titles in most areas. Chapter 15, Illness and Disease, provides titles dealing with specific diseases and groups of diseases.

Allport, Susan. *Explorers of the Black Box: The Search for the Cellular Basis of Memory*. Norton 1986 $17.95. A very interesting account of the inroads made by neurobiologists to explain the mechanisms of memory.

Amsterdam, Ezra A., and Ann M. Holmes. *Take Care of Your Heart*. Facts on File 1984 $14.95. Discusses the major risk factors for coronary heart disease and includes guidelines for changing one's life-style accordingly. Sections on anatomy, physiology, diagnostic tests, and treatments.

Barnard, Christiaan, and John Illman, eds. *The Body Machine: Your Health in Perspective*. Crown 1981 o.p. An important, wide-ranging, thought-provoking report on body systems and how they function together as a machine.

Berkley, George. *On Being Black and Healthy: How Black Americans Can Lead Longer and Healthier Lives*. Prentice-Hall 1982 $11.95 pap. $5.95. A sensible, readable, and recommended book that dispenses good advice for healthy living, regardless of skin color. Berkley describes symptoms of diseases that affect black Americans more than whites and discusses treatment through diet rather than drugs.

Blakeslee, Thomas R. *The Right Brain: A New Understanding of Our Unconscious Mind and Its Creative Power*. Doubleday 1980 pap. $14.95. Blakeslee offers some unusual theories on brain function laterality and sex differences. He advances in a cogent style the position that left brain functions may no longer play the critical, dominant role they have historically assumed.

Bloom, Floyd E., and others. *Brain, Mind, and Behavior*. W. H. Freeman 1985 text ed. $23.95. Broad in scope, this important book presents information about brain organization and its role in body function, emotions, learning, and so on. Aimed at interested readers with little or no scientific background.

Brody, Jane E. *Jane Brody's The New York Times Guide to Personal Health*. Times Bks. 1982 $19.95. Based on Brody's popular columns, this is a very useful compilation of information on some of the most popular topics in health and medicine. Includes recommended readings and organizations for further information.

Brown, Arthur M., and Donald W. Stubbs. *Medical Physiology*. Wiley 1983 $35.95. Valuable for academic or public libraries as a handy reference because this well-organized survey of the field can be used independently as a self-guide to modern medical physiology.

Bursztajn, Harold. *Medical Choices, Medical Chances: How Patients, Families, and Physicians Can Cope with Uncertainty*. Delacorte 1981 $14.95; Dell 1983 pap. $10.95. Well written and of interest to professionals and the general public, this book presents in clear-cut terms the uncertainty of life with particular reference to disease states, medical care, and choices for patients.

Changeux, Jean-Pierre. *Neuronal Man: The Biology of Mind*. Pantheon 1985 $19.95. A fascinating award-winning book by a molecular neurobiologist who aims at a basic understanding of the human nervous system from a multidisciplinary stance encompassing anatomy, physiology, biology, and chemistry.

Coleman, Richard M. *Wide Awake at 3:00 A.M.: By Choice or By Chance*. W. H. Freeman 1986 $21.95. A comprehensible book on circadian rhythms and their relationship to normal body function.

Conwell, Russell. *Acres of Diamonds*. Revell 1975 $2.50. A substantial book that describes the fundamentals of dental care for the whole family.

Creager, Joan G. *Human Anatomy and Physiology*. Wadsworth 1983 $29.95. Valuable as a quick reference for accurate information on the structure and function of the human body.

Davis, Goode P., and Edwards Park. *The Heart: The Living Pump*. U.S. News 1981 $18.75. Excellent blend of historical and current information in a series of well-illustrated essays.

Denholz, Melvin, and Elaine Denholz. *How to Save Your Teeth and Your Money: A Consumer's Guide to Better, Less Costly, Dental Care*. Van Nostrand 1980 $6.95. A nontechnical and practical book describing techniques and procedures one can employ to minimize the expense of dental care.

Desowitz, Robert S. *The Thorn in the Starfish: The Immune System and How It Works*. Norton 1987 $16.95. Written by a parasitologist and a World Health Organization researcher, this superb book unravels the mysteries of the body's immune system in an authoritative and very readable fashion.

Diagram Group. *The Brain: A User's Manual*. Berkley Pub. 1983 pap. $4.95. Concise but thorough introduction to the anatomy and functions of the various regions of the human brain.

Donovan, Bernard T. *Hormones and Human Behaviour*. Cambridge Univ. Pr. 1985 $39.50. A clear, readable but not overly simplified introduction to the complex interactions among the fields of neuroendocrinology, physical psychology, and psychiatry.

Dvorine, William. *A Dermatologist's Guide to Home Skin Care*. Scribner 1984 $12.95 pap. $6.95. An easy-to-read guide to the prevention and treatment of simple skin disorders. Contains information about skin physiology, as well as advice about creams, aging skin, common diseases, when to see a doctor, and so forth.

Ehrlich, David, with George Wolf. *The Bowel Book*. Schocken 1981 $6.95. Using authoritative information from medical experts, the authors present in an interesting way the medical physiology and psychology of the gastrointestinal system.

Fasciana, Guy S. *Are Your Dental Fillings Poisoning You?* Keats 1986 $12.95. The hazards of the mercury controversy written by a dentist who was forced out of practice by the toxic effects of dental mercury. Occasional lapses into polemics, but overall well done.

Fields, Willa L., and Karen M. McGinn-Campbell. *Introduction to Health Assessment.* Reston 1982 text ed. $28.95. Valuable for both beginning and advanced students, this work, arranged by systems and body regions, provides basic information on standard assessment procedures (inspection, palpation, and percussion).

Fincher, Jack. *The Brain: Mystery of Matter and Mind.* U.S. News 1981 $18.75. An excellent, well-illustrated basic guide to the anatomy and physiology of the brain.

Freymann, Robert, with Leslie Holzer. *What's So Bad about Feeling Good?* Jove 1983 pap. $2.95. Freymann uses doctor-patient dialogues to illustrate common health problems and the way they can be treated. He advocates the position that the doctor-patient relationship can be used to motivate patients to change bad health habits.

Galton, Lawrence. *1,001 Health Tips.* Simon & Schuster 1984 $17.95 pap. $7.95. A useful collection of remedies, hints, and guidelines on a variety of medical subjects, presented in nontechnical language.

Gatchel, Robert J., and Andrew Baum. *An Introduction to Health Psychology.* Random 1983 text ed. pap. $17.95. A good overview of the psychological aspects of health and the interrelationship between mind and body.

Goldberg, Kathy E. *The Skeleton: Fantastic Framework.* U.S. News 1982 $18.75. A comprehensive, easily understood introduction to historical and current advances in science involving the skeleton, bone growth, and healing.

Goldman, A. Richard, with Virginia McCullough. *TMJ Syndrome: The Overlooked Diagnosis.* Congdon & Weed 1987 $15.95. Presented in a clear, nontechnical style, this first book written for the layperson does an excellent job of covering the manifestations and clinical problems associated with this common disorder—temporomandibular joint pain dysfunction syndrome. The author is the Director of the Institute for the Treatment and Study of Headaches in Chicago.

Goldstein, Marc, and Michael Feldberg. *The Vasectomy Book: A Complete Guide to Decision Making.* Houghton Mifflin 1982 o.p. A highly recommended and long overdue book that provides useful and objective information on the benefits and risks of vasectomies.

Hamburg, David A., Glen R. Elliott, and Delores L. Parron. *Health and Behavior: Frontiers of Research in the Biobehavioral Sciences.* Natl. Acad. Pr. 1982 pap. $17.50. A one-of-a-kind book giving broad coverage of present knowledge of how human behavior influences health. Because the language is not highly technical, the book is appropriate for readers at many levels.

Harth, Erich. *Windows on the Mind: Reflections on the Physical Basis of Consciousness.* Morrow 1982 $15.50 1983 pap. $9.95. A synthesis of facts, theories, and paradoxes from several disciplines, this book provides a valuable overview, understandable to nonspecialists, of the nature of human consciousness.

Hausman, Patricia. *The Calcium Bible: How to Have Better Bones All Your Life.* Rawson 1985 $13.95. Not a study of osteoporosis, but rather a convincing and readable discussion of the role calcium plays in general health.

Haymes, Emily M., and Christine L. Wells. *Environment and Human Performance.* Human Kinetics 1986 $22.00. An excellent resource offering practical and theoretical information on how the environment affects the cardiovascular, respiratory, renal, muscular, and neural systems.

Jensen, Karen. *Reproduction: The Cycle of Life.* U.S. News 1982 $18.75. An extremely informative, well-illustrated, historical, and current perspective on human reproduction.

Johnson, G. Timothy, and Stephen E. Goldfinger. *The Harvard Medical School Health Letter Book.* Harvard Univ. Pr. 1981 $18.50. An excellent resource for the layperson on a wide array of important health topics.

Kals, W. S. *Your Health, Your Moods, and the Weather.* Doubleday 1982 o.p. Written from the viewpoint that one-third of the population is weather sensitive, this book successfully describes the common components of the weather (temperature, wind, and so on) that can affect human comfort and shows practical ways to avoid or ameliorate unfavorable conditions.

Lillyquist, Michael J. *Sunlight and Health: The Positive and Negative Effects of the Sun on You.* Dodd 1985 $15.95 1987 pap. $7.95. A handy compilation of scientific information concerning the sun, skin types, and the physiology of the skin.

Louria, Donald B. *Stay Well.* Scribner 1982 $14.95. Proposing that a sensible program of preventive health care can save lives, reduce medical expenses, and prevent illness, Louria sets forth a series of simple but effective strategies for minimizing risk factors and detecting early symptoms of major disease. Straightforward, practical, and well-researched.

Lynch, James J. *The Language of the Heart: The Body's Response to Human Dialogue.* Basic Bks. 1985 $19.95. An excellent example of serious science made interesting, this book talks about the heart and how its health is affected by emotions and social interactions. Scholarly but readable.

Marshall, Daniel P., and others. *Staying Healthy Without Medicine: A Manual of Home Prevention and Treatment.* Nelson-Hall 1983 lib. bdg. $28.95. A manual of preventive medicine, this book is divided into two sections: general principles of healthy living and common health problems.

Masiak, Mary J., and Mary D. Naylor. *Fluids and Electrolytes Through the Life Cycle.* Appleton 1985 $18.00. Well-researched, well-organized, and lucidly written, this book, designed for nurses, provides for any reader with some science background fundamental information on fluid, electrolyte, and acid-balance homeostatis in health and disease.

Medical Tribune Editors. *Questions Patients Most Often Ask Their Doctors.* Bantam 1983 o.p. An especially well-written question-and-answer book combining the skills of medical writers with the expertise of medical specialists. Emphasis is on preventive maintenance and major health problems of body systems.

Ottoson, David. *Physiology of the Nervous System.* Oxford 1983 $45.00 pap. $28.95. A highly recommended, readable, and understandable sourcebook on the very complex subject of the functional organization of the nervous system.

Page, Jake. *Blood: The River of Life.* U.S. News 1981 $18.75. A first-class, well-illustrated, blend of introductory historical and current information on blood.

Perkins, D. N. *The Mind's Best Work.* Harvard Univ. Pr. 1981 $20.00. A highly readable account of how the mind works.

Proctor, Donald F. *Breathing, Speech, and Song.* Springer-Verlag 1980 $22.00. A generally readable discussion of the normal and abnormal situations associated with developing sounds in humans.

Restak, Richard M. *The Brain.* Bantam 1985 $27.95. An outgrowth and expanded version of the popular eight-part public television series on the brain.

Samuels, Mike, and Hal Z. Bennett. *Well Body, Well Earth: The Sierra Club Environmental Health Sourcebook.* Sierra 1983 $22.50 pap. $12.95. Interesting and clearly written, this book is based on the premise that the earth is a living entity and that its functions are closely interconnected to human health. Well-illustrated with appendixes of toxic substances, political action groups, and recommended readings.

Sorochan, Walter D. *Promoting Your Health.* Wiley 1981 pap. $25.95. A stimulating presentation on health promotion, awareness of life-style behaviors, and self-assessment of health.

Sydney, Sheldon B. *Ignore Your Teeth and They'll Go Away: The Patient's Complete Guide to the Prevention and Treatment of Periodontal (Gum) Disease.* Devida 1982 $6.95. A very clear and well-illustrated description of warning signs, clinical examinations, and treatment methods for most common gum diseases. Written by a practicing periodontist.

Vickery, Donald M. *Take Care of Yourself: The Consumer's Guide to Medical Care.* Addison-Wesley 3d ed. 1986 $14.95. A popular and well-written compendium.

Wertenbaker, Lael T. *The Eye: The Window of the World.* U.S. News 1981 $18.75. An informative, well-illustrated, and easily understandable introduction to the human eye and its functions.

Wood, Norman. *The Complete Book of Dental Care.* Hart 1979 $6.95. A highly recommended informative guide to dentistry from the consumer's point of view. Of special value is information on how to choose and evaluate a dentist and when to seek a dental specialist.

HEMATOLOGY

[SEE the section on The Healthy Body in this chapter;
for blood (hematologic) diseases see Chapter 15 in this volume.]

HISTOLOGY

[SEE the section on The Healthy Body in this chapter.]

HISTORY OF THE HEALTH SCIENCES

[SEE the section on Biography and History of Medicine in this chapter.]

MEDICINE AND THE LAW

The application of medical knowledge to questions of law and vice versa has received greater attention during the past decade. Consequently, the number of books that has been published in the area continues to rise. The following titles include collections of pathological case studies as well as introductions to malpractice law.

Annas, George J., Leonard H. Glantz, and Barbara F. Katz. *The Rights of Doctors, Nurses and Allied Health Professionals: A Health Law Primer.* Ballinger 1983 $12.95. An American Civil Liberties Union (ACLU) handbook, this work offers a wealth of detail on medico-legal issues not found in such a convenient form elsewhere. Included is a useful glossary of legal terms.

Browne, Douglas, and Thomm Tullett. *Bernard Spilsbury: Famous Murder Cases of the Great Pathologist.* Academy Chicago 2d ed. 1983 $5.95. A fascinating collection of actual murder cases and the role of medicine, specifically pathology, in their solution.

Champagne, Anthony, and Rosemary N. Dawes. *Courts and Modern Medicine.* C. C.

Thomas 1983 $29.95. Somewhat scholarly but an interesting analysis of the interplay between the American legal and health care systems.

Christoffel, Tom. *Health and the Law: A Handbook for Health Professionals.* Free Pr. 1982 text ed. $29.95. An excellent resource and guide for persons interested in the law and health care in general, this book provides an overview, historical perspective, and issues analysis on a wide range of topics.

Corea, Gena. *The Hidden Malpractice: How American Medicine Mistreats Women.* Harper 1985 updated ed. $7.95. Called the definitive book on malpractice against women and racial minorities, this work provides a historical overview in accessible terms of sex discrimination and its results in medical care.

Eisenberg, John F. *Medical Malpractice Litigation.* Mason 1982 $32.50. A compendium that includes the applicable laws and the resolution of landmark cases in medical malpractice.

King, Joseph H. *The Law of Medical Malpractice in a Nutshell.* West 2d ed. 1986 $9.95. A succinct exposition of U.S. laws relating to liability-producing conduct arising from the delivery of professional medical services. A handy guide with sections on standards of care, proof of negligence, mental distress, and so on.

Smyth, Frank. *Cause of Death: The Story of Forensic Medicine.* Van Nostrand 1980 $12.95. A readable history of the topic with useful summaries of different categories of the causes of death.

NEUROLOGY

[SEE the section on The Healthy Body in this chapter; for the diagnosis and treatment of nervous system diseases see Chapter 15 in this volume.]

NURSING

[SEE the section on Health Professions, Nursing in this chapter.]

NUTRITION AND DIET

This section contains books on the science of food, the nutrients, and other substances contained therein, their assimilation, utilization, action, interaction, and balance in relation to health and disease. This aspect of health care has a very active publishing history with several new diet titles being published weekly. This list therefore is extremely selective, with subsections on Childhood Nutrition and Nutrition and Aging.

Aubert, Claude, and Pierre Frapa. *Hunger and Health.* Rodale Pr. 1985 $14.95. A successful discussion of the problems caused by modern techniques of food production and processing and by the Western diet emulated by other parts of the world.

Bennett, William, and Joel Gurin. *The Dieter's Dilemma: Eating Less and Weighing More.* Basic Bks. 1982 $14.95 1983 pap. $7.95. A valuable compendium of diet information and guidelines that challenges both the professional and lay communities to reevaluate basic assumptions about the biological basis of obesity.

Berger, Stuart M. *Dr. Berger's Immune Power Diet.* NAL 1985 $14.95. A convincing multipart program to strengthen the body's immune system so that it does its work properly.

Brisson, Germain J. *Lipids in Human Nutrition: An Appraisal of Some Dietary Concepts*. Burgess 1981 text ed. $22.50. Concise and well written, this work addresses the role of fats in the diet and the advisability of dietary intervention to lower the blood cholesterol level in the mass population.

Brody, Jane E. *Jane Brody's Good Food Book: Living the High Carbohydrate Way*. Norton 1985 $19.95. A useful and practical guide to carbohydrates and healthy eating.

Calabrese, Edward J., and Michael W. Dorsey. *Healthy Living in an Unhealthy World: Food for Survival in a Polluted World*. Simon & Schuster 1984 $15.95 1985 pap. $7.95. A balanced selection of information from the scientific literature concerning the health hazards present in the environment due to substances introduced by modern technology.

Carroll, David. *The Complete Book of Natural Foods*. Summit Bks. 1985 $8.95. Sensible, very readable text focusing on getting away from unhealthy foods.

Cataldo, Corinne B. *Nutrition and Diet Therapy: Principles and Practice*. West 1986 $26.95. A textbook on the role of diet therapy in proper nutritional practice.

Cheraskin, Emanuel, and others. *The Vitamin C Connection*. Harper 1983 $12.95. A well-documented book that updates earlier works on the therapeutic role of vitamin C and reviews the research literature in popular language.

Colgan, Michael. *Your Personal Vitamin Profile*. Morrow 1982 $14.95 pap. $8.95. Written in a clear and interesting style, this controversial book suggests that nutrients in much higher amounts than Recommended Daily Allowances (RDAs) are necessary to prevent disease and to maintain optimum health.

DeBakey, Michael E., and others. *The Living Heart Diet*. Raven 1984 text ed. $29.95; Simon & Schuster 1986 pap. $9.95. An excellent guide designed to promote a healthy heart. Information is technical but presented in an understandable fashion.

Fried, John. *Vitamin Politics*. Prometheus Bks. 1984 pap. $11.95. Essentially an update of his earlier *The Vitamin Conspiracy*, this book details the controversy between vitamin enthusiasts and medical researchers over the testing, use, and hazards of vitamin and megavitamin therapies. Well written and informative.

Gaby, Alan. *The Doctor's Guide to Vitamin B-6*. Rodale Pr. 1984 $15.95 pap. $8.95. A review in nontechnical language of the research on the efficacy of vitamin B6 in disease treatment. Exceptionally well-documented.

Garrison, Robert H., and Elizabeth Somer. *The Nutrition Desk Reference*. Keats 1985 $29.95. A clear and easy-to-understand book that presents information on the fundamentals of human nutrition and highlights topics of current interest and/or controversy.

Gibney, Michael J. *Nutrition, Diet, and Health*. Cambridge Univ. Pr. 1986 $29.95. A technical treatment but accessible to the educated reader.

Gurr, Michael I. *Role of Fats in Food and Nutrition*. Elsevier 1984 $36.00. An unbiased approach to a controversial topic, this book aimed at undergraduates discusses the nature, occurrence, and characteristics of biologically important fats and their metabolic and nutritional roles.

Haas, Robert. *Eat to Win: The Sports Nutrition Bible*. Rawson 1984 o.p. Aimed primarily at the athlete, the goal of this book is to improve performance, reduce the effects of aging, and promote faster and stronger healing of athletic injuries.

Hamilton, Eva M. N. *Nutrition: Concepts and Controversies*. West 3d ed. 1985 $30.95. The latest edition of a standard textbook that presents in a readable and balanced way a comprehensive view of the field of nutrition.

Hausman, Patricia. *Jack Sprat's Legacy: The Science and Politics of Fat and Choles-

terol. Richard Marek Pubs. 1981 $12.95. A well-written, well-documented book that discusses nutrition research and the controversies that have risen among nutritionists, medical researchers, farmers, milk producers, politicians, and the government.

Herbert, Victor, and Stephen Barrett. *Vitamins and Health Foods: The Great American Hustle.* G. F. Stickley 1981 $11.95. A cogent discussion of how the American public has been victimized by health hucksters who exploit people's insecurities.

Hunter, Beatrice T. *Food Additives and Federal Policy: The Mirage of Safety.* Scribner 1975 o.p. A presentation of the toxicological hazards of food additives, valuable to those interested in the regulatory process and the interplay of the regulatory agencies, industry, and the consumer.

————. *The Sugar Trap and How to Avoid It.* Houghton Mifflin 1982 o.p. A carefully documented book on the discovery and processing of refined (cane sugar), traditional (honey), artificial (saccharin), and rare natural (sorbitol) sweeteners.

Jacobson, Michael, and others. *Salt: The Complete Brand Name Guide to Sodium Content.* Workman 1983 pap. $5.95. Despite the title, this is also a well-researched guide to the dietary effects of sodium with substantial information on low- or reduced-sodium foods.

Jelliffe, E. F. Patrice, and Derrick B. Jelliffe, eds. *Adverse Effects of Foods.* Plenum 1982 $65.00. Of value to food scientists, nutritionists, and persons concerned with public health, this book presents an overview of the subject followed by detailed topical chapters prepared by recognized authorities.

Katahn, Martin. *Beyond Diet: The 28-Day Metabolic Breakthrough Plan.* Norton 1984 $15.95. Katahn proposes, convincingly, that dieters can break the low-calorie diet cycle by reprogramming the body's metabolic processes and making a commitment to daily physical activity.

LeRiche, W. Harding. *A Chemical Feast.* Facts on File 1982 $13.95. A nonemotional and well-documented discussion of what LeRiche considers to be the real hazards in our food supply—microbiological infection, poor nutrition, and accidental environmental contamination—as opposed to the hysterical claims regarding the danger of food additives.

Lindberg, Gladys, and Judy L. McFarland. *Take Charge of Your Health: The Complete Nutrition Book.* Harper 1982 $14.95. By the founder and owner of Lindberg's health food store chain, this book presents a comprehensive nutritional program to overcome poor health resulting from a vitamin, mineral, protein, or fiber deficient diet.

Long, Patricia J., and Barbara Shannon. *Nutrition: An Inquiry into the Issues.* Prentice-Hall 1983 text ed. pap. $26.95. Written for college students interested in but not majoring in nutrition, this book discusses the principles of nutrition and presents information on current issues and controversies.

Marshall, Charles W. *Vitamins and Minerals: Help or Harm?* Stickley 1983 $14.95. A discussion of each vitamin and mineral, its usefulness, the quantity needed, and symptoms of overdosage.

Michael, Jane W. *Breakfast, Lunch, and Dinner of Champions: Star Athletes' Diet Programs for Maximum Energy and Performance.* Morrow 1984 pap. $8.95. Accurate and informative about sports and nutrition, this book covers the dietary regimens of famous people in many athletic activities.

Mirkin, Gabe. *Getting Thin: All About Fat—How You Get It, How You Lose It, How You Keep It Off for Good.* Little, Brown 1983 $18.95 1986 pap. $8.95. A highly recommended and interesting book about the theories of why people get fat, why exercise is a key factor in maintaining ideal weight, and why certain popular diet plans are faulty or dangerous.

Morgan, Brian L. G. *The Lifelong Nutrition Guide: How to Eat for Health at Every Age and Stage of Life.* Prentice-Hall 1983 $14.95 pap. $7.95. A clearly written overview of the typical American diet with a discussion of vitamin and mineral requirements and specialized nutrition information for vegetarians, pregnant women and so forth.

Natow, Annette B., and JoAnn Heslin. *Nutrition for the Prime of Your Life.* McGraw-Hill 1983 $17.95 1984 pap. $8.95. In a question-and-answer format, this book covers basic facts about essential nutrients, caffeine, alcohol, and so on. Recent scientific research is quoted.

Novin, Donald, Wanda Wyrwicka, and George A. Bray. *Hunger: Basic Mechanisms and Clinical Implications.* Raven 1976 $57.00. Extensive coverage of the factors related to the control of food intake.

Null, Gary. *The Complete Guide to Health and Nutrition.* Delacorte 1984 $24.95. A comprehensive handbook for the general reader.

Passwater, Richard A., and Elmer M. Cranton. *Trace Elements, Hair Analysis, and Nutrition.* Keats 1983 $18.95. An authoritative book that describes each trace element, its role in nutrition, diagnostic techniques for establishing levels in the body, and specific case studies of ill health relating to undesirable levels of trace elements in the system.

Polivy, Janet, and C. Peter Herman. *Breaking the Diet Habit: The Natural Weight Alternative.* Basic Bks. 1983 $16.50. Interesting and well-documented, this book advocates the position that overweight people should not diet but should remain at their "natural" weight by eating only when hungry.

Pritikin, Nathan. *The Diet for Runners.* Simon & Schuster 1985 pap. $5.95. The health and diet theories that Pritikin presented in his earlier work have been expanded to cover the needs of runners, who need to be especially aware of cholesterol levels during exercise.

————. *The Pritikin Promise: 28 Days to a Longer, Healthier Life.* Pocket Bks. pap. $4.95; Simon & Schuster 1983 $20.95. A basic plan for a controlled regimen of diet and exercise.

Sanjur, Diva. *Social and Cultural Perspectives in Nutrition.* Prentice-Hall 1982 text ed. $27.95. Sanjur adroitly presents the multifaceted issues involved in nutrition behavior within a biocultural context.

Simonson, Maria, and Joan R. Heilman. *The Complete University Medical Diet.* Rawson 1983 $13.95; Warner Bks. 1985 pap. $3.50. A safe, sane diet and exercise regimen.

Smith, Lendon. *Feed Yourself Right.* Dell 1984 pap. $7.95; McGraw-Hill 1983 $14.95. By a respected expert on nutrition, this book describes the effects of diet and life-style on behavior, personality, and physical well-being.

Tobias, Alice L., and Patricia J. Thompson. *Issues in Nutrition for the 1980s: An Ecological Perspective.* Wadsworth 1980 o.p. An excellent reference for anyone concerned with balanced nutrition on a world scale, this book presents 55 well chosen selections by various authors.

Tracy, Lisa. *The Gradual Vegetarian.* M. Evans 1985 $17.95. In a wonderful, clearly written book, Tracy aims to help readers learn their way from eating refined, overprocessed foods to a health-inducing diet.

Wright, Jonathan V. *Dr. Wright's Guide to Healing with Nutrition.* Rodale Pr. 1984 $19.95. A persuasive argument that many common ailments are caused by digestive disorders, food allergies, or dietary deficiencies.

Yetiv, Jack Z. *Popular Nutritional Practices: A Scientific Appraisal.* Popular Medicine Pr. 1986 $17.95. An authoritative and readable text that provides a clear understanding of what is known and not known in a critical and often neglected area of human health.

Childhood Nutrition

Atwood, Stephen J. *A Doctor's Guide to Feeding Your Child: Complete Nutrition for Health Growth*. Macmillan 1982 $12.95. A guide to children's nutrition from the prenatal stage of development through adolescence.

Baggett, Nancy, and others. *Don't Tell 'Em It's Good for 'Em*. Times Bks. 1984 $15.50. Offering a reasonable, commonsense approach to a serious problem, this book fills a gap in diet-book literature in that it is suited for all members of an average American family.

Cohen, Mindy, and Louis Abramson. *Thin Kids*. Beaufort Bks. NY 1985 $17.95 pap. $9.95. A successful outline for a balanced nutritionally sound diet for children similar to those offered by some of the national weight loss programs for adults.

Cohen, Stanley A. *Healthy Babies, Happy Kids*. Putnam 1982 $14.95 pap. $8.95. A comprehensive and practical guide to nourishing babies and children, including more than the usual information on early childhood digestive disorders.

Goulart, Frances S. *Beyond Baby Fat: Weight-Loss Plans for Children and Teenagers*. McGraw-Hill 1985 $15.95. A compilation of several different diets aimed at specific weight problems, this book also offers solid information on childhood nutrition.

Hirschmann, Jane R., and Lela Zaphiropoulos. *Are You Hungry? A Completely New Approach to Raising Children Free of Weight and Food Problems*. Random 1985 $15.95. An innovative book in which the authors set forth a plan for self-demand feeding that they feel will allow children to develop a comfortable relationship to food.

Kamen, Betty, and Si Kamen. *Kids Are What They Eat: What Every Parent Needs to Know about Nutrition*. Arco 1983 $14.95. A warmly written, well-documented book that suggests a childhood diet rich in whole grains, sprouts, fresh fruits, and vegetables.

Lambert-Legace, Louise. *Feeding Your Child: From Infancy to Six Years Old*. Beaufort Bks. NY 1983 pap. $9.95. A practical guide based on the premise that if parents teach their children to eat and enjoy healthful food, the youngsters will do so into adulthood and thus avoid junk food, obesity, and illness.

Mahan, L. Kathleen, and Jane M. Rees. *Nutrition in Adolescence*. Mosby 1984 text ed. $11.95. A comprehensive book that combines not only nutritional facts but also knowledge of the physical and social needs of the adolescent.

Packard, Vernal S. *Human Milk and Infant Formula*. Academic Pr. 1982 $39.50. Emphasizes the nutrient content of human breast milk and various types of infant formulas.

Ritchey, S. J., and L. Janette Taper. *Maternal and Child Nutrition*. Harper 1983 text ed. $23.50. A sound sequencing of the relationship of nutrition to the health of the child at various developmental stages.

Silberstein, Warren P., and Lawrence Galton. *Helping Your Child Grow Slim: Dieting for Overweight Children and Adolescents*. Simon & Schuster 1982 $12.95 1983 pap. $8.95. Through a system of retraining, an overweight child can continue to grow and redistribute the excess weight until normal weight for the age is reached.

Weiner, Michael E., and Kathleen Goss. *The Art of Feeding Children Well*. Warner Bks. 1982 o.p. This work promotes the maintenance and recovery of children's health through good nutrition with practical information on balancing diets and incorporating a variety of nonprocessed foods into the diet.

Winick, Myron. *Feeding the Mother and Infant.* Wiley 1985 $49.95. An excellent reference source for practitioners and students in the health sciences, this book is a comprehensive state-of-the-art review of nutrition and child development.

Wunderlich, Ray, and Dwight Kalita. *Nourishing Your Child.* Keats 1986 $18.95. Advocating a bioecologic approach to child nutrition, Wunderlich and Kalita emphasize the use of appropriate vitamins, minerals, amino acids, and enzymes in addition to a healthful diet for children.

Nutrition and Aging

Armbrecht, H. James, John M. Prendergast, and Rodney M. Coe. *Nutritional Intervention in the Aging Process.* Springer-Verlag 1984 $42.50. A significant contribution to the field, this book compiles current knowledge of the field and proposes applications of the knowledge to the care of the elderly.

Feldman, Elaine B. *Nutrition in the Middle and Later Years.* PSG Pubns. 1983 o.p. Various aspects of nutrition as they pertain to the aging individual are covered by investigators working in this area.

Hendler, Sheldon P. *The Complete Guide to Anti-Aging Nutrients.* Simon & Schuster 1985 $16.95. A balanced and moderate, though somewhat uneven, attempt to sort out the conflicting claims for and against many vitamins and amino acids.

Kart, Gary S., and Seamus P. Metress. *Nutrition, the Aged, and Society.* Prentice-Hall 1984 pap. $16.95. A strong comprehensive book on aging and nutrition with appeal to a wide spectrum of professional and lay interests.

Kenton, Leslie. *Ageless Aging: The Natural Way to Stay Young.* Grove 1986 $17.95. Advocating a low-calorie diet, this book provides a useful summary of information on the nutritional aspects of longevity.

Watkin, Donald M. *Handbook of Nutrition, Health, and Aging.* Noyes Pr. 1983 $32.00. An excellent multidisciplinary review of geriatric nutrition.

OBSTETRICS

[SEE the section on Women's Health, Pregnancy
and Childbirth in this chapter.]

OCCUPATIONAL MEDICINE AND HEALTH

[SEE the section on Public, Environmental,
and Occupational Health in this chapter.]

OPHTHALMOLOGY

[SEE the section on The Healthy Body in this chapter; for books on the
medical and surgical treatment of its defects and diseases, and blindness
(eye disorders), see Chapter 15 in this volume.]

OTOLARYNGOLOGY

[SEE Ear and Throat Disorders in Chapter 15 in this volume.]

PEDIATRICS

[SEE the section on Childcare and Development in this chapter.]

PHARMACOLOGY AND TOXICOLOGY

Pharmacology is the study of the origin, nature, properties, and actions of drugs and their effects on living organisms. Toxicology is a science concerned with the detection and action of chemicals and poisons. Public interest has been focused on toxic chemicals in the environment and also on the development of new drugs to combat disease and to maintain health. This section contains representative titles for each discipline.

Altschul, Siri von Reis. *Drugs and Foods from Little-Known Plants: Notes in Harvard University Herbaria.* Harvard Univ. Pr. 1973 $35.00. A scholarly but readable compendium of folklore on food, drug, and aromatic plants, culled from the field notes on 2,500,000 specimens.

Apfer, Roberta J., and Susan M. Fisher. *To Do No Harm: DES and the Dilemmas of Modern Medicine.* Yale Univ. Pr. 1984 $15.95. A well-researched and probing work that examines the events attending the use of DES without either muckraking or denying their seriousness.

Beyer, Karl H. *Discovery, Development, and Delivery of New Drugs.* Spectrum Bks. 1978 o.p. A historically important work, a statement of how things were done at Merck, Sharp & Dohme, and a chronicle of the development of several new drugs.

Blum, Kenneth. *Handbook of Abusable Drugs.* Gardner Pr. 1984 $79.95. A compilation of information on the spectrum of abused substances, including their histories, biochemistry, pharmacology, toxicity, and behavioral and psychological aspects.

Burger, Alfred. *Drugs and People: Medications, Their History and Origins, and the Way They Act.* Univ. Pr. of Virginia 1986 $17.50. An explanation, in readable terms, of medications and their backgrounds. A wealth of interesting facts.

Carlton, Peter L. *A Primer of Behavioral Pharmacology: Concepts and Principles in the Behavioral Analysis of Drug Action.* Freeman 1983 text ed. $25.95 pap. $16.95. Destined to become a standard guide for students of behavioral pharmacology, this text provides a comprehensive analysis of the general principles of the science of drug-behavior interactions.

Carson, Bonnie L., Harry V. Ellis, and Joy L. McCann. *Toxicology and Biological Monitoring of Metals in Humans: Including Feasibility and Need.* Lewis Pubs. 1986 $49.95. A one-stop source in a brief, uniform format for information on the toxicity of the 52 elements and rare earths. *Webster's New Collegiate Dictionary* (1980) defines "rare earth" as "any of a group of similar oxides of metals or a mixture of such oxides occurring together in widely distributed but relatively scarce materials."

Dreyfus, Jack. *A Remarkable Medicine Has Been Overlooked.* Simon & Schuster rev. ed. 1983 pap. $4.95. Claims that DPH (diphenylhydantoin usually marketed under the trade name Dilantin), an anticonvulsant drug, is also efficacious in treating disorders of the nervous system.

Folb, Peter I. *The Safety of Medicines: Evaluation and Prediction*. Springer-Verlag 1980 $12.95. A comprehensive approach to a difficult subject, the book outlines the general principles of evaluation and prediction that are available for the developers of new medicines, the pharmaceutical industry, drug regulatory agencies, medical practitioners, and the lay public.

Friedman, Robert M. *Interferons: A Primer*. Academic Pr. 1981 $22.50. A useful addition to the literature that provides basic, easy-to-understand information about this new therapy. Appropriate for the student, scientist, or educated layperson.

Gabe, Jonathan, and Paul Williams. *Tranquillisers: Social, Psychological and Clinical Perspectives*. Methuen 1986 $39.95. An extremely valuable book that effectively deals with a topic of current concern.

Griggs, Barbara. *Green Pharmacy: A History of Herbal Medicine*. Viking 1982 o.p. A useful, well-written introduction to the history of herbal medicines from the early Greeks to modern pharmacology and current chemical derivatives from plants.

Hallenbeck, William H., and Kathleen M. Cunningham-Burns. *Pesticides and Human Health*. Springer-Verlag 1985 $24.80. A brief digest of human health effects and the toxicology of human exposure to pesticides.

Halstead, Bruce W., and Sylvia A. Youngberg. *The DMSO Handbook: A Complete Guide to the History and Use of DMSO*. Golden Quill Pr. 1981 $10.95 pap. $5.95. A clearly written introduction to the diversified pharmacological effects of the controversial agent dimethyl sulfoxide.

Jones-Witters, Patricia, and Weldon L. Witters. *Drugs and Society: A Biological Perspective*. Wadsworth 1983 text ed. $15.25. An interesting treatment of drug abuse from the biological standpoint rather than the psychological or sociological view.

Kaufman, Joel, and others. *Over-the-Counter Pills That Don't Work*. Pantheon 1983 $12.45 pap. $6.95. Identifies various over-the-counter drugs and discusses their use and alternatives to their use.

Kehrer, James P., and Daniel M. Kehrer. *Pills and Potions: New Discoveries about Prescription and Over-the-Counter Drugs*. Arco 1983 lib. bdg. $14.95 1984 pap. $9.95. Details developments in drugs and pharmaceuticals. Covers not only new drugs and new uses for old drugs, but also the technological, economic, and social changes regarding drugs.

Lappe, Marc. *Germs That Won't Die: Medical Consequences of the Misuse of Antibiotics*. Doubleday 1982 pap. $14.95. Traces the use and misuse of penicillin and other antibiotics and the development of antibiotic resistant strains of organisms.

Leber, Max. *The Corner Drugstore*. Warner 1983 pap. $6.95. A handy well-written book with first-aid information and drug interaction precautions for 17 categories of drugs.

Lewis, Walter H., and P. F. Elvin-Lewis. *Medical Botany: Plants Affecting Man's Health*. Wiley 1977 o.p. A carefully prepared review of injurious, healing, nourishing, and psychoactive plants.

Melville, Arabella. *Cured to Death: The Effects of Prescription Drugs*. Ed. by Colin Johnson, Stein & Day 1983 $16.95. A convincing argument that Western medicine has allowed itself to become too reliant on the use of drug therapy.

Meyers, Robert. *D.E.S.: The Bitter Pill*. Putnam 1983 $16.95. A less evenhanded though still important contribution to the literature on DES. Focus is on its use to control miscarriage.

Mindell, Earl. *Earl Mindell's Pill Bible.* Bantam 1984 pap. $8.95. A guide to pharmaceutical nutrition. Bridges the gap between vitamins and drugs.

Roffman, Roger A. *Marijuana as Medicine.* Madrona Pubs. 1982 $11.95 pap. $8.95. A well-written, carefully documented discussion of the use of marijuana in treatment, especially to counter side effects resulting from cancer therapies.

Silverman, Milton M., Philip R. Lee, and Mia Lydecker. *Prescriptions for Death: The Drugging of the Third World.* Univ. of California Pr. 1982 o.p. An important little book documenting how international drug manufacturers operate in Third World nations as compared to the way they are forced to operate under federal regulations in the United States.

Smith, John E., and M. O. Moss. *Mycotoxins: Formation, Analysis, and Significance.* Wiley 1985 $27.00. Mycotoxins are substances formed by molds that cause illness and sometimes death. This is a technical (less so than others available on the topic) book about this important medical and biological topic.

Smith, Richard B. *The Development of a Medicine.* Stockton Pr. 1985 $60.00. A brief synopsis of the process by which medicines are developed, from the discovery of a substance to its evaluation, approval, marketing, and ultimate prescription.

Sneader, Walter. *Drug Discovery: The Evolution of Modern Medicines.* Wiley 1985 $21.95. Provides substantial information, in an easy-to-read format, on the evolution of chemical substances in the therapeutic agents used in clinical biomedicine.

Wedeen, Richard P. *Poison in the Pot: The Legacy of Lead.* Southern Univ. Pr. 1984 $24.95. A fascinating history of lead poisoning, including a discussion of the economic importance of lead and how that importance has reinforced resistance to wide recognition of lead's dangers.

PHYSIOLOGY

[SEE the section on The Healthy Body in this chapter.]

POISONS

[SEE the section on Pharmacology and Toxicology in this chapter.]

PUBLIC, ENVIRONMENTAL, AND OCCUPATIONAL HEALTH

Public health is the branch of medicine concerned with the prevention and control of disease and disability, and the promotion of physical and mental health of the population on the international, national, state, or municipal level. As such, it encompasses a wide variety of concerns. This section primarily includes books dealing with environmental and occupational issues. Epidemiological titles, which demonstrate disease patterns and transmission, are included in Chapter 15 in this volume.

Burgess, William A. *Recognition of Health Hazards in Industry: A Review of Materials and Processes.* Wiley 1981 $36.00. Of excellent quality, this work provides the reader with an understanding of industrial operations and the physical contaminants and stresses present in such operations.

Cairncross, Sandy, and Richard G. Feachem. *Environmental Health Engineering in the Tropics: An Introductory Text.* Wiley 1983 $42.95. An interesting book for those seeking information about public health and environmental health in the tropics, especially in the developing countries.

Doyle, Rodger Pirnie. *The Medical Wars.* Morrow 1983 $13.95. The status of 16 of today's most publicized medical controversies, from megavitamin therapy and dietary fiber to Masters and Johnson and the Love Canal. Doyle assesses these controversies through the application of "good" research criteria.

Drake, Alvin W., and others. *The American Blood Supply: Issues and Policies of Blood Donation.* MIT 1982 $30.00. A description of the history, development, structure, and problems of the American blood banking system.

Editorial Research Reports. *Environment and Health.* Congr. Quarterly 1981 pap. $10.95. A distillation of a vast quantity of materials on environmental health issues into a slim manageable report. Easily read by the layperson.

Fisher, Albert L. *Health and Prevention of Disease in a Free Society.* North Country 1980 o.p. Some very interesting and provocative views on health and disease prevention and their relationship to political, economic, and social forces.

Gersuny, Carl. *Work Hazards and Industrial Conflict.* Univ. Pr. of New England 1981 $16.00. A study of the ongoing conflict over issues of occupational health and safety within the context of a changing legal framework.

Graham, Horace D. *The Safety of Foods.* AVI 2d ed. 1980 lib. bdg. $50.00. Includes chapters concerned with spoilage, control of infectious agents, food-borne diseases of animal origin, heavy metal contaminants, food additives, food regulations, and the safety of food provided in institutional settings.

Henderson, George, and Martha Primeaux. *Transcultural Health Care.* Addison-Wesley 1981 $24.50 pap. $19.95. A knowledgeable discussion of the cultural factors that have an impact on the behavior of providers as well as consumers of health care.

Hinds, William C. *Aerosol Technology: Properties, Behavior, and Measurement of Airborne Particles.* Wiley 1982 text ed. $47.00. A practical book with a public health orientation. Implicates aerosols in public health concerns.

Kunitz, Stephen J. *Disease Change and the Role of Medicine: The Navajo Experience.* Univ. of California Pr. 1983 text ed. $29.95. Examines the Navaho experience with modern medicine and the impact that medicine has had on Navaho morbidity and mortality rates since the late nineteenth century.

Ng, Lorenz K. Y., and Devra Lee Davis, eds. *Strategies for Public Health: Promoting Health and Preventing Disease.* Van Nostrand 1981 $24.50. A compilation of a variety of offerings that address the theme of health promotion through a better understanding of the nature of health and the way in which it is affected by individual attitudes, the health care industry, and the environment. Lucid and easily readable.

Norris, Ruth, ed. *Pills, Pesticides, and Profits: The International Trade in Toxic Substances.* North River Pr. 1982 pap. $12.95. A well-documented examination of the sale and distribution of drugs, pesticides, and other chemicals in Third World nations by multinational corporations and the problems such activities pose for the inhabitants.

Pelletier, Kenneth R. *Healthy People in Unhealthy Places: Stress and Fitness at Work.* Delacorte 1985 pap. $8.95. A thorough documentation of health hazards in the workplace with a discussion of stress reactions and management.

Russell, Louise B. *Is Prevention Better Than Cure?* Brookings 1986 $26.95 pap. $9.95. In this review of the policy debates that surround several preventive health measures, Russell demonstrates by cost-effective analysis the complexities involved in evaluating these attempts to improve health.

Stellman, Jeanne, and Mary Sue Henifin. *Office Work Can Be Dangerous to Your Health: A Handbook of Office Health and Safety Hazards and What You Can Do about Them*. Pantheon 1984 $15.45 pap. $6.95. A thorough review of the available literature, this useful work explores various aspects of known and suspected office hazards.

Trieff, Norman M., ed. *Environment and Health*. Ann Arbor Science 1980 o.p. The authors deal with the adverse effects on health of toxic environments, the adverse effects themselves, and the solutions. A good book for the uninitiated.

Turiel, Isaac. *Indoor Air Quality and Human Health*. Stanford Univ. Pr. 1985 $24.95. A rather good book on indoor air quality that provides general information on indoor air pollution sources and pollutants, with potential health effects arising from exposure.

Urquhart, John, and Klaus Heilmann. *Risk Watch: The Odds of Life*. Facts on File 1984 $16.95. A readable, commonsense discussion of the many variables that have the potential for limiting both the length and quality of our lives.

RADIOLOGY

[SEE the section on Diagnostic Testing in this chapter.]

TOXICOLOGY

[SEE the section on Pharmacology and Toxicology in this chapter.]

UROLOGY

[SEE Chapter 15 in this volume.]

WOMEN'S HEALTH

Gynecology and obstetrics are two distinct medical specialties which, in turn, have distinct but related literatures, both very large. This section contains representative titles from each, with Pregnancy and Childbirth included as a separate section.

Anderson, Mary M. *An A-Z Gynecology: With Comments on Aspects of Management and Nursing*. Harper 1986 pap. $7.95. A compact introductory manual/handbook to the topic.

Asso, Doreen. *The Real Menstrual Cycle*. Wiley 1983 $42.95 pap. $16.95. Discusses the origin and operation of biological cycles and hormone interplay during the menstrual cycle. Because of the depth of subject matter and comprehensive format, the book is recommended for use at the undergraduate level rather than at the senior high school level.

Boston Women's Health Book Collective. *The New Our Bodies, Ourselves*. Simon &

Schuster 1985 $19.95 pap. $12.95. Provides an update to their earlier volume of current and useful information on the physiology and psychology of women.

Buchsbaum, Herbert J., ed. *The Menopause*. Springer-Verlag 1983 $39.50. An edited volume of articles by authorities describing various facets of menopause and postmenopause. Well-written and well-researched.

Budoff, Penny Wise. *No More Hot Flashes and Other Good News*. Putnam 1983 $14.95. Aimed at mature women over 40, Budoff details the hormonal changes that occur as women age and the effect of these changes on health. Informative, well-documented, and readable.

Cutler, Winnifred Berg, and others. *Menopause: A Guide for Women and the Men Who Love Them*. Norton 1983 $15.00. A basic and useful guide to information about menopause written for the general public.

Fuchs, Nan Kathryn. *The Nutrition Detective: A Woman's Guide to Treating Your Health Problems Through the Foods You Eat*. Houghton Mifflin 1985 $9.95. A very good book written for women suffering from symptoms that can be eliminated through diet and diet supplements.

Gluckin, Doreen, with Michael Edelhart. *The Body at Thirty: A Woman Doctor Talks to Women*. Berkley Pub. 1983 pap. $3.50; M. Evans 1982 $12.95. Gluckin believes that women in their thirties are experiencing a rich and stimulating period of their life, but it is also a time when women begin to confront great change. This theory is explored in depth.

Graham, Hilary, and others. *Women, Health, and Healing: Toward a New Perspective*. Methuen 1985 $12.95. A stimulating collection of sociological essays analyzing women's health policy issues from the perspective of women as health consumers and providers.

Greenwood, Sadja. *Menopause, Naturally: Preparing for the Second Half of Life*. Volcano Pr. 1984 $10.00. In addition to providing extensive information on how to promote good health, this book discusses interesting and controversial questions on all aspects of menopause, osteoporosis, estrogen therapy, exercise, and so on.

Harrison, Michelle. *Self-Help for Premenstrual Syndrome*. Random rev. ed. 1985 $9.95. Harrison describes self-help strategies including diet modification, exercise, and stress reduction, and discusses medical treatment.

Holt, Linda H., and Melva Weber. *The American Medical Association Book of Womancare*. Random 1982 o.p. An exceptionally well-written and easy-to-read work covering the gamut of women's health problems and concerns from youth to old age. Clear and concise.

Hongladarom, Gail G., Ruth McCorkle, and Nancy F. Woods, eds. *The Complete Book of Women's Health*. Prentice-Hall 1982 $21.95 pap. $12.95. Comprehensive and accurate sourcebook that serves equally well as a primary instructional aid to teenagers and as a resource for mature women.

Keyser, Herbert H. *Women Under the Knife: A Gynecologist's Report on Hazardous Medicine*. Stickley 1984 $9.95; Warner Bks. 1986 pap. $3.95. Educated, interesting, and wholesomely opinionated.

Lauersen, Niels H., and Eileen Stukane. *Listen to Your Body: A Gynecologist Answers Women's Most Intimate Questions*. Simon & Schuster 1982 pap. $9.95. A delightfully informative book using excerpts from letters as a means to present factual data. Easy to read and well illustrated.

————. *PMS: Premenstrual Syndrome and You: Next Month Can Be Different*. Pinnacle Bks. 1984 pap. $3.95; Simon & Schuster 1983 $8.95. Includes an overview of female physiology and case histories, along with information on the causes, physical and emotional symptoms, and diagnois of PMS.

Lewin, Ellen, ed. *Women, Health, and Healing: Toward a New Perspective.* Methuen 1985 pap. $12.95. The focus of this collection of original essays by North American and British feminist scholars is women's health in a comprehensive sociocultural context.

Lichtendorf, Susan S. *Eve's Journey: The Physical Experience of Being Female.* Putnam 1982 o.p. This book brings together medical authorities and ordinary women who discuss the physical aspects of womanhood with personal comments and histories.

Morgan, Susanne. *Coping with a Hysterectomy: Your Own Choice, Your Own Solutions.* NAL rev. ed. 1985 pap. $7.95. Morgan is a medical sociologist who carefully examines the current status of hysterectomy in Western medical practice.

Nactigall, Lila. *Estrogen: The Facts Can Change Your Life.* Harper 1986 $15.45. A useful book on the therapeutic use of estrogen.

Norris, Ronald V., with Colleen Sullivan. *PMS: Premenstrual Syndrome.* Rawson 1983 $15.95. Describes the physical and psychological symptoms, possible causes, therapies, and the social and legal implications of PMS.

Older, Julia. *Endometriosis: A Women's Guide to a Common but Often Undetected Disease That Can Cause Infertility and Other Major Medical Problems.* Scribner 1984 $15.95. Using information from popular and scholarly publications and interviews with experts, Older provides a good overview of the subject, including surgical options and drug therapies.

Schrotenboer, Kathryn, and Genell J. Subak-Sharpe. *Freedom from Menstrual Cramps.* Pocket Bks. 1981 pap. $2.95. Up-to-date, medically accurate information on the etiology, diagnosis, and treatment of menstrual abnormalities. Concise and well-organized.

Shephard, Bruce D., and Carroll A. Shephard. *The Complete Guide to Women's Health.* NAL rev. ed. 1985 $11.95. A comprehensive, well-organized problem-oriented guide to health strategies, birth control methods, pregnancy and childbirth, as well as information on diseases of the female reproductive tract. One of the best general female health references available.

Stoppard, Miriam. *Being a Well Woman.* Holt 1982 $19.95. Intended as a guide to maintaining general well-being, this book emphasizes taking responsibility for those aspects of her health that a woman can control.

Winick, Myron. *For Mothers and Daughters: A Guide to Good Nutrition for Women.* Berkley Pub. 1985 pap. $3.50; Morrow 1983 $12.95. A comprehensive, easy-to-read discussion of the specific nutritional requirements of women during adolescence, the reproductive years, pregnancy, lactation, menopause, and aging.

Witt, Reni L. *PMS: What Every Woman Should Know about Premenstrual Syndrome.* Stein & Day 1983 $14.95 1984 pap. $2.95. A very readable description of the causes, symptoms, and diagnosis of PMS. Includes a useful glossary of terms.

Pregnancy and Childbirth

[SEE ALSO the related section, Childcare and Development, in this chapter; for books on abortion, see Chapter 20, Ethics of Science, Technology, and Medicine, in this volume.]

Andrews, Lori B. *New Conceptions: A Consumer's Guide to the Medical, Emotional and Legal Aspects of Genetic Counseling, New Infertility Treatments, Artificial Insemination, In Vitro Fertilization, and Surrogate Motherhood.* St. Martin's 1984 $13.95. This guide covers the more traditional treatments for infertility as well as the newer possibilities.

Ashford, Janet Isaacs, ed. *Birth Stories: The Experience Remembered.* Crossing Pr. 1984 $18.95 pap. $7.95. Ashford solicited birth stories from three generations of women.

————. *The Whole Birth Catalog: A Sourcebook for Choices in Childbirth.* Crossing Pr. 1983 $32.95 pap. $15.95. An impressive collection of material on pregnancy, childbirth, and the postpartum period. Emphasis is on exploring alternatives to the medical model of pregnancy and childbirth.

Bellina, Joseph H., and Josleen Wilson. *You Can Have a Baby: Everything You Need to Know About Fertility.* Crown 1985 $17.95. Provides comprehensive information on causes, diagnosis, and treatments for infertility. Special topics include selection of professionals for treatment; miscarriage; pregnancy after 35; contraceptives; and religious, moral, and legal issues.

Brown, Judith E. *Nutrition for Your Pregnancy: The University of Minnesota Guide.* Univ. of Minnesota Pr. 1983 $12.95 1984 pap. $7.95. A highly recommended and well-respected guide to good nutrition during pregnancy and the postpartum period.

Caplan, Ronald. *Pregnant Is Beautiful.* Pocket Bks. 1985 pap. $3.95. Explains how to keep in shape during pregnancy for a more comfortable pregnancy as well as a quick return to pre-pregnancy fitness. Concise and easy to read.

Corea, Gena. *The Mother Machine: Reproductive Technologies from Artificial Insemination to Artificial Wombs.* Harper 1985 $17.95. An in-depth look at historical, social, legal, and medical trends combined with descriptions of the state of the art in eugenics, cloning, surrogate motherhood, and so forth.

Edwards, Margot, and Mary Waldorf. *Reclaiming Birth: History and Heroines of American Childbirth Reform.* Crossing Pr. 1984 $19.95 pap. $8.95. An impressive contribution to women's history.

Eheart, Brenda, and Susan Martel. *The Fourth Trimester: On Becoming a Mother.* Ballantine 1984 pap. $3.50. This book treats the changes caused during the first three months of motherhood. An exceptionally thorough book.

Eisenberg, Arlene. *What to Eat When You're Expecting.* Workman 1986 pap. $7.95. A well-balanced guide to the nutritional aspects of pregnancy and how to adjust the diet accordingly.

Fay, Francesca C., and Kelly S. Smith. *Childbearing After 35: The Risks and the Rewards.* Balsam Pr. 1985 $17.95 pap. $9.95. A thorough comprehensive guide for older pregnant women. In addition to the basic topics found in most pregnancy guides, this book covers the concerns specific to women over the age of 35 and the many advantages of becoming an older parent.

Feinbloom, Richard I., and Betty Y. Forman. *Pregnancy, Birth, and the Early Months: A Complete Guide.* Addison-Wesley 1985 $16.95. A complete and well-balanced guide that covers every medical and emotional aspect of childbirth and the first few months of life.

Freeman, Roger K., and Susan Pescar. *Safe Delivery: Protecting Your Baby During High Risk Pregnancy.* Facts on File 1982 $14.95; McGraw-Hill 1983 pap. $7.95. A comprehensive well-written guide to high-risk obstetrics and neonatology. Reassuring and sensitive presentation.

Fried, Peter. *Pregnancy and Life-Style Habits.* Beaufort Bks. 1983 $9.95. A carefully researched study of the effects of exogenous substances on the developing fetus. Detailed sections on the effects of various substances, for example, alcohol and prescription and nonprescription drugs.

Glass, Robert H., and Ronald J. Ericsson. *Getting Pregnant in the 1980s: New Advances in Infertility Treatment and Sex Preselection.* Univ. of California Pr. 1982 $10.95. An infertility specialist and a research biologist present clear, concise chapters on infertility and the infertility workup, as well as detailed sections on new reproductive technology. A skillful combination of clinical medicine and basic research for the layperson.

Goldberg, Larry H., and Joann M. Leaby. *The Doctor's Guide to Medication During Pregnancy and Lactation.* Morrow 1984 $16.95 pap. $6.70. Easy to read and not oversimplified, this guide answers many of the questions women ask during pregnancy.

Hales, Dianne, and Robert K. Creasy. *New Hope for Problem Pregnancies: Saving Babies Before They're Born.* Berkley Pub. 1984 pap. $3.95; Harper 1982 $14.95. Contains superior sections on nutrition and drugs during pregnancy; includes excellent tables on food additives and drugs. Complete, up-to-date, and medically accurate.

Harper, Michael J. K. *Birth Control Technologies: Prospects by the Year 2000.* Univ. of Texas Pr. 1983 text ed. $27.50 1985 pap. $10.95. Details proposed improvements in existing methods of contraception as well as a number of proposed new techniques. Derived from extensive high-level research.

Katz, Jane. *Swimming Through Your Pregnancy.* Doubleday 1984 $10.95. A complete swimming program for pregnant women, this enthusiastic and logical presentation should provide an inspirational approach to exercise for some pregnant women.

Klaus, Marshall H., and Phyllis H. Klaus. *The Amazing Newborn.* Addison-Wesley 1985 $10.95. A product of the new interest in research on infancy, this book focuses on the characteristics and abilities of newborns. Well-illustrated, this book also translates clinical research into useful observations for parents.

Korte, Diana, and Roberta Scaer. *A Good Birth, A Safe Birth.* Bantam 1984 pap. $7.95. A summary of current medical research on childbirth and mothers' preferences for birthing.

Lauersen, Niels H. *Childbirth with Love: A Complete Guide to Fertility, Pregnancy, and Childbirth for Caring Couples.* Putnam 1983 $19.95. This highly recommended book presents detailed information on all aspects of pregnancy and childbirth, including choosing an obstetrician.

McCutcheon-Rosegg, Susan, with Peter Rosegg. *Natural Childbirth: The Bradley Way.* Dutton 1984 pap. $14.95. Provides comprehensive information on preparing for childbirth, the three stages in delivery, and controversies in childbirth.

Mitchard, Jacquelyn. *Mother Less Child.* Norton 1985 $15.95. An autobiographical account of one family's struggle with infertility.

Noble, Elizabeth. *Childbirth with Insight.* Houghton Mifflin 1983 $15.95 pap. $8.95. Well-written, thought-provoking, and controversial, this book argues "that the value and appropriateness of mechanical practice of classroom techniques designed for a reflex voluntary experience such as labor needs to be examined" (*LJ*).

Norwood, Christopher. *How to Avoid a Caesarean Section.* Simon & Schuster 1984 $14.95 1985 pap. $7.95 Norwood summarizes the current research and documents that over half of C-section deliveries are not necessary.

Rinzler, Carol Ann. *The Safe Pregnancy Book.* NAL 1985 pap. $6.95. Although this book presents information that can be found in numerous other books on pregnancy, it has unique value because of its simple organization and format.

Robinson, Susan, and H. F. Pizer. *Having a Baby Without a Man: Single Woman's Guide to Alternative Fertilization.* Simon & Schuster 1985 pap. $7.95. A clear explanation of the various methods of alternative fertilization, their history, and their success rates.

Rothman, Barbara K. *In Labor: Women and Power in the Workplace.* Norton 1982

$14.95. Rothman, a social scientist, examines the current status of Western obstetrics in this well-written, well-researched study.

Sandelowski, Margarete. *Pain, Pleasure, and American Childbirth: From the Twilight Sleep to the Read Method.* Greenwood Pr. 1984 lib. bdg. $27.95. An erudite work that traces the history of childbirth in the United States from 1914 through 1960. Very readable, excellent history.

Scher, Jonathan, and Carol Dix. *Will My Baby Be Normal? Everything You Need to Know about Pregnancy.* Dial 1983 $15.95. A general up-to-date compendium of information about each stage of pregnancy and delivery.

Schrotenboer, Kathryn, and Solomon Weiss. *Dr. Kathryn Schrotenboer's Guide to Pregnancy over 35.* Ballantine 1985 pap. $7.95. A guide that addresses the issues and problems faced by pregnant women over the age of 35. An inspiring book.

Shapiro, Howard I. *The Pregnancy Book for Today's Woman: An Obstetrician Answers All Your Questions about Pregnancy and Childbirth and Some You May Not Have Considered.* Harper 1983 $17.45 pap. $11.95. A unique, refreshing guide for pregnant women.

Sidenbladh, Erik. *Water Babies: The Igor Tjarkovsky Method for Delivering in Water.* St. Martin's 1983 $12.95. A narrative description of the beliefs of Tjarkovsky, i.e., that if infants are born and fed underwater their potential for physical and mental development is greatly enhanced.

Simkin, Penny, and others. *Pregnancy, Childbirth, and the Newborn.* Ed. by Tom Grady, Meadowbrook Pr. 1984 pap. $9.95. An excellent, clearly written book covering all aspects of pregnancy.

Sirota, Adair. *Preparing for Childbirth: A Couple's Manual.* Contemporary Bks. 1983 pap. $8.95. A basic outline of typical hospital childbirth procedures, with a focus on the Lamaze breathing method.

Tilton, Nan, and others. *Making Miracles: In Vitro Fertilization.* Doubleday 1985 $16.95. Written by the parents of the first test-tube twins, this book provides current information about in vitro fertilization.

Wood, Carl, and Ann Westmore. *Test-Tube Conception.* Prentice-Hall 1984 $14.95 pap. $6.95. A guide for prospective parents, doctors, and anyone interested in this exciting new method of treating infertility.

CHAPTER 15

Illness and Disease

Daniel T. Richards and Jodith Janes

Most men form an exaggerated estimate of the powers of medicine, founded on the common acceptance of the name, that medicine is the art of curing diseases. That this is a false definition is evident from the fact that many diseases are incurable, and that one such disease must at last happen to every living man. A far more just definition would be that medicine is the art of understanding diseases, and of curing or relieving when possible. Under this acceptation our science would, at least, be exonerated from reproach, and would stand on a basis capable of supporting a reasonable and durable system for the amelioration of human maladies.
—JACOB BIGELOW, *Nature in Disease*

Old Wine is a true panacea
    For every conceivable ill,
When you cherish the soothing idea
    That someone else pays the bill.
—WILLIAM SCHWENCK GILBERT, *The Grand Duke*, Act II, Baroness' song

Open a newspaper, news magazine, or popular journal; turn on the radio or television and more than likely there will be some segment or feature dealing with a health-related topic. There is virtually no section of the mass media that does not carry some kind of information about health, be it news of a new drug, a research hypothesis on what happens to the brain cells in patients with Parkinson's disease, a theory about fragile chromosomes, or the escalating cost of health care delivery. It has been estimated that several thousand titles are published each year on health-related subjects. Newsletters and magazines on self-health care proliferate on every magazine stand. This flood of information on the diagnosis, treatment, prognosis, and incidence of disease continues unabated, as does discussion of the financing and method of delivery of health services. There is widespread awareness of such problems as substance abuse, mental illness, sexually transmitted disease, as well as concern over industrial, occupational, and environmental health hazards. Hospitals are reaching out into the communities they serve to offer classes on diet and nutrition; exercise regimes paced to the age and level of participants, from baby massage to low impact aerobics; and sponsorship of support groups for patients, families, and friends of those afflicted with cancer, diabetes, or such disorders as Alzheimer's, Parkinson's, or cardiovascular disease. Patients are demanding and receiving a greater say in the decision making regarding their care and consumer advocacy groups are flourishing. The Peoples' Medical Society, founded in Emmaus, Pennsylvania, in February 1983, has grown from its initial membership of some 12,000 to more than 85,000 members today.

This compilation of books is not intended to be an exhaustive review but rather an indication of the range and variety of information available. Most of the books listed were published in the past six years mainly because the cutting edge of medicine moves so quickly that information on diagnosis and treatment modalities, in particular, is in a constant state of revision. Trends in publishing and public interest have created what might be described as a "disease of the year" phenomena. Of the numerous books on AIDS that appeared during 1985 and 1987; on osteoporosis and Alzheimer's disease in 1984 and 1985; herpes and sexually transmitted diseases in 1983 and 1984; and the hospice movement in the early 1980s, only a representative sampling of titles have been listed. Other diseases are not being neglected: witness the number of recent books on cancer, diabetes, cardiovascular diseases, and anorexia nervosa. It should be noted that no attempt has been made to list more than one or two of the many books available on headache or back pain. Titles dealing with this subject generally fall into the self-help genre. Books on disorders of the blood, gastrointestinal and urologic disorders, and many neurologic and musculoskeletal diseases that are neither of the how-to-cope category, textbooks, nor personal narratives are difficult to find. Comparatively speaking these disorders are written about less frequently than the big three—cancer, heart disease, and diabetes. Our aim has been to list resources concerning diagnosis, treatment, prognosis, incidence, and rehabilitation for the many disorders and diseases to which the body is heir. For the most part only those that discuss current orthodox therapy have been included.

In addition to commercially available books, there are many associations and organizations that have as a principal goal the education of the public about the disease for which they exist. These groups publish booklets and pamphlets that provide a succinct and clearly written explanation of the medical background and treatment for the disease. This type of publication is frequently distributed free or at little charge. Lists of such organizations can be found in several of the general reference books listed at the beginning of Chapter 14 in this volume. Lastly, physicians frequently can suggest publications that in their experience have been of help to their patients.

REFERENCE BOOKS

Dictionaries

Diseases: Causes, and Diagnosis, Current Therapy, Nursing Management, Patient Education. Springhouse 1984 $26.95. Provides simpler explanations than do major medical texts of the signs and symptoms of most diseases and disorders. Details expected clinical courses, diagnostic tests, treatment, possible complications, and nursing interventions.

Dorland's Illustrated Medical Dictionary. Saunders 26th ed. 1985 text ed. $35.95. The best-known medical dictionary. Excellent illustrations.

Firkin, B. G., and J. A. Whitworth. *Dictionary of Medical Eponyms.* Parthenon 1987 $48.00. Provides a description of the disease and short background notes on the person who identified it.

Logan, Carolynn M., and M. Catherine Rice. *Logan's Medical and Scientific Abbreviations.* Lippincott 1987 $22.50. Coverage includes symbols, Latin abbreviations, alternative terms, and tumor, node, and metastasis cancer staging. Over 20,000 entries.

Magalini, Sergio I., and Euclide Scrascia. *Dictionary of Medical Syndromes.* Lippincott 2d ed. 1981 text ed. $54.50. Concise descriptions, including synonyms, symptoms, diagnostic procedures, treatment, and prognosis of more than 2,700 syndromes.

Webster's Medical Desk Dictionary. Merriam-Webster 1986 $18.95. All entries are in a single alphabetical list, with a part-of-speech; places British spellings in their own alphabetical place; includes over 1,000 brief biographies.

Directories

ABMS Compendium of Certified Medical Specialists. Amer. Bd. of Med. Spec. 7 vols. 1986 lib. bdg. $200.00. Revised biennially. The only biographical directory authorized by ABMS. Lists more than 320,000 specialists certified by the 23 U.S. specialty boards. Information includes internship, residency training, fellowships, professional associations, and so on.

American Hospital Association Guide to the Health Care Field. Amer. Hospital 1986 pap. $72.50. Revised yearly. Statistics on numbers of beds, facilities and services, type of ownership (government, nonfederal or federal, nongovernment, not-for-profit, investor-owned, osteopathic), length of stay, and occupancy rates. Listings are alphabetical by state, then city.

American Medical Directory. AMA 4 vols. 30th ed. 1986 $400.00. Current information on more than 490,000 physicians, including name, address, type of practice, medical school and year of graduation, and primary specialty.

Encyclopedias

Galton, Lawrence. *Med Tech: The Layperson's Guide to Today's Medical Miracles.* Harper 1985 $19.45. Information on state-of-the-art procedures and techniques—from adoptive pregnancy to zona-free hamster egg test. Includes potential problems and history of development.

Walton, John, and Ronald B. Scott, eds. *The Oxford Companion to Medicine.* Oxford 2 vols. 1986 $95.00. A collection of definitions and short essays, including biographies "Covering topics such as diagnosis, experimental method, health insurance in the United States, law and medicine in the United Kingdom, medical microbiology, physiology, rehabilitation, and veterinary medicine, these often include short bibliographies and illustrations. The one-paragraph biographies of more than 1,000 physicians and other contributors to medical knowledge provide, albeit diffusely, historical background beyond that provided in some of the long articles" (*Wilson Library Bulletin*).

BIOGRAPHIES

These titles are by no means an exhaustive list, but rather a selection from the many titles dealing with illness and disease from a professional or personal point of view. (See also Chapters 2 and 14 in this volume.)

Astor, Gerald. *The Disease Detectives: Deadly Medical Mysteries and the People Who Solved Them*. NAL 1983 $14.95 1984 pap. $6.95. "Tells about the feelings, thoughts, and procedures of the men and women from the Centers for Disease Control who are responsible for investigating and studying outbreaks of cholera, bubonic plague, toxic shock syndrome and other medical problems" (*LJ*).

Austrian, Robert. *Life with the Pneumococcus: Notes from the Bedside, Laboratory and Library*. Fwd. by Lewis Thomas, Univ. of Pennsylvania Pr. 1985 $25.00. "The history of this fascinating bacterial pathogen and of the gradual recognition of its great diversity and disease-producing capacity is recounted lucidly. Woven into the fabric of the book, without much in the way of emphasis, is the story of Austrian's own considerable contribution to the modern developments in the control of pneumococcal disease" (*Amer. Scientist*).

Beckler, Alfred W. *A Gift of Life: The Powerful True Story of How Family Love and One Man's Indomitable Spirit Brought Him Back from Death to a Joyous Life*. Rawson 1983 o.p. "Gives hope that a diabetic can face the absolute worst and eventually conquer. Beckler is special because he is walking around with a new kidney and a new pancreas—both medical wonder operations" (*LJ*).

Clapesattle, Helen. *Dr. Webb of Colorado Springs*. Colorado Assoc. 1984 $19.50 pap. $9.95. "One of the nation's most prominent tuberculosis practitioners of the early twentieth century. Webb established a research laboratory, now the Webb-Waring [Lung] Institute [Denver, Colorado], in which several important discoveries were made" (*Choice*).

Kendall, Edward C. *Cortisone: Memoirs of a Hormone Hunter*. Scribner 1971 $7.95. "[Much] more than an exciting autobiography of the scientist Edward C. Kendall, [rather an] account of happenings in the medical sciences in the United States. Most of Kendall's book is concerned with research on the adrenal cortex. The most dramatic part of Kendall's story pertains to his collaboration with the rheumatologist, Phillip S. Hench and the administration of cortisone to a patient severely afflicted with rheumatoid arthritis" (*Amer. Scientist*).

McGill, Frances. *Go Not Gently: Letters from a Patient with Amyotrophic Lateral Sclerosis*. Ed. by Lillian G. Kutscher, Ayer 1980 lib. bdg. $18.00. Letters to a group of friends, written between July 1974 and June 1979, dealing with the author's perceptions of her terminal illness.

Paul, Olgesby. *Take Heart: The Life and Prescription for Living of Dr. Paul Dudley White*. Harvard Univ. Pr. 1986 text ed. $18.95. "A captivating biography about a preeminent physician whose outspoken views against the unnecessary invalidism of patients with heart disease bettered the lives of millions of persons world-wide during his 60-plus years of medical practice" (*LJ*).

Springarn, Natalie Davis. *Hanging in There: Living Well on Borrowed Time*. Stein & Day 1982 $14.95 pap. $8.95. "Encouragement for people living with the knowledge that they have a serious illness, typically cancer, who because of the protracted course of the illness are neither well nor completely disabled for an undefined period" (*LJ*).

Wertenbaker, Lael. *To Mend the Heart: The Dramatic Story of Cardiac Surgery and Its Pioneers*. Fwd. by Dwight E. Harken, Viking 1980 o.p. "Details the history of cardiac surgery, primarily by following the career of Dwight Emary Harken, one of the pioneers" (*LJ*).

Zola, Irving Kenneth, ed. *Ordinary Lives: Voices of Disability and Disease.* Apple-Wood 1982 $12.95. "This anthology brings together powerful and touching stories expressing individuals' feelings about chronic disease and disability" (*Choice*).

AIDS

[SEE the section on Immunology in this chapter.]

ALLERGY

[SEE the section on Immunology in this chapter.]

ANESTHESIOLOGY

Anesthesiology is the science concerned with the pharmacological, physiological, and clinical basis of anesthesia. There are few titles on this topic written for a general audience.

Brown, Robert C. *Perchance to Dream: The Patient's Guide to Anesthesia.* Nelson-Hall 1981 $14.95. An outline of the history of anesthesia. Discusses types of anesthetic agents, their actions, and possible complications.

Pernick, Martin S. *A Calculus of Suffering: Pain, Professionalism and Anesthesia in Nineteenth-Century America.* Columbia Univ. Pr. 1985 $38.00 1987 text ed. pap. $14.50. "This book can be recommended to a reader seeking to learn more about the social and professional aspects of pain relief in the half-century following the discovery of anesthesia" (*Amer. Scientist*).

ARTHRITIS

[SEE the section on Rheumatic Diseases in this chapter.]

ARTIFICIAL AND TRANSPLANTED ORGANS, PROSTHESES, AND IMPLANTS

Books listed in this section describe biotechnological advances in medicine, including implants, transplants, artificial hearts and joints, as well as the ethical, social, and economic impact of this technology.

Bigelow, W. G. *Cold Hearts: The Story of Hypothermia and the Pacemaker in Heart Surgery.* McClelland 1984 o.p. "Dr. Bigelow's story makes research look just plain fun and gives credit where credit is due" (*Anesthesiology*).

Cauwels, Janice M. *The Body Shop: Bionic Revolutions in Medicine.* Mosby 1986 $14.95. "Skillfully interweaves human interest vignettes, technical explanations, and in-depth interviews with researchers in such fields as artificial joints; artifi-

cial hearts; post-surgery prostheses for faces, breasts, and limbs; and rehabilitation of patients devastated by neuromuscular disease" (*LJ*).

Cook, Albert M., and John G. Webster, eds. *Therapeutic Medical Devices: Application and Design.* Prentice-Hall 1981 $52.95. "Reviews in some detail the medical devices that are presently available" (*Choice*).

Davis, Audrey B. *Medicine and Its Technology: An Introduction to the History of Medical Instrumentation.* Greenwood 1981 lib. bdg. $45.00. "Emphasis is placed on the major pioneering areas of medical technology: thermometry, stethoscopy, and the more varied instrumentation used to measure pulse rate, blood pressure, and other specialized cardiovascular functions" (*Choice*).

Lynch, Wilfred. *Implants: Reconstructing the Human Body.* Van Nostrand 1982 $31.95. "Provides a review and explanation of many types of surgical-implant devices and biomaterials" (*Amer. Scientist*).

Pekkanen, John. *Donor.* Little, Brown 1986 $15.95. "An absorbing and moving book that follows the donation of organs from a young woman after her death in an automobile accident" (*LJ*).

Plough, Alonzo L. *Borrowed Time: Artificial Organs and the Politics of Extending Lives.* [*Health, Society, and Policy*] Temple Univ. Pr. 1986 $24.95. "Examines federal programs for the treatment of kidney failures as well as the problem of chronic and catastrophic illness, and the cultural and political forces that have come to shape policies concerning new technologies" (*Choice*).

Reiser, Stanley J., and Michael Anbar, eds. *The Machine at the Bedside: Strategies for Using Technology in Patient Care.* Cambridge Univ. Pr. 1984 $65.00 pap. $15.95. "Examines the social, ethical, and economic impact of the diagnostic, therapeutic, palliative, and rehabilitative technologies that constitute the armamentarium of modern health care" (*Amer. Scientist*).

BLINDNESS

[SEE the section on Eye Disorders in this chapter.]

BLOOD DISEASES

[SEE the section on Hematologic Diseases in this chapter.]

BONE DISEASES

[SEE the section on Orthopedics in this chapter.]

CANCER

Cancer is not a single disease, but it is a term frequently used to indicate any of various types of malignant neoplasms, most of which invade surrounding tissues, may spread (metastasize) to other sites, and are likely to recur after attempted removal and to cause death unless adequately treated. This is neither an exhaustive nor a comprehensive list of the many books on cancer.

Included are descriptions of specific cancers, their detection, treatment, prognosis, and incidence. The personal and psychosocial impact of this disease is also explored.

Berger, Karen, and John Bostwick, III. *A Woman's Decision: Breast Care, Treatment and Reconstruction.* Ballantine 1985 pap. $9.95; Mosby 1984 $14.95. "Compiled with the aid of Reach to Recovery and the American Cancer Society. Couples personal accounts with information on this special surgery" (*LJ*).

Bracken, Jeanne M. *Children with Cancer: A Comprehensive Reference Guide for Parents.* Oxford Univ. Pr. 1986 $22.95. "Includes chapters on specific cancers; standard treatments; coping; and lists of international, national, and regional organizations and clinics" (*LJ*).

Bruning, Nancy. *Coping with Chemotherapy.* Ballantine 1986 pap. $3.95; Doubleday 1985 $15.95. "Gives possible causes of cancer, the therapies, side effects, emotional impact of chemotherapy and ways to cope with the treatment. In-depth and understanding coverage of all aspects of the physiological and emotional aspects of chemotherapy" (*LJ*).

Cancer Risk: Assessing and Reducing the Dangers in Our Society. Westview Pr. 1982 o.p. "Summarizes what is known about carcinogens; reviews related legislation and regulations; traces trends on overall age-specific and cancer rates; discusses detection and identification of carcinogenic substances; details quantitative techniques by which data from study populations are employed to estimate risk in human populations; and describes both the means and the rationale for federal regulations of carcinogens" (*Choice*).

Creasey, William A. *Diet and Cancer.* Lea & Febiger 1985 pap. $14.50. "Covers nutrition and cancer patients, protein and caloric intake, fibers, fats, vitamins, minerals, alcohol, and coffee" (*LJ*).

Edelhart, Michael, and Jean Lindenmann. *Interferon: The New Hope for Cancer.* Addison-Wesley 1981 $11.95. "What interferon is and how it works" (*Choice*).

Farmer, Peter B., and John M. Walker, Jr., eds. *The Molecular Basis of Cancer.* Wiley 1985 pap. $29.95. "Emphasizes that the action of carcinogenesis and the nature, detection and treatment of cancer can only be understood and achieved by a thorough knowledge of the basic biochemical and molecular biological mechanisms involved" (*Choice*).

Fjermedal, Grant. *Magic Bullets: A Revolution in Cancer Treatment.* Macmillan 1984 $15.95. "The inside story of major cancer research funded by the NIH" (*LJ*).

Goldberg, Richard T., and Robert M. Tull. *The Psychosocial Dimensions of Cancer.* Free Pr. 1983 $19.95. "Includes discussion of children's comprehension of disease and death at various ages; special problems of adolescent patients; drug-related issues; physical and psychological causes of nausea; issues in pain control and drugs used for this purpose" (*Choice*).

Graham, Jory. *In the Company of Others.* Fwd. by John M. Merril, Harcourt 1981 o.p. Graham, a syndicated columnist right up to the time of her death from metastasized cancer, writes of her own experiences.

Holleb, Arthur I., and others, eds. *The American Cancer Society's Complete Book of Cancer: Prevention, Diagnosis, Treatment, Rehabilitation, Cure.* Doubleday 1986 $22.50. An excellent compilation; covers topics such as smoking and cancer, monoclonal antibodies, genetic factors, specific cancers and their treatment, aids to early detection, and decision making regarding treatment and aftercare.

Kessler, I. *Cancer Control: Contemporary Views on Screening, Diagnosis, and Therapy, Including a Colloquy on the Delaney Clause.* Univ. Park Pr. 1980 text ed. $32.00.

"Specific chapters cover immunodiagnosis, chemotherapy, and cytohistopathy (the study of cancer mechanisms in cells as individuals and groups). The practical as well as the theoretical aspects of control are discussed" (*Choice*).

Levenson, Frederick B. *Causes and Prevention of Cancer*. Stein & Day 1986 $16.95 pap. $7.95. "Understanding both the genetic and psychoanalytic bases of the disease is necessary to formulate an effective therapy, the author states" (*LJ*).

Livingston-Wheeler, Virginia, and Edmond G. Addeo. *The Conquest of Cancer: Vaccines and Diet*. Watts 1984 $16.95. "A personal narrative chronicling the author's research and continuing struggle for recognition. Also a description of the regimen prescribed by her San Diego cancer clinic, complete with recipes and food lists" (*LJ*).

Margolies, Cynthia P., and Kenneth B. McCredie. *Understanding Leukemia*. Scribner 1983 $16.95 1987 pap. $9.95. "A rigorous discussion of possible causes and treatment protocols (chemotherapy, radiotherapy, bone marrow transplants, etc.)" (*LJ*).

Morra, Marion, and Eve Potts. *Choices: Realistic Alternatives in Cancer Treatment*. Avon rev. ed. 1987 pap $10.95. Supplements the information a physician provides. Educates readers in how to choose a doctor, the nature of cancer, diagnostic tests, treatment modalities, experimental investigation, unproven treatments, and more.

Petrek, Jeanne A. *A Woman's Guide to the Prevention, Detection and Treatment of Cancer*. Macmillan 1985 $14.95. "Provides an overview of cancer, with sections on diagnosis, treatment, and a discussion of risk factors" (*LJ*).

Prescott, David M., and Abraham S. Flexer. *Cancer: The Misguided Cell*. Sinauer 2d ed. rev. 1986 text ed. pap. $18.95. "A well-documented review of the basic approaches to cancer research conducted over the past decade" (*LJ*).

Rettig, Richard. *Cancer Crusade: The Story of the National Cancer Act of 1971*. Princeton Univ. Pr. 1977 $37.00. "[Details] the evolution of the 1971 legislation that provided greatly increased funding for a 'moon' shot at cancer" (*Amer. Scientist*).

Shamberger, Raymond J. *Nutrition and Cancer*. Plenum 1984 $59.50. "Reviews the role of nutrition in carcinogenesis, notes certain mutagens formed during processing or cooking, or naturally occurring carcinogens in relation to causation. Also covered are additives, artificial sweeteners, antioxidants, and food contaminants. Reviews unproven cancer diet claims" (*Amer. Scientist*).

Siegel, Mary-Ellen. *The Cancer Patients's Handbook: Everything You Need to Know about Today's Care and Treatment*. Walker 1986 $24.95 pap. $14.95. "Provides a clear description of each of the therapeutic approaches to treating cancer, including immunologic therapies with biologic-response modifiers. Discusses 'unproved' cancer treatment. Defines tests and examinations" (*New England Journal of Medicine*).

Spletter, Mary. *A Woman's Choice: New Options in the Treatment of Breast Cancer*. Beacon 1981 $14.50. "Provides descriptions of treatments, explanations of medical terminology, survival statistics, and other information that will enable a woman to know her own cancer risk, ask questions of physicians, and make informed choices" (*LJ*).

CARDIOVASCULAR DISEASES

This section includes information on the anatomy and actions of the heart, symptoms, diagnosis, treatment (including the role of diet and exercise) and prevention of stroke, heart attack, and hypertension. Below is a selective list compiled to provide historical and current information on the normal and abnormal functions of the heart and cardiovascular system.

The American Heart Association. *Heartbook: A Guide to the Prevention and Treatment of Cardiovascular Diseases.* Dutton 1980 o.p. Excellent, comprehensive information for the layperson on the causes, prevention, and treatment of heart attack, stroke, hypertension, and cardiac emergencies.

The American Medical Association Book of Heart Care. Random 1982 $12.95. "Details how the individual can prevent heart disease. Emphasizes preventive care, problems and symptoms" (*LJ*).

Caris, Timothy N. *A Clinical Guide to Hypertension.* PSG Pubns. 1985 $24.50; Warner Bks. 1986 pap. $3.95. "Describes pathophysiology, risk factors indicated by research findings and signs and symptoms. Methods of nonpharmacological treatment are presented—diet, weight control, physical conditioning and abstention from alcohol. The stepped-care method of drug therapy (from diuretics to vasodilators) is explained" (*Choice*).

Comroe, Julius H., Jr. *Exploring the Heart: Discoveries in Heart Disease and High Blood Pressure.* Norton 1984 $18.95. Discusses modern advances in the diagnosis and treatment of diseases of the heart and arterties and of high blood pressure.

Cranton, Elmer, and Arline Brecher. *Bypassing Bypass: The New Technique of Chelation Therapy.* Intro. by H. Richard Casdorph, Stein & Day 1984 $16.95. "Explains the controversial form of therapy in which EDTA (ethylene-diamine-tetra-acetic acid) is given intravenously" (*LJ*).

Dawber, Thomas R. *The Framingham Study: The Epidemiology of Atherosclerotic Disease.* Harvard Univ. Pr. 1980 text ed. $20.00. "A concise history of the 24-year Framingham study of the epidemiology of atherosclerotic disease. Valuable for the light it sheds on the problems of conducting clinical epidemiological investigations of chronic diseases" (*Choice*).

Eisenberg, Mickey, and Judy Pierce, eds. *Sudden Cardiac Death in the Community.* Praeger 1984 $30.95. "The authors argue that quick treatment delivered by skilled people who have the training and equipment to stabilize the victim of a cardiac arrhythmia/arrest in the field is currently the principle around which prehospital cardiac care is/should be organized" (*Choice*).

Garrett, R. C., and U. G. Waldmeyer. *The Pill Book of High Blood Pressure.* Bantam 1985 pap. $3.95. "Provides information on specific illnesses and the drugs commonly prescribed to treat them" (*LJ*).

Geddes, L. A. *Cardiovascular Medical Devices.* Wiley 1984 $49.95. A concise overview of the devices used in medicine for the diagnosis and treatment of blood pressure; both the invasive and noninvasive methods of accomplishing these measurements are included.

Halperin, Jonathan L., and Richard Levine. *Bypass: A Cardiologist Reveals What Every Patient Needs to Know.* Times Bks. 1985 $16.95. "Traces [the] historical development of cardiology, provides an interesting behind-the-scenes glimpse into the world of medicine—the actual bypass operation, post-operative care in the intensive care unit, and cardiac rehabilitation" (*LJ*).

Herd, J. Alan, and Stephen M. Weiss, eds. *Behavior and Arteriosclerosis.* Plenum 1983 o.p. "Reviews current knowledge of sociocultural factors associated with arteriosclerotic heart disease and patient characteristics that influence outcomes of treatment" (*Choice*).

Hoffman, Nancy Y. *Change of Heart: The Bypass Experience.* Harcourt 1985 $17.95 1987 pap. $7.95. "Drawn from the experiences of 800 questionnaire respondents and 200 interviewees, all of whom have undergone coronary bypasses" (*Journal of the American Medical Assn.*).

Johnson, Stephen L. *The History of Cardiac Surgery 1896–1955*. Johns Hopkins Univ. Pr. 1970 o.p. "Trace[s] the crucial technological breakthroughs [such as] the first successful suture of a human heart wound, by Ludwig Rehn in 1896; extracardiac surgery, pioneered in the 1930s by Robert Gross and others; and in the late 1940s and 1950s, the attack of valvular heart disease" (*Amer. Scientist*).

Kaplan, Norman M. *Prevent Your Heart Attack*. Pinnacle Bks. 1984 pap. $3.50. "A practical commonsense guide to help decrease the chances of having cardiovascular disease" (*LJ*).

Kotchen, Theodore A., and Jane M. Kotchen. *Clinical Approaches to High Blood Pressure in the Young*. PSG Pubns. 1983 text ed. $34.00. "Findings from recent laboratory and population studies are incorporated into the existing body of knowledge of childhood hypertension. The focus is on factors that lead to hypertension and on clinical approaches to assessment and treatment" (*Choice*).

Kra, Siegfried. *Coronary Bypass Surgery: Who Needs It?* Norton 1986 $16.95. "Discusses alternatives to surgery that he feels are better, in some cases, than surgery" (*LJ*).

Richardson, Robert G. *The Scalpel and the Heart*. Scribner 1970 o.p. "Includes a historic review of the circulation; operations for the relief of patients with angina pectoris; and the pioneering efforts of Drs. Hufnagel, Harken and Starr in developing the valvular prostheses" (*Amer. Scientist*).

Seymour, Roger J. *Heart Attack Survival Manual: A Guide to Using CPR in a Crisis*. Prentice-Hall 1981 o.p. "Describes the signs of heart attack, as well as how to administer CPR to adults, children, and infants who are victims of electric shock, drowning, smoke inhalation, or heart attack" (*LJ*).

Shaw, Margery W., ed. *After Barney Clark: Reflections on the Utah Artificial Heart Program*. Univ. of Texas Pr. 1984 $22.00. Proceedings of a conference, held October 13 to 15, 1983, in Alta, Utah, sponsored by the University of Utah and the University of Texas Health Science Center at Houston. "Represents papers presented at a conference held to explore the medical, legal, social, and ethical implications of this type of medical treatment with those directly involved and with a group of noted experts in areas related to this issue" (*Choice*).

Sonnenberg, David, and others. *Understanding Pacemakers*. Scribner 1982 pap. $12.95. "Deals simply with cardiac physiology and pacing technology, and addresses many of the problems and anxieties faced by pacemaker patients" (*LJ*).

Sorrentino, Sandy, and Carl Hausman. *Coping with High Blood Pressure*. Dembner Bks. 1986 $16.95. "Stresses personal responsibility for managing high blood pressure. An excellent guide to the medications prescribed for hypertension" (*LJ*).

Walker, Morton, and Garry Gordon. *The Chelation Answer: How to Prevent Hardening of the Arteries and Rejuvenate Your Cardiovascular System*. Fwd. by Robert Atkins, M. Evans 1982 $14.95. "An argument for the value of a controversial treatment (infusion of a man-made amino acid, EDTA, into the body to rid it of calcium and other minerals)" (*LJ*).

Warren, James, and Genell Subak-Sharpe. *Managing Hypertension: The Complete Program Developed by the Cleveland Clinic*. Doubleday 1986 $14.95. "Presents sound advice regarding hypertension therapy, extensive information on diagnosis, nondrug therapy, weight control, stress, and cigarette smoking among other topics" (*LJ*).

———. *Surviving Your Heart Attack: The Duke University Complete Heart Treatment*

Program. [*Frontiers of Medicine Ser.*] Doubleday 1984 $13.95. "A comprehensive discussion of the Duke University Preventive Approach to Cardiology, a program that treats the whole patient and not just the heart condition" (*LJ*).

Wilson, Philip K. *Policies and Procedures of a Cardiac Rehabilitation Program: Immediate to Long-Term Care.* Lea & Febiger 1978 o.p. "Divided into five areas: scientific foundations, organizational procedures, evaluation process, exercise prescription, and future directions" (*Choice*).

Yalof, Ina L. *Open Heart Surgery: A Guidebook for Patients and Families.* Random 1983 $9.95. "Describes the anatomy and actions of the heart and various heart diseases and conditions. Outlines diagnostic tests and exams, basic types of surgery, pre- and post operative care, the recovery and convalescent periods, and possible complications" (*LJ*).

CHILDHOOD DISEASES

This section deals with a few specialized aspects of childhood disorders, including fetal alcohol syndrome, sudden infant death syndrome (SIDS), and the psychosocial impact of birth defects or critical illness on families and children. (See also Chapter 14 in this volume.)

Abel, Ernest L. *Fetal Alcohol Syndrome and Fetal Alcohol Effects.* Plenum 1984 $27.50. "Reviews the vast amount of research that has been published in the past ten years. Describes the relation between alcohol consumption during pregnancy and the health of the newborn infant" (*Choice*).

Bergman, Abraham B. *The "Discovery" of Sudden Infant Death Syndrome: Lessons in the Practice of Political Medicine.* Praeger 1986 $42.95. "SIDS kills approximately 10,000 infants a year. Its cause is still unknown, but suspected causes, such as viruses, have been ruled out. Rarely does a book offer so much insight into human need and into political medicine" (*Choice*).

Colen, B. D. *Born at Risk.* Pocket Bks. 1982 pap. $2.95. "The fictionalized account of sick newborn infants and how their struggle for life affects the parents who hope for their survival and the physicians and nurses who treat them" (*LJ*).

Darling, Rosalyn B. *Families Against Society: A Study of Reactions to Children with Birth Defects.* Sage 1979 o.p. "Explores the attitudes and experiences of parents of children with 'discredited' stigmas, i.e., visible handicaps which impede the integration and acceptance of these children into society" (*LJ*).

Froman, Katherine. *Chance to Grow.* Dodd 1983 $13.95. "Describes a number of children with severely handicapping conditions and varying degrees of successful habilitation" (*LJ*).

Golding, Jean, and others. *Sudden Infant Death: Patterns, Puzzles, and Problems.* Univ. of Washington Pr. 1985 $25.00. "Two British epidemiologists and a research pediatrician sum up clearly what is known in a fascinating and human account, a fine case study in epidemiology and its problems" (*Scientific Amer.*).

Goodman, Richard M., and Robert J. Gorlin. *The Malformed Infant and Child: An Illustrated Guide.* Oxford 1983 text ed. $39.50 pap. $25.95. "Presents 200 malformation syndromes grouped according to fetal environment syndromes, developmental defects, or genetic syndromes. Each syndrome is discussed in terms of clinical features, prenatal diagnosis, differential diagnosis, postnatal basic defects, genetics, prognosis and age-related progress, prevention, and treatment" (*Choice*).

Hilgard, Josephine R. *Hypnotherapy of Pain in Children with Cancer.* Kaufmann 1984

$18.95. "Innovative clinical study of hypnotherapy for children in pain from cancer. Describes limitations and techniques utilized" (*Choice*).

Shanks, Susan J., ed. *Nursing and the Management of Pediatric Communication Disorders.* College-Hill 1983 pap. $29.50. "Concerned with children having speech, language, and hearing disorders. Basic information, definitions, examples, practical approaches and references" (*Choice*).

CHRONIC DISEASES AND LONG-TERM CARE

The psychological, physiological, and practical aspects of providing care for those with chronic or long-term illness is addressed here. Included are books written for health care professionals and general readers.

Burish, Thomas G., and Laurence A. Bradley. *Coping with Chronic Disease: Research and Applications.* Academic Pr. 1983 $49.95. "Covers the general issues in chronic disease care and research. Specific diseases discussed include obesity, epilepsy, spinal cord injuries, cancer, respiratory disorders, heart disease, and stroke" (*Choice*).

Coombs, Jan. *Living with the Disabled: You Can Help—A Family Guide.* Sterling 1984 o.p. "Includes selection of medical and rehabilitation care, finances, accepting a disability, dealing with stress, and adaption of the environment" (*LJ*).

Covell, Mara B., and Eileen Hanley. *The Home Alternative to Hospitals and Nursing Homes: Creating Your Own Home Health Care Center.* Rawson 1983 $15.95. "A thoughtful, compassionate, and detailed treatment of home health care, this runs the gamut from how to set up an appropriate health care environment for different age groups to dealing with a wide variety of health problems" (*LJ*).

Friedman, Jo Ann. *Home Health Care: A Guide for Patients and Their Families.* Fwd. by Jane E. Brody, Fawcett 1987 pap. $12.95; Norton 1986 $22.50. "Complete and readable handbook for anyone involved in, planning for, or contemplating home care. Succinct yet inclusive information of the practical and psychological aspects, specific advice on disease and type of care needed, daily living tips and insurances and equipment guidelines" (*LJ*).

Gohlke, Mary. *I'll Take Tomorrow: The Story of a Courageous Woman Who Dared to Subject Herself to a Medical Experiment; The First Successful Heart-Lung Transplant.* Ed. by Maureen Heffernen, M. Evans 1985 $12.95. "Although typical of inspirational success stories, realistically recounts the pain and psychological pressure of chronic disease as well as the consequences of transplantation for the human body" (*LJ*).

Hastings, Diana. *A Complete Guide to Home Nursing.* Ed. by Helen L. Maule, Barron 1986 text ed. $14.95. "Basic nursing observation techniques and procedures such as lifting the patient, taking vitals, changing bedclothes, and giving bed baths" (*LJ*).

Holzman, Arnold D., ed. *Pain Management: A Handbook of Psychological Treatment Approaches.* Pergamon 1986 $38.50. "A review of contemporary psychological approaches to treating pain. Presents the state of the art in regard to theory, treatment rationale, and data" (*Choice*).

Kerson, Toba S., and Lawrence A. Kerson. *Understanding Chronic Illness: The Medical and Psychosocial Dimensions of Nine Diseases.* Free Pr. 1985 $24.95. "Discusses financial and other sources of assistance for the chronically ill, describes the medical, social, and psychological aspects of cancer, dementia, diabetes, epilepsy, heart diseases, respiratory diseases, stroke and substance abuse" (*Choice*).

Locker, David. *Disability and Disadvantage: The Consequences of Chronic Illness.* Methuen 1984 pap. $15.95. "Presents data obtained from interviews with 24 persons severely disabled by rheumatoid arthritis in Great Britain" (*Choice*).

Milunsky, Aubrey, ed. *Coping with Crisis and Handicap.* Plenum 1981 $32.50. "Vivid and cogent writing about the coping efforts of children and families faced with serious crisis, death, and/or handicap; the impact on professionals working with them; and the rich range of creative helping approaches and strategies" (*Choice*).

Murphy, Lois B. *The Home Hospital: How the Family Can Cope with Catastrophic Illness.* Basic Bks. 1982 o.p. Drawing on her own experience in caring for her severely ill husband, Lois Murphy tells how to decide to care for a loved one at home. Practical suggestions on how to arrange a room, where to find equipment, and how to mobilize help from professionals.

Nassif, Janet Z. *The Home Health Care Solution: A Complete Consumer Guide.* Harper 1985 $17.45. "A thorough handbook for anyone looking for home care services, resources, alternatives, equipment, personnel, financial advice, and all the nitty-gritty practical aspects of arranging for someone's care" (*LJ*).

Slaby, Andrew Edmund, and Arvin Sigmund Glicksman. *Adapting to Life-Threatening Illness.* Praeger 1985 $29.95. "Demonstrates how biological, psychological, and social factors combine to create certain styles of adaptation in three life-threatening conditions: cancer, heart attack, and trauma" (*Choice*).

Steinberg, Franz U. *The Immobilized Patient.* Plenum 1980 $32.50 "A concise and well-written review of the effects of immobilization in patient care. Provides chapters on the general effects of immobilization, as well as specific effects related to circulation, respiration, bone, skeletal muscles, joints, skin, and psychological health" (*Choice*).

Tallmer, Margot, ed. *Sexuality and Life-Threatening Illness.* C. C. Thomas 1984 $27.25. "A thought-provoking discussion of the sexual needs of individuals who have been disabled, have a debilitating illness or are dying" (*Choice*).

Webster, John G., and Gregg C. Vanderheiden. *Electronic Devices for Rehabilitation.* Wiley 1985 $46.00. "A comprehensive and authoritative treatment of the design and application of electronic devices currently used in rehabilitation" (*Choice*).

COMMUNICABLE DISEASES

[SEE the section on Infectious Diseases in this chapter.]

COSMETIC SURGERY

[SEE the section on Plastic Surgery in this chapter.]

DEAFNESS

[SEE the section on Ear and Throat Disorders in this chapter.]

DEATH AND DYING

The majority of titles in this section examine the philosophy and evolution of the hospice concept of care in the United States. The question of euthanasia is also discussed. (See also Chapter 20 in this volume.)

Buckingham, Robert W. *The Complete Hospice Guide.* Harper 1983 $13.45. Covers the history and philosophy, types of care, and costs. Stresses hospice as a system of support.

Corr, Charles A., and Donna M. Corr, eds. *Hospice Care: Principles and Practice.* [*Death and Suicide Ser.*] Springer Pub. 1983 text ed. $26.95. "A comprehensive collection of 26 essays regarding the hospice concept of care. An excellent resource with extensive bibliographic references" (*Choice*).

Dubois, Paul. *The Hospice Way of Death.* Human Sciences Pr. 1980 $26.95. Case studies of three hospices—two successful and one unsuccessful. Good description of the state of the hospice movement in the late 1970s.

Hamilton, Michael P. *A Hospice Handbook.* Intro. by Edward M. Kennedy, Eerdmans 1980 pap. $7.95. An excellent resource, especially for planners of hospice care within the community. Includes a review of what hospice care is and is not, the patient and his or her family, and the care-team share in decision making as equals.

Humphry, Derek, and Ann Wickett. *The Right to Die: Understanding Euthanasia.* Harper 1987 pap. $8.95. "Co-founders of the Hemlock Society in Los Angeles argue for the right of terminally ill people to be delivered from their condition. May help to sway public opinion on an emotional level, but is of limited value as a philosophical and moral approach" (*N.Y. Times Bk. Review*).

Kohut, Jeraldine M., and Sylvester Kohut, Jr. *Hospice: Caring for the Terminally Ill.* C. C. Thomas 1984 $27.25. "Topics discussed include: hospice care models; attitudes toward death and dying; the actual development of a community-based program; staff training to include volunteers; community support systems; case studies of individuals and families; and ethical and legal issues" (*Choice*).

Kübler-Ross, Elisabeth. *Living with Death and Dying.* Macmillan 1981 $10.95 pap. $5.95. "Advocates open expression of feelings about death—denial, anger, fear and guilt—as an important step in achieving acceptance" (*PW*).

——, ed. *Death: The Final Stage of Growth.* [*Human Development Ser.*] Prentice-Hall 1975 pap. $3.95; Simon & Schuster 1986 pap. $6.95. Essays by various contributors on the philosophic, religious, and sociological approaches to death. A landmark work.

Kübler-Ross, Elisabeth, and M. Warshaw. *To Live Until We Say Good-Bye.* Prentice-Hall 1978 $12.95 pap. $5.95. A beautiful and moving book. Splendid photography and sensitive text portray how Beth, Jamie, Louise, and Jack cope with terminal illness.

Kutscher, Austin, and Margot Tallmer, eds. *Hospice U.S.A.* Columbia Univ. Pr. 1983 o.p. "A joint effort of 45 authorities who have had various experiences in establishing hospice alternatives. Topics include the hospice movement; ethical and human issues; helping the dying; alternatives to in-hospice care; and a look to the future" (*Choice*).

Mannon, James M. *Caring for the Burned: Life and Death in a Hospital Burn Center.* C. C. Thomas 1985 $31.75. "Provides a rich description and analysis of the setting and of burn patients and their families as well as such issues as pain, work among the burned, patient compliance, the dying patient, recovery and improving the care of the burned" (*Choice*).

Mumley, Annie. *The Hospice Alternative: A New Context for Death and Dying.* Basic Bks. 1983 $17.50. "A well-organized and comprehensive report on the hospice concept of care and support for the dying" (*LJ*).

Wentzel, Kenneth B. *To Those Who Need It Most, Hospice Means Hope.* Charles River Bks. 1981 $9.95 pap. $5.95. Excellent explanation of hospice philosophy and practice.

DIABETES

[SEE the section on Endocrine Diseases in this chapter.]

DIET

[SEE the section on Nutritional Disorders in this chapter and see also Chapter 14 in this volume.]

EAR AND THROAT DISORDERS

This list provides information on anatomy, physiology, treatment, and preventive measures as well as social and psychological aspects of speech and hearing problems.

Benderly, Beryl L. *Dancing Without Music: Deafness in America.* Doubleday 1980 $15.95. "Covers deafness as a social role, but adds discussions of language acquisition and learning by deaf people, the adventitiously deaf, and mainstreaming, and gives a detailed history of attitudes towards the deaf" (*LJ*).

Boothroyd, Arthur. *Hearing Impairments in Young Children.* Prentice-Hall 1982 $28.95. "Deals with the nature of hearing impairments, consequences of hearing loss, normal and abnormal communication development, intervention, and management techniques" (*Choice*).

Evered, David, and Geralyn Lawrenson. *Tinnitus.* CIBA Foundation, dist. by Wiley 1981 $49.95. Discusses "definitions and classification, epidemiology, matching and masking tests for the nature of tinnitus (its pitch, loudness, bandwidth), neurophysiological studies in cats and in human beings, personality correlates, causative drugs, surgical therapy, therapy by masking sources of noise and finally the condition as it stands in courts of law" (*Scientific Amer.*).

Freese, Arthur S. *You and Your Hearing: How to Protect It, Preserve It, and Restore It.* Scribner 1980 $3.95. "Describes the hearing process and the complex physiological system which makes it possible; causes, cures and preventive measures for some of the most common forms of hearing loss" (*LJ*).

Higgins, Paul C. *Outsiders in a Hearing World: A Sociology of Deafness.* Sage 1980 $28.00 pap. $14.00. "Discusses the identity deviance, and stigma associated with members of the deaf community. A major work concerning the sociological aspects of deaf individuals living in a deaf community interacting with a hearing world" (*Choice*).

Lane, Harlan. *When the Mind Hears: A History of the Deaf.* Random 1984 $24.95. "Traces the controversy which developed between advocates of signing and advocates of oral speech, and takes the position that the signing community constitutes a linguistic minority. This book reveals ways in which the deaf have been denied their rights to bear children, to educate themselves, to support themselves" (*LJ*).

Martin, Frederick N., ed. *Medical Audiology: Disorders of Hearing*. Prentice-Hall text ed. 1981 $57.33. "Four basic areas (outer ear, inner ear, and auditory nerve and central pathways) are each subdivided into five sections: auditory anatomy and physiology, prenatal development, etiology and pathology, audiological evaluation and management, and otological diagnosis and treatment" (*Choice*).

Rezen, Susan V. *Coping with Hearing Loss: A Guide for Adults and Their Families*. Fwd. by Kennan Wynn, Dembner Bks. 1985 pap. $15.95. "A good balance between the social, psychological, physical, and practical aspects of hearing loss" (*LJ*).

Schubert, E. D. *Hearing: Its Function and Dysfunction*. Springer-Verlag 1980 $31.50. "Concerns normal and abnormal aspects of hearing. Covers anatomy and physiology of the auditory system, psychoacoustics, and hearing loss" (*Choice*).

Sommers, Ronald K. *Articulation Disorders*. Prentice-Hall 1983 $32.67. "A succinct and complete discussion of articulation disorders and related issues. Presents a framework for understanding and treating aberrant articulatory behavior in children and adults" (*Choice*).

EMERGENCY MEDICINE

Books in this section provide information on how to distinguish whether or not injured or acutely ill patients may or may not need immediate medical treatment; basic first aid, and the organization and management of emergency medical services.

American Medical Association. *The American Medical Association's Handbook of First Aid and Emergency Care*. Random 1980 o.p. Authoritative advice on numerous common emergency medical situations: describes how to distinguish between true emergencies and problems which are alarming to the victim but do not require immediate emergency help, and when and how to call the doctor, emergency room, and ambulance.

American Red Cross. *Standard First Aid and Personal Safety*. Doubleday 2d ed. 1980 o.p. Offers concise and positive directions on wounds and severe bleeding; treating specific injuries, such as head injuries; managing choking, shock, and poisoning. Also covers bandages and dressing and emergency rescue.

Auerbach, Paul S. *Medicine for the Outdoors: A Guide to Emergency Medical Procedures and First Aid for Wilderness Travelers*. Little, Brown 1986 $24.95 pap. $12.95. Concise explanations of a whole range of medical problems. General information precedes sections on the procedures of specific situations.

Carey, Katherine, and Alice Perkins, eds. *Shock*. Springhouse 1984 text ed. $13.95. "Covers pathophysiology; major types of shock: hypovolemic, cardiogenic, and vasogenic, and common complications; adult respiratory distress syndrome; disseminated intravascular coagulation; and renal failure" (*Choice*).

Franklin, Jon, and Alan Doelp. *Shock-Trauma*. St. Martin's 1980 o.p. "Chronicles the establishment of the Maryland Institute of Emergency Services and the obstacles, both political and financial, that threatened it" (*LJ*).

Heimlich, Henry J., and Lawrence Galton. *Dr. Heimlich's Guide to Emergency Medical Situations*. Simon & Schuster 1980 $10.95. Heimlich, the inventor of the Heimlich Maneuver, provides information on more than 250 emergency situa tions. Describes how to recognize what is wrong, how to cope, and when to seek medical help.

Lefevre, M. J., ed. *First Aid Manual for Chemical Accidents: For Use with Nonpharmaceutical Chemicals*. Trans. by Ernest I. Becker, Van Nostrand 1980 pap. $23.95. "A ready reference for emergency treatment of chemical accidents. The procedures given are based on those developed by recognized authorities and a major chemical producer" (*Choice*).

Newkirk, William, and William Linden. *Managing in the Emergency Medical Services: Principles and Practice*. Reston 1984 text ed. $22.95. "Divided into five sections: techniques for management by objectives, project evaluation and review; organization of personnel and finances; effective communication, negotiating, delegation, and handling of change; quality control; and survival as an EMS manager in terms of coping with stress" (*Choice*).

Waller, Julian A. *Injury Control: A Guide to the Causes and Prevention of Trauma*. Lexington Bks. 1984 $59.00. "Presents an overview of concepts, methods, and problems of injury control and discusses models for analyzing injury events, contributing factors, and guidelines for evaluating countermeasures" (*Choice*).

Wilkerson, James A., and others. *Hypothermia, Frostbite and Other Cold Injuries: Prevention, Recognition, and Pre-Hospital Treatment*. Mountaineers 1986 pap. $8.95. "Written for outdoor enthusiasts and attendant emergency medical personnel. Explains the stages of physiological deterioration of the human body as its core temperature decreases. Discusses recognizing hypothermia and procedures for rewarming" (*LJ*).

Williams, Susan, and Barbara McVan, eds. *Giving Emergency Care Competently*. Springhouse 2d ed. 1983 text ed. $13.95. "Deals with all types of emergency situations from triage to cardiovascular, neuro, respiratory, and psychiatric emergencies" (*Choice*).

ENDOCRINE DISEASES

Endocrine diseases are diseases that occur as a result of the abnormal functioning of the endocrine glands (for example, thyroid, pituitary, pancreas). The majority of books about endocrine diseases are written by and for health care professionals. However, numerous books for the general reader on diabetes, a condition caused by a malfunction of the pancreas, have been published. A representative selection of these titles are described here.

Addanki, Sam, and S. V. Cherukuri. *Diabetes Breakthrough: Control Through Nutrition*. Pinnacle Bks. 1982 pap. $2.95. "A reiteration of the well-known fact that many over-weight diabetics would be able to produce enough insulin to meet their body's needs if they reduced to a normal weight" (*LJ*).

Anderson, James W. *Diabetes: A Practical New Guide to Healthy Living*. Arco 1982 $12.95 pap. $7.95; Warner Bks. 1983 pap. $3.50. "A comprehensive guide to the treatment of diabetes through the High Carbohydrate High Fiber diet. Also discusses insulin, obesity, and complications of diabetes" (*LJ*).

Bayliss, R. I. S. *Thyroid Disease: The Facts*. Oxford 1982 $12.95. Describes the working of the thyroid gland, how it manufactures hormones, and the complex interaction of the thyroid and pituitary gland. Discusses diagnosis, treatment, and prognosis for thyroid disorders such as hyperthyroidism, Hashimoto's (autoimmune) thyroiditis, goiter, hypothyroidism, and cancer of the thyroid gland.

Bliss, Michael. *The Discovery of Insulin.* Univ. of Chicago Pr. 1982 lib. bdg. $25.00 1984 pap. $10.95. "Re-creates the complex and dramatic series of events at the University of Toronto in 1921–22. Describes the treatment of diabetes before insulin and the research of earlier scientists and concludes by outlining the treatment of diabetes with insulin and the current production of human insulin through the development of genetic engineering" (*LJ*).

Diabetes Education Center. *Diabetes: The Comprehensive Self-Management Handbook.* Ed. by John R. Aloia, Doubleday 1984 $19.95. "A reference text for people who have diabetes: self-testing, control of insulin, meal preparation, exercise . . . everyone can learn a great deal from it in the general areas of nutrition, weight control, stress, food labeling, how the body works and more" (*LJ*).

Edelwich, Jerry, and Archie Brodsky. *Diabetes: Caring for Your Emotions as Well as Your Health.* Addison-Wesley 1987 $17.95 pap. $10.95. "Covered extensively are diet, exercise, work, medications, sexuality, and new technology. Emphasis is on changes in life-style and family relations resulting from the disease" (*LJ*).

Hamilton, Helen, and Minnie B. Rose, eds. *Endocrine Disorders.* Springhouse 1984 text ed. $19.95. "Reviews the anatomy and physiology of the endocrine system and the pathophysiology of endocrine imbalance; nursing assessment and guidelines for developing a nursing diagnosis; diagnostic tests; and specific disorders" (*Choice*).

Subak-Sharpe, Genell. *Living with Diabetes: The Revolutionary Self-Care Diabetes Program Developed by Rockefeller and Cornell University Researchers.* Doubleday 1985 $16.95. "Intended to provide a better understanding of the disease and the manner in which the treatment can be adjusted to fit one's lifestyle" (*LJ*).

Wood, Lawrence C., and Chester E. Ridgway. *Your Thyroid: A Home Reference Guide.* Houghton Mifflin 1982 o.p. "Devotes individual chapters to such problems as goiter, disorders associated with hyper- and hypothyroidism, thyroid cancer in adults and children, and the effects of drugs, food, stress, and radiation on the thyroid" (*LJ*).

EPIDEMIOLOGY

Epidemiology is a field of medicine concerned with the determination of causes, frequency, and characteristic behavior of diseases affecting human populations; also the interrelationships of host, agent, and environment as related to the distribution and control of disease. (See also Chapter 14 in this volume.)

Basu, R. N., Z. Jezek, and N. A. Ward. *The Eradication of Smallpox from India.* World Health 1979 $18.00. "In 1966 war was declared on smallpox by India. Three veterans of the National Smallpox Eradication Programme here record the success verified on April 23, 1977, when an international commission declared India free of smallpox" (*Scientific Amer.*).

Brilliant, Lawrence B. *The Management of Smallpox Eradication in India.* Univ. of Michigan Pr. 1985 text ed. $18.50. "Using a case study approach, the author documents the chronology of smallpox eradication in India, analyzes aspects of program management, and summarizes management lessons learned from this program." (*Choice*).

Cipolla, Carlo M. *Cristofano and the Plague: A Study in the History of Public Health in the Age of Galileo.* Univ. of California Pr. 1973 o.p. "Information from Tuscan archives enabled the author to analyze the demographic and economic consequences of the epidemic of plague which ravaged northern Italy around 1630. He speculates that all the epidemics of plague which occurred during the entire period 1613–66 belonged to one single pandemic cycle which swept across the subcontinent [and] concludes that besides medical ignorance and the absence of cooperation from the mass of the people, the lack of adequate economic resources was perhaps the most important factor in frustrating the work of the public health officers" (*Amer. Scientist*).

Culyer, A. J., ed. *Health Indicators: An International Study for the European Science Foundation.* St. Martin's 1983 $32.50. Papers from three workshops held at the University of York from 1979 to 1981, established by the British Social Science Research Council. "An attempt to find more subtle ways of measuring health than by death or obvious disability, so that such measures can be used affirmatively for the health of the nation" (*Choice*).

Goodfield, June. *Quest for the Killers.* Birkhauser 1985 $24.95; Farrar 1987 pap. $8.95. "Links medical progress over epidemic disease with social philosophy. Brings a sense of personal immediacy to the story of the triumphs over smallpox, leprosy and schistosomiasis" (*LJ*).

Greenberg, Michael R. *Urbanization and Cancer Mortality: The United States Experience, 1950–1975.* Oxford 1983 $45.00. "Analyzing cancer mortality data by age, race, and sex for each of the five-year periods extending from 1950 to 1975, this book provides information showing that whereas 25 years ago central U.S. cities had much higher rates of many types of cancer than the rest of the country, the difference between urban and rural areas has diminished considerably over the period examined" (*Choice*).

Gruenberg, Ernest M., and others, eds. *Vaccinating Against Brain Dysfunction Syndromes: The Campaign Against Measles and Rubella.* Oxford 1986 $29.95. "Thirty well-recognized authorities in the fields of epidemiology, public health, immunology, bacteriology, pediatrics and psychiatry tell the success story of the near eradication of rubella and measles in the U.S." (*Choice*).

Rothschild, Henry R., ed. *Biocultural Aspects of Disease.* Academic Pr. 1981 $83.00. "Excellent reviews of how prevalent worldwide diseases, such as malaria, trypanosomiasis, leishmaniasis, schistosomiasis, amebiasis, cholera, diarrhea, and thalassemia (to name only a few), interact with the culture, habitat, and genotypes of people around the globe. . . . Chapters on disease susceptibility, prevalence of disease, rare hereditary diseases, cultural beliefs associated with disease and health care, and social impacts of diseases" (*Choice*).

Rouechè, Berton. *The Medical Detectives.* Dutton vol. 2 1984 $22.50; Times Bks. vol. 1 1980 $15.00; Washington Square Pr. vol. 2 1982 pap. $4.95. The 45 essays in these collections originally appeared in *The New Yorker* between 1947 and 1984. The detectives of these tales are epidemiologists, public health officers, hospital staff members, and family doctors. The case histories range from the tragic (organic mercury in a hog farmer's family) to the whimsical (the man who turned orange from eating too many carrots and tomatoes) and involve strange illnesses, rare diseases, and the threat of plague.

Tartakow, I. Jackson, and John H. Vorperian. *Foodborne and Waterborne Diseases: Their Epidemiological Characteristics.* AVI 1981 pap. $35.00. "Specific disease entities are well discussed. . . . Outlines and discusses specific techniques of epidemiology, epidemic investigation, and preventive measures" (*Choice*).

Thomas, Gordon, and Max Morgan-Witts. *Anatomy of an Epidemic.* Doubleday 1982 o.p. "Effectively interweaves the tragic human story of some of the victims of the epidemic of Legionnaire's Disease that occurred in the summer of 1976 in Pennsylvania, with the hard work and good science that eventually solved the mystery" (*LJ*).

Vogt, Thomas M. *Making Health Decisions: An Epidemiologic Perspective on Staying Well.* Nelson-Hall 1983 $22.95. "Readable, entertaining, and thoughtful examination of personal health decisions based on a careful review of epidemiological data. Begins with a brief and entertaining survey of what epidemiology has done, and can(cannot) do" (*Choice*).

EYE DISORDERS

Most monographs on eye disorders are written for a professional audience, therefore the limited number of entries in this section.

Dobree, John H., and Eric Boulter. *Blindness and Visual Handicap: The Facts.* Oxford 1982 $13.95. "Deals primarily with diseases causing blindness, the effects of blindness and how the blind and partially sighted can be helped. Relates primarily to practices and programming in England, with a few international components" (*Choice*).

Hutchinson, R. Anthony. *Computer Eye-Stress: How to Avoid It, How to Alleviate It.* M. Evans 1985 pap. $4.95. "A purely elementary look at VDTs and the problems that can result from frequent use" (*LJ*).

Kelman, Charles D. *Cataracts: What You Must Know About Them.* Crown 1982 $12.95; G. K. Hall 1983 $11.95. "Lucid descriptions of surgical techniques. What to expect after surgery and methods for achieving visual correction after surgery" (*LJ*).

Rosenbloom, Alfred A., and Meredith Morgan. *Vision and Aging: General and Clinical Perspectives.* Prof. Pr. Bks. NYC 1986 $60.00. "A comprehensive treatment of the relationship between aging and vision changes. Explores the assessment and correction of visual problems in the elderly, also looks at the psychosocial environment as it pertains to visual function" (*Choice*).

Shulman, Julius. *Cataracts: The Complete Guide from Diagnosis to Recovery for Patients and Families.* Amer. Assn. of Retired Persons 1985 pap. $7.95; Simon & Schuster 1984 $16.95. "Reviews the fundamentals of cataracts, the parts of the eye and probable causes of cataracts. Details cataract surgery, with an in-depth discussion of the three major types: intracapsular, extracapsular, and phaecoemulsification" (*LJ*).

FIRST AID

[SEE the section on Emergency Medicine in this chapter.]

GASTROINTESTINAL DISEASES

Most materials on diseases of the digestive system are written for professionals who provide patient care, therefore the limited focus of entries here.

Ehrlich, David, and George Wolf. *The Bowel Book: A Practical Guide to Good Health.* Intro. by Peter Albright, Schocken 1981 $12.95 pap. $6.95. "Addresses such subject areas as the way the gastrointestinal system works, the effects of emotion on it, methods of improving bowel function, and bowel disorders" (*LJ*).

Jeter, Katherine. *These Special Children: The Ostomy Book for Parents of Children with Colostomies, Ileostomies, and Urostomies.* Bull 1982 $19.95 pap. $13.95. Excellent, insightful text.

Mullen, Barbara D., and Kerry A. McGinn. *The Ostomy Book: Living Comfortably with Colostomies, Ileostomies, and Urostomies.* Bull 1980 pap. $9.95. "A wealth of information concerning the psychological as well as medical aspects of ostomy surgery, care of the body after the procedure, equipment, diet and exercise" (*LJ*).

Mylander, Maureen. *The Great American Stomach Book.* Fwd. by Howard Spiro, Ticknor & Fields 1982 o.p. "Explores the range of digestive diseases from such common problems as indigestion and hiccups to such serious afflictions as hepatitis and gastrointestinal cancer" (*LJ*).

National Foundation for Ileitis and Colitis. *The Crohn's Disease and Ulcerative Colitis Fact Book.* Ed. by Penny Steiner, Scribner 1983 $15.95. "Traces the causes, symptoms and diagnosis of the diseases, discusses the various treatment options from medication to surgery and concludes with advice on coping with the illnesses" (*LJ*).

Phillips, Robert. *Coping with an Ostomy: A Guide to Living with an Ostomy.* Avery 1985 pap. $8.95. "Explains ostomy surgery and care of the ostomy. Greatest value lies in its coverage of the emotional and life-style changes caused by an ostomy" (*LJ*).

Plaut, Martin E. *The Doctors' Guide to You and Your Colon: A Candid, Helpful Guide to Our Number One Hidden Health Complaint.* Harper 1982 o.p. "In this highly readable guide, Plaut explains how the bowel works, the process of digestion, and how stool is formed" (*LJ*).

HEARING DISORDERS

[SEE the section on Ear and Throat Disorders in this chapter.]

HEART DISEASES

[SEE the section on Cardiovascular Diseases in this chapter.]

HEMATOLOGIC DISEASES

Hematologic diseases are diseases of the blood and blood-forming tissues. Most books on diseases affecting the blood are very technical, therefore the paucity of entries.

Callender, Sheila T. *Blood Disorders: The Facts.* Oxford 1986 $13.95. "Discusses the various blood abnormalities and disorders resulting from variances in normal function; disease mechanisms, diagnosis, relevant blood tests, and the rationale behind the treatment" (*Choice*).

Johnson, Mohamed Ismail. *The World and the Sickle-Cell Gene: A Study in Health Education.* Trado-Medic 1984 $15.95 text ed. pap. $7.50. "Brings together essential information related to sickle-cell disease. Covers the relationship of sickle-

cell disease and malaria, the inheritance process and geographic distribution of
the disease, personal and community health and education problems associated
with sickle-cell disease, and diagnostic and management approaches" (*Choice*).

IMMUNOLOGY

Immunology is the study of the response of the body's immune system to
pathogenic (disease causing) organisms and other foreign bodies. The immune system recognizes self from nonself. It is the immune system that must
be suppressed if a transplanted organ (kidney, heart, or lung) is to be accepted by the body. Immunization is the process by which we are rendered
immune to disease (for example, whooping cough, diphtheria, tetanus) by
injection of a killed culture of a specific microbe. Allergies are an acquired
sensitivity in susceptible persons to allergens (for example, a specific drug,
chemical, pollen, and so on). Asthma is a condition in which there is widespread narrowing of the airways in the lungs in the course of an allergic
reaction. The first half of this section deals mainly with allergies and asthma.
The second half, which is devoted to Acquired Immune Deficiency Syndrome
(AIDS), is by no means a comprehensive list as new facts and discoveries
appear so frequently that any compilation is quickly out-of-date.

Berland, Theodore, and Lucia Fischer-Pap. *Living with Your Allergies and Asthma.* St.
  Martin's 1983 $5.95. "Meant to help the allergy sufferer understand the afflic-
  tion and be able to find solutions and proper methods of treatment" (*LJ*).
Davis, Calvin Lewis. *Insects, Allergy and Disease: Allergic and Toxic Responses to
  Arthropods.* Davis 1979 o.p. "Well written and beautifully illustrated; useful
  background information" (*Choice*).
Faelton, Sharon. *The Allergy Self-Help Book: A Complete Guide to Detection and Natural Treatment of Allergies.* Rodale 1983 $19.95. "An exhaustive treatment of the
  controversial subject of allergy identification and treatment" (*LJ*).
Frazier, Claude A. *Coping with Food Allergy: Symptoms and Treatment.* Intro. by
  Charles A. Hoffman, Times Bks. rev. ed. 1985 pap. $8.95. "Includes the RAST
  test; new medications such as cromolyn sodium; allergies to the food preserva-
  tives and additives BHA, BHT, MSG and sulfites; and the efforts to get all food
  ingredients labeled" (*LJ*).
Levin, Alan Scott, and Merla Zellerbach. *The Type 1/Type 2 Allergy Relief Program.*
  Berkley Pub. 1985 pap. $3.50; Tarcher 1984 pap. $6.95. "Defines each type,
  explains the symptoms, allergens, and treatment, and presents case histories"
  (*LJ*).
Reisman, Barry. *Jared's Story: A Boy in a Bubble and How His Family Saved His Life.*
  Crown 1984 $10.95. "About a baby who after 18 months of normal behavior
  became incapacitated by a mysterious ailment" (*LJ*).
Stevens, Laura J. *The Complete Book of Allergy Control.* Macmillan 1983 $14.95;
  Pocket Bks. 1986 pap. $4.95. "Informs sufferers of the environmental causes of
  allergies, helps them identify allergens, and teaches them how to manage these
  problems" (*LJ*).
Young, Stuart H. *The Asthma Handbook: A Complete Guide for Patients and Their
  Families.* Bantam 1985 o.p. "An excellent guide which covers environmental and

dietary factors that contribute to the disease, drug and physical therapies and the role of stress in attacks" (*LJ*).

AIDS

Baker, Janet. *A.I.D.S.: Everything You Must Know About Acquired Immune Deficiency Syndrome—The Killer Epidemic of the 80's*. R & E Pubs. 1983 pap. $7.95. "Briefly reviews the current situation on causes, symptoms, treatment, and prevention of AIDS. Much of the text consists of quotations" (*LJ*).

Baumgartner, Gail H. *AIDS: Psychosocial Factors in the Acquired Immune Deficiency Syndrome*. C. C. Thomas 1985 $20.50. "A brief three-chapter monograph which includes case studies of two AIDS patients, brief vignettes of psychosocial factors and AIDS, and a brief conclusion reviewing the research problem" (*Choice*).

Cahill, Kevin, ed. *The AIDS Epidemic*. St. Martin's 1983 o.p. A collection of papers delivered at a medical meeting in New York in April 1983. Covers a wide range of topics, including immunology, epidemiology, and infectious disease control.

Cantwell, Alan, Jr. *AIDS: The Mystery and the Solution*. Ed. by Jim Highland, Aries Rising Pr. 2d ed. rev. 1986 $14.95 pap. $9.95; Trado-Medic Bks. 1984 $14.50. "One more example of the effort to explain AIDS. Asks some fundamental questions about the assumptions used by the medical and scientific community in evaluating the nature and cause of the illness" (*Choice*).

Corless, Inge, and Mary Pittman-Lindeman. *AIDS: Principles, Practices, and Politics*. Hemisphere 1987 $19.95. A collection of essays, including one by Surgeon General C. Everett Koop, on many aspects of AIDS, such as education, alternatives to hospital care, and legal considerations.

Fettner, Ann Giudici, and William A. Check. *The Truth about AIDS: Evolution of an Epidemic*. Holt 1985 pap. $8.95. A medical detective story narrating the discovery, by physicians from the Centers for Disease Control and other leading medical centers, of AIDS or Acquired Immune Deficiency Syndrome.

Fromer, Margot Joan. *AIDS: Acquired Immune Deficiency Syndrome*. Pinnacle Bks. 1983 pap. $3.95. "A straightforward account of what is generally known and hypothesized about AIDS" (*LJ*).

Gong, Victor, and Norman Rudnick, eds. *AIDS: Facts and Issues*. Rutgers Univ. Pr. 1986 text ed. $25.00 pap. $10.95. "Twenty-five essays, contributed by experts in the fields of health care, social welfare, education, and law, provide current information about AIDS" (*LJ*).

Jacobs, George, and Joseph Kerrins. *The AIDS File*. Cromlech Bks. 1987 pap. $7.95. Focuses on techniques for prevention of AIDS transmission and provides answers to frequently asked questions about AIDS.

Martelli, Leonard, and others. *When Someone You Know Has AIDS: A Practical Guide*. Crown 1987 $15.95 pap. $9.95. A useful and substantive guide to providing assistance to AIDS patients, including sections on insurance, health maintenance, wills, and grieving.

Miller, David, and John Green, eds. *The Management of AIDS Patients*. Sheridan 1986 text ed. $45.00. "A British publication with 11 senior hospital staff contributing information regarding AIDS patients" (*Choice*).

Shilts, Randy. *And the Band Played On: Politics, People and the AIDS Epidemic*. St. Martin's 1987 $19.95. Written in very accessible terms, this is the most comprehensive chronicle of the AIDS epidemic since the disease was first diagnosed in 1981. Scientific but disjointed chronologies trace the clinical and epidemiologi-

cal story of AIDS, scientific research, and the impact of the disease on both
individuals and society at large.

Siegal, Frederick P., and Marta Siegal. *AIDS: The Medical Mystery.* Grove 1983
$19.50 pap. $7.95. "Provides an authoritative description of the disease, its physical manifestations, social dilemmas, possible causes, available but as yet unsuccessful forms of therapy" (*Choice*).

INFECTIOUS DISEASES

Infectious diseases are due to organisms ranging in size from viruses to
parasitic worms. They may be contagious in origin, result from nosocomial
infection (that is, hospital-acquired infection) or they may be due to endoge-
nous microflora (normal bacteria residing in the body) from the nose and
throat, skin, or bowel. Communicable diseases are diseases transmitted
from one human to another or from an animal or insect to a human either
directly or indirectly. Below are works on the history, epidemiology, treatment, and prevention of infectious and communicable diseases.

Balfour, Henry H., Jr., and Ralph C. Heussner. *Herpes Diseases and Your Health.*
Univ. of Minnesota Pr. 1984 $14.95 1985 pap. $8.95. "Describes the transmission, clinical course, treatment and after effects of genital herpes, chicken pox,
shingles, mononucleosis, and cytomegalovirus infection" (*LJ*).

Baxby, Derrick. *Jenner's Smallpox Vaccine: The Riddle of Vaccinia Virus and Its Origin.* Fwd. by Frank Fenner, Heinemann 1981 $25.00. "A fascinating account of
the many confusing aspects of the control of smallpox. Includes some of the
history of smallpox, cowpox (both true and spurious), and horsepox. Deals with
inoculation, variation, and vaccination" (*LJ*).

Beveridge, W. I. *Influenza, the Last Great Plague: An Unfinished Story of Discovery.*
Watson Pub. Intl. 2d ed. 1977 $12.50. "Develops the reasons why influenza
differs from other major worldwide infectious diseases. Notes how evidence has
gradually shown the mechanism by which major waves of infection spread
across the countries of the world" (*Choice*).

Brandt, Allan M. *"No Magic Bullet": A Social History of Venereal Disease in the United
States Since 1880.* Oxford 1985 $19.95. "More a study of social attitudes and
medicine than a social history, this book shows how attitudes affect attempts to
control disease" (*LJ*).

Brettle, R. P., and M. Thomson. *Infection and Communicable Diseases.* Heyden 1984
pap. $12.00. "Gives up-to-date accounts of management and control including
specific therapy and nursing care involved with the common bacterial and viral
infections as well as rarer conditions such as those acquired by travellers"
(*Choice*).

Chase, Allan. *Magic Shots: A Human and Scientific Account of the Long and Continuing Struggle to Eradicate Infectious Diseases by Vaccination.* Intro. by D. A. Henderson, Morrow 1982 $19.95. "Descriptions include the work of Jenner on small-
pox, Pasteur on rabies, Theiler on yellow fever" (*LJ*).

———. *The Truth about STD: The Old Ones—Herpes and Other New Ones—The Primary Causes—The Available Cures.* Morrow 1983 $11.95 pap. $5.70. "An overview
of the sexually transmitted disease problem in the U.S. today. Of particular
interest is the historic perspective on the sexually transmitted disease problem"
(*Choice*).

Croll, Neil A., and John H. Cross, eds. *Human Ecology and Infectious Diseases.* Academic Pr. 1983 $59.00. "A contemporary collection of articles relevant to the field of human disease ecology with a specific emphasis on parasitic and zoonotic diseases. Represents current observation and methodological issues associated with research on the human-parasite interaction complex" (*Choice*).

Donaldson, R. J. *Parasites and Western Man.* Univ. Park Pr. 1979 text ed. $32.00. "Deals mainly with parasites in the Western, developed countries. Covers all aspects of both internal and external parasites as well as the interrelations of man and other animals" (*Choice*).

Freudberg, Frank. *Herpes: A Complete Guide to Relief and Reassurance.* Intro. by Paul R. Gross, Running Pr. 1982 $12.95 lib. bdg. $15.90 pap. $6.95. "A comprehensive and easy-to-understand summary of what is known about the diagnosis and management of herpes virus infections" (*Choice*).

Gregg, Charles T. *A Virus of Love and Other Tales of Medical Detection.* Univ. of New Mexico Pr. 1985 pap. $12.95. "An introduction to the likes of swine flu, Legionnaire's disease, Reye syndrome, and herpes. A fascinating account as seen by epidemiologists, researchers, physicians, and the afflicted" (*Choice*).

Gurevich, Inge, and Burke A. Cunha. *The Theory and Practice of Infection Control.* Praeger 1984 $43.95. "An excellent compilation of information on the most commonly encountered infectious diseases. Comprehensive and in sufficient detail to serve as a valuable reference" (*Choice*).

Hamilton, Richard. *The Herpes Book.* St. Martin's 1980 o.p. Essential facts on how herpes is contracted and prevented, and symptoms and course of the disease. Reviews the history, evolution, and progress of knowledge about herpes virus infections in people.

Hopkins, Donald R. *Princes and Peasants: Smallpox in History.* Fwd. by George I. Lythcott, Univ. of Chicago Pr. 1983 $25.00 1985 pap. $12.95. "Proceeding civilization by civilization, European, African, Asian, and New World, Hopkins has made extensive literary and documentary searches to discover when smallpox was first noted and how it affected the impacted culture. Traces the history of inoculation and then the development of vaccination" (*Choice*).

Jones, James H. *Bad Blood: The Tuskegee Syphilis Experiment.* Free Pr. 1981 $14.95 1982 pap. $8.95. The Tuskegee study, conducted by the Public Health Service from 1932 to 1972, was set up to follow the course of syphilis. Most of the subjects, some 400 black men, thought they were being helped by the various tests they underwent. Sharply critical of participating physicians and health personnel for withholding information and treatment from patients.

Jordan, Peter. *Schistosomiasis: The St. Lucia Project.* Cambridge Univ. Pr. 1985 $49.50. "Represents a synthesis of the 150 published papers that describe the St. Lucia Project on schistosomiasis. The West Indies project, which was sponsored by the Rockefeller Foundation from 1966 to 1981, was designed to investigate all facets of schistosomiasis through controlled studies in a variety of natural areas" (*Choice*).

Langston, Deborah P. *Living with Herpes: The Comprehensive and Authoritative Guide to the Causes, Symptoms, and Treatments of Herpes Viruses.* Doubleday 1983 o.p. "Describes the various viruses, the types and methods of infection, and the varieties of treatment. Discusses the relation between herpes and cancer and pregnancy, birth and the postnatal period" (*LJ*).

Meltzer, Alan S. *Sexually Transmitted Disease: Guidelines for Physicians and Health Workers.* Eden Pr. 1981 $5.95. "Highlights some practical aspects of the problem of the increasing incidence of sexually transmitted diseases" (*Choice*).

Neustadt, Richard E., and Harvey V. Fineberg. *The Epidemic That Never Was: Policy-Making and the Swine Flu Scare (The Swine Flu Affair).* Random rev. ed. 1983 pap. $7.95. "The 1976 swine flu crisis prompted a massive federal immunization program which had questionable benefits and serious side effects in a small number of cases. Well written, indeed it is more like a novel than a complex government document" (*Choice*).

Ostrow, David G., and Yehudi M. Felman, eds. *Sexually Transmitted Diseases in Homosexual Men: Diagnosis, Treatment, and Research*. Plenum 1983 $39.50. "Material ranges from general considerations, to discussions of specific types of sexually transmitted diseases" (*Choice*).

Paul, John Rodman. *A History of Poliomyelitis*. Yale Univ. Pr. 1971 o.p. Paul, who headed the Yale Poliomyelitis Study unit for almost 40 years after its foundation in 1931, here tells "the history [of the disease], starting with ancient records in Egypt and Greece, to the observations of Dr. Caufield on an epidemic of 'lame distemper' in New England in 1771–72; the tragic premature vaccine trials in 1935; the futile attempts to control epidemics with convalescent serum; and finally the various contributions of virology and statistical epidemiology that led to the triumphant success of the inactivated and attenuated live virus vaccines" (*Amer. Scientist*).

Riemann, Hans, and Frank L. Bryan, eds. *Food-Borne Infections and Intoxications*. Academic Pr. 1969 o.p. "Organized into four subject areas: epidemiology, infections, intoxications, and control" (*Choice*).

Saunders, Paul L. *Edward Jenner—The Cheltenham Years, 1795–1823: Being a Chronicle of the Vaccination Campaign*. Univ. Pr. of New England 1982 o.p. "A first rate account of the final years of the man responsible for vaccination against smallpox" (*LJ*).

Semmelweis, Ignaz. *The Etiology, Concept and Prophylaxis of Childbed Fever*. Trans. by K. Codell Carter [*History of Science and Medicine Ser. No. 2*.] Univ. of Wisconsin Pr. 1983 text ed. $35.00 pap. $11.95. "The painstaking attention to empirical detail and the persuasive urgent tone were the products of a man frustrated by his inability to convince his peers and administrative superiors that they were allowing the deaths of thousands of mothers" (*Choice*).

Van der Heyningen, W. E., and John Seal. *Cholera: The American Scientific Encounter, 1947–1980*. Westview Pr. 1982 o.p. "Chronicles a 30-year war against the spread of 'Vibrio Cholerae.' A war waged by a shifting international team of men and women, largely Americans who knew little of cholera but much of physiology and biochemistry, allied with the experienced doctors of the cholera countries" (*Scientific Amer.*).

Zinner, Stephen H. *STD: Sexually Transmitted Diseases*. Summit 1985 $14.95. "Discusses 18 diseases, includes background material, symptoms, treatment and preventive measures. Handy quick reference for the layperson" (*LJ*).

MUSCULOSKELETAL DISORDERS

[SEE the sections on Orthopedics and Sports Medicine in this chapter.]

NEUROLOGICAL DISEASES

Neurological diseases and disorders may be caused by infection or may be of uncertain origin. Whatever their cause, they affect the functioning of nerves and muscles. Alzheimer's Disease, a degenerative brain disorder of uncertain pathogenesis, which does not manifest itself until middle age, received much media attention beginning in 1984 and 1985. A selection of the numerous books for nonspecialists that appeared on this subject are listed. The causes, prognosis, etiology, and treatment of this and other, equally destructive, neurological diseases are described. Also listed are practical manuals for professionals and families and personal narratives that describe the psychological impact of these diseases.

Baier, Sue, and Mary Zimmeth. *Bed Number Ten.* Henry Holt 1986 $16.95. "Baier chronicles her severe bout with Guillain-Barre syndrome, a puzzling illness that can occur after a viral infection, causing degeneration of nerve sheaths and resulting in temporary paralysis" (*LJ*).

Cohen, Donna, and Carl Eisdorfer. *The Loss of Self: A Family Resource for the Care of Alzheimer's Disease and Related Disorders.* NAL 1987 pap. $9.95; Norton 1986 $18.95. "Discussions of practical information include criteria for recognizing serious memory problems, obtaining a thorough diagnosis, working effectively with a patient, dealing with financial and legal problems in institutionalizing a patient. Case-study accounts tie theory to reality" (*Choice*).

Critchley, Macdonald. *The Citadel of the Senses and Other Essays.* Raven 1986 text ed. $29.50. "Subjects include aphasia, migraine, neurosyphilis, Samuel Johnson, John Hughlings Jackson and Alphonse Daudet" (*Journal of the American Medical Assn.*)

Dement, William C. *Some Must Watch While Some Must Sleep: Exploring the World of Sleep.* Norton 1978 text ed. pap. $5.95. "A balanced account of the basic landmarks in the realm of human sleep. An overview of the behavioral and physiological correlates of sleep and sleep loss is followed by discussions of dream content, sleep disorders and their treatment, sleep disturbance and mental illness, and creativity during sleep" (*Amer. Scientist*).

Doernberg, Myrna. *Stolen Mind: The Slow Disappearance of Ray Doernberg.* Intro. by Barry W. Rovner, Algonquin Bks. 1986 $14.95. "Ray Doernberg suffered from a form of dementia known as 'Binswanger's disease.' Subcortical arteriosclerotic encephalopathy, as it is officially known, results in progressive degeneration of the subcortical region of the brain, leading to diminished intellectual capacity, loss of judgment, and problems with memory, orientation, language, and other essential skills" (*LJ*).

Dorros, Sidney. *Parkinson's: A Patient's View.* Pref. by Donald Galne, Seven Locks Pr. 1981 $14.95; Warner Bks. 1985 pap. $3.95. A personal narrative of a patient's experience with Parkinsonism over a period of 30 years.

Dreifuss, Fritz E., and others. *Pediatric Epileptology: Classification and Management of Seizures in the Child.* PSG Pubns. 1983 $39.50. "An up-to-date classification of, and guide to, the management of seizures in children. Describes various types of seizures, their prognosis, management, and psychosocial implications" (*Choice*).

Dryer, Bernard, and Ellen S. Kaplan. *Inside Insomnia: How to Get a Good Night's Sleep.* Random 1986 pap. $8.95. "Coverage of numerous perspectives including sleep physiology, biorhythms, effects and interactions of drugs and alcohol on sleep, sleeping problems, and the role of relaxation therapies and other nondrug techniques" (*LJ*).

Dudley, Rosemary, and Wade Rowland. *How to Find Relief from Migraines.* Beaufort Bks. 1982 $12.95. "An in-depth guide to the causes, treatment and prevention of migraine headache in adults and children" (*LJ*).

Fletcher, Sally. *The Challenge of Epilepsy.* Intro. by Sidney Kurn, Aura Pub. Co. 1986 pap. $9.95. "Serves the dual purpose of educating the general public about the nature of epilepsy and of helping the epilepsy sufferer and family members cope with the disorder" (*LJ*).

Franklin, Jon, and Alan Doelp. *Not Quite a Miracle: Brain Surgeons and Their Patients on the Frontier of Medicine.* Doubleday 1983 o.p. "The main events in this fascinating book are the operations to reconnect a nerve and to remove various tumors" (*LJ*).

Gino, Carol. *Rusty's Story.* Bantam 1986 pap. $3.95. "Rusty was a teenager when she was stricken with epilepsy. Misdiagnosed as a paranoid schizophrenic, for years she suffered more from inappropriate medical treatment than her condition" (*LJ*).

Hales, Dianne. *The Complete Book of Sleep: How Your Nights Affect Your Days.* Addison-Wesley 1981 pap. $7.95. "Describes normal and abnormal sleep patterns and the effect on sleep of factors such as lifestyle and health" (*LJ*).

Hayden, M. R. *Huntington's Chorea.* Springer-Verlag 1981 $49.50. "Describes the history, geographical distribution, and epidemiology of the disease, and analyzes its genetic implications. Covers the major problem of diagnosis and describes the management of the disease through medication" (*Choice*).

Lance, James W. *Migraine and Other Headaches: A Renowned Physician's Guide to Diagnosis and Effective Treatment.* Scribner 1986 pap. $7.95. "Briefly describes the various types of headache then proceeds with further explanation of migraine, cluster, and tension headaches and other headache-causing conditions including tic douloureux, brain tumor and sinusitis" (*LJ*).

Litel, Gerald R. *Neurosurgery and the Clinical Team: A Guide for Nurses, Technicians, and Students.* Springer Pub. 1980 o.p. "Outlines the fundamental aspects of neuroanatomy, neurophysiology, and neuropathology. Discusses clinical evaluation and diagnosis, and describes most neurosurgical procedures" (*Choice*).

Mace, Nancy L., and Peter V. Rabins. *The Thirty-Six Hour Day: A Family Guide to Caring for Persons with Alzheimer's Disease, Related Dementing Illnesses and Memory Loss in Later Life.* Johns Hopkins Univ. Pr. 1982 $17.50 pap. $7.95; Warner Bks. 1984 pap. $3.95. "An excellent practical manual for families and professionals involved in the care of persons with progressive dementing illnesses" (*LJ*).

Martin, Russell. *Matters Gray and White: A Neurologist, His Patients, and the Mysteries of the Brain.* Holt 1987 $18.95. "Medical terminology and explanations are skillfully intertwined with patient vignettes and heartfelt conversations over the approach to the patient with a chronic disabling neurological disease" (*LJ*).

Meinhart, Noreen T., and Margo McCaffrey. *Pain: A Nursing Approach to Assessment and Analysis.* Appleton 1983 $24.95. "Includes discussion of the neurophysiology of pain, the cultural and psychological factors that influence pain perception, and the various pain syndromes" (*Choice*).

Melzack, Ronald, and Patrick D. Wall. *The Challenge of Pain.* Basic Bks. 1983 $20.95 1985 pap. $10.95. "Incorporates findings on pain in sensory physiology, neurochemistry, and behavioral medicine, and serves to remind us of our ignorance regarding certain kinds of pain and treatments used to alter pain" (*Choice*).

Middleton, Allen H., and Gregory Walsh. *Epilepsy.* Little, Brown 1982 $16.45. "An attempt to demystify the diagnosis and management of epilepsy, particularly for parents of epileptic children" (*LJ*).

Neurological Disorders. Springhouse 1984 o.p. "Complex anatomical information and pathophysiological processes are described with thoroughness and clarity" (*Choice*).

Olshan, Neal H. *Power Over Your Pain: The 14-Day Pain Control Program Without Drugs.* Beaufort Bks. 1983 pap. $7.95; Rawson 1981 pap. $3.95. "Detailed information about chronic pain and the program of the Southwest Pain Treatment Center" (*LJ*).

Powell, Lenore, and Katie Courtice. *Alzheimer's Disease: A Guide for Families.* Addison-Wesley 1983 pap. $9.95. "Discusses knowledge of the disease, the practical and psychological challenges of caring for and understanding the patient, and the emotional and other problems of caregivers themselves" (*LJ*).

Rabin, Roni. *Six Parts Love: A Family's Battle with Lou Gehrig's Disease (ALS).* Scribner 1985 o.p. "Dr. David Rabin was a successful scientist working in the area of male contraception when in 1979 he learned he had ALS (amyotrophic lateral sclerosis). His daughter chronicles his progressive disease and the family's resolve to fight back" (*LJ*).

Sacks, Oliver. *The Man Who Mistook His Wife for a Hat: And Other Clinical Tales.* Harper 1987 pap. $7.95; Summit 1986 $16.95. "One man who could not recognize common objects at a glance, another who suddenly developed an acute sense of smell, and retarded brothers who could juggle huge prime numbers are among the subjects of these essays" (*N.Y. Times Bk. Review*).

————. *Migraine: The Evolution of a Common Disorder.* Fwd. by William Goodely, Univ. of California Pr. 2d ed. rev. 1985 $22.50 pap. $8.95. "Anyone having any interest in migraine will profit from and enjoy reading this book" (*Amer. Scientist*).

Sarno, Martha T., and Olle Hook, eds. *Aphasia: Assessment and Treatment.* Masson 1980 $42.00. Reports from a joint symposium of the Research Committees on Aphasia and on Neurological Rehabilitation of the World Federation of Neurology. "Deals with analysis of aphasia behavior, rehabilitation and research into recovery" (*Choice*).

Selby, George. *Migraine and Its Variants.* PSG Pubns. 1983 $24.00; Williams & Wilkins 1983 $27.00. "Covers the historical aspects with discussion of the etiology, trigger factors, [and] pathology related to the changes in vessel caliber, differential diagnosis of the various types of the disorder, treatment by drug and nondrug remedies and prognosis" (*Choice*).

Severo, Richard. *Lisa H: The True Story of an Extraordinary and Courageous Woman.* Harper 1985 $13.45; Penguin 1986 pap. $6.95. The story of a 21-year-old woman suffering from neurofibromatosis, who in her quest for normalcy underwent a radical life-threatening operation to remove the tumors and reconstruct her face.

Smoller, Bruce, and Brian Schulman. *Pain Control: The Bethesda Program.* Zebra 1983 pap. $3.95. "[Describes] in detail the causes and effects of pain (being careful to balance physical and psychological considerations) and the process of learning to cope with it" (*LJ*).

Soll, Robert W., and Penelope B. Genoble. *MS—Something Can Be Done and You Can Do It.* Contemporary Bks. 1984 $14.95. "Soll believes that multiple sclerosis may involve a hypersensitivity to one's own myelin, exacerbated by infections and hidden food allergies. He claims remarkable success in rehabilitating MS patients through a program of diet, motivation, behavioral self-management, and physical therapy" (*LJ*).

Tarlov, Edward, and David D'Costa. *Back Attack: A Neurosurgeon's Advice on the Best and Latest Methods for Diagnosis and Treatment.* Little, Brown 1985 $17.45 1987 pap. $9.95. Includes " 'a brief but necessary anatomy course' of back and neck, explains diagnostic tests, [and] touches on many surgical and nonsurgical therapies" (*LJ*).

Temkin, Owsei. *The Falling Sickness: A History of Epilepsy from the Greeks to the*

Beginnings of Modern Neurology. Johns Hopkins Univ. Pr. 2d ed. rev. 1971 o.p.
"(The) definitive account of the varying concepts of epilepsy, 'the falling sickness,' from the brave Hippocratic rejection of the disease as 'sacred' to the study
of the syndrome inaugurated chiefly by John Hughlings Jackson (1835–1911).
Temkin considers the broad spectrum of epileptic disorder, from severe convul-
sions to mild transitory amnesias, as it has been debated from ancient times.
[An] informative introduction to our knowledge of epilepsy in the Western
world from antiquity to the early twentieth century" (*Amer. Scientist*).

Trieschmann, Roberta B. *Spinal Cord Injuries: Psychological, Social and Vocational
Adjustment.* Pergamon 1980 $25.00. "Myths are laid to rest on emotional and
grief processes following disability, and attention is turned to environmental
and personnel influences on rehabilitation" (*Choice*).

White, Augustus A., III. *Your Aching Back: A Doctor's Guide to Relief.* Bantam 1984
pap. $3.95. Provides a wealth of information on the causes, prevention, and
treatment of back pain.

Zarit, Steven H., and others. *The Hidden Victims of Alzheimer's Disease: Families
under Stress.* New York Univ. Pr. 1985 $30.00 pap. $14.95. Examines causes and
symptoms, provides guidelines for assessment, describes possible interventions,
and offers useful strategies to effect optimal functioning in the patient and
family.

NUTRITIONAL DISORDERS

This section includes information on adverse reactions to foods and the role
of nutrition in disease and health. The wide cross-section of titles encompasses professional publications, some requiring an understanding of biology and chemistry; orthodox and unorthodox views on links between physical disorders and diet; and personal narratives about anorexia nervosa, a
disorder, mainly affecting young women, which began to receive much media attention only a few years ago.

Adverse Reactions to Foods. USGPO 1984 pap. $9.50. "Discusses history and preva-
lence of adverse reactions to foods, the chemistry of selected food antigens, the
fate of ingested antigens in the intestinal tract; reviews reported adverse reactions both to foods that involve or are suspected of involving immune mechanisms, diagnosis and treatment. Includes recommendations for future studies"
(*Choice*).

Bland, Jeffrey, ed. *Medical Applications of Clinical Nutrition.* Keats 1983 $25.00.
"Emphasizes the preventive and management role on nutrition for degenerative
diseases such as cardiovascular disease, diabetes, and gastrointestinal dysfunction" (*Choice*).

Bruch, Hilde. *The Golden Cage: The Enigma of Anorexia Nervosa.* Harvard Univ. Pr.
1978 $12.50; Random 1979 pap. $3.95. Case histories of patients treated by the
author/psychiatrist are recounted. Possible causes and treatments are explored.
A landmark book.

Carpenter, Kenneth J. *The History of Scurvy and Vitamin C.* Cambridge Univ. Pr.
1986 $39.50. "About two thirds of this book is devoted to scurvy and early
medical attempts to understand its etiology. The other third chronicles the
discovery of vitamin C" (*Choice*).

Diet, Nutrition, and Cancer. National Academic Pr. 1982 pap. $19.95 1983 text ed.
pap. $7.95. Prepared by the National Research Council Committee on Diet,

Nutrition, and Cancer. "A comprehensive study of the scientific information concerning the relationship of diet and nutrition to cancer. Summarizes the most relevant scientific information of diet and cancer and recommends several interim dietary guidelines" (*Choice*).

Emmett, Steven Wiley, ed. *Theory and Treatment of Anorexia Nervosa and Bulimia: Biomedical, Sociocultural, and Psychological Perspectives.* Brunner-Mazel 1985 $30.00. "Includes a great deal of historical, empirical, and demographic data. Highly technical medical language, frequent statistical data in tables, graphs or illustrations" (*Choice*).

Fredericks, Carlton. *Carlton Fredericks' Nutrition Guide for the Prevention and Cure of Common Ailments and Diseases.* Fireside 1981 pap. $8.95. "States [that] many physical disorders and diseases may be prevented, cured, or improved by the use of vitamins, minerals and other nutrients, and correct diet" (*LJ*).

Garfinkel, Paul E., and David M. Garner. *Anorexia Nervosa: A Multidimensional Perspective.* Brunner-Mazel 1982 $30.00. "A most comprehensive yet cautious treatment of the topic of anorexia nervosa. A source of valuable information" (*Choice*).

Hui, Yiu H. *Human Nutrition and Diet Therapy.* Jones & Bartlett 1983 text ed. $37.50. "Basic information about normal and therapeutic nutrition in humans. A background in biology and chemistry would help the reader to a more in-depth understanding of the chemical and biological basis of the information presented" (*Choice*).

Mitchell, James E. *Anorexia Nervosa and Bulimia: Diagnosis and Treatment.* [*Continuing Medical Education Ser.*] Univ. of Minnesota Pr. 1985 $25.00. "Detailed coverage from past research and treatments, to current diagnostic methodologies and care, to future research possibilities. Minimal use of technical language" (*Choice*).

Orbach, Susie. *Hunger Strike: The Anorectic's Struggle for Survival as a Metaphor for Our Age.* Norton 1986 $15.95

Palmer, R. L. *Anorexia Nervosa: A Guide for Sufferers and Their Families.* Penguin 1981 pap. $4.95. "Palmer's hypothesis is that anorexia nervosa is a psychobiological regression disorder" (*LJ*).

Romeo, Felicia F. *Understanding Anorexia Nervosa.* C. C. Thomas 1986 $19.75. "Clearly points out the major symptoms. A concise and accessible treatment" (*Choice*).

Rose, John, ed. *Nutrition and Killer Diseases: The Effects of Dietary Factors on Fatal Chronic Diseases.* Noyes Pr. 1982 $25.00. Focuses on the effects of dietary factors on atherosclerosis (coronary heart disease), cancer, and diabetes.

Rumney, Avis. *Dying to Please: Anorexia Nervosa and Its Cure.* McFarland 1983 pap. $13.95. "Written from personal experience. Discusses a variety of therapeutic approaches used for anorexia (psychoanalysis, behavior modification, drug therapy, hypnotherapy, and family therapy)" (*Choice*).

Sours, John A. *Starving to Death in a Sea of Objects.* Aronson 1980 $25.00. "An unusual device is a novella that occupies 192 pages of the book. Analyzes the condition from a variety of historical, psychodynamic and developmental aspects" (*Choice*).

Trowell, H. C., and others, eds. *Dietary Fibre, Fibre-Depleted Foods and Disease.* Academic Pr. 1985 $78.00. "A comprehensive perspective on the relationship of food fiber, or the lack of it, in the diet to various disease processes. Ranges from the basic chemistry and physiology of fiber to risk factors and symptoms of disease to the diseases themselves" (*Choice*).

Winick, Myron. *Nutrition in Health and Disease.* Krieger repr. of 1980 ed. 1986 text ed. $29.50. A comprehensive compilation of nutrition knowledge regarding both healthy and diseased states.

ONCOLOGY

[SEE the section on Cancer in this chapter.]

ORTHOPEDICS

Orthopedics is the medical specialty that utilizes surgical and physical methods to treat and correct deformities, diseases, and injuries to the musculoskeletal system. The majority of books on the treatment of bone and joint diseases are written for physicians, physical therapists, and other health care personnel. Books for the general reader on any bone disorder other than osteoporosis are difficult to find. The books here on osteoporosis are a representative selection from the many published. (See also the section on Sports Medicine in this chapter.)

Cantu, Robert C. *Exercise Injuries: Prevention and Treatment.* Stone Wall Pr. 1983 pap. $12.95. "Recommends fitness as a desirable and obtainable goal, and deals with sports injuries" (*Choice*).

Fardon, David F. *Osteoporosis: Your Head Start to the Prevention of Fractures.* HP Bks. 1987 pap. $8.95; Macmillan 1985 $15.95. "Coverage of all pertinent aspects: causes; the role of nutrition, exercise and lifestyle; detection methods; and how osteoporosis and fractured bones are treated" (*LJ*).

Notelovitz, Morris, and Marsha Ware. *Stand Tall!: Every Woman's Guide to Preventing Osteoporosis.* Bantam 1985 $7.95. "Well-documented scientific information on prevention, diet, exercise, hormone therapy and diagnostic screening techniques" (*LJ*).

Smith, Wendy, and Stanton Cohn. *Osteoporosis: How to Prevent the Brittle-Bone Disease.* Simon & Schuster 1985 pap. $5.95. "Heavy concentration on the nutritional component, offers a 30-day diet" (*LJ*).

Steinmann, Marion. *The American Medical Association's Book of Back Care.* Random 1982 o.p. "Well-illustrated description of the anatomy of the back and the changes that occur during the aging process. Discusses diseases and treatment regimens of back problems" (*LJ*).

OSTEOPOROSIS

[See the section on Orthopedics in this chapter.]

PLASTIC SURGERY

Books on plastic surgery are either very technical or written for a lay audience. Listed are four recent examples of the latter type.

Cirillo, Dennis P., and Mark Rubinstein. *The Complete Book of Cosmetic Facial Surgery: A Step-by-Step Guide to the Physical and Psychological Process.* Simon & Schuster 1984 $16.95. "Gives commonsense guidelines for choosing a surgeon. Discusses types of surgery and nonsurgical treatment" (*LJ*).

Goldwyn, Robert M. *Beyond Appearance: Reflections of a Plastic Surgeon.* Dodd 1986

$16.95. Goldwyn comments in the introduction to his book that "this book is about the process of plastic surgery, about some of my patients and myself, and about our relationship."

Reardon, James J., and Judi McMahon. *Plastic Surgery for Men: The Complete Illustrated Guide*. Dodd 1981 o.p. "Explains complicated techniques in easy-to-understand language" (*LJ*).

Snyder, Marilyn. *An Informed Decision: Understanding Breast Reconstruction*. M. Evans 1984 $17.95. "A very personal account of her own double mastectomy and subsequent chemotherapy and breast reconstruction. A manual on how to explore the options of this special surgery" (*LJ*).

PSORIASIS

[SEE the section on Skin Diseases in this chapter.]

PROSTHESES

[SEE the section on Artificial and Transplanted Organs, Prostheses, and Implants in this chapter.]

RADIOLOGY

Radiology is the use of X-rays for diagnostic or therapeutic purposes. Books on radiological examination and therapy accessible to the nonspecialist are difficult to find.

Gofman, John W., and Egan O'Connor. *X-rays: Health Effects of Common Exams*. Sierra 1985 $25.00. "Provides the data needed for evaluating the effects of diagnostic X-rays and possibly reducing dosage. Organized by type of X-ray, body part, sex and age of patient, and risk of future disease (especially cancer)" (*LJ*).

Laws, Priscilla W., and The Public Citizen Health Research Group. *The X-Ray Information Book: A Consumers' Guide to Avoiding Unnecessary Medical and Dental X-Rays*. Farrar 1983 $14.50 pap. $7.25. Explains what X-rays are, how they can harm, and major sources of unnecessary exposure. The authors' purpose is to assist consumers in minimizing risks associated with unneeded exposure without reducing the benefits of diagnostic X-ray examination.

RESPIRATORY DISEASES

Any disease that affects the ability of the lungs to function properly is a respiratory disease. This brief list includes lung anatomy and function in health and disease, a discussion of how airborne particles affect our lungs, and care and treatment of patients with respiratory diseases.

Hamilton, Helen, and Minnie B. Rose, eds. *Respiratory Disorders*. Springhouse 1984 text ed. $19.95. "Provides a general overview of the care of the patient with pulmonary dysfunctions. Reviews pulmonary anatomy and physiology" (*Choice*).

Perera, Frederica P., and A. Karim Ahmed. *Respirable Particles: Impact of Airborne Fine Particulates on Health and the Environment.* Ballinger 1979 $29.95. "A useful, compact reference book about tiny airborne particles of all sorts" (*Choice*).

Shayevitz, Myra, and Berton Shayevitz. *Living Well with Emphysema and Bronchitis: A Cardiopulmonary Fitness Program for a Healthier More Active Life.* Doubleday 1985 $15.95. "A step-by-step program for the COPD patient to follow daily; everything from diet, exercise and medication charts to recreation, sex, and cooking tips" (*LJ*).

Williams, Chris. *Lung Cancer: The Facts.* Oxford 1984 $13.95. "A basic overview of lung cancer—epidemiology, diagnostic and staging procedures, and treatment modalities" (*Choice*).

Youtsey, John W., and Kanute P. Rarey. *Respiratory Patient Care.* Prentice-Hall 1981 text ed. $29.95. "Presents respiratory care information in a well-organized form. The various pieces of equipment and their uses are described concisely and clearly" (*Choice*).

RHEUMATIC DISEASES

Rheumatic diseases are various conditions with pain and/or other symptoms that affect the joints or musculoskeletal system. Listed here are a few of the recent publications for the general reader that provide current information on the different types of rheumatic disease, their course, and their treatment.

Arthritis Foundation. *Understanding Arthritis: What It Is, How It's Treated, How to Cope with It.* Scribner 1985 $18.95 pap. $10.95. "An overview of diagnosis, accepted treatments and emotional and financial strains of arthritis. Details the 16 most common rheumatic diseases" (*LJ*).

Davidson, Paul. *Are You Sure It's Arthritis: A Guide to Soft-Tissue Rheumatism.* Macmillan 1985 $15.95. "Soft-tissue rheumatism, which includes bursitis, tendonitis, carpal tunnel syndrome, tennis elbow, and a host of other frequently treatable conditions, often is confused by the layperson with arthritis" (*LJ*).

Gadd, Irna, and Laurence Gadd. *Arthritis Alternatives.* Facts on File 1985 $16.95. "An excellent sourcebook, with emphasis on self-help groups and physicians that provide nontraditional therapies" (*LJ*).

Jetter, Judy, and Nancy Kadlee. *The Arthritis Book of Water Exercise.* Fwd. by Herbert M. Rubinstein, Holt 1985 $12.95. "An Arthritis Foundation approved program of aquatic exercise suitable for those with joint or limb impairment, whether from arthritis, stroke, surgery or accident" (*LJ*).

Keough, Carol. *Natural Relief for Arthritis.* Rodale Pr. 1984 $16.95. "Discusses the different kinds of arthritis and related disorders and summarizes in popular form the many treatments available, including arthritis diets, exercise, folk remedies, acupuncture, drugs, and surgery" (*LJ*).

Riggs, Gail Kershner, and Eric P. Gall, eds. *Rheumatic Diseases: Rehabilitation and Management.* Butterworth 1984 text ed. $39.95. "Covers the interdisciplinary team approach, techniques in the care of patients with rheumatic diseases, and rehabilitation techniques for regional disorders and specific diseases" (*Choice*).

Sernaque, Vivienne. *The Pill Book of Arthritis.* Bantam 1985 pap. $3.95. "Provides information on the various types of arthritis and detailed information on the specific drugs used in treatment" (*LJ*).

SKIN DISEASES

Books dealing with skin problems tend to fall into one of two categories—texts written for physicians and others involved in patient care and self-help books—many of which offer advice on facial skin care. The six books listed below are illustrative of these types.

Aldhizer, T. Gerard, and others. *The Doctor's Book on Hair Loss.* Prentice-Hall 1983 $14.95 pap. $7.95. "Discusses what it means to be bald, how hair grows and the types and causes of hair loss, and the use of 'cover-ups,' treatments (medical, surgical, and quack) and hairpieces" (*LJ*).

Goodman, Thomas. *The Skin Doctor's Skin Doctoring Book.* Sterling 1984 pap. $7.95. "Focuses on the most common skin problems, clearly identifies signs and symptoms, and then gives advice on how to treat these problems with over-the-counter products. Cautions that not all skin problems can be cured at home—some will need the attention of the physician" (*LJ*).

Litt, Jerome Z. *Your Skin and How to Live In It.* Corinthian 2d ed. 1982 pap. $6.95. Easy-to-understand descriptions of the most common dermatological conditions, and the physiology of the skin.

Maibach, H., and R. Aly, eds. *Skin Microbiology: Relevance to Clinical Infection.* Springer-Verlag 1981 $44.50. "A review of developments in the field of skin microbiology since 1965 and a summary of the status of research. Emphasizes the clinical aspects of skin infections" (*Choice*).

Marks, Ronald. *Acne: Advice on Clearing Your Skin.* Arco 1984 $12.95 pap. $7.95. A useful book containing practical advice on the most effective over-the-counter remedies for skin problems, including the use and application of these products. Explains how to recognize when a physician should be consulted, and describes treatments that might be prescribed.

———. *Psoriasis: A Guide to One of the Commonest Skin Diseases.* [*Positive Health Guides*] Arco 1981 pap. $6.95. A comprehensive review including the various forms of psoriasis, how skin reacts to the disease, psychological and sociological effects, possible psoriasis, and treatments (ointments, sun, ultraviolet light).

SPORTS MEDICINE

This section provides information on the importance of conditioning and training in sports, the physiological and psychological effects of anabolic steroids (used by athletes to increase muscle bulk), and the care and treatment of sports injuries. (See also the section on Orthopedics in this chapter.)

Benjamin, Ben, and Gale Borden. *Listen to Your Pain: The Active Person's Guide to Understanding, Identifying and Treating Pain and Injury.* Penguin 1984 pap. $10.95. "Helps weekend athletes understand the physiology of injury and will assist them in making informed decisions regarding treatment" (*LJ*).

Bridge, Raymond. *Running Without Pain: Avoiding and Treating Injury.* Doubleday 1980 pap. $6.95. "Covers preventive techniques for both experienced and beginning runners" (*LJ*).

Goldman, Bob. *Death in the Locker Room: Steroids and Sports.* Pref. by John B. Zeigler, HP Bks. 1987 pap. $9.95; Icarus Pr. 1984 $19.95. "Marshals an abundance of evidence that the use of anabolic steroids has severe, long-lasting physiological and psychological effects which vitiate any immediate benefit to the athlete" (*LJ*).

Griffith, H. Winter. *Complete Guide to Sports Injuries.* HP Bks. 1986 $12.95. "Discussions of injuries help the athlete and/or coach understand the anatomy involved as well as appropriate care, possible complications, and outcomes of treatment. Injuries are arranged alphabetically by body part, ailments by common name" (*LJ*).

Halpern, Alan A. *The Runner's World Knee Book: What Every Athlete Needs to Know About the Prevention and Treatment of Knee Problems.* Macmillan 1985 $13.95 pap. $7.95. "Covers all types of knee problems, with detailed evaluations and therapies" (*LJ*).

Hoffman, Marshall, and William Southmayd. *Sports Health: The Complete Book of Athletic Injuries.* Putnam 1981 pap. $14.95. "A comprehensive study of the injuries that can plague all athletes, professional and amateur. Concentrates on the care and treatment rather than the prevention of sports-related injuries" (*LJ*).

Jackson, Douglas W., and Susan C. Pescar. *The Young Athlete's Health Handbook: A Guide to Sports Medicine and Sports Psychology for Parents, Teachers, Coaches, and Players.* Dodd 1981 o.p. "Conditioning, training, physical and psychological traits, alcohol and drugs, nutrition, aggressiveness, the female athlete, levels of competition, the physically and mentally handicapped, orthopedic considerations, predicting injuries, diagnostic procedures, medications, general safety and first aid are thoroughly covered" (*LJ*).

Sandweiss, Jack H., and Steven L. Wolf, eds. *Biofeedback and Sports Science.* Plenum 1985 $24.50. "Offers several ideas and applications about biofeedback techniques used in the psychological and rehabilitative aspects of athletics as well as in enhancing athletic performance" (*Choice*).

Shangold, Mona, and Gabe Mirkin. *The Complete Sports Medicine Book for Women.* Simon & Schuster 1985 $16.95 pap. $9.95. "Concentrates on exercise-related injuries common among women and on the effects of exercise on women of all ages" (*LJ*).

Taylor, William N. *Anabolic Steroids and the Athlete: With a Chapter on Human Growth Hormone.* McFarland 1982 pap. $13.95. Factual and straightforward account of this controversial issue.

STRESS AND DISEASE

Though stress has long been recognized as an exacerbating factor in many disease states, Hans Selye in the 1950s developed the idea that animals react to stress or injury by a certain sequence of physiological reactions, called the "general adaptation syndrome." This concept he later applied to humans in his book *Stress Without Distress* (see below), and in other works. Selye now advocates a constructive management approach to stress.

The links between stress and disease have come into and gone out of fashion. Twenty years after Selye, Herbert Benson advocated meditation to relieve the harmful effects of stress on health. More recently, Meyer Friedman recommended behavior modification if "Type A" personalities were to avoid an early death from stress. Current research in this area focuses on the effects of stress in specific systems and as an underlying cause of some disease states.

Antonovsky, Aaron. *Health, Stress, and Coping: New Perspectives on Mental and Physical Well-Being.* [*Social and Behavioral Sciences Ser.*] Jossey-Bass 1979 $21.95. Antonovsky argues that researchers should ask why people stay healthy not why they get sick.

Benson, Herbert, and Miriam Z. Klipper. *The Relaxation Response.* Morrow 1975 o.p. Advocates the use of meditation to protect against the destructive effects of stress. A landmark work.

Brown, Barbara B. *Between Health and Illness: New Notions on Stress and the Nature of Well-Being.* Houghton Mifflin 1984 $14.95. Analyzes the structure of the psyche. Describes the stress of life in terms of psychic hurts and bruises and how various techniques can relieve the unease of mind and body.

Friedman, Meyer, and Diane Ulmer. *Treating Type A Behavior—and Your Heart.* Knopf 1984 $15.95. "Uses information obtained through a major study project as the basis for a program of behavioral modification" (*LJ*).

Matarazzo, Joseph D., and Sharlene M. Weiss. *Behavioral Health: A Handbook of Health Enhancement and Disease Prevention.* Wiley 1984 $79.95. "A collection of significant behavioral and medical insights in health promotion and disease prevention strategies written by noted experts in their respective fields" (*Choice*).

Milsum, John H. *Health, Stress and Illness: A Systems Approach.* Praeger 1984 $35.95. "Uses a systems approach to clarify existing knowledge and to present a broad perspective on health-stress relationships" (*Choice*).

Pelletier, Kenneth R. *Mind as Healer, Mind as Slayer: A Holistic Approach to Preventing Stress Disorders.* Delacorte 1977 $10.00; Dell 1977 pap. $9.95. Well-documented exploration of the relationship between heart, respiratory or pulmonary disease and stress. Includes techniques for stress reduction such as meditation, biofeedback, autogenic training and visualization. A holistic milestone.

Selye, Hans. *Stress Without Distress.* Harper 1974 $11.00; NAL 1975 pap. $3.50. A classic guide to the constructive management of stress.

SUBSTANCE ABUSE

Substance abuse is an issue that is of major concern to contemporary society because of the effects such addiction has on the quality of life and individual health. Numerous titles are available for the layperson describing the causes, effects, and possible treatments for such abuse.

Blum, Kenneth. *Handbook of Abusable Drugs.* Gardner Pr. 1984 $79.95. A compilation of information on the spectrum of abused substances, including narcotics, sedatives, hallucinogens, psychotropics, alcohol, tobacco, and over-the-counter drugs. Includes an overview of the history, biochemistry, pharmacology, toxicity, and behavioral and psychological aspects of each group of abused drugs.

Bush, Patricia J. *Drugs, Alcohol and Sex.* Marek 1980 o.p. Examines the impact of drugs, licit and illicit, on sexual activity.

Milkman, Harvey B., and Howard J. Shaffer. *The Addictions: Multidisciplinary Perspectives and Treatments.* Lexington Bks. 1985 $26.00. Proceedings of a 1983 conference offers readers an opportunity to consolidate often conflicting theoretical information regarding the etiology and treatment of addictions. Includes etiology of addictive behavior and therapeutic approaches.

Alcoholism

Beauchamp, Dan E. *Beyond Alcoholism: Alcohol and Public Health.* Temple Univ. Pr. 1980 o.p. Reviews the history of alcoholism; Prohibition, America's failure to legislate temperance; contemporary ideas and myths of disease causation; and the emerging trends in international alcohol consumption.

Clark, P. M. S., and L. J. Kricka, eds. *Medical Consequences of Alcohol Abuse.* Wiley 1981 o.p. Information regarding the prevalence of alcohol-related problems primarily centered around statistics gathered in Great Britain.

Deutsch, Charles. *Broken Bottles, Broken Dreams: Understanding and Helping the Children of Alcoholics.* Teachers College Pr. 1982 $13.95. This book is divided into two parts, the first of which defines alcoholism and considers its effect on members of the family. Part 2 concentrates on the helping process for the children of alcoholic parents.

Elkin, Michael. *Families Under the Influence: Changing Alcoholic Patterns.* Norton 1984 o.p. An interesting, albeit quite limiting, theoretical explanation of alcoholism.

Galanter, Marc, ed. *Recent Developments in Alcoholism.* Plenum vol. 2 1984 $65.00 vol. 4 1986 $59.95. Volume 2 covers learning and social models, alcohol and the liver, aging and alcoholism, and anthropology and is organized under five main headings: Experimental Social and Learning Models of Drinking Alcohol; Alcohol and the Liver; Recent Developments in Preclinical and Clinical Research; Aging and Alcoholism; and Contributions from Anthropology to the Study of Alcoholism. Volume 4 covers combined alcohol and drug abuse, typologies of alcoholics, the withdrawal syndrome, and renal and electrolyte consequences and a useful feature is the seven-to-ten page overview chapter that serves as an introduction to each section.

Heather, Nick, and others, eds. *The Misuse of Alcohol: Crucial Issues in Dependence, Treatment and Prevention.* New York Univ. Pr. 1985 $42.50. Deals with the appropriateness of the designation of alcoholism as a syndrome. Discusses what constitutes treatment and prevention of alcoholism.

Light, William J. Haugen. *Neurobiology of Alcohol Abuse.* Thomas 1986 $26.97. Surveys neurobiology and the chemistry of human consciousness. Addresses depression, antidepressant drugs, alcohol, and the relation of depression to alcohol and the working of the brain.

Marlin, Emily. *Hope: New Choices and Recovery Strategies for Adult Children of Alcoholics.* Harper 1987 $15.95. "A thorough, sympathetic psychotherapeutic guide to recovering from the trauma of having an alcoholic parent. . . . [Marlin] speaks from a knowledgeable point of view, experimental and scholarly, and is able to pass on both theoretical information and practical help" (*Kirkus Reviews*).

Mendelson, Jack H., and Nancy K. Mello. *Alcohol Use and Abuse in America.* Little, Brown 1985 $25.00. Overview of alcoholism, problems arising from its use and abuse, and its impact on all aspects of life.

Meryman, Richard. *Broken Promises, Mended Dreams: An Alcoholic Woman Fights for Her Life.* Little, Brown 1984 $16.95. The process of residential treatment for one alcoholic woman is painstakingly documented here based on the experiences of several individuals.

Moran, Megan. *Lost Years: Confessions of a Woman Alcoholic.* Doubleday 1985 $16.95. A vivid portrayal of life as an alcoholic.

Mumey, Jack. *Sitting in the Bay Window: A Book for Parents of Young Alcoholics.* Contemporary Bks. 1984 $12.95. Short readable guide offers specific suggestions for effective limit-setting; makes clear recommendations.

Olson, Steve, and Dean R. Gerstein. *Alcohol in America: Taking Action to Prevent Abuse.* Natl. Acad. Pr. 1985 $9.95. A distillation of a 1981 report initiated by the National Research Council and papers from a 1984 National Institute of Alcohol Abuse and Alcoholism conference.

Pace, Nicholas, and Wilbur Cross. *Guidelines to Safe Drinking.* McGraw-Hill 1984 $16.95. A guide for drinking intentionally, if one chooses to drink. The key is choice: of locations, times, and types of drink. Encourages alcoholics to abstain.

Plaint, Moira L. *Women, Drinking, and Pregnancy.* Tavistock 1985 $32.00. Presents historical and current information about alcohol consumption and its effects on pregnancy.

Rachel V. *Family Secrets: Life Stories of Adult Children of Alcoholics.* Harper 1987 $10.95. Fifteen stories of people who have experienced trauma or abuse as children of alcoholics. Stories provide tools for recovery and suggest ways of forgiving the alcoholic parent and giving up behavior patterns that might be self-destructive.

———. *A Woman Like You: Life Stories of Women Recovering from Alcoholism and Addiction.* Harper 1985 $15.95. In this fascinating collection women tell of their drinking and its effects on their lives, and of their attainment of sobriety.

Rosett, Henry L., and Lyu Weinder. *Alcohol and the Fetus: A Clinical Perspective.* Oxford 1984 $24.95. Reviews the literature on fetal alcohol syndrome and examines the clinical, experimental, and epidemiologic experience at the Boston City Hospital prenatal clinic.

Sexias, Judith S., and Geraldine Youcha. *Children of Alcoholism: A Survivor's Manual.* Crown 1985 $14.95. A sympathetic exploration of the psychological and physical scars that can result from growing up in an alcoholic home. Provides advice on how to come to terms with the past and where to seek professional help.

Wholey, Denis. *The Courage to Change: Personal Conversations about Alcoholism with Denis Wholey.* Houghton Mifflin 1984 $15.95. Celebrities' accounts of their struggles with alcohol and other drugs are grouped by theme: the beginning of alcoholism, the progression, quitting, a new life, the woman alcoholic, and alcoholism and homosexuality.

Drug Abuse

Baron, Jason D. *Kids and Drugs: A Parent's Handbook of Drug Abuse Prevention and Treatment.* Perigee 1984 $7.95. Covers drugs and their dangers, the factors leading to drug use, and preventive techniques and treatment.

Courtwright, David T. *Dark Paradise: Opiate Addiction in America Before 1940.* Harvard Univ. Pr. 1982 $20.00. A meticulous account of the demography of American opiate addiction before 1940.

Gold, Mark S. *800-Cocaine.* Bantam 1984 pap. $2.95. Taken primarily from Dr. Gold's experience with the callers to the toll-free cocaine hotline he founded in May 1983. Contains case reports demonstrating the problems with, and Gold's recommended solutions to, cocaine abuse.

Goulart, Frances Sheridan. *The Caffeine Book.* Dodd 1984 $8.95. Provides references to medical studies and reports concerning caffeine addiction and its effects on the body.

Green, Bernard. *Getting Over Getting High: How to Overcome Dependency on Cocaine, Caffeine, Hallucinogens, Marijuana, Speed, and Stimulants the Natural and Permanent Way.* Morrow 1984 $14.95. Identifies why people become addicts, how patterns of abuse develop, and the nature of psychological dependency. Recommends proper nutrition, megavitamins, minerals, relaxation, meditation, and mind expansion to replace psychological and physiological cravings for drugs of abuse.

Jones, Helen C., and Paul W. Lovinger. *The Marijuana Question and Science's Search for an Answer.* Dodd 1985 $24.95. Gathers together a massive amount of information about the potential physiological and psychological effects of marijuana. Thoroughly referenced.

Maddux, James F., and David P. Desmond. *Careers of Opioid Users.* Praeger 1981 $36.95. Provides a wealth of much-needed data on the life history of opioid addicts, including family background, social adjustment, initial drug and polydrug use, and mortality and morbidity.

Mann, Peggy. *Marijuana Alert.* McGraw-Hill 1984 o.p. A comprehensive, well-documented book about the use, abuse, and harmful effects of marijuana.

Platt, Jerome J. *Heroin Addiction: Theory, Research and Treatment.* Krieger 2d ed. 1986 $31.95. Begins with a detailed review of changes in the legal status of narcotic use in the United States. Describes the physiology and associated medical complications of heroin addiction, theories of addiction, an addict profile, and various treatments.

Reilly, Patrick. *A Private Practice.* Macmillan 1984 $14.95. More than just another personal account of overcoming drug addiction. Not only describes the intense physical and psychological struggle to master addiction to tranquilizers and sleeping pills, but also puts into perspective how Reilly's profession—medicine—contributed to the problem.

Rolling Stone Editors. *How to Get Off Drugs.* Simon & Schuster 1984 $16.95 pap. $6.95. A guide for drug users who are thinking about kicking their habit and for the friends and families who plan to assist them. Illicit psychoactive drugs, alcohol, prescription drugs, and other substances are all included.

Smoking

The federal office of the U.S. Department of Health and Human Services, Public Health Service, Office on Smoking and Health, issues very useful periodic reports on smoking and related topics, including *The Health Consequences of Smoking: A Report of the Surgeon General*, which is issued annually and focuses on specific aspects of smoking (1982, Cancer; 1984, Lung Disease; 1986, Involuntary Smoking; etc.); and *Smoking Tobacco & Health: A Fact Book* (1987). Another recent and useful title is *Review and Evaluation of Smoking Cessation Methods: United States and Canada, 1978–1985*, published in 1987. These reports can be found in most public libraries, or they can be purchased from the Superintendent of Documents, U.S. Government Printing Office, Washington, DC. Additional titles on smoking follow.

Ashton, Heather, and Rob Stepney. *Smoking: Psychology and Pharmacology.* Tavistock 1982 $8.95. An informative summary of the psychological, sociological, pharmacological, commercial, and medical aspects of smoking.

Balfour, D. J. K. *Nicotine and the Tobacco Smoking Habit.* Pergamon 1984 $65.00. Reviews various aspects of the pharmacology of nicotine and tobacco smoking. Most of the articles cited were published before 1981.

Fried, Peter, and Harry Oxorn. *Smoking for Two: Cigarettes and Pregnancy.* Free Pr. 1980 $10.95. An especially useful book on the effects of smoking on the unborn child, including "passive smoking," where the pregnant woman inhales other people's smoke.

Nash, Joyce. *Taking Charge of Your Smoking*. Bull 1981 $10.95. One of many books on quitting smoking, this text by a behavioral psychologist describes a wide variety of methods and strategies for breaking the habit.

Tollison, Robert D., ed. *Smoking and Society: Toward a More Balanced Assessment*. Lexington Bks. 1986 $15.95. An up-to-date compilation of essays on the social, economic, physiological, and political aspects of smoking.

Winter, Ruth. *The Scientific Case Against Smoking*. Crown 1980 $4.95. A compilation and discussion of scientific data derived for and from the 1979 *Surgeon General's Report on Smoking and Health*.

SURGERY

Surgery is a medical specialty in which operative or chiropractic procedures are used in the treatment of diseases, injuries, or deformities. As most books about surgery are written by and for physicians and not for the general reader, there are a limited number of entries in this section.

Christian, Rebecca, and others. *The Prevention Guide to Surgery and Its Alternatives*. Rodale 1980 o.p. "Covers seeking a second opinion, hospital choice, preoperative care, and operating and recovery room procedures as well as descriptions of common operations such as gallbladder removal, hysterectomy and surgery for ulcers" (*LJ*).

Eiseman, Ben. *What Are My Chances?* Saunders 1980 o.p. Statistics on the probabilities of cures and the complications of diseases arranged in a flowchart with explanatory annotations.

Kra, Siegfried J., and Robert S. Boltax. *Is Surgery Necessary*. Macmillan 1981 $11.95. "Covers choices available to patients for whom surgery has been recommended" (*LJ*).

Schneider, Robert G. *When to Say No to Surgery: How to Decide If You Need the Most Often Performed Operations*. Prentice-Hall 1982 $10.95. "Examines 21 of the most commonly performed operations in America, discusses when they are or are not indicated, and the risks, complications, alternatives, financial guidelines, and other information not generally publicly available" (*LJ*).

THERAPEUTICS

Therapeutics is a plan of treatment for a disease or defect based on a correct interpretation of the symptoms and a knowledge of the physiological action of the remedy used. Because most of the books on treatment are extremely technical, there are few entries in this section.

Berkow, Robert, ed. *The Merck Manual of Diagnosis and Therapy*. Merck 14th ed. 1982 $19.75. Organized by organ system primarily affected or on the basis of discipline, includes symptoms, complications, diagnosis, treatment, and prognosis.

Mangel, Charles, and Allen Weisse. *Medicine: The State of the Art*. Doubleday 1984 o.p. "Describes advances in cardiology, orthopedics, organ transplants, burn treatment, and cancer" (*LJ*).

Napoli, Maryann. *Health Facts: A Critical Evaluation of the Major Problems, Treatments and Alternatives Facing Medical Consumers.* Fwd. by James W. Long, Overlook Pr. 1983 $22.95 pap. $8.95. "A critical but relatively fair evaluation of some of the major health problems and treatments. Will help readers to choose more intelligently from the available alternatives" (*Choice*).

Robin, Eugene. *Matters of Life and Death: Risks vs. Benefits of Medical Care.* W. H. Freeman 1984 $21.95 pap. $11.95. "Analyzes the risk versus benefit of various diagnostic or therapeutic tests (procedures), the inter-relationship between patient and physician, the factors affecting the decision to accept risky procedures or heroic therapy, and, finally, basic principles for the care of the terminally ill patient" (*Choice*).

UROLOGIC DISEASES

Books on diseases of the urinary system (kidneys, bladder, and so on) that are not of an extremely technical nature are hard to find. Listed are a few recent titles written for a lay audience.

Gillespie, Larrian, and Sandra Blakeslee. *You Don't Have to Live with Cystitis! A Woman Urologist Tells How to Avoid It—What to Do About It.* Rawson 1986 $18.95. "Discusses causes, diagnosis, treatment and prevention. Covers childhood, pregnancy, and menopause as they relate to cystitis" (*LJ*).

The Human Body. The Kidneys: Balancing the Fluids. Torstar Bks. 1985 $20.95. The survival of the human depends to a large degree on the functions and processes of the kidneys. The kidneys, in a series of complex interactions with the brain and pituitary gland, blood vessels, and the adrenal glands, keep body fluids in balance. Includes physiology, anatomy, disease and disorders, transplantation, and dialysis.

Managing Incontinence: A Guide to Living with the Loss of Urinary Control. Ed. by Cheryle Gartley, Green Hill Pubs. 1985 $12.95. "Personal recollections, revealing and often humorous, of men and women with continence problems stemming from a variety of causes. Deals with anatomy and physiology of the urinary tract, medical treatments frequently used, devices and products and coping strategies" (*LJ*).

Scharf, Martin. *Waking Up Dry: How to End Bedwetting Forever.* Writers Digest 1986 pap. $7.95. Based on the successful program Scharf developed as a specialist at the Sleep Disorders Laboratory of Mercy Hospital (Cincinnati).

Seidick, Kathryn. *Or You Can Let Him Go.* Delacorte 1984 $15.95; Dell 1985 pap. $3.95. "The compelling valiant struggle of the [Seidick] family when faced with the sudden onset of end-stage renal disease in their eight-year-old son" (*LJ*).

CHAPTER 16

Clinical Psychology and Psychiatry

Amedeo Giorgi

The psychiatric patient stands apart from the rest of the world. . . . Loneliness is the central core of his illness, no matter what his illness may be. Thus, loneliness is the nucleus of psychiatry. If loneliness did not exist, we could reasonably assume that psychiatric illness could not occur either, with the exception of the few disturbances caused by anatomical or physiological disorders of the brain.

—J. H. van den Berg

Psychology, it has been said, has a long past but a short history. It has a long past because the subject matter of psychology—how individuals experience, behave in, and make sense of the world—was studied and written about by the ancient Greeks. However, it has a short history because only in modern times have psychology and psychiatry been able to access this material as modern sciences. Thus, in the modern sense, psychology and psychiatry began with their institutionalization within the framework of science. Signs indicate that the meaning of science may itself undergo evolution as it grows and expands to meet the pressures of concrete problems.

The modern era of psychology dates from 1879, when Wilhelm Wundt founded a laboratory at the University of Leipzig in Germany. It began by studying the phenomenon of consciousness—trying to determine its individual elements and how these elements were synthesized. Essentially, this type of psychology consisted of many introspective studies and experiments in sensation and perception. However, psychology in its scientific phase did not remain within the limits of this definition for very long. Around 1915, three important differentiations took place. What today is known as Gestalt psychology, reacting to the elementism of the Wundtian study of consciousness, emphasized that the experience of the world was organized and structured and that the task of psychology was to study these experiential structures. At the same time, JOHN B. WATSON (see Vol. 3), an American psychologist, thought that the study of consciousness was too narrow and elusive, and declared that psychology should study the behavior of organisms because it was more tangible, more robust, and practically speaking, workable. Finally, Sigmund Freud's influence began to infiltrate academic circles. Because of his studies of hysterics and dreams, Freud emphasized a psychology based on the unconscious, not consciousness. These three basic perspectives and their offshoots competed for dominance within scientific psychology for about 40 years.

In the mid-1950s, two more differentiations took place. One was the return of the mind and its characteristics in the form of cognitive psychology, currently the dominant perspective of mainstream psychology. This perspective emphasizes the study of how the mind gets information about the world. The other was the emergence of humanistic psychology, founded to fill a perceived gap in mainstream psychology, namely, the study of the human person as a unique individual and of the human species as possessing unique characteristics.

The above overview is meant to show that psychology is not all of one piece. This should not be surprising given the complexity of human existence and the brief time that modern psychology and psychiatry have had to discover their niches and accomplish their tasks. Nevertheless, the subject is even more complicated if clinical psychology and the professional dimensions of the fields are considered, because they pressure psychology in a wholly different way: How helpful is psychology to people suffering various experiential and behavioral maladies and conflicts?

Clinical psychology developed from the need to help people who were functioning poorly in their everyday world but were not primarily physically ill. Two major developments resulted: the establishment of clinics for dealing initially with retarded or handicapped individuals and later with purely psychological disturbances; and the invention and refinement of measuring and testing instruments, first for sensory and motor capacities, then for assessing intelligence and personality. Thus, clinical psychology was always concerned both with practical issues and the amelioration of either social or personal problems. Today, clinical psychologists still follow in this tradition, but in a highly expanded way. They are interested in theoretical issues of personality development, such as normal and abnormal functioning, personal capacities, skills and interests, and in such practical work as psychotherapy, diagnostic testing, educational and vocational evaluation of individuals and groups, and in general, the use of techniques and practical strategies to help people help themselves. Of all these interests, testing and psychotherapy seem to be the major ones. There are many types of tests and many competing forms of psychotherapy—behavioral therapy, Gestalt therapy, psychoanalysis, cognitive therapeutic approaches, and humanistic orientations—which more or less parallel the academic differentiations discussed above.

Psychiatry, like medical psychology, goes back to the ancient Greeks with whom the discipline reached a high level of sophistication. It declined, however, after the fall of Rome and continued to do so through the Middle Ages. Resurrected during the Renaissance by the work of Vives, PARACELSUS (see also Vol. 4), Weyer, and others, it finally became a specialty in its own right in the nineteenth century, especially with the classificatory system of Emil Kraepelin.

Psychiatry has its roots in and continues to be involved with "abnormal psychology," that is, with behavior or experience that is in some way or another bizarre or inappropriate to the circumstances. Everything else in psychiatry revolves around this primitive but concrete fact. Given this inappropriate or ineffective manifestation, one can look for the causes in the body—in the nervous or endocrine systems—or in the depths of the unconscious psyche or preconscious infantile experiences, or in the individual's relation to significant others or to culture as a whole. Once these abnormalities are discovered, one can describe, typify, and rank them. One can then also develop a therapy to address the assumed cause: shock therapy for neurological causes, drugs for chemical malfunctions, psychoanalysis for unconscious causes, and other forms of psychotherapy to deal with cultural deprivations.

Thus, psychiatry is not all of one piece either. Indeed, conflict has long been the norm in psychiatry, and today the disunity is compounded by the presence of "antipsychiatrists"—that is, those wishing to break away from the medical model altogether. Whether this movement is the beginning of a true answer to the perennial quest of psychiatry, or just another element in the conflict, only time will tell. Having found itself in the nineteenth century, perhaps psychiatry can find a way of interpreting its various dimensions in the twentieth century.

GENERAL PSYCHOLOGY

Abramson, Paul. *Personality*. Henry Holt 1980 text ed. $28.95. "Interesting, readable, and thereby appealing to both the nonmajor and major in psychology" (*Contemporary Psychology*).

Atwater, Eastwood. *Psychology of Adjustment: Personal Growth in a Changing World*. Prentice-Hall 3d ed. 1987 $28.67. This "excellent text for introductory courses on psychology of adjustment, employs a humanistic, growth-oriented approach" (*Contemporary Psychology*).

Averill, James R. *Anger and Aggression: An Essay on Emotion*. Springer-Verlag 1982 $34.00. "Ought to be read by anyone who is seriously interested in theories of emotion" (*Contemporary Psychology*).

Bandura, Albert, ed. *Psychological Modeling: Conflicting Theories*. [*Controversy Ser.*] Lieber-Atherton 1971 o.p. "Nine chapters, each written by an expert scientist well known for his research in modeling. . . . The reference features are exceptionally good with each article having its own bibliography" (*Choice*).

Beigel, Hugo G. *Dictionary of Psychology and Related Fields*. Ungar 1971 $15.00. "Indispensable for those doing research based on original works of Freud, Jung, Adler, Binswanger, Bleuler, et al." (*Choice*).

Boring, E. G. *A History of Experimental Psychology*. Prentice-Hall 2d ed. 1950 $42.95. The classic text of the field giving plenty of biographical information plus good discussions of substantive issues.

Coon, Dennis. *Introduction to Psychology: Exploration and Application*. West Publishing 4th ed. 1986 text ed. $32.95. " 'Instructionally engineered' should be emblazoned on the cover of this introductory book, whose design includes as many features intended to facilitate learning the contents as any nonprogrammed text I have seen" (*Contemporary Psychology*).

Corsini, Raymond J., ed. *Encyclopedia of Psychology*. Wiley 4 vols. 1984 $249.95. An up-to-date summary of psychological terms.

Gilligan, Carol. *In a Different Voice: Psychological Theory and Women's Development.* Harvard Univ. Pr. 1983 pap. $5.95. "Gilligan treats her subject clearly and concisely" (*Bk. Review Digest*).

Goldenberg, Herbert. *Contemporary Clinical Psychology.* [*Psychology Ser.*] Brooks-Cole 2d ed. 1982 text ed. $22.50. Good introduction for nonclinical professionals.

Harriman, Philip L. *Dictionary of Psychology.* Citadel Pr. repr. of 1960 ed. 1971 o.p.

———. *Handbook of Psychological Terms.* [*Quality Pap. Ser.*] Littlefield, repr. of 1965 ed. 1977 pap. $6.95. A guidebook to the technical vocabulary of scientific psychology.

The Harvard List of Books in Psychology. Harvard Univ. Pr. 4th ed. 1971 pap. $2.75. Contains 744 entries arranged by basic subject areas and selected by 40 specialists in their respective fields.

Haynes, Stephen N., ed. *Psychosomatic Disorders: A Psychological Approach to Etiology and Treatment.* Henry Holt 1981 $47.95. "A scholarly, readable volume on an array of disorders" (*Contemporary Psychology*).

Hillman, James. *Revisioning Psychology.* Harper 1977 pap. $7.95. "As an explorer of the imaginal realm of the psyche, faithful to the reality of the archetypes rather than to one theory about them, Hillman has no living peer" (*LJ*).

Lifton, Robert J. *Boundaries: Psychological Man in Revolution.* Simon & Schuster 1976 pap. $2.95. Contains reflections on man's changing sense of self in relation to the complex themes of life, such as death, destruction, and revolution.

Miller, Jean B. *Toward a New Psychology of Women.* Beacon 1986 lib. bdg. $16.00 pap. $6.95. "[An] excellent social psychological analysis of the role and status of women, [it] focuses on women as a minority group" (*LJ*).

Nordby, Vernon J., and Calvin S. Hall. *A Guide to Psychologists and Their Concepts.* [*Psychology Ser.*] W. H. Freeman 1974 text ed. pap. $9.95. "Each concept is individually treated, in a logical order, and then explained . . . in laymen's terms" (*Bk. Review Digest*).

Sanford, Nevitt. *Issues in Personality Theory.* [*Social and Behavioral Sciences Ser.*] Jossey-Bass 1970 o.p. "In the Preface, Sanford states the intent to organize his book not around a single theory or stages of development but rather in terms of issues ordered according . . . 'to a broad, theoretically neutral conceptual scheme' " (*Contemporary Psychology*).

Shaffer, John B. *Humanistic Psychology.* [*Foundations of Modern Psychology Ser.*] Prentice-Hall 1978 text ed. pap. $19.95. Good supplementary reader.

Tarczan, Constance. *An Educator's Guide to Psychological Tests: Descriptions and Classroom Implications.* C. C. Thomas 1975 pap. $12.75. Makes psychological testing and its implications of use to the teacher or school counselor.

Vander Zanden, James W. *Human Development.* Random 3d ed 1985 text ed. $27.95. "This is a very readable text designed to show students how individuals develop across the life span. . . . A good introductory developmental text, well written, carefully documented, and broad in its approach" (*Contemporary Psychology*).

Watson, Robert I. *The Great Psychologists.* Harper 4th ed. 1978 text ed. pap. $20.50. Covers important figures and historical problems in the development of psychology.

Wheelis, Allen. *How People Change.* Harper 1974 pap. $5.95. "This is a well-written, even poetic book that defines in direct human terms the meaning of freedom and the importance of the exercise of free choice in the creative growth and fulfillment of the individual" (*LJ*).

———. *Quest for Identity.* Norton 1966 pap. $6.95. An essay on modern man and his quest for identity as well as a critique of the role of psychoanalysis in this quest.

Wolman, Benjamin B. *Dictionary of Behavioral Science.* Van Nostrand 1973 $24.50.

Contains 1,200 short entries on terms, persons, and tests in psychology, psychiatry, and neurology.

Zusne, Leonard. *Names in the History of Psychology: A Biographical Sourcebook.* Wiley 1975 o.p. "Biographical information about the most eminent psychologists" (*LJ*).

PSYCHIATRY

American Psychiatric Association. *Biographical Directory of the American Psychiatric Association.* Bowker 7th ed. 1977 o.p. This authoritative biographical record of psychiatrists in the United States and Canada is a guide to the 20,000 members of the American Psychiatric Association as of 1977. Members are listed alphabetically with a geographical index for convenient cross-reference. An excellent sourcebook and an essential for all libraries.

Arieti, Silvano, and others, eds. *American Handbook of Psychiatry.* Basic Bks. 8 vols. 2d ed. rev. 1974–87 set $395.00 vol. 7 (1981) $45.50 vol. 8 (1987) $75.00. A complete encyclopedia of psychiatric forms and concepts.

Brussel, James A. *The Layman's Guide to Psychiatry.* Barnes & Noble 2d ed. 1971 pap. $2.75

Brussel, James A., and George L. Cantzlaar. *The Layman's Dictionary of Psychiatry.* Harper 1967 o.p. "The approximately 1,500 descriptive psychiatric terms (including names of famous psychoanalysts and psychiatrists) found in this dictionary are defined in an understandable, jargon-free style" (*Choice*).

Grinker, Roy R., Sr. *Psychiatry in Broad Perspective.* Human Sciences Pr. 1975 $34.95. "This book is largely a personalized, multidisciplinary overview of aspects of psychiatric research by a psychiatrist who has spent 40 years in the field. It considers topics such as the qualities of a researcher, designing a research program [and] aspects of biological, psychoanalytic and clinical research" (*LJ*).

Grob, Gerald, ed. *The Inner World of American Psychiatry, 1890 to 1940: Selected Correspondence.* Rutgers Univ. Pr. 1985 text ed. $25.00. "Selected correspondence from the men who helped shape American psychiatry, but organized in such a way that light is thrown on many of the contemporary issues and problems of psychiatry" (*Contemporary Psychology*).

Hinsie, Leland E., and Robert Campbell. *Psychiatric Dictionary.* Oxford 4th ed. 1970 $26.50. "This fourth edition is a continuing version of the Dictionary by Leland E. Hinsie and Jacob Shatzky, first published in 1940. . . . About five hundred entries have been deleted and some fourteen hundred new listings included. In making changes, the editor has been guided by several factors: 'clinical relevance, with the assumption that much basic knowledge is readily available in specialised texts; the frequency with which items recur in general texts and psychiatric journals; and the degree to which a new concept or method appears to have received confirmation in subsequent investigations' " (*Contemporary Review*).

Horton, Paul C. *Solace: The Missing Dimension in Psychiatry.* Univ. of Chicago Pr. 1981 $15.00 1983 pap. $7.95. "Useful introduction to the concept of transitional phenomena" (*Contemporary Psychology*).

Melges, Frederick T. *Time and the Inner Future: A Temporal Approach to Psychiatric Disorders.* Wiley 1982 $38.95. Well organized and enjoyable.

Miller, Milton H. *If the Patient Is You (Or Someone You Love): Psychiatry Inside Out.* Scribner 1977 o.p. For the layperson.

Strecker, Edward Adam. *Basic Psychiatry.* Random 1952 o.p. Excellent survey for the general reader.

Tseng, Wen-Shing, and John McDermott, Jr. *Culture, Mind and Therapy: An Introduction to Cultural Psychiatry.* Brunner-Mazel 1981 $27.50. A well-written pioneer work in the discipline of cultural psychiatry.

Wing, John K., and Brenda Morris, eds. *Handbook of Psychiatric Rehabilitation Practice.* Oxford 1981 text ed. pap. $15.95. A practical manual for professionals and their staffs who currently provide rehabilitative services for the mentally ill.

Zilboorg, Gregory, and George W. Henry. *A History of Medical Psychology.* Norton 1967 pap. $5.95. A fascinating account of the development of psychiatry from the ancient Greeks to the twentieth century. It has depth and breadth and is good reading for anyone interested in cultural history, not just psychiatry.

SPECIAL READING LISTS

Children

Aichhorn, August. *Wayward Youth.* Intro. by Sigmund Freud, Northwestern Univ. Pr. repr. of 1936 ed. 1983 pap. $7.95. An important early interpretation of the application of psychoanalytic theory to problems of children.

Chess, Stella. *An Introduction to Child Psychiatry.* Grune 2d ed. 1969 $40.00

Coles, Robert. *Children of Crisis.* Little, Brown 5 vols. 1967–78 pap. ea. $10.00–$19.95. The classic studies on children's perspectives on life by a respected psychiatrist. Engaging and insightful.

Conners, C. Keith. *Food Additives for Hyperactive Children.* Plenum 1980 $22.50. Written for a well-informed adult.

Copeland, Donna R., and others, eds. *The Mind of the Child Who Is Said to Be Sick.* C. C. Thomas 1983 $32.75. "This is an effective book. It is poetic and touching, as well as broadly informative about the situation of the chronically ill, cancer-stricken child or adolescent" (*Contemporary Psychology*).

Corsini, Raymond J., and Genevieve Painter. *The Practical Parent: The ABC's of Child Discipline.* Harper 1975 $15.45. This book presents "the Dreikurs/Adlerian method of family living and child rearing" (*LJ*).

Finkelhor, David. *Sexually Victimized Children.* Free Pr. 1979 $19.95 text ed. pap. $12.95. "For anyone interested in the child sexual abuse/incest question" (*Contemporary Psychology*).

Frude, Neil, ed. *Psychological Approaches to Child Abuse.* Rowman 1981 $13.95. "Presents a quite good selection of papers; recommended for anyone who wants an overview of a diversity of approaches to understanding the etiology and effects of abusive care-taking" (*Contemporary Psychology*).

Jenkins, Richard L., and Ernest Harms, eds. *Understanding Disturbed Children: Professional Insights into Their Psychiatric and Developmental Problems.* Special Child Pubns. 1976 o.p. "Multi-authored text for students of child psychiatry—provides excellent presentation of the 'state of the art' of this subspecialty as it is currently practiced" (*Contemporary Psychology*).

Josephson, Martin M., and Robert T. Porter. *Clinician's Handbook of Childhood Psychopathology.* Aronson 1980 $35.00. "Pediatricians, teachers, and other professionals who work with children and require only a broad, but shallow, exposure to child psychopathology will find the book helpful" (*Contemporary Psychology*).

Kagan, Jerome, and Robert Coles, eds. *Twelve to Sixteen: Early Adolescence.* Norton 1972 $15.00 text ed. pap. $7.95. "In this very uncommon collection of essays, a group of experts from a variety of social science disciplines talk about the young adolescent. It is an uncommon collection both because of the uniformly high quality of the contributions and because of the way in which diverse pieces nonetheless hang together as a meaningful whole" (*Contemporary Psychology*).

Kanner, Leo. *Child Psychiatry*. C. C. Thomas 4th ed. 1979 $22.75

————. *Childhood Psychosis: Initial Studies and New Insights*. Halsted Pr. 1973 o.p.

Lahey, Benjamin B., and Alan E. Kazdin, eds. *Advances in Clinical Child Psychology*. Plenum 7 vols. 1980–1986 ea. $39.50–$45.00. Up-to-date readable reviews.

Moustakas, Clark E. *The Child's Discovery of Himself*. Aronson 1974 $12.50

Poussaint, Alvin, and James Comer. *Black Child Care*. Simon & Schuster 1975 o.p. Written in a question-and-answer format, this book studies the development of the black child from infancy through adolescence.

Starr, R. H., Jr., ed. *Child Abuse Predictions: Policy Implications*. Ballinger 1982 $32.95. Readable and well researched.

Walker, Sydney, III. *Help for the Hyperactive Child*. Houghton Mifflin 1979 o.p. "His examples, for the most part, are drawn from cases that clearly demonstrate medical or emotional problems other than what has been called 'minimal brain dysfunction' or the 'hyperkinetic-learning disability syndrome' " (*LJ*).

Whiting, Beatrice B., and John Whiting. *Children of Six Cultures: A Psycho-Cultural Analysis*. Harvard Univ. Pr. 1974 text ed. $16.50 pap. $6.95. "A study of the observed social behavior of 134 children from the ages of three to eleven in Okinawa, Kenya, India, Mexico, and the United States" (*LJ*).

Zimbardo, Philip G., and Shirley Radl. *The Shy Child: A Parent's Guide to Preventing and Overcoming Shyness from Infancy to Adulthood*. McGraw-Hill 1981 $11.95. "Presents a conceptualization of shyness based primarily on survey data, anecdotal case material, and clinical experience and intuition" (*Contemporary Psychology*).

Methods and Approaches in Counseling and Therapy

Beck, Aaron T. *Cognitive Therapy and the Emotional Disorders*. International Univ. Pr. 1976 text ed. $30.00; New Amer. Lib. 1979 pap. $6.95. "Case illustrations and a review of cognitive approaches to therapy" (*Contemporary Psychology*).

Bellack, Alan S., Michael Hersen, and Alan E. Kuzdin, eds. *International Handbook of Behavior Modification and Therapy*. Plenum 1982 $95.00. An indispensable book for libraries and reference collections.

Binder, Virginia, Arnold Binder, and Bernard Rimland, eds. *Modern Therapies*. Prentice-Hall 1976 pap. $5.95. A general panorama of therapies including the innovations of the 1970s. Prepared for the lay reader.

Blocher, Donald H., and Donald A. Biggs. *Counseling Psychology in Community Settings*. Springer Pub. 1983 text ed. $23.95. "A treatise that offers a reservoir of clear ideas that will help students understand and prepare for the challenges of this profession" (*Contemporary Psychology*).

Bockus, Frank. *Couple Therapy*. Aronson 1980 $27.50. "Leaves the reader with an excellent understanding of what the experimental approach has to offer" (*Contemporary Psychology*).

Burks, Herbert M., Jr., and Buford Stefflre, eds. *Theories of Counseling*. McGraw-Hill 3d ed. 1979 o.p. "Useful for beginning counselors and personnel workers who have need for basic information on theories of counseling" (*Counseling Psychology*).

Chertok, Leon. *Sense and Nonsense in Psychology: The Challenge of Hypnosis*. Pergamon 1981 $40.00 pap. $19.75. "The reader will learn much that is of value about hypnosis and its ability as a therapeutic and research tool" (*Contemporary Psychology*).

Collier, Helen V. *Counseling Women: A Guide for Therapists*. Macmillan 1982 text ed.

$24.95. "Addressed to mental health workers, psychiatrists, psychologists, and social workers, but also will be useful to others who serve or are interested in women's needs" (*LJ*).

De Schill, Stefan, ed. *The Challenge for Group Psychotherapy: Present and Future.* International Univ. Pr. 1974 text ed. $40.00. Eleven different authors provide several interesting glimpses of analytic therapy.

Dinkmeyer, Don C., and James J. Muro. *Group Counseling: Theory and Practice.* Peacock Pubs. 2d ed. 1979 o.p. A useful introduction for anyone interested in learning about group work.

Engelkes, James R. *Introduction to Counseling.* Houghton Mifflin 1982 $29.95. "Simple, but useful introduction to difficult concepts of counseling" (*Contemporary Psychology*).

Feder, Bud, and R. Ronall, eds. *Beyond the Hot Seat: Gestalt Approaches to Group.* Brunner-Mazel 1980 o.p. "A reflection of the current mental health gestalt, with all its promise of great benefits, its multidirectional development, and its ambiguities" (*Contemporary Psychology*).

Forsyth, Donelson R. *An Introduction to Group Dynamics.* [*Psychology Ser.*] Brooks-Cole 1982 text ed. $25.00. Good introduction to the field.

Frank, Jerome D. *Persuasion and Healing: A Comparative Study of Psychotherapy.* Schocken rev. ed. 1974 pap. $8.95. An attempt to tease out what is common to many forms of psychotherapy. Very comprehensive.

Freeman, Dorothy R. *Marital Crisis and Short-term Counseling: A Casebook.* Free Pr. 1982 $22.95. "Recommended to the novice, the general reader, and the experienced clinician alike" (*Contemporary Psychology*).

Freeman, Harrop A. *Counseling in the United States.* Oceana 1967 $15.00. "A very detailed study on the most elementary aspects of counseling as a distinct profession" (*LJ*).

Getz, William L., and others. *Brief Counseling with Suicidal Persons.* Lexington Bks. 1982 $26.00. A logical and clear exposition, presenting concrete examples along with concepts.

Gibson, H. B. *Hypnosis: Its Nature and Therapeutic Uses.* Taplinger repr. of 1978 ed. 1980 $8.95 pap. $4.95. "For the person who is reading about hypnosis for the first time, this book immediately captures the interest and holds the attention of the reader" (*Choice*).

Glasser, William. *Reality Therapy: A New Approach to Psychiatry.* Harper 1965 $11.45 1975 pap. $6.95. Glasser attacks the Freudian method of concentrating on the past life of an individual in therapy and builds his new therapy on showing patients how to manage their present and future lives. He has wide experience as a psychiatrist in Los Angeles and a consultant to school systems.

Greenhill, Maurice H., and Alexander Gralnick, eds. *Psychopharmacology and Psychotherapy.* Free Pr. 1982 text ed. $29.95. Readers with clinical interests will find this book especially appealing.

Guerin, Philip J., Jr., ed. *Family Therapy: Theory and Practice.* Gardner Pr. 1976 text ed. $29.50. "Covers a rich variety of clinical and theoretical issues in 31 articles on technique, approaches, and significant clinical issues in family therapy" (*Contemporary Psychology*).

Gustafson, James Paul. *The Complex Secret of Brief Psychotherapy.* Norton 1986 $34.95. This work is marvelously readable, but still notes the profound differences separating different therapies and how some of these differences can be reconciled.

Haley, Jay. *Ordeal Therapy: Unusual Ways to Change Behavior.* [*Social and Behavioral*

Sciences Ser.] Jossey-Bass 1984 text ed. $19.95. "Ordeal therapy, which builds on the work of Milton Erickson, has one central idea: to impose an ordeal that is more severe than the problem behavior the person is trying to change. Thus changing becomes easier and more attractive than continuing the problem behavior. The book consists of 13 case histories demonstrating this approach. . . . The descriptions are quite engaging and entertaining" (*Choice*).

————. *Problem-Solving Therapy: New Strategies for Effective Family Therapy.* Harper 1984 pap. $6.95. A "how-to book whose goal is to teach therapists specific techniques in dealing with family relationships" (*Contemporary Psychology*).

Harper, R. *The New Psychotherapies.* Prentice-Hall 1975 o.p. A survey of treatment methods that have developed since 1959. "The student of behavioral science as well as the intelligent layman would find the book a helpful map for the existing psychotherapy maze" (*Contemporary Psychology*).

Horewitz, James S. *Transactional Analysis and Family Therapy.* Aronson 1979 $30.00. For the paraprofessional who does not have extensive training in psychiatry.

Kahn, Marvin W. *Basic Methods for Mental Health Practitioners.* Little, Brown 1981 text ed. $18.95. "Directly helpful to workers in community mental health programs and those involved in training, supervising, and working with paraprofessionals" (*Contemporary Psychology*).

Korchin, Sheldon. *Modern Clinical Psychology.* Basic Bks. 1976 text ed. $22.95. A broad overview of modern techniques and approaches to clinical psychology.

Kovel, Joel. *A Complete Guide to Therapy: From Psychotherapy to Behavior Modification.* Pantheon 1976 $10.00 1977 pap. $5.95. "Recommended to the ordinary consumer of therapeutic services" (*Contemporary Psychology*).

Krippner, Stanley, and Alberto Villoldo. *The Realms of Healing.* Celestial Arts 1986 pap. $9.95. A survey of types of therapies and healings, including those of other cultures and primitive societies.

Kroger, William S. *Clinical and Experimental Hypnosis: In Medicine, Dentistry and Psychology.* Lippincott 2d ed. 1977 $36.75. "A convenient beginning library for anyone becoming intrigued by hypnosis" (*Contemporary Psychology*).

Lanyon, Richard I., and Barbara P. Lanyon. *Behavior Therapy: A Clinical Introduction.* [*Topics in Clinical Psychology Ser.*] Addison-Wesley 1978 text ed. pap. $11.95. Excellent introduction to the subject.

Marlatt, G. Alan, and Peter E. Nathan, eds. *Behavioral Approaches to Alcoholism.* Rutgers Center of Alcohol Studies Pubns. 1978 pap. $6.00. A good, stimulating introduction.

Morse, Stephen J. *Psychotherapies: A Comparative Casebook.* Henry Holt 1977 text ed. $27.95. A good reference book with 24 case studies.

Naar, Ray. *A Primer of Group Psychotherapy.* Human Sciences Pr. 1982 $24.95 pap. $14.95. "Presents marvelous case material that illustrates his approach to group treatment . . . should be of particular interest to beginning group psychotherapists interested in the practical aspects of group leadership" (*Contemporary Psychology*).

Okun, Barbara F., and Louis J. Rappaport. *Working with Families: An Introduction to Family Therapy.* Dunbury Pr. 1980 o.p. A good introduction to systems and developmental theory; a solid survey of different approaches to family systems therapy.

O'Leary, K. Daniel, and G. Terence Wilson. *Behavior Therapy: Application and Outcome.* Prentice-Hall 1975 $29.95. Suitable for use by undergraduates.

Patterson, C. H. *Theories of Counseling and Psychotherapy.* Harper 3d ed. 1980 text ed. $30.95. A thorough overview of different counseling and therapy theories.

Paul, Norman L., and Betty Paul. *A Marital Puzzle: Trans-generational Analysis in Marriage Counseling.* Gardner Pr. rev. ed. repr. of 1975 ed. 1986 pap. $16.95. Includes transcripts of eight therapy sessions.

Perez, Joseph F. *Family Counseling.* Van Nostrand 1979 o.p. Should be read by anyone interested in social injustice.

Perls, Frederick S. *Gestalt Therapy Verbatim.* Bantam 1971 pap. $3.50; Real People Pr. 1969 $10.00 pap. $6.50. "The book is essential for understanding recent developments in this school of existentialist therapy" (*Bk. Review Digest*).

Peszke, Michael A. *Involuntary Treatment of the Mentally Ill: The Problem of Autonomy.* C. C. Thomas 1975 $21.50. "Valuable for those uninformed about the basis of traditional worlds of mental disorders" (*Contemporary Psychology*).

Rossi, Ernest Lawrence. *The Psychobiology of Mind-Body Healing: New Concepts of Therapeutic Hypnosis.* Norton 1986 $25.95. An excellent review of the neurophysiological dimensions of body-mind reactions and an elaboration of how hypnosis may help normal functioning.

Segraves, R. Taylor. *Marital Therapy: A Combined Psychodynamic-Behavioral Approach.* Plenum 1982 $24.50. " 'Must' reading for students of marital therapy. . . . [The] author presents volumes of information on the topic in a well-organized style" (*Contemporary Psychology*).

Seligman, Milton. *Group Counseling and Group Psychotherapy with Rehabilitation Clients.* C. C. Thomas 1977 $22.00 pap. $17.00. "Effective combination of scholarly work and practical methods that results in a very readable book" (*Contemporary Psychology*).

Shear, Howard J. *Understanding Psychotherapy: A Paradox of Being.* Dabor Science Pubns. 1977 o.p. Good for the undergraduate or general reader.

Stephenson, F. Douglas, ed. *Gestalt Therapy Primer: Introductory Readings in Gestalt Therapy.* Aronson 1978 $20.00; C. C. Thomas 1975 pap. $22.75. A collection of articles about the history, philosophy, methods, and practice of Gestalt therapy written by 11 first- and second-generation practicing Gestalt therapists.

Tjosvold, Dean, and Mary Tjosvold. *Working with Mentally Handicapped Persons in Their Residences.* Free Pr. 1981 text ed. $24.95. Useful resource for professionals.

Usdin, Gene, ed. *Overview of the Psychotherapies.* Brunner-Mazel 1975 $12.50. The use of drugs in the treatment of mental illness. Recognized experts in the field of psychiatry write about different approaches to therapy.

Watkins, Mary. *Invisible Guests: The Development of Imaginal Dialogues.* Analytic Pr. 1986 $24.95. An important contribution to the life of the imagination. Watkins shows that imaginal dialogues—dialogues with imaginary others—have value for individuals throughout their lives.

Watzlawick, Paul. *The Language of Change: Elements of Therapeutic Communication.* Basic Bks. 1978 text ed. $13.95. "Psychotherapists and those interested in interpersonal influence will appreciate and benefit from this work" (*Contemporary Psychology*).

———. *The Situation Is Hopeless, But Not Serious: The Pursuit of Unhappiness.* Norton 1983 $10.95. Watzlawick's style is engaging, intriguing, and thought-provoking. Lay readers will find him accessible and encouraging.

Wedding, Dan, and Raymond J. Corsini, eds. *Great Cases in Psychotherapy.* Peacock Pubs. 1979 text ed. pap. $14.95. Intended for the student with little background in the field.

Weiner, Irving B., ed. *Clinical Methods in Psychology.* Wiley 2d ed. 1983 $49.95. "Surveys assessment and intervention methods in a way that addresses the needs of both beginning and experienced clinicians" (*Contemporary Psychology*).

Weiner, Myron F. *Therapist Disclosure: The Use of Self in Psychotherapy.* Univ. Park

Pr. 2d ed. 1983 text ed. $26.00. Recommended for therapists and readers interested in psychotherapy.

Wolberg, Lewis R. *The Technique of Psychotherapy*. Grune 3d ed. 1977 $99.50. Valuable compendium for students and professionals.

Yablonsky, Lewis. *Psychodrama: Resolving Emotional Problems Through Role-playing*. Gardner Pr. repr. of 1976 ed. 1981 text ed. pap. $14.95. A practicing psychodramatist writes about his profession in a clear and readable way.

Yalom, Irvin D. *Existential Psychotherapy*. Basic Bks. 1980 $21.95. Students, teachers, and practitioners will benefit from Yalom's presentation of concepts and his lucid explanations.

Miscellaneous

Arieti, Silvano. *The Will to Be Human*. Dell 1975 o.p.; Times Bks. 1972 o.p. "Makes a forthright plea for the individual's right to determine his own life. . . . Humanistic examination of the capacity of man to grow by conscious willing places Arieti—despite some specific disagreements with their theories—in the same school with Fromm and Erikson" (*PW*).

Askenasy, Alexander. *Attitudes Toward Mental Patients*. [*New Babylon Studies in the Social Sciences*] Mouton 1974 text ed. $23.20. Ideally suited for public officials who have the influence to bring about necessary changes.

Axline, Virginia M. *Dibs: In Search of Self*. Ballantine 1976 pap. $2.50. The story of the transformation of a disturbed child into a healthy personality.

Back, Kurt W. *Beyond Words: The Story of Sensitivity Training and the Encounter Movement*. Russell Sage 1972 $9.95. An "excellent attempt at appraising sensitivity training as a social movement without uncritically accepting it or irrationally denouncing it. Back puts sensitivity training into historical perspective" (*Choice*).

Baruch, Dorothy W. *One Little Boy*. Dell 1983 pap. $3.95. Describes the world of a typical boy with insight.

Bellak, Leopold. *Overload: The New Human Condition*. Human Sciences Pr. 1975 $26.95. "Bellak attempts to integrate clinical and research psychiatry into a method by which the crises faced by contemporary society may be treated, in much the same manner as a psychiatrist treats a patient" (*LJ*).

Bloom, Bernard L., and Shirley J. Asher, eds. *Psychiatric Patient Rights and Patient Advocacy: Issues and Evidence*. [*Community Psychology Ser.*] Human Sciences Pr. 1982 $34.95. "This book brings together in one place a collection of data-oriented chapters on major issues in mental health law: stigma, involuntary treatment, the insanity defense, prediction of dangerousness, behavior of discharged patients, confidentiality and informed consent, and community treatment. . . . A compact and useful resource for everyone interested in the validity of the factual assumptions on which law-and-psychiatry policies are grounded" (*Contemporary Psychiatry*).

Blum, Richard H. *The Dream Sellers: Perspectives on Drug Dealers*. [*Social and Behavioral Sciences Ser.*] Jossey-Bass 1972 o.p. A highly detailed look at drugs and the world of the drug dealer.

Bowlby, John. *Maternal Care and Mental Health*. [*Monograph Ser.*] World Health 2d ed. 1952 $7.20. Constitutes the most comprehensive and integrated summary of the literature.

———. *Separation: Anxiety and Anger*. [*Attachment and Loss Ser.*] Basic Bks. 1973 text ed. $22.50 pap. $10.95. "Written in clear, well-organized style . . . an authoritative contribution to the field" (*Bk. Review Digest*).

Burton, Arthur. *Twelve Therapists: How They Live and Actualize Themselves.* [*Social and Behavioral Sciences Ser.*] Jossey-Bass 1973 o.p. "For the first time a group of well-known psychotherapists have made available biographical material which affords important insights into the art of mental healing and those who practice it. This is a rare event in an otherwise fairly obscure and private undertaking" (*Choice*).

Caplan, Gerald. *Support Systems and Community Mental Health.* Human Sciences Pr. 1974 text ed. $29.95. "Caplan's insights and examples are a welcome addition to the recent explosion of literature on volunteerism that is illustrating the need and readiness of most of us to respond to opportunities to be helpers in areas where we have resources from which others can benefit" (*Contemporary Psychology*).

Cohen, Raquel E., and Frederick L. Ahearn, Jr. *Handbook for Mental Health Care of Disaster Victims.* Johns Hopkins Univ. Pr. 1980 text ed. $18.50. "Organization is direct and strong, style is brisk . . . language is clear" (*Contemporary Psychology*).

Coles, Robert. *The Mind's Fate: Ways of Seeing Psychiatry and Psychoanalysis.* Little, Brown 1976 o.p. "A collection of occasional pieces, book reviews, articles, etc." (*N.Y. Times*).

De Beauvoir, Simone. *A Very Easy Death.* Warner Bks. 1973 pap. $1.95. Includes elements of De Beauvoir's autobiography and her own philosophical interpretation of death's meaning.

Deutsch, Helene. *Confrontations with Myself.* Norton 1973 $6.95. "A psychiatrist who received her training from Freud and then went on to become the first director of the Vienna Training Institute, Deutsch reminisces about her experiences and insights over a long career in analysis" (*LJ*).

Deutsch, Morton. *The Resolution of Conflict: Constructive and Destructive Processes.* [*Carl Hovland Memorial Lectures*] Yale Univ. Pr. 1973 $38.00 pap. $12.95. "This approach is clearly written and argued" (*Bk. Review Digest*).

Diamond, Edwin. *The Science of Dreams.* Doubleday 1962 o.p. Ranging from the beliefs of primitive man to the theories of psychoanalysis, this is "science reporting at its best, information-packed and eminently readable with no sacrifice of scientific accuracy or overstress on the sensational" (*LJ*).

Fingarette, Herbert. *On Responsibility.* Basic Bks. 1967 o.p. "A brave work, a brilliant analysis, an exciting experience" (*Bk. Review Digest*).

———. *Self-Deception.* [*Studies in Philosophical Psychology*] Humanities Pr. 1969 text ed. $17.50. "This is a brief philosophical analysis of the processes of rationalization and repression. Instances are drawn from the literature of clinical psychopathology, fiction, drama, and other sources" (*Contemporary Psychology*).

Fisher, Seymour, and Rhoda L. Fisher. *Pretend the World Is Funny and Forever: A Psychological Analysis of Comedians, Clowns, and Actors.* Erlbaum 1981 text ed. $24.95. "Presentation is simple, straightforward, and aimed at the general reader" (*Contemporary Psychology*).

Fromm, Erich, and Michael Maccoby. *Social Character in a Mexican Village.* Prentice-Hall 1970 o.p. "An empirical study of Mexican peasants by two distinguished psychoanalysts" (*Choice*).

Gedo, Mary M. *Picasso: Art As Autobiography.* Univ. of Chicago Pr. 1980 lib. bdg. $20.00 pap. $12.50. Gedo "examines the role played by personal experience in . . . Picasso's stylistic innovations" (*Bk. Review Digest*).

Gibson, H. B. *Pain and Its Conquest.* Dufour 1982 $17.95. "Clear and psychologically comprehensible book; intended as a practical manual for those who suffer pain" (*Contemporary Psychology*).

Gilkey, Langdon. *Shantung Compound.* Harper 1975 pap. $8.95. Observations, recorded daily by the well-known American theologian, in a Japanese internment camp during World War II. "The thing that differentiates this personal account from others is that it tells what the residents did and did not do as individuals, not what the Japanese did to them. What makes it distinguished, though, is Mr. Gilkey's penetrating observations on the behavior of individuals when they are stripped of social status, wealth, and freedom, and put under protected, confining, and crowded conditions" (*LJ*).

Glasser, William. *Identity Society*. Harper 1975 pap. $8.95. The search for identity is seen as the cause of many social problems.

Goethals, George R., and Stephen Worchel. *Adjustment and Human Relations*. Knopf 1981 o.p. A nontechnical and effective introduction for students to the rudiments of personality, developmental, and social psychology.

Goldenson, Robert M. *The Encyclopedia of Human Behavior: Psychology, Psychiatry, and Mental Health*. Doubleday 2 vols. 1970 o.p. More than 1,000 articles on such topics as dream interpretation, phobia, and Parkinson's disease, alphabetically arranged.

Haight, M. R. *A Study of Self-Deception*. Humanities Pr. 1980 text ed. $30.50. "Readable and makes good use of a variety of methods and considerations" (*Contemporary Psychology*).

Hall, Calvin S., and Gardner Lindzey. *Theories of Personality*. Wiley 3d ed. 1978 $39.95. An excellent, readable overview of several approaches to personality theory.

Halleck, Seymour. *The Politics of Therapy*. Aronson 1971 $20.00. "Of particular importance to mental health professionals and teachers as well" (*Choice*).

Harding, M. Esther. *I and the "Not-I."* [*Bollingen Ser.*] Princeton Univ. Pr. 1965 $25.00 pap. $7.95. "Harding is usually lucid enough for any reader who has followed the better popular psychological works" (*LJ*).

Herr, Stanley S., Stephen Arons, and Richard E. Wallace. *Legal Rights and Mental Health Care*. Lexington Bks. 1983 $24.00. A "fine book for the beginner in the area of patients' rights with respect to the law and mental health sciences" (*Contemporary Psychology*).

Jacoby, Russell. *Social Amnesia: A Critique of Contemporary Psychology from Adler to Laing*. Beacon repr. of 1975 ed. 1976 pap. $7.95. "Provocative commentary on contemporary psychology, written from the juncture of Marxism and classical psychoanalysis" (*Contemporary Psychology*).

Kastenbaum, Robert, and Ruth Aisenberg. *The Psychology of Death*. Springer Pub. 1976 text ed. pap. $22.95. Stimulating and comprehensible.

Kiell, Norman, ed. *Psychoanalysis, Psychology and Literature: A Bibliography*. Scarecrow 2d ed. 1982 $75.00. "The first extensive attempt at a bibliography of works approaching literature from a psychoanalytic or psychological point of view" (*Bk. Review Digest*).

Kubler-Ross, E. *On Death and Dying*. Macmillan 1969 $11.95 pap. $4.95. The book that broke the taboo. A necessity for the lay reader who is interested.

Lane, Harlan, and Richard Pillard. *The Wild Boy of Burundi*. Random 1978 o.p. "Main purpose is to convey to the scientifically untrained reader an appreciation of scientific method within this extraordinary context" (*Contemporary Psychology*).

Levinson, Daniel. *The Seasons of a Man's Life*. Ballantine 1979 pap. $5.95; Knopf 1978 $18.95. A study of the phases of the adult male development.

Lifton, Robert J. *Death in Life: Survivors of Hiroshima*. Basic Bks. 1982 $19.95 pap. $10.50; Simon & Schuster 1976 pap. $5.95. With this book, Lifton won the 1969 National Book Award in the Sciences. His citation reads in part: "This perceptive analysis in depth by a psychiatrist of the survivors of the first atomic bomb serves to remind us of an event too easily forgotten. It establishes that the tragedy of Hiroshima did not end with the destruction of the city but had a profound and lasting effect on the lives of all those involved in it. It makes vivid to us in literary form the social and ethical consequences of a single act of war."

Lingeman, Richard R. *Drugs from A to Z: A Dictionary.* [*McGraw-Hill Pap.*] 2d ed. 1974 text ed. $9.95 pap. $5.95. "The whole history of drugs and addicts . . . from amphetamines to zonked, from Miltown to STP" (*Choice*).

Lomas, Peter. *The Case for a Personal Psychotherapy.* Oxford 1981 $19.95. Its "greatest strength is the book's way of bringing to life, via clinical vignettes, ideas that have become stale through repetition, such as the openness and trust in the clinical relationship" (*Contemporary Psychology*).

Love, Jean O. *Virginia Woolf: Sources of Madness and Art.* Univ. of California Pr. 1978 $26.50. "Love's book has been thoroughly researched, both in secondary and in primary sources, some of which were previously untapped. In spite of the fact that there have been at least 13 books published in the last decade on Woolf's life, letters, personality, friends, and literary accomplishments, this study probably deserves to be added to the crowded Woolf shelves of college libraries" (*Choice*).

Luber, Raymond F., ed. *Partial Hospitalization: A Current Perspective.* Plenum 1979 $32.50. "Succeeds as both a primer for the uninitiated and as a beacon for those interested in making partial hospitalization a viable treatment" (*Contemporary Psychology*).

Lundberg, Margaret J. *The Incomplete Adult.* Greenwood 1974 lib. bdg. $29.95. "Lundberg argues that degree of personality development is directly related to social class membership" (*Contemporary Psychology*).

Lynd, Helen M. *On Shame and the Search for Identity.* Harcourt repr. of 1958 ed. 1970 o.p. Brings expertise to the relationship between shame and identity.

Moustakas, Clark E. *Loneliness and Love.* Prentice-Hall 1972 pap. $4.95. "This book will reaffirm those who have been through loneliness and will hopefully reawaken those out of step with their inner selves who flee loneliness because they feel 'safer' in the herd. Highly recommended" (*LJ*).

Neisser, Edith G. *Mothers and Daughters: A Lifelong Relationship.* Harper rev. ed. 1973 o.p. Well-documented, carefully researched, and an enjoyable work.

Quinnett, Paul G. *The Troubled People Book: A Comprehensive Guide to Getting Help.* Continuum 1982 $14.95. Useful guide for the lay reader.

Rachman, Stanley J. *Fear and Courage.* [*Psychology Ser.*] W. H. Freeman 1978 text ed. $19.75 pap. $12.95. "Clear and graceful prose; presents a diversity of source material" (*Contemporary Psychology*).

Reason, James, and Klara Mycielska. *Absent Minded?: The Psychology of Mental Lapses and Everyday Errors.* Prentice-Hall 1982 $13.95 pap. $6.95. Of interest to both the general reader and the psychologist.

Reisman, John M. *A History of Clinical Psychology.* Irvington repr. of 1976 ed. 1983 text ed. pap. $14.95; Krieger 2d ed. repr. of 1976 ed. 1982 $24.50. Easy to read and very informative.

Rennie, Ysabel. *The Search for Criminal Man: A Conceptual History of the Dangerous Offender.* Lexington Bks. 1978 pap. $15.00. Good for lay readers interested in the history of criminology.

Reynolds, David K., and Norman Farberon. *Endangered Hope: Experiences in Psychiatric Aftercare Facilities.* Univ. of California Pr. 1978 $23.00. "Should be read by persons interested in helping former patients make a successful transition back to society" (*Contemporary Psychology*).

Ricks, David, Alexander Thomas, and Merrill Roff, eds. *Life History Research in Psychopathology.* Univ. of Minnesota Pr. 1970 o.p. A "collection of papers presented at Columbia University Teachers College and a verbatim transcript of questions/answers and discussion following each paper" (*Contemporary Psychology*).

Roback, Abraham A. *History of Psychology and Psychiatry*. Greenwood repr. of 1961 ed. 1969 lib. bdg. $22.50. An excellent survey.

Sadoff, Robert L. *Violence and Responsibility: The Individual, the Family and Society*. Halsted Pr. 1978 o.p. "Overview of relatively current thinking on topics such as family violence, child abuse, juvenile violence, etc." (*Contemporary Psychology*).

Seabrook, Jeremy. *Loneliness*. Universe Bks. 1975 o.p. "Conveys more about the nature of loneliness than many studies full of statistics and case histories" (*LJ*).

Seeley, John. *The Americanization of the Unconscious*. International Science Pr. 1967 o.p. Seeley's thesis is that revolutionary changes in American psychiatry and sociology are producing a "distinctly American Unconscious." "A brilliant and persuasive argument against this overconfident 'boxing off' of disciplines because their approaches seem to dictate mutual exclusion. Seeley's address here is to sociology (his own specialty) and psychoanalysis, two bodies of thinking with an apparent polarity in the explanation of man's behavior" (John Bright, *SR*).

Shostrom, Everett. *Man, the Manipulator*. Bantam 1968 pap. $2.75. Shostrom, director of the Institute of Therapeutic Psychology at Santa Ana, California, discusses the differences between "manipulation," or the exploitation involved in relationships to which one does not give oneself, and "actualization," its opposite, with a discussion of the application of these concepts to various forms of psychotherapy.

Singer, Kenneth S., and J. L. Pope, eds. *The Power of Human Imagination: New Methods in Psychotherapy*. Plenum 1978 $32.50. "An eye-opener for people relatively uninformed about this vantage point" (*Contemporary Psychology*).

Stein, Leonard, and Mary Ann Test, eds. *Alternatives to Mental Hospital Treatment*. Plenum 1978 $42.50. Readable overview.

Straus, Murray A., and Richard J. Gilles. *Behind Closed Doors: Violence in the American Family*. Doubleday 1980 $12.95 1981 pap. $8.95. Highly readable; good for the lay reader.

Vonnegut, Mark. *The Eden Express*. Bantam 1976 pap. $2.75. "His descriptions of his schizophrenic experiences are not only convincing from a clinical standpoint but are written in an engaging style, with an admirable lack of self-pity. His story is worth reading, even though his illness short-circuits his search for the answers to problems which weigh heavily on the minds of many young people, and his relief at being cured of schizophrenia by biochemical approaches causes him to underestimate the complexities of the phenomenon" (*LJ*).

Walker, Lenore. *The Battered Woman Syndrome*. Harper 1977 $10.95 pap. $6.95; [*Focus on Women Ser.*] Springer Pub. 1984 text ed. $21.95. Good reading for anyone concerned with social injustice.

Watts, Alan W. *The Book: On the Taboo Against Knowing Who You Are*. Random 1972 pap. $3.95. This authority on comparative religions brings "insights from the Eastern religions . . . to bear upon the problems of Western man's misuse of his technological knowledge to the point of his imminent destruction. A timely, thoughtful, relevant book" (*LJ*).

———. *Psychotherapy East and West*. Random 1975 pap. $3.95. A search for common ground between Western psychotherapy and Eastern philosophy.

World Health Organization. *Advances in the Drug Therapy of Mental Illness: Proceedings*. World Health 1976 pap. $12.00. A collection of 21 papers.

Zimbardo, Philip G., and Shirley Radl. *Shyness: What It Is, What to Do about It*. Jove 1984 pap. $3.95. Aimed at the general reader.

Psychoanalysis

Alexander, Franz. *Fundamentals of Psychoanalysis.* Norton 1968 o.p. A well-organized, readable, and compact outline.

Alexander, Franz, Samuel Einstein, and Martin Grotjahn, eds. *Psychoanalytic Pioneers.* Basic Bks. 1966 o.p. "The editors try to give as rounded a view as possible. . . . Ferenczi, Rank, Jung, Federn, Briehl, W. Reich, M. Klein, K. Horney, H. Hartmann, E. Kris, Anna Freud, and others are among the workers described. Contributors in addition to the editors are such excellent analysts as M. Romm, N. Loewenstein, E. Pumpian-Mindlin and others. The volume unreservedly belongs in all collections in the psychological and psychiatric-psychoanalytic fields" (*LJ*).

Berne, Eric. *A Layman's Guide to Psychiatry and Psychoanalysis (The Mind in Action).* Ballantine 1982 pap. $3.50. "Dr. Berne spells it all out in an entertaining, jargon-free way that will hold anybody's interest. . . . One of the fine things about this book is the skillful use of anecdote; the examples are always informative as well as intriguing, and most of the people in them seem like characters in search of a novelist" (*PW*).

Console, William A., Richard C. Simmons, and Mark Rubinstein. *The First Encounter: The Beginnings in Psychotherapy.* Aronson 1977 o.p. Discusses psychoanalytic psychotherapy.

Eidelberg, Ludwig, ed. *Encyclopedia of Psychoanalysis.* Free Pr. 1968 $45.00. "A fairly comprehensive compendium of the more important concepts of the classical or orthodox Freudian school. The book is also liberally sprinkled with non-Freudian originated concepts which bear upon the theories of Freud. There are 643 entries . . . a bibliography of 1,500 titles, and an index of 6,000 items. The material is clearly and concisely written" (*LJ*).

English, Horace B., and Ava C. English. *A Comprehensive Dictionary of Psychological and Psychoanalytical Terms.* Longman 1958 o.p. Useful for medical, academic, and many categories of special libraries.

Fingarette, Herbert. *The Self on Transformation: Psychoanalysis, Philosophy and the Life of the Spirit.* Harper 1965 o.p. Fingarette gives an enlightened description of the phases of a self being transformed.

Frosch, John, and Nathaniel Ross, eds. *The Annual Survey of Psychoanalysis: A Comprehensive Survey of Current Psychoanalytic Practice and Theory.* 1965. International Univ. Pr. 10 vols. o.p. Summaries of studies on the history, theory, and applications of psychoanalytic psychiatry, therapy, and training. The best single source of information about psychoanalytic literature.

Greenson, Ralph R. *Explorations in Psychoanalysis.* International Univ. Pr. 1978 text ed. $40.00. A work that "provides convenient access to Greenson's abundant, authoritative, clinical wisdom" (*Contemporary Psychology*).

Grinstein, Alexander, ed. *The Index of Psychoanalytic Writings.* Pref. by Ernest Jones, International Univ. Pr. vols. 1–5 (1956–60) $200.00 vols. 6–9 (1963–66) $200.00 vols. 10–14 (1973) $200.00. A revision and update of John Richmann's *Index Psychoanalyticus* (1893–1926).

Guntrip, Harry. *Psychoanalytic Theory, Therapy, and the Self.* Basic Bks. 1973 pap. $9.95. "The basic philosophy of Guntrip, who is a world leader in psychological theorizing, is that 'to care for people is more important than to care for ideas'. . . . An important contribution to a human rather than mechanistic view in personality growth and treatment" (*Choice*).

Kohut, Heinz. *How Does Analysis Cure?: Contributions to the Psychology of the Self.* Univ. of Chicago Pr. 1984 lib. bdg. $27.50. An in-depth, yet readable, essay on the dynamics of analysis.

Kris, Ernst. *Psychoanalytic Explorations in Art.* International Univ. Pr. 1962 text ed. $37.50. The study of art and creative processes from a psychoanalytic perspective.

Liebert, Robert S. *Michelangelo: A Psychoanalytic Study of His Life and Images.* Yale Univ. Pr. 1983 text ed. $37.50. "Recommended as a humane and informed meditation on the complex personality of a great artist" (*Contemporary Psychology*).

Malcolm, Janet. *Psychoanalysis: The Impossible Profession.* Knopf 1981 $9.95; Random 1982 pap. $4.95. "An excellent essay on personality . . . which transcends reportage" (*N.Y. Times Bk. Review*).

Muensterberger, Werner, ed. *The Psychoanalytic Study of Society.* Analytic Pr. 1983 text ed. $36.00; International Univ. Pr. 1960 text ed. $20.00; Psychohistory Pr. 1981 $32.50; Yale Univ. Pr. 1979 $47.00. "The wide area of applicability of psychoanalytic concepts and the vitality of contemporary psychoanalytic thinking are well documented in this volume" (*Contemporary Psychology*).

Neumann, Erich. *Depth Psychology and a New Ethic.* Trans. by E. Rolfe, Putnam 1970 o.p. "Neumann has dealt very effectively with the ethical implications of the unconscious, noting the old and new ethic, the stages of ethical development, and the aims and values of the new ethic" (*Choice*).

Wyss, Dieter. *Psychoanalytic Schools from the Beginning to the Present.* Trans. by Gerald Onn, Aronson 1973 $30.00. A good historical survey.

Psychological Disorders

Alvarez, Alfred. *The Savage God: A Study of Suicide.* Random 1972 o.p. A reflection on the meaning of suicide with references to classical literature and some case histories.

Alvarez, Walter C. *Minds That Came Back.* Lippincott 1961 o.p. A prominent writer and emeritus professor of medicine at the University of Wisconsin offers "a unique project to physicians, jurists, clergymen, social workers, and to 'thoughtful adults'—his own reviews of outstanding autobiographies of about 75 abnormal personages. He quotes from, comments on, and summarizes the memoirs of Beers, Dostoevsky, Lucy Freeman, Maupassant, Nietzsche . . . and others, who successfully returned from the strange limbo of insanity, alcoholism, neurosis, epilepsy, phobia, or psychoanalysis" (*LJ*).

Angyal, Andras. *Neurosis and Treatment: A Holistic Theory.* [*Psychoanalysis Examined and Re-examined Ser.*] Da Capo 1982 lib. bdg. $27.50. A jewel of a book presenting Angyal's formulations about the origins of neuroses and psychological health.

Arieti, Silvano. *Interpretation of Schizophrenia.* Basic Bks. 2d ed. 1974 $39.95. Awarded a 1975 National Book Award "for its scientific content and profound humanism."

———. *Understanding and Helping the Schizophrenic: A Guide for Family and Friends.* Basic Bks. 1979 $12.95; Simon & Schuster 1981 pap. $7.75. "An excellent portrait of the world of the schizophrenic . . . in language directed toward the lay reader" (*Bk. Review Digest*).

Barnes, Mary, and J. Berke. *Mary Barnes: Two Accounts of a Journey Through Madness.* Ballantine 1978 o.p. "The book will provide absorbing reading" (*Bk. Review Digest*).

Blatt, Sidney J., and Cynthia M. Wild. *Schizophrenia: A Developmental Analysis.* Academy Pr. 1976 $41.00. "The book covers a wealth of material and the concept of boundary disturbances shows promise as an integrative touchstone" (*Contemporary Psychology*).

Brenner, Charles. *The Mind in Conflict.* International Univ. Pr. 1982 text ed. $27.50.

"Extraordinarily well-suited as a teaching text for students at any level of academic or clinical training" (*Contemporary Psychology*).

Brown, George W., and Tirril Harris. *Social Origins of Depression: A Study of Psychiatric Disorder in Women.* Free Pr. 1978 $24.95. "Massive data presented for those interested in social and psychological aspects of depression" (*Contemporary Psychology*).

Bruch, Hilde. *The Golden Cage: The Enigma of Anorexia Nervosa.* Harvard Univ. Pr. 1978 $10.00; Random 1979 pap. $3.95. "Based on clinical observations from the author's own extensive casework" (*Contemporary Psychology*).

Cegelka, Patricia T., and Herbert J. Prehm. *Mental Retardation: From Categories to People.* Merrill 1982 $26.95. "Focuses on descriptive accounts of casework and will provide students of special education with a solid framework of basic and applied facts surrounding retardation" (*Contemporary Psychology*).

Clarke, Ann M., and Alan D. Clarke, eds. *Mental Deficiency: The Changing Outlook.* Free Pr. 4th ed. 1986 $45.00. Definitive work.

Duke, Marshall, and Stephen Nowicki, Jr. *Abnormal Psychology.* Holt 1986 text ed. $33.95. A good introduction for students without a strong background in the subject.

Eysenck, H. J., ed. *You and Neurosis.* Sage 1979 o.p. "Highly readable and lucid pioneer on the theory, practice, and results of behavioral therapy" (*Contemporary Psychology*).

Fadiman, James, and D. Kawman. *Exploring Madness: Experience, Theory, and Research.* [*Psychology Ser.*] 1973. Brooks-Cole 2d ed. 1979 o.p.

Fann, W. E., and others, eds. *Phenomenology and Treatment of Schizophrenia.* Spectrum 1978 o.p. Offers a good deal of information to anyone with an interest in schizophrenia.

――――. *Phenomenology and Treatment of Depression.* Spectrum 1977 o.p. Interesting book with something for everyone.

Fingarette, Herbert. *The Meaning of Criminal Insanity.* Univ. of California Pr. 1972 pap. $6.95. "An excellent book—well written and well argued" (*Bk. Review Digest*).

Forrest, Gary G. *How to Live with a Problem Drinker and Survive.* Atheneum 1980 $18.95. A self-help book written for the families of people with drinking problems.

Friedrich, Otto. *Going Crazy.* Simon & Schuster 1976 $9.95. "Dozens of stories told efficiently by the author. . . . Conveys that we are all at the mercy of various forces" (*Contemporary Psychology*).

Gottesfeld, Harry. *Abnormal Psychology: A Community Health Perspective.* Science Research Associates 1979 o.p. Well written.

Grant, Brian W. *Schizophrenia: A Source of Social Insight.* Westminster 1975 $10.00. A "scholarly work, written with an exceptional understanding" (*LJ*).

Ingalls, Robert P. *Mental Retardation: The Changing Outlook.* Macmillan 1978 $29.00. The best introductory level text.

Kaplan, Berton H., ed. *The Inner World of Mental Illness: A Series of First Person Accounts of What It Was Like.* Harper 1964 text ed. pap. $23.50. A collection of 31 pieces, all but two previously published elsewhere, that make personal statements describing the experience of patients under the influence of psychoses and neuroses. "It will offer students first hand and first person reports of pathological experience as a supplement to the more standard fare available in abnormal psychology textbooks" (*Contemporary Psychology*).

Kisker, George W. *The Disorganized Personality.* McGraw-Hill 3d ed. 1977 text ed. $36.95. Undergraduate text.

Kuiper, Pieter C. *The Neuroses.* International Univ. Pr. 1972 text ed. $27.50

Levitt, Eugene E. *The Psychology of Anxiety.* Erlbaum 2d ed. 1980 text ed. $19.50.

"An almost excellent first undergraduate reference for a course in which anxiety is the central issue" (*Contemporary Psychology*).

Lidz, Theodore. *Origin and Treatment of Schizophrenic Disorders*. Basic Bks. 1973 $11.95. An analysis of the world of schizophrenia.

McCall, Raymond J. *The Varieties of Abnormality: A Phenomenological Analysis*. C. C. Thomas 1975 $59.50 pap. $21.75. A book, intended for undergraduates, that relies completely on clinical description.

McKeller, Peter. *Mindsplit: The Psychology of Multiple Personality and the Dissociated Self*. Biblio Dist. 1979 o.p. Well written, scholarly, and entertaining.

Mathew, Andrew M., Michael G. Gelder, and Derek W. Johnston. *Agoraphobia: Nature and Treatment*. Guilford Pr. 1981 $25.00. Of interest to lay readers, students, and mental health professionals.

Matson, Johnny L., and James A. Mulick, eds. *Handbook of Mental Retardation*. [*General Psychology Ser.*] Pergamon 1983 $82.50. "Valuable service for the serious student or professional who needs exposure to the wide range of current knowledge in a burgeoning field" (*Contemporary Psychology*).

Meyer, Robert G., and Yvonne Hardaway Osborne. *Case Studies in Abnormal Behavior*. Allyn & Bacon 1982 text ed. $17.15. "Presents cases and the therapist's perspective of pathology, diagnosis, and treatment in a way that is understandable to the student or novice" (*Contemporary Psychology*).

Nathan, Peter E., and Sandra L. Harris. *Psychopathology and Society*. McGraw-Hill 2d ed. 1980 text ed. $35.95. "Social learning perspective appropriate to integrate etiology, treatment, and description" (*Contemporary Psychology*).

Neale, John M., and Thomas F. Oltmanns. *Schizophrenia*. Wiley 1980 $43.95. Excellent survey of the field.

Neale, John M., Thomas F. Oltmanns, and G. C. Davidson. *Case Studies in Abnormal Psychology*. Wiley 1982 pap. $14.95. Case studies containing important clinical descriptions.

Page, James D. *Psychopathology: The Science of Understanding Deviance*. Oxford 2d ed. 1975 $18.95. Excellent text with a good introduction to abnormal psychology.

Perlin, Seymour, ed. *A Handbook for the Study of Suicide*. Oxford 1975 text ed. pap. $14.95. Eleven contributions examining suicidal behavior in the contexts of history, literature, philosophy, anthropology, sociology, biology, psychiatry, and epidemiology.

Polich, J. Michael, and David J. Armor. *The Course of Alcoholism: Four Years after Treatment*. Ed. by Harriet B. Braiker, Wiley 1981 $37.50. "Recommended that everyone interested in alcoholism read the study with an open mind. It is thorough and well-written" (*Contemporary Psychology*).

Price, Richard H., and S. J. Lynn. *Abnormal Psychology*. Dorsey 2d ed. 1986 $31.00. An excellent volume that brings the realm of the "abnormal" into the realm of understanding.

Reid, William H., ed. *The Psychopath: A Comprehensive Study of Antisocial Disorders and Behaviors*. Brunner-Mazel 1978 $27.50. Comprehensive; presents both the clinical and experimental perspectives.

Reynolds, David K., and Norman Farberon. *The Family Shadow: Sources of Suicide and Schizophrenia*. Univ. of California Pr. 1981 $25.50. "Should be compulsory reading" (*Contemporary Psychology*).

Rowe, Dorothy, ed. *The Experience of Depression*. Wiley 1978 o.p. A large portion of the text is devoted to transcripts of therapy sessions with depressed patients.

Sacks, Oliver. *The Man Who Mistook His Wife for a Hat and Other Clinical Tales*. Summit 1986 $16.95. A highly readable and informative series of stories revealing the mysterious depths of human existence and the concrete problems that psychiatry and clinical psychology must face. This is both good literature and good science and can be recommended for all readers.

Salzman, Leon. *Treatment of the Obsessive Personality*. Aronson 1985 $45.00. "Dr. Leon Salzman, professor of clinical psychiatry, Georgetown University School of Medicine, merits a prize for this jargon-free discussion of the obsessive-compulsive personality, 'today's most prevalent neurotic character structure' " (*LJ*).

Scharfetter, Christian. *General Psychopathology: An Introduction*. Trans. by Helen Marshall, Cambridge Univ. Pr. 1980 $62.50 pap. $19.95. "Provides a detailed descriptive, phenomenological survey of mental disorders. . . . The clinical examples provide an unusually rich and varied source of descriptive case material. . . . Particularly useful for advanced undergraduate and introductory graduate level courses in psychopathology" (*Contemporary Psychology*).

Scheper-Hughes, Nancy. *Saints, Scholars, and Schizophrenics: Mental Illness in Rural Ireland*. Univ. of California Pr. 1979 $24.00 pap. $10.95. Very readable study.

Shean, Glenn. *Schizophrenia: An Introduction to Research and Theory*. Little, Brown 1978 text ed. $13.95 pap. $10.95. Introductory text.

Shneidman, Edwin S. *Definition of Suicide*. Wiley 1985 $22.95. A series of ideas about suicide are put forward in order to help forge a new understanding of this tragic phenomenon.

Smith, Robert J. *The Psychopath in Society*. Academic Pr. 1978 $29.00. "Offers fluid writing, penetrating thinking, and sound scholarship" (*Contemporary Psychology*).

Snyder, Solomon H. *Biological Aspects of Mental Disorder*. Oxford Univ. Pr. 1980 $19.95 pap. $9.95. Good for the undergraduate reader.

Spitzer, Robert L. *Psychopathology: A Case Book*. McGraw-Hill 1983 text ed. pap. $18.95. "Contains 54 case descriptions, 50 of which were selected as models of specific diagnostic categories in that classification compendium. . . . Accompanying most of the case descriptions is a discussion of the psychopathology and diagnosis, etiology, treatment, and prognosis" (*Contemporary Psychology*).

Stein, Laszlo K., Eugene D. Mindel, and Theresa Jabaley, eds. *Deafness and Mental Health*. Grune 1981 $34.50. Good for training teachers and professionals.

Sutherland, N. S. *Breakdown*. Stein & Day 1977 $10.00. "Case study of author's own experience and layperson's guide to the mental health disciplines" (*Contemporary Psychology*).

Thorman, George. *Incestuous Families*. C. C. Thomas 1983 $21.75. A highly readable work for the general concerned public.

Thornberry, Terence P., and Joseph E. Jacoby. *The Criminally Insane: A Community Follow-Up of Mentally Ill Offenders*. Univ. of Chicago Pr. 1979 lib. bdg. $24.00. A book that will "appeal to a wide variety of audiences concerned with related policy, scientific, and theoretical issues" (*Contemporary Psychology*).

Torrey, E. Fuller. *Surviving Schizophrenia: A Family Manual*. Harper 1983 $19.50 1984 pap. $8.95. "Valuable resource for families of schizophrenics. Has the aim of educating the layperson and providing tools for coping" (*Contemporary Psychology*).

Val, Edwardo R., Moises Gaviria, and Joseph Flaherty. *Affective Disorders: Psychopathology and Treatment*. Year Book Medical 1982 $55.00. The audience for this book should be students.

Westermeyer, Joseph. *A Primer on Chemical Dependency*. Williams & Wilkins 1976 o.p. "Rigorous and elegant research; an excellent primer" (*Contemporary Psychology*).

White, Robert W., and Norman F. Watt. *The Abnormal Personality*. Wiley 5th ed. 1981 $37.95. A textbook on abnormality, but a good one.

Williams, Robert L., and Ismet Karacan. *Sleep Disorders: Diagnosis and Treatment.* Wiley 1978 $70.00. Essential reading.

Yochelson, Samuel, and Stanton Samenow. *The Criminal Personality: The Drug User.* Aronson 3 vols. 1976–86 ea. $40.00. A unique interpretation of the criminal personality with plenty of supporting data.

Zarit, Steven H. *Aging and Mental Disorders: Psychological Approaches to Assessment and Treatment.* Free Pr. 1980 $24.95 1983 $13.95. Provides useful information for the general reader.

Sexuality

Adelson, Edward T., ed. *Sexuality and Psychoanalysis.* Brunner-Mazel 1975 o.p. "This collection of essays presents . . . physiological, anatomical, biochemical, and psychological research in sexuality and relates it to classical and modern psychoanalytic thinking. . . . It helps formulate the directions contemporary psychoanalysis can follow" (*LJ*).

Bootzin, Richard R., and Joan Acocella. *Abnormal Psychology: Current Perspectives.* Random 4th ed. 1984 text ed. $28.00. Clearly slanted toward undergraduates and nonpsychology majors.

Brecher, Edward M. *The Sex Researchers.* Specific Pr. 1979 $9.50. "This account combines a readable, non-technical style with scientific accuracy. Quotations from the original works are used extensively to illustrate accurately the sex-researchers' position. Brecher's major theme is the gradual convalescence of our culture from the debilitating sexual disease of Victorianism" (*Contemporary Psychology*).

Brierly, Harry. *Transvestism: A Handbook with Case Studies for Psychologists, Psychiatrists, and Counselors.* Pergamon Pr. 1979 o.p. "A good beginning for the comprehension of a complex issue" (*Contemporary Psychology*).

Bullough, Vern L., and Bonnie Bullough. *Sin, Sickness, and Sanity: A History of Sexual Attitudes.* New Amer. Lib. 1977 pap. $9.95. For the general reader.

Carlton, Eric. *Sexual Anxiety: A Study of Male Importance.* Barnes & Noble 1980 $27.50. For the intelligent lay reader.

Ellis, Albert, and Albert Abarbanel, eds. *The Encyclopedia of Sexual Behavior.* Hawthorn Bks. 1961 o.p. More than 100 articles by international authorities on the biology, physiology, and anatomy of sex. An excellent reference work.

Gillan, Patricia, and Richard Gillan. *Sex Therapy Today.* Grove 1977 pap. $4.95; State Mutual Bk. 1976 $25.00. "Excellent and highly readable introduction to current sex therapy practices" (*Contemporary Psychology*).

Masters, William H., and others. *The Pleasure Bond: A New Look At Sexuality and Commitment.* Bantam 1976 pap. $3.95; Little, Brown 1975 $13.95. "Considers in a more personal way, the values of sexual relations" (*Contemporary Psychology*).

Moore, Donna M., ed. *Battered Women.* [*Focus Eds.*] Sage 1979 o.p. "Useful guide for workers in shelters for battered women" (*Contemporary Psychology*).

Szasz, Thomas S. *Manufacture of Madness: A Comparative Study of the Inquisition and the Mental Health Movement.* Harper 1977 pap. $7.95. "This book is addressed to a less technical reading audience" (*Choice*).

ADLER, ALFRED. 1870–1937

This Austrian psychiatrist founded the school of individual psychology. He was associated with the early group of Freud's followers; he later left it, rejecting Freud's emphasis on the (biological) sexual drives as the chief psychological determinants of personality. Adler saw personality disorders as arising from feelings of inferiority or inadequacy in the ability to reach one's life goals. For Adler the processes of socialization within one's culture are the important factors in determining a character style.

After his break with Freud in 1911, Adler founded his own school. In 1919 he set up the first child guidance clinic within the Vienna school system. In 1935 he moved to the United States where he spent the rest of his life in psychiatric practice and in lecturing. He, with Jung, was one of the two most important contemporary dissenters from Freud.

BOOKS BY ADLER

The Individual Psychology of Alfred Adler: A Systematic Presentation in Selections from His Writings. Ed. by Heinz L. Ansbacher and Rowena R. Ansbacher, Harper 1964 pap. $11.95. A systematic and authentic presentation of Adler's thought by his foremost disciples.

Superiority and Social Interest: A Collection of Later Writings. Ed. by Heinz L. Ansbacher and Rowena R. Ansbacher, Northwestern Univ. Pr. 2d ed. rev. 1970 $19.95; Norton repr. 1979 pap. $8.95. A continuation of the systematic presentation of Adler's own thought interpreted by his disciples.

The Practice and Theory of Individual Psychology. 1923 [*Quality Pap. Ser.*] Littlefield 2d ed. repr. of 1929 ed. 1973 pap. $5.95. The presentation of individual psychology as a separate science by its originator.

The Neurotic Constitution. 1926. [*Select Bibliographies Ser.*] Ayer repr. of 1926 ed. 1972 $31.00

Understanding Human Nature. 1927. Trans. by W. B. Wolfe, Fawcett 1978 pap. $2.25. A presentation of the fundamentals of individual psychology and demonstrations of its practical applications for the layperson.

The Problems of Neurosis: A Book of Case Histories. 1929. Harper 1964 o.p. Running comments on case material briefly presented to illustrate special points.

The Science of Living. 1929. Ed. by Heinz L. Ansbacher, Doubleday 1969 o.p. "A surprisingly clear and simple statement of the fundamental principles of psychology" (*N.Y. Times*).

The Education of Children. 1930. Trans. by E. F. Jensen, Regnery-Gateway 1978 pap. $3.95. "Many a child will be better understood by those who acquaint themselves with Dr. Adler's wise counsel" (*Boston Transcript*).

What Life Should Mean to You. 1931. Ed. by Alan Porter, Little, Brown o.p. A consistent application of the principles of individual psychology to all aspects of life.

Education of the Individual. Greenwood repr. of 1958 ed. 1970 lib. bdg. $22.50. This book deals with four major problems every individual has to face: his/her relationship with others, his/her sense of equality, the escape of the ephemeral, and the meaning of his/her actions.

The Problem Child. Capricorn Bks. 1963 o.p. Treats the style of a problem child with specific cases.

BOOKS ABOUT ADLER

Brachfeld, F. Oliver. *Inferiority Feelings in the Individual and the Group.* Trans. by Marjorie Gabain, Greenwood repr. of 1951 ed. 1973 lib. bdg. $22.50. An exhaustive survey of the literature pertaining to unorganized inferiority (inferiority of the individual) and organized inferiority (inferiority of the group) arranged around such topics as inferiority in relation to the newborn, crime, sex, racial inferiority.

Mosak, Harold H., ed. *Alfred Adler: His Influence on Psychology Today*. Noyes Pr. 1973 o.p. An evaluation of Adler's work and influence by disciples and followers.

Sperber, Manes. *Masks of Loneliness: Alfred Adler in Perspective*. Macmillan 1974 $7.95. "The reader will gain insight into the conflict between Adler and Freud, the influence of Marxist ideas on Adler, the flavor of Austria and Vienna in the early days of psychoanalysis and the personalities of Adler and Freud" (*Choice*).

ALLPORT, GORDON W(ILLARD). 1897–1967

Allport, professor of psychology at Harvard University from 1942 until his death, did important work in the study of social attitudes and in the study of personality and its measurement. As a youth he visited Sigmund Freud in Vienna and, according to the *N.Y. Times*, though impressed by Freud he nevertheless felt there was "room for one more behavioral scientist in the world." Allport believed that the Freudian personality theories were fitted for only a small minority of individuals. He once called his own ideas a form of empiricism restrained by reason.

Allport was especially concerned with, and outspoken against, religious and racial prejudice. He shared "with William James and John Dewey the resolute capacity to see man as human regardless of whatever particular scientific trends may hold sway at any given moment. Allport helps fulfill his own prediction, that 'soon . . . psychology will offer an image of man more in accord with the democratic ideals by which psychologists as individuals live' " (Rollo May, *SR*). He served as president of the American Psychological Association in 1937, receiving its Gold Medal Award in 1963. He was editor of the *Journal of Abnormal and Social Psychology* for 12 years. (See also Volume 3, Chapter 4.)

BOOKS BY ALLPORT

(with Philip E. Vernon). *Studies in Expressive Movement*. 1933. Hafner repr. 1966 o.p. "The authors believe that their work demonstrates that gesture and handwriting both reflect an essentially stable and constant individual style, and that the theories of specificity and identical elements are wholly inadequate to account for the consistency obtained" (*Psychological Abstracts*).

(and Handley Cantril). *Psychology of Radio*. Ayer repr. of 1935 ed. 1971 $23.50

The Use of Personal Documents in Psychological Science. 1942. [*Social Science Research Council Bulletin*] Kraus repr. of 1942 ed. pap. $4.50. "The book seeks to improve the appraisal of the self-revealing records of personal experience through an analysis of the form and content value of examples illustrating the various types of personal documents" (*Social Forces*).

(and Leo Postman). *The Psychology of Rumor*. Russell repr. of 1947 ed. 1965 $20.00. "Though scholarly, it is easy and interesting to read . . . essential to any library which accepts the social obligation of furthering human good by encouraging understanding" (*LJ*).

The Individual and His Religion: A Psychological Interpretation. 1950. Macmillan 1967 pap. $4.95. "An interpretation of the significance of religion from a psychological standpoint" (*Annals of the Amer. Academy of Political and Social Science*).

The Nature of Prejudice. 1954. Addison-Wesley 1979 $7.64 pap. $5.95; Anti-Defamation League repr. pap. $8.95. "The book can be used as a text, but it will almost surely find its way into discussion groups and eventually to the general reader" (*Social Forces*).

Becoming: Basic Considerations for a Psychology of Personality. [*Terry Lectures Ser.*] Yale Univ. Pr. 1955 $12.50 pap. $4.95. An instructive comparison of two very different approaches to the field of psychology.

Pattern and Growth in Personality. Holt 1961 o.p. "We need a name for the Allportian position for it is now apparent that it is a true theory of personality and not just a point of view or a set of attitudes about how personality should be described or assessed. It is not a system in the grand architectonic tradition—constructed block by block and brick by brick, with deliberate intention and self-congratulatory commentary—but rather an organic emergent, a compelling, structured, and articulated perspective on the nature of man and his functioning" (*Contemporary Psychology*).

Personality and the Social Encounter: Selected Essays. Univ. of Chicago Pr. 1981 text ed. pap. $17.00. "Twenty-one reprints, covering the period 1931 to 1960 . . . range from the open system of personality theory to the problems of war and peace, from ethics to ego-psychology, from metaphysics to metapsychology" (*Contemporary Psychology*).

(ed.). *Letters from Jenny.* Harcourt 1965 pap. $3.95. "Mr. Allport shows us how existentialist philosophers and therapists would see Jenny's daily life and explain it" (*N.Y. Times Bk. Review*).

The Person in Psychology. Beacon Pr. 1968 o.p. Selected essays (1939–67) "dealing with the applications of varieties of psychological theories, the influence and relationship between personality development and social institutions, prejudice as a personality trait, and finally a biographical section which provides a biographical approach to the psychological theories of individual psychologists. The separate parts are held together by Mr. Allport's consistent interest in individual development" (*LJ*).

Books about Allport

Evans, Richard I. *Gordon Allport: The Man and His Ideas.* Dutton 1971 o.p. "Evans had a lengthy filmed interview with Dr. Allport shortly before his death, and this book is the transcript. Evans offers as well a brief sketch of Dr. Allport's career and appends the transcript of an extremely interesting seminar involving some of the late psychologist's foremost students. Dr. Allport emerges as a witty and marvelously balanced man, befitting his role as one of the fathers of the psychology of the 'whole personality' " (*PW*).

Ghougassian, Joseph P. *Gordon W. Allport's Ontopsychology of the Person.* Philos. Lib. 1972 $10.00. "It is contended that Allport's humanistic psychology with its emphasis on the uniqueness of the individual personality and on the principle of functional autonomy is a revolutionary force in American psychology" (*Psychological Abstracts*).

BERNE, ERIC LENNARD. 1910–1970

Eric Berne was a practicing psychiatrist and the author of the bestselling work *Games People Play* (1964), which remained on the bestseller lists until 1967. In it Berne argued that people tend to play games with each other in their interpersonal relationships for a number of reasons, namely, to escape from reality, to hide ulterior motives, and to avoid actual participation in real life. A few of these games are destructive but most are desirable and necessary. Berne demonstrated to his readers how to recognize these games and how to play the most socially useful roles.

A native of Montreal, Berne received a medical degree from McGill University and later studied at the New York Psychiatric Institute. At the time of his fatal heart attack in 1970, he was a lecturer in group therapy at the Langley-Porter Neuropsychiatric Institute and a consultant at the McAuley Clinic in San Francisco.

BOOKS BY BERNE

Layman's Guide to Psychiatry and Psychoanalysis (The Mind in Action). 1957. Ballantine 1982 pap. $3.50. An introduction to psychoanalysis for laypersons by a "young Freudian."

Transactional Analysis in Psychotherapy: A Systematic Individual and Social Psychiatry. Grove 1961 o.p. This book outlines Berne's unified system of individual and social psychiatry. Berne sees structural analysis as a more general theory than orthodox psychoanalysis.

Intuition and Ego States: The Origins of Transactional Analysis. Ed. by Paul McCormick, Harper 1977 o.p. A series of papers discussing intuition, diagnosis, communication, ego states, etc., from a transactional perspective.

Games People Play: The Psychology of Human Relationships. 1964. Ballantine 1978 pap. $2.75. "A compendium of unconscious maneuvers nearly everyone makes in his relationships with other people, and its forthright language and somewhat acid style understandably appeal to laymen who may easily recognize themselves as adept life-game players" (*Newsweek*).

Structure and Dynamics of Organizations and Groups. Grove 1966 o.p. "Berne's approach to a theory of group structure and function is bold and creative" (*Amer. Journal of Public Health*).

Principles of Group Treatment. Oxford 1966 o.p. "Meets a need by sharpening some of the basic issues involved in group methods of treatment. The author makes conceptual comparisons among different methods and schools and presents his views of a variety of related topics" (*Contemporary Psychology*).

Happy Valley. Grove 1968 o.p. A python named Shardlu rolls down the hill one day into a flowery valley and has many adventures with the strange animals and people who live there.

Sex in Human Loving. Simon & Schuster 1970 o.p. "Delves amusingly into the male-female relationship in many aspects, from the coy euphemisms most of us employ as a 'sexual vocabulary' to the sex act itself, its biology, its psychology, its deviations, and the guises and disguises under which the old Adam-and-Eve game is played in our time" (*PW*).

What Do You Say after You Say Hello: The Psychology of Human Destiny. 1972. Ballantine 1975 pap. $4.50. "As a psychiatrist, Dr. Berne found that each person—under the powerful influences of his parents—writes in early childhood his own script that will determine the general course of his life. . . . [Dr. Berne] demonstrates how each life script gets written, how it works, and how each of us can break free of it to help us attain real autonomy and true fulfillment" (Publisher's note). "One strong point of the book and its approach is that the layman can plug into the analysis of his own script as well as those of others" (*Best Sellers*).

(and C. Steiner). *Beyond Games and Scripts*. Ballantine 1978 pap. $2.50. "Selections range from the by now familiar 'games' and 'scripts' that influence behavior to

telltale words and gestures, group dynamics, sex and TA, and games psychotherapists (and their patients) play. Useful to people actively involved with TA"
(*PW*).

Book about Berne

Jorgenson, Elizabeth Watkins, and Henry Irvin Jorgenson. *Eric Berne: Master Games-
man—A Transactional Biography*. Grove 1984 pap. $7.95. A sympathetic biogra-
phy of the founder of transactional analysis.

BETTELHEIM, BRUNO. 1903–

Bruno Bettelheim has had remarkable success in treating very deeply
emotionally disturbed children. He is a vehement opponent of the "operant
conditioning" methods of B. F. Skinner (see Vol. 3) and other behaviorists. He
himself once studied with Sigmund Freud. Austrian-born, Bettelheim was
profoundly influenced by the year he spent in a German concentration camp
during World War II. His famous *Individual and Mass Behavior* (1943, o.p.),
first published in a scientific periodical and then in pamphlet form, is a study
of the human personality under the stress of totalitarian terror and concentration camp living. Bettelheim sees a relationship between the disturbances of
the concentration camp survivors and those of the autistic (rigidly with-
drawn) children he describes in *The Empty Fortress* (1967) because both have
lived through "extreme situations."

The Children of the Dream (1969) describes with considerable enthusiasm
the absence of neurosis in children brought up on kibbutzim in Israel in
groups of other children and cared for by adults who are not their parents.
Bettelheim believes that American ghetto children would benefit from this
kind of experience in preference to the at best partial help of present Head
Start or other programs designed to accelerate educational progress for the
deprived.

Bettelheim was the principal of the Sonia Shankman Orthogenic School,
a residential laboratory for the treatment of disturbed children at the University of Chicago. He is currently Distinguished Professor of Education,
Emeritus, and Professor of Psychology and Psychiatry, Emeritus, at the
University of Chicago. While he is officially retired and currently divides his
time between Chicago and California, he has remained active in his scholarly pursuits.

Books by Bettelheim

Love Is Not Enough: The Treatment of Emotionally Disturbed Children. 1950. Avon
1971 pap. $3.50; Free Pr. 1950 $20.95. Bettelheim points out in this study that
parents, besides loving their children, should "create a setting in which both
their own legitimate needs and the needs of their children can be satisfied with
relative ease"; he describes the methods of his own school in this light.

Symbolic Wounds: Puberty Rites and the Envious Male. Free Pr. 1954 o.p. Bettelheim
points out the need for a revision of Freudian theories in light of more recent
knowledge.

Truants from Life: The Rehabilitation of Emotionally Disturbed Children. Free Pr. 1955
$18.95 pap. $10.95. Case studies of four psychotics successfully treated at Bettelheim's school.

The Informal Heart: Autonomy in a Mass Age. 1960. Avon 1971 pap. $3.95; Free Pr. 1960 $17.95. How people can achieve self-realization in spite of present barriers.

Paul and Mary: Two Case Histories of Truants from Life. Free Pr. 1961 o.p.

Dialogues with Mothers. 1962. Avon 1971 pap. $2.50; Free Pr. 1962 text ed. $16.95. "Consisting of reports of group discussions with parents, this book is basically concerned with 'getting them [parents] to analyze a particular situation in their own words, on the basis of their own anxieties, notions and ideas' " (*Psychological Abstracts*).

(and Morris Janowitz). *Social Change and Prejudice.* Free Pr. 1964 $18.95. "Represents a highly creative and systematic attempt at synthesis of psychoanalytic and sociological method and interpretations" (*SR*).

The Empty Fortress: Infantile Autism and the Birth of the Self. 1967. Free Pr. repr. 1972 $10.95 text ed. pap. $10.95. In this "striking combination of casebook, plea for charity, and medical polemic, Bettelheim analyzes the nature of infantile autism with exhaustive care, describes (only to dismiss) rival theories of its origins, explodes some myths that have arisen about this form of psychosis, charts courses of treatment, and offers some tentative theories of his own. The most beautiful, most heart-rending, and . . . most enduring part of his book consists of three case histories" (Peter Gay, *The New Yorker*).

The Children of the Dream. 1969. Avon 1970 pap. $2.50; Macmillan 1969 $7.95. An appraisal of childrearing in the Israeli kibbutz.

A Home for the Heart. 1973. Univ. of Chicago Pr. 1985 pap. $14.95. "At once a summation and a further expansion of both his basic psychological concepts and his practical application of his ideas about institutional care. It may be Bettelheim's most lucid exposition of his notion of the 'therapeutic community,' and as such is indispensable to professionals, students and concerned lay readers. . . . An important work" (*PW*).

The Uses of Enchantment: The Meaning and Importance of Fairy Tales. Knopf 1976 $19.95; Random 1977 pap. $5.95. A thoughtful, humane, and sensitive approach to the fairy tale.

Surviving and Other Essays. 1979. Knopf 1979 $15.00; Random 1980 pap. $6.95. "Superbly written essays—penetrating and incisive. . . . Highly recommended for general collections" (*LJ*).

Freud and Man's Soul. 1983. Knopf 1983 $11.95; Random 1984 pap. $6.95. "The main thrust of his analysis of Freud's mistranslation is a critique of American psychoanalysis and the American approach to psychology in general" (*Nation*).

BINSWANGER, LUDWIG. 1881–1966

Ludwig Binswanger was born in Kreuzlingen, Switzerland, to a family of physicians and psychiatrists. He studied medicine in Lausanne, Heidelberg, and Zurich, receiving his medical degree in 1907. While at Zurich he studied with Jung and was a psychiatric intern under Eugene Bleuler. His father, Robert Binswanger, was the director of the sanatorium "Bellevue" at Kreuzlingen, and Ludwig served as his associate from 1908 to 1910. He succeeded his father in 1921 and remained as medical director until his retirement in 1936.

Binswanger was friends not only with Freud, but also with MARTIN HEIDEGGER (see Vol. 4), the existential philosopher, who visited "Bellevue" and discussed Binswanger's concept of "existential analysis" with him. Unfortunately, Binswanger's work is largely untranslated and of what is, most is very technical. However, his small book of reminiscences reveals a great deal about both Binswanger and Freud.

BOOK BY BINSWANGER

Sigmund Freud: Reminiscences of a Friendship. Grune & Stratton 1957 o.p.

BOSS, MEDARD. 1903–

Born in St. Gallen, Switzerland, Boss was educated at the University of Zurich and served in many capacities ranging from staff psychiatrist to head psychiatrist at many hospitals and clinics in the Zurich area. He was appointed professor of psychotherapy at the University of Zurich's medical faculty in 1954 (he is currently emeritus) and has had his own private practice since 1935.

During his career, he has been closely associated with Freud, Jung, Eugene Bleuler, H. W. Maier, Binswanger, and Martin Heidegger. In addition, he has taught and has been therapist for numerous psychotherapists throughout the world. He founded the Institute for Daseinanalytic Psychotherapy and Psychosomatics in Zurich in 1971, which is based on his own synthesis of Heidegger's concept of being and Freud's psychoanalysis.

BOOKS BY BOSS

The Analysis of Dreams. Philos. Lib. 1958 o.p. "A large part of the book is devoted to a critical analysis of other dream theories, notably those of Freud and Jung. . . . For Boss, dreams are not symbolic of behavior in waking life or of objects in the external environment, nor are dreams projections. What are they then? . . . A dream is reality" (*Contemporary Psychology*).

Psychoanalysis and Daseinanalysis. 1963 Da Capo repr. of 1963 ed. 1982 $25.00. "The exposition of the philosophy of *Daseinanalysis* represents necessary reading for all American psychologists because of its searching inquiry into philosophic issues created by what Boss perceives as the invasion of Man's inner sanctum by science-based concepts and techniques, i.e., psychotherapy and/or psychoanalysis" (*Contemporary Psychology*).

A Psychiatrist Discovers India. Dufour 1965 o.p. "Sets out the results of his investigation into the relevance to western psychiatric practice of the psychological assumptions of oriental sages and saints" (*TLS*).

I Dreamt Last Night. Gardner Pr. 1977 $23.95. "A casebook . . . the theory is presented painlessly and piecemeal in the discussion of specimen dreams" (*Contemporary Psychology*).

(ed.). *Existential Foundation of Medicine and Psychology.* 1977. Aronson 1983 $30.00. "If one is willing to persevere and follow Boss's perspectives, the effort will be a rewarding one" (*Contemporary Psychology*).

BOOK ABOUT BOSS

Scott, Charles, ed. *On Dreaming: An Encounter with Medard Boss.* Scholars Pr. GA 1982 text ed. pap. $9.95. "Contains seven papers by two philosophers, two theologians, two psychologists, and Medard Boss. . . . Boss's paper utilizes some other theorists' published dreams to illustrate his disagreements with their interpretations and to explain his own daseins-analytical, phenomenological dream theory" (*Religious Studies Review*).

BRILL, A(BRAHAM) A(RDEN). 1874–1948

Brill was the founder of psychoanalysis in America. He first brought Freud's teaching to this country, and first translated his works into English. He also translated Jung. He was born in Austria and came to the United States alone at the age of 13. He graduated from New York University, took his medical degree at Columbia University, taught at both universities, and was a practicing psychoanalyst. His *Basic Principles of Psychoanalysis* (1949) is the classic handbook of psychoanalysis for lay readers.

BOOKS BY BRILL

Psychoanalysis, Its Theories and Practical Application. [*Medicine and Society in America Ser.*] Ayer repr. of 1913 ed. 1972 $20.00

Fundamental Conceptions of Psychoanalysis. Ayer repr. of 1921 ed. 1973 $22.00

Freud's Contribution to Psychiatry. 1944. Peter Smith 1972 $11.25. "An excellent set of lectures by an American pioneer in the field of psychoanalysis" (*The New Yorker*).

Basic Principles of Psychoanalysis. 1949. Univ. Pr. of Amer. repr. of 1949 ed. 1985 text ed. pap. $10.75

DEWEY, JOHN. 1859–1952

[SEE Volume 3, Chapter 5.]

ELLIS, ALBERT. 1913–

Albert Ellis is a clinical psychologist and a marriage counselor. "I usually work with psychotherapy and marriage counseling," he told the editors of *Contemporary Authors*, "from 9:45 A.M. to 11 P.M., including the holding of six different psychotherapy groups every week." Ellis originated the rational-emotive therapy movement, which ignores Freudian theories and advocates the belief that emotions come from conscious thought "as well as internalized ideas of which the individual may be unaware."

Ellis was educated at the City College of New York and at Columbia University where he received a Ph.D. in psychology in 1943. He taught for a number of years at Rutgers University, New Jersey, and the Union Graduate School. Presently, he is executive director of the Institute for Rational Living, Inc., in New York City.

BOOKS BY ALBERT ELLIS

The Art and Science of Love. Lyle Stuart 1960 o.p.

(and Robert Harper). *A New Guide to Rational Living.* Wilshire 1961 pap. $3.00. "Presents the basics of Ellis' Rational-Emotive Therapy (RET) which is directed toward helping people change their emotions and actions by changing their attitudes and their thinking. . . . This is one of the most useful books in the self-help genre" (*LJ*).

(and Robert Harper). *A Guide to Successful Marriage.* Wilshire 1962 pap. $5.00. "Practical handbook for improving communication, resolving disagreements, handling anger and frustration, coping with kids, and enhancing sex and love feelings" (Publisher's catalog).

Reason and Emotion in Psychotherapy. 1962. Citadel Pr. 1984 pap. $7.95; Lyle Stuart 1962 $15.00. "Describes its [rational-emotive therapy] origins, differences from other major psychotherapeutic methods, and explains how this kind of holistic approach can achieve good results in a wide range of disturbances" (Publisher's catalog).

Sex without Guilt. 1966. Lyle Stuart rev. ed. 1966 $4.95; Wilshire 1958 pap. $5.00. "Famous classic which covers every phase of human sex relations, from masturbation to sexual variety" (Publisher's catalog).

Is Objectivism a Religion? Lyle Stuart 1968 o.p. "An assessment of the philosophy of objectivism as espoused by Ayn Rand and Nathaniel Branden. His analysis is thorough and scholarly in nature, and it deals forthrightly with the major tenets of objectivist philosophy . . . should be of interest to those concerned with objectivist philosophy, as well as those who would like to see a deft literary surgeon at work" (*LJ*).

(and Roger O. Conway). *The Art of Erotic Seduction.* Lyle Stuart 1968 o.p. "A step-by-step method of physical tactics for seducing an initially reluctant or unwilling female . . . it does succeed in the chapters where the authors discuss the technique of erotic arousal; the chapter on how to establish a long relationship is excellent" (*LJ*).

How to Live with a Neurotic. 1969. Wilshire 1957 pap. $5.00. "Shows how to ease the strain of living, working or associating with neurotics or psychotics; also useful as a treatment adjunct for therapists" (Publisher's catalog).

(and John M. Gullo). *Murder and Assassination.* Lyle Stuart 1971 o.p. "In a popular and graphic style, the authors trace case histories of a number of vivid murders from Nero to Stalin and Hitler" (*Choice*).

Growth through Reason: Verbatim Cases in Rational-Emotive Therapy. Wilshire 1971 pap. $7.00. "Listening in on these actual dialogues between patient and therapist is a fascinating experience, both for the professional and for the layperson interested in personal growth" (Publisher's catalog).

Executive Leadership: A Rational Approach. 1972. Institute for Rational-Emotive Therapy repr. of 1972 ed. 1978 pap. $5.95. "In this book he outlines the applications of his growth-through-reason principles for the normal executive" (*LJ*).

How to Master Your Fear of Flying. 1972. Institute for Rational-Emotive Therapy 1977 pap. $3.95. "Deals both with specific fears about flying, and general fears about dying" (Publisher's catalog).

Humanistic Psychotherapy: The Rational-Emotive Approach. 1973. Ed. by Edward Sagarin [*McGraw-Hill Pap.*] 1974 pap. $5.95. Shows how rational-emotive therapy differs from psychoanalytic, behavioral, and other therapies in theory, method, and effectiveness.

(and Albert Abarbanel, eds.). *The Encyclopedia of Sexual Behavior.* Hawthorn Bks. 1961 o.p. "An authoritative encyclopedia, written with clarity and good taste . . . still a standard in the field and . . . frequently cited" (*Wilson Library Bulletin*).

The Sensuous Person: Critique and Corrections. Lyle Stuart 1973 o.p. "With some wit leavening his blunt language, Ellis not only points out the follies of the sex-book writers but makes an earnest pitch for full sexual self-acceptance 'with whatever actual or potential weaknesses you have' " (*PW*).

How to Raise an Emotionally Healthy, Happy Child. Wilshire 1966 pap. $5.00. "Shows parents how to help their offspring develop self-acceptance and frustration tolerance" (Publisher's catalog).

Sex and the Liberated Man. Lyle Stuart 1976 $12.95. "Covers the art of sexual persuasion and how to relate to, arouse, and satisfy your partner and yourself, both physically and emotionally" (Publisher's catalog).

A Garland of Rational Songs. Institute for Rational-Emotive Therapy 1977 $3.50. "Songs satirizing people's irrational philosophies are set to popular tunes with lyrics by Albert Ellis" (Publisher's catalog).

Anger: How to Live with and without It. 1977. Citadel Pr. repr. of 1977 ed. 1985 pap. $5.95. "Presents an easily mastered step-by-step technique which will help you explore and understand the roots and nature of your anger" (Publisher's catalog).

(and Russell Grieger). *Handbook of Rational-Emotive Therapy.* Springer 1977 text ed. $29.95 pap. $12.95. "Geared for the novice in the cognitive-behavioral world" (*Contemporary Psychology*).

(and Eliot R. Abrahms). *Brief Psychotherapy in Medical and Health Practice.* Springer Pub. 1978 pap. $16.95. "Provides brief RET techniques for helping patients deal with their health-related anxiety, anger, and depression" (Publisher's catalog).

(and William J. Knaus). *Overcoming Procrastination.* New Amer. Lib. 1979 pap. $2.95. "Provides specific, practical techniques for changing old delay tactics into more self-disciplined, creative living" (Publisher's catalog).

(and Jeff Slaton). *Death Jag.* Woodhill 1980 pap. $1.95

(and Irving Becker). *A Guide to Personal Happiness.* Wilshire 1982 pap. $5.00. "Specifically demonstrates how to use RET and other methods to undo the main blocks to personal happiness and achieve self-acceptance" (Publisher's catalog).

(and Michael E. Bernard, eds.). *Rational-Emotive Approaches to Problems of Childhood.* Plenum 1983 $45.00. "Twenty-four authorities apply RET to the problems of childhood. Topics include the assessment and treatment of conduct disorders, low frustration tolerance, under-achievement, anxiety and phobias, obesity, and sexual problems" (Publisher's catalog).

Overcoming Resistance: Rational-Emotive Therapy with Difficult Clients. Springer Pub. 1985 text ed. $23.95. "Cognitive, emotive, and behavioral techniques for helping turn around negative client patterns" (Publisher's catalog).

(and Michael E. Bernard, eds.). *Clinical Applications of Rational-Emotive Therapy.* Plenum 1985 $39.50. "Leading RET therapists on love, sexuality, athletic performance, midlife problems, dying, marriage and divorce, women, substance abuse, and healthy living" (Publisher's catalog).

ELLIS, HAVELOCK. 1859–1939

Ellis's works fall under many heads: science, art, travel, poetry, essays. He has achieved distinction in many differentiated fields. His most important work was *Studies in the Psychology of Sex* (1898), which, when first published in England, was the subject of legal battles as to its "obscenity." However, the book helped to change public attitudes toward sex and greatly contributed to the study of sexual problems. Ellis interpreted his data from a biological rather than a clinical viewpoint. Freud, who drew from his material, regarded Ellis's conclusions as "happy anticipations of our own deductions." Ellis's most popular philosophical work is *The Dance of Life* (1923), a survey of modern civilization giving the author's own outlook on life. Many of his earlier books are out of print. The son of a British ship's captain, he spent much of his childhood in the Pacific. He became a teacher in New South Wales, then studied medicine in London, eventually devoting himself to research and writing in England.

BOOKS BY HAVELOCK ELLIS

Studies in the Psychology of Sex. 1898. Random 2 vols. 1936 o.p.

The World of Dreams. 1922. Darby repr. of 1922 ed. 1981 lib. bdg. $40.00; Gale repr. of 1922 ed. 1976 $40.00

The Dance of Life. 1923. Greenwood repr. of 1923 ed. 1973 lib. bdg. $32.50; Richard West repr. of 1923 ed. 1978 lib. bdg. $37.50

The Psychology of Sex: A Manual for Students. 1933. Emerson 1939 $15.95; Harcourt 2d ed. 1978 pap. $4.95. "Makes appeal to the lay reader and renders common property many details and instances which had better be reserved for the professional office" (*Booklist*).

From Rousseau to Proust. 1935. [*Essay Index Repr. Ser.*] Ayer repr. of 1935 ed. 1968 $18.00. A collection of biographical and critical essays and introductions dating from 1904 to 1934.

ERICKSON, MILTON H. 1901–1980

Born in Nevada, in 1901, Erickson grew up on a farm in Wisconsin. Both a psychiatrist and a psychologist, he was a member of many national and international professional organizations. At the time of his death, he was the world's leading practitioner of medical and therapeutic hypnosis.

BOOKS BY ERICKSON

Advanced Techniques of Hypnosis and Therapy: Selected Papers of Milton H. Erickson, M.D. Ed. by Jay Haley, Grune 1967 $68.50

The Nature of Hypnosis and Suggestion. Irvington 1980 text ed. $37.50 pap. $19.95

Teaching Seminar with Milton H. Erickson, M.D. Ed. by Jeffrey K. Zeig, Brunner-Mazel 1980 $27.50

(and Ernest L. Rossi). *Experiencing Hypnosis: Therapeutic Approaches to Altered States.* Irvington 1981 text ed. $39.50

BOOKS ABOUT ERICKSON

Bandler, Richard, and John Grinder. *Patterns of Hypnotic Techniques of Milton H. Erickson, M.D.* META Pubns. 1975 pap. $8.95

Haley, Jay. *Uncommon Therapy: The Psychiatric Techniques of Milton H. Erickson, M.D.* 1973. Norton 1986 $19.95. "Valuable reading for both graduate and undergraduate students who are interested in the outcomes of hypnotic training—namely skill in observing people and the complex ways they communicate, skill in motivating people to follow directives, and skill in using one's own words, intonations, and body movements to influence other people" (*Choice*).

Zeig, Jeffrey K. *Experiencing Erickson: An Introduction to the Man and His Work.* Brunner-Mazel 1985 $25.00. Personal record of working with Milton Erickson and his ideas. Close-up report.

ERIKSON, ERIK H. 1902–

American youth by the thousands have taken up Erikson's concern with their "identity" and "identity crisis." He is a practicing psychoanalyst whose theory of human development views the ego as evolving through the classical Freudian stages, which are each affected by cultural and social, as well as biological, factors. In adolescence, according to Erikson, the search for an "identity" becomes crucial. The conflicts between the self and its new view of parents as well as the world at large cause an "identity crisis"—

which Erikson finds a phenomenon affecting whole peoples in ways analogous to its effect on single individuals. Most of his writings explore this theme and its ramifications.

Born in Germany, Erikson graduated from the Vienna Psychoanalytic Institute and came to the United States in 1933. He holds an honorary degree from Harvard University, where he was professor emeritus of human development and lecturer on psychiatry. He has done extensive research at various American universities and was for a decade a senior staff member at the Austen Riggs Center, an institute in Stockbridge, Massachusetts, for the study and treatment of neuroses. He now lives in southern California. (See also Volume 3, Chapter 4.)

BOOKS BY ERIKSON

Childhood and Society. 1950. Norton 1986 $19.95 pap. $7.95. "Erikson's approach is basically that of psychoanalysis, but of psychoanalytic theory sophisticated with the insight of cultural anthropology and with a keen sense for history" (Clyde Kluckhohn).

Young Man Luther: A Study in Psychoanalysis and History. 1958. Norton 1962 pap. $5.95. "A unique integration of psychoanalysis, history, and the problem of the Great Man" (Margaret Mead).

Insight and Responsibility. Norton 1964 $14.95 pap. $7.95. Six lectures dealing with the ethical implications of psychoanalytic insight and people's responsibility to succeeding generations.

Identity and the Life Cycle: Selected Papers. 1967. [*Psychological Issues Monograph Ser.*] International Univ. Pr. 1967 $20.00; Norton 1980 $14.95 pap. $4.95. "Three influential articles ... detail the progress of the author's thinking as he advanced from clinical evidence to theoretical outline to therapeutical applications via the employment of his psycho-history technique" (*Booklist*).

Identity: Youth and Crisis. Norton 1968 $12.95 pap. $5.95. An adaptation of major essays over the period 1958 to 1968, this "offers a tremendous richness of ideas. It illuminates the striving for identity—one of the fundamentals of personality growth. It analyzes the influences on the youthful individual of social conditions and mores which create norms and tensions often harmful to psychic development. It discusses the 'inexorable standardization of American adolescence' and pinpoints *identity confusion* as leading young people into pseudointimacies, intellectual stagnation and impoverished interpersonal relationships" (Hillel A. Schiller, *Book-of-the-Month Club News*).

(and Huey P. Newton). *In Search of Common Ground*. Ed. by Kai T. Erikson, Norton 1973 $12.95

Dimensions of a New Identity. Norton 1974 $10.95 1979 pap. $3.95. "Provocative and readable ... should be in libraries where Jefferson scholars and those concerned with the interaction of the individual psyche history are likely to seek it" (*LJ*).

Life History and the Historical Moment. Norton 1975 $14.95 pap. $3.95. "A collection of previously published essays which cover a wide range of Erikson's interests ... most date from the late 1960's and early 1970's" (*LJ*).

The Life Cycle Completed: A Review. Norton 1982 $11.95 1985 pap. $4.95. "There is a freshness and vitality in the presentation of the life cycle that would lead one to feel the insights were being discovered for the first time" (*Choice*).

BOOKS ABOUT ERIKSON

Coles, Robert. *Erik H. Erikson: The Growth of His Work.* Little, Brown 1970 o.p. "This is not a conventional biography but rather an intellectual odyssey of perhaps the most seminal, living, psychoanalytical practitioner of our day. Coles examines the intellectual thrust of Erikson's work in a lively, systematic fashion; he is free enough to be both sympathetic and critical; and he is scholarly without being pedantic" (*Choice*).

Evans, Richard I. *Dialogue with Erik Erikson: And Reactions from Ernest Jones.* Praeger 1981 $33.95. "A psychologist and teacher of psychology at the University of Houston has attempted to extract [Erikson's] underlying philosophies and conceptualizations by utilizing the Socratic method—that is, teaching his audience through questioning his subjects. As a corollary to Erikson's work the dialogue has value; read without previous knowledge of Erikson's theories it would be more frustrating than fruitful" (*N.Y. Times*).

Maier, Henry W. *Three Theories of Child Development.* Longman 3d ed. 1978 o.p. "The theorists concerned are Piaget, Erikson, and Sears. . . . There are distinct advantages as well as problems in restricting study to three theorists, but for an individual beginning in the field to study child development, this is a compelling and a somewhat simpler approach" (*Choice*).

FOUCAULT, MICHEL. 1926–1984

One of the most prominent French thinkers of his generation, Foucault was educated at the École Normale Superieure and the Sorbonne, obtaining his diploma in 1952. He later held a chair as professor of the history of systems of thought at the Collège de France in Paris. Foucault wrote on a wide variety of topics, including madness, its historical determinants, and its forms of treatment. (See also Volumes 2 and 4.)

BOOKS BY FOUCAULT

Madness and Civilization: A History of Insanity in the Age of Reason. 1965. Random 1973 pap. $4.95. "Rather than to review historically the concept of madness, the author has chosen to recreate, mostly from original documents, mental illness, folly, and unreason as they must have existed in their time, place, and proper social perspective" (*Christian Century*).

The Order of Things: An Archaeology of the Human Sciences. 1970. Random 1973 pap. $5.95. "The ostensible attempt is to show under what conditions the human sciences arose; but the real value of the book is in the distinctions it establishes among the styles of thought and expression in the late Renaissance, the classical period, and the modern period (the types of each are, respectively, Paracelsus, Condillac, and Nietzsche and Mallarmé)" (*LJ*).

The Birth of the Clinic: An Archaeology of Medical Perception. Pantheon 1973 $8.95; Random 1974 pap. $3.95. "There is so much in this book . . . that it is impossible to do more than hint at its interest or at the counter arguments that it stimulates" (*New Statesman*).

Mental Illness and Psychology. Harper 1976 o.p.

BOOKS ABOUT FOUCAULT

Hoy, David. *Foucault: A Critical Reader.* Basil Blackwell 1986 $45.00 pap. $14.95

Rajchman, John. *Michel Foucault: The Freedom of Philosophy.* Columbia Univ. Pr. 1985 $22.00

FRANKL, VIKTOR. 1905–

Viktor Frankl was born in Austria where he subsequently studied medicine and became a psychiatrist. Under the Nazis, Frankl and most of his immediate family were placed in concentration camps; only Frankl himself survived. Having observed that the prisoners who were able to survive the suffering and humiliation of the concentration camps were those who could find some spiritual meaning in their suffering, Frankl was led to posit the "will-to-meaning" as the basic struggle of human existence, and he built his therapy around this idea.

Frankl is currently professor of neurology and psychiatry at the University of Vienna Medical School and distinguished professor of logotherapy at U.S. International University. Frankl states that "logotherapy . . . makes the concept of man into a whole . . . and focuses its attention upon mankind's groping for a higher meaning in life."

BOOKS BY FRANKL

Man's Search for Meaning: An Introduction to Logotherapy. 1962. Washington Square Pr. 1985 pap. $3.95. "Today we hear a great deal about disaffiliation, alienation, existential emptiness and identity crises. All these seem to include the problem of a self that finds no reason for being, and it is precisely to this problem that Frankl, in simplicity and eloquence, addresses his quest and directs his therapeutic answer" (*Contemporary Psychology*).

The Doctor and the Soul: From Psychotherapy to Logotherapy. 1965. Random 1973 pap. $4.95. "Set[s] forth his theory of Logotherapy, a concept of the existential form of life as the goal of psychotherapy. An important contribution to psychoanalysis, and, as well, to the fields of religion and philosophy" (*PW*).

Psychotherapy and Existentialism: Selected Papers on Logotherapy. Washington Square Pr. 1967 o.p. "The concepts of 'life purpose,' 'noögenic neurosis,' and 'paradoxical intention' are well described and illustrated by impressive case studies" (*Choice*).

The Will to Meaning: Foundations and Applications of Logotherapy. 1969. New Amer. Lib. 1970 pap. $6.95. "Presents little new for the professional, but in combination with *Man's Search for Meaning*, it may be a very good introduction to logotherapy for the undergraduate or interested layman" (*Choice*).

The Unheard Cry for Meaning: Psychotherapy and Humanism. Simon & Schuster 1979 pap. $8.95. In this work Frankl extends the discussion of logotherapy to its philosophical bases and talks about the light it sheds on ordinary life.

FREUD, ANNA. 1895–1982

Anna Freud, daughter of the famous Sigmund Freud, was instrumental in carrying on the work and studies of her father. An exponent of orthodox Freudian theory, she wrote *Psychoanalysis for Teachers and Parents* (1935) to explain his basic theory to the general public. It is a charming exposition and reminds us, in part by the fact that we recognize so much of it as familiar, of the tremendous impact Freud has had on the general culture of the twentieth-century Western world as well as the understanding and healing his work made possible for troubled human beings. Deeply interested in the problems of children, Anna Freud organized a residential war nursery for homeless youngsters during World War II and for many years directed the Hampstead Child Therapy Clinic in London, where she made her home.

Although she lacked medical training, her vast experience and lucid writing earned her the respect of many physicians and medical institutions. Some of her most important work was on the functioning of the ego in normal as well as disturbed children.

BOOKS BY ANNA FREUD

Writings. International Univ. Pr. 7 vols. 1937–74 various prices. "[The author's] range of knowledge is topped off by a fine literary style which makes the articles a very real pleasure to read" (*Choice*).

Psychoanalysis for Teachers and Parents. 1935. Trans. by Barbara Low, Emerson 1935 $8.95; Norton repr. 1979 pap. $4.95. "It expresses in simple terms the basic principles of analysis and explains the terminology" (*Survey*).

(and Dorothy T. Burlingham). *War and Children.* 1943. Greenwood repr. of 1943 ed. 1973 lib. bdg. $40.00. "It is the most gripping and moving volume this reviewer has read in the vast literature of WWII" (*Boston Globe*).

The Psycho-Analytical Treatment of Children: Lectures and Essays. 1946. International Univ. Pr. 1965 text ed. $17.50. "Anna Freud deals in detail with the differences in analytic work with child as opposed to adult. . . . Combines sophistication with clear explanation, and is readable and valuable" (*Contemporary Psychology*).

(and Thesi Bergmann). *Children in the Hospital.* International Univ. Pr. 1966 text ed. $17.50 pap. $12.95. "A number of brief sketches of children with various kinds of difficulties provide a basis for insightful commentary" (*Contemporary Psychology*).

Difficulties in the Path of Psychoanalysis: A Confrontation of Past with Present Viewpoints. International Univ. Pr. 1969 text ed. $30.00

Introduction to Psychoanalysis: Lectures for Child Analysts and Teachers. [*Writings of Anna Freud*] International Univ. Pr. 1974 text ed. $22.50

Introduction to the Technic of Child Analysis. [*Classics in Child Development Ser.*] Ayer repr. 1975 $17.00

Psychoanalytic Psychology of Normal Development (1970–1980). [*Writings of Anna Freud*] International Univ. Pr. 1981 text ed. $37.50. "Throughout this volume, the language is clear, the style is informal and almost conversational" (*Science Books and Films*).

BOOK ABOUT ANNA FREUD

Peters, Uwe H. *Anna Freud: A Life Dedicated to Children.* Schocken 1984 $24.95. "This straightforward, chronological account of the life and work of Anna Freud aptly matches the clarity and simplicity of Miss Freud's own work. . . . For those in the field, this biography should become a highly valued source ranking with the very finest historical accounts of the development of psychoanalysis" (*LJ*).

FREUD, SIGMUND. 1856–1939

Few men can claim a wider or deeper influence on their age than Sigmund Freud. His was the revolutionary theory of the unconscious, that strange submerged part of the human mind. His was the new method of treating mental and emotional illness, which he called psychoanalysis—the beginning of modern psychiatry. His theories and concepts have influenced anthropology, education, art, and literature. He was born in Moravia of a middle-class Jewish family and lived most of his life in Vienna. He died in London, a refugee from Hitlerism.

With his collaborator Josef Breuer, Freud worked originally toward curing patients of hysteria by uncovering their "unconscious" through hypnosis. He later substituted his own method of free association for the same end. His theories of personality were not well received by the medical profession or the general public until about 1909, when he first explained himself in the United States, and many of Freud's contemporaries (such as Adler, Jung, and later Karen Horney and Erich Fromm) disagreed with his emphasis on the infantile sexual instinct and the Oedipus complex. But whatever new developments occur, Freud's work will remain basic. (See also Volume 3, Chapter 4.)

BOOKS BY SIGMUND FREUD

The Complete Psychological Works: Standard Edition. Ed. and trans. by James Strachey, Norton 24 vols. 1976 $595.00

The Collected Papers of Sigmund Freud. Trans. by Joan Riviere and others, ed. by Ernest Jones, Basic Bks. 5 vols. 1959 ea. $36.00 set $175.00. "This is a great service to American students of human behavior. It may result in a large number of them reading much of Freud himself" (*Amer. Journal of Sociology*).

The Basic Writings of Sigmund Freud. Trans. by A. A. Brill, Modern Lib. 1938 $12.95. "The introduction is offensively egotistic. Otherwise, a fine job" (*The New Yorker*).

General Selection from the Works of Sigmund Freud. Doubleday 1957 pap. $4.95

The Interpretation of Dreams. 1900. Avon 1986 pap. $4.95; trans. and ed. by James Strachey, Basic Bks. 1954 $22.50; Buccaneer Bks. repr. of 1900 ed. 1983 lib. bdg. $23.95; Modern Lib. 1950 $6.95. The Strachey edition is the variorum edition, "incorporating all the alterations, additions, and deletions made by the author in the German text over a 30-year period, copiously annotated by the translator, with completely recast bibliographies, new appendixes, indexes of dreams, and a massive general index. . . . An essential acquisition" (*LJ*).

The Psychopathology of Everyday Life. 1904. Norton 1971 pap. $6.95. "The annotations . . . are indispensable. In addition, Strachey has provided a concordance, a system of cross-references reminding the reader when a point, a theme, or an incident has been mentioned before" (*Contemporary Psychology*).

Three Essays on the Theory of Sexuality. 1905. Trans. and ed. by James Strachey, Basic Bks. 1982 $18.95 pap. $8.95

Selected Papers on Hysteria and Other Psychoneuroses. 1909. Trans. by A. A. Brill [*Nervous and Mental Disease Monographs*] Johnson Repr. repr. of 1912 ed. $19.00

Introductory Lectures on Psychoanalysis: A General Introduction to Psychoanalysis. 1910. Liveright repr. of 1966 ed. 1977 pap. $5.95. "The *Lectures* cover all Freud's major theories: paraphrases (a more neutral translation of *Fehlleistungen* than the English term 'Freudian slip,' biased by long years of popular usage), dream theory, and the general theory of neuroses, for example, but also many other themes of general cultural interest, such as occultism and femininity" (*TLS*).

Totem and Taboo. 1913. Norton 1962 $6.00 pap. $3.95; Random 1960 pap. $2.95. Freud attempts to trace the origins of religion and morality.

The History of the Psychoanalytic Movement. 1917. Trans. by A. A. Brill [*Nervous and Mental Disease Monographs*] Johnson Repr. repr. of 1917 ed. $14.00; Macmillan 1985 pap. $4.95; Norton 1967 pap. $5.95

Beyond the Pleasure Principle. 1920. Norton repr. of 1961 ed. 1975 $6.95 pap. $3.95

Group Psychology and the Analysis of the Ego. 1922. Trans. by James Strachey, Norton repr. 1975 $6.95 pap. $2.95

The Ego and the Id. 1923. Trans. and ed. by James Strachey. Norton 1962 pap. $2.95. "The serious student of Freud will appreciate Strachey's lengthy introduction to the book, which sets the historical context, discusses the issues that led Freud to write it and traces the development of some of the significant ideas that are elaborated in it" (*Contemporary Psychology*).

The Future of an Illusion. 1927. Trans. by W. D. Robson-Scott, Norton 1975 $10.95 pap. $2.95

Leonardo da Vinci: A Study in Psychosexuality. 1932. Amereon 1971 $9.95; Norton 1965 pap. $4.95; Random 1966 pap. $2.95. "An interesting study of one genius by another" (*N.Y. Review of Bks.*).

Inhibitions, Symptoms, and Anxiety (Problem of Anxiety). 1936. Norton 1977 $6.95 pap. $3.95. A detailed account of Freud's thinking on the role of anxiety on the neurosis.

Moses and Monotheism. 1939. Ed. by Katherine Jones, Random 1955 pap. $4.95. "An epoch-making work. Professor Freud here ventures into fields hitherto unexpected" (*Living Age*).

Freud: A Dictionary of Psychoanalysis. 1950. Ed. by Nandor Fodor and Frank Gaynor, Greenwood repr. of 1950 ed. 1969 lib. bdg. $29.75. "Basic terms of psychoanalysis defined for psychologists, psychiatrists, and psychoanalysts" (*Christian Century*).

On Aphasia. Trans. by E. Stengel, International Univ. Pr. 1953 text ed. $25.00

Selections from Three Works by Freud. Ed. by John Richman, Hogarth Pr. & The Institute of Psychoanalysis 1939 o.p.

Origin and Development of Psychoanalysis. Regnery-Gateway 1960 pap. $3.95

Cocaine Papers. Ed. by Robert Byck, New Amer. Lib. 1975 pap. $8.95. "Provides access to some psycho-pharmacologic notes of 19th century authors who first studied cocaine" (*LJ*).

Delusion and Dream and Other Essays. Beacon 1966 o.p.

Infantile Cerebral Paralysis. Trans. by Lester A. Russin, Univ. of Miami Pr. 1968 $19.95. "As a recognized authority on the paralyses of children he was invited to prepare a treatise on the subject for Nothnagel's *Handbuch* (1897). Well received at that time, it is still considered to be one of the most thorough and complete expositions of a subject which even today is replete with controversy, disagreement, and uncertainty; and which remains refractory to any generally successful treatment" (*Choice*).

A Young Girl's Diary. Gordon Pr. $75.00

Letters of Sigmund Freud. Trans. by James Stern and Tania Stern, ed. by Ernst L. Freud, Basic Bks. 1960 $22.50. From approximately 4,000 letters, Freud's youngest son selected 315 of a personal kind to present a portrait of the man. The letters are arranged chronologically from June 1873 to September 1939. Recipients include friends and disciples, members of Freud's family, and such noted persons as Einstein, Thomas Mann, Rolland, Schnitzler, H. G. Wells, and Arnold Zweig and Stefan Zweig. "There is a greatness, a consistency of style. Those virtues which mark Freud's genius—his manifold curiosity, his swiftness of judgment, his tenacity—are exhibited throughout his letters, though in a minor, private key" (*Nation*).

The Origins of Psychoanalysis: Letters to Wilhelm Fliess, Drafts and Notes, 1887–1902. Ed. by Marie Bonaparte, Anna Freud, and Ernst Kris, Basic Bks. 1954 $20.00 pap. $11.95. "Students and scholars will be grateful for the publication in this book of the material on which Jones based his study" [*The Collected Papers of Sigmund Freud*] (*LJ*).

Psychoanalysis and Faith: The Letters of Sigmund Freud and Oskar Pfister. Trans. by Eric Mosbacher, Basic Bks. 1963 o.p. The correspondence between Freud, the "unrepentant heretic," and a Protestant clergyman.

A Psycho-Analytic Dialogue: The Letters of Sigmund Freud and Karl Abraham, 1907– 1926. Trans. by Bernard Marsh and Hilda C. Abraham, ed. with pref. by Hilda C. Abraham and Ernst L. Freud, intro. by Edward Glover, Basic Bks. 1966 o.p. "In their letters—which Dr. Glover points out read 'like the index to a textbook of abnormal (and normal) psychology'—the two analysts traded ideas about many of the principal ideas and subjects Freud was investigating. . . . Richly rewarding" (*LJ*).

The Letters of Sigmund Freud and Arnold Zweig. Ed. by Ernst L. Freud, Harcourt 1971 o.p. "This correspondence, which includes 42 letters by Freud and 77 by Zweig, and covers the fateful years from 1927 to 1939, presents an interesting human document of the last and tragic period of Freud's life" (*LJ*).

Sigmund Freud and Lou Andreas-Salomé: Letters. Ed. by Ernst Pfeiffer, Harcourt 1972 o.p. "These letters (covering the years from 1911, when Andreas-Salomé attended a psychoanalytic meeting in Weimar, to 1936, the year before her death) cast much light on the history of psychoanalysis and on the characters of both Freud and Andreas-Salomé. . . . The correspondence reveals her to be a passionate, optimistic, brave, and unselfish woman, and Freud himself seems less remote" (*LJ*).

The Freud-Jung Letters: The Correspondence between Sigmund Freud and C. G. Jung. 1974. Ed. by William McGuire, trans. by Ralph Manheim and R. F. C. Hull [*Bollingen Ser.*] Princeton Univ. Pr. 1974 $45.00 pap. $14.95. "Read sequentially, the letters convey the inexorable quality of tragic drama: two honest and devoted men gripped by a revolutionary insight into the human mind struggle to be true to that insight while grappling with their own unconscious reactions to each other" (*LJ*).

BOOKS ABOUT SIGMUND FREUD

Abramson, Jeffrey B. *Liberation and Its Limits: The Moral and Political Thought of Freud.* Beacon Pr. 1986 text ed. pap. $7.95; Free Pr. 1984 $14.95. "Offering a fresh interpretation of the nature of Freud's work, he contends that our contemporary view of liberation represents a radical and dangerous departure from Freud's original conception of what constitutes healthy freedom. . . . This study is much needed as a counterbalance to hedonistic interpretations of Freudian psychology" (*Booklist*).

Anzieu, D. *Freud's Self-Analysis and the Discovery of Psychoanalysis.* International Univ. Pr. 1986 text ed. $60.00

Appignanesi, Richard, and Oscar Zarate. *Freud for Beginners.* Pantheon 1979 pap. $4.95. An intellectual/biographical cartoon introduction to Freud. Combines "refreshing slapstick with a remarkable amount of fairly sophisticated and tightly compacted—but lucid—information" (*Village Voice*).

Berliner, Arthur K. *Psychoanalysis and Society: The Social Thought of Sigmund Freud.* Univ. Pr. of Amer. 1983 lib. bdg. $24.75 text ed. pap. $12.25

Bersani, Leo. *Baudelaire and Freud.* [*Quantum Ser.*] Univ. of California Pr. 1978 $18.50 pap. $2.65

Brandell, Gunnar. *Freud: A Man of His Century.* Trans. by Iain White, Humanities Pr. 1979 text ed. $18.75

Brill, A. A. *Freud's Contribution to Psychiatry.* 1944. Peter Smith 1972 $11.25. "An excellent set of lectures by an American Pioneer in the field of psychoanalysis" (*The New Yorker*).

Brome, Vincent. *Freud and His Disciples: The Struggle for Supremacy.* Longwood 1984 pap. $5.95

————. *Freud and His Early Circle.* Apollo 1969 o.p. "Mr. Brome's book concentrates not on the theoretical divergences between rival schools, though he handles them competently enough, but on the tangle of motives, temperaments, and misunderstandings of which this complex story is composed. On a subject that has generated much heat he writes with the dispassion of a historian. . . . He has produced an excellent book" (J. W. Burrow, *SR*).

Chabot, C. Barry. *Freud on Schreber: Psychoanalytic Theory and the Critical Act.* Univ. of Massachusetts Pr. 1982 lib. bdg. $17.50. "No mere reading of Freud's 'case study' on paranoia, this significant work cogently argues the necessity of a psychological theory to the interpretive processes of literary criticism" (*Choice*).

Dilman, Ilham. *Freud and the Mind.* Basil Blackwell 1985 $29.95 pap. $9.95. "In addition to philosophic readers, [many] will find Dilman's book an excellent and thoughtful guide" (*Contemporary Psychology*).

Fancher, Raymond E. *Psychoanalytic Psychology: The Development of Freud's Thought.* Norton 1973 pap. $6.95. "Fancher has indeed made Freudian psychology clear, with more grace and less dogmatism than Calvin Hall. But he has also achieved a mix of biography and exegesis that constitutes first-rate history of science" (*Choice*).

Fine, Reuben. *Development of Freud's Thought: From the Beginnings (1886–1899) Through Id Psychology (1900–1914) to Ego Psychology (1914–1939).* Aronson rev. ed. 1973 $25.00

Freeman, Lucy, and Herbert S. Strean. *Freud and Women.* Ungar 1981 o.p. "Freud emerges from this examination as a well-intentioned investigator of the female psyche. . . . General readers will enjoy reading about Freud's studies in this fast-moving, jargon-free narrative peopled with fascinating characters, chief of whom is Freud" (*LJ*).

Freud, Martin. *Sigmund Freud: Man and Father.* Aronson 1983 $25.00. Freud's eldest son recalls events of his childhood in a refreshing series of episodes.

Fromm, Erich. *Sigmund Freud's Mission: An Analysis of His Personality and Influence.* Peter Smith 1978 $11.25. "Brilliantly written" (*N.Y. Times*).

Grinstein, Alexander. *Sigmund Freud's Dreams.* International Univ. Pr. 1980 text ed. $40.00. "[The author] has limited himself to 19 dreams Freud had from 1895 to 1900 when Freud analyzed himself and made some of his greatest discoveries. . . . An important contribution to both Freudiana and the science of dream interpretation" (*LJ*).

Hale, Nathan G., Jr. *Freud and the Americans: The Origin and Foundation of the Psychoanalytic Movement in America, 1876–1918.* Oxford 1971 $27.50. In dealing with Freud's impact on America, Hale "proposes to deal with . . . the state of psychiatry, neurology and sexual morality in this country before Freud's appearance at the Clark University Conference in September 1909" (*America*).

Hall, Calvin S. *A Primer of Freudian Psychology.* Hippocrene Bks. repr. of 1954 ed. 1978 lib. bdg. $18.00; New Amer. Lib. 1979 pap. $2.95

Isbister, J. N. *Freud: An Introduction to His Life and Work.* Basil Blackwell 1985 $45.00 pap. $8.95

Jones, Ernest. *The Life and Works of Sigmund Freud.* Ed. and abr. by Lionel Trilling and Steven Marcus, Basic Bks. 3 vols. 1953–57 o.p. The author of this great biography, "a dauntingly stupendous task," was a member of Freud's small circle of coworkers and his close friend for 40 years. Permanent President of the International Psycho-Analytic Association and founder and former editor of *International Journal of Psychoanalysis*, Ernest Jones had at his disposal from the Freud family all the personal records and correspondence including 1,500 letters, among them the love letters written by Freud to his future wife. On the publication of the last volume, Charles Rolo of *Atlantic* said: "Dr. Jones's great achievement is that—in addition to setting on record so detailed, lucid and informed a study of Freud's personal history and his work—he has projected to the layman the inner drama that pervades Freud's life, the excitement of a revolutionary adventure of the mind." In their laudable attempt to make the three-volume monumental work more accessible to the general reader, Trilling and Marcus "have eliminated the documentation and deleted various whole chapters, most of the excursive footnotes, and some letters, but have retained whatever material is relevant to an understanding of Freud's life and character."

Kanzer, Mark, and Jules Glenn, eds. *Freud and His Patients.* Aronson 1979 $30.00

Kline, Paul. *Fact and Fantasy in Freudian Theory.* [*Methuen's Manuals of Modern Psychology Ser.*] 2d ed. 1981 $49.95. Wilhelm Reich, a student of Freud, made many contributions of his own to the field of psychoanalysis and later founded his own cult. "Amidst some of Reich's hyperbolic exaggerations, one finds here pungent descriptions of Freud's courage, his intellectuality, his Jewishness, his marriage, as well as his inner harshness and lack of interest in saving the world. . . . Much the most interesting part of [the book] consists of tape-recorded interviews which Dr. Kurt Eissler conducted in 1952 on behalf of the Freud archives [with] the surviving early analysts about their contact with Freud" (*Nation*).

Krull, Marianne. *Freud and His Father.* Norton 1986 $18.95

McCaffrey, Phillip. *Freud and Dora: The Artful Dream.* Rutgers Univ. Pr. 1984 text ed. $20.00

Miller, Jonathan, ed. *Freud: The Man, His World, His Influence.* Little, Brown 1972 o.p. "Portrayed are Freud's Vienna—sensual, anti-Semitic, a crucible of intellect and art; as well as Freud's relationship to Marx, philosophy, child rearing, anthropology, aesthetics, morality, and surrealist art" (*LJ*).

Oring, Elliott. *The Jokes of Sigmund Freud: A Study in Humor and Jewish Identity.* Univ. of Pennsylvania Pr. 1984 $15.95. "An interesting investigation of a relatively little studied aspect of Freud's life that ought to have appeal not only in relation to Freud but as a prototypical study of Jewish identity" (*LJ*).

Roazen, Paul. *Freud and His Followers.* Knopf 1975 $15.95; New York Univ. Pr. 1985 pap. $15.00. "[Roazen's] book is scholarly but not forbidding, well-written, of importance to specialists, but also fascinating for anyone interested in the history of psychology or in the personalities of Freud's circle" (*LJ*).

———. *Freud: Political and Social Thought.* [*Psychoanalysis Examined and Re-examined Ser.*] Da Capo repr. of 1968 ed. 1986 lib. bdg. $32.50. A political scientist, in "an endeavor to develop the relationship between psychoanalysis and political science [examines] Freud's own application of his concepts and their political and social implications" (*LJ*).

———. *Sigmund Freud.* Prentice-Hall 1973 $6.95. A collection of ten papers that discuss Freud as a pioneer in psychoanalysis and the effect of psychoanalysis on the social sciences. Contributors include Fromm, Riesman, Marcuse, Parsons.

Ruitenbeek, Hendrik, ed. *Freud As We Knew Him.* Wayne State Univ. Pr. 1973 $27.50. "A selection of 60 pieces . . . which bring alive a vivid picture of Freud the man as he appeared to a remarkable set of individuals, including James

Putnam, Thomas Mann, Stefan Zweig, Roy Grinker, Sr., and Hilda Doolittle (H.D.)" (*Contemporary Psychology*).

Salome, Lou A. *Freud*. [*Austrian-German Culture Ser.*] Black Swan 1986 $20.00

Shepherd, Michael. *Sherlock Holmes and the Case of Doctor Freud*. Methuen 1985 pap. $5.95

Stewart, Walter. *Psychoanalysis: The First Ten Years, 1888–1898*. Macmillan 1967 o.p. "A delineation of Freud's theories which led to his blind alleys and an outlining of how Freud resolved his difficulties. Dr. Stewart is scholarly, detached, and dedicated to the task he has assigned himself" (*LJ*).

Wittels, Fritz. *Freud and His Time*. Liveright 1931 repr. 1956 o.p. This book is important not because of the originality or excellence of its material but because it is one of the best statements of the Freudian theories yet to appear in English.

———. *Sigmund Freud: His Personality, His Teaching and His School*. Trans. by Eden Paul and Cedar Paul [*Select Bibliographies Repr. Ser.*] Ayer facsimile ed. repr. of 1924 ed. 1977 $20.00

FROMM, ERICH. 1900–1980

Born in Frankfurt, Germany, Erich Fromm studied sociology and psychology at the universities of Heidelberg, Frankfurt, and Munich, and received a Ph.D. from Heidelberg in 1922. After training in psychoanalysis in Munich and Berlin, he devoted himself to consultant psychology and theoretical investigation. He first visited the United States in 1933 and later became an American citizen. His *Man for Himself* (1947) brought a "new trend in the study of man." *Escape from Freedom* (1941) studies the causes of totalitarianism. In *The Art of Loving* (1956), he discussed love generally and came to the conclusion that although the "principle underlying capitalistic society and the principle of love are incompatible . . . love is the only sane and satisfactory answer to the problem of human existence." In *May Man Prevail?* (1961), he wrote that what is required above all is a drastic change in the U.S. attitude: "What can save us and what can help mankind is a renaissance of the spirit of humanism, of individualism, and of America's anticolonist tradition." Fromm was a humanist and a socialist in the pure sense. In *Beyond the Chains of Illusion* (1962), he shows that socialism had been badly distorted from its Marxian ideals. He believed that bureaucratic capitalism, toward which the West seemed to be heading, offered the best probability for the avoidance of nuclear war. In his later years, Fromm was no longer a practicing analyst, but taught at New York University as well as at the National University of Mexico.

Books by Fromm

Escape from Freedom. 1941. Avon 1971 pap. $3.95; Henry Holt 1963 pap. $5.95. An important and challenging book; it bridges the gap between economics and psychology.

Man for Himself: An Inquiry into the Psychology of Ethics. 1947. Fawcett 1978 pap. $2.95. "The thesis is developed that the clinician must reject modern ethical relativism (values are matters of culturally-determined preferences) and accept humanistic ethics in the study of personality whether viewed theoretically or therapeutically" (*Psychological Abstracts*).

The Forgotten Language. 1951. Grove 1956 pap. $4.95. "Fromm develops the theme of symbolism as 'the only universal language the human race ever developed.'. . . Freud's views on dreams are broadened to include 'the significant expression of any kind of mental activity under the condition of sleep' " (*Psychological Abstracts*).

The Sane Society. 1955. Fawcett 1977 pap. $2.95

The Art of Loving. 1956. Harper 1974 pap. $3.80. "Provocative, challenging, the book aims to discuss love in all its aspects" (*Springfield Republican*).

Marx's Concept of Man. [*Milestones of Thought Ser.*] Ungar 1961 $14.95 pap. $6.95. "The texts made available here are extremely interesting to anyone who wants to arrive at his own image of Marx's system" (*LJ*).

May Man Prevail? Doubleday 1961 o.p. "An intelligent and masterful analysis of the problem, assuredly controversial" (*Kirkus*).

Beyond the Chains of Illusion. 1962. Simon & Schuster 1985 pap. $7.95. "Fromm bares his own battle to come to terms with Marx and Freud, both of whom, he writes, 'have given us the intellectual tools to break through the sham of rationalization and ideologies, and to penetrate to the core of individual and social reality' " (*Saturday Review*).

The Dogma of Christ, and Other Essays on Religion, Psychology, and Culture. Henry Holt 1963 o.p. His projection of the concept of fatherhood found in psychoanalysis to the experience of early Christianity, with its emphasis on the role of the Son and the doctrine of a God-made man.

You Shall Be As Gods: A Radical Interpretation of the Old Testament and Its Traditions. 1966. Fawcett 1977 pap. $2.50. "The legitimacy of this method is extremely questionable, but his conclusion and clear presentation [are of] . . . interest" (*LJ*).

The Revolution of Hope: Toward a Humanized Technology. Harper 1968 o.p. "[This] will undoubtedly become another classic" (*LJ*).

The Heart of Man: Its Genius for Good and Evil. 1968. Harper 1980 pap. $5.95. "This book is in some respects a counterpart to 'The Art of Loving.' While the main topic there was man's capacity to love, the main topic here is his capacity to destroy, his narcissism and his incestuous fixation" (Erich Fromm).

(and Ramón Xirau, eds.). *Nature of Man: A Reader.* [*Problems of Philosophy Ser.*] Macmillan 1968 $7.95 pap. $5.95. Some 70 selections ranging from the Upanishads to David Riesman. "After analyzing past efforts to identify the essence of man, [the editors] put forward their own provocative suggestion, that man's capacity 'to become aware, to give account to himself of himself and of his existential situation . . . is fundamentally his nature' " (*LJ*).

The Crisis of Psychoanalysis. Fawcett 1971 o.p. "This important collection of Fromm's essays presents his views on the development of Freud's theories and the ineffective use of them by many psychoanalysts today" (*LJ*).

(and Michael Maccoby). *Social Character in a Mexican Village.* Prentice-Hall 1970 o.p. "An empirical study of Mexican peasants by two distinguished psychoanalysts" (*Choice*).

The Anatomy of Human Destructiveness. 1973. Fawcett 1978 pap. $3.50; Holt 1973 $10.95. "Writes with brilliant insight in attempting to break the deadlock in the struggle between the instinctivism of Konrad Lorenz, who affirms man's 'innate' aggressiveness, and behaviorist B. F. Skinner's 'social engineering' stance" (*PW*).

To Have or To Be? Bantam 1981 pap. $4.50; Harper 1976 $13.41. "Fromm's richly coherent discourse beautifully seeks out the meaning of 'being' as it illuminates or underlies Biblical writings, the thought or lives of Master Eckhart, the Buddha and later figures like Spinoza, Schweitzer and others—including Marx and Lenin, about whom his insights are remarkably acute" (*PW*).

The Greatness and Limitations of Freud's Thought. Harper 1980 $11.45; New Amer. Lib. 1981 pap. $2.95. "Fromm, characteristically, turns complex material into easily readable passages, enhancing his viewpoints with historical, anthropological, and mythological references" (*Critic*).

On Disobedience and Other Essays. Winston Pr. 1981 $12.95. "A collection of nine essays . . . [that] elaborates in various ways on his well-known humane socialism and socially responsible neo-Freudian ideas" (*Choice*).

BOOKS ABOUT FROMM

Evans, Richard I. *Dialogue with Erich Fromm.* Praeger 1981 $29.95. His ideas as elicited by a professor from the University of Houston "in an eminently readable manner" (*LJ*).

Funk, Rainer. *Erich Fromm: The Courage to Be Human.* Continuum 1982 $19.50. "The most comprehensive and detailed exposition of Fromm's thought to appear in any language" (*Choice*).

Gotesky, Rubin. *Personality: The Need for Liberty and Rights.* Libra 1967 $3.50

Hammond, Guyton B. *Man in Estrangement: Paul Tillich and Erich Fromm Compared.* Vanderbilt Univ. Pr. 1965 o.p. "Some readers may find the most valuable (and easiest) portion of the book to be the earlier chapters in which Hammond traces the concept of estrangement to its origin in Hegel. Tillich's conception of it derives more directly from Hegel's earlier writings, Fromm's from the Marxian inversion of Hegel. This historical approach brings the notion of estrangement into clear focus, and highlights the fundamental difference between Fromm and Tillich" (*Contemporary Psychology*).

Hausdorff, Don. *Erich Fromm.* Twayne 1972 o.p. "Brief but very informative. Provides an evaluation of Fromm's work in a spirit of 'critical sympathy and intellectual curiosity' " (*Choice*).

HORNEY, KAREN. 1885–1952

Horney was born in Hamburg, Germany, the daughter of a Norwegian father and a Dutch mother. While attending medical school at the University of Berlin, she became interested in psychoanalysis. She came to the United States in 1932 to be assistant director of the Chicago Institute of Psychoanalysis. She then became a practicing analyst and lecturer at the New School for Social Research in New York. In 1941 she helped found the American Institute of Psychoanalysis and held the post of dean until her death. Like that of other analysts, much of her work involved a restatement of Freudian theory. "I believe," she wrote in her first book, "that deference for Freud's gigantic achievements should show itself in building on the foundations that he has laid, and that in this way we can help to fulfill the possibilities which psychoanalysis has for the future, as a theory as well as a therapy." The *N.Y. Times* has said of her, however: "Much of Karen Horney's psychological theorizing has passed into common currency. . . . During the thirties and forties, [she] was a revolutionary thinker, pitting her culturally embedded, female-accented psychology against what she considered Freud's excessively male, materialistic and biologically determined theories."

BOOKS BY HORNEY

The Neurotic Personality of Our Time. 1937. Norton 1965 pap. $4.95. "Clearly written; for intelligent laymen, social workers, teachers, and psychiatrists" (*Booklist*).

New Ways in Psychoanalysis. 1939. Norton 1964 pap. $3.95. "The material is presented with lucidity and, if read in conjunction with *The Neurotic Personality*, should present no difficulties to the lay mind" (*Churchmen*).

Self-Analysis. 1942. Norton 1968 pap. $3.95. "Dr. Horney's book contains a great deal of interesting new material" (*Survey Graphic*).

Our Inner Conflicts: A Constructive Theory of Neurosis. 1945. Norton 1966 pap. $3.95. "I know of no other writer today in the field of psychoanalysis with a directness, a clarity, a reasonableness devoid of professional jargon and technical trim which equals that of Karen Horney, whose *New Ways in Psychoanalysis* was an important modern contribution" (*Kirkus*).

Neurosis and Human Growth: A Study of Self-Realization. 1950. Norton 1970 pap. $3.95. "Karen Horney's book is an important and constructive document in the growing controversy" (*N.Y. Times*).

Feminine Psychology. 1967. Ed. by Harold Kelman, Norton 1973 pap. $3.95. Horney's "humanism, her ability to reason clearly and write simply are evident in this collection, which reveals her gradually evolving ideas about feminine psychology and her level-headed solutions to the problems created by distrust between the sexes. Those familiar with her books will want to add 'Feminine Psychology' to their collection. Those unfamiliar will find this an admirable introduction" (*N.Y. Times*).

BOOK ABOUT HORNEY

Kelman, Harold. *Helping People: Karen Horney's Psychoanalytic Approach.* Aronson 1971 $35.00. "An extensive presentation of Kelman's modification of Horney's theory of neurosis, psychoanalytic concepts and techniques, and stages of the treatment process" (*LJ*).

JAMES, WILLIAM. 1842–1910

William James, the brilliant and readable Harvard "pragmatic" philosopher and the first Harvard professor of psychology (1889–1897), is one of the "fathers" if not *the* father of American psychology. After brief personal investigation of the work of Helmholtz, Hering, and Wundt in Germany, he introduced experiments in psychology in a Harvard graduate course on "The Relations between Physiology and Psychology" in 1875. His *Principles of Psychology* (1890) became a standard textbook. James saw human psychology as a biological adjustment to the changing environment—with the state of consciousness as a "selecting agency." His student G. Stanley Hall, later himself a pioneer of distinction in the field, recalled (says Gay Wilson Allen) how in the early days James kept "in a tiny room under the staircase of the Agassiz museum . . . a metronome, a device for whirling a frog," and other novel research tools for the period. His philosophical and psychological studies had each an effect on the other, but in 1897 he took the Harvard Chair in Philosophy and devoted the rest of his life to that discipline. (See also Volumes 3 and 4.)

BOOKS BY JAMES

The Writings of William James: A Comprehensive Edition. Ed. by John J. McDermott, Modern Lib. 1968 $5.95; Univ. of Chicago Pr. 1978 pap. $20.00. "A valuable contribution to the current William James revival.... Mr. McDermott has chosen not only the well-known James classics but has also drawn from unpublished papers and from newspaper interviews, and combined all into a comprehensive portrait of our greatest American philosopher" (*LJ*).

William James on Psychical Research. Ed. by Gardner Murphy and Robert Ballou, Kelley repr. of 1960 ed. 1973 $27.50. "James' writings on psychical phenomena are presented under the following headings: 'Early Impressions'; 'General Statements'; 'Clairvoyance, Levitation and the Astral Body'; 'William James and Mrs. Piper'; 'William James and Frederic Meyers'; 'Religion and the Problems of the Soul and Immortality'; and 'The Last Report' " (*Psychological Abstracts*).

The Principles of Psychology. 1890. Dover repr. of 1890 ed. 1950 text ed. pap. $9.95; Harvard Univ. Pr. 1983 text ed. $25.00 pap. $17.50; Peter Smith $32.50. Authorized unabridged editions. "This critical text of the preeminent classic of American psychology incorporates the results of the highest standards of textual scholarship to present James's intentions in a definitive edition" (*Choice*).

Talks to Teachers on Psychology: And to Students on Some of Life's Ideals. 1899. [*Works of William James*] Harvard Univ. Pr. 1983 text ed. $25.00; Norton 1958 pap. $6.95. "James's fifteen lectures to teachers and three addresses to college students, first published in book form in 1899. Includes James's preliminary notes and drafts, descriptions of source documents and editing procedures, and a historical account of the original lectures and their publication" (*Contemporary Psychology*).

The Varieties of Religious Experience: A Study in Human Nature. 1902. Harvard Univ. Pr. 1985 text ed. $45.00; Modern Lib. 1978 $8.95; New Amer. Lib. 1958 pap. $4.50; Penguin 1982 pap. $4.95. "For James *The Varieties of Religious Experience* was an occasion to summarize many of his ethical and philosophical views, but also an opportunity to show what he believed the human mind is all about, and not least, how psychologists and psychiatrists ought think about their work" (*The New Republic*).

Psychology: The Briefer Course. 1892. Harvard Univ. Pr. 1984 text ed. $35.00

BOOKS ABOUT JAMES

Eisendrath, Craig R. *The Unifying Moment: The Psychological Philosophy of William James and Alfred North Whitehead.* Harvard Univ. Pr. 1971 $22.50. "Fulfills a real need for a comparison of the thought of James and Whitehead.... A very good book for those interested in epistemological issues arising in process philosophy" (*Choice*).

Linschoten, Hans, ed. *On the Way Toward a Phenomenological Psychology: The Psychology of William James.* Trans. by Amedeo Giorgi [*Philosophical Ser.*] Duquesne Univ. Pr. 1968 o.p. The Professor of Experimental and General Psychology at the University of Utrecht (until his early death in 1964) "finds multitudes [of contradictions] in the philosophy of William James but insists that, transcending ostensible internal contradictions, a synthesis of a great philosophy may nevertheless be detected.... Notwithstanding that this is a psychologist writing for psychologists and his book is by no means a bedside reader, a certain freshness breaks through. Hans Linschoten's study leaves no doubt that a brilliant if controversial career, perhaps not yet at its height, was tragically halted" (Alan W. Miller, *SR*).

Wilshire, Bruce. *William James and Phenomenology: A Study of "The Principles of Psychology."* AMS Pr. repr. of 1968 ed. 1979 $24.00

JUNG, C(ARL) G(USTAV). 1875–1961

The Swiss Dr. Jung was one of the most famous of modern psychologists and psychiatrists. Jung met Freud first in 1907 and became his foremost associate and disciple. The break came with the publication of Jung's *Psychology of the Unconscious* (1916), which did not follow Freud's theories of the libido and the unconscious. Jung eventually rejected Freud's system of psychoanalysis for his own "analytic psychology." This emphasizes present conflicts rather than those from childhood; it also takes into account the conflict arising from what Jung called the "collective unconscious"—evolutionary and cultural factors determining individual development. Jung was considered by Freud's followers as a "deserter" and a "mystic"; his theories have continued to be the topic of heated discussions. He invented the association word test and contributed the word "complex" to psychology. He first described the "introvert" and "extrovert" types. Jung's interest in the human psyche, past and present, led him to study mythology, alchemy, oriental religions and philosophies, and primitive peoples. Later he became interested in parapsychology and the occult. He thought that unidentified flying objects might be a psychological projection of modern people's anxieties.

Jung was elected a fellow of the Royal Society of Medicine and received an honorary D.Sc. by Oxford University, the first psychologist to receive such an honor in England. He also received honorary degrees from Harvard University, the University of Calcutta, the Banaras Hindu University, the University of Allahabad in India, and the University of Geneva.

BOOKS BY JUNG

The Collected Works of C. G. Jung. Ed. by Herbert Read, M. Fordham, and Gerhard Adler, trans. by R. F. C. Hull [*Bollingen Ser.*] Princeton Univ. Pr. 20 vols. 1953–85 ea. $17.50–$40.00

The Basic Writings of C. G. Jung. Ed. by Violet de Laszlo, Modern Lib. 1977 $9.95. "A representative selection from Jung's writings . . . covering the entire period of his production up to the present" (*Psychological Abstracts*).

Psychological Reflections: A New Anthology of His Writings, 1905–1961. Ed. by Jolande Jacobi and R. F. C. Hull [*Bollingen Ser.*] Princeton Univ. Pr. 1970 $34.50 pap. $8.95. "This new edition of the 1953 book draws on over 30 additional sources, including interviews and posthumously published works" (*LJ*).

Psyche and Symbol: A Selection from the Writings of C. G. Jung. Ed. by Violet de Laszlo, Doubleday 1958 pap. $6.50

The Portable Jung. Ed. by Joseph Campbell [*Viking Portable Lib.*] Penguin 1976 pap. $7.95. A collection of Jung's major writings, spanning his entire career.

The Psychology of Dementia Praecox. [*Nervous and Mental Disease Monographs*] Johnson Repr. repr. of 1909 ed. $19.00. "A re-translation by A. A. Brill of the study originally published in 1906 and translated by him into English in 1909. In the first chapter the author critically reviews the previous psychological theories of schizophrenia and indicates that Freud's contribution of the concepts of repression and conversion adds greatly to the understanding of the phenomena of the psychosis" (*Psychological Abstracts*).

The Theory of Psychoanalysis. Johnson Repr. repr. of 1915 ed. $14.00

Modern Man in Search of a Soul. 1933. Harcourt 1955 pap. $3.95. "Involved as the book is, it will repay a careful reading on the part of those who have some knowledge of what has been done in analytical psychology" (*Churchmen*).

Analytical Psychology, Its Theory and Practice: The Tavistock Lectures. 1935. Random 1970 pap. $4.95. "This book of five lectures by Jung is a summary of his views, delivered to a London professional audience in 1935" (*LJ*).

(and Carl Kerenyi). *Essays on a Science of Mythology: The Myths of the Divine Child and the Mysteries of Eleusis.* 1949. [*Bollingen Ser.*] Princeton Univ. Pr. rev. ed. 1963 $14.00 pap. $6.95. "Kerenyi presents two myths and Jung relates them to psychological experience. The divine child, at once helpless infant and godlike being, born and reared in parentless and perilous circumstances is nonetheless able to survive and be nurtured, emerging triumphant. . . . The divine maiden (koré) is at once eternal maiden, eternal mother, and eternal woman who is part of the man-woman relationship which enables mankind to continue" (*Contemporary Psychology*).

The Undiscovered Self. Little, Brown 1958 $12.45 pap. $4.70; New Amer. Lib. 1974 pap. $2.50. "Wise, witty, and forthright counsel for the reflective reader" (*Booklist*).

The Freud-Jung Letters: The Correspondence between Sigmund Freud and C. G. Jung. Ed. by William McGuire, trans. by Ralph Manheim and R. F. C. Hull [*Bollingen Ser.*] Princeton Univ. Pr. 1974 $45.00 pap. $14.95. "The reader of these letters will find in them, or read out of them, whatever his personal inclinations dictate. They are, of course, a gold mine for the historian. . . . Virtually every person who reads these letters will be looking for tidbits of scandal and slander. He will find them, plus some pretty racy language. Personalities are discussed with candor" (*Contemporary Psychology*).

C. G. Jung: Letters, 1906–1950. Ed. by Gerhard Adler and Aniela Jaffe, trans. by R. F. C. Hull [*Bollingen Ser.*] Princeton Univ. Pr. 1973 $42.00. "Over 900 letters have been selected from over 1,600 written between 1906 and 1950 to more than 500 different persons of prominence. The letters were often the medium for communicating his ideas to the outside world and for rectifying misinterpretations that might have no other means of correction" (*Choice*).

Memories, Dreams, Reflections. Pantheon rev. ed. 1963 $22.00; ed. by Aniela Jaffe, Random 1965 pap. $6.95. This profound and absorbing autobiographical book, described as an "interior biography," is accessible in its language and its thought to the lay reader as well as to psychologists. It is mostly written from interviews, which the editor began with Jung in 1957, but four chapters, including those on his childhood and his skepticism about theology, were written by Jung himself.

BOOKS ABOUT JUNG

Bennett, E. A. *What Jung Really Said.* Schocken 1971 pap. $4.95. "Bennett, a psychotherapist and friend of the late Dr. Jung, reviews Jung's work as it developed: first with Bleuler and Janet; then with Freud, who had the most influence on him; and finally, his own independent work, as creator and leader of a new influential school of thought and therapy. . . . A well-written book, highly recommended" (*LJ*).

Brome, Vincent. *Jung: Man and Myth.* Atheneum 1978 $11.95 pap. $6.95. "The best biography of C. G. Jung ever written. . . . This British author has done a good job of presenting a balanced portrait of a complicated man; he has neither oversimplified nor become lost in trivial psychological analysis" (*Choice*).

Cohen, Edmund D. *C. G. Jung and the Scientific Attitude.* [*Quality Pap. Ser.*] Littlefield 1976 pap. $4.95; Philosophical Lib. 1975 $8.95. "A standard review of Jungian principles, never seriously criticizing Jungian concepts" (*Choice*).

Cowan, Lyn. *Masochism: A Jungian View.* Spring Pubns. 1982 pap. $12.00

Cox, David. *Modern Psychology: The Teachings of Carl Gustav Jung.* Barnes & Noble 1958 pap. $3.95. "Cox presents a good overview of a relevant psychological approach to life, and provides a depth perspective into the nature of oneself that will be extremely helpful in search for a deeper appreciation of one's intricate life" (*Choice*).

Hall, Calvin, S., and Vernon J. Nordby. *A Primer of Jungian Psychology.* New Amer. Lib. 1973 pap. $2.95; Taplinger 1973 o.p. "The aim of this little book is 'to present Jung's concepts and theories clearly, simply, and accurately.' This the authors have done—and very competently" (*LJ*).

Homans, Peter. *Jung in Context: Modernity and the Making of a Psychology.* Univ. of Chicago Pr. 1979 lib. bdg. $17.50 1982 pap. $6.95. "The analysis of the psychological influences that shaped Jung's work is given the most attention" (*Contemporary Psychology*).

Jacobi, Jolande F. *The Psychology of C. G. Jung.* Trans. by Ralph Manheim, Yale Univ. Pr. 1973 $16.50 pap. $8.95

———*The Way of Individuation.* New Amer. Lib. 1983 pap. $7.95. "Jacobi is well known as a systematic expositor of Jung's ideas. This book presents in nontechnical fashion for the educated layman a discussion of Jung's concept, individuation, the innate tendency of an individual to realize himself as a unique, whole person" (*LJ*).

Jaffe, Aniela. *The Myth of Meaning.* 1971. Trans. by R. F. C. Hull, Humanities Pr. 1977 text ed. $20.50 pap. $9.25. "The author, an analytical psychologist and personal secretary to Carl Jung during his last years, devotes herself to the problem of explaining Jung's main interest—the meaning and aim of human existence" (*LJ*).

Matton, Mary Ann. *Jungian Psychology in Perspective.* Free Pr. 1985 pap. $10.95

Neumann, Erich. *The Great Mother: An Analysis of the Archetype.* Trans. by Ralph Manheim [*Bollingen Ser.*] Princeton Univ. Pr. 1964 $40.00 pap. $10.95. "A major study of the way women have been regarded since prehistory" (*PW*).

Nichols, Sallie. *Jung and Tarot: An Archetypal Journey.* Weiser 1984 pap. $12.95

Samuels, Andrew. *Jung and Post-Jungians.* Routledge & Kegan 1984 $24.95

Staude, John-Raphael. *The Adult Development of C. G. Jung.* Methuen 1981 $16.95. "Staude's book puts Jung's adult development into the framework of 'life-span developmental psychology.' It thus makes valuable contrasts between academic and Jungian psychology: the former concentrates on the ego and the latter revitalizes it and relates it to the Jungian self" (*Choice*).

Stein, Murray, ed. *Jungian Analysis.* Open Court 1982 $19.95; Shambhala 1984 pap. $10.95. "This book, with its distinguished roster of contributors, its clinical orientation, and its useful list of references at the end of each chapter, will certainly be important to those who are actively involved with Jungian practice" (*Contemporary Psychology*).

Storr, Anthony. *C. G. Jung.* [*Modern Masters Ser.*] Viking 1973 o.p. This book "explains Jung's complex theories of analytical psychology in a clear, simple, understandable prose. . . . Storr refers to the *Collected Works* frequently and in this way provides a useful guide to them on such topics as individuation, self, archetype, and other Jungian formulations. Enjoyable reading for the layman or the beginning student" (*Choice*).

Ulanov, Ann Belford. *The Feminine in Jungian Psychology and in Christian Theology.* Northwestern Univ. Pr. 1971 o.p. The author's work "revolves around Jung's approach to and the structure of the psyche, his concept of the feminine in both male and female, and the concept of the feminine as it relates to the religious function and the doctrine of man, God and Christ, and the Spirit" (*Choice*).

Van der Post, Laurens. *Jung: And the Story of Our Time.* Random 1977 pap. $6.95. "Loaded with rich perceptions. . . . A most stimulating book" (*PW*).

LACAN, JACQUES. 1901–1981

Jacques Lacan was born into an upper-middle-class Parisian family. He received psychiatric and psychoanalytic training, and his clinical training began in 1927. His doctoral thesis, "On Paranoia and Its Relation to Personality," already indicated an original thinker; in it, he tried to show that no physiological phenomenon could be adequately understood without taking into account the entire personality, including its engagement with a social milieu.

Lacan led a "back to Freud" movement in the most literal sense, at a time when others were trying to interpret Freud broadly. He emphasized the role of the image and the role of milieu in personality organization. He also believed that Freud's greatest insight was his understanding of the "talking cure" as revelatory of the unconscious as being structured like a language. By taking Freud literally, Lacan led a psychoanalytic movement that evolved into a very specific school of interpretation. He is difficult to read, but provocative and rewarding.

Books by Lacan

Ecrits: A Selection. Trans. by Alan Sheridan, Norton 1982 pap. $10.95. "These nine essays, chosen by Lacan himself, are the first sizable chunk of Lacan's work to be available in English. . . . Readers with the necessary background and energy will find in *Ecrits* important insights into structuralism and Freud's theories" (*LJ*).

The Language of the Self: The Function of Language in Psychoanalysis. Dell 1975 pap. $3.95

The Four Fundamental Concepts of Psycho-Analysis. Trans. by Alan Sheridan, Norton 1978 $19.95 1981 pap. $9.95. "Enigmatic, provocative, at times too cute, but in the end very rewarding to read" (*Choice*).

Speech and Language in Psychoanalysis. Trans. by Anthony Wilden, Johns Hopkins 1981 pap. $9.95

Feminine Sexuality. Ed. by Juliet Mitchell and Jacqueline Rose, Norton 1983 $19.50 1985 pap. $9.95. "Lacan sees sexuality as a psychic rather than a biological construct, which is why many feminists have been attracted to his work. It is not the penis as biological organ that is superior for Lacan, but rather the penis in its symbolic significance as the phallus within culture. . . . What Mitchell and Rose's selections make clear is that Lacan doesn't so much look at feminine sexuality as he does at women in male fantasy (a worthy undertaking in itself)" (*The New Republic*).

Book about Lacan

Mueller, J. P., and W. J. Richardson. *Lacan and Language: A Reader's Guide to Ecrits.* International Univ. Pr. 1982 $30.00. A useful guide in which the authors render Lacan accessible to the novice.

LAING, R(ONALD) D(AVID). 1927–

R. D. Laing is a prominent British psychoanalyst who has won wide attention in the United States, especially among young people, for his questioning of many of the old concepts of what is "normal" and what is "insane" in a world that he sees as infinitely dangerous in the hands of "normal" people. In *The Politics of Experience* (1967), an excellent introduction to his thinking, he writes: "A little girl of seventeen in a mental hospital told me she was terrified because the Atom Bomb was inside her. That is a delusion. The statesmen of the world who boast and threaten that they have Doomsday weapons are far more dangerous, and far more estranged from 'reality' than many of the people on whom the label 'psychotic' is affixed."

Much of Laing's work has been done in the field of schizophrenia. Philosophical and humanist in approach, he questions many of the cut-and-dried classifications for the mentally ill, whom he regards with great compassion; he looks beyond the "case" to the man or woman trying to come to grips with life in the broadest human context. He is a compelling writer of great literary skill who brings to his studies a worldview that reaches far beyond the confines of his profession. Born in Glasgow, Laing practices at the Tavistock Institute of Human Relations and directs the Langham Clinic—both in London.

Books by Laing

The Divided Self. 1960. Penguin 1965 pap. $4.95. "Any therapist who wants to deepen his feeling for man will profit from the hours in Laing's stimulating company" (*Critic*).

The Self and Others. 1961. Penguin rev. ed. 1972 pap. $4.95 "Essentially an essay on human relationships from a standpoint midway between psychoanalysis and existentialism" (*TLS*).

(and David G. Cooper). *Reason and Violence: A Decade of Sartre's Philosophy, 1950–1960.* 1964. Fwd. by Jean-Paul Sartre, Random 1971 pap. $5.95. "The publication of *Reason and Violence* does . . . convey some sense of the contemporary relevance of Sartre's *Critique*" (*Journal of Philosophy*).

(and Herbert Phillipson and A. Russell Lee). *Interpersonal Perception.* Springer Pub. 1966 o.p. "This book contains a theory, a method, and an instrument for the study of how two persons perceive each other. . . . The authors compared in great detail the average responses of 12 disturbed and 10 nondisturbed married couples. . . . On the face of it, the authors seem to have developed an ingenious and sensible way of measuring psychological relationships between two persons" (*Contemporary Psychology*).

The Politics of Experience. 1967. Ballantine 1978 pap. $2.50. A most interesting discussion of his psychological theories—for lay people—in the context of the modern world. Brief and beautifully written.

Knots. Pantheon 1970 $3.95; Random 1972 pap. $2.95. "Of interest to followers of Laing, therapy group members, and students of behavior in general" (*LJ*).

The Politics of the Family and Other Essays. Random 1972 pap. $4.95. "Laing, a psychoanalyst . . . here questions assumptions about the family" (*Canadian Forum*).

The Voice of Experience. Pantheon 1982 $12.00. "Both coherent in its design and sustained in its intensity" (*TLS*).

Conversations with Adam and Natasha. Pantheon 1984 pap. $3.50. "The short dialogues recorded here actually took place among Laing, his wife and their two children. . . . The conversations reflect the emotional development of fairly healthy children within the context of a secure, reciprocal relationship with their parents" (*PW*).

The Facts of Life: An Essay in Feelings, Facts and Fantasy. Ballantine 1984 pap. $3.95; Pantheon 1984 pap. $3.95. "His metaphoric, cryptic and elliptic style leaves much to the reader but is appropriate for the complex discussion of psyche-soma interrelations" (*LJ*).

Wisdom, Madness and Folly: The Making of a Psychiatrist, 1927–1957. McGraw-Hill 1985 $14.95 1986 pap. $4.95

BOOKS ABOUT LAING

Boyers, Robert, and Robert Orrill, eds. *R. D. Laing and Anti-Psychiatry.* Hippocrene Bks. repr. of 1971 ed. 1974 $24.50. "[A] collection of critical essays and transcripts of interviews and symposiums by psychiatrists, sociologists, literature professors and psychologists . . . many-faceted, well-rounded treatment" (*PW*).

Friedenberg, Edgar Z. *R. D. Laing.* [*Modern Masters Ser.*] Viking 1974 $9.95. "Friedenberg discusses the limitations of Laing's research, the ambiguity of much of his writing, the rejection of scientifically controlled observation, and the influences of Eastern philosophy" (*LJ*).

LEWIN, KURT. 1890–1947

[SEE Volume 3, Chapter 4].

MASLOW, ABRAHAM H(AROLD). 1908–1970

In its first edition, Abraham Maslow's *Toward a Psychology of Being* (1962) sold more than 100,000 copies. Like R. D. Laing, Maslow questioned the old psychoanalytic notions of being well or ill "adjusted" to the world and spoke from a broadly human base. Human nature—the inner nature of every individual which is uniquely his own—"seems not to be . . . necessarily evil; . . . the basic human capacities are on their face either neutral, premoral or positively 'good.' What we call evil behavior appears most often to be a secondary reaction to frustration of this intrinsic nature." On this foundation Maslow built an affirmation of people and people's potentialities for self-fulfillment and psychological health. He considered his "humanistic" or "Eupsychian" approach to be part of the revolution then taking place in psychology, as in other fields, toward a new view of people as sociable, creative, and loving beings whose welfare is not in the cure of "neurosis" or other ills but on the development of their most socially and personally constructive potentials.

Maslow was chairman of the psychology department at Brandeis University, Waltham, Massachusetts. He taught for 14 years at Brooklyn College and was president of the American Psychological Association from 1967 to 1968. His wife, Bertha, helped edit his journals and last papers after his death as well as assisting with a memorial volume about him.

BOOKS BY MASLOW

(ed.). *Motivation and Personality.* 1954. Harper 2d ed. 1970 text ed. pap. $19.95. "In this book Maslow presents a systematic theory and application of motivation and personality which he has derived from a synthesis of 3 approaches: holistic, dynamic, and cultural" (*Psychological Abstracts*).

(ed.). *New Knowledge in Human Values.* 1959. Regnery-Gateway repr. 1970 pap. $5.95. "The reader will be well advised to read and judge these papers on their individual merits and to disregard the dubious attempt to glean from them a 'scientific' indication of 'creative altruism' " (*Annals of the Amer. Academy of Political and Social Science*).

Toward a Psychology of Being. 1962. Van Nostrand 2d ed. 1968 $17.95 pap. $10.95

Religions, Values and Peak-Experiences. 1964. Penguin 1976 pap. $3.95; Peter Smith 1983 $12.75 "[A] small but powerful book. . . . His observations and reflections lead him not so much to deny once and for all that any two-dimensional world and experience exist, as to assert that this formulation of reality is obscurantist" (*Contemporary Psychology*).

Eupsychian Management: A Journal. Irwin 1965 o.p. "Throughout the reader is confronted with Maslow's unique blend of values and science as he sketches the possibility of moving toward Utopia (or Eupsychia) through improved management" (*Contemporary Psychology*).

The Psychology of Science: A Reconnaissance. 1966. Regnery-Gateway repr. 1969 pap. $3.95. "A criticism of Western science, especially psychology, with its focus on solving problems that are often of trivial value" (*LJ*).

The Farther Reaches of Human Nature. 1971. Penguin 1976 pap. $5.95. "A collection of papers from the leading spokesman of humanistic psychology . . . a source book for ideas, concepts, hypotheses, and theories that will probably occupy psychologists, other social scientists, and laymen for many years to come" (*Choice*).

Dominance, Self-Esteem, Self-Actualization: Germinal Papers of A. H. Maslow. Ed. by Richard J. Lowry, Brooks-Cole 1973 o.p. "The editor has expertly woven into a coherent text eight of the important early papers spanning the years from 1936 to 1950 by A. H. Maslow, one of the founders of the third force or humanistic psychology" (*Choice*).

The Journals of A. H. Maslow. 1973. Ed. by Bertha G. Maslow and others, Brooks-Cole 1979 o.p. "Reading through this 11-year accumulation (thousands of handwritten pages) of Maslow's frequent entries in his personal journals provides a depth of understanding of the man and his ideas not otherwise available" (*Choice*).

BOOKS ABOUT MASLOW

Lowry, Richard J. *A. H. Maslow: An Intellectual Portrait.* Brooks-Cole 1973 o.p. "In this short, well crafted volume, the author provides a sympathetic but scholarly treatment of Maslow as a theorist. . . . Lowry seeks to offer a brief intellectual portrait, and he succeeds admirably" (*Contemporary Psychology*).

Maslow, Bertha G., and others, eds. *Abraham H. Maslow: A Memorial Volume.* Brooks-Cole 1972 o.p.

MAY, ROLLO. 1909–

"The development of an existential psychology in America is in good part the work of Rollo May. He helped bring existentialism to psychology some fifteen years ago, and since then his impact has increased each year. As he says here, he isn't an existentialist in a 'cultist' sense. In American psychology the existential approach is part of a wider trend which includes many views" (Eugene T. Gendlin, *Psychology Today*). May's psychology is sometimes referred to as humanistic—he is one of the affirmative, "third force"

American psychologists who are also critical of the society in which we live. Gendlin writes further: "In . . . *Psychology and the Human Dilemma* [1966], May offers a wealth of valid and stimulating ideas in a totally engaging and readable fashion. [The human dilemma is that] man is always both an active subject and a passive object . . . May [says]: 'Only in knowing ourselves as the determined ones are we free.' This last sentence and his many similar discussions seem to mean that we can't help what happens, but only what attitude we take toward what happens. In fact, he means more than this—in taking an attitude toward what happens we change what happens." In late 1968, May was the subject of an article in the *N.Y. Times* in which he was said to feel that "one sign that the modern age is dying is that its myths are dying." We are at present in a "limbo" between myths—the situation in which people become disoriented and "alienated." "In the new myths," he said, "I would think that racial variation will be seen as a positive value, that emphasis on one world will replace fragmented nationalism, and that things will be valued more for their intrinsic worth rather than in use— what they can be banked for."

As a young man, Rollo May taught for a period at the American College in Saloniki, Greece. He received his Ph.D. at Columbia University in 1949. He worked as Supervisory and Training Analyst at the William Alanson White Institute in New York City and adjunct professor of clinical psychology at the New York University Graduate School of Arts and Sciences for many years. Currently May lives in the San Francisco area, writes, still sees clients, and was instrumental in establishing the Rollo May Center for Humanistic Studies at Saybrook Institute in San Francisco.

BOOKS BY MAY

The Meaning of Anxiety. 1950. Norton 1977 $14.95; Washington Square Pr. 1979 pap. $4.95. "This volume is not only a lucid compendium of the modern theories of anxiety; it also presents some aspects of the phenomenological approach in psychiatry" (*U.S. Quarterly Booklist*).

Man's Search for Himself. 1953. Dell 1973 pap. $8.95; Norton 1953 $16.95. "This volume was written for laymen, and it is altogether successfully adapted to a lay audience" (*Chicago Sunday Tribune*).

The Art of Counseling. Abingdon, 1978 o.p.

(and others, eds.). *Existence: A New Dimension in Psychiatry and Psychology*. 1958. Simon & Schuster 1967 pap. $10.95. "This is a book which gives a compelling hint of what is coming in psychological therapy and psychological science" (*Contemporary Psychology*).

(ed.). *Symbolism in Religion and Literature*. Braziller 1960 $6.95

(ed.). *Existential Psychology*. Random 2d ed. 1961 text ed. pap. $5.00. "This is a book which undergraduates and professional psychologists of varying persuasions can pick up, read readily, and use to satisfy curiosity about the concept 'existentialism' as it is related to psychology" (*Contemporary Psychology*).

Psychology and the Human Dilemma. 1966. Norton repr. of 1978 ed. 1980 pap. $6.95. An "existential discussion of the dichotomy between reason and emotion and the resulting isolation of the individual" (*LJ*).

(and Leopold Caligor). *Dreams and Symbols: Man's Unconscious Language*. Basic Bks. 1969 o.p.

Love and Will. Norton 1969 $14.95. The "focus is man vis-a-vis his contemporary world. And he finds that man is a very troubled soul, not because of his world but because of himself" (*Choice*).

My Quest for Beauty. Saybrook 1985 $18.95. This book weaves art and clinical insight together to demonstrate a more humane psychotherapy.

Power and Innocence: A Search for the Sources of Violence. Dell 1976 pap. $7.95; Norton 1972 $14.95. "His jargon-free inquiry is an exploration of the human need for dignity, significance and self-assertion—and the dire social consequences of humiliation, debasement and impotence" (*PW*).

Paulus. Harper 1973 o.p. "The well-known author and psychotherapist has written a striking personal portrait of Paul Tillich in which he combines his personal respect and love for his friend with psychological and theological insight" (*Choice*).

The Courage to Create. Bantam 1976 pap. $3.95; Norton 1975 $13.95. "[The author] provides a lucid and highly concentrated analysis of the creative process in the course of covering a good deal of familiar territory" (*SR*).

The Discovery of Being. Dell 1983 pap. $7.95; Norton 1983 $13.95. "May ... provides the reader with principles of his existential psychotherapy; delineates his view of the cultural-historical context that gave rise to both psychoanalysis and existentialism; and sets forth what he considers to be the contributions to therapy of an existential approach" (*Choice*).

Freedom and Destiny. 1981. Dell 1983 pap. $7.95; Norton 1981 $14.95. "He insists that freedom is intertwined with the idea of destiny, or a pattern of limits and potentials that make up the givens of one's life. . . . May picks lively arguments with Gay Talese, Christopher Lasch, Fromm and B. F. Skinner in a wise, courageous and inspiring essay that offers fresh hope for individuals and society" (*PW*).

MENNINGER, KARL AUGUSTUS. 1893–1966

The Menninger Clinic was founded in Topeka, Kansas, in 1920 by Karl and his father, Charles Frederick, and in 1926 they were joined by Karl's brother William. The Menninger Foundation, started in 1941, was established for the purpose of research, training, and public education in psychiatry. Karl Menninger was instrumental in founding the Winter Veterans' Administration Hospital, also in Topeka, at the close of World War II. It functioned not only as a hospital but as the center of the largest psychiatric training program in the world. *The Crime of Punishment* attracted much attention (and some controversy) when it was published in 1968. A former professor of criminology and an officer of the American League to Abolish Capital Punishment, Menninger felt that there may be less violence today than there was 100 years ago, but that it is now better reported. "We need criminals to identify ourselves with," he has said, "to secretly envy and to stoutly punish." The "controlling" of crime by "deterrence," he says, makes "getting caught the unthinkable thing" for offenders (quoted in the *N.Y. Times*). His plea is for humane, constructive treatment in place of vengeance and an end to public apathy. The books of both Karl Menninger and William Menninger are written with great clarity and human sympathy. They have done much to dispel misunderstandings about mental illness and its treatment.

BOOKS BY MENNINGER

The Human Mind. 1930. Knopf rev. ed. 1945 o.p. "An absorbing book, which is easy
to read, profusely illustrated with illuminating examples of the cases cited, and
one well calculated to appeal both to the casual reader and to the person who
would have a more serious purpose" (*Annals of the Amer. Academy of Political
and Social Sciences*).

Man Against Himself. 1938. Harcourt 1956 pap. $7.95. "It is valuable because it
presents in readable and complete form the psychoanalytic theory of suicide,
heretofore buried piecemeal in psychoanalytic journals and books" (*Amer. Sociological Review*).

(and Martin Mayman and Paul Pruyser). *The Vital Balance: The Life Process in Mental
Health and Illness.* 1963. Peter Smith 1983 $21.25. With two psychologists at the
Menninger Clinic, Menninger presents to the lay reader his hopeful new unitary
concept of mental illness, which treats all mental health problems as aspects of
the same basic disorder.

The Crime of Punishment. 1968. Penguin 1977 pap. $5.95; Viking 1968 $13.95. "This,
an expansion and rewriting of the Isaac Ray Award lectures given by Dr. Menninger at Columbia University in 1963 and 1964, and at the University of Kansas in 1966, indicts the U.S. penal system and presents proposals for its reform.
Menninger speaks out persuasively against this system with facts about police,
courts, judges, jails, lawyers, psychiatrists, many case histories and, above all,
with the immense background and mature wisdom of an eminent psychiatrist"
(*LJ*).

(and Jeanetta Lyle Menninger). *Love Against Hate.* 1942. Harcourt 1959 pap. $5.95.
An analysis of the war of emotions within each of us. The authors show how the
power of love can shape our aggressiveness.

PAVLOV, IVAN PETROVICH. 1849–1936
    [SEE Volume 3, Chapter 4.]

PIAGET, JEAN. 1896–1980
    [SEE Volume 3, Chapter 4.]

RANK, OTTO. 1884–1937

Considered one of the most gifted psychotherapists of his time, Rank
investigated matters "beyond psychology," and became known for his energy, intellectual curiosity, and self-awareness. In the years of his association with Freud from 1905 to 1925, he served as secretary to the psychoanalytic movement and it was generally assumed that Freud regarded him as
his successor. Rank, however, eventually came to see the roots of all psychoneuroses in the experience of birth. This theory he described in *The Trauma
of Birth* (1924). Such differences caused his break with Freud in the middle
1920s, after which he lived in Paris and then New York. He first formulated
his theories about art and neuroses in the series of remarkable daybooks
(1903–1904). In 1912 he helped to found *Imago,* the first European journal
of psychoanalysis.

BOOKS BY RANK

Art and the Artist: The Creative Urge and Personality Development. 1907. Agathon repr. of 1932 ed. 1975 $15.00. "The author presents a more matured consideration of a problem which engaged him about twenty-five years ago, viz., that of the psychological bases for the production of artistic works. The discussion is of a theoretical sort, copiously illustrated with material from the history of art" (*Psychological Abstracts*).

The Myth of the Birth of the Hero: A Psychological Interpretation of Mythology. 1909. [*Nervous and Mental Disease Monographs*] Johnson Repr. repr. of 1914 ed. 1971 o.p.; Random 1959 pap. $3.95

(and Hans Sachs). *The Significance of Psychoanalysis for the Mental Sciences.* 1916. [*Nervous and Mental Disease Monographs*] Johnson Repr. repr. of 1916 ed. 1971 $19.00

The Don Juan Legend. 1924. Trans. and ed. by David G. Winter, Princeton Univ. Pr. 1975 o.p. "An *interpretation* of the theme, drawing on psychoanalysis (before and after his break with Freud), literature, history, and anthropology to examine some of the psychological processes that operate within the legend" (*Choice*).

The Trauma of Birth. 1924. Brunner-Mazel 1952 o.p. "Analysis turns out to be a belated accomplishment of the uncompleted mastery of the birth trauma. . . . Psychoanalysis replaces for the patient the lost primal object—mother—by a surrogate whom he will be able to renounce the more easily by being made constantly conscious of the surrogate as such. Severance from the analyst, which is the essential aim of analysis, is accomplished by reproductions of the birth trauma in which the patient gives up his doctor in order to lose his suffering" (*Psychological Abstracts*).

Modern Education: A Critique of Its Fundamental Ideas. Knopf 1932 o.p. "Presents a sociological and metaphysical consideration of the relations of education to psychology, the nature and needs of the child, the place of sex in development and education, leadership, the influence of current ideology, vocational choice and fitness, family relationships, and self guidance" (*Psychological Abstracts*).

Will Therapy and Truth and Reality. 1936. Norton 1978 pap. $7.95. "Fundamentally a philosophical treatise, dealing with the problems of the mind from a psychoanalytical point of view. . . . Will is discussed as a psychological and a moral problem and its power as a therapeutic agent in psychoanalysis is treated theoretically" (*Psychological Abstracts*).

Beyond Psychology. 1941. Dover 1959 text ed. pap. $5.95. "He argues for an acceptance of 'the fundamental irrationality of the human being and life in general with allowance for its dynamic functioning in human behavior' and for a more balanced evaluation of the irrational as against the rational" (*Psychological Abstracts*).

Psychology and the Soul. 1950. Amer. Inst. Psych. 1986 2 vols. $147.55. "In this major work the author sketches his views of the origin, development and nature of mental life on the basis of his experience of 30 years and his studies in the fields of psychoanalysis and racial psychology" (*Psychological Abstracts*).

Double: A Psychoanalytical Study. Ed. by Harry Tucker, Jr., Univ. of North Carolina Pr. 1971 o.p. "Rank's unique, pioneer psychoanalytic study on the double in literature is a splendid contribution to the field of books relating psychology to literature" (*LJ*).

BOOKS ABOUT RANK

Lieberman, E. James. *Acts of Will: The Life and Work of Otto Rank.* Free Pr. 1985 $24.95. "Affords an excellent introduction—for both scholars and informed lay readers—to the work of a brilliant psychoanalytic innovator whose seminal theories on birth trauma, separation anxiety, and time-limited therapy (to name just a few) are still central issues today" (*LJ*).

Menaker, Esther. *Otto Rank: A Rediscovered Legacy*. Columbia Univ. Pr. 1982 $27.50. "Dr. Menaker is right in her contention that Rank anticipates all the 'separation anxiety theories,' ranging from Klein to Bowlby, Mahler, and Kohut.... [She] has done a splendid service in resuscitating the work of a man unjustly neglected for so many years, and to read her book is to share some of the excitement of Rank's agile mind" (*TLS*).

REIK, THEODOR. 1888–1969

The Viennese-born psychoanalyst became Freud's pupil in 1910, completed the first doctor's dissertation on psychoanalysis in 1911, and received his Ph.D. in psychology at the University of Vienna in 1912. He lectured at the Vienna Psychoanalytic Institute in Berlin and at The Hague. He came to the United States in 1938 and became an American citizen. He founded the National Psychological Association for Psychoanalysis in 1948, which accepts lay analysts for membership and has programs for their training. Reik never had any medical training. His *Listening with the Third Ear* (1948) is a stimulating discussion of Freud's development of psychoanalysis, and describes in detail his own cases during 37 years of active practice. His books show great erudition and, written with literary skill, sparkle "with insights and with witty profundities." He may be regarded as "the founding father of *archaeological psychoanalysis*," a branch of depth psychology dedicated to the probing of archaeological data from psychoanalytic viewpoints.

BOOKS BY REIK

Listening with the Third Ear: The Inner Experience of a Psychoanalyst. Farrar 1948 pap. $11.95. Provides the answers to the layman's question: "What is psychoanalysis?"

Dogma and Compulsion. Greenwood repr. of 1951 ed. 1973 lib. bdg. $45.00. "Reik gives a detailed account of the development of the dogma of the godhead of Christ in order to show that dogma is the most important expression of the people's obsessional thinking, with the same mechanisms as the obsessional neurosis of individuals" (*Psychological Abstracts*).

The Secret Self: Psychoanalytic Experiences in Life and Literature. Greenwood repr. of 1953 ed. 1973 o.p. "It is probably the most mature and sophisticated book of this prolific psychoanalytic author" (*SR*).

Of Love and Lust: On the Psychoanalysis of Romantic and Sexual Emotions. Farrar 1957 pap. $12.95; Jove 1976 pap. $2.25. "The freshest, most charming pages are those discussing the emotional differences between the sexes. You must read these for yourself. *Love and Lust* is thoughtful and profound; and these final pages, on the differences between men and women, are pure gold" (*Contemporary Psychology*).

Compulsions to Confess: On the Psychoanalysis of Crime and Punishment. [*Essay Index Repr. Ser.*] Ayer repr. of 1959 ed. $30.00. "[The book] is distinguished by Reik's ability to convey his recondite concepts with such charm and humor as to make them not only informative, but vastly entertaining" (*Kirkus*).

The Creation of Woman: A Psychoanalytic Inquiry into the Myth of Eve. 1960. Mc-

Graw-Hill 1973 o.p. Insights and literary skill make the reading of this new book an exciting experience" (*LJ*).

Jewish Wit. Gamut Pr. 1962 o.p. Reik "has written . . . a kind of analytic joke book to illustrate a comparative social psychology of [the Jewish] people. . . . The book is fascinating reading and at the very least gives some unusual insights into the psychological aspects of the cultural heritage of a people" (*LJ*).

The Need to Be Loved. Farrar 1963 o.p. An examination of the many aspects of the problems from infancy to old age.

Fragment of a Great Confession. Greenwood repr. of 1965 ed. 1973 lib. bdg. $24.75

The Search Within: Inner Experiences of a Psychoanalyst. 1968. Aronson 1974 o.p. "This, the first of a series of volumes of selections from Theodor Reik's works, is a synthesis of his frank reminiscences of his personal life, his training, practice and the development of his philosophy" (*Psychological Abstracts*).

Myth and Guilt. Braziller 1957 o.p. "Collective human guilt may be traced back to the prehistoric killing and eating of a father whose rule was experienced as divine" (*Psychological Abstracts*).

The Unknown Murderer. Intl. Univs. Pr. 1978 text ed. pap. $19.95. "A psychoanalytic study of some aspects of murder and the judicial process. The author shows that what passes for logical evidence in the investigation of murder crimes is oftentimes psychological evidence" (*Psychological Abstracts*).

ROGERS, CARL RANSOM. 1902–1987

Educated at the University of Wisconsin and Columbia University (Ph.D., 1931), Carl Rogers taught at several large universities for many years and conducted a private practice as a counseling psychologist. *Current Biography* states that "he is best known as the originator of the nondirective 'client centered' theory of psychotherapy. This prescribes a person-to-person, rather than a doctor-patient relationship between therapist and client, and allows the client to control the course, pace, and length of his own treatment." Rogers incorporated many of the elements of this theory into the basic structure of encounter groups.

The author of many books and articles, Rogers received many professional awards in official recognition of his high achievements, most notably the presidency of the American Psychological Association (1946–47).

BOOKS BY ROGERS

Carl Rogers on Personal Power. Dell 1977 o.p. Rogers extends his therapeutic views to education, business, politics, and international affairs, always affirming the inherent goodness of human nature.

Measuring Personality Adjustment in Children Nine to Thirteen Years of Age. 1931. AMS Pr. repr. of 1931 ed. 1982 $22.50. "The development of a 40-minute pencil and paper group test—yielding '4 diagnostic scores, indicating the degree of the child's Personal Inferiority, Social Maladjustment, Family Maladjustment, and Daydreaming'—and its application to 52 problem children and to a larger group of normal children" (*Psychological Abstracts*).

Counseling and Psychotherapy. Houghton Mifflin 1942 o.p.

Client-Centered Therapy. Houghton Mifflin 1951 text ed. pap. $23.50. "The recent development of the techniques of client-centered counseling is interpreted, the attitude and orientation of the counselor, the relationship as experienced by the client, and the process of therapy are discussed" (*Psychological Abstracts*).

(and Rosalind F. Dymond, eds.). *Psychotherapy and Personality Change*. Univ. of Chicago Pr. 1954 o.p. "Describes and explains a large-scale research program in client-centered psychotherapy, carried out at the Counseling Center of the University of Chicago" (*Psychological Abstracts*).

Therapist's View of Personal Goals. Pendle Hill 1960 pap. $2.50. "In his therapeutic work Rogers sees clients take such directions as: away from façades; away from 'oughts'; away from meeting expectations; away from pleasing others; toward being a process; toward being a complexity; toward openness to experience; toward acceptance of others; toward trust of self" (*Psychological Abstracts*).

On Becoming a Person. Houghton Mifflin 1961 $10.95 pap. $8.95. "A therapist's view of personality problems in general, with psychotherapy a special case within this larger and (even to Rogers) more interesting set of problems" (*Contemporary Psychology*).

(and Barry Stevens). *Person to Person: The Problem of Being Human*. Real People Pr. 1967 pap. $6.50. "An excellent job of presenting the Rogerian philosophy. For those who would like data or science, this book will be disappointing; for those who prefer humanism this book will be exciting" (*Choice*).

Carl Rogers on Encounter Groups. Harper 1970 o.p. "In this highly readable book, richly endowed with actual examples, Rogers presents information about what goes on within the encounter group, what should characterize the facilitator (leader) of such a group, the outcomes of intensive group experiences, research evidence, and future trends and applications" (*LJ*).

Becoming Partners: Marriage and Its Alternatives. 1972. Dell 1973 pap. $9.95. "Rogers' summary of the qualities of a lasting relationship—commitment, communication, dissolution of roles, becoming a separate self—is not new, but what is significant is his idea that modern couples should think of themselves as pioneers free to explore all possibilities" (*LJ*).

A Way of Being. Houghton Mifflin 1980 text ed. pap. $8.95. "This is a book rich in theoretical insights and experiential sharing, and full of invigorating optimism. . . . The reader has a vivid sense of a man reviewing his life and taking stock" (*LJ*).

Freedom to Learn for the Eighties. Merrill 1983 text ed. $16.95. "A powerful statement on behalf of the kind of enlightened teaching that many prominent educators have been urging for some time" (*Contemporary Psychology*).

BOOK ABOUT ROGERS

Evans, Richard I. *Carl Rogers: The Man and His Ideas*. Dutton 1975 pap. $3.95. "This volume may be seen as a valuable asset to a general understanding of Rogers' thought. . . . The book's primary contribution, besides an insight into Rogers the man, will probably be the whetting of academic appetites for further study in Rogerian thought" (*Choice*).

ROYCE, JOSIAH. 1855–1916

[SEE Volume 4, Chapter 5.]

SCHAFER, ROY. 1922–

Roy Schafer is adjunct professor of psychology and psychiatry at Cornell University Medical College, a training analyst at Columbia University Center for Psychoanalytic Training and Research, and also maintains a private practice. He received the American Psychological Association's Award for Distinguished Professional Contribution to Knowledge in 1983.

BOOKS BY SCHAFER

(and David Rapaport and Merton Gill). *Diagnostic Psychological Testing: The Theory of Statistical Evaluations and Diagnostic Application of a Battery of Tests*. 1944. Intl. Univs. Pr. 1968 text ed. $40.00. "Designed to be a 'focused and theoretically oriented handbook of diagnostic psychological testing' " (*Contemporary Psychology*).

The Clinical Application of Psychological Tests. 1948. [*Menninger Foundation Monograph Ser.*] Intl. Univs. Pr. 1967 text ed. $35.00. "Considered a sequel to *Diagnostic Psychological Testing*, this volume presents primarily a collection of concrete, individual case records, designed to show how the data comprising the final test report are carefully elicited from both separate and overall test findings" (*Psychological Abstracts*).

Psychoanalytic Interpretation in Rorschach Testing: Theory and Application. Grune 1954 $31.00. "Brief summary statements of defenses, each followed by a review of expected Rorschach test indicators and illustrative case protocols. Differences and similarities between Rorschach responses and dreams are discussed. Individual differences in defense style are emphasized" (*Psychological Abstracts*).

Projective Testing and Psychoanalysis. Intl. Univs. Pr. 1967 text ed. $25.00. "A collection of nine articles published originally between 1953 and 1960. This collection is not a systematic statement of a new theoretical position, nor can it serve as an independent diagnostic textbook" (*Contemporary Psychology*).

A New Language for Psychoanalysis. Yale Univ. Pr. 1976 $30.00 pap. $12.95. "Should be of considerable interest to a wider public since it proposes a radical reformulation of psychoanalytic theory" (*N.Y. Review of Bks.*).

Language and Insight: The Sigmund Freud Lectures at University College London. Yale Univ. Pr. 1978 $25.00. "The book is always provocative and thoughtful, often brilliant" (*Contemporary Psychology*).

The Analytic Attitude. Basic Bks. 1983 $21.95. "Readers of various degrees of philosophic and psychological sophistication may be stimulated by reading this book" (*Contemporary Psychology*).

SKINNER, B. F. 1904–

[SEE Volume 3, Chapter 4.]

STRAUS, ERWIN. 1891–1975

Erwin Straus was born in Frankfurt, Germany. He received a comprehensive classical education and in 1910 began to study medicine and philosophy. His studies were interrupted by World War I, during which he served as a field doctor on the Polish front.

Straus's teachers and acquaintances form a veritable list of notables of twentieth-century German intellectual life. Among the former were Jung, HUSSERL (see Vol. 4), Reinach, SCHELER (see Vol. 4), Pfander, Kraepelin, and Geiger, and his friends included CASSIRER (see Vol. 4), von Gebsattel, Binswanger, Zutt, and Minkowski.

Straus first lectured at the University of Berlin in 1927, but because of his partial Jewish background had to cease teaching in 1934 after the Nazis came to power. He fled the Nazis in 1938 and taught at the experimental community of Black Mountain College in North Carolina. In 1946 Straus went to the Veterans Administration Hospital in Lexington, Kentucky, as

Director of Research and Education, and remained there for the rest of his life. In addition to authoring many creative and original articles, Straus played a formative role in introducing the anthropological and phenomenological orientation to psychiatry in this country.

BOOKS BY STRAUS

The Primary World of the Senses. Trans. by J. Needleman, Free Pr. 1963 o.p. A critique of Pavlov's views in order to restore the value of sensory experience for the interpretation of human existence.

Phenomenological Psychology. Trans. in part by E. Eng, Basic Bks. 1966 o.p. A series of essays by Staus on phenomenological psychology, written with erudition and style. Makes sense of many common experiences.

Man, Time and World: The Anthropological Psychology of Erwin Straus. Duquesne Univ. Pr. 1982 text ed. $15.50. "English translation of *Event and Experience* (1930) and *The Archimedian Point* (1957). . . . The works point out inadequacies in reductionist psychological theories, and propose a holistic, anthropological account of psychological phenomena based on the individual's experience of time and becoming" (*Contemporary Psychology*).

SULLIVAN, HARRY STACK. 1892–1949

Conceptions of Modern Psychiatry (1940) was originally published as articles in the periodical *Psychiatry,* of which Sullivan was an editor. He contributed greatly to the understanding of schizophrenia and obsessional states. As head of both the William Alanson White Foundation (1934–1943) and of the Washington School of Psychiatry (1936–1947), he brought to public and professional attention his view that psychoanalysis needed to be supplemented by a thoroughgoing study of the impact of cultural forces on the personality.

BOOKS BY SULLIVAN

Conceptions of Modern Psychiatry. 1940. Norton 1966 pap. $8.95. "This series of 5 lectures constitutes a comprehensive survey of modern psychiatric thought" (*Psychological Abstracts*).

The Interpersonal Theory of Psychiatry. Norton repr. of 1953 ed. 1968 pap. $4.95. "This may well turn out to be the most seminal look in its field in this decade" (*SR*).

Psychiatric Interview. Norton repr. of 1954 ed. 1970 pap. $3.95. "Although the lectures were directed primarily towards psychiatrists, Sullivan also meant them for all those who engage in dynamic interviewing" (Preface).

Schizophrenia as a Human Process. Norton repr. of 1962 ed. 1974 pap. $8.95. The contents of this volume posthumously gathered, consist of the early work of Sullivan when he was associated with the Sheppard and Enoch Pratt Hospital near Baltimore. He was thoroughly familiar with Freud, but was free to develop new approaches to diagnose and treat mental illness.

The Fusion of Psychiatry and Social Science. Intro. by Helen Swick Perry, Norton repr. of 1964 ed. 1971 o.p. Here Sullivan "makes some sorties into sociology and tries to tie his psychoanalytic theories into the workings of society as a culture made up of subcultures with interaction of one on the other and vice versa" (*LJ*).

Personal Psychopathology: Early Formulations. Norton repr. of 1972 ed. 1984 pap. $9.95. "An unsystematic and somewhat fragmented presentation of the Sullivan-ian approach to mental illness and treatment. However, the . . . student and layman will profit from the many valuable clinical insights offered here" (*Choice*).

Clinical Studies in Psychiatry. Norton repr. of 1956 ed. 1973 pap. $8.95. "A representative selection from the clinical lectures given at Chestnut Lodge" (Preface).

BOOKS ABOUT SULLIVAN

Mullahy, Patrick, ed. *Psychoanalysis and Interpersonal Psychiatry: The Contributions of Harry Stack Sullivan.* Aronson 1967 o.p.

Pearce, Jane, and Saul Newton. *Conditions of Human Growth.* Citadel Pr. repr. of 1963 ed. 1969 $6.95. pap. $4.95. It "should prove stimulating, not only to the followers of Sullivan's evolution, but to non-Sullivanians as well. The volume suffers from the lack of an index, a curious omission from an otherwise careful and thoughtful piece of work. It is recommended for all collections in the psychiatric and clinical psychological fields, as well as general collections for the informed layman who wants an overview of the interpersonal theory of the Sullivan school" (*LJ*).

THORNDIKE, EDWARD LEE. 1874–1949

[SEE Volume 3, Chapter 5.]

VAN DEN BERG, J. H. 1914–

Born in Deventer, The Netherlands, van den Berg began his career as a high school teacher of mathematics, and then studied medicine and decided to specialize in psychiatry at the University of Utrecht. He did his doctoral dissertation under H. C. Rumke and was introduced to phenomenology and trained as a psychotherapist. In 1947, he began private practice and was appointed head of the Psychiatric Clinic at the University of Utrecht. In 1954, he was appointed professor of conflict psychology at the University of Leiden. In the course of his own research, he found it necessary to develop a "metabletic" method that investigates the meaning of cultural and human changes that occur within the same time period. Currently professor emeritus at the University of Leiden, he continues his private practice.

BOOKS BY VAN DEN BERG

The Psychology of the Sickbed. Humanities Pr. 1967 o.p. "Presents 'an existential approach to the meaning of illness . . .' with a discussion of lying and its various forms, recommendations to visitors, the sickbed recovery of the patient, and the patient and his physician" (*Psychological Abstracts*).

The Changing Nature of Man: Introduction to a Historical Psychology. Norton repr. of 1961 ed. 1983 pap. $5.50. "Dealing with such issues as child-rearing practices, belief in God, the status of women, the kinds of neurotic symptoms people show, and the delaying of maturity, he makes a case for his thesis which is well worth attention" (*Contemporary Psychology*).

Dubious Maternal Affection. Duquesne Univ. Pr. 1972 o.p.

Divided Existence and Complex Society: An Historical Approach. Duquesne Univ. Pr. 1974 text ed. $12.50. "Discusses the relationship of 'divided existence' (i.e., multiple personality) to culture" (*Psychological Abstracts*).

A Different Existence: Principles of Phenomenological Psychopathology. Duquesne

Univ. Pr. 1972 text ed. pap. $8.00. This is an excellent introduction written in a lively style to show the differences between psychoanalytic and existential-phenomenological interpretations of a client.

WOLPE, JOSEPH. 1915–

Joseph Wolpe received his medical degree from the University of Witwatersrand, South Africa. After medical and surgical internships, he went into private practice, and then in 1946 decided to enter psychiatric training and research. During this time, he did the research on which his behavioral therapy is based.

Wolpe was professor of psychiatry at the University of Virginia School of Medicine from 1960 to 1965. Since then, he has been director of the Behavior Therapy Unit at Temple University Medical School and a senior research psychiatrist at Eastern Pennsylvania Psychiatric Institute in Philadelphia.

BOOKS BY WOLPE

The Practice of Behavior Therapy. Pergamon 3d ed. 1982 $43.00 pap. $13.95. "Wolpe's significance, and our enduring respect for him as an interpreter of behavior therapy, come less from the rightness of his particular theories . . . than from regard for his values: that psychological principles derived from the laboratory can be adroitly adapted to clinical concerns and that the performance, though always improvisational, can be evaluated by the standards of scientific method" (*Contemporary Psychology*).

Psychotherapy by Reciprocal Inhibition. Stanford Univ. Pr. 1958 o.p. "Taking a reductionist position, Wolpe begins his argument with a description of 'the making and unmaking of functional neural connections,' from which he moves to a behavioral learning theory, presumably after having established a neural basis for such a theory" (*Contemporary Psychology*).

CHAPTER 17

Engineering and Technology

Patricia Davitt Maughan

Give me . . . the engineer; and take your saints and virgins, relics and miracles. The spinning-jenny and the railroad, Cunard's lines—and the electric telegraph, are to me . . . signs that we are, on some points at least, in harmony with the universe.
—CHARLES KINGSLEY, *Yeast* (1848)

The open society, the unrestricted access to knowledge, the unplanned and uninhibited association of men for its furtherance—these are what may make a vast, complex, ever growing, ever changing, ever more specialized and expert technological world, nevertheless a world of human community.
—J. ROBERT OPPENHEIMER, *Science and the Common Understanding* (1953)

It is hard to imagine a single area of modern life that has not been affected in some way by developments and advancements in the fields of engineering and technology. Through them, we are able to reproduce, at will, among other things, light, images, sound, and movement. It is as a result of engineering and technology that we now have at our disposal everything from explosives to motion pictures.

Engineering and technology continue to generate a great deal of excitement and controversy, for they not only remain the embodiment of our ability to direct the formidable forces of nature for the use and convenience of humankind, but, at times, they may also create a series of problems equal to those they seek to alleviate. Robert Nesbit put it well when he wrote in *The New York Times Magazine* (September 28, 1975), "It is hard to think of an area of modern physical welfare that cannot be traced in some way to science and technology."

The existence of modern society is powerful evidence of our ability to "engineer," that is, to create systems, devices, and processes useful to society. The history of humans closely parallels their ability to invent. Had it not been for our skill in making tools, harnessing fire, developing pottery, and inventing the wheel—all accomplishments of engineering—it is doubtful that our early predecessors would have survived, let alone prospered.

There followed on these early technological accomplishments other engineering benchmarks: the Egyptian water clock, the Roman arch, the extraction of metals for weaponry and coinage, the development of movable type (one of the most influential inventions in the history of society thus far), the discovery of steam engines, the telegraph, the electric light, the internal combustion engine, the automobile, and the airplane, all of which have pushed forward the limits of people's mastery over their environment.

This spirit of excitement continues to capture the popular imagination in such recent developments as the microchip, which has not only allowed for the miniaturization of electronic devices but has served as the driving force behind many areas of technology in recent years including manned space flight, weather and communication satellites, planetary probes, and most recently, industrial robots.

As a result of the ever-increasing uses of engineering and technology, people and their environment have been affected in a variety of ways, some good and some bad. The quickening development of the ability to alter the environment has added new responsibilities to the job of the engineer and the technologist. In the past, sound science and practical economics comprised the ingredients for good engineering. Today, both environmental effects and sound sociology must be added to the "technological equation."

A wide range of general and popular works incorporating current engineering and technological findings and exploring the effects of technological advances are introduced in this chapter.

GENERAL WORKS

Baynes, Ken, and Francis Pugh. *The Art of the Engineer.* Overlook Pr. 1981 $85.00. "This book reproduces and discusses a selection of mechanical engineering drawings made for the transport industries between the late sixteenth century and the present day. It contains many superb examples of draughtsmanship, a number of which are equal in quality to the finest drawings of any kind" (Introduction).

Borgmann, Albert. *Technology and the Character of Contemporary Life: A Philosophical Inquiry.* Univ. of Chicago Pr. 1987 pap. $12.95. Puts forth the opinion that technology and the new products resulting from it constitute a major influence on the quality of modern life, causing people to become distanced from production and susceptible to technological distractions. Borgmann maintains that technology is not a neutral tool and that it constitutes only a limited component of a rewarding life in our day and age.

Congdon, R. J., ed. *Introduction to Appropriate Technology: Toward a Simpler Life-Style.* Rodale Pr. 1977 o.p. A work by technical revolutionaries who believe appropriate technology offers a humanistic counterweight to the mechanistic view of the world that has prevailed for the last few centuries. The text presents a lively critique of Western technology and explores the spirit of appropriate technology as it is found in revolutionary societies such as China, Cuba, and North Vietnam.

Cotterill, Rodney. *The Cambridge Guide to the Material World.* Cambridge Univ Pr. 1985 $37.50. Covers the physical, chemical, and biological properties of many materials including glass, plastics, ceramics, metals, minerals, and crystals in a large-format and beautifully illustrated text. Useful in exploring the topics of materials science, mineral, and chemical engineering.

Cross, Hardy. *Engineers and Ivory Towers.* [*Essay Index Repr. Ser.*] Ayer repr. of 1952 ed. 1980 $17.00. A collection of technical and nontechnical articles, transcribed

speeches, classroom notes, society papers, and graduate lectures on the philosophy of engineering edited by a former student of Cross at Yale University.

Davidson, Frank Paul. *Macro: Reindustrializing America and the World.* Morrow 1983
$17.95. Davidson argues that "particular projects, such as a transcontinental
supersonic subway . . ., are quite feasible, not science-fiction dreams; that they
are necessary; that planning for them must begin now, even if the ground-
breaking is decades away" (*N.Y. Times Bk. Review*).

DeGregori, Thomas R. *A Theory of Technology: Continuity and Change in Human
Development.* Iowa State Univ. Pr. 1985 text ed. pap. $19.50. Attempts to gener-
ate a clear, coherent, consistent definition of technology and argues that the
impact of technology on human life is a primary and continuing cause of human
betterment.

Dorf, Richard C. *Technology, Society, and Man.* Boyd & Fraser 1974 o.p. Provides an
introduction to engineering as a discipline and examines its influence in such
areas as history, trade, agriculture, human safety, ecology, technology assessment, the state, and the military; lastly, it explores technology and the future.

Dorf, Richard C., and Yvonne L. Hunter, eds. *Appropriate Visions, Technology, the
Environment and the Individual.* Boyd & Fraser 1978 $16.00 pap. $12.50. Documents a series of programs held in late 1977 devoted to the problems of growing
technology, the need for energy conservation, and the maintenance of human
values. Records the presentations made at the conference featuring well-known
speakers E. F. Schumacher (*Small Is Beautiful*) and Barry Commoner, of Washington University.

Feibleman, James. *Technology and Reality.* Kluwer Academic 1982 $25.00. Explores
the historical impact of technology on philosophy and suggests what positive
effects on philosophy the daily advances in the physical sciences might currently have.

Florman, Samuel. *Blaming Technology: The Irrational Search for Scapegoats.* St. Martin's 1981 $12.95 1982 pap. $6.95. A compendium of anecdotes gathered during
the author's lecture tour of college campuses following the publication of his
earlier volume, *The Existential Pleasures of Engineering*, and a series of articles
written for *Harper's* focusing attention on issues that constitute the public debate on technology.

———. *The Civilized Engineer.* St. Martin's 1987 $15.95. Written by a civil engineer
who studied literature under both Trilling and Krutch at Columbia, this is a
collection of essays covering a wide range of topics of interest to engineers and
humanists alike, including the contribution of women to engineering, the loss of
the Challenger, and emerging fields of specialization in engineering today.

———. *The Existential Pleasures of Engineering.* St. Martin's 1977 pap. $5.95. "Valu-
able reading for engineers given to self scrutiny" (*Time*).

Goulet, Denis. *The Uncertain Promise.* Overseas Dev. Council 1977 pap. $5.95. Exam-
ines whether modern technology is the key to successful development, if technology will deliver on its promise to bring development to the Third World,
whether technology can be "transferred" from one cultural setting to another
with beneficial rather than deleterious effects, and how policies for "moderniz-
ing" relate to broader national goals and concerns.

Greenhill, Ralph. *Engineer's Witness: A Photographic Panorama of Nineteenth Century
Engineering Triumphs.* Godine 1985 $35.00. "Visually, the 90-plus photographic
plates are a worthy complement [to nineteenth century engineering] . . . the
steel and stone memorials spread across the continent, attest to the ingenuity
and vision of the American engineer, and Mr. Greenhill's dramatic pictorials

and informative texts celebrate the imagination, industry, and sheer exuberance of 19th-century America" (*Christian Science Monitor*).

Krohn, Wolfgang, and others, eds. *The Dynamics of Science and Technology.* Kluwer Academic 1978 lib. bdg. $36.50 text ed. pap. $18.50. Examines science and technology in their social context, the "scientification" of technology, and the conceptual distinctions to be made between science and technology.

Kursunoglu, Behram, and Arnold Perlmutter, eds. *Impact of Basic Research on Technology.* [*Studies in the Natural Sciences*] Plenum 1973 $49.50. Seven essays on scientific and technical developments by contributors such as Vladimir Zworykin, Edward Teller, John Bardeen, and P. A. M. Dirac.

Lawless, Edward W. *Technology and Social Shock.* Rutgers Univ. Pr. 1977 pap. $15.00. Presents the results of a study funded by the National Science Foundation of the kinds of episodes of public alarm over technology that have inspired major news stories in the media in recent years.

Layton, Edwin T. *The Revolt of the Engineers: Social Responsibility and the American Engineering Profession.* Johns Hopkins Univ. Pr. repr. of 1971 ed. 1986 text ed. $29.50 pap. text ed. $9.95. Traces the development of a sense of professional identity and social responsibility among American engineers. Describes the conflict between progressive and conservative factions within the profession, and focuses on engineering professionalism and ethics.

Mazur, Allan. *The Dynamics of Technical Controversy.* Broadcasting Pubns. 1981 $11.95 text ed. pap. $8.95. Attempts to explain the controversies arising over a variety of scientific and technological products and suggests how they might be used as effective means for technology assessment. Mazur suggests regularities in behavior that occur across classes of technological controversies, and indicates the kinds of data needed in order to advance our understanding.

Merkel, James A. *Basic Engineering Principles.* AVI Pub. 2d ed. 1983 text ed. $24.50. A basic introduction to the principles of engineering written for nonengineers interested in developing an appreciation for and understanding of engineering knowledge. Covers such topics as fluid mechanics, heat transfer, air conditioning, and basic electricity.

Nussbaum, Bruce. *The World after Oil: The Shifting Axis of Power and Wealth.* Simon & Schuster 1984 pap. $7.95. "Nussbaum argues that 'the world is poised to take a quantum leap to a higher technological plateau.' He outlines the possible efforts on the world of three burgeoning technologies: robotics, bioengineering, and telecommunications. . . . With stakes so high, Nussbaum argues, these high-techs will encourage international spying, industrial crime . . . and a shift in world power" (*LJ*).

O'Neill, Gerard K. *The Technology Edge: Opportunities for America in World Competition.* Simon & Schuster 1984 $16.95. "Microengineering, robotics, genetic engineering, magnetic flight, private aircraft, and space science are the technologies discussed in this book. [O'Neill] . . . describes each area from a business and science perspective and compares progress made in the United States with . . . other countries. . . . His goal is to determine which of the six technologies offer real promise for the next decade" (Publisher's note).

Petroski, Henry. *Beyond Engineering: Essays and Other Attempts to Figure Without Equations.* St. Martin's 1986 $17.95. A collection of essays and articles, many of which have appeared elsewhere, on the nature of engineering and technology. Describes some of Petroski's experiences at the Argonne National Laboratory and includes his observations on engineering education, the effects of technology on family life, and some whimsical pieces with a technological bent.

Rybczynski, Witold. *Paper Heroes: A Review of Appropriate Technology.* Doubleday

1980 o.p. Takes a critical look at the Appropriate Technology Movement, which attempts to grapple with, among other things, the relationship between technology and development, ideology and industrialization, and people and machines.

———. *Taming the Tiger: The Struggle to Control Technology.* Penguin 1985 pap. $6.95. A worldwide treatment that includes anecdotes illustrating the sociological and environmental impact of technology. Historical as well as current perspectives are provided, supporting Rybczynski's central theme that if we are to control technology, we must first control ourselves.

Seurat, Silvere. *Technology Transfer: A Realistic Approach.* Gulf Pub. 1979 $19.00. Fully explores and conveys the complexity of technology transfer, which the author defines as the capacity to store and transmit to people both industrial know-how and the accumulated experience and understanding of others.

Susskind, Charles. *Understanding Technology.* San Francisco Pr. 1985 pap. $7.50. "It discusses how technology developed, how inventions like electronic equipment and the computer ushered in a new era, and the relationship of society to the technologist. Many modern inventions and processes are described in terms the reader with little technical background could easily grasp" (*LJ*).

The Techno/Peasant Survival Manual: The Book That Demystifies the Technology of the 80's. Bantam 1980 o.p. A consciousness-alerting book that describes selected major new technological advances and tells, in simple language, how they work. Also covers the potential for liberation and potential harmful effects, and points to the cogent political and social issues associated with each particular advance.

Wenk, Edward, Jr. *Tradeoffs: Imperatives of Choice in a High-Tech World.* Johns Hopkins Univ. Pr. 1986 $19.95. A scholarly treatment of the costs and benefits of technological progress as well as the influence of government in fostering technological developments. Case studies provided along with the text include, historically, the invention of the steam engine, and, currently, the disposal of nuclear power waste products.

GENERAL REFERENCE WORKS AND GUIDES

Abbott, David, ed. *The Biographical Dictionary of Scientists: Engineers and Inventors.* Bedrick Bks. 1986 $28.00. Provides a collection of short biographical sketches, following a brief introduction to the chronology of technology from prehistory to the age of the microchip. Includes an 8-page subject index and a 14-page glossary of engineering terminology.

Anthony, L. J., ed. *Information Sources in Engineering.* Butterworth 2d ed. 1985 text ed. $89.95. Brings together in one volume both published information sources and the known channels of access to these sources, thus presenting a picture of the international scene in engineering. Provides an introduction to the structure of engineering information, covers primary and secondary sources, includes 18 chapters on specialized subject fields, and ends with 16 pages of indexes to subjects, information services, and organizations.

Bell, S. P., comp. *A Biographical Index of British Engineers in the 19th Century.* Garland 1975 lib. bdg. $37.00. Gives access to the obituary notices of some 3,500 British engineers who died prior to 1900 and lists many of those responsible for the major developments in British engineering in the second quarter of the nineteenth century and for its influence throughout the world in the second half of the nineteenth century.

Brown, John F. *A Student Guide to Engineering Report Writing.* United Western Pr. 2d ed. 1985 $14.95. "It provides information regarding the reasons why technical writing is important, report format, presentation of technical data ... photography, and writing style and grammar" (*Automotive Engineering*).

Ernst, Richard. *Comprehensive Dictionary of Engineering and Technology*. Cambridge Univ. Pr. 2 vols. 1985 vol. 1 $105.00 vol. 2 $115.00. "Entries are alphabetical. The author has placed each term within its own specialized field. All branches of modern industry are covered. These range from raw materials and their extraction to the processing industries with their products, research, development, and manufacture" (*Mining Engineering*).

Gieck, Kurt. *Engineering Formulas*. McGraw-Hill 5th ed. 1986 $19.95. Organized in a classified arrangement with an eight-page subject index. Provides a "brief, clear and handy guide to the more important technical and mathematical formulae" (Introduction).

Grogan, Denis. *Science and Technology: An Introduction to the Literature*. 4th ed. Shoe String 1982 $27.50 pap. $18.50. "Intended for the would-be practitioner who is familiar with the general sources of information and wishes to learn about the literature of science and technology. Emphasis is on the general structure and pattern of this literature ... each of 22 chapters is devoted to specific sources, e.g., guides to the literature, encyclopedias. ... Criteria for selecting items in these lists was accessibility and value to students" (Introduction).

Hicks, Tyler G., and S. D. Hicks. *Standard Handbook of Engineering Calculations*. McGraw-Hill 2d ed. 1985 $68.00. "Revised, updated, and considerably expanded, this edition provides step-by-step calculation procedures for solving the kinds of engineering problems encountered most frequently. It contains more than 1,100 comprehensive, numbered, procedures—each with a typical worked-out practical design problem, plus more than 4,000 related procedures" (*Automotive Engineering*).

Lesko, Matthew. *Lesko's New Tech Sourcebook: A Directory to Finding Answers in Today's Technology Oriented World*. Harper 1986 pap. $19.95. Covers more than 170 high-tech topics and lists government, commercial, and not-for-profit organizations that do research in these fields. Also lists relevant databases and journals that are available. Provides a helpful list of people who are willing to respond to mail and telephone requests for information.

McGraw-Hill Dictionary of Engineering. McGraw-Hill 1984 $36.00. Drawn from the vocabularies of ten major engineering disciplines: aerospace engineering, civil engineering, design engineering, industrial engineering, materials science, mechanical engineering, metallurgical engineering, mining engineering, petroleum engineering, and systems engineering; each of the 16,000 terms is identified by its field of primary use.

McGraw-Hill Dictionary of Science and Engineering. McGraw-Hill 1984 $32.50. Aimed at the general public; covers more than 35,000 terms spanning some 100 subject disciplines. Like other McGraw-Hill reference sources, includes an indication of the general discipline from which the term is derived in advance of providing a definition.

McGraw-Hill Dictionary of Scientific and Technical Terms. McGraw-Hill 3d ed. 1984 $70.00. Over 115,000 definitions are provided in this reference source, which is thought to be among the best scientific and technical dictionaries currently available. Identifies each term by general discipline before providing its definition. Includes many illustrations along with the definitions and provides several useful appendixes including a listing of biographical entries, periodic chart of the elements, and metric system units.

Malinowsky, H. Robert, and Jeanne M. Richardson. *Science and Engineering Literature: A Guide to Reference Sources*. Libraries Unlimited 3d ed. 1980 lib. bdg.

$33.00 text ed. pap. $21.00. Lists and describes some 1,273 reference sources in science and engineering with particular emphasis given to current, in-print titles, major bibliographies, and abstracting and indexing services. Each reference's annotation includes information on the work's scope, intended audience, and special features. Covers both primary and secondary sources in the scientific and technical literature and includes separate chapters on a variety of scientific and technical subject disciplines.

Matschoss, Conrad. *Great Engineers*. Trans. by H. S. Hatfield [*Essay Index Repr. Ser.*] Ayer repr. of 1939 ed. $27.50. An illustrated biography of engineers from antiquity to the twentieth century. "This book is addressed to lovers of technical achievement, and of the men responsible for it, who show by their lives that great deeds are brought about by ideals which are far beyond the mere material valuation of technical work" (Preface).

Mount, Ellis. *Guide to Basic Information Sources in Engineering*. [*Information Resources Ser.*] J. Norton Pubs. 1976 o.p. A nonexhaustive "sourcebook of information about engineering and allied fields, and in particular about how to find this information in the reference room or information center once those at the reference desk have been queried and the card catalog consulted" (Preface).

Myers, Robert A., ed. *Encyclopedia of Physical Science and Technology*. Academic Pr. 15 vols. 1987 $2,500.00. A monumental work covering all major aspects of the physical sciences and technology. Contains over 400 original articles written by experts, each containing a table of contents, glossary of unusual terms, and concise definition of the subject, followed by an in-depth presentation. All articles are juried by peer groups of the authors. Well illustrated, the set includes over 3,300 bibliographic entries and 45,000 subject index entries.

Parker, Sybil P., ed. *Concise Encyclopedia of Science and Technology*. McGraw-Hill 1984 $89.50. Covers more than 7,000 topics in a single volume, many of which are extracted from the larger 15-volume set of the *McGraw-Hill Encyclopedia of Science and Technology*. A useful index comprising some 30,000 entries is also included.

———. *Modern Scientists and Engineers*. McGraw-Hill 3 vols. 1980 $135.00. Presents "extended biographical data on contemporary leaders of science and engineering around the world in a form possessing reference value for the librarian and educational value for the students" (Preface).

Rolt, L. T. *Great Engineers*. G. Bell 1962 o.p. Celebrates some of the great but less famous engineers whose work influenced the course of engineering history. Tells, through ten biographies of British engineers, the history of the Industrial Revolution in England.

Roysdon, Christine M., and Linda A. Khatri. *American Engineers of the Nineteenth Century: A Biographical Index*. Garland 1978 lib. bdg. $39.00. Provides for the first time in a single source, personal-name indexing to brief biographies of several thousand American engineers and technologists that appeared in the technical and trade press of the nineteenth century. Those persons indexed were largely engaged in activities that characterized the mid and late nineteenth century, especially the development of railroads and canals and the beginning of industrialization.

Schenk, Margaret T., and James K. Webster. *What Every Engineer Should Know About Engineering Information Sources*. Marcel Dekker 1984 o.p. A selective, noncomprehensive review of a variety of engineering information formats including periodicals, nonbibliographic databases, standards and specifications, patents, trade literature, audiovisual materials, statistical sources, software, and technical reports.

Smiles, Samuel. *Lives of the Engineers.* Intro. by L. T. Rolt, Kelley 3 vols. repr. of 1861 ed. 1968 $95.00. Traces the influence and contributions of foreign engineers and the development of indigenous engineering in Great Britain through a collection of biographies of engineers.

Subramanyam, Krishna. *Scientific and Technical Information Resources.* Dekker 1981 o.p. An examination of the various phases of scientific information including its generation through research and development, its recording, surrogation, synthesis, and dissemination. An overview of the structure and characteristics of scientific and technical literature including over 1,500 sources arranged in a classed system.

Turner, Roland, and Steven L. Goulden, eds. *Great Engineers and Pioneers in Technology.* St. Martin's vol. 1 1981 $69.50. A projected three-volume series that intends to bring together information on many engineers from all fields of engineering, in a variety of cultures and time periods, from the beginning of recorded history to the present. Volume 1 begins with builders mentioned in the earliest records of civilization through the Industrial Revolution.

Who's Who in Technology Today. Res. Pubns. CT 5 vols. 4th ed. 1981–82 $425.00. Biographical summaries subdivided by specific areas within a volume that also contains an index of principal expertise and an index of names.

Young, Margaret Labash, ed. *Scientific and Technical Organizations and Agencies Directory.* Gale 2 vols. 1985 $150.00 supp. 1986 $80.00. "More than 12,000 entries are divided into 13 broad categories such as R & D centers, federal and state agencies and programs, patent and standard organizations, [etc.].... A master name and keyword index to all thirteen chapters is provided ... the orientation of STOAD is national, although some foreign organizations are listed" (Preface).

AERONAUTICS AND AVIATION

Begun as an offshoot of mechanical engineering, the field of aeronautics expanded dramatically following World War II. Flight propulsion has developed from simple propellers to such technologies as turboprops, ramjets, turbojets, and rockets. Air speeds have correspondingly increased from several hundred miles per hour to the velocities of space vehicles and satellites.

Current design techniques make extensive use of a variety of fields including mathematical analysis, metallurgy, and computing.

Apostolo, Giorgio. *The Illustrated Encyclopedia of Helicopters.* Bonanza 1984 $19.95. Provides data on engines, size, weight, maximum speed, and so on, for military and civilian helicopters from around the world. Color drawings are supplied for most models. Includes indexes by country of origin, designer, model number, and other information.

Bergman, Jules, and David Bergman. *Anyone Can Fly.* Doubleday 3d ed. rev. 1986 $19.95. Provides instructions on how to fly and describes what it is like to pilot a plane. Covers foundations of flight, takeoffs, landing, soaring, cross-country flight, solo flying, and weather conditions. Heavily illustrated. Includes a glossary of flight terminology.

Etkin, Bernard. *Dynamics of Atmospheric Flight.* Wiley 1972 text ed. $52.95. "This work has excited great interest and appreciation among leaders in the field" (*Choice*).

Gollin, Alfred. *No Longer an Island: Britain and the Wright Brothers, 1902–1909.* Stanford Univ. Pr. 1984 $39.50. "Gollin has provided a fascinating survey of British reactions to the advent of aviation. As an essay of weapons procurement, it is, however . . . inconclusive" (*AHR*).

Hart, Clive. *The Prehistory of Flight.* Univ. of California Pr. 1985 $40.00. Examines people's concept of flight beginning with classical Greek culture. Tracks the development of the design and construction of heavier-than-air flying machines from the ninth century B.C. through the eighteenth century. The heavily illustrated text includes a listing of more than 50 historical attempts at flight.

Jackson, Robert. *Flying Modern Jet Fighters.* Sterling 1986 pap. $7.95. Explores what it is like to fly modern combat planes and discusses training and air-superiority tactics. Examines the F-111, Hawk, F-14 Tomcat, F-15, F16, F-104, and Harrier, among other aircraft. Ends with a discussion of the future of manned combat aircraft.

Lomax, Judy. *Women of the Air.* Dodd 1987 $15.95. A complete, colorful, and detailed history of women's involvement in aviation beginning with Mme Thible's balloon flight in 1784 and ending with Jeana Yeager's 1987 flight aboard the Voyager. The lives of such early pioneers as Amelia Earhart are chronicled in separate biographical chapters.

Millspaugh, Ben P. *Ultralight Airman's Manual.* TAB Bks. 1986 pap. $14.95. Modern composite materials have permitted the construction of a new type of airplane, the ultralight, an improbably frail-looking experimental craft weighing only a few hundred pounds complete with engine. This book introduces the basics of ultralight engines and aerodynamics, basic chart reading, meteorology, and significant legal and operational restrictions. Contrasts the operation of conventional planes with that of ultralight craft.

Montgomery, M. R., and Gerald L. Foster. *A Field Guide to Airplanes of North America.* Houghton Mifflin 1984 $12.95. Provides a description and illustration for more than 300 civilian and military planes in an easy-to-handle, pocket-size volume.

Simonson, G. R., ed. *The History of the American Aircraft Industry.* MIT 1968 $35.00. "This collection brings together some of the important 'classic selections' on the industry, many [of which] are out of print or available in scattered copies only" (*LJ*).

Sweetman, Bill. *High Speed Flight.* Jane's Pub. 1983 o.p. Supplements the literature of aviation by providing a thorough and heavily illustrated review of international high-speed aircraft. Particular emphasis is given to the years following World War II. Provides extensive statistical information on each plane and examines the importance of various aviation developments to the history of aviation.

Wescott, Lynanne, and Paula Degen. *Wind and Sand: The Story of the Wright Brothers at Kitty Hawk Told Through Their Own Words and Photographs.* Abrams 1984 $19.95. "An enthralling addition to the accounts of what the Wright Brothers wrought at Kitty Hawk . . . [Wescott and Degen] have balanced words that are mostly those of the sensitive geniuses from Dayton, Ohio, with photographs that are as much works of art as they are historic documents" (*N.Y. Times Bk. Review*).

Yeager, Chuck, and Leo Janos. *Yeager: An Autobiography.* Bantam 1985 $17.95 1986 pap. $4.95. Chronicles Yeager's many aviation achievements, including breaking the sound barrier, and describes both the private and public life of this well-known supersonic aviator. Includes anecdotes about fellow pilots as well.

Yeager, Jeana, and Phil Patton. *Voyager*. Knopf 1987 $19.95. Yeager (no relation to
    Chuck) and Dick Rhutan flew their craft nonstop around the world without
    refueling. The book reveals the very human side of this great technological feat.

AGRICULTURAL FOOD ENGINEERING

Worldwide, agriculture is both the largest and the oldest of our industries. In
the United States, agriculture and its peripheral industries account for some
40 percent of the gross national product (GNP) and one-third of the labor force.
Agricultural engineering concerns itself with the design and implementation
of improved methods of providing food and fibers. Although significant progress has been made in the use of mechanical power to increase the production
and harvesting of crops, the demand for new equipment and techniques to
increase efficiency and reduce costs is ever present.

Harlander, Susan K., and Theodore P. Labuza, eds. *Biotechnology in Food Process-
    ing*. Noyes 1986 $48.00. "This volume presents the proceedings of a 1985 sympo-
    sium ... this symposium explored the current status of the economic, techno-
    logical, and regulatory impact of evolving areas of high technology on food and
    food-related industries. The references are current and extensive ... this volume
    provides an excellent current reference source in a rapidly developing field"
    (*Choice*).
Powledge, Fred. *The Fat of the Land: What's Behind Your Shrinking Food Dollar and
    What You Can Do About It*. Simon & Schuster 1984 $15.95. "This book examines
    the food system from farm to grocery store, concentrating on the economic
    additives that increase the cost of food. Powledge discusses the effects of agricul-
    tural practices and marketing on food quality and quantity, points out the costs
    that highly processed and fabricated foods add, and describes the roles played
    by the distributors. . . . Concluding chapters focus on food and nutrition organi-
    zations that perform watchdog or consumer education functions" (*LJ*).

AUTOMOTIVE ENGINEERING

[SEE under Transportation and Automotive Engineering in this chapter.]

BIOTECHNOLOGY

The origins of biotechnology rest with the use of fermented foods and the
development of food preservation techniques by Neolithic man. Microbial
activity was not discovered until much later, during the nineteenth century,
when scientists such as Theodor Schwann, LOUIS PASTEUR, and Eduard Buchner pioneered the fields of alcohol bioconversion, microbial fermentation,
and cell-free metabolism.
    Further advances in industrial fermentation were brought about as a
result of food shortages during the twentieth-century war years, and industrial microbiology and fermentation later expanded to include exploration
into antibiotics, enzymes, pesticides, vitamins, and solvents. Currently, biotechnology concerns itself not only with these areas of study, but also with

the fields of waste treatment, sterilization, textile microbiology, and petroleum processes.

Antébi, Elizabeth, and David Fishlock. *Biotechnology: Strategies for Life.* MIT 1986
$39.95. A collection of 24 chapters that include original essays by scientists and
technologists in the field addressing topics, problems, and noted names in biotechnology. Much of the original work in the field is described along with descriptions of current and potential future applications. Also included is a separate chapter that reviews the machinery currently in use to run the new technology. The text is well illustrated and has a complete glossary, bibliography, and
chronology of hallmarks in biotechnology.

Calder, Nigel. *The Green Machines.* Putnam 1986 $16.95. "Calder's awesome com-
mand of information covering all aspects of current biotechnology makes this
prophetic and visionary book an instructive delight to read. The major portion
of it constitutes a late-20th century review of what has been and is on the brink
of being achieved ... from the point of view of the early 21st century. What is
embedded ... is the capability of avoiding a nuclear winter, chaos, and much
worse by the advent of an enlightened king of social revolution ... an exem-
plary, practical blueprint for an optimistic future" (*Choice*).

Cheremisinoff, Paul N., and R. P. Ouellette, eds. *Applications of Biotechnology.*
Technomic 1985 pap. $35.00. "In 49 chapters written by people who really know
their fields, the reader is treated to a very broad survey of biotechnology ... as
it stands today, as well as a glimpse of what one futurist is thinking. ... The
chapters are very readable and understandable by persons with an average
background in biology and biochemistry" (*Food Technology*).

Higgins, I. J., and Jennifer Jones, eds. *Biotechnology: Principles and Applications.*
Blackwell Pubns. 1985 text ed. $50.00 pap. $27.00. The text assumes a general
background in biology, chemistry, and enzymology and discusses materials,
chemical engineering, food, genetics, medicine, agriculture, and energy, as well
as a wide range of other topics and their relationship to biotechnology. Organized into nine chapters; an index and suggested further readings are included.

Olson, Steve. *Biotechnology: An Industry Comes of Age.* National Academic Pr. 1986
pap. $9.95. A compact synthesis of the state-of-the-art thinking on biotechnology's
accomplishments and future as put forth at the 1985 Symposium on Biotechnology sponsored by National Academies of Science and Engineering, Institute of Medicine, and Academy Industry Program.

CHEMICAL ENGINEERING

The field of chemical engineering concerns itself with the development and
production of industrial and consumer products from a variety of raw materials including ores, salt, natural gas, petroleum, water, air, sulfur, and
coal. Through a variety of chemical processing techniques, these materials
are converted to an equally diverse range of products, which include aluminum, fuels, solvents, fertilizers, antibiotics, paper, and petrochemicals.

Grayson, Martin, ed. *Kirk-Othmer Concise Encyclopedia of Chemical Technology.*
Wiley 1985 $99.95. "A one volume summary of the monumental 26-volume
third edition of *Kirk-Othmer* .... A handy, compact reference which is ex-
tracted from the 'bible' of chemical technology incorporating over 1,100 entries" (*Metal Finishing*).

Miles, Wyndham D., ed. *American Chemists and Chemical Engineers*. Amer. Chemical Society 1976 $29.95. "Contains both informative and evaluative biographical material for more than 500 men and women who have made prominent contributions in one or more fields of chemistry. . . . The time span is more than 300 years—from early colonial alchemists to truly contemporary individuals" (*Choice*).

Professional Directory of Chemists and Chemical Engineers. Amer. Inst. of Chem. Eng. $25.00

CIVIL ENGINEERING

Along with military engineering, civil engineering comprises one of the two original branches of engineering as it was historically constituted. The Englishman John Smeaton, who built the Eddyston lighthouse, was the first to call himself a "civil engineer," in 1782. Today, civil engineers have a major role to play in both urban and regional planning. They tackle air-, water-, and land-pollution problems, and the result of their efforts can be seen in a variety of public works (highways, tunnels, parking facilities), special structures, transportation facilities, water resource development projects, and other facilities that enhance our environment. Because civil engineering is so diverse a field, its subdisciplines, such as construction, sanitary, and transportation engineering, are covered elsewhere in this text.

Bracegirdle, Brian, and Patricia H. Miles. *Thomas Telford*. David & Charles 1973 $15.95. "It presents, in 112 superb photographs and a minimum of explanatory text, a fascinating selection of Telford's achievements. The well-known items are all there—St. Mary's, Bridgnorth, Chirk and Pontcysyllte aqueducts, Ellesmere Port warehouses, the Caledonian and Göta canals, the Menai, Conway and Waterloo bridges and St. Katharine's Dock. . . . This is a book to appeal to the artist as much as to the engineer or industrial archaeologist" (*TLS*).

Kannappan, Sam. *Introduction to Pipe Stress and Analysis*. Wiley 1986 $39.95. "Kannappan has written a clear and useful guide or handbook for the designer and stress analyst of industrial piping systems . . . it is a reference volume . . . the book will be useful to engineering or engineering technology students who are designing or building piping systems as part of design or laboratory projects as well as to graduate engineers and technologists in design offices" (*Choice*).

Kissam, Philip. *Surveying for Civil Engineers*. McGraw-Hill 2d ed. 1981 $42.95. "An in-depth work that works well as an instructional guide or as a reference. The five major sections of the book cover instruments and methods for large surveys, operations, procedures for precise control, photogrammetry for construction and land surveys, and the appendix . . . there are numerous drawings, diagrams, tables, charts, and other illustrations" (*Public Works*).

Sayenga, Donald. *Ellet and Roebling: Their Friendship and Rivalry*. Amer. Canal and Transport 1983 $4.00

Schodek, Daniel L. *Landmarks in American Civil Engineering*. MIT 1987 $50.00. "This handsome volume traces the history of a number of projects—bridges, dams, roads, tunnels, railroad cuts and the like—formally designated as significant landmarks by the American Society of Civil Engineers. The list includes some of the most beautiful built objects in the American environment . . . by bringing to his chronicle the same balance of precision and passion one would hope for in a fine engineer, Mr. Schodek comes close to persuading his reader to invest heavily in bridge bonds and municipal sewer systems" (*N.Y. Times Bk. Review*).

Schultz, Marilyn Spigel, and Vivian Loeb Kasen. *Encyclopedia of Community Planning and Environmental Management*. Facts on File 1983 $50.00. "Basic, short definitions are provided here for nonspecialists in the fields of land use, transportation, housing, planning, urban design, census, and social surveys. The entries are concise, and a complex system of cross-references is included. . . . Schultz and Kasen's book is useful . . . for public, high school, and beginning college collections" (*Choice*).

Schuyler, Hamilton. *The Roeblings: A Century of Engineers, Bridge-Builders and Industrialists*. AMS Pr. repr. of 1931 ed. 1972 $29.50. "A century ago, John A. Roebling, a native of Muhlhausen, Germany, immigrated to this country, and founded a line of Roeblings who have ever since been important figures as engineers, bridge-builders, and industrialists. Founders of a great wire cable industry, three generations of the family have been connected with the building of suspension bridges, from the famous Brooklyn Bridge projected in 1867, to the 'George Washington Bridge' over the Hudson, opened in 1931" (*Journal of American History*).

Scott, John S. *Dictionary of Civil Engineering*. Halsted Pr. 3d ed. 1981 $28.95. Published originally in Great Britain, this book contains more than 300 pages of definitions for terms commonly used in civil engineering. Excludes terminology of building and construction, but provides cross-references to a companion volume entitled *The Penguin Dictionary of Building* (Penguin 1986 pap. $8.95). Includes a units and conversion factors chart and list of abbreviations.

CONSTRUCTION AND MAINTENANCE

Involved with the planning, execution, and control of building projects, construction engineering is itself a specialized branch of civil engineering. Topics investigated by this field include work scheduling, construction methods, equipment selection, and cost estimating.

Bianchina, Paul. *Illustrated Dictionary of Building Materials and Techniques*. TAB Bks. 1986 $22.95 pap. $14.95. "A complete listing of some 4,000 terms dealing with building materials and techniques is the backbone of this fine book. Areas covered include electrical, tools, plumbing, solar, moldings, finishes, stairs, roofs, and heating. Methods, products, materials, applications, and equipment are enhanced by 800 clear line drawings. . . . More than 60 pages of appendixes provide additional helpful information: abbreviations, conversions/tables/weights; sections about building, framing, lumber, plywood, hardware, electrical, and plumbing" (*Choice*).

Boyer, Lester L., and Walter T. Grondzik. *Earth Shelter Technology*. Texas A&M Univ. Pr. 1987 lib. bdg. $32.50 pap. $14.95. Provides an introductory discussion of the fundamental variables that determine successful earth-sheltered designs. Not a "how-to" manual, the text nonetheless presents many examples of interesting and thought-provoking earth-sheltered designs and includes a complete and up-to-the-minute list of additional readings on the subject.

Brumbaugh, James E. *Complete Roofing Handbook: Installation, Maintenance, Repair*. Macmillan 1986 $29.95. Reviews the major types of roofs and their methods of construction, roofing materials, and techniques for application. Includes discussion of minor structural repairs to complete re-roofing projects. Special problems are also treated, including ventilation, dormers, and skylights. A listing of trade and professional organizations and roofing manufacturers is included along with a large number of drawings and photographs.

Cushman, Robert F., and J. P. Bigda, eds. *McGraw-Hill Construction Business Handbook.* McGraw-Hill 1984 $65.00. "Contains a wealth of information that is very useful to public works officials, engineers, consultants, and others in the public sector who may be involved in contracts, specifications, bonding, arbitration, and so forth . . . recommended reference book" (*Public Works*).

Lenchek, Tom, and Chris Mattock. *Superinsulated Design and Construction: A Guide for Building Energy-Efficient Homes.* Van Nostrand 1986 $34.95. Using information garnered from Canadian and U.S. government programs, the text presents four approaches to building energy-efficient housing and discusses the pros and cons of each method. Covers insulation, sealing, controlling interior humidity, blocking air infiltration, and air/vapor barrier systems. Useful to homebuilders and contractors alike.

Lewis, Bernard T. *Building Maintenance Engineering Price Book: 1986–1987.* Methuen 1986 $39.95. A basic authoritative reference text for maintenance costs, estimation of costs, and standard time data. A fully validated compilation of information, it will give accurate cost or standard time data for performing maintenance jobs of all sorts. Intended for use by building maintenance staff to reduce time spent estimating time and cost data.

Rollwagen, Mary, and others. *The Consumer's Guide to Earth Sheltered Housing: A Step-by-Step Workbook for Prospective Owners.* Van Nostrand 1984 $25.50. An illustrated guide covering the advantages and disadvantages of underground homes and including advice to homeowners on dealing with architects and contractors.

Schepp, Brad, and Stephen M. Hastie. *The Complete Passive Solar Home Book.* TAB Bks. 1985 $24.95 pap. $16.95. Accompanied by many photographs and illustrations, the text covers the topics of passive heating and cooling, energy conservation, solar water heating, wood stoves, and financing. Focuses primarily on the design of new housing; includes a list of manufacturers of solar equipment for the home market.

Swanson, Theodore D., and others. *Active Solar Thermal Design Manual.* ASHRAE 1985 $35.00. "Deals with applications in the areas of residential and commercial space heating, potable hot water heating, process water heating, and space cooling. It presents fundamentals and methodologies in solar system design that have emerged and have proven true through practical applications" (*Heating/Piping/Air Conditioning*).

Wade, Herb. *Building Underground: The Design and Construction Handbook for Earth-Sheltered Houses.* Rodale Pr. 1983 $19.95 pap. $14.95. Explores a variety of topics related to the construction of houses that are partially covered by earth, including site analysis, use of passive solar mechanisms, building, plumbing, and wiring techniques. Discusses, through the use of case studies, eight typical underground houses. The text is heavily illustrated and includes sample layouts and drawings.

EDUCATION AND CAREERS

Beakley, George C., and Deloss H. Bowers. *Careers in Engineering and Technology.* Macmillan 4th ed. 1987 text ed. pap. $25.00. An introductory text that reviews career fields and employment opportunities in engineering and technology. Following a short history of engineering, it discusses the professional responsibilities of engineers, oral and written technical communication, computers and engineering, modeling and the design process, and the technical work team.

Kemper, John D. *Engineers and Their Profession.* Holt 1982 pap. $22.95. A comprehensive review of the profession covering the environment; public responsibility; energy issues; engineers in private practice, industry, and government; engineering management; creativity, salaries; professional registration; unions; engineering societies; and the various branches of engineering.

Laithwaite, Eric. *Invitation to Engineering.* [*Invitation Ser.*] Basil Blackwell 1985 o.p. "Written to give as good an insight as possible into what the daily life of a practicing engineer is really like, whether it be in industry . . . or as an academic" (Preface).

Pletta, Dan H. *The Engineering Profession: Its Heritage and Its Emerging Public Purpose.* Univ. Pr. of Amer. 1984 lib. bdg. $29.00 text ed. pap. $14.25. Covers the history and organization of the engineering profession along with a review of the purpose and obligations of professions, economic and political constraints on the field, engineering education, the law and public interest, and engineering management and societal leadership. Pletta is an emeritus professor at the Virginia Polytechnic Institute.

Red, W. Edward. *Engineering: The Career and the Profession.* Brooks-Cole 1982 o.p. Designed to assist students in determining if their interests and talents are compatible with an engineering career and to help them decide what branches of engineering they might want to specialize in. Also assists students in understanding the distinctions between educational and professional engineering careers. Includes selective bibliography of introductory readings.

Winkler, Connie. *Careers in High Tech: Exciting Jobs in Today's Fastest-Growing Fields.* Prentice-Hall 1986 pap. $9.95. "A useful guide to the types of jobs available in the high-tech industry . . . describes the kind of training and education usually deemed suitable for successful careers . . . chapters outline specific types of positions in various disciplines such as data processing, personal computers, artificial intelligence, biotechnology and publishing" (*Booklist*).

ELECTRICAL ENGINEERING AND ELECTRONICS

The history-making advances in electrical engineering closely parallel the landmark discoveries and inventions of the past, such as the development of the electric battery by Alessandro Volta in 1800, the demonstration of electrolysis a few weeks later by William Nicholson and Sir Anthony Carlisle, the discovery of electromagnetic induction by Michael Faraday, Samuel F. B. Morse's patenting of the telegraph, and the development of the high-resistance carbon filament lamp by Thomas Edison in 1880.

Electrical engineering research today is no longer carried out by distinct individuals working over long periods of time in isolation; it is instead big business, conducted by highly organized teams of researchers on university campuses and in industrial and corporate settings. Great strides have been made in the years since World War II with the invention of the transistor, which has permitted the miniaturization of many electrical and electronic components. Many of the discoveries associated with the military effort of the war years have now become part of our daily lives. These include microwaves, integrated circuits, and even lasers.

Electronics, the study and application of charge carriers' motion under the influence of radiant energy or externally applied current, now pervades a multitude of human endeavors. Counted among these are satellite communications, electronic banking, medical devices and implants, national defense and aerospace research, and home entertainment. Since the 1960s, solid state electronics has dominated the field, with increased interest in transistors and semiconductor assemblies and devices.

Aitken, Hugh G. J. *The Continuous Wave: Technology and American Radio, 1900–1932*. Princeton Univ. Pr. 1985 $67.50 pap. $19.95. "Aitken's accounting . . . provides an unprecedented cohesiveness, many new details, and a few challenges to older interpretations. During the period covered, business and government were learning which organizational forms and managerial techniques worked best for technological innovation. Because radio makes a revealing case study in this process, this book is important for a wide range of readers" (*Science*).

Alber, Antoine F. *Videotex/Teletext: Principles and Practices*. McGraw-Hill 1985 $43.95. "Designed for professionals in the field or those who want to become professionals. It covers the gamut from videotex history to distribution-system design to the corporate structure necessary to operate a successful videotex service" (*Byte*).

Baylin, Frank. *Satellites Today: The Complete Guide to Satellite Television*. ConSol 1983 pap. $9.95. Discusses the nature, design, history, and cost of communication satellites and earth stations. Operating problems, available programs, legal issues, and the future of satellite television are all explored in some detail.

Clifford, Martin. *Your Telephone: Operation, Selection and Installation*. Howard Sams 1983 pap. $13.95. Heavily illustrated text that explains the parts of the telephone, different types of phones, telephone security issues, mobile telephones, and the use of new technologies in the field. Particularly useful to home consumers, now that so many people own or are considering purchase of their own phones.

Decareau, Robert V., and R. A. Peterson. *Microwave Processing and Engineering*. VCH 1986 $62.00. "The authors begin with a general discussion of microwave applications and design philosophies, then follow with chapters on microwave power sources; power supplies and microwave plumbing; typical applicators; materials of construction; design measurements and equipment; control systems; and microwave leakage and its measurement and control. Material for this volume is drawn from the author's extensive knowledge and experience as well as from the substantial patent and technical literature" (*Choice*).

Eargle, John. *Handbook of Recording Engineering*. Van Nostrand 3d ed. 1986 $54.95. A logical review of all of the elements required for successful recording, including microphones, audio transmission, loudspeakers, signal processing devices, and monitoring systems. Discusses analog magnetic, disc, and digital recording.

Faber, Rodney B. *Essentials of Solid-State Electronics*. Wiley 1985 $33.95. "A traditional and conventional 'bottom up' approach to solid-state electronics . . . summaries provide a compact statement of the main equations and definitions which have been developed . . . a very supportive text minimizing the level of mathematical skill required" (*IEEE Proceedings*).

Freeman, Roger L. *Reference Manual for Telecommunications*. Wiley 1985 pap. $85.00. "This book is a compilation . . . for telecommunication system engineers . . . the aim of [which] is to provide a central source of basic information that will have repeated application" (*Telephone Engineer & Management*).

Friedel, Robert, and others. *Edison's Electric Light: Biography of an Invention.* Rutgers Univ. Pr. 1986 $27.95. An attempt to examine in some depth, based on a careful study of the Edison archives, the invention of the electric light, which the authors characterize as a complex human achievement and one of the most important agents for change in the last two centuries.

Grayson, Martin, ed. *Encyclopedia of Semiconductor Technology.* Wiley 1984 $99.95. Reprinted from the well known *Kirk-Othmer Encyclopedia of Chemical Technology.* Full texts, tables, figures, and reference materials from the original are reproduced unchanged. Includes heavily illustrated articles authored by industrial and academic experts on nearly every aspect of semiconductors, including their manufacture and use, integrated circuits, magnetic materials, and superconductors.

Guide to Electronics in the Home. Consumer Reports Bks. 2d ed. 1986 pap. $7.00. Provides product descriptions, ratings, and recommendations for a variety of home electronic products including stereo systems, cassette recorders, calculators, smoke detectors, video cameras, and VCRs. Most of the material provided has been extracted from previously published issues of *Consumer Reports.*

Hoenig, Stuart A., and Leland Payne. *How to Build and Use Electronic Devices Without Frustration, Panic, Mountains of Money, or an Engineering Degree.* Little, Brown 2d ed. 1980 pap. $18.50

Holzman, Harvey N. *Modern Residential Wiring.* Goodheart 1986 $18.00 text ed. pap. $12.75. Covers introductory concepts of electricity and explains complicated wiring tasks. Very well illustrated. Contains a wealth of information for the homeowner interested in doing his or her own wiring.

Hughes, Thomas Parke. *Elmer Sperry: Inventor and Engineer.* Johns Hopkins Univ. Pr. 1971 $39.50. A readable account of a most useful life. In addition to the gyroscopic work that made his fame and fortune, Sperry invented a variety of other devices and founded the American Institute of Electrical Engineers.

Isailovic, Jordan. *Videodisc Systems: Theory and Applications.* Prentice-Hall 1987 $51.00. "A most-welcome addition to a seriously limited group of books on videodisc systems. This field is obviously in an expansive mode and will become an integral part of everyone's life in a very short time. Isailovic treats both theoretical and practical aspects of videodisc systems . . . detailing the principles and descriptions of optical and capacitive playback systems . . . discuss-[ing] recording and production . . . programmable optical videodisc systems . . . signal processing and frequency modulation techniques" (*Choice*).

Kybett, Harry, and Delton T. Horn. *The Complete Handbook of Videocassette Recorders.* TAB Bks. 3d ed. 1986 $21.95 pap. $14.95. The text, which includes many diagrams, explains how to use VCRs, how they work, and discusses portable VCRs and camcorders. Suitable for the professional and layperson alike.

Linggard, Robert. *Electronic Synthesis of Speech.* Cambridge Univ. Pr. 1985 $34.50. "Describes how speech can be generated artificially using computers and special electronic circuits" (*Mechanical Engineering*).

McGraw-Hill Dictionary of Electrical and Electronic Engineering. McGraw-Hill 1985 $17.50. Contains close to 490 pages of concise definitions of terms used in the fields of electrical and electronic engineering.

Pehl, Erich. *Microwave Technology.* Artech House 1985 o.p. "Deals with wave propagation in various media, including coaxial cable, waveguide, and transmission lines, and the circuit elements that can be formed of these media. . . . Pehl's style is straightforward. He introduces a concept, presents the mathematical background for the idea, and then offers a practical example to illustrate the concept" (*Microwaves & RF*).

Rains, Darell L. *Major Home Appliances: A Common Sense Repair Manual.* TAB Bks. 1987 $21.95 pap. $14.95. This clearly written and well-illustrated text provides extensive diagnostic and repair procedures for washers, dryers, refrigerators, and dishwashers. Also covered are methods to prolong the life of major home appliances, safety factors, warranties, and parts suppliers.

Read, Oliver, and Walter L. Welch. *From Tin Foil to Stereo.* Howard Sams 1976 o.p. The most comprehensive and best-illustrated story of the phonograph from 1877 up to the complex mechanical, acoustical, and electronic inventions that gave us the stereophonic disk process of the late 1950s.

Reid, T. R. *The Chip: How Two Americans Invented the Microchip and Launched a Revolution.* Simon & Schuster 1985 $15.95 1986 pap. $7.95. Provides a detailed history of the development of the integrated circuit and studies its two inventors, Robert Noyce and Jack Kilby, showing how each independently came up with the same idea. Includes selected illustrations and a reading list.

Roberts, R. S. *Dictionary of Audio, Radio and Video.* Butterworth 1981 $44.95. Provides 240 pages of illustrated definitions and explains the meanings and applications of terms common to audio, radio, and video engineering. Appendixes cover classifications of radio frequencies and emissions, a list of common acronyms and abbreviations, and European and American television system standards.

Roberts, Steven, ed. *International Directory of Telecommunications.* Longman 1986 $84.50. "Fulfills well the object of its compiler: to produce a reference companion for use by managers and researchers who want a general overview of the international telecommunication and broadcasting organisations and industries . . . will serve well those who have an interest in the international telecommunication scene" (*British Telecommunications Engineering*).

Ryder, John Douglas. *Engineers and Electrons: A Century of Electrical Progress.* IEEE Pr. 1983 $33.35. This book is "not intended as a scholarly history, but it does provide, in an informal and readable way, the story of how electrical engineering began and grew over the decades to provide the technology that is a part of our daily lives. . . . The illustrations are excellent, and each chapter provides a list for further reading" (*Science Books & Films*).

St. Maur, Suzan. *The A-Z of Video and Audio-Visual Jargon.* Methuen 1986 pap. $17.95. Clarifies some 800 jargon terms used in audiovisual technologies and explains the techniques and concepts behind them. Written in clear, encyclopedic style for those involved in publicity work and media studies as well as for the home video enthusiast. Explores and defines the language of video, slides, tape, and film.

Salsberg, Art. *First Book of Modern Electronics Fun Projects.* Howard Sams 1986 $12.95. This heavily illustrated text describes projects involving audiovisual equipment, computers, telephones, test equipment, and security devices that appeared previously in *Modern Electronics* magazine and elicited a good deal of reader interest. The projects are practical in nature, and lists of parts required to complete them are provided.

Singleton, Loy A. *Telecommunications in the Information Age: A Non-Technical Primer on the New Technologies.* Ballinger 2d ed. 1986 $19.95. Background information, an explanation of how each works, and a look into the future are provided on the topics of videodisks, communications satellites, cable television, videotex, and other telecommunications technologies, in easy-to-understand language. A glossary and list of recommended readings are included.

Watson, John. *Mastering Electronics.* McGraw-Hill 2d ed. 1985 pap. $19.95. Explains the workings of devices such as digital circuits, television, radio, and amplifiers to the lay reader. Suggests and describes home projects for each of these devices, with particular emphasis on understanding the ABCs of how they work.

Williams, Gene B. *Chilton's Guide to Large Appliance Repair and Maintenance.* Chilton 1986 pap. $13.50. Presents an introductory overview of the tools needed for maintenance and repair, fundamentals of electricity, and the basics of electric motors, thermostats, heating elements, and safety. Discusses the repair of ranges, dishwashers, refrigerators, washers, and dryers. Also provides advice on the purchase of major appliances.

———. *Chilton's Guide to Small Appliance Repair and Maintenance.* Chilton 1986 $12.50. Presents an introductory overview of the tools needed for maintenance and repair, fundamentals of electricity, and the basics of electric motors, thermostats, heating elements, and safety. Discusses the repair of irons, coffee makers, toasters, vacuum cleaners, blenders, and fans. Provides advice on purchasing small home appliances.

ENGINEERING—HISTORY

Clark, Ronald W. *Works of Man.* Viking 1985 $29.95. Surveys the history of engineering and technology with particular focus on developments in Western civilization since the invention of the steam engine. Includes a detailed index, many colored photographs, and a short list of suggested readings.

Corn, Joseph J., ed. *Imagining Tomorrow: History, Technology and the American Future.* MIT 1986 $17.50. An extensive examination of technology that assesses innovations against changing times and covers a variety of inventions such as radio and plastics, technological happenings including world's fairs, and the impact of technology on commercialism.

De Camp, L. Sprague. *The Ancient Engineers.* Ballantine 1980 pap. $2.95. A most readable popular history of technology. "Mr. de Camp has written a detailed but anecdotal history of how mechanical things got done in the ancient civilizations—how the pyramids were built, and the Great Wall of China, what ancient siege engines were like and how they operated, and much more. For all history buffs as well as modern technicians" (*PW*).

Donohue, Jack. *Wildcatter: The Story of Michel T. Halbouty and the Search for Oil.* Gulf Pub. repr. of 1979 ed. 1983 $24.00

Flaxman, Edward, ed. *Great Feats of Modern Engineering.* [*Essay Index Repr. Ser.*] Ayer repr. of 1938 ed. rev. ed. $20.00

Morison, Elting E. *Men, Machines, and Modern Times.* MIT 1966 pap. $6.95. "A series of essays and lectures giving historical perspective on technological change" (*LJ*).

Nortlock, J. R. *Just an Engineer.* State Mutual Bk. 1986 $45.00

Pacey, Arnold. *The Maze of Ingenuity: Ideas and Idealism in the Development of Technology.* Holmes & Meier 1975 text ed. $30.00; MIT 1976 pap. $9.95. Presents the changes in outlook that accompanied the development of technology in Europe between 1100 and 1870, and discusses the humanitarian, social, and intellectual ideals and objectives of technology in the 1970s.

Parsons, William Barclay. *Engineers and Engineering in the Renaissance.* MIT 1968 pap. $16.50. "The topics include Da Vinci, machines and mechanism (not clocks), mining, the engineering of cities, of rivers, canals and harbors, of bridges and domes. Here is the famous account of how Domenico Fontana moved the obelisk to St. Peter's, and the story of the design and construction of the Rialto Bridge in Venice, the Pont Neuf over the Seine, the Santa Trinità across the Arno, the great domes of Florence and of Rome" (*Scientific American*).

Robinson, Eric H., and A. E. Musson. *James Watt and the Steam Revolution: A Documentary History*. Kelley 1969 $29.50. A selection of reprinted documents, produced on the occasion of the bicentenary of Watt's first patent, including a good deal of previously unpublished material on the work of the inventor.

Susskind, Charles. *Twenty-Five Engineers and Inventors*. San Francisco Pr. 1977 $7.50

Turner, Roland, and Steven L. Goulden, eds. *Great Engineers and Pioneers in Technology: From Antiquity Through the Industrial Revolution*. St. Martin's Vol. 1 1982 $69.50. "Entries for individual engineers are arranged in chronological order by actual or presumed date of birth and include a brief biographical sketch, a discussion of outstanding engineering achievements, and suggestions for further reading. . . .Reference and research use is enhanced by inclusion of an alphabetical index of biographical entries, a brief glossary of technical terms, a chronological table of significant engineering events, a bibliography of major historical studies on engineering, a list of illustrations, and a general index" (*Choice*).

Wasserman, Neil H. *From Invention to Innovation: Long Distance Telephone Transmission at the Turn of the Century*. Johns Hopkins Univ. Pr. 1985 $17.50. A twofold study in technological innovation—one engaging in the examination of a particular, significant innovation in telephone transmission, the second, exploring how large enterprise in the United States went about developing the capability of using modern science and engineering.

Weitzman, David. *Traces of the Past: A Field Guide to Industrial Archaeology*. Scribner 1980 o.p. Provides a heavily illustrated look at the history of railroads, bridges, iron industry and trade, and oil wells in America's past.

York, Neil Longley. *Mechanical Metamorphosis: Technological Change in Revolutionary America*. Greenwood 1985 $35.00. "York's investigation covers the era of the American revolution, roughly from 1760 to 1790. . . . The book's sixth chapter 'Limits to innovation: the Pennsylvania rifle,' presents a superb account of an instance when institutional resistance to an invention . . . frustrated its adoption. . . . York is at his best when discussing the work and vision of specific inventors in the context of a largely indifferent and occasionally hostile society" (*Science*).

ENGINEERING GEOLOGY

[SEE under Petroleum Engineering and Engineering Geology in this chapter.]

FLIGHT

[SEE under Aeronautics and Aviation in this chapter.]

HOLOGRAPHY

[SEE under Lasers and Holography in this chapter.]

INDUSTRIAL ENGINEERING
AND ENGINEERING MANAGEMENT

The first awakening of industrial engineering as a field of study is most often associated with the Industrial Revolution in the nineteenth century, when factory production replaced household or cottage industries. The frontier-breaking efforts of Frederick Taylor (1856–1915), often referred to as the father of scientific management, formed the basis on which industrial engineering was conceptualized and grew. From his pioneering late nineteenth- and early twentieth-century study in work design, measurement, planning, and scheduling grew later research efforts in cost reduction, inventory control, assembly line balancing, work-place design, and productivity improvement. Modern industrial engineering builds on these efforts and interests itself in such areas as computer analysis, management information systems, human factors engineering, and biomechanics.

Bain, David L. *The Productivity Prescription: The Manager's Guide to Improving Productivity and Profits*. McGraw-Hill 1986 $29.95 pap. $10.95. "A timely work on a topic that currently is generating a great deal of interest. . . . What sets this 'how to' book apart . . . is the author's emphasis on increasing productivity without increasing capital investment. . . . He suggests that by making use of contemporary behavioral theory productivity can be increased. . . . The case studies Bain includes are a particularly valuable feature" (*LJ*).

Clark, Forrest D., and A. B. Lorenzoni. *Applied Cost Engineering*. Dekker 2d ed. rev. 1985 $32.50. "A very well written textbook that ranges from the bare basics in cost engineering to the latest techniques in cost engineering and project controls . . . very easy to follow. . . . there are 10 'case studies' at the end of the 25 formal chapters" (*Chemical Engineering*).

Grove, Andrew S. *High Output Management*. Random 1985 pap. $3.95. "The author deals with basic management techniques rather than with a new management method . . . by means of . . . simple analogies he [seeks to] enable the reader to comprehend the complexities of managing both small and large organizations" (*LJ*).

Kendrick, John W. *Improving Company Productivity: Handbook with Case Studies*. Johns Hopkins Univ. Pr. 1986 pap. $10.95. A summary of "the current state of the art with respect to the measurement of company productivity, the various practical uses to which productivity measures may be put, and the development of productivity improvement programs" (Introduction).

Melman, Seymour. *Profits Without Production*. Univ. of Pennsylvania Pr. 1987 pap. $15.95. "The thesis of this book strikes at the heart of a much debated current issue, the relative decline in U.S. productivity compared with that of Japan, West Germany, and other developed countries. . . . [Melman] carefully reevaluates much of the territory addressed by . . . others . . . who contend American managers have been overly preoccupied with short-term profits at the expense of long-run product quality . . . [a] well documented, scholarly work" (*LJ*).

Meredith, Dale D., and others. *Design and Planning of Engineering Systems*. Prentice-Hall 1973 $34.95. "Presents techniques for problem solving and discusses such items as systems modeling, optimization concepts, evaluations, linear graph analysis, calculus methods, linear programming, decision analysis, network planning, and others" (*Public Works*).

Schonberger, Richard. *Japanese Manufacturing Techniques: Nine Hidden Lessons in Simplicity*. Free Pr. 1982 $18.95. Schonberger's book is "eminently readable and clearly organized into nine chapters, each containing a lesson from Japanese experience, especially Just-In-Time production and Total Quality Control, the implications of which are well explained. . . . The stress is on production management . . . the author . . . enriches the book by interesting case-study examples" (*Choice*).

INVENTORS AND INVENTING

Arnold, Tom, and Frank S. Vaden. *Invention Protection for Practicing Engineers*. Van Nostrand 1971 $16.95 pap. $11.95. "Discussed are the problems of what is patentable and what is not, patent searching, securing a patent, evaluating patents for purchase or sale, litigation and enforcement, licensing, the function of a patent attorney, and trends in patent law" (*LJ*).

Botkin, James, and others. *The Innovators: Rediscovering America's Creative Energy*. Univ. of Pennsylvania Pr. 1986 pap. $13.95. A collection of case studies illustrating technological and educational issues affecting innovation in American and international businesses. Explores both high-tech developments and the absorption of new technologies into basic industries.

Jewkes, John, and others. *Sources of Invention*. Norton 2d ed. 1971 o.p. Part 1 of the text presents modern views on invention, reviews inventors and inventions of the nineteenth century, and traces industrial research developments. Parts 2 and 3 are a varied compendium of case studies covering such technological inventions as diesel-electric railways, the cyclotron, freon refrigerants, and the long-playing record.

Josephson, Matthew. *Edison: A Biography*. McGraw-Hill 1959 pap. $8.95. Drawn from original sources, this volume is interesting not only for its coverage of Edison, but also for the material on Jay Gould, George Westinghouse, J. P. Morgan, and other of his entrepreneurial and financial associates.

Lasson, Kenneth. *Mouse Traps and Muffling Cups: One Hundred Brilliant and Bizarre United States Patents*. Arbor House 1986 $9.95. A catalog of inventions compiled from the records of the U.S. Patent and Trademarks Office that includes such well-known creative accomplishments as the airplane and sewing machine, lesser known but nonetheless successful inventions such as the parking meter, and unsuccessful patents for items such as luminous hats and tapeworm traps.

Leslie, Stuart W. *Boss Kettering*. Columbia Univ. Pr. 1986 $32.50 pap. $14.50. A biography of Charles F. Kettering, acknowledged in his lifetime as America's greatest living engineer and inventor. Some of the fields to which he contributed include inventory control systems, nontoxic refrigerants, high-speed diesel engines, solar energy, four-wheel brakes, and leaded gasoline.

MacCracken, Calvin D. *A Handbook for Inventors: How to Protect, Patent, Finance, Develop, Manufacture, and Market Your Ideas*. Scribner 1983 $14.95. Describes all of the steps required to get a patent and methods for protecting your invention until patent coverage is obtained. Financing and manufacturing methods are also discussed by MacCracken, who is a professional inventor. Directed to the nonspecialist.

Runes, Dagobert D., ed. *The Diary and Sundry Observations of Thomas Alva Edison*. Greenwood 1968 $32.50. Includes excerpts from Edison's personal diary and

Edison's observations on motion pictures and the arts, war and peace, education and work, people and machines, "a better world," life after death, and spiritualism.

LASERS AND HOLOGRAPHY

Since the introduction of lasers (*Light Amplification by Simulated Emission of Radiation*) in 1960, their scope of application has increased steadily to include high-speed scanners such as we now encounter in libraries and supermarket checkout stands, laser surgery and welding, materials processing, holography, and videodisk reading.

Though invented much earlier (in 1948 by Dennis Gabor), holography, a technique for recording and later recreating the amplitude and phase distributions of coherent wave disturbances, is widely used as a means of optical image formation. As in laser technology, there exists a plethora of emerging holographic applications, including everything from microscopy to state-of-the-art advertising techniques and artistic expression.

Broad, William J. *Star Warriors*. Simon & Schuster 1985 $16.45 1986 pap. $8.95. "Broad takes us into the world of the O-Group at Lawrence Livermore Labs, where advances in computer science and laser technology are being shaped into Star Wars weapons" (*Science*).

Laurence, Clifford L. *The Laser Book: A New Technology of Light*. Prentice-Hall 1986 $19.95. Reviews the history of laser technology, discusses the common types of lasers, and chronicles the increasing fields in which the laser is used in our contemporary world, including optics, holography, medicine, the military, and communications. Basic definitions are provided for terms such as the index of refraction, frequency, wavelength, and coherence. Information is also provided about careers in laser technology.

Wenyon, Michael. *Understanding Holography*. Arco 1984 $14.95 pap. $8.95. Provides a basic introduction to the holograph, a device that produces a three-dimensional image of an object through the use of lasers. Discusses principles and applications of holography, the future of holography, and how to make your own holograms.

MECHANICAL ENGINEERING

This subspecialty of engineering interests itself with the design and production of machinery and borrows heavily from the study of mathematics, mechanics of materials, statics, dynamics, thermodynamics, and fluid mechanics.

Del Vecchio, Alfred. *Dictionary of Mechanical Engineering*. Philos. Lib. 1961 $10.00. Provides more than 300 pages of definitions of terms used in the fields of architecture, automatic controls, engineering mechanics, combustion, and power plants. Selective definitions are provided in the related fields of electricity, heat treatment of metals, mathematics, and welding. Includes 20 pages of conversion factors following the main text.

Hine, Charles R. *Machine Tools and Processes for Engineers.* Kreiger repr. of 1971 ed. 1982 $39.50. "The author covers all the important tools with a descriptive and analytical treatment that shows how they should be used, what they can and cannot be expected to do" (*LJ*).

Nayler, G. H. *Dictionary of Mechanical Engineering.* Butterworth 3d ed. 1986 text ed. $65.00. Provides over 400 pages of partially illustrated definitions for terms commonly used in the fields of mechanical power in engines, transport, and mechanisms. Excludes definitions that pertain to hand tools and to many fields that are allied to mechanical engineering such as welding and metallurgy. Appendixes include definitions of units.

Reader, G. T., and C. Hooper. *Stirling Engines.* Methuen 1982 $65.00. A coherent and readily intelligible account of the Stirling engine, which is experiencing renewed popularity because of its potential for reducing conventional fuel consumption.

Walker, Graham. *Stirling Engines.* Oxford 1980 text ed. $105.00. A comprehensive treatise on the Stirling engine, a mechanical device that operates on a closed regenerative thermodynamic cycle and embraces a large family of machines with different functions, characteristics, and configurations.

Whitt, Frank Rowland, and David Gordon Wilson. *Bicycling Science: Ergonomics and Mechanics.* Fwd. by James McCullagh, MIT 2d ed. 1982 $27.50 pap. $10.95; State Mutual Bk. 1982 $39.00. Directed to mechanically inquisitive bicyclists, teachers of introductory mechanics and physiology, and engineers and others interested in exploring approaches to lessen our dependence on high-energy-consumption transportation. Includes a short chapter on the history of bicycles and tricycles. The subtitle reflects engineering's recent awareness of ergonomics—designing machines that take account of how the human body will interact with them.

MILITARY ENGINEERING

Traditionally, the discipline of engineering was composed of two branches: military engineering and civil engineering. With time, civil engineering was subdivided into a variety of more specialized areas now recognized as formal fields of study and research in and of themselves (e.g., mechanical engineering, electrical engineering, industrial engineering, nuclear engineering, and so on). Military engineering itself has expanded to include new areas of interest. Among these are airborne radar, antisubmarine warfare, electronic warfare, guided missiles, and fire-control systems.

Brodie, Bernard, and Fawn M. Brodie. *From Crossbow to H-Bomb.* Indiana Univ. Pr. rev. ed. 1973 $20.00 pap. $8.95. A wealth of information written in an easy style that chronicles the contributions of science to warfare.

Macksey, Kenneth. *Technology in War: The Impact on Science of Weapon Development and Modern Battle.* Arco 1986 $19.95. "Traces the influence of scientific and technical developments on weapons over several centuries up to the present. Ranges from the design of forts to missiles. It is a handsome book with many photographs and drawings . . . but it is also a sobering book in considering the effects of modern weapons, including firearms, submarines, and aircraft" (*LJ*).

MINING AND METALLURGY

Mining, the extraction of minerals from the earth, dates back to the earliest experiences in human history; the usable products garnered from mining are fundamental to society. In the face of continued demand for mineral products, mineral exploration has taken on greater importance and has become highly technical and expensive. With increasing demand for mined materials, systematic exploration has replaced accidental discovery and the size of mining sites has increased correspondingly. Additionally, there is a growing concern in the field over the issues of conservation, pollution, and public policy.

Metallurgy has played an equally important role in the course of human history. Dating back some 6,000 years, metallurgy had its genesis in the artistic and decorative arts but soon evolved to include pragmatic applications. Today, the area of concern of metallurgy has widened considerably and includes the fields of physics, chemistry, mechanical engineering, and chemical engineering. Today's metallurgical plants supply metals and alloys to the construction and manufacturing industries in a variety of forms. The emerging technologies of nuclear power generation, space exploration, and telecommunications require new techniques of metal production and processing. Of equal concern to the modern metallurgist are the areas of energy and materials conservation, recycling of secondary metals, and environmental pollution.

American Society for Metals. *Metals Handbook Desk Edition.* ASM 1985 $96.00. "A new addition to the *Metals Handbook* series in a format which complements rather than replaces the current ninth edition ... its publication represents a response to the demand for a single-volume, readily accessible, practical first reference to metals technology" (*International Journal of Production Research*).
Sawkins, Frederick J. *Metal Deposits in Relation to Plate Tectonics.* Springer-Verlag 1984 $49.20. "The author ... was one of the first to realize the potential impact of the theory of plate tectonics on our understanding of how mineral deposits are formed and how we can find more. He has written a book that is clear and terse.... there is something for everyone, whether general reader or specialist" (*Science*). Well-known mines and mining districts are covered.
Smallman, R. E. *Modern Physical Metallurgy.* Butterworth 4th ed. 1985 $59.95 pap. $39.95. "The flavour of the new edition has remained unaltered. The original aims were to bring together, to illustrate, and to make comprehensible at undergraduate students' level the ways in which physical metallurgy has developed" (*British Corrosion Journal*).

NAVAL ENGINEERING

With the passage of time, the field of naval architecture and engineering has evolved to become as much a science as it was once considered an art. It involves not only the design of hulls, structures, and cargo-handling systems, but also propulsion, electrical, and hydrodynamic systems as well as economic analysis, given the increasing costs of ship construction and available fuels.

Beaver, Paul. *Nuclear-Powered Submarines.* Sterling 1986 pap. $7.95. Primarily a collection of well-chosen, captioned photographs of nuclear submarines. Some of the photographs illustrate rare views of everyday life for shipboard personnel.

Jackson, John. *An Illustrated Guide to Modern Destroyers.* Prentice-Hall 1986 $10.95. Provides narratives, technical data, and profuse color illustrations for 54 classes of postwar destroyers from 19 navies worldwide. A readable, good overview presented in a compact volume of less than 200 pages.

Marshall, Roger, and Paul Larsen. *A Sailor's Guide to Production Sailboats.* Morrow 1986 pap. $17.95. Begins by reviewing the principles for selecting and inspecting sailboats, and continues by providing manufacturer-supplied data on engines, propellers, fuel capacity, steering, safety, rigging, beam width, displacement, ballast, draft, and interior fittings, among other things. Essentially a buyer's guide. The text covers more than 400 production sailboats and provides interior diagrams, photographs, and sketches along with the text.

Vego, Milan. *Soviet Navy Today.* Sterling 1986 pap. $7.95. A little under 70 pages of photographs illustrating destroyers, submarines, minesweepers, aircraft carriers, and other ocean-going military vessels from the Soviet Union with a limited text accompanying them.

Verney, Michael. *The Compleat Book of Yacht Care.* Sheridan 1986 $34.95. A thorough review of boat maintenance, which discusses the tools and materials needed to do a good job. The text covers general mechanics, engines, deck work, sails, painting and varnishing, rigging and ropes. A separate chapter is provided on dinghies and trailers.

NUCLEAR ENGINEERING

A large, complex, and controversial field, nuclear engineering concerns itself with the design, development, construction, and operation of facilities that produce such useful forms of energy as heat and electricity from fission and fusion processes. The work of nuclear engineers involves the solution of complex mechanical, electrical, and materials problems. The handling and storage of large quantities of radioactive materials used as reactor fuel, produced as by-products, or left as waste touch on problems of public concern such as the protection of human life, environmental pollution, and equipment contamination.

Adato, Michelle, and others. *Safety Second: The NRC and America's Nuclear Power Plants.* Indiana Univ. Pr. 1987 $22.50. The text sets about answering four basic questions about the Nuclear Regulatory Commission (NRC), the federal agency charged with being the nation's nuclear watchdog: Has the Nuclear Regulatory Commission tackled the most difficult and wide-ranging safety issues? Does the NRC enforce its own rules consistently and to the letter of the law? Is the public allowed to influence NRC decision making? Has the NRC maintained objectivity and distance from the industry in its regulatory functions?

Craig, Paul P., and John A. Jungerman. *The Nuclear Arms Race: Technology and Society.* McGraw-Hill 1985 $23.95. Reviews the history of the arms race, civil defense, the effects of nuclear weapons, and verification. Covers most technical aspects of nuclear arms and their control.

Green, Jonathon. *A-Z of Nuclear Jargon.* Methuen 1986 text ed. $34.95. Clarifies and demystifies the technology behind nuclear jargon. Covers all aspects of nuclear warfare: arms control, personnel and weapons systems, tactics and strategies, and disarmament talks. Provides background, context, and implications of nuclear technology so that the underlying meaning of the words and abbreviations becomes understandable.

Jastrow, Robert. *How to Make Nuclear Weapons Obsolete.* Little, Brown 1985 $15.95. Jastrow, formerly affiliated with the National Aeronautics and Space Administration (NASA), explains how "Star Wars" is supposed to work. Represents a point of view that is opposed by many respected scientists, and is therefore likely to be controversial. Portions of the text, which defends President Reagan's view on "Star Wars" as a viable defense against nuclear weapons, have already appeared in *The New York Times.*

League of Women Voters Education Fund. *The Nuclear Waste Primer: A Handbook for Citizens.* N. Lyons Bks. 1985 $11.95 pap. $5.95. Provides a concise, balanced introduction to the nuclear waste issue. Defines the forms, sources, and dangers of radiation and reviews history, key legislation, and current status of high- and low-level waste management. Identifies sources for further information and points out to citizens how they can influence the decision-making process.

Leclercq, Jacques. *The Nuclear Age.* Le Chene 1986 $53.00. Translated from the French, the text describes nuclear reactor design, fabrication, and installation; the fuel cycle; the history of nuclear engineering; and nuclear safety issues. Approximately half of the book is comprised of colored maps, diagrams, photographs, and drawings.

Nitske, W. Robert. *The Life of Wilhelm Conrad Röntgen: Discoverer of the X-Ray.* Univ. of Arizona Pr. 1971 o.p. "The book can be appreciated by the general reader, as well as by scientists and scholars. It contains an extensive bibliography and several appendixes providing a chronology, a genealogy, and English translations of Röntgen's three original publications on x-rays" (*LJ*).

Tirman, John, ed. *The Fallacy of Star Wars: Based on Studies Conducted by the Union of Concerned Scientists.* Vintage 1984 pap. $4.95. Discusses the technical difficulties inherent in "Star Wars," the likely ease with which Soviet offensive measures to counteract American weapons might be undertaken, and the probability of an escalation of the weapons race. Argues for dropping President Reagan's Strategic Defense Initiative plan and appends a model treaty drafted by the Union of Concerned Scientists, a public interest group that deals with nuclear arms control and nuclear power safety.

Union of Concerned Scientists. *Empty Promise: The Growing Case Against Star Wars.* Beacon 1986 $19.95 pap. $7.95. Contains ten chapters covering various issues related to the Strategic Defense Initiative, or "Star Wars." Explores the political ramifications of the program as well as unusual technical problems.

Walker, Charles A., and Edward J. Woodhouse, eds. *Too Hot to Handle? Social and Policy Issues in the Management of Radioactive Wastes.* Yale Univ. Pr. 1983 text ed. $25.00 pap. $6.95. A thorough examination of the technical and political ramifications of handling nuclear wastes. Reviews the nature of radioactive waste, current disposal methods, and those under consideration for future use. Also includes public views on the topic for readers' consideration.

PATENTS

[SEE under Inventors and Inventing in this chapter.]

PETROLEUM ENGINEERING
AND ENGINEERING GEOLOGY

More attention has been directed at petroleum engineering as increasing demands are made on crude oil and natural gas supplies as sources for meeting our growing energy needs. Petroleum engineers involve themselves in the exploration and analysis of existing reservoirs, assessing production rates, and planning and executing projects directed at earth penetration and the recovery of natural gas and oil. Current efforts are focused on more economic retrieval methods and on developing new recovery techniques necessitated by current exploration in arctic and ocean regions.

Klein, George de Vries. *Sandstone Depositional Models for Exploration for Fossil Fuels*. Intl. Human Resources 3d ed. 1985 $48.00. "While the basic principles of depositional systems described in the 1980 second edition are still valid, the revision includes new sedimentological concepts and newly released information on the application of sandstone models to exploration for oil, coal, uranium, and mineral deposits" (*Journal of Petroleum Technology*).

Shaffer, Ed. *The United States and the Control of World Oil*. St. Martin's 1983 $27.50. Shaffer presents a mass of information on the subject of American control of oil. He demonstrates the relationship between the rise of oil as a world commodity and the growth of the United States as a world power, and the problems the United States faces now that it is no longer the dominant force in the world oil market.

Sherrill, Robert. *The Oil Follies of 1970–1980: How the Petroleum Industry Stole the Show (and Much More Besides)*. Doubleday 1983 o.p. "Sherrill offers one chapter on the energy development of each year from 1970 to 1980—and then includes an appendix . . . that consists of background essays on the history of Standard Oil, the industry's consistent pattern of underestimating supply, the Government's efforts to regulate natural gas, etc." (*N.Y. Times Bk. Review*).

Whittaker, Alan, ed. *Field Geologist's Training Guide*. Intl. Human Resources Development 1985 text ed. $34.00. "Designed for oil industry people who are interested in petroleum geology, drilling procedures, formation evaluation, but at an introductory level . . . a basic book that conveniently assembles . . . a lot of well established facts" (*Geophysics*).

ROBOTICS

The technology is available at present to produce the most complex of robots capable of performing materials handling tasks in industry, increasing productivity, and relieving human operators from functions that are routine, burdensome, or threatening to human safety. Counted among these are functions associated with welding, painting, assembly, and loading and unloading of potentially hazardous materials. The enormous quantity of currently published material dealing with robotics reflects the rapidly growing scientific and popular interest in this field.

Asimov, Isaac, and Karen A. Frenkel. *Robots: Machines in Man's Image*. Harmony 1985 $19.95. A well-illustrated, easy-to-understand overview of robotics that touches on the origins of robots; pioneers in and uses of industrial robots; how robots work; personal and hobby robots; jobs, the economy, and research and development; and robots and society.

Deken, Joseph. *Silico Sapiens: The Fundamentals and Future of Robots.* Bantam 1986 pap. $4.50. An easy-to-understand answer book about robots and their implications for the human race. Tackles: What are robots? How will they evolve in the near and distant future? How will they coexist with people? Does robot intelligence endanger or enhance the human species?

Hanafusa, Hideo, and Hirochika Inoue, eds. *Robotics Research.* MIT 1985 $52.50. "Sixty-two contributions . . . provide a unique opportunity to view the future shape of robotics in such areas as arm and hand design, dynamics, image understanding, locomotion, touch and compliance, systems, kinematics, visual inspection, control, assembly, and sensing" (*Automotive Engineering*).

Kelly, Derek. *A Layman's Introduction to Robotics.* Petrocelli Bks. 1986 $27.95. An attempt to describe in a general way some central features of robotics such as what robotics is, the history of robotics, robotic concepts, hardware and software, implications of robotics, careers in robotics, and the future of robotics.

Logsdon, Tom. *The Robot Revolution.* Simon & Schuster 1984 pap. $9.95. A well-illustrated historical description of the development of robots that also includes a peek at the future. Provides a vision of the factory of the future and discusses both civilian and military applications of robotics.

Miller, Richard K. *Industrial Robot Handbook.* Fairmont Pr. 1986 pap. $99.00. A collection of 79 articles describing the use of robots in a wide range of industrial settings. Easy to read, the text includes a list of robot manufacturers and many helpful illustrations.

Nof, Shimon Y., ed. *Handbook of Industrial Robotics.* Wiley 1985 $85.00. "In 77 highly illustrated, informative chapters, this volume presents the most current relevant information on the research, development, design, and application of industrial robots . . . should serve as a guidebook for courses in mechanical, electrical, and industrial engineering, and production/operations management" (*Automotive Engineering*).

Todd, D. J. *Fundamentals of Robot Technology: An Introduction to Industrial Robots, Teleoperators and Robot Vehicles.* Halsted Pr. 1986 $29.95. Written by a mechanical engineer, the text covers most types of robots in operation in the world today as well as those in early-, mid-, and late-developmental stages. One of the most comprehensive and best-presented books on the subject currently available.

Waldman, Harry. *Dictionary of Robotics.* Macmillan 1985 $34.95. International in scope, this is among the most comprehensive dictionaries on robotics, listing more than 2,000 terms and providing more than 100 illustrations. Includes terms, major manufacturers, publications, and individuals in the field. The preface includes a brief review of highlights in the development of industrial robots from 1939 to the present.

SAFETY ENGINEERING

At one time, the only important criteria when designing and building a machine were that it work reliably and economically. Safety, if considered at all, meant little more than putting a guard around the most dangerous parts and hoping that everyone would be careful. Today that is much changed. The demands of consumers and industrial unions have led to a host of federal, state, and local laws, such as the Federal Occupational Safety and Health Act, that have created standards of performance and safety for almost every workplace and machine in our society. These laws, coupled with an increasing willingness on the part of the public to sue corporations, has made safety a prime design consideration. The tragedies of Bhupal, Chernobyl, and the *Challenger* demonstrate that much more needs to be done, but the progress of recent years has been considerable.

De Grazia, Alfred. *A Cloud over Bhopal: Causes, Consequences and Constructive Solutions.* South Asia Bks. 1985 $12.00. Explores all aspects of the Union Carbide accident in Bhopal, India, and explores questions concerning the impact of multinational corporations on developing countries, responsibility and negligence in relation to corporate and government involvement, and the extent to which we can reasonably expect technology to save the world.

Ferry, Ted S., ed. *New Directions in Safety.* ASSE 1985 $45.00. "Twenty-seven articles . . . have been compiled in this book to represent the best readings in safety over the past two years" (*Occupational Hazards*).

Kletz, Trevor A. *What Went Wrong: Case Histories of Process Plant Disasters.* Gulf Pub. 1985 $42.00. "A much more informative book than its title would imply. The author has collected hundreds of case records of accidents or near-accidents in process and chemical plants . . . cause and effect are described. The book then examines many tragedies and provides details of remedial actions that could have prevented most, if not all, of these events" (*Chemical Engineering*).

Morone, Joseph G., and Edward J. Woodhouse. *Averting Catastrophe: Strategies for Regulating Risky Technologies.* Univ. of California Pr. 1986 $25.00. Attempts to understand why, despite close calls, risky technologies have thus far produced no major catastrophes in the United States. Explores strategies now in use and questions whether we could be doing better.

Perrow, Charles. *Normal Accidents: Living with High-Risk Technologies.* Basic Bks. 1984 $21.95. A review of the phenomenon that, as technology expands, we create systems that increase risks to ourselves and to future generations. Explores a variety of these systems such as nuclear power plants, space missions, and genetic engineering with the hope that in better understanding their risky nature we can reduce their attendant dangers.

Petroski, Henry. *To Engineer Is Human: The Role of Failure in Successful Design.* St. Martin's 1985 $16.95. Citing examples of many well-known incidents and newsworthy disasters, suggests that engineering failures have been instrumental in improving engineering designs and projects over the years. The text is enlivened by many unexpected literary references.

SANITARY ENGINEERING

A subspecialty of civil engineering, sanitary engineering concerns itself particularly with water treatment, distribution, and supply, sewage handling, water pollution prevention and control, air and water quality, and environmental factors affecting the comfort, safety, and health of the population. This is an area of increasing interest and concern to the public and one in which growing consumer activity has been observed.

Sheaffer, John R., and Leonard A. Stevens. *Future Water: An Exciting Solution to America's Resource Crisis.* Morrow 1983 $14.95. Examines the problems associated with current procedures for purifying sewage and describes their effects, such as the tainting of ground and surface water supplies. Proposes purifying these water supplies rather than "dumping" waste into existing bodies of water.

Twort, A. C., and F. M. Law. *Water Supply*. Arnold 3d ed. 1985 $54.95. "Introduces new approaches and techniques while reemphasizing the old tried and true methods and processes and continuing to deal with those aspects of supply that are of concern to the water engineer: ensuring an adequate supply and safeguarding its quality" (*Journal of the Amer. Water Works Association*).

Walski, Thomas M. *Analysis of Water Distribution Systems*. Van Nostrand 1984 $43.95. "Provides field-tested, practical advice for examining and solving problems with water distribution systems.... Well illustrated with photographs, diagrams, drawings, charts, graphs, and is suitable as a reference or textbook" (*Public Works*).

STRUCTURAL ENGINEERING

The four areas of concern in structural design as practiced by the engineer are functional requirements, structural scheme, stress analysis, and internal forces. The introduction of computerization to the field now permits structural engineers to devote more time to creative planning for aesthetics, function, and structural layout, and to entertain more complex structures than were possible before the advent of computer programs capable of handling cost estimates and construction drawings.

Cowan, Henry J. *The Master Builders: A History of Structural and Environmental Design from Ancient Egypt to the Nineteenth Century*. Krieger repr. of 1977 ed. 1985 $40.00. A thorough examination of the history of building science.

———. *Science and Building: Structural and Environmental Design in the Nineteenth and Twentieth Centuries*. Wiley 1978 o.p. A companion to the preceding book that brings the history up to the present day.

Epstein, Samuel, and Beryl Epstein. *Tunnels*. Little, Brown 1985 $14.45. Covers the history and methods of tunnel construction and discusses aqueducts, railway tunnels, subway tunnels, sewers, and tunnels for underwater use by automobiles. Fills a gap in the literature for a subject area that is only rarely written about for the layperson.

Loyrette, Henri. *Gustave Eiffel*. Rizzoli 1985 $40.00. "This is a biography of the French structural engineer. Eiffel's family background is described, as is his education and training, and his role in advancing the state of the art in ... engineering throughout his life.... [Among the works described are] the Budapest Station, the Douro Bridge ... the Garabit Viaduct ... the iron framework of the Statue of Liberty, and ... the Eiffel Tower" (*Choice*).

Plowden, David. *Bridges: The Spans of North America*. Norton 1984 $29.95 1987 pap. $19.95. "This book is not about the social or environmental consequences that attend any form of construction; it is simply about bridges—how, when, where, and by whom some of the most important ones have been built in North America, and what they look like" (Preface).

Trachtenberg, Alan. *Brooklyn Bridge Fact and Symbol*. Univ. of Chicago Pr. 1979 o.p. A well-illustrated review of the facts and symbolism associated with the Brooklyn Bridge, a major construction in one of America's leading cities, which became a vehicle for ideas and feelings associated with new conditions in an industrialized America.

TRANSPORTATION AND AUTOMOTIVE ENGINEERING

Transportation engineering, a field that concerns itself with the movement of goods and people, is a dynamic field encompassing water, rail, automotive, air, highway, and subway transport systems. The introduction of the automobile in the early part of the twentieth century revolutionized the way we live. Water transportation systems have increasingly been distinguished by emphasis on larger equipment, necessitating larger waterways. Though commercial movement has been often dominated by water transportation, intercontinental passenger travel now more often involves air transport. Developments in air travel have been significant since its introduction by the now famous Wright Brothers. The railroad industry continues to develop faster and safer methods of operating trains and moving cargo. The merger of numerous railway corporations has fostered developments in this area. Population growth and rapid urbanization have brought about the design and construction of rapid transit and subway systems in many of the world's leading metropolitan areas. Dramatic developments in the movement of people and goods have been realized over the past century and are well documented in the literature of transportation.

Allen, G. Freeman. *Railways: Past, Present and Future.* Morrow 1982 o.p. A beautifully illustrated worldwide study of the evolution of modern railways from their earliest days to the present.

Altshuler, Alan, and James Womack. *The Future of the Automobile: The Report of MIT's International Automobile Program.* MIT 1986 $9.95. This book, originally published in 1984, "is a study of the world automotive industry. An international team of 130 authors spent four years looking into . . . industrial efficiency, labor relations, international competition, organizational trends . . . as well as into technological innovations and . . . the question of the automobile's future status" (*Choice*).

Automobile Club of Italy. *World Cars.* Herald Bks. 1973–81 ea. $45.00–$95.00. "The world's latest automotive offerings with their pictures and specifications together with a review of the technical advances written by recognized authorities . . . a marvelous compilation" (*Blue Horn*).

Bishop, George, and others. *Grand Marques.* Exeter 1984 $12.95. A collection of primarily color photographs documenting the development of Rolls Royce, Ferrari, Porsche, and Mercedes automobiles. The text provides a history of each car shown.

Bobrick, Benson. *Labyrinths of Iron: A History of the Subways.* Ed. by Danielle Bobrick, Newsweek 1981 $13.95. Written for the layperson, this volume combines aspects of a sociological study and an engineering history to provide a comprehensive understanding of the development of subway transport worldwide.

Brady, Robert N. *Automotive and Small Truck Fuel Injection Systems: Gas and Diesel.* Reston 1985 text ed. $34.95. Describes most of the current fuel injection systems and discusses combustion chamber designs, fuel characteristics, and system components. Notes similarities and differences between current systems, reviews their design and operation, but excludes coverage of problem diagnosis, service, and repairs. Concludes with a chapter on turbocharging.

Gabbard, Alex. *Vintage and Historic Racing Cars.* Ed. by Dean Batchelor, HP Bks. 1986 $25.00. Provides detailed descriptions and photographs of Ferraris, Bugattis, Porsches, Jaguars, and other racing cars built during the last 60 years. Appeals to more than just car buffs.

Ingram, Arthur, and Martin Phippard. *Highway Heavy Metal: The World's Trucks at Work*. Sterling 1986 $19.95. Provides thorough documentation of the features of an international selection of trucks of all types and sizes. Contains numerous photographs, many in color, and fills the gap in the literature on this topic. Includes discussions on trends in future truck design and information on truck-line ownership.

Itzkoff, Donald M. *Off the Track: The Decline of the Intercity Passenger Train in the United States*. Greenwood 1985 $27.95. "The classic passenger trains are gone, and this book is the first to analyze their demise in clear and penetrating detail . . . although short, it gives comprehensive coverage, including an impressive list of sources" (*Choice*).

Lacey, Robert. *Ford: The Men and the Machine*. Bantam 1987 $5.95; Little, Brown 1986 $24.95. The first half of the book contains an excellent history of not only the first Henry Ford and his company, but the development of the American automobile industry as well. The second half follows the fortunes of the company as control passed to his descendants.

Lud, Ned. *Automagic: The Secret Life of Machines*. Golemacher 1985 $20.00. "A book for everyone who ever gave a motor car a personal name, coaxed a new one into reluctant life on a cold morning, or nursed an ageing one through its umpteenth nervous breakdown . . . [the reviewer] heartily endorse[s] Martin Gardner's enthusiastic review in the *Skeptical Inquirer*, where he describes *Automagic* as 'absolutely metal bending' " (*New Scientist*).

Miller, William H. *The Last Atlantic Liners*. St. Martin's 1985 $15.95. Provides full descriptions of more than half of the approximately 200 ocean liners that regularly sail or have sailed. Arranged by nationality of the liners, the text provides stories about voyages as well as many photographs. Appendixes include information on length, tonnage, and events of interest.

Philip, Cynthia Owen. *Robert Fulton: A Biography*. Watts 1985 $18.95. The "best current biography of Fulton. There are 32 high quality plates that illustrate the man, his machines, friends, and foes. American landscape, he argued, required transportation for goods, services, and defense. . . . Fulton's imagination pulsed with steam engine-like enthusiasm that he hoped would be contagious throughout his country" (*Choice*).

Potter, Stephen. *On the Right Lines: The Limits of Technological Innovation*. St. Martin's 1987 $35.00. A very readable account of what shaped the railroad's growth and subsequent decline. Examines the technical aspects of what can be done to improve railroad performance.

Reynolds, J. F. *Brakes*. Reston 1986 text ed. $32.00. Provides the basics of automotive and truck brakes, including how they are made, how they work, and how to repair them. Separate chapters are provided on brake diagnosis, electric brakes, and antiskid brakes. Also covered are principles of shop safety and equipment for servicing brakes.

Sikorsky, Robert. *Drive It Forever: Your Key to Long Automobile Life*. McGraw-Hill 1983 $12.95 pap. $6.95. Directed to the average car owner, this volume discusses the preservation, maintenance, and repair of cars to extend their life and improve gas mileage in the short run.

Small Air-Cooled Engines Service Manual. Intertec Pub. 15th ed. 1986 $14.95. Arranged alphabetically by manufacturer's name. The text describes some 500 air-cooled engines and provides instructions on how to repair each one of them. Step-by-step instructions are provided and augmented with hundreds of exploded views and photographs. An introduction on the fundamentals of air-cooled engines is also included.

CHAPTER 18

Energy

Peter Meier

> If, then, you ask me to put into one sentence the cause of that recent, rapid, and enormous change and the prognosis for the achievement of human liberty, I should reply, *It is found in the discovery and utilization of the means by which heat energy can be made to do man's work for him.*
> —ROBERT A. MILLIKAN, *Freedom*

In late 1980, the energy situation of the United States, and the Western World in general, appeared bleak. In the space of a few years, oil prices had risen from $2.00 per barrel to more than $30.00, and the member countries of the Organization of Petroleum Exporting Countries (OPEC) were amassing great wealth at our expense. Many of the economic problems of the late 1970s, such as high interest rates and high inflation, were blamed on the great increase in oil prices. Motorists had spent hours at gas stations waiting in line. Natural gas shortages in recent winters had caused widespread disruptions in the Northeast as industries and schools had to close. President Carter had addressed the nation wearing a sweater, talking of shortage and sacrifice, and Congress spent years bickering over the president's proposals. The Central Intelligence Agency (CIA) was predicting that the Soviet Union, whose own oil production was beginning to decline, would become much more aggressive in the Middle East in order to secure the region's oil resources for itself, a prediction that some believed to be borne out by the Soviet invasion of Afghanistan. Iran, one of the major oil producers in the Shah's time, was in revolutionary turmoil, and locked in a bitter struggle with the United States over the Embassy hostages. The use of the one energy resource of which the United States has almost unlimited quantities, coal, encountered great resistance from environmentalists, and a wider use of nuclear energy in the United States had been dealt an almost fatal blow by the accident at Three Mile Island. Yet, at the same time, many of the new technologies such as coal gasification and wind that seemed so promising in the immediate aftermath of the first oil embargo in 1973 and 1974 were encountering numerous problems despite billions of dollars of research sponsored by the newly created U.S. Department of Energy.

Seven years later, the situation appears to have changed dramatically. Oil prices fell as low as $9 per barrel in 1986, OPEC is in disarray, and even years of war and tanker sinkings in the Persian Gulf have had little impact on oil prices. The media speak of the "oil glut." Natural gas in the United

States is in abundant supply, and the worldwide coal supply surplus favors consumers. The Soviet Union now relies on energy exports as a major source of foreign currency, and few now believe that a Russian invasion of Iran, were it to come, would be motivated by a need for oil.

But even today all is not as rosy as it seems. Some of the developing countries that had looked to oil exports as a path to economic development, such as Nigeria, Indonesia, and Mexico, have suffered devastating blows as the oil price collapsed. The question of nuclear safety is far from resolved, as demonstrated by the accident at Chernobyl in the USSR. Indeed, nuclear plants have become so expensive to build that the economic feasibility of nuclear power, that President Eisenhower once thought would produce "electricity too cheap to meter," remains in grave doubt. As the Texas oil and gas industry collapsed, oil imports to the United States are again on the rise, and many knowledgeable observers predict a resurgence of OPEC in the 1990s as world oil demand begins to eliminate the current glut. The Middle East remains in chaos, with the forces of Islamic Fundamentalism threatening the conservative regimes in the region. And with the severe cutbacks in federal research spending in energy, the prospects for new energy technologies remain as bleak as in the 1970s.

Domestic energy policy remains in disarray. The nuclear industry says nuclear power is safe, antinuclear advocates say that the risks of nuclear power, however small, do not justify the benefits. Environmentalists continue to argue the virtues of solar energy, yet the economics are such that few companies can stay in business very long making solar equipment. The administration argues that more research is needed on acid rain before huge expenditures on pollution control at coal burning power plants are warranted, others argue that one must act immediately if irreversible damage to the environment is to be avoided. Oil consuming states continue to oppose an oil import fee, while oil producing states, and many noted energy experts, argue that an oil import fee (perhaps used to buy oil from Mexico to fill the Strategic Petroleum Reserve and at the same time help Mexican hard currency earnings) is vitally necessary to avoid the devastating impact of a future oil shock.

How does one begin to inform oneself on a topic so beset with controversy, subject to so many uncertainties, and yet so important to our lives? For almost every expert opinion there is likely to exist a contrary view, espoused by an equally eminent expert. Even "facts" are hard to establish. For example, the actual quantity of oil, coal, and nonrenewable resources still remaining is difficult to establish for three main reasons: (1) most such resources are underground, and therefore subject to the uncertainties of geology; (2) there exists an intrinsic relationship between price and availability, for example, given a high enough price, an almost infinite amount of oil could be produced from shales and tar sands (consequently every statement about resources should be [but rarely is] accompanied by their cost); and (3) even if the information were known with reasonable certainty, those who possess the data may have political, tax, or economic reasons for hiding, distorting, or falsifying published data.

GENERAL BIBLIOGRAPHY

The following general titles will provide the reader with a good overview of the major issues. Many are regarded as classics, many are controversial, but all illustrate important aspects of the problems society faces in dealing with energy questions.

Energy Transition in Developing Countries. World Bank 1983 $6.00. The two oil price shocks of the 1970s were particularly hard on developing countries, many of which had to borrow from American and European banks to finance the additional costs of oil (since the dollar surpluses that the oil exporters gained were largely entrusted to dollar denominated accounts, this process was sometimes described as "petrodollar recycling"). Thus the already widespread problems of developing country debt were made much worse. In this report the World Bank presents an excellent overview of the energy problems of developing countries, and how the international financial institutions can help.

Markun, Patricia M. *Witnesses for Oil*. Intro. by Frank N. Ikard, Amer. Petroleum 1976 o.p. The big oil companies were held to blame by large segments of the public and many liberal politicians for the sharp rise in prices following the first oil embargo of 1973, and a number of Committees of Congress held hearings on the desirability of breaking up the oil companies. "Vertical Integration," a term used to describe the characteristic organization of the big multinational oil companies that embraces all the steps from production, transport, refining, distribution, and marketing, came under particular attack. This book presents the oil industry case, presented as excerpts from testimony presented at the hearings. The perspective is as to be expected (one section is called "Divestiture and OPEC," a response to Anthony Sampson [see below]), but the book has much valuable information.

Mosley, Leonard. *Power Play: Oil in the Middle East*. Random 1973 o.p. Immensely entertaining, highly readable bestseller that tells the story of the fight by nations and oil companies to develop Middle Eastern oil resources from the early days of the Baku fields on the Caspian Sea to the early 1970s when OPEC first began to wield its power.

Pimentel, David, and Marcia Pimentel. *Food, Energy, and Society*. Halsted Pr. 1979 o.p. An excellent, nontechnical presentation of the interdependencies between food, energy, and their impacts on society. Compares the energy inputs for grain versus livestock production, and examines the role of energy in fisheries, food packaging, and food preparation.

Sampson, Anthony. *The Seven Sisters*. Bantam 1976 pap. $4.95. A bestseller by a British journalist, the "Seven Sisters" refers to the major multinational oil companies—Exxon, Mobil, Shell, BP, Texaco, Standard, and Gulf.

Wells, Malcolm, ed. *Notes from the Energy Underground*. Van Nostrand 1980 $10.95. A series of essays that challenge some of the cherished beliefs of our culture with wit and originality. Includes contributions by Isaac Asimov and Russell Baker.

THE GEOPOLITICS OF ENERGY

The basic geopolitical dilemma for the West is that a substantial part of the world's energy resources, and oil in particular, is controlled by either openly or potentially hostile countries, such as the Soviet Union, Libya, and

Iran, or by countries whose reliability and relations with the West are at best uncertain, such as Saudi Arabia, South Africa, and Poland. Japan and Western Europe import most of their energy, and the United States is again expected to increase its dependence on oil exports by the 1990s. These realities have a profound influence on the conduct of foreign policy of nations, as witnessed by the recent steps taken by the United States and its allies to secure the freedom of navigation, and the safe passage of oil to Japan and the West, in the Persian Gulf.

The struggle over the world's energy resources remains one of the key factors in our lives. History teaches us that wars are fought over resources, not ideology, and the outcome of modern wars is frequently decided by the logistics of fuel. The loss of the Romanian oil fields and the American bombing of German synthetic fuel plants in World War II brought that conflict to a quick end: Hitler's tanks and planes simply ran out of gasoline. And the brilliant German General Rommel was defeated in the North African desert not by the fighting abilities of his opponents, but because British submarines sank his tankers bringing fuel across the Mediterranean.

The works included in this section have been selected from a huge volume of recent writing. The energy resources and consumption trends in the USSR, China, and the Third World are stressed here since they are fundamental to an understanding of the dynamics of international energy politics. A separate section covers the energy policy of the United States (see below). The reader interested in the role of energy in international affairs is also directed to the periodical *Foreign Affairs*, published by the Council on Foreign Relations (New York), which has carried some of the most influential articles on energy policy.

Dienes, Leslie, and Theodore Shabad. *The Soviet Energy System: Resource Use and Policies*. Halsted Pr. 1979 $24.95. An excellent overview of the energy resources of the Soviet Union.

Hewett, Ed A. *Energy, Economics, and Foreign Policy in the Soviet Union*. Brookings 1984 text ed. $28.95 pap. $10.95. Complements the earlier Dienes and Shabad work (see above) with a more extensive discussion of the foreign policy implications of the analysis. Examines such issues as the role of western technology in developing Siberian resources, and the importance of oil exports to Soviet hard currency needs. The Soviet Union is one of the world's major producers, and a major consumer of energy, and an understanding of its problems is central to the long-term global energy outlook.

Landis, Lincoln. *Politics and Oil: Moscow in the Middle East*. Intro. by Kurt L. London, Assoc. Faculty Pr. 1973 $22.95. Whether or not one subscribes to the view that access to the warm water ports is a central objective of Soviet policy, Soviet-Arab relations are a key aspect of the Middle East turmoil. This book provides a good history of Soviet policy in the area until the early 1970s. The extensive bibliography alone merits inclusion in our list.

Mabro, Robert. *World Energy, Issues and Policies: Proceedings of the First Oxford Energy Seminar*. Oxford 1980 $44.00. A collection of papers presented at the first Oxford Energy Seminar held to debate the world energy situation. A good survey of the major problems.

Turner, Louis. *Oil Companies in the International System*. Allen & Unwin 3d ed. 1983 text ed. pap. $11.95. Similar in scope to Anthony Sampson's book (see under

General Bibliography above), but comes to a largely opposite conclusion: despite their size and notoriety, the multinational oil companies have actually been relatively unimportant as players in international politics.

Woodward, Kim. *The International Energy Relations of China*. Stanford Univ. Pr. 1980 $65.00. Despite its considerable length, strongly recommended as a starting point for any study of energy issues in China. Examines energy problems in the context of China's relationships with the USSR, Japan, and the West, and the ongoing modernization process. Also includes nearly 100 tables in a comprehensive statistical profile.

THE ENERGY POLICY OF THE UNITED STATES

The energy policy of the United States has undergone significant changes over the past 20 years. The conservation and interventionist-oriented policy of the Carter years has been replaced by a more oriented policy of the Reagan Administration, whose central assumption is that the marketplace, not the government, is the most effective mechanism for ensuring the optimal use of resources. Again, there is a huge volume of material and the selections here serve only as a starting point for further reading.

In addition to the works cited below, the reader will find the proceedings of the Congressional Hearings, published by the U.S. Government Printing Office, to be most useful in researching the federal energy policy. While these contain a great deal of "filler" material, often papers by industry or academics whose views happen to coincide with those of a committee member, and introduced into the record by that member, there is usually much of interest to the general reader.

Burrows, James C., and T. Domenich. *An Analysis of the United States Oil Import Quota*. Lexington Bks. 1970 o.p. Written before the oil embargo of 1973, it examines the oil import quota program that was in effect throughout the 1960s.

Byrne, John, and Daniel Rich, eds. *The Politics of Energy Research and Development*. Transaction Bks. 1986 $14.95. A collection of papers on how decisions are made to fund research and development in particular energy technologies and the impact of this process on the energy system.

Conant, Melvin A. *The Oil Factor in U.S. Foreign Policy: 1980–1990*. Lexington Bks. 1981. o.p. Outlines a strategy for the United States to reduce its vulnerability to disruptions in international oil markets. Stresses the importance of cooperation rather than competition with Europe and Japan.

Energy Policy Project Staff. *A Time to Choose: America's Energy Future*. Ballinger 1974 $25.00 pap. $12.95. Launched in the immediate aftermath of the first oil embargo, this well-known and widely cited study argues the need for an energy policy, and examines the choices that must be made, particularly with respect to changing the rate of growth of overall energy consumption (per unit of GNP).

Federal Energy Administration. *Project Independence Blueprint: Final Task Force Report, Solar Energy*. Solar Energy repr. of 1974 ed. $59.50. In response to the oil embargo of 1973 and 1974, and the realization that the United States would be dependent for some time on foreign sources of oil, the president established the goal of energy independence by 1980, and the Federal Energy Administration (FEA) was charged with conducting a comprehensive study of how this goal might be achieved. The goal was quickly found to be unattainable: even if domestic resources could have been mobilized to substitute for all imports in some seven years, the economic costs would have been far too high (in terms of inflation, fall in GNP, environmental factors, and so on). However, the study merits attention in that it is the first comprehensive examination of energy policy options for the United States.

Stobaugh, Robert, and Daniel Yergin, eds. *Energy Future: The Report of the Harvard Business School Energy Project*. Random House 1982 pap. $6.36. Widely publicized report of the Energy Project at the Harvard Business School. Argues the case for much greater emphasis on conservation and low-technology solar.

U.S. Department of Energy. *Report of the Alcohol Fuels Policy Review*. Solar Energy 1979 pap. $19.95. The degree to which Congress should grant tax advantages to alcohol producers, particularly to make gasahol, a blend of ethanol and gasoline, is a perennial issue in Congress; this report illustrates the arguments for and against federal subsidies for renewable energy.

ENERGY ECONOMICS

Most of the books listed here should be comprehensible to the non-economist and contain a minimum amount of mathematical analysis. The interested reader is also directed to *Energy Journal*, published by the Energy Economics Educational Foundation, Inc., which is the journal of the International Association of Energy Economists. *Energy Journal* covers almost all aspects of energy policy and economics, and has a coverage of international issues commensurate with the worldwide membership of its association.

Cuff, David J., and William J. Young. *The United States Energy Atlas*. Free Pr. 1980 $85.00. Comprehensive presentation of the energy resources of the United States, covering everything from the distribution of coal resources to geothermal energy and the location of nuclear fuel processing facilities. An exceptional reference volume.

Lind, Robert C., and others. *Discounting for Time and Risk in Energy Policy*. [*Resources for the Future Ser.*] Johns Hopkins Univ. Pr. 1982 text ed. $42.50; RFF Assocs. 1982 $42.50. The question of the discount rate to be used for investment planning is of course not unique to the energy sector, but because of the capital intensity of most energy sector projects it has special importance. This volume is a collection of technical papers on the subject presented at a conference convened by the Electric Power Research Institute. While some papers are quite mathematical, several excellent introductory chapters pose the salient issues in less technical terms.

MacAvoy, Paul W. *Energy Policy: An Economic Analysis*. Norton 1983 $17.50 pap. $4.95. An excellent objective presentation of pricing, taxation, and regulation of oil, gas, and electricity.

Merklein, Helmut A., and W. Carey Hardy. *Energy Economics*. Gulf Pub. 1977 $20.00. An easy book for the lay reader that serves as an excellent introduction to the subject.

Pindyck, Robert S., ed. *The Production and Pricing of Energy Resources*. Volume 2 in *Advances in the Economics of Energy and Resources*. Jai Pr. 1979 $42.50. The ten somewhat diverse papers in this volume provide a good starting point for researching mathematical models of energy supply, particularly oil and coal.

Tussing, Arlon R., and Connie Barlow. *The Natural Gas Industry: Evolution, Structure, and Economics*. Ballinger 1984 $32.00. Good presentation of the history of the natural gas industry in the United States and of the role of federal government regulation of the interstate pipelines.

Webb, Michael G., and Martin J. Ricketts. *The Economics of Energy.* Halsted Pr. 1981 pap. $23.50. A more advanced text than Merklein and Hardy (see above), with a particularly good discussion of energy tax policy.

COAL, OIL, AND GAS

There is little question that the development of modern industrial nations, and rapid growth in prosperity of the western nations in the first half of the twentieth century, was due to the availability of apparently limitless amounts of cheap oil. Indeed, until the oil embargo of 1973 and 1974, the finite nature of the world's oil resources attracted little attention outside the oil industry itself. This section includes titles that focus on the physical and technical issues; where and how to find oil, the transformation of crude oil to useful products (petroleum refining), and the operation of world oil markets.

For geological reasons, natural gas is usually found in the same places as oil, and most oil fields produce so-called "associated gas"; indeed, until recently, very little exploration effort was directed explicitly to natural gas fields. Moreover, for many of the oil producing countries of the Third World, finding a use for natural gas is one of the big problems since they lack the large residential and commercial markets that account for most natural gas consumption in the United States and Europe. Much natural gas in Nigeria and the Middle East is simply flared (i.e., burned off at the well site) as the pace of development of industries that can use gas (fertilizers, steel manufacture, and so forth) has lagged. Algeria and the Soviet Union have benefited from the proximity of markets in Europe that can be reached by pipeline, and Indonesia exports gas in liquefied form to Japan.

Finally, mention should be made of two leading periodicals: *The Petroleum Economist,* published in the United Kingdom (Box 105, 107 Charterhouse St., London EC1M 6AY), with good coverage of oil and gas economics and policy issues, and *The Oil and Gas Journal,* published by PennWell (Tulsa, Oklahoma), with coverage of policy issues, drilling/production, exploration, transportation, and refining.

Adelman, M. A. *The World Petroleum Market.* [*Resources for the Future Ser.*] Johns Hopkins Univ. Pr. 1973 $37.00. A classic exposition of the industry written long before the subject came to the forefront of public attention. Contains excellent analyses of the evolution of the world market since World War II.

Berger, Bill D., and Kenneth E. Anderson. *Modern Petroleum: A Basic Primer of the Industry.* Petro. Mktg. Educ. Found. 1971 $33.95. A good, nontechnical presentation of oil exploration, refining, distribution, and consumption patterns that requires no more than high school physics.

Gary, James H., and Glenn E. Handwerk. *Petroleum Refining: Technology and Economics.* Dekker 1975 o.p. For those who have mastered the material in Leffler's book (see below), and who require greater engineering detail.

Leffler, William L. *Petroleum Refining for the Nontechnical Person.* Petro. Mktg. Educ. Found. 1979 $33.95. Petroleum refining, in which crude oil is converted into such familiar products as gasoline and jet fuel, is a highly complex technology, and most books on the subject are filled with technical jargon familiar only to experts and petroleum engineers. But this book is highly recommended as a first introduction.

Megill, Robert E. *An Introduction to Exploration Economics.* PennWell Bks. 2d ed. 1979 $44.95. As mentioned in the cover notes, this book is written for those "who know little about the subject and have forgotten most of their college math." An excellent introduction to the methods used in the industry to evaluate potential oil fields.

OECD Staff. *Coal Prospects and Policies in IEA Countries: 1983 Review.* OECD 1984 pap. $22.50. Examines domestic resources, trade, and prices for each of the IEA countries (Western Europe, Japan, United States, and Canada).

Valencia, Mark J. *South East Asian Seas: Oil under Troubled Waters.* Oxford 1985 $18.95. An excellent brief history of oil resources and international relations in such disputed areas as the Gulf of Tonkin, the South China Sea, and the Gulf of Thailand.

Verleger, Phillip K., Jr. *Oil Markets in Turmoil: An Economic Analysis.* Ballinger 1982 $35.00. Analyzes the international oil market in the 1970s and makes an excellent companion to Adelman's book (see above).

Wijetilleke, Lakdasa, and Anthony J. Ody. *The World Refinery Industry: Need for Restructuring.* World Bank 1985 $20.00. A review of world petroleum supply and demand and the consequences of the worldwide refining industry. Only basic familiarity with economics and science is necessary.

Wilson, Carroll L., ed. *Coal-Bridge to the Future.* Ballinger 1980 $29.95. Report of the World Coal Study, an international project involving 16 major coal producing and consuming countries; concludes that coal will have to supply between one-half and two-thirds of the additional energy needed by the world through the year 2000. Controversial, reflecting the bias of coal proponents.

Zimmerman, Martin B. *The U.S. Coal Industry: The Economics of Policy Choice.* MIT 1981 text ed. $37.50. "This well-organized and relevant book gives an econometric view of factors that can be expected to determine the future of coal. . . . Information on the structure of the coal industry, on marketing, and on environmental trade-offs is incorporated in a conceptual model dealing with supply, demand, and regional transportation" (*Choice*).

ELECTRICITY AND NUCLEAR POWER

The problems of the nuclear industry in the United States are well known. From early expectations that atomic energy would produce "electricity too cheap to meter" has come the reality that not a single reactor has been ordered by U.S. electric utilities since 1978. Moreover, of plants that were ordered in the 1973 to 1978 period, most have since been canceled: of 28 units ordered in 1974, 27 have since been canceled by the utilities themselves, and one (the Jamesport 2 unit on Long Island) was rejected by New York State in 1980. Nevertheless, even if no more units were ever built, there is still a great concern about the safety of existing reactors, and about the problem of nuclear waste disposal. Moreover, as evidenced by the continental scale impacts of the Chernobyl accident in the USSR, what happens in other countries where the nuclear power industry has suffered less of a downturn remains of global interest. Japan, France, the USSR, and even such developing countries as Taiwan and South Korea have nuclear power programs that continue at a rapid pace. Thus, while nuclear power accounts for some 17 percent of electricity generated in the United States, in France it exceeds 60 percent.

In addition, there is the uncertainty of radioactive waste disposal, one of the most urgent energy problems at the national level. Yet, finding a site for long-term storage of wastes from commercial reactors has dragged on for decades without a successful resolution. The problems are as much political as technical.

Institute for Energy Analysis. *Economic and Environmental Impacts of a U.S. Nuclear Moratorium.* Ed. by Alvin M. Weinberg, MIT 2d ed. 1979 $35.00. With nuclear power accounting for some 15 to 20 percent of electricity generation, the economic impacts of a nuclear moratorium (having various definitions from closing all existing reactors to not allowing any new reactors) are likely to be substantial, particularly in those regions such as the Northeast, where nuclear power accounts for a much higher share of electricity.

International Atomic Energy Agency Publications Catalog. Unipub 1985 (free). Annotated catalog of the hundreds of reports on nuclear power prepared for and by this United Nations agency.

Kaku, Michio, and Jennifer Trainer, eds. *Nuclear Power, Both Sides: The Best Arguments for and against the Most Controversial Technology.* Norton 1982 $16.95 1983 pap. $8.95. Presents both sides of questions such as reactor safety, waste disposal, economics, and the future of nuclear energy, including articles by Nobel laureates in physics, Ralph Nader, and Amory Lovins. An excellent starting point for becoming familiar with the nuclear debate.

Katz, James E., and Onkar S. Marwah. *Nuclear Power in Developing Countries: An Analysis of Decision Making.* Lexington Bks. 1982 o.p. Examines the increasingly controversial subject of nuclear power commercialization in developing countries and the possible relationship to weapons proliferation. Has good reviews of the nuclear programs of some 15 countries including China, India, Pakistan, Iran, and Egypt.

Keeny, Spurgeon M., Jr. *Nuclear Power Issues and Choices.* Ballinger 1977 o.p. Report of a major and well-known study sponsored by the Ford Foundation to clarify the issues underlying the debate on nuclear power at home and abroad.

New Electric Power Technologies: Problems and Prospects for the 1990's. USGPO 1985 pap. $12.00. A comprehensive presentation of the financial problems of electric utilities, the forces that are leading them to explore new technologies, and, in some detail, the prospects for the technologies themselves. Strongly recommended as a starting point for any research on the future of the electric power industry.

Nuclear Power in an Age of Uncertainty. USGPO 1984 pap. $10.00. One of the main reasons for the many cancellations of nuclear power plants in the last ten years is the dramatic decline in electricity growth. For example, in 1974 the projected peak power demand for 1984, as estimated by the North American Reliability Council, was over 750 gigawatts: the actual demand was some 425 gigawatts! This study examines this and other uncertainties facing the nuclear power industry in the United States.

Starr, Philip, and William A. Pearman. *Three Mile Island Sourcebook: Annotations of a Disaster.* Garland 1983 $53.00. A comprehensive bibliography of all government documents, coverage by the major news media, and assessments of pro-

and antinuclear groups of the 1979 accident at Three Mile Island. An excellent start for someone wishing to research all sides of the story.

U.S. Department of Energy. *Impacts of Financial Constraints on the Electric Utility Industry.* Energy Information Administration 1981 consult publisher for information. With a number of electric utilities in extreme financial difficulties (such as the Long Island Lighting Company struggling under the burden of the Shoreham plant, or the utilities in New England struggling under the burden of Seabrook), the ability of utilities to raise capital for continued system expansion is being questioned. Here is an introduction to the subject, including nontechnical discussions of bond ratings, the role of "construction work in progress" in utility financial statements, and the dependence of investor-owned utilities on Wall Street.

RENEWABLE ENERGY TECHNOLOGIES

With conventional energy technologies based on nonrenewable fossil resources beset by strategic, environmental, and safety concerns, and, in the wake of the oil price shocks of the 1970s, and economic problems, the potential of renewable energy technologies appeared to many to be worth much more serious attention than had been the case. Critics noted that the response of governments to the energy problems of the 1970s was to throw ever larger amounts of money at conventional, fossil-based technologies, such as nuclear and coal, despite the realities that the prospects for these technologies at the level of local implementation remained poor in light of environmental and siting problems (for example, see the section on Electricity and Nuclear Power above). However, even under the most optimistic assumptions about the economics of solar energy, it has been clear to most that small-scale solar technology cannot substitute for conventional fossil energy in the foreseeable future, particularly to supply the energy needs of the world's big cities. Nevertheless, it is also clear that there are numerous applications where renewable energy provides cost-effective solutions at the local scale that should be exploited.

Probably the best source of current information on renewable energy technologies are the publications of the Solar Energy Research Institute (best known by its acronym SERI), created by the federal government in the late 1970s as the center for the nation's research and development efforts in solar energy. A useful periodical is *Alternate Sources of Energy* (107 South Central Ave., Milaca, MN 56353), which has excellent coverage of recent developments in cogeneration, minihydro, wind, and other renewable technologies.

Goodman, Louis J., and Ralph N. Love, eds. *Biomass Energy Projects: Planning and Management.* Pergamon 1981 $33.00. A collection of papers on selected biomass systems—wood to ethanol in New Zealand, the Hawaii Bagasse project, biogas projects in Fiji and the Philippines.

Keisling, Bill. *The Homeowner's Handbook of Solar Water Heating Systems.* Rodale 1983 $16.95 pap. $12.95. "Covers systems over a broad range of complexity, from the most simple to those which require professional handling. Includes tables and formulas for determining system requirements as well as plans for different types of heaters" (*LJ*)

Knight, H. Gary, and others, eds. *Ocean Thermal Energy Conversion: Legal, Political and Institutional Aspects.* Lexington Bks. 1977 o.p. This technology harnesses the temperature differences between the warm surface and the colder deep layers of the ocean to generate electricity: potentially endlessly rekindled from the sun, and without major pollution problems of thermal plants, or land-use conflicts of hydroelectric plants, it has long caught the imagination of scientists and industry innovators. Here is a good introduction to the technology and the economic, legal, and institutional problems that must be overcome for the technology to become commercial reality.

Kreider, Jan F., and Frank Kreith, eds. *Solar Energy Handbook.* McGraw-Hill 1981 $75.00. A definite compendium for the assessment and design of solar systems.

Lovins, Amory B. *Soft Energy Paths: Toward a Durable Peace.* Harper 1979 pap. $4.95. Lovins argues the case for a so-called "soft" energy strategy that emphasizes conservation and small-scale decentralized technology rather than one based on a heavy reliance on large-scale, centralized technology, especially nuclear power. Lovins is particularly concerned with the relationship between nuclear power and nuclear weapons proliferation. Dismissed by some as an amateur, Lovins nevertheless had a profound influence on the energy policy initiatives of the Carter administration.

Morris, David. *Be Your Own Power Company.* Rodale 1983 $15.95 pap. $9.95. "An understandable account of the technical and legal aspects of producing one's own electricity and selling it. Includes wind, hydroelectric, and photovoltaic generating devices, co-generation (producing both heat and electricity at once), and solar power" (*LJ*).

Ross, D. *Energy from the Waves.* Pergamon 2d rev. ed. 1981 text ed. pap. $12.00. The first book entirely devoted to wave energy, written for the lay reader.

U.S. Department of Commerce, Economic Development Administration. *Solar Heating and Cooling of Buildings: Sizing, Installation and Operation of Systems.* USGPO 1980. An excellent "how to" manual, prepared originally as a text for a training course on solar heating and cooling of residential buildings. Contains a wealth of practical information, as well as statistical and engineering data.

U.S. Department of Energy. *Estimates of U.S. Wood Energy Consumption from 1949 to 1981.* Energy Information Administration 1982 pap. $3.00. In the immediate aftermath of the oil crises, as heating oil and electricity prices increased sharply, the use of wood as a fuel in the residential and commercial sectors also increased sharply as consumers sought to minimize home heating costs. This report provides excellent statistical information on wood consumption and how to calculate the heating demand of different types of homes in different parts of the country.

White, L. P., and L. G. Plaskett. *Biomass as Fuel.* Academic Pr. 1982 $46.50. Examines the technical and economic considerations of using crop, animal, wood, and municipal wastes as energy sources and the prospects for tree farming and aquaculture and marine harvesting. Includes an excellent bibliography.

ENERGY DEMAND AND CONSERVATION

We have noted in the Electricity and Nuclear Power section (see above) how electricity growth has declined dramatically in the United States over the past decade. In the period from 1972 to 1981, industrial energy use fell by about 6 percent, while production in paper, aluminum steel, and cement increased by some 13 percent, implying that the energy intensity of these basic materials fell by over 15 percent. Similar progress has been made in transportation fuels (as evidenced by the increasing fleet average miles per gallon) and in the household sector. Yet, the United States has a long way to go: some estimates suggest that homes in Sweden have, on average, twice the insulation values of homes in northern Minnesota.

Council on Economic Priorities. *Jobs and Energy: The Employment and Economic Impacts of Nuclear Power, Conservation, and Other Energy Options.* Ed. by Wendy C. Schwartz, CEP 1979 $35.00. Uses the Shoreham Nuclear Power Plant as a case study to examine employment impacts. Argues that a conservation strategy produces a far greater number of permanent local jobs than does nuclear power.

Dick-Larkham, Richard. *Cutting Energy Costs.* Beekman 1977 $24.95. How to save energy and reduce energy costs in all types of U.S. agriculture from energy-saving ideas for berry growers to the manufacture of farm alcohol and gas.

Nivola, Pietro S. *The Politics of Energy Conservation.* Brookings 1986 $32.95 pap. $12.95. Examines the role of Washington politics, special interest groups, and public opinion in shaping congressional voting patterns that led to compromises that delayed an effective conservation response to the oil price shocks of the 1970s.

Office of Technology Assessment. *Residential Energy Conservation.* Allanheld 1980 text ed. $18.95. There are many "how-to" books on energy conservation options in the household sector, but here is a comprehensive discussion by a technically well-respected office of the government.

Reay, David A. *Industrial Energy Conservation: A Handbook for Engineers and Managers.* Pergamon 2d ed. 1979 $72.00 pap. $31.00. A more advanced book than that by Thumann (see below) that examines the conservation potential in specific industry groups that are especially energy intensive—iron and steel, aluminum, chemicals, pulp and paper, glass, food processing, and textiles.

Stein, Richard G. *Architecture and Energy.* Doubleday 1977 o.p. Buildings in which we live and work consume about 33 percent of the energy used in the United States, and building those buildings consumes another 10 percent of energy used in manufacturing. The book examines, from an architect's perspective, the importance of what has become known as "passive" solar technology—building structures in better harmony with the environment.

Thumann, Albert. *Plant Engineers' and Managers' Guide to Energy Conservation: The Role of the Energy Manager.* Van Nostrand 1982 $31.95. A comprehensive, easy-to-read guide to be used in reducing energy costs in both existing facilities and new plants. Although the audience is technical, following the exposition requires nothing more than freshman physics and math.

CHAPTER 19

Science, Technology, and Society

Judith A. Adams, Stephen H. Cutcliffe, and Christine M. Roysdon

> No matter how completely technics relies upon the objective procedures of the sciences, it does not form an independent system, like the universe: it exists as an element in human culture and it promises well or ill as the social groups that exploit it promise well or ill. The machine itself makes no demands and holds out no promises: it is the human spirit that makes demands and keeps promises.
>
> —LEWIS MUMFORD, *Technics and Civilization*

Lewis Mumford's early recognition that technology "exists as an element in human culture," presaged our contemporary understanding that at root science and technology are processes driven primarily by value judgments separate from the scientific and technical knowledge bases on which they draw. Science and technology, of course, also have societal impacts affecting, in turn, cultural and institutional values, forming a dynamic relationship of constant and complex recursive interactions. The academic study of this complex set of relationships has coalesced as the field of Science, Technology, and Society studies.

Emerging in consort with, and in many ways out of, the widespread social upheavals of the 1960s and early 1970s, the field has for the past two decades tried to raise our collective social consciousness regarding the complexity of relationships between science, technology, and society. It has done so by noting the positive and negative (both expected and unexpected) impacts of science and technology, by analyzing the modes by which scientists and engineers conduct their work, by scrutinizing the ways in which societal institutions—governmental, industrial, financial, and economic—shape the environment for and development of science and technology, and by suggesting mechanisms for better control over the scientific and technological process. The field approaches its subject matter from an interdisciplinary perspective, as well as from a variety of more specific disciplinary approaches including history, philosophy, sociology of science and technology, environmental and economic impact analyses, science and technology policy studies, and the reflection of science and technology in art and literature, to name some of the more prominent. In short, the study of science, technology, and society is a broad and multifaceted field.

The literature that embodies the research and comments on the field's issues is large and still growing, and it is found in a wide range of monographs, journals, and other materials. This chapter focuses primarily on those interdisciplinary books dealing with science and technology in the context of societal values. It leaves for other chapters ethics per se and the history of science and technology, but readers should consult those chapters, especially Chapter 20, for overlapping and related material. It does, however, include some general works in the philosophy of technology, and the sociology of science and technology. Because much of the literature pertaining to science, technology, and society is found in the periodical literature, included here are a number of anthologies that contain the best of such essays.

Finally, it should be recognized that much of the early faith in science and technology as providers of social and economic progress has waned in recent years. Questions concerning the problematic impact of science and technology on the environment, both social and ecological, and the ability of humankind to control technology have largely dominated the contemporary literature. However, to the greatest degree possible, this chapter attempts to provide a cross-section and balance of statements on specific issues and general attitudes.

GENERAL BIBLIOGRAPHY

Agassi, Joseph. *Science and Society: Selected Essays in the Sociology of Science.* Kluwer Academic 1981 $79.00. Thirty-four essays covering such concerns as scientific methodology, the nature of scientific revolutions, scientific discovery, science and culture, scientific publishing, science and religion, and science and technocracy.

———. *Technology: Philosophical and Social Aspects.* Kluwer Academic 1986 lib. bdg. $39.50 text ed. pap. $19.95. A philosophical analysis of technology in which Agassi argues for a harmonization of social and physical technology involving broad public participation through the political process. "In brief, this book is meant to be one small addition to the campaign for the intensification of the search for better tools for the democratic control of technology."

Barbour, Ian G. *Issues in Science and Religion.* Harper 1971 pap. $8.95. Scientific parallels in the methods of science and religion are elucidated. A historical investigation defends the necessity for an integrated worldview rather than the conceptualization of science and religion as separate modes of knowledge. They are instead "complementary languages."

———. *Myths, Models, and Paradigms.* Harper 1976 text ed. pap. $8.95. Symbolic models in science are considered to be meaningful in understanding religious reality. Even in science, metaphors or models need not be taken literally but should be symbolically apprehended. An acceptance that absolute claims need not be made in science can lead to an enhanced appreciation of the plurality of religious experiences.

———. *Technology, Environment and Human Values.* Praeger 1980 $17.95 pap. $16.95. An excellent survey of the relationship of values and technology as it pertains to environmental concerns. A general discussion of values is followed by chapters on environmental policies, including cost-benefit analysis and technology assessment, and on scarce resources, population, growth, and food production.

Barbour, Ian G., and others. *Energy and American Values*. Praeger 1982 $34.95 pap. $14.95. In an analysis of the attitudes that promoted acceptance of electricity, petroleum, and nuclear power as energy sources, these scholars concentrate on the accommodation of values in conflict, such as rationing and consumerism, independence and centralization, equity and efficiency.

Barnes, Barry. *About Science*. Basil Blackwell 1985 $24.95 pap. $8.95. Barnes is concerned with "science as an activity, with the way science is ordered and organized, and particularly with the relationship of science to the rest of society." He argues against a simplistic notion of "technological determinism," suggesting instead that science and technology should be understood in the social context that engenders them.

Barnes, Barry, and David Edge, eds. *Science in Context: Readings in the Sociology of Science*. MIT 1982 text ed. pap. $10.95. Readings address five themes: scientific communication, scientific knowledge, science-technology interplay, the interaction of science and society, and science as expertise. Authors selected for the anthology are scientists of yesteryear, contemporary sociologists of science, and popular writers.

Barrett, William. *The Illusion of Technique: A Search for Meaning in a Technological Civilization*. Doubleday 1978 $12.95 pap. $6.95. In an empirical challenge to rationalism, Barrett surveys modern philosophy, focusing on the thought of Wittgenstein, Heidegger, and William James. Mathematical philosophy, as seen by Wittgenstein, is considered to be useless as an explanation of scientific and technological creativity, while Heidegger is found to illuminate an understanding of technology.

Bell, Daniel. *Coming of Post-Industrial Society: A Venture in Social Forecasting*. Basic Bks. 1976 $18.95 pap. $10.95. An examination of the changes in the social framework of the United States caused by the transformation from a manufacturing culture to an information society. The preeminent position of science and technology industries both generates a technical elite that holds a central position in the political process and creates tension between populism and elitism.

Ben-David, Joseph. *The Scientist's Role in Society: A Comparative Study*. Univ. of Chicago Pr. repr. of 1971 ed. 1984 $20.00 text ed. pap. $8.95. A classic analysis of the transformation of scientist from leisured amateur (seventeenth century) to academic professor (eighteenth and nineteenth centuries) to member of an institutional or industrial team (twentieth century). Insofar as responsibility is related to social role, recognition of these historical changes is crucial. The ethical consequences of such changes are investigated in Jerome R. Ravetz, *Scientific Knowledge and Its Social Problems* (see Chapter 20 in this volume.)

Benthall, Jonathan. *The Body Electric: Patterns of Western Industrial Culture*. Thames & Hudson 1976 o.p. Drawing on the contradiction between humankind's desire to order the world through technology and the "recoil of the body," Benthall provides a "framework for understanding the interactions between Western technology and Western civilization since about 1750" (Introduction) through an analysis of art and literature.

Bereano, Philip L., ed. *Technology as a Social and Political Phenomenon*. Wiley text ed. 1976 $49.95. A collection of essays dealing with general and theoretical concepts regarding the relationship between technology and society. Seven themes organize the readings: The Nature of Technology, Technology and Social

Change, Technology and Values, On Being a Technocrat and the Alternatives, Defining the Problem, Technology: The Past and the Future, and Technological Planning: The Politics of Choice.

Beres, Louis Rene. *Apocalypse: Nuclear Catastrophe in World Politics.* Fwd. by Paul C. Warnke, Univ. of Chicago Pr. 1980 $20.00 1982 pap. $8.95. Sketches three paths to catastrophe—superpower confrontation, nuclear proliferation, terrorism—and considers strategies for averting each.

Billington, David. *The Tower and the Bridge: The New Art of Structural Engineering.* Basic Bks. 1983 $24.95; Princeton Univ. Pr. 1985 pap. $12.95. Uses examples from the historical development of structures since the late eighteenth century to support an analysis of the integral relationship between good engineering design and pleasing aesthetics, an art form Billington refers to as "structural art."

Bleier, Ruth, ed. *Feminist Approaches to Science.* [*Athene Ser.*] Pergamon 1986 $27.50 pap. $12.50. Nine essays that explore "the nature of contemporary science and [attempt] to extend our visions toward a science that is different, better, feminist, and emancipating" (Preface). Includes a bibliography highlighting recent feminist critiques of scientific theory and practice.

Bolter, J. David. *Turing's Man: Western Culture in the Computer Age.* Univ. of North Carolina Pr. 1984 $19.95 pap. $8.95. The computer is considered to be the technology that defines our age. Bolter carefully elucidates the links—metaphorical, social, scientific, and otherwise—forged by this technology with its culture. It is clear that the computer provides the sturdiest bridge between the worlds of science, history, art, and philosophy.

Borgmann, Albert. *Technology and the Character of Contemporary Life: A Philosophical Inquiry.* Univ. of Chicago Pr. 1985 lib. bdg. $25.00. Borgmann suggests that the traditional technological paradigm that blames problems not on technology but on political indecision, social injustice, or environmental constraint is inadequate. He argues instead that technology creates a "controlling pattern" dividing our lives into labor and leisure, leading, once basic needs have been satisfied, to thoughtless consumption and a lack of enduring meaning. Not a rejection of technology per se, but rather a call for more visionary goals by a thoughtful citizenry.

Boyle, Charles, Peter Wheale, and Brian Sturgess. *People, Science and Technology: A Guide to Advanced Industrial Society.* Barnes & Noble 1984 $26.50 1986 pap. $11.95. Written primarily as a text for science and engineering students. The authors are concerned with why science and technology have failed truly to liberate the human race and what can be done to achieve such a liberation. Part 1 offers historical, philosophical, sociological, political, and economic perspectives on science and technology; Part 2 includes topical chapters on food and agriculture, health and medicine, energy, war, communications, and work. The concluding section examines questions of social control of science and technology.

Braun, Ernest. *Wayward Technology.* [*Contributions in Sociology Ser.*] Greenwood 1984 lib. bdg. $29.95. Includes both historical material on the development of our technologically-based society and an analysis of the contemporary process of technological innovation. Braun argues for a sensitive technology policy and suggests technology assessment may hold out the answer to individuals who fear the uncontrollability of technology.

Bronowski, Jacob. (See his main entry in this chapter.)

Brown, Lester R. *Building a Sustainable Society.* Norton 1981 $14.95 pap. $6.95. The purpose of this Worldwatch Institute study is prescriptive, to outline the steps to a sustainable society, to describe its essential character, and to provide direction for planners. Creating such a society will require fundamental economic and social changes and will affect every aspect of human existence.

Brzezinski, Zbigniew. *Between Two Ages: America's Role in the Technetronic Era.* Greenwood repr. of 1970 ed. 1982 lib. bdg. $35.00; Penguin 1976 pap. $4.95. The coming "technetronic society" will be determined by technology, most specifically by computers and communications. A tyranny is forecast in which exploiters of the media will control an easily swayed populace. To counter such abuses, Brzezinski outlines plans for international cooperation and widespread citizen participation in the political arena.

Cowan, Ruth S. *More Work for Mother: The Ironies of Household Technology from the Open Hearth to the Microwave.* Basic Bks. 1983 text ed. $17.95 1985 pap. $8.95. While technology has alleviated the drudgery of housework, Cowan believes it has further isolated the housewife in her unspecialized and unpaid work. New chores have been added, such as transportation, and additional work must be done to achieve the new standards of domesticity made possible by household technologies.

Cutcliffe, Stephen H., Judith A. Mistichelli, and Christine M. Roysdon, eds. *Technology and Values in American Civilization: A Guide to Information Sources.* [*Amer. Information Guide Ser.*] Gale 1980 $62.00. An extensive interdisciplinary bibliography with more than 2,400 annotated entries covering both books and articles that discuss the interactions of human values and technology. Topical chapters include the history of technology, industrialization, labor and the work process, economics of technology, urbanization, sociology and psychology, education, technology policy, transportation, communications, environment, energy, appropriate technology, philosophy and ethics, literature, art, architecture, music, and futures.

Czitrom, Daniel J. *Media and the American Mind: From Morse to McLuhan.* Univ. of North Carolina Pr. 1982 $19.95 pap. $7.95. A comprehensive analysis of cultural and psychological reactions in the contemporary United States to communications media focusing specifically on the telegraph, motion pictures, and radio. Progressive, behavioral, and radical intellectual theories regarding media impact are also surveyed.

DeGregori, Thomas R. *A Theory of Technology: Continuity and Change in Human Development.* Iowa State Univ. Pr. 1985 text ed. pap. $19.50. DeGregori develops 30 principles of technology and technology transfer that form a theory of technology. His positive interpretation views technology as creative in its use of resources and supportive of humanity's range of choice. Useful bibliographies. Interesting counterpoint to Denis A. Goulet's *The Uncertain Promise.*

DeVore, Paul W. *Technology: An Introduction.* [*Technology Ser.*] Davis Mass. 1980 text ed. $18.95. A broad-based, yet concisely written, introduction to technology in its social context. The first half of the book takes a historical or "evolutionary" look at technological development, while the remainder of the volume explores the essence of technology, its problems (population, food, energy, resources, environment), and its potential future.

Dickson, David. *The New Politics of Science.* Pantheon 1984 o.p. An examination of the patterns of control over science determines that decisions are concentrated in a class of "corporate, banking, military, and university leaders," who use this control for "political as well as economic objectives." The removal of science policy from direct democratic control has been assisted by such measures as tax incentives, patent reform, and links between universities and business.

———. *The Politics of Alternative Technology.* Universe 1975 $8.00 1977 pap. $4.50.

Technological change is interpreted as a political process, thus the problems associated with technology result from social and political factors as well as the nature of technology. Alternative technologies can therefore only be developed within the framework of an alternative society.

Dubos, René. *A God Within.* Irvington 1972 text ed. $29.50; Scribner 1973 pap. $8.95. Through the recognition of the "entheos," or the spirit within a system, perhaps a balance can be created between civilization and the natural environment. Dubos considers humankind's responses to environmental crises and champions an attitude that fosters the development of the inherent qualities of a place rather than thoughtless exploitation.

———. *Reason Awake: Science for Man.* Columbia Univ. Pr. 1970 $26.00 pap. $11.00. A "despairing optimist" considers the implication of the "penetration of science into all aspects of human life" (Foreword). Dubos calls for increasing concern regarding the direction of scientific effort as well as a greater emphasis on human values instead of technological imperatives.

———. *So Human an Animal.* Scribner 1984 pap. $7.95. Explores the effects of the external world, not only natural surroundings, but also technologies, cities, and social attitudes, on a person's biological and mental being. Dubos believes that a holistic understanding of the effect of surroundings on human development provides a rational basis for confronting problems, especially consequences of technology.

Durbin, Paul T., ed. *A Guide to the Culture of Science, Technology, and Medicine.* Free Pr. 1980 $65.00 rev. ed. 1984 pap. $19.95. A major guide to the field, including descriptive essays on the history, philosophy, and sociology of science, technology, and medicine. Also includes a chapter on science and technology policy. Extensive, although unannotated, bibliographies supplement each chapter. Revised 1984 edition includes a bibliographic update of titles published since 1980.

———. *Research in Philosophy and Technology.* Jai Pr. 1979–84 vol. 7 1984 $52.50. An outstanding collection of philosophical essays inspired by the occasion of the Orwellian year of 1984 and organized around the theme of Conflicting Interpretations of Technology and Society. The collection is divided into four sections: Technology Pro and Con, Mediating the Dispute, Technology and Politics, and Concrete Issues: Feminism, the Third World, and the Computer Revolution.

Eiseley, Loren. *The Firmament of Time.* Atheneum rev. ed. 1960 pap. $5.95. The central thesis of these lectures is the changes in the human conception of nature and the effect of these changes on a person's relationship to the natural world. With a style that is poetic, Eiseley describes the steps that have led people to substitute natural science for a worldview dominated by divine creation. He moves eloquently from Newton and Galileo to Darwin and Kierkegaard.

Ellul, Jacques. (See Ellul's main entry in this chapter.)

Feibleman, James K. *Understanding Human Nature: A Popular Guide to the Effects of Technology on Man and His Behavior.* Horizon Pr. 1978 $8.95. This collection of self-contained essays on the physical and social forces acting on contemporary humankind is organized according to the complexity of the surroundings in which humankind finds itself: from the individual to the cultural to the global.

Florman, Samuel. *Blaming Technology: The Irrational Search for Scapegoats.* St. Martin's 1982 pap. $6.95. A rebuttal of antitechnological writing rejects technological determinism and dismisses the "technocratic elite" as a myth. In other essays, Florman argues that engineers are politically important, denies that small is beautiful, and attempts to explain why there are not more women becoming engineers.

———. *The Existential Pleasures of Engineering.* St. Martin's 1977 pap. $5.95. Vigorously confronting critics of technology, particularly Ellul, Dubos, Mumford, and Roszak, Florman describes the intellectual and spiritual rewards of engineering. He argues that because they have not been granted the politician's power nor the historian's hindsight, engineers cannot be held responsible for damages done by technology.

Ford, Daniel F. *Three Mile Island: Thirty Minutes to Meltdown.* Penguin 1982 pap. $5.95; Union of Concerned Scientists 1981 $4.95. A summary account, by the former Executive Director of the Union of Concerned Scientists, of the TMI nuclear disaster—its causes and how it was handled.

Ford, Daniel F., Henry Kendall, and Steven Nadis. *Beyond the Freeze: The Road to Nuclear Sanity.* Beacon Pr. 1982 pap. $6.95. Termed a "primer" on the basic issues surrounding the nuclear arms race, this volume provides a background on the key forces that have resulted in the present level of nuclear weapons, analyzes the heightened buildup of the 1980s, and presents the pros and cons of the freeze proposal.

Gendron, Bernard. *Technology and the Human Condition.* St. Martin's 1977 text ed. pap. $12.95. A critical review of three perspectives on the social role of technology—utopian, dystopian, and socialist—questioning whether technology's impact is harmful or beneficial. Gendron finds the last perspective most compelling with the potential for societal benefit pending optimum political conditions.

Gibbons, Michael, and Philip Gummett, eds. *Science, Technology and Society Today.* Longwood 1984 $16.00 pap. $7.50. Designed primarily as a text for STS courses. The essays in this anthology are divided into four groups: an examination of the origins and verification of scientific knowledge, ways in which this knowledge can be utilized, relationships between science and technology including the impact of technological change, and the control of science and technology.

Goulet, Denis. *The Uncertain Promise: Value Conflicts in Technology Transfer.* [*International Documentation Ser.*] Overseas Dev. Council 1977 $12.95 pap. $5.95. Goulet questions whether modern technology can readily be transferred from rich to poor countries because of inherent cultural and value conflicts. "Technology is portrayed as a 'two-edged sword,' simultaneously the bearer and destroyer of values" (Introduction). Latin American focus.

Gray, Mike, and Ira Rosen. *The Warning: Accident at Three Mile Island.* Norton 1982 $14.95. Contains all the facts and characters of Ford's *Three Mile Island*, but written in the almost novelistic "new journalist" form. Exciting and very readable.

Heidegger, Martin. *The Question Concerning Technology and Other Essays.* Garland 1978 lib. bdg. $24.00; Harper 1977 pap. $6.95. In intricate philosophical prose, Heidegger explores the "essence" of technology. Technology is not an instrument of people's making, but is instead a phenomenon that is centrally determining of Western history. Technology, as "enframing" or destining, precedes and is more fundamental than science because it serves as the "essence" that demands that nature be identifiable and orderable.

Hickman, Larry, ed. *Philosophy, Technology and Human Affairs.* Ibis Pr. 1985 pap. $15.95. A collection of 81 essays designed primarily as a reader for technology and human values, as well as philosophy of technology. Major topic headings include "Toward a Philosophy of Technology," "The Phenomenology of Everyday Affairs" (automobiles, television, technology and sex, clocks), "Stages of Technological History," "Technology and Embodiment," "Technology and Determinism," "Technology, Man, and Society," "Technological Aesthetics," and "Technological Ethics." Contributions are by many leading thinkers in the field.

Hirschhorn, Larry. *Beyond Mechanization: Work and Technology in a Post-Industrial Age.* MIT 1984 text ed. $17.50. Hirschhorn argues that for the workplace to move beyond mechanization people must circumnavigate three discontinuities—machine design, the relationship of worker and machine, and the relationships among people at work. This may be achieved by recognizing the flexibility of machine systems and the worker's integral participation in the process.

Horwitch, Mel. *Clipped Wings: The American SST Conflict.* MIT 1982 $35.00. Depicts the bureaucratic intrigue, technical problems, public protest, and managerial snafus that characterized the political conflict over the supersonic transport from the 1950s to the 1970s. Horwitch shows how a technical research and development project was transformed into debates about government funding of commercial interests and about environmental quality.

Ihde, Don. *Existential Technics.* State Univ. of New York Pr. 1983 $39.50 pap. $14.95. Includes a set of four essays on "technics" grouped around a theme of experiential or "existential" involvement with technology. Ihde, a phenomenologist, holds that contemporary life and, hence, our perceptions and interpretations of it are "technologically textured."

———. *Technics and Praxis.* Reidel 1979 o.p. A pioneering collection of essays analyzing technology from the philosophical perspective. Draws heavily on Heideggerian themes regarding the primacy of technology and argues that "the use of . . . any technological artifact is *non-neutral*" (from Chapter 2, *Technics and Praxis*).

Kahn, Herman, William Brown, and Leon Martel. *The Next Two Hundred Years.* Morrow 1976 pap. $7.95. Eschewing the doomsayers, these forecasters present an optimistic view of a superindustrial society of continued growth that benefits from priorities emphasizing technological advancement. Today's problems regarding population, energy sources, raw materials, food, and pollution are solvable, but boredom may be a consequence in the future.

Kasson, John F. *Civilizing the Machine: Technology and Republican Values in America 1776–1900.* Penguin 1977 pap. $6.95. The transformation of the machine from a symbol of social evil to its intellectual equation with republican virtues is skillfully analyzed. Kasson focuses on various subjects, including Emerson, the introduction of domestic manufactures, the factory town of Lowell in Massachusetts, artistic responses to the machine, and utopian novels.

Kidder, Tracy. *The Soul of a New Machine.* Avon 1982 pap. $3.95; Little, Brown 1981 $16.45. The close-knit work relations of a group of engineers are explored in this study of the development of a new super minicomputer at Data General in the late 1970s. Describes the competition, obsession, camaraderie, and peculiar managerial and technical talents involved in high-pressure, high-tech projects.

Knorr-Cetina, Karin, and Michael Mulkay, eds. *Science Observed: New Perspectives on the Social Study of Science.* Sage 1983 $27.50. Essays in this collection discuss new empirical approaches to the sociology of science that concentrate on scientific discourse and on the laboratory as the site for sociological and ethnographic study of scientific work.

Kouwenhoven, John A. *Made in America.* Octagon repr. of 1948 ed. 1975 lib. bdg. $20.50. American art is considered to be indigenous, evolving from the functional pattern of the frontier and from the prevalence of technology. The "vernacular" forms are traced in architecture, literature, railroads, bridges, jazz, painting, automobiles, and factories.

Kuhn, Thomas S. *The Structure of Scientific Revolutions.* [*Foundations of the Unity of Science Ser.*] Univ. of Chicago Pr. 2d ed. 1970 $17.50 pap. $6.95. Kuhn scrutinizes the nature of reactions of the scientific establishment to anomalies that subvert the existing tradition of scientific practice. He pays careful attention to the roles of seemingly arbitrary or accidental personal, cultural, and historical elements in scientific revolutions.

Lamont, Lansing. *Day of Trinity*. Atheneum 1985 pap. $9.95. The basic history of the Manhattan Project and the creation of the first atomic bomb. Describes the moral attitudes of the scientists and engineers involved.

Lapham, Lewis H., ed. *High Technology and Human Freedom*. [*International Symposia Ser.*] Smithsonian 1986 $19.95 pap. $9.95. Taking as its point of departure George Orwell's *1984*, this collection of essays, originally delivered at a conference "The Road After 1984," probes "major issues in the ethics and potentialities of technology." Topics include the impact of such technologies as robotics, computerization, databases, and electronic communications on education, employment, class structure, and politics.

Lawless, Edward W. *Technology and Social Shock*. Rutgers Univ. Pr. 1977 pap. $15.00. Forty-five case studies examining "episodes of public alarm over technology-social shock" (Preface). Each case study provides an abstract of the events, author's comment, and references. Final overview discusses characteristics and commonalities of the cases.

Lowrance, William W. *Of Acceptable Risk: Science and the Determination of Safety*. Kaufmann 1976 $11.95 pap. $7.95. Based on the premise that "risks to health and safety are becoming more acute in nature and degree," this volume reviews the processes through which policy decisions on safety are reached. A case study of DDT illustrates the issues introduced.

Mackenzie, Donald, and Judy Wajcman, eds. *The Social Shaping of Technology: How the Refrigerator Got Its Hum*. Taylor & Francis 1985 $53.00 pap. $21.00. The editors are particularly interested in "the *social* factors that shape technological change." Following several general essays on this theme are sections devoted to production, domestic, and military technology.

Mandelbaum, Michael. *The Nuclear Future*. Cornell Univ. Pr. 1983 $22.50 pap. $5.95. An introductory overview of the nuclear era. Mandelbaum discusses Soviet and American weapon systems and nuclear policy, and analyzes the genesis and growth of the American and European antinuclear movement, which reflects a loss of faith in nuclear deterrence as a means of preserving peace.

——. *The Nuclear Question: The United States and Nuclear Weapons, 1946–1976*. Cambridge Univ. Pr. 1979 $29.95 pap. $11.95. A history and political analysis of American nuclear weapons policy in which Mandelbaum argues that "the main lines of nuclear weapons policy were laid down between 1961 and 1963" (Introduction). He believes a nuclear weapons "regime" has emerged in which a system of international obligations and doctrines governs the role of nuclear weapons in peace, war, and diplomacy.

——. *The Nuclear Revolution: International Politics Before and After Hiroshima*. Cambridge Univ. Pr. 1981 $37.50 pap. $11.95. Complementing his study of American nuclear weapons policy (see above), Mandelbaum addresses the question of how nuclear weapons have affected international politics. He considers such topics as the comparison of nuclear versus chemical and biological weapons, the balance of power, the arms race, NATO, the nuclear presidency, and the nuclear apocalypse.

Marcuse, Herbert. *One-Dimensional Man*. Beacon Pr. 1966 pap. $6.95. An advanced industrial society dominated by technology is visualized. The totalitarian rule of a technical elite manipulates the "false consciousness" of the society so that the multidimensional human personality is reduced to a single facet. Technology serves to institute pleasant forms of social control.

Marx, Leo. *Machine in the Garden: Technology and the Pastoral Ideal in America.* Oxford 1964 pap. $9.95. The tension between the innocence of the primitive garden and the corruption of cities and the machine is explored through a study of the American literary response to technology. Many writers attempt to reconcile the competing values through a metaphor of "the middle landscape," but myths are inadequate and people are left with a dislocation of mind and emotion.

Mazur, Allan. *The Dynamics of Technical Controversy.* Comm. Pr. Inc. 1981 $11.95 text ed. pap. $8.95. Technologically based controversies "can be extremely useful for society by providing an effective means for identifying and evaluating the problems and advantages of technologies which are not always in clear view." By comparing such controversies as the antiballistic missile, fluoridation, and nuclear power, Mazur identifies a general "life cycle" for such controversies.

Meadows, Donella H., and others. *The Limits to Growth: A Report for the Club of Rome's Project on the Predicament of Mankind.* New Amer. Lib. 1972 pap. $3.95; Universe 2d ed. 1974 $10.00 pap. $5.00. From projections generated by a computer-based world model, this report concludes that the persistence of growth trends would culminate in "limits" being reached within ten years.

Meehan, Richard. *Getting Sued and Other Tales of the Engineering Life.* MIT 1981 $22.50 pap. $6.95. Meehan captures the essence and spirit of the civil engineer through a series of autobiographical anecdotes tracing his career from his MIT student days, through dam building projects in Thailand and Chile, to getting sued for his role in the building of a California high school. Revealing and good reading at the same time.

Merton, Robert K. *The Sociology of Science: Theoretical and Empirical Investigations.* Univ. of Chicago Pr. 1973 $30.00 1979 pap. $11.00. A collection of Merton's significant papers over 40 years on the social and cultural context of science, including the reward system, normative structure, processes of evaluation, and the sociology of knowledge.

Mesthene, Emanuel G. *Technological Change: Its Impact on Man and Society.* [*Studies in Technology and Society*] Harvard Univ. Pr. 1970 $10.00. An extended essay, based on experience with the Harvard Program on Technology and Society, in which Mesthene argues for an interpretation of technology as a "neutral" force that can be used for good or harm. Mesthene is generally perceived as a conservative voice speaking in favor of technology's potential for good over its potential for harm.

Mitcham, Carl, and Jim Grote, eds. *Theology and Technology: Essays in Christian Analysis and Exegesis.* Univ. Pr. of Amer. 1984 lib. bdg. $34.50 text ed. pap. $20.25. A collection of 20 essays centered on the assumption that at root questions in the philosophy of technology are theological in character. The essays explore "themes which emerge in the theological reassessment of Christian heritage from the perspective engendered by modern technological development" (Introduction). Includes an annotated bibliography of over 800 entries.

Mitcham, Carl, and Robert Mackey. *Bibliography of the Philosophy of Technology.* Univ. of Chicago Pr. 1973 o.p. The basic bibliographical starting point for studies in the philosophy of technology. Periodic updates to this central resource have appeared in selected volumes of Paul T. Durbin, *Research in Philosophy and Technology.*

——, eds. *Philosophy and Technology: Readings in the Philosophical Problems of Technology.* Free Pr. 1983 text ed. pap. $12.95. A good introductory collection of essays in the philosophy of technology divided into five sections: conceptual issues, ethical and political critiques, religious critiques, existentialist critiques, and metaphysical studies. Excellent updated bibliography focusing on English language works.

Muller, Herbert J. *The Children of Frankenstein: A Primer on Modern Technology and Human Values.* Indiana Univ. Pr. 1970 o.p. As an appreciator of the contributions of technology, Muller believes people can control the Frankenstein monster and employ it for "saner, more civilized purposes." He surveys effects of technology on science, government, business, and mass media, and reviews its consequences, such as the stifling of curiosity, artistic sensibility, and self-realization.

Mumford, Lewis. (See his main entry in this chapter.)

Nelkin, Dorothy. *Controversy: Politics of Technical Decisions.* [*Focus Eds.*] Sage 2d ed. 1984 $29.00 pap. $14.95. Motives, assumptions, and actions of public officials, citizens, and scientists are revealed in 12 original case studies of the siting of large-scale projects (nuclear power plants, airports, factories), the implementation of technologies (automobile airbags), the regulation of drugs (DES, laetrile, smallpox vaccine), and the limits of research (fetuses, recombinant DNA).

———. *Science As Intellectual Property: Who Controls Scientific Research.* [*A.A.A.S. Ser. on Issues in Science and Technology*] Free Pr. 1983 text ed. $15.95 pap. $7.95. Examines structural changes in the profession of science generated by the emergence of basic research as a commodity that is vulnerable to commercial interests, public concerns, and military controls. The impacts of restrictions on the Freedom of Information Act and of the industry support of academic research are reviewed.

Nelson, J. Robert. *Science and Our Troubled Conscience.* Fortress Pr. 1980 pap. $8.95. An attempt to suggest ways in which Christianity can offer insights into scientific and technological developments.

Norman, Colin. *The God That Limps: Science and Technology in the Eighties.* Norton 1981 $14.95 pap. $6.95. The social, economic, and political forces that shape technological innovation are explored. Many of the technologies developed in the postwar era are shown to be inappropriate in the 1980s and reforms are suggested for the resolution of global problems. Norman identifies recent trends that influence technologies.

Ogburn, William F. *On Culture and Social Change: Selected Papers.* [*History of Sociology Ser.*] Univ. of Chicago Pr. 1964 pap. $2.95. Several papers in this collection by a major sociologist include the relationship between technological and social change. Topics include technology and government, technology and standard of living, and technology as an environment.

Pacey, Arnold. *The Culture of Technology.* MIT 1985 $20.00 pap. $7.95. A general investigation of the links between technology and social, cultural, political, and scientific values. Examples selected for values exploration include nuclear weapons proliferation, automation, medicine, and Third World development.

Perrow, Charles. *Normal Accidents: Living with High-Risk Technologies.* Basic Bks. 1984 $21.95. Perrow argues that the *systems* characteristics of modern technologies are so complex that potentially catastrophic accidents must now be considered "normal." Nonetheless, better management of high-risk technologies should be possible through improved design of organizations that respond to malfunctions. Perrow also warns against the "new shamans," the current crop of elite risk-assessors.

Petroski, Henry. *To Engineer Is Human: The Role of Failure in Successful Design.* St. Martin's 1985 $16.95. Popular explanation by an engineer of why failure and risk are a necessary aspect of modern engineering practice.

Pirsig, Robert M. *Zen and the Art of Motorcycle Maintenance: An Inquiry into Values.* Bantam 1976 pap. $4.95; Morrow 10th ed. repr. of 1974 ed. 1984 $35.00. Pirsig relates an accordant relationship with technology, as revealed in the peace he achieves through methodical tuning of his motorcycle and the logical solving of mechanical problems. There is also a lengthy consideration of the relationship of quality and technology.

Polanyi, Michael. *Science, Faith and Society.* Univ. of Chicago Pr. 1964 pap. $4.95. The process of scientific intuition and the nature of authority in science are explored. Polanyi refutes the notions that scientists abandon theories when faced with conflicting evidence from new observation, and that "progress" in science affects only the interpretation of facts.

————. *The Tacit Dimension.* Peter Smith repr. 1983 $11.50. A series of lectures by a scientist-philosopher who attempts to bridge the chasm of Charles P. Snow's *Two Cultures.* Polanyi demonstrates that scientist and humanist search for knowledge in similar ways. New values or truths are bred from tacit thought, that is, inspiration from an inner center, and we cannot deny responsibility for them.

Pulos, Arthur J. *American Design Ethic: A History of Industrial Design.* MIT 1983 $50.00 1986 pap. $22.50. Surveys the interaction of U.S. industrial design and cultural patterns from the colonial period to the 1930s. Pulos is particularly strong in demonstrating the connections in material culture between economic, technological, advertising, and artistic history. The 350 illustrations are particularly well chosen.

Pytlik, Edward C., and others. *Technology, Change and Society.* Davis Mass. rev. ed. 1985 text ed. $17.95. A brief introduction to technology and societal issues based on existing secondary materials. Part I treats general topics, while Part II covers such specific subjects as population, energy, ecology, medicine, work, technology assessment, and forecasting.

Ramo, Simon. *What's Wrong with Our Technological Society—and How to Fix It.* McGraw-Hill 1983 $21.50. A lack of coincidence is seen to exist between technological advances and social progress. Ramo contends a balance must be developed among three foci: society, technology, and liberty. The implications of the role of various forces in this triangle are explored, including nuclear power, information technology, regulation, free enterprise, and national security.

Rapp, Friedrich. *Analytical Philosophy of Technology.* Kluwer Academic 1981 $34.00. "The aim of this work is to present a philosophical analysis of technology that takes into account the historical and systematic aspects of technological development, provides a thematically ordered overview of the pertinent problems and basic solutions, and at the same time, makes a contribution of its own to the relevant issues" (from Chapter 1, *Analytical Philosophy of Technology*). A good survey of developments, especially European, in the philosophical analysis of technology.

Richter, Maurice N., Jr. *Technology and Social Complexity.* State Univ. of New York 1982 $42.50 pap. $14.95. A brief sociologically based conceptualization of the complex interrelationships between technology and the way in which societies evolve. Contrasts "premodern," or traditional, and "modern" societies in order to reach an integrated understanding of the process of technological modernization.

Rosenberg, Nathan. *Inside the Black Box: Technology and Economics.* Cambridge Univ. Pr. 1983 $34.50 pap. $14.95. Rosenberg sheds light on a hitherto largely unexamined phenomenon, the black box of technology, by analyzing how individual technologies have influenced the rate of productivity, the nature of the learning process underlying technical change, the speed of technology transfer, and the effectiveness of government policies designed to influence the development of these technologies.

Rosenberg, Nathan, and Claudio Frischtak, eds. *International Technology Transfer: Concepts, Measures, and Comparisons.* Praeger 1985 $45.95. Collects nine studies analyzing the general character of technology transfer from industrially advanced to developing countries and the specific situations in key countries such as India, Korea, and Japan. Good notes, references, and index.

Rothschild, Joan, ed. *Machina Ex Dea: Feminist Perspectives on Technology.* [*Athene Ser.*] Pergamon 1983 $30.00 pap. $10.95. Twelve essays attempt to redefine women's relationship with technology. Articles document inventions by women, contributions to engineering, effects of office automation, household technology, gender differences in scientists, significance of reproductive technology, feminist utopias and dystopias, and needs for further research.

Roy, Rustum. *Experimenting with Truth: The Fusion of Religion with Technology Needed for Humanity's Survival.* [*Hibbert Lecture Ser.*] Pergamon 1981 $32.00 pap. $10.00. Contains the 1979 Hibbert lectures in which Roy attempts to show "the coupling of the worldview of the modern enterprise of science *and technology* with the worldview of the 'radical,' 'avant-garde' Christian community."

Rybczynski, Witold. *Taming the Tiger: The Struggle to Control Technology.* Penguin 1985 pap. $5.95. Rybczynski argues that "we must learn to live with the machine," for technology is an inherent part of human culture, and that when we view it as such "we shall discover that the struggle to control technology has all along been a struggle to control ourselves."

Salomon, Jean-Jacques. *Science and Politics: An Essay on the Scientific Situation in the Modern World.* Trans. by Noel Lindsay, MIT 1973 $32.50. Salomon presents a philosophical critique of science policy. The term "technonature" is coined to express the worldwide identification of scientific endeavor with political instrumentality. Salomon believes that the potentiality of science to be irrevocably joined to politics has been present in modern science from its origins. "Science tenders its services to power and becomes a partner in its decisions; power makes use of science and becomes a partner in its destiny" (Introduction).

Schumacher, E. F. *Small Is Beautiful: Economics As If People Mattered.* Harper 1976 $12.45 pap. $7.50. Conventional socialist and capitalist economics are challenged in these essays by the father of appropriate technology. Instead of "progress" accompanied by cataclysmic social change, Schumacher advocates the use of technologies that promote decentralization, preservation, compatibility with nature, self-reliance, and provide work that has creative value and is nonexploitative.

Shapley, Deborah, and Rustum Roy. *Lost at the Frontier: U.S. Science and Technology Policy Adrift.* ISI Pr. 1985 $19.95 pap. $13.95. "An experiment in science criticism" in which Shapley and Roy argue for a science policy that attaches more weight to purposive basic research, applied science, engineering, and technology in contrast to our current excessive emphasis on undirected basic research.

Sills, David L., and others, eds. *Accident at Three Mile Island: The Human Dimension*. Westview 1981 lib. bdg. $25.00 pap. $12.50. Nineteen essays by 28 authors, a semiofficial, interdisciplinary outgrowth of the President's Commission on the accident at Three Mile Island. The writers analyze public perceptions, local responses, institutional responsibilities, sociotechnical interactions, and policy implications of this key event. Good notes and annotated bibliographies on each of the topics covered.

Slack, Jennifer D. *Communication Technologies and Society: Conceptions of Causality and the Politics of Technical Intervention.* [*Communication and Information Science Ser.*] Ablex 1984 $29.50. Slack argues that traditional approaches to technological criticism and intervention—technology assessment, alternative technology, and Luddism—fail to deal adequately with causality in the complex relationship of technology and society. She proposes an alternative model of "structural causality" to analyze the invention and innovation of communications technologies.

Snow, Charles P. *Two Cultures: And a Second Look*. Cambridge Univ. Pr. repr. of 1964 ed. 1969 $24.95 pap. $6.95. Snow's classic plea for interdisciplinary education centers on the inability and unwillingness of scientists and humanists to communicate. His eloquent call for the meeting of the two cultures was the catalyst for many interdisciplinary programs in science, technology, and society.

Spiegel-Rosing, Ina, and Derek de Solla Price, eds. *Science, Technology and Society: A Cross-Disciplinary Perspective*. Sage 1977 $37.50. A significant collection of original papers on contextual values of science and technology, social studies of science and technology, and science policy studies. Useful bibliographies.

Stanley, Manfred. *The Technological Conscience: Survival and Dignity in an Age of Expertise*. Free Pr. 1978 $17.95; Univ. of Chicago Pr. 1981 pap. $9.95. "Linguistic technicism," the misuse of scientific and technological vocabularies as well as metaphor and imagery in other areas of human activity, is carefully studied. For example, Stanley details the problems created by using cybernetics as a metaphor for order.

Stilgoe, John R. *Common Landscape of America: 1580–1845*. Yale Univ. Pr. 1982 $42.00 1983 pap. $12.95. Common design, that is "understood and agreed upon by all," is Stilgoe's interest in his cultural analysis of the patterns of building in this period. Looking at landscape, planting patterns, cities and grids, turnpikes, canals, roads, farmland and farmhouses, fences, fairs, furnaces, mills and factories, churches, and even graveyards, he demonstrates that democratic tendencies to accept the generally understood predominated while unique ventures were viewed with distrust. While innovation was praised, it had to evoke respected traditions and standards. Extensive bibliography.

Teich, Albert H., ed. *Technology and Man's Future*. St. Martin's 4th ed. 1986 text ed. $17.95 pap. $13.95. A usefully updated anthology designed to stimulate student thinking about purpose and direction in technological development. Includes a wide range of perspectives from Jacques Ellul and Robert Pirsig to Emanuel Mesthene and Samuel Florman, and from Peter Drucker and William Lowrance to E. F. Schumacher and Langdon Winner.

Thompson, E. P., ed. *Star Wars: Science Fiction, Fantasy, or Serious Probability?* Pantheon 1986 pap. $5.95. Contributors assess the scientific and technical merits of the Strategic Defense Initiative, its cost and economic impact, political effects both domestic and international, and the resultant changes in the concept of nuclear deterrence.

Toffler, Alvin. *Future Shock*. Bantam 1971 pap. $4.95; Random 1970 $18.95. Toffler's thesis is that moral and technological change is accelerating beyond the adaptive skills of human beings. The result is "future shock," a peculiar amalgam of stress, mental illness, family problems, and "information overload."

———. *The Third Wave*. Bantam 1981 pap. $4.95; Morrow 1980 $14.95; Telecom Lib. 1980 $14.95. An assemblage of anecdotes, studies, and mass media clippings is presented to support Toffler's contention that society is on the brink of a new age of individuality and decentralization in entertainment, information, technology, education, and other cultural forms.

Tribe, Lawrence H., and others, eds. *When Values Conflict: Essays on Environmental Analysis, Discourse and Decision*. [*Amer. Academy of Arts and Sciences Ser.*] Ballinger 1976 text ed. $29.95. The contributors explore avenues to improve adequate legal, political, and technical decision-making methodologies in order to give greater recognition to conflicts between values. The role of values in the Tocks Island Dam controversy serves as a case study in this attempt to develop alternative assessment modes.

Turkle, Sherry. *The Second Self: Computers and the Human Spirit.* Simon & Schuster 1984 $17.95 1985 pap. $8.95. Turkle investigates the changes in modes of thinking experienced by individuals, especially children, as they are exposed to computers. Since the impact is primarily mental and personal, the computer may dissolve the traditionally strong division between physics and psychology.

Wenk, Edward, Jr. *Margins for Survival: Overcoming Political Limits in Steering Technology.* Pergamon 1979 $32.00 pap. $13.25. Identifies "pathologies of [a] short run" perspective, including, for example, the reward structures in politics and industry, pressures for rapid returns on investments, temporal provincialism, scarcity of time, pressures to reduce conflict, media pressure for the "quick fix," and bureaucratic resistance to change. Such mind-sets must be overcome if long-term political solutions to "steering" technology are to be found.

Wiener, Norbert. *The Human Use of Human Beings: Cybernetics and Society.* Avon 1967 pap. $2.95. A collection of essays using the concept of cybernetics as a takeoff point for more general discussions of communication processes in society, scientific discovery, technology and religion, and militarism.

Winner, Langdon. *Autonomous Technology: Technics-Out-of-Control As a Theme in Political Thought.* MIT 1977 pap. $9.95. In characterizing technology Winner argues that technological change is out of human control and hence the political sphere is now being shaped by the needs of technological activity.

Wolfe, Tom. *The Right Stuff.* Bantam 1984 pap. $4.50; Farrar 1983 $15.95. A "new journalism" account of the U.S. space program that contrasts the daring heroism of individual pilots who raced to break the sound barrier with the stumbling beginnings of Project Mercury and the passive role initially conceived for the astronauts. In following the astronaut selection and training process, Wolfe shows how both the public image and the roles of the astronauts were created and transformed.

Ziman, John M. *The Force of Knowledge: The Scientific Dimension of Society.* Cambridge Univ. Pr. 1976 $49.50 pap. $19.95. A course of illustrated lectures portraying science as a social activity. Topics range from an analysis of who scientists are to styles of research, financial support of science, methods of communication, and the role of science in war.

——. *An Introduction to Science Studies: The Philosophical and Social Aspects of Science and Technology.* Cambridge Univ. Pr. 1985 $22.95. A valuable summary of science, technology, and society studies relying in part on Ziman's earlier work, especially *Public Knowledge.*

——. *Public Knowledge: An Essay Concerning the Social Dimension of Science.* Cambridge Univ. Pr. 1976 $15.95. An introductory sociological analysis of science written by a leading theoretical physicist in which it is argued that science is a form of public knowledge based on "a *consensus* of rational opinion over the widest possible field." Ziman distinguishes between scientific and nonscientific disciplines, discusses the role of education and the significance of creativity, and analyzes the structure of the scientific community and its institutions.

——. *Teaching and Learning About Science and Society.* Cambridge Univ. Pr. 1980 $27.95. Ziman provides a rationale for science, technology, and society education and outlines an approach for its study. Following a critique of conventional science education, he offers a graphically depicted, theoretical model of science as a social phenomenon. A fine introduction to science, technology, and society education.

Zimmerman, Jan, ed. *The Technological Woman: Interfacing with Tomorrow.* Praeger 1983 $26.95. Thirty-one papers explore the impact of new technologies on the lives of women at home and at work. Contributors generally fear that computer technology will create further sex stereotyping, will add to the clerical burden of housewives, and will shrink job opportunities for less-skilled clerical and manual female laborers.

BRONOWSKI, JACOB. 1908–1974

A scientist and author, Bronowski was born in Poland, moved to England at the age of 12, and was educated at Cambridge University, where he earned a Ph.D. in mathematics in 1933. At Cambridge, he also edited a literary magazine and wrote verse. Until joining the government service in 1942, he served as lecturer at University College in Hull.

His participation in research during World War II was critical to his career; Bronowski pioneered developments in operations research, and was specifically concerned with how to study the effects of bombing. In 1945 he viewed the ruins of Hiroshima and Nagasaki and authored a report on the devastating effect of the atomic bomb. This "universal moment" provided the genesis for his book *Science and Human Values* (1965). After the war Bronowski joined the Ministry of Works and served in various government posts concerned with research in power resources.

In 1964 he came to the United States as Senior Fellow (1964–70), later Director (1970–74), of the Council for Biology in Human Affairs at the Salk Institute for Biological Studies, in La Jolla, California. He also taught or lectured at a number of American universities, including MIT, Columbia, and Yale.

Bronowski's writing career is clearly divided into two periods. Prior to World War II, he authored a number of mathematical papers, poetry, and literary criticism. After the war, along with occasional technical work, Bronowski's writing consisted primarily of numerous essays on scientific values, science as a humanistic enterprise, language, and creativity.

In 1973, Bronowski's acclaimed 13-part BBC television series, "The Ascent of Man," chronicled attempts to "understand and control nature" from the earliest times to the present and called for a democracy of intellect wherein "knowledge sits in the homes and heads of people with no ambition to control others, and not up in the isolated seats of power."

David R. Topper, in an issue of the journal *Leonardo*, traces five major themes developed in Bronowski's writings: (1) that the fundamental concepts of science are intelligible to lay people; (2) that science involves values and is not neutral; (3) that scientific development is open-ended; (4) that science, like art, is creative; and (5) that the uniqueness of human beings derives from imagination.

Neither naive nor utopian, Bronowski remained a consistent optimist and defender of science. In *A Sense of the Future* (1977), Bronowski states that as science becomes more preoccupied with relations and arrangement, it too becomes engaged in the search for structure that typifies modern art. He believed that "knowledge is our destiny. Self-knowledge, at last bringing together the experience of the arts and the explanations of science, waits ahead of us." Although no full-length biography of Bronowski has as yet appeared, in 1985 an issue of *Leonardo* (vol. 18, no. 4) was devoted to a retrospective; in addition to a lengthy and thorough biography and bibliography, there were essays on his life and work and excerpts from his writings.

BOOKS BY BRONOWSKI

The Common Sense of Science. 1953. Harvard Univ. Pr. 1978 pap. $4.95. Essays on science and sensibility; the scientific revolution and the machine; Isaac Newton; the eighteenth century and the idea of order; the nineteenth century and the idea of causes; the idea of chance; the common sense of science, truth, and value; science as destroyer or creator.

(and Bruce Mazlish). *The Western Intellectual Tradition: From Leonardo to Hegel.* Ayer repr. of 1960 ed. $37.00; Harper pap. $8.95. An intellectual history from the Renaissance to the nineteenth century, each chapter focusing on the outlook of a representative man or group of men.

(and others). *Technology: Man Remakes His World.* Macdonald 1964 o.p. Encyclopedic, heavily illustrated survey of technology, ranging from transportation and energy technologies to the manufacture and use of textiles, metals, ceramics, and other products and materials. Still useful despite its age.

(and Millicent E. Selsam). *Biography of an Atom.* Harper 1965 $10.89. Basic atomic theory for children. Traces the journey of a carbon atom from the origins of the earth to its incorporation into a steak dinner.

The Identity of Man. 1965. Natural History Pr. rev. ed. 1971 pap. $3.50. A series of essays first presented at the American Museum of Natural History, which discuss the nature of man as machine or as self, interpretations based on two modes of knowledge: the knowledge of the physical world and the knowledge of experience.

Science and Human Values. 1965. Harper 1972 pap. $4.95. Broad-ranging lectures exploring the relationship between science and art, touching on the origins of knowledge, perception, language, scientific discourse, and method. The final essay explores the values of science, concluding that science "has created the values of our intellectual life and, with the arts, has taught them to our civilization. Science has nothing to be ashamed of even in the ruins of Nagasaki. The shame is theirs who appeal to other values than the human imaginative values which science has evolved."

The Ascent of Man. Little, Brown 1974 $34.00 pap. $19.45. Thirteen essays derived from Bronowski's acclaimed television series about man's progressive attempts to understand and control nature, from agriculture to relativity. Personal, optimistic; heavily illustrated. Bronowski concludes: "The ascent of man is always teetering in the balance. There is always a sense of uncertainty. . . . And what is ahead for us? At last the bringing together of all that we have learned, in physics and in biology, towards an understanding of where we have come: what man is."

A Sense of the Future: Essays in Natural Philosophy. Ed. by Piero Ariotti and Rita Bronowski, MIT 1977 pap. $6.95. A collection of previously published essays spanning 20 years. Contends that science, like art, employs creativity and imagination, though it must be faithful to facts. Bronowski urges that the division between science and everyday living and thinking be set aside. Research is viewed as a form of altruism: "Every scientist looks forward; what else is research but to begin what others will finish and enjoy?"

Magic, Science and Civilization. [*Bampton Lectures*] Columbia Univ. Pr. 1978 $15.00 pap. $8.00. Notes that science and humanism have grown together since the Renaissance era; contends that the decline of magic between 1500 and 1700 stimulated the development of both.

The Origins of Knowledge and Imagination. [*Silliman Lectures Ser.*] Yale Univ. Pr. 1978 $17.50 pap. $5.95. Interprets the growth of science as a decoding of messages of the universe, drawing parallels between the linguistic skills of the poet and the scientific imagination.

The Visionary Eye: Essays in the Arts, Literature, and Science. Ed. by Piero Ariotti and Rita Bronowski, MIT 1978 $22.50 pap. $5.95. A collection of 1969 lectures devoted to the creative process. Art is distinguished from science as a way of articulating values and entering into the lives of others, as communication, not explanation.

ELLUL, JACQUES. 1912–

Jacques Ellul is arguably the most widely recognized contemporary critic of modern technological society. Born in Bordeaux, France, Ellul received a doctorate in the history of law and social science in 1936 from the University of Bordeaux where, after serving in the Resistance during World War II, he taught until his retirement in 1980. Ellul also worked for several years for the Bordeaux mayor's office. Although influenced strongly by his early reading of both the Bible and Marx, Ellul has been unable to synthesize Marxist thought with Christianity. These readings and experiences have left their mark on his own later thought and writing.

In addition to teaching and writing in his areas of specialization—Roman law, the history and sociology of institutions, Marxism, propaganda, and technique in society—Ellul has also served as a lay pastor and been active with various theological organizations including the World Council of Churches. He has also taken a role in the environmental movement and in working for the prevention of juvenile delinquency and violence. Since 1969 he has served as editor of *Foi et Vie* (*Faith and Life*). His active retirement is devoted to continued writing including an autobiography to be published after his death.

In his more than 30 books and 600 articles Ellul has provided a sociopolitical as well as a theological analysis of contemporary society. *The Technological Society* established Ellul as a social critic. Written in 1954, but not translated into English for another decade, it made a major impact on the collective consciousness of a society just coming to recognize the central role and force of technology. Here Ellul develops the notion of "technique," a concept much broader than technology per se. "Technique is the totality of methods arrived at and having absolute efficiency . . . in every field of human activity." Technology is thus all encompassing for Ellul, and his subsequent books, especially *The Political Illusion* (1965) and *Propaganda* (1962), further develop elements of this central theme.

This "trilogy" of books reflects Ellul's desire to arouse his readers to the dangers of technological determinism, hoping to help them transcend it. Because of a dialectical approach separating his sociopolitical and theological studies, Ellul has often been criticized as overly pessimistic in his sociologically based writings. However, his theological works do provide a more helpful perspective and counterpoint to his sociological work. Most notable are *The Politics of God and the Politics of Man* (1966), *The Meaning of the City* (1970), and especially *The Ethics of Freedom* (1973). Ellul's most recent sociological critique of technology, *The Technological System* (1977), is likewise countered theologically by *Hope in Time of Abandonment* (1972).

Together then these four volumes—*The Technological Society, The Political Illusion, Propaganda,* and *The Technological System*—are the main corpus of Ellul's sociopolitical critique of technical society. Among his other works touching on important subthemes, *Autopsy of Revolution* (1969) questions what kind of revolution is realistically possible.

While a deep and full understanding of Ellul requires reading major portions of his extensive scholarship, one can facilitate the process by reading *In Season, Out of Season* (1981), an extended interview with Ellul, and Darrell Fasching's excellent systematic introduction, *The Thought of Jacques Ellul.*

Historian, theologian, sociologist—Ellul is all these and much more. Whether one finds Ellul overly pessimistic or insightfully revealing, the reader interested in the societal context of contemporary technology must come to grips with the central themes of his work—"technology as a threat to human freedom and hope as the foundation of a Christian ethic of freedom" (Fasching, *The Thought of Jacques Ellul*).

BOOKS BY ELLUL

The Technological Society. 1954. Trans. by John Wilkinson, Random 1967 pap. $4.95.
A critical, largely pessimistic, sociological analysis of contemporary society, in which Ellul analyzes the central shaping and controlling role of technology, defined more broadly and all encompassingly as "technique." "Technique is not an isolated fact in society (as the term would lead us to believe) but is related to every factor in the life of modern man; it affects social facts as well as all others" (Author's Note to Reader). Ellul's central sociological work and the starting point for any serious review of this major scholar.

Propaganda: The Formation of Men's Attitudes. 1962. Trans. by Konrad Kellen and Jean Lerner, Random 1973 pap. $5.95. An analysis of the sociological character and the psychological and sociopolitical effects of propaganda. The technological society promotes propaganda and at the same time depends on its "integration" capacity to adjust people to desired patterns. "Propaganda is called upon to solve problems created by technology, to play on maladjustments, and to integrate the individual into a technological world" (Preface).

The Political Illusion. 1965. Trans. by Konrad Kellen, Knopf 1967 o.p. With the growing centralization of the technological state, political action, especially popular democratic participation and control, in response to the crisis of contemporary society is an "illusion." The greatest pitfall is the notion of "political solutions." Genuine political problems consist of contradictory facts that are not amenable to "political" solutions, only to equitable settlements. The answer is to demythologize politics, putting it in its proper place, focusing instead on productive "tensions" based on legitimate interests and concerns. The theological counterpoint is *The Politics of God and the Politics of Man.*

The Politics of God and the Politics of Man. 1966. Trans. by Geoffrey W. Bromiley, Eerdmans 1972 o.p. "The theological counterpart of *The Political Illusion*" according to Joyce Hanks and John Wilkinson, well-known scholars of Ellul and translators of some of his works.

Autopsy of Revolution. 1969. Trans. by Patricia Wolf, Knopf 1971 o.p. Ellul wonders whether we are really aware of the change, the revolution, that is necessary to transform modern technological society.

The Meaning of the City. 1970. Trans. by Dennis Pardee, Eerdmans o.p. For Ellul the city symbolizes the ultimate secular world of humankind and hence the rejection of God; however, the heavenly city of Jerusalem represents a place of communication between God and humankind. The "theological counterpoint" to *The Technological Society,* according to John Wilkinson's introduction.

The Ethics of Freedom. 1973. Trans. and ed. by Geoffrey W. Bromiley, Eerdmans 1976 o.p. Ellul notes that he "planned that *The Ethics of Freedom* would be the dialectical counterpoint to my studies of Technique."

The Technological System. 1977. Trans. by Joachim Neugroschel, Continuum 1980 $19.50. Technology is all encompassing and has become the "determining factor" in culture. We are integrated in a technological milieu and can no longer choose. "Our choices are therefore never real, they bear solely on what the technological society makes available to us." Special attention is paid to the computer.

In Season, Out of Season: An Introduction to the Thought of Jacques Ellul, Based on Interviews by Madelaine Garrigou-Lagrange. 1981. Trans. by Lani K. Niles, Peter Smith 1983 $16.00. Many of the questions in this "autobiographical" interview were originally formulated by Ellul. Excellent introduction to Ellul.

Perspectives on Our Age: Jacques Ellul Speaks on His Life and Work. Ed. by William H. Vanderburg, trans. by Joachim Neugroschel, Winston Pr. 1981 $10.95. Ellul's response to questions posed by the editor. More focused on his thought than *In Season, Out of Season,* which is somewhat more personal and theologically oriented.

BOOKS ABOUT ELLUL

Christians, Clifford G., and Jay M. Van Hook, eds. *Jacques Ellul: Interpretive Essays.* Univ. of Illinois Pr. 1981 $29.95 pap. $9.95. Includes essays on Ellul's intellectual debts to Marx, Barth, and Kierkegaard; his sociopolitical perspective; and his theological thought.

Cranmer, John. *Jacques Ellul: The Major Works.* Hexagon Pr. 1980 o.p. A brief bibliographic survey of Ellul's books translated into English as well as some of his English-language articles.

Fasching, Darrell J. *The Thought of Jacques Ellul: A Systematic Exposition.* [*Toronto Studies in Theology*] E Mellen 1982 $49.95. According to the publisher, Ellul calls this book "the best introduction that I know for understanding my work." It is.

Gill, David W. *The Word of God in the Ethics of Jacques Ellul.* Scarecrow Pr. 1984 $17.50. An overview of Ellul's work and an analysis of the place of Christ and Scripture in contemporary Protestant ethics.

Hanks, Joyce Main, and Asal Rolf. *Jacques Ellul: A Comprehensive Bibliography.* Supp. 1 to *Research in Philosophy and Technology.* JAI Pr. 1984 $47.50. An extremely comprehensive, annotated bibliography of Ellul's lifework: books, articles, interviews, reviews, dissertations, and a valuable section of works, mostly articles, about Ellul and his thought. Also includes helpful author, title, and subject indexes. Updates included in *Research in Philosophy and Technology* (1986, vol. 9).

Holloway, James Y., ed. *Introducing Jacques Ellul.* Eerdmans 1970 o.p. Originally published as a special issue of *Katallagete: Be Reconciled* in 1970, this was the first book devoted to Ellul.

MUMFORD, LEWIS. 1895–

Mumford pioneered the creation of an "organic" method of cultural analysis. The interdisciplinary nature of the American Studies movement derives from Mumford's many-faceted studies elucidating connections in American art, city development, architecture, history, literature, politics, social trends, and above all, demonstrating the prevailing influence of technology.

Witness to an extraordinary century, he accurately assesses technology "as an integral part of man's higher culture," at the same time testifying to the inadequacy of the mechanistic "idea of progress," which systematically associates technological innovation with human improvement. Instead, Mumford, with a genius for synthesizing meaningful patterns from widely separated observations, ceaselessly demands a "new humanism," a merging of imagination and creativity with the physical forms of civilization.

Lacking a formal university degree, Mumford is a novel renaissance man in this age of specialization. A desire to be a writer led him to journalism, playwriting, and studies at the City College of New York, Columbia University, and the New School of Social Research, where he was motivated by Thorstein Veblen. After brief stints in the textile industry, as a laboratory assistant, and as a radio electrician with the Navy, Mumford became associate editor of *Dial*, the most distinguished literary magazine of its era, and then in 1920, in London, served as editor of *Sociological Review*.

Strongly influenced by the Scottish botanist, sociologist, and town planner Sir Patrick Geddes, in 1923 Mumford became a charter member of the Regional Planning Association of America, an experimental group that approached city problems from a regional, ecological point of view. He also served as a consultant for the New York Housing and Planning Commission and later for the park board in Honolulu. In 1925 he edited the regional planning issue of *Survey Graphic* and began contributing architectural criticism to a number of popular journals in the 1930s. In the last four decades, Mumford has devoted his energies to teaching and writing.

In his first book, *The Story of Utopias* (1922), Mumford introduces his approach to social change, which relies on an understanding of history both to deal with the present and to plan for the future, and he begins to formulate his awareness of the dominance of the machine in the West. Mumford's assessment of our technological civilization is focused in four volumes produced between 1934 and 1970: *Technics and Civilization* (1934); *Art and Technics* (1952); *The Myth of the Machine*, vol. 1, *Technics and Human Development* (1967), and vol. 2, *The Pentagon of Power* (1970). These studies present an integrated cultural perspective on the place of technology in civilization and challenge firmly embedded assumptions regarding Western material culture.

Throughout his career, Mumford has stressed how important it is to balance the needs of the human spirit against the demands of the objective world. Despite evident pessimism over nuclear weapons and the influence of "megatechnics," Mumford continues to express confidence that the personal and objective worlds can be complementary to each other, and that the "good life," which he has defined as "to be alive, to act, to embody significance and value, to be fully human," can be more than a vision.

BOOKS BY MUMFORD

The Story of Utopias. 1922. Peter Smith 1959 $17.25. From Plato to H. G. Wells, utopias are seen to be attempts to make reality over in a more human pattern. Attention is given to the mechanical utopias of the industrial age. A final chapter surveys how science, technology, and art have escaped from the service of mankind and presents suggestions for their humanization so that they may form a foundation for "eutopia," the good place.

Sticks and Stones: A Study of American Architecture and Civilization. 1925. Dover rev. ed. 1955 pap. $3.95. A groundbreaking study in the history of American architecture, the volume places architecture within a cultural or social context. Mumford demonstrates that civilization and architecture develop together by discussing the influences, including industrialization, which shaped buildings of various periods and locales from the New England village to Monticello to pioneer settlements.

The Brown Decades: A Study of the Arts in America, 1865–1895. 1931. Dover 2d ed. 1955 pap. $3.00. The works of Eakins, Howells, Dickinson, the Roeblings, Sullivan, Wright, and others demonstrate that while art and architecture, in these 30 years, generally mirror the sooty browns and the functionalism of industrialization, the products of these creative minds gleam and enrich the prevalent sordidness.

Technics and Civilization. 1934. Harcourt 1963 pap. $8.95; Peter Smith repr. 1984 $16.75. A historical study of the machine, covering 1,000 years, presents the first extensive examination of the reciprocal nature of the relationship between technical forces and the social milieu.

Art and Technics. [*Bampton Lectures*] Columbia Univ. Pr. 1952 $22.50 1960 pap. $11.50. A series of lectures surveys the merging of art and technics into a working relationship in an attempt to readapt the machine to the human personality by integrating the autonomy and spontaneity of art.

The City in History: Its Origins, Its Transformations and Its Prospects. 1961. Harcourt 1968 $19.95 pap. $9.95. The city, from ancient agricultural village to modern megalopolis and suburbia, is viewed in regard to its form, function, and purpose within its culture. Mumford argues the necessity of organic unity between man and the urban environment. Contains an especially lengthy and helpful bibliography.

The Highway and the City. Greenwood repr. of 1963 ed. 1981 lib. bdg. $25.00. The contemporary city, its problems and goals, is considered in a collection of previously published essays. Topics include the UNESCO house, skyscrapers and traffic congestion in London, Wright and the Guggenheim Museum, the interior design of Pennsylvania station, and the automobile and highway systems.

The Myth of the Machine. 1967–70. Harcourt 2 vols. 1971–74 pap. $5.95–$7.95. Vol. 1, *Technics and Human Development;* Vol. 2, *The Pentagon of Power.* In this "revision of obsolete technological stereotypes," our present commitment to technical and scientific progress as an end in itself is questioned. By tracing the course of human development, Mumford casts doubt on theories that present man as essentially a toolmaker. The second volume deals with "megatechnics" and the misdirection of our energies that has made us incapable of experiencing satisfying lives.

The Urban Prospect. Harcourt repr. of 1968 ed. 1969 pap. $4.95. In a collection of articles from the 1950s and 1960s, Mumford finds fault with many of the urban planners of this century. Innovators such as Wright, LeCorbusier, and Doxiadis have perpetuated dispersal, suburban sprawl, and inefficient transportation systems. Also included is Mumford's statement before the Senate Committee on Government Operations, later titled "A Brief History of Urban Frustration."

Interpretations and Forecasts, 1922–1972: Studies in Literature, History, Biography,

Technics, and Contemporary Society. 1973. Harcourt 1979 pap. $5.95. The selection of 42 essays and reviews serves as a stimulating overview of Mumford's thought and style. Drawing examples from Leonardo, Kepler, philosophers, and inventors, Mumford demonstrates that new technologies become part of a complex, interdependent, totalitarian system. Mechanical devices are seen to be symptoms of man's failure to appreciate essential human values.

Architecture As a Home for Man: Essays for Architectural Record. Ed. by Jeanne M. Davern, McGraw-Hill 1975 o.p. A collection of 24 essays originally published from 1928 to 1968 evaluating architectural principles and concepts as they relate to human and moral goals. Essays range from the future of the city and urban transportation to domestic architecture and building for the aged.

Findings and Keepings: Analects for an Autobiography. Harcourt 1975 o.p. An idiosyncratic but charming collection of writings largely from Mumford's early career, the volume contains letters, articles, a short story, a play on the building of the Brooklyn Bridge, and "Prologue to Our Time, 1895–1975," which is a summary of Mumford's thought. He also discusses the process of writing *Technics and Civilization.*

My Works and Days: A Personal Chronicle, 1895–1975. Harcourt 1979 $13.95. In these selected writings spanning from 1914 to 1977, Mumford's evolving thought is evident. Biographical narratives of life, adolescence, marriage, and children join concerns about the technological society, nuclear war, and the place of art in society.

Sketches from Life: The Autobiography of Lewis Mumford—the Early Years. 1982. Beacon Pr. 1983 pap. $13.95. The events and the personalities that shaped Mumford's career and thought are chronicled, ranging from New York City itself to individuals such as members of his family, a lover, Patrick Geddes, and Frank Lloyd Wright. Although one reviewer finds here the "tone of an urban Thoreau," the volume suffers from nostalgia.

The Lewis Mumford Reader. Ed. by Donald Miller, Pantheon 1986 $22.50 pap. $12.95. The scope of Mumford's thought and contribution is achieved in this fine selection of his writings. The pieces are arranged under five primary themes: architecture, urban history, the future of the city, American culture, and technology. The editor is Mumford's official literary executor.

BOOKS ABOUT MUMFORD

Conrad, David R. *Education for Transformation: Implications in Lewis Mumford's Ecohumanism.* ETC Pubns. 1976 $14.95. Beyond a consideration of the implications of Mumford's concepts of wholeness and interrelatedness for education, Conrad examines Mumford's ideas of organic technology and architecture as well as his devotion to the creation of life-affirming urban and suburban environments.

Morley, Jane, comp. *On Lewis Mumford: An Annotated Bibliography.* [*Program for Assessing and Revitalizing the Social Sciences*] Univ. of Pennsylvania Pr. 1985 free. This introductory compendium of secondary works is a helpful guide to the major Anglo-American sources on Mumford. Most of the well-annotated entries focus on humanities and social science books and articles, including architecture and city planning published since about 1950, that analyze Mumford and his work. Included are references to doctoral dissertations on Mumford, several bibliographies, and a list of scholarly reviews of Mumford's books.

Newman, Elmer S. *Lewis Mumford: A Bibliography, 1914–1970.* Harcourt 1971 o.p. Covers publications by Mumford, including books, articles, book reviews, letters to the editor, prefaces and introductions, edited works. Newman collaborated with Mumford in the preparation of this volume.

CHAPTER 20

Ethics of Science, Technology, and Medicine

Carl Mitcham

Modern war, the bomb, and other discoveries present us with . . . a problem not of physics but of ethics.

—ALBERT EINSTEIN, *Einstein On Peace*

Not counting the insanity of a sudden, suicidal atomic holocaust, which sane fear can avoid with relative ease, it is the . . . peaceful and constructive use of worldwide technological power . . . that poses threats much harder to counter.

—HANS JONAS, *The Imperative of Responsibility*

Ethics is the study and judgment of human conduct. Such study has, at least peripherally, always entailed some discussion of science, technology, and medicine. In the *Nicomachean Ethics* of ARISTOTLE (see also Vols. 3 and 4) science and *techne* (the Greek root of our "technics" and "technology") are described as intellectual virtues, and in exploring the nature of such qualities illustrations are often drawn from the arts and medicine. The Hippocratic Oath of the same period applies general ethical principles to professional medical conduct. More than 2,000 years later, Immanuel Kant was still considering the relation of ethics to science and technique, although he sought radically to distinguish ethical from scientific knowledge and categorical or moral imperatives from technical ones.

Substantively, however, one can identify in the course of history two broad ethical attitudes toward science, technology, and medicine. From PLATO (see Vols. 3 and 4) and Aristotle to the Renaissance, science and its correlates were subject to widely accepted political and religious constraints. Science and technology were generally judged defective forms of knowledge or socially destabilizing, if not morally pernicious, activities.

Beginning in the Renaissance, however, and with gathering strength by the time of the Enlightenment, the traditional constraints were effectively removed and replaced by a new ethical commitment to the unfettered pursuit of science and technology for "the relief of man's estate" (FRANCIS BACON [see Vol. 1]). Science was put forth as the one true form of knowledge; its applications in medicine and industrial technology were argued to produce material benefits for all.

Since the mid-eighteenth century, in reaction first to modern science and then to the Industrial Revolution, there has been a series of ethical reevaluations of science, technology, and medicine. The continuing debate about the relationship of ethics to science can be associated with a series of technological developments, such as nuclear energy, environmental pollution, biomedical manipulation, and advanced information technologies. The present bibliography is designed to highlight precisely these four main areas of ethical concern as well as to provide references to literature on the ethics of science in general, professional engineering ethics, and the ethics of technology.

Many of these discussions assume knowledge of the science, technology, society relation elucidated by works surveyed in Chapter 19, and by studies in the history of science, technology, and medicine cited in Chapter 2. Indeed, some works mentioned in the present chapter are further studies by authors also listed in these other chapters.

Another rich source for insights into developing moral perceptions, especially in environmental ethics and bioethics, can be found in civil court cases. Expansion in corporate liabilities for industrial accidents, environmental legislation associated with the U.S. Natural Environment Policy Act of 1969, consumer protection legislation, and court decisions in biomedical cases, such as those of Karen Ann Quinlan, Baby Jane Doe, Baby Faye, etc., all contribute to our ethical engagement with technology. Those case studies volumes that deal with these fields are not, however, included in the present survey.

ETHICS IN SCIENCE

There are three different but related discussions concerning ethics in science. First, in light of a distinction between science and ethics that has often been expressed as one between facts and values, there are books that try to analyze or to bridge this hiatus either by arguing the "fact" that human beings have and need values, or that to promote the investigation of scientific facts is itself a "value." The latter approach is illustrated by a good deal of work in the sociology of science. Second, there are works that simply explore the professional ethics of scientific practice, for example, the moral principles and values of scientists as scientists. Third, there are books that argue that because of the social impact of modern science, scientists should adopt some form of social ethics, a subject that shades into public policy of science, technology, and medicine.

Barnes, J. A. *Who Should Know What? Social Science, Privacy and Ethics.* Cambridge Univ. Pr. 1980 $24.95 pap. $7.95. On ethical issues that arise for the professional social scientist.

Bayles, Michael D. *Professional Ethics.* Wadsworth 1981 text ed. pap. $13.00. Focuses on consulting professionals (physicians, lawyers, consulting engineers, architects) rather than on scholarly professionals (scientists, nonconsulting engineers, teachers). Notwithstanding the growing social impact of the latter, the analyses are often relevant. Good references and bibliography.

Beauchamp, Tom L., and others, eds. *Ethical Issues in Social Science Research.* Johns

Hopkins Univ. Pr. 1982 $35.00 pap. $14.95. Essays by philosophers and social scientists examining moral dilemmas, the research imperatives that lead to conflicts, and proposals for regulation.

Berg, Kare, and Knut Erik Tranoy, eds. *Research Ethics*. A. R. Liss 1983 $68.00. Although biomedical research receives the major emphasis, many of the issues—regulations protecting experimental subjects, fraud, ultimate goals, and universality of principles—have wide implications.

Born, M. *Physics in My Generation*. [*Heidelberg Science Lib*.] Springer-Verlag 2d ed. rev. 1969 pap. $12.95. Most of this book is simply about developments in nuclear physics, but Born is one of the physicists who has maintained most consistently that nuclear weapons require a new responsibility on the part of scientists, and the three concluding essays present aspects of this argument.

Bronowski, Jacob. *Science and Human Values* 1965. Harper 1972 pap. $4.95. A classic text.

Chalk, Rosemary, Sallie B. Chafer, and Mark S. Frankel. *Professional Ethics Activities of Scientific and Engineering Societies: AAAS Professional Ethics Report*. Amer. Assn. for the Advancement of Science 1980 pap. $4.00. A document including the professional ethics statements of a number of AAAS affiliate societies, reports on issues, and recommendations for future development.

Glass, Hiram B. *Progress or Catastrophe: The Nature of Biological Science and Its Impact on Human Society*. Ed. by Ruth N. Anshen, Praeger 1985 $29.95 pap. $9.95. A collection of essays. The first set analyzes the nature of biological science, culminating with a restatement of the conclusions from *Science and Ethical Values* (see below) regarding the four ethical commandments of science: "to cherish complete truthfulness; to avoid self-aggrandizement at the expense of one's fellow-scientist; to defend fearlessly the freedom of scientific inquiry and opinion; and to communicate fully one's findings through primary publication, synthesis, and instruction." A second set of essays goes on to consider the social issues raised by contemporary biology and by what biology tells us would be the consequences of nuclear war.

———. *Science and Ethical Values*. Greenwood repr. of 1965 ed. 1981 lib. bdg. $22.50. A classic argument that "ethical values . . . grow out of the biological nature of man and his evolution."

Graham, Loren R. *Between Science and Values*. Columbia Univ. Pr. 1981 $28.00 pap. $14.00. Historical study of how recent transformations in the sciences of physics and biology have had a fundamental impact on epistemological and ethical values, respectively.

Haller, Rudolf, ed. *Science and Ethics*. Humanities Pr. 1981 text ed. $32.50. Nineteen original papers from an international symposium focusing on the evaluation of rationality and methodology in the social and natural sciences, and especially on the question of whether research should ever be restricted.

Hill, A. V. *The Ethical Dilemma of Science*. Rockefeller Univ. Pr. 1960 $10.00. A collection of essays. The "ethical dilemma" of the title is that good science often seems to entail bad social consequences.

Holton, Gerald, and Robert S. Morison, eds. *Limits of Scientific Inquiry*. Norton 1979 $19.95 pap. $5.95. Should science be limited, for either ethical or other reasons? Important symposium with 15 scientists, philosophers, and historians; originally published as a special issue of *Daedalus* (1979).

Hook, Sidney, and others, eds. *The Ethics of Teaching and Scientific Research*. Prometheus Bks. 1977 $17.95. The third section of this book contains ten essays mostly by scientists on the ethical dimensions of their work.

Lakoff, Sanford A., ed. *Science and Ethical Responsibility*. Addison-Wesley 1980 text ed. pap. $31.95. Proceedings from a student Pugwash conference stressing the social responsibility of science.

Lowrance, William W. *Modern Science and Human Values.* Oxford 1985 $24.95. Sophisticated study of interactions between values (including ethics) and science-technology. Chapter 1 argues that science cannot dictate values, although it can influence them. Chapter 4 considers the professional responsibility of scientists.

Margenau, Henry. *Ethics and Science.* Krieger repr. of 1964 ed. 1979 $22.50. A physicist defends the factual achievements of ethics and argues for methodological parallels with science. "The method of science as well as that of ethics is rooted deep in human nature.... If science progressively reveals one part of human nature, ethics progressively reveals another."

Nelkin, Dorothy. *The University and Military Research: Moral Politics at MIT.* Braziller $7.95 pap. $1.95. A study of the 1970 MIT decision to divest itself of the Instrumentation Laboratory, known for its military-related research.

Passmore, John. *Science and Its Critics.* [*Mason Welch Gross Lecture Ser.*] Rutgers Univ. Pr. 1978 $15.00. In response to the antiscience movement of the 1970s, this book defends science as an intellectual pursuit that "does not destroy uniqueness ... is not hostile to the imagination ... does not falsify by being abstract; [and] is as objective as the human condition permits."

Ravetz, Jerome R. *Scientific Knowledge and Its Social Problems.* Oxford 1971 $42.00 pap. $9.95. Distinguishes between the amateur (seventeenth century), academic (nineteenth century), and industrial (twentieth century) forms of science, each with its own appropriate ethics. Part 4 sketches an ethics for the new industrialized form.

Reagan, Charles E. *Ethics of Scientific Researchers.* C. C. Thomas 2d ed. 1971 o.p. General analysis of the scientific pursuit of knowledge as one intrinsic good among others, followed by a series of case studies. Includes a good bibliography.

Rescher, Nicholas. *The Limits of Science.* Univ. of California Pr. 1984 $32.95. On the internal (cognitive) and external (economic) constraints on science.

Singer, Peter. *The Expanding Circle: Ethics and Sociobiology.* Farrar 1981 $10.95. Though this is a defense of the sociobiological theory that all social ethics have a biological basis, it also considers most of the arguments leveled against this view.

Sperry, Roger W. *Science and Moral Priority: The Merging of Mind, Brain, and Values.* Intro. by Ruth N. Anshen [*Convergence Ser.*] Columbia Univ. Pr. 1982 $17.00; Praeger 1984 pap. $9.95. Argues for an ethics based on the knowledge provided by the modern scientific understanding of the brain and the brain-mind relationship.

Stent, Gunther S., ed. *Morality as a Biological Phenomenon: The Presuppositions of Sociobiological Research.* Univ. of California Pr. 1980 $25.50 pap. $5.95. Proceedings from a critical symposium on Edward O. Wilson's *Sociobiology: The New Synthesis* (Harvard Univ. Pr., 1975), and on the idea that morality has an evolutionary basis in biology.

Thackray, Arnold, and Everett Mendelsohn, eds. *Science and Values: Patterns of Tradition and Change.* Humanities Pr. 1974 text ed. $11.50. Eight historical essays on science as a "cultural phenomenon" influenced by different sets of social values.

Weingartner, Paul, and Gerhard Zecha, eds. *Induction, Physics, and Ethics: Proceedings of the 1968 Salzburg Colloquium in the Philosophy of Science.* [*Synthese Lib.*] Humanities Pr. 1970 text ed. $21.50. Section three contains six papers and a discussion on "Science and Ethics: The Moral Responsibility of the Scientist."

NUCLEAR ETHICS

For both scientists and the general public, the practical application of theoretical physics to the harnessing of nuclear energy for weapons and power generation has been the single greatest stimulus to a reassessment of the Enlightenment faith in modern science. The resulting debate has gone through two major stages.

First, the original concern voiced by nuclear scientists and engineers in the late 1940s and early 1950s gave birth to the *Bulletin of the Atomic Scientists* and the Pugwash movement. The *Bulletin,* which for a time changed its name to *Science and Human Affairs,* remains a necessary reference source; for two valuable collections of articles from it, see listings below for Grodzins and Rabinowitch, and Ackland and McGuire. For the Pugwash movement, which takes its name from Pugwash, Nova Scotia, where the originating conference took place in 1957, see the book by Joseph Rotblat (also below). In the late 1950s and early 1960s these movements contributed to a public protest against nuclear weapons that led eventually to the limited nuclear test ban treaty of 1963.

Second, the late 1970s witnessed the development, in association with the environmental movement, of extensive concern about nuclear power and a renewed protest against nuclear weapons. The nuclear energy issue was dramatized by the partial meltdown at Three Mile Island in the United States in 1979 and the even more serious disaster at Chernobyl in the U.S.S.R. in 1986. The nuclear weapons issue was given impetus by the breakdown of détente, by President Reagan's Strategic Defense Initiative (announced in March 1983), and by a pastoral letter of the U.S. Conference of Catholic Bishops critical of nuclear weapons (May 1983).

The fundamental ethical issues concern whether or not nuclear weapons have altered the human condition, the moral status of deterrence theory and of the use of nuclear weapons, and the question of properly apportioning responsibility and risk with respect to both nuclear weapons and nuclear power.

Ackland, Len, and Steven McGuire, eds. *Assessing the Nuclear Age.* Univ. of Chicago Pr. 1986 $29.00 pap. $12.95. An important later collection of articles from the *Bulletin of the Atomic Scientists.* See also the listing for Grodzins and Rabinowitch (below).

Allison, Graham T., and others, eds. *Hawks, Doves, and Owls: An Agenda for Avoiding Nuclear War.* Norton 1985 $14.95 1986 pap. $6.95. Nine studies on how best to achieve the objective of assuring that U.S. nuclear weapons policy serves to defend and preserve U.S. values and institutions by avoiding nuclear war. Grew out of the Harvard Nuclear Study Group.

Anzovin, Steven, ed. *The Star Wars Debate.* [*Reference Shelf Ser.*] Wilson 1986 pap. $9.50. A collection of recent substantive journal articles. Includes two presidential documents.

Blake, Nigel, and Kay Pole, eds. *Dangers of Deterrence: Philosophers on Nuclear Strategy.* Methuen 1984 pap. $9.95. (See entry below.)

——. *Objections to Nuclear Defence: Philosophers on Deterrence.* Methuen 1984 pap. $11.95. Both *Dangers of Deterrence* (above) and *Objections to Nuclear Defence* take, as their titles indicate, a decidedly skeptical view of deterrence theory. *Dangers* contains seven papers on political and strategic questions. *Objections* has nine essays on moral issues. All authors represent the Anglo-American analytic philosophical tradition.

Bracken, Paul. *The Command and Control of Nuclear Forces.* Yale Univ. Pr. 1983 $27.50 1985 pap. $8.95. The proper management of nuclear weapons presents as many ethical issues as it does military ones.

Castelli, Jim. *The Bishops and the Bomb: Waging Peace in a Nuclear Age.* Doubleday 1983 pap. $7.95. An approving account of the writing of the U.S. Catholic bishops' pastoral letter "The Challenge of Peace: God's Promise and Our Response." Some analysis of the issues. An appendix reprints the pastoral letter itself.

Cohen, Avner, and Steven Lee, eds. *Nuclear Weapons and the Future of Humanity: The Fundamental Questions.* [*Philosophy and Society Ser.*] Rowman & Allanheld 1986 $39.50 pap. $16.95. Twenty-four original essays on the history and dimensions of the nuclear arms race, living with nuclear threats, the paradoxes of nuclear strategy, morality and deterrence, and future prospects. The "fundamental questions" of the subtitle—e.g., Do nuclear weapons alter the human condition? Is deterrence theory morally justified?—underlie all specific questions about MX deployment, the nuclear freeze, Strategic Defense Initiative, and so on. One of the two primary collections on nuclear weapons.

Davidson, Donald L. *Nuclear Weapons and the American Churches: Ethical Positions on Modern Warfare.* Westview Pr. 1983 $21.50. A description of the positions on nuclear weapons and policies held by the major American religious denominations.

Dwyer, Judith A., ed. *The Catholic Bishops and Nuclear War: A Critique and Analysis of the Pastoral, the Challenge of Peace.* Intro. by Cardinal Joseph Bernardin, Georgetown Univ. Pr. 1984 pap. $6.50. Five critical essays on the U.S. Catholic bishops' pastoral letter.

Dyson, Freeman. *Weapons and Hope.* Harper 1984 $17.45 1985 pap. $6.95. A mathematician and physicist holds out the hope of realizing a peaceful resolution of the nuclear dilemma.

Dyson, Freeman, Raymond Aron, and Joan Robinson. *Values at War: Selected Tanner Lectures on the Nuclear Crisis.* Univ. of Utah Pr. 1983 pap. $5.95. Three lectures by Dyson expand on the theme that cultural patterns endure longer than weapons technologies and political arrangements. Aron finds the work of peace research institutes wanting. Robinson discusses such obstructions to peace as international economic complicity, nationalistic aspiration, and the lack of political morality.

Ehrlich, Paul R., and others. *The Cold and the Dark: The World after Nuclear War.* Fwd. by Lewis Thomas, Norton 1984 $12.95 1985 pap. $7.95. Readable presentation of the "nuclear winter" thesis that nuclear war would have long-term biological and climatic consequences. Principal papers are by Ehrlich and Sagan; also included are the text of an exchange between Soviet and American scientists, and technical papers supporting the major conclusions.

English, Raymond, ed. *Ethics and Nuclear Arms: European and American Perspectives.* Ethics and Public Policies Center 1985 pap. $7.00. Nine of the ten authors support American policies and criticize the German Greens, British unilateralists, U.S. Catholic bishops, and the World Council of Churches.

Faulkner, Peter T., ed. *Silent Bomb: A Guide to the Nuclear Energy Controversy.* Random 1977 $12.50. An adversarial collection of 23 articles criticizing nuclear energy. Appendixes include testimonies before the U.S. Atomic Energy Commission, bibliography, glossary, and list of organizations and periodicals.

Fisher, David. *Morality and the Bomb: An Ethical Assessment of Nuclear Deterrence.* St. Martin's 1985 $25.00. An analysis of NATO deterrence policy concluding that it is morally justifiable, while arguing for the simultaneous pursuit of the utopian ideal of complete disarmament.

Fox, Michael, and Leo Groarke, eds. *Nuclear War: Philosophical Perspectives.* Peter Lang 1985 text ed. $23.00. Twelve papers and 14 commentaries, followed by an unannotated but helpful bibliography. The second of the two primary collections on nuclear weapons (see also Cohen and Lee, *Nuclear Weapons and the Future of Humanity* [above]). The editors are Canadians, and over half the contributors are not U.S. citizens, which gives a special tone to the volume.

Goodwin, Geoffrey. *Ethics and Nuclear Deterrence.* St. Martin's 1982 $22.50. Eight essays commissioned by the Council on Christian Approaches to Defence and Disarmament of the British Council of Churches.

Grinspoon, Lester, ed. *The Long Darkness: Psychological and Moral Perspectives on Nuclear Winter.* Yale Univ. Pr. 1986 text ed. $25.00 pap. $7.95. Eight essays, not all equally related to the theme. Carl Sagan summarizes the nuclear winter hypothesis. J. Bryan Hehir outlines the reasoning behind the U.S. Catholic bishops' criticism of nuclear weapons. Psychologists Robert Jay Lifton, John E. Mack, and Jerome D. Frank make the case for nuclear weapons as a psychological phenomenon.

Grodzins, Morton, and Eugene Rabinowitch, eds. *The Atomic Age: Forty-Five Scientists and Scholars Speak.* Simon & Schuster 1965 o.p. The first collection of articles from the *Bulletin of the Atomic Scientists* and the best source for the views of scientists during the early nuclear period. See also the listing for Ackland and McGuire (above).

Hardin, Russell, and others, eds. *Nuclear Deterrence: Ethics and Strategy.* Univ. of Chicago Pr. 1985 $25.00 pap. $10.95. Twenty articles, drawn from three different issues of the journal *Ethics.*

Hollenbach, David. *Nuclear Ethics: A Christian Moral Argument.* Paulist Pr. 1983 pap. $3.95. Part 1 reconsiders "just war" theory, Part 2 nuclear weapons policy from the point of view of theological ethics.

Jaspers, Karl. *The Atom Bomb and the Future of Man.* Trans. by E. B. Ashton, Univ. of Chicago Pr. 1984 pap. $10.95. Originally published in German in 1958 (first trans. as *The Future of Mankind,* 1961), this was the first sustained philosophical attempt to argue that nuclear weapons alter the human condition, and thus, as Einstein said, require us to develop a "new way of thinking."

Kahn, Herman. *On Thermonuclear War.* Greenwood repr. of 1961 ed. 1978 lib. bdg. $60.50. Dated but classic systems analysis of the military options in nuclear war.

Kaku, Michio, and Jennifer Trainer, eds. *Nuclear Power, Both Sides: The Best Arguments for and against the Most Controversial Technology.* Norton 1982 $16.95 1983 pap. $6.95. Twenty original essays on the history of nuclear power, radiation dangers, reactor safety, nuclear waste disposal, economics, alternative reactor technologies, and future prospects. The single best collection on nuclear power.

Kenny, Anthony. *The Logic of Deterrence.* Univ. of Chicago Pr. 1985 lib. bdg. $20.00 pap. $6.95. Analyzes the ethics of nuclear war and critiques deterrence theory and practice.

Lackey, Douglas P. *Moral Principles and Nuclear Weapons.* [*Philosophy and Society Ser.*] Rowman & Allanheld 1984 $32.50 1986 pap. $11.95. A comprehensive moral critique of nuclear weapons policies from a utilitarian perspective.

Lawler, Philip F. *The Ultimate Weapon.* Regnery 1984 pap. $8.95. A traditionalist response to the U.S. Catholic bishops' pastoral letter on nuclear weapons. The "ultimate weapon" is not bombs but prayer.

Lefever, Ernest W., and E. Stephen Hunt, eds. *The Apocalyptic Premise: Nuclear Arms Debated.* Ethics & Public Policy Center 1982 $22.00 pap. $14.00. Outlines alternative positions.

MacLean, Douglas, ed. *The Security Gamble: Deterrence Dilemmas in the Nuclear Age.* [*Maryland Studies in Public Philosophy*] Rowman & Allanheld 1984 $29.95 pap. $14.95. Part 1 details U.S. nuclear deterrence policies; Part 2 contains eight essays considering the moral justification of these policies.

Nelkin, Dorothy. *Nuclear Power and Its Critics: The Cayuga Lake Controversy.* Braziller $6.50 pap. $1.75. A sociologist's study highlighting moral issues in the context of a specific debate.

Nelkin, Dorothy, and Michael Pollak. *The Atom Besieged: Extraparliamentary Dissent in France and Germany.* MIT 1981 $30.00 pap. $17.50. A comparative study of the antinuclear power movements in France and West Germany. Argues that such movements are part of a general socioethical critique of modern technology.

Novak, Michael. *Moral Clarity in the Nuclear Age.* Fwd. by Billy Graham, Nelson 1983 o.p. A critique of the U.S. Catholic bishops' pastoral letter and a defense of deterrence.

Nye, Joseph S., Jr. *Nuclear Ethics.* Free Pr. 1986 $14.95. Seeks to define a middle position between the extremes of nuclear advocacy and abolition, with an appeal to both consequences and intentions. Concludes with five ethical maxims to guide nuclear policymaking. By an ethicist and former Deputy Undersecretary of State. Good notes and partially annotated bibliography.

Paul, Ellen Frankel, and others, eds. *Nuclear Rights, Nuclear Wrongs.* Basil Blackwell 1986 text ed. $24.95. On the fundamental ethical principles that should inform defense policies, on obligations between nations, and on the dilemmas created by advanced weapons technology and strategic theory.

Ramsey, Paul. *The Just War: Force and Political Responsibility.* Univ. Pr. of Amer. repr. of 1968 ed. 1983 lib. bdg. $36.25 text ed. pap. $17.75. Important argument by a conservative Protestant theologian from an early stage of the nuclear weapons debate.

———. *War and the Christian Conscience: How Shall Modern War Be Conducted Justly?* Duke Univ. Pr. 1985 pap. $9.95. Unlike many theologians, Ramsey believes it might be possible under certain conditions to have a just nuclear war.

Roberts, L. E. J. *Nuclear Power and Public Responsibility.* Cambridge Univ. Pr. 1984 $24.95. The nuclear power industry has responsibilities during normal operation to protect human beings against toxic emissions, against accidents, and against environmental pollution. In fact, it is failing its responsibility in all three areas. By the director of the Atomic Energy Research Establishment at Harwell, England.

Rotblat, Joseph. *Scientists in Quest for Peace: A History of the Pugwash Conferences.* MIT 1972 o.p. The best treatment of the subject.

Russell, Bertrand. *Common Sense and Nuclear Warfare.* AMS Pr. repr. of 1959 ed. 1985 $18.00. A standard work from the initial public debate about nuclear weapons by a Nobel Prize-winning mathematician and philosopher turned propagandist.

Schell, Jonathan. *The Abolition.* Avon 1986 pap. $3.95; Knopf 1984 $11.95. Vigorous argument for the abolition of nuclear weapons.

———. *The Fate of the Earth.* Avon 1982 pap. $3.95; Knopf 1982 $11.95. Graphic, popular presentation of the consequences of a full-scale nuclear war.

Shrader-Frechette, Kristin S. *Nuclear Power and Public Policy: The Social and Ethical*

Problems of Fission Technology. [Pallas Paperbacks Ser.] Kluwer Academic 1980 lib. bdg. $20.00 2d ed. 1983 text ed. pap. $10.50. Best monograph on ethical issues related to nuclear power. Considers reactor radiation emission standards and core meltdown dangers in relation to due process, nuclear waste disposal policy as exemplifying the argument from ignorance, the problem of externalities in nuclear economics, and nuclear safety and the naturalistic fallacy.

Sider, Ronald J., and Richard K. Taylor. *Nuclear Holocaust and Christian Hope: A Book for Christian Peacemakers.* Paulist Pr. 1983 pap. $6.95. An action-oriented biblical analysis critical of nuclear weapons. Appendixes contain a bibliography and lists of peace organizations, audiovisual materials, and study guides.

Sterba, James, ed. *The Ethics of War and Nuclear Deterrence.* Wadsworth 1985 pap. $11.00. Nineteen reprinted articles covering "just war" theories, the history of deterrence, and conflicting positions on nuclear strategy. Identifies the basic ethical questions of whether nuclear weapons can ever be legitimately used, and whether threatening use is justified only if use itself is justified.

Teller, Edward. *Better a Shield Than a Sword: Perspectives on Defense and Technology.* Free Pr. 1987 $19.95. Strong statement of views on nuclear technology, science and the military, and nuclear ethics.

Weinberg, Alvin, and others, eds. *The Nuclear Connection: A Reassessment of Nuclear Power and Nuclear Proliferation.* Pref. by Peter Auer, Paragon 1985 $27.95 pap. $19.95. Six essays, each with commentary, on the specific problems of nuclear proliferation.

Woolsey, R. James, and Michael Quinlan, eds. *Nuclear Arms: Ethics, Strategy, Politics.* ICS Pr. 1984 $22.95 pap. $8.95. Fifteen original studies, with three devoted explicitly to ethics: Charles Krauthammer's "On Nuclear Morality," Patrick Glynn's "The Moral Case for the Arms Buildup," and Michael Quinlan's "Thinking Deterrence Through."

ENVIRONMENTAL ETHICS

In contrast to the ethical discussion of nuclear weapons, which has often been promoted by and identified with Christian institutions, environmental ethics was at its inception in the late 1960s associated with an intense criticism of Christianity. In "The Historical Roots of Our Ecologic Crisis" (*Science*, 1967), an article that became the rallying cry of the early environmental movement, medieval historian Lynn White, Jr., charged that the Judeo-Christian belief in human beings as created in the image of God to practice dominion over the earth was a major factor contributing to environmental pollution. Biologist Garrett Hardin's seminal "The Tragedy of the Commons" (1968) also became the basis for an ethical challenge concerning "the limits of altruism." (One irony is that the Apollo moon landing of 1969, which can be viewed as a major achievement of the "domination project," may also have been a chief galvanizer of public awareness; pictures of a blue-green earth rising above the barren lunar landscape did much to raise consciousness of the earth as a complex but fragile ecosystem on which human life depends.)

Subsequent discussion—developed in conjunction with a plethora of analyses of natural ecology, the population explosion, resource depletion, and pollution—has shifted debate toward a number of key ethical questions.

Among these are: Is nature valuable only in relation to its human use, or does it have some value in itself? Is an environmental ethic properly based on human nature and its needs or on the nonhuman natural order and its requirements? Do human beings have duties toward future generations, or toward animals, plants, and nonliving things? Alternatively, do any of these have rights? Is moral concern properly directed toward individuals or species or even ecological systems?

There exist two bibliographies on environmental ethics, both by Mary Anglemyer and others, cited below. The journal *Environmental Ethics* is a primary outlet for articles in the field.

Anglemyer, Mary, and Eleanor R. Seagraves, eds. *The Natural Environment: An Annotated Bibliography in Attitudes and Values.* Smithsonian 1984 $25.00. Eight hundred fifty-seven annotated entries covering 1971–1983. No entries duplicate those in the 1980 Anglemyer bibliography (below).

Anglemyer, Mary, and others, eds. *A Search for Environmental Ethics: An Initial Bibliography.* Smithsonian 1980 text ed. $14.95. Four hundred forty-six annotated entries covering 1945–1979.

Attfield, Robin. *The Ethics of Environmental Concern.* Columbia Univ. Pr. 1983 $28.00 pap. $14.00. Good historically oriented overview covering many of the same themes as Passmore (below).

Berry, Wendell. *The Unsettling of America: Culture and Agriculture.* Sierra Club Bks. 1977 $14.95. pap. $7.95. Criticizes agribusiness and argues that the ecological crisis is "a crisis of character." By a poet and farmer.

Blackstone, William T., ed. *Philosophy and Environmental Crisis.* Univ. of Georgia Pr. 1974 pap. $6.00. Eight papers from the proceedings of a 1971 conference. The first environmental ethics book, and a minor classic in the field.

Elliot, Robert, and Arran Gare, eds. *Environmental Philosophy: A Collection of Readings.* Pennsylvania State Univ. Pr. 1983 $24.50 pap. $10.95. Twelve original essays by 14 authors, and centered in three topics: the environment and human interests, development of an environmental ethics, and historical studies. High-quality work. The editors are Australian, and the volume strongly reflects thought outside the United States.

Evernden, Neil. *The Natural Alien: Humankind and Environment.* Univ. of Toronto Pr. 1985 $19.95. An examination of the affairs of the mind (art, literature, philosophy, biology, photography, etc.) that makes it so difficult to espouse the causes of the environment. Not crisis oriented, but a subtle study of the worldview that underlies crises.

Glacken, C. J. *Traces on the Rhodian Shore: Nature and Culture in Western Thought from Ancient Times to the End of the Eighteenth Century.* Univ. of California Pr. 1973 pap. $15.50. A much more detailed study than Passmore (below).

Goldfarb, Theodore, ed. *Taking Sides: Clashing Views on Controversial Environmental Issues.* Dushkin 2d ed. 1987 pap. $9.50. Good collection of alternative views.

Hardin, Garrett. *Filters against Folly: How to Survive Despite Ecologists, Economists, and the Merely Eloquent.* Penguin 1986 pap. $6.95. Environmental problems are caused not by vice but foolishness. Three ways to filter out the follies of our natural inclinations and simplified ideologies are literacy (examining the meanings of words), numeracy (quantifying information), and ecolacy (assessing complex interactions). Criticizes both free market capitalism and radical ecology.

———. *Stalking the Wild Taboo.* Kaufmann 2d ed. 1978 pap. $8.95. A collection of essays, using the author's biology-ecology interests to defend abortion and attack various aspects of religion, technology, competition, and the idea of "human needs."

Hardin, Garrett, and John Baden, eds. *Managing the Commons.* W. H. Freeman 1977 text ed. pap. $12.95. Twenty-six essays, half of them by the editors, including Hardin's "The Tragedy of the Commons" (*Science*, 1968), a seminal influence on the ecology movement.

Hargrove, Eugene C., ed. *Beyond Spaceship Earth: Environmental Ethics and the Solar System.* Sierra 1986 $25.00. Fifteen papers from a 1985 conference on the social, human, and political dimensions of space exploration from scientific-technological, philosophical, and theological perspectives.

————. *Religion and the Environmental Crisis.* Univ. of Georgia Pr. 1987 $25.00 pap. $12.00. Eleven papers covering pagan, Amerindian, Jewish, Christian, Taoist, and Islamic environmental ethics.

Hart, John. *The Spirit of the Earth: A Theology of the Land.* Paulist Pr. 1984 pap. $8.95. Presents a Catholic theology and ethics of the land.

Kohak, Erazim. *The Embers and the Stars: A Philosophical Inquiry into the Moral Sense of Nature.* Univ. of Chicago Pr. 1984 $17.50. Personal reflections on the experience of building and living in an isolated mountain cabin, and on humanity as part of the order and unity of nature.

Leopold, Aldo. *A Sand County Almanac: With Other Essays on Conservation from Round River.* Oxford 1966 $17.75; intro. by Hal Borland, Tamarack Pr. 1977 $25.00. The chapter titled "The Land Ethic" is the Bible of environmental ethicists. See also the chapter titled "Wilderness."

McCloskey, H. J. *Ecological Ethics and Politics.* [*Philosophy and Society Ser.*] Rowman 1983 text ed. $30.95. Rejects scientific predictions of ecological disaster as based too much on projections of past trends, argues for an anthropocentric environmental ethics, and expresses optimism about international political solutions to environmental problems.

MacLean, Douglas, and Peter G. Brown, eds. *Energy and the Future.* Rowman 1983 text ed. $37.50 pap. $18.50. The most philosophical analysis of energy policy issues. Stresses social justice, environmental ethics, and responsibilities to future generations.

Norton, Bryan G., ed. *The Preservation of Species: The Value of Biological Diversity.* Princeton Univ. Pr. 1986 text ed. $29.50. Eleven original papers focused on the key question: Why preserve an endangered species? Good interdisciplinary collection, with bibliography.

Partridge, Ernest, ed. *Responsibilities to Future Generations: Environmental Ethics.* Prometheus Bks. 1981 $19.95 pap. $13.95. Twenty-five quality essays by professional philosophers on the question, "What moral responsibilities do the living have to future generations?"

Passmore, John. *Man's Responsibility for Nature: Ecological Problems and Western Traditions.* Macmillan 1978 text ed. pap. $10.95. Still the best one-volume, historically oriented introduction to the field. Part 1 contrasts the "man as despot" and "cooperation with nature" traditions in the West. Part 2 considers in detail problems of pollution, resource depletion, destruction of species, and human overpopulation. Part 3 concludes that "if the world's ecological problems are to be solved . . . it can only be by that old-fashioned procedure, thoughtful action."

Regan, Tom, ed. *Earthbound: New Introductory Essays in Environmental Ethics.* Random 1984 text ed. pap. $11.00; Temple Univ. Pr. 1984 $29.95. Ten original essays on key topics by principal figures in the field. A good introduction to the field (by Regan), analyses of pollution and political theory (Machan), energy and

ethics (Shrader-Frechette), responsibilities to future generations (Baier), ethics
in agriculture (Aiken), environmental ethics theory (Johnson), and so on.

Rolston, Holmes, III. *Philosophy Gone Wild: Essays in Environmental Ethics.* Prometheus Bks. 1986 $19.95. Previously published essays by a philosopher-scientist.
His "Is There an Ecological Ethic?" (he argues yes, based on an appreciation of
nature) is a minor classic in the field.

Santmire, H. Paul. *The Travail of Nature: The Ambiguous Ecological Promise of Christian Theology.* Fortress Pr. 1985 pap. $16.95. The most comprehensive Protestant
theological response to the challenge of Lynn White, Jr., and others. Also a
study of Christian attitudes and resources neglected by Passmore and Attfield
(cited above).

Scherer, Donald, and Thomas Attig, eds. *Ethics and the Environment.* Prentice-Hall
1983 pap. $15.95. An introductory anthology.

Shrader-Frechette, Kristin S. *Environmental Ethics.* Boxwood 1981 $12.50 pap.
$9.95. This cross between a monograph and a reader is composed of 12 chap-
ters, each followed by readings, a third of which are in fact by the author.

Stone, Christopher D. *Should Trees Have Standing? Toward Legal Rights for Natural
Objects.* Kaufmann 1974 pap. $5.95. The classic argument that nonhuman en-
tities can have natural rights and therefore "standing" in a court of law.

Taylor, Paul W. *Respect for Nature: A Theory of Environmental Ethics.* [*Studies in
Moral, Political, and Legal Philosophy*] Princeton Univ. Pr. 1986 text ed. $35.00
pap. $12.50. A monograph defending a biocentric theory of environmental ethics.

Van de Veer, Donald, and Christine Pierce, eds. *People, Penguins, and Plastic Trees:
Basic Issues in Environmental Ethics.* Wadsworth 1986 pap. $15.00. Well orga-
nized little volume, and the best general introductory anthology. Part 1 focuses
on other animals and Part 2 focuses on plants, species, and wilderness—in each
case asking in what ways they have values other than to be of human use. Part 3
deals with the environmental ethics theory and Part 4 deals with the conflicts
between ethics, economics, and ecology. Select, unannotated bibliography.

White, Lynn, Jr. *Machina Ex Deo: The Virgin and the Dynamo Reconsidered and Other
Essays.* MIT 1969 o.p. A collection of influential popular essays by an important
historian of technology.

ETHICS IN MEDICINE AND BIOETHICS

Each year the United States spends more on health care than on nuclear
weapons and power plants combined, or on automobiles and gasoline, one
of the primary sources of pollution. Medicine is also the field in which
technological advancements have the most immediate impact on large numbers of people. It is not surprising then that bioethics is the single most
highly developed area of interaction between ethics and technology. It is a
field with many good textbooks, with its own encyclopedia—*Encyclopedia
of Bioethics*, edited by Warren T. Reich—and a voluminous list of publications, surveyed annually in *Bibliography of Bioethics*, edited by LeRoy Walters and others (both cited below). (Some hint of the diversity of relevant
journals is provided by the annotations in this section.) At the same time,
because of its necessary involvement with professional medical ethics,
bioethics has roots that go deeper than other contemporary debates about
aspects of technology and ethics.

The field of bioethics may conveniently be divided into the various moral issues associated with different stages of human life. Abortion, in vitro fertilization, fetal experimentation, surrogate motherhood are all related to the beginning of life. The physician-patient relationship and questions of confidentiality and informed consent relate to the human adult. Organ transplants and euthanasia are associated with the end of life. Covering all periods are issues of the allocation of scarce medical resources and health care policy, the protocols of biomedical research (including experimentation on animals), and the special perspectives of nurses, psychologists, and social workers. In each of these areas, bioethical issues tend to be framed in terms of competing claims, appealing variously to personal rights, social utilities, and natural law.

Because of the wealth of books in this field, the present section is the most selective of this chapter.

Abrams, Natalie, and Michael D. Buckner, eds. *Medical Ethics: A Clinical Textbook and Reference for the Health Care Professions.* MIT 1982 text ed. $50.00 pap. $29.50. Articles dealing with conceptual foundations, clinical ideals and behaviors, and issues in clinical cases. "The editors . . . have taken on—and succeeded at—the difficult task of compiling a book that is, at once, a practical handbook for clinical use, a reference work for scholars and theorists, and a collection of thoughtful philosophical discourses on the role of medicine" (*Science, Technology, and Human Values*).

Beauchamp, Tom L., and James F. Childress. *Principles of Biomedical Ethics.* Oxford 2d ed. 1983 $29.95 pap. $16.95. The first systematic philosophical discussion of basic principles. Presents biomedical ethics as the application of general ethical theories, principles, and rules to problems of therapeutic practice, health care delivery, and medical and biological research. Considers only utilitarian and deontological theories of moral deliberation, and analyzes four core principles— autonomy, beneficence, nonmaleficence, and justice. "Selections of principles, rules, and issues are apropos, and the cases are wide ranging and provocative" (*Journal of the American Medical Association*).

Beauchamp, Tom L., and LeRoy Walters, eds. *Contemporary Issues in Bioethics.* Wadsworth 2d ed. 1982 text ed. $35.25. Among the earliest, and still one of the best, collections.

Bloch, Sidney, and Paul Chodoff, eds. *Psychiatric Ethics.* Oxford 1981 text ed. $32.50 pap. $12.95. Eighteen original papers covering the whole range of psychiatric ethics. Appendix includes a number of relevant professional codes.

Bullough, Vern L., and others, eds. *Issues in Nursing: An Annotated Bibliography.* Garland 1986 $60.00. Includes both primary and secondary sources from books, journals, and dissertations, with a wide focus that includes ethical, legal, educational, and professional issues.

Callahan, Daniel. *The Tyranny of Survival: And Other Pathologies of Civilized Life.* Univ. Pr. of Amer. repr. of 1973 ed. 1985 text ed. pap. $10.75. Obsessions with individualism and survival can lead to technological tyranny. Drawing on readings of Freud and Philip Rieff, and utilizing population growth and genetic engineering as case studies, Callahan seeks a settlement based on an ethic of public morality and a science of technological limits.

Childress, James F. *Who Should Decide? Paternalism in Health Care.* Oxford 1982 $27.50 pap. $14.95. The conflict between professional paternalism and patient autonomy pervades health care. To understand it, we must examine some of the ideas behind it, such as the principles of beneficence and respect for persons and the metaphors of father or parent (from family life) and autonomy (from political life).

Christie, Ronald J., and C. Barry Hoffmaster. *Ethical Issues in Family Medicine.* Oxford 1986 $24.95. A collaborative work by a physician and a philosopher. Focuses not on the sensational issues (abortion, genetic engineering, etc.) but on pervasive ethical questions of everyday medical practice—whether or not to impose changes on a patient's life-style, how to treat difficult patients, and so on.

Duncan, A. S., and others, eds. *Dictionary of Medical Ethics.* Crossroad NY 1981 $24.50. "This volume aims simply to define and to serve as an introduction to the burgeoning and increasingly complex field of medical ethics. It provides both an informed guide for the layperson seeking information, and, for the professional, detailed bibliographies with cross references" (*Journal of Bioethics*).

Engelhardt, H. Tristram, Jr. *The Foundations of Bioethics.* Oxford 1986 $27.95. The first systematic treatment by a single author, and one who holds doctorates in both medicine and philosophy. Begins with a history of the rise of secular bioethics, then provides a thorough treatment of its foundations and applications. Makes the basic principle a Kantian conception of "the person" as a moral agent: "Persons, not humans, are special."

Faden, Ruth R., and Tom L. Beauchamp. *A History of Theory of Informed Consent.* Oxford 1986 $29.95. A definitive account.

Fletcher, Joseph. *Humanhood: Essays in Biomedical Ethics.* Prometheus Bks. 1979 $18.95 pap. $10.95. A collection of essays vigorously presenting one of the most avowedly secular humanist positions on a range of issues.

Goldstein, Doris Mueller. *Bioethics: A Guide to Information Sources.* Gale 1982 $62.00. A selective, annotated index emphasizing publications prior to 1973, when LeRoy Walters's *Bibliography of Bioethics* begins. Excellent one-volume survey not just of literature but of organizations, library collections, journals, bibliographies, and textbooks.

Gorovitz, Samuel. *Doctors' Dilemmas: Moral Conflict and Medical Care.* Oxford 1985 pap. $7.95. General introduction to those areas of health care most frequently beset by moral difficulties, and a study of how philosophical reflection can help deal with them.

Holmstrom, Lynda Lytle, and Jeanne Guillemin. *Mixed Blessings: Intensive Care for Newborns.* Oxford 1986 $20.80. "In this inside account of the work accomplished in the neonatal intensive care unit, two medical sociologists focus on . . . medical decision making" in the United States, England, the Netherlands, and Brazil (*American Journal of Public Health*).

Hunter, Edna, and Daniel Hunter. *Professional Ethics and Law in the Health Sciences.* Krieger 1984 $15.95. A practitioner's guide.

Jameton, Andrew. *Nursing Practice: The Ethical Issues.* Prentice-Hall 1984 text ed. pap. $20.95. "At least the fourth book on nursing ethics in recent years, and . . . extremely rich in coverage and resources cited" (*Journal of Religious Ethics*). Actually, more like the tenth book on the subject in recent years.

Jennett, Bryan. *High Technology Medicine: Benefit and Burdens.* Oxford 1986 pap. $11.95. Descriptive but critical survey of medical technologies in diagnosis and treatment with analysis of options in future assessment and use.

Kass, Leon R. *Toward a More Natural Science: Biology and Human Affairs.* Free Pr. 1985 $23.50. Considers the ethical meaning of new biomedical technologies of reproduction and genetics, the relation between modern medicine and the traditional art of healing, and then proposes a new view of nature as a basis for an ethics of scientific technology. "Different in many ways from anything else in the field. Well written and provocative" (*Hastings Center Report*).

Kieffer, George H. *Bioethics: A Textbook of Issues.* Addison-Wesley 1979 text ed. $24.95. A well-written and widely used text.

Kleinig, John. *Ethical Issues in Psychosurgery.* Allen & Unwin 1985 $19.50 pap. $7.50. Highlights the problem of objective evaluation in psychosurgery because of inadequate follow-ups, diversity of procedures, placebo effects, etc. "Kleinig's chief contribution is to pose clearly a series of relevant questions that permit intelligent ethical debate" (*Hastings Center Report*).

Levine, Carol, ed. *Taking Sides: Clashing Views on Controversial Bioethical Issues.* Dushkin 2d ed. 1987 $9.50. Well-edited collection; topical and provocative, as the title implies.

Levine, Robert J. *Ethics and Regulation of Clinical Research.* Urban & Schwarzenberg 2d ed. 1986 $45.00. Comprehensive survey of the ethical and legal responsibilities of clinical investigations and institutional review boards.

Lockwood, Michael, ed. *Moral Dilemmas in Modern Medicine.* Oxford 1985 $9.95. Nine original papers from a seminar and lecture series. Mary Warnock, chair of the British Committee of Inquiry into Human Fertilisation and Embryology, contributes reflections on some discussions that went into the "Warnock Report"; Lockwood analyzes some of the issues highlighted by the report; and an appendix describes legal and political developments in Britain as a result of this controversial inquiry.

McCormick, Richard A. *How Brave a New World: Dilemmas in Bioethics.* Georgetown Univ. Pr. repr. of 1981 ed. 1985 pap. $12.95. Good introductory overview of the issues.

Mappes, Thomas A., and Jane S. Zembaty, eds. *Biomedical Ethics.* McGraw-Hill 2d ed. 1986 $28.95. A well-organized collection of readings.

Meier, Levi, ed. *Jewish Values in Bioethics.* Human Sciences Pr. 1986 $24.95. Presents the Jewish perspective.

Nicholson, Richard H., ed. *Medical Research with Children: Ethics, Law, and Practice.* Oxford 1986 $27.95. Not a collection of articles but the report of a British Institute of Medical Ethics working group of 19 physicians, lawyers, ministers, hospital administrators, etc. Identifies key risks and benefits in pediatric research and discusses the dilemmas of child consent (age of competency and adequacy of parental or guardian consent). "As society moves further from the codes of an established religion, it looks increasingly to the moralist for a set of rules" (*Lancet*).

Pence, Terry. *Ethics in Nursing: An Annotated Bibliography.* National League for Nursing 2d ed. 1986 pap. $16.95. A restricted bibliography of articles by nurses in nursing journals explicitly on ethics.

Rachels, James. *The End of Life: Euthanasia and Morality.* Oxford 1986 $17.95 pap. $9.95. Rejects traditional, especially religious, criticisms of euthanasia and argues for an alternative, qualified acceptance. "The alternative view begins by pointing out that there is a deep difference between *having a life* and merely *being alive.*" The latter is not important in itself, as traditional prohibitions of euthanasia seem to imply.

Reich, Warren T., ed. *Encyclopedia of Bioethics.* Free Pr. 4 vols. 1978 $250.00; Macmillan 2 vols. 1982 lib. bdg. $145.00. The standard reference work in the field.

Reiser, Stanley J., ed. *Ethics in Medicine: Historical Perspectives and Contemporary Concerns.* MIT 1977 text ed. $60.00 pap. $29.95. The best and most wide-ranging sourcebook available. Includes over 100 documents and articles, classic and contemporary, and numerous illustrative cases on the physician-patient relationship, foundations of medical ethics, regulation and public health, truth-telling, human experimentation, procreation, suffering and death, and health care allocation.

Shannon, Thomas A., and Jo Ann Manfra. *Law and Bioethics: Selected Cases.* Paulist Pr. 1981 pap. $14.95. Makes readily available the texts of over 20 major U.S. court cases, together with commentary.

Shelp, Earl E. *Theology and Bioethics: Exploring the Foundations and Frontiers.* Kluwer Academic 1985 lib. bdg. $39.50. Eighteen original papers mostly by leading religious ethicists who have already played a role in the development of bioethics. But the conclusion seems to be, as John Cobb, Jr., writes in an epilogue, that "Christianity does not provide a set of moral principles distinct from . . . [those of] post-Christian thinkers."

Singer, Peter, and Deane Wells. *Making Babies: The New Science and Ethics of Conception.* Scribner 1985 $14.95. A revision of *The Reproduction Revolution* (1984). A "valuable introduction to the new reproductive technologies and to at least some of the moral quandaries which they create" (*Ethics*).

Steere, Jane. *Ethics in Clinical Psychology.* Oxford 1984 $15.95. The only volume specifically to address the issues of clinical psychology. Includes chapters on ethics in psychotherapy, psychological assessment, research, and "the South African context" (the author is a lecturer at the University of Cape Town's Child Guidance Clinic). Good unannotated bibliography.

Thompson, Joyce, and Henry O. Thompson. *Bioethical Decision Making: Who Owns the Problem.* Appleton & Lange 1985 pap. $24.95. Part 2 purports to provide a step-by-step process for decision making. Contains a good annotated bibliography of over 80 titles.

Tooley, Michael. *Abortion and Infanticide.* Oxford 1984 $29.95. Highly philosophical defense of the liberal position on the morality of abortion.

Vaux, Kenneth, ed. *Powers That Make Us Human: The Foundations of Medical Ethics.* Univ. of Illinois Pr. 1986 $16.95. The powers at issue include morality (Leon Kass), honor (William May), subsistence (Ivan Illich), feelings (Willard Gaylin), reason (H. Tristram Engelhardt, Jr.), justice (Joseph Fletcher), hope (Vaux), virtue (Stanley Hauerwas). "Draws our attention to the rich complexities of the moral life in medicine" (*Journal of Medicine and Philosophy*).

Veatch, Robert M. *A Theory of Medical Ethics.* Basic Bks. 1981 $9.95. Criticizes paternalism and argues that the theory of a social contract among equals produces the most satisfactory medical and human decisions.

Walters, LeRoy, and others, eds. *Bibliography of Bioethics.* Free Pr. 1981 $55.00; Gale 6 vols. 1975–80 ea. $68.00; Kennedy Institute 3 vols. 1984–86 ea. $25.00; Macmillan 1982 $60.00. This annual series is the most comprehensive index to the field. The first volume focused on materials from 1973; subsequent volumes have covered periods progressively more contemporaneous with their dates of publication. One weakness is that there are no annotations, only a complex descriptive thesaurus until Vol. 9 (1983, focusing on 1980–82) when annotations were added, but only for articles from 15 selected journals.

Weir, Robert F. *Selective Nontreatment of Handicapped Newborns: Moral Dilemmas in Neonatal Medicine.* Oxford 1984 $27.95 pap. $11.95. An important and generally well-reviewed study constituting "the first full-length analysis . . . since the famous Baby Doe case of 1982" (*New England Journal of Medicine*).

ETHICS IN INFORMATION SCIENCE AND COMPUTER TECHNOLOGIES

The relation of ethics to information science and computer technologies is often called "computer ethics." The term is, however, unnecessarily limiting, since the basic issues in computer ethics can be found associated with other information media—from print to electronic technologies. The ethical issues in question include responsibility in information handling, fair public access, privacy, confidentiality, and security.

Computer ethics was initially restricted to concerns about threats to individual privacy and corporate security. More recently, as indicated by Deborah Johnson in *Computer Ethics* (cited below), it has broadened to address the issues of ethical codes for computer professionals, liability for the malfunctioning of computer programs, and the relation between computers and power. Still other discussions focus on the anthropological implications of artificial intelligence.

Christians, Clifford, and others. *Media Ethics: Cases and Moral Reasoning.* [*Annenberg Communication Ser.*] Longman 1983 $24.95 text ed. pap. $16.95. Deals with news reporting, advertising, and entertainment in both print and electronic media. Case studies focus on issues of censorship, child education, confidentiality, conflicts of interest, deception, economic pressures, explicit sex, fairness, health and safety, law-bending, being an accessory to criminal actions, media self-criticism, minorities and the elderly, privacy, sensationalism, stereotyping, and violence.

Hoffman, W. Michael, and Jennifer Mills Moore, eds. *Ethics and the Management of Computer Technology.* [*Proceedings of the Fourth National Conference on Business Ethics*] Oelgeschlager 1982 text ed. $30.00. Good collection of 12 original articles.

Johnson, Deborah. *Computer Ethics.* Prentice-Hall 1985 text ed. pap. $13.95. Opens with a chapter on ethical theory, then works its way through ethics codes for computer professionals, corporate liability for malfunctioning programs, privacy, influence of computers on centralization of power, and ownership of software. Stresses legal issues.

Johnson, Deborah, and John W. Snapper, eds. *Ethical Issues in the Use of Computers.* Wadsworth 1985 $23.00. The basic collection of readings in this area. Thirty-three articles divided into sections on ethical codes for computer professionals, general responsibility, privacy and security, computers and power, and software as property. Makes good use of legal cases.

Kemnitz, Thomas, and Philip Vincent. *Computer Ethics.* Trillium Pr. 1985 $9.95. A beginner's introduction to the issues, making use of 17 scenarios with questions for discussion.

Mitcham, Carl, and Alois Huning, eds. *Philosophy and Technology II: Information Technology and Computers in Theory and Practice.* Kluwer Academic 1986 lib. bdg. $59.00. Includes articles on automation and workers' rights, computers in medicine, privacy, responsibility for "data pollution," and so forth. Includes a 40-page annotated bibliography.

Parker, Donn B. *Fighting Computer Crime.* Scribner 1983 $19.95. Overview of the empirical phenomena of computer crime, the various responses, and some ethical issues (see especially Part 4, "Ethical Conflicts in Computing"). By an internationally known computer security consultant.

Roszak, Theodore. *The Cult of Information: The Folklore of Computers and the True*

Art of Thinking. Pantheon 1986 $17.95. Critical of the computer revolution, Roszak attacks the cybernetic model of the human mind, debunks the notion of an information economy, and criticizes the computer industry for its opportunistic invasion of the schools.

Schellenberg, Kathryn, ed. *Computer Studies: Computers in Society.* Dushkin 1986 pap. $8.95. Reprints a wide variety of articles, mostly from the more popular press, on social and ethical issues.

Shallis, Michael. *The Silicon Idol: The Micro Revolution and Its Social Implications.* Schocken 1984 $15.95. What is unique about Shallis is that he gives arguments about the moral dangers of computers a religious dimension.

Weizenbaum, Joseph. *Computer Power and Human Reason: From Judgment to Calculation.* W. H. Freeman 1976 text ed. $16.95 pap. $13.95. In attempting to define what computers can and cannot be expected to do, Weizenbaum argues against the "imperialism of instrumental reason." Valuable for its eloquent skeptical review of potential substitutions of computers for human interaction in such functions as counseling, law, and language translation.

ENGINEERING ETHICS AND ETHICS OF TECHNOLOGY

Engineering ethics is the attempt to apply ethical principles to the profession most intimately involved with modern technologies. The ethics of technology refers to the general attempt to come to terms with technology as a whole—without being limited to nuclear weapons and power plants, industries that create chemical pollutants, biomedical technologies that challenge traditional understandings of life, and machines designed to manipulate information. The ethics of technology, that is, seeks to relate all more restricted discussion of particular technologies. Since engineers are also involved across the whole spectrum of technologies, professional engineering ethics and the general ethics of technology are thus properly associated. The two have, in fact, undergone dramatic and related development over the last two decades.

The easiest development to sketch is that in professional engineering ethics. In the early 1900s it was commonly assumed that the primary obligation of the engineer was to an employer. In the 1960s, however, such a presumption began to be questioned, and it was argued instead that an engineer's primary responsibilities were to society as a whole. This was associated with the development of alternative technologies and with attempts to protect engineers from the power of employers, neither of which has been wholly successful.

As with the development of engineering ethics, that of a more general ethics of technology has behind it several concerns. In addition to the specific ethical issues already surveyed, one might name the consumer advocacy movement, special concerns about worker health in various industrial or office settings, and technological disasters such as airplane accidents and failures in bridges, dams, and other civil engineering structures. As a result, the concepts of safety and risk have become an increasing aspect of ethical discourse. Perhaps the central transformation taking place in ethics as a result of technological advance is precisely the articulation and expansion of the notion of moral responsibility to meet these increasingly crucial factors of safety and risk. Outside the developed world, issues of social justice and cultural dislocation as a result of technological transfer or development also play a prominent role.

Ballard, Edward G. *Man and Technology: Toward the Measurement of a Culture.* Duquesne Univ. Pr. 1978 text ed. pap. $10.00. A general critique of technological culture that argues that too deep an involvement in technology ignores the human self.

Baum, Robert J. *Ethics and Engineering Curricula.* Pref. by Sissela Bok [*Teaching of Ethics Ser.*] Hastings Center 1980 pap. $4.00. Overview of work in this area.

Berger, Peter L. *Pyramids of Sacrifice: Political Ethics and Social Change.* Doubleday 1976 pap. $4.95. Compares the developmental strategies of Brazil (capitalist) and China (socialist). Finding that both cause unjustified human suffering, Berger argues for a third way.

Douglas, Mary. *Risk Acceptability According to the Social Sciences.* [*Social Science Perspectives: Occasional Reports of Current Topics*] Russell Sage 1986 text ed. pap. $6.95. A critical overview based on the thesis that risk perception is influenced by social and cultural institutions as much as by personal or individual sensitivities.

Fischhoff, Baruch, and others. *Acceptable Risk.* Cambridge Univ. Pr. 1981 $24.95 1984 pap. $10.95. Best general overview of the problem of risk in a technological society and the various methods used to evaluate it.

Goodpaster, K. E., and K. M. Sayre, eds. *Ethics and Problems of the 21st Century.* Univ. of Notre Dame Pr. 1980 text ed. pap. $7.95. Papers on the concept of morality and methods of moral reflection, followed by applications to food distribution, technology and the sanctity of life, historical preservation, and the rights of nonhumans.

Goulet, Denis. *The Cruel Choice: A New Concept in the Theory of Development.* Univ. Pr. of Amer. repr. of 1971 ed. 1985 text ed. pap. $14.75. "The aim of this work is to thrust debates over economic and social development into the arena of ethical values," according to the introduction. Develops the key concepts of "vulnerability" and "existence rationality," and describes a series of "ethical strategies for development" based on the three principles of adequate means, universal solidarity, and popular participation.

Grant, George. *English-Speaking Justice.* Univ. of Notre Dame Pr. 1986 $11.95 pap. $4.95. Argues that modern technology is based on the English-speaking peoples' ideas of justice, freedom, and equality. Criticizes these views.

Gunn, Alastair, and P. Aarne Vesilind. *Environmental Ethics for Engineers.* Lewis 1986 $18.95 pap. $13.95. Part 1 contains a brief analysis of environmental ethics and engineering practice in general. Part 2 is an anthology of nine readings.

Iannone, A. Pablo, ed. *Contemporary Moral Controversies in Technology.* Oxford 1987 $29.95 pap. $12.95. A reader with 33 articles oriented toward specific problems. Not even the first section, "Technology, Ethics, Technology Ethics," contains any general theory, yet the sections on moral controversies in technology assessment, technology management, technology research and development, technology transfer, and technology policymaking are all quite good. The most extensive, on technology management, has six subsections dealing with the technologies of information, gene splicing, health care, space development, energy, and materials. Select bibliography.

Illich, Ivan. *Tools for Conviviality.* Harper 1973 o.p. A classic and influential attempt to spell out moral standards for the evaluation of technological development.

Jonas, Hans. *The Imperative of Responsibility: In Search of an Ethics for the Technological Age.* Univ. of Chicago Pr. 1985 lib. bdg. $23.00 pap. $9.95. The single most
important philosophical text in the general ethics of technology. Argues that the
character of human action has been fundamentally altered by the powers of
modern technology, and that responsibility, especially toward future generations, calls for a slowing down of technological change. Also provides a theoretical grounding for responsibility as a moral concept.

———. *Philosophical Essays: From Ancient Creed to Technological Man.* Univ. of
Chicago Pr. 1980 $18.00. Part 1 (the longest of three) contains eight essays on
"Science, Technology, and Ethics." The first and fifth—"Technology and Responsibility: Reflections on the New Tasks of Ethics" and "Philosophical Reflections
on Experimenting with Human Subjects"—are especially important. Also considers the Jewish perspective on the ethics of technology.

Kranzberg, Melvin, ed. *Ethics in an Age of Pervasive Technology.* Westview Pr. 1980
$32.00. Proceedings from a symposium held in Israel in 1974. Good collection of
short articles by such important thinkers as Gershom Scholem, Isaiah Berlin,
Daniel Bell, Robert Gordis, René Dubos, Jacques Ellul, Hans Jonas, Alvin Weinberg, and others. Includes the "Mount Carmel Declaration on Technology and
Moral Responsibility."

Layton, Edwin T. *The Revolt of the Engineers: Social Responsibility and the American
Engineering Profession.* Johns Hopkins Univ. Pr. 1986 text ed. $29.50 pap. $9.95.
An excellent and influential overview (originally published in 1971) of the rise of
engineering as a profession, with professional codes and special values, in the
United States.

Lossing, Larry D., and Edward J. Bayer, eds. *Technological Powers and the Person:
Nuclear Energy and Reproductive Technology.* Pope John Center 1983 pap. $15.95.
Considers the moral status of nuclear power and reproductive techniques—that
is, the "positive" sides of nuclear weapons and artificial contraception—from
the Catholic Christian perspective. Somewhat pro nuclear and con artificial
insemination.

Lydenberg, Steven D., and others. *Rating America's Corporate Conscience: A Provocative Guide to the Companies behind the Products You Buy Every Day.* Addison-
Wesley 1986 $21.95 pap. $14.95. An example of grass-roots ethics of technology.

MacLean, Douglas, ed. *Values at Risk.* Rowman & Allanheld 1986 $28.50 pap. $15.95.
Eight original papers considering risk and risk analysis in technological society.

Martin, Michael, and Roland Schinzinger. *Ethics in Engineering.* McGraw-Hill 1983
text ed. pap. $22.95. A philosopher (Martin) and an engineer (Schinzinger) ex-
plore a range of ethical issues from an analytic perspective.

Mitcham, Carl, and Robert Mackey, eds. *Philosophy and Technology: Readings in the
Philosophical Problems of Technology.* Free Pr. repr. of 1972 ed. 1983 text ed.
pap. $12.95. The largest section of the book is devoted to "Ethical and Political
Critiques." Reprints a number of important texts not easily found elsewhere by
Jacques Ellul, Emmanuel Mesthene, Gunther Anders, C. S. Lewis, Yves Simm,
George Grant, Nicholas Berdyaev, Eric Gill, Lynn White, Jr., and others.

Monsma, Stephen V., and others. *Responsible Technology: A Christian Perspective.*
Eerdmans 1986 pap. $12.95. The product of a year-long study group at Calvin
College (Michigan). Moves from analyzing the spiritual nature of technology to
developing moral guidelines for Christian engineers and others. Good annotated
bibliography.

Papanek, Victor. *Design for the Real World: Human Ecology and Social Change.* Academy Chicago 2d rev. ed. 1985 pap. $10.95. Strongly worded moral argument by
an industrial engineer. "Design must become an innovative, highly creative,

cross-disciplinary tool responsive to the true needs of man. It must be more research oriented, and we must stop defiling the earth itself with poorly-designed objects and structures."

Porter, A. R., and others. *A Guidebook for Technology Assessment and Impact Analysis.* Elsevier 1980 $33.75. A reference book overview of what technology assessment is all about.

Rescher, Nicholas. *Risk: A Philosophical Introduction to the Theory of Risk Evaluation and Management.* Univ. Pr. of Amer. 1983 lib. bdg. $29.75 text ed. pap. $12.25. See especially chapters on "The Ethical and Legal Dimension of Risk" and "Risk and Technology."

————. *Unpopular Essays on Technological Progress.* Univ. of Pittsburgh Pr. 1980 $12.95. On the economic and social ramifications of technological progress.

Sapolsky, Harvey M. *Consuming Fears: The Politics of Product Risks.* Basic Bks. 1986 $18.95. Highlights problems, but short on moral analysis or alternatives.

Schaub, James H., and others, eds. *Engineering Professionalism and Ethics.* Krieger repr. of 1983 ed. 1986 text ed. pap. $29.50. Good general collection of over 70 readings.

Shrader-Frechette, Kristin S. *Science Policy, Ethics, and Economic Methodology: Some Problems of Technology Assessment of Environmental Impact Analysis.* Kluwer Academic 1985 text ed. lib. bdg. $39.50 pap. $19.50. The subtitle indicates the primary focus of this critical study of weaknesses in certain methods of technology assessment.

Unger, Stephen H. *Controlling Technology: Ethics and the Responsible Engineer.* Henry Holt 1982 pap. $20.95. Engineers are often forced to choose between loyalty to a corporate employer and loyalty to conscience. This book argues that loyalty to conscience and the "whistle blowing" that often results need to be supported by the professional engineering organizations. Good case studies. Appendixes also include a number of engineering ethics codes. "A book that must be read by all engineers" (*IEEE Technology and Society Magazine*).

Winner, Langdon. *The Whale and the Reactor: A Search for Limits in an Age of High Technology.* Univ. of Chicago Pr. 1986 lib. bdg. $17.50. Technologies are forms of life, so that choices about the kinds of technical systems we construct should be understood as choices about who we want to be and what kind of world we want to live in.

Name Index

In addition to authors, this index includes the names of persons mentioned in connection with titles of books written, whether they appear in introductory essays, general bibliographies at the beginnings of chapters, discussions under main headings, or "Books About" sections. Persons mentioned in passing—to indicate friendships, relationships, and so on—are generally not indexed. Editors are not indexed unless there is no specific author given; such books include anthologies, bibliographies, yearbooks, and the like. Translators, writers of introductions, forewords, afterwords, etc., are not indexed except for those instances where the translator seems as closely attached to a title as the real author, e.g., FitzGerald's translation of the *Rubáiyát of Omar Khayyám*. Main name headings appear in boldface as do the page numbers on which the main entries appear.

Title Index

Titles of all books discussed in *The Reader's Adviser* are indexed here, except broad generic titles such as "Complete Works," "Selections," "Poems," "Correspondence." Also omitted is any title listed with a main-entry author that includes that author's name, e.g., *Collected Prose of T. S. Eliot*, and titles under "Books About," e.g., *Eliot's Early Years* by Lyndall Gordon. The only exception to this is Shakespeare (Volume 2), where all works by and about him are indexed. To locate all titles by and about a main-entry author, the user should refer to the Name Index for the author's primary listing (given in boldface). Whenever the name of a main-entry author is part of a title indexed here, the page reference is to a section other than the primary listing. In general, subtitles are omitted. When two or more identical titles by different authors appear, the last name of each author is given in parentheses following the title.

Subject Index

This index provides detailed, multiple-approach access to the subject content of the volume, employing the subject headings as entry terms. Arrangement is alphabetical. Collective terms for authors are included, e.g., *Astronomers, Mathematicians, Physicists,* but the reader is reminded to use the Name Index to locate individual writers.

Abstracts, information and library science, 136–37
Aeronautics, engineering and technology, 556–58
Aging
in medicine and health, 398–400
nutrition and, 432
Agricultural food engineering, 558
AIDS, 465–66
Alcoholism, 480–81
Algebra, 88–91
Allergy. *See* Immunology
Alternative health care, 401–3
Analytical chemistry, 292–93
Anatomy
in biology, 323–25
in medicine. *See* Healthy body
Ancient period—science, technology, and medicine in, 38–40
Anesthesiology, 447
Animal behavior, 371–75
in sociobiology, 375–77
writers, 373–75
Applied science, in earth sciences, 218–20
Art, computer applications in, 153–55
Arthritis. *See* Rheumatic diseases
Artificial and transplanted organs, 447–48

Artificial intelligence, 156–61
collections and anthologies, 159–60
introductions, 156–59
philosophy, background, and context, 160–61
Astronomers, 173–74, 184–96
Astronomy, 168–96
astronomers, 173–74, 184–96
cosmology in, 178–80
equipment and persons in, 173–74
general works in, 170–72
history of, 30–32, 173–74
planets and solar system in, 175–77
reference works in, 170–72
and search for extraterrestrial intelligence, 183–84
space program and, 180–82
stars and galaxies in, 177–78
techniques in, 173–74
without instruments, 174–75
Astrophysics, 239–40
Atmospheric science, in earth sciences, 216–18
Atomic physics, 237–38
history of, 238
Automotive engineering, 580–81

Aviation, engineering and technology, 556–58

Bibliographic tools, history of science, technology, and medicine, 25–27
Bibliography
biographical and historical, information and computer science, 164–67
biology, 307–12
chemistry, 278–82
directories, dictionaries, encyclopedias, 279–81
guides to chemical literature, 282
energy, 584
history of science, technology, and medicine, 25–27
information and library science, 136–37
philosophy of science and pseudoscience, 54–58
probability, 122–26
science and society, 595–609
statistics, 122–26
technology and society, 595–609
Biochemistry, 288–89, 325–26
Bioclimatology, 326

717